the Colorado Guide

Bruce Caughey & Dean Winstanley

Fifth Edition

Fulcrum Publishing
Golden, Colorado

To Brian, Maura, Shannon and Julia

The information in *The Colorado Guide, Fifth Edition,* is accurate as of February 2001. However, prices, hours of operation, addresses, phone numbers, websites and other items change rapidly. If something in the book is incorrect, please write to the authors in care of Fulcrum Publishing, 16100 Table Mountain Parkway, Suite 300, Golden, Colorado 80403; fulcrum@fulcrum-books.com.

The Colorado Guide provides many safety tips about weather and travel, but good decision making and sound judgment are the responsibility of the individual. Neither the publisher nor the author assumes any liability for injury that may arise from the use of this book.

Library of Congress Cataloging-in-Publication Data

Caughey, Bruce.
  The Colorado guide / Bruce Caughey, Dean Winstanley.— 5th ed.
     p. cm.
Includes index.
  ISBN 1-55591-006-8
  1. Outdoor recreation—Colorado—Guidebooks. 2. Colorado—Description and travel. 3. Colorado—Guidebooks. I. Winstanley, Dean, 1960- II. Title.
  GV191.42.C6 C37 2001
  917.88'0434—dc21

                     2001001536

Printed in Canada
0 9 8 7 6 5 4 3 2 1

Project manager: Daniel Forrest-Bank
Editorial: Don Graydon, Amy Timms, Erin Lawson
Design and formatting: Michelle Taverniti
Maps: Marge Mueller, Gray Mouse Graphics
Front cover photograph: Summertime wildflowers in full bloom below Treasury Mountain (left) and Treasure Mountain, Maroon Bells–Snowmass Wilderness, Elk Mountains, Colorado. Copyright © Eric Wunrow.
Back cover photograph: Sunlight filters through aspen trees on a perfect ski day. Photo by Burnie Arndt, courtesy of Aspen Skiing Company.
Title page photograph: A magical reflection on Lake San Cristobal captures the natural beauty of the surrounding peaks. Photo by Bruce Caughey.

Fulcrum Publishing
16100 Table Mountain Parkway, Suite 300, Golden, Colorado 80403
(800) 992-2908 • (303) 277-1623
www.fulcrum-books.com

Contents

Acknowledgments

Neither of us could have known back in 1987 that we were embarking on a writing partnership that would last this long. Our indebtedness to family, friends and acquaintances runs deep. We especially want to thank the locals around the state who shared their secrets about favorite places and to readers of the book for comments and suggestions for improving the guide.

The sheer volume of information and subject areas covered in our guide requires us to rely on subject experts around the state. Special thanks to those who manage our public lands, often working for the National Forest Service, National Parks, Bureau of Land Management, Colorado State Parks and Colorado Division of Wildlife. Their careful review and input has been invaluable. We also must thank the many individuals at chambers of commerce and business organizations who went out of their way to help us. As always we depended heavily on destination tourism experts and ski area representatives (special thanks to Harry Graham for his invaluable help).

The staff at Fulcrum has a catchy enthusiasm about our guide that keeps us coming back for each revised edition. Thanks to our editor Daniel Forrest-Bank for his efforts and Don Graydon (the "cyber tweaker") who pored over the book with an intelligence and thoroughness that greatly improved the final copy.

Especially from Bruce

Many people helped make the fifth edition a reality. First, I'd like to recognize and thank my parents, Ken and Judith Caughey, whose love, support and encouragement instilled a lifelong curiosity about the state.

A crew of associate researchers, writers and friends captured the essence of many destinations. Special contributions to the book by Kirstin Bebell, Dave Donley, Rich Sharp, Lisa Bunse and Kevin Day helped immensely. Your sharp eyes and keen intuition helped make this guide possible. Marybeth Smith and Cindy Murphy also helped ensure the chapter information was up-to-date by fact checking information all around the state.

Shannon and Julia brought back many fond childhood remembrances while on the road, including word games and backseat turf battles. Love you girls!

Especially from Dean

I am indebted to Wendy Newman, our research associate, for her invaluable role in maintaining our connectedness to a state that continues to change at lightning speed. Her good humor, enthusiasm and love for the land is infectious! Thanks also goes out to friends and associates on-site including April Darrow, Rich Grant, Barb Bowman, Kathleen Brown, Nicole DePriest, Annie Kuhles, Elizabeth Youngquist and Gary Nichols for their suggestions and other invaluable assistance.

Spencer Winstanley provided fine companionship on the road and exhibited a deft touch with those alligators in the San Luis Valley! Sheila hung in there, especially when it finally sunk in that our "spare time" was indeed disappearing for the foreseeable future. And special thanks to my son, Brian, the "Road Warrior," for accompanying his dad along so many trails and backroads of the state.

Introduction

This Is Colorado

No one summed up Colorado better than Teddy Roosevelt when he said, "The scenery bankrupts the English language." The Rocky Mountains dominate this striking landscape as they run through the middle of the state, constituting a mountainous area three times as large as the Swiss Alps. Colorado's peaks are legendary: more than 1,100 of them rise to 10,000 feet or higher; 54 mountains top off at over 14,000 feet.

The state's colorful history becomes most apparent at the ancient cliff dwellings of Mesa Verde National Park and in former mining boomtowns such as Leadville and Silverton. Woven into the historical fabric are the unmistakable impacts of Anglo, Hispanic and Native American culture, all indelibly etched into Colorado's character. Colorado is a rich and varied land; its 4 million residents appreciate the healthy mix of recreation and culture combined with a dash of the Wild West.

More than 20 million visitors make their way to the state each year, not only for personal adventure and wilderness travel but also to enjoy some of the best powder skiing in the world. As "Winter Sports Capital of the Country," Colorado offers 25 major ski areas.

Colorado is a place with so much to do that up-to-date, accurate advice is a precious commodity—and that's the main reason for creating this newly revised fifth edition of *The Colorado Guide*. As native Coloradans, we enjoy sharing tips about the state with friends who come to visit. We hope our guidebook accomplishes the same by capturing the essence and spirit of Colorado for you. With an insider's perspective of Colorado cities, small mountain towns and areas far from civilization, we try to unlock some of the state's best-kept secrets. Included are specifics that guide the way to many popular activities, such as hiking, skiing, fly-fishing and whitewater rafting. We also offer information about mountain resorts, the arts and museums of Denver and the region's many hot springs.

When we first set to work on this massive guidebook project in 1987, we had a feeling it would strike a chord with our readers. More than a dozen printings and five editions later, we are still going strong. But when we consider all the revisions to this guide during the past 12 years, it's mind-boggling. Along with continually updating the 1,600 or so business descriptions in the book, we've encountered a host of changes in the life of our state. In Denver, the Lower Downtown historic district (better known as LoDo) and the bustling, attraction-packed Central Platte Valley have become the heart and soul of a city that needed a vibrant

Spring runoff flows down from the Continental Divide. Photo by Bruce Caughey.

center of activity and discovery. And Denver, the capital city of Colorado, has added Major League baseball (the Colorado Rockies) and National Hockey League action (the Colorado Avalanche) to its attractions, joining football's Denver Broncos and basketball's Denver Nuggets.

With tremendous growth continuing in Colorado and a noticeable loss of solitude on our public lands, it has been heartening to see the steps taken in recent years to preserve and provide access to more outdoor areas. State lottery funds and local open-space and park taxes are helping to pay for this effort. The way we have fun in the outdoors continues to change as well. Snowboarding was barely a concept when we first started this guide, but now some 35 percent of ski area lift tickets are sold to boarders. Snowshoeing, likewise, has taken off in a big way, thanks in part to new, lightweight equipment.

Among other changes in Colorado, legalized low-stakes gambling has become a major presence in Central City, Black Hawk and Cripple Creek, as well as on the Ute reservations. And over the years an incredible number of bed and breakfast inns have opened (and some have closed), enriching the lodging options of travelers throughout the state. Colorado's economy has been on a steady upswing since the late 1980s—booming along with the state's population. This growth, along with open-space acquisition and other methods of preserving Colorado's high quality of life, continue to be dominant issues.

We have tried to stay up with as many changes, big and small, as is humanly possible in order to keep this guidebook accurate and up-to-date. We're thankful to have a strong network of contacts throughout the state, including many readers who write, e-mail or call us with ideas for interesting and offbeat places to include in the book (and sometimes with suggestions for deletions, too). Among the significant additions are website addresses for hundreds of businesses and attractions, pointing you to the new wealth of information available on the Internet. In preparation for this new edition, we revisited the statewide destination areas in the book,

always with an eye toward improving and enriching our coverage. This research effort has again resulted in a more complete and easy-to-use guide, which we hope will impart some of the fascination and love we feel for the state of Colorado.

History

This land called Colorado, to which so many people now come for rest and relaxation, meant something much different to its first inhabitants. Nomadic hunters of bison and woolly mammoths may have roamed the area as far back as 15,000 years ago. Archaeologists continue to learn more about these prehistoric residents (Folsom Man) from their stone spearheads and other artifacts. Close on the heels of Folsom Man came the more advanced Anasazi civilization—Colorado's first farmers. They inhabited the mesa tops and cliffs of southwestern Colorado from approximately A.D. 1 until their mysterious disappearance in A.D. 1300. The Anasazi are known for their basket making and, in later periods, for pottery and stone masonry (the latter can be witnessed in the stunning cliff-hanging citadels at Mesa Verde National Park; see the **Cortez** chapter).

In the centuries following the disappearance of the Anasazi, bands of nomadic Native American tribes (most notably Utes and Comanche in the mountains and Arapaho and Cheyenne on the plains) wandered the state in search of game. The buffalo was an integral part of their way of life. By the late 1500s the arrival of Anglos forever changed the Indians' lifestyle in Colorado. For one thing, these newcomers brought horses, enabling the Indians to travel greater distances and to hunt more effectively.

By many accounts, the first European to enter Colorado was the Spanish explorer Francisco Coronado. In 1540 he and other conquistadors made their way north from Mexico in search of the mythical "Seven Cities of Cibola," where it was said the streets were paved with gold. No such luck for Coronado, who arrived in northern New Mexico only to find Pueblo Indians living in poverty. Perhaps to rid themselves of him, the Indians suggested to Coronado that he head to what is now Kansas: there he would find the riches he sought. Many historians believe he traveled through southeastern Colorado on his way to Kansas. He never found his gold. At about this time, the Spanish gave the area its name: *Colorado,* which means "reddish" or "ruddy."

Over the next few hundred years, as the Spanish moved north and settled in the Rio Grande Valley of New Mexico, they played a major role in the history of Colorado. Although they never established any permanent settlements in the state, Spain claimed all the land south of the Arkansas River and west of the Continental Divide. The Spanish friars Dominguez and Escalante provided one of the first written accounts of Colorado. These men left Santa Fe (northern New Mexico) in the summer of 1776, looking for a route to the new Spanish settlement in San Francisco, California. Their journey took them through much of southwestern Colorado. Poor relations with the Indians persisted throughout Spain's colonization of the New World—perhaps stiff taxes and enslavement had something to do with it! This disregard for Native American culture on the part of the Spanish was repeated in later years by Anglo-Americans.

After the Louisiana Purchase in 1803, the United States doubled in size. This largely uncharted land was acquired from Napoleon Bonaparte, ruler of the French empire, in one of the best real estate deals of all time. Expeditions were sent west to explore the new territory, which included northeastern Colorado. In 1806 Lt. Zebulon Pike led the first expedition to Colorado via the Arkansas River. Though a rather inept pathfinder, Pike did manage to explore much of southern Colorado before being captured in Spanish territory along the Rio Grande in the San Luis Valley (he thought he was on the Red River of Texas).

Another significant expedition was conducted in 1820 by Maj. Stephen H. Long. Entering Colorado on the South Platte River, Long explored much of the Front Range—which is the region lying just east of the Colorado Rockies—before leaving along the Arkansas River. Unimpressed with the land along the Front Range, Long called it the "Great American Desert" and "unfit for cultivation." He was wrong, though, as eastern Colorado went on to support some of the most productive agricultural land in the western United States. Later expeditions in the 1840s by John C. Frémont and in 1853 by Capt. John Gunnison added knowledge about Colorado's complex geography.

In the 1820s the trading and trapping era began, as beaver hats became the rage in Europe and the eastern United States. High prices paid for beaver pelts swayed a number of adventurous trappers to venture into the wilds of Colorado. These men were the real pioneers and included Jim Bridger, Jim Beckwourth, Jedediah Smith and Kit Carson. After Mexico achieved independence from Spain in 1821, trade between this new country and the United States blossomed. To facilitate trade, the Santa Fe Trail was established between St. Louis, Missouri, and Santa Fe. In the late 1820s traders William and Charles Bent and Ceran St. Vrain built Bent's Fort along the Mountain Branch of the Santa Fe Trail that passed through southeastern Colorado. For almost 20 years the fort served as a base for western trade with Mexico and the Pacific Coast.

When beaver hats fell out of fashion in the 1830s, trappers looked around for an alternative income and found it in hunting buffalo. The Plains Indians were concerned, and rightly so, that the buffalo slaughter threatened their way of life. Short-term relations were soothed by trading trinkets, guns and liquor. Even so, within a few short decades the buffalo were hunted almost to extinction.

By 1846 relations between the United States and Mexico deteriorated to such a point that the Mexican War broke out. Two years later, Mexico ceded its land in present-day Colorado to U.S. victors in the Treaty of Guadalupe Hidalgo. The United States, however, agreed to honor Mexican land grants in extreme southern Colorado. These grants had been given by the Mexican government to individuals who agreed to establish settlements in remote northern areas of the Mexican frontier. In 1852 Hispanic settlers, moving into what is now southern Colorado, established San Luis, the first permanent town in the state. A number of other settlements followed. Today this area is still a cradle of Hispanic culture.

Colorado's most notable modern era kicked into gear in 1858 when William Green Russell and his party from Georgia discovered gold along Dry Creek near present-day Denver. Hundreds of anxious miners made their way to the mining camps of Denver City and Auraria in the Pikes Peak Gold Rush. Many returned east in disgust calling the strike a hoax, but gold strikes by George Jackson near Idaho Springs and by John Gregory near Central City in the spring of 1859 proved the early rush was well founded and thousands more streamed into the territory. Publicity in eastern newspapers also prompted fortune seekers to head west, and in the early 1860s towns sprang up along the Front Range and in the mountains at Breckenridge, Fairplay and Georgetown, among other places. Denver quickly grew as a supply town for the mining camps.

In February 1861 the Colorado Territory was established, which was a step toward statehood and self-rule for the new residents. When the Civil War broke out in 1862, however, the Colorado Territory fell on hard times. Many miners left to fight, and the Plains Indians used this preoccupation with the war to begin a series of raids on new settlers. Angered by the encroachment on their hunting grounds and disregard for Indian culture, Arapaho and Cheyenne intensified their strikes between 1862 and 1864. The conflict reached a bloody climax when over 100 Indians, including women and children, were slaughtered by volunteer troops in the Sand Creek Massacre (see the **Southeast Plains** chapter). Although there were a few more uprisings, Sand Creek was really the death knell for the Indians of Colorado's eastern plains.

By the late 1860s most of the easily obtainable gold from streambeds in the territory had been snatched up. Miners were now forced to dig shafts into the mountains to get at the gold ore. The problem was that gold proved difficult to extract from the ore; a cheap processing method was badly needed. In 1868 Prof. Nathaniel Hill solved the ore reduction problem and opened his Boston and Colorado smelter in Black Hawk.

In the 1870s and 1880s Colorado mining really boomed. Prospectors pushed farther west into the mountains, discovering new mining areas. Silver was mined and soon became more dominant than gold. After Colorado achieved statehood in 1876, it received the nickname "Silver State." Georgetown and Silver Cliff were large silver mining towns, but nothing could compare to the deposits near Leadville. When silver was discovered in Leadville in 1877, the population soared from less than 100 to more than 24,000 within a few months. Many fortunes were made.

The quest for new mining areas created a conflict with another of Colorado's Indian tribes—the Utes. The Utes roamed the mountains of Colorado following herds of deer, elk, buffalo and antelope. At first they were friendly with the Anglo settlers, especially since these strange-looking newcomers made war on the Arapaho and Cheyenne, the Utes' bitter enemies on the plains. Under the guidance of Chief Ouray, the Utes accepted a series of treaties with the U.S. government, which continued to reduce their territory. Finally, after a band of northern Utes killed Indian agent Nathan Meeker in the Meeker Massacre of 1879 (see the **Meeker** chapter), the tribe was relocated to Utah and a small reservation in southwestern Colorado. Anglo settlers now reigned over the whole state.

Another major factor in Colorado's development was the arrival of the railroads. In 1870 the Denver Pacific spur was completed, connecting Denver to the Union Pacific's transcontinental line at Cheyenne, Wyoming. Soon after, other railroads snaked through the state, including the Denver & Rio Grande. Well-engineered narrow-gauge railroads chugged along to out-of-the-way mountain mining towns, providing an inexpensive means of shipping ore to the smelters and supplies to the towns. Remnants of these mountain rail lines can be found in many locations throughout the state.

In addition to the mining industry, cattle ranching on the eastern plains helped fuel the state's economy for a couple of decades before homesteaders began farming much of the land. Ambitious irrigation projects turned the arid land along the Lower Arkansas River Valley and the South Platte Valley near Greeley into lush farmland by the late 1880s. This diversification of Colorado's economy came not a moment too soon, as troubling times for the mining industry were just around the corner.

In 1893 the U.S. government abandoned the silver standard, causing silver prices to plummet. Colorado's economy was hit heavily—mines shut down and, in a span of a few days, 10 banks closed in Denver. Despite a large gold strike at Cripple Creek that produced through the 1890s and into the 1900s, Colorado's glory days of mining were over. With the new century came an increased emphasis on agriculture and a new industry—tourism.

During the Great Depression of the 1930s, projects by the Civilian Conservation Corps (CCC) and the Works Progress Administration (WPA) helped develop Colorado's national forest land and highway system, making it easier for visitors to enjoy the state's beauty. Irrigation projects, including the enormous Big Thompson diversion in north-central Colorado, brought water from the state's Western Slope of the Continental Divide through tunnels in the mountains to the more heavily populated Eastern Slope.

With World War II came an interest in Colorado by the Air Force. High altitude and good weather made Colorado an ideal training area for pilots. Some bases have closed, but military facilities continue to be important in Colorado—most notably the Air Force Academy in Colorado Springs. Although the extremely cyclical oil and gas industry put a damper on the state's economy in the 1980s, Colorado has rebounded with its steady base in transportation, light manufacturing, ranching, agriculture and high-tech industry. But none of these is as exciting to a visitor as downhill skiing and other components of the tourism boom.

For more information on Colorado history, contact the **Colorado Historical Society, 1300 Broadway, Denver, CO 80203; 303-866-3355; www.coloradohistory.org.**

Suggested Reading

A Colorado Reader (Pruett Publishing, 1995), edited by Carl Ubbelohde, Maxine Benson and Duane Smith, is the best complete history we've been able to find. While driving through the state, carry along James McTighe's well-organized and lively *Roadside History of Colorado* (Johnson Books, 1989). *The Colorado Book* (Fulcrum Publishing, 1993) is an excellent collection of writings on the state by famous authors, celebrities and others. For an in-depth look at the state's ghost towns and mining camps, as seen through the eyes of artist Muriel Sibell Wolle, read her classic *Stampede to Timberline* (second revised edition, Swallow, 1974). For a historical travel perspective, it's tough to match *The WPA Guide to 1930s Colorado* (University Press of Kansas, 1987). *The Archaeology of Colorado* (Johnson Books, 1983) by E. Steve Cassells provides a useful and readable account of human prehistory in Colorado.

Geography and Geology

Some residents say if Colorado were ironed out, its area would be larger than that of Texas. This may be an exaggeration, but it does draw attention to Colorado's most distinctive feature—the Rocky Mountains. The Rockies slice north-south through the state with 54 peaks rising higher than 14,000 feet, including the highest "14er," Mt. Elbert at 14,433 feet. The Great Plains, covering the eastern third of Colorado, extend east to Kansas and Nebraska and north into Wyoming. On the western side of the Rockies, the Colorado Plateau is characterized by great canyons and valleys.

A collection of weathered wagons near Guffy. Photo by Bruce Caughey.

Along the spine of the Rockies lies the Continental Divide, which acts as a watershed for North America. All waters on the Western Slope drain into the Pacific, while Eastern Slope waters eventually drain into the Gulf of Mexico. Colorado encompasses the headwaters for more than 10 major rivers, including western giants such as the Colorado, Rio Grande, Arkansas and Platte.

Looking at the rugged peaks, deep canyons and windswept plains of Colorado, one doesn't have to be a scientist to guess that the state has had a long, active geologic past. This history began 300 million years ago with the uplift of the Ancestral Rockies. These mountains consisted of two ranges similar to the present-day Rockies, located 100 miles west of today's Front Range. After 20 million years, the uplift ceased and erosion began. A million years of exposure to water, wind and ice eroded away the Ancestral Rockies to small hills similar to the Appalachian Mountains of the eastern United States. Remnants of these ancient mountains can be seen in the red formations throughout the mountains of Colorado (Red Rocks, Garden of the Gods and the area around Vail are good examples).

During this period of erosion, a shallow inland sea covered most of North America, including Colorado. The water level of this sea varied greatly, causing the formation of huge coastal plains, which, because of a very dry climate, sometimes resembled a desert with wind-blown sand and dunes. This was especially true in western Colorado.

Later the climate became more humid. Rivers meandered over the coastal plains, and the "desert" was transformed into a lush, green, sometimes swampy environment. This period, between 200 and 65 million years ago, was the age of the dinosaurs. Fossils of more than 70 dinosaur species have been found in the Morrison Formation of Colorado, including the bones of the largest brontosaurus ever excavated. Near the end of this period, the inland sea once again engulfed most of Colorado, depositing thick layers of shale over most of the state.

The present-day Rockies began to form 65 million years ago and continued forming for 20 million years during an event called the Laramide Orogeny. Forces within the earth pushed up the Precambrian "basement" rock by 15,000 to 25,000 feet. The previously deposited layers on top of the much older Precambrian rock folded, buckled and cracked. Today these soft layers have been eroded away to expose the harder, more resistant Precambrian rock. Evidence of this monumental event can be seen throughout Colorado, where layers that had once lain flat have been violently forced up to almost vertical positions.

Forty million years ago in southwestern Colorado, volcanoes erupted over and over again, expelling immense amounts of gas, lava and ash. This period continued for 30 million years. Before some of the magma could reach the surface, it solidified into dikes, sills and laccoliths. Today erosion has exposed these features. Sleeping Ute Mountain near Cortez is a good example of a huge laccolith, as are the dikes radiating from the Spanish Peaks near La Veta. This highly volcanic area includes the San Juan Mountains, the West Elk Mountains and the Flat Tops Plateau. Beginning 28 million years ago (and lasting 23 million years), Colorado land was uplifted by 5,000 feet, yet the overall make-up of the region really didn't change.

From 75,000 to 10,000 years ago, glaciers helped carve and shape the mountains of Colorado. Many glaciers in the higher mountains created cirque valleys, characterized by the U-shaped walls and floor instead of the normal V shape of a stream-formed valley. This U shape forms because the glacier scours out the bottom of the valley.

Suggested Reading

One of the best sources for detailed geological information is *Roadside Geology of Colorado* (Mountain Press Publishing Co., 1986) by Halka Chronic.

Flora and Fauna

Colorado's terrain varies enormously, stretching from grassland to glacier, from 4,000 feet above sea level to over 14,000 feet. With such dramatic variances, there are no less than eight separate ecosystems in the state. These conditions set the stage for Colorado's diversity of plant and animal life. Within an hour's drive you can go from viewing prairie dogs on the high plains near Denver to looking at mountain goats and rare alpine plants high on the slopes of Mt. Evans.

The eastern plains grasslands are home to a community of songbirds, including Colorado's state bird, the lark bunting, as well as to raptors such as red-tailed hawks and bald eagles. Game birds include grouse, ducks, geese and pheasants. Among the yucca and prickly pear cactus you'll also find pronghorn antelope, prairie rattlesnakes, coyotes, foxes and badgers.

In the mountains, black bears, bighorn sheep and elk are among the leading citizens. The predominant trees of the high country are pines, spruce and aspens. Autumn brings the shimmering gold, red and purple hues of the changing aspen leaves, while summer produces a plethora of columbine, Indian paintbrush, fairy slipper and other colorful wildflowers.

A great variety of fish species live within Colorado's reservoirs, lakes and rivers. Bass, walleye, catfish, bluegills and wipers inhabit the lower elevations. Trout and kokanee salmon are among the fish swimming in the mountain streams and lakes.

Throughout the book we have tried to include information about the predominant flora and fauna in different parts of the state, but you may want to learn more. The State of Colorado manages more than 250 wildlife areas, which serve as prime observation points, especially for bird-watchers. The **Colorado Division of Wildlife (6060 Broadway, Denver, CO 80216; 303-297-1192; www.wildlife.state. co.us)** will be happy to answer questions about wildlife or provide brochures and pamphlets. The **U.S. Fish and Wildlife Service (P.O. Box 25486, Denver Federal Center, Denver, CO 80225-0207; 303-236-7904; www.fws.gov)** stands ready with information about the national wildlife refuges in the state.

Suggested Reading

An excellent source of information is *From Grassland to Glacier: The Natural History of Colorado* (Johnson Books, 1984), by Cornelia Fleischer Mutel and John C. Emerick. This highly readable book describes the ecosystems of Colorado in easy-to-understand terms. *Explore Colorado— A Naturalist's Notebook* (Denver Museum of Natural History and Westcliffe Publishers, 1995), by Frances Alley Kruger and Carron A. Meaney, is an appealing collection of photos and drawings of Colorado-specific flora and fauna. *The Guide to Colorado Birds* (Westcliffe Publishers, 1998), by Mary Taylor Gray, provides a well-organized companion with crisp color photos of the state's many birds. *Guide to Colorado Wildflowers* (Westcliffe Publishers, 1995), by G. K. Guennel, comes in two volumes: *Plains and Foothills* and *Mountains*. Both volumes are colorful and comprehensive.

Climate

Colorado's weather varies enough to suit anyone's tastes and is therefore tough to generalize. Because the Rocky Mountains cut through the middle of the state, creating their own uncertain weather patterns, forecasting is something of a nightmare. These high peaks attract snow flurries almost any time of year, but once November arrives, large quantities of snow stick around for winter. Thanks to crisp winter weather and powder snow, skiing rules the high country from November through April; Colorado is an outdoor playground for hikers, campers, anglers and sightseers the rest of the year. Snow cover remains at the highest locations until summer when long, pleasant days finally melt away winter's residue. Driving in the mountains during or after a snowfall can be treacherous. For **road conditions** contact **303-639-1111; www. dot.state.co.us.**

You can count on cool nights even in midsummer as the thin mountain air loses its heat. The dry climate, however, takes some of the swelter out of summer and some of the bite out of winter, making it a pleasant place despite temperature extremes. Denver, at the eastern foot of the Rockies, almost qualifies as a desert, with merely 15 inches of annual precipitation. Once in a while a heat wave comes through and the temperatures rise over 100° F. The Front Range of the Rockies enjoys more than 300 days of sunshine each year, but afternoon rain showers are commonplace in summer.

In Colorado you can experience all four seasons in one day, so dressing for unpredictable weather is something of an art. A good rule is to be prepared for anything by wearing layers. In summer be prepared for cool mornings and evenings, hot midday temperatures and afternoon rainstorms. Winter requires a warm jacket, hat and gloves. When you're exploring the high country, summer or winter, be sure to take along sunscreen. For a quick Denver and Front Range **weather forecast,** check television station websites; perhaps the best is **www.9news.com,** with many live cameras around the city.

Visitor Information

For visitor information, the **Colorado Travel and Tourism Authority (CTTA)** is perhaps the best place to begin. The CTTA offers good general information about the state and can refer you to many clubs and organizations for more specifics. Contact them at **1-800-COLORADO; www.colorado.com.**

Stop in at the **Welcome Centers** at the major entry points when you drive into Colorado. These centers, generally open daily in summer from 8 A.M. to 5 P.M. (winter hours may vary greatly), are located in **Ft. Collins, Burlington, Cortez, Dinosaur, Fruita, Julesburg, Lamar** and **Trinidad; www.dola.state.co.us/ fs/welcome.htm.** Local volunteers and some staff members serve as great resources for the whole state (you will leave swamped with pamphlets and new travel ideas).

Other excellent information can be found on the Internet. Many destinations and resorts offer websites—we have included many addresses in each chapter—and of course you can use a search engine to find relevant information. Exceptional

A marmot peeks out from its rocky, high-alpine home on Mount Evans. Photo by Bruce Caughey.

information is available from the **State of Colorado (www.state.co.us), National Park Service (www.nps.gov), Bureau of Land Management (www.blm.gov), U.S. Forest Service (www.fs.fed.us), U.S. Fish and Wildlife Service (www.fws.gov)** and **Colorado Ski Country USA (www.skicolorado.org),** as well as from many ski resorts and area chambers of commerce.

For specific destinations, it's a pretty safe bet to start with each area's chamber of commerce (see the Services section at the end of each chapter). One of the largest organizations offering information about the entire state is the **Denver Metro Convention and Visitors Bureau, 1555 California, Suite 300, Denver, CO 80202; 1-800-233-6837; 303-892-1112; www.denver.org.**

Tips for Visitors

Health and Safety

It might be helpful to understand a few common maladies that sometimes plague visitors to Colorado.

Altitude Sickness (pulmonary edema)— If you feel a persistent headache, nausea or dizziness (or in severe cases a buildup of fluid in your lungs), you might be experiencing problems due to rapid elevation gain. Mountain climbers and skiers especially need to be aware that your body needs time to adjust (especially above 8,000 feet). If untreated by an increase in oxygen levels, altitude sickness can be potentially life threatening.

Dehydration—It's important to replace body fluids, especially when engaging in Colorado's many strenuous outdoor activities. If you feel symptoms such as intense thirst, dizziness and higher heart and breath rates, increase your intake of fluids.

Giardia—Hikers and backpackers should be sure to purify stream and lake water before taking a single sip. A single-cell parasite, *Giardia lamblia,* can make your life miserable (severe cramps and diarrhea are common symptoms) within a day or two of drinking contaminated water.

Hypothermia—Prolonged exposure to the cold may cause your body temperature to drop, inducing a slowed heart rate, lethargy and confusion. Get immediate medical help and try to get to a warm place.

Sunburn—Colorado's higher elevation provides less protection from the sun's ultraviolet rays. Lather up with sunscreen, even if there's cloud cover, or you'll be sorry. Skiers should be really careful because the snow's reflective power increases the intensity of the sunlight.

Telephones

Four area codes in Colorado serve as prefixes for long-distance telephone numbers; as a general rule the Denver metro region is 303, but newer Denver-area numbers begin with 720; northern Colorado is 970; the southern region is 719. When calling within metro Denver, you must dial the area code before the seven-digit phone number. When calling long distance from within each region, you need to dial 1 plus the desired area code. For long-distance directory assistance, dial the area code plus 555-1212; within Denver dial 1-411. The operator will answer if you dial 0. For emergency assistance, dial 911.

Traffic

Colorado traffic has morphed into a troublesome problem, especially from the Denver area to the mountain resorts along Interstate 70 and back. The interstate gets backed up with skiers and summer travelers heading up to the hills on weekend mornings and almost every Sunday evening as travelers return to town. Of course the traffic is worse during peak ski season and long holiday weekends. Avoid the rush by staying in the hills a bit longer, commuting in off-hours or trying for a midweek escape.

Time

Mountain Standard Time (Colorado) is two hours earlier than Eastern Standard Time (New York) and one hour later than Pacific Standard Time (California).

Getting There

Colorado lies virtually at the geographic center of the United States, and Denver is the largest city in the Rocky Mountain region. It's natural for the city to be an important transportation hub. **Denver International Airport** makes a strong statement about the direction of the city's future and provides a visual connection to the snowcapped peaks to the west. Lying 24 miles northeast of downtown, Denver International is the largest in size (53 square miles) and one of the busiest of the airports in the world. Five runways and 94 gates enable daily nonstop flights to more than 100 cities (more than 1,300 flights), including nonstops to Europe. From Denver International you can make connecting flights to destinations in Colorado, including Aspen, Colorado Springs, Pueblo, Grand Junction, Durango, Steamboat Springs, Telluride, Gunnison and Crested Butte.

The vast concourses, sprawling layout and tentlike architecture of the airport can be intimidating, but its logic reveals itself after a couple of visits. An underground transit system whisks people from the gate area over to the main terminal, where rental cars, taxis and hotel reservations await. For a bargain on parking, pull off at the outlying lots and take a bus into the terminal. For more information, contact the airport's main information number, **1-800-247-2336,** or visit **www.flydenver.com.** To reach the airport from downtown Denver, head east on I-70 past Chambers Rd. and turn north on Peña Blvd. From the southern metro area, the toll road E-470 whisks travelers directly to the airport.

Air travelers to and from Colorado are discovering **Colorado Springs Airport (719-550-1900; www.flycos.com),** located about 70 miles south of Denver. It offers service to many regional and national destinations. The airport handles more than 100 direct flights per day and is served by most major carriers. **Black and White Transportation Services** offers shuttle service between the two airports; **719-227-9201; 719-499-0301; www.black-n-white-trans-inc.com.**

Trains are no longer a way of life in the West, but the **Amtrak** East Coast to West Coast route, passing through Denver and Glenwood Canyon, is one of the prettiest rides imaginable. For information, stop in at downtown Denver's Union Station or contact **1-800-872-7245** or **www.amtrak.com.**

A restored barn reminds visitors of simpler days in the Crystal River Valley. Photo by Bruce Caughey.

From virtually any point in the country, you can take a **Greyhound** bus into Denver. From there you can ride a bus to many towns in the state. **1055 19th St., Denver; 1-800-231-2222; 303-293-6555; www.greyhound.com.**

Getting Around

To really experience the back roads of Colorado away from the major highways, you should have your own vehicle; many national rental companies can help you. Try **Budget Rentals (1-800-527-0700; www.drivebudget.com)** or **Hertz (1-800-654-3131; www.hertz. com).** On a tight budget, consider renting at **Cut Rate,** where they will rent you a late-model American car (with snow tires and ski racks if necessary) by the day, week or month (two-day minimum in peak seasons); **8000 E. Colfax, Denver; 303-393-0028.** A side note: hitchhiking in Colorado is legal, but rides come infrequently. You can easily use van service from Denver to the mountain resorts by contacting any number of van companies. For frequent service to Summit County and Vail, try **Colorado Mountain Express; 1-800-222-2112; www. cmex.com.**

Additional ways of getting around include catching a connecting flight from Denver International Airport or Colorado Springs Airport to mountain resorts. **Greyhound Bus Lines** makes daily runs to many Front Range and mountain towns and offers frequent buses from the airport to the downtown bus station; **1055 19th St., Denver; 1-800-231-2222; 303-293-6555.** The **Ski Train** makes runs from Denver to Winter Park Ski Area every Sat.–Sun. in winter (except Dec. 23, 24 and 31); **1701 Wynkoop at Union Station; 303-296-ISKI; www.skitrain.com.**

Information for Persons with Disabilities

Colorado is continually improving services to disabled travelers. Perhaps that's one reason that Colorado is home to a larger percentage of physically challenged citizens than any other state. Many organizations do exemplary jobs of providing outdoor recreation for people with special needs. **Winter Park** has the largest handicapped ski program in the country. **Wilderness on Wheels** (see the **South Park and 285 Corridor** chapter) offers a system of wide, wooden boardwalks along a trout-filled creek. **The Colorado State Parks, U.S. Forest Service and National Park Service** have all worked to create more accessible campgrounds and facilities. Lodging opportunities have opened up, and most smaller lodges and bed and breakfasts now feature rooms for guests who use wheelchairs. Persons with disabilities may receive helpful information from the **Colorado Association of Community Centered Boards** at **303-832-1618** or **www. caccb.org.**

How This Book Is Organized

The Colorado Guide is designed to be visitor-friendly. The book is arranged in six geographic regions: Northwest, North Central, Northeast, Southwest, South Central and Southeast. Each region, with a map pinpointing its location in the state, is divided into destination areas, 40 in all. Background information about each destination sets the scene: general introduction, history and directions on getting there. Specific information is then provided on the major attractions, festivals and events, outdoor activities, sightseeing highlights, lodging and camping, restaurants and services. Website information is included throughout. Within each chapter, you will find all you need to plan a terrific trip. The index at the back of the book is an added help.

Following is a look at the principal subject areas that we cover in each chapter:

Festivals and Events

A full calendar of festivals and events takes place throughout Colorado; from these, we have selected some of the most outstanding to include in each chapter. The mountain towns have beefed up their festival and entertainment options to help attract more visitors. Some

events are worth planning your vacation around, while others may merit only a detour. In summer, **Telluride** is known for its wide array of artistic events, including the renowned bluegrass festival. Any mention of music must include **Aspen,** which is the best place for a summer's worth. Rodeo is another Rocky Mountain favorite—the National Western Stock Show in **Denver** should not be missed, and mountain towns often have their own summer rodeos. Just south of Denver, in Castle Rock, the Castle Pines Golf Club is home to the annual (PGA) international golf tournament. Colorado is also known for any number of marathons, ultramarathons, triathlons and bike races throughout the year. Check *Rocky Mountain Sports Magazine,* free at sporting goods stores, for information on events; also at **www.rockymountainsports.com.**

Outdoor Activities

BIKING
Mountain Biking
Colorado, with its maze of backcountry logging and mining roads, is ideally suited for this hugely popular sport. Indeed, the state has even hosted the world championships. Mountain bikes, equipped with up to two dozen gears, a sturdy alloy frame and wide, knobby tires, are perfectly suited for rough rides. Some adventurous souls prefer single-track riding, which essentially involves riding on hiking trails. As long as mountain bikers respect the rights of people on foot, this is fine. Mountain bikes are allowed on most public land, but remain strictly prohibited in wilderness areas and other posted areas. Since fat-tire riding has become so popular, many extensive trail systems have been developed, and rentals are available in many towns. **Crested Butte, Durango, Winter Park** and **Steamboat Springs** in particular have become well-known centers for the sport. For an extended ride from alpine to desert terrain, consider the **San Juan Hut System** (see the **Telluride** chapter) between Telluride and Moab, Utah, or the Kokopelli Trail (see the **Grand Junction**

chapter), which follows the Colorado River through mesa and canyon country.

Bicycle Touring

With a good road map you can bicycle tour anywhere in the state. Of course, there are some outstanding rides, such as at the **Colorado National Monument** (see the **Grand Junction** chapter) and along the maintained **bike path between Breckenridge and Vail** (see the **Summit County** chapter). Hard-surface, greenway trails throughout and between many communities have exploded in number over the past 10 years, earning Colorado praise and a reputation as one of the most bike-friendly places in the nation. Taking advantage of the state's topography and natural beauty, many multi-day ride events attract participants from around the country and the world. Some of the standout occasions include *The Denver Post* **Ride the Rockies** weeklong event and the **MS-150** from Denver to the Royal Gorge.

Suggested Reading

For a selection of mountain bike rides across the state, with topographic maps, pick up a copy of William Stoehr's *Bicycling the Backcountry* (Pruett Publishing, 1987). You might also try *Mountain Biking Colorado's Historic Mining Districts* (Fulcrum Publishing, 1991), by Laura Rosseter. A good bet for touring is the *Colorado Cycling Guide* (Pruett Publishing, 1990), by Jean Alley and Hartley Alley. In addition, many books can be found for specific destinations around the state.

FISHING

Colorado, with more than 65,000 miles of streams and nearly 2,500 coldwater lakes and reservoirs (and 36 warmwater lakes and reservoirs), provides a kaleidoscope of fishing opportunities. Getting away from it all, clearing your brain of every thought except landing a big brown trout, is what Colorado angling is all about—no matter if you are into fishing with a minuscule dry fly or with a No. 6 hook and a worm. We have carefully selected better-than-average public waters to include in each chapter—but as you know, this is no guarantee of good fishing.

We mention the following special designations throughout: **Gold Medal water,** the highest-quality trout water in Colorado, offering the greatest potential for catching large numbers of fish, including trophy-sized trout; and **Wild Trout water,** which supports self-sustaining trout populations. A Colorado fishing license is a must for fishing on all public water; resident and nonresident licenses are available at most sporting goods stores. These stores are also a great source of information—as long as you keep in mind that they would love to sell you armloads of tackle. When buying your license, be sure to pick up a copy of *Colorado Fishing and Land and Water Use Information* for specific details on restrictions and regulations throughout the state. For more information contact the **Colorado Division of Wildlife, Central Regional Office, 6060 Broadway, Denver, CO 80216; 303-297-1192.** The Division of Wildlife provides up-to-date fishing and stocking reports by region: **Denver Metro area, 303-291-7535; Northeast, 303-291-7536; Southeast, 303-291-7538; Northwest, 303-291-7537; Southwest, 303-291-7539; general information, 303-291-7533; www.wildlife. state.co.us.**

Suggested Reading

For a comprehensive look at Colorado's fly-fishing opportunities, full of useful reference materials, check out Marty Bartholomew's *Flyfisher's Guide to Colorado* (Wilderness Adventures Press, 1998).

FOUR-WHEEL-DRIVE TRIPS

Jeeping in the Colorado Rockies is big. Logging and mining roads built as far back as the 1860s provide access to ghost towns and some of the most spectacular scenery in the country. Jeep tour and rental companies are scattered throughout the mountain towns. No matter whether you take to the back roads on a guided trip or are driving your own vehicle, be sure to pack out all your trash. Please don't drive off existing roads, as this promotes erosion; it's especially important above treeline where the fragile alpine tundra will quickly die if driven on. A number of standout four-wheel-drive trips are discussed in the chapters of this book, especially around **Ouray, Telluride, Silverton** and **Creede.** Information about jeeping on public land is available from the **U.S. Forest Service, P.O. Box 25127, Lakewood, CO 80225; 740 Simms St., Golden, CO 80401; 303-275-5350; www.fs.fed.us/r2.** The **U.S. Bureau of Land Management** is another great source of information at **2850 Youngfield St., Lakewood, CO 80215; 303-239-3600; www.blm. gov.** And you can't beat the trail ideas and descriptions provided by the Colorado Off-Highway Vehicle Coalition at **www.cohvco.org.**

Suggested Reading

The Colorado Pass Book (Pruett Publishing, 2000), by Don Koch, offers terrific descriptions of many of Colorado's back-road mountain passes. Refreshingly, there's even a section on responsible back-road driving! One of the best guides to the ghost towns of Colorado is *Jeep Trails to Colorado Ghost Towns* (Caxton Press, 1972), by Robert L. Brown.

GOLF

With 300 days of sunshine per year, challenging topography and drop-dead beautiful scenery, Colorado's a perfect location for golfers. And indeed, Colorado offers plenty of opportunities, with some courses rivaling any in the country. If you plan to play golf in the mountains, practice your putting ahead of time—the difficult break in mountain greens continues to baffle pros and amateurs alike. Also keep in mind that at this high altitude, the ball travels much farther than at sea level—you may want to club down. Although the mountain courses are open only in summer and early fall, many courses on the Western Slope and along the Front Range (including Denver) are open year-round. Greens fees for 18 holes can vary anywhere from approximately $15 to $200; the mountain resorts tend to charge much more than city courses. Due to the constantly changing fees, we do not list specific prices in this book. But don't worry—we'll warn you if the greens fees are steep.

A number of celebrity and PGA tournaments take place throughout the state. For information about tournaments, course locations, golf schools, course dress codes or anything else connected with golfing in Colorado, contact the comprehensive website **www.golfcolorado.com.** Another information source is the **Colorado Golf Association, 7465 E. 1st Ave., Suite C, Denver, CO 80230; 303-366-GOLF; www. golfhousecolorado.org.**

HIKING AND BACKPACKING

For our money (or lack of it), one of the best ways to experience the varied and beautiful country of Colorado is by getting into the backcountry for a hike. The state is set up for it. Public lands include 11 national forests, 33 wilderness areas, Bureau of Land Management domain, 3 national parks, 4 national monuments, more than 200 state and federal wildlife areas and 41 state parks.

National forest land is administered by offices scattered throughout the state. Destinations bordering on national forest land will have the local address for the ranger office. These folks provide a wealth of information for hiking and other outdoor pursuits. They also offer printed material, including the useful *Recreational Opportunity Guide* and Forest Service maps. For general information about the national forests in Colorado, contact the **U.S. Forest Service, P.O. Box 25127, Lakewood, CO 80225; 740 Simms St., Golden, CO 80401; 303-275-5350; www.fs.fed.us/r2.**

Wilderness areas, located within the national forests, are so designated to retain their pristine nature. They differ primarily from the rest of the national forest land in that no motorized vehicles or mountain bikes are allowed. Aside from that, a few extra rules apply, as well as some very important wilderness ethics. Maintaining the unspoiled beauty of these areas is a monumental task; everyone needs to help.

Here are a few suggested outdoor practices (known as Leave No Trace ethics) that you should apply to any trip, whether it's in a wilderness area or at a roadside picnic table:

- Stay on existing trails. Straying off the trails kills vegetation and promotes erosion, especially on alpine tundra.
- Use gas stoves, especially at high altitudes where firewood is scarce and slow to replenish itself. If you absolutely need a fire, use an existing fire ring.
- Wash at least 100 feet from water sources; use biodegradable soap.
- Carry a small shovel or trowel to bury human waste 6 to 8 inches below the ground.
- Pack out all trash: don't bury it.
- Leave pets at home: they disturb the wildlife.
- Camp at least 100 feet from trails, streams and lakes. Choose a site in the woods rather than in an open meadow, for protection of the meadow as well as for your own privacy and that of other hikers.
- Use existing campsites to protect unused areas.
- Take only pictures and leave only footprints. Leave your camp in better shape than you found it.

The **Bureau of Land Management,** which oversees an enormous amount of acreage in Colorado, has been focusing more on use of its land for recreation; there are some incredible opportunities, from high alpine climbs to desert canyon hikes. Contact the **BLM** at **2850 Youngfield, Lakewood, CO 80215; 303-239-3600; www.co.blm.gov.** For information about hiking opportunities at **Colorado State Parks: 1313 Sherman St., Room 618, Denver, CO 80203; 303-866-3437; www.coloradoparks.org.**

Colorado's ever-changing weather conditions can be a real problem for unprepared hikers. You should always have warm clothing and waterproof rain gear in the high country to help avoid hypothermia. Speaking of the high country, altitude sickness (pulmonary edema) can strike anyone, especially those unaccustomed to higher elevations. Take time to adjust to the high altitude—don't go out and climb a 14,000-foot peak the day after arriving from sea level. Afternoon thunderstorms frequent the mountains in summer; lightning strikes above treeline are common. Another precaution involves the hundreds of old, abandoned mines scattered throughout the state. It's very likely that you'll come across one or two of them. If you do, stay out! They are very dangerous and can contain toxic gases, hidden shafts and rotten timbers, among other hazards.

One of the most exciting developments in Colorado is the tremendous effort going into regional and statewide trail planning and projects. One highlight is the **Colorado Trail.** This 469-mile trail stretching from Denver to Durango was 15 years in the making. It crosses national forest and private land, winding through low-lying valleys and over high passes along the Continental Divide. Sections of the trail are mentioned in appropriate chapters throughout this book. If you want more information about this trail or are considering hiking its entire length, contact the U.S. Forest Service. Pick up a copy of the excellent book *The Colorado Trail: The Official Guidebook* (Westcliffe, 1994), by Randy Jacobs. It comes in handy along the trail and in planning your trip; the book includes stunning photos by John Fielder and maps.

For topographic maps of Colorado, stop in at sporting goods stores or visit the **U.S. Geological Survey** at the Denver Federal Center; **P.O. Box 25286, DFC Building 810, Denver, CO 80225; 303-202-4700; www.edc.usgs.gov/webglis.** The *Colorado Gazetteer* is an excellent and comprehensive resource for all topo maps in Colorado; it's available at most outdoor recreation stores.

Suggested Reading

One of our favorites for nontechnical route information and a relaxed, informative style is

A young visitor plays with snakes while soaking in a natural hot spring on the Yampa River. Photo by Bruce Caughey.

Rocky Mountain Walks (Fulcrum Publishing, 1993), by Gary Ferguson. *Best Hikes with Children in Colorado* (The Mountaineers, 1991), by Maureen Keilty, is an outstanding resource for families. *Colorado's Fourteeners* (Fulcrum Publishing, 1996), by Gerry Roach, provides interesting information about Colorado's highest peaks. Check out the *Guide to the Colorado Mountains* (Colorado Mountain Club, 1992) for great background and route information throughout the state. *Colorado BLM Wildlands* (Westcliffe Publishers, 1992) offers insights into hiking opportunities in lesser-known areas. Many quality hiking books deal with specific regions of the state. *The Complete Guide to Colorado's Wilderness Areas* (Westcliffe Publishers, 1994), by John Fielder and Mark Pearson, includes excellent background about the state's many wilderness areas. *Colorado's Best Wildflower Hikes* (Westcliffe Publishers, 1998), by Pamela Irwin and David Irwin, includes two volumes, covering Colorado's Front Range and High Country with attractive color photos and hiking descriptions.

HORSEBACK RIDING

Colorado is horse country, and you'll feel comfortable wearing a cowboy hat and boots in most towns. We have listed stables in each chapter where applicable; most offer trail rides, breakfast rides and overnight pack trips. If you want a chance to ride every day for a week, consider a dude ranch vacation. For more information about horseback riding, get in touch with the **Colorado Outfitters Association (970-876-0543; www.colorado-outfitters. com)** or the **Colorado Dude and Guest Ranch Association (P.O. Box 2121, Granby, CO 80446; 970-887-3128; www.colorado ranch.com).**

LLAMA TREKKING

In South America, llamas have been domesticated beasts of burden for more than 1,000 years; now they've become the rage in Colorado. You can't hop on the back of a llama and ride off into the sunset, but these lovable cousins of the camel can carry up to 100 pounds of gear on their backs. Just drape a tether over your shoulder and start hiking up a trail—your llama will follow. It's an exotic way to spend an afternoon or, better yet, a few days of vacation. We have listed llama packers at destinations around the state.

RIVER FLOATING

There you are, paddling through a stretch of calm water within a beautiful rock-walled canyon. Suddenly you hear the roar of the approaching rapids. Charging furiously down through the whitewater and maneuvering over a small waterfall, you finally reach calm water once again and have time to catch your breath. If you have the chance, a raft trip down one of Colorado's rivers promises to be an unforgettable part of your vacation.

From the high Rocky Mountains of Colorado, more major rivers begin their long journeys to the ocean than in any other state in the country. When the snow begins to melt each spring and the water levels in the rivers swell, thousands of rafters and kayakers take to the frigid waters for calm floats and hair-raising runs down some of the most challenging rivers in the world. Desert canyon sections of the **Dolores River** and action-filled floats down the **Upper Arkansas, Green** and **Colorado Rivers** are definite highlights. Descriptions of rivers and a few outfitters are listed in appropriate chapters of this book.

Although some people take their own rafts down the rivers, most trips are run through private outfitting companies. Outfitters vary greatly, offering different types of trips, so it's important to decide ahead of time what kind of river experience you are looking for. Colorado's rivers offer the full gamut, from leisurely floats (Class I—easy) to demanding (Class IV—very difficult) multi-day expeditions. A great source is the **Colorado River Outfitters Association; 303-280-2554; www.croa.org.**

Suggested Reading

If you are planning to arrange your own rafting or kayak trip or just want further information about rivers in Colorado, we can still suggest the timeless book *The Floater's Guide to Colorado* (Falcon, 1983), by Doug Wheat.

SKIING

Cross-Country Skiing and Snowshoeing

In wintertime, an almost limitless network of backcountry trails and roads lie concealed beneath a thick blanket of snow. And they are getting used. Gliding across freshly fallen snow on cross-country skis or lightweight snowshoes, away from crowds and expensive lift tickets, is an increasingly attractive alternative for many people. Before heading into the backcountry, find out about **avalanche conditions** at **303-275-5360** or **www.caic.state.co.us.**

There are many groomed trail systems throughout the state that usually charge a small fee. All the mountain resorts have cross-country ski and snowshoe rental shops, which also can be gold mines of valuable advice. Check at a local Forest Service office for additional information, but remember they are usually closed on weekends in winter. Extended backcountry trips can be taken on the **10th Mountain Trail Association Hut System** (see the **Aspen** chapter or **www.huts.org**) and other smaller hut operations. For information online, try **www.colorado-xc.org** for nordic centers, guides, guest ranches, weather and other links.

Downhill Skiing and Snowboarding

Few places in the world rival the abundance of light powder snow, vertical drop and striking views that Colorado provides. With 25 areas to choose from, you should plan your winter getaway with these factors in mind: size and difficulty of the mountain, base village amenities and cost. **Vail** and **Aspen** are world-class resorts in every respect. The four ski areas in Summit County are fast approaching that status, and with **Breckenridge** and **Keystone** resorts owned by Vail, they are on the fast track. Another Summit County resort, **Copper Mountain,** is seeing big changes as a base village springs up at the bottom of the mountain. In a refreshing difference from many other resorts, **Arapahoe Basin,** just up the road from Keystone, remains almost unchanged. If you are in search of a low-key, western atmosphere in a destination with as much mountain as you'd ever desire, make arrangements at **Steamboat Springs, Winter Park, Crested Butte** or **Telluride.** Near Denver, **Loveland** attracts hordes of snowboarders to its wide-open terrain. Smaller family areas such as **Ski Cooper, SolVista** and **Monarch** offer low-cost vacations.

We have written in this guide about all the major ski areas in the state. Turn to the table of contents to find out if there is a full chapter covering the area you are interested in; otherwise, check the index. Almost all ski areas maintain excellent websites with snow reports, lodging deals and statistics (check the Downhill Skiing and Snowboarding section in each chapter). With expanded snow-making capabilities, Colorado's ski season is well under way in November. It peaks during Christmas week and lasts into April (Arapahoe Basin usually stays open until late May or June). Almost every area offers discounted lift tickets early and late in the season. Quite often, reduced-price tickets can be purchased at Denver-area grocery stores and gas stations throughout the season. Many areas offer discount cards in order to build loyalty; Vail's Colorado Card is one of the best available to Colorado residents; **www.coloradocard. com.** It's usually less expensive to rent downhill and snowboard equipment in Denver before heading into the mountains. All-inclusive vacation package deals offered through travel agents are sometimes a bargain.

For more information about downhill skiing, contact **Colorado Ski Country USA, One Civic Center Plaza, 1560 Broadway, Suite 2000, Denver, CO 80202; 303-837-0793; www.coloradoski.com.** Call **303-825-SNOW** for a complete snow report; **303-639-1111** for mountain road conditions.

Suggested Reading

For an excellent guide to trails and tours in Colorado's northern mountains, pick up a copy of *Skiing Colorado's Backcountry* (Fulcrum Publishing, 1989), by Brian Litz and Kurt Langford. Get the lowdown on backcountry hut skiing in *Colorado Hut to Hut: A Guide to Skiing and Biking Colorado's Backcountry* (Westcliffe Publishers, 1992), by Brian Litz. For information on downhill skiing, don't miss Claire Walter's excellent resource, *Rocky Mountain Skiing* (Fulcrum, 1996). Claire Walter also has written a popular guide for snowshoers: *Snowshoeing Colorado* (Fulcrum, 2000).

Seeing and Doing

DINOSAURS

More than 60 million years ago, dinosaurs roamed Colorado, eating plants and each other. Some of the world's most significant dinosaur fossils have been found in Colorado. It's not that the state had more dinosaurs; it's just that the geologic upheaval that formed the Rockies exposed many dinosaur remains. Some of the best places to learn about dinosaurs are in **Grand Junction, Cañon City, Dinosaur National Monument** and the **Denver Museum of Nature and Science.**

HOT SPRINGS

Native Americans found spiritual well-being in Colorado hot springs. Then came the spas for well-to-do tourists in the late 1800s. Colorado is home to many natural hot springs—some are highly developed, while others present a more natural setting. We have tried to uncover the best places to take a relaxing soak. See the Hot Springs section in the chapters on **Glenwood Springs, Pagosa Springs, Ouray** and **Steamboat Springs** for some great ideas. Check out *Colorado's Hot Springs* (Pruett Publishing, 1996), by Deborah Frazier, as a good statewide resource.

MUSEUMS AND GALLERIES

We have included most museums (worth their salt) in the appropriate chapters. With our first-hand descriptions, you should be able to decide if you want to stop for a visit. As far as galleries are concerned, we have tried to cover only those

The San Juans rise suddenly from the close confines of Lake City. Photo by Kirstin Bebell.

that are truly outstanding. In places like **Aspen** or **Denver,** it would be absurd to list the scores of possibilities for viewing and buying art. Check with the chamber of commerce in each destination. The staff, and in many cases the chamber website, will be happy to help you locate galleries and antiques shops.

NIGHTLIFE

So you've tired of museums and sightseeing, and you want to find out where Coloradans hang out. You may want to zero in on some "pints of interest," in the form of brewpubs. Per capita, no place beats Colorado in terms of beer production (it helps that Coors and Budweiser are brewed here, too). Many towns and mountain resorts have brewpubs to quench your thirst. Nightlife options also include comedy clubs, live music, country and western dancing, sporting events and cultural happenings. These activities and more are covered in the Nightlife section of each chapter.

SCENIC DRIVES

It's tough to avoid beautiful scenery while driving in Colorado. We've still managed to find some atypical routes that offer vibrant scenery and often some historically relevant attractions along the way. Unlike the outings described in the Four-Wheel-Drive Trips sections, all of the routes we include under Scenic Drives can be traveled in passenger cars. Colorado's more spectacular roadways have been designated as Scenic and Historic Byways. Anytime you find a distinctive sign emblazoned with a blue columbine, you've managed to find a designated Scenic Byway. A few of these routes are destined for fame, including our favorites: the San Juan Skyway (see the **Durango** chapter) and Trail Ridge Rd. (see Major Attractions in the **Estes Park** chapter). For further information about Colorado's two dozen Scenic Byways, visit the terrific website **www.dot.state.co.us/public.** A really good book is *Colorado's Scenic Guide— Southern and Northern Regions* (Johnson Books, 1996), by Lee Gregory.

Where to Stay

ACCOMMODATIONS

We have gone out of our way to select unique accommodations that you'll remember (fondly, we hope) well into the future. No one has paid for inclusion in the book and, while our narrowed-down list of selections may be subjective, we have given honest evaluations. Each write-up should provide you with enough information to decide whether a particular hotel, motel or bed and breakfast is for you. Whenever possible, we have avoided national chains—not because these places are bad, but simply because most people already know what to expect when checking into a Hilton, Holiday Inn, Best Western or Motel 6. To find the toll-free **reservation numbers** for these chains, call **1-800-555-1212.** If you would like a complete listing of what is available in an area, give the chamber of commerce a call (listed under the Services section in each chapter). They will be more than happy to answer your query. The larger resorts offer toll-free central reservations numbers (also listed under the Services section in each chapter).

Because prices are constantly changing, we have used a price guideline throughout the book that shows approximately how much a night's lodging (double occupancy) will cost:

$	under $40
$$	$40–$80
$$$	$80–$120
$$$$	$120 and up

For those of you who have never stayed at a bed and breakfast inn, it's time to step in from the cold. This European idea has caught on in Colorado in a big way; a multitude of wonderful "escapes" are discussed in nearly every chapter in this book. Bed and breakfasts generally operate on a smaller scale than other lodging establishments, and the owner's personal touch is always evident. You can stay in a small, immaculate Victorian; a sprawling log mansion, a castle or a rustic lodge. In the morning you'll have the chance to meet and talk with other guests during a complimentary breakfast. A number of organizations represent Colorado's B&Bs; here are two of the best: **Distinctive Inns of Colorado, 1-800-866-0621, www.bedand breakfastinns.org;** and **Bed and Breakfast**

Innkeepers of Colorado, 1-800-265-7696, www.innsofcolorado.org.

Historic hotels provide another unique getaway. During their boom days, many of the mining towns built grandiose hostelries that eventually fell into disrepair. Quite a few have now been beautifully refurbished—for example, you might stay at the Peck House in **Empire,** the Imperial Hotel in **Cripple Creek** or the Hotel Boulderado in **Boulder.** Perhaps the best-known hotel in Colorado is the Brown Palace Hotel in **Denver.** Not quite as many people know about the impressive Strater Hotel in **Durango,** the Hotel Jerome in **Aspen** or the Hotel Colorado in **Glenwood Springs.**

Guest (dude) ranches can be found throughout the state. Normally guests stay for a week, and everything (including meals) is provided. If you have ever had a longing for the Wild West (riding horses each day, singing around the campfire and more), but also like sleeping on a comfy mattress, you should consider a ranch vacation. Families seem to take very well to the wide list of activities and somewhat structured environment. Some ranches also specialize in fishing, cross-country skiing and outdoor-skills vacations. For information on some of Colorado's best, read about the Home Ranch or Vista Verde in the **Steamboat Springs** chapter, Latigo Ranch in the **North Park** chapter, Skyline Ranch in the **Telluride** chapter or the C-Lazy-U in the **Winter Park and Middle Park** chapter. You may also want to contact the **Colorado Dude and Guest Ranch Association, P.O. Box 2121, Granby, CO 80446; 970-887-3128; www.coloradoranch.com.**

When on a budget, there is no better place to find shelter than at a youth hostel. Hostels are also great places to meet other travelers. Sometimes restrictive rules are enforced and a quick morning chore is required, but the price is right. Despite the name, people of all ages are welcome. Though the **American Youth Hostel (AYH)** system is not as developed as its European counterpart, several accommodations are available in Colorado. For a complete listing and membership information, contact **American**

Youth Hostels, Rocky Mountain Council, 1310 College Ave., Suite 315, Boulder, CO 80306; 303-442-1166; www.hostels.org.

People over 60 years of age (with companions age 50 or older) may want to inquire about **Elderhostel** programs, which flourish in Colorado. For a brochure, contact **Elderhostel, 75 Federal St., Boston, MA 02110-1941; 1-877-426-8056.**

CAMPING

Camping opportunities in Colorado are diverse and numerous. Variations in terrain, amenities and price are key considerations. Throughout this book, we have listed most campgrounds in the national forests, monuments and parks, state parks and recreation areas as well as many private campgrounds. Most of the listings are designated sites that can be reached by a regular passenger car or RV.

Whether you're camping in the wilderness or just off the highway, minimum-impact camping ethics should always be practiced. Leave your campsite in better shape than you found it. The following is a brief explanation of possible camping experiences in Colorado.

In the National Forests

Not everyone realizes this simple fact about camping in the national forest: you can camp anywhere you want to unless it's posted otherwise. Most designated campgrounds charge a fee between $5 and $8 per site per night. Amenities usually include picnic tables, fire pits, pit toilets, pump water and trash cans. Campsites that don't charge a fee usually don't supply drinking water. Most campgrounds have a maximum-stay limit of two weeks; sites are assigned on a first-come, first-served basis. Some of the most popular areas of the national forests get extremely crowded in summer; **reservations** are taken for many of these campgrounds at least 10 days in advance at **1-800-280-2267** or **www.reserve usa.com.** For more information about camping in the national forests, contact the **U.S. Forest Service, P.O. Box 25127, Lakewood, CO 80225; 740 Simms St., Golden, CO 80401; 303-275-5350; www.reserveusa.com.**

In the National Parks, Monuments and Recreation Areas

Camping in these areas is usually allowed only at designated sites; most charge a fee and offer the same amenities as national forest campgrounds. An entrance fee to these areas is also required. With the exception of two campgrounds in Rocky Mountain National Park that are available with advance reservations, all campground sites are available on a first-come, first-served basis. For additional information about camping in the national parks, monuments and recreation areas, contact the **National Park Service, P.O. Box 25287, Denver, CO 80225; 303-969-2000; 303-969-2020; www.nps.gov.** As in the national forests, reservations can be made at **1-800-280-2267** or **www.reserveusa.com.**

In Colorado State Parks

These areas have some very civilized campgrounds that often include rest rooms with hot showers. An entrance fee is required as well as a fee for camping. Reservations can be made at least three days in advance at **1-800-678-2267, 303-470-1144** or **www.reserveamerica.com.** For further information about camping in the state parks, contact the **Colorado Division of Parks and Outdoor Recreation, 1313 Sherman St., Suite 618, Denver, CO 80203; 303-866-3437; www.coloradoparks.org.**

On BLM Land

Camping on land administered by the federal Bureau of Land Management is possible in many places throughout Colorado. Here and there are some relatively primitive campgrounds that often include picnic tables and outhouses; only a few charge a fee. Some of these campgrounds are mentioned in this book. For additional information about camping on BLM land, contact the **Bureau of Land Management, 2850 Youngfield St., Lakewood, CO 80215; 303-239-3600; www.co.blm.gov.**

At Private Campgrounds and Cabins

Most camping sections end with a listing of at least one private campground. These are the plush places with all the amenities you could ask for, including shower rooms, laundry facilities and RV hookups. For further information about private campgrounds, contact the **Colorado Agency for Cabins, Campgrounds and Lodges, 5101 Pennsylvania Ave., Boulder, CO 80303-2799; 303-499-9343; www.colorado directory.com.**

Where to Eat

There's a reason we gain so much weight during these book updates: constant research to find the best restaurants. In addition to this firsthand work, we narrowed down the list of restaurant choices in each destination by asking countless locals about their favorite places to eat. The restaurants we've listed in each chapter also constitute what we consider to be an accurate representation of available price ranges, foods and dining styles. We personally visited each of the establishments to see if they were worthy of mention; we accepted no payment for inclusion in the book. If there was a particular specialty in an area, we have given it more play: Mexican food in the San Luis Valley, for instance. You may

also notice that we have an aversion to chains: does anyone need to explain what's in store for you under the golden arches?

Most people like to know how much their meal will cost, so we provide a guideline for every restaurant, based on the price of an entrée per person:

$	under $5
$$	$5–$10
$$$	$10–$20
$$$$	$20 and up

An additional resource worth looking into for restaurant selections is **www.zagat.com,** with reviews and other dining information for most areas of the state.

Now What?

That's all there is to it. Just throw this book into your car, SUV, bike pannier or backpack and hit the road. We hope you find the book enormously useful and that while reading it and using it, you experience some of the fun and excitement we enjoyed in creating *The Colorado Guide*.

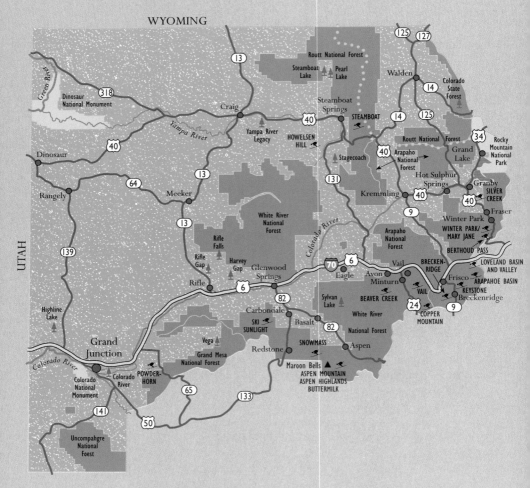

WYOMING

UTAH

Creek River

Dinosaur
National Monument

318

40

Dinosaur

Rangely

40

64

139

Highline
Lake

141

Grand
Junction

Colorado River

Colorado
National
Monument

Colorado River

POWDER-
HORN

65

50

Uncompahgre
National
Forest

Yampa River

Craig

13

Meeker

13

13

Rifle
Falls

Rifle
Gap

Harvey
Gap

Rifle

6

Glenwood
Springs

82

Carbondale

SKI
SUNLIGHT

Vega

Grand Mesa
National Forest

133

Redstone

Basalt

82

SNOWMASS

Aspen

Maroon Bells
ASPEN MOUNTAIN
ASPEN HIGHLANDS
BUTTERMILK

Sylvan
Lake

White River

National Forest

Eagle

6

70

Yampa River
Legacy

HOWELSEN
HILL

Steamboat
Springs

40

STEAMBOAT

Stagecoach

131

Kremmling

White River
National Forest

Routt National Forest

Steamboat
Lake

Pearl
Lake

13

Colorado River

Arapaho
National
Forest

Arapaho
National
Forest

Vail

Avon
Minturn

BEAVER CREEK

VAIL

24

COPPER
MOUNTAIN

Walden

14

Colorado
State
Forest

14

125

125

Routt National Forest

Hot Sulphur
Springs

40

9

Grand
Lake

Granby

40

Winter Park

WINTER PARK/
MARY JANE

BERTHOUD PASS

BRECKEN-
RIDGE

Frisco

9

Breckenridge

KEYSTONE

ARAPAHOE BASIN

LOVELAND BASIN
AND VALLEY

125

127

34

Rocky
Mountain
National
Park

SILVER
CREEK

Fraser

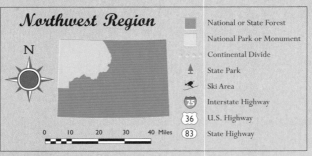

Northwest Region

N

National or State Forest

National Park or Monument

Continental Divide

State Park

Ski Area

25   Interstate Highway

36   U.S. Highway

83   State Highway

0   10   20   30   40 Miles

Northwest Region

A skier enjoys some of Steamboat's famous powder.
Photo courtesy of Steamboat Ski & Resort Corporation.

Aspen

Colorado's premier ski resort town, Aspen, sits mountain-locked at the head of the beautiful Roaring Fork Valley. Historic mining town, laid-back mountain retreat, cultural mecca, elitist playground for the superrich: Aspen's images vary greatly, quite often in what would seem to be direct conflict. You don't need to look hard for the town's eccentricities—some might say absurdities—to reveal themselves.

Aspen's allure comes in part from its intriguing and sometimes tumultuous history. Beginning as a remote mining camp in 1879, the town quickly prospered and grew to be one of the richest silver-producing areas in the world, until the crash of the silver market in 1893. Today Aspen's Victorian-era prosperity still makes up a large part of its personality. Reminders of Aspen's past range from the many beautifully restored homes to restaurants and bars named after famous mines and residents.

The visionaries who developed Aspen as a winter ski resort and summer intellectual/cultural retreat in the late 1940s set the tone for what exists today. Winter activities revolve around Aspen's four distinctive ski areas, which uphold an international reputation for fine powder skiing and runs suited to all abilities. Of the four, only Snowmass provides a condo-style planned community right on the mountain; Aspen Mountain's lifts rise right from the edge of the historic town. Cross-country skiing is excellent in the area, and the range of après-ski partying is unmatched.

In summer the town comes together around the arts: the Aspen Music Festival, Theatre in the Park, DanceAspen and other events attract performers from around the world. With public forest lands and nearby wilderness areas, hiking, backpacking and fishing opportunities are limitless. In autumn, as far as the eye can see, aspen trees transform into burnished coats of gold and red. Aspen quiets down and many of the businesses close in the spring (mud season) and late

fall (after the leaves have fallen), though these can be ideal times for a visit.

Over the years Aspen has drawn a very educated and sophisticated group of residents. Add to this a complex mix of values and lifestyles, and the result is explosive. The vast majority of political issues still hinge on the long-running conflict between development and slow growth. Aspen politics remain a fractious part of life for many locals. More substantial issues include the scarcity of affordable housing and frequent bottlenecks of cars in town and down-valley.

Aspen's image as a hangout for jet-setters and international celebrities is valid, though it has been blown out of proportion. Aspen naturally provides unlimited ways for vacationers to part with large stacks of cash; the average house costs about $2 million. However, you don't necessarily need to take out a loan to eat at many of the restaurants—budget travelers can actually find some surprisingly affordable vacation options. In summer you can track down deals on hotel rates, many of the festivals are free and you can stay at campgrounds around the area for practically nothing.

History

Like its beautiful surroundings, Aspen's history has a generous share of peaks and valleys. For centuries the Roaring Fork Valley had been a prime hunting ground for the Ute Indians, who tenaciously fought to keep the area off-limits to settlers. But a treaty in 1868 forced the Utes to move west out of the valley they loved so dearly. It wasn't until more than 10 years later that prospecting began in the area.

In June 1879 Walter Clark and three others made their way over Independence Pass from Leadville. For more than a year they had studied geological maps that led them to believe the remote Roaring Fork Valley might contain as much silver ore as the rich Leadville area. They weren't disappointed, as silver was found in abundance. Word of the silver strikes quickly spread, and other anxious miners arrived to stake their claims (mainly on Aspen Mountain) before winter set in. As snow fell that first winter, three camps had already been established: Independence, Ashcroft and Aspen, the latter of which was originally called Ute City. While the first camp leader, H. B. Gillespie, was away in Washington, D.C., petitioning for postal service for Ute City, a newcomer named B. Clark Wheeler arrived. Wheeler proceeded to organize the miners and rename the town Aspen.

By the summer of 1880 Aspen boasted a population of more than 1,000. Over time the Mollie Gibson, Chamberlain, Venus and famous Smuggler mines produced some of the richest silver ore ever found. But one big obstacle remained between the miners and fantastic profits: the lack of a nearby smelter. Transporting the silver ore by pack mules over Independence Pass to the smelters in Leadville, Pueblo and Denver was costly and inconvenient. Aspen needed someone with very deep pockets willing to finance construction of a smelter. In 1883 the answer to the miners' dreams materialized in the form of eastern businessman Jerome B. Wheeler (no relation to B. Clark Wheeler). This onetime partner in Macy's department store in New York City came to Aspen, bought up some mining claims

and built the much-needed smelter. This spurred Aspen's growth, and things started to boom.

The Denver & Rio Grande Railroad arrived in 1887, followed a year later by the Colorado Midland Railroad. (Unfortunately, Colorado Midland's depot location—on brothel-strewn Fanny Hill St.—left a bit to be desired; "nice" women of the town stayed away, thereby saving themselves from the embarrassment of being confused with the "soiled doves.") The railroads provided the vital link with the outside world, thereby helping transform Aspen into a hopping town of 12,000 inhabitants by 1893, the third-largest community in the state.

From 1887 to 1893 Aspen was the richest silver mining area in the United States. It boasted six newspapers, two banks, a waterworks, telephone service and the distinction of being one of the first towns in the United States to run on

---

Getting There

The shortest route from Denver to Aspen (162 miles) can be taken only in summer. Drive west on Interstate 70 for 79 miles to Copper Mountain, then follow Hwy. 91 south past Leadville to the junction with Hwy. 82. Turn west and drive on the narrow, winding road over Independence Pass to Aspen. (For more information about the pass, see the Scenic Drives section.) In winter you must take a 200-mile route via Interstate 70 to Glenwood Springs and then south on Hwy. 82.

*Fly from Denver International Airport on a connecting flight to the Aspen/Pitkin County Airport (some fly into Eagle County Airport, an hour and 15 minutes away). Direct service is available from many major cities. From Denver International it's also possible to rent a car, hire a limo or arrange van service. You can also take an **Amtrak** train into Glenwood Springs (40 miles from Aspen) from Chicago (via Denver) or from San Francisco. Call Amtrak at **1-800-872-7245**.*

electricity. During this heyday Jerome Wheeler built the Wheeler Opera House and the magnificent Aspen showpiece, the Hotel Jerome. The hotel opened on Thanksgiving Eve, 1889, with Aspen's biggest social event to date. Guests came from as far away as Europe. This soirée helped bring Aspen into the national spotlight, but the attention was short-lived.

In 1893 the silver crash caused prices to plummet. Within a week the mines had closed and people were moving out. The Smuggler II Mine on Smuggler Mountain managed to stay open for a while longer and in 1894 produced the largest silver nugget in the world, weighing in at over a ton. But not even the richest silver mine in the world could afford to stay open. Aspen was on the skids and would not see the end of economic hard times for decades.

By 1930 the population had dwindled to 700. But before long the Aspen area began to draw attention as a potentially great winter resort. Ironically, Aspen Mountain was not the first slope eyed for development. Alpine ski experts initially decided on nearby Ashcroft as the best location for the envisioned resort. In the meantime, the Works Progress Administration (WPA) had constructed a lift on Aspen Mountain in 1936. The 10-cent-per-ride lift was actually a 10-passenger boat tow, consisting of a half-inch cable, two mine hoists and a gas motor.

World War II put Aspen's ski area development plans on hold. As the United States was drawn into the war, the 10th Mountain Division ski troops, stationed at Camp Hale, held maneuvers near Aspen. Many fell in love with the town and its skiing, vowing to come back after the war. A number of these men returned to help transform Aspen into a winter resort.

Raising the money needed to develop Aspen into a major ski resort proved difficult. In 1947 Walter Paepcke, founder of Container Corporation of America, arrived with his checkbook open to save the day. Ironically, Paepcke was initially drawn to Aspen for the purpose of establishing a summer retreat for business leaders to "revitalize body and soul." He thought the retreat would make money, but was eventually convinced

by a local businessman, Austrian Friedl Pfeiffer, that the winter resort idea would be even more lucrative. So Paepcke helped locate investors, and soon Aspen was a year-round attraction.

Very quickly Aspen gained worldwide recognition. The 1949 Goethe bicentennial festival lured more than 2,000 people, including many celebrities. The following winter Aspen Mountain hosted the World Ski Championships and was catapulted into the league of world-class ski resorts. Aspen Highlands Ski Area opened in 1958, soon followed by the opening of Buttermilk Mountain, the teaching mountain. The last piece fell into place when Snowmass Ski Area opened in 1967. Today the Aspen Skiing Company continues to thrive, expanding and adapting since its humble beginnings.

Major Attractions

Maroon Bells Scenic Area

The Maroon Bells, thought to be the most photographed peaks in North America, offer one of the most beautiful views on the planet. From Maroon Lake at the end of a scenic 9-mile road, gaze up at several 14,000-foot peaks that rise within the short span of the Maroon Bells–Snowmass Wilderness.

Because the incredible, above-treeline beauty of the peaks attracts so many people to a fragile alpine ecosystem, access to the Maroon Creek Valley is restricted, but an efficient bus system can whisk you from Aspen. No cars are allowed up the Maroon Lake Rd. between 8:30 A.M. and 5 P.M. in summer (June through Labor Day and Sept. weekends), except for campers with permits and physically handicapped individuals. Once at the famous Bells, you can hike on the 100 miles of trails or just simply kick back and enjoy the view. Bring along your fishing pole and camera, too. If you are expecting a man- or woman-in-the-wilderness experience, this is probably not the place. For more information contact the **Aspen Ranger District Office, 806 W. Hallam, Aspen, CO 81611; 970-925-3445; www.whiteriver/r2.com.**

Fountains on the Hyman Street Walking Mall delight children on a summer afternoon. Photo by Bruce Caughey.

Hiking

Maroon Creek Trail—Several short hikes can be taken from the bus drop-off, but this is one of our favorites. Maroon Creek Trail is a 3.25-mile downhill stroll to East Maroon Portal, where the bus will pick up hikers at the roadside. Those unaccustomed to the altitude may want to start out on this mellow trail.

West Maroon Pass—Take a 13-mile hike to Crested Butte past beautiful Crater Lake and over West Maroon Pass. Take the spectacular hike after the snow melts in mid-June and be prepared for the trip. Contact **Crested Butte Taxi, 970-349-5543,** if you want to be met at the terminus of the trail and shuttled back.

Other Hikes—See the Hiking and Back-packing section.

Interpretive Tours

The **Aspen Center for Environmental Studies** offers nature tours at Maroon Lake each hour from 10 A.M to 2 P.M. In addition, a powerful telescope at the lake may help you spot some of the resident elk, deer, bighorn sheep, eagles and other wildlife.

Camping

Up Maroon Creek Road—It's very hard to find a campsite in this valley during midsummer. You should definitely make reservations: **1-877-444-6777; www.reserveusa.com.**

Forest Service Campgrounds—Maroon Lake (44 sites), **Silver Bar** (4 sites), **Silver Bell** (4 sites) and **Silver Queen** (6 sites)—are open from early June until mid-Sept. depending on the snowpack. Private vehicles need to secure a camping permit at the entrance station before heading up the road. Silver Bar and Silver Bell do not accommodate trailers; fee charged.

Getting There

Since summer access is restricted, the best way to get a view of the Bells is via the efficient bus system from Aspen. Buses depart from Rubey Park Transit Center every half hour from 9 A.M. to 4:30 P.M. daily. Round-trip fare is very reasonable; children under 5 ride free. Once there, stay as long as you wish and take any bus back to Aspen between 9:30 A.M. and 5 P.M. Once the snow begins to fall, Maroon Lake Rd. is not plowed above the T-Lazy-7 Ranch due to extreme avalanche danger. For further information call **970-925-8484.**

Festivals and Events

Check out happenings in the Aspen area all year long. The **U.S. Comedy Arts Festival** in Jan. attracts big names, the **paragliding festival** in early Sept. astounds and the **Food and Wine Classic** in Oct. brings chefs and fine-food aficionados to the area. Snowmass offers a free **summer concert series** on Thurs. nights. Annual sporting competitions range from rugby to golf to volleyball. For information check with the **Aspen Chamber Resort Association** at **1-800-262-7736;www.destinationaspen. com.** Here are a few of the true standouts:

Snowmass Balloon Festival

mid-June This high-altitude event has attracted increasing numbers of spectators since it began in 1975. More than 50 balloonists compete in races and maneuvers. An added attraction for spectators is the champagne breakfast served at the launch site to the sounds of classical music. Don't miss the nightglow event when the balloons turn into giant luminaria. **1-800-598-2003; 970-923-2000; www.snowmassvillage.com.**

Aspen Music Festival

late June through Aug. For the past four decades live music has drifted across the summer hills of Aspen, ranging from jazz to symphonic, opera to avant-garde. Music emanates not only from formal concerts but from intense rehearsals, informal sessions and private practice. This wonderful festival helps provide a perfect learning environment for students at the Aspen Music School. An idyllic summer afternoon at the music tent might feature a famous guest artist such as Itzhak Perlman on violin or James Galway on flute. The concerts are reasonably priced, but the unique tent-enclosed setting also allows the music to reach nonpaying patrons seated comfortably on the grass outside. For more information call **970-925-3254; www.aspenmusicfestival.com.**

Colorado Mountain Fair

end of July More than 10,000 people cut loose each summer at this very popular festival in Carbondale, 30 miles northwest of Aspen on Hwy. 82. Since 1971 the fair has offered many kinds of food, music and booths with everything from massage to jewelry making. Music and special contests like log splitting keep the valley locals and outsiders flocking here each summer. **Carbondale Chamber of Commerce, 970-963-1890.**

Janus Jazz Aspen/Snowmass

Labor Day weekend A range of musical tastes that go far beyond jazz can be heard at this annual rite. Since 1990, in a meadow below Snowmass Village, thousands have enjoyed music from the likes of Lyle Lovett, Joe Cocker, Jimmy Cliff and Hugh Masekela. An outdoor market is set up for food, drinks and unusual products from around the world. A great scene for four straight days. **970-920-5770; www.jazz aspen.com.**

Outdoor Activities

Biking

MOUNTAIN BIKING

Need you ask? When the snow melts off the surrounding mountain trails and jeep roads, locals put away their skis and bring out their mountain bikes. Actually, a few fanatic bikers start riding around town before the snow has even melted. Snowmass also has a terrific on-mountain trail system and a new top-of-the-mountain bike terrain park. Here are a few trail ideas in the Aspen area:

Government Trail

This demanding route traverses the Snowmass Ski Area and eventually leads to Buttermilk Ski Mountain. Meadows, peaks and panoramic views make it worth the effort. Inquire at Blazing Adventures in Snowmass Village for exact trail directions.

Maroon Creek Road

This paved road climbs 1,000 feet in 9 miles (18 miles round trip). The constant yet gentle uphill ride provides an outstanding view of the Maroon Bells from Maroon Lake. To reach Maroon Creek Rd., take Hwy. 82 out of Aspen for 1 mile north and turn left at the Aspen Highlands sign. See the Major Attractions section for more information.

Pearl Pass

This tough ride shouldn't be considered unless you are in good shape. The 12,700-foot Pearl Pass crosses over into the Crested Butte area to the south. The road was originally built to ship silver from Ashcroft to the nearest railroad down-valley from Crested Butte. To reach the pass, head up Castle Creek Rd. to Ashcroft, 13 miles from Aspen. From Ashcroft, at 9,500 feet, the road follows the river up 3,200 vertical feet and 8 miles to the pass. From the pass you can head back to Aspen or proceed down to Crested Butte 12 miles away.

10th Mountain Trail Association Hut System

More than 300 miles of gorgeous single-track and dirt roads connected by huts (see the Skiing section for more information).

Rentals and Tours

Try **Blazing Adventures,** which offers downhill bicycle tours as well as rentals: **105 Village Sq., Snowmass Village, CO 81615, 970-923-4544;** or in **Aspen** at **Hyman and Mill St., 970-925-5651, www.blazingadventures.com.**

Dog Sledding

Krabloonik's Kennels

In 1947 Stuart Mace, who handled sled dogs for the 10th Mountain Division during World War II, began offering sled rides from Toklat, his lodge up in the nearby ghost town of Ashcroft. His tradition carries on at Krabloonik's, where you can take full- and partial-day sled rides up the valley toward Mt. Daly and the towering 14,130-foot Capitol Peak. The sleds, pulled by teams of 13 dogs, are designed similarly to those made by Eskimos from bone and rawhide.

Caution: the rides are quite pricey. Reservations essential; full prepayment required. Follow Brush Creek Rd. past the Snowmass Ski Area for about half a mile to the parking lot. **970-923-3953.**

Fishing

With long stretches of Gold Medal water on two of Colorado's best trout streams in addition to countless high-country lakes and tributaries, Aspen is a natural destination for anglers. For guided wade trips and float fishing in McKenzie-style boats, try **Frying Pan Anglers, 123 Emma Rd., Unit 100, Basalt, 970-927-3441;** or **Taylor Creek Fly Shop, 183 Basalt Center Circle, Basalt, 970-927-4374, www. taylorcreek.com.**

Fryingpan Lakes

A 5-mile hike is required to reach the three small lakes at 11,000 feet. The reward is not only the beautiful scenery but a chance at the multitude of small brook trout. This unstocked natural habitat yields many fish from a mere 2 surface acres of water. From Basalt follow County Rd. 105 along the Fryingpan River until it turns into Forest Rd. 505. From the end of Forest Rd. 505 the trail sets out.

Fryingpan River

This river is legendary for large browns and rainbows from Ruedi Reservoir down to Basalt. Due to its "legend" status and Gold Medal designation, you can expect competition along the river, especially on weekends. The river never gets muddy, thanks to a controlled water flow from the dam. Use artificial flies or lures only. Catch and release all trout on the Upper Fryingpan (beginning at Ruedi Dam and continuing downstream 4 miles). You can keep two fish over 16 inches on the Lower Fryingpan (beginning at Basalt and continuing upriver 9 miles). For solitude, try fishing the Fryingpan in winter and early spring. Use small (size 18 to 20) green and brown elk hair caddis in spring when the water is still a bit murky and dry flies in summer. In late Aug.

An early sled lift that was once used to haul skiers up the mountain. Photo by Bruce Caughey.

lots of top action results from the green drake mayfly hatch.

Hunter Creek

This smallish creek flows into the Roaring Fork on the northeast edge of Aspen. Catch small brook, brown and cutthroat trout with small flies in the evening hours. Access can be difficult, but a dirt road (Hunter Creek Rd.) from Aspen loosely follows the creek 6 miles to the boundary of the Hunter–Fryingpan Wilderness Area.

Ivanhoe Lake

To reach this moderately fished lake, head 5 miles up the rough dirt road (Forest Rd. 105 and 527) that follows Ivanhoe Creek from east of Ruedi Reservoir. Ivanhoe Lake, pushed up against the Continental Divide in a beautiful setting, is stocked with rainbows, and rainbows are what you'll catch.

Roaring Fork River

After the spring runoff calms down, fishing within the city limits can be good. Be aware of the mix of public and private land on the river. Just to the north of town is a good area to catch both rainbow and brown trout. You can fish all the way from Independence Pass down to Glenwood Springs. We tend to focus on the stretch downstream from the Woody Creek Bridge to Carbondale where you'll find premium trout-fishing water and beautiful scenery.

It's also Gold Medal water from Carbondale, where the Crystal River joins, down to the Roaring Fork's confluence with the Colorado. This heavily fished stretch yields rainbows, browns and whitefish. There is a two-fish limit; only artificial lures and flies may be used from Apr. through Oct.

Willow Lake

This above-treeline lake at 11,705 feet provides good fishing for large brook and cutthroat. A longtime Aspen fishing expert once saw a dozen bighorn ewes on a trip to this area. Willow Lake is a 5-mile trek from Maroon Bells Lake, high in the Maroon Bells–Snowmass Wilderness Area (see Major Attractions for directions).

Four-Wheel-Drive Trips

There is some terrific jeeping on the former mining roads and ski area roads, now maintained by the county, that crisscross Ajax ski mountain. You can go on your own or hire a guide. If you want to make it over the passes to Crested Butte, be sure to have good shock absorbers, because the roads are extremely rocky. For jeep tours, check out **Blazing Adventures** at the **corner of Mill St. and Hyman Ave., Aspen; 970-925-5651; www.blazingadventures. com.** For many more ideas in the area, read the **Glenwood Springs** and **Redstone and Crystal River Valley** chapters.

Golf

Aspen Golf Course

Although it's a municipal course, the Aspen Golf Course has a high rating and relatively cheap greens fees. This fine 18-hole course poses a pretty good challenge, even to scratch golfers. The holes are laid out fairly flat, making some of the hazards difficult to see. Watch out for irrigation ditches and lakes on this course, as there are more of them than seems fair. If the golf gods will it, snow in the valley clears enough to open the course by May 1. Restaurant and pro shop; carts available. **22475 W. Hwy. 82, 970-925-2145 (summer); in winter call Aspen Sports, 970-925-6331.**

River Valley Ranch

Situated in Carbondale, this 7,300-yard, 18-hole championship course was designed by Jay Moorish, the 1996 Golf World Architect of the Year. The course is very open, offering unbelievable views of Mt. Sopris around every bend. It's a residential real estate development, so you may encounter some construction, but it's tastefully done and most fairways are not lined on both sides by homes. The Crystal River flows along one side of the course and there's even a resident bald eagle in a special conservation area. Great final 4 holes to finish play.

One caution: practice your woods before arriving at the range—they don't allow 'em. Nice clubhouse with deck and the upscale confines of the Rock Creek Grill. **424 River Valley Ranch Dr., Carbondale; 970-704-1100.**

The solitary profile of Mt. Sopris towers over the River Valley Ranch Golf Course. Photo by Bruce Caughey.

The Snowmass Golf Club

This sculpted course rolls along in the valley down below the ski mountain. Brush Creek runs through the middle of the fairly treeless course. While greens fees are rather steep, the Snowmass Lodge and Club offers reduced fees and choice tee times for guests. Pro shop, carts and club rentals available. **239 Snowmass Club Cir., Snowmass Village; 970-923-3148; www. snowmassclub.com.**

Hiking and Backpacking

White River National Forest surrounds Aspen, tempting lovers of the outdoors with three wilderness areas: Collegiate Peaks, Hunter–Fryingpan and Maroon Bells–Snowmass. Within the jagged Elk Mountains are no fewer than six 14,000-foot peaks. Mountaineers, backpackers and families wanting to take a stroll converge on Aspen's mountains each summer. It's still possible to get away from humanity. The **10th Mountain Trail Association Hut System** also serves hikers in summer months (see the Skiing section for more information).

It's difficult to condense a list of the trail opportunities in the Aspen area. For more trail ideas, contact the **Aspen Ranger District, 806 W. Hallam St., Aspen, CO 81611, 970-925-3445;** or the **Sopris Ranger District, 620 Main, P.O. Box 309, Carbondale, CO 81623, 970-963-2266, www.fs.fed.us/r2/ whiteriver.**

For maps, equipment and informed advice, visit the **Ute Mountaineer, 308 S. Mill St., Aspen; 970-925-2849; www.utemountain eer.com.**

American Lake

This daylong, 7-mile round-trip hike is steep but worth the trouble. The lake is beautiful and the fishing for rainbow trout can be surprisingly good. Views of surrounding peaks are also stunning. Plan on about 5 hours of hiking time. Camping is not permitted on the east end of the lake. To reach the trailhead, turn left onto Maroon Creek Rd. from Hwy. 82 just west of Aspen. Take another quick left onto Castle Creek

Rd. and drive 10 miles to the trailhead, which is on the right side of the road across from the Elk Creek Lodge.

Braille Trail

Approximately 2 miles farther up Hwy. 82 from the Grottos turnoff (10 miles east of Aspen), the quarter-mile-long Braille Trail offers blind hikers a chance to experience the natural surroundings. Guided by a nylon cord, hikers can decipher the more than 20 signs, which are in both braille and print. A miniature tape player and cassette, to enhance the sensory experience, can be borrowed (no charge) from the **Aspen Ranger District** at **806 W. Hallam St.** The tape was designed specifically for use on the Braille Trail. Look for the turnoff on the right side of Hwy. 82.

Conundrum Creek

See the Hot Springs section for specifics on this 9-mile (18 miles round trip) hike.

Four Pass Loop

This well-known route passes through the heart of the Maroon Bells–Snowmass Wilderness Area. It's a beautiful and demanding 28-mile loop taking you over four major passes (West Maroon, Frigid Air, Trail Rider and Buckskin), all of which are at about 12,500 feet. Allow four to five days for your journey and don't hurry. Be sure to check in at the Forest Service office to learn about any backcountry restrictions. The loop takes you by Maroon, Crater and Snowmass Lakes. The trail begins and ends at Maroon Lake. Parts of the trail are usually snow-covered until July. Get a topographic map for this hike. If you get an urge to bag some of the 14ers along the way remember that many climbers have died on the treacherous slopes of Pyramid Peak and the Maroon Bells—they have been named the "Deadly Bells" by some.

Grottos

The Grottos are located about 8 miles up Independence Pass (east from Aspen on Hwy. 82), just a short walk along the Roaring Fork

River from the parking area. It's a popular picnic and sunning spot in the summer. Grottos gets its name from its interesting rock formations, including the granite "ice caves" that were carved out when the river flowed through here. The area is close to town and very scenic. Look for the dirt road on the right side of Hwy. 82 about a half-mile past mile-marker 50. A footbridge crosses the river near the parking area. No camping.

Maroon Bells
See the Major Attractions section for additional information.

Midway Pass to Hunter Creek
Located in the Hunter–Fryingpan Wilderness, this 20-mile hike (allow three days) is less known than the trails in the Maroon Bells–Snowmass Wilderness Area. Both elk and deer make their homes here in summer. Start at about 10,000 feet and enjoy views to Independence Pass as you work your way northwest into the Hunter Creek drainage, which leads back to Aspen. The trail begins 14 miles east of Aspen on Hwy. 82 on the left side of the road across from Lost Creek Campground. There is a fork about half a mile up the trail. Take the left fork up Midway Creek Trail. After crossing Midway Pass, the trail drops and snakes through marshy areas until it intersects Hunter Creek Trail. Take a left onto Hunter Creek Trail and proceed down to the outskirts of Aspen. Snow remains on the upper part of this trail until July.

Horseback Riding

T-Lazy-7 Ranch
The T-Lazy-7 offers a 4-hour lunch ride up to the scenic Maroon Bells. **3129 Maroon Creek Rd.; 970-925-7040; 970-925-4614.**

Ice Skating
The Ice Garden, a public indoor ice rink, provides skating and rentals throughout the week. Special events may preclude public use of the ice. **233 W. Hyman Ave.; 970-920-5141; www.aspengov.com.** You can also find the outdoor **Silver Circle Ice Rink** directly **across from Rubey Park.**

Llama Trekking
From July to Sept., **Ashcroft** and the **Pine Creek Cookhouse** offer daily llama treks up into White River National Forest. Treks (a bit pricey) begin at the cookhouse and include a gourmet lunch. Overnight trips are available on request. Be sure to call for reservations. Located 12 miles up Castle Creek Rd. from Hwy. 82. **312 G. Aspen Airport Business Center, Aspen, CO 81611; 970-920-4093.**

River Floating

Crystal River
See the **Redstone and Crystal River Valley** chapter.

Roaring Fork River
The upper Roaring Fork River is a popular river for kayaking, even though parts of it can be treacherous. This well-named river surges angrily out of the Sawatch Range east of Aspen. Just before reaching town, the river mellows, providing good beginner stretches all the way through Aspen. West of Aspen down to Basalt (12 miles), the water can be dangerous, and novices are warned to keep out, especially during high water. The 12-mile section below Basalt to Carbondale is much easier. For information about floating downstream from Carbondale, see the River Floating section of the **Glenwood Springs** chapter.

Outfitters
Colorado RiffRaft—These folks offer trips down the Roaring Fork, Colorado, Crystal and other rivers. Located at the base of the gondola. **555 E. Durant St., Aspen; 1-800-759-3939; 970-925-5405; www.riffraft.com.**
Blazing Adventures—They offer trips on the Roaring Fork, Colorado, Gunnison and Arkansas Rivers. At the **corner of Mill St. and Hyman**

Ave., Aspen; 970-925-5651; www.blazing adventures.com.

Skiing

CROSS-COUNTRY SKIING AND SNOWSHOEING

Aspen serves as a choice destination not only for downhill enthusiasts but for cross-country skiers as well. Everything from extensive groomed trail systems to demanding backcountry trails can be found here. Roughing it overnight in a unique backcountry hut is a peaceful alternative to the town's highly charged atmosphere. Snowshoers can certainly take advantage of the trail systems, but also consider calling the **Aspen Center for Environmental Studies (ACES)** about walks at its Hallam Lake Wildlife Sanctuary and on all four ski mountains. Call ACES at **970-925-5756; www.aspen.com/aces.** For those of you headed off on your own, remember to call **Avalanche Information** at **970-920-1664.** For more backcountry ski ideas and information, contact the **Aspen Ranger District Office, 806 W. Hallam St., Aspen, CO 81611; 970-925-3445; www.fs.fed.us/r2/whiteriver.** Or contact **Ute Mountaineer, 308 S. Mill St., Aspen, CO 81612; 970-925-2849; www. utemountaineer.com.**

Backcountry Trails

Braun Hut System—Colorado's original, this series of seven high-mountain huts stretches as far south as Pearl Pass and is accessible via Ashcroft (12 miles up Castle Creek Rd. from Aspen). Isolation, difficult trail conditions and avalanche danger make it necessary for skiers to have advanced skills. Guides can be arranged through several companies, including **Aspen Alpine Guides, P.O. Box 659, Aspen, CO 81612; 970-925-6618; www.aspen alpine. com.**

The Braun huts are a bit more spartan than the 10th Mountain Trail Association huts (see next entry) and were not truly designed to be skied hut to hut. Built to accommodate from 6 to 18 people, these year-round huts can best be

reached via separate trails. Fred Braun, an Austrian ski trooper in the early 1920s who later lived in Aspen, remembered that when he arrived in the United States in 1928, he had to send to Norway for ski boots! For information and reservations, contact the 10th Mountain Division Hut Association address given in the next entry.

10th Mountain Trail Association Hut System—For adventurous and experienced skiers, an impressive series of European-style backcountry ski huts stretches between Aspen and the Vail Valley. The hut system all started after Fritz Benedict, a veteran of the 10th Mountain Division ski troops, traversed Europe's Haute Route in the Alps. Beginning in 1980 Benedict began working with a group of volunteers to construct a similar hut system in the backcountry between Aspen, Leadville and Vail.

Currently 10 overnight huts and 7 private lodges extend north by northeast through the spectacular Hunter–Fryingpan and Holy Cross Wilderness Areas along a 250-mile route. Ski all or part of the hut system.

The huts (each sleeps about 16 people) offer many conveniences and supplies, such as mattresses, pillows, stoves and other kitchen necessities. You will need to bring a sleeping bag, food and emergency gear. Two of the private lodges along the trail (**Diamond J Ranch** and the **Polar Star Inn**) provide more creature comforts, such as running water and saunas. The Diamond J Ranch is a full-blown ski-touring resort that can be reached via County Rd. 105 from Basalt.

The 10th Mountain Division hut system attracts people from all over the world who want to experience the beauty of Colorado's high country in winter. Strong intermediate to advanced skills are needed as well as heavy-duty equipment. Guides and maps are available. To arrange transportation back to your car after a one-way ski on the west side of the system, call **Timberline Tours** at **970-920-3217.** Full payment is required when reservations are made. Reserve very early for winter weekends. Open late Nov.–May, depending on conditions. For

Sunlight filters through aspen trees on a perfect ski day. Photo by Burnie Arndt, courtesy of Aspen Skiing Company.

information and reservations, contact the hut association at **1280 Ute Ave., Aspen, CO 81611; 970-925-5775; www.huts.org.**

Groomed Trails

Ashcroft Ski Touring Center—For a relatively remote groomed trail system, try this one, which starts in Ashcroft 12 miles up Castle Creek Rd. south of Aspen. The center **(970-925-1971)** offers several warming huts and 30 kilometers of groomed trails. How about a gourmet lunch or dinner at the Pine Creek Cookhouse? For details see the Where to Eat section.

Aspen/Snowmass Nordic Trail System— This fine nordic system offers a 48-mile network of groomed cross-country trails within a 15-mile area in the valley. Coordinated by the nonprofit Aspen/Snowmass Nordic Council to facilitate ski connections between the two towns, the free trail system is accessible from many points in and around town. Pick up a map of the trail system at the Aspen Visitors Center in the Wheeler Opera House (see the Services section) or at a sports store. For more information contact the **Aspen Cross-Country Ski Center, 39551 W. Hwy. 82, Aspen, CO 81611; 970-925-2145.**

Ski Rentals

Aspen Cross-Country Ski Center (see previous entry) has what you need. Another choice for equipment, including heavy-duty backcountry gear, is the **Ute Mountaineer, 308 S. Mill St., Aspen, CO 81611; 970-925-2849.** In Snowmass try the **Snowmass Club Touring Center, P.O. Box G-2, Snowmass Village, CO 81654; 970-923-3148.**

DOWNHILL SKIING AND SNOWBOARDING

Life in Aspen still revolves around downhill skiing, despite the wealth of peripheral activities. Since 1936, when trees were cut to make room for Roch Run on Aspen Mountain, the ski industry has flourished. Today there are four excellent ski mountains to choose from. Each mountain has a personality of its own, and taken together they offer an incredible range of supreme skiing. The key to your enjoyment is to correctly match the mountain with your ability and mood. Aspen

Mountain finally relented in 2001 to allow snow-boarders for the first time. Tickets for all four areas are interchangeable. All areas offer a range of services including rentals, child care and lessons. For further information contact **Aspen Skiing Company, P.O. Box 1248, Aspen, CO 81612; 1-800-525-6200; 970-925-1220; www.skiaspen.com; www.rideaspen.com.**

Aspen Highlands

Aspen Highlands is an all-around ski area with what many consider the ideal division of terrain: half intermediate and the rest split between advanced and beginner. It has a tremendous 3,800-feet vertical drop, which is easier to get up with the addition of high-speed quads. Since it was not part of the Aspen Skiing Company until recently, it has always been seen as some-thing of a rebel, with its jeans-clad skiers not conforming to the glitzy standards of the neigh-boring areas. Experts will appreciate Highlands Bowl—a walk-in, guided, powder adventure that plunges an amazing 4,300 feet. My favorite attribute of the area still has to be the view as you ride up the Olympic Chairlift: your eyes fol-low up Maroon Valley to the impressive 14,000-foot summits of the Maroon Bells and Pyramid Peak. A new base village, with an impressive mix of retail and residential develop-ment, opens in 2001.

Aspen Mountain

The runs on this mountain are designed for the enjoyment of expert and strong intermediate skiers. Since there are no "green" runs, there should be no worries about novice skiers making tentative tracks across your fall line. Because of the mountain's orientation, skiers and boarders may consider taking advantage of the sun. Stick to the eastern flanks in the morning before mov-ing to western exposures later in the day. The Silver Queen gondola whisks skiers from the base to the 11,212-foot summit of Aspen Moun-tain in a mere 14 minutes; check out the new two-person, high-speed Ruthy's lift. Locals call the mountain Ajax, after a now-defunct silver mine. By whatever name, it is steep, challenging

and definitely not for beginners. The new on-mountain Sun Deck is a perfect place to chill out with great views, warm up by the round fire-place and have lunch or a drink.

Buttermilk Mountain

Two miles west of Aspen, Buttermilk is widely known as a great teaching mountain and a snow-boarder's paradise, thanks to endless miles of gentle, rolling terrain. Southerly views to Pyramid Peak in the Maroon Bells–Snowmass Wilderness Area make skiing here even more of a pleasure. Families (especially the kids) will enjoy cruising smooth trails; advanced skiers can head for the more difficult Tiehack Parkway and Tiehack Trail runs on powder days. The long, groomed runs are perfect for telemarking—lessons are available.

Snowmass Ski Area

A staggering variety of slopes for every ability is just 12 miles from Aspen in a perfect family envi-ronment. Four contiguous peaks and more than 2,000 skiable acres eliminate the need to ski the same run twice. Intermediate runs make up 65 percent of the total. The most notable of these is Big Burn—a mile-wide swath of white space, broken only by occasional stands of evergreen trees and served by a poma lift. This run down to the base stretches over 4 miles. Supposedly Big Burn is the result of an 1870s fire set by the Ute Indians to spite white settlers. Check out the gorgeous glades at Two Creeks. Slope names provide more than a hint of what's to come: take your pick from, say, the steep challenge of Hanging Valley Wall or the gentle incline of Fanny Hill. You can enjoy fine dining on this mountain at Gwyn's. Or, for a truly interesting lunch, make a reservation and ski into Krab-loonik's restaurant by way of Dawdler Trail (see the Where to Eat section).

Sleigh Rides

Take a mellow, intimate sleigh-ride dinner, end-ing at the **Pine Creek Cookhouse** near Ashcroft. See the Where to Eat section for details.

Seeing and Doing

Ballooning

Not every high alpine area is suited to ballooning, but in Aspen it's a popular adventure. The panorama of 14,000-foot peaks takes on a new dimension from the hanging basket of a hot-air balloon. Most ballooning companies depart shortly after sunrise and stay aloft for an hour or two. We suggest **Unicorn Balloon Company of Colorado, 300B, Aspen Airport Business Center, Aspen, CO 81611; 1-800-468-2478; 970-925-5752.**

Ghost Towns

Ashcroft

This shadow of a town once rivaled Aspen in importance. In the summer of 1882 Ashcroft had two main streets, three hotels, a jail and a newspaper. Horace Tabor plowed millions of dollars of his Leadville silver profits into Ashcroft's Tam O'Shanter and Montezuma mines, with modest success. It is said that when he brought his young bride, Baby Doe, to Ashcroft, a 24-hour holiday ensued, with all drinks on Tabor.

Once Aspen found its place on the map in 1883, Ashcroft started to wane. The transport of silver ore was far easier from Aspen, due to its location in the Roaring Fork Valley. Ashcroft's only route was over Pearl Pass on a rough road to Crested Butte. When the D&RG Railroad puffed into Aspen in 1887, the quiet fate of Ashcroft was secured. Today only nine buildings remain of the town that once boasted a population of 2,500. But it is still nestled in a beautiful location surrounded by the Elk Mountains.

To get to Ashcroft from Aspen, follow Hwy. 82 west to Castle Creek Rd. Turn left and continue up Castle Creek Rd. for 12 miles until reaching the sign for Toklat gallery. Ashcroft is in the valley east of Toklat. An interpreter (from the Aspen Historical Society), known as the "ghost of Ashcroft," may be there to make your visit more meaningful. Small admission charged to provide upkeep.

Independence

See the Scenic Drives section.

Gondola Rides

Climb aboard Aspen Mountain's Silver Queen gondola and enjoy on-mountain activities with a stunning mountain backdrop. You can hike up and ride back down to town for free. On top, check out the new Sun Deck restaurant or play a round of disk golf, take a guided nature walk or enjoy occasional classical music concerts. Runs daily from mid-June to late Sept., and on weekends before and after the peak season. For information contact the **Gondola Ticket Office** at **970-920-0719.**

Hot Springs

Conundrum Hot Springs

These springs in the Maroon Bells–Snowmass Wilderness Area receive visitors year-round. Most people show up in midsummer. To avoid crowds, the best time to make the fairly long (9 miles one way) but not overly steep hike is in spring and fall. Wintertime sees ambitious and skillful cross-country skiers visiting for a quick soak before returning in the afternoon. Beware of avalanche danger in this area.

Conundrum Hot Springs is located on Conundrum Creek, a couple of miles down the valley from Triangle Pass, which leads over into the Gunnison/Crested Butte area. Two pools, one about 3 feet deep and the other 4 feet deep, provide an excellent soaking temperature between 99° and 103° F.

Conundrum is overused, so please camp at designated sites only. Fires are restricted. To reach the trailhead from Aspen, head about 5 miles up Castle Creek Rd. toward Ashcroft. Turn right onto Forest Rd. 128 and drive about a mile to the trailhead parking lot.

Museums and Galleries

Anderson Ranch Arts Center

At one time a working ranch, this place has gained quite a reputation in the arts community as a place to come and learn from the best. Each summer photographers, painters, woodworkers and furniture designers, among others, enroll in one- or two-week courses taught by visiting masters. The ranch offers self-guided tours of the galleries and grounds during weekdays. **5263 Owl Creek Rd., P.O. Box 5598, Snowmass Village, CO 81615; 970-923-3181; www. andersonranch.com.**

Aspen Art Museum

Featuring changing exhibitions with an emphasis on contemporary art, this museum provides stimulating year-round programming, including art classes for children and adults, free lectures, members' art trips and more. The museum is in a historic brick building in a park area near the Roaring Fork River, with views to Red and Aspen Mountains. Open Tues.–Sat. 10 A.M–6 P.M., Sun. noon–6 P.M., closed Mon. A free reception and gallery tour is offered each Thurs. 5–7 P.M. Saturday admission is free. **590 N. Mill St., Aspen, CO 81611; 970-925-8050; www. aspenartmuseum.org.**

Aspen Galleries

Paintings, sculpture, Eskimo and Native American art, gemstones, photography, jewelry, pottery, weavings—Aspen galleries run the gamut. This town is one of the best places to gallery-hop this side of Rodeo Drive. *Aspen* magazine has a rundown of galleries that belong to the Aspen Fine Arts Association. Or check in with the Aspen Visitors Center in the Wheeler Opera House.

Rocky Mountain Institute (RMI)

With the help of more than 100 volunteers, Amory and Hunter Lovins built a 4,000-square-foot research center near Old Snowmass. In keeping with RMI philosophy, their showpiece is built with super insulation and an earth-sheltering, passive solar design, but without a conventional heating system. Low-energy appliances are used whenever possible. Showers and toilets are designed to drastically reduce water consumption. The researchers employed at RMI seem to understand the perils of our energy-squandering lifestyles and are out to make a difference. There are small group tours, or you can take a self-guided weekday tour. Contact RMI at **1739 Snowmass Creek Rd., Snowmass, CO 81654-9199; 970-927-3851; www. rmi.org.**

Wheeler Stallard House Museum

The Aspen Historical Society is located in the spacious house Jerome B. Wheeler built in 1888 in a futile effort to entice his wife to Aspen from Manitou Springs. (She never budged.) Inside you'll find authentic Victorian furnishings that have been donated by various families. A re-created living room, dining room and kitchen occupy the main floor. The upstairs features collections of photos, clothing and children's toys. The museum gift shop sells books and other items of interest.

An interesting staff adds life to an otherwise quiet and musty museum. On one visit we heard incredible stories about the Aspen of old; Hilder Anderson reminisced about growing up on her ranch in Snowmass: "Back in 1914 a Swedish classmate taught me how to ski. And we took some ribbing at school from kids who said that 'only a dumb Swede would ski!'" The times have changed a bit. Ask about historical walking tours in the west end as well as downtown. Open 1–4 P.M. daily, in summer and during ski season. Small admission fee. **620 W. Bleeker St.; 970-925-3721.**

Nightlife

The nightlife in Aspen is not to be missed. Whether you want a quiet night in a piano bar or an all-night binge, you'll find it here.

Caribou Club

This members-only nightclub offers weeklong memberships with a price tag that'll make you wince. Once past the snobbish hostess, you'll see a relaxed and exclusive crowd hanging out on overstuffed furniture, drinking at the bar or dancing in the smallish but lively disco room. Call for information and hours: **970-925-2929.**

Crystal Palace Dinner Theatre

Okay, so this place is rather expensive and touristy. But for more than four decades this cabaret revue has entertained with its high-energy, satirical fun and multitalented performers. Backlit stained glass, a mammoth chandelier and a balcony railing formed from wrought-iron bedsteads whimsically decorate the Crystal Palace. Two seatings nightly in winter; reservations strongly recommended. **300 E. Hyman Ave.; 970-925-1455; www.aspen. com/crystalpalace.**

Double Diamond

Top-notch live music can be heard in this small club setting that seems to have had more names than Elizabeth Taylor has had husbands. A well-placed dance floor just in front of the stage draws an energetic crowd to its feet. **450 S. Galena St.; 970-920-6905.**

Explore Bookstore and Bistro

For dessert and gourmet coffees in a refined Victorian setting, this is the choice. Besides the usual espresso and cappuccino, Explore also offers a wide selection of teas, juices and mineral waters. Check out the extensive vegetarian menu. Open daily 10 A.M–midnight. **221 E. Main; 970-925-5336.**

The J Bar

Located in the historic Hotel Jerome, built in 1889, this bar goes back a few years. It attracts a diverse crowd of elbow-benders. In Aspen's early ski days, John Wayne brawled here, and playwright Thornton Wilder impressed local ranchers with his legendary drinking capacity. The ceiling is decorated with pressed-tin designs, and there is a great old wooden bar. Belly up to the bar for an après-ski drink or stop in after dinner when things pick up. **330 E. Main St.; 970-920-1000.**

The Little Nell

Listening to strains of live jazz in peak summer and winter seasons with a perfectly mixed cocktail makes you feel like a million (even if you're not!). See the Where to Stay section for more information.

Ultimate Taxi

You won't forget this ride in an old Checker cab, decked out with a computerized sound system, fog machine, laser show, spinning disco ball and 160 lights. It's better than a disco. Jon Barnes, owner of the taxi, cranks up the tunes before pulling down a microphone and banging away at a couple of keyboards. **970-925-0361.**

Wheeler Opera House

Jerome B. Wheeler built this three-story Victorian showpiece in 1889. For many years the opera house languished in disrepair, a burned-out reminder of better days. Today, nicely restored, it is home to Aspen's artistic and cultural community. Natural wood is used lavishly throughout, contrasted by plush velvet stage curtains, red carpeting and gold stars painted on the ceiling; an elegant chandelier dominates the interior. Enjoy a year-round program of music, theater, dance and film. Check with the ticket office at **970-920-5770** for the performance schedule or a historic tour. **320 E. Hyman Ave.; www.wheeleroperahouse. com.**

Woody Creek Tavern

For information on this rustic bar/restaurant, see the Where to Eat section.

Scenic Drives

Independence Pass

This narrow, winding route, braced on one side by a stone guardrail, provides a bit of excitement for flatlanders unaccustomed to mountain driving. It is unquestionably at its colorful best during autumn and is impassable in winter. The pass, with its barren summit at 12,500 feet on the Continental Divide, provides the best route through the Sawatch Range; when the pass is closed, the drive to Aspen from the east is substantially longer.

The story goes that the pass is named Independence because of a gold strike on July 4,

1879, 4 miles west of the pass. A town quickly grew on that site. In the early 1880s Independence had daily stage service to Leadville. (Reportedly, the population of only 2,000 supported 10 saloons.) The treacherous road over Independence Pass fell into disuse soon after the arrival of railroads into the lower valleys. Going over the pass required 10 to 25 hours, several changes of horses and payment at three tollgates. Since no railroad ever made its way to Independence, the town was all but a memory by the turn of the century.

You might pull off at the Grottos, a series of granite caverns 8 miles east of Aspen (see the Hiking and Backpacking section). To reach Independence Pass, follow Hwy. 82 east from Aspen. About 15 miles from Aspen, before reaching the summit, look to your right. You will see the remains of Independence down below the road. At the summit you'll find a parking area and a short walking trail. Closed in winter.

Wildlife

Aspen Center for Environmental Studies

In 1968 Elizabeth Paepcke founded this non-profit foundation to preserve Hallam Lake, on the north edge of town. The Aspen Center for Environmental Studies (ACES) provides environmental programs for local schoolkids and offers a series of summer programs aimed at enhancing awareness of the environment around Aspen. Year-round tours are available of Hallam Lake Wildlife Sanctuary. ACES has a range of interesting and informative programs, including tours of the ski mountains in summer and in winter (snowshoes required). **100 Puppy Smith St., Aspen, CO 81611; 970-925-5756; www. aspen.com/aces.**

Where to Stay

Accommodations

The array of lodging choices in Aspen runs the gamut from ritzy, full-service hotels to small, European-style ski lodges to luxury condominiums. You will not, however, find many large chain hotels, due to strict zoning requirements. Down-valley in the emerging towns of **Carbondale** and **Basalt,** you can find some chains, including a Best Western and a Days Inn. Staying overnight in Aspen is generally more expensive than in other parts of the state, especially in high season when rooms are at a premium. We have listed some of the more outstanding accommodations in Aspen, geared to suit a variety of tastes and budgets. For a more complete listing, contact **Aspen Central Reservations; 1-800-262-7736; 970-925-9000; www.destinationaspen.com.**

Hotel Jerome—$$$$

Only the Jerome truly reflects the limelight Aspen experienced during its prosperous silver boom. After a decades-long slide into disrepair, a major renovation completed in 1989 put the Jerome back where it belongs—in a league with the finest historic hotels in the country. Layers of paint were stripped, revealing sandstone and beautiful wood that had not seen daylight for the better part of 60 years. Furniture was restored and priceless tile and solid-iron door fixtures were polished for reuse. The end result is a comfortable, plush hotel that's worth a look around even if you aren't spending the night.

Jerome B. Wheeler, the onetime president of Macy's department store in New York City and Aspen's major benefactor, took over the unfinished hotel project after the original developers fled town. He opened the grand hotel on Thanksgiving Eve, 1889. Today the Jerome offers 27 luxurious rooms, including 7 guest suites in the original hotel building. The new wing offers an additional 67 guest rooms (no two rooms are the same). The hotel lobby is marvelously plush with restored antique sofas and chairs. An open core in the center of the building rises three stories to a glass-covered ceiling. The original bar, restaurant and ballroom are worth visiting. For a unique après-ski scene, check out the pool on the west side of the building or head to the J Bar (see the Nightlife section). Reserve far in advance

A red fox pauses on a winter day. Photo by James Prout, courtesy of Aspen Skiing Company.

for peak times. **330 E. Main St., Aspen, CO 81611; 1-800-331-7213; 970-920-1000; www. hoteljerome.com.**

The Little Nell—$$$$

This 92-room luxury hotel at the base of Ajax provides the easiest ski-in/ski-out location in town. It takes a while to fully appreciate the muted interior colors, but the logic of this hotel's soothing, contemporary design soon becomes obvious. After mixing a drink at your own private wet bar, cranking up the gas fireplace and sinking into a down-filled chair, this hotel will grow on you. All of the spacious rooms and suites come equipped. Hidden away in an armoire lies a remote-controlled TV/ VCR. Most rooms have balconies offering views up the mountain and overlooking the year-round heated pool and whirlpool bath. Leave your skis with the ski concierge, who will, for a fee, wax them and sharpen the edges overnight.

The oversized marble bathrooms (fitted with brass) have functional spaces to eliminate any tie-ups. The Little Nell also features a state-of-the-art exercise facility as well as a nice bar, a highly regarded restaurant and plush common living room. This five-star, five-diamond property has no problem booking rooms well in advance. **675 E. Durant St., Aspen, CO 81611; 1-800-525-6200; 970-920-4600; www. thelittlenell.com.**

St. Regis Hotel—$$$$

The "Hotel Formerly Known as the Ritz" offers truly elegant accommodations to those who can afford it. The size by Aspen standards is monolithic—some 257 rooms occupy the horseshoe-shaped structure built to provide mountain views from every room. The hotel feels like it's been around for a long while thanks to the Colorado red brick exterior and classic design. The upper-crust style, luxury features and round-the-clock service has a place in Aspen. The lobby comes off surprisingly warm with its detailed attention to sights, sounds and textures; fresh flowers, lush wood, soft music and fabulous art and sculpture can be found throughout the hotel. Rooms, with every conceivable amenity, include three phones, a safe, a bathroom scale and, of course, a stocked bar and fridge. The beauty salon appears larger than the spa, although there is also an inviting outdoor pool and hot tub. Your choice of restaurants and bars. Reserve rooms far in advance. **315 E. Dean St., Aspen, CO 81611; 1-888-454-9005; 970-920-3300; www.stregisaspen.com.**

Sardy House—$$$$

Bordered by two towering blue spruces, Sardy House is a beautifully restored Queen Anne Victorian mansion steeped in history. As you pass the red brick Sardy House on Main St., its gables, turrets and balcony will provoke you into taking a second look. Inside, oak staircases lead to well-appointed guest rooms and suites. The many amenities at the Sardy House more than make up for the sometimes smallish rooms, but you will find more space in any of the six suites.

You'll find TVs and VCRs only by looking inside the cherry wood armoires. Laura Ashley prints overlay the feather comforters, and many of the hardwood ceilings are vaulted and multiangled. White-tiled bathrooms have new fixtures done in the old style and heated towel racks. A connected carriage house offers newer rooms; those on the upper floor have unique angled ceilings. Outside you'll find a heated swimming pool and a whirlpool bath. A full table-served breakfast is included in the room rate. **Jack's Restaurant,** on the main floor, serves gourmet dinners (**$$$ to $$$$**) to the public in a cozy, romantic atmosphere. **128 E. Main St., Aspen, CO 81611; 1-800-321-3457; 970-920-2525; www.aspen. com/sardylenado.**

St. Moritz Lodge—$$ to $$$

"Sometimes I feel more like a bartender than a desk clerk," said the guy behind the counter at Aspen's most reasonably priced, loud and lively lodge. Not that he pours drinks—but he does dispense advice, and most travelers tend to hang out in the somewhat worn lobby and get to know one another. Choose from a condo, a smallish private room or a dorm room (this is Aspen's unofficial youth hostel). Enjoy the deck and small heated pool. Continental breakfast available in winter and summer; consider sticking around for the après-ski party after a day on the slopes. Weekly and monthly rentals available. While you will find refrigerators in every room, they don't come stocked. **334 W. Hyman Ave., Aspen, CO 81611; 1-800-817-2069; 970-925-3220; www.stmoritzlodge.com.**

IN BASALT
Shenandoah Inn—$$$ to $$$$

The Frying Pan River will become a part of your everyday experience at this inn due to its backyard proximity. Every room has a river view. Better yet, enjoy the sounds of rushing water from a lounge chair on the wooden deck or from the riverside hot tub. Guests are welcome to fish the private frontage on this touted stream. This tastefully decorated inn complements the wooded surroundings; you'll appreciate the airy common areas and 16-foot flagstone fireplace. Four guest rooms have private baths; all feature hand-sewn down comforters and plenty of space. Enjoy the western decor of the original homestead on the property. This stand-alone cabin, with a full kitchen, is rented for up to four people. Bob and Terri Zeits will welcome you into their beautiful home. Bob, a professional chef, treats you to a multicourse gourmet breakfast. "Just come and hang out," says Terri. **P.O. Box 560, Basalt, CO 81621; 1-800-804-5520; 970-927-4991; www. shenandoahinn.com.**

IN CARBONDALE
Mt. Sopris Bed and Breakfast—$$$$

With magnificent views of Mt. Sopris from atop a bluff near Carbondale, this B&B will seduce you into returning time and again. In three log buildings situated around a pool and hot tub, you will find 13 guest rooms, each with private bathroom. Decorated tastefully and impeccably clean, with conveniences such as TV and telephones, this place should be on your radar if you want to take an adult retreat from the everyday. A full breakfast is served in the open dining room each morning at 8:30 so that guests have a chance to get to know each other. The spacious great room features a river-rock fireplace and grand piano and views out of a wall of windows to Mt. Sopris. A flagstone patio entices you outdoors during warmer months. The owner, now in her eighties, has turned over day-to-day operations to a caretaker. No children, no smoking and no pets. **0165 Mt. Sopris Rd., P.O. Box 126, Carbondale, CO 81623; 1-800-437-8675; 970-963-2209; www.mtsoprisinn.com.**

Ambiance Inn—$$$

Stretch out and enjoy one of the four large, comfortable rooms with private baths in this contemporary house off Main St. in Carbondale. It's an absolute bargain by Aspen standards. The huge Aspen Suite with its ski motif and knotty pine walls was our favorite. While comfortable, none of the rooms are going to win any interior design awards. An excellent full breakfast is provided downstairs at 8 A.M. sharp. Your hosts,

Norma and Robert, are friendly, knowledgeable and nonintrusive. Norma will fix dinner with a day's notice. **66 2nd St., Carbondale, CO 81623; 1-800-350-1515; 970-963-3597; www. ambianceinn.com.**

IN SNOWMASS VILLAGE

A number of fine attributes (besides the skiing) entice people to venture to Snowmass, but unique or historical lodging opportunities are not among them. Those seeking a full-service resort atmosphere should check into the **Snowmass Club Lodge ($$$$),** which offers plush accommodations along with an athletic club, restaurant, golf course and indoor tennis courts. **P.O. Box G-2, Snowmass Village, CO 81615; 1-800-525-0710; 970-923-5600; www. snowmassclub.com.**

Another nice slopeside hotel, the **Silver Tree,** offers full-service amenities including three restaurants. **P.O. Box 5009, Snowmass Village, CO 81615; 1-800-837-4255; www. silvertree.com.**

Most of the Snowmass condo buildings stair-step right up the ski mountain. This ski-in/ski-out accessibility enables you to buckle your ski boots in your living room. The condos are an especially good option for families and people who want to escape the hurly-burly of Aspen. A small village at the base of the mountain will meet your dining and shopping needs. For reservations contact the **Snowmass Village Resort Association; 1-800-332-3245; www.snow massvillage.com.**

Camping

White River National Forest

In the Aspen area are 15 Forest Service camp-grounds equipped with a variety of facilities ranging from primitive to plush. Most campsites are assigned on a first-come, first-served basis. Selected campgrounds in the area accept reservations at least 10 days in advance at **1-877-444-6777** or **www.reserveusa.com.** For more information: **Aspen Ranger District Office, 806 W. Hallam St., Aspen, CO** **81611; 970-925-3445; www.fs.fed.us/r2/ whiteriver.**

Toward Independence Pass

Up the valley on Hwy. 82 are five campgrounds to choose from before you reach the pass. **Difficult Campground** (47 sites, fee charged) is the closest to Aspen—5 miles. Farther up Hwy. 82 you'll find **Weller** (11 sites, fee charged), **Lincoln Gulch** (7 sites, fee charged) and **Lost Man** (9 sites, fee charged) **Camp-grounds,** located 9 miles, 11 miles and 14.5 miles, respectively, from Aspen. Up Hwy. 82, 11 miles from Aspen, turn south up Lincoln Creek Rd. for 7 miles to reach **Portal Camp-ground** (7 sites, no fee) on Grizzly Reservoir. This road is not maintained and may be tough going for trailers and passenger cars. For reservations check **1-800-820-CAMP** or **www. reserveusa.com.**

Up Maroon Creek Road

See the Major Attractions section for information.

Up the Fryingpan River

Although a bit far from Aspen, the drive may be worth it if you seek solitude and great fishing. From Aspen drive northwest on Hwy. 82 for 18 miles to Basalt. From Basalt, head upriver on Fryingpan Rd. (County Rd. 105) to Ruedi Reservoir. Four campgrounds at **Ruedi** charge a fee: **Mollie B** (26 sites), **Little Maud** (22 sites), **Little Mattie** (20 sites) and **Dear-hamer** (13 sites). A few miles above the reservoir are two other campgrounds: **Elk Wallow** (8 sites, no pump water, no fee) and **Chapman** (42 sites, fee charged).

Private Campgrounds

BRB Crystal River Resort—Provides shaded sites for tents and RVs in a nice location along the Crystal River. Offers a couple dozen log cabins (studios and one-bedrooms) during summer. **7207 Hwy. 133, Carbondale, CO 81623; 970-963-2341; www.coloradovacation.com/ cabins/brb.**

Where to Eat

More than 100 restaurants, ranging from five-star masterpieces to dive diners, call Aspen home. Surprisingly, unlike the revolving door of most resort towns, the Aspen area manages to keep a stable of consistent eateries. Following are some of the best.

Pine Creek Cookhouse—$$$$

Imagine a light falling snow under a full moon. Place yourself on cross-country skis or in a horse-drawn sleigh in the Castle Creek Valley, 12 miles from Aspen, and head to an offbeat dining experience. Starting at the ghost town of Ashcroft, the 1.5-mile jaunt through the woods to a tastefully decorated backcountry restaurant heightens your senses and creates a certain camaraderie among guests. You have a choice of entrées each evening. Cornish game hen, herbed Rocky Mountain trout and roast leg of lamb were served during our visit. The set dinner price includes a guide, cross-country ski rental and a miner's lamp. The sleigh ride is an extra. When skiing at the Ashcroft Touring Center stop in for **lunch ($$$)**, served noon–2:30 P.M. In summer it is possible to drive or hike to the cookhouse and enjoy a nice buffet lunch. Reservations a must. **Ashcroft Touring Center; 970-925-1044.**

Butch's Lobster Bar—$$$ to $$$$

Unless you know what you're looking for, this Snowmass restaurant can be tough to find, but definitely worth it. It's a slice of the Eastern seaboard. The well-trained staff serves up plates of excellent steamers, mussels, scallops and fried clams. You can, of course, order lobster, or try the hot spiced garlic shrimp, softshell crab or any of the six nightly fish specials. You'll get to know Butch's fish-loving friends in the various pictures on the walls—he's a former Cape Cod lobsterman. Kids' menu and full bar. Open nightly from 5:30 P.M. in winter, 6 P.M. in summer. Reservations recommended. Located at the Timberline Condos in Snowmass directly across from free parking in Lot 13. **970-923-4004.**

Krabloonik's—$$$ to $$$$

As a working sled-dog kennel, Krabloonik's has to be one of the most unusual places to dine in the Aspen area, if not in the entire country—due in part to the 300 yipping dogs near the entrance. Located up the road from Snowmass Ski Area, this atmospheric log cabin offers a spectacular view up the valley to Mt. Daly and 14,130-foot Capitol Peak. The decor is Alaskan rustic, but white tablecloths and fine crystal immediately clue you in to the fact that gourmet-caliber fare will be served. Wild game selections include moose, caribou, elk and wild boar shipped in from as far away as New Zealand. Choose from more than 200 wines and a European beer list. Open for lunch 11 A.M.–2 P.M. and dinner from 5:30 P.M. daily in winter (dinner-only in summer). Skiers at Snowmass can reach the restaurant via Dawdler Trail. Reservations are essential (months in advance for the peak holiday period). For information about a dogsled ride, see the Dog Sledding section. Located a quarter-mile above Snowmass Ski Area on **4250 Divide Rd., Snowmass Village; 970-923-3953.**

Campo de Fiori—$$ to $$$$

Elizabeth and Luigi Giordani founded this restaurant, which has zoomed into the forefront of excellent nouvean Italian fare. Pull up at the small bar and watch the hip crowd and the intense action in the open kitchen. Taking in the earthy surroundings and wonderful aromas, you won't mind waiting for a table. Campo celebrates life, food and wine. We suggest the seafood entrées, especially the grilled dishes, but you may just want to linger over a steaming plate of pasta. The authentic Italian flavors, starting with fresh bread dipped in a little olive oil, will make you savor each bite. Get a reservation. **205 S. Mill St.; 970-920-7717.**

Takah Sushi—$$ to $$$$

Only in Aspen would you find a long-running sushi war as well as a newspaper war. Here Takah Sushi edges the chic Kenichi, due to local loyalty. It's the casual, friendly atmosphere along with the creative Japanese and Pacific Rim menu that keeps people coming back. Try their tempura, or head straight to the sushi bar, where the chefs will amaze you with their artistry. Open nightly from 5 P.M. On the **Hyman Ave. Mall; 970-925-8588.**

La Cocina—$$

Since 1971 this has been a consistent and deserving favorite among locals. La Cocina offers creative New Mexican-style food; its good value makes it a highlight in Aspen. The owners, Nick and Sarah Lebby, work seven days a week, Sarah in the kitchen and Nick greeting and seating guests. La Cocina's menu favorites include the Cocina bean dip appetizer, any enchilada plate and the blue corn tortilla dinner. Don't miss the Chocolate Velvet dessert. New Mexican decor and a friendly, down-to-earth atmosphere. Hours are 5–10 P.M. daily. No reservations, but they now accept credit cards. **308 E. Hopkins Ave.; 970-925-9714.**

Wienerstube—$ to $$

A couple of talented Austrian chefs opened the Wienerstube in 1965. Breakfast at this popular restaurant has become something of an Aspen tradition. Enjoy the light garden setting, which is complemented by lots of stained glass. A "stammtisch" table serves as a gathering place for regular customers. Breakfast choices include traditional bacon and eggs as well as eggs Benedict, crêpes, Belgian waffles with fruit and homemade Viennese pastries. Open for breakfast 7–11 A.M. The extensive lunch menu is served 11 A.M.–2:30 P.M.; closed Mon. **633 E. Hyman Ave.; 970-925-3357.**

Woody Creek Tavern—$ to $$

When the glitz of Aspen starts to get to you, stop in at the Woody Creek Tavern for a game of pool, a burger and a cheap beer on tap. You might ask about the house drink: the Biff. Occasionally Don Henley or Hunter S. Thompson has been known to stop by this local hangout. Nice patio in summer. Mexican food, burgers and chicken make up the menu—the hot chicken wings are great. To get there take Hwy. 82 down-valley from Aspen for a few miles and turn right on Woody Creek Rd. Follow the road across a bridge and turn left at the fork. The tavern is just down the road from there. Serving lunch and dinner 11:30 A.M.–10 P.M. **2 Woody Creek Plaza, Woody Creek; 970-923-4585.**

Popcorn Wagon—$

Calming classical music, crêpes and a nice little outdoor seating area can be found along with inexpensive drinks and, yes, popcorn. It's a great value right in the center of town. The historic wagon, built in Chicago in 1913, has been in operation for more than three decades—a long time for any Aspen restaurant. Located across from the Wheeler Opera House on **Hyman Ave. and Mill St.**

IN BASALT
Chefy's—$$$ to $$$$

Heading down-valley to Basalt may seem like a pain if you're staying in Aspen, but the food at Chefy's is worth it. Owner/chef Claude Van Horton puts major effort into his cuisine, which ranges from innovative pasta and seafood dishes to perfectly grilled steaks. The delicate sauces, artistic presentation and precision service make special meals a common occurrence. Don't even think about skipping the wild mushroom soup. Though simple, this small restaurant with an outside deck has a pleasant atmosphere that enhances your experience. Couples may want to try reserving a table in the quiet nook behind the bar. Lunch is served Mon.–Fri. 11:30 A.M.–2:30 P.M.; cocktails and appetizers are served 2:30–5:30 P.M. Open seven nights a week 5:30–9:30 P.M. for dinner; Sun. brunch. **166 Midland Ave., Basalt; 970-927-4034.**

IN CARBONDALE
Six 89—$$$$

Mark Fischer, the talented chef/owner of one of the valley's finest restaurants, cooks what can be purchased fresh at the markets, adjusting the menu as needed. Here you can describe your likes and let him create specially tailored meals in what he calls "random acts of cooking." Or you can pick from the well-considered menu, with items such as sassafrass-seared North Atlantic salmon, roasted artichoke risotto or grilled New Zealand rack of lamb. The intimate dining occurs on the main floor of a rambling brick, turn-of-the-century house. You can enjoy the patio or the polished interior, featuring woodwork, soothing lighting, fresh flowers and pressed white tablecloths. The carefully chosen wine list focuses on New World wines that complement the fresh food. Open nightly from 5:30 P.M. **689 Main St., Carbondale; 970-963-6890.**

The Village Smithy—$ to $$

If you are driving into or out of Aspen, stop in at the Village Smithy. This is without a doubt one of the finest, if not the finest, breakfast place in the valley. Located down-valley from Aspen in Carbondale, this restaurant is, appropriately, housed in an old blacksmith's shop. Eggs Benedict are the house specialty, but the huevos rancheros are a favorite with regulars. Homemade lunch items also keep locals coming back for more. Full bar available. Breakfast and lunch served 7 A.M.–2 P.M. weekdays; breakfast served until 2 P.M. on weekends. At **3rd and Main in Carbondale; 970-963-9990.**

Services

Visitor Information

Aspen Resort Association—Stop in at the Wheeler Opera House for information and advice on what to see and do in the Aspen area: **328 E. Hyman Ave., Aspen, CO 81611; 970-925-1940.** You can also check in at **425 Rio Grande Pl., Aspen, CO 81611; 1-800-262-7736; 970-925-9000; www.destinationaspen.com; www.aspen4you.com.**

Snowmass Resort Association—38 Village Sq., P.O. Box 5566, Snowmass Village, CO 81615; 1-800-332-3245; 1-800-598-2004; 970-923-2010; www.snowmassvillage.com.

Basalt Area Chamber of Commerce—P.O. Box 514, Basalt, CO 81621; 970-927-4031; **www.basaltonline.com.**

Carbondale Chamber of Commerce—0590 Hwy. 133, Carbondale, CO 81623; 970-963-1890.

Day Care

Care services—Aspen Sprouts, 970-920-1055; or **Big Burn Bears, 970-925-1220 ext. 4570** or **970-923-0570.** You can also check with the ski company at **1-800-525-6200.**

Transportation

Free shuttle buses—Buses begin at **Rubey Park** (on Durant Ave. between Mill St. and Galena St.) before whisking skiers to each of the surrounding ski mountains, the airport and business park. The buses run at least every 30 minutes and more frequently during the morning and afternoon skier rush hour. Check the Roaring Fork Transit Agency schedule before heading down-valley to Glenwood. Park-and-Ride works really well up- and down-valley. The buses come equipped with bike racks.

Free city buses—These buses serve Aspen, running four different routes from 7 A.M. to 1 A.M. All bus routes originate at Rubey Park. See the Major Attractions section for buses to the Maroon Bells. For schedules and routes: **970-925-8484; www.aspengov.com/transportation.**

High Mountain Taxi—24-hour taxi service; specializes in luxury four-wheel-drive vehicles and limousine service; **970-925-TAXI.**

Public Parking—For a reasonable fee you can park at the **Rio Grande Parking Plaza** one block from Main St. off North Mill St. **on Rio Grande Pl.** just behind the county courthouse. Another pay lot, closer to the mountain, sits at the **corner of Hyman Ave. and Original St.** Park for free at many of the Park-and-Ride lots up- and down-valley: **970-920-5267; www.aspengov.com/parking.**

Dinosaur National Monument

Remote and often overlooked, Dinosaur National Monument is a recreationist's mecca and a stunning, beautiful geological exhibit. Located in the unforgiving, arid Colorado Plateau country in the extreme northwestern corner of the state, this three-pronged, 300-square-mile monument straddles the Utah–Colorado border. In its southwestern corner, where an ancient river once flowed, lies the Dinosaur Quarry, representing one of the highest concentrations of Jurassic-period fossilized dinosaur bones in the world. Sprawled across the monument, the Uinta Mountains are one of just a few mountain ranges in the western hemisphere that run east-west. At the center of the monument at Echo Park lies the confluence of two of the West's mightiest rivers: the Green and the Yampa.

Dinosaur is a land of rugged plateaus and deep, hidden canyons that are deceptive from a distance. Like other western canyon country, the monument's parks and side gorges are best viewed and discovered from within. By far the best way to see the monument is from the river. Rafters and kayakers spend days floating through the narrow rock canyons, carved as deep as 3,300 feet over millions of years. Tranquil for a few miles, then violent and angry, the Green River pinches together for steep drops down the narrow rapids sections. Driving the back roads and hiking the backcountry of Dinosaur are other ways to experience the canyons, plateaus and mountains. If you make the effort to reach Dinosaur National Monument, you won't be disappointed.

Getting There

The two main entrances to the monument are located at Dinosaur, Colorado, and at Jensen, Utah. To reach Dinosaur (295 miles northwest of Denver), head west via Hwy. 40 through northern Colorado. From the south (Grand Junction), head west on Interstate 70 for 16 miles and turn north on Hwy. 139 to Rangely and then northwest on Hwy. 64 to Dinosaur. The northern end of the park at the Gates of Lodore can be reached via Hwy. 318, which heads northwest out of Maybell.

History

More than 140 million years ago, during the Jurassic period, dinosaurs and other creatures roamed around the area that today is Dinosaur National Monument. Many of these beasts' bones were covered and preserved over the eons until they were discovered in 1909 by paleontologist Earl Douglass. On a search for large fossils for the Carnegie Museum in Pittsburgh, Douglass was excited, to say the least, when he discovered eight apatasaurus (a.k.a. *brontosaurus*) vertebrae imbedded in what was once a sandbar

Caged dinosaurs try to escape à la Jurassic Park. Photo by Kirstin Bebell.

along an ancient river. The dinosaur bones had collected in the silt of the river and had been covered up by accumulating sand and mud.

Over the next 15 years, 350 tons of dinosaur bones and associated rock were excavated from this area and taken to the Carnegie Museum and other institutions around the world. Today 12 different species have been unearthed in what has proven to be one of the world's most productive dinosaur digs. In 1915 President Woodrow Wilson proclaimed the dinosaur dig and 80 acres around it a national monument. President Franklin D. Roosevelt expanded the monument land by adding more than 300 square miles in 1938.

At least as far back as 7000 B.C., primitive humans were making their way over the plateaus and through the canyons of northwestern Colorado. More recently (A.D. 200–1300), Fremont Man, the prehistoric hunter-gatherer and horticulturist, left marks throughout the area in the form of rock art. Petroglyphs are etched into scores of canyon walls in the shape of humans, sheep, lizards and numerous other renderings of life as seen through the eyes of these ancients.

Whether these etchings are a form of written language or of art is still not known.

Modern humans' first recorded ventures into the area began in 1776 with the Franciscan friars Dominguez and Escalante, who traveled just south of Dinosaur on their search for a safe route to the West Coast from Santa Fe. When the beaver pelt business was booming in the early 1800s, trappers who fanned out in the Wyoming, Utah and Colorado area met periodically at a rendezvous spot along the Green River called Brown's Park. This area is just north of the monument boundary.

With people entering the area to trap and later to search for gold, it was only a matter of time before they discovered the canyons on the Green and Yampa Rivers. In 1825 Gen. William H. Ashley, a fur trader from Missouri, floated through perhaps the most treacherous section of the Green River—Lodore Canyon. The group of men he assembled in Missouri for one of his many trips west read like a Who's Who of mountain men, including Jim Beckwourth, Jim Bridger, John Colter and Jedediah Smith. In 1869 Maj. John Wesley Powell brought news of the Dinosaur area and its river to the world through his compelling journal entries, written during his much-publicized survey and exploration trip west. A few years later, he again floated the upper Green River down through its narrow canyons in northwestern Colorado. These accomplishments become even more significant given the fact that Powell had only one arm.

Due to Dinosaur's remote location and rough terrain, sections of the area remained wild and unexplored until well into the 1900s. At the turn of the century, some settlers entered the region to homestead the remote canyons and parks. Cattle rustlers, highwaymen and bank robbers also found the area a perfect place to hide out between jobs while the heat wore off. Butch Cassidy and his Wild Bunch frequented Brown's Park (then called Brown's Hole).

Dinosaur National Monument has the distinction of being one of the first sites in the country where environmental interests outstripped those of developers. From about 1950 to 1955 intense debates raged over two proposed dams that would have flooded the canyons and covered up forever the ancient rock art. Largely due to efforts by the Sierra Club to increase public awareness, the proposed site was canceled. Today the rivers in the northwestern corner of the state remain free flowing, though civilization's need for water constantly threatens the fragile desert with new dam proposals.

Facts About the Monument

Dinosaur Quarry
Come and visit the place where the first dinosaur bones were discovered in 1909. This is the only place in the monument to see dinosaur bones. An enormous structure encloses the quarry where, until 1991, technicians worked to uncover and extract dinosaur remains. Visible from within the building is an exposed hillside with fossilized remains of at least one Jurassic

critter. Visitors can browse through the displays and ask questions of the park ranger on duty. The entrance is 7 miles north of Jensen, Utah. From the parking lot, a shuttle bus, which operates from Memorial Day to Labor Day, takes you up to the quarry; you can drive up yourself during the rest of the year. The quarry visitor center is open 8 A.M.–7 P.M. daily from Memorial Day to Labor Day, 8 A.M.–4:30 P.M. the rest of the year. Fee charged. Jensen, Utah, is 20 miles west of Dinosaur, Colorado, on Hwy. 40. For more information, call the quarry at **435-789-2115.**

Monument Headquarters
The headquarters is located 2 miles east of the town of Dinosaur at the intersection of Hwy. 40 and Harper's Corner Rd. There is an audiovisual program as well as exhibits. Free admission. Obtain backcountry camping permits and any information you need here. Open daily, 8 A.M.–6 P.M. Memorial Day to Labor Day, 8 A.M.–4:30 P.M. the rest of the year; closed holidays; **970-374-3000.**

Services and Information
Gas, food and lodging are not available within Dinosaur National Monument. The towns of Dinosaur and Rangely offer the closest services

Rock art decorates many canyon walls in Dinosaur National Monument. Photo by Kirstin Bebell.

in Colorado; Jensen (no lodging) and Vernal have what you need on the Utah side. There are two well-equipped visitor information centers on the fringe of the national monument: one on Route 64 in the town of **Dinosaur, 970-374-2205;** and the other in **Jensen, Utah, 801-789-4002; www.nps.gov/dino.**

Weather

The Dinosaur area is arid, but this doesn't necessarily mean hot. In the summer it can get very hot during the day, but it cools down at night. Thunderstorms are common during June, July and Aug. Snow usually falls by Oct., with cold weather continuing into the spring—temperatures below 32° F are common. Dress accordingly.

Outdoor Activities

Biking

MOUNTAIN BIKING
Yampa Valley Trail

The opening of this multiple-use, single- and double-track trail is beginning to attract mountain bikers along its 85-mile length. The rugged trail extends through Craig to Dinosaur National Monument along the Yampa River for the most part, but unfortunately it also tracks the shoulder of Hwy. 40 for a portion of the trip. Our recommendation for mountain bikers is to check out the section between Maybell and Echo Park. For more information contact the Bureau of Land Management (BLM) office in Craig at **970-826-5000.** For a guided tour of this or other backcountry trails contact **Holiday River and Bike Expeditions** in Salt Lake City: **1-800-624-6323; 801-266-2087; www.bikeraft.com.**

Fishing

With a fishing license, you can head out to sections of the Green and Yampa Rivers. See the Jones Hole write-up in the Hiking and Backpacking section or check with the sources at the end of this chapter for more information.

Four-Wheel-Drive Trips

Exploring the back roads in the Dinosaur area is a great way to experience the country. But be forewarned that when rain starts to fall in canyon country, some of the roads are not passable even with a four-wheel-drive vehicle. If you get stuck at the bottom of a muddy hill, you may have a long wait while the road dries—or an even longer hike out. Be sure to have plenty of gasoline, food, water and tools with you.

For road ideas in and around Dinosaur National Monument, visit the rangers at monument headquarters near the town of Dinosaur. Bureau of Land Management land surrounds practically the entire monument, offering some fascinating country just waiting to be explored. For more information about back-road possibilities, contact the BLM at the **Little Snake Field Office, 455 Emerson St., Craig, CO 81625; 970-826-5000; www.co.blm.gov.**

Crouse Canyon

Although Crouse Canyon can be driven in a passenger car in good weather, it is a very rough road for the first few miles. The route begins in Colorado, then quickly curves over into Utah for the duration of the 25-mile, dirt road trip. The Crouse Canyon Rd. begins dramatically by crossing a swinging bridge over the Green River. Once across, the road follows the river upstream for a while, on the southern edge of Brown's Park National Wildlife Refuge. Suddenly the road turns southwest and propels you into a narrow canyon. Towering rock walls and a cool stream lined with cottonwood groves await. The road eventually climbs up onto a plateau.

Be on the lookout for some of the most memorable residents of the area, the Mormon crickets. These huge, wingless grasshoppers swarm across the road, devouring their comrades who've been tragically crushed under the wheels of passing cars. When the Mormons first settled in Utah, their crops were set upon by these creatures. By "divine intervention," a flock of California gulls came to the rescue, gorging themselves on these tasty insects. The Mormons were so thankful to the birds that the California seagull was made the state bird of Utah.

To reach Crouse Canyon, head northwest from Maybell on Hwy. 318 for 62 miles to the turnoff to Brown's Park National Wildlife Refuge. Turn left and proceed on the dirt road down to and over the swinging bridge. After 25 miles, you hit a paved road that goes to Vernal, Utah, or to the Dinosaur Quarry.

Yampa Bench Road

This rough dirt road bumps and bounces its way for 42 miles through the monument and adjacent BLM land. Through canyons and over open country covered with sage, juniper and piñon, Yampa Bench Rd. offers a rugged look at the area. To reach Yampa Bench Rd., head north from monument headquarters on Harper's Corner Rd. for 25 miles to Echo Park Rd. Turn right and drive 8 miles down to the fork in the road. The right fork is Yampa Bench Rd. It comes out on Hwy. 40 at Elk Springs, 32 miles northeast of monument headquarters.

Hiking and Backpacking

Although the number of established hiking trails within the monument is rather limited, routes into side canyons are endless. Backcountry camping is allowed in the monument, but you need to obtain a free permit issued at either the quarry, monument headquarters or some of the field ranger stations. Be very careful if you venture out on your own. Take plenty of water and consult the rangers about the area you intend to backpack. Following are a few hiking and backpacking ideas.

Irish Canyon

This multicolored canyon, not more than 400 feet wide, is located outside the northern entrance of the monument. Steep walls with green, red and gray layers tower above the piñon pines in the canyon. An exhibit, petroglyphs and three

campsites are at the entrance to the canyon. Side canyons beckon to hikers. Near the north end of the canyon are two natural ponds known as the Irish Lakes. You need to bring your own drinking water for camping or hiking in this area. This is a secluded place, even though it is accessible by road. To reach Irish Canyon, head northwest from Maybell on Hwy. 318 for 41 miles and turn right on County Rd. 10N. Proceed 4 miles to the canyon entrance.

Jones Hole

Follow this 4-mile trail down along Jones Hole Creek into Whirlpool Canyon, one of the few remote parts of the **Green River** accessible on foot rather than by water. Here you can find excellent fishing for brown, rainbow and cutthroat trout, but be sure to have a valid Utah fishing license. Plenty of trees and steep rock walls (some with pictographs) along the way keep you somewhat cool in the summer heat. The trailhead is on the north side of the river, 40 miles east of Vernal. For directions and a map, stop in at monument headquarters or the quarry.

Nature Trails

There are short, interpretive nature trails at the following spots: **Split Mountain Campground, Gates of Lodore, Harper's Corner, Plug Hat Butte,** and **Sounds of Silence Trail.** The trail at Harper's Corner is 2 miles round trip and offers a fantastic view.

Willow Creek Canyon, Skull Creek Canyon and Bull Canyon

Located in a BLM Wilderness Study Area fairly close to monument headquarters, these three canyons provide spectacular backcountry hiking opportunities without marked trails. Bull Canyon, characterized by many draws, creeks, colorful cliffs and unique rock formations, is accessible from Plug Hat Picnic Area, 4 miles north on Harper's Corner Rd. from monument headquarters. Trails into Willow Creek and Skull Creek Canyons, located to the northeast of monument headquarters, can be accessed from

Hwy. 40. The upper reaches of Willow Creek offer intermittent 200-foot waterfalls in early spring. For information and maps pertaining to these beautiful, secluded canyons, contact the BLM office in Craig, **970-826-5000,** or monument headquarters, **970-374-3000; www.co.blm.gov.**

River Floating

Some of the best floating in the state can be found on several sections of the Green and Yampa Rivers, namely Cross Mountain and Split Mountain gorges, and the canyons of the Whirlpool, Lodore and Yampa Rivers. Each year commercial and private rafters and kayakers submit applications to obtain the limited permits. The best way to experience the monument is definitely from the water. Floating allows access to many places inaccessible by any other means.

Green River

The Green River flows peacefully into northwestern Colorado below Flaming Gorge, then turns south and enters the magnificent, colorful Gates of Lodore at the northern tip of the monument. It's here that the Green cuts through the Uinta Mountains, exposing 2,300-foot-deep Lodore Canyon. Once inside the 17-mile-long canyon, the river picks up speed, crashing down through the narrow passageway that has frightened and captivated so many boaters over the years. In 1869 Maj. John Wesley Powell described the scenery of Lodore Canyon as "even beyond the power of pen to tell." The Gates of Lodore, like most of the landmarks along the river, was named by Powell. It refers to a passage from a 19th-century poem by Robert Southey that Powell liked to recite to his crew as they started down the rapids in their stiff wooden boats.

Once through Lodore Canyon, the Green is met at Steamboat Rock at Echo Park by the meandering Yampa River from the east. The swollen Green then heads southwest through Whirlpool Canyon and Split Mountain Gorge, before emerging onto the desert plateau.

Gates of Lodore, a popular put-in for rafters down the Green River. Photo by Bruce Caughey.

Yampa River

Intersecting Hwy. 318 at Sunbeam, 7 miles northwest of Maybell, the Yampa River meanders west for 15 miles until it reaches the treacherous Cross Mountain Canyon. An incredibly demanding stretch of river for kayakers, Cross Mountain Gorge is only for rafters with a death wish. For 3.5 terrible miles, a virtually unending maelstrom eats rafts as it continually scours the rock canyon. The gorge comes out in Lily Park and continues to Deerlodge Park, a put-in point at the east end of Dinosaur National Monument. This is where most rafters put in for the Yampa River trip down through the Yampa River Canyon. Past alcoves and overhangs of canyon walls rising 1,000 feet, Yampa River Canyon twists and turns its way farther west. Along the banks in sheltered spots under rock overhangs, ancient campsites still show signs of fire pits, food caches and cryptic rock art. Downriver, Warm Springs Rapids shakes, rattles and rolls river mariners down to the confluence with the Green River at Echo Park. From here on it's a relatively relaxing ride down the Green.

Outfitters

More than 10 commercial outfitters offer float trips on the Green and Yampa Rivers through Dinosaur. Trips vary from one to five days in length. If you just want a day trip through Split Mountain Gorge, check with monument headquarters to see which outfitters have been granted that concession. For multi-day trips, be sure to book far in advance, because the trips fill up. Following are some of the better-known outfitters.

Adrift Adventures—One-, three- and four-day trips down the Green River, as well as five-day trips on the Yampa. **P.O. Box 192, Jensen, UT 84035; 1-800-824-0150; www. adrift.com.**

Don Hatch River Expeditions—First outfitter in the area. Bus Hatch, the father of the current owner, began running trips for "dudes" back in 1936. **P.O. Box 1150, Vernal, UT 84078; 1-800-342-8243; 801-789-4316; www. hatchriver.com.**

Holiday River and Bike Expeditions— 544 E. 3900 S., Salt Lake City, UT 84107; 1-800-624-6323; 801-266-2087; www.bike raft.com.

Mountain Sports Kayak School—Barry Smith takes kayakers down the treacherous Cross Mountain Gorge section of the Yampa River. Only advanced kayakers should consider this trip. **P.O. Box 1986, Steamboat Springs, CO 80488; 970-879-8794; 970-879-6910.**

Further Information

For more information about the rivers and obtaining permits, write the superintendent at **Dinosaur National Monument, 4545 Hwy. 40, Dinosaur, CO 81610; 970-374-3000; www.nps.gov/dino.**

Seeing and Doing

Scenic Drives

Although some of the dirt roads around the area can be driven in a regular passenger car, if it rains heavily, the desert clay becomes very slick and can make the roads impassable, even for four-wheel-drive vehicles.

Cañon Pintado

Located in Douglas Creek Valley, just south of Rangely on Hwy. 139, Cañon Pintado is an excellent area for observing the rock art left by ancient cultures. More than 50 sites on the canyon walls in the area display rock art created by the Fremont people who lived here from roughly A.D. 600 to 1300. Evidence shows that other humans inhabited the area as far back as 9000 B.C.

The canyon gets its Spanish name ("painted canyon" in English) from friars Dominguez and Escalante, who admired the artwork while riding through the canyon. To reach the canyon from Dinosaur, head south 18 miles on Hwy. 64 to Rangely. From Rangely head south into the canyon on Hwy. 139. For more information about the canyon, contact **BLM White River Field Office, 73544 Highway 64, Meeker,**

CO 81641; 970-878-3601; www.co.blm.gov./wrra/wrraindex/htm. A brochure identifying and explaining the rock art sites in the area can be obtained from the **Rangely Chamber of Commerce; 970-675-5290.**

Cub Creek

From the entrance to the Dinosaur Quarry 7 miles north of Jensen, Utah, begin this scenic 12-mile drive to Josie Morris's Cabin. Morris moved to this homestead nestled at the foot of Split Mountain in 1914 to raise livestock, vegetable crops and fruit. For 50 years she lived here, visited only occasionally by friends and relatives.

On the drive in, the view of Split Mountain is as spectacular as the rock formations along the way. About 10.5 miles from the entrance, stop and inspect the impressive array of petroglyphs. A road guide can be purchased at the entrance or at monument headquarters.

Echo Park Road

This is a highlight of the monument, offering beautiful canyons, panoramic views, rock art, history and even a cave. To get there, head north from monument headquarters on Harper's Corner Rd. for 25 miles, then turn right on Echo Park Rd. Almost immediately this dirt road begins a steep descent down into the canyons; many rocky side gorges head off from it. This section is impassable when the road is wet. After 8 miles on the dirt road there is a fork. Turn left.

After about 4 miles, you can pull off on the left side of the road to inspect the petroglyphs, which are chiseled into the rock at least 30 feet above the ground. You have to wonder how ancient people were able to get up there, but park rangers are convinced that over the years Pool Creek has eroded the canyon bottom, stranding the petroglyphs high up on the cliff. After another mile or so down the road, there is a turnoff at Whispering Cave. Once inside the arch-shaped entrance, the cool air of the cave may keep you there a while. A crack in the rock at least 100 feet high—and just wide enough to squeeze through—extends into the dark for a long distance. Bring a flashlight and see how far you get.

Another mile down the road, you come to the end of the drive, about three-quarters of a mile downstream from the confluence of the Green and Yampa Rivers. Echo Park gets its name from Maj. John Wesley Powell, who was the first to notice the incredible echoing qualities of the rock walls. Echo Park was better known at one time as Pat's Hole, named after the old Irish hermit who lived here until the early 1900s. Pat Lynch, who died in 1917 at the ripe old age of 98, was a loner who lived in the caves along the river. According to many stories, Lynch made pets of wild animals in the area, including a mountain lion, which he would screech at—and then get a far-off reply. Perhaps the original conservationist of the Dinosaur area, Lynch left these words scribbled on a piece of paper found by a local rancher's wife in a nearby cave:

If in these caverns you shelter take
Plais do to them no harm
Lave everything you find around
Hanging up or on the ground

Harper's Corner Road

The view from the overlook at Harper's Corner is one of the best into the central canyon area. A 2-mile round-trip hiking trail follows a knife-edge ridge to an overlook perched 2,500 feet above Echo Park. Harper's Corner is named after a rancher who used to keep his herd in this natural corral. Steep cliffs served to enclose most of the corral, and all he needed was a short stretch of fence to contain his herd. The 31-mile drive on Harper's Corner Rd. begins at monument headquarters. At the headquarters be sure to pick up a copy of *Journey Through Time,* a guide to interesting points along the road.

Where to Stay

Accommodations

You can't find lodging within the monument, but there are a few small, grotty motels in the town of Dinosaur, and a couple of decent ones in Rangely. If you are traveling through Craig, you might stop at the **Taylor Street Bed and Breakfast ($$).** Gary and Diana Cook have beautifully redecorated the eight guest rooms using themes such as fishing or ducks to create a comfortable atmosphere. Most rooms have private baths, though a few share. One room is wheelchair accessible. **403 Taylor St., Craig, CO 81625; 970-824-5866.** For a bigger (and better) selection try Vernal, Utah, 13 miles northwest of Jensen, Utah, on Hwy. 40. One place worth noting in Vernal is the **Rodeway Inn ($$ to $$$); 590 W. Main, Vernal, UT 84078; 801-789-8172; www.vernal rodeway.com.** Don't miss a chance to stop in at **McCarty's Rocky Mountain Soda Fountain** right next to the hotel office for a scoop of ice cream.

Camping

All of the monument's great campgrounds are available on a first-come, first-served basis. There is usually no problem finding a site, except sometimes on holidays and summer weekends. Although some of these campgrounds provide drinking water (none in the winter months), you should pack in your own to use for washing. RVs can use some of the campgrounds, but there are no hookups. Fires are allowed in designated fire rings only. If you don't want to stay in one of the designated campgrounds, talk to the rangers at monument headquarters for other car-camping and backpacking ideas.

Deerlodge Park Campground (8 primitive sites) is located just above the Yampa River Canyon. Most Yampa River floaters put in here for the trip downriver. No water and no fee. To reach Deerlodge Park, head northeast on Hwy. 40 from monument headquarters for 39 miles and turn left on Deerlodge Park Rd. Proceed 12 miles to the campground. From Maybell head southwest on Hwy. 40 for 16 miles and take a right onto Deerlodge Park Rd.

Echo Park Campground (15 sites, a group site, and 4 walk-in sites; fee in summer; drinking water in summer) lies at the confluence of the Green and Yampa Rivers. This small meadow borders the river and is surrounded by sandstone walls and Steamboat Rock, a monstrous fin of sandstone around which the river flows. Echo Park Campground is reached by following Harper's Corner Rd. 25 miles from monument headquarters. Take a right onto Echo Park Rd. (dirt) and go 13 miles. Echo Park Rd. is very steep in spots and impassable when wet. Big RVs and trailers should not attempt the drive. For more information about Echo Park, see the Scenic Drives section.

Gates of Lodore Campground (17 sites) is located at the north end of the park at the entrance to Lodore Canyon on the Green River. Most rafters put in here for a float down through the monument. To reach the campground from monument headquarters, head northeast on Hwy. 40 for 55 miles to Maybell. At Maybell turn northwest on Hwy. 318 and proceed 41 miles to a turnoff, heading left on a dirt road for 10 more miles to the campground. Fee and drinking water in summer; open year-round.

Rainbow Park Campground (2 sites) is located on the north side of the Green River, 26 miles from the Dinosaur Quarry. The primitive **Ruple Ranch Campground** (camping is allowed, but there are no designated sites) is located another 5 miles up on the north side of the Green River. The road in to these campgrounds is rough and impassable when wet. No fee. Rainbow Park has a put-in for rafters taking day trips through Split Mountain Gorge and the famous S.O.B. Rapids.

Split Mountain Campground (33 sites), open to groups only in summer, and **Green River Campground** (88 sites) are the only modern campgrounds, located 4 and 5 miles east of the Dinosaur Quarry, respectively. Fee charged. This is where many rafters take out after a trip downriver. Split Mountain itself is quite a geologic wonder. The Green River has somehow scoured and scraped away at the rock, splitting the mountain down the middle and baffling geologists at the same time. Green River Campground is open from Memorial Day to Labor Day. When Green River Campground closes, Split Mountain accepts individual campers.

Services

Visitor Information

Dinosaur National Monument—Super-intendent, 4545 Hwy. 40, Dinosaur, CO 81610; 970-374-3000.

Dinosaur Nature Association—For books, maps and other information sources. **1291 E. Hwy. 40, Vernal, UT 84078; 1-800-845-DINO; 435-789-8807; www.dinosaurnature.com.**

Colorado Welcome Center—Staffed by volunteers, this place is an excellent source of statewide information. Located at the **inter-section of Hwy. 40 and Route 64 in Dinosaur; 970-374-2205.**

Utah Visitors Center—Just south of the Dinosaur Quarry, this place is worth stopping by. Located at the **intersection of Route 40 and Hwy. 149 in Jensen, UT; 435-789-4002; 801-789-4002.**

Glenwood Springs

Indians, prospectors, gamblers, health nuts—throughout the years Glenwood Springs has attracted many types of souls, giving the area a colorful history matched only by the surrounding natural beauty.

Located at the confluence of the Colorado and Roaring Fork Rivers, Glenwood Springs is best known for its massive hot springs pool. Originally used by the Ute Indians, the hot mineral springs began attracting wealthy miners and aristocrats from around the world when the resort was built in the 1880s. These bluebloods who came to "take the waters" received first-class service at the famous Hotel Colorado. For over 100 years, people have come to Glenwood Springs to get out and enjoy numerous recreational possibilities.

Sunlight Mountain Resort and nearby Aspen attract downhill skiers. The surrounding White River National Forest offers a backcountry par-

adise. The Colorado River running through spectacular Glenwood Canyon to the east of town has some reasonably exciting stretches for rafters and kayakers. The canyon bike trail also draws in-line skaters to its super smooth "champagne concrete." The newly reopened Glenwood Caverns and Historic Fairy Caves now bring an added attraction to a town already brimming with possibilities. The list goes on.

Tourism still dominates the local economy. In contrast to its up-valley neighbor, Aspen, Glenwood is a resort town characterized by more affordable prices and friendly, down-to-earth people. Noteworthy lodging and memorable dining make Glenwood Springs a highly recommended destination for Coloradans and out-of-staters alike.

History

Long before the first Anglo settler entered the Glenwood Springs area, the Utes returned to the hot springs each season to bathe in the waters and enjoy the rejuvenating steam of the

Getting There

Glenwood Springs lies conveniently along Interstate 70, 160 miles west of Denver. It is easily accessible by car or train. **Amtrak** *trains stop in Glenwood Springs twice a day: one heads east and one heads west. Call Amtrak for more information at* **1-800-USA-RAIL** *or check* **www.amtrak.com.** *Reasonably priced commuter buses run between Glenwood Springs and Aspen and all stops in between. For schedule information call the* **Roaring Fork Rapid Transit Agency, 970-925-8484.** *Aspen's airport, 40 miles up the Roaring Fork Valley, and the Eagle County airport, 30 miles east on Interstate 70, offer daily flights from Denver year-round.*

vapor caves. The Utes called the hot springs Yampah, meaning "Big Medicine," and jealously protected them from other tribes. The site held religious significance for the Utes, and they believed the waters had magical healing powers. Isolated from the Anglo settlements to the east, the springs were not officially "discovered" until 1860. Capt. Richard Sopris was in the area to prospect, survey and explore. When a member of his party was hurt in a fall, the Utes welcomed the group to the hot springs and helped nurse the injured man back to health. Sopris named the spot Grand Springs.

In 1880 James Landis, from Leadville, claimed the hot springs as his property. This took a lot of guts (or stupidity), because the Glenwood area was still Ute territory. But the Utes were soon driven out by settlers who liked the rich, easily irrigated land.

The town's name was changed to Glenwood Springs in honor of an early pioneer's hometown, Glenwood, Iowa.

In 1885 Walter Devereux began his effort to put Glenwood Springs on the map as a hot springs resort. Devereux was an engineer, educated at both Princeton and Columbia Universities, who had been sent to Aspen to work for silver magnate and town benefactor Jerome B. Wheeler. He made his fortune quickly in the silver strikes at Aspen and then turned his attention to Glenwood Springs. Devereux incorporated the town and purchased the hot springs along with 320 acres on the south side of the Colorado River. Then, with the help of some English investors, he began building the resort he hoped would bring a little class and culture to the area.

The influx of big money into Glenwood attracted many questionable characters, and by 1887 there were no less than 22 bars within a two-block area. Among these high-profile low-lifes was Doc Holliday, the card-dealing, gun-toting dentist of Wild West fame.

In 1887 the Denver & Rio Grande Railroad arrived in Glenwood Springs to much celebration, after blasting its way through the last 20 miles of Glenwood Canyon. The town now had contact with the outside world and developed rapidly. By 1888 the world's largest hot springs pool was completed. Measuring 615 feet by 75 feet, the brick-lined pool was created by diverting the Colorado River. This unenviable task was given to the local jail inmates, who pounded away at "jailbird rock" in order to earn meals. The bathhouse was completed in 1890; it featured, among other things, a beautiful casino upstairs (used today as offices).

The icing on the cake was the completion of the Hotel Colorado in 1893, two months before the silver crash and the onset of nationwide economic troubles. However, the hotel survived well, as many of the guests were foreigners or the superrich Astors and Vanderbilts. For more about Hotel Colorado history, see the Where to Stay section.

In the late 1800s a strange phenomenon developed in Glenwood Springs—the "dude cowboy." Many European aristocrats visited the resort and thought it only fitting to take a trip into the wilderness before returning home. Local cowboys made good money as guides and quite often tried to play tricks on these rich "city slickers." Sometimes the tricks backfired.

Al Anderson, a famous local guide, tried to make a fool of his customer, Lord Rathbone, by losing him in the wilderness. Miles from nowhere, Anderson took off on his horse through some impossibly thick brush. To his great surprise, Lord Rathbone kept up with him, saying only, "By jove, that was a lively canter!" Today, of course, dude ranches exist all over the West.

After World War I, hot springs resorts went out of fashion and Glenwood's glamorous days faded into a memory. Things weren't necessarily quiet though. During Prohibition, the town achieved a questionable distinction by becoming a haven for Al Capone and other Chicago mobsters on the run.

History is everywhere in Glenwood Springs, and the town takes great pains to keep historical buildings intact and renovated. With its hot springs, Glenwood remains a perfect spot for a relaxing vacation.

Major Attractions

Glenwood Canyon

Okay, so it's not visible from outer space like the Great Wall of China. But the 12-mile stretch of four-lane freeway squeezed into the narrow Glenwood Canyon—the final piece in the interstate highway system—is surely an engineering Wonder of the World.

Completed after 13 years of steady work, the Glenwood Canyon project represents an impressive collaboration/compromise between ardent environmentalists and those eager to see the pristine canyon confines tamed by a superhighway. Engineers marvel at the impressive 6 miles of above-ground viaduct and 2 miles of tunnel that lie along the way. "Enviros" helped ensure any rock blasted away from the 2,000-foot walls was resculpted, revegetated and stained to match the natural surroundings. In addition, trees and other vegetation were purposely worked around and over to avoid any damage.

Although it's heavily traveled by trains, bikes, rafts and cars, Glenwood Canyon remains one of the most beautiful canyons in the state. This 1,800-foot-high canyon was carved by the Colorado River through layers of sedimentary rock, the oldest being 600-million-year-old Precambrian granite.

Biking and In-line Skating

The drive through the canyon is spectacular in its own right, but for an unforgettable, river's edge experience, head east into the canyon from Glenwood Springs along the cement bike path. The spectacular 20-mile bike path follows the Colorado River through the canyon. Bikers share the route with in-line skaters who love the smooth surface. Go the entire route or at least to the Hanging Lake Cutoff (see the Hiking and Backpacking section). To reach the path head east from the Vapor Caves on 6th St.

Glenwood Caverns and Historic Fairy Caves

Closed to the public since 1917, this cave system is again wowing visitors to Glenwood. The

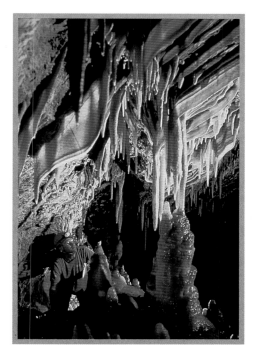

King's Row at Glenwood Caverns and Historic Fairy Caves amazes visitors with its myriad geologic formations. Photo by David Harris.

Rafters float down the Colorado River past the world's largest outdoor mineral hot springs pool in Glenwood Springs. Photo by Bruce Caughey.

grottos, caverns and labyrinths bring to light wondrous formations, including rare crystals, long strands of so-called "cave bacon" attached to the ceiling and many stalagtites and stalagmites. Newly opened sections include a five-story-high room with descending steps that access a fantastic side cavern called King's Row. The caves are in limestone, deposited about 325 million years ago, 3 miles up a winding dirt road in the mountain just behind the historic Hotel Colorado. With the help of amateur spelunkers, new passageways continue to be discovered. The newly discovered areas drip with the moisture that causes new formations to build in a continuously evolving environment. There is a marked contrast with the old section, which has dried out after being open for decades to the impacts of air and light. Visitors take a bus on the bumpy Transfer Trail up to the cave entrance, where it's always a cool and comfortable 52° F. Open Apr. 15–Nov. 1, weather permitting. Reservations suggested. Adventurous cave explorers (13 or older) may want to try the 3- to 4-hour Wild Tour. **508 Pine St., Glenwood Springs, CO 81601; 1-800-530-1635; 970-945-4CAV; www.glenwoodcaverns.com.**

Glenwood Hot Springs Pool

Completed more than 100 years ago, this facility has been soothing everyone from saddle-sore cowboys to skiers ever since. You'd be foolish not to come and relax at the "world's largest outdoor mineral hot springs pool." Open year-round, visitors suntan on the grassy area in summer; in winter, the pool provides a steamy haven from the surrounding snow. There are two pools: the large one (which can hold more than 1,000 swimmers) is heated to 90° F, and the smaller, therapeutic pool is maintained at 104° F. The hydro-tube water slide is a kick. Towels and swimsuits can be rented. Also accessible are the athletic club, bathing suit shop and restaurant. The pools are closed the second Wed. of each month during Sept. through May. Hours are 9 A.M.–10 P.M. in winter and 7:30 A.M.–10 P.M. in summer. **401 N. River St., Glenwood Springs, CO 81601; 970-945-7131.**

Yampah Spa and Vapor Caves

For hundreds of years before settlers "discovered" Glenwood Springs, the Utes brought their sick and ailing to partake in the healing qualities of the vapor caves. These caves, formed by hot mineral water percolating up through fissures in the rocks, supposedly have curative powers for ailments from asthma to constipation. The original Ute cave was on the south side of the river. Last used in 1887, it was sealed over and now lies under the railroad tracks. The caves were quite luxurious when first developed in the 1880s, with marble benches and electric lighting. Back then men and women had separate bathing times and wore linen bags with a drawstring at the neck as suits.

The Vapor Caves have been fully renovated and now you can opt for services ranging from private hot tubs to massages to facials to leg waxing. Soothing, New-Age tunes waft throughout the facility. Three separate caves are heated to a piping hot 110° F. Open every day of the year 9 A.M.–9 P.M. Located next to the hot springs pool at **709 E. 6th St., Glenwood Springs, CO 81601; 970-945-0667.**

Festivals and Events

Strawberry Days

third weekend in June Since 1898 area residents have celebrated what is now the oldest civic festival in the state—Strawberry Days. The festivities have been expanded over the years to include carnival rides, live bands and 5-kilometer and 10-kilometer footraces. One thing that hasn't changed over the years is the free strawberries and ice cream. **970-945-6589; www.glenwood chamber.com.**

Summer of Jazz

Wed. evenings in summer On summer Weds. starting at about 6:30 P.M., top musicians gather to perform an appealing mix of Dixieland, progressive and traditional jazz sounds, depending on the night. Pick up a sandwich and head for **Two Rivers Park,** at **Hwy. 6 and Two Rivers**

Park Rd.; 970-945-6589; www.glenwood chamber.com.

Outdoor Activities

Biking

MOUNTAIN BIKING

Many of the trails listed as cross-country skiing and hiking routes are also fine for mountain biking. One area worth checking out is located northwest of **Dotsero.** Head east 18 miles on Interstate 70 to Dotsero and go north. Two roads, Coffee Pot Rd. and Sweetwater Rd., both head off to the left within a few miles, providing access to the **Flat Tops area** of the White River National Forest. According to an avid Glenwood mountain biker, "The Flat Tops is like a little northern Michigan plopped down at 10,000 feet, man." Remember that no bikes are allowed in wilderness areas.

You might also try a ride up **Red Mountain,** an old ski area located on the end of West 9th St. Bike to the top of the dirt road for a great view of town and the valley. Another nearby possibility is **Red Canyon Rd.** (County Rd. 115) about 2 miles south of town on the west side of Hwy. 82. The road climbs steeply for 2 miles and then levels off a bit for the next 1.8 miles to the trailhead for Lookout Mt. Park. Scrub oak dominates the surroundings as do far-off views to Mt. Sopris and the valley south to Aspen. Or enjoy the trail system up **Four-Mile Rd.** near Ski Sunlight. The road climbs from just below the Sunlight Inn Lodge for 4 miles up to **Four Mile Park,** where you will find a network of roads and single-track trails waiting. Here you'll see tons of wildflowers in summer and changing aspen for beautiful autumn cruises.

For additional ideas, pick up (for a nominal fee) a copy of the *Hiking and Bike Trails* brochure that contains information on 19 trails. It's available from the **White River National Forest Office, 9th and Grand Ave., www.fs.sed.us/r2/whiteriver;** or the **Glenwood Springs Chamber Resort** Association, 1102 Grand Ave., www.glen woodchamber.com.

Rentals and Information

Check out any of the numerous shops in town.

BICYCLE TOURING
Glenwood Canyon
See the Major Attractions section.

Fishing

For local information about where the fish are biting, visit **Roaring Fork Anglers, 2114-B Grand Ave., Glenwood Springs, CO 81601; 970-945-0180; www.rfanglers.com.** The guys here also run a fishing guide service that includes float trips down rivers in the state. If you want a close-up view along with an education on the feeding habits and life cycles of local fish, stop by the **Glenwood Springs Fish Hatchery** at the end of Mitchell Creek west of town. These places tend to be consistently good:

Fryingpan River

Arguably one of the finest stretches of Gold Medal water in the state, the Fryingpan flows into the Roaring Fork River at the small town of Basalt, 24 miles southeast of Glenwood Springs. For more information, see the Fishing section in the **Aspen** chapter.

Rifle Gap State Park

No question that when the water level is up, this is a pretty place to throw a line: clear blue water hemmed in by sandstone and shale cliffs. You have a good chance to catch browns, rainbows, walleyes and bass. Keep an eye out for underwater spear fishers, who like this area for the exceptionally clear water. Snagging one of them would not be a pretty sight. To reach Rifle Gap Reservoir from Glenwood Springs, take Interstate 70 west for 26 miles to Rifle. Head north for 5 miles to a junction with Hwy. 325. Turn right and continue 5 miles to the state park. For information about how the fish are biting, contact the **Park Office: 970-625-1607; www. coloradoparks.org.**

Four-Wheel-Drive Trips

Transfer Trail
Climbing the mountains toward the Flat Tops to the north of town is Transfer Trail. This extremely rough road (four-wheel-drive-only after 2 miles!) was once part of the Ute trail system and then a toll road that at one time crossed the Flat Tops to the Meeker area. The first section of the road provides spectacular views down on Glenwood Springs as well as No Name Canyon. Transfer Trail also connects with other four-wheel-drive roads in the Flat Tops area. From Glenwood Springs drive west on Hwy. 6 toward West Glenwood and turn north (right) onto Transfer Trail (Forest Rd. 6020). An easier route up into the Flat Tops is Coffee Pot Rd. (Forest Rd. 600), which can be accessed 2 miles north of Dotsero, just east of Glenwood Canyon. Hard cores can eventually reach Coffee Pot Rd. from Transfer Trail and do a loop back to town.

Nearby
For some spectacular four-wheel-drive opportunities, see the **Gunnison and Crested Butte** and the **Redstone and Crystal River Valley** chapters.

Golf

Glenwood Springs Golf Club
This mature nine-hole course enjoys a commanding view up the Roaring Fork Valley to Mt. Sopris. Pro shop and restaurant; carts available. **193 Sunny Acres Rd.; 970-945-7086.**

Johnson Park Miniature Golf
That's right, miniature golf. This place, boasting two 18-hole putt-putt courses, is definitely worth a visit if you are with the family or just want to kill a couple of hours. Water cascades down a waterfall, winding its way through one of the only naturally landscaped putt-putt courses in the country. Skee-ball, picnic tables and snacks are available. Open Memorial Day to Labor Day, 9 A.M.–10 P.M.; the months of May and Sept., noon–9 P.M.; Apr. and

Oct., Fri.–Sun., noon–9 P.M. **51579 Hwy. 6** (between Glenwood and West Glenwood); **970-945-9608.**

Rifle Creek Golf Course
Avid golfers from around the state rank Rifle Creek high on their list of mountain courses, and with good reason. It's highly scenic, with strange lava dike formations of the Hogback Range running throughout the course. This 18-hole championship course is plenty challenging—especially the hilly front 9, with its canyons and spectacular elevated tee boxes. The creek comes into play on many of the back 9 holes, where you'll also see numerous woolly marmots. A memorable mountain course but, alas, the greens fees are rather steep. Open Mar.–Nov. Located 5 miles north of Rifle on Hwy. 13, and then right on Hwy. 325 for about 4 miles. **3004 Hwy. 325, Rifle, CO 81650; 970-625-1093.**

Westbank Ranch Golf Course
This nine-hole, par 70 course nests in the Roaring Fork Valley, about 5 miles south of Glenwood, just off Hwy. 82 on Old Hwy. 82. It has a pro shop and restaurant. It plays 6,264 yards from the men's tees. **1007 Westbank Rd.; 970-945-7032.**

Hiking and Backpacking
Up the Roaring Fork Valley from Glenwood Springs, no less than four wilderness areas can be reached for day hikes and extended overnight trips within White River and Gunnison National Forests. Possible trails in these areas are discussed in the **Aspen** and **Redstone and Crystal River Valley** chapters. Contact the **White River National Forest Headquarters** for maps and trail ideas, at **900 Grand Ave., Old Federal Building, Glenwood Springs, CO 81601; 970-945-2521; www.fs.sed.us/r2/whiteriver.** The National Forest Office and the Chamber of Commerce Visitors Center stock copies of the *Hiking and Bike Trails* brochure (19 trail ideas). **Summit Canyon Mountaineering (732 Grand Ave.; 970-945-6994; www.shopatsummitcanyon.com)** has

The magical waterfalls and pools at Hanging Lake make the hike worth every step. Photo by Bruce Caughey.

rental equipment and any information you may need. In the immediate vicinity, here are a few memorable day hikes:

Boy Scout Trail

This is a relatively short, moderate hike that offers great bird's-eye views of the town, the Roaring Fork Valley and Glenwood Canyon. Near the turn of the century, an observatory was built at the top of the hill, and in 1910 people flocked here for a view of Halley's Comet. The observatory burned shortly thereafter and was never rebuilt. The 1.5-mile trail begins at the dead end at the east end of 8th St. Follow the signs.

Doc Holliday's Grave

Just about anyone can take this easy half-mile hike to Linwood Cemetery. Lying on an eastern promontory, the cemetery overlooks town and a large portion of the valley. The second person to be buried here was Doc Holliday, famous gambler and gunman from the Old West. Holliday came to Glenwood Springs in the spring of 1887 to relieve his tuberculosis. It didn't help. Holliday died in Nov. of that year at the age of

35. Friends pitched in to buy a casket and bury him in this hilltop cemetery. Controversy still rages about whether or not he was really buried in the cemetery or in a plot in town. At any rate, a stone marker in the cemetery commemorates Doc Holliday and says he died in bed, a distinction Holliday would have been proud of.

Few people know that another famous (infamous, perhaps) character from the Old West is also buried in the cemetery. In the pauper grave section, a stone with the name "Harvey Logan" marks the resting place of Kid Curry. He was a bank robber and a onetime member of Butch Cassidy's legendary Hole-in-the-Wall Gang. The trail to the cemetery begins at 12th St. and Palmer Ave. A sign marks the trailhead. The hike takes about 15 minutes.

Hanging Lake

An extremely popular hiking destination, Hanging Lake is both scenic and easily accessible. It was formed by a geologic fault that caused the lake to drop down from the valley floor above, from where it is currently fed by a series of cascading waterfalls. The 1.2-mile trail, which climbs 930 feet from the floor of Glenwood Canyon, takes about 1 hour and is definitely worth the climb. Views of the falls and back down Deadhorse Canyon are spectacular. Tip: be sure to hike an extra 200 yards above the lake to Spouting Rock, where the full force of the creek shoots directly out of a hole in the cliffside. Hanging Lake's large number of visitors make it important that you help preserve the beauty of the surrounding environment by sticking to the designated trails. To reach the trailhead, head east 10 miles into Glenwood Canyon on Interstate 70 from Glenwood Springs. Look for the exit to the parking area.

Horseback Riding

AJ Brink Outfitters

These nice folks can set you up for one to five days depending on your wishes. Located 38 miles from Glenwood Springs, north of Gypsum; **970-524-7344.**

Sunlight Mountain Resort

Located 10 miles from downtown Glenwood Springs. From Hwy. 82 at the south end of Glenwood Springs, follow the signs up County Rd. 117 (Four Mile Rd.). **10901 County Rd. 117, Glenwood Springs, CO 81801; 970-945-7491.**

River Floating

Colorado River

As you probably know by now, the Colorado River flows right through Glenwood Springs, paralleling Interstate 70 on its way west. A 20-mile stretch of river that is very popular for rafters and kayakers begins just below Shoshone Power Plant (in Glenwood Canyon), crashes down through the canyon, through Glenwood Springs and downriver to New Castle. The Glenwood Canyon stretch has some exciting rapids, petering out at the mouth of Grizzly Creek. The calm water down through town offers just a few ripples. Below Glenwood Springs the river enters South Canyon, which

offers some exciting rapids for the remainder of the way to New Castle.

Roaring Fork River

The 13.5-mile stretch from Carbondale on down to Glenwood Springs along the Roaring Fork River is popular with many kayakers, rafters and canoeists. The rapids are fairly mellow (Class I and Class II) but offer a few surprises, especially for people just out for a leisurely float. The river drops an average of 27 feet per mile along this stretch, with many good places to take out on the north end of Glenwood Springs.

Outfitters

Blue Sky—With its office located on the ground floor of the Hotel Colorado, Blue Sky has been offering trips on the Colorado and Roaring Fork since 1975. **970-945-6605; www.blueskyadventures.com.**

Rock Gardens—Locals consistently give high praise to Rock Gardens Rafting, which offers trips down the Colorado from Shoshone Power Plant in Glenwood Canyon and along the Roaring Fork. Located just off the No Name exit in Glenwood Canyon at **1308 County Rd. 129; 970-945-6737; www.rockgardens.com.**

Skiing

CROSS-COUNTRY SKIING AND SNOWSHOEING

As with hiking and mountain biking, the area's cross-country skiing and snowshoeing possibilities are plentiful. Whether it's track skiing or a backcountry adventure, you'll find it nearby. For further information about trail possibilities, maps and avalanche danger, contact the **White River National Forest Headquarters, 9th and Grand Ave., Glenwood Springs, CO 81601; 970-945-2521; www.fs.sed.us/r2/whiteriver.**

Backcountry Trails

Sunlight Peak and Four Mile Park—Trails in these areas are among the nearby possibilities.

From the 10,603-foot summit of Sunlight Peak Trail, views up and down the Roaring Fork Valley are fantastic. Four Mile Park trails are well maintained in winter for snowmobile use. If you don't mind sharing the trails with machines, you may like the area. The Four Mile Park trails extend to Grand Mesa, about 30 miles to the west. Both are located near Sunlight ski area. Take the right fork just below the ski area onto Forest Rd. 300. From the fork go about 2 miles to the Forest Rd. 318 turnoff to the right. The Sunlight Peak Trail begins here. About 2 miles farther up Forest Rd. 300, Four Mile Park trails begin.

West Elk Creek—The West Elk Creek area, located about 16 miles northwest of Glenwood Springs, has a number of good trails on White River National Forest land. The trails head north, eventually reaching the Flat Tops Wilderness. To get to the trails, head west on Interstate 70 from Glenwood Springs for 11 miles and turn northwest on Elk Creek Rd. at New Castle. Drive a few miles to West Elk Creek Rd. (County Rd. 244) and take a right. Trails leading to the right off this road begin after a mile or so.

Groomed Trails

Sunlight Nordic Center—Located at the Sunlight ski area, this center has an extensive trail system integrated with its downhill facilities. Cross-country trails can be reached from the base area as well as from the top of the Primo and Segundo chairlifts. It's ideal for telemarking. Equipment rental and cross-country skiing lessons (including telemark) are available; track fee. Less than half a mile down the trail from the parking lot is the **Back Country Cabin ($$),** available for overnight stays for up to six people. **10901 County Rd. 117 (Four Mile Rd.), Glenwood Springs, CO 81601; 1-800-445-7931; 970-945-7491; www.skisun lightmtn.com.**

Rentals and Information

Sturdy backcountry cross-country skiing equipment, including telemark skis and snowshoes, can be rented at **Summit Canyon Moun-** taineering, 732 Grand Ave., Glenwood Springs; 970-945-6994.

DOWNHILL SKIING AND SNOWBOARDING

Aspen

Forty-two miles south of Glenwood Springs on Hwy. 82. See the Skiing section of the **Aspen** chapter.

Sunlight Mountain Resort

Just 10 miles from downtown Glenwood Springs, Sunlight offers good value in a laid-back, family atmosphere. With few lifts and an area map that an 8-year-old can read, you can all go skiing and snowboarding without fear of getting lost. The mountain features 2,010 vertical feet of mostly beginner and intermediate trails, although there are some great steeps off Fryingpan and Wishbone alleys, and even some powder caches in the Upper Glades. Okay, so you won't find high-speed, detachable quad chairlifts, but you will find an unpretentious, friendly environment. And the lift ticket prices have held for years. Besides, where else can you ski all day and then soak your sore muscles in the world's largest hot springs pool? Don't miss taking a run on Ute, a 2.5-mile-long cruiser along the perimeter. If you're tired of the glitz and high lift prices at bigger resorts, try this place. Free shuttles from town. Rentals, child care and buffet-style restaurant. **10901 County Rd. 117 (Four Mile Rd.), Glenwood Springs, CO 81601; 1-800-445-7931; 970-945-7491; www.skisunlightmtn.com.**

Rentals

In Glenwood, downhill rentals are available at several shops.

Seeing and Doing

Museums and Galleries

Frontier Historical Museum

This is a good place to get a feel for the history of Glenwood Springs and the surrounding area.

Sunlight Mountain Resort, just outside Glenwood Springs, is one of the best family ski destinations in Colorado. Photo by Bruce Caughey.

Information and artifacts about the development of Glenwood's Yampah Hot Springs, coal mining in the area and Teddy Roosevelt's visits highlight the displays. Upstairs in the Tabor Room is a hand-carved bed and dresser that once belonged to H.A.W. and Baby Doe Tabor of Leadville silver-boom fame. Small fee for visitors over 12. Mon. and Thurs.–Sat. 1–4 P.M. in winter; Mon.–Sat. 11 A.M.–4 P.M. during summer. **1001 Colorado Ave.; 970-945-4448.**

Nightlife

Buffalo Valley

The state's largest dance floor has replaced what used to be a local museum. Check out live rock and country bands in the Old West saloon atmosphere. The bar features inlaid silver dollars—a thousand of 'em! Good restaurant, especially for

steaks and, as you may have guessed, buffalo. At the south end of town at **3637 Hwy. 82; 970-945-5297.**

Scenic Drives

Glenwood Canyon

See the Major Attractions section.

Rifle Falls State Park

Located about 40 miles northwest of Glenwood Springs, Rifle Falls stands out as an oasis in this semi-arid part of the state. At the base of the 50-foot falls, lush green ferns, flowers and moss flourish. It's an attractive place to visit. Below the cliffs from which the falls plummet are a number of limestone caves ideally suited for novices (no pits or brain-twisting labyrinths). Coyote Trail leads to an observation point at the top of the falls.

To reach Rifle Falls State Park from Glenwood Springs, drive west on Interstate 70 for 26 miles to Rifle. At Rifle, head north on Hwy. 13 for 5 miles to a junction with Hwy. 325. Turn right and continue 11 miles (past Rifle Gap Reservoir) to Rifle Falls State Park on the right. The campground has 19 sites; fee charged. You'll find a good map of the area here. Be sure to take the short hike to the falls. Check the state park website at **www.coloradoparks.org.** Camping reservations at **1-800-678-CAMP** or **www.reserveamerica.com.**

Where to Stay

Accommodations

Glenwood is generally not a place to show up without a lodging reservation; during many times of the year things can get tight. On the north side of town, stretching toward West Glenwood, you'll find a lengthy row of motels including a Best Western, Ramada and Affordable Inn, just to name a few. Reservations can be made quickly and easily through **Glenwood Central Reservations: 1-800-221-0098; www.glenwoodchamber.com.** For some unique accommodations nearby, check the **Redstone and Crystal River Valley** and **Aspen** chapters. Below are a number of suggested standouts that range from historic to romantic.

Four Mile Creek Bed and Breakfast— $$$ to $$$$

This charming, historic log home occupies a quiet bend in the creek just 6.5 miles south of Glenwood Springs. Originally homesteaded in 1885, this B&B is on the National Register of Historic Places. You will recognize it from the road because of the big red barn (home to several llamas) on the lovely grounds. The main house has two rental rooms, which feature folk art and timeless furniture (queen bed in each; shared bath; terry-cloth robes provided). If you want more privacy, ask about the cabin, with its heavy wood beams and its own small kitchen. The cushy cabin sleeps up to four. In the former ranch bunkhouse, you'll find a small mercantile, with a selection of folk art, farm and garden products and collectibles. Owners Sharill and Jim Hawkins are friendly and knowledgeable folks who will make you feel at home. On the road to Sunlight Mountain Resort. **6471 County Rd. 117, Glenwood Springs, CO 81601; 970-945-4004; www.fourmilecreek.com.**

Hotel Colorado—$$$ to $$$$

Since its illustrious opening in June 1893, Hotel Colorado has lodged and entertained notables from all over the world, including six U.S. presidents. Walter B. Devereux opened the hotel as the final stage of his dream of a world-class spa in the mountains. Built in the Italian Renaissance style, rooms went for $5 per night ($320 by today's standards). No detail was overlooked in making this a hotel for royalty.

In 1905 the hotel became the White House of the West when Teddy Roosevelt came and stayed while bear hunting in the surrounding mountains. President William Howard Taft visited the hotel a few years later and greatly enjoyed the accommodations—especially the oversized bathtubs. As the heaviest president, Taft reportedly had gotten stuck in a bathtub at the Brown Palace

Hotel in Denver. As the 20th century pushed on, the hotel relaxed its decorum and admitted the common man, including gangsters of the late 1920s. During World War II the Navy turned the hotel into a naval hospital. Wide hallways, therapeutic waters and good rail connections to the coast made it an obvious choice.

Today this 126-room hotel has undergone much-needed renovation, which has greatly improved the appearance of the lower-priced rooms as well as the hallways. If you decide to stay at the hotel, take note: spend a few extra dollars on a deluxe room or suite; they are decorated with antiques and generally are in nicer shape. History buffs should ask for Room 230, where both Presidents Taft and Roosevelt made speeches to the people in the courtyard below. The Bell Tower Room at the top of the hotel contains a spiral staircase and a sundeck with a commanding view. The hotel also offers dining in the Devereux Room. **526 Pine St., Glenwood Springs, CO 81601; 1-800-544-3998; 970-945-6511;** Denver **303-623-3400; www.hotelcolorado.com.**

Hotel Denver—$$$ to $$$$

The Hotel Denver, built in 1906, is arguably the plushest, most amenity-conscious lodging you'll find in Glenwood. Located across the street from the Amtrak train station, the hotel offers 60 well-appointed, soundproof rooms with special touches throughout. The hotel sports an attractive art deco style, featuring a three-story glass atrium near the front desk. Now that the hotel has added its own brewpub (see **Glenwood Canyon Brewing Company** in the Where to Eat section), it's definitely the place to be! Besides, it's centrally located, just a short walk from the hot springs pool. Special weekend/low season rates and package rates are plentiful; kids stay free. **402 7th St., Glenwood Springs, CO 81601; 1-800-826-8820; 970-945-6565; www.thehoteldenver.com.**

Brettelberg Condominiums—$$$

Located on the mountain at Sunlight Mountain Resort, the Brettelberg condos have gone downhill. Even though the place features a great on-mountain setting, these battered places feel a lot like college dorms. But the price is still right for a place on the mountain where you can ski in and ski out. Rec room, hot tub (when working) and laundry facilities. **11101 County Rd. 117, Glenwood Springs, CO 81601; 1-800-634-0481; 970-945-7421; www.brettelberg condos.com.**

Glenwood Springs Hostel—$

Offering dormitory-style accommodations, private and semiprivate rooms, this American Youth Hostel facility provides a friendly alternative to those traveling on a budget. Gary, the owner, is particularly helpful to visitors who want information about what to do in the area, but the place is not exactly ready for the "white glove" dust test. Gary shares his collection of more than 2,000 vinyl records with guests in the funky common room. Mountain bike rentals are available. Limited check-in times; closed during certain midday hours. **1021 Grand Ave., Glenwood Springs, CO 81601; 970-945-8545; www.rof.net/yp/ gwhostel.**

Camping

Rifle Falls State Park

Located 6 miles beyond Rifle Gap State Park on Hwy. 325. For more information see the Scenic Drives section.

Rifle Gap State Park

Located northwest of Glenwood Springs. Head west on Interstate 70 for 26 miles to Rifle and then north for 5 miles on Hwy. 13. Turn right on Hwy. 325 and proceed for 5 miles. There are 46 sites, and a fee is charged. For reservations: **1-800-678-CAMP; www.reserve america.com.**

White River National Forest

Drive east on Interstate 70 for 18 miles to Dotsero. Head north for 2 miles and take a left on Forest Rd. 600 (Coffee Pot Rd.) and proceed

about 16 miles to **Coffee Pot Spring Campground** (7 sites, no water, fee charged). On up at the end of the road, another 15 miles, are **Supply Basin Campground** (7 sites), **Kline's Folly Campground** (4 sites) and **Deep Lake Campground** (35 sites). None of these has drinking water; all charge a fee. Supply Basin and Kline's Folly are on Heart Lake; Deep Lake Campground is on the shore of Deep Lake.

About 8 miles north of Dotsero, take a left on Sweetwater Lake Rd. and drive 10 miles to **Sweetwater Lake Campground** (9 sites, drinking water, fee charged).

Northwest of Glenwood Springs, about 7 miles north of Rifle Falls State Park (see the Scenic Drives section) is **Three Forks Campground** (4 sites, no fee).

Many beautiful camping opportunities exist south, up-valley from Glenwood. For ideas see the Camping sections of the **Aspen** and **Redstone and Crystal River Valley** chapters. Some campsites can be reserved at **1-877-444-6777** or **www.reserveusa.com.**

Private Campgrounds

The Hideout—For cushy camping this place offers close proximity to town, RV hookups and tentsites. Twelve rental cabins **($$ to $$$)** with maid service are just the thing for people who can't decide whether they want a weekend in town or one in the woods. Laundry, showers and a gift shop; reservations suggested; open year-round. **1293 County Rd. 117; 970-945-5621; www.toski.com/hideout.**

Rock Gardens—Located along the Colorado River in Glenwood Canyon at No Name exit, Rock Gardens offers both hookups and tentsites. **1308 County Rd. 129; 970-945-6737.**

Where to Eat

Sopris Restaurant and Lounge—$$$

This is perhaps the finest restaurant in the Roaring Fork Valley. Owner and chef Kurt Wigger spent 17 years tickling customers' taste buds at the Red Onion Restaurant in Aspen before opening the Sopris in 1974. Originally from Lucerne, Switzerland, Wigger has professional chef credentials that include membership in the elite Confrérie de la chaîne des rôtisseurs of France. After serving celebrities such as Clint Eastwood, George C. Scott, Cybill Shepherd and Vince Bzdek, Wigger surely must have felt his life was complete when Jill St. John announced, "Kurt, I love your crazy cooking." The impressive fare includes oysters Rockefeller, lobster Newburg, veal piccata, Milanese and pepper steak flambé. The restaurant is a bit dark, unfortunately, with no view up the valley to Mt. Sopris. Located about 7 miles south of Glenwood Springs on Hwy. 82. Open 5 P.M.–midnight daily. **7215 Hwy. 82; 970-945-7771.**

Florindo's—$$ to $$$

Although initially skeptical of the local ravings about the fine northern Italian cuisine at Florindo's, we were very impressed with this classy little place in downtown Glenwood Springs. Since 1989 Florindo's has offered ample portions of seafood, veal, pasta and chicken dishes, preceded by plates of delicious Italian bread. Italian wines dominate the wine list. Italian owner Florindo Gallicchio and his Hungarian-born wife, Roza, have really made an impression here with their food. As our eastern-transplant waitress said, "It's to die for!" Open for lunch Mon.–Fri. 11:30 A.M.–3 P.M.; dinner Mon.–Sat. 5–10:30 P.M.; closed Sun. **721 Grand Ave.; 970-945-1245.**

Glenwood Canyon Brewing Company—$$ to $$$

With eight of its own brews stored in the on-site tank farm and a very pleasant setting in the Hotel Denver, this brewpub seems destined to become "the place" in Glenwood Springs. Tasteful exposed brick and light wood touches throughout highlight the restaurant and separate bar (both are nonsmoking). Locals seem to most enjoy the Hanging Lake Honey Ale, but the Oatmeal Stout proved to be delicious. The restaurant serves up light sandwiches, burgers and salads or dinner entrées that include fiery Southwest ravioli and grilled baby back ribs. Don't skip the decadent bread pudding. Open for lunch and dinner from 11 A.M. daily. **402 Seventh St.; 970-945-1276.**

Italian Underground—$$

Florindo's has the northern Italian, but the Underground is the place to go for southern Italian. With checkered tablecloths, Chianti bottles and an abundance of marinara sauce, you expect to see a Sicilian grandmother busy at work in the kitchen. What you'll find instead is Gregory Durrant (whose grandparents ran a similar restaurant in New Castle years ago) preparing the sausage and all bread and pizza dough from scratch. The Underground is well named, occupying a dimly lit, attractively decorated basement room along Grand Ave. The menu features lasagna, pizza, spaghetti and great homemade cannolis. Each of the main entrées comes with salad and bread, and ice cream for dessert; popular with families. Open 5–10 P.M. daily. **715 Grand Ave.; 970-945-6422.**

Los Desperados—$$

The best all-around Mexican restaurant in town, "Los Dos," as locals call it, is very popular, especially at lunchtime. Margaritas are good but not world-class. House specialties include the macho burrito, enchilada plate and relleno royale. They also feature several seafood specialties. It's best to keep Glenwood's Mexican dining opportunities in perspective. When asked where the best Mexican food in town was, more than one person responded, "At my house." Open Tues.–Sun. 11 A.M.–10 P.M., Mon. 5–10 P.M. **0055 Mel-Rey Rd.; 970-945-6878.**

Daily Bread Cafe and Bakery—$ to $$

Home-cooked meals with large portions characterize this popular breakfast and lunch spot. Each day all of the breads and delicious pastries are made from scratch. In addition to traditional breakfast fare, creative daily specials are served along with notables like granola and Huevos Extraordinaire. For lunch try their monstrously large salads and bowls of homemade soup. Top off your meal with a piece of one of their locally famous pies. Wholesome food and a welcome atmosphere have earned the Daily Bread a very loyal and far-flung clientele. Open Mon.–Fri. 7 A.M.–2 P.M., Sat. 8 A.M.–2 P.M., Sun. 8 A.M.–noon. **729 Grand Ave.; 970-945-6253.**

Delice—$ to $$

Since 1978 Swiss chef Walter Huber has been tantalizing Glenwood Springs palettes with his European pastries, fresh bread, soups and deli-style sandwiches. This is definitely the stop to make when thinking about packing a hearty picnic lunch. Or pull up a chair at this little restaurant. If you're still hungry after lunch, try one (or a pair) of his Dolly Parton pastries. Open Mon.–Fri. 10 A.M.–3 P.M. **1512 Grand Ave.; 970-945-9424.**

19th Street Diner—$

The atmosphere and most of the food is a blast from the past. 19th Street Diner, with its black-and-white checkered linoleum floors, booths and counter seating, serves up Americana with its blue plate special, chicken-fried steak, honey-dipped southern fried chicken and hamburgers. Prices are very reasonable at this casual eatery. Full bar at the back. Dining area open Mon.–Sat. 7 A.M.–9 P.M., Sun. 7:30 A.M.–8 P.M. **1908 Grand Ave.; 970-945-9133.**

Services

Visitor Information

Central Reservations—1-800-221-0098.

Glenwood Springs Chamber Resort Association—Staffed during business hours with someone to answer questions; self-serve brochure racks accessible after hours. **1102 Grand Ave., Glenwood Springs, CO 81601; 970-945-6589; www.glenwoodchamber. com.**

Transportation

Glenwood Trolley—For a couple of bucks during summer you can buy an all-day pass to a trolley that plies a frequent route between west and south Glenwood Springs. **970-945-6589.**

Grand Junction

With the tremendous growth in Colorado over the past decade or so, it's difficult to explain why more visitors aren't aware of the Grand Junction area. It has so much to offer. Located in the fertile Grand Valley of western Colorado, Grand Junction is surrounded by diverse, rugged country just waiting to be explored. To the southwest is the stark beauty of Colorado National Monument and the slickrock canyon country of the Colorado Plateau. Grand Mesa, with its many forests and lakes, towers to the east. To the north the bleak allure of the Book Cliffs captures your attention.

Exposed strata of the surrounding canyons and buttes attract geologists from around the country—but these layers of shale, sedimentary rock and red slickrock sandstone are so riveting they catch everyone's eye. From within these layers, fossilized dinosaur bones have long been unearthed. Discoveries continue almost daily, giving paleontologists more work than they can handle. The sheer number of significant fossil finds and the popularity of dinosaurs in general have turned Grand Junction into a major dinosaur center; museums, natural sites and on-site digs await (see the Major Attractions section).

To fully appreciate Grand Junction you'll want to get out into the natural surroundings. The whitewater kayaking, rafting and canoeing are outstanding. Nearby, wind- and water-scarred plateau country caters perfectly to hikers and

ever-growing numbers of mountain bikers. With almost unlimited single-track trails at its doorstep (300 miles at last count), the nearby town of Fruita has transformed itself into a mountain biking center that rivals Moab, Utah. Fruita recently was chosen by *Bicycling* magazine as one of America's 10 best bike towns. Driving the many scenic highways or back-road routes through the area's orchards offers another excellent way to enjoy your stay in Grand Junction. Or pay a visit to one of the area's wineries that have garnered increasing raves from wine connoisseurs throughout the country.

All of the enticements listed above, as well as mild winter weather, account for Grand Junction's claim as western Colorado's largest town (just over 100,000 residents). With many people continuing to relocate here, Grand Junction's future looks bright.

History

The Northern Ute Reservation occupied most of the Grand Valley until 1881, when the Utes

---

Getting There

Located on Interstate 70, 258 miles west of Denver, Grand Junction is serviced by **Greyhound Bus Lines. Amtrak** rolls through Grand Junction on its way to the West and East Coasts. **Walker Field Airport** is becoming popular with visitors thanks to many direct flights from locations around the country.

were forcibly expelled from their lands and pushed into Utah to allow Anglo settlement. Ironically, the town of Ute was established in 1881, only three months after the Utes moved west. The town's name soon changed to West Denver—a mere 258-mile commute to downtown Denver. Residents eventually settled on a name taken from the town's location at the junction of the Grand and Gunnison Rivers. In 1921 the Grand River was renamed the Colorado, and to this day Grand Junction remains a misnomer.

In 1881 settlers were initially drawn to the valley for the semiarid land, which was perfect for pasturing cattle. By the end of that year, however, irrigation enabled the rich red valley soil to spring to life. With new emphasis placed on agriculture, cattle ranchers were soon relegated to the high mesas. The young town began carving a niche as a trade center for western Colorado when the Denver & Rio Grande Railroad's main line started service in 1887.

Over the years apricots, cherries, grapes and peaches have provided an economic mainstay for the town as well as the nearby orchard towns of Palisade and Clifton. Although the economy has diversified over time, Grand Junction has gone through several boom-and-bust cycles. Nearby uranium and oil-shale mining once promised to turn Grand Junction into a major city, and hopes and regional pride ran high. (During the uranium boom of the 1950s, one travel writer even referred to the uranium mining as "a radioactive icing" on your "vacation cake.") But neither the uranium nor the oil-shale development panned out. Both went bust, leaving Grand Junction with little more than dreams about what might have been.

These days, a growing tourism industry and reputation as an excellent place to relocate are drawing increasing numbers of people to this understated yet spectacular area of the state.

Major Attractions

Colorado National Monument

Five-hundred-foot-deep red canyons and solitary sandstone monoliths characterize this monument and serve as an example of the force of wind and water erosion. Sheer cliffs and wide vistas have created a unique patchwork of colors, textures and shapes. To fully appreciate the muted contrasts of this national treasure, it's better to visit during low sun—in early morning or late afternoon. Once within the canyons, civilization seems light-years away, even though Interstate 70 is only a few miles in the distance.

History

Although many folks were involved in the designation of Colorado National Monument, we need to focus much of the credit on a dedicated recluse. For many years in the early 1900s, John Otto lived alone in the canyons while waging a one-man letter-writing campaign urging the creation of a national park. The rest of his time was spent cutting trails and guiding adventurous tourists over the rugged terrain. Many of the trails Otto created are still in use today. In 1911 President Taft proclaimed the area a national monument, and Otto was made the first superintendent. Later that year he was married at the base of 450-foot-high Independence Monument.

Getting There

To reach the east entrance to the park from the center of Grand Junction, head west on Grand Ave. to Hwy. 340. Follow the signs across the Colorado River and turn left at the first intersection. The west entrance of the monument can be easily reached from Interstate 70 by taking the Fruita exit and following the signs south. Pick up a map of the monument and its hiking trails at either entrance. Open year-round; small entrance fee.

Biking

Rim Rock Dr. became known to professional and novice cyclists thanks to professional race classics. It is an ideal touring ride, especially in the early morning when road traffic and heat are at a minimum. The smooth asphalt road draws cyclists fit enough to handle the heat and severe change in elevation—2,300 vertical feet during

Colorado National Monument from the rim. Photo by Dean Winstanley.

the 35-mile loop from Grand Junction. For an easier 10-mile ride, start at the visitor center, ride to Artist's Point and return. Off-road mountain biking is not permitted in the monument, but several adjoining areas are ideal for it. See the Biking section in the Outdoor Activities section.

Camping

Saddlehorn Campground—Located near the visitor center, Saddlehorn has 80 semiprimitive sites and a picnic area. Fee charged; open year-round. Backcountry camping is permitted throughout the monument; register (no fee) at the visitor center.

Hiking

Take a memorable hike down into the deep canyons to soak up the sights and sounds of this place. The desert is alive in small ways that require a closer look and more patience than

city dwellers are used to. Many trails snake their way down into the inner sanctum of Colorado National Monument.

Short trails such as **Coke Ovens, Window Rock** and **Otto's Trail** offer good views in an hour or less. Especially well suited to families is **Alcove Nature Trail,** across the road from the visitor center. Guide booklets with information about geology, flora and fauna of the monument are available here. A hike down popular **Monument Canyon Trail** requires 4 hours of your time. It is a well-maintained 6-mile trail that descends 600 feet and provides a close look at massive cliff walls and looming rock monoliths. **Serpent's Trail,** near the east entrance, follows an old roadbed around 54 switchbacks in only 2.5 miles. The steep trail allows for sweeping views to Grand Junction and beyond.

Bring your own water for hikes into the canyons. In summer carry at least a gallon per day for each person. No pets or fires are permitted in the backcountry.

Rim Rock Drive

Beginning in the 1930s and, after a couple of lengthy work stoppages, finishing in the 1950s, National Park Service crews, the Civilian Conservation Corps (CCC) and others shoveled dirt and blasted rock for 23 miles through the monument to complete Rim Rock Dr. Today the road offers motorists and bicyclists dramatic views from the northern edge of the Uncompahgre Plateau. The road, with its many turnouts, descriptive plaques and scenic overlooks, is a worthwhile and easy way to see the broad expanse of desert canyon terrain. There is a 35-mile circuit over Rim Rock Dr. from Grand Junction and back.

Visitor Center

Located 4 miles from the west entrance, the center has exhibits and a slide show on the geology, history, plants and wildlife in the area. Staff members answer any questions you may have. Rest rooms and water fountains are available. Open daily 8 A.M.–6 P.M. in summer and 9 A.M.–5 P.M. Oct.–May. **Colorado National**

Monument, Fruita, CO 81521; 970-858-3617; www.nps.gov/colm.

Dinosaurs

Western Mesa County is, quite simply, a dinosaur lover's dream. It has quickly developed into a destination for paleontologists and others interested in learning more about these creatures that roamed through western Colorado 150 million years ago. More than 30 species—including bones from supersaurus and ultrasaurus, the largest dinosaurs yet discovered—have been unearthed in the vicinity. Listed below are some ways that you (and the kids) can get into the action.

Field Sites

Walk down the "Trail Through Time" in Rabbit Valley, located west of Grand Junction. Many sites en route feature uncovered dinosaur bones; several areas nearby are under current excavation by professionals. Rabbit Valley is 24 miles west of Grand Junction. Take a marked turnoff north from Interstate 70. Brochures, maps and information about **Riggs Hill** and **Dinosaur Hill,** two of western Colorado's most historically significant fossil areas, can be found at any of the dinosaur museums or the Grand Junction Visitors Center.

Dinamation International Society offers opportunities to go out in the field and work at an actual dinosaur dig. Multi-day expeditions led by paleontologists are available in the Grand Junction area, Dinosaur National Monument, Utah, Wyoming and abroad. For information: **1-800-DIG-DINO.**

Museum of Western Colorado— Dinosaur Journey

This is the best of Mesa County's dinosaur museums. Aside from an actual dig, it's hard to imagine a better place to learn about geology and dinosaurs. Twenty incredibly creative and educational interpretive/interactive displays enable kids (and adults) to experience an earthquake, dig dinosaur fossils, witness the effects of water erosion and more. Numerous robotic dinosaurs draw well-deserved attention: check out the life-size Utahraptor that was discovered nearby. This vicious carnivore was two times the size of velociraptor, made famous in the movie *Jurassic Park.* Check out the dilophosaurus that spits! The 20,000-square-foot museum also features mounted dinosaur skeletons, a working lab and gift shop. Highly recommended. Open 9 A.M.–5 P.M. daily year-round. Located south of Interstate 70 from Fruita at **550 Jurassic Ct., Fruita, CO 81521; 1-800-DIG-DINO; 970-858-7282.**

Grand Mesa

East of Grand Junction, 11,000-foot-high Grand Mesa rises more than a mile above the valley floor. Its 53 square miles make it the largest flat-topped mountain in the country. Lava flows, 400 feet thick, helped form the flat surface and protected the underlying sedimentary rock from the erosion so evident in this area. Dotted with more than 200 lakes and covered with thick pine forests and aspen groves, Grand Mesa attracts a lot of summer visitors. With its magnificent views and many recreational opportunities, it's easy to see why.

The entire mesa is part of Grand Mesa National Forest. Heavy snow in winter closes all roads except Skyway Drive (Hwy. 65), which runs north-south across the mesa. In summertime after the snow melts, activity on Grand Mesa reaches "grand" proportions. As one Grand Junction local says, "It turns into one big Winnebago parking lot." Although that's an exaggeration, an autumn visit will avoid crowds while providing a look at the changing aspen.

History

To the Ute Indians, Grand Mesa was known as *Thigunawat,* meaning Home of Departed Spirits. Ute legend says the many lakes on the mesa were created by vicious thunderbirds that lived along the rim. Apparently an irate Ute pitched several baby thunderbirds out of their nests and into the waiting jaws of a giant serpent in the valley below.

The vengeful thunderbirds reacted by ripping the serpent to pieces and dropping the remains from high over the mesa. These falling chunks of serpent caused indentations, which filled with water and created the lakes. A more scientific explanation suggests the lakes were formed by erosion.

In 1879, following the nearby massacre of Indian agent Nathan Meeker and some of his men, the Utes took five hostages up onto the mesa. Shortly thereafter, the U.S. cavalry arrived to negotiate a hostage release. The Utes surrendered and the hostages were freed.

In 1881, when significant numbers of settlers began to arrive in the valleys below Grand Mesa, a need for a summerlong water supply led to the building of many reservoirs on the mesa top. Nowadays these reservoirs and lakes not only supply water to the thirsty valley below but also double as fishing holes. The mesa has developed into a cool summer retreat from the hot, arid valley floor.

Getting There

See the Grand Mesa Scenic and Historic Byway and the Land's End Road write-ups in this section.

Visitor Information

Visit the **Grand Junction Ranger District Office, 2777 Crossroads Blvd., Grand Junction, CO 81506; 970-242-8211.** In summer try the two visitor centers on the mesa; one is located at Carp Lake and the other is at the edge of the mesa on Land's End Rd.

Camping

There are 13 public campgrounds on the mesa with more than 250 sites equipped with a variety of amenities. Those with more comforts charge a small fee; the more primitive campgrounds without water are free. Some sites are wheelchair accessible. All the campgrounds open in late June and close for the winter on Oct. 15. Reservations available at **1-877-444-6777.**

Fishing

All of the more than 220 lakes and streams on Grand Mesa are actively stocked by the Division of Wildlife. Rainbow trout (up to 18 inches) are the primary fish you'll run across, but brook and cutthroat also swim these waters. The fish begin feeding as soon as the ice melts from the perimeter of the lakes. Unless you fish early or late in the season you will have plenty of company. In winter, ice fishing is popular as well as productive.

Hiking

Crag Crest Trail—This is an ideal 10-mile circular trail for short day trips or full-day hikes. The trail winds its way past lakes and through stands of fir, spruce and aspen. The northern section of Crag Crest (11,189 feet) is the highest part of the trail. On a clear day you'll have great views in all directions: the Book and Roan Cliffs to the north, the West Elk and San Juan Mountains to the south and the La Sal Mountains far to the west in Utah.

Crag Crest Trail is restricted to foot and horse travel. Be sure to bring your own water or a means for purifying what you find along the way. Camping is allowed at least 300 feet off the trail. Keep a close eye on children when approaching the northern section, as there are a number of sheer drop-offs on both sides. The west trailhead parking lot is located just off Hwy. 65 next to Island Lake; the east trailhead can be reached by taking Forest Rd. 121 from Hwy. 65 near Island Lake and driving to Eggleston Lake (about 5 miles). For maps and more information, go to the visitor center at Carp Lake, which is open in summer 9 A.M.–6 P.M. daily.

Scenic Drives

Grand Mesa Scenic and Historic Byway—This magnificent 78-mile (one-way) drive takes you from the orchard country of Grand Junction and up across the 11,000-foot-high terrain of Grand Mesa. If you have the time to explore this route, do so!

Canoeists on one of Grand Mesa's many small lakes. Photo courtesy of Grand Junction Visitors and Convention Bureau.

Starting in Grand Junction, drive 23 miles northeast on Interstate 70 to the Hwy. 65 turnoff at Plateau Canyon. After you have driven 10 miles through the picturesque canyon, the road angles south and begins climbing up through the town of Mesa, past Powderhorn Ski Area and eventually onto Grand Mesa. Once on the mesa, you'll shortly reach an intersection with Land's End Rd. (a nice circle tour back to Grand Junction; see write-up below). Continue across the mesa on Hwy. 65 and drop down to the end of the byway at the town of Cedaredge. (For information about attractions in Cedaredge, see the **Black Canyon Country** chapter.) To loop back to Grand Junction continue down on Hwy. 65 and then turn right onto Hwy. 92. At Delta head north on Hwy. 50 to Grand Junction. Brochures with byway information and maps can be picked up at the visitor center in Grand Junction.

Land's End Road—In the summertime a drive on Land's End Rd. can be spectacular as well as hair-raising. Land's End is located on the western edge of Grand Mesa, where it snakes its way down a sloping cliff on a series of seemingly endless switchbacks. To reach the road from Grand Junction, head south on Hwy. 50 about 14 miles and turn left on the road marked as an access to Land's End Rd. The pavement ends after about

7 miles as you reach the Grand Mesa National Forest boundary. Follow the bumpy dirt road as it winds up the side of the mesa. Eventually you'll reach an observation site, just to the left of the road as you reach the rim. From here the view down to the valley floor, thousands of feet below, is dizzying. Once on top of the mesa, continue to the Hwy. 65 intersection (see the Grand Mesa Scenic and Historic Byway write-up above).

Lodging

Several lodges occupy the mesa, but most of them are open only during summer and early fall. After seeing a picture of winter snowdrifts covering the two-story Grand Mesa Lodge, it's easy to see why. Here are a few possibilities:

Alexander Lake Lodge ($$ to $$$)— Alexander Lake offers six small cabins, three with kitchenettes. Each is furnished with queen-size beds. The lodge has a restaurant (known for its steaks) and bar, as well as a small store. **P.O. Box 900, Cedaredge, CO 81413; 970-856-2539.**

Grand Mesa Lodge ($ to $$)—The lodge sits beside Island Lake near the northern end of the mesa. Ken and Conne run a friendly place with motel units and housekeeping cabins. Rental boats are available for fishing; no restaurant. Pets okay. Open year-round. **P.O. Box 49, Cedar-edge, CO 81413; 970-856-3250; www.color adodirectory.com/grandmesalodge.**

Mesa Lakes Resort ($ to $$$)—Located near the north rim of the mesa, Mesa Lakes provides 12 housekeeping cabins with fireplaces and a number of rustic motel units. This place is also well known for its tasty home-cooked meals. **P.O. Box 230, Mesa, CO 81643; 1-888-420-MESA; 970-268-5467.**

Powderhorn Resort—Just down the north rim of the mesa, Powderhorn offers a nice lodging alternative near the ski slopes and closer to town. **Valley View Condominiums ($$$ to $$$$)** offers fully equipped one- or two-bedroom condos with attractive furnishings, views to the valley or mountain and cable TV, phone and VCR. Efficiencies have no windows. Sauna and whirlpool bath available. Powderhorn also offers recently renovated rooms with ski-in/ski-out access at **The Inn at Wildwood ($ to $$)**; double bed and private bath in each room. Both places can be reached at **P.O. Box 370, Mesa, CO 81643; 970-268-5700.**

Winter on the Mesa

The mesa virtually closes up in winter. Hwy. 65 (Skyway Dr.) stays open, but Land's End Rd. is closed to cars until June. You can cross-country ski on most parts of the mesa, but be warned—snowmobilers love this place. A number of cross-country trail systems are maintained along Hwy. 65. You can park at Skyway (mile-marker 32), County Line (mile-marker 30) or Ward Creek (mile-marker 25) to set out on your trips. Pick up a trail map at the Grand Junction Visitors Center or a Forest Service office. Powderhorn offers cross-country as well as downhill skiing (see the Skiing section). In winter, ice fishing on the lakes is very popular.

Festivals and Events

Fruita Fat Tire Festival

late Apr. On a weekend in late Apr., learn from seasoned Grand Valley trail riders just exactly why this area is becoming so popular with mountain bikers. Join participants on rides along Kokopelli's Trail and other standout rides. Other activities include a mountain bike merchandise display, issues forum, bike rodeo, dinners and live entertainment. **1-800-873-3068; www.edgecycles.com.**

Junior College Baseball World Series

end of May Though not the Big Leagues, this popular tourney brings together the finest junior college teams in the country for a week of competition, culminating in the crowning of the national champ. Major League scouts and baseball fans enjoy these games in Grand Junction at Suplizio Field and Lincoln Park. **970-245-9166; www.grand-junction.net.**

Palisade Peach Festival

weekend in mid-Aug. If you are lucky enough to be in the Grand Valley during the Aug. peach harvest, make your way to the orchard town of Palisade for this celebration. A parade, food and crafts fair and peach recipe contests highlight the festival. Gorge yourself on what many believe to be Colorado's finest produce. **970-464-7458.**

Colorado Mountain Winefest

late Sept. This celebration of the wineries in the valley has emerged as an annual highlight. It's held jointly in Grand Junction and the orchard town of Palisade. Great food and music as well as wine tastings dominate the three-day event. Wine-making seminars and winery tours round things out. **1-800-704-3667; www.grand-junction.net.**

Outdoor Activities

Biking

MOUNTAIN BIKING

With more than 1,000 miles of single-track trails in the Grand Valley alone, the Grand

Junction vicinity is perfect for mountain biking. Many trails have been developed in the canyon country over the past few years.

Kokopelli's Trail

Officially opened in the summer of 1989, this highly rugged and scenic trail stands as the product of hard work by hundreds of volunteers and cooperation between the BLM offices in Grand Junction and Moab, Utah. Named after the humpbacked, flute-playing deity familiar to many Native Americans of the Colorado Plateau, Kokopelli stretches 128 miles through canyons and slickrock mesas between Loma (20 miles west of Grand Junction) and Moab.

Though some sections of the trail are quite mellow and flat, a 4,500-vertical-foot climb over the La Sal Mountains does indeed separate the serious pedaler from the novice. Sections of the trail range from single-track to well-graded county roads. Those who plan overnight trips along the trail should be familiar with mountain bike ethics and low-impact camping techniques. Important—there is no water available along the trail. Maps can be purchased throughout Grand Junction. For more information contact the **Colorado Plateau Mountain Bike Trail Association, P.O. Box 4602, Grand Junction, CO 81502;** or **Over the Edge Sports, 202 E. Aspen, Fruita, CO, 1-800-873-3068; www.edgecycles.com.**

Little Park Road

This popular ride, with its canyons and many junipers, attracts riders due to its proximity to Grand Junction. To reach Little Park Rd., enter Colorado National Monument from the east entrance and proceed about 4 miles to the Glade Park Rd. junction. Turn left and continue a few more miles and take another left onto Little Park Rd. The road loops back toward town.

Tabeguache Trail

This 142-mile trail winds its way south from Grand Junction through beautiful sections of public land along the Uncompahgre Plateau to Montrose. Elevations range from 5,500 to just under 10,000 feet. The trailhead is located a couple miles from the east entrance to Colorado National Monument on Monument Rd. Maps and information are available at BLM offices in Grand Junction and Montrose, visitor centers and area bike shops.

Rentals and Trail Information

Pick up a copy of the *Biking Guide to the Grand Valley,* available at outdoors shops throughout the county. Try a mountain bike for a day or a few days at **The Board & Buckle, 2822 North Ave.; 970-242-9285. The Bike Peddler,** at **710 N. 1st St., 970-243-5602,** also offers rentals and information. Another excellent place for rentals and tours is **Over the Edge Sports** at **202 E. Aspen, Fruita; 1-800-873-3068; 970-858-7220; www.edgecycles.com.** You can also check in at the **BLM office** at 2815 H Rd.; 970-244-3000; www.co.blm.gov.

BICYCLE TOURING

Colorado National Monument

See the Major Attractions section.

Colorado River Trails

Since the late 1970s Colorado State Parks and dedicated folks in Grand Junction have been working hard to create a trail system running along the Colorado River through town. Eventually the trail will extend from Clifton (east of town) to the Loma boat launch, west of Fruita. For now, enjoy a number of trail sections and loops accessible from various points. Great rides are available on the Audubon, Blue Heron, Connected Lakes, Watson Island and Corn Lake Trails. For information and a helpful map brochure, contact the **Colorado River State Park office** at **Corn Lake, 32 Rd. and the Colorado River in Clifton; 970-434-3388; www.coloradoparks.org.**

Fishing

Even though two of the state's largest rivers converge at Grand Junction, the river fishing is not something you should go out of your way for.

Fishing is much better on Grand Mesa (see the Major Attractions section) and upriver in the Gold Medal trout water of Gunnison Gorge (see the Fishing section of the **Black Canyon Country** chapter).

Four-Wheel-Drive Trips

John Brown Canyon/Moab Loop

For a mellow day's drive, this is a bit ambitious. But for someone fascinated with the canyon country of the Colorado Plateau, it's time well spent. John Brown Canyon is a remote, steep-walled slickrock canyon that winds its way to the Utah border. This area is closed in winter. Once in the canyon, there are no facilities for car or driver. For the necessary details, visit the **BLM office** at **2815 H Rd., Grand Junction, CO 81506; 970-244-3000.** We strongly recommend that you use BLM or USGS topographic maps.

To reach the canyon from Grand Junction, head south on Hwy. 50 for 9 miles to White-water and take a right on Hwy. 141. Drive 44 miles to the town of Gateway and turn left after crossing the Dolores River. The canyon road is just upriver on the right. A four-wheel-drive dirt road leads west into Utah, following the north slope of the La Sal Mountains and providing a view of the Wingate sandstone of Fisher Towers to the north. The road eventually comes out on Hwy. 128 along the Colorado River northeast of Moab. Take a left to Moab or just turn right, following alongside the river until you rejoin Interstate 70. Turn east on the interstate and return to Grand Junction, about 60 miles down the highway.

Golf

Adobe Creek National Golf Course

This enjoyable links-style course lies in the countryside near Fruita. You won't find many trees, but hazards do exist. Copious grass and sand bunkers, as well as water on eight of the holes, provide plenty of challenge. Full-service pro shop. Call for tee times and directions. **876 18¹/₂ Rd., Fruita, CO 81521; 970-858-0521.**

Battlement Mesa Golf Club

Beautiful, expansive views of the surrounding mesas help pass the time at this excellent 18-hole public course, 41 miles northeast of Grand Junction just off Interstate 70. Water, large cottonwoods and treacherous roughs all come into play—unless you want to go through a bag full of balls, keep your shots on the fairway. Watch for package deals on lodging and golf. Located in Parachute (Exit 75); **970-285-PAR4.**

Lincoln Park Golf Club

A mature, nine-hole course with pro shop and driving range. Located in Lincoln Park at **14th St. and Gunnison Ave.; 970-242-6394.**

Tiara Rado Golf Course

Nestled at the foot of Colorado National Monument's towering red rock walls, this relatively interesting 18-hole course provides spectacular views of the area. Though not very challenging, postage-stamp greens, elevated tee boxes and strategically placed water keep things interesting. The great flagstone patio at Piñon Grill makes a perfect place for a drink and a chance to add scores. Full pro shop and other services. On the west end of town. **2063 S. Broadway; 970-245-8085.**

Hiking and Backpacking

There's no question about it: the Grand Junction area is the place to come in Colorado for desert canyon hiking and backpacking. Many of these remote canyons of the Colorado Plateau are as beautiful as Canyonlands and Arches National Parks in Utah—there are just a lot fewer people. For hiking among pines in a mountain setting try the Crag Crest Trail on Grand Mesa (see the Hiking section for Grand Mesa, in the Major Attractions section) or dozens of other trails on the mesa. Listed below are several hiking areas west of Grand Junction in the BLM's vast 72,000-acre Black Ridge Canyons Wilderness Study Area. Canyon hiking in the spring and summer is thirsty work, and the black gnats can be quite bothersome—bring lots of water and bug repellent. Also, keep a lookout for desert

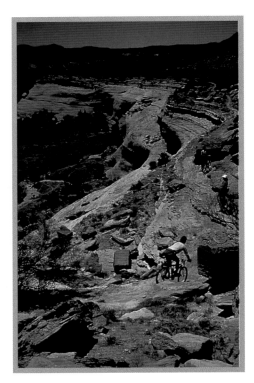

Bikers along Kokopelli's Trail. Photo by Stuart Macdonald.

bighorn sheep, successfully reintroduced into the area. For more information and maps, contact the **BLM office** at **2815 H Rd., Grand Junction, CO 81506; 970-244-3000; www. co.blm.gov.**

Rattlesnake Canyon

One of the best-kept secrets in Colorado, Rattlesnake Canyon offers the second-largest concentration of natural rock arches in the world, next to Utah's Arches National Park. At least 12 arches await you, carved by erosion in the Entrada sandstone of the canyon walls. The largest, Rainbow Bridge, is about 80 feet by 120 feet. The canyon's remote location, underdevelopment and intimidating name keep many people away, so if you make the effort you may not see many folks.

From Grand Junction head west on Interstate 70 to Exit 19 (the Fruita exit), then south to the west entrance of Colorado National Monument. Enter the monument and go about 11 miles and turn right (west) on a dirt road marked with the sign "Glade Park Store 5 Miles." Proceed 0.2 mile, cross a cattle guard and turn right at the Black Ridge Hunter Access Rd. sign. From there continue about 8.2 miles to a junction. Turn right, drive 2 miles down the Old Ute Trail and park your vehicle. This road, especially the last 2 miles, should be attempted only by four-wheel-drive vehicles with high clearance and only during good weather. When it rains the road becomes a slippery, muddy mess.

From the parking area a marked half-mile trail leads down to the canyon rim where the southernmost arch, Rainbow Bridge, can be seen. Though a bit tricky for some people, the Lower Arches Trail can be reached quickly by climbing down the slickrock under Rainbow Bridge. Otherwise you must follow the rim three-quarters of a mile north and work your way down from there. Rattlesnake Canyon can also be reached by Pollock Canyon Trail (6 miles one way). To reach the Pollock Canyon trailhead, drive south from Fruita toward the Colorado National Monument entrance and turn right at the marked sign. Proceed 3 miles.

Other Canyon Hiking Possibilities

To many people who have hiked and backpacked in canyon country, the scenery and positive overall experience are unparalleled. However, this deceptive country can quickly turn hostile and deadly to even the most experienced desert rats. The following backpacking trips should be undertaken only by seasoned hikers familiar with desert camping.

Mee Canyon, Knowles Canyon and **Jones Canyon,** located in the BLM's Black Ridge Wilderness Study Area, offer miles of remote hiking. Red sandstone walls and cottonwood groves characterize this desert canyon terrain. The trailhead for Mee Canyon can be reached from the Black Ridge Hunter Access Rd., on the way to Rattlesnake Canyon (see previous entry). Mee Canyon is known for its steep slickrock canyon walls and large 300-foot by 320-foot cave. Knowles and Jones Canyons are approached by taking the Glade Park Store Rd. out of Colorado National Monument. One mile north of Glade Park Store turn on BS Rd. and continue 12 miles to the Knowles trailhead and 15 miles to the Jones trailhead.

River Floating

Colorado River

The stretch of the Colorado River running through Grand Junction is, for the most part, extremely calm. Kayakers, inner tubers, canoeists and rafters cool off in summer by taking leisurely floats west to the Loma take-out.

However, downriver from Loma is a different story. The Colorado turns northwest and enters Horsethief Canyon (9 miles long), then heads southwest through Ruby Canyon (6 miles long) to the Colorado-Utah border. Both of these canyons, rimmed by gigantic slickrock cliffs, have fairly rough water. This stretch of the Colorado River allows excellent hiking access to spectacular side canyons, including Rattlesnake, Mee and Knowles.

In Utah, Westwater Canyon, stretching almost 30 miles to the take-out at Dewey Bridge, offers one of the wildest stretches on the Colorado River. Included here is the famous Skull Rapid and the nightmarish giant whirlpool known to floaters as the Room of Doom—at high water its outer perimeter can be as high as 3 feet above the vortex. In one section of Westwater, ancient black Precambrian rock is exposed, not to reappear again until the river enters the Grand Canyon hundreds of miles downstream. A permit for Westwater Canyon may be obtained at the **Moab District BLM Office, 82 E. Dogwood, Moab, UT 84532; 801-259-7012; www.blm.gov/utah/moab.**

Gunnison River

The lower Gunnison offers fairly challenging, intensely beautiful stretches of water as it flows northwest to Grand Junction before emptying into the Colorado River. For more information see the River Floating section of the **Black Canyon Country** chapter.

Outfitters

Adventure Bound—For one-day and multi-day trips down the Colorado River, including Westwater and Cataract Canyons and trips to the Green and Yampa Rivers, contact Adventure Bound at **2392 H Rd., Grand Junction, CO 81505; 1-800-423-4668; 970-245-5428.**
Rimrock Adventures—Families may want to consider a full-day trip with Rimrock Adventures, offering mild canoe floats and wild rides down Ruby, Horsethief and Westwater Canyons of the Colorado. Canoe and raft rentals as well as shuttle service are available. **P.O. Box 608, Fruita, CO 81521; 970-858-9555.**

Skiing

CROSS-COUNTRY SKIING AND SNOWSHOEING

The lifts at Powderhorn take cross-country skiers to the rim of Grand Mesa, where an organized trail system heads into the backcountry. The Powderhorn Nordic Center machine-grooms about 10 kilometers of trails within ski area boundaries. Gentle ski area slopes are excellent for telemark skiing. Rentals and instruction are available. Grand Mesa is a snowmobiler's paradise, but many good cross-country trails exist and are kept fairly separate. For trail locations see Grand Mesa under the Major Attractions section.

DOWNHILL SKIING AND SNOWBOARDING
Powderhorn

Logic would have it that downhill skiing near an area called Grand Mesa would be less than thrilling. Yet, surprisingly, there is a generous vertical drop of 1,650 feet at this ski mountain, only 35 miles east of Grand Junction. If you are looking for a family-friendly area with a majority of intermediate runs, Powderhorn is perfect.

The stunning views you'll see while skiing any-where on the mountain are completely different from those in any other area in Colorado. The ski area boasts far more trees, primarily spruce and aspen, than either the barren plateau in the distance or the valley below. Ski rentals and lessons are available. For lodging options at the ski area as well as on Grand Mesa, see the Major Attractions section. **P.O. Box 370, Mesa, CO 81643; 1-800-241-6997; 970-268-5700; www. powderhorn.com.**

Seeing and Doing

Museums

Cross Orchards Historic Farm

Listed on the National Register of Historic Places, Cross Orchards was a 243-acre working fruit farm from 1896 to 1923. Today it's a great place to learn about the historic importance of the orchards to Grand Junction through daily living-history demonstrations. Stroll the grounds and inspect the buildings and orchard. Also of note are the Cross Orchards Country Store, Swanson Farm, Uintah Railway exhibit and the collection of antique road-building equipment. Fee charged. Open 9 A.M.–3 P.M. Tues.–Sat. and 11 A.M.–5 P.M. on Sun., Apr. 1–Oct. 30. **3079 F (Patterson) Rd., Grand Junction, CO 81504; 970-434-9814; www.mwc.mus.co.us/crossorchards.**

Dinosaur Museums

See the Dinosaurs write-up in the Major Attractions section.

Museum of Western Colorado

Stop by this excellent museum where you'll learn about the history of western Colorado and, more specifically, of Grand Junction. The history begins with the woolly mammoth-spearing Folsom Man of 15,000 years ago and ranges to the present-day fruit farmers. The gun section includes flintlocks from the early 1800s. Exhibits change frequently; fee charged. Open Apr. 1–Sept. 30, Mon.–Sat. 9 A.M.–5 P.M.; open the rest of the year Tues.–

Sat. 10 A.M.–4 P.M., closed Sun. and Mon. **248 S. 4th St.; 970-242-0971.**

Nightlife

Rockslide Brewery and Restaurant

Although it's a tough call to say whether the Rockslide's biggest draw is its microbrew or decent-enough pub food, we'll have to go with the brew. We especially liked the Widow Maker Wheat and the Cold Shivers Pale Ale. Keep an eye out for the daily brew specials as well.

Located in a spacious historic building on Main St. in downtown Grand Junction, the Rockslide packs folks into its pub, restaurant area and outdoor patio. High ceilings, exposed brick walls and comfortable table and booth seating provide a relaxing spot after a day out exploring the area. Menu items **($ to $$)** are numerous, ranging from lighter lunch fare such as salads and sandwiches to steaks, pizza and tasty pasta dishes. The restaurant is open Mon.–Sat. 11 A.M.–9 P.M.; Sun. at 8 A.M. for breakfast; bar is open till 11 P.M. on weekdays and midnight on weekends. **401 Main St.; 970-245-2111.**

Scenic Drives

Grand Mesa Scenic and Historic Byway

For information about this beautiful drive, as well as a possible trip along the steep, switch-backing Land's End Rd., see the Grand Mesa write-up in the Major Attractions section.

The Orchards

Though these are wonderful places to explore, a word of advice: get a map before you set out. East of Grand Junction the rich peach, apricot, grape and cherry orchards in and around the town of Palisade are especially active during the harvest season: mid-July–Aug. You'll find many roadside fruit stands from which to choose. Spring is particularly beautiful when the trees are blossoming. Also stop in at one of the wineries located in this area (see the Wineries section). To reach the orchards from Grand Junction, head east on F Rd., or take Interstate 70 to the Palisade exit.

Rim Rock Drive

See the Colorado National Monument write-up in the Major Attractions section.

Unaweep/Tabeguache Scenic and Historic Byway

If you have some time on your hands, this trip is well worth your while. Head south from Grand Junction for 9 miles on Hwy. 50 to the junction of Hwy. 141 at Whitewater. Turn west on Hwy. 141 and head into Unaweep Canyon. It was through Unaweep Canyon (44 miles long and 2,500 feet deep) that the waters of the Gunnison and Colorado Rivers once flowed. When the Uncompahgre Plateau began to push up through the shale about 8 million years ago, the water found a new course, leaving Unaweep high and dry. The canyon's steep rock walls and groves of cottonwood and pine make it a pleasant drive.

About 14 miles west of Whitewater, a dirt road (Divide Rd.) heads off to the left, leading up to the rim of the canyon for a good view. Continuing west on Hwy. 141, you'll eventually hit the town of Gateway.

From Gateway, Hwy. 141 takes a swing south and begins winding its way up along the Dolores River in one of the state's most beautiful sandstone canyons. Over the years the Dolores has cut its way down through sedimentary rock, sandstone, mudstone and shale, revealing many-colored layers—a geologist's dream. The looming bulk of the Entrada and Wingate sandstone walls is a monument to time and weather.

Twenty-nine miles south of Gateway is a turnout on the right side of the road where you can get a bird's-eye view of the **Hanging Flume.** Constructed from 1889 to 1891, the Hanging Flume was built into the canyon walls to carry water to Mesa Creek Flats for hydraulic gold mining. During construction, workers clung to swinging ropes lowered as much as 400 feet from the canyon rim above. The 6-foot by 4-foot, 6-mile-long flume was an engineering success but a financial disaster.

Continuing south on the highway leads you into uranium country. Beginning in the late 1800s the world began to see a use for uranium ore. In 1898 an order came from France for several tons of ore, which was then refined into radium by Pierre and Marie Curie. At Uravan, 6 miles south of the Hanging Flume turnout, ore was mined during World War II to supply the Manhattan Project, the U.S. government operation to develop the world's first atomic bomb. Mining boomed in Uravan during the 1950s but died out in 1962, with the town soon following suit. Other abandoned mines can be seen in the vicinity.

From Uravan continue south through Norwood to Placerville and then east on Hwy. 62 to Ridgway. From Ridgway, head north on Hwy. 50 through Montrose and Delta on the way back to Grand Junction. Total round-trip distance is 151 miles. Before heading out on this route, pick up a byway brochure at the visitor center in Grand Junction.

Wineries

In Colorado? Yes. The Western Slope of Colorado has proven to have a long, cool growing season and suitable soil, making it fine vineyard country. In comparing Colorado's Grand Valley wineries to Napa Valley, a favorable *Sunset Magazine* article advised visitors to "check your snobbery at the door." Many of the wineries continue to garner awards, giving Napa a run for its money. Seven wineries, all with tasting rooms, can be found in the orchards east of Grand Junction. Here are our favorites:

Carlson Vineyards

This very small but renowned winery specializes in peach, cherry, apple and plum wines. Also try the chardonnay select. Open 11 A.M.–6 P.M. daily. Check out their dinosaur series. **461 35 Rd., Palisade, CO 81526; 970-464-5554.**

Colorado Cellars

This interesting operation run by Richard and Padte Turley has been producing wine commercially since the late 1970s. Their standout wines include riesling and chardonnay. Tours and tastings are available year-round 9 A.M.–4 P.M. Mon. through Fri.; from noon on Sat. **3553 E Rd., Palisade, CO 81526; 1-800-848-2812; 970-464-7921.**

Grande River Vineyards

Grande River offers mainly traditional-style grape wines including meritage, chardonnay and syrah. Tasting room hours vary; call ahead. **787 Elberta Ave., Palisade, CO 81526; 1-800-CO-GROWN; 970-464-5867.**

Plum Creek Cellars

Located just outside of Palisade, the winery's tasting room is open daily 9:30 A.M.–6 P.M. for samplings of its standout chardonnay, merlot and cabernet sauvignon. **3708 G Rd., Palisade, CO 81526; 970-464-PLUM.**

Where to Stay

Accommodations

The Grand Junction area is still primarily set up for motel stays, many of which you'll find just off Interstate 70 at the Horizon Dr. exit. Easily identifiable and accessible chains include the **Adam's Mark,** the **Ramada Inn, Days Inn** and the **Holiday Inn.** (Ideas for lodging on Grand Mesa can be found in the Grand Mesa write-up under the Major Attractions section.) In Fruita, try the **Super 8 Motel** just off of the I-70 exit.

Other ideas and phone numbers can be obtained from the **Grand Junction Visitors Center** at **1-800-962-2547; www.grand-junction.net.** Listed below are a few standout bed and breakfast inns.

Orchard House Bed and Breakfast—$$$ to $$$$

A beautiful orchard-country locale, comfortable rooms, delicious and creative food and the owner's local perspective—all combine to provide an unbeatable night in the Grand Junction

A very solid tunnel along Rim Rock Drive in Colorado National Monument. Photo by Dean Winstanley.

area. Peach and cherry trees surround Stephanie Schmid's 4,000-square-foot inn, just 20 minutes east of Grand Junction. Four beautifully decorated rooms, named after Stephanie's pets, meet the needs of everyone from families to honeymooners. The latter will enjoy Conrad's Room, the upstairs suite with private bath and tremendous views of orchards, vineyards and mountains. Stephanie's delicious breakfasts feature local produce. Consider splurging for one of her gourmet dinners as well. Highly recommended. **3573 E½ Rd., Palisade, CO 81526; 970-464-0529; www.theorchardhouse. com.**

Mt. Garfield Bed and Breakfast—$$$

Four guest rooms of various sizes all include private baths and attractive furnishings. Todd and Carrie McKay prove to be warm hosts at this orchard-country bed and breakfast inn. Stroll the 7-acre grounds to the peach orchard or the livestock pen with a few resident buffalo. The buffalo theme continues into breakfast where you'll enjoy the house specialty—the Buffalo Breakfast Casserole or lighter fare. **3355 F Rd., Clifton, CO 81520; 1-800-547-9108; www. gj.net/mckayinn.**

Stonehaven Bed and Breakfast—$$$

Located just north of Fruita, Stonehaven provides a relaxing escape from the hustle and bustle of Grand Junction. Enjoy wonderful views of the Colorado National Monument from the spacious veranda that skirts the south side of this distinctive stone home, built in 1906. Four rooms, which vary considerably in size, furnishings and price, are available. At the high end, try the Grey Room (honeymoon suite) on the second floor with whirlpool tub, fireplace and other niceties; the other two rooms on the second floor are decorated much more modestly and share a bath down the hall. The full breakfast will definitely fill you up. Kids will enjoy the playground equipment and chickens. **798 N. Mesa St., Fruita, CO 81521; 1-800-303-0898; 970-858-0898; www.gj.net/~stone hvn.**

Los Altos Bed and Breakfast—$$ to $$$$

If you are looking for a room with a view, you will be hard-pressed to find a better one than what's available at Los Altos. From its commanding hilltop location west of Grand Junction, enjoy the 360-degree views of the Colorado National Monument, Bookcliffs, Grand Mesa and other area features. Lee and Young-Ja Garrett custom-built the inn with six comfortable guest rooms, each with a private bath. Features vary considerably from the top-end Vista Suite with its private deck, fireplace and reading room, down to more meager but memorable rooms. A delicious homemade breakfast is served in the dining room; tea is served each afternoon at 4 P.M. Be sure to pay careful attention to the directions that you receive to this inn or you'll likely get lost. **375 Hillview Dr., Grand Junction, CO 81503; 1-888-774-0982; 970-256-0964; www. colorado-bnb. com/losaltos.**

Camping

For information on campgrounds at Colorado National Monument and Grand Mesa, see the Major Attractions section.

State Parks

Colorado River State Park—This park, 30-plus miles long, offers two opportunities for overnight stays. **Island Acres** lies along the Colorado River 15 miles east of Grand Junction on Interstate 70, with 80 tent and RV sites available; fee charged. **Box B, Palisade, CO 81526; 970-464-0548.** The 65 sites at the park's newly opened **Fruita** site are an excellent option as well; **970-434-3388.** Reservations for both campgrounds can be arranged by calling **1-800-678-CAMP** or via the Internet at **www.reserveamerica.com.**

Highline State Park—Located 7 miles north of Loma, Highline offers 27 grassy campsites for both tents and RVs. Shower building; fee charged. For reservations call **1-800-678-CAMP; www.reserveamerica.com, 1800 11.8 Rd., Loma, CO 81524; 970-858-7208; www.coloradoparks.org.**

Private Campgrounds

Junction West RV—This campground offers RV hookups in western Grand Junction. **793 22 Rd., Grand Junction, CO 81531; 970-245-8531. RV Ranch Grand Junction**—This refurbished RV park garnered the highest rating in *Trailer Life 2000* for Colorado campgrounds. It definitely has all the bells and whistles: 132 sites (mostly pull-through hookups), nine rental **cabins ($)**, computer room, concierge, etc. This ain't your typical RV park. Located 3 miles east of Grand Junction at **3238 E. Interstate 70 Business Loop, Clifton, CO 81520; 970-434-6644.**

Where to Eat

Chefs'—$$$

New to town, Chefs' is reaping kudos from its well-heeled clientele. The "New World cuisine" features seafood, poultry, meat and nightly pasta specials. The intimate atmosphere and soft music contribute to the restaurant's reputation for romance. Open Tues.–Sat. 5–10 P.M.; reservations are a must. **936 North Ave.; 970-243-9673.**

The Winery—$$$

The Winery continues to be the place where residents go to celebrate special occasions. Low lighting, interior walls of weathered wood and comfortably spaced tables provide an intimate setting. The menu is limited, yet carefully chosen. Dinners of freshly cooked prime rib, shrimp tempura, sirloin steak or even lobster are prepared in an open kitchen. Wine is available by the carafe or bottle, though the list is not as extensive as you might expect. Open daily 5–10 P.M. **642 Main St.; 970-242-4100.**

W W Peppers—$$ to $$$

Innovative Southwestern cuisine is featured at this extremely popular restaurant. Shredded beef or lobster enchiladas, Santa Fe burritos and chimichangas keep the locals coming back. Also available are sandwiches, burgers and chicken dishes. A word of warning: they charge for the chips and salsa. The light Southwestern decor is enhanced by skylights and many plants. Reservations not accepted, so be prepared to wait a while during prime dinner hours. Open Mon.–Fri. 11 A.M.–10 P.M., Sat. and Sun. 5–10 P.M. **753 Horizon Dr.; 970-245-9251.**

Fiesta Guadalajara—$$

Though we were initially skeptical about another "concept" Mexican restaurant, this new arrival to Grand Junction was a pleasant surprise. Spacious, brightly colored and upbeat, it's no wonder Fiesta Guadalajara consistently packs in the locals. Choose from an enormous menu of burritos and other standards, as well as the specials. Roving musicians entertain dinner patrons on weekends. Especially recommended for families. Open Mon.–Thurs. 11 A.M.–10 P.M., Fri.–Sat. 11 A.M.–11 P.M., Sun. noon–9 P.M. **710 North Ave., 970-255-6609; 970-255-6628.**

Los Reyes—$$

Although sporting a more polished atmosphere since a rebuild, the excellent food at Los Reyes hasn't changed. Chips with three kinds of salsa (green chili, red chili and chunky red tomato and onion) go perfectly with a cold cerveza Mexicana. Los Reyes offers numerous choices of Mexican beer. The large combination dinners are filling but not cheap. Most menu items may be ordered à la carte—for something different try their stuffed oro sopapilla. Open till 9 P.M. on weekdays, 10 P.M. weekends. **811 S. 7th St.; 970-245-8392.**

Crystal Cafe and Bake Shop—$ to $$

The light, airy atmosphere and friendly owners provide icing on the cake for your visit to this charming cafe along Main St. in downtown Grand Junction. The terrific food is reason enough to go out of your way to visit the Crystal. Peruse the specials listed on the chalkboard or dive into the menu, highlighted by breakfast omelettes, soups and tasty sandwiches. The main draw for many repeat customers are the huge breakfast pastries (try the cinnamon rolls) and other fresh-baked goods, which are also available for take-out. Don't forget to leave room for one of their creative desserts. Open Mon.–Fri. 7 A.M.–3 P.M. and Sat. 8:30 A.M.–3 P.M. **314 Main St.; 970-242-8843.**

Junct'n Square—$ to $$

Though the decor is a bit antiseptic, aside from some art on the walls and the trellises over the booths, Junct'n Square serves up some of the best deep-dish pizza we've tasted. Located near the Main Street Mall downtown, this restaurant is hopping at lunchtime when specials are offered. In addition to the pizza, calzones and antipasto, try the quiche, soups, submarines and salads. Full bar; free delivery. Open Mon.–Thurs. 11 A.M.–8 P.M.; Fri.–Sat. 11 A.M.–10 P.M.; Sun. 4–8 P.M. **119 N. 7th St.; 970-243-9750.**

Starvin' Arvin's—$ to $$

Starvin' Arvin's continues as the standout rib-stickin', down-home restaurant choice in the

Grand Junction area. The prices are reasonable and the portions ample. Arvin's biscuits and gravy are well known around town. In addition to the breakfast items, try the burgers and prime rib. The waitress lingo is laced liberally with "Honey" and "Sweetie." Now at three locations in the Grand Junction area, including the original just off Interstate 70 on Horizon Dr. Open daily 6 A.M.–9 P.M., till 10 P.M. on weekends. **752 Horizon Dr.; 970-241-0430.** Also at **337 S. 1st St.; 970-242-1600.** In Fruita (no breakfast) at the **I-70 Fruita exit truck stop; 970-858-7698.**

Main Street Bagels—$

Nothing fancy, just 17 varieties of fresh bagels and hot cups of joe. Oh yes, the full gamut of trendy coffee drinks and juices; bagel sandwiches are worth mentioning as well. This very popular place in downtown Grand Junction opens Mon.–Fri. at 6:30 A.M., Sat. at 7 A.M., and Sun. at 7:30 A.M.; closes in late afternoon. **559 Main St.; 970-241-2740.**

Services

Visitor Information

Colorado Welcome Center—This well-staffed visitor center offers racks of brochures and information about what to do in the area. **340 Hwy. 340, Fruita, CO 81521; 970-858-9335.**

Fruita Area Chamber of Commerce—325 E. Aspen, P.O. Box 117, Fruita, CO 81521; 970-858-3894; www.fruitachamber.org.

Grand Junction Visitors Center—740 Horizon Dr., Grand Junction, CO 81506; 1-800-962-2547; 970-244-1480; www.grand-junction.net.

Transportation

Amtrak—970-241-2733; www.amtrak.com.

Greyhound Bus Lines—230 S. 5th St.; 970-242-6012; www.greyhound.com.

Sunshine Taxi Service—1331 Ute; 970-245-TAXI.

Grand Lake

Wedged between Rocky Mountain National Park and the shores of Colorado's largest natural lake, this alluring mountain village is a vintage throwback to Colorado's past. Creaky wooden boardwalks, rough-hewn summer cabins, false-fronted stores and a well-used hitching post in front of a local bar force you to think about the past while wandering around town.

For more than 100 years, Grand Lake village has been a popular summer retreat. The community of 350 full-time residents swells during the peak summer travel season when each day sees 3,000 visitors pass near town. This surge of visitors has spawned too many T-shirt shops and miniature golf courses along Grand Ave. Despite Grand Lake's prime location at the west entrance of Rocky Mountain National Park, most people come here unaware of exactly what the area has to offer.

Outdoor recreation is the primary draw: consider the exceptional backcountry trails in Arapaho National Forest or Rocky Mountain National Park, or the fishing, waterskiing and boating on Grand Lake, Shadow Mountain Reservoir and Lake Granby. If all that doesn't get your heart pumping, try a round of golf at your choice of two of the top 18-hole public courses in the state. At an elevation of 8,369 feet, Grand Lake's cool summer weather enhances most outdoor activities. When the summer sun fades

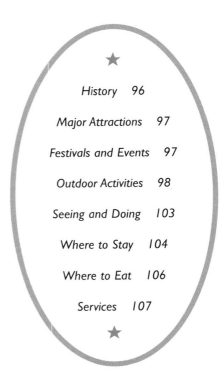

behind the peaks, an evening of surprisingly good repertory theater can be found in the rustic Community House. Or maybe you'd prefer dancing the two-step to live country and western music in a local saloon.

In winter Grand Lake shows an even quieter side when many of the businesses shut down for the season. The closure of Trail Ridge Rd. along Hwy. 34, which climbs to 12,183 feet, stops the flow of traffic through Rocky Mountain National Park and turns Grand Lake into a town at the end of the road. A thick blanket of snow transforms the town into its pastoral best, attracting many cross-country skiers, snowshoers and snowmobilers. Nearby Winter Park and SolVista ski areas make Grand Lake an ideal and less expensive base for a winter escape, without all the trappings.

Getting There

Grand Lake is located 102 miles (about 2 hours) northwest of Denver. Take Interstate 70 west to Hwy. 40 and turn north. Just past Granby head north on Hwy. 34 toward Rocky Mountain National Park. A highly recommended alternative, in summer, is a drive through Rocky Mountain National Park on Trail Ridge Rd. (see the Major Attractions section in the **Estes Park** chapter).

History

Ute Indians living near Grand Lake used trails along the North Inlet and Tonahutu Creek to travel east across the Continental Divide on hunting expeditions. At the same time, the Arapaho and Cheyenne came to Grand Lake from the plains to hunt elk and deer and to fish in the lake. Conflicts between the Utes and these visiting tribes were inevitable. After one legendary fight the Utes began calling the lake "Spirit Lake."

As the story goes, the Utes were camping by the lake when a party of Arapaho attacked them. Greatly outnumbered, the Utes put their women and children on a fishing raft and told them to paddle to the middle of the lake, where they would be safe. During the fight a storm blew off the water, capsizing the makeshift raft and drowning all aboard. Legend has it that the early morning mists seen rising from the lake are the spirits of the dead Utes.

The first settler in Grand Lake was Joseph (Judge) Wescott, who arrived in 1867. Homesteading 160 acres on the shore of the lake, Wescott made a living by trapping and fishing. Supposedly each morning he caught about 100 trout, which he kept alive and periodically packed off to hotels in Georgetown. Except for an occasional hunting party or band of Utes, with whom he was on friendly terms, Wescott had Grand Lake pretty much to himself.

In 1879 gold was discovered on the Colorado River about 15 miles north of Grand Lake. To reach the goldfields, well-provisioned prospectors crossed the Continental Divide from the east, near present-day Trail Ridge Rd. Those needing supplies followed a trail into Grand Lake, where they could load up before continuing their search for riches. By the end of 1879 Grand Lake had a hotel, a general store, a sawmill and many commercial buildings and residences. Along with this progress came gambling, prostitution and gunfights. A reputation for lawlessness kept many people away.

The boom was short-lived as the gold soon played out. By fall 1883 mining camps such as Lulu City were almost deserted. In Grand Lake, with bankruptcies the order of the day, only one business and a handful of people remained.

Gradually word spread of the area's beauty and its excellent fishing and hunting. As the

1880s drew to a close, Grand Lake prospered. By 1902 the area was attracting wealthy families from Colorado and surrounding states, who built summer homes along the shores of the lake. In 1905 the highest registered yacht club in the world (at 8,369 feet) was formed.

A big boost to tourism came in 1952 when the Colorado–Big Thompson Project was dedicated. The project created a series of dams, reservoirs, channels and a 13.1-mile-long tunnel beneath the Continental Divide to deliver much-needed irrigation water to the eastern plains. In addition to smaller reservoirs, the project created Shadow Mountain Reservoir and Lake Granby, making the Grand Lake area an ideal water sports playland.

Major Attractions

Rocky Mountain National Park
Perhaps the largest number of visitors to the area are drawn to Grand Lake for one reason: close proximity to Rocky Mountain National Park. With beautiful scenery, spectacular hiking and an abundance of wildlife, it's easy to see why. Information about the park has been interspersed at appropriate places throughout this chapter. Perhaps the best local stop for information about the park is the **Kawuneeche Visitor Center,** on Hwy. 34 about 1 mile north of Grand Lake. The center provides a wealth of information about the park and available services. The lion's share of details and background about the park, however, can be found in the Major Attractions section of the **Estes Park** chapter. Also try the park's website at **www.nps.gov/romo.**

Festivals and Events

High Altitude Sled Dog Championships
late Feb. Topping off Grand County's "Triple Crown" of sled-dog races, this annual event draws over 100 mushing teams from the United

High Altitude Sled Dog Championships. Photo courtesy of Grand Lake Chamber of Commerce.

States and Canada. Races begin midmorning at the Winding River Resort Village adjacent to Rocky Mountain National Park. Footpaths and cross-country ski trails provide access to choice viewing sites along the race routes. **970-627-3402; 970-627-3372; www. grandlake chamber.com.**

Buffalo Barbeque and Western Weekend

weekend in mid-July   For more than 50 years this summertime event has been packing them in with its Old West theme and focus on Grand Lake's heritage. Oh, and there's also the enormous buffalo barbecue roast on Sun. Other events include a 5-kilometer run, pancake breakfast and musical performances in the town park. **970-627-3402; www.grandlake chamber.com.**

Grand Lake Regatta and Lipton Cup Races

early Aug.   Shortly after the founding of the Grand Lake Yacht Club in 1905, several of the club's members wined and dined English tea baron Sir Thomas Lipton. They convinced him their annual regatta needed a trophy, and he donated a solid sterling silver cup. Each year members of the Grand Lake Yacht Club compete for the prestigious Lipton Cup while spectators cheer them on. **970-627-3402; www.grand lakechamber.com.**

Outdoor Activities

Biking

MOUNTAIN BIKING

In summer, a growing number of fat-tire enthusiasts make their way to Grand Lake for leisurely excursions and training rides. More than 100 miles of marked single-track trails and dirt roads provide enough terrain to keep you happy for days. Mountain bike information is available at the **Sulphur Ranger District Office** on Hwy. 40 in Granby, **970-887-4100,** and at the **Grand Lake Area Chamber of Commerce** visitor center as you enter Grand Lake; **970-627-3402.**

In nearby Winter Park there are over 600 miles of marked trails, making it one of the top mountain bike centers in the state. For more information see the Biking section in the **Winter Park and Middle Park** chapter.

Rentals

Rocky Mountain Sports—Christina Gill, the French owner of this shop, rents mountain bikes, helmets and child carriers. Familiar with the area, she can suggest many good trails and provides trailhead drop-offs if needed. If you own a bike, the shop will watch it while you eat lunch or wander around the village. Open Memorial Day–mid-Sept. **711 Grand Ave., Grand Lake, CO 80447; 970-627-8124.**

Fishing

The Grand Lake vicinity, known as the Three Lakes Area, is famous for its fishing. With **Grand Lake, Shadow Mountain Reservoir** and **Lake Granby,** the angler has a vast area from which to choose. Arapaho National Recreation Area, which encompasses several lakes, provides 340 overnight campsites as well as public boat access. The recreation area head-quarters is at **62429 Hwy. 40, P.O. Box 10, Granby, CO 80446; 970-887-4100.** Though the Colorado River and many other smaller streams flow nearby, the best fishing is in the lakes. Some experts believe record-breaking fish are cruising the cold depths of these lakes. Majestic views and the possibility of trophy fish make these lakes a paradise.

Colorado River

The stretch from Granby Dam down to the juncture with the Fraser River offers good fishing for brown and rainbow trout. Some browns up to 15 pounds have been taken in this area, but nearly all of the surrounding land is private.

Grand Lake

As the largest natural body of water in Colo-rado, this 300-foot-deep lake offers rainbow trout, kokanee salmon and some of the largest mackinaw in the state. Mackinaws weighing more than 20 pounds are taken almost every year. Because most of the shoreline is private property, a boat is recommended. Rainbows are more active in spring. Trolling and inlet fishing usually produce the best results, especially from early spring through mid-July. Wet flies and lures are good for brown and rainbow while sucker meat can tempt those mackinaw. Spear fishing can also be good, if you don't mind cold (64° F) water. When the lake freezes over in winter, ice fishing rules. Boat rentals, including outboards, canoes and pontoons, are available at **Boaters Choice, 1246 Lake Ave.; 970-627-9273; 970-627-3401;** in winter call **970-627-8918.** This business also offers tours and dinner cruises.

Lake Granby

The largest of the three lakes, Granby offers 41 miles of shoreline when full. Mostly rainbow, kokanee and an occasional big brown trout are caught. Mackinaw fishing has picked up in recent years with lucky trollers catching some over 30 pounds. **Gala Marina** at **928 Grand County Rd. 64, 970-627-3220,** offers rentals for fishing boats, pleasure boats and pontoons. Crewed sailboat charters and rentals are available

Catching some good wind on Lake Granby. Photo by Bruce Caughey.

from **Captain Spongefoot Sailing Co., 970-887-2746.**

Shadow Mountain Reservoir

This shallow reservoir offers rainbow, kokanee and some mackinaw as its prizes. Because of its 20-foot depth, it is often choked with weeds in late summer, but the fish are there. The reservoir is best for rainbows and browns through July, with kokanee hitting later in the summer. The most popular areas for fishing are the submerged Colorado River channel and the shoreline. Ice fishing is often good. Boat rentals, including fishing, pleasure boats, pontoons and canoes, can be arranged through **Trail Ridge Marina, 12634 Hwy. 34,** 2.5 miles south of Grand Lake; **970-627-3586.**

Golf

Grand Lake Golf Course

At an altitude of 8,420 feet, this 18-hole course offers a challenge even to the best players. Carved out of aspen and pine forests and surrounded by the rugged peaks along the Continental Divide, the course has tight, tree-lined fairways. An errant shot will leave you with a lost ball, so play conservatively and stay on the fairways! Leave the driver in the bag at this course and don't expect to putt well the first time out. The break of the greens can be confusing. From Grand Lake take Hwy. 34 north about a quarter of a mile. Turn left on County Rd. 48 and follow it about a mile to the course. **P.O. Box 590, Grand Lake, CO 80447; 970-627-8008.**

Pole Creek Golf Club

See the **Winter Park and Middle Park** chapter for information on this award-winning public course.

Hiking and Backpacking

Grand Lake, surrounded by Arapaho National Forest and Rocky Mountain National Park, offers some of the most accessible and magnificent hiking in the state.

For more information, backpacking supplies (including rentals) and maps, check with Tim or Marilou Randall at **Never Summer Mountain Products.** Open year-round, daily in summer and Fri.–Mon. in winter. **919 Grand Ave., P.O. Box 929, Grand Lake, CO 80447; 970-627-3642.** Hiking information and maps of hikes in **Rocky Mountain National Park** can be obtained at the **Kawuneeche Visitor Center,** just inside the park on Hwy. 34; **970-627-3471.** The **Sulphur Ranger District Office** can also help. **9 Ten Mile Dr., Granby, CO 80446; 970-887-4100.**

Indian Peaks Wilderness Area

Since the Indian Peaks Wilderness Area receives heavy use from Front Range visitors, a backcountry permit is required for overnight camping. They are available at the Sulphur Ranger District Office in Granby. Call for reservations or check in to see if there are any last-minute permits available. Many trails leave from Monarch Lake into the wilderness area. For more hikes in the Indian Peaks, see the Hiking and Backpacking section of the **Winter Park and Middle Park** and **Boulder** chapters. Here are two good hikes near Grand Lake:

Arapaho Pass Trail—This relatively easy trail follows Arapaho Creek to the top of the pass (approximately 11,900 feet). It's about 10 miles one way. The first 8 miles are easy hiking, with the last 2 miles uphill. The trailhead is at Monarch Lake (see directions to the Buchanan Creek Trail, in the next entry).

Buchanan Creek Trail—A 9- to 10-mile hike of intermediate difficulty, the Buchanan Creek Trail parallels the north shore of Monarch Lake, then follows Buchanan and Cascade Creeks to Crater Lake. You can camp and fish at Crater Lake, making the trip back the next day. Several opportunities exist for side trips off this trail. If you care to go to the top of the divide you can take Buchanan Pass Trail (veer north at the confluence of Buchanan and Cascade Creeks) to 12,304-foot Buchanan Pass. It's about an 8-mile trip (not an easy hike) from the trailhead to the top of the pass. Another way to the top of the divide is Pawnee Pass Trail. Instead of turning south to Crater Lake, continue east 3 miles to the top of the 12,541-foot pass. To get to the Buchanan Creek trailhead from Grand Lake, take Hwy. 34 south to County Rd. 6. Turn left and follow the road about 10 miles to the trailhead at Monarch Lake.

Rocky Mountain National Park

A permit is required for all backcountry overnight stays in the park. These free permits, limited in number, are available at the Kawuneeche Visitor Center on Hwy. 34. (See the Major Attractions section of the **Estes Park** chapter for more information or visit the park website at **www.nps.gov/romo**). Here are four standout trails within the national park:

Colorado River Trail—The Colorado River Trail is an easy "up and back" hike that can be as long or as short as desired. It's a 2-mile walk to Shipler Park and 3.7 miles to Lulu City, an early mining town. When the national park was established, all the structures were removed as part of an effort to restore the area to its natural state. To get to the trailhead from Grand Lake, take Hwy. 34 north 10 miles into the park. The Colorado River trailhead is marked on the left side of the road.

East Inlet Trail—This trail offers the day hiker several alternatives. Those wanting a short hike can stop at Adams Falls (0.3 mile one way). These crashing falls offer beautiful scenery with awesome mountain backdrops. Those who continue along the relatively flat trail another 15 minutes will find themselves in a high-country meadow, a great place to have a picnic and photograph Mt. Baldy. Those who can handle more uphill hiking can take the 4.5-mile trail to Lone Pine Lake, or to Lake Verna, another three-quarters of a mile. To get to the trailhead from Grand Lake, follow W. Portal Rd. to the end, about 1.5 miles from the Grand Ave. junction.

Timber Lake Trail—The 4.8-mile hike to Timber Lake is a little more challenging than the Colorado River Trail. And the trail is well named—you hike through a thick pine forest for most of the way. After climbing steadily for the first 2 miles (with views to the lofty peaks on the park's western boundary) you reach the Timber Creek drainage. From here the trail contours up the valley on a more level grade. This area is the only place in the United States where the Continental Divide forms a horseshoe, thus surrounding the Kawuneeche Valley, including this trail and the Colorado River Trail. The Timber Lake trailhead is across the road from the Colorado River Trail trailhead (see Colorado River Trail write-up for directions).

Tonahutu Creek/North Inlet Loop—A challenging 27-mile, three-day hike (downright difficult in two days) is the Tonahutu Creek/North Inlet Loop, which takes you deep into Rocky Mountain National Park. The best way to hike it is to head east up North Inlet Trail. Proceed over Andrews Pass (in the neighborhood of 12,000 feet) to Ptarmigan Pass and Ptarmigan Point (12,363 feet) through Bighorn Flats to the Tonahutu Creek Trail and then back to the trailhead. The hike from Andrews Pass through Bighorn Flats (all above 11,000 feet) takes you along the Continental Divide for spectacular views. This trip is not for the beginner. Camp in designated areas only. To reach this trailhead, take West Portal Rd. about three-quarters of a mile to the Shadowcliff Lodge turnoff. Turn left; the road dead-ends at the trailhead in less than a mile.

Horseback Riding

Sombrero Stables

Horses are rented by the hour, day or week for guided rides into Rocky Mountain National Park. Special breakfast and dinner steak-fry rides are available as well as all-day Continental Divide trips. Reservations are necessary. Pony rides are offered for the kids. Open from the week before Memorial Day to mid-Sept. **304 W. Portal Rd., Grand Lake, CO 80447; 970-627-3514.**

Winding River Resort

For a selection of horse-related family options, from trail rides to hay rides, check with the folks at Winding River Resort. Located just north of town in the Kawuneeche Valley. For reservations and information call **970-627-3215.**

River Floating

Although the headwaters of the Colorado River begin on the Continental Divide just north of Grand Lake, the best floating stretch is about 50 miles away. Numerous outfitters make the trip from Pump House to State Bridge on the Colorado. Here are a couple of outfitters:

Mad Adventures

Located in Winter Park, they offer beginning to advanced river trips. **1-800-451-4844; 970-726-5290.**

Rapid Transit Rafting

Rapid Transit Rafting offers trips of moderate difficulty—perfect for the beginner but exciting enough to keep the experienced rafter interested. Though not mandatory, reservations are recommended. **P.O. Box 4095, Estes Park, CO, 80517; 1-800-367-8523; 970-586-8852.**

Skiing

CROSS-COUNTRY SKIING AND SNOWSHOEING

Numerous cross-country and snowshoeing trails wind their way into Rocky Mountain National Park and Indian Peaks Wilderness Area, providing serene backcountry opportunities. Trails in Grand Lake are readily accessible along with many other fine trail systems in the Winter Park area. Before heading into the backcountry, be sure to check out the latest snow conditions with the **Sulphur Ranger District Office** in Granby, **970-887-4100,** or with **Kawuneeche Visitor Center,** just inside Rocky Mountain National Park on Hwy. 34, **970-627-3471.**

Backcountry Trails

Rocky Mountain National Park—A ski in to Lulu City on the **Colorado River Trail** (see the Hiking and Backpacking section) makes for a pleasant, scenic day trip. In winter, the road

(Hwy. 34) is plowed to Timber Lake trailhead, about 10 miles into the park. From here, continue on the fairly easy snowed-in road up to Milner Pass for excellent views. Watch out for snowmobilers!

Another trail idea in the park is **Green Mountain Trail.** For this one-way trail, you may want to use two cars to shuttle between the beginning and ending points. Take one car to the Green Mountain Trail, about 3 miles north of Grand Lake on Hwy. 34 into Rocky Mountain National Park. Ski along Green Mountain Trail east (uphill) about 2 miles. When you hit the Tonahutu Creek Trail, turn right (south) for a nice 4-mile downhill run. Total distance one way is 6 miles. Pick up your other car at the **Tonahutu Creek/North Inlet trailhead.** To reach this trailhead, take West Portal Rd. about three-quarters of a mile to the Shadowcliff Lodge turnoff. Turn left; the road dead-ends at the trailhead in less than a mile. If you want a longer, more strenuous trip, start at the Tonahutu Creek trailhead and do the trip in reverse and then return (6 miles each way).

Groomed Trails

Grand Lake Touring Center—Based at the Grand Lake Golf Course, this center features 30 kilometers of groomed and skating trails on and around the course. Rentals and lessons are available at the pro shop. Be sure to contact the center for information on moonlight skiing and other special programs. **P.O. Box 590, Grand Lake, CO 80447; 970-627-8008.**

Rentals and Information

Never Summer Mountain Products—The shop provides rental skis and snowshoes and trail information. Open daily, but the owners tend to vary hours and days in winter. **919 Grand Ave., P.O. Box 929, Grand Lake, CO 80447; 970-627-3642.**

DOWNHILL SKIING AND SNOWBOARDING

See the Outdoor Activities section of the **Winter Park and Middle Park** chapter.

Snowmobiling

Come winter, snowmobiles take to the streets of Grand Lake with the same rights as conventional street vehicles—so don't be surprised. Grand Lake boasts the largest groomed trail system in the state with approximately 130 miles of trails, in addition to deep-powder riding. The system provides everything from simple trail riding to hill climbing.

Numerous shops in the area that rent snow-mobiles can give you information on where to ride. One rental shop to consider is **Spirit Lake Rentals,** offering 2-, 4- or 8-hour unguided rides. They are located on Main St. as you enter town; **1-800-894-3336; 970-627-9288; www.grandlakecolorado.com/polaris.** You may also call the **Grand Lake Area Chamber of Commerce** at **970-627-3402** for other ideas.

Water Sports

In addition to attracting anglers, the lakes also bring in many other water sports enthusiasts. Public boat ramps and marinas are spread throughout the Three Lakes Area, providing access for boaters and water-skiers. Along Hwy. 34 are numerous rental outfits on the shores of Shadow Mountain Reservoir, Grand Lake and Lake Granby. Lake Granby, with its constant afternoon winds, is a favorite of windsurfers and sailors. For more information about tour and rental companies, see the write-ups under the Fishing section.

Seeing and Doing

Museums

The Kauffman House

In 1892 Ezra Kauffman built the Kauffman House in downtown Grand Lake and ran it as a hotel until his death in 1921. The restored, two-story log house features displays depicting life in the late 19th and early 20th centuries. Open in summer for free tours. Contact the **Grand Lake Area Chamber of Commerce** at

970-627-3402 or the **Historical Society** at **P.O. Box 656, Grand Lake, CO 80447** for information.

Nightlife

E.G.'s Garden Grill

For a relaxed atmosphere and perhaps the best Bloody Mary in western Colorado, stop in at E.G.'s (see the write-up in the Where to Eat section).

The Lariat Saloon

Another local favorite is the Lariat Saloon, a rustic western classic. Food available; live music on weekends. Open year-round 11 A.M.–2 A.M. daily; grill 11 A.M.–1 A.M. **1121 Grand Ave.; 970-627-9965.**

Rocky Mountain Repertory Theatre

A talented cast performs entertaining musical revues and comedy from mid-June to Sept. These summer and fall weekend shows take place at the Community House in the town park on Grand Ave. Reservations suggested. **970-627-3421.**

Stagecoach Inn

Founded in 1923, this rustic local favorite has a warm, friendly atmosphere and features live country and western music on summer weekends. The Stagecoach Inn boasts the only dance floor in Grand Lake. Open all year 11 A.M.–2 A.M. **920 Grand Ave.; 970-627-8079.**

Scenic Drives

Trail Ridge Road

This incredible 48-mile road through Rocky Mountain National Park crosses the Continental Divide at a lofty 12,183 feet. Driving over during the short summer season is an absolute must! If you do it in early morning or at dusk, watch out for elk on the road as you drive through Kawuneeche Valley. See the Major Attractions section of the **Estes Park** chapter or check the park's website at **www.nps.gov/romo.**

Where to Stay

Accommodations

Grand Lake offers a multitude of places to stay—from rustic cabins and 80-year-old lodges to modern condominiums. For a fairly complete listing of lodging possibilities check out the **Grand Lake Area Chamber of Commerce** website at **www.grandlakechamber.com**. To request a vacation planner, call **1–800–531–1019**. Also try **www.grandlakecolorado.com**.

E.G.'s Country Inn—$$$$

The inn is located just above the popular restaurant of the same name (see the Where to Eat section). Three immaculate, plush rooms are somewhat eclectically decorated with mahogany items and some antiques. Each room is equipped with a king-size bed, private bath and other creature comforts. Innkeeper and 30-year Grand Lake resident Judy Lorens relies on her son (the restaurant's chef) for preparation of one of the inn's main enticements—gourmet breakfast in bed. **1000 Grand Ave., P.O. Box 1618, Grand Lake, CO 80447; 970-627-3080.**

Spirit Mountain Ranch—$$$$

Secluded on 72 acres of beautiful aspen forest, Spirit Mountain offers plush accommodations and terrific hospitality. Built by innkeepers Sandy Wilson and Beth Wasmer, the four guest rooms are uniquely decorated with antiques and feature king-size beds and private marble baths. Three of the rooms have private decks. Guests relax in two great rooms decorated with Mission-style furniture, or in the library, on the main deck or in the hot tub. Hiking trails start right at the front door (llamas and rental snowshoes available). Full breakfast served in the dining room or out on the sundeck. **P.O. Box 942, Grand Lake, CO 80447; 970-887-3551; www.fcinet.com/spirit.**

Lemmon Lodge—$$$ to $$$$

Set on the banks of Grand Lake, this hideaway, excellent for families, offers a private sand beach and 26 cabins on five wooded acres. Each of the cabins is unique: some offer full kitchens and cable TV, while others are more basic (and cheaper to rent). Aside from fishing and the use of a private dock, the lodge has a playground, horseshoe pit, volleyball court and enough barbecue grills to keep everyone happy. Lemmon Lodge has too many good sides to mention and, accordingly, cabins are usually booked a year in advance. Open from the end of May to mid-Sept. For reservations (minimum stay requirement) contact the Lemmon Lodge, **P.O. Box 514, Grand Lake, CO 80447; 970-627-3314** in summer and **970-725-3511** in winter.

Soda Springs Ranch Resort—$$$

If the closest you want to get to "roughing it" is out on the area's hiking trails, then consider staying at one of the comfortably modern condominium units at Soda Springs. One-, two- and three-bedroom units are available complete with kitchens, fireplaces and other comforts of home. Families love this place for the use of its pool, hot tub and tennis courts. Located about 5 miles south of Grand Lake. **9921 Hwy. 34, #20, Grand Lake, CO 80447; 970-627-8125; www.sodaspringsranch.com.**

Grand Lake Lodge—$$ to $$$$

Although kudos are reserved primarily for Grand Lake Lodge's outstanding restaurant with its awesome views down to Grand Lake and Shadow Mountain Reservoir (see the Where to Eat section), many folks still enjoy a stay at this historic lodge. Constructed from lodgepole pine in 1925, the lodge allows guests to relax and enjoy the stunning views from the front porch or from a lounge chair at the best poolside spot in the state. Others head inside the main lodge on brisk mornings to sit by the large round fireplace.

Simple (some bordering on spartan) cabins are scattered in the woods above the main lodge. Most cabins are one- or two-bedroom units with private bath; several offer kitchenettes. Larger families or groups are invited to stay in a cabin once used by Henry Ford. Henry would still feel at home at the lodge thanks to its small collection of vintage Model Ts. The lodge entrance is a quarter-mile north of the Grand Lake turnoff on Hwy. 34. Open from the first weekend in June to the second weekend in Sept. For summer reservations contact Grand Lake Lodge, **15500 Hwy. 34, P.O. Box 569, Grand Lake, CO 80447; 970-627-3967; www.grandlake lodge.com.** Off-season call in Denver at **303-759-5848.**

Rapids Lodge—$$ to $$$$

Built on the banks of the Tonahutu Creek around 1910, the Rapids Lodge is the oldest existing lodge in Grand Lake. Owners Lou and Toni Nigro have worked hard to restore the main split-pine building in a way that preserves its historic integrity while allowing guests the use of modern conveniences. Highlighted by a warm country decor, each of the six upstairs rooms offers creature comforts such as four-poster beds, thick quilts and color TV. Each room has a private bathroom; some feature claw-footed tubs. The rooms vary in size and in price, but each provides much more than just a simple night's rest. Those who enjoy being serenaded by the sounds of rushing water may request stream-side rooms. No young kids are allowed at the lodge. Nearby, several small cabins and some plush, modern condominium units are available. Try the excellent restaurant located downstairs (see the Where to Eat section). Open year-round. **209 Rapids Ln., P.O. Box 1400, Grand Lake, CO 80447; 970-627-3707; www.rapidslodge.com.**

Western Riviera Motel and Cabins— $$ to $$$

If lodging recommendations were based on convenient location alone, the Western Riviera would win hands down. Situated right in town, overlooking Grand Lake and the town's shore-side park, this is the best motel-style accommodation we've found. The Western "Riv" is a great family place, featuring 13 motel rooms and two suites in the main complex. Across the street you may want to book one of the rooms in the cabin duplexes, with kitchenettes, or one of the four cabins right on the lake. Guests also enjoy

the outside deck with its tables and hot tub. **P.O. Box 1286, Grand Lake, CO 80447; 970-627-3580; www.westernriv.com.**

Shadowcliff Lodge—$ to $$

On a cliff overlooking Grand Lake and North Inlet Stream, Shadowcliff Lodge clings to its spectacular perch. Two large, three-story lodges offer basic, American Youth Hostel–approved accommodations. Most lodge rooms sleep four to eight people on bunk beds, and there is a spacious common room for meeting others. In addition to hostelers, many large groups and families use the lodge or rent several good-sized cabins with full kitchens. No pets allowed. Family-style meals available for an extra price. Open June 1–Oct. 1. **W. Portal Rd., P.O. Box 658, Grand Lake, CO 80447; 970-627-9220** in summer; in winter call **303-355-1012** in Denver.

Camping

Arapaho National Forest

From Granby head 3 miles northwest on Hwy. 40 and turn right on Hwy. 125. Proceed 10 miles to **Sawmill Gulch Campground** (6 sites, fee charged). Another 2 miles up Hwy. 125 leads to **Denver Creek Campground** (22 sites, fee charged).

Arapaho National Recreation Area

Nearly 328 campsites are located within the recreation area and all require a fee. From Grand Lake go south on Hwy. 34 about 3 miles to County Rd. 66. Turn left and go another mile to **Green Ridge Campground** (78 sites) next to Shadow Mountain Reservoir. **Stillwater Lake Campground** (129 sites) is located 6 miles south of Grand Lake on Hwy. 34, just off the highway on the shores of Lake Granby. Another mile south from Stillwater Lake Campground, turn left on County Rd. 66 and proceed 1 mile to **Sunset Point Campground** (25 sites). Continue 7 miles to **Arapaho Bay Campground** (84 sites), also on the shores of Lake Granby. To reach **Willow Creek Campground** (35 sites) from Grand

Lake, head south on Hwy. 34 for 8 miles and turn right on County Rd. 40. Proceed 3 miles to the shores of Willow Creek Reservoir. Reservations for Green Ridge, Stillwater and Arapaho Bay Campgrounds can be made at **1-877-444-6667** or **www.reserveusa.com.** Group camping is available at **Cutthroat Bay Group Campground,** on the shores of Lake Granby; reservations at **1-800-416-6992.**

Rocky Mountain National Park
To reach **Timber Creek Campground** (100 sites, fee charged) from Grand Lake, go north on Hwy. 34 for 8.4 miles into the park. Some wheechair-accessible sites are available. For reservations call **1-800-365-CAMP.**

Private Campgrounds
Elk Creek Campground—Open year-round, with RV hookups (summer only) and tentsites. Facilities available include showers, laundry and groceries. Located just off Hwy. 34 north of Grand Lake at the Grand Lake Golf Course Rd. **P.O. Box 549, Grand Lake, CO 80447; 1-800-355-2733; 970-627-8502.**
Winding River Resort Village—Spread out in a beautiful, thickly wooded location adjacent to Rocky Mountain National Park, this family-oriented resort offers 160 campsites, half of which offer full RV hookups. Hot showers, a small country store and laundry facilities are available. You may want to inquire about staying in one of the three extremely plush **bed and breakfast rooms ($$$);** a couple of small **cabins ($$$),** each with a private deck, are also available. There is a huge list of activities for families and even a Frisbee golf course. Entrance across from the Kawuneeche Visitor Center on Hwy. 34. **Box 629, Grand Lake, CO 80447; 970-627-3215** or Denver direct **303-623-1121.**

Where to Eat

Caroline's Cuisine—$$$ to $$$$
Popular with locals and return visitors, this comfortable, six-sided restaurant offers haute cuisine. Owners Jean-Claude and Caroline met while working at the Ritz-Carlton in Boston, and their top-notch training shows through in the food. Start off with an appetizer such as steamed mussels in garlic butter sauce or onion soup au gratin. Entrée highlights include the slow-roasted duck with pears and surf-and-turf with filet mignon and shrimp in addition to nightly specials. Be sure to try the decadent desserts. Full bar. Children's menu. Open for dinner Tues.–Sun. 5–9 P.M. (until 9:30 P.M. Fri. and Sat.). Weather permitting, dine from the new outdoor deck. Located 5 miles south of Grand Lake on Hwy. 34 at the Soda Springs Ranch turnoff; **9921 Hwy. 34, #27; 970-627-9404.**

The Rapids Restaurant—$$$ to $$$$
This historic lodge offers fine Italian dining, with large picture windows looking out to Tonahutu Creek. Favorite dishes among patrons include lasagna and manicotti (all pasta is imported from Italy) as well as prime rib of beef. Excellent dessert choices change nightly. Children's menu offered. Open Jan.–late Nov. daily 5–9:30 P.M. **209 Rapids Ln.; 970-627-3707.**

Grand Lake Lodge Restaurant—$$ to $$$
This restaurant offers one of the most spectacular views in Colorado along with fine dining. Look out on Grand Lake, Shadow Mountain Reservoir and the surrounding mountains while enjoying your meal. The deck tables are best for this, but reservations are not accepted. The restaurant serves breakfast, lunch and dinner as well as a Sun. champagne brunch. A rough-hewn interior and the mesquite-grilled specialties add to the atmosphere. Children's menu offered. In addition to a full bar the lodge has an excellent selection of microbrewed beers on tap. Breakfast 7:30–10 A.M. Mon.–Sat.; lunch 11:30 A.M.– 2:30 P.M. Mon.–Sat.; dinner 5:30–10:30 P.M. daily. Champagne brunch served Sun. 9:30 A.M.–1:30 P.M. Open Memorial Day–Labor Day week. Located just off Hwy. 34 north of Grand Lake; **970-627-3967.**

E.G.'s Garden Grill—$ to $$$

A reliable dining option in Grand Lake village, E.G.'s offers a creative menu and terrific ambience throughout the year. A fireplace, soft music and local art on the walls accentuate the cozy indoor seating. Weather permitting, grab an outdoor patio table either under an umbrella or larger shelter, and start off with a drink from the full bar. Lunch highlights include homemade soups, Baja fish tacos, sandwiches, pizza and salads; dinner features a number of seafood items, baby back ribs, steaks and roasted duck with grand marnier sauce. The daily specials are highly recommended. Open daily 11:30 A.M.– 9:30 P.M. **1000 Grand Ave.; 970-627-8404.**

Grand Lake Golf Course Restaurant and Lounge—$ to $$

This spacious restaurant/lounge provides pretty views while serving up tasty sandwiches, homemade soups, salads and Mexican food for a great price. Appetizers are also popular, especially with the ravenous golfers and cross-country skiers who have just come in from a day on the course and trails. Open year-round: breakfast served Mon.–Fri. 8–11 A.M. and Sat.–Sun. 7–11 A.M.; lunches served Mon.–Fri. 11 A.M.–4 P.M., until 5 P.M. Sat.–Sun. See the Golf section for directions; **970-627-3922.**

Services

Visitor Information

Grand Lake Area Chamber of Commerce—The Chamber of Commerce Visitors Center is located at the intersection of Grand Ave. and Hwy. 34 as you enter town. **P.O. Box 57, Grand Lake, CO 80447; 970-627-3402; www.grandlakechamber.com.** For a vacation planner, contact **1-800-531-1019.**

Other information—www.grandlakecolorado.com.

Relaxing on the Grand Lake Lodge porch swing. Photo by Bruce Caughey.

Meeker

Every autumn hunters crowd into Meeker before setting off into the Flat Tops Wilderness Area to the southeast, their hearts set on bagging some of the area's plentiful game, which includes the largest indigenous herd of elk in the world. Lodging in and around Meeker fills up in Sept. and Oct. as the area is flooded with hunters. During the rest of the year, with the exception of July 4th weekend, this small town in the White River Valley of northwestern Colorado quiets down. The only traffic jams occur when ranchers move herds of cattle and sheep to and from summer ranges by way of local roads.

An offbeat, outdoor lover's vacation destination, Meeker also entices families with its nearby guest ranches. Some offer expert fly-fishing instruction and access to private water, while others impart a western feel with a strong focus on horses. Or set out on your own because camping, fishing and hiking opportunities are limitless in the White River National Forest and Flat Tops Wilderness Area. Sections of the White River boast thousands of trout per mile. Also of note is that the national Wilderness Area concept was first conceived by a group of visitors enjoying the beauty of nearby Trappers Lake.

Meeker's apparent resistance to change adds to its charm. Most ranchers in this wide valley enjoy a way of life similar to that of previous generations. This continuity, coupled with the fact that Meeker remains remote and undeveloped, causes a rich local flavor to emerge. You'll quickly learn residents are proud of their rock-solid community.

History

Meeker was named after Indian agent Nathan C. Meeker, who was killed on the afternoon of Sept. 29, 1879, during a Ute uprising at the White River Indian agency. The incident was not

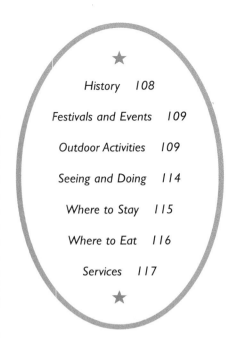

solely the result of a local problem; rather, it was the culmination of inevitable conflict between Indians and settlers.

Nathan Meeker accepted the job as White River Indian agent in the spring of 1878. An idealist, he had been at various times a Greenwich Village poet, war correspondent, columnist and founder of a Colorado agricultural cooperative (now the town of Greeley). He wanted the Utes to stop their migratory hunting expeditions and adopt the plow. The Utes, of course, had a different opinion about the sedentary life of farming. Distrust and resentment simmered as Meeker imposed his will during the first growing season. The next year he made a fatal mistake when he ordered an irrigation channel to be built through a field where the Utes raced their horses. He also had some of their best horse pastures plowed under.

Getting There

Meeker is 227 miles northwest of Denver. Drive west on Interstate 70 for 185 miles to the Rifle exit. Turn north on Hwy. 13 and continue 42 miles to Meeker.

War clouds gathered over the White River Indian agency in the late summer of 1879. Meeker finally understood that his safety was in peril when his favorite Ute chief, Johnson, threw him against the wall of his cabin for his offensive suggestion that some of the Utes' ponies be killed to free more farmland. After this assault Meeker sent a formal request for troops. A detachment of army troops, led by Maj. Thomas T. Thornburgh, moved in to support the agency. They were ambushed at Milk Creek by a small band of Utes, who swiftly killed Thornburgh and many of his men.

The Utes' anger turned on Meeker. In a rage, this band of Native Americans descended on the agency later the same day, setting fire to the buildings and killing all of the men at the post. Meeker was found stripped and mutilated. The women, including Meeker's wife, Arvilla, and daughter, Josephine, were kidnapped and held captive for nearly a month on Grand Mesa. During this time they were raped, according to Ute custom, but eventually released. As a result of the White River Ute uprising, all Utes in Colorado suffered: the southern bands were relocated to reservations in extreme southwestern Colorado, while the northern Utes were banished to an area in Utah.

The massacre took place 3 miles west of present-day Meeker by way of Hwy. 64. A roadside marker points the way to the exact location of the White River Indian agency. A military camp was established at the present site of Meeker after the massacre. The army maintained order until 1883, when it closed the post and sold its buildings to settlers coming into the valley.

Festivals and Events

Range Call

July 4th weekend More than a century ago cowboys started competing in the rodeo at Meeker. The annual tradition continues during the July 4th weekend with professionals and local ranch hands. In addition to the rodeo, Range Call offers fireworks, dances, concerts, footraces and, most importantly, the Meeker Massacre pageant—a historical reenactment that illustrates the painful clashing of Native Americans with the intruding settlers. The Meeker Chamber of Commerce is happy to give details for the current year's lineup: **970-878-5510; www.meekerchamber.com.**

Meeker Classic Sheep Dog Championship Trials

Second weekend in Sept. Since 1987 the Meeker Classic Sheep Dog Championship Trials have attracted sheep ranchers, dog lovers and neophytes who want to see real working sheep dogs in action. Some of the world's best handlers and their dogs compete in a five-day event that pits them against a challenging course and local sheep. In addition to the trials, a wool festival features spinning and weaving, sheep-shearing demonstrations and product displays. For information contact the Meeker Chamber of Commerce at **970-878-5510; www.meeker chamber.com.**

Outdoor Activities

Biking

MOUNTAIN BIKING

Once you are up in the White River National Forest, single-track and dirt roads provide endless possibilities. Please remember, however, that riding is strictly prohibited within the wilderness boundaries. A couple of excellent riding areas include the Miller Creek drainage as well as all or part of the 36-mile route from Ripple Creek Pass to Yellowjacket Pass. For more trail ideas, contact the **Blanco Ranger District Office, 317 E. Market St., Meeker, CO 81641; 970-878-4039; www.wilder net.com.**

Fishing

The best fishing in the Meeker area is east of town. Nearly all lakes and streams discussed in this section are located in the **Flat Tops**

Far-reaching views characterize the Flat Tops Wilderness Area. Photo by Dean Winstanley.

Wilderness and other parts of White River National Forest. Meeker offers easy access to the Flat Tops, which encompass some of the finest fishing territory in the state. This 9,600-foot plateau is laced with high-country lakes and streams. Since there are no roads in the wilderness, getting to the best fishing requires some effort on foot or by horseback. One word of caution: the fish in the Flat Tops are well fed by multitudes of insects that flourish in the waterlogged environment. From spring through fall, be prepared to encounter thick clouds of mosquitos.

We have chosen to include bodies of water that provide relatively good fishing year after year. Remaining are countless fisheries in the backcountry, known only to longtime residents and guides. While many hidden lakes and ponds provide excellent fishing, some are unstocked and others face a yearly winterkill. For up-to-date fishing information call the Colorado Division of Wildlife's stocking report at **303-291-7531** or condition report at **303-291-7534.** You can reach the division's Grand Junction office at **970-255-6100.** If you have ever considered hiring a guide or an outfitter, this is the place to do it.

If you're in Meeker and looking for some advice from the locals, stop by **Wyatt's Sport Center** at **223 8th St.; 970-878-4428.** They have an excellent selection of rods and lures, as well as essentials for hunting.

The Orvis-endorsed fly-fishing masters at **Elk Creek Lodge ($$$$),** located about 18 miles east of Meeker, offer fishing on more than 6 miles of private White River access, 6 miles on Marvine Creek and 100-plus pools along the lodge's 3-mile stretch of Elk Creek. If you tire of the excellent fishing in the area, climb into the lodge's plane for a guided day trip to the Gold Medal water of the Fryingpan River near Basalt, or the trout-infested waters of the Green River below Flaming Gorge in Utah. Brett Harvey runs a first-class operation that includes comfortable accommodations for 12 people. As you may have guessed, Elk Creek Lodge can provide plenty of fond memories, but it ain't cheap. For information contact Steve at **P.O. Box 130, Meeker, CO 81641; 970-878-4565; www.colorado-west/elkcreek.** For another exclusive fishing and lodging experience you may also wish to contact the folks at **7 Lakes Lodge ($$$$); 1-800-809-4772; 970-878-4772; www. sevenlakeslodge.com.**

Bailey Lake

If you want a smaller lake in the backcountry, try this one. A 5-mile hike from Buford is required to reach **Bailey Lake.** It's another half-mile to **Swede Lake.** Both lakes are considered good fisheries for brook and rainbow trout. To reach the trailhead, take Hwy. 13 for 2 miles east of Meeker. Turn right on River Rd. (County Rd. 8) and head 21 miles to Buford. The trail leads south from the community center in Buford.

Marvine Creeks

Eight miles northeast of Buford, Marvine Creek flows into the White River on private land. County Rd. 12 follows the creek upstream 7 miles to the Flat Tops Wilderness boundary at Marvine Campground. Below the campground much of the creek flows through private land. Above the campground the creek splits into West, Middle and East Forks with good trails following each. The West Fork of Marvine Creek provides ideal water for catching small brook, rainbow and cutthroat trout on small flies. The Middle Fork is wider and therefore easier to fish. The East Fork can be good, if you can put up with the brush along the narrow banks. From Meeker take Hwy. 13 east for 2 miles. Turn right on River Rd. (County Rd. 8) and continue for 28 miles. Turn right on Marvine Creek Rd. and travel 7 miles to the campground.

South Fork of the White River

Flowing into the White River near the town of Buford is the South Fork. A road parallels the river for 11 miles to the Flat Tops Wilderness boundary at South Fork Campground. From the boundary a good trail follows the river 16 miles to its origin. The farther you hike, the more beautiful the water and the better the fishing. Though the river is fast, there are many deep pools with lunker cutthroat and rainbows. Six miles of the upper section are limited to flies only. Stop in at the **Buford Store, 970-878-4745,** and ask about their selection of small dry flies. One local suggested we use a minuscule size-22 hook on the upper South Fork. Take Hwy. 13 for 2 miles east of Meeker. Turn right on River Rd. (County Rd. 8) and proceed for 20 miles. Turn right on South Fork Rd. and continue to the campground.

Trappers Lake

Located near the northeast Flat Tops Wilderness boundary, this beautiful and easily accessible lake remains one of the best fisheries around. A pure strain of cutthroat trout reproduces naturally in the deep water of Trappers Lake. Boats without motors are allowed and may be rented at the Trappers Lake Lodge (see the Where to Stay section). To allow native trout to safely spawn, fishing is prohibited in all inlets to the lake and upstream for half a mile and the outlet is closed downstream to the first falls. Only artificial flies and lures are allowed; all fish longer than 10 inches must be released; bag and possession limit for cutthroat trout is eight fish, but you can keep any brook trout you catch. Four campgrounds with a total of 53 developed sites are located near the lake. To get to Trappers Lake, take Hwy. 13 for 2 miles east of Meeker. Turn right onto River Rd. (County Rd. 8) and proceed 39 miles to Trappers Lake Rd., which ends at the lake 10 miles farther.

White River

This river's headwaters begin at Trappers Lake (see previous entry), then flow west through Meeker and eventually into Utah. The upper portion of the river, for 6 miles from Trappers Lake down to Himes Peak Campground, offers good fishing for brook, rainbow and cutthroat trout. Big Fish Creek flows into the White River at the campground and can be excellent for small rainbow trout. Below Himes Peak Campground, the river enters a long, narrow swath of private property. The next stretch of public fishing is located on the river near North Fork Campground. West of Meeker, fishing on the White River is poor, and whitefish are the only catch. To reach the upper portion of the White River, take Hwy. 13 for 2 miles east of Meeker. Turn right onto River Rd. (County Rd. 8) and travel 39 miles to Trappers Lake Rd., which ends at the lake 10 miles farther.

Four-Wheel-Drive Trips

Dead Horse Road

This rough and narrow four-wheel-drive road rises and falls some 2,500 feet during its 12-mile duration. Also known as the Long Park Loop, it offers incredible views of the North Fork Valley and the Flat Tops. The west terminus of the loop can be found 35 miles east of Meeker on County Rd. 8. Follow the switchbacks up the southern slope of the valley into Long Park. Take the right fork and follow the divide for 3 miles before dropping back into the White River drainage. As you proceed down the road, take the east fork (the west fork ends at Missouri Creek) back to County Rd. 8.

Hiking and Backpacking

To the east of Meeker is one of the most under-rated recreation areas in the state—the northern section of the White River National Forest. If you hope to hike and backpack among the state's tallest peaks, this isn't the place. It's a land of rolling hills surrounding the vast plateau known as the Flat Tops Wilderness Area, which never rises above 12,000 feet. It offers relatively few people, plentiful wildlife, excellent fishing and beautiful scenery. Thick stands of aspen and pine are interspersed with fields of wildflowers. Since the terrain is virtually devoid of readily identifiable landmarks, it is easy to get lost or confused. Maps and a compass are essential.

Just after the turn of the century, Teddy Roosevelt came to the Meeker area on a hunting expedition in country that is still home to herds of deer and elk as well as mountain lions and black bears. If you plan a multi-day backpack trip in this area, pack a fishing rod.

Vegetation is lush and for a very good reason—it rains a lot here in the summer. Be sure to pack adequate rain gear. The mosquitos and flies can get thick, so bring some effective insect repellent. In autumn this is a popular hunting area, so it would be wise to dress in bright clothing. In addition, many sheep graze in the Flat Tops area, so be sure to boil or otherwise purify all of your drinking water.

Once up on the Flat Tops, the trails criss-cross, making route possibilities endless. For more trail ideas, contact the **Blanco Ranger District Office, 317 E. Market St., Meeker, CO 81641; 970-878-4039; www.wilder net.com.**

Chinese Wall Trail

This trail begins at about 10,000 feet and runs south by southeast for 18 miles along the northwest border of White River National Forest. It then loops back around north for 7 miles to Trappers Lake. Along the way enjoy far-reaching views into the White River drainage to the west and the Williams Fork drainage to the east. The trail winds its way through stands of trees and high plateau meadows. Quite a few trails branch off from the Chinese Wall along the way. Be sure to bring a topographic map. To reach the trailhead from Meeker, drive east 2 miles on Hwy. 13 and turn right on County Rd. 8. Drive 44 miles to the trailhead on the right, 0.2 mile from the summit of Ripple Creek Pass.

Marvine Trail

This fairly long hike (11.5 miles) gives you a good sample of the Flat Tops Wilderness Area: excellent fishing, the rolling hills of the Flat Tops plateau and lots of pine and aspen groves. The gradual hike up Marvine Creek rises from 8,000 feet up to about 10,800 feet. A couple of stream fords are necessary on the hike, and they can be tricky during spring runoff. This highly popular valley is also a good place to cross-country ski and snowshoe in wintertime. To reach the trailhead from Meeker, head east 2 miles on Hwy. 13, then turn right onto County Rd. 8 and drive 28 miles to Marvine Creek Rd. (County Rd. 12). Turn right, cross the bridge and take a left; proceed 6 miles to Marvine Campground and the trailhead.

Mirror Lake

Located in a basin below some 1,000-foot cliffs, Mirror Lake, with its blue water and fantastic brook trout fishing, is one of the best short hikes in the area. The 2.5-mile trail climbs from 8,500 feet up to 10,000 feet, crossing private land in the process (stay on the trail). After about 2 miles you reach a lake with green water. This is Shamrock Lake. Continue on up the trail to Mirror Lake. To reach the trailhead from Meeker, drive east 2 miles on Hwy. 13 and then turn right onto County Rd. 8. Drive 39 miles to Trappers Lake Rd. (Forest Rd. 205). Turn right at Trappers Lake Rd. and drive half a mile to the Mirror Lake trailhead access road. Turn right and drive a quarter-mile to the trailhead.

Peltier Lake Trail

This 6.5-mile trail (one way) climbs through oak brush and aspen groves as it rises to about 9,000 feet. After 3.5 miles, the trail passes Peltier Lake and continues another 3 miles to Bailey Lake. Both lakes offer good fishing for brookies and rainbow trout. To reach the trailhead from Meeker, head east on Hwy. 13 for 2 miles and then right on County Rd. 8 for 18 miles. Turn right on South Fork Rd. and drive 10 miles to the Peltier Lake trailhead on the left.

Skinny Fish Lake/McGinnis Lake Trail

This 2.5-mile trail (one way) branches to the two lakes half a mile below Skinny Fish Lake. Located in the Flat Tops Wilderness Area, these lakes get heavy use from horse packers and hikers because the fishing is good. Either of the lakes makes for a great day hike, though you must endure many beetle-killed pine trees in the area. Also, be on the lookout for aspen trees that have been written on. In the late 1940s a Greek shepherd named Nick "Theo" Theopolis killed time (and maybe a few trees) by writing a daily diary entry on the aspen. ("Today I saw a coyote—but not a problem—looks like rain.") To reach the trailhead from Meeker, drive east 2 miles on Hwy. 13. Take a right at County Rd. 8 and drive 39 miles to Trappers Lake Rd. (Forest Rd. 205). Turn right and continue 8 miles. Pull in at the Skinny Fish Lake trailhead parking area on the left. Walk a mile up the Lost Lakes Trail to the Skinny Fish Lake Trail intersection, which heads off to the right.

Spring Cave Trail

A half-mile hike from South Fork Campground leads to Spring Cave, the second-largest cave in Colorado. Many of its passages are believed to be unexplored. Deep within its recesses is an underground passage known as Thunder Road, which contains one of the largest underground waterways in the United States. From the campground the trail crosses the White River through blue spruce and climbs into aspen about halfway to the cave. Exploring the cave (spelunking) is definitely not suggested unless you are experienced! It's easy to get lost. To reach the trailhead from Meeker, drive 2 miles east of town on Hwy. 13 and take the right fork onto County Rd. 8. Proceed 18 miles to South Fork Rd. (County Rd. 10) and turn right. Drive 12 miles to the South Fork Campground. The trailhead begins here.

Trappers Lake Trail

This trail begins at Trappers Lake. It follows the pine forests along Fraser Creek up into the high country of the Flat Tops plateau, about 5.5 miles from the lake. The trail extends about 16 miles (one way) and offers good campsites along most of the way. You can make your trip as long or as short as you want. Numerous trails intersect the Trappers Lake Trail, so a good map of the area can let you play it by ear and take side trips. Fishing in the endless potholes on the plateau can be worth your while. To reach the trailhead from Meeker, drive 2 miles east on Hwy. 13 and turn right onto County Rd. 8. Drive 39 miles to Trappers Lake Rd. (Forest Rd. 205). Turn right and drive 10 miles to Trappers Lake and the trailhead.

Horseback Riding

White River National Forest has more than 250 miles of maintained trails that are perfect for riding. Many outfitters can take you into the

Hiking near Stillwater Reservoir in the Flat Tops Wilderness. Photo by Dean Winstanley.

backcountry for hunting and fishing expeditions as well as for shorter rides, or you may consider staying at a local guest ranch.

Fritzlan's Guest Ranch

Pick your pleasure from guided trail rides and guided fishing trips, as well as the opportunity to rent your own horse. **1891 County Rd. 12, Meeker, CO 81641; 970-878-4845.**

Sombrero Horse Rentals

These stables possess the largest herd of saddle horses in the nation. They offer guided rides and pack trips and horse rentals, and are one of the few outfitters with a permit for the White River National Forest. Reservations recommended. Located 12.5 miles up County Rd. 8 at **12900 County Rd. 8, Meeker, CO 81641; 970-878-4382; www.sombrero.com.**

Trappers Lake Lodge

For details, see the Where to Stay section.

Skiing

CROSS-COUNTRY SKIING AND SNOWSHOEING

For trail ideas see the Hiking and Backpacking section or contact the **Blanco Ranger District Office, 317 E. Market St., Meeker, CO 81641; 970-878-4039; www.wildernet.com.** Also see Trappers Lake Lodge and Sleepy Cat Guest Ranch in the Where to Stay section.

Seeing and Doing

Museums

White River Museum

A visit to this museum is far better than climbing up into Grandma's attic. Housed in a former U.S. cavalry garrison, it features a hodgepodge of artifacts and historic memorabilia. "We've got a little bit of everything," said the friendly museum curator. You'll see a jar of carrots from 1938, a bottle collection, a bear coat and a copper still from the 1920s. Don't miss the Spanish war axe or the carving in aspen bark of a pretty woman by local sheepherder Pacino Chacon. In the back room are a bright-red fire truck, horse-drawn carriages and a mounted two-headed calf. No fee charged, but donations are accepted. Open daily May–Oct., 9 A.M.–5 P.M.; Nov.–Apr., 11 A.M.–3 P.M. **565 Park, P.O. Box 413, Meeker, CO 81641; 970-878-9982.**

Scenic Drives

Flat Tops Trail Scenic Byway

As the name suggests, this drive provides extremely scenic views as it makes its way up the White River Valley from Meeker and then over 10,000-foot Ripple Creek Pass toward the town of Yampa. About 40 miles of this 82-mile route are unpaved, but any vehicle can make the trip. It's even open in winter. Along the way are many places to fish, hike and take photos. One of the many worthwhile side trips is Trappers Lake (see the Where to Stay and Fishing sections). From

Meeker, head 2 miles west on Hwy. 13 and turn right onto County Rd. 8. Continue on this road and follow the signs. Stop by the **Meeker Chamber of Commerce Visitors Center** for a detailed map with information about what to do and see along the way; **970-878-5510.**

Where to Stay

Accommodations

Heaps of guest ranches and small cabins are scattered throughout the area. For a clean, comfortable and fully refurbished motel in town, you may want to stay at the **White River Inn ($ to $$), 219 E. Market St., Meeker, CO 81641; 970-878-5031.** For a fairly complete list of lodging opportunities, contact the **Meeker Chamber of Commerce** at **970-878-5510; www.meekerchamber.com.** Here are a few true highlights:

Trappers Lake Lodge—$$$

Check out this collection of 16 rustic cabins on the banks of one of Colorado's most productive fisheries (see the Fishing section). Though an upgrade replaced some of the woodstoves in the cabins with gas stoves and heat, you still must rely on a central bathhouse for rest rooms and hot showers. Check out the general store and a remodeled lodge building where delicious family-style meals ($$) can be found. Guests are welcome to soak out the day's troubles in the hot tub. Guided horseback trips are also available. In addition to the fishing on Trappers Lake, they have a number of fishing camps up on the Flat Tops; catch-and-release is emphasized. Rowboats, canoes and horses are available to rent by the hour or by the day. The lodge lies adjacent to the northeast Flat Tops Wilderness boundary. Open in winter for snowmobiling and cross-country skiing. To get there take Hwy. 13 for 2 miles east of Meeker. Turn right at River Rd. (County Rd. 8) and head 41 miles to Trappers Lake Rd., which ends near the lodge 8 miles away. **7700 Trappers Lake Rd., P.O. Box 1230, Meeker, CO 81641; 970-878-3336; www.trapperslake.com.**

Meeker Hotel—$$ to $$$$

Even if you are just passing through, stop off at this old hotel and take a look around the restored lobby. Once inside, your every move is watched by the beady glass eyes of 15 stuffed elk, buffalo, deer and bighorn sheep heads mounted on the walls. Separated by an etched glass partition, the lobby reveals Meeker's history in newspaper accounts as well as the hotel's exposed brick walls and oak floors.

This hotel, built in 1896, once offered high-class accommodations, including a restaurant and a barbershop. The 24 rooms have been enlarged and modernized from the originals; they range from suites with private bathrooms to small rooms with a bath down the hall. The slightly funky decorator schemes will remind you of another era. It's an interesting place to wander around. You can even stay in the two-room suite where Teddy Roosevelt slept during a visit in 1900 to hunt bears. Open year-round; be sure to call ahead in winter. **560 Main St., Meeker, CO 81641; 970-878-5255; www.meekerhotel.com.**

Sleepy Cat Guest Ranch—$$ to $$$

Located 18 miles east of Meeker in the White River Valley, Sleepy Cat has been putting up families and sportsmen since 1946. Twenty-one cabins with kitchenettes are rented by the night or by the week. The restaurant attracts people from miles away for great food and drink (see the Where to Eat section). Unlike some guest ranches, Sleepy Cat does not have an organized plan of activities for the week. The ranch sits near the edge of the Flat Tops Wilderness and offers outstanding fishing, hunting and cross-country skiing. The people running Sleepy Cat are friendly, and the price is a pittance for what you get. The only drawback: Sleepy Cat is fairly close to a main road. From Meeker take Hwy. 13 east for 2 miles. Turn right on County Rd. 8 and continue for 16 miles. **16064 County Rd. 8, Meeker, CO 81641; 970-878-4413; www.colorado-west.com/cat.html.**

Camping

White River National Forest

Several campgrounds are spread out near the White River Valley east of Meeker. For reservations contact **1-877-444-6777** or **www.reserve usa.com.** To reach all of the listed camping areas, drive east on Hwy. 13 for 2 miles. Turn right on River Rd. (County Rd. 8) and proceed to the campground turnoff.

For **South Fork Campground** (17 sites, fee charged), drive 18 miles east on River Rd. (County Rd. 8), turn right on South Fork Rd. and head 12 miles over rough road to the campground. For **East Marvine Campground** (7 sites, fee charged, horse site available), take River Rd. 28 miles east and then turn right onto Marvine Creek Rd. and proceed 6 miles. Another mile up Marvine Creek Rd. is **Marvine Campground** (18 sites, fee charged). To reach **North Fork Campground** (39 sites, fee charged), drive 33 miles east of Meeker on River Rd. to the campground. For **Himes Peak Campground** (9 sites, fee charged), drive 39 miles east on River Rd.; turn right on Trappers Lake Rd. and continue 6 miles to the campground. Continue another 4 miles to Trappers Lake to find **Bucks, Shepherds Rim, Trapline** and **Cutthroat Campgrounds** (total of 53 sites). The campgrounds are located past Trappers Lake Lodge.

Private Campground

Rim Rock Campground—For hearty souls this campground provides 30 full RV hookups even in the cold winter months. Seven rental units are available as well. From Meeker head west for 2 miles on Hwy. 13 and then a half-mile northwest on Hwy. 64. **73179 Hwy. 64, Meeker, CO 81641; 970-878-4486.**

Where to Eat

Dade's Family Restaurant—$$ to $$$

After Pizza Hut moved in, the owners of Dade's decided to expand their repertoire from pizza to a year-round, dinner-only, family operation. Formerly known as Pizza Pro, the place will still serve you a piece of marinara-and-cheese pie, but those with an appetite for steak (regular or chicken-fried) or a breakfast-as-dinner specialty will also find themselves satisfied by this modest restaurant and the attentive staff. Mon.–Sat., 6–9 P.M. **975 W. Market St.; 970-878-4625.**

Sleepy Cat Guest Ranch—$$ to $$$

Nearly everyone we talked with in Meeker raved about the good food and atmosphere at Sleepy Cat. It's definitely worth the short and scenic trip 18 miles east of town. The hand-hewn log lodge is divided into several small dining rooms. Some tables look out over a grassy meadow to the White River. The heavy pine walls of the restaurant are lined with the requisite hunting and fishing trophies. The menu dwells on steaks and chops; on weekends try the rib specials. Some seafood and chicken entrées are served, along with lighter meals such as hamburgers and a salad and soup bar. A separate bar area fills up with ranch hands from the area and can be a fun place to spend some time. Dancing to tunes from the jukebox or occasional live bands often takes place on weekends. From Meeker take Hwy. 13 east for 2 miles. Turn right on County Rd. 8 and continue 16 miles to the ranch. Open daily Memorial Day–Nov., 8 A.M. for breakfast, 11 A.M.–2 P.M. for lunch and 5:30–9 P.M. for dinner; Fri.–Sat. in winter for dinner only. The bar stays open all day and into the night. **16064 County Rd. 8; 970-878-4413.**

Meeker Bakery and Cafe—$$

For a simple start-me-up, check out the Meeker Bakery with its fresh donuts and an inexpensive menu, to eat in or take out. Open from 5 A.M. daily. **265 5th; 970-878-5500.**

Trappers Lake Lodge—$$

The lodge serves three meals daily; the burgers are excellent. Located in a spectacular spot on the banks of Trappers Lake at the Flat Tops Wilderness Area boundary. See the Where to Stay section.

Meeker Cafe—$ to $$$

Next to the historic Meeker Hotel you can find a double-sided restaurant that serves as the small-town cafe of note. For breakfast, slip into a booth or find a counter seat and enjoy your egg or skillet breakfast and cup of java. Lunch and dinner items shift to sandwiches, burgers and some slightly more elaborate picks. The owners have taken care to preserve the integrity of the place while providing a hearty meal at a fair price. Full bar. Open 6 A.M.–9 P.M. Mon.–Sat.; till 10 P.M. Fri. **560 Main St.; 970-878-5062.**

Services

Visitor Information

Meeker Chamber of Commerce—This staffed visitor center provides information and advice on the area. **710 Market St., P.O. Box 869, Meeker, CO 81641; 970-878-5510; www.meekerchamber.com.**

North Park

This is indeed a special place. While driving through North Park, which is a geographic area that essentially follows the Jackson County lines, most visitors are drawn to the lofty peaks that surround this central high-mountain basin. The Medicine Bow Range to the east, the Rabbit Ears Range and Never Summer Mountains to the south and the Park Range to the west beckon all who appreciate the natural beauty of Colorado. North Park is reminiscent of Wyoming to the north: big views, a major ranching influence and just a touch wilder than most areas of the state.

Nowhere is this "wild" sense more evident than in the tremendously plentiful and diverse wildlife of North Park. Locals are quick to mention the Gold Medal fishing, excellent hunting and wildlife viewing throughout North Park. Well-stocked waters of Delaney Butte Lakes, Lake John and the North Platte River, among others, keep many anglers returning year after year. Colorado's largest concentration of moose (about 600) feed along the willow-covered streams and ponds of North Park.

North Park definitely qualifies as a Colorado back-road destination—instead of a neon cityscape, you look west to an array of peaks rising to over 12,000 feet in the Mt. Zirkel Wilderness. An extensive network of trails and

dirt roads crisscross public land throughout the entire North Park area, beckoning visitors to explore. The immense Colorado State Forest provides excellent access to such trails and roads along the base and into the Medicine Bow Range.

With a population of less than 1,000, the ranch supply center of Walden is the primary town in North Park offering motel accommodations and meals.

History

In the first half of the 1800s Ute Indians would summer in North Park while hunting buffalo and an abundance of other wild game. Beginning in the 1820s trappers made sojourns into North Park for the easy fur-bearing game. Despite the Anglo presence, life for the Native Americans was relatively routine until settlement to the east, near present-day Fort Collins, began. Utes made raids on the new settlements, stealing horses and returning to North Park over Ute Pass in the Medicine Bow Range. The Anglo settlers rarely followed them into the mountains.

When John Frémont visited North Park on his second expedition in 1844, he called it a

---

Getting There

The approximate center of North Park is the town of Walden, 150 miles northwest from Denver. The most direct route is to drive west on Interstate 70 for 42 miles to Hwy. 40. Follow the highway to Granby before heading north on Hwy. 125 to North Park. Another choice is to follow the Cache la Poudre–North Park Scenic Byway, a picturesque 101-mile drive between Fort Collins and Walden (see the **Fort Collins and West** chapter).

Well-equipped backcountry yurt in the Colorado State Forest. Photo courtesy of Colorado State Parks.

"paradise to all grazing animals." But it wasn't ranching that drew the first wave of settlement in North Park—it was prospecting. James O. Pinkham, a short Canadian old-timer, began panning for gold in the early 1870s. Other men followed but never struck the rich placer gold they were searching for. By 1880 silver was the draw, and in only two years the new town of Teller City had a population of 1,300. The miners, however, soon learned that transporting the ore was too expensive, and by 1885 Teller City, in the Never Summer Mountains, was deserted. Many of the men who ventured to North Park for mining eventually settled here and began raising livestock. John Frémont had been on the mark back in 1844: the future of the valley was to be found in ranching. Although locals still rely on ranching for their livelihood, tourism continues to make an ever-increasing impact.

Festivals and Events

Never Summer Rodeo and Parade
late June This annual amateur rodeo draws people in from near and far to Walden. Highlights include barbecues, dances and a parade. **970-723-4600.**

North Park Fair
mid-Sept. This event takes place in Walden over an autumn weekend. Check out the livestock, crafts, 4-H sale, barbecue and dance. **970-723-4298.**

Outdoor Activities

Biking

MOUNTAIN BIKING
Colorado State Forest
With over 112 miles of trails, this is an excellent place for mountain biking. Many routes roll along through stands of lodgepole pine, spruce and aspen. The best way to reach the majority of riding opportunities is through the main entrance to the forest.

To really experience the State Forest backcountry without having to carry a lot of extra weight, consider an overnight stay along the **Never Summer Nordic Yurt System.** With a

State Forest trail map, which you can pick up at the terrific Moose Visitors Center, explore some of the prime trails such as Grass Creek Loop. On this difficult 16-mile round trip, you will pass North Michigan Reservoir and 10,000-foot Gould Mountain before finally coming out on Hwy. 14. Yurts are located in various places along trails throughout the forest. What's a yurt? For an explanation see the Cross-Country Skiing and Snowshoeing section and the photo on the previous page. For directions, see the Colorado State Forest write-up in the Hiking and Backpacking section.

Fishing

Along with hunting, fishing is the major tourist attraction in North Park. Not only is the angling good on the dozens of streams flowing out of the surrounding mountains, but there are many popular lakes in the bottomland. So take your time and enjoy the mixture of plains and mountains while fishing in North Park. Don't hesitate to pursue some of the smaller tributaries and beaver ponds, for they sometimes offer the best fishing. Although much of the land in the park is privately owned and posted against fishing, miles of streams are open, due to fishing leases with landowners. These areas are marked; if you need more information on public water, stop by **Sportsman's Supply in Walden, 466 Main St.,** and talk with Steve or Glenda Knight. Or contact them at **970-723-4343, www.sports manssupply.xtcom.com,** for an update on local conditions. Also try the **Division of Wildlife** information line at **303-291-7537; www.dnr.state.co.us/wildlife/fishing/fish cond.html.**

Delaney Butte Lakes

Cold spring water feeds this series of three lakes, and ample hatches of insects help the brown, rainbow and Snake River cutthroat trout grow to the size of small imported sports cars. Okay, that's an exaggeration, but they do get big. The fishing is so good for browns that North Delaney Butte Lake has been designated as Gold Medal water. Fishing tends to be better in spring and fall, especially early and late in the day. In Aug. the moss and weeds can get to be a problem for people who are fishing. Motorboats are allowed at Delaney Butte but cannot be rented. Camping is permitted around the lakes, but it's bleak— there is little to no tree cover or protection from the often gusty wind. To reach the lakes, head west 5.3 miles from Walden on County Rd. 12W and then another 4.5 miles on County Rd. 18 until the road reaches a T. Turn right on the well-marked road to Delaney Butte and drive north to the lakes.

Lake John

A local favorite, this very shallow lake is well stocked with cutthroat and rainbow trout. The 550-acre Lake John is easier to fish from a boat, and rentals are available at Lake John Resort, **970-723-3226; www.coloradodirectory.com/ lakejohnresort.** Camping is available on the western shore. To reach Lake John from Walden, head west for about 5 miles on County Rd. 12W and then north on the same road for about 7 miles.

Michigan River

Locals seem to prefer the conditions and setting of the Michigan River to those of the North Platte. Fairly wide, the Michigan offers many good holes as it flows north through the park toward its confluence with the North Platte. Many lunker browns can be caught on the Michigan with lightweight fly or spin tackle. Three forks of this river flow into North Park from the Colorado State Forest to the east and Routt National Forest to the south. Much of the river southeast of Walden runs parallel to Hwy. 14, providing many access points along the way.

North Platte River

This meandering Gold Medal stream, flowing north into Wyoming, presents many deep pools and riffles where the predominant population of North Park brown trout feeds. Most of the fish are about a foot long, but some really large ones are pulled from the North Platte every year. Spinners can be effective early in the year, despite muddy water during the spring runoff;

casting toward the banks is very good as long as you hunker down low enough to avoid showing yourself to the fish. The North Platte is also excellent for wading with fly-fishing gear. At times in late summer, irrigation demands severely reduce the flow. To get through irrigated plots, be sure to bring your waders and some mosquito repellent. Private land is interspersed with public access fishing. Seventeen miles north of Walden, a narrow canyon off Hwy. 125 is designated Wild Trout water; 1 mile after crossing the North Platte on Hwy. 125, turn right on a public access road to reach this stretch of river in the Routt National Forest.

Four-Wheel-Drive Trips

Upper Jack Creek

This demanding but scenic road along Upper Jack Creek climbs high to the southeast into the **Never Summer Mountains.** Near the upper end of the creek the rough road forks, the right fork leading into the wide-open Jack Basin, the other to the Never Summer Wilderness boundary and the trailhead to Baker Pass.

There are a couple of ways to reach Upper Jack Creek. From Gould, head south on Forest Rd. 740 for about 6 miles over Calamity Pass and down to an intersection at the site of Teller City, a thriving mining town in the 1880s. Today only a few remnants of Teller City's log cabins remain. At the intersection, turn left on Forest Rd. 758 and head up-valley. The wilderness boundary is about 5 miles from Teller City. Another way to access the area is to turn east onto County Rd. 21 about 2 miles south of Rand on Hwy. 125. Drive about 3 miles to the forest boundary onto Forest Rd. 740 and proceed about 4 miles to Teller City.

Hiking and Backpacking

North Park provides seldom-used trail access away from the crowds and into some of Colorado's finest mountain country. Many roads run west out of the park and butt up against the boundary of the Mt. Zirkel Wilderness. Encircled by Routt National Forest, this wilderness area offers hikers an expanse of beautiful terrain. Stop by the **Parks District Ranger Office** for information and maps; **100 Main St., Walden, CO 80480; 970-723-8204.** For more information on trails from the other side of the Mt. Zirkel Wilderness, see the Hiking section of the **Steamboat Springs** chapter.

Colorado State Forest also offers some excellent hikes. With over 70,000 pine-covered acres, this striking 28-mile-long strip of remote land extends from near the Wyoming border south to the Never Summer Mountains with elevations ranging from 8,000 to 12,900 feet. By far the most popular hikes in the forest are the ones leading up into the mountain lakes. Numerous trails climb into bowls in the Medicine Bow Range; try trips to **Clear Lake** (5 miles one way), **Kelly Lake** (4 miles) or **Ruby Jewel Lake** (1.5 miles). On the southern end of the forest are trails leading past the spectacular Nokhu Crags to **Lake Agnes** (1 mile) and the barren summit of Mt. Richtoffen. From here you can also access the seldom-used **Thunder Pass Trail** into the remote north end of Rocky Mountain National Park. Another such trail into the national park is via **Baker Pass.** The 1-mile trail leads to the pass summit for spectacular views into Jack Basin, south into Rocky Mountain National Park and north into an adjacent drainage and the magnificent peaks of the Never Summer Range. For directions to the trailhead, see the Upper Jack Creek write-up in the Four-Wheel-Drive Trips section.

For information about the Colorado State Forest, visit the **Moose Visitors Center** (state forest headquarters), along Hwy. 14 about 23 miles southeast of Walden. The main park entrance is about 20 miles southeast of Walden (2 miles northwest of Gould) along Hwy. 14; the southern entrance is another 5 miles southeast (toward Cameron Pass). **2746 Jackson County Rd. 41, Walden, CO 80480; 970-723-8366; www.coloradoparks.org.**

River Floating

See the River Floating section in the **Winter Park and Middle Park** chapter.

Nokhu Crags on the edge of the Never Summer Wilderness Area. Photo by Dean Winstanley.

Skiing

CROSS-COUNTRY SKIING AND SNOWSHOEING

Colorado State Forest

Many miles of the roads and trails in the forest are transformed into excellent cross-country and snowshoe routes when the winter blanket of snow arrives. The state forest has an extensive network of trails available in winter. For trail ideas, you may want to call or stop in at the state forest headquarters at the Moose Visitors Center (directions in the Hiking and Backpacking section) or check out trail ideas and descriptions on the park's website, **www.coloradoparks.org.**

Never Summer Nordic Yurt System

Cross-country skiers, bikers and hikers interested in comfortable huts on a multi-day backcountry trip definitely should check out the Never Summer Nordic Yurt System. Actually, they aren't huts—they are yurts, portable dome-shaped dwellings used by nomadic Mongols and Turks in central Asia. Located in the state forest, this yurt system offers great skiing along the Medicine Bow Range and Never Summer Mountains as well as a fairly comfortable night's stay along the trail. Not quite as rustic as their Asian cousins, these yurts feature a sundeck and are reinforced to withstand the elements. Each sleeps six and is equipped with bunk beds and foam mattresses, a cookstove, lantern, utensils and firewood. Reasonable nightly rates, especially during the week. Reservations are a must. **P.O. Box 1983, Ft. Collins, CO 80522; 970-482-9411; www.neversummer nordic.com.**

Seeing and Doing

Museums

Park Pioneer Museum

This museum, located west of the courthouse in Walden, keeps going and growing. Take your time and you'll gain a better understanding of the ranch heritage of Jackson County. Guns, saddles, carriages, kitchen items and antiques fill the museum. Small fee. Open mid-June through mid-Sept., Tues.–Sun. noon–5 P.M.; by appointment in winter. **365 Logan St., Walden, CO 80480; 970-723-8371; 970-723-4212.**

Scenic Drives

Cache la Poudre–North Park Scenic and Historic Byway

This picturesque 101-mile drive between Fort Collins and Walden on Hwy. 14 follows the Cache la Poudre, Colorado's first Wild and Scenic River, and heads over 10,276-foot Cameron Pass before dropping into North Park. See the **Fort Collins and West** chapter for more information.

Nearby

See the **Steamboat Springs** chapter for information on **Buffalo Pass** and **Rabbit Ears Pass,** which cut through Routt National Forest over the Park Range south of the Mt. Zirkel Wilderness. This is a beautiful loop trip, especially in fall.

Wildlife

Arapaho National Wildlife Refuge

There are few better spots in Colorado for catching a glimpse of wildlife, especially waterfowl. During the migratory months of May and Oct., up to 8,000 waterfowl can be found throughout the 24,804-acre refuge. This magnificent, protected wetland habitat is best experienced at dawn and dusk when things can really come to life. In addition to waterfowl, the wildlife you may see practically runs the gamut: golden eagles, great blue herons, owls, beavers and, of course, moose.

To reach the refuge from Walden, drive south on Hwy. 125 for 8 miles and turn left (east) at the main entrance sign. Continue on the dirt road to the refuge headquarters; here you can take off on trails or pick up a brochure for the

self-guided auto tour. For additional information contact the **Refuge Manager** at **P.O. Box 457, Walden, CO 80480; 970-723-8202; www.fws.gov.**

Colorado State Forest

Wildlife viewing in the state forest is excellent; if you are patient you can catch a glimpse of deer, elk, raptors and, more recently, moose. Until 24 moose were transplanted to North Park in 1978, Colorado essentially had seen the last of this magnificent animal. Today the North Park herd is flourishing, numbering about 600. The state forest is home to at least 120 moose. For the best viewing, be out looking at dusk and dawn when the moose tend to spend most of their time in the willow-covered clearings by the streams and ponds. Stop by the Moose Visitors Center along Hwy. 14 to learn about these enormous critters and where you might catch a glimpse of one. (Another great place to see moose in North Park is along the Illinois River,

Sentinel outside the Moose Visitors Center, Colorado State Forest. Photo by Dean Winstanley.

2 miles south of Rand on Hwy. 125, then left at the Old Homestead Lodge and 6 miles southeast on Forest Rd. 740.)

Where to Stay

Accommodations

Basic motel rooms can be found in Walden or south of the park in Kremmling. For a listing of motels in and around Walden, call **970-723-4344** or **970-723-4600**. Consider a stay in one of the refurbished backcountry cabins at Colorado State Forest (see the Camping section). Many camping areas in the surrounding mountains lie in wait, as well as a few guest ranches.

Latigo Ranch—$$$$

With tremendous views of the Indian Peaks and unlimited trails for horseback riding and hiking, this small ranch northwest of Kremmling on Gore Pass is a perfect secluded getaway. Riding is emphasized; guests are paired with compatible horses for the duration of their stay. After a week under the instruction of experienced wranglers, your riding skills and horse knowledge should improve greatly. Take off on morning and afternoon trail rides, fish in the private pond or nearby rivers or just relax by the swimming pool. Latigo is also open in winter, attracting cross-country skiers (lessons offered) to more than 65 kilometers of groomed ski trails (tracks set nightly) and some of the best backcountry terrain you'll ever encounter.

Accommodations feature comfortable duplex cabins with modern amenities. The family atmosphere at Latigo encourages guests to get to know one another. Food is ample "gourmet-ranch" style—if there is such a thing. **P.O. Box 237, Kremmling, CO 80459; 1-800-227-9655; 970-724-9008; www.latigotrails.com.**

Camping

Colorado State Forest

The state forest charges a fee not only to access its land but also to stay at one of its four developed campgrounds (154 sites). All of the state forest's campgrounds are accessible from the north and south entrances to the park along Hwy. 14 near Gould. To reach **North Michigan Reservoir Campground** turn right off Hwy. 14 (2 miles northwest of Gould) at the north entrance to the state forest. This is a heavily used campground since boating is permitted at North Michigan Reservoir. To reach **Bockman Campground,** continue east for just over a mile on the road past North Michigan Reservoir. At the south end of the park (about 3 miles east of Gould on Hwy. 14) sits **Ranger Lakes Campground.** Some 4 miles beyond the turnoff to Ranger Lakes, the twisting road to the **Crags Campground** takes off from the right side of the road. Crags has 27 campsites (large rigs may think twice about attempting this steep road).

The state forest also offers rustic, though recently renovated, **cabins ($ to $$).** All six cabins lie on the shores of North Michigan Reservoir and come equipped with wood-burning stoves, bunks with mattresses, picnic tables and grills; they have no electricity or running water. To reserve a campsite or cabin, contact **1-800-678-CAMP; 303-470-1144** in Denver or **www.reserveamerica.com.**

Routt National Forest

Many campsites in the Routt National Forest may be reserved days in advance by calling **1-877-444-6777**; all charge a fee. To reach **Grizzly Creek Campground** (12 sites) from Walden, drive southwest on Hwy. 14 for 13 miles and turn right (west) onto County Rd. 24. Continue 11 miles to the edge of the national forest and this campground. Three miles north of Grizzly Creek on Forest Rd. 615 is **Teal Lake Campground** (17 sites). Four miles south of Grizzly Creek Campground on Forest Rd. 20 you'll come to **Hidden Lakes Campground** (9 sites). **Big Creek Lakes Campground** (54 sites) is on the 400-acre Big Creek Lake at the edge of the Mt. Zirkel Wilderness. Near the Wyoming border, Big Creek Lakes can be reached from Walden by heading north on Hwy. 125 to Cowdrey and then west on County Rd. 6 to Pearl. After that, follow the signs southwest on Forest Rd. 600.

Aspen Campground (7 sites), in the southeast corner of North Park, is 1 mile southwest of Gould on Forest Rd. 740. **Pines Campground** (11 sites) is 3 miles farther south on Forest Rd. 740.

Private Campground

North Park KOA Kampground—People who take their RV amenities seriously can rest assured that this KOA has every creature comfort possible. In addition to 27 RV sites, campsites and cabins are available. Located just off Hwy. 14 at the entrance to the Colorado State Forest (just outside of Gould). **Star Route, Box 90A, Walden, CO 80480; 970-723-4310.**

Where to Eat

Howlin' Coyote Inn—$$ to $$$

Situated in the woods of Gould, near the entrance to the Colorado State Forest, the Howlin' Coyote is reminiscent of a rustic roadhouse along the Alaska Highway. An occasional moose even appears in the surrounding forest. The inn was opened a few years back by Sandi Hinrichsen, who managed the famous Bucksnort Saloon (see the Nightlife section of the **Denver and Environs** chapter) for 12 years. This roadside restaurant offers hearty lunches and dinners in a cozy dining room with an impressive stone fireplace. Choose from burgers, steak sandwiches and burritos for lunch; filling dinnertime options range from steaks (of course) and ribs to barbecued chicken breast. The bar offers a great place to stop in after a day outside enjoying the state forest. Open daily 11 A.M.–10 P.M. May–Oct.; Fri.–Sun. the rest of the year. **55278 Hwy. 14; 970-723-8282; www.howlincoyoteinn.com.**

Rand Yacht Club—$$ to $$$

Alongside Hwy. 125 in the blink-and-you'll-miss-it burg of Rand you'll find this attractive little bar and grill. From the game-trophy mounts and ranch implements covering the weathered-wood walls to the laminated coin-filled bar, the Yacht Club exudes North Park charm. Though you may be coaxed into ordering one of the many seafood entrées, stick to the burgers and steaks. Dinner salad ingredients are surprisingly fresh for this neck of the woods. The Yacht Club is only open Thurs. through Sun. for dinners, but hopes are to expand. Located 22 miles south of Walden in Rand at **10178 Hwy. 125; 970-723-8400.**

The Coffee Pot Cafe—$ to $$

This quintessential down-home cafe is *the* place in Walden to grab some tasty (and cheap) eats and catch up on the local scoop. Slide into a booth or a chair at one of the numerous tables and peruse the menu that includes highly recommended breakfast, lunch and dinner specials. Many of the items, from breakfast rolls to the soups, are homemade. Try the all-you-can-eat soup and salad bar. After lunch or dinner, consider a piece of their "award winning, world famous, etc." pie. Open daily 6 A.M.–10 P.M. **460 Main St., Walden; 970-723-4670.**

Services

Visitor Information

North Park Chamber of Commerce—Staffed for most of the year; plenty of brochures and information. Located just off Main St. next to the town library, at **416 4th St., P.O. Box 68, Walden, CO 80480; 970-723-4600; www.northparkcoc.com.**

Redstone and Crystal River Valley

An ideal mountain retreat, the Crystal River Valley captures the essence of the Rockies. Away from large resort towns, it offers exactly what many people hope to find while visiting Colorado: impressive natural beauty, fascinating history, genuine people and a long list of year-round outdoor activities. This place also offers a welcome contrast to its fast-paced neighbor Aspen—yet Aspen is close enough for visitors to head up the Roaring Fork Valley for great downhill skiing and nightlife.

Hemmed in from the east by peaks reaching above 14,000 feet, the Crystal River flows through this pristine valley. From Carbondale, Hwy. 133 winds along the Crystal River. The lower part of the valley is completely dominated by the broad shoulders of Mt. Sopris (12,953 feet), which looms like a much higher peak. The tree cover thickens and the scenery becomes more beautiful along the upper reaches, which lie under the prominent Elk and Ragged Mountains.

Caught between the Maroon Bells–Snowmass Wilderness and the Ragged Wilderness, hikers find virtually unlimited access to pristine backcountry. Fishing, kayaking, mountain biking and horseback riding draw others. In winter the focus shifts to cross-country and downhill skiing. In an area of spectacular beauty, the entire valley looks its best in fall, when red, rocky cliffs are contrasted with broad strokes of golden aspen.

The small towns of Redstone and Marble and the ghost town of Crystal City bring an enduring past to light. Redstone, a charming one-street community of about 100 residents, lies 12 miles upriver from Carbondale. Now many of the miners' homes have been refurbished for summer use. Redstone is also home to a number of fine art galleries and antique shops. At the south end of town, the distinctive Redstone Inn stands much as it did in the early 1900s. Two miles south of town, the magnificent Redstone Castle (Cleveholm) appears like a misplaced storybook fantasy. Farther upriver the ramshackle village of Marble, long dependent on its namesake, has found hope again with the reopening of the quarry.

Getting There

From Denver take Interstate 70 west for 166 miles to Glenwood Springs. Turn onto Hwy. 82 and go 10 miles southeast to Carbondale. Turn right onto Hwy. 133 and head up the Crystal River Valley. Flights are available from **Denver International Airport** to the Aspen/Snowmass Airport. Redstone is located 42 miles from the airport.

For a change of pace, take an Amtrak train into Glenwood Springs from Chicago (via Denver) or from San Francisco. Contact **Amtrak** for reservations and information: **1-800-872-7245; www.reservations. amtrak.com.** From Glenwood rent a car for the 27-mile ride to Redstone.

History

For many hundreds of years nomadic Utes spent summers hunting in the Crystal River Valley. They were later promised by treaty that this land would be theirs forever. However, by 1872 prospectors began trickling over the mountains into the southern end of the secluded valley from Gothic and Crested Butte. The land was officially opened to settlement in 1881 when the Utes were forced to depart for distant reservations in Utah. Small ranches and farms began to flourish, especially in the wide northern end of the valley near the confluence of the Crystal and Roaring Fork Rivers.

In 1882 John Osgood, founder of Pueblo's Colorado Fuel & Iron (CF&I), purchased coal claims in the area. Two decades later he founded the model coal village of Redstone with mixed success. In an attempt to avoid the labor problems of other coal towns, Osgood provided each worker with relatively good conditions. But the miners resented their loss of independence, as they were forced to join in the community and obey Osgood's many rules. For instance, the men were to shower before appearing on the streets after work, and a "no treating" rule prevented workers from buying drinks for friends.

The Redstone Inn was created as an upscale community hall and bachelor rooming house. Miners with families were put up in small houses, each built slightly different from the next. A couple of miles up-valley Osgood built his opulent $2.5 million, 42-room dream palace called Cleveholm. Rooms were paneled with solid mahogany woodwork, gold leaf, silk brocade and elephant hide; imported chandeliers, rugs and furniture were throughout. Osgood entertained industrialists, celebrities and even President Theodore Roosevelt. By 1903 Osgood was virtually forced out of business by economic difficulties and the incursions of eastern tycoons J. P. Morgan and John D. Rockefeller, but he remained a millionaire until his death in 1926.

In the late 1800s marble was quarried with some success at the upper end of the Crystal River Valley. The marble, with its glistening white color veined with pale browns, rivaled the best Italian varieties. With the opening of the Yule Marble Quarry in 1905, the entire valley underwent an economic revival. Trains of 40 mules brought marble to the railhead in the town of Marble until an electric train began service to the quarry in 1908. The town grew quickly and by 1916 boasted a population of over 1,500. The largest piece of marble ever quarried at Marble was a 100-ton block, for the Tomb of the Unknown Soldier, which took one year to pare down to 56 tons. The construction of the Lincoln Memorial in Washington, D.C., also depended on marble from here. In 1941 a flood and resultant mudslide destroyed much of the town and caused the railroad to stop service. The quarry reopened and now ships marble to markets including Italy.

Many developers have come into the Crystal River Valley to promote tourism. But most people come to this isolated valley because it has remained relatively undeveloped.

Festivals and Events

Annual Stone Carver's Exhibition
mid-July The Marble Institute of Colorado and the Redstone Art Center team up to support the Stone Carver's Exhibition. Watch marble-cutting masters at work, or purchase a block of marble and try it yourself. If you don't like what you've created, try again; marble is a surprisingly affordable medium in Redstone. All the necessary tools are provided. **1-888-963-3790.**

See the Festivals and Events section in the **Aspen** and **Glenwood Springs** chapters for other information on nearby happenings.

Outdoor Activities

Biking

MOUNTAIN BIKING
Many demanding jeep roads and single-track trails are ideal for strenuous mountain bike routes. The best rides leave from Marble. A great 4-mile ride heads up to the historic marble

quarry on a recently improved road. Now that the quarry has reopened, you'll encounter more activity along the way. Another favorite is a 5-mile ride up to the ghost town of Crystal (see the Schofield Pass write-up in the Four-Wheel-Drive Trips section) and its picturesque mill. Adventuresome (and physically fit) riders can continue from Crystal to Lead King Basin and back to Marble.

For rentals and backcountry information, contact **Life Cycles, 0902 Hwy. 133, Carbondale, 970-963-2453;** or the **Sopris Ranger District Office, 620 Main St., Carbondale, CO 81623, 970-963-2266.**

BICYCLE TOURING

The 31-mile ride up the Crystal River Valley on Hwy. 133 from Carbondale to Marble has long been a favorite of bicyclists. Not only is the scenery fantastic but the narrow valley protects you from the wind.

Fishing

Outstanding fishing on three main rivers— **Crystal, Roaring Fork** and **Fryingpan**—has lured many an angler to this part of the state. For reliable information about accessible stretches on the three rivers, pick up a free fishing guide at area businesses as well as at the **Carbondale Chamber of Commerce** and the **Sopris Ranger District Office.** For further information about fishing the Gold Medal waters of the Roaring Fork and the Fryingpan, see the Fishing section in the **Aspen** chapter.

Beaver Lake

Located in the town of Marble, this small, heavily fished lake is filled by the Crystal River. Though a bit weed-choked at the shoreline, the occasionally stocked lake offers fairly consistent fishing for rainbow and brook trout. It's a great place for a canoe or a small rowboat, but no motors are allowed. Easily accessible at the east end of town.

Crystal River

At the near-ghost town of Crystal, the North and South Forks converge, and the fast-running Crystal River begins its 35-mile tumble down the valley. The beautiful, stocked river eventually flows into the Roaring Fork River a couple of miles below Carbondale. But because it's easily accessible and full of trout, it can get crowded. You'll find fewer people as you move up-valley toward Marble, and chances are you'll get more action from brook trout there. Be sure to steer clear of private property.

Dinkle Lake

Rainbow and brook trout are frequent catches at this high-country lake situated near the edge of White River National Forest northeast of Redstone. It's a good place for a leisurely picnic. A 3.5-mile hike from Dinkle Lake, with a 1,600-foot elevation gain, will land you at Thomas Lakes. There you'll be challenged by feisty cutthroat trout. The two lakes are about a quarter of a mile apart and have several designated campsites near their perimeters. The marked turnoff to Dinkle Lake (Prince Creek Rd.) is located a mile south of Carbondale, across from the fish hatchery on Hwy. 133.

Yule Creek

Yule Creek flows into the town of Marble from the south. It's quick and narrow and can provide good fishing for small cutthroat. Cascading over remnants of quarried white marble, the creek takes on a translucence. The dirt road to the marble quarry parallels the creek for 4 miles through private property. After the quarry a hiking trail follows the creek southeast toward Yule Pass. To reach Yule Creek from Marble, turn right on 3rd St. and drive to a parking area for the mill. Walk or drive across the one-lane bridge for 2.75 miles to the parking lot on the left.

Four-Wheel-Drive Trips

Jeep Tours

Crystal River 4x4 Tours offers several different trips in the area, including tours to the Yule Marble Quarry, Lead King Basin and the Crystal Mill. You can also peruse their handcrafted marble wares before departing for your tour. **620 W. Park St., Marble, CO 81623; 970-963-1991.**

Schofield Pass

Beginning in Marble, a rough dirt road heads east to the ghost town of Crystal before a treacherous ascent to the top of Schofield Pass (10,707 feet). After zigzagging on the main road through Marble to Beaver Lake, continue 1.5 miles to the intersection for Lead King Basin and Crystal City. Turn right on Forest Rd. 314 and continue 5 miles to Crystal. The first man-made structure you will see is the photogenic Sheep Mountain Mill; since 1892 it has been clinging to its rocky perch above the Crystal River. Just beyond the mill, over a slight rise, are the wood-frame houses of Crystal City. In 1881 Crystal was a bustling town of 650 residents, who used the town as a jumping-off point for prospecting in the area. It had its own newspaper, hotel, general store and post office. Today a dozen original, well-preserved buildings remain as summer homes. The section of the road from Crystal to the top of the pass is suited only to small jeep-type vehicles and experienced drivers.

After Crystal, Forest Rd. 317 leads southwest on a precipitous route toward the pass. At the top of the steep grade a lush meadow marks the site of the abandoned town of Schofield. It was founded in 1879 by a group of miners who didn't seem to care that they were inside Indian territory. After the summit, wind down the other side to Gothic and eventually to Crested Butte. If you are staying in Redstone or Marble, try a scenic loop trip from Crested Butte: return over Kebler Pass and McClure Pass, dropping back into the Crystal River Valley.

Hiking and Backpacking

The hiking in this area is surprisingly diverse but primarily steep. There are little-used access points to the Maroon Bells–Snowmass Wilderness Area and hikes into historic locales. You'll always be accompanied by a vista of tall peaks. For more information and maps, contact the **Sopris Ranger District Office, 620 Main St., Carbondale, CO 81623; 970-963-2266.**

Avalanche Creek

This trail leads from Avalanche Campground on a southwestern route into the Maroon Bells–Snowmass Wilderness Area. Hike in as far as you wish for a day trip. This is also a good choice for a two-day backpack trip, since the elevation gain is fairly gradual. The trail merges with **East Creek Trail** after about 6 miles. East Creek Trail, an extremely demanding route that climbs 4,000 vertical feet, eventually heads west back to Redstone. If you continue on **Avalanche Creek Trail,** you'll end up in the heart of the Maroon Bells–Snowmass Wilderness Area near Capitol Peak, Capitol Lake and Avalanche Lake. These are gorgeous hikes, especially when the wildflowers are at their peak, starting in mid-July. Good maps are essential. To reach the trailhead, drive south on Hwy. 133 for 12 miles from Carbondale. Turn east on County Rd. 10

A famous mill near Crystal. Photo by Bruce Caughey.

and continue for 3 miles on a rough dirt road to Avalanche Campground.

Crystal

Bring your camera on this easy 5-mile walk along a jeep road to the ghost town of Crystal. The walk is shaded by aspen and evergreens most of the way. In summer you'll enjoy the cooling effect of walking beside the rushing waters of the Crystal River. Before long you'll see the famous mill, waterfall and the dozen remaining buildings of the old town. (See the Four-Wheel-Drive Trips section for more information.) To reach the road from Marble, head east from Beaver Lake for 1.5 miles to the junction of the roads to Lead King Basin and Crystal City. Park near the junction, unless you have a four-wheel-drive vehicle, and walk down the right fork (Forest Rd. 314) to Crystal.

Thomas Lakes and Mt. Sopris

From Dinkle Lake the 3.5-mile hike to Thomas Lakes is a beautiful introduction to hiking trails in the area. The two lakes are located on the northwestern side of the massive twin peaks of Mt. Sopris (both reach 12,953 feet). The hike to the lakes can be done easily in a day; bring your fishing pole. Many hikers spend the night at primitive campsites near the lakes before making the 2,700-foot climb from the lakes to the top of Mt. Sopris. The hike is nontechnical, but you should be in good shape. The trail leads due south from the southeast side of Thomas Lakes. A mile south of Carbondale near the fish hatchery on Hwy. 133, take the Prince Creek Rd. turnoff to Dinkle Lake. Start walking. Note: the Prince Creek Rd. becomes impassable when wet, so keep your eye on the weather.

Yule Marble Quarry

A fascinating but short hike leads from a parking area next to Yule Creek to the actual quarry. See the Scenic Drives section for information.

Horseback Riding

A good option for hour-long, daylong and overnight pack trips is **Chair Mountain**

Stables in Redstone. Ira, the owner and a real cowboy, will entertain you with the lore and legends of the area. They also offer breakfast and steak dinner rides. Located behind the old coke ovens at **17843 Hwy. 133; 970-963-1232.**

River Floating

Roaring Fork

See the **Aspen** chapter.

Skiing

CROSS-COUNTRY SKIING AND SNOWSHOEING

Many nordic skiers come to this peaceful valley to make tracks on old forgotten roads, mountain trails and organized trail systems. The only conceivable drawback to skiing in this narrow valley is the short-lived sunshine. Many trails, however, avoid this by climbing high above the valley. For more trail ideas and information on the extensive 10th Mountain Division hut system, see the Skiing section of the **Aspen** chapter. Check with the **Sopris Ranger District Office in Carbondale** for current avalanche conditions; **620 Main St.; 970-963-2266.** Or call the **avalanche hot line** at **970-920-1664.** Rentals are available at the **Redstone Inn** front desk, **970-963-2526,** or at the **general store** across from the town park, **970-963-3126.**

Backcountry Trails

McClure Pass—From the top of McClure Pass (8,755 feet), enjoy spectacular views of the Ragged Mountains and back to the Crystal River Valley. Above the valley floor, you'll have a chance to bask in the sun. A moderately easy forest road sets out to the south from the summit. Dogs allowed. To reach McClure Pass drive 8 miles southwest on Hwy. 133 from Redstone. **Town Trail**—Starting at the Redstone Inn, this easy 2-mile round-trip route tracks along behind town, passing by the old schoolhouse and many former miners' homes. The Town Trail is perfect if you are interested in skiing the flats with the opportunity for a warm cup of hot chocolate at the end of the trail. You can rent skis at the inn and inquire about other trail possibilities. For information call **970-963-2526.**

Groomed Trails

Ute Meadows Nordic Center—More than 10 kilometers of groomed trails await. For the more adventurous, there are also plenty of ungroomed trails for snowshoers and cross-country skiers. Ski lessons are available by appointment. The ice skating rink also provides winter fun. At an elevation of 7,750 feet, this winter wonderland usually benefits from frequent snow. Open daily; rentals not available. Located next to the Ute Meadows Inn Bed and Breakfast at **2880 County Rd. 3, Marble, CO 81623; 1-888-883-6323; 970-963-7088.**

DOWNHILL SKIING AND SNOWBOARDING

Aspen and Snowmass

You can ski at any of four world-class mountains located about an hour from Redstone. See the **Aspen** chapter for more information.

Ski Sunlight

Consider a day of skiing at this uncrowded smaller area. From the Crystal River Valley, Sunlight is a bit closer than Aspen. See the **Glenwood Springs** chapter for additional information.

Seeing and Doing

Hot Springs

Hot Springs Pool at Glenwood Springs

Only 27 miles away is the world's largest hot springs pool. See the Major Attractions section of the **Glenwood Springs** chapter.

Penny Hot Springs

Long used by Ute Indians and later by settlers, Penny Hot Springs still bubbles forth. Depending on the Crystal River's water level and the amount of boiling source water, you might enjoy a couple of shallow pools that mix to a good soaking temperature. Because it's a bit difficult to find and occasionally sabotaged by unknown locals, our advice is to ask locally about the status of Penny Hot Springs and, if you decide to soak, wear a suit. The springs are located 1.5 miles north of Redstone on Hwy. 133, hidden down along the river on a wide bend in the road. Park on the turnout on the road's shoulder.

Museums and Galleries

Lined with many fine galleries, Redstone Blvd. is an extremely popular street for window shopping. Among other things you'll see stained glass, original oils and watercolors and even wearable art. The aesthetically pleasing valley has long inspired artists; well-known painters such as Frank Mechau and Ben Turner have spent time here.

Redstone Art Center

Don't miss this gallery. Nationally known sculptor Bev Goss can be seen transforming huge pieces of local marble into remarkable human forms in a building adjacent to the gallery. Some people might imagine marble as having a certain coldness to it; Goss somehow creates a softness and warmth from the stone and she encourages you to reach out, touch and feel her work. In addition to sculpted marble you can see other Colorado artists' work in pottery, jewelry, woodwork, watercolor and other media. Stop in on a "Summer Sunday" to observe art demonstrations from wood turning to chainsaw carving. See the Festivals and Events section for information on the Annual Stone Carver's Exhibition. **0173 Redstone Blvd., Redstone, CO 81623; 1-888-963-3790; 970-963-3790.**

Redstone Museum

Located in a small log cabin that once housed one of John Osgood's offices for the Coal Basin mines, this tiny museum has an interesting collection of historical memorabilia. Open in summer 10 A.M.–4 P.M. daily, on **Redstone Blvd.** across from the Redstone General Store.

Scenic Drives

Crystal River Valley and Yule Marble Quarry

The scenery on this drive won't disappoint you. Begin by following Hwy. 133 south past the coke ovens of Redstone for 5 miles to a marked turnoff for Marble (County Rd. 3). Once in the town of Marble (5 miles farther down the road), turn right at the 3rd St. stop sign and go a block to the remains of the marble mill. At the site are tons of rejected pieces of the gleaming stone and white marble support columns reminiscent of classical Greek ruins.

From the marble mill cross a one-lane bridge over the Crystal River onto a very good dirt road—fit for any vehicle except perhaps a Winnebago. Open in summer only, this road parallels Yule Creek for 4 miles on its southern route toward the slopes of Treasure Mountain (13,462 feet). The pretty drive ends at a small parking lot where a 5-minute walk along the creek will take you to the bottom of an avalanche of refuse marble. From here, take a short but steep (and lung-searing) 20- to 30-minute hiking trail to the 100,000-square-foot quarry. The deep pit bears the scars of the process that still removes huge slabs of the crystalline rock. During the quarry's prime, one "room" could produce 3,000 cubic feet of marble per day. Since the quarry resumed operation, much of the quarry area is restricted. But it's still a great place to explore, as long as you are aware of the inherent dangers. Please leave all the marble where you find it.

West Elk Loop

Arguably one of the most dramatic and least-traveled of Colorado's outstanding Scenic and Historic Byways, the 205-mile West Elk Loop is especially beautiful in autumn when the aspen are at their colorful best. Hwy. 133 through the Crystal River Valley constitutes the northern stem of the West Elk Loop, which extends south over 8,755-foot **McClure Pass.** From Redstone, head 8 miles south on Hwy. 133 to the pass summit. From here, be sure to pull off and take a long look south to the Ragged Mountains

Remnants of a mill near the Yule Marble Quarry. Photo by Bruce Caughey.

and back north to Mt. Sopris at the head of the valley. Continuing on from here, the highway drops into the quiet orchards of the North Fork Valley. The loop also includes trips over the beautiful **Kebler Pass** and along the remote Hwy. 92 near the north rim of the **Black Canyon of the Gunnison National Park.** For more information about these stretches of the West Elk Loop, see the Scenic Drives sections of the **Gunnison and Crested Butte** and **Black Canyon Country** chapters.

Where to Stay

Accommodations

The Crystal River Valley certainly offers some fine (and we mean rather upscale) bed and breakfasts and standout inns. The moderately priced **Redstone Cliffs Lodge ($$ to $$$$)** is a motel with the feel of mountain cabins. Amenities include an outdoor hot tub and cable TV. **0433 Redstone Blvd.; 1-888-652-8005.** For tighter budgets, consider staying down-valley in Carbondale or Glenwood Springs, where you'll find a number of more affordable motels.

Avalanche Ranch—$$$ to $$$$

First off, innkeeper Sharon Boucher knows how to make you (and your family) feel welcome and comfortable at her marvelous country inn. The 45-acre spread lies 7,000 feet above the Crystal River with views to the distinctive slopes of Mt. Sopris. The Homestead House has three bedrooms that will accommodate up to 10 people. This quaint ranch house features a large stone fireplace and is furnished with antiques—only fitting since Sharon sells antiques as well. Families love the 12 small cabins (breakfast not included). All cabins have expansive views over the valley, including the llama pasture. Couples will also enjoy the cozy cabins, particularly No. 6, which offers a bit more space and ambience. In addition to kitchens and other self-contained features, each cabin has a barbecue pit and a picnic table.

Kids love it here! They can feed pigs, sheep and llamas and go exploring in the apple orchard. There's a tree house and a tire swing, plus badminton, horseshoes, hiking, fishing and plenty of animals to pet, including a donkey and several goats. One rule: absolutely no smoking allowed indoors. **12863 Hwy. 133, Redstone, CO 81623; 1-877-963-9337; 970-963-2846; www.avalancheranch.com.**

Cleveholm Manor,
Historic Redstone Castle—$$$ to $$$$

Though recently sold, the castle still offers its spacious 42-room interior as a bed and breakfast when groups have not booked the entire place. The castle cost John Osgood $2.5 million when he built it in 1903 to impress his friends and enemies alike. It is said that Osgood and Teddy Roosevelt, during the president's visit, sat on the front lawn while the gamekeeper let loose captive deer, one at a time, for them to shoot. Other guests included John D. Rockefeller, J. P. Morgan, Jay Gould and John "Bet a Million" Gates. John Osgood's second wife, Alma, was

known as Lady Bountiful. Each Christmas she asked the children of Redstone to write letters to Santa. She then collected the mail, left on her private railcar for a New York City shopping spree and returned with presents for the kids.

It's easy to feel the castle's history as you walk around the library, the armory and the main living room with its massive fireplace. The 16 enchanting bedrooms are carefully appointed with antiques; all beds have feather comforters. For a honeymoon, few places rival these accommodations, especially the Lady Bountiful Suite. Enjoy the fabulous views across the well-tended grounds to the Crystal River. This is an ideal place for a retreat or wedding; the entire castle can be reserved. Other ways to experience the castle are to take a tour of the premises ($10 per person on weekends only) or enjoy a leisurely gourmet dinner in the elegant dining room (served most Fri. and Sat. nights throughout the summer). Reservations essential. Located 1 mile south of Redstone at **0058 Redstone Blvd.,**

Redstone Inn. Photo by Bruce Caughey.

Redstone, CO 81623; 970-704-1430; www. theredstonecastle.com.

Mt. Sopris Inn—$$$ to $$$$

This exceptional inn is located 2 miles up the Crystal River from Carbondale on Hwy. 133. See the Where to Stay section in the **Aspen** chapter.

Redstone Inn and Spa—$$$ to $$$$

Nestled beside the Crystal River on the south end of town, this distinctive Tudor-style inn is a perfect destination. You can't miss the four-faced clock tower—an exact replica from a Dutch inn in Rotterdam. In 1902 John Osgood built the inn as a place for his unmarried coal workers to live. Today word has spread about the inn, forcing early reservations for summer weekends. If you haven't been here for a few years, you'll be impressed with the many upgrades and improvements. Not only do the rooms sport new furnishings, fresh paint, carpet and wallpaper, but there is also a classy little health spa right on the bank of East Creek.

The rooms vary quite a bit in size, with some on the small side. To ensure a romantic setting, reserve the large bridal suite. People on a tight budget will be glad to know that inexpensive dormer rooms with half-baths are available; showers are down the hall. All rooms have a classy and subtle decor. A heated lap pool, large outdoor hot tub and tennis courts are available for guests, along with 22 acres to explore. This inn has that old European feel: rich, strong colors, a comfortable lobby, reading rooms and a popular bar. With several packages throughout the winter including activities such as ice climbing, cross-country ski lessons, or a full-moon sleigh ride, you'll surely find a weekend perfectly designed for you. Cross-country ski rentals are available at the front desk. You will want to visit the elegant restaurant or more reasonably priced grill for breakfast, lunch or dinner. Don't miss the Sun. brunch (see the Where to Eat section). **0082 Redstone Blvd., Redstone, CO 81623; 1-800-748-2524; 970-963-2526; www. redstoneinn.com.**

Ute Meadows Inn Bed and Breakfast— $$ to $$$

"Serenity in the Crystal River Valley" is the very suitable slogan for this exquisite bed and breakfast. Whether you want to horseback ride, hike, fish, mountain bike or relax in front of a fireplace, Ute Meadows is the ideal location. The retreat is located on 200 acres of private property, which has been in the Darien family since the 1920s. The inn also boasts a nordic center with 10 kilometers of groomed trails and an ice-skating rink (see the Cross-Country Skiing and Snowshoeing section). All seven bedrooms are spacious and comfortable, featuring down comforters, split log furniture from local artisans and private bathrooms. The breakfast menu changes frequently, but always centers around locally produced items such as tortillas from Carbondale. Boarding is available for horses, and kennels can accommodate dogs. **2880 County Rd. 3, Marble, CO 81623; 1-888-883-6323; 970-963-7088; www.utemeadows.com.**

Camping

White River National Forest

For reservations at the U.S. Forest Service campgrounds, call **1-877-444-6777** or **www. reserveusa.com.** All listed campgrounds charge a fee.

Avalanche Campground (10 sites) is located 12 miles south of Carbondale on Hwy. 133. Turn east on County Rd. 10, cross a bridge and continue 3 miles to the campground. Trailers over 20 feet long are not allowed due to the rough dirt road on the final half-mile.

Bogan Flats Campground (37 sites) enjoys a beautiful setting near the Crystal River south of Redstone. From Redstone, take Hwy. 133 for 5 miles, turn left at the turnoff to Marble (County Rd. 3) and continue 1.5 miles to the campground.

McClure Pass Campground (19 sites) is located about 11 miles southwest on Hwy. 133 from Redstone, a few miles past McClure Pass.

Redstone Campground (19 sites) is located a mile north of Redstone. It offers shaded campsites next to the Crystal River and is very popular. Drinking water, showers and electric hookups available.

Where to Eat

With only a few (though quite good) restaurants in Redstone, you may want to try down-valley. A local favorite for breakfast and lunch is in Carbondale, only 10 miles away: the **Village Smithy** at **3rd and Main.** Another superb choice for a special meal is **Six89** in **Carbondale,** offering gourmet intercontinental cuisine, **970-963-6890** (see the **Aspen** chapter for information on this and other excellent restaurants). Another option is to head farther down-valley to Glenwood Springs.

Cleveholm Manor,
Historic Redstone Castle—$$$$
On most Fri. and Sat. nights Redstone Castle offers gourmet dining in a fabulous setting. The castle also offers special dances and wine tastings from time to time. See the Where to Stay section.

Redstone Inn—$$ to $$$
The classic setting of the inn matches the excellent food. In the gracious dining room you can enjoy carefully prepared continental cuisine and first-class service. Entrées include classic cuisine with regional dishes as well: samples include grilled duck breast, wild mushroom pasta and succulent Colorado prime rib. The dining room is also open for breakfast and lunch. If you are lucky enough to be staying at the inn over a weekend, make certain you stay for the brunch buffet (Sun. 8–11:30 A.M.), which includes fresh-squeezed orange juice and all the delectables you care to eat. For a slightly more low-key atmosphere and lower-priced options, eat in the grill, with its indoor pub seating or poolside patio tables. Grill specialties include stone-baked pizzas, salads and sandwiches. Both dining venues include daily specials. Open daily 7:30 A.M.–9:30 P.M. **0082 Redstone Blvd., Redstone, CO 81623; 970-963-2526.**

The Crystal Club Cafe—$ to $$$
Billy and Kim Amicon have made this restaurant into a local legend. This is where the locals come for homemade breads, scrumptious entrées and a plentiful bar. From incredible subs to delicious Italian dishes, the menu is diverse and affordable, a welcome sight in Redstone. Sit outside on the patio or beside the Crystal River as you relax with a cold drink in hand. View wildlife from the porch or enjoy the warm fireplace in the dining room. Open daily for lunch and dinner in the summer; weekends in the winter. **0467 Redstone Blvd.; 970-963-9515.**

Dorle's Cafe—$ to $$
Though they serve dinners, this attractive little cafe has a loyal following for its fresh, homemade breakfasts and lunches. Weather permitting, grab a table on the front or back porch. Inside, you'll find plenty of wooden tables with local artwork gracing the walls. Fairly standard breakfast dishes such as omelettes are available, but choose from a selection of their excellent European-style pastries and baked goods. Lunch highlights include the homemade soups and salads; creative daily specials, such as a tasty fish pie stuffed with halibut, tuna and salmon, are not to be missed either. Terrific desserts. Open May–Dec., 8 A.M.–8:30 P.M. **0167 Redstone Blvd., Redstone, CO 81623; 970-963-9220.**

Services

Visitor Information
Basalt Area Chamber of Commerce— P.O. Box 514, Basalt, CO 81621; 970-927-4031.

Carbondale Chamber of Commerce—499 Weant Blvd., P.O. Box 1645, Carbondale, CO 81623; 970-963-1890; www.carbon dale.com.

Redstone Information—www.redstone colorado.com.

Steamboat Springs

Despite the growing pains that are felt by many resort areas in Colorado, Steamboat Springs remains a major ranch-supply center in the midst of some of the best skiing in the world. The imposing ski mountain is the reason people head to Steamboat Springs in winter. It offers what many downhillers consider to be the pinnacle of Colorado skiing: deep powder, aspen glades and the second-highest vertical drop in the state. Thanks to the massive mountain and its 3-hour drive from Denver, lift lines are usually short.

Lincoln Ave., the 12-block main street of Old Town, is the perfect place to buy a bridle for your horse, get a hot wax for an old pair of skis or a good meal. Staid western-wear stores share space with an occasional T-shirt shop. The blending of old and new gives Steamboat a permanence and personality beyond many other Colorado ski resorts. Three miles south of the town center at the base of the ski mountain lies Steamboat Village—a planned development with hotels, condos, restaurants and shops.

Getting There

Steamboat Springs is located 160 miles northwest of Denver. Travel time varies depending on the weather, but the drive takes about 3 to 3$^1/_2$ hours. From Denver head west on Interstate 70 to Silverthorne, north to Kremmling on Hwy. 9 and then northwest over Rabbit Ears Pass on Hwy. 40. **Greyhound Bus Lines** *services Steamboat.*

About 22 miles from Steamboat Springs, the **Yampa Valley Regional Airport** *has nonstop flights from many cities in the country (during ski season only); express flights from Denver and Colorado Springs are available year-round.*

Steamboat Springs, now with a full-time population of almost 8,500, has a long tradition of competitive skiing. Since the Winter Olympics began in 1924, Steamboat has provided 43 competitors for the U.S. team—8 at the 1994 winter games alone!

Cross-country skiing trails are virtually unlimited in the surrounding valleys, on top of Rabbit Ears Pass and at an organized nordic center near the mountain village. Be sure to take a plunge in the steaming hot spring pools after a day in the cold. The Strawberry Park Hot Springs pools lie just 7 miles north of downtown.

The long days of a Steamboat summer can be filled with any number of activities, and should be—this place lends itself to exploring the surrounding country. Set out on foot, horse or mountain bike. Bring along a picnic lunch or your fishing rod. Or perhaps try a float on the Yampa River through town. If you are inclined to take part in a guest ranch vacation, the experience can range from rustic to cushy.

Local tourist magazines talk of the "Yampa Valley Curse." According to local lore, the valley casts a spell over all visitors, compelling them to return year after year. Legend or not, Steamboat Springs does have an indelible allure, making it difficult to stay away—many people have

Steamboat Lake in summer. Photo by Dean Winstanley.

relocated here permanently. And these transplants, not always possessing the same values and beliefs of the Steamboat old-timers, are increasingly making their presence known. As a matter of fact, a town ordinance passed in the mid-1990s bestowed a new county bridge with the name James Brown Soul Center of the Universe Bridge. The "Godfather of Soul" himself showed up at the dedication ceremony sporting an electric blue jumpsuit and announced "I feel good!"

History

With more than 150 hot springs and bountiful game in the Steamboat area, the northern Utes (Yampatika) began summering here as early as the 1300s.

According to most accounts, Steamboat Springs got its name in 1865 when three French trappers riding horseback along the Yampa River heard a chugging sound they thought was a steamboat. It turned out to be a hot spring that continued to chug until 1908 when the railroad blasted out the rock chamber over it.

In 1875 James Crawford, the first settler in the valley, built his homestead. Although a treaty in 1868 took away the land around Steamboat from the Ute Indians, they still made frequent trips to the valley. Soon Crawford was a good friend with the Utes. In the summer of 1879, when the Meeker Massacre erupted southwest of Steamboat and the Utes attacked settlers after provocation by the inept Indian agent Nathan Meeker, Crawford's homestead remained unscathed. By 1880 the Utes were forced onto a reservation in Utah. This was followed by a sharp increase of homesteaders flocking to the Steamboat area, filling the broad valley with farms and ranches.

At about the same time, a late mining boom was in full swing 30 miles to the north at Hahn's Peak. Although the area produced a relatively meager $4 million in gold, eager miners scoured the hillsides and creeks until the early 1900s. During this period miners and ranchers would converge on Steamboat Springs for a good time.

Although the locals relied on skis in winter as a means of transportation, it was not until a wiry Norwegian came to town in 1913 that people started to ski for fun. Carl Howelsen, a champion jumper and cross-country skier from Norway, organized Steamboat Springs' first Winter Carnival, during which he amazed the townsfolk by heaving himself more than 110 feet off a jump he had built. It was not long before locals were trying it themselves. Howelsen Hill, just west of town, became the jumping hill. Legend has it that early jumpers would occasionally land among a startled herd of wintering elk. By the 1940s downhill skiing had also become a passion for the townsfolk, so much so that it became part of the school curriculum in 1943. During the late 1940s and into the 1950s Steamboat Springs produced more downhill champions and Olympic team members than any other town in the country. Among them were Gordy Wren, Skeeter Werner and her brother Buddy Werner.

In the late 1950s many locals, particularly Jim Temple, began scouting out Storm Peak, the mountain south of town, as a possible site for a new ski area. In January 1963 the mountain opened for business. It was Temple who coined the often-used phrase "champagne powder" to describe Steamboat's light, fluffy snow. In 1964, when Buddy Werner died tragically in an avalanche in Switzerland, the mountain was renamed Mt. Werner. Since the early days of the ski area, expansion of the facilities and growth of the town have been dramatic.

Festivals and Events

Winter Carnival

early Feb.　Like many snowbound communities that get "cabin fever" about midwinter, Steamboat has a remedy: Winter Carnival. Since 1914 the town has let loose with a weeklong celebration highlighted by traditional events such as ice sculpture competitions, a hockey tournament and ski jumping. When snow-covered Lincoln Ave. is blocked off, thrill seekers sit on snow shovels pulled down the street by galloping horses as the crowd cheers. The high school band makes an appearance on skis at the parade, as does the famous (at least locally) All Broads Kazoo Band. At night fireworks explode and the "lighted man" skis down Howelsen Hill. **970-879-0695; 970-879-0880.**

Pro Rodeo Series

mid-June through late Aug.　Since the late 1800s Steamboat area ranch hands have pitted their rodeo skills against one another. The tradition continues at the nation's largest weekly pro rodeo. Every Fri. and Sat. night the Howelsen Hill Rodeo Grounds fills up for this genuine exhibition of talent and luck. **970-879-0880.**

Rainbow Weekend

mid-July　A hot-air balloon rodeo and Art in the Park (150 artists) highlight Rainbow Weekend. One of the ballooning events demands that the balloonists negotiate their craft close enough to a mock steer to rope it. Good luck. Chamber music performances add to the fun. **970-879-0880.**

Outdoor Activities

Biking

MOUNTAIN BIKING

Mountain bikers have found a welcome home in Steamboat. An infinite number of ride possibilities spread out from Steamboat like bent spokes from a hub. Check out seldom-used dirt roads in the rolling ranch country or steep single tracks in the high mountains. For maps and additional information, contact the **Hahns Peak Ranger District Office, 925 Weiss Dr., Steamboat Springs, CO 80487; 970-879-1870; www.fs. fed.us/mrnf/hpbe/hpbewel.htm.** The District Office also has information about the Routt Divide Blowdown, which may affect your trail choice. Or contact the Steamboat Chamber of Commerce visitor center.

Fish Creek Falls

For a relatively short but steep ride on a twisting 4-mile road, consider a ride up to Fish Creek Falls. For information, see the Hiking and Backpacking section.

Rabbit Ears Pass to Buffalo Pass

This 20-mile trail through Routt National Forest provides a great look at the beautiful backcountry along the Continental Divide (the elevation gain is less than 800 feet). To reach the trailhead from Steamboat Springs, drive south on Hwy. 40 to Rabbit Ears Pass, turn left to Dumont Lake and take the first left after the campground entrance. Head north on Trail 311 to Divide Trail (Trail 1101). This single track then heads north past Lake Elmo and Round Lake. Turn left onto the Percy Lake Trail and head to Long Lake. From there continue north on Trail 310 to Buffalo Pass and descend into Steamboat Springs. An alternative is to continue on Trail 1101 from Long Lake, joining up with Trail 310 about 1 mile before reaching Buffalo Pass—there is more single-track trail this way. You may want to get dropped off at the trailhead.

River Road

This cruising ride follows a fairly flat, improved gravel road (and some pavement) alongside the Yampa River south of Steamboat as far as 9 miles from town. Great views! Return via the same route or on Hwy. 131. To reach River Rd. cross the 5th St. Bridge in town and turn left.

Steamboat Ski Area

The ski mountain has really developed into an excellent place to test your mountain biking skills. Fifteen trails, including the challenging **Pete's Wicked Trail** (single track) wind their way from the top of the gondola on Thunderhead Peak. **Thunderhead Trail,** a steady 3-mile climb, is one of the most popular rides. If you'd rather just practice your downhill skills, buy a ticket for the Silver Bullet gondola. The gondola runs 10 A.M.–4 P.M. daily in summer. Tickets are good for multiple gondola rides. Bike rentals are available at the summit as well as the base of the gondola. **970-879-6111.**

BICYCLE TOURING

Town Trail System

Miles of paved bike trails wind their way through the Steamboat area, but one of the most accessible and enjoyable stretches has to be the **Yampa River Core Trail.** This 3-mile paved trail follows the Yampa River south from downtown. Along the way you'll find small parks and see anglers and floaters enjoying the river. For information and a map, stop by the Chamber of Commerce Visitors Center or check with area bike shops.

Rentals and Information

There are several full-service mountain bike shops in town. Here are a couple of shops offering repairs, rentals and advice.

Ski Area—Those riding up the gondola may want to rent at the ski area base. Bikes, helmets, etc. **970-879-6111.**

Ski Haus—In addition to rentals, Ski Haus also publishes a biking magazine, complete with area maps. Located in front of Safeway at **Hwy. 40 and Pine Grove Rd.; 970-879-0385.**

Sore Saddle Cyclery—**1136 Yampa St.; 970-879-1675.**

Fishing

Colorado State Parks

The following fisheries represent the best flatwater fishing in the Routt County area. For fishing conditions and other information, call **970-879-3922.**

Pearl Lake—Only 3 miles east of Steamboat Lake, this smaller lake is well worth the minimal effort of getting there—but it's restricted to flies and lures only. To get there from Steamboat, take County Rd. 129 north 24 miles to the marked right turn for Pearl Lake.

Stagecoach State Park—Once known for its feisty rainbow trout as well as browns and cutthroat, Stagecoach is currently known by anglers more for its enormous northern pike. You'll find two boat ramps at this 3-mile-long fishery on the Yampa River. **Stagecoach Lake Marina** rents fishing boats as well as practically every other craft imaginable. Slips available for rent. Fishing licenses and tackle, groceries and camping supplies available. **970-736-8342.** To reach the reservoir from Steamboat, head south on Hwy. 131

for about 5 miles and then turn left onto County Rd. 14 for 5 more miles. **970-736-2436; www. coloradoparks.org.**
Steamboat Lake State Park—This popular and scenic fishery is stocked with hundreds of thousands of fingerling trout. The average size is about 12 inches, but much larger fish are taken regularly. Both shore and boat fishing often result in good catches on the large lake. You may talk with the park manager about where the fish are biting. Steamboat Lake is open to fly, lure and bait fishing with a limit of eight fish. From Steamboat Springs drive north on County Rd. 129 for 27 miles to reach the lake. **970-879-3922; www.coloradoparks. org.Steamboat Lake Marina** rents fishing, pontoon and paddleboats as well as canoes; they also have fishing supplies and licenses. Located on the northwest shore of Steamboat Lake; **970-879-7019.**

Dumont Lake

Each year plenty of catchable trout are stocked at Dumont. The lake offers good fishing and the kind of beauty that makes any fishing trip worthwhile. Your best bet is with bait or spin gear. Dumont Lake is the first in a series of small backcountry lakes that reach north from Rabbit Ears Pass all the way to Fish Creek Reservoir on Buffalo Pass. Dumont Lake is located near the top of Rabbit Ears Pass. Take Hwy. 40 east of Steamboat for 24.5 miles and watch for a brown and yellow sign on the north side.

Elk River

The Elk flows out of the northwest side of the Mt. Zirkel Wilderness Area, and its upper portions are excellent for small rainbows and some brooks. You'll find the best fishing in late summer when runoff waters recede. To reach the **upper Elk,** take County Rd. 129 north of Steamboat for 18 miles to the small town of Clark. A couple of miles north of Clark turn right on Seedhouse Rd. and parallel the Elk River into Routt National Forest. After turning on Seedhouse Rd., the best fishing is 5 miles upriver between Hinman Campground and Seedhouse Campground.

The smaller tributaries flowing into the Elk River in the Routt National Forest are normally quite good for brooks, rainbows and mountain whitefish. The **North Fork of the Elk** is brimming with small brook and rainbow trout, especially in its upper portions. From Seedhouse Campground head north on Forest Rd. 431 (four-wheel drive) along the North Fork to the boundary of the Mt. Zirkel Wilderness Area. Fly-fishers may want to pursue the even smaller creeks flowing into both the North and South forks.

Flat Tops Wilderness

See the Fishing section in the **Meeker** chapter for information on the maze of productive lakes, ponds and streams spread out over this high plateau only a short distance from Steamboat.

Mt. Zirkel Wilderness

Remote and wonderfully beautiful are the many backcountry lakes and streams of the Mt. Zirkel Wilderness. The farther you hike, the better the fishing tends to be. A few ideas for backcountry lakes include **Three Island Lake, Mica Lake** and **Gold Creek Lake.** These lakes tend to remain unaffected by winterkill and offer excellent fishing for small trout. These lakes receive heavy impact; to prevent shoreline damage, don't camp within a quarter-mile of the lakes. To reach the Mt. Zirkel Wilderness from Steamboat, travel north on County Rd. 129 for 18 miles to Clark. A mile or so north of Clark, turn right on Seedhouse Rd. and continue until the road forks. A right turn on Forest Rd. 443 takes you to the trailhead for Three Island Lake; continue on Seedhouse Rd. and you'll be at the trailhead for Mica and Gold Creek Lakes. The Routt Divide Blowdown impacted these areas (see the Hiking and Backpacking section for information).

Yampa River

The Yampa flows east out of the Flat Tops but eventually changes course and passes directly through Steamboat Springs before turning west for its long run to the confluence with the Green

River. During the heavy runoff, which can extend into July, spin and bait casters do quite well. The fishing near Steamboat has been improved by a kayak course just south of town; pools and eddies provide a good habitat for rainbows, browns, natives and whitefish. There have even been a number of large northern pike caught within the town limits. On this section of the Yampa, a catch-and-release policy has been implemented.

Outfitters

Buggywhip's Fish & Float Service—These folks offer guided fishing trips and floats to most of the major rivers in Colorado as well as the Green River in Utah. Lessons available as well. Located at **20 Lincoln Ave.** and at **1102 Lincoln Ave., P.O. Box 770479, Steamboat Springs, CO 80477; 1-800-759-0343; 970-879-8033; www.buggywhips.com.**

Straightline—Provides guide services, rentals, float trips, fly-fishing and spin casting schools and fishing information. **744 Lincoln Ave., P.O. Box 4887, Steamboat Springs, CO 80477; 1-800-354-5463; 970-879-7568; www.straightlinesports.com.**

Other Resources—For insider tips from a guy who's fished the Steamboat area since 1962, pick up a copy of Scott Ford's guidebook *Fishing the 'Boat.*

Golf

Haymaker Golf Course

Opened in the summer of 1997, this fantastic, Scottish-links-style course just south of town definitely has the mountain golf community buzzing. Deep bunkers, wide-open fairways, native grasses and a plethora of wetlands distinguish this gem that was nominated as one of *Golf Digest*'s 10 best new public golf courses. Other accolades for the course include its recognition as an environmentally friendly course—one of only 12 courses nationwide to achieve Audubon Signature status. This challenging course, with its broad views of the ski area and surrounding mountains, is highly recommended. **34855 Hwy. 40 E.; 1-800-494-1818; 970-870-1846; www.haymakergolf.com.**

Sheraton Steamboat Golf Club

Designed by Robert Trent Jones Jr., this 18-hole golf course is one of the finest and most challenging mountain courses in the state. Groves of aspen and pine combine with far-reaching views of the Yampa River Valley and Mt. Werner. Guests staying at the Sheraton Hotel get a break on greens fees. This course is first class and charges accordingly. Walk-ons are welcomed seven days a week, but reservations 24 hours in advance are strongly recommended. Drive south of downtown on Hwy. 40, turn left toward the ski area on Mt. Werner Rd. and take another left onto Steamboat Blvd. Turn right onto Clubhouse Dr. and follow the signs. **1-800-848-8878; 970-879-2220; www.steamboat-sheraton.com.**

Steamboat Golf Club

For a course with more down-to-earth prices, try the nine-hole Steamboat Golf Club, located 6 miles west of town on Hwy. 40. Greens fees are higher on weekends. **970-879-4295.**

Hiking and Backpacking

Tree-covered ridges of aspen, lodgepole pine, fir and spruce, meadows packed with colorful wildflowers and quiet streams meandering through scenic valleys: these have historically been the characteristics of Routt National Forest near Steamboat. Though it hasn't nearly the rugged terrain or soaring peaks other parts of the state possess, Routt, with its ample wildlife and great fishing, has its own allure. Some of the peaks rise above 12,000 feet, but overall the forests and mountain meadows are closer to 10,000.

Within the national forest, directly east of Steamboat Springs, lies the Park Range. Extending more than 50 miles, this range runs north from Rabbit Ears Pass all the way to the Wyoming border. Straddling the Continental Divide for much of the way, the Mt. Zirkel Wilderness beckons many hikers and backpackers. At the divide, hikers are rewarded with spectacular views of the Yampa River Valley to the west, North Park and the Medicine Bow Range to the east. Many trailheads into the wilderness branch off from Buffalo Pass Rd., which cuts east from Steamboat over the divide and into North Park.

In October 1997 an unusual event altered sections of the forest for years to come. Winds over 120 miles per hour roared across the Continental Divide from the east, leveling some 4 million trees in an area 5 miles wide by 30 miles long. Known as the **Routt Divide Blowdown,** this event has changed the forest and some of its recreational opportunities. Forest Service crews have cleared some trails but it is wise to check with the district office before setting out on a hike. For maps and additional information, contact the **Hahns Peak Ranger District Office, 925 Weiss Dr., Steamboat Springs, CO 80487; 970-879-1870; www.fs. fed.us/mrnf/hpbe/hpbewel.htm.** A special number for blowdown information is **970-870-2192.**

Topographic maps, supplies and rental equipment can be found at a number of stores in the Steamboat area, including **Ski Haus,** in front of Safeway at **1450 S. Lincoln Ave.; 970-879-0385.** In Clark pick up a map at the **Clark General Store; 970-879-3849.** You can't miss it. When you're at the Clark store be sure to get a "Clark single" ice cream cone. It's the best deal in the state.

Fish Creek Falls

Fish Creek Falls and the trail heading east from there are good areas for day hikes and extended backpack trips. This has to be the most popular tourist spot in the Steamboat area, and with good reason. Each year thousands of people drive the 4 miles up Fish Creek Falls Rd. to the recreation area and look in awe at the 283-foot waterfall. During the late spring and early summer, when the snow melt-off is particularly high, the falls are torrential.

Originally homesteaded in 1901 by the Crawford family, the falls area was aptly named for the whitefish and brook trout spawning here

in autumn. The townspeople used to have a picnic each year during the spawn. Using pitchforks, hooks and gunnysacks, they would collect the fish to be salted and stored for winter.

A small footbridge, reached via a quarter-mile trail leading from the parking lot (fee charged), crosses the creek right in front of the falls. Picnic tables, rest rooms, interpretive signs and wheelchair accessibility make things easier for visitors.

The upper **Fish Creek Falls Trail** leads to an overlook above the falls. The lower trail leads to the bridge across the creek and climbs another 2 miles to a second set of falls, eventually reaching the Continental Divide. About 5 miles above the lower falls is **Long Lake,** where good campsites can be found. For a longer hike, turn south on Trail 1101, which eventually reaches **Dumont Lake Campground** on Rabbit Ears Pass, 10.5 miles from Fish Creek Falls.

To reach Fish Creek Falls from Lincoln Ave. (Hwy. 40) in town, turn north onto Third Ave. and drive one block to the four-way stop at Oak St. Turn right and continue 4 miles on Fish Creek Falls Rd. to the parking lot.

Flat Tops Wilderness

For information about the Flat Tops, see the Hiking and Backpacking section in the **Meeker** chapter.

Mt. Werner (Ski Area)

Many people who visit Steamboat overlook one of the most obvious places to hike in the area: Mt. Werner. Not only are there cut trails and great views, but less ambitious hikers can take a gondola up the mountain. From the top of the gondola you can continue to the top of Storm Peak. A number of trails can get you back down to the bottom of the mountain, including the popular 3-mile **Thunderhead Trail.** Fee charged for the gondola; open 10 A.M.–4 P.M.; **970-879-6111 ext. 233.**

Seedhouse Road Trails

Just north of Clark, Seedhouse Rd. (Forest Rd. 400) turns northeast, following the Elk River

13 miles to the old mining camp of Slavonia. From this road many people begin day hikes and backpack trips into the beautiful lakes and craggy mountains of the Mt. Zirkel Wilderness Area. **Gilpin Lake, Gold Creek Lake** and **Three Island Lake** are overused. Backpackers should not camp any closer than a quarter-mile from the lakes—day hikes for fishing and sightseeing are a better idea. Up above Gilpin and Gold Creek Lakes, Ute Pass crosses the Continental Divide at a low spot that the Utes used to frequent when traveling back and forth between the Yampa Valley and North Park and hunting buffalo and deer.

One good possibility for backpacking in this area is a trip up to **North Lake** and the Continental Divide. The trail climbs, steeply at first, about 2,400 vertical feet in just under 5.5 miles. You'll reach the lake after about 4 miles of tree-covered hiking; from the lake you'll find meadows and easier hiking up to the divide. The trailhead is located just another 1.5 miles past the Three Island Lake trailhead (see the Mt. Zirkel Wilderness listing in the Fishing section).

Wyoming Trail

Feeling ambitious? How about taking the Wyoming Trail (No. 1101), which follows the Continental Divide for over 50 miles from Buffalo Pass near Summit Lake Campground, north through the Mt. Zirkel Wilderness Area and on up to Medicine Bow National Forest just over the Wyoming border. Views down into North Park and the Yampa River drainage are spectacular from the trail, which is above treeline for much of the way.

The trail can be indistinguishable in many sections and difficult to follow, due to late snowpack and boggy areas. Much of the trail is still used by local ranchers as a stock driveway. If you just want to hike part of the way, it's possible to get back out on Seedhouse Rd. near Slavonia, about 15 miles from Clark. To reach the trailhead on Buffalo Pass, take Strawberry Park Rd. 4 miles out of Steamboat Springs, turn right on Buffalo Pass Rd. and proceed 9 miles to the pass.

Horseback Riding

In case you've forgotten, here's a reminder: Steamboat Springs is a great area for horseback riding. The Yampa River Valley and nearby Elk River Valley are packed full of working ranches, guest ranches and some combinations of both. The ranching way of life has been vital to the Steamboat area. Even the ski area used to be part of a ranch.

Del's Triangle 3 Ranch

Del's, located in a secluded area north of Steamboat, offers all you could want from a horseback outfit. It's common to spot many elk grazing in meadows and forests near the ranch. Rides range from 1 hour to multi-day pack trips into the nearby national forest. Winter rides also available. Drive north on Elk River Rd. about 20 miles to the Clark Store. Turn left (west) and continue for 2 miles. **P.O. Box 333, Clark, CO 80428; 970-879-3495.**

Dutch Creek Guest Ranch

Journey into the nearby Routt National Forest for a short ride or for the entire day from the Dutch Creek Guest Ranch. Riders of all abilities are welcome at this ranch 25 miles north of Steamboat, near Steamboat Lake. **P.O. Box 846, Clark, CO 80428; 1-800-778-8519; 970-879-8519; www.cmn.net/~dutch.**

High Meadows Ranch

Located about an hour south of Steamboat, this remote guest ranch offers partial and full-day rides, as well as multi-day pack and hunting trips. Open year-round. **P.O. Box 771216, Steamboat Springs, CO 80477; 1-800-457-4453; 970-736-8416; www.hmranch.com.**

River Floating

Although some floaters, especially kayakers, find stretches of the Elk River to float, the majority of river activity in the Steamboat Springs area happens on the Yampa. The Yampa River flows 170 miles from its headwaters and through the town of Steamboat Springs before turning west and building steam on its way to the spectacularly carved canyons of Dinosaur National Monument.

Originally called Bear River by early settlers, the Yampa got its present name from the potato-like root that grows along its banks. The Utes relied on it as a food source.

With the help of city funds, locals have fixed up a section of the river in town for kayakers, canoeists and inner tubers. Along certain stretches, boulders have been placed in the river, forming a kayak course. Folks float this stretch all through the late spring and summer. Farther downriver, mellow sections attract canoers while exciting stretches provide perfect rafting opportunities.

To help preserve the Yampa while providing recreational access to the river, **Colorado State Parks** began management of the **Yampa River State Park.** The park includes a series of river access put-ins and take-outs, a visitor center and campground near Hayden (see Camping section) and improved facilities at Elkhead Reservoir near Craig. For more information, contact park headquarters in Hayden at **970-276-2061; www.coloradoparks.org.**

Outfitters

Backdoor Sports—Offers inner tube rentals for floats through town. **9th and Yampa St.; 970-879-6249; www.steamboatextreme. com.**

Buggywhip's—Provides half-day to four-day guided raft-floating trips on the Yampa, Green, Colorado, North Platte, Arkansas and Eagle Rivers. **4th and Lincoln Ave., P.O. Box 770479, Steamboat Springs, CO 80477; 1-800-759-0343; 970-879-8033; www.buggy whips.com.**

Mountain Sports Kayak School—Barry Smith has been kayaking for years, cultivating a national reputation along the way. If you want to learn how to kayak, this is the guy to teach you. His company offers lessons, focusing on first-time kayakers. Kayak and inner-tube rentals are available. Located in Ski Haus Sports at **Hwy. 40 and Pine Grove Rd.; 970-879-8794; 970-879-6910.**

Skiing

CROSS-COUNTRY SKIING AND SNOWSHOEING

The cross-country skiing in the Steamboat area is ideal from a nordic skier's perspective. Rolling hills make it easy to do circle tours, as opposed to skiing up and down a steep river canyon. Heavy snowfall makes for a long touring season, which attracts the U.S. Olympic nordic team in early fall and late spring. Local people like Sven Wiik, the "guru of American cross-country skiing," have been instrumental in fueling enthusiasm for the sport.

For trail maps and other information, contact the **Hahns Peak Ranger District Office, 925 Weiss Dr., Steamboat Springs, CO 80487; 970-879-1870; www.fs.fed.us/mr nf/hpbe/hpbewel.htm** or the **Chamber of Commerce Visitors Center** in town.

Backcountry Trails

Rabbit Ears Pass—Cross-country skiers from the state are familiar with the Rabbit Ears Pass trail system. Rolling hills at 10,000 feet offer beautiful views and miles of circuitous, marked trails through the pine and aspen. The terrain is great for everything from gliding to telemarking.

Stay on the trails, as it's deceivingly easy to lose your way in the forest, and there are not many distinguishable landmarks. Rabbit Ears Peak, however, with its two crumbly, rose-colored granite spires, is a notable exception. In winter you can ski to the base of the rocks from the top of the pass. All trailheads lie along Hwy. 40 on Rabbit Ears Pass, about 10 miles southeast of Steamboat Springs.

Seedhouse Road—This road follows the path of the Elk River down from the Mt. Zirkel Wilderness in a beautiful mountain valley. Routt National Forest has a marked trail system that begins 4.5 miles northeast of Clark in the Hinman Park area. You may also follow Seedhouse Rd. up from Hinman Park, as it remains unplowed but groomed for snowmobilers—good skate skiing. The trails are mostly of the rolling hill variety, with views to Mt. Zirkel in the distance. For information and maps, contact the Forest Service office in Steamboat. To reach Seedhouse Rd., take County Rd. 129 north of Steamboat for 18 miles to Clark. A couple of miles north of Clark turn right on Seedhouse Rd. and parallel the Elk River into Routt National Forest. There is also a trail system in and around Clark.

Groomed Trails

Home Ranch and **Vista Verde Guest Ranch**—These full-service guest ranches offer public access to miles of groomed trails on their property. See the Where to Stay section.

Howelsen Ski Area—About 5 miles of groomed and track trails (2.5 miles lighted) await at the base of Howelsen Hill in town. Rentals not available. **970-879-8499.**

Steamboat Ski Touring Center—Over 30 kilometers of trails (both tracked and skating) wind along Fish Creek and the surrounding areas near the base of Mt. Werner, offering something for novices to experts. Lessons, backcountry guided trips and rentals are available. The Picnic Basket sandwich shop offers warm drinks and lunches. Head south from town and turn east on Mt. Werner Rd. Turn left onto Steamboat Blvd. and follow the signs. **P.O. Box 775401, Steamboat Springs, CO 80477; 970-879-8180; www.nordicski.net.**

Rentals and Information

Ski Haus—The Ski Haus rents a full selection of track and backcountry equipment. They can also provide you with good trail ideas. Located in front of Safeway at **Hwy. 40 and Pine Grove Rd.; 970-879-0385.**

Straightline Outdoor Sports—Located in town; rents all types of cross-country equipment at reasonable prices. **744 Lincoln Ave.; 970-879-7568; www.straightlinesports.com.**

DOWNHILL SKIING AND SNOWBOARDING

Howelsen Ski Area

Howelsen Ski Area, owned by the town of Steamboat Springs, offers a vertical drop of only 440 feet and is served by a chairlift, a poma lift and a pony tow. In addition to downhill skiing, the hill now has six different ski jumps that are used for Olympic-level qualifying meets and training—it's the largest ski jumping complex in North America. The hill is open to the public each day; night skiing also offered till 10 P.M. nightly. Located **across the 5th St. Bridge** from downtown; **970-879-8499.**

Steamboat Powder Cats

Powder lovers (with spare cash) who want to get away from the world of groomed runs and lift lines should try this service. Enter a new dimension of skiing, boarding or backcountry telemarking by taking a snow cat into the high country near Buffalo Pass and cutting the first tracks. An overnight stay in a secluded cabin is also an option. **P.O. Box 2468, Steamboat Springs, CO 80477; 970-879-5188; www.powdercats.com.**

Steamboat Ski Resort

Colorado offers plenty of world-class skiing, and Steamboat stands out among some of Colorado's best. From the base of Steamboat, the initial 1,000-foot rise of Christie Peak provides you only an inkling of what kind of skiable terrain lies beyond. But as the eight-passenger gondola carries you swiftly over the first hill, you are on the verge of discovery. Each year an average of 351 inches of Colorado powder drops on 2,800 skiable acres. This ample, light snow has helped Steamboat develop a reputation for superb powder skiing.

Spread out among five interconnected mountains, the area offers 3,600 vertical feet (second-highest in Colorado) and diverse terrain for all abilities. With its long bump runs, Storm Peak is the choice of many mogul and powder aficionados. Many advanced skiers are drawn to Priest Creek, where they can pick a run down through the challenging aspen-studded glades of Shadows and Twilight. Steamboat's newest addition to its already ample list of choice runs is Pioneer Ridge—260 tree-covered acres adjacent to Storm Peak. Incredibly, lift lines still remain short.

The legacy of champions continues as Billy Kidd, 1964 Olympic silver medalist and 1970 world champion, serves as the director of skiing at the Steamboat Ski Area. Most days at 1 P.M., you can meet Kidd at the top of Thunderhead Mountain for an informal ski clinic and run to the bottom. **2305 Mt. Werner Cir., Steamboat Springs, CO 80487; 1-800-922-2722; 970-879-6111.** The terrific website for the area, **www.steamboat-ski.com,** provides hundreds of pages of information, from ski schools to where to stay.

Sleigh Rides

Windwalker Tours

At 1 P.M. daily Windwalker Ranch loads up its sleighs with passengers and rides near large herds of feeding elk. The photo opportunities are fantastic, so be sure to bring your camera. Allow 2 hours and dress warmly. Transportation to the sleighs is provided and reservations are required. For additional information and reservations, contact at **1-800-748-1642; 970-879-8065; www.wind walkertours.com.**

Seeing and Doing

Ballooning

Pegasus

A reliable, longtime company (since 1983). In summer, rides are offered in the morning; winter rides are given both in morning and afternoon. Reservations required. **1-800-748-2487; 970-879-9191.**

Hot Springs

Beginning with the Ute Indians, hot springs around Steamboat have been used for medicinal and recreational purposes. Indians believed the Great Spirit who lived below the surface of the earth would rejuvenate their strength. In addition to using the mineral springs for health reasons, the Utes may also have used a sulfurous vapor cave across the river for torturing prisoners. Stories indicate that enemies of the Utes, especially captured Arapaho and Cheyenne, were put in the cave and slowly asphyxiated.

In 1875 James Crawford, the first settler in Steamboat, shoveled out a hole in the sand so his

Bugling bull elk. Photo by John Geerdes.

family could enjoy a good hot soak at Heart Spring—now the location of the Steamboat Springs Health and Recreation Association. Crawford counted more than 150 springs in the Steamboat vicinity. Though many of the natural springs have disappeared as the town has grown, you'll likely smell an occasional burst of sulfur gas emitted from thermal waters coming up from faults deep in the earth. Iron Spring, Steamboat Spring, Lithia Spring, Soda Spring and Sulfur Spring are the names of a few that still bubble to the surface. A couple of great soaking opportunities remain at year-round swimming holes.

Steamboat Springs Health and Recreation Association

Starting with James Crawford, many bathers have enjoyed bathhouses and pools at this location. Today there are several concrete and tile pools, a hydro water slide, a snack bar and workout facilities. The hot mineral soaking pool is kept at a steady 100° F. Though this site has been heavily developed, it is a great place for families to come and enjoy an in-town soak. Open year-round 6:30 A.M.–10 P.M. Mon.–Fri.; 8 A.M.–10 P.M. on weekends. Fee charged. **136 Lincoln Ave.; 970-879-1828.**

Strawberry Park Hot Springs

Longtime Steamboat residents bemoan the changes at Strawberry Park Hot Springs. Only a few years ago the springs were known by locals as a great place to ski into for a private soak. Now the road is plowed (though treacherous, requiring chains or four-wheel drive) in winter and admission is charged. But the rock-lined pools remain a fine place for those in search of a natural location. Three 3- to 5-foot-deep pools are fed by source water of 146° F and mixed with cold creek water to temperatures ranging from 70° F to 106° F. On hot summer days the water is kept cooler. The important rules are: bring no glass; bring no pets unless you are camping there; bring no kids after dark and wear a bathing suit during daylight hours (optional after dark). Reservations required for Fri. and Sat. night visits. There are five **cabins ($$)** and

Relaxing in Strawberry Park Hot Springs. Photo by Bruce Caughey.

a caboose for rent and 10 **tentsites ($)** spread around the property. Open daily 10 A.M.–midnight. To reach Strawberry Park Hot Springs, drive 7 miles north of Steamboat on County Rd. 36 (Strawberry Park Rd.). The road ends at the gate. **P.O. Box 773332, Steamboat Springs, CO 80477; 970-879-0342.**

Museums and Galleries

Depot Art Center

The historic railroad depot, built in 1906, now serves as a hub for the artistic community. Dance programs, music programs, plays and gallery displays are featured. For information and a schedule of events, call **970-879-9008.** Hours vary greatly. Located at **1001 13th St. in Steamboat Springs; www.steamboat springsarts.com.**

Tread of Pioneers Museum

With the exception of the small Ute Indian display, nearly all of the items in this museum came from pioneer families in Routt County. It is a worthwhile stop for those interested in the early history of the area. The living room is filled with worn furniture and old photos; check out the piano that was shipped around Cape Horn on a voyage beginning in New York City in 1868 and ending in Steamboat Springs 18 years later. You will gain a new respect for the origins of ski jumping when you look at the heavy leather ski-jumping boots that Carl Howelsen (alias the Flying Norseman) used in the early 1900s. Be sure to see the extensive ski memorabilia, ranch relics and furniture created from the horns of moose, elk and bighorn sheep—illuminating the eccentric taste of the Anglo settlers. Open year-round Tues.–Sat. 11 A.M.–5 P.M. **800 Oak St.; 970-879-2214.**

Nightlife

Blue Cat Jazz Club

For information about this weekend jazz club, see the In-Season Bakery and Cafe write-up in the Where to Eat section.

The Inferno

A wild après-ski spot at the base of the gondola, the Inferno is a great place to unwind after a day on the slopes. Their famous shot wheel is spun periodically (à la *Wheel of Fortune*) to determine special drink prices for the next few minutes. The Inferno has a reputation for being a "meat market" and is also known for its great live rock music, which can be heard Mon.–Sat. Deck seating, weather permitting. **2305 Mt. Werner Cir.; 970-879-5111.**

Steamboat Brewery and Tavern

Award-winning microbrew (especially the Alpenglow) can be found at the Steamboat Brewery and Tavern in downtown Steamboat. Definitely not a rowdy nightlife hot spot, the Brewery provides a relaxing atmosphere and a terrific menu. Dining selections **($$ to $$$)** change four times per year. Open 11:30 A.M.–10 P.M. daily for food; bar open until 2 A.M. **5th and Lincoln Ave.; 970-879-2233.**

The Tugboat Grill and Pub

This local favorite has been around forever and is an integral part of "The Triangle" of popular restaurants and bars at Ski Time Square. A casual sports bar, the Tugboat offers live rock and blues music on summer weekends (Tues.–Sat. in winter). Lunch, dinner and après ski. Open daily 11:30 A.M.–1:30 A.M. year-round. On the mountain at **1860 Mt. Werner Rd.; 970-879-7070.**

Scenic Drives

Buffalo Pass

This is the only road crossing the Continental Divide through the Park Range just east of Steamboat Springs. It offers great views of the Yampa River basin and North Park. Buffalo Pass gets its name from the time when Ute Indians used to wait in ambush for the herds of buffalo migrating between North Park and the Yampa Valley. In summertime the higher meadows are blanketed with a spectacular and diverse selection of wildflowers, including columbine and Indian paintbrush; autumn offers a memorable golden aspen tour. The dirt road is pretty rough, but passenger cars can make it. Snow usually prohibits crossing the pass until after July 4th. Hiking trails branch off to the north of the road into the Mt. Zirkel Wilderness Area. To reach Buffalo Pass, take Strawberry Park Rd. 4 miles out of Steamboat to the intersection of Buffalo Pass Rd. (County Rd. 38). The summit of the pass is about 12 miles up the road. Continue approximately 16 miles down into North Park to Hwy. 14, turn right and return to Steamboat over Rabbit Ears Pass.

Elk River Valley

It's hard to match the beauty of this valley as it traces the path of the Elk River down from the Mt. Zirkel Wilderness. In July the wildflowers create a patchwork of colors in the high meadows. Routt National Forest encompasses much of the valley, where you may enjoy camping, fishing and hiking (see the appropriate sections for more information). After about 13 miles, at

Slavonia, the road ends at a wilderness access point, with views of snowcapped peaks along the Continental Divide. To reach the Elk River Valley, take County Rd. 129 north of Steamboat for 18 miles to Clark. A mile or so north of Clark, turn right on Seedhouse Rd. and proceed into Routt National Forest. Note: the Routt Divide Blowdown has impacted this area. For up-to-date information on how the blowdown may affect your visit, contact the **Hahns Peak Ranger District Office, 925 Weiss Dr., Steamboat Springs, CO 80487; 970-879-1870; www.fs.fed.us/mrnf/hpbe/ hpbewel.htm.**

Another excellent option is to continue north on County Rd. 129 to **Steamboat Lake State Park** near the historic mining town of Hahns Peak. Steamboat Lake offers swimming, boat rentals, camping and picnic sites. Be sure to visit Steamboat Lake's terrific new visitor center, with interpretive displays, maps, books and heaps of information about the area.

Fish Creek Falls

This highly scenic 283-foot waterfall, only 4 miles east of Steamboat Springs, provides an excellent bang for your gasoline buck. For history, hiking information, directions and other details, see the Hiking and Backpacking section.

Flat Tops Trail Scenic Byway

Wonderful drive from the nearby town of Yampa over 10,000-foot Ripple Creek Pass and down along the White River to Meeker. Highly recommended! For information see the Scenic Drives section of the **Meeker** chapter.

Where to Stay

Accommodations

Condominium complexes, many of which boast a ski-in/ski-out location to lifts, dominate accommodations in Steamboat, as in other large resorts in Colorado. There are some wonderful places to stay that can meet just about every taste and budget.

Hotels of note include the plush **Sheraton Steamboat ($$$ to $$$$),** offering first-class accommodations right at the base of the Silver Bullet Gondola; **1-800-848-8877.** In downtown Steamboat, the **Harbor Hotel ($$$ to $$$$),** somewhat of a landmark, offers refurbished rooms (some rather small) in the old hotel as well as comfortable, modern condominium units out back. A health spa and complimentary continental breakfast are available. **703 Lincoln Ave., P.O. Box 774109, Steamboat Springs, CO 80477; 1-800-543-8888 nationwide; 1-800-334-1012 Colorado; 970-879-1522.**

All lodging needs ranging from condominiums to cabins can be met by calling the efficient and helpful **Steamboat Central Reservations** at **1-800-922-2722** or **970-879-0740.** For a terrific source for higher-end slopeside condos (such as the plush Torian Plum) and private homes, contact **Steamboat Premier Properties** at **1-800-228-2458** or **970-879-8811; www.steamboat-premier.com.** For more specific suggestions for overnight stays, see below.

GUEST RANCHES

With the Steamboat area's rich ranching history, the plethora of guest ranches/dude ranches should come as no surprise. Among our top choices are the following.

High Meadows Ranch—$$$$

For seclusion that's slightly more affordable than the ranches listed above, consider a stay at High Meadows, about 1 hour south of Steamboat Springs. High Meadows gears itself to families and offers what they term à la carte pricing to provide flexibility. Activities abound, especially horseback riding into the nearby Routt National Forest, cross-country skiing on 15 kilometers of groomed trails and fishing for small brookies in the nearby ponds and streams. Three log lodges provide 10 comfortable guest rooms. For more information, contact **Denny Stamp, P.O. Box 771216, Steamboat Springs, CO 80477; 1-800-457-4453; 970-736-8416; www.hm ranch.com.**

Home Ranch—$$$$

On the high end, few places in Colorado compare with the Home Ranch. This spacious, exclusive spread, located in the Elk River Valley at the edge of Routt National Forest 20 miles north of Steamboat, offers guests the chance to enjoy a mountain lifestyle with many comforts found at five-star hotels. Each cabin, furnished with handmade furniture, Indian rugs and a woodstove, features a private outdoor whirlpool bath. In addition to the cabins and six lodge rooms, an enormous three-bedroom, three-bath cabin is available. Carefully prepared, delicious meals are served three times daily. There's plenty to keep you busy, from horseback riding to fly-fishing to a heated year-round pool. Forty kilometers of cross-country ski trails are the main attraction in winter. In July and Aug. guests must reserve their stays on a weekly basis, with all meals included. The rest of the year is more flexible but usually requires a three-day minimum stay. For information contact Ken and Cile Jones, **P.O. Box 822, Clark, CO 80428; 970-879-1780; www.homeranch. com.**

Vista Verde Guest and Ski Touring Ranch—$$$$

Winter or summer, this wonderful ranch hideaway attracts guests from around the country who enjoy the perfect combination of activities and pure relaxation. Located 25 miles north of Steamboat, the 540-acre working cattle and horse ranch is bordered by 1.2 million acres of Routt National Forest and the Mt. Zirkel Wilderness Area. Vista Verde's impressively wide assortment of featured activities includes horseback riding, hiking, mountain biking, fishing, whitewater rafting, rock climbing and hot-air ballooning. In winter the ranch is used as a nordic center, getting 300-plus inches of snow. Miles of groomed trails on the ranch include skating trails and a ski-in cabin; adjacent Forest Service terrain provides unlimited touring. The ranch's sizable staff includes full-time guides and instructors to aid guests who want to learn to toss the perfect fly or cut a telemark turn. After a day on the trails, enjoy the log-and-glass-enclosed spa with outdoor whirlpool, sauna and deck. Eight hand-hewn, renovated cabins (some with hot tubs) spread out among the aspen trees at Vista Verde serve as extremely comfortable escapes from the ranch activities. A gourmet chef serves three heaping meals each day at the attractive main lodge; two lodge rooms are available as well. Meals are included in the weekly summer price; shorter stays can be arranged in winter. **P.O. Box 465, Steamboat Springs, CO 80477; 1-800-526-RIDE; 970-879-3858; www.vistaverde.com.**

BED AND BREAKFASTS

Rooms on the Mountain—$$$ to $$$$

Closer to the ski area, try a night at the intimate **Rooms on the Mountain.** Three rooms are available and kimonos are provided (and encouraged) as proper breakfast attire. **2685 Apres Ski Way, Herbage C-5, P.O. Box 88-2086, Steamboat Springs, CO 80488-2086; 970-879-5223.**

Sky Valley Lodge—$$$ to $$$$

Out of town, the Sky Valley Lodge, though not technically a bed and breakfast, offers 24 comfortable rooms spread out between two lodges partway up Rabbit Ears Pass. Terrific continental breakfast included; outdoor hot tub; shuttle provided to town and ski area. **31490 E. Hwy. 40, P.O. Box 3132, Steamboat Springs, CO 80477; 1-800-499-4759; 970-879-7749; www. steamboat-lodging.com.**

Steamboat Valley Guest House—$$$ to $$$$

This guest house provides a cozy hilltop view of town. Four guest rooms with private baths and an outdoor hot tub are the main features. Innkeepers George and Alice Lund provide a delicious Swedish breakfast each morning and are a great source of information for what to see and do in the area. **1245 Crawford Ave., P.O. Box 773815, Steamboat Springs, CO 80477; 1-800-530-3866; 970-879-9017.**

Steamboat Bed and Breakfast—$$$

This spacious and comfortable B&B continues as one of the bright spots of a trip to Steamboat.

When lightning struck the Euzoa Church (built in 1891) and burned half of the roof, the former owner painstakingly undertook a renovation project that lasted two and a half years. The result is an updated version of the church with a perfect layout for a small inn. Each of the seven rooms has a private bath and is decorated with antiques/neo-antiques. The highlight may be the Sunrise Room with its king-size bed and three windows. Guests can enjoy the music conservatory and living room, complete with a large fish tank, and the inviting outdoor deck and hot tub. Conveniently located and reasonably priced. No smoking; well-behaved kids okay. **442 Pine St., P.O. Box 775888, Steamboat Springs, CO 80477; 970-879-5724; www.steamboat b-b.com.**

RUSTIC CABINS

Columbine Cabins—$ to $$$

Remote and rustic, yet recently renovated, the comfortable Columbine Cabins are an added treat to Steamboat area accommodations. Located a few miles north of historic Hahn's Peak on County Rd. 129, these 12 cabins once provided shelter to miners in the area's short-lived gold rush of 1897. Each cabin includes kitchens, towels and linens; other than that, amenities vary significantly. Open year-round for access to nearby Routt National Forest, Steamboat Lake and the Mt. Zirkel Wilderness. **P.O. Box 716, Clark, CO 80428; 970-879-5522; www.coloradovacation.com/cabins/columbine.**

Perry-Mansfield Log Lodges—$ to $$

Hidden in the pine and aspen trees just northeast of town in Strawberry Park, Perry-Mansfield offers six rustic cabins for those who want to escape the resort atmosphere of Steamboat. Perry-Mansfield Camp began in 1913 as a performing arts camp for girls. Today there is a six-week summer program for girls, but some cabins can still be booked during this time. These rustic cabins, which can sleep up to 10 people, are available for very reasonable prices. All contain complete kitchens including utensils

and cookware; each has at least one bedroom on the main floor and more sleeping space in a loft. The cabins are winterized. Reservations are a must. **40755 Routt County Rd. 36, Steamboat Springs, CO 80487; 970-879-7125.**

Steamboat Lake—$

Recently constructed, the bare-bones cabins at Steamboat Lake are definitely a terrific option for those who do not mind roughing it a bit. The half dozen cabins can be booked year-round through Steamboat Lake Marina at **970-879-7019.** Also check information about the cabins at the Steamboat Lake State Park website, **www.coloradoparks.org.**

Camping

Routt National Forest near Steamboat Springs

This area offers a host of camping options. All the listed sites charge a fee. **Dry Lake Campground** (8 sites) can be reached by heading 4 miles north of Steamboat Springs on Strawberry Park Rd., then east for 3.5 miles on Buffalo Pass Rd. Another 8.5 miles up Buffalo Pass Rd. is **Summit Lake Campground** (16 sites), located at the summit of the pass. Check to see if the road is open before planning a trip up here. From the summit of Buffalo Pass, **Granite Campground** (6 sites) can be reached by heading 5 miles south to Fish Creek Reservoir.

Hinman Park Campground (13 sites) can be reached by driving 18 miles north from Steamboat on Elk River Rd. to Glen Eden. Turn northeast on Seedhouse Rd. for 6 miles. **Seedhouse Campground** (25 sites) is just another 3.5 miles up Seedhouse Rd. from the turnoff to Hinman Park Campground.

Hahn's Peak Lake Campground (26 sites) is located 25 miles north of Steamboat up Elk River Rd. At the sign for the campground, turn left and proceed 2.5 miles on Forest Rd. 486. Sites at Hahn's Peak may be reserved by calling **1-888-444-6777.**

Heading southeast from Steamboat Springs on Hwy. 40 eventually leads you to **Meadows Campground** (30 sites), 15 miles from town. Two miles farther up the road is **Walton Creek Campground** (16 sites). At the summit of Rabbit Ears Pass (22 miles from Steamboat), head north for a mile on the old Hwy. 40 road to **Dumont Lake Campground** (22 sites).

For other camping ideas in Routt National Forest, talk to **Hahns Peak Ranger District Office, 925 Weiss Dr., Steamboat Springs, CO 80487; 970-879-1870; www.fs.fed.us/mrnf/hpbe/hpbewel.htm.**

State Parks

Reservations at the four state parks listed below can be made at least three days in advance by calling **1-800-678-2267** or in Denver **970-470-1144** or at **www.reserveamerica.com.** Fee charged at all sites.

Pearl Lake—Offers 36 wooded sites near the shores of Pearl Lake. Recently added are two **yurts ($)** for rent year-round. Located in the Elk River Valley 26 miles north of Steamboat. A side road leads 2 miles to the park.

Stagecoach State Park—You'll find 92 modern sites at this popular reservoir state park. Showers available. To reach the park, drive about 5 miles south from Steamboat Springs on Hwy. 131 and then left on County Rd. 14 for 5 miles.

Steamboat Lake State Park—Steamboat Lake, 25 miles north of Steamboat Springs on Elk River Rd., offers terrific camping opportunities at 238 recently renovated sites. **Sunrise Vista Campground** lies on the north side of the lake and **Dutch Hill Campground,** including the enormously popular Bridge Island, is also on the north side. Camper cabins are available for rental year-round (see Steamboat Lake, in the Accommodations section). There are shower buildings, laundry facilities and a wonderful new visitor center.

Yampa River State Park

Fifty-plus sites are found at this former hay meadow along the Yampa River a few miles west of the town of Hayden on Hwy. 40. Included are a shower building, state park visitor center and river access. **970-276-2061.**

Private Campgrounds

Steamboat Springs KOA—Located 2 miles west of town on Hwy. 40, KOA offers the ultimate in fat camping, including a hot tub, swimming pool and fishing. Cabins, tentsites and RV hookups available. Open all year. **3603 Lincoln Ave., Steamboat Springs, CO 80487; 970-879-0273; www.koacampground.com. Strawberry Park Hot Springs**—Along with the fantastic natural hot springs, four cabins (sleeping bags necessary) and 10 tentsites are available. See the Hot Springs section.

Where to Eat

Hazie's—$$$$

The experience of taking a gondola to the top of Thunderhead Peak for dinner, as well as the starlit return trip, is one to remember. While enjoying a bottle of wine and an elegant meal, gaze out of the picture windows as the sun sets on the Yampa Valley to the west. Although the food (probably the most expensive in Routt County) is, quite frankly, inconsistent, not many places can match Hazie's for atmosphere and spectacular views. A full meal and round-trip gondola ticket are included in one package price. In winter, lunch is served daily and dinner is served Tues.–Sat.; in summer, dinner is served Fri. and Sat. and there also is a Sun. brunch. Reservations strongly suggested. On the mountain, at the top of the **Silver Bullet Gondola; 970-879-6111 ext. 465.** In summertime, for a more affordable mountaintop dining alternative, try lunch at the **BK Corral ($ to $$$),** also located at the gondola building. Enjoy the drop-dead views from the outside patio while sipping a beer and enjoying a burger, sandwich or one of their daily specials. **970-879-6111.**

Giovanni's Ristorante—$$$ to $$$$

A proven survivor in Steamboat's topsy-turvy restaurant business, Giovanni's continues to provide delicious Italian cuisine in an intimate atmosphere. Exposed brick, wood paneling and photos add to the meal. The menu primarily features veal, chicken and seafood dishes; nightly specials are also a nice option. Giovanni's takes pride in its impressive selection of Italian wines. This is a great place for a romantic dinner for two. Open 5:30–10 P.M. in winter; 6–9 P.M. in summer. Reservations recommended. Located at **127 11th St.; 970-879-4141.**

La Montaña—$$$ to $$$$

La Montaña stacks up against the finest regional restaurants with its creative award-winning Southwestern dishes. This restaurant offers table seating under a peaked solarium with nice views. The light Southwestern feel goes well with the food. Unique and spicy concoctions range from elk fajitas and red chili pasta to more traditional enchilada and burrito dinners. You'll love the service. Restaurant hours: 5–10 P.M. in winter, 5:30–10 P.M. in summer. Bar (can eat here, too) hours: 4:30 P.M.–closing. On the mountain at the corner of Apres Ski Way and Village Dr. **2500 Village Dr.; 970-879-5800.**

L'Apogee—$$$ to $$$$

Muted pastels in this restaurant's dining room provide an elegant setting for a special night out. A small blackboard menu displays the nightly offerings of traditional and contemporary French cuisine. Thankfully, the staff patiently translates dishes for the linguistically challenged. L'Apogee has put together an award-winning wine cellar to complement the carefully prepared food of owner/chef Jamie Jenny. The wine list offers 875 choices; more than 38 selections are available by the glass. You may want to ask about their collection of single-malt scotch. Reservations recommended. Open 5:30–10:30 P.M. nightly. In town, **911 Lincoln Ave.; 970-879-1919.**

Old West Steak House—$$$ to $$$$

In cattle country it's a good idea to follow the locals to the best steak house in town. The Old West is a no-nonsense eatery specializing in choice cuts of charbroiled beef. Prime rib, filet mignon and top sirloin are served, along with more exotic cuts of elk steak. If your taste leans toward seafood or chicken, there are several selections. Owners Barb and Don Silva personally greet nearly every guest walking into their establishment. Don, the macho construction worker in a series of Winston cigarette ads a few years back, raved about his prime rib tacos, proclaiming, "I've eaten tacos all over the world and mine are the best." And we all know how tough it is to get a good taco in Bangkok. The upstairs bar menu offers a lighter version of the restaurant menu at more affordable prices **($$).** Reservations recommended. Dinner 5–10 P.M. nightly. A late-night bar menu is served until midnight. In town, **11th St. and Lincoln Ave.; 970-879-1441.**

Cugino's—$$ to $$$

Asked what makes his Philly-style pizza so good, owner "Angie" Angelaccio hinted that it has something to do with the dough. Whatever it is, it keeps attracting locals. The inside of this small restaurant has the feel of an East Coast pizzeria; outside patio seating as well. The kitchen is easily visible from the tables, and you almost feel as though you are in there with them as they toss the dough and cook the pasta. Cugino's does specialize in pizza, but they also are known for their strombolis, calzones and Philly steak sandwiches. More upscale entrées include eggplant parmesan and tortellini Genovese. At lunchtime, pizza by the slice is available. Daily specials; no reservations. Open daily 11 A.M.–10 P.M. Delivery available 5–9:30 P.M. **825 Oak St.; 970-879-5805.**

Harwig's Grill—$$ to $$$

Located next to its swank sister restaurant, L'Apogee, the popular Harwig's offers lighter, more affordable food with an international presentation. The all-star lineup of chefs each uses a wide-open theme to perfect personal dream dishes. Finger-food items on the menu alone could constitute a meal; these range from Shumei dim sum to filo triangles. Along with a tasty

Aspen leaves at their most colorful. Photo by Dean Winstanley.

ample-sized speakers. The menu is extensive and so is the beer list. For an escape from Steamboat and a fun meal, you might want to try it. Open Tues.–Sun. 5–10 P.M. On the main street in Oak Creek; **970-736-8538.**

In-Season Bakery and Cafe—$ to $$

Located just off Lincoln Ave. in town, this gourmet cafe/deli serves fresh-ground coffee and other coffee drinks, Belgian waffles and elegant egg dishes. Although the In-Season is best known for its breakfast items, it also offers great soups, salads, sandwiches and dessert pastries. Outside seating in summer alongside Soda Creek. Open Mon.–Sat. 7 A.M.–2 P.M.; elaborate **Sun. brunch ($$$)** 9 A.M.–2 P.M. On Thurs.–Sat. nights after 8, the cafe undergoes a transformation to the intimate Blue Cat Jazz Club. Enjoy drinks and live jazz music. **131 11th St.; 970-879-1840.** Another popular breakfast option is the all-you-can-eat buffet located in the Steamboat Sheraton's **Sevens** restaurant at the base of the ski hill at Ski Time Square.

Winona's—$ to $$

This attractive cafe in downtown Steamboat Springs offers standard breakfast and lunch entrées but with a healthy flair. You'll find many vegetarian dishes along with egg omelettes, pancakes and waffles. Their cinnamon rolls received raves from *Bon Appétit* magazine in 1997. Lunches include deli sandwiches, hoagies, burgers, salads, homemade soups and desserts. Sidewalk seating when weather permits. Open Mon.–Sat. 7 A.M.–3 P.M.; Sun. 7 A.M.–1 P.M.; dinner hours vary greatly. **617 Lincoln Ave.; 970-879-2483.**

Azteca Taqueria—$

Nothing fancy; this is simply the best wrap joint in Steamboat. Choose from a wide variety of enormous burritos as well as more standard Mexican fare such as enchiladas, tacos, chimichangas and quesadillas. Conveniently located at **4th and Lincoln Ave.** in downtown Steamboat. Dine in or take out. Open daily 9 A.M.–8 P.M. **970-870-9980.**

selection of salads, Harwig's features interesting entrées ranging from Tuscan fish chowder to the wonderful gaeng pet gai Thai dish. Be sure to check the nightly specials. Access to L'Apogee's drink selections. Pub atmosphere; highly recommended. Open 5:30–11 P.M. for dinner; bar open 5 P.M.–2 A.M. **911 Lincoln Ave.; 970-879-1980.**

Chelsea's—$$

An institution in the area? Well, maybe. Chelsea's, located in nearby Oak Creek (22 miles south), has been around since the late 1970s, when the town was enjoying a boom. Specializing in Szechuan Chinese food, Chelsea's is a small, laid-back place with a lot of character and good food. Named after a previous owner's daughter, the restaurant is decorated with a mishmash of Chinese trinkets, and rock music blasts from

Services

Visitor Information

Steamboat Central Reservations—Can arrange everything from condominium rentals to ski rentals. **1475 Pine Grove Rd., Suite 202, P.O. Box 774728, Steamboat Springs, CO 80477; 1-800-922-2722; 970-879-6111; www.steamboat-ski.com.**

Steamboat Springs Chamber Resort Association—Terrific visitor center at **1255 S. Lincoln Ave., P.O. Box 774408, Steamboat Springs, CO 80477; 970-879-0880; www.steamboat-chamber.com.**

Day Care

Babies, Etc.—Baby-sitting services for infants on up. **970-879-3263.**

Kids' Vacation Center—Summer and winter activities and day care for kids, run by the ski area. **970-879-6111 ext. 218.**

Transportation

Alpine Taxi-Limousine Inc.—A taxi/limousine shuttle service back and forth from Yampa Valley Regional Airport, Denver International Airport and other ski areas and Steamboat. **30475 W. Hwy. 40, Steamboat Springs, CO 80477; 1-800-343-RIDE; 970-879-8294.**

Steamboat Springs Transit—For a schedule of this free local bus service, call **970-879-3717.**

Storm Mountain Express—Shuttle service between airports and Steamboat Springs. **P.O. Box 882057, Steamboat Springs, CO 80488; 877-844-8787; 970-879-1963.**

Summit County

Summit County sits high in the mountains 70 miles west of Denver. Taken as a whole, it's the undisputed king of recreation and winter resorts in Colorado. For sheer size and number of visitors, Summit County wins the prize with four ski areas and numerous resorts—not to mention the beauty of the surrounding White River National Forest.

The spectacular setting encompasses towering mountains along the Continental Divide, which rims the eastern and southern borders of the county, while the magnificent peaks of the Tenmile and Gore Ranges lie to the west. Tenmile Creek, the Blue River and the Snake River all converge from different valleys at the focal point of the county—Dillon Reservoir, an immense water storage area for Denver since the early 1960s. The Blue River exits Dillon Reservoir and meanders north to Green Mountain Reservoir, eventually dumping into the Colorado River after 36 miles.

The Breckenridge gold rush of 1859 created the need for Summit County's first settlements. Later, silver strikes near Montezuma in 1863 brought even more people to the area. After the mining boom petered out, many towns died as people moved on, although Breckenridge, Dillon and Frisco hung on. With its unique charm, Breckenridge stands out above the rest. Streets in this Victorian town are lined with attractively restored buildings, earning a National Historic District designation.

Getting There

Summit County is located 70 miles west of Denver on Interstate 70. Van and limousine companies provide regular shuttle service between Denver International Airport and Summit County. **Greyhound Bus Lines** makes a stop in Silverthorne; **1-800-231-2222; www.greyhound.com.**

Summit County boasts four ski areas, each with its own personality. Breckenridge is the best known of the four, with diverse terrain on four separate mountains. Steep runs at Arapahoe Basin, one of Colorado's oldest ski areas, complements the terrain at Keystone, a planned resort, which stands out particularly for its fine accommodations, restaurants and first-class service. As the dust settles on the recent, massive base development at Copper Mountain, the resort's off-mountain amenities—dining, shopping and lodging—now fall in line with its superb skiing.

In addition to downhill skiing, a number of nordic centers and dozens of backcountry trails attract cross-country skiers and snowshoers. When the snow melts and the wildflowers start to bloom, summer activity in Summit County nearly matches the peak winter season. Hiking in the surrounding mountains, mountain biking the back trails, cruising along the outstanding paved Summit County bike trail system, jeeping to old ghost towns and golfing on one of the exceptional courses are just some of the attractions.

During the busy winter and summer seasons the county's population swells with vacationers and seasonal workers, and a growing year-round population often strains county resources.

Clustered around Dillon Reservoir, the towns of Frisco, Dillon and Silverthorne can provide an escape from the resorts and their higher-priced accommodations. If you want a total escape from the adult-Disneyland atmosphere, you might also consider staying near the old mining town of Montezuma, one of those rare mountain towns that has managed to hold onto its past, without dramatic development and change.

Summit County covers a huge area. Having spent a lot of time there over the years, we've narrowed this chapter down to include what we consider the features, and the hidden gems, that you may find most appealing in your travels.

History

In August 1859 a small group of prospectors found gold while panning along the Upper Blue River near present-day Breckenridge. Excited by their finds, the miners spread out along the river and up French Gulch, looking for rich veins. Fearing an attack by the local Ute Indians, they built a stockade and named it Fort Meribeh. During that first winter, these prospectors made their first major discovery under 8 feet of snow at Gold Run. Working with just a shovel and a pan, one man could extract up to $500 worth of gold a day in this gulch.

Word got out and by spring the rush was on. When the town of "Breckinridge" was established that spring, it was the first permanent Colorado settlement on the Western Slope of the Continental Divide. Hoping to get a post office, the town fathers named it in honor of Vice President John C. Breckinridge. When the Civil War broke out, the townspeople, angered by the vice president's support for the Confederacy, altered the spelling to *Breckenridge,* changing the first *i* to an *e.*

Over the next 40 years prospectors and mining companies used every conceivable method to extract gold and silver from surrounding streams and mountains, including panning, placer mining and dredging. From 1898 to 1942 large dredging machines tore up miles of streams and rivers while gleaning gold from the sand and leaving ugly piles of rock in their wake (still visible today).

Breckenridge grew quickly, experiencing economic ups and downs along the way. Perhaps the biggest shot in the arm came in 1882 when the Denver South Park & Pacific Railroad arrived in town via Boreas Pass. In 1897 miner Tom Groves unearthed "Tom's Baby"—at 13 pounds, said to be the largest gold nugget ever discovered. (Tom, acting like a doting father, tenderly wrapped it in velvet before showing it off to the townsfolk.)

The town attracted its share of characters. Perhaps the best known was "Father" Dyer, the itinerant Methodist minister who traveled unceasingly to the surrounding mining camps, delivering the mail along with the word of God. His church still stands in Breckenridge. Another local character was "Captain" Sam Adams, who established the ill-fated Breckenridge navy. Adams, a real schemer, convinced the locals to supply him with four boats and a crew of 10 men to float down the Blue River to the Colorado River and eventually to the Pacific Ocean. The attempt failed miserably and Adams was run out of town.

Although Breckenridge was the largest and most successful mining region in Summit County, it was just a matter of time before settlers spread out into other parts of the county. In the 1860s prospectors made rich silver strikes in the Montezuma mining district. Settlements such as Montezuma, Saints John, Peru, Chihuahua and Decatur yielded ore on and off through the turn of the century. In 1873 the town of Frisco got its start due to mining at nearby Mt. Royal. Frisco eventually grew as a central supply link and railroad stop between Georgetown and Leadville. As in other areas of Colorado, the 1900s brought hard times as most mines shut down and populations dwindled. But Summit County was perfectly suited for its 20th-century savior: skiing.

Skis were used for transportation in Summit County during the early mining days. However, it was not until after 1910 that skiing started being treated as a sport. A group of locals living in Old Dillon (now at the bottom of Dillon Reservoir) built a ski jump on which Anders Haugen, a Norwegian, set a world record in 1919. As downhill skiing caught on in the 1930s, people looked closely at Summit County for its potential ski area development. After World War II, the county's first modern ski area took form at Arapahoe Basin. Trails were cut and a lift installed before the ski area opened for business in 1948. Skiing's popularity increased, and the next area, Breckenridge, opened in 1962.

With the development of ski areas and the completion of Dillon Reservoir in the early 1960s, Summit County started building its reputation as a great place to get away from it all. The 1970s saw dramatic growth with the opening of Keystone Resort and Copper Mountain Resort in 1972. When the Eisenhower Tunnel on Interstate 70 was completed in 1973, cutting the driving time from Denver by half an hour, many day visitors from along the Front Range began flocking to Summit County.

With the financial backing of major ski corporations, Summit County will undoubtedly see continued growth, evolution and development. Whatever your opinion of this change, the county will continue to be home to many of Colorado's most-visited year-round resort destinations.

Festivals and Events

In Summit County you can plan your stay around the many winter and summer events. Complete year-round listings can be obtained by contacting individual resorts or the **Summit County Chamber of Commerce** (see the Services section). Here are a few of the best.

Ullr Fest

mid-Jan. This weeklong winter carnival in Breckenridge is one of the Summit County highlights. In celebration of Ullr, the Norse god of winter, people really get into the party spirit. Snow sculptures left over from the **American International Snow Sculpture Champion-**

A fortresslike playground in Frisco creates the perfect play environment for children. Photo by Bruce Caughey.

ships (the week preceding Ullr Fest) now in Riverwalk Center only. The infamous Ullr parade, bonfire and dance can get very rowdy. For more information call **970-453-2913; www. gobreck.com.**

Heeney Tick Festival

mid-June This bizarre festival got its start in 1981 when a Heeney local recovered from a bout with tick fever. Friends decided this called for some sort of celebration. The first year's festivities consisted of miniature floats on a table. Big deal. But the celebration has expanded into a parade (about 10 minutes), a dance, food booths and the crowning of the annual Tick King and Queen. If you have nothing else to do, join in on this unique celebration of summer's arrival to the high country. Located 23 miles north of Silverthorne on County Rd. 30 off Hwy. 9 at Green Mountain Reservoir. Contact Debbie and Dale at the Melody Lodge for information; **970-468-8497.**

Breckenridge Festival of Music

late June through mid-Aug. This standout music festival attracts professional classical musicians from around the country who participate in workshops and performances. The highly acclaimed National Repertory Orchestra has joined the event, a move sure to attract even more visitors. Music lovers can purchase tickets for two orchestras, four string quartets, a brass quintet, woodwind quartet and vocal quartet. Other events include workshops, camps and other programs. Some events are free. **970-453-2120.**

No Man's Land Celebration

late August In the early 1930s the federal government learned that a tract of land, including Breckenridge, had accidentally been left off the map in several historic treaties. To commemorate this oversight, the town has been celebrating the "Kingdom of Breckenridge" for some 60 years. The event is highlighted by historical tours, musical performances and even ice-cream socials. **970-453-6018.**

Outdoor Activities

Biking

MOUNTAIN BIKING

Endless miles of old jeep roads and single-track trails provide anything from easy cruises to bone-jarring odysseys. The best areas to concentrate on are around Breckenridge and Montezuma. You can also ride select areas of Copper Mountain and Breckenridge ski mountains via chairlift. For a complete rundown on various trail ideas in the area, drop by the visitor centers in Frisco and Dillon or the **Dillon Ranger District Office, 680 Blue River Pkwy., Silverthorne, CO 80498; 970-468-5400;** recorded message at **970-468-5434; www.fs.fed.us/ r2/whiteriver.** Check out the *Mountain Bike Guide to Summit County,* by Laura Rossetter.

Argentine Pass

For the ultimate mountain bike challenge, consider a frightening trip over 13,207-foot Argentine Pass. Back in the 1800s a toll road crossed over Argentine Pass, connecting the Summit County area with Georgetown. The road has deteriorated since then and is only 2 feet wide in spots. As a local biker put it, "One false move and you're hamburger." From Keystone head up Montezuma Rd. about 3 miles and look for the Peru Gulch trailhead on your left. Park here and begin your ride up the trail, which gets increasingly steep and hazardous. From the summit of Argentine Pass, make your way northeast down to the ruins of Waldorf, an old ghost town (see the **Georgetown and Idaho Springs** chapter). From here the road takes you down to Guanella Pass Rd. and into Georgetown; a shuttle is necessary to get back. Before attempting this trail, consult with the Forest Service at the **Dillon Ranger District Office** in Silverthorne. Be sure to carry good maps and supplies. Good luck.

Boreas Pass Road

This moderate 10-mile ride makes its way to the summit of Boreas Pass from Breckenridge. You may continue down the other side of the pass to the town of Como. In summer car traffic gets heavy. Ride in the morning or early evening to avoid traffic. For a description and directions, see the Cross-Country Skiing and Snowshoeing section.

Deer Creek/Webster Pass Loop

This difficult 15-mile trail takes you to the Continental Divide, with views of the Tenmile and Gore Ranges, Grays and Torreys Peaks and sprawling South Park. In midsummer the tundra wildflowers are blooming above 12,000 feet. The trail possibilities in this area are limitless. Get maps and advice at the **Dillon Ranger District Office.** From Keystone, drive southeast on Montezuma Rd. 2.5 miles past the town of Montezuma. Deer Creek Rd. climbs up to the divide. From here head east over to Radical Hill and down to Webster Pass Rd., which returns to Montezuma.

Georgia Pass

Highly scenic and fairly challenging, 11,598-foot Georgia Pass crosses over the mountains southeast of Breckenridge, dropping down into South Park near Jefferson. See the Four-Wheel-Drive Trips section for details.

Peaks Trail

Intermediate riders can negotiate the uphill stretches and stream crossings required on this 9-mile ride along the Tenmile Range between Frisco and Breckenridge. From Frisco head south on the bike path along Hwy. 9 for a mile or so and turn right on Miner's Creek Rd. Proceed to Rainbow Lake and then south on the trail. You'll come out at the Breckenridge Ski Area.

Saints John

Near Saints John (an old town near Montezuma), a fantastic network of trails awaits. For information see the Saints John write-up in the Cross-Country Skiing and Snowshoeing section.

Rentals and Information

You shouldn't have any trouble finding a rental bike or trail information in Summit County.

BICYCLE TOURING

If you are planning a summer vacation in Summit County, strap your touring bike onto the car because the area is a cyclist's dream. Miles of paved bike paths connect most of the towns in Summit County, including the 10-mile **Blue River Bikeway** between Breckenridge and Frisco, the 6-mile **Tenmile Canyon Bikeway** between Frisco and Copper Mountain and the 13.5-mile **Vail Pass Bikeway** between Copper Mountain and Vail. A paved spur also connects Keystone to the rest of the trails. A *Bike the Summit Trail Map* showing the various routes in the area is available at local bike shops, visitor centers and at the **Dillon Ranger District Office.** Additional information on the bike paths can be obtained at the town halls in Breckenridge, Dillon, Silverthorne and Frisco. This is unquestionably one of the best ways to enjoy Summit County.

Boating

Dillon Reservoir

Surrounded by three mountain ranges, with 26 miles of shoreline and constantly shifting winds, this reservoir—also known as Lake Dillon—is a challenge for sailors. "If you can sail here, you can sail anyplace in the world," says Bob Evans, harbormaster at Dillon Marina. Sailors also appreciate the pristine environment and terrific views. Because the reservoir serves as a main water source for Denver, the deep, cold waters are off-limits to swimming and other immersion activities. You can, however, still head out on a charter cruise, a pontoon boat or a motorized fishing vessel if you don't want to count totally on wind power. No matter what you choose to get you around the lake, you'll amazed by the beauty of this place. Just be prepared for unpredictable afternoon winds that can be dangerous at times. Two marinas serve the boating population and provide rentals. **Dillon Marina (970-468-5100; www.dillonmarina. com)** on the northeast shore remains the best. It sponsors sailing regattas and even offers a sunset cruise with a five-course gourmet dinner. To the

Many boaters visit Dillon Reservoir, which is known for its strong, sometimes unpredictable, winds. Photo by Bruce Caughey.

west, **Frisco Bay Marina (970-668-5573)** provides services, boat rentals (including canoes) and launching ramps. On a much smaller scale, you may wish to rent a paddleboat on pretty **Keystone Lake** at the Keystone resort.

Fishing

Fishing in one of the area's lakes or streams should not be overlooked. "Hot spots" do, of course, change with the seasons, so get some current advice from the **Division of Wildlife's Northwest Region Office** in Grand Junction at **970-248-7175,** or check **www.wildlife. state.co.us.** Visitor centers in Summit County have a couple of excellent fishing brochures.

Blue River

The Blue River begins its 45-mile run through Summit County (along Hwy. 9) from Hoosier Pass just south of Breckenridge. A number of small tributaries converge, and by the time the Upper Blue River reaches Breckenridge, the fishing can be pretty good. Downstream from Breckenridge the river runs through an area that was dredged during the mining days, leaving large piles of river rock along the banks. You may try early in the season for rainbows and in the fall for browns and brookies. This section (3 miles north of Breckenridge down to Dillon Reservoir) is closed to fishing Oct. 1–Jan. 31. Below Dillon Reservoir the **Lower Blue River** is designated Gold Medal water; catch-and-release only. Many curse this stretch of the river, complaining that the fish are too hard to catch for it to be designated Gold Medal. There are five designated parking areas along Hwy. 9 as the river moves toward Green Mountain Reservoir. Try to fish the stretches that are as far away as possible from the road. Depending on the hatch, locals have had luck with No. 14 and No. 16 elk hair caddis imitations.

Dillon Reservoir

Dillon Reservoir is the focal point of Summit County, and many seem content to look no farther for fishing. Casting from the 26-mile shore is not quite as effective as fishing from a boat, but it can be worthwhile. There are boat launching ramps at **Frisco Bay, Frisco Marina, Dillon Marina, Blue River Inlet** and **Pine Cove Campground.** Both the **Frisco Marina** and the **Dillon Marina** rent boats. Try fishing just as the ice recedes from the reservoir and after the lake has been stocked with small kokanee salmon and cutthroat and brook trout. Also, some 4- and 5-pounders have been reeled in at this time. A few hog-sized brown trout cruise the waters during the autumn spawn but are hard to catch. Trolling slowly with a Kastmaster lure has been quite alluring to many species, but, of course, the time-tested worm will also do the trick.

Green Mountain Reservoir

Although its waters yield many good-sized trout, Green Mountain Reservoir is best known for its excellent kokanee salmon. Among the biggest in the state, the kokanee weigh 2 pounds and up; snagging is permitted Sept. 1–Dec. 31. The water level at Green Mountain Reservoir fluctuates greatly throughout the summer. Boat ramps are located at the south end of the reservoir and at the town of Heeney. Ice fishing is popular in winter. Located 23 miles north of Silverthorne on Hwy. 9.

Mountain Lakes

Dozens of lakes in Summit County offer good fishing. Some lie beside major thoroughfares, while others require a vigorous hike. **Mohawk Lakes** can be reached by heading west on Spruce Creek Rd., 5 miles south of Breckenridge on Hwy. 9. Drive up Spruce Creek Rd. about 3 miles and walk up to the three lakes (about 1 mile to the first lake and another mile to the others). You'll need a high-clearance vehicle to reach the Mohawk Lakes trailhead. Fairly sizable cutthroat inhabit these lakes. **Officer's Gulch Pond,** located just off Interstate 70, 4 miles west of Frisco, is stocked with rainbow and brook trout. In the Eagles Nest Wilderness, **Salmon Lake** and **Willow Lakes** are 6- and 7-mile hikes, respectively. Although they are a bit hard to reach, the fishing can be quite good. Ten-inch cutthroat are the common catch with lures

and flies. The trailhead begins up in Wildernest, just west of Silverthorne. See the Willow Lakes write-up in the Hiking and Backpacking section.

Four-Wheel-Drive Trips

Old wagon roads connecting the many mining settlements in Summit County provide great four-wheeling along with spectacular backcountry scenery. No fewer than 11 major roads were built over high mountain passes in the area and many are open for jeepers today. Be sure to stay on the designated jeep roads, especially in the fragile high alpine tundra. Also, don't attempt to cross the Continental Divide roads until at least June, when the snow has had a chance to melt. For other trip ideas contact the **Dillon Ranger District Office, 680 Blue River Pkwy., Silverthorne, CO 80498; 970-468-5400; www.fs.fed.us/r2/whiteriver.**

Georgia Pass

This original wagon road connects the Breckenridge mining district with South Park. At 11,598 feet, Georgia Pass presents great views of the Tenmile Range, Grays and Torreys Peaks and South Park. To reach the pass road from Breckenridge, drive 4 miles north on Hwy. 9 to Tiger Rd. and turn right. Follow the road along Swan River past North Fork Rd. and keep bearing right. Follow the south fork of the river. You will pass through the remains of **Parkville,** which was the county seat back in the early mining days. One night some residents of Breckenridge snuck into the county hall and stole the county records. Possession being nine-tenths of the law, the county seat was moved to Breckenridge.

The road meanders along the South Fork of the Swan River, eventually leading to the summit of Georgia Pass. From the pass it descends down into South Park along Michigan Creek, eventually reaching Hwy. 285 at the town of **Jefferson.** From Jefferson you can return to Breckenridge via Boreas Pass or Hoosier Pass (Hwy. 9).

Webster Pass

This vintage 1880s wagon road links the Montezuma mining district with the Eastern Slope of the Continental Divide. The road begins just above the town of **Montezuma** and heads up 4 fairly easy miles to the pass at 12,108 feet. From the pass the steep and extremely tricky road descends the eastern side down Handcart Gulch into **Hall Valley** (see the Four-Wheel-Drive Trips section of the **South Park and 285 Corridor** chapter). To get to this road from Keystone, drive southeast on Montezuma Rd. through the town of Montezuma; it begins about 2.5 miles above the town.

Tours and Information

Tiger Run 4x4 Tours—Tiger Run Resort offers rather pricey guided tours from 2 to 4 hours in length. Snowmobile tours in winter. Office located in Breckenridge at **0056 County Rd. 450; 970-453-2231; www.tigerrun tours.com.**

Golf

Breckenridge Golf Club

This 18-hole course, designed by Jack Nicklaus, is laid out following the natural contours and terrain of its surroundings. Recent additions are 9 new holes and a new clubhouse. The course plays through forests, valleys, mountainsides, streams and even beaver ponds. Tee times should be made at least two days in advance. Located just east of Hwy. 9 on Tiger Rd. at **200 Clubhouse Dr., P.O. Box 168, Brecken-ridge, CO 80424; 970-453-9104; www.golf colorado.com/breckenridge.**

Copper Creek Golf Course

At 9,650 feet this championship 18-hole course boasts the highest altitude of any PGA course in the country. Designed by Perry Dye, the course features great views of the Tenmile Range to the east. Dye's trademark railroad ties bulkhead the tees, lakes and greens. Holes play near the ski mountain and along Tenmile Creek. Copper Mountain Resort guests get a break on the greens fees. **104 Wheeler Pl., Copper Mountain, CO 80443; 970-968-2339; www. ski-copper.com.**

Keystone Ranch Golf Club

This outstanding Robert Trent Jones Jr. course offers a wide range of terrain and spectacular views. The front 9 plays through trees; holes 4 through 8 are patterned after old Scottish courses with lots of sagebrush and streams. The back 9 is very open, with water hazards and few trees. The 60-year-old clubhouse (the old ranch house) is a beautiful facility with a fine pro shop and restaurant. Carts are required. Resort guests are strongly encouraged to reserve tee times at least four days in advance; space-avail-able-only for nonguests. The course opens at the end of May. Guests pay reduced greens fees. You might also want to try a round on the challeng-ing new **River Course** at Keystone, which opened in the summer of 2000. The 18-hole course winds around the Snake River, offering impressive views of the Continental Divide and the Gore Range. Native plant species are incor-porated in the design. Yes, greens fees are steep, depending on the season. Both courses are located at Keystone Ranch, near Keystone Resort, at **1437 Summit County Rd. 150, Box 38, Keystone, CO 80435; 970-468-4250; www.keystoneresort.com.**

Raven Golf Club

After a major multi-year development and ren-ovation, this challenging 18-hole course remains a major golf challenge. It has a lot of hills, doglegs and narrow fairways. Set back from the Blue River Valley, it offers incredible views of the valley and the Gore Range. Greens fees tend to be lower before the end of May. Don't miss having a libation at the swanky new $12 million clubhouse. Located in Silverthorne, 2 miles north on Hwy. 9 from the Silverthorne exit on Interstate 70. **2929 Golden Eagle Rd., P.O. Box 25420, Silverthorne, CO 80498; 970-970-262-3636; www.ravengolf.com.**

Hiking and Backpacking

It's hard to justify going to Summit County in summer without getting onto one of the numer-ous trails into the backcountry. Plenty of trails, for the novice and experienced backpacker

Golfing at the base of Copper Mountain with far-reaching mountain vistas. Photo by Bruce Caughey.

alike, extend into the White River National Forest, offering spectacular hiking through pine and aspen forests, fields of wildflowers and high alpine basins. To the west of Silverthorne, the Eagles Nest Wilderness straddles the lofty Gore Range, providing a quick escape from the crowds and condos of the resorts. Residents of the county are quick to share some of their favorite hiking trails. Stop in at the **Dillon Ranger District Office, 680 Blue River Pkwy., Silverthorne, CO 80498; 970-468-5400; www.fs.fed.us/r2/whiteriver.** You might want to pick up a copy of Mary Ellen Gilliland's *The Summit Hiker,* an excellent book containing historical details and precise directions for dozens of area hiking trails.

Argentine Pass

In 1869 workers finally finished the dangerous wagon road over 13,207-foot Argentine Pass. Many lives had been lost in the process, but the much-needed link between the mines in Peru Gulch and Georgetown was complete. This 2.3-mile hike to the summit is difficult but worth the effort. The first part is very steep, but the trail eventually mellows into a steady pitch. The rocky scree and talus slopes require sturdy hiking boots. From the summit on the Continental Divide you'll have views as far west as the Sawatch Range and east to Georgetown and Mt. Evans. To reach the trailhead from Keystone, drive 4.6 miles southeast on Montezuma Rd. and turn left onto Peru Creek Rd. Continue about 5 miles and park at the Shoe Basin Mine building on the right. Hike up the trail a third of a mile to the Argentine Pass trailhead.

Masontown Trail

This easy 1.4-mile hike (one way) is great for the whole family. It starts near Frisco and climbs up the lower reaches of Mt. Royal. Along the trail many old mining sites scar the forested slopes. Views of the Blue River Valley and Dillon Reservoir are superb. The trail ends at the battered remains of the old mining camp of Masontown. Local legend has it that on New Year's Eve, just after the turn of the century, Masontown residents were down in Frisco whooping it up when an avalanche roared down the mountain, completely demolishing their small settlement. Reach the trailhead from the west end of Main St. in Frisco (near Interstate 70), head east into Frisco and find a place to park on the right. Cross the footbridge over Tenmile Creek and turn left onto the paved bike path. After a half-mile hike you'll see the Mt. Royal/Masontown trailhead on the right.

Mohawk Lakes

This fine 2.8-mile day hike takes you past Mayflower Lakes and beyond to Lower and Upper Mohawk Lakes at 12,100 feet. Mining ruins abound. At Lower Mohawk Lake an old mill site still stands, with an aerial tram leading up the mountain above. Be sure to look for Continental Falls to the north above the old mill. Views from the lakes are spectacular. To reach the trailhead from Breckenridge, drive south on Hwy. 9 for 2.4 miles and turn right into "The Crown" subdivision and then left onto Spruce Creek Rd. Drive 1.2 miles up to the trailhead. There is another trailhead 1.6 miles farther up the road that cuts the hike down to 1.2 miles, but you need a high-clearance vehicle.

Monte Cristo Gulch/Blue Lakes

Although we suggest hiking through this steep-walled, mining-rich valley, you can cheat and drive almost all the way to the reservoir between Upper and Lower Blue Lakes. On the north side of the valley rises Quandary Peak (14,264 feet). The steep mountainsides are marked with remains of mine shafts and cabins built into seemingly vertical rock walls. It's a wonder the miners were able to get to the sites. For a short 1.1-mile hike, drive along the left fork in the road below the lower lake and park your car. Begin hiking along the trail on the south side of the lake, past a few old mining buildings (now inhabited), including the enormous Arctic Mine. With its five tunnels, tram and stamp mill, the Arctic was one of the biggest gold producers in the area and operated until 1936. The trail follows the lakeshore and ends up at a cascading waterfall just below the upper lake. To reach this valley from Breckenridge, drive south on Hwy. 9 for 7.5 miles and turn

right onto Blue Lakes Rd. Drive 2.2 miles to the lower lake.

Mounts Lincoln, Democrat and Bross

This hike is probably the only one in Colorado in which you can realistically climb three 14,000-foot peaks in one day. Located just south of Breckenridge over Hoosier Pass. For information see the Hiking and Backpacking section of the **South Park and 285 Corridor** chapter.

Quandary Peak

Located near Breckenridge, Quandary Peak (14,264 feet) is one of the most accessible 14,000-foot peaks in the state. Mining was undertaken all over the mountain and many remnants are still visible, even near the summit. A couple of routes can be taken up the mountain, but the easiest is along the wide east ridge. From this approach, the last half-mile or so is a fairly steep rock scramble. Enjoy views from the summit to the Blue River Valley, South Park and Grays and Torreys Peaks. To reach the trail from Breckenridge, head south on Hwy. 9 for 7.5 miles and turn right (west) on Blue Lakes Rd. Drive about a third of a mile and look for a dirt road on the right. Park and begin hiking west and then north for about half a mile, and then head left on a trail that climbs up the east ridge for 2.5 miles to the summit.

Ski Areas—Chairlifts to the Top

For those unaccustomed to the high altitude of Summit County, even a short hike can take your breath away. Breckenridge, Copper Mountain and Keystone ski areas offer chairlift rides in summer. Once at the top of the lift you have a number of options: hike up even farther, hike down to the bottom or enjoy a peaceful lunch and ride the lift back down. At Breckenridge the lift is open late June–early Sept. 10:30 A.M.–3:30 P.M. daily. Tickets can be purchased at the base of Peak 8. From town head west at the traffic light and up Ski Hill Rd. to the base of Peak 8. At Copper Mountain, E and American Eagle lifts are open daily 10 A.M.–3 P.M. July–Labor Day, and on fall weekends only. No fee. The gondola at Keystone is open daily throughout the summer 9 A.M.–3 P.M. A small fee is charged.

Willow Lakes

Located high in the Eagles Nest Wilderness, Willow Lakes can be a beautiful overnight getaway, but can get quite crowded on weekends and holidays. The 8.5-mile trail leads to a series of four lakes at about 11,400 feet. There is camping at the lakes, and fishing for small cutthroat can be good. The trail begins at Mesa Cortina above Silverthorne and climbs up through dense forests of lodgepole pine. Wildlife is plentiful up here; the last time we hiked this trail we saw a bear paw print. Above the lakes is a very steep, rocky trail to a saddle high in the Gore Range that offers fantastic views over into the Vail area. Firewood is limited, so packing a stove is a good idea. To reach the trailhead from Silverthorne, turn left off Hwy. 9 onto Wildernest Rd. (across from Wendy's). Go a short distance to a fork, turn right and then immediately left onto Royal Buffalo Dr. (No. 1240). Drive less than a mile and turn right onto Lakeview Dr. (No. 1245). Proceed to the fork with Aspen Dr. and turn left, negotiating the curve to the trailhead parking area. The trailhead is marked Mesa Cortina.

Horseback Riding

If you want to ride a horse in Summit County, find out where rides are offered away from developed areas. You might try **Bar T Outfitters,** in Silverthorne, **970-468-6916,** with hourly, half-day and full-day rides as well as overnight pack trips. Try a winter ride, too. Or check out **Breckenridge Stables** for a 90-minute ride on the Breckenridge Trail or a Sunrise Cowboy Breakfast ride; **970-453-4438.**

Ice Skating

In winter **Keystone Lake,** in the middle of Keystone Village, is transformed into one of the largest outdoor, groomed skating rinks in the country. Lace up a pair of rental skates and give it a try; lessons also available. A small fee is charged for use of the rink. If you prefer the passive approach, sit at one of the nearby cafes and watch the action. Open 10 A.M.–10 P.M. daily; **970-468-2316.** You can also check out **Breckenridge's** new $5 million indoor and outdoor **ice rinks, on Boreas Pass Rd.,** 100 yards off Main St. The rinks offer year-round training opportunities, rentals, open skating and recreational hockey time for those needing to cool off; fee charged. In winter you can also try the great outdoors at **Maggie Pond,** south of the Village at Breckenridge. Open from 8 A.M. to 10 P.M. Rental skates; small fee.

River Floating

Blue River

Below Dillon Reservoir (Lake Dillon), the Blue River snakes its way 38 miles north, where it dumps into the Colorado River near Kremmling. The Blue River is not particularly well known to river floaters; Green Mountain Reservoir limits the navigable stretches, and the floating season is very short. The nearby stretches of the **Upper Colorado River** and the **Upper Arkansas River** are worth serious consideration as well. For detailed information about the Arkansas River, see the **Upper Arkansas Valley** chapter.

Consider contacting **The Adventure Company,** in Breckenridge at **1-800-497-RAFT** or **970-453-0747,** and **American Adventure Expeditions,** near Buena Vista at **1-800-288-0675.**

Skiing

CROSS-COUNTRY SKIING AND SNOWSHOEING

In addition to four nordic centers, limitless trails entice you into the backcountry. To get out on a backcountry trail, obtain information from the **Dillon Ranger District Office, 680 Blue River Pkwy., Silverthorne, CO 80498; 970-468-5400;** recorded message at **970-468-5434; www.fs.fed.us/r2/whiteriver.** You should also seriously consider calling the **avalanche information** number for Summit County, which is updated twice daily at **970-668-0600.**

Backcountry Trails

Boreas Pass—Beginning just south of Breckenridge, the trail up Boreas Pass follows the old Denver South Park & Pacific Railroad bed, which connected Breckenridge to the outside world back in the mining days. Views of the Tenmile Range from points along the trail are superb. The fairly easy trail follows Boreas Pass Rd. 3.5 miles up to Baker's Tank, which stored water for railroad locomotives from 1882 to 1937. This is a great place for lunch. Ambitious skiers can continue up the trail another 3.5 miles to the summit of the pass. A settlement on the pass back in the late 1800s included the highest post office in the country. To reach the trailhead from Breckenridge, drive south on Hwy. 9 just past the Breckenridge Inn, then turn left and proceed about 3.5 miles to the end of the plowed road (Forest Rd. 223).

Peru Gulch Trail—Beautiful high alpine views and old mining ruins highlight a trip up heavily used Peru Gulch Trail. It starts out as fairly easy terrain for the first 2 miles and then gradually climbs more steeply for 4 miles to the Pennsylvania Mine. Some skiers continue up from here through the ruins of the ghost town of Decatur and up into Horseshoe Basin, with views to Grays Peak (14,270 feet) and Argentine Pass. The avalanche danger can be high at the upper end of the valley. To reach the trailhead from Keystone, head east 4.6 miles on Montezuma Rd. and look for the trailhead and parking lot on the left.

Quandary Peak—Though the peak is extremely avalanche-prone during the winter, springtime turns the eastern basin of this 14,000-foot peak into a telemarker's dream. For information see the Hiking and Backpacking section.

Saints John Trail—Named for two saints, John the Baptist and John the Evangelist, Saints John is the locale of one of the first major silver discoveries in the Colorado Territory. In 1864 John Coley rigged up a primitive smelter, which was later replaced by a state-of-the-art version made with bricks imported from Wales. The townspeople of Saints John boasted that they had no bars (unheard of for a mining town), but they did maintain a fine library with more than 300 volumes of classics.

Located within the Arapaho National Forest at 11,000 feet elevation, Saints John commands a fantastic view of Grays and Torreys Peaks (both over 14,000 feet), Glacier Mountain and a number of nearby (and active!) avalanche chutes. The valley and surrounding peaks and ridges are especially well suited to backcountry skiing. Miles of trails spread out on terrain that includes many narrow downhill stretches. An abandoned cabin at the Wild Irishman Mine, 2 miles above Saints John, is a good place to eat lunch.

To reach Saints John from Keystone, drive 7 miles southeast on Montezuma Rd. to the town of Montezuma and park just off the road, on the right. You'll see the signs and the trail (a road in summer) heading up into the pines. In summer you can drive the remaining 1.4 miles up to the old townsite of Saints John with a four-wheel-drive vehicle. In winter you'll have to ski in.

Summit Huts and Trails Association—Four cabins have been built or restored, providing a range of perfect backcountry overnight retreats with capacities ranging from 3 people at little Ken's Cabin to 20 people at Janet's Cabin. Janet's was the first completed cabin in an ambitious, long-range plan for huts throughout the county.

Located southwest of Copper Mountain at 11,618 feet, Janet's is also one of our favorites. From Interstate 70 the trail to Janet's heads 5.5 miles up Guller Gulch to 11,618 feet. The cabin comes equipped with many items, including kitchen utensils and mattresses. Janet's Cabin also connects with the extremely popular 10th Mountain Division hut system to the west (see the Skiing section of the **Aspen** chapter for details). For information about all the huts, including Janet's Cabin, Francie's Cabin, Section House and Ken's Cabin, contact **P.O. Box 2830, Breckenridge, CO 80424; 970-453-8583; www.huts.org.**

Webster Pass—See the Four-Wheel-Drive Trips section for information on this easy 4-mile trail.

Groomed Trails

Breckenridge Nordic Ski Center—More than 35 kilometers of trails are available for track skiing, skating and snowshoeing through the pines. One of the oldest of its kind in Colorado, this center provides everything you need, from rentals to lessons (individual or private). Guided skiing is available for the blind. Telemarking terrain/lessons are available only at the Breckenridge Ski Area. Open daily 9 A.M.–4 P.M. Located 1 mile west on Ski Hill Rd. from Main St. in Breckenridge. **1200 Ski Hill Rd., P.O. Box 1776, Breckenridge, CO 80424; 970-453-6855; www.breckenridge.com.**

Copper Mountain/Track Cross-Country Center—This center has a wide reputation as an excellent facility. Owned and operated by Copper Mountain Resort, it has more than 25 kilometers of machine-set tracks, skating lanes and, for more advanced cross-country skiers, rolling hills. The K lift takes skiers uphill for runs down challenging trails. A range of lessons is available, from beginning track skiing to telemarking (telemark lessons are given on the ski mountain). Clinics are offered throughout the winter on skiing techniques, waxing, snow safety and many more subjects. Moonlight tours, back-country trips and overnight trips can be arranged. Rentals available. Hours are 8:30 A.M.–3:30 P.M. daily. **P.O. Box 3001, Copper Mountain, CO 80443; 1-800-458-8386; 970-968-2882 ext. 6342; www.ski-copper.com.**

Frisco Nordic Center—In a pine forest near the shores of Dillon Reservoir (Lake Dillon), skiers can explore 35 kilometers of set trails. The center, designed by Olympic silver medalist Bill Koch, provides rentals and lessons. Open daily 9 A.M.–4 P.M. Located 2 miles south of Frisco along Hwy. 9; **P.O. Box 532, Frisco, CO 80443; 970-668-0866.**

Keystone Cross-Country Center—More than 29 kilometers of set trails provide easy skiing around Keystone Resort. The center has a nordic ski school run by Jana Hlavati, a former U.S. Olympic team member. They even teach telemark techniques at the ski area. Mountain Top Trail (intermediate/expert) can be reached via the ski area gondola for a charge. Guided full-moon tours. Open 8 A.M.–5 P.M. daily. Located 2.2 miles east of Keystone on Montezuma Rd., next to Ski Tip Lodge; **P.O. Box 38, Keystone, CO 80435; 1-800-345-4FUN; 970-468-4275; www.keystoneresort.com.**

Rentals and Information

Each nordic center has rental equipment, as do a large number of area shops.

DOWNHILL SKIING AND SNOWBOARDING

Summit County's four ski areas host over 3 million skiers each winter. More than 4,800 acres of slopes, 60 lifts and 358 trails should have the terrain you are looking for—whether it's easy ballroom skiing or steep, ungroomed mogul runs. Front Range skiers should keep in mind that Summit County ski area tickets are sold at a discount by many outlets along the Front Range, including supermarkets.

Arapahoe Basin

The top of Arapahoe Basin, perched at a lofty 13,050 feet, is the country's highest ski area summit. This allows it to stay open into June (sometimes July and Aug. depending on the snowpack) each year, much to the delight of sun-seeking, die-hard skiers. Of the four ski areas in Summit County, Arapahoe is the oldest, getting its start back in the 1940s when Max Dercum and a handful of cronies installed the first chairlift. Much of the equipment they used was army surplus, acquired from Camp Hale, near Leadville, where the 10th Mountain Division ski troops trained during World War II. Cables and pulleys were liberated from old mines.

The area has come a long way and now has more than 490 acres of skiable terrain. But it's not the best area for beginners; only 10 percent of the mountain is for novices. However, intermediate and advanced skiers love it. The Pallavicini lift services a slew of black runs on the right side of the mountain—and they are steep! Convenient shuttle bus to Keystone. Child care available. Located a few miles east of

Keystone on Hwy. 6, at the western base of Loveland Pass. **970-496-7077.**

Breckenridge Ski Area

The growth of Breckenridge, especially in the past 10 years, has been phenomenal. And the expansion should continue with the ongoing infusion of development money from its parent company, Vail Resorts. At more than 1,600 acres, Breckenridge comprises 4 interconnected mountains: Peaks 7, 8, 9 and 10. Together they offer plenty of terrain for skiers of all abilities. Peak 10 features intermediate and advanced terrain. The lower part of Peak 8 and most of Peak 9 keep beginners and intermediates happy with well-groomed runs. Advanced skiers usually head to the back bowls of Peak 8 and to the exacting double-black-diamond bump runs on the North Face of Peak 9. Runs such as Devil's Crotch and Hades are extremely challenging.

There are two main bases. The one at the bottom of Peak 9 is accessible right in town; the base at Peak 8 can be reached by a shuttle bus that runs every few minutes. Breckenridge's ample number of lifts, including several high-speed Superchairs, helps keep lift lines relatively short, even during peak season. In addition to open skiing in Imperial bowl, accessible via a half-hour hike to the top of 13,000-foot Peak 8, an additional 200 acres of bowl skiing has been opened on Peak 7. On-mountain restaurants, such as the Vistahaus on Peak 9, have spacious sundecks and spectacular views of the Blue River Valley and the towering mountains to the east. With its excellent teaching program, Breckenridge offers especially good lessons to kids. Child care available. Snowboarders should check out this mountain: the World Snowboard Championships have been held here. **970-453-5000; www.breckenridge.com.**

Copper Mountain Resort

Not only are the runs at Copper Mountain well designed, but geographically the mountain is a natural. For the most part, you'll find separate domains for beginner, intermediate and advanced skiers at the immense 2,324-acre ski

The new base development at Copper Mountain brings welcome amenities to the resort. Photo by Bruce Caughey.

resort. This provides peace of mind to skiers who don't want to accidentally end up on a run that is either too easy or too difficult. Advanced skiers stick to the left (east) side of the area, which offers challenging bump runs and bowl skiing near the top of the mountain. Runs at the Union Peak side, on the right (west) side of the area, are well-groomed intermediate and beginner terrain.

Twenty-three lifts, including a six-pack and four high-speed quads, provide quick access to the many runs. Because of its fine reputation, 2,601 vertical feet and easy access, Copper Mountain receives a lot of day skiers from the Denver area. Now, with a major new base development, you may want to book a place for the weekend instead of fighting the I-70 traffic. Ski school and day care available. With limited close-in parking, our advice is to park in the outlying lots and take the shuttle to the mountain. Located about 6 miles southwest of Frisco on

Interstate 70. **1-800-458-8386; 970-968-2882; www.ski-copper.com.**

Keystone Resort

Keystone continues to host more skiers per year than practically any other resort in Colorado. Award-winning accommodations, facilities and excellent service can take most of the credit. In addition, sophisticated snow-making machines crank up in late Sept., allowing Keystone to open in Oct., much earlier than most other areas. The area also offers night skiing on 40 percent of the runs, which keeps the slopes open for more than 12 hours a day. Keystone has long been a mountain for beginners and intermediates. The well-groomed runs provide worry-free skiing that is especially attractive for families. The holdout mountain started allowing snowboarders during the 1996–1997 season. The teaching programs are first-rate and include the Mahre Training Center. The Mahre twins (Phil and Steve), former world champions and Olympic gold and silver medalists, operate exclusively at Keystone, offering weeklong lessons.

During its early years of operation, Keystone drew the wrath of advanced skiers, frustrated with the area's lack of challenging runs. To diversify and attract more advanced and expert skiers, Keystone developed the challenging North Peak, accessible from the top of Keystone Mountain. But the best news to advanced skiers is that a number of high-speed quad lifts and two gondolas are ready to whisk you up the mountain (including the steeper terrain of North Peak). Be sure to check out the impressive 26,000-square-foot Outpost Restaurant and the demanding runs of the Outback. After a snowstorm, the Outback's advanced and expert terrain provides top-notch tree skiing. Located about 10 miles east of Dillon on Hwy 6. **970-468-2316; www.keystoneresort.com.**

Sleigh Rides

Dining in the Woods

Taking off from Union Creek at Copper Mountain, the sleigh makes its way along a torchlit trail to a tent in the woods where a down-home dinner of brisket, chicken and ribs is served. The meal changes nightly. This is a guaranteed romantic outing—that is, unless you take the kids. Open Tues.–Sun. nights; **970-968-2882; www.ski-copper.com.**

Two Below Zero Sleigh Rides

Two mule-drawn red oak sleighs depart nightly from the Frisco Nordic Center to a heated tent in the woods near Lake Dillon. Enjoy a combo of top sirloin, chicken breast and marinated shrimp kebobs with all the trimmings; vegetarian dinners are provided with advance notice. Closed Sun. **P.O. Box 845, Frisco, CO 80443; 970-453-1520.**

Seeing and Doing

Alpine Slide

On the **Super Slide** at Breckenridge you can glide down one of two tracks on Peak 8 in your specially designed sled. You control the brake lever so the ride can be as easy or as scary as you want. The sled is big enough for an adult and a small child. No. 5 chairlift takes you to the top of the track. One-ride tickets are available as well as all-day passes. To reach the lift from the stoplight in town, head west up Ski Hill Rd. for about 1.5 miles. Open daily from mid-June to Labor Day., 9 A.M.–5 P.M. **970-453-5000; www.breckenridge.com.**

Chairlift Rides

During the summer you can ride chairlifts up the mountains at Breckenridge, Copper Mountain and Keystone ski areas. See the Hiking and Backpacking section.

Mining Tours

Country Boy Mine

Just 2 miles from downtown Breckenridge, head 1,000 feet underground for a new perspective on the 110-year-old local mining industry. A tour of the mine doesn't come free, but it does come with many interesting exhibits and a chance to do some gold panning. Pull on your hard hat and a warm jacket for the tour. Open 10 A.M.–5 P.M. daily in summer; shorter winter hours. **542 French Gulch Rd., Breckenridge, CO 80424; 970-453-4405.** The **Washington Mine** can be seen with the Summit Historical Society (see the Museums section).

Museums

Frisco Historic Park

Established in 1982, Frisco Historic Park consists of seven completely restored buildings from Frisco and the surrounding area. The **Frisco Schoolhouse Museum,** the largest of these, is located on its original site. It was first used as a saloon before becoming a schoolhouse. It now houses artifacts and information about the Ute Indians, mining and Dillon Reservoir. The other buildings include private residences and the old Frisco jail. Open Tues.–Sat. 11 A.M.–4 P.M. in winter; open through Sun. in summer. No fee. **120 Main St., Frisco; 970-668-3428.**

Summit Historical Society Tours

The Summit Historical Society, through local funding, has been able to restore a number of interesting sites around the county. Both self-guided tours and tours with a knowledgeable guide are available. For information: **970-453-9022 or www.summithistorical.org.** Here are a couple of the more interesting tours.

Washington Mine, near Breckenridge, operated from 1880 to 1973. Visitors are led into the horizontal shaft with miner's candles. Many artifacts are on display to help you gain a better understanding of gold and silver mining in Colorado. Tours begin June 1 and run through the summer, Mon.–Sat. at 1 P.M.; small fee. **Breckenridge Briggle House** is a fine Victorian home built in 1896. Its main attraction is an art collection that includes "hair" art. This unusual medium features small bobbles, made from women's hair, which were popular accessories in the Victorian era. The Briggle House

tour, along with stops at the 1880 **Alice G. Milne House** and the 1875 **Edwin Carter Museum,** are offered Wed.– Sat. at 10 A.M.; small fee.

Nightlife

Narrowing down the long list of nightlife options in Summit County is no easy task. Because it contains the largest collection of winter resorts in the country, Summit County offers an abundance of après-ski spots where people dance to live music into the wee hours. You can easily pick a new place (or three or four for that matter) during each night of your vacation. Briefly, here are the highlights:

Breckenridge

For après ski many people converge on the Village area, and the margaritas at **Mi Casa (600 Park Pl., 970-453-2071),** offering happy hour every day 3–6 P.M. The massive outdoor porch is ideally suited for a post-skiing margarita bonanza. For country dancing, pool playing and generally wild times, stop by the second-floor **Salt Creek Saloon (110 E. Lincoln St., 970-453-4949).** How about live theater? The **Backstage Theater (Pond Level at the Village at Breckenridge, 970-453-0199)** gives evening performances in winter and summer. Call for reservations. Beer lovers should try **Downstairs at Eric's (111 S. Main St., 970-453-1401),** where you'll find an incredibly large variety of beer on tap, including their excellent house brew. Last time we visited, an inebriated gentleman kept ramming his Ford Explorer into an occupied PortaPotty across the street! If you're looking for a loud, smoky place to soak up a Broncos game, this is it. Another great stop is the **Breckenridge Brewery and Pub (600 S. Main St., 970-453-1550).** They provide fresh beer and a lively après-ski and nightlife scene with great views to the ski mountain (see the Where to Eat section).

Copper Mountain

Après ski kicks into high gear at the newly built **Molly B's Rocky Mountain Tavern (in the**

East Village, 970-968-2318), with what seems to be the longest bar in this hemisphere. It's a great scene with a roaring fire and frequent live music. The bar stays open until midnight. **Farley's (970-968-2577, in the East Village at the Mountain Plaza)** provides a more soothing atmosphere with many drink specialties. In the West Village, near the American Eagle lift, stop in at **Endos (970-968-2318)** for wild times with a younger crowd, including an occasional frozen T-shirt contest.

Dillon

While the faux-profane Dam-everything paraphenalia gets a little old at the **Dillon Dam Brewery and Restaurant,** the eight brews crafted on the premises are something else. Try their beer sampler platters for a taste of what's inside the giant on-premises brew kettles. Particularly worthwhile is Brewmaster Matt Luhr's Slowpitch Pilsner. The restaurant part of the Brewery provides some eclectic selections, from a Greek quesadilla to a truly magnificent salmon chowder. Open 11:30 A.M.–10:30 P.M. **100 Little Dam Rd.; 970-262-7777.**

Frisco

At **208 Main St., Moose Jaw, 970-668-3931,** offers cheap beer, burgers and a game of pool. This has been the local favorite for years.

Keystone

The **Snake River Saloon** offers good dining, and the rowdy bar scene in the next room often features great live rock music late into the night. **23074 Hwy. 6; 970-468-2788.** The **Goat-Soup and Whisky** offered no soup while we visited but did serve as an ideal place to swill on some severely cheap drinks while playing foosball, pool and a Pinball Wizard game and munching on some affordable "goat wings" (bar menu 4–10 P.M.)—and catching some live music, too. In Keystone **just off Hwy. 6; 970-513-9344.**

Silverthorne

The **Old Dillon Inn** was an institution in Summit County even before it was moved from the old townsite of Dillon, which was flooded by the reservoir in 1962. Both the restaurant (Mexican food) and bar pack people in for live music, cervezas and margaritas. If you don't mind crowds, give it a try. **311 Blue River Pkwy. (Hwy. 9); 970-468-2791.**

Scenic Drives

Boreas Pass/Hoosier Pass

From the comfort of your Chrysler or Ford, cross two of the most historic passes in the area, which were barely navigable by mule just over a century ago. Boreas Pass Rd. (Forest Rd. 223) begins at the south end of Breckenridge and heads southeast along the old (1882) Denver South Park & Pacific Railroad bed. The grade was so steep that the engine could pull only three cars at a time. One story has it that P. T. Barnum's circus train was on its way to Breckenridge when it started to stall. The elephants were let out of the cars and helped push the train to the summit. Historic sights along the way include Baker's Tank (a restored water tank) and the remains of a settlement on the 11,482-foot summit. When it was built, this line of train track was the highest in the country. Enjoy the spectacular panorama of the Tenmile Range along the route.

From the summit of the pass (10 miles from Breckenridge), continue down the other side of the Continental Divide and take in the views of the wide expanse of South Park. After about 13 miles you'll reach the old town of Como (see the **South Park and 285 Corridor** chapter). From Como turn right on Hwy. 285 and head to Fairplay, then take another right onto Hwy. 9. The road almost immediately begins climbing northward to the 11,541-foot summit of Hoosier Pass. Homesick prospectors from Indiana gave the pass its name around 1860. From the summit return to Breckenridge, about 10 miles north.

Loveland Pass

It wasn't too many years ago that every motorist driving between Denver and Summit County had to ascend the skyscraping Loveland Pass. Since completion of the Eisenhower Tunnel in 1973, people have forgotten how beautiful the views are from the 11,992-foot summit of the pass. Granted, the drive takes longer, but at the summit you can get out and walk along ridges of the Continental Divide. Views to both sides are spectacular. Visitors who want to see alpine tundra without having to walk up to it should make this drive. To reach Loveland Pass from Keystone, head east on Hwy. 6 past Arapahoe Basin Ski Area and follow the switchbacks to the summit. Either return the same way or descend the east side of the pass and return via Interstate 70 through the Eisenhower Tunnel.

Shopping

While you are walking the quaint streets of Breckenridge, alluring shops try to get you inside with tempting window displays. The shopping ranges from high-end galleries to bookstores to the inevitable T-shirt shops. Frisco also features a shopping district along its main drag.

Prime Outlets at Silverthorne

One of the biggest anomalies in Summit County has been the Silverthorne development of three shopping malls full of well-known retail brands at reduced prices. For those who can't get shopping out of their system (even with all of the beautiful distractions), these factory stores are a welcome respite from the premium prices commanded at the nearby resorts. Over 70 stores; open daily. Located just off of Interstate 70 in Silverthorne at **145 M Stephens Way; 970-468-9440.**

Where to Stay

Accommodations

With distinct personalities, we have divided out excellent lodging options at each destination. If you're just not sure where to begin, you may want to contact **Summit County Central Reservations: 1-800-365-6365; www.skier**

In-line skaters and bikers enjoy the new concrete terrain park in Silverthorne. Photo by Bruce Caughey.

lodging.com. For a look at about 20 smallish inns spread around the county, you can also contact **Summit County Bed and Breakfast, www.summitcountybnbs.com.**

IN BRECKENRIDGE

The majority of Breckenridge accommodations are deluxe lodges and condominium rentals. At the base of Peak 9 the magnificent **Breckenridge Hilton, Beaver Run Resort** and the **Village at Breckenridge** all offer modern, luxurious rooms right at the ski mountain. Contact **Breckenridge Central Reservations: 1-800-221-1091; 1-800-800-BREC; www.gobreck.com.**

A number of excellent bed and breakfasts have opened in and around Breckenridge over the past couple years. For a truly memorable night, try **Muggin's Gulch Inn ($$$ to $$$$),** a sensational place built with massive post and beam construction, with lots of knickknacks on display. It lies a few miles out of town on 160 acres surrounded by national forest land, at **4023 Tiger Rd., P.O. Box 3756, Breckenridge, CO 80424; 970-453-7414; www.mugginsgulch.com.** Another excellent choice in a convenient location is the Bavarian-style **Hunt Placer Inn ($$$$).** They describe it as "comfortable elegance" and we'd have to agree that their eight rooms (three with fireplaces) featuring private baths and balconies fit the bill. **275 Ski Hill Rd., P.O. Box 4898, Breckenridge, CO 80424; 970-453-7573; www.huntplacerinn.com.** The most elegant and expensive of the newer B&Bs has to be the **Little Mountain Lodge ($$$$).** The lodge features expansive common areas and unique rooms designed with an eye for detail in addition to private baths and decks. Take your shoes off and enjoy your surroundings. **98 Sunbeam Dr., P.O. Box 2479, Breckenridge, CO 80424; 970-453-1969; www.littlemountainlodge.com.**

Allaire Timbers Inn—$$$ to $$$$

It's difficult to find anything not to like at this luxury bed and breakfast inn. Built in 1991 by innkeepers Jack and Kathy Gumph in a wooded location at the south end of Breckenridge, the Allaire is an attractive wood-and-stone structure, offering 10 guest rooms, each with a private bath and balcony. Named after Colorado mountain passes, each room has a creatively expressed theme. For a special occasion, consider staying in one of the two deluxe suites, which include their own fireplace and hot tub. Guests spend a lot of their time in the enormous common room where they enjoy a crackling fire, afternoon treats and a full breakfast each morning. Take in the view of the Tenmile Range from the whirlpool bath on the large deck. No smoking. **9511 Hwy. 9, P.O. Box 4653, Breckenridge, CO 80424; 1-800-624-4904; 970-453-7530; www.allairetimbers.com.**

The Lodge at Breckenridge—$$$ to $$$$

If you have the financial wherewithal, a stay at the Lodge at Breckenridge is recommended for one simple reason—the superb views.

Unbelievable views, actually. Large picture windows in most of the 45 rooms and suites look out to the Breckenridge ski area and the Tenmile Range, Hoosier Pass or Mt. Baldy. The renovated rooms provide spacious, attractive western decor with comfortable furniture. Some of the rooms have a sunken bedroom area and a small kitchen. After a long day of exploring, hiking or skiing, pay a visit to the indoor pool, whirlpool bath or weight room; facials, body treatments and massages are available for an extra charge at the spa. Breakfast (at a reduced rate for guests) and dinner **($$$ to $$$$)** are served at the **Top of the World** restaurant. Package deals available. When reserving, be sure to ask for a room with a view. Located 2 miles up Boreas Pass Rd. from the south end of town. **112 Overlook Dr., P.O. Box 391, Breckenridge, CO 80424; 1-800-736-1607; 970-453-9300; www.thelodgeatbreck.com.**

Bed and Breakfasts on Main St.—$$ to $$$

Here, in the heart of Breckenridge, you can choose from three different styles of accommodations. Choose the recently built **"Barn"** on the banks of the Blue River, with its spacious, high-ceilinged rooms, phones, TVs and gas fireplaces. Go to the front of the property and you'll find **The Williams House** (1885), a small mining-era home filled with antiques. The five guest rooms in the Williams House, each with private bath, are smallish but tasteful. Enjoy relaxing in the Victorian front parlor and the more casual sunroom, which provides a view to Peaks 7 and 8. Then be sure to check out the adjacent **Willoughby Cottage** (built in 1880 and perfect for a romantic retreat), which was completely gutted and restored by owners Diane Jaynes and Fred Kinat. Three rooms include a sitting area, fireplace, whirlpool bath, enclosed TV/VCR and antique furniture; there is a minimum stay requirement. Full breakfast for all guests is served in the Barn; it includes fresh-ground coffee, homemade bread and an entrée that varies daily. The owners' personal touches, in-depth knowledge of the area and warm hospitality are reasons for staying here—connoisseurs of bed and breakfasts will enjoy this place. **303 N. Main St., P.O. Box 2454, Breckenridge, CO 80424; 1-800-795-2975; 970-453-2975; www.breckenridge-inn.com.**

Fireside Inn—$ to $$$$

Originally built in 1879, this home has been added on to over the years, resulting in an eclectic and very popular inn. Rates vary quite a bit among the four private rooms with baths and five dorm rooms, which constitute some of the least expensive lodging in town. The owners have spiffed up the private rooms with antiques, including brass beds. The Brandywine Suite is the finest, with one queen bed and a trundle bed. There used to be a decanter of fine brandy in the room, but it was removed after the maid kept getting bombed while cleaning! At day's end guests tend to collect downstairs for conversation around the fireplace or, quite often, in the hot tub. Continental breakfast comes with the room rate in summer. **114 N. French St., P.O. Box 2252, Breckenridge, CO 80424; 970-453-6456; www.firesideinn.com.**

IN COPPER MOUNTAIN

Accommodations in Copper Mountain have shifted dramatically with a massive new base area development. For years, Copper's hodge-podge of scattered amenities has never quite matched the wonderful skiing. But now, a thoughtful approach and a huge infusion of cash have helped a superb village area with a major shift in lodging and amenities. You'll find shops, restaurants, bars, open plazas (one with a climbing wall) and The Beach, a gathering place right at the base of the ski mountain. Take your pick from many primarily first-class lodge rooms and condominiums. Descriptions and prices can be obtained at **1-800-458-8386** or **www.ski-copper.com.**

Club Med—$$$$

This was the first Club Med in North America. Offering "the antidote to civilization," this glitzy international resort provides weeklong vacation packages that include lodging in their lavish hotel, dining, cabaret entertainment and all the skiing you want. Club Med at Copper Mountain is not strictly for swinging singles—programs for kids are provided. Open during winter only. **50 Becker Pl., Copper Mountain, CO 80443; 1-800-CLUB-MED; 970-968-2161; www.clubmed.com.**

IN FRISCO

With its location alongside Interstate 70, Frisco has quite a number of motel chains to choose from. In addition, condominiums and private homes can be rented. Call the **Lake Dillon Resort Association: 1-800-365-6365; 970-468-6222.**

Creekside Inn—$$$ to $$$$

Most newly constructed B&Bs don't make it into our book for a couple of reasons: (1) who knows if they'll be here next year, and (2) new construction often doesn't have a unique charm or appeal. But we bet you'll be pleased with this contemporary inn, and with the new owners, who have traveled the world and filled the place with interesting treasures. Its functionality reveals itself underneath the charm of the furnishings; each of the seven rooms features a private bath. The massive rock fireplace and large windows with mountain views make it easy to meet other guests in the common areas. At the edge of the backyard the soothing sounds of Tenmile Creek will put you to sleep, especially after a stint in the outdoor hot tub. Full breakfast served with hot entrée, fresh fruit and baked goods. **51 W. Main St., P.O. Box 4835, Frisco, CO 80443; 1-800-668-7320; 970-668-5607; www.creeksideinn-frisco.com.**

Galena Street Mountain Inn—$$$ to $$$$

Located just off Main St. in Frisco, this inn provides comfortable accommodations in 15 spacious rooms. Each room comes complete with a private bathroom and cable TV; the Mission-style furniture, attractive decor and down comforters are the same in each room. For a special occasion, the Tower Room is worth remembering with its turret and large windows.

Two common rooms (one with a large selection of books) and a refreshment bar are available to guests, as are the hot tub and sauna. Breakfast served each morning in the large dining room. No smoking. **1st Ave. and Galena St., P.O. Box 417, Frisco, CO 80443; 970-668-3224; www.colorado.bnb.com/galena.**

Hotel Frisco—$$$

Of the many bed and breakfasts in Summit County, the former Twilight Inn remains a personal favorite. Open since December 1987, this inn features 12 unique and carefully furnished rooms. Eight have private bathrooms, while the others share baths. The largest room sleeps eight people comfortably. The library/TV room is an excellent place to relax and visit with other guests after a day of hiking or skiing. Don't overlook the hot tub and a steam room. Continental breakfast included. It has remained a comfortable, handsome and reasonably priced place. **308 Main St., P.O. Box 397, Frisco, CO 80443; 970-668-5009; www.hotelfrisco.com.**

IN KEYSTONE

Accommodations at Keystone Resort are all handled through a central reservations number, **1-800-222-0188.** You have three main choices—a room at plush **Keystone Lodge** in the village, a condominium or a luxury home rental. For a charming, historical lodging opportunity, read on.

Ski Tip Lodge—$$$ to $$$$

Those wishing to avoid slick, modern accommodations should think about staying at comfortably rustic Ski Tip Lodge. Located east of the Keystone ski area in a relatively isolated pine forest (isolated for Keystone, that is), the lodge, without the distractions of telephones and TVs, is the perfect escape. Originally built as a stagecoach stop in the 1880s, Ski Tip was transformed into Colorado's first skiing guest ranch by Max and Edna Dercum in the 1940s. Max, an avid skier, developed Arapahoe Basin Ski Area just up the valley. Even though the Dercums sold Ski Tip to the Keystone Resort in 1983, the charm lives

on. Decorated like a Swiss chalet, with colorful flowers blooming in window boxes in summer, this hand-hewn log lodge features interior wooden beams. Fourteen rooms are furnished with antiques, quilts and lace curtains—some have private baths, while others share. Ski Tip Lodge is famous for its excellent food (see the Where to Eat section), and winter lodging prices include breakfast and a four-course dinner. In summer, lodging includes breakfast only. Bus transportation for skiers to Keystone (a mile or so west) is provided every half hour. Reservations recommended. **Box 38, Keystone, CO 80435; 1-800-222-0188.**

IN MONTEZUMA

Western Skies Bed and Breakfast—$$$ to $$$$

Just three-quarters of a mile from the mountain burg of Montezuma is the former Paradox Lodge, now owned by Kent Lange and Lynne Wagner-Lane. Western Skies' 22-acre spread is surrounded by miles of national forest land and across the road from the Peru Gulch trailhead. With four lodge rooms and three cabins, the place can easily suit your mood. The two upstairs rooms are especially spacious, with king-size beds and gas fireplaces. Many of the lodge's customers forgo the traditional downhill ski vacation to take advantage of the proximity to excellent cross-country skiing, snowshoeing, hiking and mountain biking. Renovations to the lodge include a breakfast nook that capitalizes on the tremendous views. Efforts to add light to the cozy cabins scattered around the main lodge make them more welcome; each cabin comes with necessities, but you can also request breakfast delivered to your door. Check out their website for a 360-degree virtual tour of the rooms. **5040 Montezuma Rd., Dillon; 970-468-9445; www.colorado-bnb.com/western skies.**

IN SILVERTHORNE AND HEENEY

Melody Lodge—$$ to $$$

Settling into a mountain cabin has such a different feel than that of a condo, and if it's your thing, this could be the place you'd be interested in. Melody Lodge offer two comfortable cabins as well as a spacious two-bedroom suite in the old lodge building. It's located right on the shores of Green Mountain Reservoir, about 18 miles north of Silverthorne. All accommodations come equipped with small kitchens. Debbie and Dale Mitchener, who run the place, also can coordinate activities such as hiking, boating, fishing and horseback riding. This is a very relaxing alternative to the resort scene. **1534 Summit County Rd. 30, Heeney, CO 80498; 800-468-8495; 970-468-8497; www.coloradovacation.com/cabins/melody.**

Alpine Hutte—$ to $$
When Fran Colson and her son, Dave, opened their low-cost lodge in the fall of 1987, they let out a sigh of relief—financing had not been easily obtained. As Fran puts it, "The bankers were trying to tell me tourists expected and wanted to spend a lot of money for lodging." Luckily she convinced one bank otherwise. The result is a European-style lodge offering a startlingly low nightly rate for a bed.

The lodge sleeps 66 people in spacious rooms with four to eight bunks each and two large bathrooms on each floor. The only private room has a queen-size bed but costs three times as much per night. Downstairs, guests spend time either in the TV room or the main living room with its stone fireplace, dining room table and overstuffed sofas. For a very small fee, breakfast, lunch and dinner are offered; guests may cook their own meals in summer and off-season. The bedrooms are closed for cleaning each day from 9:30 A.M. to 3:30 P.M., but the downstairs rooms remain open. There is also an evening curfew. If you don't mind a few regulations, the Alpine Hutte is definitely worthwhile. American Youth Hostel discount; wheelchair accessible; reservations recommended. For additional information and reservations, **471 Rainbow Dr., P.O. Box 919, Silverthorne, CO 80498; 970-468-6336.**

Camping

White River National Forest
Dillon Reservoir—The national forest campgrounds at Dillon Reservoir (Lake Dillon) are plentiful but extremely crowded during the summer months. You might also stop in at the Forest Service office in Silverthorne to get an idea of where you'll have the best chance to find a site. Although many sites are available on a first-come, first-served basis, about half can be reserved at least 10 days in advance at **1-877-444-6777** or **www.reserveusa.com.**

Heaton Bay Campground (72 sites), **Peak One Campground** (79 sites), **Pine Cove Campground** (50 sites) and **Prospector Campground** (107 sites) are located along the northwest shore and along Hwy. 9 south of Frisco. Group camping is available at **Windy Point Campground** (72 sites); reservations required. **Blue River Campground** (24 sites) is located on the Blue River, 7 miles north of Silverthorne on Hwy. 9.

Green Mountain Reservoir—**McDonald Flats Campground** (13 sites), **Prairie Point Campground** (31 sites), **Elliot Creek Campground** (primitive camping) and **Cataract Creek Campground** (4 sites) are located next to Green Mountain Reservoir, 23 miles north of Silverthorne on Hwy. 9. A fee is charged at these campgrounds; sites can be reserved at **1-877-444-6777** or **www.reserveusa.com.**

Private Campground
Tiger Run Resort—Believe it or not, though large, Summit County offers only one private RV campground. And it's pricey. Tiger Run, one of only a few five-star RV resorts in the country, offers RV sites, tennis courts, a large clubhouse, an indoor swimming pool, a hot tub, a laundry and a game room. It even has some nice cabin-type accommodations as well. No tents are allowed. Tiger Run is located along Hwy. 9 between Frisco and Breckenridge. From Frisco drive south about 6 miles and turn left at the Tiger Run sign. **85 Tiger Run Rd.,**

Breckenridge, CO 80424; 970-453-9690; www.tigerrunresort.com.

Where to Eat

IN BRECKENRIDGE
Briar Rose Restaurant—$$$ to $$$$
In the early 1960s this restaurant was built in tribute to the legacy of good food and drink at the historic Briar Rose Boarding House. Both the fine food and the historic atmosphere make this a really fun place to eat. The dining area is decorated in Victorian style with antiques. The old wooden bar was moved from the Breckenridge Opera House, where for years it helped reluctant operagoers tolerate *Madama Butterfly* a little more easily. Game trophies line the walls, and the portrait of a reclining nude behind the bar seems to fit perfectly. Menu items range from steak to seafood; occasionally, game dishes such as elk, venison and buffalo are available. The prime rib has a good reputation around town. Pages of the menu are interspersed with an extensive wine selection, featuring straightforward descriptions of each vintage. Reservations are a good idea. Open daily in winter 5–10 P.M.; Mon.–Sat. in summer 6–10 P.M. Briar Rose is located just off Main St. at **109 E. Lincoln St.; 970-453-9948.**

Cafe Alpine—$$ to $$$$
Chef/owner Keith Mahoney puts a major emphasis on creative cuisine made with fresh ingredients and an extensive, well-chosen wine list at his cozy, four-level restaurant. The attention to detail can be found in the folded linen napkins and an extraordinarily well-trained and knowledgeable wait staff. The sophistication of the place creates romantic vibes with a fire glowing in the corner, original contemporary art works and a display of a vast wine selection of mostly French and California vintages. The eclectic menu cannot be described in detail, because every day new specials appear and four times yearly it undergoes complete revision. Despite the menu's changeability, locals swear

this place has consistently great food. For lighter appetites, the second-floor Tapas bar should be your only stop for everything from sashimi to Chesapeake Bay crab cakes. Breakfast Mon.–Fri. 8–11 A.M. (till 2 P.M. weekends); lunch 11 A.M.– 5 P.M.; dinner starts at 5 P.M. **106 E. Adams Ave.; 970-453-8218.**

Breckenridge Brewery and Pub—$$ to $$$
For an outstanding glass of freshly brewed ale and a picture-perfect view of the ski mountain, try to get an upstairs seat at the Breckenridge Brewery. This comfortable place continues to be the hot spot in town. In addition to six varieties of brew made on the premises (locals seem to prefer the India Pale Ale), you can fill up on pub food; lunch and dinner standards include burgers, wings, sandwiches and salads. You might want to order the fresh pasta or fish special in the evening. Great deck in summer. Open 11 A.M.–2 A.M. daily. **600 S. Main St.; 970-453-1550.**

Mi Casa—$$ to $$$
The Mexican food at this very popular Breckenridge restaurant is nothing exceptional, but the atmosphere is lively and the enthusiasm of the wait staff spills over to the customers. The decor reminds you of certain other large Mexican restaurants with its tile floors, white stucco walls and hanging flower baskets. Aside from variations on the standard burrito, enchilada, etc., Mi Casa does offer some fairly interesting chicken dishes as well as a fish-of-the-day special. Also, take advantage of the many varieties of salsa, asking for one with a chili rating to suit your taste.

Adjacent to the restaurant is the extremely popular Mi Casa bar, which has been an après-ski hangout for years (happy hour 3–6 P.M. daily). The 16-oz. margaritas here have attracted a loyal following. Restaurant open 5–9:30 P.M. **600 Park Pl.; 970-453-2071.**

Poirrier's Cajun Cafe—$$ to $$$
Although hundreds of miles from the bayou country of Louisiana, make no mistake: the cajun

food at Poirrier's is excellent. Cajun artwork/ decor, including obligatory pennants of Louisiana sports teams (Geaux Tigers!), and potent Hurricane drinks served during Mardi Gras all get you in the mood. For starters, try some Cajun popcorn: peeled crawfish dipped in corn flour and then deep fried. Entrée standouts include seafood gumbo, poisson hymel and many other seafood dishes. *Attention!*—do not leave without trying a piece of the exquisite bread pudding, served hot with rum butter sauce and chantilly cream. Open for lunch 11:30 A.M.–2 P.M. (3 P.M. in summer); dinner 5:30–9 P.M. (10 P.M. in winter). **224 S. Main St.; 970-453-1877.**

Rasta Pasta—$$

While Rasta Pasta offers some traditional fare like spaghetti with marinara and garlic bread, the real winners at this popular Breckenridge eatery are the Caribbean-influenced pasta dishes. You have to respect any restaurant daring enough to pair grapes, bananas, garlic and tortellini and make it taste phenomenal. If the long wait is any indicator, it is obvious Rasta's willingness to experiment has created quite a strong following among the locals. From the Rastafari-influenced decor to the laid-back staff, this place remains an interesting step off the well-worn Italian path. Open daily for lunch 11 A.M.–4 P.M. and dinner 4 P.M. to close. **411 S. Main St.; 970-453-7467.**

Blue Moose Restaurant—$ to $$$

Known primarily for its tasty breakfasts, the Blue Moose attracts a loyal local crowd along with vacationers. Sit inside the small restaurant or at a picnic table out front and enjoy breakfast standards such as omelettes, pancakes or lighter fare including fruit bowls, granola and home-made muffins. Standouts include eggs Benedict, huevos rancheros and the breakfast burrito. Lunch and dinner entrées run the gamut from burgers to fresh pasta to chicken Moroccan. Full bar. Open 7 A.M.–2 P.M. in summer; in winter, dinner is served 5–10 P.M. **540 S. Main St.; 970-453-4859.**

IN COPPER MOUNTAIN

Molly B's Rocky Mountain Tavern— $$ to $$$$

This newly opened spacious, warm dining establishment is pretty much the kind of place you envision eating at on your ski vacation—with hardwood floors, wood fire, solid menu of American-style favorites, hearty portions and a great selection of single-malt scotches. The bartender says it has "the longest bar in the state," which gets packed for après ski. In the summertime for lunch, their outdoor porch offers a great view of the slopes, while you munch a juicy burger or a Cobb salad. While the complete absence of booths was a bit disconcerting, Molly B's presents one of Copper Mountain's best semiaffordable dining options. Located in the East Village. Open 7 A.M.–10 P.M.; the bar stays open till midnight. **970-968-2318.**

Farley's—$ to $$$$

An institution in Copper Mountain since 1973, Farley's excels in both its fine food and après-ski entertainment. The restaurant gets its name from the owner's German shepherd, who's no longer with us. Fireplaces, beer kegs in the walls and vaulted ceilings characterize this comfortable place. Prime rib, steaks and fresh seafood highlight the menu. Appetizers, including barbecued ribs and artichoke parmesan, appease the après-ski crowd. Extensive wine list; good margaritas. Located at the base of the B lift, the tavern opens daily in mid-afternoon and stays open till 2 A.M. Restaurant is open 5:30–10 P.M. daily. **Snowflake Building; 970-968-2577.**

IN DILLON

Ristorante Al Lago—$$$

The Ottoborgo family continues to wow locals with their excellent northern Italian cuisine. After their highly praised restaurant in Berthoud Falls burned down, the family moved to Dillon and opened Ristorante Al Lago. The father, Alessandro, is from Italy and spends most of his time tending bar. His son, Ivano, studied the culinary arts in Italy and picked up secrets from New York chefs. Ivano prepares everything from scratch and even cuts his own veal and fish. The veal entrées are creative and considered by many locals to be the restaurant's highlight. Also offered are chicken, fresh seafood and a daily special. Delicious bread and desserts round out the meal. The dining room is very comfortable with a stone fireplace, wood beams, brick floors, candlelight and a spectacular view up to Buffalo Mountain. In the backyard deer and chickens roam (the deer can be fed from the balcony). Open Tues.–Sun. 5–10 P.M. **240 Lake Dillon Dr.; 970-468-6111.**

IN FRISCO
The Blue Spruce Inn—$$$ to $$$$
Strangely enough, this old establishment has traveled through more of Summit County than some vacationers have. Opened 50 years ago as a roadhouse between Old Dillon and Breckenridge, the building was moved to Frisco in the 1960s to avoid the rising waters of the reservoir. It continues to be one of the consistently fine restaurants in Summit County. The Blue Spruce Inn is cozy and intimate, with pine paneling, hanging plants and a lichen-covered stone fireplace. Specialties include slow-roasted prime rib, continental dishes and fresh seafood. Try their daily specials, such as poached salmon with tomato-hollandaise sauce or baked marlin with blackberry-hazelnut butter sauce. Service is superb. Dinners nightly 5–10 P.M.; call for reservations. **20 Main St.; 970-668-5900.**

The Butterhorn Bakery and Cafe—$ to $$
From the decidedly healthy Frisco skillet to the disgustingly unhealthy (woooahhh sticky buns!), everything we ate, smelled and tasted at this fine eatery was fabulous. The portions are huge, the prices are cheap and their vegetarian offerings are ample. They seem to do a little bit of everything—cramming a bakery, a full-service cafe, an ice cream shop and a coffee bar into one space. Most impressive is the create-your-own grilled-cheese sandwich, addressing a long underestimated segment of cafe society: the grilled-cheese aficionado. Open daily 7:30 A.M.– 4 P.M. **408 Old Main St.; 970-668-3997.**

The Moose Jaw—$ to $$
Serving heaping baskets of burgers and fries, the Moose Jaw is a great place for a cheap beer and a game of pool. Primarily locals hang out here. It's not fancy; it's just an inexpensive alternative. Open daily noon–2 A.M. **208 Main St.; 970-668-3931.**

IN HEENEY
The Green Mountain Inn—$ to $$$
If you are down at Green Mountain Reservoir and get hungry, stop in at the Green Mountain Inn. It serves as the meeting place for locals in the Heeney area and leans a bit toward the rustic side. Menu items are of the usual steak-and-fried-chicken variety, but there are a few house specials to investigate. Open in winter 4:30– 9 P.M. on weekdays, 9 A.M.–9 P.M. on weekends; summer hours 4:30–9 P.M. weekdays and 7 A.M.– 9 P.M. weekends. Closed Mon. year-round. In Heeney, 23 miles north of Silverthorne on County Rd. 30 off Hwy. 9. **7101 Summit County Rd. 30; 970-724-3812.**

IN KEYSTONE
Keystone Ranch—$$$$
Keystone Ranch had been a working cattle ranch for more than 30 years when it closed down operations in 1972. Now the restaurant provides beautiful views of the Tenmile and Gore Ranges as well as some of the finest gourmet food in Summit County. The six-course meal changes nightly but always features homemade soups, wild-game dishes and excellent desserts. Enjoy a cocktail in the living room beside the two-story stone fireplace. With only two seatings, reservations are recommended. 5:30–9 P.M. nightly. Three miles from Keystone Village; **1437 Summit County Rd. 150; 970-496-4386.**

Ski Tip Lodge—$$$$
Located in a rustic cabin east of the Keystone Resort ski area, Ski Tip Lodge is well known for what many people consider to be the best food in Summit County. A stagecoach stop in the 1880s, the lodge has been operating as a ski lodge and restaurant since the 1940s. Warm

yourself by the stone fireplace before being seated in the dining room. Each evening a choice of meat, fowl or fish is offered, with items changing nightly. The sauces are wonderful. Four-course dinners are served 5:45–10 P.M. nightly with soup, salad and freshly baked bread. Reservations required. One mile east on Montezuma Rd. from Keystone; **970-496-4950.**

Raz's Good Food Cafe—$ to $$

While you may have to grab the ketchup from another table or remind your server to bring silverware, this tiny dive specializing in warm, cheap breakfast standards (eggs, bacon, potatoes) presents one of Keystone's only non-resort-owned breakfast options. The cafe's location (right next to the local Texaco) and espresso drinks are a little lacking, but it's worth a visit just to soak up the local vibe and remind yourself that breakfast needn't be prepared by a classically trained chef to be tasty. Across from Keystone Village on Hwy. 6; **970-468-9454.**

IN MONTEZUMA

The Soul House—$ to $$

As the only place to eat or get something warm to drink in Montezuma—in fact, the only business in town—Sadie Stunkel's legendary Soul House serves as a sort of community center for the tiny population. In winter, Sadie skis 2 miles from her mountain cabin to serve up coffee, chai, fresh-baked goods and sandwiches to the local populus. Some nights the place doubles as a gathering place for potlucks and parties, providing some needed relief from the treacherous mountain weather. The hours are fairly unpredictable off-season, but in the cold of winter, it's open 8 A.M.–5 P.M. The bright and disarmingly comfortable decor can lull you into a state of unparalleled relaxation, so it might take a crowbar to remove you from the warmth and goodness of this true original. **970-468-1716.**

IN SILVERTHORNE

Silverheels—$$$

Located in the woods of Wildernest high above Silverthorne, this hacienda-style Southwestern restaurant features extremely creative dishes as well as one of the most attractive and romantic dining rooms in Summit County. The appealing decor includes hand-hewn wood beams set in white stucco, with bunches of chilis and Indian corn decorating the walls. Silverheels' menu is really quite something, consisting primarily of steak, seafood and a variety of Southwestern specialties, all of which are exquisite in color, presentation and taste. Some entrées entail tabletop "stone age cookery" in which customers cook their own meal on a sizzling granite slab. Be sure to try for a table in the main dining room for views out the picture windows to the lodgepole pine forest. This is a special place. Reservations highly recommended during peak seasons and on weekends. Open 4:30–10 P.M., but the bar stays open till midnight. **81 Buffalo Dr.; 970-468-2926.**

Old Dillon Inn—$$

The Old Dillon Inn has done its share of moving around. Built in 1869 in Montezuma, it was first moved to Old Dillon piece by piece. When Dillon Reservoir was completed in 1962, the building was loaded on a flatbed and moved to its present location. The owners supposedly had the kegs retapped before the beer had a chance to get warm. The Old Dillon Inn serves tasty New Mexican–style food; the specialty is blue-corn crab enchiladas. The nightlife here is locally famous and can get rowdy. Live music (usually country-western) plays Fri.–Sun. The margaritas are excellent. Although the restaurant gets incredibly crowded, reservations are not accepted. Open for dinner 4:30–10:30 P.M.; bar stays open till 1 A.M. Located along Hwy. 9 in Silverthorne at **311 Blue River Pkwy.; 970-468-2791.**

Services

Breckenridge

Breckenridge Central Reservations— 1-800-221-1091 or **1-800-800-BREC** out of state, and **1-800-822-5381** in state.

Breckenridge Children's Centers—The ski area offers a bunch of programs and attractions designed especially for kids. A recently installed pony lift on Peak 9 and the new Kid's Kastle are a couple of examples. **970-453-5000.**

Breckenridge Resort Chamber of Commerce—311 Ridge St., P.O. Box 1909, Breckenridge, CO 80424; 970-453-2913; www.gobreck.com.

Breckenridge Trolley—Provides free daily transport around Breckenridge.

Copper Mountain

Copper Mountain Resort—P.O. Box 3001, Copper Mountain, CO 80443; 1-800-458-8386; www.ski-copper.com.

Day Care—**Belly Button Bakery and Babies** provides day care for kids two months of age and older. Reservations required; **970-968-2882.**

Frisco

Information—The town offers a free vacation planner by contacting **1-800-424-1554** or **www.townoffrisco.com.**

Keystone

Keystone Children's Center—This 8,000-square-foot facility provides day care for infants and children up to age 12. It's also where kids as young as 3 can begin to learn how to ski. **1-800-255-3715; 970-486-4181; www.keystone.com.**

Keystone Resort—Be sure to visit the **Activities Center (1-800-354-4FUN)** for information and reservations on a range of adventures, dining and events during your stay. Also: 1-800-222-0188; www.keystoneresort.com.

Summit County

Summit County Central Reservations—1-800-365-6365; www.skierlodging.com.

Summit County Chamber of Commerce—Two visitor centers: one in **Frisco (970-668-2051)** and one in **Silverthorne (970-262-0817).** Also: **www.summitcham ber.org.**

Summit County Online Vacation Planner—For condo reservations: **www.summit net.com.**

Transportation

Colorado Mountain Express—This service offers vans between Summit County resort destinations and Eagle County Airport and Denver International Airport; **1-800-222-2112; www. cmex.com.**

Resort Express—Provides airport shuttles. **273 Warren Ave., P.O. Box 1429, Silverthorne, CO 80498; 1-800-334-7433; 970- 468-7600.**

Summit Stage—This free public bus system provides year-round transportation between all the resorts and major towns in Summit County. Pick up a schedule at a visitor center or wherever you're staying. Ski and bike racks provided. **970-668-0999.**

Vail Valley

Considered by many to be the Colorado ski area with the finest snow conditions and most varied terrain, Vail has made quite a name for itself in a very short period of time. Vail Mountain has remained king of ski hills as the biggest ski resort in North America. Not resting on its laurels, the mountain expanded to include Blue Sky Basin, with a fabulous assortment of runs and excellent, long-lasting, soft-snow conditions.

Located 100 miles west of Denver along Interstate 70, the town, which extends nearly 7 miles through the valley, offers 5,289 acres of skiable terrain inside its boundaries. Although established in 1962, Vail firmly established itself in early 1989, and again in 1999, when it played host to the World Alpine Ski Championships. Often called the Alpine Olympics, this biennial competition is the single most important event in alpine skiing.

There couldn't be a more worthy site for the championships than Vail, consistently voted one of North America's top resorts by readers of ski magazines. Tucked away behind massive Vail

Telemark turns on Vail's world-famous snowy slopes. Photo by Jack Affleck.

Getting There

Vail Valley is 100 miles west of Denver on Interstate 70. Regular and chartered ground transportation is available directly to and from **Denver International Airport** *as well as via bus, taxi, limo and van. The* **Vail/Beaver Creek Jetport** *in Eagle can be reached by air from Denver and other major cities. Some shuttle flights add only a nominal charge to the cost of a ticket to Denver International Airport.*

Mountain are the legendary back bowls, Colorado's own Shangri-la of schuss. The combination of sun, altitude and dry air on the back bowls is perfect for Dom Perignon powder. More than ever Vail appears committed to courting more of Colorado's Front Range skiers by offering special lift ticket pricing.

Vail's main sister resort, Beaver Creek, alone adds over 1,625 acres of skiable terrain to the Vail Valley empire. (Lift tickets are interchangeable.) Challenging runs at Grouse Mountain provide for a more exciting, well-rounded skiing experience featuring double-black-diamond terrain. Sometimes called the "Last Resort," Beaver Creek is Colorado's swankiest. Exclusive hotels and condo developments, a shopping plaza and an air of European sophistication have developed in a beautiful valley setting. The connection of the base villages of Beaver Creek, Bachelor Gulch and Arrowhead adds the feeling of village-to-village skiing. Beaver Creek now boasts the Vilar Center for the Performing Arts (see the Nightlife section), which is somehow located right beneath the ice rink in the heart of town. Super-exclusive Bachelor Gulch will see a five-star hotel opening soon.

Nearby towns of Edwards, Minturn and Redcliff offer visitors a down-to-earth atmosphere steeped in mining history; a smattering of small businesses, including affordable restaurants and a couple of choice B&Bs, can be found by the curious. Along with Avon, Eagle and Gypsum, these towns are where most Vail/Beaver Creek employees can still afford to live, offering a laid-back realism that remains a welcome part of the Vail Valley experience.

Not to be ignored in all of the skiing hype is the beautiful backcountry of the White River National Forest, complete with two wilderness areas that flank Vail Valley. Within a cross-country run of Vail to the southwest is the popular Holy Cross Wilderness. To the north, at the heart of soaring Gore Range, lies Eagles Nest Wilderness. Sunsets in the valley turn the craggy range into a spectacular tangerine curtain. This national forest land contains an abundance of trails for hiking, mountain biking and cross-country skiing. Plenty of high mountain lakes and rushing streams await anglers.

Facing this striking alpine scenery in a front-row seat is the quaint Bavarian-style village of Vail itself. Skiers who prefer archrival Aspen call Vail a glitzy, prefab storybook village that lacks the historic charm of Aspen. And even Vail locals admit it can be a mountain Disneyland of sorts. But Disney does have its pluses—convenience, no cars in the center of town and five-star service. Vail entices you with many options for running your gold card to the limit within its Tyrolean labyrinth of shops, lodges and eateries.

Even so, behind all of Vail's glamour beats the heart of a real town. There isn't a single stoplight, a fact that makes arriving a bit tricky. As you pull off the highway the roundabout baffles you the first time, but gets easier thereafter. Instead of trying to navigate the town in a car, just park in structures at either Vail or Lionshead and walk or take the shuttle bus. Don't panic: the town quickly reveals its meandering logic.

History

Vail is barely a baby boomer in Colorado history—many of its skiers are older than the four-decades-old area. But the narrow valley was home to the Ute Indians in the 19th century, before gold prospectors prompted their angry exit. Despite their unceremonious ouster, the Utes later helped bring snow to the very back bowls they are so often falsely accused of torching in spite fires. On opening day of the new ski area in 1962, there was one problem: no snow. So the Utes were summoned back. Minnie Cloud led a ceremonial rain dance (renamed a snow dance for the occasion) on the deck of the new lodge at Vail. Within a week a blizzard hit, launching a successful season. By the way, the price of a full-day lift ticket back then was $5.

French trappers and explorers were the first Europeans in the valley. But perhaps the most memorable explorer of all was Lord Gore, a wealthy baronet from Ireland who put together a hunting party in the mid-1850s for a three-year hunting expedition in the wilds of America. Gore had a veritable hunting army, with nearly 50 men, 100 horses, 50 hunting dogs, 6 wagons, 16 carts, a carpeted silk tent, a fur-lined commode, a few prostitutes and a three-month supply of trade whiskey (180-proof grain alcohol mixed with red pepper). He took along renowned mountain man Jim Bridger as a guide and the two exchanged stories along the way—Bridger's tales of the frontier for Gore's Shakespearean dramas. When they got into the mountains near Vail, Gore and his party proceeded to shoot every buffalo, deer and elk within range, killing literally thousands of them. Gore took a few trophies and left the rest to rot.

The trip finally came to an end after many misadventures in the Black Hills of South Dakota, when local Indians decided they'd had enough. Bear's Rib, an Uncpapa Sioux, and his war party surrounded Gore and his men, then stripped them of their horses, supplies and all their clothes. Gore was left wandering in the wild until friendly Hidatsa Indians took him in. Later he quietly made his way back to Ireland. According to historians, Bridger came back later and named a mountain range and creek after Gore.

Another landmark—Mount of the Holy Cross—became famous in 1873 when William Henry Jackson took a photo of the cross with swirling clouds; it inspired pilgrimages up the mountain, which continue today. Henry Wadsworth Longfellow saw the photo and penned a poem about the mountain.

In 1942 more than 15,000 men were stationed at Camp Hale, about 25 miles south of Vail, in preparation for winter fighting in Europe. After World War II, many of these 10th Mountain Division troopers became prime players in Colorado's burgeoning ski industry. Vail's modern history began with Pete Seibert, a 10th Mountain veteran.

Earl Eaton, who had been prospecting for uranium in Vail Valley, had met Seibert in Aspen. Eaton approached Seibert one day in Loveland (where Seibert worked) to tell him about a new prospect: the perfect ski mountain. Seibert took one look at the glorious slopes and agreed. They immediately began soliciting investors and, so as not to tip off anyone, formed the Trans Montane Rod & Gun Club to buy up land. Once permits were cleared and investors found, the ski area was built in a single year.

Vail got its name from Charlie Vail, chief engineer for Colorado's highway department in the late 1930s. Vail originally lent his name to present-day Monarch Pass, but locals who preferred Monarch protested. As a compromise, the moniker was transferred to the unnamed pass that is now Vail Pass.

Vail, which served as Gerald Ford's western White House during his presidency in the 1970s, is approaching middle age in the grand style befitting Colorado's and the United States' premier ski resort.

Festivals and Events

American Ski Classic

early Mar. Pros and amateurs descend on Vail for three events in a short period: the **World Cup,** the **Gerry Ford Invitational Ski Classic** and the **Legends of Skiing,** featuring the sport's greats. **970-949-1999; www. vvf.com.**

Fourth of July Celebrations

This area features a concentration of Independence Day celebrations. The festivities include **VailAmerica Days,** the **Vail Hill**

A statue stands tribute to the 10th Mountain Division ski troops in the center of Vail. Photo by Bruce Caughey.

Climb and a mountaintop fireworks display. Down-valley, the **Salute to the USA** fireworks display in Avon is the biggest and brightest in the valley (well worth the short trip, say locals); the **Minturn** celebration includes a concert and kayak races. **970-476-1000.**

Bravo! Vail Valley Music Festival

late June In summer the Vail Valley fills with the sounds of music. Styles range from classical to jazz, but the quality of the sounds never varies. Concerts are held variously at the **Ford Amphitheater** in Vail and **Vilar Center** in Beaver Creek. **970-827-5700; www.vail musicfestival.org.**

Eagle County Rodeo

early Aug. This popular rodeo usually kicks off with a concert and bull rider event. Here you'll have a chance to watch cowhands in this sanctioned pro-rodeo event. **970-328-8779; www.eagle-county.com.**

Outdoor Activities

Biking

MOUNTAIN BIKING

Vail is a good place to two-wheel—good and tough. The steep valley makes for mostly challenging, uphill rides. Vail and Beaver Creek Mountains are also open to mountain biking. Rentals are available at the top of the Lionshead gondola at Eagles Nest every day during summer as well as at locations at Beaver Creek. In addition, many of the town's ski shops do double duty by offering bike rentals and repair when the snow melts. Cyclists can take the gondola up and ride down to return bikes in Lionshead. Bikes may also be taken up the gondola for a fee.

Red Sandstone Road

This moderate 15-mile ride north to scenic Piney Lake from Vail starts off steep, then levels out with plenty of downhill stretches sprinkled amid the uphill. Especially fun is a roller-coaster set of small hills near the end; the only drawback to this pretty ride is occasionally heavy automobile traffic along the way. At Piney Lake (9,342 feet), you can claim your reward: a dramatic view of the full measure of Gore Range. Also at the end of the trail is Piney River Ranch, where you can rent boats and drop a fishing line. Red Sandstone Rd. (Forest Rd. 700) leaves Vail's N. Frontage Rd. a mile west of the Vail Village exit from Interstate 70.

Shrine Pass Road

See the Scenic Drives section for information.

10th Mountain Trail Association Hut System

This remarkable hut system opens its arms to summer travelers on bike or on foot. See the Cross-Country Skiing section.

Tigiwon Road

For a taste of what a ride in the lunar rover must have felt like, try this bumpy 6-mile trail. The pitted road leads to the stone Tigiwon Hut south of Minturn and provides excellent views to Vail's back bowls. Most cyclists find this ride more than enough, but—depending on when the road was last graded—it's possible to continue another 2.5 miles to the edge of the Holy Cross Wilderness. But remember, mountain bikes aren't allowed in wilderness areas. To reach Tigiwon Rd. (Forest Rd. 707), drive or ride 2.8 miles south of Minturn on Hwy. 24 and turn right.

Vail Mountain

A true fat-tire enthusiast will want to ride up the mountain rather than take a relaxing trip up on the gondola or chairlift. The dirt road from Vail Village to mid-Vail is a tough 2-hour test. Look for the beginning of the road right behind the Vista Bahn lift. Taking a detour down a section of the ski hill when descending the road is discouraged.

Rentals and Information

Christy Sports—For a varied supply of mountain bikes and 24-speed touring bikes, check this company at **293 Bridge St., Vail, 970-476-2244**, and at **182 Avon Rd., Avon, 970-949-0241; www.christysports.com.**

BICYCLE TOURING

The **Vail Pass Bikeway** from Vail to Frisco has quickly become a favorite with cyclists of all abilities. But why ride a bike up a 10,666-foot pass, enduring a grueling hour or more of hairpin twists and killer inclines? For the thrill of speeding down the other side, of course. Tip: ascending the paved path from the Vail side (elevation gain: 2,206 feet) is a lot tougher than from the Copper Mountain side (elevation gain: 1,400 feet). (For more information see the Biking section of the **Summit County** chapter.) Another possibility for visitors is to ride the fairly flat recreational trails that connect the lifts along the base of Vail Mountain.

Fishing

Eagle River

Although the once-proud Eagle River seems to be losing the battle to developers, stretches of classic trout fishing remain. The Eagle flows north through a narrow, scenic canyon near Redcliff and continues downstream past the contaminated mines and townsite of Gilman. A couple of miles northwest of Minturn, Gore Creek joins the flow. From there the Eagle River flows west down the valley between Hwy. 6 and Interstate 70 through ranches and pasture, where it is fed further by Brush and Gypsum Creeks. Rainbow and brown in the 10- to 14-inch range can be found in the Eagle on designated public water between Wolcott and Gypsum. The river is easy to get to from Hwy. 6, but stay off private land. Just below the confluence, you can fish on public water for about a mile. The fish seem to be a little bigger downriver near Eagle. Look for pools of deep, flat water. Locals recommend fly-fishing with a size 12 to 16 elk hair caddis imitation or perhaps a prince nymph.

Gore Creek

Gore Creek originates near Red Buffalo Pass in the Eagles Nest Wilderness, runs right through Vail and joins the Eagle River 2 miles northwest of Minturn. Although much of it is surrounded by civilization and its trappings, the creek is still swimming with rainbow, brook, brown and cutthroat trout. In fact, within the town's borders (from Red Sandstone Creek to the Eagle River 3 miles downstream) the creek is designated Gold Medal water; flies and lures only. Try fishing just east of the Vail Golf Course, but do not fish on the course itself. The rushing creek with its large, smooth bottom rocks can be tough to wade in places but is usually worth the trouble. The upper reaches of the creek in Eagles Nest Wilderness—north of Gore Creek Campground in East Vail—offer fishing away from the highway and condos.

Homestake Reservoir

Though steep, rocky banks make fishing tricky, Homestake is a popular spot. Rainbow, brook and cutthroat trout swim in this reservoir adjacent to the Holy Cross Wilderness. Controversy over the reservoir and an ongoing sister project,

Homestake II, have resulted in lengthy legal battles. Meantime, the fishing's great on the reservoir as well as down below on Homestake Creek, which is stocked and surprisingly uncrowded. From Hwy. 24, 3 miles south of Redcliff, turn right onto Homestake Rd. (Forest Rd. 703) at Blodgett Campground and drive 11 miles up to the 300-acre reservoir.

Mountain Lakes

Near the summit of Vail Pass are the heavily fished and easily accessed **Black Lakes.** The two lakes, which feed into Black Gore Creek, are generally well stocked and easy to reach from Interstate 70. **Lost Lake,** on the edge of the Eagles Nest Wilderness, is a popular lake in a beautiful setting at the headwaters of Red Sandstone Creek. Follow Red Sandstone Rd. north from Vail for 6 miles toward Piney Lake. The marked trailhead is on your right just past some private cabins. The upper three of the four **Missouri Lakes** in the Holy Cross Wilderness have brook and cutthroat trout. To reach the lakes from Redcliff, drive 3 miles south on Hwy. 24 and turn right on Homestake Rd. to Gold Park Campground. Follow the rough road southwest up Missouri Creek. The lakes are about a 3-mile hike from the end of the road.

    Beaver Lake on the upper reaches of Beaver Creek in the Holy Cross Wilderness has a good supply of brook and cutthroat. Get a parking pass and directions at the Beaver Creek Resort guard station to the Beaver Creek Nature Center. An easy hiking trail follows the creek to Beaver Lake. **Sylvan Lake State Park,** 16 miles south of Eagle on West Brush Creek Rd., is worth the short trip for the scenery alone. The brook and rainbow trout found in Sylvan Lake are an added bonus, and they bite throughout the year. Bring your boat along if you want to catch the big ones in this 40-acre lake.

Piney Lake

This 60-acre lake about 15 miles north of Vail at the end of Red Sandstone Rd. (Forest Rd. 700) has fair to good brook trout fishing, with good to great views of the Gore Range. On the private, southwest side of the lake is Piney River Ranch, which can provide canoes and other small craft for float fishing. Virtually the entire shoreline is open to the public (for a small fee) for catching a variety of trout, including native and cutthroat. The ranch also rents rods for children. **P.O. Box 3460, Vail, CO 81658; 970-477-1171.**

Four-Wheel-Drive Trips

Most of the back roads around Vail do triple duty as jeep roads and mountain biking trails in summer and cross-country ski routes in winter. For trip ideas contact the **Holy Cross Ranger District Office, 24747 Hwy. 24, Minturn, CO 81645; 970-827-5715; www.fs.fed.us/r2/whiteriver.**

Holy Cross City

The former stage route from Gold Park Campground to Holy Cross City has a reputation as one of the best, and most difficult, four-wheel-drive roads in the state. It's a particularly challenging drive that requires steady nerves. People from across the country come to navigate the road's coils, which are spiced by plunging chasms below. One negative result of the popularity was a huge bog dug by stuck jeeps near the ghost town. Recently, however, the bog was reclaimed through a massive volunteer effort from 25 jeep clubs. Provided that vehicles stay on the hardened road, the Forest Service has no plans to close the route. For historical information about Holy Cross City, see the Hiking and Backpacking section. To reach the road from Interstate 70, take the Minturn exit and drive 13 miles south on Hwy. 24. Turn right onto Homestake Rd. (Forest Rd. 703) and go 8 miles to the marked jeep road.

Mill Creek Road

Starting on the maintenance road from behind the Lodge at Vail, this rugged road ascends through the ski area. Stay to the left as the road passes a gate about a mile up. Keep heading east up to the top of China Bowl and along the China Wall to 360-degree views of the surrounding ranges. The real jeeping begins on an old logging road that starts at another gate at about 10,500 feet. Drive until you can't go any farther. The road ends at the top of the Benchmark (some people still call it "Benchmark Road") summit at 11,716 feet. In winter the challenging cross-country Commando ski run follows this road down (see the Skiing section). Allow for about a 3-hour round trip.

Rentals and Tours

Timberline Tours—These folks offer guided backcountry trips in custom-built, off-road vehicles. In addition to half-day and full-day trips, there are several variations on the theme: night tours, sunrise and sunset tours and packages that combine jeeping and caving, or jeeping and rafting. **23698 Hwy. 24, Minturn; 970-476-1414; www.timberlinetours.com.**

Golf

Six 18-hole courses provide a good variety of high-altitude (and high-priced) golfing in Vail Valley. The golfing season opens in mid-May and closes in mid-Oct. Spring weather in Vail has on occasion allowed the ultimate recreational day: skiing in the morning and a round of 9 in the afternoon. Most courses are long, narrow affairs due to the geography of the steep-walled valley. A Hale Irwin–designed course at **Cordillera** is coming into its own now that it has been around for a while. It offers tremendous views to the Sawatch and Gore mountain ranges. **970-926-2200; www.cordillera-vail.com.**

Beaver Creek Resort Golf Club

This course, designed by Robert Trent Jones Jr., is preeminent among the links in the Vail Valley. It twists down the secluded Beaver Creek Valley from the foot of the ski mountain. Though not as long as the other courses in the area, rolling hills, large, irregular traps and undulating, basketball-court-sized greens promise a challenging round. Along the way are great views of the surrounding ranges in the White River National Forest. Many of the resort's multimillion-dollar homes line the fairways, and an antique barn stands in the middle of the course. Greens

fees are higher for nonguests; public tee times are limited. The course opens in mid-May. Located on the road up to Beaver Creek Ski Area, off the Avon exit on Interstate 70. **103 Offerson Rd., Beaver Creek, CO 81620; 970-949-7123.**

Eagle-Vail Golf Course

Designed by PGA pros Bruce Devlin and Bob Van Hagge, Eagle-Vail is a very challenging course wedged in between the Eagle River and White River National Forest. Along with the obvious river hazard, water holes and 60 sand traps wreak havoc upon even the best players. This course, located midway between Vail and Beaver Creek, offers the best deals on golf in the valley, including bargain-rate greens fees during spring and fall. The club features a pool and tennis courts as well as a driving range. Located just off Interstate 70 at Exit 171 at Avon. **0431 Eagle Dr., Avon; 970-949-5267; www.eagle vail.org.**

Sonnenalp Golf Club

Sonnenalp's location 7 miles down-valley from Beaver Creek allows for a longer season than other courses in Vail. This Scottish course—its name means "sun on the mountain"—features few trees and many pothole-type traps. Opening date recently has been Apr. 1. The course's rolling layout was designed in 1980 by Golf Force, formerly a Jack Nicklaus company. Reserve tee times at this semiprivate resort seven days in advance. **1265 Berrycreek Rd., Edwards; 970-477-5370; www.sonnenalp.com.**

Vail Golf Club

This 18-hole golf resort just east of Vail Village is the area's oldest, dating back to 1967, just five years after the ski area opened. The head pro described it as "a good test of golf," with fairways that dip in and out of the flanks of Vail Mountain and Golden Peak. Gore Creek cuts through the course, coming into play on more than half the holes, as do a number of sand traps. Nearly every tee has a view of the spectacular Gore Range. Be sure to call for tee times. **1778 Vail Valley Dr.; 970-479-2260; www.vailrec.com.**

Looking out on the Gore Range from the Vail Golf Club. Photo by Bruce Caughey.

Hiking and Backpacking

Patiently hunched around the glamorous town of Vail is some great country known well by veteran hikers. Not 20 miles from the glitz and glamour, elk and marmots ply the Eagles Nest and Holy Cross Wilderness Areas. Holy Cross, which boasts over 100 miles of trails for hikers, is the second-most-used wilderness area in the state. In fact, it used to be a national monument but lost its designation in 1954 because of its poor accessibility and short summer season, according to rangers. Others say it's because the natural shape of a cross on the namesake mountain is crumbling. The enigmatic area remains popular, nonetheless, and the Forest Service is worried about overuse. Hikers and backpackers are asked to practice leave-no-trace camping by staying on trails and using stoves instead of campfires.

Meanwhile, more and more hikers are discovering the terrain of the Eagles Nest Wilderness, which hunters once claimed as their own. Most hikes in this area have the stunning, 600-million-year-old Gore Range hanging above

them like a curtain on a stage. For more information stop in at the **Holy Cross Ranger District Office** at **Dowd Junction** just after turning onto Hwy. 24, **P.O. Box 190 Minturn, CO 81645; 970-827-5715; www.fs.fed.us/ r2/whiteriver.** For a walk in town, there's nothing better than the easy, rolling **Gore Trail,** which parallels the creek ending at Ford Park and the gorgeous **Botanical Gardens.**

Bighorn Creek

The 3.5-mile hike to the "Bighorn Hilton," an old homesteader's cabin, is less steep than many hikes near Vail. Wildflowers and a fern grove highlight the early part of this trail in the Eagles Nest Wilderness. At mile 2, it's hard to know what to look at first—Bighorn Falls on your left or down-valley to Vail and Bighorn Creek. From this point the trail climbs quickly up a ridge. Shortly after, a level wooded trail brings you to the cabin. The structure, which serves as a storm shelter, makes a good turnaround point for the day hike. To get to the trailhead, take the East Vail exit off Interstate 70 and drive east on

S. Frontage Rd. to Columbine Dr. Turn left and go to the end of the pavement.

Booth Falls Trail

Sixty-foot Booth Falls is a handsome reward for making this moderate 2-mile hike in the Eagles Nest Wilderness. The trail begins steeply, getting into the mountains quickly, but soon levels out to a wildflower meadow with columbines, mariposa lilies, shooting stars and great views back toward Vail. Hikers are treated to an uncountable number of waterfalls and Swiss Alps–like vistas along Booth Creek. Reach the trailhead by taking the East Vail exit off Interstate 70 and turn onto the frontage road on the north side of the highway. Drive a mile west and turn uphill on Booth Falls Rd. The trailhead is at the end of the road near the water gauging station.

Holy Cross City

History buffs will enjoy this 2-hour hike up an old stage route to the remains of Holy Cross City. The ruins of several cabins and other structures mark the treeline ghost town that had boomed and died by 1884. Shaft houses, foundations of two ore mills and skeletons of mines dot the mountainsides. During boom times the Holy Cross Mill was connected to its sister mill in Gold Park by a 2.5-mile flume. From Minturn take Hwy. 24 south 13 miles to Homestake Rd. (Forest Rd. 703). Follow this gravel road 8.5 miles west to Forest Rd. 704 and turn right. Drive 2.3 miles to a T and turn right again. Go about 2 more miles, keeping to the right, and park in the level area just before the road turns into a very rough four-wheel-drive road. The trail starts on this road, quickly joining the historic Holy Cross City Rd. Look for a signed fork a little over 1.5 miles into the hike. Take the left fork and continue staying to the left to reach the "city."

Mount of the Holy Cross

Rangers say the climb up Mount of the Holy Cross is the most popular hike in the Vail area. The trail up this 14er (barely, at 14,005 feet), about 6 miles each way, is usually climbed on an overnight trip. In the 1930s a series of "hanky healing" pilgrimages were made up the mountain, which bears the natural image of a giant cross etched in snow. People too ill to make the climb sent their handkerchiefs to a Denver pastor who promised to bless them on the peak and send them back. In 1932 the pastor received over 2,000 hankies, and two rangers had to help him carry them up the mountain. The trail starts off with a rugged, rocky climb to Half Moon Pass; hikers are rewarded by tremendous panoramas of the Gore and Mosquito Ranges. The pass alone makes a good day's climb. After crossing the narrow path over the pass, the trail drops down to Cross Creek, which is a great place to see the aspen in fall. Many hikers camp here, so they can finish the ascent up Mount of the Holy Cross before noon the next day to avoid electrical storms. When possible, however, the Forest Service encourages making the climb in a day, because of overuse in the Cross Creek area. After the trail crosses the creek and completes a series of switchbacks up through the forest, its route becomes obvious: just follow the ragged edge of the Holy Cross Ridge to the summit. Start hiking up Half Moon Pass Trail, just to the right of the Fall Creek trailhead at the end of Tigiwon Rd. (for directions see the Notch Mountain write-up below).

Notch Mountain

Clergymen still lead pilgrimages up this 5-mile trail to see the huge cross of snow etched in Mount of the Holy Cross to the west. A stone shelter was built on top of 13,100-foot Notch Mountain in 1924 to accommodate the hundreds of pilgrims. (When you're on the 35th switchback above treeline, it's hard to imagine how anybody could have brought materials up for such a structure.) The fairly difficult hike starts off in a shadowy forest that soon opens up to a meadow. From there the trail clings to a steep valley wall until reaching the posted fork for Notch Mountain at mile 2. After the killer switchbacks, Mount of the Holy Cross finally reveals itself. The 1,500-foot-high cross lies directly across the valley to the west—right in front of you as if on an easel. But alas, the right arm of the cross isn't as prominent as it once was, due to erosion and avalanches. The best time to see the cross is between June 15 and July 10 when the white of the snow-filled cross contrasts sharply with the stone summit. To reach the trailhead from Vail, take the Minturn exit off Interstate 70. South of Minturn (2.8 miles) on Hwy. 24, turn right onto Tigiwon Rd. (Forest Rd. 707). Drive 8.5 miles to the end of the road at Half Moon Campground. Take the Fall Creek Trail from there.

Ski Mountains

Top-of-the-world views can be had without working up a sweat via gondola and chairlift rides up Vail or Beaver Creek Mountains. At the top of the Lionshead gondola in Vail, seven easy hikes are laid out. The **Gore Range Loop** provides a scenic 1-mile walk to the Eagle's View turnaround and back with no elevation gain at all. **Berrypicker Trail** is all downhill. Yes, it's lined with all sorts of berries, and it gets hikers back down the mountain to Lionshead in about 2 hours. Leave the car at the Lionshead parking structure west of Vail Village and walk to the gondola building. Trail maps are available there.

10th Mountain Trail Association Hut System

See the Cross-Country Skiing and Snowshoeing section for detailed information.

Two Elk Trail

This 11-mile hike carries a National Scenic Trail designation, which means some past government official must have really enjoyed it. It's easy to see why: the summit of Two Elk Pass abounds with views of the Gore and Sawatch Ranges and the many bowls on Vail Mountain's back side. A little farther along, the trail offers a peek at Mount of the Holy Cross. But the best reason to hike the trail is to glimpse its namesake—the elk. There's always a good chance of spotting some because they are boxed into the area by highways and towns. The best time to hear them bugling is Aug. and Sept. The hike can be done in one day but is best as an overnighter. The trailhead

begins in East Vail just south of the Gore Creek Campground on old Hwy. 6 at the closed gate. It ends in Minturn, making a car shuttle necessary. Drive the second car to the bridge over Eagle River in Minturn. Cross the bridge and drive past the cemetery. Go right at the first fork and left at the second to the mouth of Two Elk Canyon, near the foot of Battle Mountain. The trail begins near Two Elk Creek.

Horseback Riding

Beaver Creek Stables

Here's where riders looking for more elaborate excursions should come. Try breakfast and lunch rides, rides combined with fishing at Beaver Lake, sunset rides to Beano's Cabin for dinner (see the Where to Eat section) or perhaps an overnighter to Trapper's Cabin with hiking side trips. Located just above Beaver Creek Village. No credit cards accepted. **970-845-7770.**

Piney River Ranch

About 15 miles north of Vail, you can really get into the backcountry by riding the trails from the ranch into the Eagles Nest Wilderness, with the 13,000-foot Gore Range as a backdrop. The ranch also offers boating and fishing on the lake, making it a great getaway destination from Vail. Check out the new hewn-log Lake View Grill, serving lunch Tues.–Sun. 11 A.M.–5 P.M. The road to Piney Lake (Forest Rd. 700) leaves Vail's N. Frontage Rd. a mile west of the Vail Village exit. The ranch is at the road's end. **Piney River Ranch, P.O. Box 7, Vail; 970-477-1171.**

Spraddle Creek Ranch

Horses are available for 1- to 3-hour rides in the former Ute stomping grounds around Spraddle Creek and the lower reaches of Bald Mountain. The ranch is definitely geared toward families on day outings rather than serious trekkers out for longer trail rides. A pony ride on the ranch is ideal for young children. Located just across Interstate 70 from the roundabout in Vail Village. **100 Spraddle Creek Rd.; 970-476-6941; www.spraddlecreekranch.com.**

Ice Skating

Black Family Ice Rink

As the centerpiece of Beaver Creek Village, this ice rink entertains visitors 10 A.M.–9 P.M. daily in winter and 6–10 P.M. in summer. Mons. during winter enjoy a skating demonstration on the 150- by 65-foot outdoor rink. Rentals available. Small fee. **970-476-9090; www.beaver creek.com.**

The John Dobson Ice Arena

This arena, on the bus route between Vail and Lionshead, holds public skating sessions daily. Children under 6 must be accompanied by an adult. Hockey and figure skates are available to rent. **321 E. Lionshead Cir., Vail, CO 81657; 970-479-2271; www.vailrec.com.**

Nottingham Lake

For an outdoor experience, head to Avon. **970-949-4280; www.avon.org.**

Vail Golf Resort

Skate at the golf course, under the white bubble. **970-479-2291.**

River Floating

Eagle River

The floating season for the Eagle River is substantially shorter than for many Colorado rafting rivers: mainly during spring runoff (May–July). During that period, however, the Eagle does churn up some pretty exciting white water on its upper reaches. It's one of the few free-flowing rivers left in the state. Families looking for more subdued trips will prefer the rides nearer Eagle on the lower reaches. With the icy-cold water, wet suits are a must in the early float season.

Outfitters

Vail's location near three of Colorado's most popular rafting rivers—the Eagle, the Colorado and the Arkansas—means there are plenty of outfitters to choose from. Here are a couple:

NOVA Guides—This widely respected guide service leads raft trips in summer (as well as a variety of winter activities, such as snowmobiling and snowcat tours). They float the Colorado, Arkansas and Eagle Rivers and offer float fishing trips on the Roaring Fork and other lakes and streams in the White River National Forest. A range of other activities (even mountain biking tours and paintball games) as well. **P.O. Box 2018, Vail, CO 81658; 970-827-4232; www.novaguides.com.**

Timberline Tours—Started in 1971, this is Vail's oldest guide service. They float the Colorado and Arkansas. **P.O. Box 131, Vail, CO 81658; 1-800-831-1414; 970-476-1414; www.timberlinetours.com.**

Skiing

CROSS-COUNTRY SKIING AND SNOWSHOEING

Nordic skiing and snowshoeing have not gotten lost in the shadow of immense Vail Mountain. Besides two centers in Vail and one at Beaver Creek, there are a number of great backcountry trails throughout the Vail Valley and surrounding White River National Forest. For information on backcountry trails, contact the **Holy Cross Ranger District Office, P.O. Box 190, Minturn, CO 81645; 970-827-5715; www.fs.fed.us/r2/whiteriver.** Incidentally, the ranger's office, located at Dowd Junction just after turning off Hwy. 24 at Minturn, has a wildlife viewing station that offers tremendous looks at wintering elk.

Backcountry Trails

Booth Falls—Check out this terrific snowshoeing trail after a snowstorm (see the Hiking and Backpacking section).

Commando Run—This is Colorado's top-rated cross-country tour, a grueling 18 miles for advanced skiers only. Avalanche danger and tough-to-follow trails are only two of the formidable obstacles to completing this daylong trek. Since it's a one-way trail, you must figure out your transportation ahead of time. The best way is to park your car in Vail and take a taxi or have someone drop you off at the Vail Pass rest area. The trail begins on the Shrine Pass Rd. and comes in three parts: the Shrine Pass–Lime Creek roads, Bowman's Shortcut to Two Elk Pass and the descent to the Golden Peak runs at Vail Ski Area. Magnificent views of Gore Range, Mount of the Holy Cross, Notch Mountain and the Tenmile and Mosquito Ranges will be seen along the way. But it's next to impossible to find the way without a topo map and detailed directions. It's best to ski it with someone who's done it before.

Shrine Pass—This fairly easy 11-mile trail has a tried-and-true formula: 3 miles up, 8 miles down and margaritas (no pre-mix here) at Reno's (at 127 W. Water St. in Redcliff). No deviations allowed. It's a great day trip, and consequently the Shrine Pass route sees heavy use on weekends from snowmobilers and skiers alike. Thankfully the trails now diverge at the pass into separate areas, so you don't need to worry as much about the inevitable conflict between two distinct user groups. The best chance for solitude on this ski tour is midweek. Leave one car up Forest Rd. 709 from Redcliff and pile in the other car for the drive up to the rest area at the summit of Vail Pass. The trail starts on Shrine Pass Rd. with a moderate climb to Shrine Pass summit. After reaching the summit, the easy-to-follow road starts downhill to Redcliff, with a great view of Mount of the Holy Cross along the way. Allow about 4 to 6 hours. For more information see the Scenic Drives section.

10th Mountain Trail Association Hut System—This extensive system is named in honor of the members of the ski troops of the 10th Mountain Division who trained in the area and fought in World War II. The system encompasses many overnight huts and other accommodations linked by more than 300 miles of backcountry trails. The Shrine Mountain Inn near the top of Vail Pass is one of the huts that you can see along the backcountry trail described in this section. On this eastern end, the system extends from Shrine Pass to Tennessee Pass near Leadville. The huts along

Skiers take a break on the Shrine Pass route. Photo by Bruce Caughey.

the way each sleep about 16 and are usually booked to capacity. Basics are supplied. For trail guides (a good idea for most people), see Paragon Guides (listed below under the Guided Tours section). For hut reservations and other details, contact the **10th Mountain Division Hut Association, 1280 Ute Ave., Aspen, CO 81611; 970-925-5775; www.huts.org.** Detailed information on the Aspen end of the system can be found in the Skiing section of the **Aspen** chapter.

Tigiwon Trail (Tigiwon Road)—Beginning and intermediate skiers will like this 8-mile run up Tigiwon Rd. to Half Moon Campground. At mile 6 there's a stone hut to warm up in and views of the Gore Range and Vail's back bowls to warm up to. The hut, built to house pilgrims on their way to Mount of the Holy Cross, can be reserved for overnight trips from May 15 to Nov. 15 by calling the **Holy Cross Ranger District Office, 970-827-5715;** other times of year it's available at no charge. Look for elk on the way since the trail crosses part of their winter range. The full 8 miles can take most of a day, but coming back down should take only a third as long. Tigiwon is a Ute word meaning "friends"—ironically, Tigiwon Rd. begins near Battle Mountain, named for a notorious fight between Utes and Arapaho Indians in 1849. Tigiwon Rd. is 2.8 miles south of Minturn off Hwy. 24. Turn right and drive a half-mile up the road, park and start skiing.

Groomed Trails

Cordillera Nordic Ski System—With soaring views to the Upper Eagle Valley and Squaw Creek stretching out in front of you, you will love this upscale retreat. The extensive trail system offers a good variety of loop trails with varying degrees of difficulty. The trails wind in and out of aspen and evergreen forests near future megahome sites. If you are going to make the short drive to Cordillera, you might as well consider a spa package that offers the benefit of luxurious trappings. Another possibility, depending on when you visit, is the moonlight ski package. Contact **1-800-877-3529; 970-926-2200; www.cordillera-vail.com;** also see the Where to Stay section.

Golden Peak Center in Vail—Vail's nordic center at the base of Chair 6 on the east side of Vail Village has 20 kilometers of trails. More than ever, snowshoers are taking advantage of the backcountry tours and short treks. For the decadent sports enthusiast, there's the gourmet tour, including hot drinks, three appetizers, three entrées and three desserts served along the way. Reservations for the gourmet snowshoe tour must be made by 10 A.M. the day before. Equipment rental, group lessons, private lessons available. Half-day snowshoe tours every morning. **970-479-4390; www.vail.com.**

McCoy Park at Beaver Creek—The top-of-the-world views make this the best place to ski and snowshoe groomed trails in the area. McCoy Park has 32 kilometers of trails, many named after mining claims in the area from the late 1800s. Twenty percent of the terrain is

beginner, 60 percent intermediate and 20 percent advanced. Telemarking, snowshoeing and cross-country skiing lessons are given on Beaver Creek Mountain. There's also a warming hut with hot drinks and boot lockers at the top of the lift. **970-845-5313; www.beavercreek. com.** If, however, you don't feel like taking the lift to McCoy Park, you might consider slipping onto the Beaver Creek Golf Course.

Vail Nature Center—The nature center has served as a nordic headquarters for East Vail since 1984. An 8-mile track with plenty of loops follows Gore Creek out from Golden Peak. Besides rental equipment and day tours, the center offers snowshoe walks and exhibits on nordic skiing and natural history. The center is four blocks east of Golden. **841 Vail Valley Dr., Vail, CO 81658; 970-479-2291; www.vail rec.com.**

Vail Nordic Center—For track or skate skiing, you can't beat the price of the nordic center at the Vail Golf Course: it's free. Try out their groomed tracks at the east end of Vail. **1778 Vail Valley Dr.; 970-476-8366.**

Guided Tours, Rentals and Information

Christy Sports—Located at **293 Bridge St., Vail, 970-476-2244,** and at **182 Avon Rd., Avon, 970-949-0241; www.christy sports. com.**

Paragon Guides—These folks offer three- to six-day trips on the 10th Mountain Trail Association Hut System between Vail and Aspen for experienced nordic skiers. See the Backcountry Trails section for more information. **P.O. Box 130, Vail, CO 81658; 1-877-926-5299; 970-926-5299; www.paragon guides.com.**

DOWNHILL SKIING AND SNOWBOARDING
Beaver Creek Ski Area

"Like Tiffany's is to jewelry stores, like Gucci is to luggage, like Cadillac is to automobiles, that's what Beaver Creek is going to be to ski areas in this country." That's the way former Colorado governor Dick Lamm described Beaver Creek at the opening ceremonies in 1980. With something suspiciously like a guard tower on the road leading up to the area, it does feel a little like you're entering a members-only club. Even so, valley residents take the sheen off by simply calling it "The Beav."

Beaver Creek was originally meant as the site for skiing events of the 1976 Olympics, which Colorado subsequently turned down, but that didn't deter the pricey development of the area. Today nearly 1,700 acres are served by 13 lifts, and the mountain experience encompasses three base villages: Beaver Creek, Arrowhead and Bachelor Gulch. It feels like a European ski experience thanks to interlocking mountains and the Swiss-style condos, restaurants and shops at Beaver Creek.

Beginning skiers like the area because many of the easiest and most spectacular runs are concentrated at the top of the mountain. Experts prefer the gladed, narrow, double-black-diamond Birds of Prey, which is tougher than most runs at Vail; this run served as the site of the men's downhill and super-G events at the World Cup competitions in December 2000. The steep pitch of the runs at Grouse Mountain also call out to expert and advanced skiers. But most of Beaver Creek has an odd fall line that makes you feel like you are skiing at a slant. Because of few traverses, open glades and terrain parks, the area also appeals to snowboarders. With the gentle terrain of Bachelor Gulch, skiers can now interconnect with the runs at Arrowhead. Generally the skiers at Beaver Creek are less aggressive than those at Vail and lift lines remain shorter; lift tickets are interchangeable between the two areas. **1-800-525-2257; 970-476-9090; www.beaver creek.com.**

Vail

According to master ski filmmaker Warren Miller, "There is no comparison" to Vail's back bowls. Now that there are seven back bowls—Sun Down, Sun Up, China, Tea Cup, Siberia, Inner Mongolia and Outer Mongolia—no other ski area in the region can compare (not even Jackson Hole has more acreage in its vast bowls). Vail's back bowls are totally ungroomed, which can make for a variety of snow conditions. Mornings on fresh-snow days are unquestionably heaven on skis.

But variety is the key to Vail's appeal, from the broad-faced back bowls to mean moguls and manicured cruising runs on the front side. This is the largest single-mountain ski area in North America, so large and varied that it's always easy to find a new, challenging path—no matter your ability. In fact, you could ski this area for a week solid and still not be able to cover all of the runs. Despite this size, the area expanded in 2000 with the opening of Blue Sky Basin—some 520 additional acres of intermediate to advanced terrain with great tree skiing, natural jumps and adventuresome, powder-laden chutes.

The mountain now has three base areas—**Vail Village, Cascade Village** and **Golden Peak.** With 33 lifts, Vail can move more skiers than ever over a total of 5,289 acres of skiable terrain. Snowboarders meet the challenge of a 400-foot halfpipe with 10-foot walls! Kids even have their own terrain at Golden Peak (renamed Whippersnapper Mountain). The top of the Eagle Bahn gondola has been transformed into an area called Adventure Ridge that appeals to nonskiers, too. After a quick ride up the new gondola, you'll find ski biking, laser tag, snowshoe rentals, a sledding hill, great views and a restaurant.

The Vail/Beaver Creek Ski School remains the largest in the world with some 800 instructors. Free Meet-the-Mountain tours give skiers a good idea of the immensity of this mountain. For information: **1-800-525-2257; 970-476-9090; www.vail. com.**

Sledding and Tubing

You can go "thrill sledding" with a specially engineered ski bike at the new Adventure Ridge area at the top of the Eagle Bahn gondola. This area caters to kids of all ages and is even open at night. For information: **970-476-9090; www. vail.com.** If you just want a great free sledding hill, head to Meadow Mountain, off Interstate 70 at the Minturn exit.

Sleigh Rides

Steve Jones Sleigh Rides

Nightly rides on the Vail Golf Course leave each evening from Thanksgiving into Mar. **970-476-8057; www.vailsleighrides.com.**

Timber Hearth Grille Sleigh Ride Dinner

If you splurge on this sleigh ride into the back-country at Cordillera, you'll be treated to a gourmet buffet in a tent. **970-926-5588.**

Swimming

Avon Recreation Center

This beautifully designed new workout facility offers an array of different pools (laps, kids, diving and leisure) and a 142-foot slide. Fee charged. **325 Benchmark Rd., Avon, CO 81620; 970-949-9191; www.avon.org.**

Seeing and Doing

Ballooning

For this natural high, try **Camelot Balloons, 970-926-2435; www.camelotballoons.com.** You can also call **Mountain Balloon Adventures, 970-476-2353.**

Museums

Colorado Ski Museum

Did you realize that skiing originated 6,000 years ago? You'll learn a lot about skiing when you visit this well-put-together museum (and Colorado Ski Hall of Fame). The museum, founded in 1976, is one of only a handful in the country dedicated to skiing. Don't miss the 12-foot-long, 2-inch-thick wooden skis that look more like logs. A theater inside shows historical and current ski films. Gift shop; small fee except for children under 12. Located in the Vail Village Transportation Center on the bus route; open 10 A.M.–5 P.M. daily except Mon. **231 S. Frontage Rd., Vail, CO 81658; 970-476-1876; www.vailsoft.com/museum.**

Vail Nature Center

This small natural history museum hosts guided nature walks and recreational activities in summer. In winter the nature center becomes a nordic center and the trails become cross-country and snowshoeing treks. Knowledgeable guides run an interpretive center in a renovated farmhouse on the preserve. Inside are seasonal displays on the Vail Valley's flora, fauna and geography. The 7-acre preserve is on the southeast side of Ford Park just east of Vail Village. Open 9 A.M.–5 P.M. daily Memorial Day to Labor Day; hours vary the rest of the year. **75 S. Frontage Rd., Vail, CO 81658; 970-479-2291; www.vailrec.com.**

Nightlife

Vail Area

For après ski if it's sunny, try the deck at either the **Red Lion (970-476-7676)** or **Pepi's (970-476-4671)** at **Gasthof Gramshammer** in Vail Village. Ask for a toe-warming Snuggler—peppermint schnapps and hot chocolate—or a hot buttered rum with a cinnamon stick in it.

During ski season the concept of weekend doesn't really exist in Vail—the joints are jumping every night. Each bar seems to have its designated night when it swells in popularity. If you stay an entire week, you might try the following rotation:

Mon.: **Vendetta's, 970-476-5070**—Upstairs from the restaurant with live music or a DJ. Its location right in the thick of the village makes it easy to bounce around to several night spots.

Tues.: **Hubcap Brewery and Steakhouse, 970-476-5757**—Vail's very own brewpub. The handcrafted beer can almost substitute for a meal, especially if you sample a few of the darker variations.

Wed.: **Club Chelsea, 970-476-5600**—The only place for a disco scene with the added feature of a cigar bar.

Thurs.: **Mickey's, 970-476-5011 ext. 115**—This Vail institution features the pop and classical music of piano man Mickey Poage in the Lodge at Vail.

Fri.: **Garfinkle's, 970-476-3789**—At a prime Lionshead location right next to the new gondola, this great spot offers frozen drinks and a large selection of imported beer, making it the perfect place to begin your afternoon attitude adjustment.

Sat.: **The Club, 970-479-0556**—Loud, young and smoky. Some local live musicians take the stage in the small basement bar and get the crowd dancing in a hurry. Generally the rowdiest people find their way here.

Outside Vail

For après ski, folks in Beaver Creek gather at the **Coyote Cafe (970-949-5001).** The cafe specializes in Mexican food and offers a happy hour. Whereas Vail is known for its nightlife, Beaver Creek is pretty quiet at night, but you should check out any programs at the **Vilar Center for the Performing Arts** in the center of town (underneath the ice rink). Everything from comedy to classical music concerts can be found here **(970-920-2787; www.beavercreek.com).**

If the serene and sophisticated Beaver Creek scene gets to you, head to Avon and **Cassidy's Hole in the Wall (970-949-9449).** It's a country and western, beer-swilling hangout with a worn wooden dance floor and a sense of humor (see the Where to Eat section for additional information).

Parks

Ford Park

At the east end of Vail right along the Gore Creek walking path lies this jewel of a park. Named for part-time Vail Valley residents Betty and Gerald Ford, the park features the usual playground and picnic areas. But you'll also find the unusual: the **Betty Ford Alpine Garden,** at 8,200 feet, represents the highest alpine botanical garden in North America. You will be impressed by the quantity of blooms at this extraordinarily beautiful place, especially in late summer. It's free! There's also an amphitheater for summer music performances. **970-476-0103; www.bettyfordaplinegardens.org.**

An explosion of color at the Betty Ford Alpine Gardens in Vail. Photo by Bruce Caughey.

Peeking out of a snowy shelter on Shrine Pass. Photo by Bruce Caughey.

Vail Nature Center

See the Museums section.

Scenic Drives

Red Sandstone Road

Though probably a little rough for Oldsmo-Buicks and similar cars, this summer-only, 30-mile round trip packs in quite a bit of scenery. And the end result—Piney Lake at the base of the Gore Range—is well worth the bumps. You might also consider taking this beautiful trip on snowmobile in winter. For more details and directions from Vail, see the Biking section.

Shrine Pass Road

This summer-only route, once temporarily named Holy Cross Trail, was christened for its terrific view of Mount of the Holy Cross. The route started out as an Indian trail when Utes hunted in the area. Indian campsites unearthed in the vicinity have been carbon-dated to 7,000 years ago. Before the Vail Pass Rd. was built in 1940, this road served as the major route between Denver and Glenwood Springs. Just east of the Vail Pass summit, turn off onto the Shrine Pass dirt road west of the rest area parking lot. The 11,000-foot summit is just 2.3 miles up, with wraparound views of the Gore Range to the north, the Sawatch Range to the southwest, the Tenmile Range to the east and the Flat Tops in the far west. Mount of the Holy Cross can be seen at mile 3.75—look for the sign. The road continues down through the canyon to Redcliff, where it joins up with Hwy. 24 for a pretty drive on pavement past Battle Mountain and Minturn north to Interstate 70. Hwy. 24 south from Redcliff over Tennessee Pass to Leadville makes a nice variation.

Where to Stay

Most people come to stay in Vail for a week or more, so condos and lodges account for many of the rooms. There's also a Marriott and a Holiday Inn. One of the more impressive hotels is the

Vail Cascade Hotel ($$$ to $$$$), 970-476-7111; www.vailcascade.com. Located in Cascade Village, this fine hotel features its own ski lift and other luxury amenities, including great workout facilities. Check out the on-premises **Chap's ($$$ to $$$$),** a fancy place for a perfectly cooked steak. You should look into one of the ski or golf package deals, depending on the season.

Vail rates during the summer generally run about half of what they are in winter. For information on hotels, condos and lodges (and last-minute reservations, often at a discount), contact the **Vail Valley Tourism and Convention Bureau: 1-800-525-3875; 970-476-1000; www.visitvailvalley.com.** If you are interested in home-stay accommodations try **Bed and Breakfast Vail: 1-800-748-2666; www.vail.net/lodging/bnb.**

Virtually all rooms in Beaver Creek are in several self-contained condominium complexes or deluxe lodges. Most of the rooms are pricey, but off-season packages can be incredible values. The most extraordinary complex is the **Hyatt Regency at Beaver Creek** (see entry below). Nearby, **The Charter ($$$$),** at **970-949-6660,** offers condo-style accommodations. You could always get away to **Trapper's Cabin ($$$$+), at 970-845-7900 ext. 102,** where your private chef and cabin keeper will make sure the wilderness isn't too hard on you (bring your platinum credit card). For information about renting these places, call them direct or contact **Vail Resorts Central Reservations, P.O. Box 915, Avon, CO 81620; 1-800-525-2257; 970-845-5745.** There's also plenty of less-expensive lodging in the nearby towns of Eagle, Avon, Minturn and Redcliff.

Hyatt Regency at Beaver Creek—$$$$

Most 300-room hotels lose something in intimacy and architectural style. Not so with the Hyatt. Phenomenal attention to detail helps this hotel capture a feeling previously reserved for European aristocracy. Do you know any other hotels that employ a full-time fire tender to keep massive stone hearths glowing in common guest areas? There is also a large, round outdoor fireplace that provides a perfect place to sip your toddy after a day on the slopes. Perched dramatically in an exclusive location only steps away from Beaver Creek's slopes, the Hyatt offers plenty of extras, including an indoor/outdoor pool with snow-melt deck and six outdoor whirlpools (the largest, measuring 16 feet in diameter, is lavishly filled by a heated waterfall). The health club and spa offer herbal body wraps and hydraulic workout equipment. "Camp Hyatt" entertains the kids while parents enjoy a real vacation. Three unique restaurants tempt your palate, including Patina **($$$ to $$$$),** which offers fine dining with a Southwestern influence, Mon.–Sat. Prices at the hotel vary dramatically with the seasons—the same room costs three times as much during the peak ski season than in May. For information and reservations contact Hyatt Worldwide at **1-800-233-1234** or the hotel directly at **136 Thomas Pl., P.O. Box 1595, Beaver Creek, CO 81620; 970-949-1234; www.beavercreek hyatt.com.**

The Lodge at Cordillera—$$$$

The contrast is striking: drive past the mobile home park at Edwards before heading up Squaw Creek toward this secluded, European-style retreat. After passing muster at the guard station, you will pass massive new homes and a Hale Irwin-designed 18-hole golf course before finally reaching the impressive Lodge at Cordillera. Perched amid 7,000 acres of private forest and alpine meadow, the lodge's slate roof, native stone accents and stately Belgian architecture make it a place fit for royalty wannabes. If you want to be pampered, you've come to the right place. At the spa, two hydrotherapy tubs, a state-of-the-art workout room and a staff of personal trainers and masseuses are at your service. In winter nothing beats swimming laps in the indoor pool while surrounded by floor-to-ceiling picture windows. Oh, except the hot tub has the same incredible view. The lodge has been expanded but still offers only 56 rooms, so you won't ever feel lost or neglected. Simple elegance best describes the rooms: some have balconies or terraces, many feature fireplaces and some have lofts (perfect for families). All are decorated with a welcome flair. You don't ever need to leave this privileged preserve, but they do offer shuttles to Beaver Creek and Vail. The natural surroundings and trail system entice you outside in summer (golf, hiking, mountain biking, swimming, tennis) or winter (cross-country skiing on 20 kilometers of groomed track). In the evening you will want to take time for a leisurely meal at the award-winning **Restaurant Picasso ($$$$)** or at two other restaurants. **P.O. Box 1110, Edwards, CO 81632; 1-800-877-3529; 970-926-2200; www. cordillera-vail.com.**

Black Bear Inn of Vail—$$$ to $$$$

In this immense log structure next to Gore Creek, you'll find 12 rooms and a couple of caring proprietors. Unlike many Vail residents, owners Jessie and David Edeen did not just move here. The large common room has comfortable, overstuffed couches, an antique woodstove and a deck with great views. The bedrooms are simple, attractive and comfortable, each with a small private bathroom. Every room has a sleeper sofa, and some top-floor rooms connect easily for families traveling together. If you stay in summer, you may want to request a room on the side opposite Interstate 70 because the highway noise isn't totally masked by the creek. Outdoor summer games include horseshoes, bocce ball, croquet and badminton. In addition to home-baked bread, granola, juice, coffee and fruit, you will get a daily special each morning. Minimum stay requirement, depending on season. Well-behaved kids okay; no smoking inside; no pets. **2405 Elliott Rd., Vail, CO 81657; 970-476-1304; www.vail.net/blackbear.**

Gasthof Gramshammer—$$$ to $$$$

Proprietor Pepi Gramshammer is known locally as Mr. Vail; his lodge could just as easily be known as Hotel Vail. The lodge, born the same year as the town, epitomizes all that's good about Vail's transplanted Tyrolean charm. The

German word for it is *Gemütlichkeit,* which means something like "friendliness and ambience." Pepi and his wife, Sheika—both transplanted Austrians—are directly responsible for the cozy inn's charm. Pepi, a former Olympic skier, might turn up to carry your bags, fix your TV or bus your table. Sheika, an alumna of an expedition to Mt. Everest, travels to Europe four times a year to find authentic supplies for the lodge. And the family dog, Aretha, makes guests feel right at home. The 27 European-style rooms and apartments come in color schemes of champagne, blue and rose. All apartments feature fireplaces and down comforters. Warning: the rooms only rent out a week at a time during ski season and are usually sold out a year ahead. Most guests are returnees. The hotel's restaurant, the **Antlers Room ($$$ to $$$$),** serves a Bavarian/continental menu, specializing in wild game. The adjacent deck is the best in Vail. **231 E. Gore Creek Dr., Vail, CO 81657; 970-476-5626; www. pepis.com.**

Sonnenalp Resort—$$$ to $$$$

The Sonnenalp is a mountain hotel in three parts: Sonnenalp Resort, the Austria Haus and Club and the Swiss Hotel and Spa. All are perched on the sunny side of Gore Creek in Vail Village. The separate houses allow this fairly large hotel to maintain a small-inn atmosphere. And this isn't imitation alpine: the Fassler family created the Sonnenalp idea at its resort near Oberstdorf, West Germany. Fourth-generation innkeepers Rosana and Johannes Fassler continue the tradition in Vail. A giant contingent of Bavarians was staying when we visited, and we were told that many guests are European, adding to the Old World ambience. The favorite of the three houses is the Swiss Hotel, with its attention to detail. All 178 rooms in the three houses are priced the same. Each features feather comforters and handcrafted furnishings imported from Germany. The hotel has an elaborate spa even by Vail standards. Among its features are a cold dip—a narrow, deep pool to plunge into before heading to the sauna or whirlpool bath—

and one hypotherapy tub. It's necessary to book rooms at least three months in advance during ski season. **20 Vail Rd., Vail, CO 81657; 970-476-5656; www.sonnenalp.com.**

Redcliff Lodge—$$$

Check out this extremely well-thought-out, comfortable but not elegant lodge. The Redcliff provides radiant heat under the wood floors; three rooms share a common kitchen. Downstairs you can pop in for a beer or a wrap at Mango's (see the Where to Eat section). **206 Eagle, Redcliff, CO 81649; 970-827-9109; www.redclifflodge.com.**

Minturn Inn—$$ to $$$$

The young owners totally refurbished this 1915 vintage home and filled it with mountain-style furniture, including log beds. **442 Main St., P.O. Box 186, Minturn, CO 81645; 1-800-MINTURN; 970-827-9647; www.minturn inn.com.**

Comfort Inn—$$ to $$$

For skiers who like Beaver Creek but don't want to add too much more to their personal budget deficit, Avon's calling. Just a mile from the Beaver Creek Ski Area, in affordable Avon, is the sturdy Comfort Inn. Inside are 150 good-sized rooms, all with queen- or king-size beds. Amenities include a pool, whirlpool bath, hospitality suites and free continental breakfast served in the wood-beamed Comfort Clubroom. **P.O. Box 5510, Avon, CO 81620; 970-949-5511; www.comfortinn.com.**

Roost Lodge—$$ to $$$

The Roost is like a Volkswagen bug: it isn't pretty but it's popular and reliable. This **A**-frame-style lodge has long been a favorite of the budget-conscious—it's just about the least expensive place to stay in the Vail Village vicinity. During ski season it's about the only place to find a room available on fairly short notice without raising your credit limit. The 72 rooms are casually comfortable. There's a whirlpool bath and a covered pool. Roost Lodge is 2 miles from Vail ski

area at the West Vail exit. A shuttle bus runs to the ski area hourly, 8 A.M.–midnight. **1783 N. Frontage Rd., Vail, CO 81657; 970-476-5451; www.roostlodge.com.**

Camping

Sylvan Lake State Park

A truly gorgeous mountain setting at an elevation of 8,500 feet awaits you at this state park. **Elk Run Campground** (30 sites, fee charged) and **Fisherman's Paradise Campground** (12 sites, fee charged) both fit the bill for tents, trailers and campers; there are some pull-through sites for larger units. You can also reserve one of nine new and very popular cabins. Located 16 miles south of Eagle on W. Brush Creek Rd. For reservations: **1-800-678-CAMP;** in Denver **303-470-1144; www. reserveamerica.com.**

White River National Forest

Most national forest campsites can be reserved at **1-877-444-6777** or **www.reserveusa.com. Gore Creek Campground** (25 sites, fee charged) is the closest to Vail and therefore the most popular in the area. It's 5 miles east of Vail Village, near the boundary of the Eagles Nest Wilderness. Take Exit 180 from East Vail onto Hwy. 6 and head east 2 miles.

Tigiwon Campground (9 sites, no fee) is 6 miles up Tigiwon Rd. off Hwy. 24, 2.8 miles south of Minturn. A stone lodge built as a resting place for pilgrimages to Mount of the Holy Cross is available to groups on a free reservation basis by calling the **Holy Cross Ranger District Office, 970-827-5715.**

Half Moon Campground (7 sites, no fee) is 2.5 miles farther up Tigiwon Rd. at two trail-heads for the Holy Cross Wilderness.

Hornsilver Campground (12 sites, fee charged) is right off Hwy. 24, 1.5 miles south of Redcliff. **Blodgett Campground** (6 sites, fee charged) is just off Hwy. 24 on Homestake Rd. (Forest Rd. 703), 12 miles south of Minturn. **Gold Park Campground** (11 sites, fee charged), 10 miles farther up Homestake Rd., used to be an old gold mining camp. Jeep and hiking trails to Holy Cross City ghost town and the Holy Cross Wilderness leave from here.

Where to Eat

Beano's Cabin (Beaver Creek)—$$$$

Taking a moonlit sleigh ride to dinner is probably not something you do every day, so here's your chance. Beano's Cabin is a rustic log cabin in the Larkspur Bowl on Beaver Creek Mountain. Large sleighs rendezvous on the half hour for the journey toward a sumptuous western-style dinner. During summer, guests ride horses to the cabin. Be sure to make reservations in advance. Rides leave Wed.–Sun. **970-949-9090; www.snow.com.**

Mirabelle's (Beaver Creek)—$$$$

This gourmet French restaurant has been referred to not only as the best restaurant at Beaver Creek but as the best restaurant in the Rockies, period. It's housed in a gorgeous restored farmhouse that dates back to 1898, when it was the biggest residence in Avon. Inside are oak furnishings and etched glass. Entrées include salmon, trout, shrimp Provençal, veal, beef and lamb. The selection of wines is palate-boggling. The restaurant is located right across from the reception house on the road up to Beaver Creek. Open for dinner Tues.–Sun. 6–10 P.M. **55 Village Rd.; 970-949-7728.**

The Left Bank (Vail)—$$$ to $$$$

A host of restaurants in Vail seems to offer the same exclusive menu of French/continental fare. According to nearly everyone we asked, the Left Bank does it best. Chef Luc Meyer apprenticed in France, and he and his wife Liz collected the restaurant's French country decor. The Meyers serve a variety of seafood and game, specializing in veal, elk steaks and chicken prepared a different way each day. Though prices are high, the Left Bank is in demand. During ski season reservations are necessary up to two weeks in advance. No credit cards accepted.

Open Thurs.–Tues. 6–10 P.M. Located in the Sitzmark Lodge at **183 Gore Creek Dr.; 970-476-3696.**

Minturn Country Club (Minturn)— $$ to $$$$

Don't bother scheduling tee times, because this is just a great little restaurant with a good sense of both humor and food. The club truly believes in letting you "Have It Your Way": you're the chef here. Pick a steak, kabob, fish or chicken from a meat case and toss it on the charcoal grill in the dining room. Sidelights include a salad bar, corn on the cob, asparagus, baked potatoes and huge slabs of Texas toast you can swab with garlic butter and throw on the grill. During ski season the club is elbow-to-elbow for dinner. Located in the former Minturn Post Office on Main St. Open daily 5:30–10 P.M. **131 Main St., Minturn; 970-827-4114.**

Sweet Basil (Vail)—$$ to $$$$

This sunny cafe is a lunch favorite of people who work in the village. One reason is that meals are served quickly, usually in a half hour or less. But speedy service alone doesn't make a successful restaurant. The continental food is also delicious, rated four stars by *The Denver Post*. What struck us most was the variety on the menu, from grilled duck-breast sandwiches to pizza to chili with corn sticks. The cooks outdo themselves with unusual garnishes, such as pink peppercorn butter and cranberry mayonnaise. Don't leave too soon and miss the Sweet Basil forte—homemade desserts. The breezy, upscale interior features works of local artists. Though best at lunch (served daily 11:30 A.M.–2:30 P.M.), Sweet Basil also offers dinner 6–10 P.M. **193 E. Gore Creek Dr.; 970-476-0125.**

Cassidy's Hole in the Wall (Avon)— $ to $$$

For a solid bite to eat in a down-home atmosphere, stop in at Cassidy's. You'll find locals mixing it up with tourists from Beaver Creek at the bar, or hunched over huge plates of food. As far as the food goes, it's basic but done right:

steaks, baby back ribs, burgers, chicken and trout are balanced with lighter dishes, such as salads and sandwiches. If you prefer eating a meal in a semiquiet setting, ask for an upstairs table. Occasional live music. Open every day 11 A.M.–2 A.M. **82 E. Beaver Creek Blvd.; 970-949-9449.**

The Gashouse (Edwards)—$ to $$$

When you've had a little too much overpriced French food, designer jeans and mink stoles, here's the perfect roadhouse-style antidote. The only fur you'll see at the Gashouse is on the deer heads mounted on the log walls of this Conoco-station-turned-restaurant. This is where many locals run to escape the tourist blitz. Service can be a bit slow and indifferent, but the price is right. Go for a steak or a large portion of fresh fish; crab cakes remain a summer favorite. The Gashouse is 4 miles west of Beaver Creek on Hwy. 6. Open daily from 11 A.M. **34185 Hwy. 6; 970-926-3613.**

Fiesta's New Mexican Cafe and Cantina (Edwards)—$ to $$

This is where locals head for excellent Mexican dishes in a casual atmosphere. Run by the Marquez sisters, you won't find a tastier relleno, burrito or chimichanga. Be sure to try the award-winning green chili or, if you want a change of pace, the white jalapeño sauce. Top it all off with cinnamon sopapillas. The margaritas absolutely passed our test! Open Mon.–Fri. 10:30 A.M.–10 P.M.; weekends at 7:30 A.M. for breakfast, until 10 P.M. In Edwards Plaza between Hwy. 6 and Interstate 70; **970-926-2121.**

Mango's (Redcliff)—$ to $$

Funky, friendly and with flavorful food. What more do you want? Named after the owner's rottweiler, this place specializes in wraps, fish tacos and chicken quesadillas, as well as other grill items. You can order a fresh Kaltenberg brew from the tap. Sometimes they have entertainment or poetry readings. It's a very local place right in front of the Redcliff Lodge. Open Mon.–Thurs. 11:30 A.M.–9 P.M.; Fri.–Sat. 8 A.M.–10 P.M.; Suns. for brunch only. **166½ Eagle St., Redcliff; 970-827-9109; www. theredclifflodge.com.**

Daily Grind (Vail)—$

During peak season, don't be discouraged by the line because the fresh hot coffee and the friendly, offbeat atmosphere is worth it. Light lunches, baked goods and strong coffee. Check it out in the evening for wines by the glass and a tapas menu. Open daily at 6:30 A.M. **288 Bridge St.; 970-476-5856.**

Services

Visitor Information

Eagle Valley Chamber of Commerce—P.O. Box 964, Eagle, CO 81631; 970-328-5220; www.eaglevalley.org.

Vail/Beaver Creek Reservations—P.O. Box 7, Vail, CO 81658; 1-800-728-2759; 970-845-5745; www.snow.com.

Vail Valley Chamber of Commerce—Stop in for information and advice about what to do in this part of the valley. **P.O. Box 1437, Avon, CO 81620; 970-949-5189; www.vailvalley chamber.org.**

Vail Valley Tourism and Convention Bureau—Serves as a reservations service and provides information about the area. **100 E. Meadow Dr.; 1-800-525-3875; 970-476-1000; www.visitvailvalley.com.**

Day Care

ABC School—This preschool located in Vail cares for children 2 to 5 years old. **149 N. Frontage Rd., Vail, CO 81657; 970-476-1420.**

Vail Recreation District—Offers activities for kids of all ages. **970-479-2292; www.camp vail.com.**

Transportation

Bus System—Vail's free bus system is second only in volume to downtown Denver's free mall shuttle. **970-328-8143; www.ci.vail.co.us.**

Colorado Mountain Express—Airport shuttles to Vail and Avon/Beaver Creek. **P.O. Box 580, Vail, CO 81658; 1-800-247-7074; 970-949-4227; www.cmex.com.**

Winter Park and Middle Park

As you descend from the 11,315-foot summit of Berthoud Pass on a winding highway, you get a true sense of the tall peaks lining the perimeter of the Fraser Valley. Many of these mountains reach above 13,000 feet. A major part of the beauty of this area lies in the million acres of Arapaho National Forest. This huge stretch of public land thankfully preserves undeveloped mountain vistas as you visit the small towns anchored along the Fraser River.

At the head of the valley lies Winter Park, a favorite ski destination. A couple of miles down-valley on Hwy. 40 you'll find the neighboring town of Fraser. As the river valley widens into the area commonly known as Middle Park, the small towns of Tabernash, Granby and Hot Sulphur Springs make their entry.

Middle Park, unlike its northern and southern counterparts, offers extremely complex geologic terrain: faults, uplifts and overthrusts have been further altered by volcanic formations and erosion. This geologic activity has created a beautiful variety of mountainous landscapes. Once a prized hunting ground of the Indians, today this region is a prized vacationing ground for people from around the country.

With good reason Winter Park is one of the state's most popular ski areas. Offering a dynamic range of terrain, the combined resort of Winter Park and Mary Jane can accommodate the crush of Front Range skiers that flock here on weekends. Nearby SolVista provides a smaller setting well suited to many families—skiing here with smaller crowds (and fewer "expert" skiers from Colorado) is a great alternative. Now that the owners of SolVista have purchased and reopened Berthoud Pass, the range of skiing and snowboarding in the area has expanded nicely.

Once the snow has melted, and "mud season" is declared over (Memorial Day), people stay in the area as a perfect base for hiking, mountain biking, golfing or simply appreciating the gorgeous surroundings. With a major base-area development partially complete, and gorgeous condos and a new village in a place where there used to be dirt parking lots, there seems to be a personality shift going on here. And yet the town of Winter Park maintains its own somewhat haphazard appeal just 2 miles north of the ski area. There, numerous mini-shopping plazas, restaurants and lodges are spread along both sides of Hwy. 40. Split in half by traffic, Winter Park misses out on some of the intimacy of other ski villages. But what it lacks in city planning, it seems to have gained back in personality.

"The coldest spot in the nation" is a phrase commonly associated with the town of Fraser, where the thermometer can dip to more than 50° F below zero on winter nights. The ring of tall peaks around the town creates stationary pockets of frigid air. The masochists living here are actually proud of their self-proclaimed designation as "icebox of the nation."

Down-valley, northwest along Hwy. 40, small ranching centers lie beyond the fray of the

Getting There

Winter Park is located 67 miles (about 90 minutes) northwest of Denver. The best route from Denver is via Interstate 70, west for 42 miles to Hwy. 40 at Exit 232. Follow Hwy. 40 over Berthoud Pass and drop into Winter Park at the head of the Fraser Valley. After Winter Park come the small communities of Fraser, Tabernash, Granby and Hot Sulphur Springs.

Greyhound Bus Lines (1-800-231-2222; www.greyhound.com) provides daily service between Winter Park and downtown Denver. You might also try an airport shuttle from **Home James (1-800-451-4844).**

On winter weekends, perhaps the best way to reach Winter Park from Denver is on the **Rio Grande Ski Train (303-296-ISKI; www.skitrain.com).** The 2-hour trip winds through South Boulder Canyon and passes under the Continental Divide by way of historic Moffat Tunnel. There is also twice-daily **Amtrak** train service **(1-800-USA-RAIL; www.amtrack.com)** to Fraser from Chicago and San Francisco on the California Zephyr.

retail shops and restaurants in Winter Park and Fraser. Hwy. 40 takes you past prime ranch land to the Gold Medal trout water of the upper Colorado River and eventually to quiet Hot Sulphur Springs. The transformation of the hot springs pools into a worthy destination have added something special to the valley to complement the old Riverside Hotel and the Grand County Historical Museum.

History

From the mid-1600s Middle Park had been a coveted Indian hunting ground because the large game herds in the valley provided easy prey. Confrontations between Ute and Arapaho hunting parties were commonplace.

When the fur trade was booming in the 1820s, trappers came into the valley. These hardy mountain men had a practical knowledge of the park, but it was not until the expedition of John C. Frémont in 1844 that any maps of Middle Park existed.

Irish nobleman Lord Gore briefly visited Middle Park while on his legendary American hunting expedition, which lasted from 1854 to 1857. Traveling with a huge entourage, Gore single-handedly killed thousands of bison and 40 grizzly bears and lost count of the elk, antelope and deer that he slaughtered. In the evening Lord Gore retired to his green-striped tent to sip vintage wines and enjoy the company of imported ladies of pleasure.

As the 1870s arrived, a smattering of Anglos had settled in Middle Park. Ute and Arapaho Indians continued to hunt in summer and did not appreciate the intrusion. By the time of the Ute Massacre in Meeker on Sept. 29, 1879 (see the Meeker chapter), tension was reaching new heights. It was a time of occasional violence and constant concern for the entire valley. A common sentiment of the times was expressed by U.S. Army Gen. Pope, who said the Utes were "worthless, idle vagabonds, who are no more likely to earn a living... by manual labor than by teaching metaphysics." After the Indians were expelled from their homeland, sheep and cattle ranching took on primary importance in Middle Park. Many prospectors came into the area but left with little reward for their efforts.

Before the turn of the century, William Byers, owner of the *Rocky Mountain News,* had modest success in trying to lure wealthy vacationers to his latest purchase: Hot Sulphur Springs. Miners and lumberjacks appreciated the soothing vapor waters in greater numbers than the moneyed. Even though the natural springs beside the Colorado River were rumored to have healing powers, Byers's spa never really got off the ground. However, by 1911 Hot Sulphur Springs began attracting tourists to skiing events at its annual Winter Carnival.

Winter has long been a popular season in the Fraser Valley. Skiers have streamed into the

Winter Park area since completion of the Moffat Railroad Tunnel in 1927. The train emerged from underneath the Continental Divide and eager skiers with 7-foot wooden skis would hike up the mountain for a meager two runs per day. The first lift on the Denver-owned watershed was a simple rope tow in 1935.

Today the train still runs on weekends, shuttling skiers and summertime visitors from Denver, but the facilities have grown steadily to create a major ski destination. Unlike nearly all ski areas, Winter Park was still managing to operate as a nonprofit entity, owned by the City and County of Denver.

Festivals and Events

Spring Splash
mid-Apr.   The end of the Winter Park ski season is ushered in with a splash. The highlight of the daylong party is a ski race down an obstacle course ending in a 40-foot-long pool of ice-cold water. Costumed skiers try to pick up speed so they can glide over the water, but many lose their momentum about halfway across. **970-726-5514; 303-892-0961** in Denver.

World Class Rock Fest and Winter Park Jazz Festival
July   Summertime at the base of Winter Park's ski slopes: lay back on your blanket, enjoy the mountain view and listen to some of the world's top musicians in a natural amphitheater. If you're tired of grumbling about high ticket prices and short concerts, don't worry—while the tickets are not cheap, each festival features four to five bands each day, during two distinctive musical events.

Those into folk and rock music will want to attend the KBCO World Class Rock Fest. In past years Bonnie Raitt, Natalie Merchant and Bare Naked Ladies have performed for large crowds. The Jazz Festival attracts a talented range of acts from the smooth fusion of David Sanborn to the Orleans sound of the Neville Brothers. Bring your own food and drink or browse the veritable tent city of food vendors. **970-726-5514; 303-892-0961** in Denver; **www.winterparkresort.com; www.kbco.com.**

High Country Stampede
Sat. nights from July to the end of Aug.   At the rodeo grounds just west of Fraser, amateur riders and ropers display their skills in front of an enthusiastic crowd. Most of the contestants are regional ranch hands; all ride competitively for their pride and a share of the purse. This popular event coincides with a western barbecue and steak fry that shouldn't be missed. For more information and tickets contact the **Winter Park/Fraser Valley Chamber of Commerce; 970-726-4118; 303-422-0666** in Denver.

Outdoor Activities

Biking

MOUNTAIN BIKING
Ranchers, loggers and the Denver Water Board have left behind a maze of dirt roads that are ideal for sturdy two-wheelers. The annual Fat Tire Classic in late June remains one of the top fund-raising events (for the American Red Cross) anywhere. Winter Park is also a regular stop on the National Off Road Biking Association (NORBA) series. For information and updates on trail conditions, contact **1-800-903-7275.** You may also want to get in touch with the **Sulphur Ranger District** at the south end of Granby, **9 Ten Mile Dr., P.O. Box 10, Granby, CO 80446; 970-887-4100; www.fs. fed.us/outernet/arnf/srd.**

Fraser River Trail
This winding, well-marked, paved trail offers 5 miles of gentle terrain between Winter Park Resort and Fraser. The trail is an excellent option for families, even good for strollers and wheelchairs. Make a day of it by stopping at any of the picnic tables along the way.

Fraser Valley Trails

The wide Fraser Valley, with its rolling hills, sprawling meadows and dense forests, makes an ideal place for all skill levels. Here you'll find a world-class trail system, featuring 600 miles of mapped and marked roads, including a good bit of single-track trails. Thousands of additional miles of unmarked trails and dirt roads, most of which started out as logging roads, get used by many in-the-know locals. For marked roads and trails, you may pick up information and a free map at the **Winter Park/Fraser Valley Chamber of Commerce** on Hwy. 40 in central Winter Park.

Rollins Pass Road (Corona Pass)

See the Four-Wheel-Drive Trips section for more information on this historic route.

Winter Park On-Mountain Biking

Another perfect option, especially for those not quite used to high-altitude riding, is to take the Zephyr Express chairlift up (many of the chairs are equipped with bike racks) and head down the 44 miles of marked trails at Winter Park Resort. If you want to skip the lift ticket you can, of course, ride up and down the mountain all you want for free. Since debuting its on-mountain trails in 1991, Winter Park Resort has continued to expand its marked trails to accommodate all skill levels—although first-timers should seriously consider sticking to the valley floor. Riders take their bikes up the ski lift (for a fee) and then get to skip most thigh-burning uphills. Stop in for an energy-boosting lunch and glorious views from 10,700 feet at the massive, hewn-log Sunspot Lodge.

In addition to the downhill experience at the ski mountain, riders can access more than 600 miles of marked, mapped trails throughout the valley. A few favorite trails: the mellow 6-mile **Northwest Passage,** the more difficult 12-mile **Zoom Loop** and the great 6-mile cruiser called **Long Trail.** On-mountain trail information is available at **www.skiwinter park.com.**

Rentals and Tours

A proliferation of mountain bike shops have opened in Winter Park, run by enthusiasts who are knowledgeable about the sport and nearby trails. If you plan on renting a bike for a long period of time, be sure to phone in an early reservation.

Ski Depot Sports—Located in Park Plaza Shopping Center on Hwy. 40; **1-800-525-6484; 970-726-8055.**

Slopeside Gear and Sport—Located in the Zepher Mountain Lodge at the base of the ski area. They offer bikes and mountain scooters with wide, knobby tires fit for dirt.

Fishing

President Eisenhower used to fish in this valley, so it should be good enough for you! For a great full-service fly shop, guided trips and access to private water, check in with **The Fly Shop** at Devil's Thumb Ranch Resort; **970-726-9231; www.devilsthumbranch.com.** Check out some of these great options:

Arapaho National Recreation Area

Shadow Mountain Reservoir, Willow Creek Reservoir, Lake Granby, Grand Lake and **Monarch Lake,** all northeast of Granby, offer excellent fishing in a beautiful setting. See the Fishing section of the **Grand Lake** chapter for more information.

Colorado River

After the Fraser River joins the Colorado River near Granby, the wide river is designated Gold Medal water. It is therefore a pity that, unless you are one of a privileged few, most of the river is off-limits. Only 5 miles of the river between Granby and Kremmling remain unfenced. The river flows through sprawling cattle ranches, and permission to fish is rarely granted. However, you might be able to gain access to private water by hiring a local outfitter who has already made arrangements with the landowner. There is a good 2-mile stretch downstream from Hot Sulphur Springs in Byers Canyon. Fishing for large rainbows and browns is popular here, despite the fact that the river is closely paralleled by the highway and the embankment is fairly steep. It is easier to wade this stretch than to try to fish it from the riverbank.

Fraser River

Flowing down from the upper reaches of Berthoud Pass, the Fraser River can be worth your time and persistence. Upper portions of the river, near Winter Park Resort, offer a chance at well-stocked rainbows and brooks. The small river flows next to Hwy. 40 for much of its upper run. One mile downstream from Tabernash, to a mile or so above Granby, the river is designated Wild Trout water. As the river enters Fraser Canyon, the fishing for rainbows and browns is rated good. This was President Eisenhower's favorite place to fish. Now you'll face a complex system of state land grants offering a limited patchwork of public water; check with the Division of Wildlife at **303-291-7533**

An angler throws a perfect fly line on the Fraser River. Photo by Rod Walker.

for current information. Popular flies include the Royal Wulff and gray caddis imitations on top; Hare's Ear and Stonefly nymphs under the surface. Mepps and Rapala lures tend to produce some bites.

Meadow Creek Reservoir

As soon as the ice melts from this high mountain reservoir, the fishing gets hot for rainbows and brooks. Dispersed camping can be found on the north shore. For a smaller, natural lake, try fishing at **Columbine Lake,** a 3-mile hike from above the reservoir. The high lake (11,100 feet) is a sure bet for pan-sized cutthroat. To reach this area, take Hwy. 40 to just east of Tabernash. Turn onto Forest Rd. 129, which winds northeast to the reservoir. Past the campgrounds, at the end of the road, is the trailhead for Columbine Lake.

Williams Fork Reservoir

This good-sized reservoir is locked between the high peaks of the Williams Fork and Vasquez Mountains at an elevation of 7,800 feet. There are a lot of rainbow and brown trout, pike and even kokanee salmon swimming around in what eventually becomes Denver's tap water. Though the water level fluctuates, this can be an excellent place to catch a stringer full of fish. A boat ramp and camping area are located on the west side. To get to the reservoir, take Hwy. 40 west of Hot Sulphur Springs 4 miles, to a point just east of Parshall. Ute Pass Rd. (County Rd. 3) branches south for the last few miles to Williams Fork Reservoir.

Four-Wheel-Drive Trips

Rollins Pass Road (Corona Pass)

The Needles Eye Tunnel east of the summit (11,671 feet) of Rollins Pass caved in years ago, blocking the way for jeeps wanting to continue much beyond the Continental Divide. Even so, the drive up the road to the summit from the west side is still beautiful. Contact the **Forest Service office** in **Boulder (303-444-6600)** or **Granby (970-887-4100)** to find out about current conditions. You can bypass the blockage on foot or by mountain bike to complete the trip to Nederland.

The entire route follows the original path of the railway over the divide. Rollins Pass was used for 24 years as the main line of the Denver, Northwestern and Pacific Railway Company until the Moffat Tunnel was completed in 1927. The railway and namesake tunnel were both the brainchild of David H. Moffat. After he made his fortune in banking and mining, he set out to find a shorter passage to Salt Lake City and the West Coast. His idea for a line due west of Denver was a 175-mile shortcut to the established routes. The route over Rollins Pass was intended only as a stopgap measure until the tunnel was completed. Built from 1923 to 1927, the 6.2-mile tunnel was finally completed at a huge cost: 19 lives and $18 million. At the Continental Divide the tunnel is bored a mile beneath the surface. The completion of the tunnel eliminated 23 miles and 2.5 hours of travel time off the "Hill" route.

From Winter Park turn right (east) from Hwy. 40 onto Forest Rd. 149 and stay on the main road. As you continue toward the pass, the condition of the road gets worse. The status of the road, once maintained as a passenger car route, has deteriorated as the result of major rock slides and the tunnel cave-in.

Rentals and Tours

Mad Adventures—This Winter Park company offers a small selection of guided jeep tours in the area. One 3-hour tour goes to the top of Rollins Pass. Reservations required. **P.O. Box 650, Winter Park, CO 80482; 1-800-451-4844; 970-726-5290; www.mad adventures.com.**

Golf

Grand Lake Golf Course
See the **Grand Lake** chapter

Pole Creek Golf Club
Highly rated by *Golf Digest* magazine and considered by many to be one of the finest mountain courses in the state, the 27 holes at Pole Creek make for very exciting play. At an elevation of 8,600 feet, the ball flies 12 percent farther than at sea level. Like other mountain courses, lodgepole pines line the fairways on many holes and majestic mountain views can be pleasantly distracting. Some holes are laid out Scottish-style with few trees and plenty of natural hazards. If you want to beware of any one hole, watch out for the 570-yard hole No. 7. "You need three well-placed shots in a row to have any hope," says golf pro Kim Anders. The contours of the course mirror the inspiring views to the Indian Peaks, which provide a backdrop on many holes. Pro shop, range and restaurant; club rentals and motorized carts available. Breakfast and lunch served daily at the Tavern on the Green. Located 11 miles northwest of Winter Park on Hwy. 40 between Tabernash and Granby; **970-726-8847.**

SolVista Resort
Golf is coming to SolVista. Check on the phased-in opening of the links-style course, with a planned completion in 2001. **970-887-3384; www.silvercreek-resort.com.**

Hiking and Backpacking
Arapaho National Forest surrounding the Fraser Valley provides a beautiful expanse for hiking and backpacking. Many backcountry trails weave their way through miles of high country. The popular Indian Peaks Wilderness Area, encompassed within the national forest, straddles both sides of the Continental Divide. Because of heavy use, a permit is required for backcountry camping. For reservations or trail information contact the **Boulder Ranger District, 303-444-6600,** or the **Sulphur Ranger District** at the south end of Granby, **9 Ten Mile Dr., P.O. Box 10, Granby, CO 80446; 970-887-4100; www. fs.fed.us/outernet/arnf/srd.** If you are unable to plan your trip to the Indian Peaks ahead of time, there are a few last-chance permits issued by the district offices.

The Vasquez Mountains and the Fraser Experimental Forest are little-used forest areas to the west of Winter Park and Berthoud Pass.

The experimental forest is not nearly as sinister as it sounds; new techniques of forest management are applied here.

Byers Peak Trail

This tough, steep 3.5-mile hike leads to the top of Byers Peak (12,804 feet). Before reaching treeline the defined trail passes through tall stands of Engelmann spruce in the Fraser Experimental Forest. Nearly constant winds buffet the upper reaches of the peak. A couple of small lakes lie a short distance from the trail and are said to have good fishing. Once at the summit enjoy far-reaching views of the mountains and valleys of northern Colorado. To reach the trailhead, head west on County Rd. 73 (Eisenhower Dr.) in Fraser toward St. Louis Creek Campground. After 4 miles take a right at the Byers Peak signpost and continue along the dirt road for 4.5 miles to the Byers Peak Trail parking lot.

Caribou Pass Trail

This trail offers a fairly difficult 4.4-mile hike to Caribou Pass (11,790 feet) and excellent views of the Indian Peaks. Those seeking a longer backpack trip can continue over Arapaho Pass to Monarch Lake. Be prepared for occasional muddy conditions as you set off on this trail. The first mile is on an old four-wheel-drive road (now closed to vehicles). As the trail tracks beside Meadow Creek, it passes a couple of crumbling log cabins that have seen better days. At a marked trail junction, follow the footpath that heads east from the Columbine Lake Trail (see below) and into a subalpine forest. For the next mile, the trail ascends sharply through the trees, interspersed in places with flowering meadows. Caribou Pass is a tiring half-mile hike from treeline. At the top, the panorama to the east is inspiring: Apache Peak (13,441 feet), Navajo Peak (13,409 feet) and down to Caribou Lake at the base of the pass. Another half-mile hike along the ridge to the north leads to the top of Satanta Peak (11,979 feet). A precarious half-mile cliff walk to the south leads to Lake Dorothy.

To reach the trailhead for Caribou Pass and Columbine Lake Trails, take Hwy. 40 northwest almost to Tabernash. A half-mile east of town, Forest Rd. 129 heads northeast to Meadow Creek Reservoir. The trailhead for both hikes is located above the reservoir at the parking area for Junco Lake.

Columbine Lake Trail

This is a great half-day hike despite the fact that your feet may get wet while passing through a low meadow area. The nearly 3-mile trail uses the same route as Caribou Pass Trail (described above) for the first mile and a half. At a marked junction, Columbine Lake Trail continues south into a thick forest before heading to the top of a plateau. The trail passes through a couple of marshy meadows before reaching the lake at treeline. Along the trail the views to Winter Park Resort and the Fraser Valley are superb. Columbine Lake (11,060 feet) is a great place for picnicking and a chance at catching cutthroat trout. To reach Columbine Lake Trail, see the directions for Caribou Pass Trail above.

Corona Trail

There are a couple of ways to reach Corona Trail, but the best is from the top of Rollins Pass (11,671 feet) at the Continental Divide. From there the spectacular above-treeline trail follows a level grade atop the divide for 6 miles. Beware of incoming thunderstorms and snowstorms. Midway along the trail is Devil's Thumb Pass, where the finger-shaped rock of the same name is clearly visible. The thumb is a favorite technical climb. From the pass Devil's Thumb Trail leads to the western and eastern sides of the divide. To reach Rollins Pass head east on Forest Rd. 149 from Hwy. 40 between Winter Park and the ski area. The road can be rough and the Forest Service does not recommend it for passenger cars, but many make it to the top without any problems.

Another access route to Corona Trail involves climbing 2,000 vertical feet in less than 2.5 miles before reaching the Continental Divide. This trail begins at Devil's Thumb Park at the junction of High Lonesome and Devil's Thumb Trails. Follow Devil's Thumb Trail to the divide. There are good camping spots after crossing to the east side of Devil's Thumb Pass, near Devil's Thumb and Jasper Lakes. To reach the trailhead requires taking a four-wheel-drive road (Forest Rd. 128) east of Hwy. 40 at Fraser.

Monarch Lake Trailheads

Many excellent trails lead into the Indian Peaks Wilderness from Monarch Lake. Some of these are described in the Hiking and Backpacking section of the **Grand Lake** chapter.

Horseback Riding

High Mountain Lodge at Tally Ho Ranch

Located near Fraser on County Rd. 50; **1–800–772–9987; 970–726–5958.**

SolVista Resort

Great views accompany you on rides that last from 1 to 4 hours. At the SolVista Resort entrance near Granby. **970–887–1454; www.silvercreek-resort.com.**

YMCA Snow Mountain Ranch

Located 12 miles northwest of Winter Park near Tabernash. **970–887–2152; www.ymca rockies.org.**

River Floating

The moderate 14-mile stretch of the Upper Colorado River downstream from Kremmling attracts crowds of floaters on weekends. The periodic rapids and canyon scenery along the way add greatly to the trip. Several other lesser-used stretches of the river downstream from State Bridge offer leisurely floats virtually devoid of people but without any exciting rapids. Kayaking and canoeing are also great options. As many as 40 commercial outfitters make the trip.

Outfitters

Mad Adventures—**1–800–451–4844; 970–726–5290; www.madadventures.com.**

Timber Rafting—In Granby, information at **970–887–2141.**

Skiing

CROSS-COUNTRY SKIING AND SNOWSHOEING

Backcountry Trails

Thanks to the hundreds of miles of logging roads, many of which are marked for mountain biking, this valley reigns supreme for those seeking backcountry experiences on skis and snowshoes. Check the Mountain Biking and Hiking and Backpapcking sections for ideas beyond the following:

Sevenmile Trail—This is actually part of the old Berthoud Pass wagon road, a route between Denver and Middle Park. To get the most out of this trail, leave a second car at the fourth switchback on the west side of Berthoud Pass. The trail begins at the top of the pass with a plummeting drop into Hell's Half Acre, which can be avoided by following down along Hwy. 40 to its first switchback. Eventually you will track out by your car on the west side of Berthoud Pass.

Groomed Trails

Devil's Thumb Cross-Country Center— The center maintains more than 100 kilometers of expert, intermediate and beginner trails. The terrain at Devil's Thumb offers stunning views of surrounding peaks, but at times you'll be hemmed in by thick woods. To reach Devil's Thumb, drive 3 miles northeast of Fraser on Hwy. 40 and turn right on County Rd. 83. Follow the signs and be sure to keep right at the fork. **970–726–8231; www.devilsthumb ranch.com.**

Devil's Thumb also features the **Ranch House Restaurant and Saloon ($$ to $$$),** where many locals go for good food in an old log cabin that takes full advantage of the scenery; the setting retains an authentic rustic charm and you'll enjoy the eclectic menu. Live acoustic music on weekends. You might also want to consider staying in a lodge room (thin walls) or reserve one of their well-appointed cabins—for a romantic retreat, reserve the **"Fox" cabin ($$$).** Open year-round. **P.O. Box 750, Tabernash, CO 80478; 970-726-5633.**

Granby—SolVista Nordic Center maintains a selection of easy, well-groomed trails just outside of Granby. It has also become a popular place for telemarking on its gentle downhill ski slopes. The trail fee at the Nordic Center includes a couple of rides on certain lifts. Views from the upper trails into Fraser Valley are breathtaking, and a few of the descents will require all of your balance. Rentals, instruction, restaurants and lodging are all available. For more information on the ski area, see the entry on SolVista. Located 17 miles north of Winter Park **on Hwy. 40; 970-887-3384; www. silvercreek-resort.com.**

Tabernash—YMCA Snow Mountain Nordic Center offers a 30-mile public trail system (with a lighted loop for night skiing) that stretches throughout their property. The Nordic Center has long offered equipment rentals, lessons and passes during its lengthy winter season. Because the snow melts late in the season, the ranch trails are used extensively for training Olympic hopefuls. The employees have a refreshing, professional attitude about the sport. Trails range from beginner to expert. (For more information on Snow Mountain Ranch see the Where to Stay section.) Located 12 miles northwest of Winter Park **off Hwy. 40; 970-887-2152;** Denver metro area **303-443-4743; www.ymcarockies.org.**

DOWNHILL SKIING AND SNOWBOARDING

Berthoud Pass

High atop 11,315-foot Berthoud Pass, just a 20-minute hop off Interstate 70, skiers and boarders can find lift-served extreme skiing, numerous powder caches and value pricing. Berthoud recently found its financial footing with the owners of the much gentler SolVista ski area about 30 miles away. Tickets between the two resorts are interchangeable. Some gentler slopes lie just beneath the chairlifts, but the real reason to ski here remains the variety of expert pitches.

A snowboarder carves wide turns at Winter Park's halfpipe. Photo by Rod Walker.

Berthoud's glade skiing/boarding is tough to match, and you end up dropping below the pass and taking one of the frequent shuttle rides back up. The area's well-trained ski patrol does avalanche control within the boundaries, which encompass 1,700 acres of terrain and a vertical drop of 1,200 feet. Make sure you do off-season workouts before attempting the long, narrow bump runs on the west side of the highway. A day lodge provides rentals, gift shop, food and warming hut. **1-800-SKI-BERTHOUD; www. berthoudpass.com.**

SolVista

This compact ski area is a perfect complement to the expansive slopes of Winter Park/Mary Jane—families won't be intimidated thanks to fairly gentle terrain, small crowds and reasonable prices. Despite the fact that you will see expert slopes at SolVista, the black-diamond designation here would indicate intermediate runs at other Colorado areas. It's also a great place to learn how to snowboard or try snowbiking for that matter. Beginners have a separate learning area. **P.O. Box 1110, Granby, CO 80446; 1-800-283-7458; 970-887-3384; www. silver creek-resort.com.**

The base area features a saloon, restaurant, ski rental shop and nursery. Many condos are springing up at the bottom of the ski mountain, and the Brazilian owners plan to greatly expand the facilities over the coming years, including a golf course nearby. The 342-room **Inn at SilverCreek ($$ to $$$)** has all the amenities just 2 miles away; call **1-800-926-4FUN.** If you want to indulge in ski-in/ski-out accommodations try the condos at **Mountainside ($$$$), 1-800-777-1700.** SolVista is located 17 miles north of Winter Park on Hwy. 40. Bus service to and from Winter Park each day.

Winter Park Resort

Since 1939 when Winter Park opened with one T-bar tow, it has grown into a large, technologically equipped resort rivaling the best in the Rockies. Its 1,413 acres of skiable terrain cover four interconnected mountains—Winter Park, Mary Jane, Vasquez Ridge and Parsenn Bowl on the slopes of North Cone. Each of the mountains attracts some of the highest snow depths of any major Colorado ski area, and lift service includes eight high-speed quads. Despite Parsenn Bowl's intermediate ranking, its above-timberline location can make conditions on its moderate slopes highly variable (from unbelievable knee-deep powder to tricky crust). Halfway down its wide-open slopes, though, you plunge into the protection of the trees on narrow runs and glades. Advanced skiers will always head for the never-ending challenge of Mary Jane, with its own base facilities and long, deeply carved bump runs. Mary Jane has steadfastly hung onto its mantle as the state's bump heaven with 60 percent of its slopes classified as Most Difficult and only 3 percent beginner terrain. With a generous vertical drop of 2,610 feet, some runs stretch to 4.5 miles in length. Another good stop for experts who want to explore a variety of terrain besides mogul fields can be found in the *off-piste* (that is, ungroomed) conditions of Vasquez

Cirque. Most novice and intermediate skiers choose from the wide selection of groomed runs at both Winter Park and Vasquez Ridge.

At the top of Winter Park Mountain, stop in at the massive new Lodge at Sunspot for great eats and views (see the Where to Eat section). Visible to the northeast, the Continental Divide cuts a high route in front of your eyes. Since the area is easily accessible from Denver and a good value, expect longer lift lines on the weekends. The Children's Center at Winter Park offers day care for kids ages 2 months to 8 years; children over 3 can participate in a ski program that takes advantage of the Discovery Park. Skiers without Buddy Passes should make a note to pick up discounted tickets at gas and grocery outlets before heading up to the hills. For more information contact **P.O. Box 36, Winter Park, CO 80482; 970-726-5514;** in Denver **303-892-0961; www.skiwinterpark.com.**

National Center for the Disabled—Since Hal O'Leary founded this skiing program in 1970, it has grown to be the largest of its kind. Children and adults with all types of disabilities enjoy instruction and adaptive equipment at a nominal fee. A racing program, started in 1984, has trained many elite racers in an intense summer and winter training regimen. **970-726-5514;** in Denver **303-892-0961.**

Tubing

Fraser Winter Sports

At the Fraser tubing hill you can enjoy the exhilaration of jumping on a custom-made inner tube

Happy children whoop and holler on a sunny sledding day near Fraser. Photo by Bruce Caughey.

and flying down the steep, snow-covered mountain. Kids and adults love the experience equally. A set fee includes tube rental and as many rides up the rope tow as you can handle. The mountain is well lighted at night, and if it gets too cold you can skip a run and go inside to a crackling fire and a cup of hot chocolate. Located on the south end of Fraser. Open Mon.–Fri. 4–10 P.M. and weekends 10 A.M.–10 P.M. **970-726-5954.**

Seeing and Doing

Alpine Slide

Unlike the playground-variety slide we all grew up with, the longest slide in Colorado requires a chairlift ride to reach the top. With its high banked curves, the Alpine Slide resembles a luge course in the way it twists down the ski mountain. Pick up a combo ticket at the Winter Park base area and you can spend an entire day on the slide (or you can pay as you go), as well as enjoying a human maze, the requisite round of mini-golf and even a few tries at a pinnacle-shaped climbing wall. Fun for a wide range of ages. Open from early June to Labor Day 9:30 A.M.– 5 P.M. daily; until 7 P.M. during most of July and Aug. **970-726-5514;** in Denver **303-892-0961; www.skiwinterpark.com.**

Hot Springs

Hot Sulphur Springs Resort and Spa

This place used to be musty and run-down—but now we can recommend it. That's because Charles Nash came along and restored the ailing resort into a low-key and satisfying destination. The unfiltered, mineral-rich water in 20 different pools is said to heal all sorts of ailments, although for some people, the sulfur smell remaining on the skin can be a bit disconcerting. Lupe's Pool, the hottest, varies from 109° F to 112° F. Down the hill as you move to other pools, the water gets cooler. Decks and walkways connect the pools, and benches provide perfect spots to kick back and enjoy the views along the Colorado River. The perennial favorite,

Ute Pool, features a natural rock overhang with a steaming waterfall. Kids are relegated to the lower, cooler pools, but adults can wander the entire premises. Suits are required except in privacy areas. In addition to hot springs, 14 spa rooms serve up massage, herbal wrap and mud bath treatments. (See the Where to Stay section for more information.) Located about 30 minutes west of Winter Park on Hwy. 40. **P.O. Box 275, Hot Sulphur Springs, CO 80451; 970-725-3306; www.hotsulphursprings.com.**

Museums

Cozens Ranch House

William Zane Cozens must have been ready for a serious change of pace in 1874 when he quit his job as sheriff of Central City and moved to the Fraser Valley. By 1881 he and his family were living in a large ranch complex that included a residence, a small hotel, a stage-stop/dining room and the first post office in the valley. The empty Cozens Ranch was gradually falling apart until the Grand County Historical Association undertook an ambitious renovation. Today the ranch displays furniture, clothes and artifacts that reflect the simple life the Cozens family enjoyed. It's worth pulling off the highway for a look around. Small fee. Open daily Memorial Day–Oct. 1 and Dec. 15–Apr. 15, 10 A.M.–5 P.M.; closed during off-season on Mon. and Tues. Look for the sign on the east side of Hwy. 40 between Winter Park and Fraser. **P.O. Box 165, Hot Sulphur Springs, CO 80451.**

Grand County Historical Museum

The old Hot Sulphur Springs School, built in 1924, provides a perfect setting for recounting the long history of Grand County. The skiing exhibit provides a choice bit of trivia: Hot Sulphur Springs Ski Area, on the mountainside behind the museum, was the first in Colorado. Looking through the old photos and ski memorabilia in the front room, you realize how much the sport has changed. Another section of the museum displays Indian artifacts from Windy Gap and more recent Indian history.

How many times have you heard about the "white man's settlement of the West"? The Grand County Museum doesn't forget that pioneer women also played an indispensable role. Other exhibits show the development of towns in Grand County including Fraser, Tabernash, Granby and Kremmling. Free admission. Open in summer 10 A.M.–5 P.M. daily; in winter Wed.–Fri. 10 A.M.–5 P.M. and the first and third weekends of the month. Located at the east end of Hot Sulphur Springs on Hwy. 40, **110 E. Byers Ave.; 970-725-3939.**

Nightlife

Crooked Creek Saloon (in Fraser)

A young and very local crowd frequents this rowdy mountain bar. The floor starts to shake on weekends when the live rock or blues music begins. A full calendar offers specials to groups every night of the week. The Crooked Creek is a great place to eat hefty fatboy burgers, a plateful of pasta, stir-fry or a 16-oz. T-bone steak. They serve full breakfasts, but the bar atmosphere and smoke never quite go away. Open daily 7 A.M.–2 A.M. **Hwy. 40; 970-726-9250.**

The Derailer Bar

Check out this après-ski scene at the base of Winter Park ski area, where live music plays Tues.–Sat. during the season. Appetizers are served. Open until 6:30 P.M. **Winter Park base area; 970-726-5514 ext. 273.**

The Slope

Quantity seems the rule with three bars and several levels of mingling space available. The Slope is renowned among locals for its large dance floor and loud bands. The time to come here is when national acts stop by on tour. Call ahead. In **old-town Winter Park; 970-726-5727.**

Scenic Drives

Rocky Mountain National Park

It is easy to forget that Rocky Mountain National Park is right around the corner from the Fraser Valley. The west entrance of the park is located northeast of Granby on Hwy. 34. Before reaching the park you will pass Lake Granby and Shadow Mountain Reservoir. If you have never driven over Trail Ridge Rd. don't miss this experience; open late May–mid-Oct. For more information on Rocky Mountain National Park see the **Estes Park** chapter.

Where to Stay

Accommodations

Most of the accommodations we have chosen are in the vicinity of Winter Park Resort. Even so, you may want to consider an inexpensive motel room a little farther down-valley. You'll find basic rooms at sensible rates along Hwy. 40 between Tabernash and Hot Sulphur Springs. If you prefer a historic, though somewhat tattered, hotel, stop in at **The Riverside ($ to $$), 970-725-3589,** 26 miles northwest of Winter Park in Hot Sulphur Springs. One reasonably priced, basic (be advised: smoking and pets are okay) motel with kitchenettes and even a hot tub is the **Fireside ($$), 970-726-4668,** in Tabernash. You may want to try one of the cabins at **Devil's Thumb Ranch ($$$)** (see the Skiing section).

A host of bed and breakfasts have opened up throughout the valley in recent years. A newly constructed luxury bed and breakfast called the **Grand Victorian ($$$$), P.O. Box 1045, Winter Park, CO 80482, 1-800-204-1170,** re-creates a turn-of-the-century look complete with a turret, but without any creaky floors or antiques. It features fairly large rooms and suites with private bathrooms. For further lodging options call the **Winter Park/Fraser Valley Chamber of Commerce: 1-800-722-4118; 970-726-4118.**

C Lazy U Guest Ranch—$$$$

This is no ordinary ranch. From the moment you are helped to your well-appointed accommodations, you'll begin appreciating the mix of five-star luxury and dude-ranch atmosphere. This mix makes the C Lazy U a popular choice among a selective crowd that tends to return year after year. Rooms can be booked either in spacious individual cabins or in separate lodge buildings. The ranch is geared to horseback riding (they have about 180 of 'em!), and you will have your own horse for the duration of your week's stay. Don your C Lazy U robe and find your way to the oversized hot tub. Other options might be to lounge by the pool, try your luck fishing in Willow Creek or retreat to the well-equipped workout center. A trained instructor supervises all children's activities. In winter, guests can take full advantage of 30 kilometers of groomed cross-country trails. Three meals a day are served family-style in the comfortable dining room. The corner bar provides a cozy place for a scotch after a hard day on the trail. Most guests book for a week, but some special, shorter packages are available. Open year-round except for the months of Oct.–Nov. and Apr.–May. Located north of Granby. Reservations a must. **P.O. Box 379, Granby, CO 80446; 970-887-3344; www.clazyu.com.** Another guest ranch in the area just up the road from the C Lazy U is the **King Mountain Guest Ranch.** Enjoying a fine location surrounded by Arapaho National Forest, this ranch offers a great mix of activities for the entire family. **1-800-476-5464; 970-887-2551; www.kingranchresort.com.**

Claddagh Inn Bed and Breakfast—$$$$

Join the Finnigans in their massive hewn-log home and you will gain a new appreciation for the Irish term *claddagh*, which means friendship, love and loyalty. Here you will find a wonderful attention to detail in each of the seven guest rooms, including the massive main floor suite. The rooms, each with a unique feel, feature a private bath, jetted tubs and a TV/VCR combo. The hosts know how to make you feel right at home in this clean, comfy place. They bring out an afternoon snack and guests get to know each other in the wooded setting. The large gourmet breakfast, served around a large dining table, may make you want to skip lunch. Enjoy the common areas, especially the back deck and the downstairs sauna. Located just outside of Fraser

in a deeply wooded and quiet area. For reservations: **P.O. Box 2350, Fraser, CO 80442; 1-888-726-0456; 970-726-0456; www.claddagh innbb.com.**

Zephyr Mountain Lodge—$$$$

In a prime location adjacent to the ski mountain, with easy lift access, Zephy Mountain offers the finest accommodations in Winter Park. Restaurants and shops are beginning to fill the ground floor of the new development, and the upper floors have 236 new condo units, all individually owned. Many of the deluxe one-, two- and three-bedroom units are available for rent. With kitchen areas, TVs hidden inside wooden armoires, gas fireplaces and comfy, upscale furniture, the units provide a fine place to relax after putting away your skis or hiking boots. Common areas are built with stone and wood and feature separate ski lockers, a lovely lobby area with stone floor and a spiffy outdoor hot tub with mountain views.

The new ski-in/ski-out Zephyr Mountain Lodge at Winter Park. Photo by Bruce Caughey.

Located right at the base of Winter Park Resort; **1-877-754-8400; 970-726-8400; www.zephyr mountainlodgewp.com.**

Iron Horse Resort—$$$ to $$$$

This "condotel" (with a handful of lodge rooms, too) boasts four outdoor hot tubs and an indoor/outdoor pool. All of the condo-type units feature a working fireplace, a functional kitchen with dining area, balcony or deck as well as a Murphy bed; one- and two-bedroom units are available. You'll enjoy the contemporary design and tasteful common areas. The **Rails Restaurant ($)** offers reasonably priced breakfast entrées as well as a solid dinner menu. For information and reservations contact **P.O. Box 1286, Winter Park, CO 80482; 1-800-621-8190.** Another option close to the base area is **The Vintage Hotel ($$$ to $$$$)** with 118 comfortable rooms and suites; **1-800-472-7017.**

Hot Sulphur Springs Resort and Spa—$$$

People looking for a five-star resort spa may not find their Shangri-la here, but those who want to experience a slightly funky place—punctuated by an occasional train whistle—should consider staying at Hot Sulphur Springs Resort. Guests are offered the opportunity to enjoy the 20 unfiltered, mineral-rich pools built into an open hillside with great views to the Continental Divide. Take a small, clean, motel-style room (sans TV and phone), and you get unlimited use of the pools. Many of the rooms feature log-type furniture and others have a retro-1940s look. A newly refurbished cabin and an upper-floor apartment near the pools remain choice romantic spots. Located about 30 minutes west of Winter Park on Hwy. 40. For reservations: **P.O. Box 275, Hot Sulphur Springs, CO 80451; 970-725-3306; www.hotsulphur springs.com.**

YMCA Snow Mountain Ranch—$ to $$$

In a spectacular mountain setting 14 miles north of Winter Park near Tabernash on Hwy. 40, a range of year-round activities are to be enjoyed by all. This ranch resort maintains a wholesome family environment and provides one of Colorado's best values. Snow Mountain Ranch offers temporary memberships to all guests for the duration of their stay, but full members are given priority in reserving prime accommodations. Still, there are enough cabins and lodge rooms to take care of everyone for the majority of the year. Perhaps the single most outstanding aspect of the ranch is the extensive trail system stretching throughout the property. The Nordic Center offers equipment rentals, lessons and passes for 30 miles of groomed trails for beginner to expert cross-country skiers. Summer use of the marked trails revolves around hiking, mountain biking or horseback riding. The ranch encourages its guests and members to use its many recreational facilities. A few other activities include indoor swimming, roller skating, basketball, tennis, miniature golf and ice skating. Try the climbing wall. The Aspen Room is open year-round for inexpensive breakfasts and dinners.

Your best bet for a family vacation at Snow Mountain is to reserve reasonably priced two- or three-bedroom **cabins ($$$;** the price goes up on larger cabins). Larger four- to seven-bedroom cabins are available for family reunions. Each well-equipped cabin comes with refrigerator, range and telephone as well as kitchen implements. The chance to gather before a large moss-rock fireplace or out on a wide balcony for views of the Indian Peaks makes each cabin a place for fond family memories. In addition, you can arrange fairly inexpensive **dorm-style and private lodge rooms ($$ to $$$),** available for families, groups and individuals in several room designs. Most rooms come with a private bathroom. The lodges are very well kept, with large common areas. The drawback: you never know if you'll be sharing the same lodge with 200 screaming 13-year-olds. During summer, **four campgrounds ($)** cater to a segregated smattering of tents and RVs. For more information: **YMCA, P.O. Box 169, Winter Park, CO 80482; 970-887-2152;** Denver line **303-443-4743; www.ymcarockies.org.**

Camping

Arapaho National Forest

Reservations at some areas can be made at **1-877-444-6777** or **www.reserveusa.com.** All listed campgrounds charge a fee. **Idlewild Campground** (24 sites) is located on Hwy. 40, just 1 mile south of Winter Park. **Robbers Roost Campground** (11 sites) is about 5 miles south of Winter Park on the east side of Hwy. 40, with sites for both tents and trailers situated under the shadow of the Continental Divide. Drive 3 miles northwest of Granby on Hwy. 40, turn right on Hwy. 125 and proceed 10 miles to **Sawmill Gulch Campground** (6 sites). Another 3 miles and you'll arrive at **Denver Creek Campground** (22 sites). Travel 4 miles southwest on Forest Rd. 160 from Fraser to **St. Louis Creek Campground** (16 sites). Another 3.5 miles down the road is **Byers Creek Campground** (6 sites).

Private Campground

YMCA Snow Mountain Ranch—See the Accommodations section for information.

Where to Eat

Dinner at the Barn—$$$

Climb into the sleigh under a cozy wool blanket and you're off to a memorable evening with a couple 2,000-pound draft horses in the lead. Just when the crisp winter air is settling into your bones, the sleigh arrives at the small, heated barn. Hot cider and coffee take the chill off, but you can bring along something stronger. Soon everyone at your table is digging into a carefully prepared gourmet meal. Knick-knacks hang on the old wood walls, and the western feel doesn't get much more real than when you have to find your way to the outhouse. It's not your typical evening out—especially when Annie breaks out her guitar and sings upbeat country and western songs. Located in the Winter Park area. **970-726-4923.**

The Lodge at Sunspot—$$ to $$$$

Few restaurants can compete with the many attributes of this tasteful mountaintop lodge. From a broad picture window at an elevation of 10,700 feet, the view to the Fraser Valley and Continental Divide could hardly be more beautiful. Located midway up the ski mountain, you'll need to take the lift to this 20,000-square-foot monument of timber and stone for a hearty lunch. You have your choice of the Provisioner, a casual food marketplace, or the more formal, upscale Sunspot Dining Room. Try the roasted chicken marinated with a Caribbean barbecue sauce or a broiled elk T-bone steak. On selected evenings, the Sunspot Dining Room features a fixed-price, six-course gourmet meal—getting up to the restaurant by sleigh makes for an especially romantic evening. Open for Sun. brunch in summer; consider working off the calories by walking or biking down the mountain. **970-726-5514, ext. 373.**

Paul's Creekside Grill—$$ to $$$$

You might not expect to find a well-run restaurant in a big ski lodge, but this one at the Inn at SilverCreek fits the bill. Paul Streiter works hard to ensure every patron has an excellent dining experience. The interior feels surprisingly intimate even though an atrium rises high above and a wall of windows looks out to the pool and distant ski hill. The full-service restaurant serves a nice breakfast buffet and also great stuff from the grill for lunch. But dinner is where the chef can really shine, with items such as pepper-seared pork loin, London broil over sautéed spinach and grilled salmon with berry salsa. As long as Paul is here, you will enjoy the meal. Full bar. Hours may adjust seasonally, but generally you can find breakfast Mon.–Sat. 7:30–10 A.M. and Sun. till 1 P.M.; lunch Mon.–Sat. 11:30 A.M.–2 P.M.; dinner daily 5:30–9 P.M. Located 15 miles north of Winter Park and 2 miles east of Granby on Hwy. 40. **970-887-2484**

Mama Falzitto's—$$ to $$$

In old-town Winter Park, you can find superb, authentic Italian country food in a cozy environment not far from the ski slopes. Order up a plate of steaming pasta, including chicken cannelloni, pasta primavera or the classic, always wonderful, Mama's bolognese. They also serve entrées such as veal piccata and rib-eye steak. For something a bit lighter, try a large Caesar salad with chicken or shrimp. Children's menu available. Open Tues.–Sat. 5–9 P.M. **1128 Winter Park Dr.; 970-726-9049.**

The Ranch House Restaurant and Saloon—$$ to $$$

A great choice, especially on a full moon. See Devil's Thumb in the Skiing section.

Carver Brothers Bakery—$ to $$$

This place is so well known that, despite the hidden, off–Main Street location, there is plenty of business. Choose from a mouth-watering array of freshly baked pastries, including cheese pockets and cinnamon raisin bagels. Take out your order or find a table in the expanded seating area. Reasonably priced full breakfasts include a light and tasty breakfast burrito and an assortment of egg dishes. Lunch items include savory homemade soups, salads, submarine sandwiches and daily specials. Dinner entrées cover a range from crispy catfish to filet mignon and sautéed pork medallions. Open daily from 7 A.M.; lunch is served 11 A.M.–3 P.M. in summer, until 5 P.M. in winter. In winter dinner is served 5–9 P.M. Located directly west behind Cooper Creek Sq.; **970-726-8202.**

Crooked Creek Saloon—$ to $$$

See the Nightlife section.

Hernando's Pizza Pub—$ to $$

Good pizza is found in abundance in Winter Park, but people tend to agree that Hernando's is the best. For a change of pace try the Roma pizza. Tables are situated near a round fireplace in the center of the room, or you can take out. The decadent pizza is served on white or whole wheat crust, with a variety of toppings. Also served are spaghetti, lasagna and antipasto salad. A terrific patio is the place to be in summer.

There's a full bar, with generous drinks served in jars and hand-decorated dollar bills tacked everywhere. No smoking; free delivery in season. **970-726-5409.**

The Kitchen—$ to $$

A small, homey cafe with marvelous breakfasts. Get to this local favorite early or you'll have a long wait. Once inside choose from a breakfast burrito, huevos rancheros, eggs Benedict or any number of "dishes for egg haters." No credit cards; smoking okay; no whining. Open 7:30 A.M.–12:30 P.M. only. Located at the north end of Winter Park off Hwy. 40; **970-726-9940.**

Services

Visitor Information

Winter Park Central Reservations— 1-800-453-2525; 970-726-5587; in Denver **303-447-0588; www.skiwinterpark.com.**

Winter Park/Fraser Valley Chamber of Commerce—Stop by and talk with one of the helpful staffers about things to see and do in the valley. Located in central Winter Park adjacent to a park and playground on Hwy. 40. **P.O. Box 3236, Winter Park, CO 80482; 1-800-722-4118; 970-726-4118;** in Denver **303-422-0666.**

Day Care

Fraser Creative Learning Center—970-726-5681.

Winter Park Children's Center—Winter Park will take care of your youngster between 8 A.M. and 4 P.M. Minimum age is 2 months. Kids 3 to 13 can be taken skiing by specially trained children's instructors. **970-726-5514.**

Transportation

The Lift Bus Service—Winter Park's free shuttle bus provides year-round transportation between town and the ski areas. During the peak hours of 8–10 A.M. and 3–5 P.M., there are frequent buses throughout town.

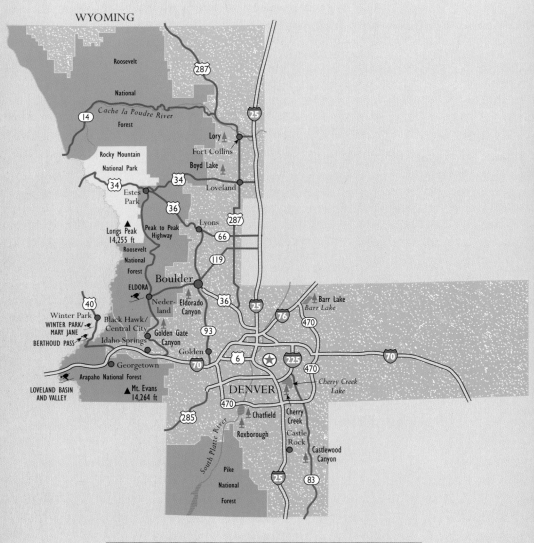

WYOMING

Roosevelt

National

Cache la Poudre River

Forest

(14)

(287)

(25)

Lory

Fort Collins

Boyd Lake

Rocky Mountain

National Park

(34)

(34)

Loveland

(34)

Estes
Park

(36)

Lyons

(287)

Longs Peak
14,255 ft

Peak to Peak
Highway

(66)

Roosevelt

National

Forest

(119)

Boulder

ELDORA

Neder-
land

Eldorado
Canyon

(36)

(25)

Barr Lake

Barr Lake

(40)

Winter Park

WINTER PARK/
MARY JANE

BERTHOUD PASS

Black Hawk/
Central City

Idaho Springs

Golden Gate
Canyon

(93)

(76)

(470)

Georgetown

Golden

(6)

(225)

(70)

Arapaho National Forest

(70)

(470)

LOVELAND BASIN
AND VALLEY

Mt. Evans
14,264 ft

DENVER

*Cherry Creek
Lake*

(470)

(285)

South Platte River

Chatfield

Roxborough

Cherry
Creek

Castle
Rock

Castlewood
Canyon

Pike

National

Forest

(25)

(83)

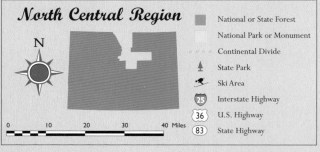

North Central Region

N

	National or State Forest
	National Park or Monument
	Continental Divide
🌲	State Park
⛷	Ski Area
(25)	Interstate Highway
(36)	U.S. Highway
(83)	State Highway

0   10   20   30   40 Miles

North Central Region

*The famous East Face of 14,255-foot Longs Peak in Rocky Mountain National Park.
Photo by Bruce Caughey.*

Boulder

Though Boulder is only a short 40-minute drive from Denver, you feel like you're entering a different realm. From the moment you drop into town from the scenic overlook on the Boulder Turnpike (Hwy. 36), the view forces your attention to the Rocky Mountains shooting up to the west and the plains stretching east toward the horizon. Boulder enjoys a supreme location, at the base of the dramatic red rock formations known as the Flatirons.

Many people consider Boulder a type of utopia, and Mork and Mindy, Boulder's most famous former "residents," didn't do much to dispell the image (you can still see their house at 1619 Pine St.). Thanks to the university population, the place retains the intimacy of a small town, and the general population tends to be young and well educated. Boulder has managed to retain many 1960s counterculture ideals with its graying boomers holding onto the reigns of power. Unlike most neighboring towns, however, Boulder also represents a cosmopolitan rainbow of humanity. Many world-class cyclists, runners and climbers live here while undergoing a high-altitude training regimen.

It's also a major high-tech center, with numerous computer and scientific institutions, often working in tandem on projects spawned at the University of Colorado's main campus. Fewer than 100,000 residents enjoy the quality of life Boulder has to offer, for which they pay a price—having to sustain an upscale economy

where everything from groceries to housing costs more than in other areas.

Boulder doesn't fight its image as an idealistic bastion of free thought. The University of Colorado at Boulder, with more than 25,000 students, is the biggest but certainly not the only place to take classes. Alternative education flourishes at Naropa University (America's only Buddhist university), Hakomi Institute, Boulder College, Rolf Institute, Boulder Graduate School and the Boulder College of Massage Therapy. Innovative entrepreneurs have made their mark with landmark businesses such as McGuckins Hardware, Liquor Mart and Celestial Seasonings.

The main thing you'll want to do in Boulder is stay outside—in fact *Outside* magazine named Boulder the number one spot in the country for outdoor sports and best place to be an Uberjock. Boulder Mountain Parks and Open Space land preserves spectacular views of the mountains and the wide-open prairies; 33,000 acres are reserved solely for public recreational use. Hiking and mountain biking trails enter the foothills from virtually any street on Boulder's western edge. A half hour farther west, Roosevelt National Forest and Indian Peaks Wilderness Area provide

---

Getting There

Boulder is located less than 40 minutes from downtown Denver. To get there drive north on Interstate 25 until you reach the Boulder Turnpike (Hwy. 36), which leads 27 miles northwest to Boulder. Frequent daily **Regional Transportation District (RTD)** buses shuttle between Denver and Boulder.

virtually unlimited opportunities for hiking, fishing, camping and cross-country skiing.

Exploring former wagon roads is another great way to spend a day in the historic high country of the Front Range. Many twisting canyons lead to old supply towns and mining camps west of Boulder. Nederland, Ward and Gold Hill are still going strong today, and other nearly forgotten towns still provide local color. Cutting across the gorgeous, 55-mile Peak to Peak Highway—one of the state's best autumn drives—should fulfill your highest expectations of the state's new Scenic and Historic Byway program.

In town, music, lectures, theater and dance proliferate. You won't find a place more conducive to walking or riding bikes and you'll never be far from a cafe or restaurant. A stroll down the Pearl Street Mall or through the beautiful University of Colorado campus shouldn't be missed.

History

In 1858 Capt. Thomas Aikins, an early prospector, said of the Boulder area: "The mountains looked right for gold and the valleys looked rich for grazing." Other settlers felt the same way. When the first gold strike was made on aptly named Gold Hill a few months later, the town of Boulder City sprang to life. Named for the numerous large rocks in the vicinity, the tag "City" was added in the hope it would actually become one someday.

Early townspeople endured the elements in dirt-floor log cabins built along Pearl St. Occupants used wool blankets to cover furnishings and supplies during rainy periods and slept under leaky roofs on mattresses made with pine needles and hay until enough straw could be grown. The newcomers had virtually no trouble with the Southern Arapaho Indians, who, under the leadership of Chief Niwot (Left Hand), let the settlers stay.

Although the town was built on a pile of rocks in the foothills, Boulder's fortunes were not to be found in minerals, which is why it didn't fall victim to the same fate of the boom-and-bust mining towns. Instead, Boulder grew up as a supply and transportation center for the gold, silver and tungsten mining operations dotting the mountains to the west. It later served as a hub for farmers on the plains.

Boulder eventually found its future in education. In 1860 the young town opened the first schoolhouse in Colorado. By the time Colorado achieved statehood in 1876, the original University of Colorado building, Old Main, was under construction. The freshman class consisted of nine men and one woman in 1878.

The arrival of the first railroad in 1879 helped ensure Boulder's continued growth. But Boulder's position as a supply and transportation center for the surrounding mining camps gradually diminished as the university grew up with the town. A dramatic leap in enrollment occurred after World War II as returning military took advantage of the GI Bill. Today, as one of four University of Colorado campuses, Boulder attracts top students from every state and 70 foreign countries.

It's hard to believe today, but Boulder was "dry" from 1907 until 1967. Absolutely no liquor was served (legally) until the Catacombs opened in the Hotel Boulderado in 1969. The sixties found Boulder on the same long-hair, barefoot, free-love circuit as progressive campuses in Berkeley and Madison—a kinship that still exists, according to some. Since then, however, Boulder has toned down its hippie image and gentrified some of its former hangouts as real estate prices have skyrocketed. Today a pleasant and diverse mix of nightspots, cafes and quality restaurants have opened in town. But despite changes it's still a place to relax and let your hair down.

Major Attractions

Pearl Street Mall

You'll miss the essence of Boulder by neglecting to visit the Pearl Street Mall. It's a place where

There is always something exciting happening on Boulder's Pearl Street Mall. Photo by Bruce Caughey.

the pulse of the city is out in the open air. The mall's wide brick walkway is bordered on both sides by restaurants, shops, galleries and bars, most of which occupy turn-of-the-century, two-story buildings. Grassy areas, flowers, sculptures and wooden benches complete the physical environment. But it's the people that electrify the mall's atmosphere, especially on summer evenings when outdoor restaurants and cafes are packed. While strolling down the mall you'll be sure to catch free performances by jugglers, magicians, acrobats, musicians, contortionists and mimes. Try to stump "Zip Code Man" who will nearly unfailingly deduce your hometown just from its zip code! Fashion statements abound. Foreign accents hang in the air. The mood changes with the seasons, but there is always something happening. If you prefer a guided walking tour of Boulder's downtown (or Mapleton Hill neighborhood), contact **Historic Boulder** at 303-444-5192; small fee charged.

Celestial Seasonings Tour of Tea

Nineteen-year-old Mo Siegel had a great idea when he started gathering herbs in 1969 in Aspen. Over the years his company, Celestial

Seasonings, has grown into one of America's best-loved and most successful companies. They provide a fascinating, free 35-minute tour that includes all of the plant's operations including R&D, marketing, the herb garden, art and the factory floor, where all of the herbs and teas are mixed and packaged (1,000 tea bags per minute). The wonderful aromas you catch are reason enough to take the tour; you won't soon forget the mint room. The factory gets quite loud, so children under 5 are not permitted on that portion of the tour. Stop in for a sandwich, salad or soup at the Celestial Cafe, which is open daily during lunch. The tea shop offers tour tickets, tea tasting and T-shirts. Guided tours are offered on the hour from 10 A.M. to 3 P.M. Mon.–Sat., Sun. 11 A.M.–3 P.M. For information and directions: **303-581-1202; www.celestial seasonings.com.**

National Center for Atmospheric Research

Anyone curious about the air, sun and weather will find the National Center for Atmospheric Research a fascinating place. Scientists there do work involving subjects such as lightning, wind shear, global warming and climate modeling. There are no classified secrets here. The center welcomes the public to take self-guided tours during regular hours, or hour-long guided tours. Don't miss the interactive model of the sun or the Cray supercomputers that can make nearly a billion calculations per second. Check out the interactive exhibits to better understand weather dynamics. A library and a cafeteria are also open to the public Mon.–Fri. Lunch is served 11:30 A.M.–1:30 P.M. The center has two art gallery areas on the second floor. A number of hiking trails lead into the Open Space land west of the facility, including some trails with wheelchair access.

Designed by architect I. M. Pei, the National Center for Atmospheric Research commands an enviable mesa-top position overlooking Boulder. The unique building resembles the cliff dwellings of Mesa Verde; few modern structures commune in such a beautiful way with a natural setting. If you make the trip to the center, you will surely see some deer along the way. The visitor center is open 8 A.M.–5 P.M. Mon.–Fri., 9 A.M.–4 P.M. weekends and holidays. Located at the west end of Table Mesa Dr., **1850 Table Mesa Dr.; 303-497-1174; www.ncar.ucar.edu.** Another stop on the science circuit is the **National Institute of Standards and Technology,** which has a number of lobby displays, the world's most accurate clock (atomic powered) and guided tours Tues. and Thurs. at 9:30 A.M. and 1:30 P.M. No fee. **325 Broadway; 303-497-3000; www. nist.gov.**

University of Colorado, Boulder Campus

To get a feel for the campus, wander by Old Main, the university's first stately building, which was already under construction when Colorado became a state in 1876. "It loomed before us gaunt and alone in the pitiless clear light—no tree nor shrub nor any human habitation was in sight," wrote Jane Sewall, daughter of CU's first president, in 1877. In the intervening years the campus has come a long way, but Old Main still stands as a spruced-up reminder of the days of yore. The initial freshman class of 10 students has grown to more than 25,000. Today enormous sandstone buildings with red tile roofs are separated by open grassy areas and long walkways. The **University Memorial Center,** with its attractive outdoor fountain, serves as the nucleus of activity. Inside the center, students and faculty spend off-time enjoying restaurants, a video game room, pool hall, bowling alley and the all-important university bookstore.

Stop by the fascinating **CU Heritage Center** in **Old Main** for displays on the history of the University, a pamphlet on some of the campus highlights and guided tours. Open Tues.–Fri. 10 A.M.–4 P.M.; Mon. and Sat. 10 A.M.–2 P.M. **303-492-6329; www.colorado.edu.**

The inspired I. M. Pei–designed National Center for Atmospheric Research lies high atop a mesa above Boulder. Photo by Bruce Caughey.

Festivals and Events

Conference on World Affairs

early Apr. Since 1948 the University of Colorado campus has transformed itself into an international oasis where flags fly and experts on every possible subject converge. Question-and-answer periods follow each presentation, which in the past have included luminaries such as Eleanor Roosevelt, Henry Kissinger, Roger Ebert and R. Buckminster Fuller. You'll be able to mingle with government officials, CIA operatives, witches, cosmonauts, refugees, journalists and radical feminists—something for everyone. **303-492-2525.**

Kinetic Conveyance Challenge

early May Every year this event embraces a silly outlook that overpowers any sense of serious drive to be the quickest to the finish line. Teams win in categories such as best newcomers, engineering, perseverance, sportsmanship and looks. Ridiculous team names—such as the Pepe Le Pew Eau de Parfum—match the sheer audacity of grown men and women sitting inside an oversized toilet or wearing special reservoir-tipped hats. The fastest teams arrive merely 45 minutes after the start, while others straggle in 3 hours later. Some don't make it past the beach or a few yards into the water. Top bands play high-energy sets for the assembled thousands of fans of this annual nonsense. Food and drink are in bountiful supply. Sponsored by KBCO radio. You might also want to catch the wacky conveyances at a prechallenge parade at the Pearl Street Mall. **303-444-5600; www. kbco.com.**

Colorado Music Festival

late June through early Aug. Though not as well known as the Aspen Music Festival, this event has everything going for it. Classical music concerts take place in the magnificent all-wood **Chautauqua Auditorium,** built in 1898. Under the direction of Giora Bernstein, musicians from symphonies around the world come together to play with renowned guest artists. Preconcert picnickers cast a cheery array of color across the expansive lawns. If you prefer dining at a table, have dinner on the commodious porch of the Chautauqua Dining Hall and enjoy this quintessentially Boulder scene (see the Where to Eat section). Since 1976 the music festival has been an important part of summertime in Boulder. **303-449-1397; www.colorado musicfest.org.**

Colorado Shakespeare Festival

late June through mid-Aug. In a beautiful garden setting at the **Mary Rippon Outdoor Theater** on the CU campus, highly entertaining productions of Shakespeare are performed each summer. Talented company members and well-known guest artists play a number of the major roles. This festival has been going strong since 1958 and is now considered one of the best in the country. Whether it is a joyful production of *A Midsummer Night's Dream* or a rendition of *The Tempest,* you will feel the emotions only Shakespeare can evoke. For ticket information (beginning in late May), call **303-492-0554.**

Athletic Events

year-round Boulder not only attracts many world-class athletes to train and live, but the town also hosts a large number of athletic events each year. The powerhouse **Colorado Buffalos** Big 12 **football** games at Folsom Field always provide a raucous experience. Ralphie (the team's buffalo) makes a traditional run around the football field. The **Colorado Buffalos** women's **basketball** team has been making waves lately. The university also stages soccer, skiing and ultimate Frisbee competitions, among others. Call **303-492-8337** for information and tickets. The **Bolder Boulder 10-kilometer race** attracts nearly 40,000 runners every Memorial Day, making it one of the largest in the world. The finish line can be found inside Folsom stadium with tens of thousands of cheering spectators. For more information: **303-444-RACE; www.bolderboulder.com.**

Outdoor Activities

Biking

MOUNTAIN BIKING

This sport has actually attracted too many people in the Boulder area. Bikes are prohibited on Boulder Mountain Park trails. In Roosevelt National Forest, however, hundreds of miles of roads and trails remain open to mountain bikes. Bring your own bike or rent at one of the shops in town. Many bike shops in town stock the useful Boulder Mountain Biking Map.

Boulder Creek Path

This 16-mile path snakes through the city from 55th St. It leads basically west along the creek, crossing several bridges and heading up pretty Boulder Canyon to Four Mile Canyon. If you want to keep going up to Gold Hill, read the next entry.

Gold Hill

A ride up to Gold Hill via either Sunshine or Four Mile Canyons should satisfy even the most avid riders. It's about a 10-mile uphill ride from the mouth of either canyon to this out-of-the-way hamlet. To get to Sunshine Canyon, ride west on Mapleton Ave.; to reach Four Mile Canyon ride west on Canyon Blvd. (Hwy. 119) for 2 miles, then turn right on County Rd. 118 and right again at the sign for Gold Hill.

Nederland

The mountainous area around Nederland is full of possible rides. The ghost town of Caribou lies at the windswept edge of treeline, making a great 5-hour round trip. There are a couple of ways to get to the townsite. The most obvious and direct route follows along the wide dirt Caribou Rd. A rougher, more challenging route, with fewer competing autos, is up the old mining roads along Sherwood Creek. Eventually they funnel out to Caribou Rd. near the once-booming silver camp of Caribou. Riders in really good shape might want to consider an all-day ride over Rollins Pass to Winter Park (see the

Four-Wheel-Drive Trips section); have someone meet you there or ride back over the next day.

BICYCLE TOURING

You're in Boulder, the home of Olympic cycling champions Connie Carpenter-Phinney and Davis Phinney and Tour of Italy winner Andy Hamsten. It's easy to get around town, thanks to one of the best bike trail systems in the United States. The number of people in Boulder who commute to work on bikes is 10 times the national average. Many riders enjoy the strenuous pull up Flagstaff Mountain (see the Scenic Drives section). Other trails and designated bike lanes make up more than 50 miles of well-maintained bikeway. Pick up a trail map at the **Boulder Chamber of Commerce, 2440 Pearl St.; 303-442-1044; www.boulder chamber.com.**

Rentals and Information

The Bikesmith—Great for adult and children's bike rentals including trailers and helmets. Also, in-line skates. **2432 Arapahoe Ave.; 303-443-1132.**
University Bicycles—These folks rent town bikes, mountain bikes and Burley trailers. **839 Pearl St.; 303-444-4196.**

Fishing

Most fishing areas near Boulder receive heavy use. After all, the area's lakes and streams are easily accessible to more than 2 million Front Range residents. A unique attraction in Boulder is the **Fish Observatory,** located on the bike path just behind the Regal Harvest House Hotel at **1345 28th St.** In a park setting, its four round windows are built into a subterranean wall bordering Boulder Creek. The windows provide an underwater view into the natural habitat of brown, brook and cutthroat trout. Look closely enough and you may learn something about their feeding patterns. Here are a few fishing ideas:

Barker Reservoir

At the east side of Nederland, this popular fishing spot remains a consistent producer for

The tranquil shore of Gold Lake. Photo by Bruce Caughey.

stocked rainbow trout in the 12-inch range. No boats are allowed on the lake, though you may see a few facetious Nederland Yacht Club T-shirts. The water line at Barker Reservoir tends to fluctuate greatly depending on downstream water needs.

Boulder Creek

Many sections of this small stream prove to be quite productive habitats. South Boulder Creek flows down from the Continental Divide near Rollins Pass. Fishing on the South Fork can be good for smallish cutthroat trout all along Forest Rd. 149 near the east portal of the Moffat Tunnel. At the tunnel a smattering of small lakes—including **Arapaho Lakes, Crater Lakes** and **Forest Lakes**—are accessible by trail. Though these lakes are heavily fished, you can usually have good success for rainbow, brown and cutthroat trout. You can also find excellent, but hard-to-reach, fishing within the steep canyon below Gross Reservoir. Some good evening fly-fishing can be found within the Boulder city limits on Boulder Creek. It is all catch-and-release, and some of the trout—brook, brown and cutthroat—grow to decent sizes.

Boulder Reservoir

Fishing for warmwater species including crappie, catfish and largemouth bass can be good at this city-owned water supply. Unless you are a Boulder resident with a permit, boating is prohibited on weekends. For bank fishing try the deep water near the dam embankment. Take the Longmont Diagonal (Hwy. 119) east of Boulder and turn left on 51st St. Travel north for a couple miles to the gatehouse. Fee charged; open year-round.

Brainard Lake

Everyone likes to spend Sun. afternoons at Brainard Lake—so many that you must now pay for parking. The lake is nestled into a beautiful mountain setting just a few miles west of Ward. Fishing can be good for pan-sized stocked rainbow and brown trout. A half-mile up South St. Vrain Creek lies **Long Lake,** which is limited to flies and lures. Another mile above Long Lake, a trail leads to **Lake Isabelle;** flies and lures only.

Four-Wheel-Drive Trips

Rollins Pass Road

This classic drive was once open to passenger cars. A tunnel on the historic route near the top

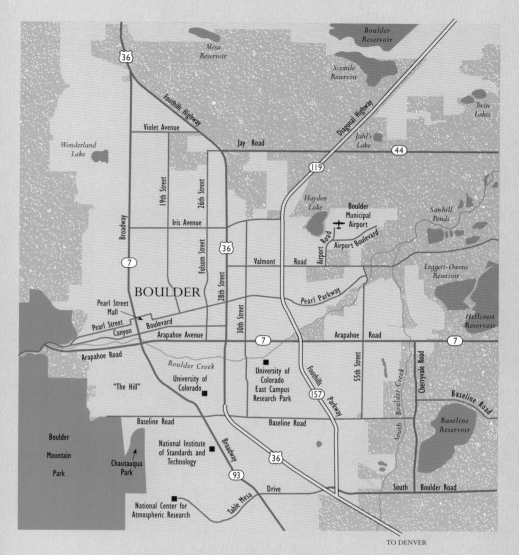

Boulder Reservoir

Mesa Reservoir

Sixmile Reservoir

Twin Lakes

36

Foothills Highway

Diagonal Highway

Violet Avenue

Jay Road

Juhl's Lake

44

Wonderland Lake

19th Street

26th Street

119

Iris Avenue

Folsom Street

36

Hayden Lake

Boulder Municipal Airport

Airport Road

Airport Boulevard

Sawhill Ponds

Leggett-Owens Reservoir

7

Valmont Road

28th Street

BOULDER

Pearl Parkway

Hillcrest Reservoir

Pearl Street Mall

30th Street

Pearl Street Boulevard

Canyon

Arapahoe Avenue

7

Arapahoe Road

7

Arapahoe Road

Boulder Creek

"The Hill"

University of Colorado

University of Colorado East Campus Research Park

Foothills Parkway

157

55th Street

South Boulder Creek

Cherryvale Road

Baseline Road

Baseline Road

Baseline Road

Baseline Road

Boulder Mountain Park

Chautauqua Park

National Institute of Standards and Technology

Broadway

36

Baseline Reservoir

93

Drive

South Boulder Road

National Center for Atmospheric Research

Table Mesa

TO DENVER

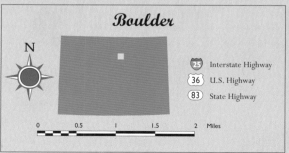

Boulder

N

25   Interstate Highway

36   U.S. Highway

83   State Highway

0   0.5   1   1.5   2   Miles

of the pass has caved in, making vehicle travel west of the divide impossible. Perhaps the tunnel will be blasted out in the future, but no one is willing to commit to a timetable. For now you can drive to within 1.5 miles of the pass, but the route is blocked from there (hikers and mountain bikers can bypass the tunnel and continue down the other side of the pass on the road). For more information on the history of the road, see the Four-Wheel-Drive Trips section of the **Winter Park and Middle Park** chapter. To get to Rollins Pass Rd. from Boulder, drive west on Hwy. 119 to Nederland and then south on Hwy. 72 to Rollinsville. Follow the signs west from Rollinsville. For information on the status of the road, contact the **Boulder Ranger District: 303-444-6600; fs.fed.us/arns.**

Switzerland Trail

This rough four-wheel-drive road follows the path of the narrow-gauge railroad that once carried rich gold ore from the mines to the smelters. In the early 1900s excursion trains also made this scenic trip into the high Front Range mountains. To reach this historic route, take Canyon Blvd. (Hwy. 119) west out of Boulder for 3 miles. Turn right on County Rd. 118, which leads into Four Mile Canyon. Stay on County Rd. 118 past Salina and Wallstreet until you reach Sunset, 17 miles from Boulder. From Sunset take a sharp right onto the Switzerland Trail, which climbs uphill, eventually emerging on County Rd. 52. From here you can pass through the old mining town of Gold Hill on the return to Boulder. Another segment of the Switzerland Trail can be reached by taking a left at Sunset. This four-wheel-drive road passes by Glacier Lake before joining Hwy. 72 between Nederland and Ward.

Golf

Flat Irons Golf Course

This challenging 18-hole course, with many lakes and mature trees, provides exceptionally well-kept greens and unobstructed views of nearby mountains. Partly because of its reason-

able fees it's also one of the most popular in Boulder. Pro shop. **5706 Arapahoe Ave.; 303-442-7851.**

Lake Valley Golf Course

Lake Valley's 18 holes have been challenging golfers since 1965. As the name implies, several lakes and other water hazards come into play. Tee times are taken two days in advance. Located 5 miles north of Boulder on Neva Rd. just east of Hwy. 36; **303-444-2114.**

Hiking and Backpacking

Boulder lies flush against the dramatic jagged uplift of the Rocky Mountains. Just west of Boulder, possibilities for hiking and backpacking abound. Many residents can walk from their front doors and be on trails in minutes. This hiking section could easily be expanded into a book of its own—instead, we have a scaled-back listing of some excellent hiking options in the Boulder Mountain Parks, Roosevelt National Forest and the Indian Peaks Wilderness. For more information and maps contact the **Boulder Ranger District Office, 2140 Yarmouth Ave., Boulder, CO 80301, 303-444-6600, fs.fed.us/arns;** or the **City of Boulder Mountain Parks, Ranger Cottage, 9th and Baseline, Boulder, CO 80302, 303-441-3408, www.ci.boulder.co.us/bmp.** Topographic maps, rental equipment, supplies and other information can be obtained at **Mountain Sports, 821 Pearl St.; 303-443-6770.**

South of Rocky Mountain National Park, the Indian Peaks Wilderness straddles both sides of the Continental Divide. Dominant peaks, alpine tundra, colorful wildflowers and a smattering of lakes set a beautiful stage for hikers. The area is so popular that backpacking access is limited by a permit system. Day hikers do not need permits, but one is required for overnight camping June 1–Sept. 15. Permits are available by reservation for a small fee by calling **303-444-6600.**

The hikes on the west side of the Continental Divide are discussed in the Hiking and Backpacking section of the **Winter Park and Middle Park** chapter.

Arapaho Glacier

This strenuous day trip in the Indian Peaks Wilderness Area begins at the same trailhead as hikes in the vicinity of Arapaho Pass (see next entry). Break right from the Arapaho Pass Trail (No. 904) onto Glacier Trail (No. 905) 2 miles after setting out. The 3.5-mile hike tracks along above treeline for most of the way, ending at the glacier at 12,700 feet. Looking up at Arapaho Peak (13,397 feet) from the glacier is irresistible—go ahead and scramble to the top for fabulous views down both sides of the Continental Divide.

Arapaho Pass

A number of exciting trips for backpackers can be found in the Arapaho Pass area, all of which leave from the Fourth of July trailhead. The steady uphill trail (No. 904) begins at 10,121 feet and climbs 3 miles to the pass at 11,900 feet. It follows an old stagecoach route for part of the way, and close to treeline you'll see the remains of the Fourth of July Mine. From the pass on the Continental Divide, enjoy views to the tall peaks of Rocky Mountain National Park to the north and Middle Park down below to the west. Options from the top of Arapaho Pass include dropping down to the west to Caribou Lake, then continuing southwest over Caribou Pass to Columbine Lake. Another longer trip takes you all the way down to Monarch Lake. Come back over Pawnee Pass, ending at Pawnee Campground, north of where you started out. If you choose this last route, you'll need to arrange for transportation back to your vehicle. The Fourth of July trailhead lies 12 miles from Nederland. Travel west to Eldora on County Rd. 130 and then onto County Rd. 111 for the remaining miles on a rough dirt road.

Boulder Falls

North Boulder Creek plummets 70 feet to join Middle Boulder Creek just a few miles up Boulder Canyon (head west on Canyon Blvd.). The short walk to the falls from the parking area is ideal for all ages. A trail leads up in back of the falls for those seeking a longer hike.

Boulder Mountain Parks and Open Space

This sweeping open land virtually encircles Boulder, offering some 100 miles of excellent hiking trails just outside the city. Since 1967 Boulder citizens have been paying a tax to preserve this land from development and to set aside more for the future. This foresight has allowed residents and visitors the luxury of hiking onto the eastern plains and into beautiful mountains to the west of Boulder. For a complete trail map to the Boulder Mountain Parks, drop by the **Boulder Convention and Visitors Bureau, 2440 Pearl St., 303-442-2911,** or any local sporting goods store.

Trails lead away from Boulder in clusters from designated trailheads. **Chautauqua Park,** located on the west end of Baseline Rd., has a parking area at a trailhead leading toward the Flatirons and Bluebell Shelter. Many trails pass near the stunning red rock strata of the Flatirons. Technical climbers are often seen hanging on these vertical rocks; inexperienced climbers should stick to walking trails to avoid becoming statistics. Other trails lead away from **Sunrise Circle Amphitheater** near the top of Flagstaff Mountain. Still others lead from the **National Center for Atmospheric Research** (see the Major Attractions section) at the west end of Table Mesa Dr.

Some of the more popular trails include **Mesa Trail,** which leads from just below Bluebell Shelter on a beautiful 6-mile southerly course to Eldorado Springs. Have a car meet you in Eldorado Springs and you won't have to backtrack. The well-defined Mesa Trail provides sweeping views of the Front Range and the Flatirons while tracking through deep woods and grassy meadows. A highly recommended short hike begins on the Mesa Trail in a northerly direction from the National Center for Atmospheric Research. Merge onto **Enchanted Mesa Trail,** which ends at Chautauqua Park in town. Another interesting hike, beginning at the west end of Mapleton Ave. (just past Boulder Memorial Hospital), is **Mt. Sanitas Trail,** which leads to the top of the 6,863-foot mountain. The round-trip hike provides great views of

Climbers hang on sheer cliff walls in Eldorado Canyon. Photo by Colorado State Parks.

Boulder and can be completed in under 2 hours. This is a good hike early or late in the year because of its low elevation.

Isabelle Glacier Trail

Each weekend hundreds of people take this hike—so if you want solitude and free parking, look elsewhere. Beginning at the ever-popular Brainard Lake, a 2-mile trail leads gradually uphill to Isabelle Glacier (12,000 feet). A longer trail (No. 907) continues from Lake Isabelle on up to Pawnee Pass at 12,541 feet. If you take the entire 4.5-mile, one-way hike be prepared for a particularly steep final 2 miles. If you're interested in a longer backpacking loop, head over the Continental Divide to Monarch Lake and return to the east side of the divide via Arapaho Pass (see entry above). To reach Brainard Lake

drive just north of Ward on Hwy. 119, turn left and take Brainard Lake Rd. (County Rd. 102) west for about 5 miles.

Horseback Riding

Gold Lake Mountain Resort and Spa

Located near Ward (see the Where to Stay section for more information); **303-459-3544**.

Sombrero Ranch

Offering hourly rides as well as pack trips. Located east of Boulder on Hwy. 34; **303-442-0258**.

Llama Trekking

Timberline Llamas

This company can take you on an extraordinary excursion you will never forget. The llamas carry your gear, taking the burden off your shoulders and adding an exotic element to your trip. For more information, contact them in Golden at **303-526-0092; www.timberlinellamas.com.**

Skiing

CROSS-COUNTRY SKIING AND SNOWSHOEING

Boulder is a jumping-off point for miles upon miles of diverse cross-country terrain. For a map of marked backcountry trails in the Roosevelt National Forest, contact the **Boulder Ranger District Office, 2140 Yarmouth Ave., Boulder, CO 80301; 303-444-6600; fs.fed. us/arns.**

Backcountry Trails

Brainard Lake Trail System—This area has proven very popular among cross-country skiers, so having tracks to follow is seldom a problem. Thankfully, no snowmobiles are allowed. Fairly difficult trails lead to Long Lake and Lake Isabelle as well as farther north on **Blue Lake Trail.** Be aware of avalanche areas, especially above Blue Lake and Lake Isabelle. For an easy trail try the CMC (Colorado Mountain

Club) southern route. More experienced skiers can make a hilly loop on **Waldrop North Trail.** To reach the trailhead, take Hwy. 72 just north of Ward to a marked turnoff for Brainard Lake Rd. (County Rd. 102). Turn left and head west as far as possible and park on the side.

Lost Lake Trail—For people with some cross-country experience, this is an excellent half-day trip that leads up an unplowed road from the town of Eldora. The 6-mile round-trip route has an elevation change of 1,000 feet. A mile after setting out, take the left fork and ski up to the townsite of Hesse. Stay on the trail for 1.5 miles and take a left cutoff on Lost Lake Trail. The trail leads south to Lost Lake in just over a half-mile. An alternative to turning left onto Lost Lake Trail is to continue straight on **King Lake Trail;** there is some avalanche danger as you come within a mile of King Lake. To reach the trailhead from Nederland, turn right on County Rd. 130 and continue west to Eldora. Take the right fork to a parking area at the west end of the town of Eldora.

Rainbow Lakes Road—This easy 4.5-mile trail works its way to Rainbow Lakes. The trail is better after a recent snow because otherwise it tends to become windblown and icy in spots. The lakes are half a mile beyond the campground. The gradual downhill return trip provides a chance to stretch out and glide. From Nederland drive 7 miles north on Hwy. 72. Turn left at a sign opposite the Colorado University Mountain Research Station and drive a little less than a mile to the fork in the road. Begin skiing on the unplowed left fork.

Groomed Trails

Eldora Nordic Center—From the southeast side of the Eldora ski area parking lot, 45 kilometers of groomed and backcountry trails take off into the woods. The center also features four new snowshoe routes. The center offers rentals as well as instruction in skating, telemarking and touring. For a longer trip, inquire about an overnight stay at Tennessee Mountain Cabin, which sleeps up to 12. A trail fee is charged;

hours are 9 A.M.–4 P.M. daily. Located 21 miles west of Boulder. Take Canyon Blvd. (Hwy. 119) west to a mile beyond Nederland and turn left at the Eldora turnoff. **1-888-235-3672; 303-440-8700.**

Rentals and Information

Eldora Nordic Center—At Eldora Mountain Resort; 1-888-235-3672; 303-440-8700. Mountain Sports—821 Pearl St.; 303-443-6770.

DOWNHILL SKIING AND SNOWBOARDING
Eldora Mountain Resort

Only 30 minutes from Boulder, Eldora offers downhill skiing only a short commute away. The modest ski area appears to be on the right track and has been expanding in recent years with two quad lifts, a triple, four double chairs and four surface lifts. They also have added lights for night skiing. They have maintained modest lift prices and there is rarely a wait. About half the terrain is intermediate, 30 percent is expert and the rest suits beginners. With 1,400 feet of vertical and a long run of about 2 miles, there's plenty of skiing. The expert Corona Bowl, on the back side of the mountain, offers a steep pitch to advanced skiers and keeps its snow thanks to strategically placed wind blocks. Also try the recently thinned Moose and Salto Glades. Wind is the only nemesis at Eldora—toward the top it can get really gusty, though much of the mountain is protected by trees. Snowboarders take note of Eldora's terrain park, featuring spines, tabletops, hits and rollers. Rentals are available at the base. The lodge serves breakfast, lunch and dinner. Upstairs the Alpenhorn is a great après-ski hangout.

Located 21 miles west of Boulder. Take Canyon Blvd. (Hwy. 119) west to a mile beyond Nederland and turn left at the Eldora turnoff. RTD bus service shuttles skiers five times daily (three times on Sun.) from Boulder. For more information contact **P.O. Box 1697, Nederland, CO 80466; 1-888-235-3672; 303-440-8700; www.eldora.com.**

Sledding

Boulder Parks

The city gives the okay for sledding on the hills at Scott Carpenter and Tantra Parks. Another good spot for a free sledding experience is on the hill near Fairview High School.

Swimming and Tubing

Boulder Creek

Stop by a local gas station and buy an inner tube for floating Boulder Creek's chilly waters just west of town. Join the locals by finding one of many put-ins along Canyon Blvd. and within Eban J. Fine Park. At the east end of the park, a whitewater course entices kayakers through its gates. Perfect for cooling off on a hot summer afternoon.

Boulder Reservoir

It's not the prettiest beach in the world, but in Colorado who's complaining. The "Res" is a fun place to swim and suntan. Many people prefer boating, canoeing and windsurfing, and many rental craft are available. Take the Longmont Diagonal (Hwy. 119) east of Boulder and turn left on 51st St. Travel north for 1.5 miles to the gatehouse; open Memorial Day–Labor Day; fee charged. **303-441-3468.**

Eldorado Artesian Springs

Once a famed resort, Eldorado Artesian Springs has slipped a bit over the years. But it has a great setting just outside the entrance to Eldorado Canyon State Park. A day here can include swimming, hiking, picnicking and watching climbers hang on the canyon's sheer rock walls (see the Scenic Drives section). The comfortably warm pool is naturally heated from geothermal waters more than a mile beneath the surface. Located 5.5 miles south of Boulder on Hwy. 93, then west on Hwy. 170 for 3 miles; open 10 A.M.–6 P.M., Memorial Day–Labor Day; fee charged. **303-499-1316; www.eldorado springs.com.**

Windsurfing

Boulder Reservoir

This is the place to learn how to windsurf or to show off your skills. Conditions are usually good, but at times the wind can be fierce. Lessons and rentals available; entry fee charged. Take the Longmont Diagonal (Hwy. 119) east of Boulder and turn left on 51st St. Travel north for 1.5 miles to the gatehouse; **303-441-3461.**

Seeing and Doing

Ballooning and Gliding

Air Boulder

For ballooning: **3345 15th St., Boulder, CO 80304; 303-442-5253.**

Mile High Gliding

Try these high-performance planes (not hang gliding) by getting in touch at **303-527-1122.**

Museums and Galleries

Boulder is a town of few museums and many galleries. You can find the best and brightest galleries along the Pearl Street Mall. A standout destination for purchasing art on the mall is the **Boulder Arts and Crafts Cooperative,** featuring the works of 150 local and national artists; **1421 Pearl St.; 303-443-3683.** To see high-quality western paintings and sculpture in a museum environment visit the **Leanin' Tree Museum, 6055 Longbow Dr.; 303-530-1442.** Another recommended stop is the **University Memorial Center** on the University of Colorado campus, which features an ever-changing collection of art from nationally recognized artists as well as CU students.

Boulder Historical Society and Museum

In a wonderful stone mansion on "the Hill" in Boulder, this fine museum houses many artifacts (dating to the 1860s). In fact, because the historical society's collection is so vast, they must rotate displays several times a year. The house, replete with its Tiffany stained-glass window and Italian-tiled fireplace, is the perfect setting for old photographs, furniture, toys, clothing and quilts. Don't miss the kitchen with its round icebox and interesting tools. Small donation suggested. Open Tues.–Fri. 10–4 P.M.; Sat. and Sun. noon–4 P.M. **1206 Euclid Ave.; 303-449-3464.**

Boulder Museum of Contemporary Art

This museum, located in a historic two-story warehouse, brings innovative exhibitions and performances to the heart of downtown. It presents contemporary art by local, regional, national and international artists in 10,000 square feet of renovated exhibition and performance spaces. Check out what is happening on the cutting edge at **1750 13th St.; 303-443-2122; www.bmoca.org.** At dusk on summer evenings, you can see movie classics just behind the museum, projected for everyone's enjoyment. Donation requested; **www.outdoor filmfestival.com.**

Collage Children's Museum

Happy shrieks and the patter of feet fill the colorful, fun-filled environment of Boulder's children's museum. Children up to preteens will love being told, "Yes! Please touch." Displays range from a hands-on magnetic sculpture table to a massive soap bubble that children can create with the help of a hula hoop. Without knowing it, your kids will undoubtedly learn something. The museum features many special events, changing exhibits and performances throughout the year. "Virtually the only time you hear a kid crying is when parents attempt to leave this place," remarked the museum director. Open 10 A.M.–5 P.M. Mon.–Sat., except closed Tues.; 1–5 P.M. Sun. **2065 30th St.** in Aspen Plaza, **Boulder, CO 80301; 303-440-9894.**

Fiske Planetarium

With state-of-the-art equipment, a 65-foot dome and highly regarded on-campus experts, Fiske rivals the best planetariums in the world. Friday-evening star talks with University of Colorado astronomers point out attributes of the heavens while sharing current research with audience members. After the program many people like to go to the observatory for a free peek through one of two large telescopes, 16 and 24 inches, at the real night sky. Other monthly events include multimedia/laser shows geared to rock and roll. The children's matinee, science discovery program and other events take place throughout the year. Located on the University of Colorado campus on **Regent Dr.** Call **303-492-5001** for a schedule of events.

Mapleton Hill Walking Tour

See some of Boulder's grandest homes on this fine historical walking tour. Pick up a self-guiding brochure at the **Boulder Convention and Visitors Bureau, 2440 Pearl St., 303-442-2911;** or check in with **Historic Boulder** at 646 **Pearl St., Boulder, CO 80302, 303-444-5192.**

University of Colorado Natural History Museum

Established in 1902, this fine museum features subjects such as Southwestern archaeology, paleontology, anthropology and botany. Terrific hands-on exhibit of animal tracks. Lectures, courses and traveling exhibits are also offered. Open Mon.–Fri. 9 A.M.–5 P.M., Sat. 9 A.M.–4 P.M., Sun. 10 A.M.–4 P.M. In the Henderson Building on campus at **15th St. and Broadway; 303-492-6892; www.colorado.edu/cumuseum.**

Nightlife

Finding nightlife shouldn't be a problem in Boulder. The free summer acts and many bars of the Pearl Street Mall (see the Major Attractions section) always draw large crowds. We have listed a few outstanding places, but don't forget the exploding cafe scene (see the Where to Eat section). For a more complete listing of area nightlife, check the *Colorado Daily* or the *Boulder Daily Camera* newspapers. For big name and regional music try **The Fox Theatre** and **Cafe on the Hill (1135 13th St., 303-443-3399,** www.foxtheatre.com) or **Boulder Theater** (2032 14th St., 303-786-7030, www.boulder theater.com). The easiest way to get the latest happenings is to call the **KBCO Information Line** at 303-444-5226 for a recorded message or check the events board at **www.kbco.com.**

Boulder Dinner Theater

Since 1976 this dinner theater has provided complete evenings of dining and entertainment. A professional acting troupe with members from around the United States puts on Broadway-style shows, including *Cabaret, West Side Story, A Chorus Line* and *Evita.* Unlike some dinner theaters, you may choose from a menu—prime rib, spinach lasagna and chicken teriyaki are a few of the entrées—and the performers also wait the tables. If a performance is sold out, go ahead and stop by; the theater will buy you a drink, and if there are any no-shows, you can buy their tickets. Open Tues.–Sun. **5501 Arapahoe Ave.; 303-449-6000.**

Brewpubs

The **Walnut Brewery** has a loyal following— on weekends, lines often form at the entrance. They serve various styles of beer, including bitter, wheat and stout (but all at the same cold temperature). With high ceilings and window-encased brew vats, this loud place is as much restaurant as pub. **1123 Walnut; 303-447-1345.** Another great bet for brewpub aficionados is the nearby **Oasis Brewing Company,** with its long bar, seasonal beers and upstairs pool tables. **11th and Canyon; 303-449-0363.**

Trios Wine Bar

With some 60 wines by the glass, classy second-floor surroundings and live jazz or blues music, it's not hard to see why Trios attracts a steady stream of well-heeled customers and many couples out for a romantic evening. With muted lighting and a well-versed serving staff wearing black and white, Trios makes you feel almost as if you were at a private club. Try reasonably priced wine flights (three 2-oz. samplers) from Colorado or Napa Valley and an excellent late

night menu. Live music starting at 7 P.M. weekdays and 8:30 P.M. weekends. **1155 Canyon Blvd.; 303-442-8400; www.triosgrille.com.**

West End Tavern

This neighborhood tavern is a great place to hang out. The 100-year-old oak bar—brought to Boulder from Miss Kitty's Saloon in Nebraska— fits into its present home in the tavern with less than a quarter-inch to spare. Jazz and blues are featured in the renovated downstairs section. The upstairs deck offers perfect views of the Flatirons. For a summer sunset, come here. Decent menu with filling selections from nachos to burgers. **Between 9th St. and 10th St. on Pearl St.; 303-444-3535.**

Scenic Drives

Eldorado Artesian Springs

Just south of Boulder at the base of a narrow, rocky canyon lies the small community of Eldorado Springs. This town enjoyed a heyday in the early 1900s, when it became known as a fashionable spa. Warm artesian spring water was funneled into pools, and guests enjoyed comfortable rooms and a choice of restaurants. Eldorado Artesian Springs has lost its glossy image, but it remains a good place to swim (see the Swimming and Tubing section). Enter Eldorado Canyon State Park just beyond Eldorado Artesian Springs. After buying an inexpensive parks pass, head into this land of sheer cliffs dotted with climbers from around the world. The technical climbing is some of the state's best, but it's also a great place to hike or relax and watch; bring along a picnic lunch. No camping allowed. To reach Eldorado Springs, take Broadway (Hwy. 93) south of Boulder for 5.5 miles. Turn right on Eldorado Springs Dr. (Hwy. 170) and continue 3 miles.

Flagstaff Mountain

This quick, winding route up Flagstaff Mountain overlooks Boulder from the west. The paved road has several pullouts; after a few miles of continuous uphill driving there is a turnoff for

A golden autumn moment on the Peak to Peak Highway. Photo by Bruce Caughey.

the Sunrise Circle Amphitheater. Turn right and continue to a magnificent overlook of Boulder. At the amphitheater there are picnic tables and several hiking trails. At night the lights of Boulder make the drive worthwhile. To reach Flagstaff Mountain, drive west on Baseline Rd. and keep going.

Peak to Peak Highway

By taking any of the canyons west of Boulder, you'll soon end up on the spectacular Peak to Peak Highway. The road, designated a Scenic and Historic Byway, stretches all the way from Blackhawk north to Estes Park, with mountain scenery and history along the whole route. In fall shimmering aspen stands provide a show of epic proportions.

A good loop trip from Boulder, taking in a section of the Peak to Peak Highway, begins at the west end of Canyon Blvd. (Hwy. 119). This old mining road was improved in 1915 by convict labor. After 8.5 miles on the twisting, paved road, there is a parking turnout on the left (south) side for **Boulder Falls.** Cross the highway and after a short distance you'll be face-to-face with North Boulder Creek cascading over eroded rocks. It's a torrent during spring runoff. After another 8 miles west on Hwy. 119, the road comes out of the canyon at **Nederland.** This small town was born as a supply center to the silver camp of Caribou a few miles to the west. In 1873 a few Dutch investors bought the Caribou Mine, which was producing $3 million a year by 1875. The glory years were short-lived, though, because of the silver market crash of 1893. Caribou is a ghost town today, but Nederland (named for the Dutch-owned mine) is still going strong. In town you'll find a couple restaurants, including the popular Pioneer Bar.

From Nederland turn right on Hwy. 72 (the Peak to Peak Highway), which provides stunning views on the way to **Ward,** 14 miles north. (A left would take you south toward Rollinsville and eventually to Central City.) Ward is an old gold camp that has survived to accommodate a new generation of residents who prefer quiet and solitude. Situated in a narrow canyon, the town is one of the more beautiful near-ghost towns in the state. Fortunately, the schoolhouse and church survived a disastrous fire in 1900.

Just north of Ward, a marked turnoff heads west for about 5 miles to **Brainard Lake.** The incredible view of the Indian Peaks from this popular mountain lake make it a worthwhile stop (parking fee). For more information about some of the trails in the area, see the Hiking and Backpacking section. From Ward continue 27 miles north to **Estes Park** on Hwy. 7 (see the **Estes Park** chapter for more information) and loop back to Boulder on Hwy. 36. Or drop back toward Boulder via Left Hand Canyon from Ward.

Shopping

McGuckins Hardware Store

For 45 years McGuckins has easily remained the king of one-stop shopping, thanks to its immense collection of eclectic stuff. The motto at this family-owned store rings true: "If we don't have it, you don't need it." You don't even have to buy anything as you wander through this collection of some 200,000 items—everything from tools and camping equipment to wheelbarrows and toasters. Buying every variety of nails, screws and bolts (up to 1-inch diameter) has never been easier, especially with the help of one of their easy-to-find, green-vested employees. This is the place to find that hard-to-buy-for a gift. McGuckins has a terrific collection of unusual Christmas ornaments. Located inside a hangar-sized store **off 23rd and Arapahoe Sts.; 303-443-1822.**

Where to Stay

Accommodations

Boulder Victoria—$$$$

In 1891 Colonel Nicholson completed building and furnishing his large, two-story home. Precisely 100 years later, new owners spruced up the place into an elegantly appointed, six-room B&B. In a convenient just-off-the-mall location, you will find large guest rooms featuring period antiques and brass beds topped with billowy down comforters. Modern private bathrooms, telephones and TVs (hidden from sight in an

armoire) provide the only exceptions to the Victorian atmosphere.

Architectural curiosities and odd angles liven up the guest rooms—especially the Nicholson Room with its archways and covered balcony. Be sure to wander out onto the canopied terrace for prime westerly views of the mountains. The only drawback to staying on the second floor is an extremely steep staircase.

On the main level, you will find three more guest rooms (including a suite) and the main common area, decorated in warm hues of green and rose. Guests are invited to linger, flip through a selection of Colorado picture books or enjoy a glass of port wine. You can take your continental breakfast—granola, yogurt, baked goods, coffee and fruit—in the adjacent breakfast room or outside on the flagstone patio. They also serve desserts and cappuccino in the evening. **1305 Pine St., Boulder, CO 80302; 303-938-1300; www.bouldervictoria.com.**

A few blocks north, check out the deluxe accommodations at the **Earl House ($$$$),** an 1882 vintage B&B run by the same owners. The Earl House features six period rooms and two larger carriage houses in back. Most feature four-poster beds; private bathrooms and period antiques throughout. **2329 Broadway, Boulder, CO 80304; 303-938-1400.**

Gold Lake Mountain Resort and Spa (Ward)—$$$$

To get away from every worldly pressure, even for a weekend, head straight to Gold Lake. You'll encounter fine dining and a full-scale spa in a secluded mountain setting, featuring decadent services ranging from aromatherapy to massage (including a dual massage, with two therapists working on you in tandem) and a hot-rocks treatment, with heated stones placed along your body. If that were not enough, then you can enjoy the warmth of lakeside hot pools, with views to the Continental Divide and surrounding forest. Your private mountain cabin continues the experience with carefully selected antiques and tasteful furnishings, including comfy beds with down comforters encased in raw silk and hemp duvets. The artistry of the furnishings is evident even in the bathrooms, where you may find oversized slate tubs backed by hammered copper. Located a half hour west of Boulder at **3371 Gold Lake Rd., Ward, CO 80481; 1-800-450-3544; www.goldlake.com.**

The Alps—$$$ to $$$$

A few miles up Boulder Canyon, the old Moose Lodge has been transformed into a romantic escape not to be missed. As you enter this charming bed and breakfast, look around because you are actually standing within a cabin dating back to the 1870s. The lodge was built up around it over the years. Each of the inn's 12 rooms features a unique, appealing decor with a sitting area, fireplace, antiques and private bathroom. You'll love the claw-foot or double whirlpool baths (some located right in the bedroom area). The common areas are accented by heavy logs, moss-rock fireplaces and the right amount of warm lodge furniture and knickknacks. On warm days the decks and verandas beckon you outside to relax. Excellent full breakfasts, afternoon tea and a selection of evening desserts will tempt you throughout the day. Located 3 miles up Boulder Canyon. **38619 Boulder Canyon Dr., Boulder, CO 80308; 303-444-5445; www.alpsinn.com.**

Hotel Boulderado—$$$ to $$$$

This historic hotel opened with a bash on New Year's Day in 1909. It's a graceful brick hotel built with a style and elegance similar to that of the Brown Palace Hotel in Denver. A stained-glass mezzanine ceiling is clearly visible from the ornate lobby. The hotel thrived from day one, as its luxurious rooms were furnished in the finest style. Many famous guests stayed at the Boulderado, including Teddy Roosevelt (where didn't he stay?), Helen Keller, Louis Armstrong and Robert Frost. Traveling evangelist Billy Sunday, deliverer of hell-fire sermons, also stayed at the Boulderado during its first year. He described the town as "a sinkhole of iniquity, crying for redemption."

The hotel declined dramatically during the 1960s and early 1970s, but was resurrected in the early 1980s. In 1985 a new expansion connected by a walkway added 61 rooms. Both the old and new portions of the hotel are reminiscent of the Victorian era. However, some of the feel of the old hotel, with its creaky floors and manual Otis elevator, is lost on the new side. Each of the rooms and suites has a unique personality, but rooms on the upper floors have better views. Staying at the Boulderado entitles guests to a complimentary pass to a nearby full-service health club. Downstairs you'll find **Q's ($$$ to $$$$),** an excellent high-end restaurant with interior and porch seating; try out the saffron-infused gazpacho or grilled asparagus prosciutto for starters. Reservations recommended. **2115 13th St., Boulder, CO 80302; 1-800-433-4344; 303-442-4344; www.boulderado.com.**

Briar Rose—$$$

You will feel right at home in this comfortable, historic 11-room bed and breakfast. The rooms are beautifully furnished in antiques, and the beds are topped with puffy feather comforters. Slipping into a relaxed mind-set comes easily when surrounded by such attention to detail, including artistic stencils painted on the walls. You can arrange for tea and cookies delivered to your room for an afternoon respite. Find a room in the main house, or in the separate, but still homey carriage house. Although it's in the heart of town, the Briar Rose is protected from the outside world by a dense shield of shrubbery and trees. An elegant continental breakfast is served each morning in your room or out on the glass-enclosed sunporch. A common room open to all guests is filled with couches and chairs arranged around a fireplace. Reservations encouraged. **2151 Arapahoe Ave., Boulder, CO 80302; 303-442-3007; www. bnbinns.com/briarrose.inn.**

Boulder Mountain Lodge—$$ to $$$

See the Camping section.

Foot of the Mountain Motel—$$ to $$$

This simple motel, with its inordinate amount of charm, sits at the base of the mountains on the outskirts of Boulder. The convenience of the city

Boulder's Foot of the Mountain Motel allows visitors to step back to a simpler time. Photo by Bruce Caughey.

blends well with unobstructed mountain views. Most rooms have bathtubs that offer spectacular window views up Flagstaff Mountain. The Foot of the Mountain conjures up the feeling of a mountain cabin with its rough bark exterior, bright red paint around the windowsills, blooming flower boxes and all-wood interior. All rooms are equipped with private baths, cable TV and small refrigerators. **200 Arapahoe Ave., Boulder, CO 80302; 303-442-5688.**

Boulder International Youth Hostel—$

You won't find a mint on your pillow at night, but for sheer value and the opportunity to meet travelers from around the world, there's no better place. With a mix of private, small group and men's and women's dorm rooms, the hostel has appealed to many since it opened in 1961. Large downstairs common area, shared kitchen and laundry facility. **1107 12th St., Boulder, CO 80302; 303-442-0522; www.boulder hostel.com.**

Camping

Boulder Parks and Recreation

Buckingham/Fourth of July Campground has only 8 tentsites, no water and no fee. Because the campground usually fills up on weekends, get there as early as possible. It is a primitive campground reached by a rough dirt road. Its proximity to the Indian Peaks Wilderness trailheads is a major advantage. To reach the campground from Nederland, travel west on County Rd. 130 past Eldora. After the pavement ends, take the right fork some 5 miles to the campground. (The left fork leads to the Hesse trailhead.)

Roosevelt National Forest

West of Boulder are a number of first-come, first-served campgrounds. Some of the campsites, however, can be reserved in advance by calling **1-877-444-6777.** All listed campgrounds charge a fee. Three miles south of Nederland on Hwy. 119 is **Kelly-Dahl Campground** (46 sites), with beautiful views of the Continental Divide. **Rainbow Lakes Campground** (18 sites) is reached by taking Hwy. 72 for 6.5 miles north of Nederland to a sign that reads Mountain Research Station; turn left and continue on a rough dirt road for 5 miles. **Pawnee Campground** (55 sites) is 5 miles west of Ward on County Rd. 102. It's an extremely popular area near Brainard Lake.

To reach **Peaceful Valley Campground** (17 sites), drive 15 miles west from Lyons on Hwy. 7 to the junction with Hwy. 72; turn left and continue southwest on Hwy. 72 for 6 miles. **Camp Dick Campground** (41 sites) is located another mile west of Peaceful Valley on a dirt road.

Private Campground

Boulder Mountain Lodge—Next to a gurgling creek, just 5 minutes away from Boulder, is a small RV and tent campground with a basic motel. The **motel rooms ($$ to $$$)** feature picnic tables out in front and are clean and comfortable; some have kitchenettes. At the far end, away from the tents, a newer building features four smallish suites. This is a really nice family place located at the former town of Orodell. The office is in the old narrow-gauge train depot. The campsites are shaded by mature trees, and guests enjoy a small outdoor pool and year-round hot tubs. Kids will love fishing in the private pond. **91 Four Mile Canyon Rd., Boulder, CO 80302; 1-800-458-0882; 303-444-0882.**

Where to Eat

Flagstaff House—$$$$

Plan on arriving at Flagstaff House before dark so you can enjoy the commanding view of Boulder as dusk settles slowly over the valley. This restaurant, with tiered decks and glassed-in seating areas, virtually hangs from the side of Flagstaff Mountain. Once darkness takes over, the twinkling lights of Boulder are a beautiful accompaniment to your meal. The menu is not necessarily traditional—more than 40 entrées are served, including grilled rack of Colorado lamb, elk with ginger sauce, Maine lobster and pheasant breast. Flagstaff House is just about the only restaurant in Boulder where you must dress up. Valet parking; reservations requested. Open for dinner from 6 P.M. Mon.–Sun. (from 5 P.M. on Sat.). To reach Flagstaff House, head west on Baseline Rd. and continue about halfway up Flagstaff Mountain and look for the sign. **303-442-4640.**

Laudisio—$$$ to $$$$

Tucked into the corner of a small shopping center, you'll find a classic piece of Italy transplanted in Boulder. Fresh ingredients, incredible pasta, premium olive oils and the sights and sounds of cooking permeate the restaurant's open kitchen. One of Boulder's top chefs recommended Laudisio to me as an excellent example of creative Italian cooking—he's right! The daily specials entice you with tastes from all over Italy, and the superior staff helps you wade through the choices. A full bar and extensive Italian wine list complement the food, as does the artistic setting. End your meal with a cappuccino and a decadent crème brûlée. Be sure to get there early or make a dinner reservation. Open for lunch Mon.–Fri. 11:30 A.M.–2:30 P.M.; dinner served daily from 5:30 P.M. In the Willow Springs Shopping Center, **28th St. and Iris Ave.; 303-442-1300.**

Mediterranean Restaurant—$$ to $$$

The "Med" will impress you with the barrage of interesting colors that emerge from the light, airy interior space. Whether you eat in the restaurant surrounded by huge displays of fresh flowers and little cozy nooks or out in the courtyard patio, you will enjoy the ambience. And the food matches the environment. Light dishes designed for sharing dominate the tapas menu. You can also order a tasty individual pizza, a plate of pasta or a wonderful Greek salad. Open for lunch Mon.–Sat. 11:30 A.M.–2:30 P.M.; dinner nightly from 5 P.M. Located just off the Pearl Street Mall at **1002 Walnut; 303-444-5335.**

Sunflower—$$ to $$$

In an airy setting east of the Pearl Street Mall, this organic-food restaurant epitomizes what many think of as Boulder-style cuisine—free of preservatives, additives or artificial ingredients. Vegans will have to think through the menu with its ample choices of carefully prepared meat-free cuisine and organic salad bar. But if you want to order something with free-range chicken or perhaps salmon, that's possible, too. "You can eat a large meal here and not feel over-stuffed, because of our recipes and ingredients," says Chef Matt Snyder, who owns the restaurant with John Pell and Alison McDonald. They all have a say in the kitchen. Careful service and an informal yet classy decor set the tone. Don't even think about skipping their best-selling triple chocolate mousse cake and a cup of coffee (soy or rice milk is an option, as is agave for sweetener). Open for lunch Mon.–Sat. 11 A.M.–2:30 P.M.; Sun. brunch 10 A.M.–2:30 P.M.; dinner nightly 5–10 P.M. **1701 Pearl St.; 303-440-0220.**

Blue Parrot Cafe—$$

Located in the small community of Louisville (residents pronounce the "s"), this landmark restaurant has been treasured for its down-home Italian cooking since opening in 1919. A plateful of thick, homemade spaghetti and an extra pot of sauce are the main reasons to eat here; top off your meal with some spumoni. In addition to serving lunch and dinner, the casual restaurant is open for breakfast; Italian food die-hards will love the option of ordering a side of spaghetti with egg dishes. Full bar. Open Mon.–Thurs. 8 A.M.–9:30 P.M., Fri.–Sat. 8 A.M.–10 P.M., Sun. 8 A.M.–8 P.M. **640 Main St., Louisville, CO 80027; 303-666-0677.**

Dushanbe Teahouse—$ to $$$

More than 40 artisans from Boulder's sister city of Dushanbe in the country of Tajikistan toiled in their homeland creating hand-carved, distinctly painted elements for this extraordinarily detailed building. Crate by crate, thousands of pieces were shipped to Boulder before being incorporated into the building we see today. The craftsmanship of the Dushanbe (pronounced doo-SHAWN-bay) can be seen in its brightly colored, elaborate rectangular structure, set amid a well-kept garden courtyard and outdoor seating area. The teahouse features a carefully selected menu for lunch, teatime, dinner and weekend brunch. Borrowed cuisines range from Indian to Mediterranean to Mexican. Dinner entrées include Persian lamb kabobs, stew and Thai curry noodle. At other times, you'll see tofu, egg dishes, pasta and unique salads—even a breakfast burrito. Menu choices are complemented by beer, wine, juices, coffee and, of course, an excellent variety of teas. The service can be sporadic and at times slow. Open 8 A.M.–9 P.M. daily, a bit later Fri. and Sat. nights. **1770 13th St.; 303-442-4993.**

Chautauqua Dining Hall—$ to $$

The atmosphere on the porch of this venerable 1898 dining hall is the main reason to eat here. A wide balcony overlooks grassy Chautauqua Park and offers gorgeous mountain views. The hall feels warm and sunny even in the depths of winter, but be sure to eat on the veranda during nice weather. It's a good choice for breakfast, brunch, lunch and dinner. The food ranges from omelettes and pancakes for breakfast, to sandwiches for lunch and full entrées for dinner. Award-winning desserts include caramel apple cobbler served with homemade ice cream. On weekends there is usually a long wait for breakfast, but you can order a cappuccino or a Bloody Mary and wait for your turn: it's the most pleasant waiting room in Boulder. Chautauqua is also the perfect place to come for dinner before a festival or event at the drafty, all-wood Chautauqua Auditorium. No reservations. Open 7 A.M.–2 P.M. for breakfast, 11:30 A.M.–2 P.M. for lunch, 5:30–9 P.M. for dinner. Chautauqua Park, **900 Baseline Rd.; 303-442-3282.**

Lucile's—$ to $$

On a side street just off the Boulder Mall is the kind of restaurant you love to happen upon. Lucile's serves breakfast and lunch in the casual confines of an old house. The covered porch is the best place to sit on warm summer mornings; inside, the small rooms create a feeling of intimacy. For breakfast it is hard to imagine a tastier dish than the Cajun breakfast—red beans, poached eggs topped with hollandaise sauce and served with grits or potatoes and a buttermilk biscuit. Spicy lunch dishes include gumbo, shrimp Creole and blackened red snapper. Don't forget to order the beignets—delicious sopapilla-like donuts. Open weekdays 7 A.M.–2 P.M., weekends 8 A.M.–2 P.M. **2124 14th St.; 303-442-4743.**

Boulder Farmer's Market—$

From May through Oct., on Sats. 8 A.M.–2 P.M. and Weds. 10 A.M.–2 P.M., the Farmer's Market should be your first destination for fresh food and produce. Find fruit and baked goods as well as restaurant meals, along with a wonderful ambience. Gazing and smelling fresh-cut flowers while listening to live local music makes this entire scene a sensory excursion. **On 13th St.** right in front of the Dushanbe Teahouse, just south of Canyon.

Tra-Ling's Oriental Cafe—$

This bargain-priced Chinese restaurant offers quick lunches and dinners. You can choose your entrée, rice and noodles from behind glass— we promise, no color photos of selections here. The food is ready before you know it; sit down, take out or have it delivered. Open Mon.–Fri. 11:30 A.M.–9:30 P.M., Sat.–Sun. 4:30–9:30 P.M. **1305 Broadway; 303-449-0400.**

Assorted Cafes

An open passageway to Boulder's best bookstore on a prime Pearl Street Mall location sets the **Bookend Cafe (1115 Pearl Street Mall, 303-440-6699)** apart. Tremendous people-watching and, if you can get a table, great coffees and fresh pastries; an excellent place to lose yourself in a good book and let the afternoon slip by; open 6:45 A.M.–11 P.M. daily. On "the Hill" stop by **Buchanans Coffee Pub (1301 Pennsylvania, 303-440-0222)** with its dark green color scheme, a wall of windows, great coffee and atmosphere; open Mon.–Fri. 7 A.M.–11 P.M.; weekends open at 8 A.M. **Trident Coffee House and Bookstore (940 Pearl St., 303-443-3133)** epitomizes a Boulder scene with its eclectic selection of used books and laid-back environment. Stop in to buy a book and then settle in for a relaxing cup of coffee, espresso or cappuccino; open Mon.–Fri. 6:30 A.M.–11 P.M., on weekends 7 A.M.–11 P.M. For exotic surroundings, don't skip the remarkable **Dushanbe Teahouse** (see write-up above).

Services

Visitor Information

Boulder Convention and Visitors Bureau—Stop in here for information and advice on the area. **2440 Pearl St., Boulder, CO 80302; 303-442-2911; www.bouldercoloradousa.com.**

Day Care

City of Boulder Child Care Support Center—Information and referrals for child care. **303-441-3180.**

YWCA and YMCA—Both of these organizations have referral lists of baby-sitters. The YWCA has emergency child care Mon.–Fri. **303-442-2778.**

Transportation

Boulder Airporter—Van service to Denver International Airport for a reasonable price. **303-444-0808.**

Boulder RTD Bus Service—For information on bus service in town and to **Denver International Airport,** call RTD at **303-299-6000** or stop by the **Boulder Convention and Visitors Bureau** and pick up a schedule (see listing above).

Boulder Yellow Cab—303-442-2277.

Central City and Black Hawk

As you drive up the mile-long road from Black Hawk to Central City and look at the many old houses perched on the steep mountainsides, it's easy to see how ill suited the surrounding area is for these two small towns. But early settlers had a very good reason for choosing this location. In the spring of 1859, gold strikes along Gregory Gulch fueled the first big rush to Colorado (at the time called the Kansas Territory). Serving as a catalyst for settlement in Colorado, Central City was also the cultural center for the state and quite nearly became the state capital. The town's tradition of theater and opera goes back to the 1860s. Many summer visitors to this Victorian mining town still attend the renowned Central City Opera.

Since 1990 when Colorado voters approved limited-stakes gambling, radical and sometimes controversial change has taken hold of these communities. For now the area's renewed vigor captures the imagination of most visitors. Ringing slots, flashing lights and the rush of coins hitting metal create a charged atmosphere inside most doorways. Dedicated gamblers with coin-blackened fingers, some paying only a nickel per pull, occasionally shout and laugh when hitting a jackpot. Others squeeze into a place at the blackjack or poker tables to try to build up their stacks of chips in the haze of cigarette smoke. With a $5 betting limit, though, high rollers should stick to Vegas and Atlantic City. (See the Major Attractions section for more specifics on gambling.)

At a glance, the false-fronted towns couldn't look better. But a closer look reveals some interesting changes. A massive rebuilding of the towns took place at first, and small, gleaming new casinos stood behind historic facades. But recently the smaller operations, by and large, have been replaced by major new developments, which

have added hotel rooms to the area. The big players have come to set up shop in Blackhawk along Hwy. 119, literally chipping away the mountainside to squeeze in more parking and bigger gaming areas. The great majority of gamblers have gravitated to Black Hawk, thanks in large measure because it's the first town you come to from the Denver area. The town of Central City, only a mile away, is in full-scale retreat; even the famous Teller House recently shut down its gaming operation.

No doubt the historical integrity of the area has been compromised, and many locals left years ago, cashing in on hyperinflated land prices. An army of construction workers has

Getting There

Central City is located 30 miles west of Denver. From Golden, head west up Clear Creek Canyon on Hwy. 6 and then northwest on Hwy. 119 to Black Hawk. Continue 1 mile west of Black Hawk on Hwy. 279 to reach Central City.

transformed the area into a sort of western theme park. Time will tell if the towns get their acts together to provide services visitors expect at a true destination resort.

If you don't like gambling or opera, don't worry; there are plenty of other things to do. Visit an interesting museum or investigate the hilly neighborhoods surrounding the downtown area. Or drive to some of the neighboring ghost towns—say, Nevadaville or Apex—and to any number of old cemeteries. It's not a good idea to take a hike on the surrounding hills because of hundreds of abandoned mines. A trip to Central City and Black Hawk is still an outstanding way to learn about a fascinating period of Colorado history.

History

In the spring of 1859, when Georgia prospector John H. Gregory made his way up a side gulch of North Clear Creek, he couldn't possibly have known just how much gold he was about to discover. At a spot between Central City and Black Hawk, he found what he was looking for at a place later named Gregory Gulch. The town of Mountain City grew around Gregory's claim, and by the end of the year thousands of miners were clamoring around the area. Colorado's first major gold rush was on, with the area eventually producing more than a half billion dollars' worth of minerals. Many camps were established, including Black Hawk, Gregory Point, Missouri City, Nevadaville, Hoosier City, Dogtown and, of course, Central City—so named for its central location in the gulch. Out of convenience, miners from the surrounding camps would meet here, and it quickly grew into the main supply center.

Placer strikes continued into the 1860s and many miners became rich. Central City continued to grow and for a few years rivaled Denver as the largest town in the territory. But by the mid-1860s the placer mining began petering out. No one doubted there was still plenty of gold left in the hills, but it was trapped in quartz formations, making it difficult and expensive to remove. In 1867 Nathaniel P. Hill came to the rescue. Hill, a chemistry professor from Brown University, built the Boston–Colorado Smelter in Black Hawk, which could economically break down the refractory gold ore. That put the mining boom back on its feet. With the smelter and the arrival of the Colorado & Southern Railroad from Denver in 1872, Black Hawk grew into quite a town of its own.

Hardrock mining proceeded at a frenzied pace. On Quartz Hill, between Central City and Nevadaville, the Mammoth vein was discovered, over the years producing millions in gold, silver, lead and copper. The largest mine along the Mammoth vein was the Glory Hole, a highly profitable open-pit mine that helped the area around Quartz Hill to become known as "the richest square mile on Earth."

Aside from mining, Central City is well known for the cultural mark it left on the state. The area drew a diverse group of immigrant miners, including Chinese, Russians, Canadians, Scots and Englishmen. The Cornish miners from England had the greatest influence on the town. To a degree their mortarless stone walls still characterize both Central City and Black Hawk. More important, they were active supporters of opera and theater. From the beginning the community supported amateur shows performed in makeshift tents. In July 1862 the Montana Theatre opened. Its debut performance went on as planned, despite the fact that on the previous day George W. Harrison, the owner, is said to have fired 35 shots into local boxer Charlie Swits. His defense at the trial was that he "didn't like Swits." The jury must have agreed, because Harrison was acquitted. He eventually went on to become a state senator. The Montana Theatre played to packed houses until 1874, when a raging fire wiped out most of the wooden buildings and homes in Central City.

Residents of Central City began to rebuild after the fire, using stone in place of wood to prevent further catastrophes. Evening entertainment resumed in 1875 with the completion of the new Belvidere Theatre, where operatic and theatrical productions received rave reviews statewide. After a performance of *Bohemia Girl* brought down the house, townsfolk began planning a new opera house worthy of such quality performances. In December 1877 the *Rocky Mountain News* reported that the opera house construction was proceeding just fine and promised "the most beautiful auditorium to be found between Chicago and San Francisco." The opera house finally opened in the spring of 1878 to sellout crowds. Numerous dramas were also performed by famous thespians of the time, such as Sarah Bernhardt and Edwin Booth.

In the 1880s the Central City area experienced a decline in fortunes. With silver prices going up, the central economic focus of Colorado shifted from the dwindling goldfields of Central City to the booming silver town of Leadville. By 1890 many townsfolk had moved on. Along with a loss of local patrons, the Central City Opera House lost business when Tabor's Grand Opera House was built in Denver.

Although some mining continued well into the 1900s, Central City was on its way to becoming another ghost town. Peter McFarlane, who had taken over control of the opera house in 1896, kept it open despite consistent losses. In 1910 he began using the building to show the latest craze—motion pictures. This continued until 1927. Then, after staying closed for more than four years, the opera house experienced a rebirth, when it reopened with a successful production of *Camille,* starring Lillian Gish.

When Coloradans voted to legalize gambling in Central City and Black Hawk, along with Cripple Creek, they changed the course of history. The dramatic pace of change will astound people with pregambling memories of these towns. But then, some 50 years ago gambling was legal, so perhaps some think of it as a return to "better days."

Major Attractions

Gambling

Dramatic, multimillion-dollar developments seem to have overtaken most of the family-owned casinos, although a few of the smaller places still survive. The extravagantly large developments, located mostly in Black Hawk, are backed by conglomerates such as Caesar's and Harrah's. These large casinos offer gamblers an array of games and incentives; hawkers line the streets shouting reasons to come inside. Tucked among the games you'll find restaurants, with some lavish buffets with absolutely incredible deals on food. Getting something to drink (for free if you are gaming) is absolutely no problem. Parents should remember this is primarily an adult playground with a 21-years-or-older rule to enter gaming areas.

Those driving will be pleased to know that parking near the casinos has eased up considerably over the past several years; many casinos now offer "free" valet parking service (sometimes with a hitch, so be sure to ask). If everything seems full in either town, you can always park above Central City and take a shuttle back into town. Harvey's provides free van service on the 1-mile route between Central City and Black Hawk.

For people staying along the Front Range, round-trip bus transportation from various pickup points can be found by calling **Ace Express** at **303-421-2780.** It's one of the safest bets you can make.

Colorado Central Station also offers limited bus service from some parts of Denver. Reserve by calling **303-279-3000; www.colorado centralstation.com.**

Here is a sampling of a few gambling establishments:

Colorado Central Station

With a railroad theme, this longtime establishment packs 'em in with incentives that include car giveaways. Try the special Boxcar Brew at their bar. **340 Main St., Blackhawk; 303-279-3000; www.coloradocentralsta tion.com.**

Harvey's

This large Central City casino also offers rooms for the night (see the Where to Stay section), several restaurants, underground parking and 40,000 square feet of gambling. Las Vegas–style entertainment most afternoons/evenings. **At Gregory and D Streets** as you enter town; **1-800-WAGON-HO.**

Isle of Capri

Bright, almost garish colors permeate the tropical environment of this gleaming new $29 million casino. A waterfall crashes down through an opening in the floor, and three restaurants vie for your winnings. It's the largest hotel in town, with 237 rooms (see the Where to Stay section). **400 Main St., Blackhawk; 1-800-THE-ISLE; www.isleofcapricasino. com.**

Jazz Alley

This small, turquoise-colored operation has survived due to its great location amid the big casinos, and a sense of fun. Last time we walked by, Elvis waved from the doorway. They schedule music on many afternoons and evenings. Great all-day breakfast special, too. **321 Main St., Blackhawk; 303-582-1125.**

Festivals and Events

Lou Bunch Day

mid-June   Although Central City had very few brothels in comparison with many other Colorado mining towns, each year the town holds a celebration in remembrance of their last known madam—Lou Bunch, who left town in 1916. On Lou Bunch Day, the townsfolk dress up in period costumes (heavy on the garters) and have a brass bed race through town. In the evening the Madams and Miners Ball takes place at the Teller House. All events are free except for the ball. For more information call **303-582-5077.**

Summer Opera Festival

early July through mid-Aug.   Since its grand reopening in 1932, the beautiful Central City Opera House has been thrilling opera and theater lovers with its fine productions. Memorable

performances (two or three different productions) in this opulent, historic setting make for a great time at the oldest summer opera series in the country. See the History section for more information on the opera house. Ask about special recitals and their lovely weekend brunch. Reserve tickets by contacting the **Central City Opera House Association, 621 17th St., Suite 1625, Denver, CO 80293; 303-292-6700.**

Outdoor Activities

Four-Wheel-Drive Trips

Central City to St. Mary's Glacier

This 10-mile drive takes you west through magnificent country rich in mining history. For detailed directions, see the Four-Wheel-Drive Trips section of the **Georgetown and Idaho Springs** chapter.

Hiking and Backpacking

Taking off on a hike around Central City is not such a good idea. Locals are very careful not to wander off established roads and trails because of the vast number of mine shafts nearby.

Golden Gate Canyon State Park

This beautiful mountain park offers miles of excellent hiking trails as well as a hut system for backcountry camping. For further information, see the Parks, Gardens and Recreation Areas section in the **Denver and Environs** chapter.

Seeing and Doing

Cemeteries

In the nearby hills lie more than 10 historic cemeteries, complete with ornate Victorian tombstones. A couple of them can be easily reached from Central City by heading west on Eureka St. to the edge of town. You can't miss 'em. Ask also about the annual Ghost Tour and Cemetery Crawl that are scheduled in the fall

Central City's "Shady Ladies" work to preserve the colorful history of the former mining district. Photo by Bruce Caughey.

each year. History buffs actually play the parts (can we call it a living history?) of the more interesting people buried near Central City. For more information go to **City Hall** at **141 Nevada St.; 303-582-5251.** Or check with the **Historical Society** at **303-582-5283; www. coloradomuseums.org/gilpin.htm.**

Museums and Galleries

Gilpin County Arts Association

Since 1947 Gilpin County has helped sponsor the oldest juried art show in the state. An impressive display of work by Colorado artists includes everything from watercolor paintings to weavings in a lovely setting just across from the opera house. You feel as though you are in an outdoor garden replete with water-falls, even though you are indoors. There is no admission charge. The art show runs from mid-June through mid-Aug. Open daily except Mon., noon–6 P.M. **117 Eureka St., Central City, CO 80427; 303-582-5952** (summer only).

Gilpin County Historical Museum

Located in an old stone school building, this museum contains a large collection of local memorabilia. The school was built in 1869 and classes were held there until 1967. The Gilpin County Historical Society now owns the building and has packed both floors with interesting artifacts. Admission fee charged. Open daily Memorial Day–Labor Day, 11 A.M.–4 P.M.; call before visiting Sept.–Oct. **228 E. High St., P.O. Box 247, Central City, CO 80427; 303-582-5283; www.coloradomuseums.org/ gilpin.htm.**

The Lace House

Built in 1863 by Lucien K. Smith, the Lace House is an excellent example of Carpenter Gothic architecture; locals refer to it as the Gingerbread House. Unfortunately, the house has been closed to the public. In a comedy of errors, the Black Hawk town council—in an effort to preserve the building—would not permit the house to be moved to make way for casino development. The casino eventually built

During some festivals, bikers mix with operagoers and gamblers in the heart of Central City. Photo by Bruce Caughey.

a paved parking lot entirely around the structure and prohibited pedestrian access. So, what used to be a wonderful piece of history is now off-limits to the public. **161 Main St., Black Hawk.**

Teller House and Central City Opera House

When the railroad from Denver finally reached Black Hawk in 1872, construction had already begun on Central City's showpiece hotel—the Teller House. Built with local stone, the four-story masterpiece was furnished exquisitely, including luxurious carpeting in each of the 150 rooms. When President Ulysses S. Grant visited town in 1873, a special walkway was created out of silver bars, leading from his coach to the front door of the Teller House. In later years other celebrities, including Mark Twain and P. T. Barnum, stayed at the hotel.

Because it was built of stone, the Teller House survived the devastating fire in 1874 that ripped through Central City, destroying most of the buildings. When the adjacent opera house reopened in 1932, the Teller House and its

famous bar also underwent restoration. Twelve layers of wallpaper were peeled off the barroom walls, revealing the original murals. It was in 1936 that Denver newspaperman Herndon Davis painted the *Face on the Barroom Floor* while attending the summer opera with a lady friend. The face is still on the floor.

You can tour the opera house daily with a knowledgeable, friendly guide throughout the summer for a small fee. Inside the hotel you'll find gorgeous upstairs rooms, with massive diamond-dust mirrors and high-end antique furnishings of the period. Next door at the opera house you can get an idea why this acoustically perfect structure still draws large crowds. **120 Eureka St., Central City; 303-582-9608.**

Thomas House Museum

This well-preserved 1874 Victorian will give you a true sense of what life was like in Central City well over a century ago. You'll find everyday stuff in addition to the well-preserved treasures of one prominent local family. Guided tours only. Small fee. Open Memorial Day–Labor Day, Thurs.–Sun. 11 A.M.–4 P.M. **209 Eureka St., Central City, CO 80427; 303-582-5283.**

Nightlife

For information on casino action, see the Major Attractions section.

Summer Opera

See the Festivals and Events section.

Scenic Drives

Oh My God Road (Virginia Canyon)

A drive over Oh My God Rd. is highly recommended. It leads south from Central City over the mountains to Idaho Springs, 9 miles away. To reach the road, follow Spring St. south past the train station and keep driving. For more information about this historic road, see the Scenic Drives section in the **Georgetown and Idaho Springs** chapter.

Peak to Peak Highway

This gorgeous route, one of Colorado's Scenic and Historic Byways, begins at Black Hawk and heads north along the Front Range of the mountains for approximately 60 miles to Estes Park. Be sure to pick up a Peak to Peak brochure at the **Central City Hall, 117 Eureka St.,** for a mile-by-mile description. For more information see the Scenic Drives section in the **Boulder** chapter.

Where to Stay

Accommodations

With the opening of Harvey's, the casinos have gotten into the hotel business. We have listed the best of the casino stays, but you may also want to try one of the historic bed and breakfast accommodations in the towns.

Harvey's—$$$ to $$$$

You'll find a choice of 118 rooms and suites at this massive casino complex on the outskirts of Central City. One floor of rooms is reserved for smokers, another for nonsmokers. The western-themed rooms are comfortable places to rest until you get your second wind. A couple of on-site restaurants. Located at the intersection of **D and Gregory Sts., Central City; 1-800-HARVEYS.**

Isle of Capri—$$$ to $$$$

If you can stand the bright color scheme, this new 237-room hotel offers clean, comfortable rooms with all the amenities. Comforts such as three TVs and telephones in every one of its small suites are provided. All rooms come with pay-per-view television, Nintendo and Internet access—for those quiet, reflective moments when you are not in the casino! All rooms have a wonderful oversized whirlpool bath, complete with the Isle of Capri logo branded onto the side. **400 Main St., Blackhawk; 1-800-THE-ISLE; www.isleofcapricasino.com.**

The Lodge Casino—$$$ to $$$$

You can't miss the large Lodge Casino located off Hwy. 119 as you enter Black Hawk. With 50 rooms above the casino floor, this place has improved its fairly standard hotel rooms with pine furniture and muted, pleasing colors. The lodge offers some suites and a massive "presidential-type" suite for the true VIPs, with a gas fireplace, mini-kitchen and hospitality area. **240 Main St., Blackhawk, CO 80422; 1-877-711-1177; www.thelodgecasino.com.**

Chateau L'Acadienne—$$$

Jim and Shirley Voorhies live in one section of their one-story 1870s vintage home, and you get the other. They know the area very well and can direct you to some highlights. Built of "Hooper" brick from the area, the old home has been upgraded and made comfortable with antique furnishings. The New Orleans room features some Bourbon St. knickknacks. Jim, a former New Orleans resident, says the Chateau is a place to *laissez le bon temps rouler!* Gourmet breakfast is served in the small area outside your room on weekends (Continental breakfast during weekdays), but is better eaten in bed or out at a small table in front. Three rooms share a common bathroom; smoking permitted; cable TV. Be sure to haggle about the room rate, because you will almost always get a discount. **325 Spring St., P.O. Box 427, Central City, CO 80427; 303-582-5209.**

High Street Inn—$$$
Built in 1890 on "Bankers Row" overlooking Central City, each room in this historic inn reflects the careful attention of the owners. Pat and Selina Hughes welcome you into a comfortable, relaxing environment. Each of the three brightly decorated and sunny rooms (private or shared bath) provide elegant surroundings for guests. Enjoy a hearty full breakfast or a healthy mix of cereals and fresh fruit in the dining room or out on the great front porch. Cable TV; no smoking in the rooms. **215 W. First High St., P.O. Box 775, Central City, CO 80427; 303-582-0622.**

Camping

Arapaho National Forest
For reservations call **1-877-444-6777** or **www.reserveusa.com.** The closest campground to Central City is **Columbine Campground** (47 sites, fee charged), 2.1 miles northwest of town on County Rd. 279. From Black Hawk head 3 miles north on Hwy. 119 and 1 mile west to **Pickle Gulch Campground** and picnic area (30 sites, no fee). This campground is reserved for groups only; for information call **303-567-2901.** Four miles north of Black Hawk on Hwy. 119 is **Cold Springs Campground** and picnic area (47 sites, fee charged).

Golden Gate Canyon State Park
Located 7 miles north of Black Hawk on Hwy. 119 and 2 miles east on Gap Rd., Golden Gate Canyon State Park has 71 sites and a fee. Also a few primitive campsites. Call **303-582-3707** or **www.reserveamerica.com** for reservations. See the Parks, Gardens and Recreation Areas section of the **Denver and Environs** chapter for more information.

Private Campground
KOA Kampground—Just 5.5 miles north of Black Hawk off Hwy. 119 you'll find a little camping oasis with places for RVs and tents in addition to five small cabins. Pool, convenience and liquor stores and laundry facilities. **661 Hwy. 46, Black Hawk, CO 80422; 303-582-9979.**

Where to Eat

Dining in Central City and Black Hawk continues to be in a state of flux as the casinos try to attract gamblers into their establishments. The Black Forest Inn and other old-time places to eat have closed their doors. The good news is that you can often find great food deals advertised on signs as you wander around the towns. We can offer a few suggestions, but please inquire locally. **Fitzgeralds,** located in a casino of the same name at **101 Main St.** in **Black Hawk (1-800-538-LUCK),** offers a cozy feeling of Ireland with comfort food, including corned beef, salads and other fare. For five-star dining, most recommend the **White Buffalo** at the Lodge Casino (see the Where to Stay section) or **Farraday's** at the Isle of Capri (see the Where to Stay section). Ask about the buffet brunch offerings, where you can really fill up at a good price.

Services

Visitor Information
Casino websites serve as a source of current information. They include **www.coloradocentralstation.com** and **www.isleofcapricasino.com.**

Transportation
Services—Van or bus service is perhaps the best way to travel between the Front Range and Central City/Black Hawk. Several casinos offer their own transportation, or try **Ace Express** at **303-433-3613.** For those who really want to go in style, call **Colorado Limousine** at **303-832-7155.**

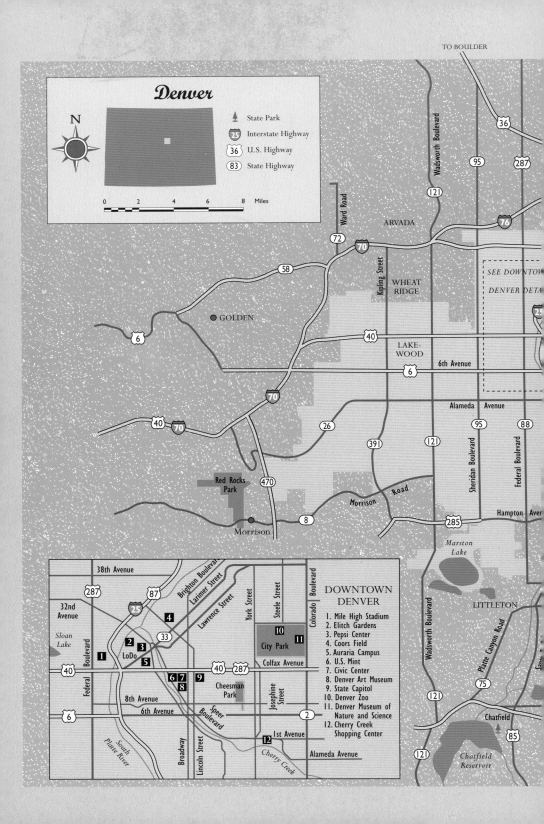

Denver

- ▲ State Park
- 25 Interstate Highway
- 36 U.S. Highway
- 83 State Highway

0 2 4 6 8 Miles

TO BOULDER

ARVADA

WHEAT RIDGE

GOLDEN

LAKE-WOOD

6th Avenue

Alameda   Avenue

Red Rocks Park

Morrison   Road

Morrison

Marston Lake

LITTLETON

Chatfield

Chatfield Reservoir

Ward Road

Wadsworth Boulevard

Kipling Street

Sheridan Boulevard

Federal Boulevard

Wadsworth Boulevard

Platte Canyon Road

Hampton Aver

SEE DOWNTOW
DENVER DETA

DOWNTOWN DENVER

1. Mile High Stadium
2. Elitch Gardens
3. Pepsi Center
4. Coors Field
5. Auraria Campus
6. U.S. Mint
7. Civic Center
8. Denver Art Museum
9. State Capitol
10. Denver Zoo
11. Denver Museum of Nature and Science
12. Cherry Creek Shopping Center

38th Avenue

32nd Avenue

Sloan Lake

Brighton Boulevard

Larimer Street

Lawrence Street

Lawrence Street

York Street

Steele Street

Colorado Boulevard

City Park

Colfax Avenue

Josephine Street

Cheesman Park

Speer Boulevard

Federal Boulevard

8th Avenue

6th Avenue

Broadway

Lincoln Street

South Platte River

Cherry Creek

1st Avenue

Alameda Avenue

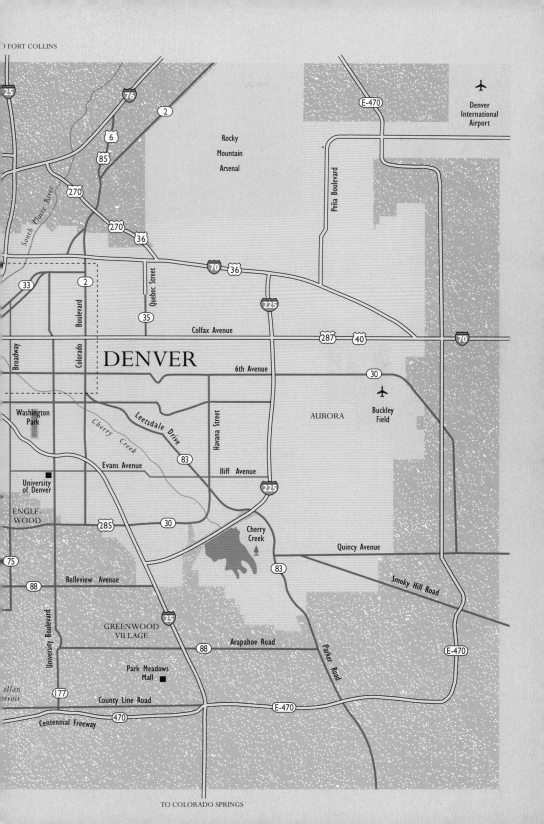

Denver and Environs

As a friend once aptly described it, "Denver is a big lawn chair facing the mountains." Looking at most maps of Denver does give you the impression that the Rocky Mountains rise abruptly about 100 yards west of the city. Actually, Denver proper sits 15 to 20 miles from the mountains, located a mile above sea level on the high, arid plains. From many points in the city, though, you can see the hills of the high plains break a bit, then the foothills, followed by mountains towering far in the distance. On summer afternoons, thunderheads mix with the high peaks in a breathtaking display, dwarfing the city's downtown office towers.

The hub of the Rocky Mountain West, Denver is the largest urban center within a 600-mile radius. Its strong economy continues to fuel growth at breakneck speed. Yet those unfamiliar with Denver might still incorrectly view it as either a dusty, riotous cow town or glamorous snow-covered capital of the mountains. Though at one time Denverites may have dreamed of parity with urban heavyweights such as Chicago, many locals now rank the metro area in a league of its own.

Denver International Airport immediately increased Denver's importance as a national transportation center when it finally opened in 1994. At 53 square miles it's the largest commercial airport in the world, also the world's 10th busiest. (Denverites are still coming to grips with the added drive time to get to the new complex, which some joke is so far east from the metro area it's in Kansas.)

Ties to western heritage and a oneness with its remarkable outdoor lifestyle have helped Denver come into its own as a major city. Nowhere, perhaps, is this more apparent than in the architecture that has dramatically changed the face of Denver in a few short years by accentuating the region's features. Coors Field, home to Major League baseball's Colorado Rockies, blends with the historic warehouse district of Lower Downtown (LoDo). Even Denver International Airport's Teflon-coated peaked roof design reminds one of the snow-covered Rockies.

Downtown Denver's Central Platte Valley, including the historically significant confluence of the South Platte River and Cherry Creek, is undergoing a tremendous renaissance. Some of the city's newest and most significant facilities lie clustered there, facing the river. The Central Platte includes Six Flags Elitch Gardens Amusement Park, the state-of-the-art Pepsi Center arena, Colorado's Ocean Journey aquarium and the REI Denver flagship store, among others—all practically a stone's throw from each other. Commons Park, being developed between LoDo and the Central Platte Valley, will include as its focal point a 30-acre park (Denver's largest park development in over a century) centered around the river.

Although Denver has traditionally served primarily as a jumping-off point to the mountains, even back in the mining days, that's no longer the case. It has truly become a worthy destination of its own. LoDo, located at the historic

Getting There

Denver International Airport *offers daily nonstop flights to more than 110 cities, including some in Europe, making it one of the busiest in the world. Flights to many towns and resorts around the state are available as well. The airport lies 24 miles east of downtown ($35 cab ride). Head east on Interstate 70 past Interstate 225 and turn north on Peña Blvd. for the final 10 miles. For information contact* **303-342-2000** *or* **www.flydenver.com.** *For flight info call* **1-800-AIR2DEN.** *Information about public transportation to and from the airport is available from the* **Regional Transportation District (RTD)** *at* **303-299-6000; www.rtd-denver.com.** *A growing number of air travelers to and from Colorado are discovering* **Colorado Springs Airport,** *located about 70 miles south of Denver.*

Greyhound Bus Lines *maintains daily bus schedules from all parts of the country to Denver and several of the larger ski resorts. Their main terminal is in downtown Denver. For information:* **1-800-231-2222; 303-293-6555; www.greyhound.com.**

Denver's historic **Union Station** *is still a railroad hub for* **Amtrak.** *Six daily arrivals and departures serve Los Angeles, San Francisco, Seattle and Chicago. Trains also make daily stops in Winter Park, Glenwood Springs, Grand Junction and other Colorado towns. For train information:* **1-800-872-7245; www.amtrak.com.**

Denver can also be reached by car from New Mexico to the south and Wyoming to the north via Interstate 25, from Utah to the west and Kansas to the east via Interstate 70 and from Nebraska to the northeast via Interstate 76.

northwestern edge of downtown, has made a dramatic comeback from skid row to the city's hippest restaurant, entertainment and gallery district (see the Historic Buildings and Districts section). Cherry Creek Shopping District, with its multitude of upscale stores, adjacent neighborhood shops (450 stores) and outstanding summertime arts festival, draws visitors from many other states, making it one of the biggest attractions in Colorado.

The Denver area features some excellent parks and what many consider to be the finest urban trail system in the country. With all of this going on, perhaps it's not surprising that Denver boasts arguably the healthiest, fittest citizens of any city in the country.

Denver hosts a diverse ethnic population. You can find well-established Italian, Jewish, Greek and Japanese communities, usually in particular neighborhoods. The western part of the city reveals Colorado's Hispanic roots in its street names and large Hispanic population. Denver also has a very strong African-American community, centered in the old Five Points area northeast of downtown. The nationally recognized Black American West Museum and Heritage Center, located in this part of the city, brings alive a long-neglected part of U.S. history. Neighborhoods such as Park Hill have about a 50-50 African-American and Anglo mix. Korean, Thai, Laotian and Vietnamese immigrants are building strong communities in the city; the excellent Asian restaurants and markets on S. Federal Blvd. are definitely worth a visit. With its diverse neighborhoods, Denver enjoys a vitality unknown in racially homogeneous cities. Various festivals celebrate ethnic heritages.

More than 2,000 restaurants can be found throughout the metro area, and the Denver Performing Arts Complex (the Plex), the second largest of its kind in the country, has given the arts community something to sing about. With a nationally envied Scientific and Cultural Facilities District tax endowing the arts throughout the region, Denver offers many other outstanding venues for enjoying the arts as well. The arrival in 1995 of the Colorado

Downtown Denver skyline. Photo by Bruce Caughey.

Avalanche hockey team helped round out an exciting year-round choice of professional Denver sports teams—along with the Denver Broncos, Denver Nuggets and the Colorado Rockies.

There are tried-and-true tourist destinations in Denver—the gold-domed state capitol, an impressive granite miniature of the U.S. Capitol; the U.S. Mint with its bullion and machine-gun turrets above a Florentine palace's passageways; the Museum of Nature and Science, which continues to do Denver proud. The abundant museums explain themselves for the most part, and serviceable bus tours leave no obvious stone unturned. But Denver also has other, hidden enjoyments. Therefore, our mission is to illuminate the unusual corners of Denver—places a Denver cousin would show you only if you never betrayed her to the relatives. Denver's history is intriguing, and many of its lessons are relevant today.

History

In the spring of 1858 Georgia prospector William Green Russell and 12 companions found gold dust on a tributary of the South Platte River, near present-day Englewood (a suburb of Denver). Though they were only panning $10 each per day and the gold soon ran out, news of a rich strike in the Rockies blew out of proportion and spread east. Enthusiastic miners began making their way west with the slogan "Pikes Peak or Bust."

When the gold played out on the Platte, members of Russell's party moved down the river to a grove of cottonwood trees at the confluence of Cherry Creek and the South Platte and erected a few cabins at Auraria (named after Russell's hometown in Georgia). Across the river from Auraria, the St. Charles Town Company, headed by Charlie Nichols, staked out another town. A group from Leavenworth, Kansas, led by Gen. William Larimer, jumped the St. Charles claim, infuriating Nichols. But Gen. Larimer and his Kansas group held firm, telling Nichols to quit complaining or they would use a noose on him. Since the area at the time was all part of the Kansas Territory, the group named their new town Denver City, after the Kansas territorial governor, James W. Denver. This was done with hopes it would stroke Denver's ego enough to ensure the group's claim to the site. These circumstances surrounding the establishment of Denver angered the residents of Auraria, and an intense rivalry between the two towns lasted for years.

At this time a band of Arapaho Indians remained in the area, observing these strange newcomers who were trespassing on Indian land. Although the land around Denver had been guaranteed to the Arapaho in the Fort Laramie Treaty of 1851, the Indians remained friendly to the settlers for the first couple of years. Historian Thomas Noel recounts, "Arapaho warriors left their women and children in Denver while they made war on the Utes in the mountains. After returning, the Arapaho invited Denverites to their dog feasts and Ute scalp dances."

Miners arriving in 1858 and early 1859 were greeted with outrageously high prices for supplies and found no gold in the streams; many returned east in disgust. In the spring of 1859, however, a rich strike at Central City in the mountains west of Denver rekindled the rush to the area (this time for real). Denver grew because it was a way station for miners headed to the mountain camps. Those who decided to stay in Denver in these early days were a tough, independent group. A noteworthy representative was William Byers, from Omaha, Nebraska, who had written a guidebook to the Pikes Peak region, compiled after hearing stories from miners returning from the Colorado goldfields. When Byers came to Denver, he brought along his printing press. Quite aware of the feud between Auraria and Denver, Byers set up a newspaper office on the banks of Cherry Creek, between the two towns. His newspaper, the *Rocky Mountain News,* made an immediate impact on Denver when it first appeared on April 23, 1859, gaining a wide readership and fueling further migration of people from the East.

As gold strikes in the mountains increased, Denver continued to grow. In these early years, Denver developed a reputation as a tough, dusty frontier town that disgusted many mannerly visitors. After a trip to early Denver, Horace Greeley, editor of the *New York Tribune,* wrote that in Denver there were "more brawls, more pistol shots with criminal intent than in any other community with equal numbers on Earth."

In the early 1860s relations with the Arapaho and Cheyenne soured when the Indians refused to comply with terms of the new Fort Wise Treaty of 1861. The Indians attacked settlements on the plains and hindered freight shipments to Denver. This clash of Anglo and Indian culture culminated with the brutal massacre of peaceful Arapaho and Cheyenne at Sand Creek in 1864 (see the **Southeast Plains** chapter). The Indians retaliated, once again attacking settlements on the plains and cutting off Denver's supply routes for a couple of months before troops squelched the uprisings once and for all.

In the mid-1860s the Union Pacific dealt Denver a severe blow when it chose to lay its transcontinental railroad tracks through Cheyenne, Wyoming, 100 miles to the north. Denverites believed their town was doomed without a railroad. Through the efforts of William Byers and Gov. John Evans, $280,000 was raised by 1867 to finance a railroad spur to the railhead in Cheyenne. The Denver Pacific Railroad was completed in June 1870, followed by the Kansas Pacific, which had laid tracks across the prairie from Kansas. With efficient rail transportation, Denver's population soared from just over 4,000 to 35,000 in one decade. Along with the gold mining towns in the mountains, silver mining districts began thriving—especially Leadville. Times were good in Denver; it was the major supply center not only for the gold mining towns and the metropolis of Leadville but also for the growing cattle industry of the plains and agricultural towns in the Platte and Arkansas River Valleys. In the 1880s many rich miners and cattle barons built mansions in the Capitol Hill area of Denver. Their deep pockets and desire to outdo their neighbors spawned unique sandstone palaces characterized by turrets, bays and leaded-glass windows. Many of these mansions still grace Denver's neighborhoods.

Despite this new money and Denver's development, an unrefined image persisted. The town had, as Walt Whitman described it, "plenty of people, business, modernness—yet not without a certain racy wild smack all its own." This wasn't helped by the town's notorious red-light district on Market St., called The Row. So seductive was this decadent area that one day, in June 1880, the town council didn't conduct any business—too many council members were attending the grand opening of a new house on The Row.

In 1893 the price of silver plummeted, and along with it, Denver's fortunes. Many mines closed and 10 Denver banks went under. Denverites were confronted with a grim reality—their future was tied too closely with that of the mining industry. If Denver was to continue to grow and prosper, it needed to diversify its economy. In the second half of the 1890s a huge gold strike at Cripple Creek gave another boost to the economy, but looking to the future, the town helped finance agricultural research and started to realize how well suited it was for tourism. With constant reminders from a new paper in town—*The Denver Post*—about the town's potential, Denver entered a new era, trying to forget the hard times that had accompanied the mining decline. One of the first things Denver did was to clean up its act. The brothels were closed and, under the direction of Mayor Robert Speer, parks (complete with statues and fountains) were built, streets were laid out and 18,000 trees were planted. When Speer died in 1918, Denver had undergone a remarkable transformation from a dusty cow town to a green, well-planned city.

Of course Denver's growth hasn't been a smooth, easy glide from 1918 to the present. Rather, it has been somewhat lurching, sometimes stagnant, but always reflective of Denver's optimism. After World War II, Denver entered a new period of expansion—one that many felt was too fast. The tide turned in 1972 when the state resoundingly voted down a chance for Colorado to host the Winter Olympics. Residents were wary of overdevelopment, higher taxes and a change in their comfortable, uncrowded lifestyle. Times were good for most

of the state, with Denver well on its way to becoming a major trade and distribution center. Vast oil and coal reserves attracted hundreds of small firms and many national giants. In the early 1980s new downtown office towers were going up at an incredible rate, with as many as 15 cranes dotting the skyline at once.

Growth seemed to be the mandate as the city teemed with a too-good-to-be-true excitement. After the oil glut in the mid-1980s, the economic vulnerability of Denver was once again exposed. An incredibly high percentage of office buildings stood vacant after the building frenzy ran its course. Today, along with its role as a manufacturing, trade and tourism center, the Mile High City has emerged as a transportation hub for the country with the opening of Denver International Airport. With a well-diversified economy and a wonderful quality of life that continues to draw droves of newcomers, Denver's current "boom time in the Rockies" is not likely to let up anytime soon.

Festivals and Events

The National Western Stock Show and Rodeo

mid-Jan. This one is big—really big. For two weeks cattlemen and cattlewomen from around North America attend the largest livestock exhibition in the world. Stetsons and cowboy boots fill the town; horse trailers pull up to the doors of the luxurious Brown Palace Hotel and the doorman doesn't bat an eye. When the stock show is on, all other bets are off. Some of the events include pro and amateur rodeos, livestock judging and horse shows. You can easily spend a few hours roaming the grounds. Kids love it. All shows take place just off Interstate 70 at the **Denver Coliseum, 4655 Humboldt St.; 303-297-1166; www.national western. com.**

Capitol Hill People's Fair

first weekend in June Each June, over 300,000 Denverites from all walks of life flock to **Civic Center Park** to enjoy the People's Fair. The huge crowd, with a life of its own, ebbs and flows around the statues, past the six music stages and up and down rows of more than 550 booths. Everyone walks these aisles, sampling Greek gyros and therapeutic teas, browsing through Krishna cookbooks and tomes on palmistry and signing petitions. You can discuss the intricacies of an embroidered dress with a seamstress and the virtues of Libertarianism with a true believer. Virtually every band in Denver spends an hour on a stage. It all happens between the capitol and the city and county building. Don't miss it. **303-830-1651; www. peoples fair.com.**

Colorado Renaissance Festival

weekends in June and July   At this re-creation of medieval England, a costumed lass or lad will ambush you for a kiss. As you approach the wooden fortifications surrounding King Henry's domain, be prepared to pay homage to His Highness as you quaff an ale and devour an enormous drumstick. And beware the fool, who makes quick work of anyone who challenges his wit. A host of merchants vie for your attention with wares from strange lands. The brave engage in feats of strength and the agile balance themselves on rope contraptions. You'd be hardpressed to find a more enjoyable place to take the kids. The festival runs on weekends only; fee charged. Drive south on Interstate 25 for 25 miles to the town of **Larkspur; 303-688-6010; www.coloradorenaissance.com.**

Cherry Creek Arts Festival

Fourth of July weekend   Located amid the blocks of shops just north of Cherry Creek Shopping Center, one of Denver's newest festivals energizes the city over the long Fourth of July weekend. Stop by to see the work of over 200 carefully selected artists, chosen from more than 2,400 applicants. This has quickly developed into one of only a handful of the finest outdoor-juried art shows in the nation. More than 300,000 people make their way to the three-day show to get a look at the work of some of the top artists in the country and internationally and listen to live music. The Creation Station arts education center for kids has been a big hit. So has the guy who performs his "art attack" by messily painting a canvas to the rhythms of Mozart and Beethoven—infinitely more enjoyable than watching Richard Simmons sweat to the oldies. **303-355-2787; cherryarts.org.**

Festival of Mountain and Plain— A Taste of Colorado

Labor Day weekend   In 1895 Denverites first gathered to celebrate the recovery from the 1893 silver crash and to pay tribute to the strengthening economies of the mountains and plains. The weeklong festival, patterned after Mardi Gras, was highlighted by a number of parades. Today the festivities last only a few days but still draw a large crowd—400,000. Scores of arts and crafts booths fill Civic Center Park just west of the state capitol. The main attraction is the Taste of Colorado, featuring food from over 50 of the area's finest restaurants. Live local and nationally known bands perform. **www. atasteofcolorado.com.**

Other Festivals

There is always some sort of festival in Denver. **Cinco de Mayo** (5th of May) is one of the biggest celebrations in town, especially among the Hispanic community. The Greeks have theirs at the annual **Greek Festival** in June on the grounds of the Greek Orthodox Cathedral. The **Old South Gaylord Street Festival** is celebrated in May, and **Oktoberfest** floods Larimer St. with beer in Sept. In late Sept., Denver hosts the **Great American Beer Festival,** the Superbowl of beer festivals with over 1,700 entries from 350 breweries around the country. In fall the **Denver International Film Festival** draws large crowds, including critics and famous actors. For information and specific dates on these and other festivals, contact the **Denver Metro Convention and Visitors Bureau: 1-800-233-6837; 303-892-1112; www.denver.org.** Another great source for week-to-week happenings in Denver is *Westword,*

A performance in the main arena at the Colorado Renaissance Festival. Photo by Bruce Caughey.

a free newspaper available virtually everywhere in town. Weekend sections of the Fri. daily newspapers *(The Denver Post* and *Rocky Mountain News)* are also good sources. Online sources include **www.westword.com, www.denver.city search.com,** and **www.insidedenver.com.**

Broncomania and Other Sports Phenomena

Each Sun. afternoon in fall, Denver's shopping malls are deserted, streets are empty and the orange sunset over the mountains takes on a slightly brighter hue. What's going on? A **Denver Broncos** football game, what else? Most Denver residents (or Colorado residents for that matter) have their eyes glued to the TV, while the lucky few (75,000) pack into the new stadium, Invesco Field, to cheer the Broncos and jeer the opponents, creating ear-splitting decibel levels. Without question, Denver fans are the most rabid pro football fans in the country. The games at Mile High Stadium were sold out for years and that is likely to continue at the new digs. People are usually selling extra tickets at the entrance gates, however. **303-433-7466; www.denver broncos.com.**

On the edge of downtown Denver's Central Platte Valley, the 18,000-seat **Pepsi Center** arena serves as home to the **Denver Nuggets** pro basketball team and the **Colorado Avalanche** pro hockey team. Games run from Oct. into June; tickets for both teams are available at the **Pepsi Center box office** or at **303-830-8497** or through their websites: **www.denvernuggets.com; www.colorado avalanche.com.**

To the delight of many a hard-core baseball fan, the **Colorado Rockies,** Denver's big-hitting Major League baseball team, have settled into their spectacular stadium at Coors Field (see the Historic Buildings and Districts section). For ticket information: **1-800-388-7625; www.coloradorockies.com.**

At the University of Denver (DU), **Magness Arena** provides an outstanding new 6,200-seat venue for the **Pioneers hockey and basketball teams.** You can also check the events line for other college athletic events, concerts and even professional boxing matches. The arena is housed in the $70 million **Ritchie Center for Sports and Wellness.** Its gold-leaf-encrusted spire (my son refers to it as the "spaceship build-ing") commands attention from **the corner of University Blvd. and I-25. 303-871-2215; www. du.edu/athletics.**

Outdoor Activities

Golf

Tee off at well over 55 public golf courses in the Denver metro area. With more than 300 days of sunshine annually in Denver, most courses stay open year-round, weather permitting. Here are a few of our favorites:

Arrowhead Golf Club

Located among the jutting cathedral-like red rocks near Roxborough State Park, this course is an unforgettable golfing experience and, frankly, its beauty can be distracting. Arrowhead was

A perfect rainbow graces the summer skyline after one of Denver's frequent afternoon "thunderboomers" that roll down from the Rockies. Photo by Dean Winstanley.

designed in 1970 by Robert Trent Jones Jr., who considers the course among his favorite six in the world. The interesting layout snakes its way through the rocks and troublesome scrub oak following the natural contours of the land. Its 76 sand traps and six lakes keep golfers challenged. The 13th hole is a standout—a par 3 that drops 95 feet to the green. Be sure to club down or you'll end up in the lake just behind the green. Reservations a must. Pro shop, driving range and restaurant. Located southwest of Denver, south of Chatfield Reservoir; pricey. **10850 W. Sundown Trail, Littleton, CO 80125; 303-973-9614.**

Fox Hollow Golf Club

This is certainly one of the finest public courses in the metro area. Its westside location and varied terrain provide challenging shots and great views. The Canyons course involves a hike up for the first two holes, ending with a number of holes working down along a river canyon. The Meadows course provides beautiful, challenging holes mixed among the mature trees along Bear Creek. Full-service pro shop; great dining, bar and outside seating at the Fox Den. **13410 W. Morrison Rd., Lakewood, CO 80228; 303-986-7888.**

Hyland Hills Golf Course

Hyland Hills is extremely popular, and with good reason. The greens crew keeps the challenging course in great shape. Holes are long, with lakes and ditches often coming into play. The eighth hole is particularly dangerous—a 526-yard straightaway is lined on the left by a lake, and a ditch crosses the fairway just in front of the green. In addition to an 18-hole course, there is another 9-hole course and two par-3 courses. **9650 Sheridan Blvd., Westminster, CO 80030; 303-428-6526.**

Lone Tree

Once an exclusive private club, this excellent course at the extreme south end of the metro area is now open to the general public. The course is well named; you'll have to contend with very few trees. But ponds, creeks and sand traps all combine to create plenty of challenge. Views from the course to the mountains west of the Denver area are fantastic. **9808 Sunningdale Blvd., Littleton, CO 80124; 303-799-9940; 303-790-0202.**

Meadow Hills Golf Course

Meadow Hills is one of the finest all-around public courses in the Denver area. The mature course has lots of cottonwoods, pines and elms lining the fairways. Greens fees are reasonable to boot. With relatively few sand traps and three lakes, you can score well if you keep to the fairways. The resident Canada geese, however, can be distracting, and they don't show much fear. Located in Aurora, just east of Cherry Creek Reservoir. **3609 S. Dawson St., Aurora, CO 80014; 303-690-2500.**

Riverdale Dunes

Although Riverdale is located near Brighton (northeast metro area), it feels as if you're out in the country. Finished in 1985 the Dunes course plays like the wide, open Scottish links with rolling hills and natural grass roughs. The older and less distinctive Knolls course is characterized by a series of irrigation canals, and water comes into play on 13 holes. Located next to the Adams County Fairgrounds at **13300 Riverdale Dr., Brighton, CO 80601; 303-659-6700; www.riverdalegolf.com.**

Wellshire Golf Course

Located in south Denver, Wellshire is another fine, mature course. One of the oldest in the city, it was a country club until Denver purchased it in the 1940s and opened it to the public. Wellshire plays long (6,592 yards), but the small number of lakes and traps helps your score. Trees are everywhere. Views west to the mountains accompany you on many of the holes. After your round, stop in at the pub or have a meal at the excellent Wellshire Inn restaurant (see the Where to Eat section). Located at the intersection of Hampden Ave. and Colorado Blvd. **3333 S. Colorado Blvd., Denver, CO 80222; 303-757-1352.**

Ice Skating

Evergreen Lake

For decades this lake has been popular for ice skating. At the skating center, you'll find a snack bar, rental skates and shelter from the cold. It usually opens by Christmas on a daily basis and remains open afternoons, evenings and weekends after the holidays, weather permitting. Fee charged. To reach Evergreen from Denver, head west on Interstate 70 about 20 miles to the Evergreen Pkwy. exit. From the exit drive 8 miles southwest on Hwy. 74 to **Evergreen. 303-674-2677.**

Parks, Gardens and Recreation Areas

City Parks

Cheesman Park has the most unified and serene landscaping in the city park system, with a wonderful view of the mountains. It's one of the nicest spots within the city to attend a free summer concert. You owe yourself a stroll around the perimeter and a nice rest in the Greek-style pavilion, a remnant of the "City Beautiful" campaign launched early this century. You'll walk past some of Denver's most impressive houses, some of which open directly onto the park. Cheesman Park is located **next to the Denver Botanic Gardens** just north of 8th Ave., between Humboldt and Race Sts.

The grounds of **City Park** contain the zoo, Natural History Museum, a golf course and three lakes. The designer of the English Gardens in Munich and Hyde Park in London also laid out this Victorian idealization of nature. Statues of Robert Burns and Martin Luther King show how much the park has stretched to contain the changing dynamics of Denver. Highlights include a stroll through a large rose garden, paddleboats (rentals) at one of the lakes, tall pine trees, grassy areas and views to the mountains. Located **north of 17th St., between Colorado Blvd. and York St.**

Springtime brings Denverites outside in eager hordes to their favorite gathering place, **Washington Park.** Not only is it a beautiful park with mature trees and wide grassy expanses but it also has a couple of lakes that provide fishing. Both kids and adults love all the diversions: recently renovated indoor swimming pool and gym facilities, several tennis courts, jogging paths and two large, fantastic playgrounds. Though speed limits have been established, bicyclists and in-line skaters whir around and around the park road in their Lycra outfits. On the west side of the park, bordering Downing St., a barrage of flowers blooms in intricate gardens. A replica of George Washington's garden at Mt. Vernon adorns the north bank of Grasmere Lake. The quaint old boathouse with its refurbished pavilion is available for most any occasion. What many consider Denver's premier park lies to the **east of Downing St. between Virginia and Louisiana Aves.**

Cherry Creek State Park

The state park at Cherry Creek Reservoir is one of Denver's most popular destinations, especially on scorching summer days. Located on the high plains about 10 miles southeast of downtown Denver, Cherry Creek offers plenty of hiking, biking and, primarily, water sports. Good warmwater fishing (especially for walleye), windsurfing, sailing and waterskiing are all very popular. Boat rentals are available at **Cherry Creek Marina, 303-779-6144.** In addition, many people hang out on the meager 250-yard strip of sand (what we in Colorado call a beach) and dip their toes in the water. Families with small kids and bikini-clad teenagers ply the sandy northeast edge of the reservoir under the watchful eye of lifeguards. On summer weekends you start feeling like a human sardine. During the week, though, this area can provide a nearby peaceful getaway. Miles of hard- and soft-surface bike trails provide terrific rides in the park as well as numerous regional trail connections. Cottonwood trees protect 102 campsites in several designated campgrounds; all charge a fee. Horseback rides available at the park's livery stable. The east entrance to Cherry Creek Reservoir is 1 mile south from Interstate 225 on Parker Rd. For more information, contact

Cherry Creek State Park, 4201 S. Parker Rd., Aurora, CO 80014; 303-690-1166; www.coloradoparks.org. Camping reservations at **1-800-678-CAMP** or **www.reserve america.com.**

Denver Botanic Gardens

The Denver Botanic Gardens offer more visual and olfactory pleasures than any other place in the city. The enormous glass honeycomb of the conservatory dominates your initial view of the grounds. Under the enclosure grows a lush forest of carob, cocoa, banana and hundreds of other trees and shrubs. In winter there is no better place to remember that spring is coming than in the orchid room when it catches the afternoon sun. If you walk to the far western end of the grounds, the Japanese garden, mountain flora path and alpine gardens offer wonderful contours, textures and scents—even in Feb.

In summer the Japanese garden is the most peaceful spot in Denver. The stream flows under a small wooden bridge, edged with irises in every shade. A lingering walk through the pine grove brings you to the alpine garden, which is particularly fine in May and early June. This is one of the most important and extensive collections of alpine plants in the world, with colors as vivid as any hybrid created with the gloved hand. You'll also see blossom-laden peonies, extensive rose beds, water lilies, a sensuous garden of the plants of the Bible, an even more sensuous herb garden, several well-conceived sculptures and fountains and, from late May through July, an explosion of irises.

On many summer nights, the Botanic Gardens host concerts in the grassy amphitheater on the grounds. Excellent gift shop. Open until 8 P.M. Sat.–Tues. May–Sept.; 9 A.M.–5 P.M. daily on other days and seasons. **1005 York St.; 303-331-4010; www.botanicgardens.com.**

Denver Greenway Trails

With all of the changes hitting the Denver metro area over the years, one of the true highlights has been the recreation trail network that has evolved. With at least 450 miles of interconnected trails winding through the region, Denver has rightly gained a national reputation for its tremendous greenway trails, many of which trace the area's waterways, connecting local and state parks and wildlife areas.

The South Platte River bursts out of **Waterton Canyon** southwest of the metro area and winds a slow, meandering course through the heart of Denver. Since 1974 an extensive redevelopment has taken place, and today the river is traced by a well-used concrete recreation trail. Numerous other recreation trails, including the outstanding **High Line Canal Trail,** feed into the **Platte River Trail** at various locations throughout the metro area. The core path currently stretches over 20 miles from **Chatfield State Park** (see write-up in this section) to the northern reaches of the metro area. Several small parks and even a wildlife sanctuary or two

The High Line Canal, with its adjacent recreation trail, winds 55 miles through the Denver metro area. Photo courtesy of Colorado State Parks.

are situated along its route as well as historic markers that share interesting tidbits about people and settlements that once occupied the riverbanks. Along the path you'll have pleasant views of the river, interspersed with thick stands of cottonwood and willows (despite problems with tree-gnawing beavers).

At historic **Confluence Park** along the river path in Denver's Lower Platte River Valley, Cherry Creek and the South Platte merge. It was here that a mining encampment in 1859 grew into a tent city and, eventually, Denver. It's because of the odd northwest angle of Cherry Creek that the downtown grid runs frustratingly askew: the streets were originally laid out to run parallel to the creek, directly facing Longs Peak. At any rate, from Confluence Park the excellent **Cherry Creek Trail** breaks away from the main **Platte River Trail,** tracing Cherry Creek, eventually reaching **Cherry Creek State Park** (see write-up in this section) and south of there to **Castlewood Canyon State Park** near Franktown. For an excellent free map of the Denver metro greenway trails, contact the **Colorado Division of Parks and Outdoor Recreation, 1313 Sherman St., Room 618, Denver, CO 80203; 303-866-3437; www. coloradoparks.org.**

NEARBY
Barr Lake State Park

Twenty miles northeast of Denver, off Interstate 76, you'll find a haven for birds and bird-watchers. More than 300 species of birds have been spotted at the lake, including herons and cormorants that nest in trees along the lakeshore. Other common sightings include owls, falcons, geese and nesting bald eagles. The visitor and nature center provides excellent information.

A 9-mile dirt trail encircles the lake (great for hiking and mountain biking), and boardwalks extend out over the water to strategic bird-watching areas and observation blinds. The gazebo is a great place for a picnic, especially on a weekday when you can have the lake to yourself. Sailboats, hand-propelled craft and boats with electric trolling motors are allowed.

A bird's-eye view from the observation deck in Castlewood Canyon State Park. Photo by Gene Schmidt.

Warmwater fishing can be good for perch, bass and an occasional trout. From Denver, drive 20 miles northeast on Interstate 76. Entrance fee charged. **13401 Picadilly Rd., Brighton, CO 80601; 303-659-6005; www.colorado parks.org.**

Castlewood Canyon State Park

Lying 30 miles south of Denver, this scenic canyon park is a bit of a surprise, contrasting with the surrounding prairie hills. The park is a great place to hike, rock climb, watch for wildlife or just get away from the city. Cherry Creek meanders north through Castlewood Canyon, which is characterized by steep sandstone walls and the remains of an old dam. Castlewood Canyon Dam, built on unstable ground in 1890 for Denver-area water storage, burst in 1933, flooding the Cherry Creek drainage all the way to the Platte River at Denver.

A series of canyon and rim hiking trails take you through ponderosa pine, Douglas fir, aspen and gambel oak, providing great views along the way. The visitor and nature center at the park's south end is worth a stop for maps, information and maybe even a ranger-led walk. To reach the main park entrance from Denver, take Hwy. 83 about 6 miles south of Franktown. The north entrance can be reached by heading a quarter-mile west from Franktown on Hwy. 86 and then left (south) on County Rd. 51 for 3 miles. Or bike to the park from the north via the Cherry Creek Trail, which links with the Denver metro greenway trail system. Picnic tables; wheelchair accessible; fee charged. **P.O. Box 504, Franktown, CO 80116; 303-688-5242; www. coloradoparks.org.**

Chatfield State Park

This reservoir, built along the South Platte River as a flood control effort, offers just about every water sport except surfing. The Army Corps of Engineers didn't foresee how popular it would become with boaters, but today there are over 250 slips for yachts, sailboats and motorboats. It's also a great place for swimmers, anglers and windsurfers. Landlubbers enjoy the foothills location for hiking, biking (along the Denver

Greenway Trails—see write-up in this section), horseback riding (rentals available), sunbathing and bird-watching. Chatfield is an excellent bird habitat—a veritable holy ground for bird-watchers. The nature trails are very nice, and the heron rookery (complete with an observation area) cement this lake's position as one of the best stops in the Denver area. In winter, try the decent ice fishing. You might want to call **B & B Livery (303-933-3636)** for horseback rides, or the **Chatfield Marina (303-791-5555).** Located along the shore are 153 campsites; all charge a fee. To get there from C-470, take the Wadsworth Blvd. (Hwy. 121) exit and go south on Hwy. 121 to the park entrance. **11500 N. Roxborough Park Rd., Littleton, CO 80125; 303-791-7275; 303-791-7547; www.coloradoparks.org.** Camping reservations at **1-800-678-CAMP** or **www. reserveamerica.com.**

Devil's Head

Located in the Pike National Forest southwest of the Denver metro area, Devil's Head is a beautiful escape for city folk, especially in the fall and especially with kids. Although a lot of people choose to make a weekend of it, Devil's Head is certainly close enough to town to do in a day. Its craggy profile is easily visible along the Front Range. The main attractions are the huge rocks strewn about the forest, thick aspen groves and the easy 1.5-mile trail up to the **Devil's Head Fire Lookout.**

The well-marked trail begins at Devil's Head Campground and climbs 948 feet through ponderosa pine and Douglas fir forests. Perched atop a giant granite outcropping at the summit is the fire lookout, an enclosed station that was the last of its kind along Colorado's Front Range. Visitors are welcome to climb the stairway and enjoy the spectacular 360-degree view from the lookout. Be sure to bring your camera.

Devil's Head Campground offers 22 sites; a fee is charged. Some other campgrounds can be found in the area also. To reach Devil's Head from Denver, head south on Hwy. 85 from Littleton for 10 miles to Sedalia. At Sedalia head

west on Hwy. 67 for 9 miles and then left (south) on Rampart Range Rd. for 9 miles. Rampart Range Rd. is closed in the winter. For information, contact the **Platte River Ranger District** at **303-275-5610; www.fs.fed.us/ r2/psicc.** Camping reservations at **1-877-444-6777** or **www.reserveusa.com.**

Dinosaur Ridge

Driving west toward the mountains from Denver on I-70, the first hill that appears, rising from the plains, is the seemingly unremarkable Hogback. At a place along the Hogback known as Dinosaur Ridge, once an ancient seashore, visitors can take a geologic and paleontologic glimpse back a few eons via dinosaur tracks and other fossilized remnants of creatures long gone. It was here at Dinosaur Ridge that the first stegosaurus bones were discovered. The staffed visitor center, interpretive hikes and the walking trail are all worth a visit. Located west off of C-470 at **16831 W. Alameda Pkwy.; 303-697-DINO; www.dinoridge.org.**

Golden Gate Canyon State Park

Within 45 minutes of Denver, you can surround yourself with beautiful, rolling, forested terrain of the Front Range. Spring brings out a barrage of wildflowers in lush meadows, including columbine; fall is highlighted by golden hillsides of aspen. Roads traverse the outer portions of this 10,550-acre park, while the unspoiled interior can be reached only on foot or horseback. Fishing for rainbow trout on its well-stocked streams can be quite good. Nearly 60 miles of marked hiking trails wind through the park, providing perfect day outings. After winter storms these trails make excellent, meandering cross-country ski routes. Stop by the visitor center on Golden Gate Canyon Rd. just inside the southeast entrance for a look at exhibits on the park's ecology, geology and plant life. Open daily 8 A.M.–4:30 P.M. year-round. Rangers at the impressive new center can help you plan your visit and give you a trail map.

Golden Gate Canyon State Park's **campgrounds** charge a fee and usually fill up on summer weekends; reservations can be made by calling **303-582-3707** in Denver. **Reverends Ridge Campground** (106 sites), in the northwest corner of the park, provides laundry and hot showers to campers. **Aspen Meadows Campground** (35 sites) in the north central portion of the park is much smaller and less developed. Twenty-three backcountry sites (including a number of Appalachian-style log huts) appeal to hikers who want to get away from camping alongside the road; permit required; no fires allowed.

To reach the park from Golden, head north on Washington Ave. (Hwy. 93) for 1.5 miles to Golden Gate Canyon Rd. Turn left (northwest) and drive 13 miles to the park entrance. **3873 Hwy. 46, Golden, CO 80403; 303-582-3707.** Camping reservations at **1-800-678-CAMP** or **www.reserveamerica.com.**

Jeffco Open Space

Jefferson County, just west of Denver, owns and manages over a dozen excellent mountain parks in the foothills. For information about these and other Jeffco parks, contact **Jeffco Open Space, 700 Jefferson County Pkwy., Suite 100, Golden, CO 80401; 303-271-5925; www.co.jefferson.co.us.** Here are some of the standouts:

The 1,400-acre **Mt. Falcon Park** offers easy day hiking and superb mountain biking. After a big snowstorm, Mt. Falcon becomes a great place to cross-country ski. Almost 10 miles of trails provide choice views of Denver, Red Rocks Park and Mt. Evans. Part of the park's interesting history includes remnants of John Brisben Walker's magnificent home, which was destroyed by fire in 1918. This wealthy founder of *Cosmopolitan* magazine dreamed of constructing a summer White House for presidential use on his 4,000-acre estate around the turn of the century. Construction never progressed beyond laying the foundation and cornerstone; its remains are also visible on trails in the park.

From Denver, head southwest on Hwy. 285 about 14 miles to the Indian Hills exit (Parmalee Gulch Rd.). Drive north for about 3.5 miles and turn right at the Mt. Falcon Park sign and proceed 2 miles to the parking area.

Another of Jeffco's excellent mountain parks, the 3,000-acre **White Ranch** northwest of Golden, provides 18 miles of multiuse trails, popular with mountain bikers and hikers. Once a working cattle ranch, the park offers great views along the Front Range and occasional wildlife spottings. Backcountry camping by permit only; call **303-271-5925** for information.

Red Rocks Park and Amphitheater

Red Rocks Amphitheater, located in Red Rocks Park just west of Denver near the town of Morrison, is a sight to behold—where else can you see golden and bald eagles perching where the Beatles once performed? This amphitheater, surrounded by towering 400-foot red rocks, was completed in 1941 by George Cranmer, Denver's legendary manager of improvements and parks. Nature had finished about three-quarters of the work in this natural bowl, but the 8,000-seat theater left something to be desired acoustically. Cranmer went to Germany at his own expense to consult with Wolfgang Wagner, son of the great Richard Wagner himself. Cranmer wanted to hear Richard Wagner's operas at Red Rocks, and he wanted to hear them right. Wolfgang Wagner came and adjusted the theater to the acoustic satisfaction of everyone, gallantly refusing to be paid.

These days, popular music concerts pack the place during summer evenings. Both musicians and spectators love the amphitheater for its unique location and the spectacular panoramic view of Denver spreading over the plains.

A number of hiking trails wind through the 2,700-acre park, and it's a great place for a picnic. Although it's tempting to climb around, stay off the rocks—park rangers are quick to dole out stiff fines to anyone challenging this rule. To reach Red Rocks Park from Denver, head west on Interstate 70 to the Morrison exit and drive south to the entrance to the park. Call the **Trading Post** at **303-697-8935** for more information.

Roxborough State Park

Spectacular razor-backed rocks marching along the face of the foothills are the dominant characteristic of Roxborough State Park. Miles of hiking trails take you through lush meadows and between rocks created over millions of years by stream-deposited sand turned reddish from iron compounds. Both prairie and mountain species grow in this unique setting—aspen next to yucca and scrub oak and, in the spring, a diversity of flowers. Bobcats, deer, elk and coyotes roam the hollows, and eagles circle overhead.

Everyone can enjoy the miles of nature trails in this dramatic environment; in winter Roxborough is a place of solitude and wonder. After a snowstorm it's best explored on touring skis. The visitor center blends perfectly into the landscape—inside you can look at the exhibits and participate in educational programs. Rangers often lead trail hikes and interpretive nature walks; cart tours available. Entrance fee charged.

Mount Evans from the south on Devil's Head Trail. Photo by Dean Winstanley.

From Denver take Santa Fe Dr. (Hwy. 85) south to Titan Rd. Turn right and proceed 3.5 miles and left (still on Titan Rd.) another 3 miles to a marked entrance to the park. **4751 N. Roxborough Dr., Littleton, CO 80125; 303-973-3959; www.coloradoparks.org.**

Waterton Canyon

This steep canyon, formed by the rushing waters of the South Platte River, has endured a number of major changes. The first was in 1877, when narrow-gauge tracks were laid through the canyon by the Denver South Park & Pacific Railroad. Then came Strontia Springs Resort, which catered to Denverites escaping the city for the weekend. The most drastic change occurred in 1983, when a large portion of the canyon was flooded by the Strontia Springs Reservoir. Though the reservoir has forever changed its character, Waterton Canyon remains an excellent recreation area close to the city.

Southwest of Denver a dirt road leads 6 miles to the base of **Strontia Springs Dam** alongside the South Platte River. Fishing for large rainbow and brown trout in the tailwaters of the dam has been excellent. The road into Waterton Canyon also marks the start of the **Colorado Trail,** which leads 469 continuous miles to Durango in the southwestern corner of the state. This road ends at the base of the dam. From here a 10-mile hiking/mountain biking trail leads to the confluence of the North and South Forks of the South Platte River (near the ghost town of South Platte). Along the way watch for bighorn sheep. From the confluence, a dirt road follows the river up Cheesman Canyon to the small town of Deckers; the entire valley is fairly heavily used with a lot of excellent trout fishing, camping and hiking on public land.

To reach Waterton Canyon, drive south on Interstate 25 to C-470; go west on C-470 to Wadsworth Blvd. (Hwy. 121). Turn south on Hwy. 121 for a few miles to the parking area just past the Lockheed Martin service road. Cheesman Canyon and the South Platte River can be reached via Waterton Canyon and the Colorado Trail or by driving south from Denver

The spectacular red rock geological display along Colorado's Front Range is at its dramatic best in Roxborough State Park. Photo by Gene Schmidt.

on Hwy. 285 for 32 miles to Pine Junction, then south on County Rd. 126 for 25 miles to Deckers.

Swimming

Six Flags Elitch Gardens
(See the Amusements section that follows.)

Water World
Surfing in Colorado? It's possible at **Water World,** a monstrously large summertime hangout. Hundreds of sun and water worshippers turn out each day for rides down slides, through the inner-tube rapids and on the waves in one of the two wave pools. This place provides excellent summer fun for kids of all ages. To help parental blood pressure, the park now features satellite-linked kid locaters—letting you see instantly where your kids are in the park by looking at their "blips" on the park map! Get into your suit and break out the suntan lotion. Open Memorial Day–Labor Day. **1800 W. 89th Ave., Federal Heights, CO 80221; 303-427-SURF;www.hylandhills.org/water world. html.**

Seeing and Doing

Amusements

Lakeside Amusement Park
Smaller than Elitch Gardens (see previous write-up), Lakeside has some great attractions, including the Cyclone Coaster and the vintage carousel. They don't make amusement parks like this one any more. Open on weekends in May and then 6–10 P.M. daily June to Labor Day, noon–11 P.M. weekends. Look for the high bell tower and the lake just south of Interstate 70 at Sheridan Blvd. **4601 Sheridan Blvd., Denver, CO 80212; 303-477-1621; www.lakeside amusementpark.com.**

Six Flags Elitch Gardens Amusement Park
Since 1890 Elitch Gardens has provided Denver with a lot of good times (amusement park rides, summer concerts and, of course, its beautiful gardens). Since opening up a few years ago at its new location in the South Platte River Valley in downtown Denver, Elitch Gardens has ensured that the fun continues. Many of the popular rides

at the original location have reappeared, including the Twister II roller coaster. But the new park is much larger and has added many new rides. True adrenaline junkies may want to shell out additional cash for a onetime fall on the XLR8R, a more restrained version of bungee jumping; others subject themselves to the terrifying, free-falling Mind Eraser. Kiddieland rides are more tame, but perfect for the kids. So is the recently added Island Kingdom Water Park, with its wave pool, water slides and other wet attractions. Other highlights include the carousel and gardens (which have not yet reached their former glory) with more than 50,000 flowers. Live entertainment nightly. Entrance fees allow unlimited rides. Open weekends Apr.–May; daily from late May to Labor Day. Located at I-25 and Speer Blvd. **299 Walnut, Denver, CO 80204; 303-595-4FUN; www.sixflags.com/ elitchgardens.**

Tiny Town

Located on 20 acres in the mountains southwest of Denver, this unique place is just what the name implies—a tiny town. Miniature churches, fire stations, houses and schools line the streets, fascinating children and, yes, adults, too. Tiny Town also features a diminutive railroad. Small fee charged. Open 10 A.M.–5 P.M. on weekends in May, Sept. and Oct.; daily Memorial Day–Labor Day. From Denver, head southwest on Hwy. 285 about 5 miles past C-470 and turn left onto S. Turkey Creek Rd. You'll see the Tiny Town sign from the highway. **6249 S. Turkey Creek Rd., Morrison, CO 80465; 303-697-6829.**

Water Parks

See the Swimming section.

Brewery Tours

Coors Brewery

Each year 350,000 visitors head to Golden for a free half-hour tour of the world's largest single brewing facility. Small groups wander through, looking at the immense 15,500-gallon copper kettles (that's 55,000 six-packs!) where the beer

is blended, heated and filtered. You'll also get a chance to look at the malting, quality control and packaging departments. The best part is saved for last: the tour ends in the tasting room where visitors (of age) can sample a fresh, ice-cold glass of free Coors on tap. With advance reservations, tours are available in foreign languages and for those with hearing and mobility limitations. Open Mon.–Sat. 10 A.M.–4 P.M. **13th St. and Ford St., Golden, CO 80401; 303-277-BEER; www.coorsandco.com.**

Buffalo Herds

Once they numbered in the millions. After settlers made their way west and their 50-year buffalo slaughter ended, barely 1,000 of the furry beasts remained. Luckily, buffalo hunting was finally outlawed. Today their numbers have increased to tens of thousands throughout the West. A couple of Denver mountain parks contain herds that are usually easy to see. The most accessible place is off Interstate 70, 20 miles west of Denver at the **Genesee Park** exit. **Daniel's Park,** 20 miles south of Denver, has the largest herd. To reach Daniel's Park from Denver, head south on Hwy. 85 about 2 miles past Sedalia and turn left on Daniel's Park Rd. Proceed about 3 miles to the park.

Historic Buildings and Districts

Denver has a cache of historic buildings, hidden away on residential streets or garishly displayed on busy avenues. Weekend and lunchtime tours of some of these gems can be arranged through the **Denver Foundation for Architecture, 303-770-9193.** Another source of information is **Historic Denver Inc., 821 17th St., Suite 500, Denver, CO 80202; 303-534-5288.** Pick up a Historic Walking Tour map of Denver at the downtown **Visitors Bureau, 225 W. Colfax.** The *Mile High Trail* offers directions for six downtown walking tours and is available for a small fee.

Colorado State Capitol

Modeled after the U.S. Capitol, this venerable building differs from its eastern cousin in its

The gold-domed state capitol building in Denver, replicated after the nation's Capitol, is worth a visit. Photo by Bruce Caughey.

spiral staircase from the third floor to the dome for spectacular views of the city and mountains as well as a dizzying view down into one of the rotundas. But the best show is inside when the legislature is in session (mid-Jan. through mid-May). In small enclosed rooms just off the Senate and House floors, lobbyists vie for the attention of legislators. Or you can go into the basement cafeteria where you'll see more of the same politicking in progress. Informative brochures available. Tours are given in summer on the half hour 9 A.M.–3:30 P.M. Mon.–Fri., 9:30 A.M.–2:30 P.M. on Sat.; call ahead for winter hours. **200 E. Colfax Ave., Denver, CO 80203; 303-866-2604.**

Coors Field

This impressive Major League baseball stadium blends nicely into the historic warehouse architecture of the LoDo district (see write-up below). There is no question it has propelled the rebirth of activity in this part of town. A visit here on game day when the Colorado Rockies have a home stand will explain why.

At Coors Field, built solely as a baseball park, it's hard to find a bad seat. A mid-level walkway encircling the field allows fans to stroll the myriad of shops, food booths and a few restaurants without ever straying far from the action. A highlight, the **Sandlot Brew Pub,** allows you to follow the game on TV before heading back to your seat with a fresh microbrew. The Sandlot is accessible from Blake St. for those who do not have tickets; **303-312-2514.**

Even if you are not a baseball fan, this place is irresistible. Where else in the United States can you simultaneously watch a Big League game and the sun setting over the Rockies? Located at **20th and Blake Sts.** Ticket information at **1-800-388-7625,** at the box office or at **www.coloradorockies.com.**

Governor's Mansion

Walter Cheesman, an early settler and Denver's first pharmacist, built this house for his family at the turn of the century. He died before its completion, but not before he had ensured that the

smaller, gold-leaf dome and gray granite. Completed in 1908, a full 18 years after the cornerstone was laid, the state capitol sits impressively on a hill overlooking Civic Center Park, commanding an excellent view of the mountains. As well it should, the law forbids high-rise buildings from blocking this view. The 13th step on the west side announces that it is precisely a mile high (a disputed measurement, by a few feet).

Inside, the workmanship is impeccable, with beautiful native marble, brass banisters and vaulted ceilings. Perhaps the most impressive detail is the rose onyx wainscoting throughout the building; so much was needed for the job that the state supply was totally depleted. Above the legislative chambers, stained-glass representations of governors and early settlers illuminate the proceedings. Informative tours begin inside the west entrance and eventually lead up the grounds were terraced to rival the most innovative gardens in Europe.

His wife and daughter lived in the house until 1926, when they sold it to Claude Boettcher, whose father founded the sugar beet industry in northern Colorado. The Boettcher family eventually donated the mansion to the state, which has recently changed the name to the Colorado Executive Residence. Most of the house remains as Cheesman designed it, including the large library and lounge off the main hall. Across the hall is an enormous dining room, which now suits the needs of all of Colorado's first families. The house has particularly striking pieces of Asian art. The chandeliers are superb works of crystal and porcelain.

The pride of the house, however, is the 60- by 70-foot Palm Room, with a white marble floor, stone columns and white furniture. Palm trees accent the room; large windows open out to Cheesman's terraced garden. Free limited 20-minute tours of the mansion are given noon–2 P.M. on Tues. May–Aug. and during the Christmas season. At the **corner of 8th Ave. and Logan St.; 303-866-3682.**

LoDo

Architecturally impressive, historical and exciting, Denver's lower downtown (LoDo) district is an absolute must for out-of-town visitors. With 26 square blocks bordered by Larimer St. and the train tracks, this area has undergone an urban renaissance unmatched by few U.S. cities in the past decade. Blocks of restored turn-of-the-century warehouses have drawn art galleries, trendy restaurants, loft dwellers and others back into the city. Whether it's an afternoon game at Coors Field (see entry in this section) to see the Colorado Rockies baseball team or a late night at one of the hopping nightspots, you'll find LoDo vibrant and alive.

Quite a story lies behind many of the historic buildings in LoDo. Thankfully, plaques affixed to these structures provide a quick synopsis of who originally financed and occupied each building as well as a snippet of other local history. These plaques provide a perfect self-guided walking tour. For a more in-depth glimpse into LoDo history and that of other downtown Denver locales, contact **Gunslingers, Ghosts and Gold** for entertaining guided walking tours; **303-860-8687.**

Museums and Galleries

Black American West Museum and Heritage Center

Did you know that nearly one-third of all cowboys in the western United States were black? This museum, located in the heart of Five Points, tells the history of blacks in the West in various roles as cowboys, doctors, barbers, legislators and teachers. It's a fine place to get a feel for this segment of our history, through artifacts, historic photos and, if you're lucky, a real live legend. When we visited, Alonzo Pettie, a spry 78-year-old decked out in a Levi's jacket and cowboy hat, told us of growing up in east Texas and breaking horses on a ranch. Stop by for a visit. Fee charged. Hours vary considerably, so call ahead. **3091 California St., Denver, CO 80205; 303-292-2566.**

Buffalo Bill's Grave and Memorial Museum

Perched atop Lookout Mountain, just west of Denver, you'll find the final resting place of William F. Cody, better known as Buffalo Bill. Cody personified the Wild West, having been a Pony Express rider, scout for the cavalry and quite a buffalo hunter. Cody achieved international fame in the late 1800s with his Wild West show, which toured throughout the United States, Canada and Europe. He died at his sister's home in Denver in 1917 and was buried on Lookout Mountain, despite protests from Nebraska and Wyoming claiming Cody had wanted to be buried in their states.

Along with his grave is a museum containing much of Buffalo Bill's memorabilia. An observation deck on top of the museum gives you a great view of the mountains to the west and the Denver area to the east. Small fee charged. To reach the grave and museum from Denver, drive west on Interstate 70 about 15 miles and get off at Exit 256. Follow the signs up Lookout Mountain Rd. to the turnoff. If you continue on scenic Lookout Mountain Rd. for about 7 miles you'll reach Golden. Open May–Oct. 9 A.M.– 5 P.M., Nov.–Apr. 9 A.M.–4 P.M.; closed Mon. in winter. **303-526-0747; 303-526-0744; www. buffalobill.org.**

Butterfly Pavilion and Insect Center

This interesting and slightly bizarre "bug zoo" has quickly evolved into one of the Denver area's most talked-about exhibits. The enormous domed butterfly pavilion, kept at a steamy 80° F, provides the perfect habitat for over 1,200 butterflies from 60 tropical species. Stroll through the pavilion or check out the insect zoo, which features such creepy critters as tarantulas, the giant sonoran centipede or the 2-inch-long Madagascar hissing cockroach. Visitors who eat any of these insects will be asked to leave. Great place for kids; soon to be expanding. Open 9 A.M.–6 P.M. daily. Located along Hwy. 36 in **Westminster** at **6252 W. 104th Ave.; 303- 469-5441; www.butterflies.org.**

Byers-Evans House

Historians never second-guess the legendary accomplishments behind the historical names Byers and Evans. The fact that both prominent Denver families occupied the same house is a quirk of fate that does not go unnoticed at this fine museum. Built in 1883 by William N. Byers, founding editor of the *Rocky Mountain News,* the home was purchased six years later by William Gray Evans, son of Colorado's second territorial governor. Kept in the Evans family for three generations, this two-story home recently fell into the caring hands of the Colorado Historical Society, which has restored the home to reflect the 1912–1924 period.

Begin the tour by viewing the 20-minute videotape of Denver's history, an interesting prelude to the home tour. Look around the deceptively large house and you begin to make sense of its many additions. Most of the Evans furniture remains, including the detailed wooden bookcases in the sitting room. Be sure to notice the parlor's intricately painted ceiling, which was discovered under layers and layers of ordinary house paint. Small admission fee. Open 11 A.M.–3 P.M. daily except Mon. **1310 Bannock St.** adjacent to the Denver Art Museum; **303-620-4933; 303-620-4795; www.colorado history.org.**

The Children's Museum

If you don't have a child of your own, borrow one and go out for a great time at one of the best museums in town. Displays here are meant to be touched, prodded, pulled and played with, all with the purpose of teaching children (and adults) the inner workings of processes and machines. Shop at the smallest grocery store in the world, complete with automatic price scanner (no coupons accepted). Check out the outdoor playground and ski hill (lessons available). The Center for the Young Child, the newest interactive exhibit, features a 3,700- square-foot playscape with areas that stimulate sensory awareness and provide hands-on exploration for newborns to 4-year-olds. Puppet shows are popular, as are various seasonal exhibits. Live family theater performances are featured every Sat. and the first Fri. evening of each month. You'll enjoy the trip as much as the kids will. Open daily 9 A.M.–5 P.M. in summer; Tues.–Sun. in winter. As you drive by on Interstate 25, you can't miss the museum, across the highway from Mile High Stadium; it's the brilliant green building with a pyramid roof. You may want to consider parking a few blocks away (along the Platte River) and taking the trolley, which passes right by the museum. **2121 Children's Museum Dr., Denver, CO 80211; 303-433-7444; www.cmdenver.org.**

Colorado History Museum

Run by the Colorado Historical Society, this well-organized museum is home to many artifacts and great dioramas depicting Colorado's colorful history—from detailed and accurate Indian gatherings to a display of Denver's disastrous flood in 1864. There are photographs and artifacts of the Indian wars, the massacres, the pioneers and miners, the bars, brothels and early residents. It's as complete a gathering of state history as can be housed under one roof. The research library is overflowing with historical newspapers from every town in Colorado. Excellent temporary exhibits; take your time and enjoy. Don't miss the fine gift shop with a wide selection of Colorado books. Located in the wedge-shaped building just southwest of the state capitol. Open Mon.–Sat. 10 A.M.–4:30 P.M., Sun. noon–4:30 P.M. **1300 Broadway; 303-866-3681; www.coloradohistory.org/home.htm.**

Colorado Railroad Museum

Train buffs will love this large collection of locomotives, cabooses and other railroad cars scattered about a 12-acre yard. Some real gems are kept in this back lot—many of the silent trains are open for anyone to climb aboard and pretend. Take a close look at the D&RG Engine No. 346, the oldest operating locomotive in Colorado, or the Galloping Goose #2, a strange-looking contraption built with various parts from a Buick, Pierce Arrow, Ford truck and a railroad engine. Inside the re-created depot, old photos and exhibits of Colorado's railroad history are displayed. Downstairs, the scale model HO train running through a miniature world is a child's dream. Open daily 9 A.M.–5 P.M. Sept.–May, 9 A.M.–6 P.M. the rest of the year. Take Exit 265 off Interstate 70 in Golden and follow the signs. **17155 W. 44th Ave., Golden, CO 80401; 303-279-4591; www.crrm.org.**

Denver Art Museum

This castlelike structure, next to the Denver Public Library, serves quite nicely as a repository of great artwork, including one of the richest Native arts collections in the country (over 19,000 items). It's also home to fine, recently upgraded displays of Asian, pre-Columbian and Spanish colonial art collections. The American exhibit houses Thomas Cole's *Dream of Arcadia,* a masterpiece of the Hudson River School. Several Picassos, Monets and a Klee add strength to the European collection. Beware of Linda, resident art critic and patron—she's the lifelike sleeper/ statue found on the floor of the contemporary section.

The wonderful **Palette's Restaurant ($ to $$$)** is open for lunch and dinner; it makes a terrific prelude or conclusion to a visit to the museum. The gift shop contains some worthwhile items, including a decent book section and merchandise that reflects traveling exhibits. Family programs and free entrance on Sat. Open Tues.–Sat. 10 A.M.–5 P.M. (till 9 P.M. on Wed.); Sun. noon–5 P.M.; closed Mon. The art museum will soon be undergoing a dramatic renovation so you may want to call ahead. **100 W. 14th Ave. Pkwy.; 720-865-5000; www.denver artmuseum.org.**

Denver Firefighter's Museum

One of the best-kept secrets in town, this place is unknown even to many natives. Learn about Denver's fire-fighting history in this museum, which houses old fire engines and fire equipment. Don't worry, you don't have to slide down the pole to the exit. Open Mon.–Sat. 10 A.M.–2 P.M. **1326 Tremont Pl.; 303-892-1436; www.firedenver.org/museum.**

Denver Museum of Nature and Science

The granddaddy of museums in Denver, this museum is probably best recognized for its traveling exhibits and innovative, extensive dioramas of animals in their natural habitats. This was the first museum to use such displays (some of which were built in the 1930s as WPA projects). It holds the world's largest mammoth fossil, scaring small children and adults alike as they round the corner to a room filled with tusks and teeth. Dinosaur skeletons—especially that of Tyrannosaurus rex—seem to roar in midstride at visitors. They serve merely as a minor introduction to the newest and most popular exhibit—Prehistoric Journey. Perhaps the most exciting and innovative dinosaur and paleontological exhibit in the country, it traces the 3- to 5-billion-year history of life on Earth, with fossils, interactive displays and other methods.

Ornithologists and butterfly enthusiasts will be delighted with the collection of North

American birds and butterflies. A walk through the mineral collection mimics a journey into an underground cavern, complete with fluorescent rocks and samples from Colorado's richest mines and mills (be sure to look for "Tom's Baby").

The museum generally hosts several major traveling exhibits (check the schedule for current offerings). Cafeteria, restaurant and gift shop; admission fee charged. Open daily 9 A.M.– 5 P.M. **2001 Colorado Blvd.; 1-800-925-2250; 303-322-7009; www.dmns.org.**

The exceptional **IMAX Theater,** located at the east entrance of the museum complex, is truly one of those places where the viewer becomes part of the film. The theater features a four-story screen with a state-of-the-art sound system. The screen can become the Grand Canyon, outer space, the stratosphere or Stonehenge. Go where the filmmaker wants to take you, and nobody will get hurt. Call **303-370-6300** for prices and show times.

Located on the west side of the building, the **Gates Planetarium** features traditional astronomical displays, including views of the night sky as it appears in all hemispheres and in all seasons. Occasionally, spectacular laser shows get the normally staid planetarium moving to rock music or whatever the laser projectionists are moved to feature. Call **303-370-6351** for prices and show times.

Denver Public Library

The relatively new central library should absolutely not be missed. This multicolored architectural masterpiece, which includes its renovated predecessor, holds a staggering 3 miles of bookshelves (three times the previous space), making it the largest library between Chicago and Los Angeles. Its features, too numerous to detail, are highlighted by a children's library and storytelling room, rows of computers with Internet access and the Gates Western History Reading Room, with its two-story wooden derrick structure. Pay it a visit or search for a book via their online catalog. Mon.–Wed. 10 A.M.–9 P.M., Thurs.–Sat. 10 A.M.– 5:30 P.M. **10 W. 14th Ave. Pkwy., Denver, CO 80204; 303-640-6200; www. denver.lib. co.us.**

Four Mile Historic Park

Just a stone's throw from the neon lights and strip joints of the Glendale area, the Four Mile Historic Park provides an interesting look into Denver's past, including the oldest structure in metro Denver. The Four Mile House, built in 1859, operated for years as a stage stop along the Cherry Creek branch of the Smokey Hill Trail and then as a farm. Today 14 acres, including the original house, outbuildings and equipment, serve as a living history museum, representative of the period 1859–1883. Stroll the farmstead, where you can see draft horses, chickens and crops in the garden. Guides in period costumes and seasonal programs add much to the visit, especially for kids. Stagecoach rides available on the weekends. Small fee. Open Apr.–Sept. Wed.–Fri. 12–4 P.M., Sat.–Sun. 10 A.M.–4 P.M. Also open Oct.–Mar. Sat.–Sun. 12–4 P.M. **715 S. Forest St.; 303-399-1859.**

Littleton Historical Museum

Your kids will beg you to return again and again to this wonderful 1860s homestead and farm museum. You'll also find three art galleries featuring changing exhibits. In addition to the farmhouse, look for the schoolhouse, blacksmith shop, smokehouse and a bunch of barnyard animals. No charge. Open Tues.–Fri. 8 A.M.– 5 P.M., Sat. 10 A.M.–5 P.M., Sun. 1–5 P.M. **6028 S. Gallup St., Littleton, CO 80120; 303-795-3950; www.littletongov.org/museum.**

Lower Downtown Galleries

It's difficult to stroll the streets of LoDo without tripping over the numerous galleries that proliferate throughout the area—40 at last count. Although you certainly can visit anytime, one of the best ways to enjoy LoDo's galleries is during First Friday. From 5 to 9 P.M. on the first Fri. of each month, more than three dozen galleries open their doors to folks who are interested in a self-guided walking tour of art. Maps available at any gallery. The success of this event has now spawned Second Sunday. For more information on LoDo, see the Historic Buildings and Districts section.

Mizel Museum of Judaica

This small museum has a fine reputation for its fascinating changing exhibits. Anyone interested in Jewish artifacts from around the world should call ahead to see what the museum is showing. Past displays have ranged from ancient Middle Eastern artifacts to a wonderful collection of hats to photos from the lost world of the European Jews. Open Mon.–Fri. 10 A.M.–4 P.M., Sun. noon–4 P.M. No fee. The entrance is located on the east side of the building. **560 S. Monaco Pkwy.; 303-333-4156; www.mizel museum.org.**

Molly Brown House Museum

Built in 1889 by one of Denver's great architects, William Lang, this Colorado sandstone and lava stone home is a Victorian masterpiece. J. J. Brown, husband of one of the state's most colorful characters, Molly Brown, bought the mansion in 1894 with money made from his famous Little Johnny gold mine. Molly's heroism during the sinking of the *Titanic* gained her international fame and the nickname "Unsinkable Molly." Today tours of the home are given by women dressed in turn-of-the-century costumes. Stone lions guard the entrance, and the interior is decorated in velvet, lace, beautiful dark wood and a significant amount of Brown's original furniture. At Christmastime the decorations transform the entire house into something more than a historical landmark. The gift shop is a great place to pick up some *Titanic* memorabilia. Open Mon.–Sat. 10 A.M.–3:30 P.M., Sun. noon–3:30 P.M.; closed Mon. in winter. Fee charged. **1340 Pennsylvania St.; 303-832-4092; www.mollybrown.org.**

Ocean Journey

With its massive, attractive glass architecture, Ocean Journey serves as a tremendous new attraction in Denver's Central Platte Valley. Yes, it's an aquarium, but if you are expecting simply a giant fishbowl you are in for a surprise. What's cool about this 106,000-square-foot facility is the way visitors are exposed to the 15,000 fish, bird and mammal specimens. Visitors can trace the journey and varying ecosystems of two of the world's most interesting waterways: the Colorado River and Indonesia's Kampar River. Begin at the Colorado's headwaters at 12,700 feet, viewing the likes of endangered greenback cutthroat. Then stroll through the arid American Southwest and view a flash flood, before eventually reaching river's end at the Sea of Cortez in the Gulf of Mexico. Next, enter the rain forest–shrouded path of the mighty Kampar. Travel downriver past Sumatran tigers, through a mangrove swamp and eventually to the ocean, dramatically represented by an enormous shark-filled blue tank above you. Don't miss the sea otter display. Kids and adults will love this place and are guaranteed to learn something; fee charged. **700 Water St., Denver, CO 80211; 303-561-4450; www.oceanjourney.org.**

U.S. Mint

This building where U.S. coins are made resembles a Florentine palace inside and out. Inside the mint you'll be treated to a guided tour that explains coin production and also stops before a stack of gold bullion—the mint is the third-largest gold repository in the country. Near the end of the tour, the guide might point out the antiquated machine-gun turrets, installed after the stock market crash of 1929 to make sure things didn't get out of hand. Forever afterward you'll check for the little "D" below the date on your pennies. Open daily 8 A.M.–3 P.M. in winter and until 2:45 P.M. in summer. Be sure to call ahead for ticket information; reservations not accepted. On the **corner of W. Colfax Ave. and Cherokee St.; 303-405-4761; 303-405-4765; www.usmint.gov.**

Nightlife

Visitors will be pleased with Denver's ever-increasing diversity of places to eat, drink and be happy. Downtown Denver is bordered by a couple of areas worth considering: LoDo and the uptown area along 17th Ave. The jazz scene is flourishing and the Denver Performing Arts Complex adds a vitality to the city's cultured side. If you feel like a night of country and western dancing or comedy, there are a number of choices. For a complete listing of events and entertainment in the metro area, pick up a free copy of *Westword* (**www.westword.com**) or consult the Fri. editions of either the *Rocky Mountain News* or *The Denver Post*. Here are a few suggestions.

Brewpubs

Colorado produces more beer than any other state. Denver offers a number of excellent microbreweries/pubs. The best conglomeration is located in LoDo. **Breckenridge Brewery** provides good views of its brewing operation from just about every seat in the place. Five tasty house brews on tap; full restaurant menu including appetizers, sandwiches, burritos and steaks. Added feature: its prime location across from Coors Field, at **2220 Blake St.; 303-297-3644.**

Wynkoop Brewing Company, a Denver institution and arguably the largest brewpub in the nation, remains our favorite of the Mile High City's brewpubs. Housed in the historic J. S. Brown Mercantile Building (**1634 18th St.; 303-297-2700),** it's known for a wide selection of homemade brews, its happy-hour prices and its relaxing atmosphere. Try the stout, wheat, amber ale or bitter brew, or a reasonably priced sampler. It's a comfortable place to knock down a couple and enjoy a meal of bangers and mashers (traditional English sausage simmered in stout beer, and mashed potatoes). If you enjoy pool, this is the place to be: a second-floor hall provides at least two dozen quality tables. Brewery tours Sat. afternoons. Open Mon.–Sat. 11 A.M.–2 A.M., Sun. 10 A.M.–midnight. You may also want to try the **Denver Chop House and Brewery,** a bit more upscale than most brewpubs (see the Where to Eat section).

Rock Bottom Brewery, with its great location on the 16th Street Mall, is extremely popular with the downtown lunch crowd and for after-work fun. In addition to a great selection of freshly brewed beer, the menu features pretty tasty items such as the portobella mushroom wrap. Live bands on most nights; outdoor patio seating, weather permitting. **1001 16th St.; 303-534-7616.**

Farther to the south, amid the steel and glass of the Denver Tech Center, you'll find the cavernous yet attractive **Great Northern Tavern.** Though more of an eatery (**$$ to $$$**) than a nightspot, the GNT offers up some terrific brews, including the outstanding amber. All brews are shipped down from their brewery in Keystone. You'll find them at **8101 E. Belleview Ave.; 303-770-4741.**

Cafes

The coffee culture has definitely filtered into Denver. New java joints continue to sprout up all over the city. They offer limitless atmospheres to fit your mood, including, of course, the omnipresent **Starbucks.** The most dense concentration of cafes can be found in Cherry Creek North, amid Denver's most exclusive shopping district. You might also head a couple of blocks southeast to **Peaberry's (3031 E. 2nd Ave.; 303-322-4111)** for a slight change of pace (22 locations in the metro area). Both places have indoor and patio seating.

Try **Vicious Rumors 6th Ave. Cafe (corner of 6th Ave. and Washington; 303-777-6060)** for a strong, steaming cup of coffee. If you're wondering where the beret-and-bongo crowd hangs out in Denver, make a beeline for **Paris on the Platte (1553 Platte; 303-455-2451).** This coffeehouse provides comfortable settings for people to sit and explore the outer limits of their intellect—or at least make it appear that way. **The Market (1445 Larimer St.; 303-534-5140)** in Larimer Square continues to be a popular gathering spot downtown.

Common Grounds (1601 17th St. at 17th and Wazee; 303-296-9248) offers board games and an upright piano available if the mood strikes; occasional live music and spoken word performances. On Capitol Hill, stop in at the

Ocean Journey, Denver's exciting new aquarium in the Central Platte River Valley. Photo courtesy of Ocean Journey.

Penn St. Perk (corner of 13th Ave. and Pennsylvania St.; 303-860-0400), next to the Molly Brown House Museum. In the Washington Park area, visit **Stella's (1476 S. Pearl St.; 303-777-1031).**

Comedy

If you feel like some laugh therapy, stop by the **Comedy Works,** featuring local acts and national headliners nightly. New talent and improvisation takes the stage on Tues.; closed Mon. Located in Larimer Square at **1226 15th St.; 303-595-3637; www.comedyworks. com.** Or consider the hugely popular and hilarious show at the **Impulse Theater,** in the Wyncoop Brewery's basement at **1634 18th St.; 303-297-2111; www.impulsetheater.com. Chicken Lips Comedy Theater** offers improvisational plays and musicals year-round at **2145 S. Logan St.; 303-534-4440; www.chickenlips.com.**

Concerts

For big-name outdoor concerts, **Red Rocks** is hard to beat; **303-640-7334; www.redrocks-online.com** (see the Parks, Gardens and Recreation Areas section for more information). **Fiddler's Green,** in the Denver Tech Center area, is also a good summertime locale; **303-220-7000.** The **Denver Botanic Gardens (303-331-4000, www.botanicgardens.com)** and the **Denver Zoo (303-376-4800, www.denverzoo.org)** host summer concerts ranging from classical to World Beat—they usually sell out.

Well-known indoor venues include the recently renovated **Fillmore Auditorium.** This outstanding 3,600-seat auditorium that was completed in 1999 to resemble its San Francisco namesake is at the **corner of Clarkson and Colfax Ave.; 303-837-1482.** On a smaller scale, the **Paramount Theatre (303-892-7016, in downtown Denver)** and the outstanding **Arvada Center for the Arts and Humanities (303-431-3080, www.arvada center.org)** attract national acts. Both locales are gorgeous places to hear music while sipping a glass of wine and polishing off a picnic dinner. The **Bluebird Theater** on E. Colfax Ave. features musicians ranging from rock to folk in an intimate setting; **303-322-2308.** Purchase tickets for most major events through

Ticketmaster, 303-830-8497; www.ticket master. com.

County and Western Dancing

With a 5,000-square-foot dance floor, the **Grizzly Rose Saloon and Dance Hall** is not only Colorado's largest country and western dance saloon but it's also by far the best place to learn the Texas two-step and other necessary dances. Lessons are offered by Bill and Kathy—you'll be struttin' your stuff in no time. Well-known national acts perform on many nights, especially on weekends, when decked-out cowboys/girls kick up their heels. Now featuring family nights on Sun. The Nashville Network tapes concerts here periodically for national TV. A very entertaining place. **5450 N. Valley Hwy.; 303-295-1330; www.grizzly rose.com.** Another western dance saloon that has come on strong in recent years is **The Stampede,** located near the corner of Havana and Parker Rd. A popular "meat market" with a younger crowd, the Stampede offers free line dancing and other country and western dance lessons. **2430 S. Havana St., Aurora; 303-337-7686; www. stampedeclub.com.**

Country Dinner Playhouse

Located near the Tech Center, off Interstate 25 at the southern end of the metro area, this dinner playhouse is consistent if not spectacular. A buffet dinner is followed by a full-scale musical production. After the "Barnstormers" perform some numbers from upcoming shows, the stage descends from the ceiling. The acting and choreography are usually good, with some productions excelling each year. This is a great family outing. Reservations recommended. Open Tues.–Sun. nights. **6875 S. Clinton St., Greenwood Village, CO 80112; 303-799-1410; www. countrydinnerplayhouse.com.**

Denver Performing Arts Complex

Beautiful and functional, this impressive four-square-block arts center has not only given Denver a cultural identity but a Tony Award to boot—a 1998 Tony for Outstanding Regional

Theatre. Its nine theaters make it the second-largest such complex in the nation, eclipsed only by New York's Lincoln Center. Whether you are interested in theater, music, ballet or opera, this series of architecturally unique buildings in downtown Denver is the place to come. The acoustically acclaimed **Boettcher Concert Hall** is home to the **Colorado Symphony Orchestra** and **Opera Colorado; 303-595-4388.** *Sunset Boulevard, Miss Saigon* and other major Broadway shows continue to pack 'em in at the contemporary **Buell Theater, 303-893-4100.** For traditional and contemporary drama as well as musicals, contact the **Denver Center Theatre Company; 303-893-4100.** National touring shows with huge casts play at the **Auditorium Theatre, 303-893-4100,** as does the **Colorado Ballet, 303-837-8888; www. coloradoballet.org.** Information on the entire complex is available at **www.denver center.org.**

El Chapultepec

No need to dress formally at this funky jazz dive. For years, this small, unassuming and smoky bar has featured some of the best bebop around. If you're into upright bass and sultry saxophone, stop by. In addition to the outstanding live jazz, the proximity of El Chapultepec ("the grasshopper") to LoDo and Coors Field guarantees that the place is usually crowded. The Mexican food is hot and the jazz is cool. Open nightly; no cover charge. **1962 Market St.; 303-295-9126.**

Herman's Hideaway

Hot. Dark. Crowded. Smoky. What more could you ask for in a blues/rock club? In this fairly small, informal setting, the music leaps out at you. To secure a seat, get here an hour or two before the bands start playing around 9:30 P.M. There's great dancing, pool and general overindulgence. **1578 S. Broadway; 303-778-9916; 303-777-5840.**

La Rumba

Located in an unassuming brick warehouse-style building, La Rumba is *the* dance place in Denver, having received accolades near and far. Well-dressed crowds line up outside every Thurs. through Sat. nights for a chance to show off their salsa moves on the large wooden dance floor. The uninitiated may want to take a salsa class as a prelude to an evening at La Rumba. Or watch the action from a large leather couch near the dance floor or in the quieter bar area. La Rumba's also known for its huge selection of tequilas and rums. Located just **west of Broadway on 9th Ave.; 303-572-8006.**

Mercury Cafe

An institution in Denver, this coffeehouse/cafe draws a wide variety of clientele. Its second-floor dance hall follows suit by booking an eclectic mix of live entertainment, ranging from punk rock to swing bands to poetry readings to comedy and theater. Never boring, the Mercury's hours vary, but it is open Mon.–Sat. for lunch and dinner; Sun. for brunch and dinner; now serving its own microbrew. **2199 California St.; 303-294-9281; 303-294-9258; www.mercurycafe.com.**

NEARBY
The Buck Snort Saloon

This is a great place for dancing, albeit in crowded quarters, to quality live bands on Sat. nights. Located near Pine Junction, about an hour's drive from Denver. (See the Where to Eat section.)

The Little Bear

This rustic mountain bar in the town of Evergreen is legendary for providing wild nights of dancing to live music. The Little Bear attracts a diverse crowd—from bikers to bankers—and everyone seems to enjoy the contrast. Top local rock, blues and country and western bands play most often, with national acts frequently making one- and two-night stops. Open nightly Tues.–Sun. until at least midnight. **28075 Hwy. 74, Evergreen, CO 80439; 303-674-9991.**

Shopping

The Denver metro area, isolated from other major cities, attracts people from around the region with its extensive shopping network. More than 25 malls and shopping centers exhibit great appeal, but as in any city, there are a few unusually good places to spend, spend, spend.

Cherry Creek Shopping District

Long before the grand opening of the upscale **Cherry Creek Mall** in 1990, this district was already the talk of the town. The arrival of such retail heavyweights as **Neiman-Marcus, Lord & Taylor** and **Saks Fifth Avenue** has helped Cherry Creek draw shoppers from around the Rocky Mountain region. In addition to all of the stores in the main mall, the surrounding neighborhood is bursting with small shops, art galleries, cafes and restaurants. This is a great place to take a stroll, window-shop and peek into some of the city's best small businesses. Located at **E. 1st Ave. and University Blvd.**

The Tattered Cover Book Store, in the Cherry Creek district, is perhaps the best bookstore in the United States. Denver's largest and best-known bookstore puts forth an offering of more than 500,000 books—probably more than were lost at the burning of the library in Alexandria. This is not a used bookstore. Even so, Joyce Meskis, the owner, encourages leisurely browsing and reading. Feel free to plop down in a comfortable armchair and leaf through a few interesting titles. You could easily spend hours wandering through the four-story assortment of books perched on tidy, well-stocked shelves. The Tattered Cover offers worldwide mailing and free gift wrapping. If they don't have it stocked, and the book is in print on the planet, the helpful staff has the best ability to retrieve it. Also a selection of magazines, calendars, maps, globes and greeting cards near the main-floor cafe. Free parking in the covered lot next to the store. For a good meal or a glass of wine in a window-encased setting, try the **Fourth Story Restaurant ($$ to $$$).** The Tattered Cover is at **2955 E. 1st Ave. (at Milwaukee); 1-800-833-9327; 303-322-7727; www.tatteredcover.com.** Though somewhat smaller than its famous sibling, the excellent **Tattered Cover Historic LoDo** bookstore provides a wide assortment of volumes that you can peruse in any number of cozy chairs, a full-service coffee shop and an enormous newsstand. **1628 16th St.; 303-436-1070.**

FlatIron Crossing

Situated between Boulder and the Denver area along Hwy. 36, this gigantic, brand-spankin'-new mall offers a twist. In addition to over 180 stores and restaurants, its design features include bikeway connections and retractable glass walls to enable breezes to blow through the mall. **One W. FlatIron Cir., Broomfield, CO 80021; 720-887-9900; www.flatiron crossing.com.**

Larimer Square

Located in the historic 1400 block of Larimer St., Larimer Square is a must-visit in Denver. Housed in 1880s vintage buildings, a variety of distinctive shops, restaurants and bars line one of Denver's oldest and, at one time, seediest streets. In 1959 Kent Ruth, in his book *Colorado Vacations,* called Larimer St. "pretty much a skid-row slum." Today the mood is both romantic and exuberant, especially in the evening when twinkling tree lights and street globes cast a warm glow on the restored three-story, brick Victorians. During the Oktoberfest celebration in Sept., Larimer St. is blocked off and kegs are tapped; brass bands and lederhosen are nearly as common as jeans and T-shirts. Celebrations in Larimer Square mark other occasions as well, including Halloween, St. Patrick's Day and Cinco de Mayo. The architectural integrity has been maintained, even though wares are displayed in a bold, modern manner. From the Market's excellent cappuccino to Williams-Sonoma's exotic cookery utensils, Larimer Square is a treasure to be enjoyed. **303-534-2367; www.larimersquare.com.**

Park Meadows

Touting itself as a "retail resort" rather than a mall (what's in a name?), this upscale shopping area south of Denver offers a mix of stores and entertainment housed in a setting reminiscent of a Colorado mountain lodge. Stone fireplaces, cozy sofas and wonderful Colorado art scattered throughout indeed set this enormous place apart from the competition. Many of the stores are three to four times the size of their typical locations. Retail giants including Nordstrom and Dillard's serve as anchors among the 130-plus shops, stores and restaurants. Located at Interstate 25 and C-470. **8401 Park Meadows Center Dr., Littleton, CO 80124; 1-888-333-PARK; 303-792-2999; www.parkmead ows.com.**

REI—Denver Flagship

The outstanding retail space created by outdoor-recreation giant REI is difficult to describe and best visited firsthand. The historic Denver Tramway Powerhouse Building—a red-brick behemoth built in 1901 and now listed on the National Register of Historic Places—provides a sprawling, airy venue for REI's retail concept: interactive shopping. Determine the effectiveness of a heavy jacket by entering the Cold Room, with temperatures that can drop to 30° F below zero. Or test a water purifier by filtering water from an indoor stream. Try out a mountain bike on the store's outdoor single-track trails or ascend one of 14 climbing routes on the indoor 45-foot-high Pinnacle, designed to resemble the sandstone of Boulder's Flatirons. Stroll by the outdoor recreation booth to plan your next trip to the hills. Whether you actually purchase anything is beside the point—a visit here is an event. Conveniently located on the Platte River at Confluence Park and accessible via the greenway trail system. Free parking. Open weekdays 10 A.M.–9 P.M.; Sat. until 7 P.M. and Sun. until 6 P.M. **1416 Platte St., Denver, CO 80202; 303-756-3100; www.rei.com.**

The 16th Street Mall

The tree-lined 16th Street Mall slices through the center of the downtown shopping district. Outdoor cafes, historic buildings, shops and restaurants can be found along its length; free shuttle buses run up and down the mall connecting the Market St. and Civic Center bus stations. The crown jewel of the mall is the recently opened **Denver Pavilions,** between Glenarm and California Sts. The facility landed a few big-name anchors including **Wolfgang Puck Cafe, Virgin Megastore, Hard Rock Cafe** and **Nike Town. 500 16th St.; 303-260-6001; www.denverpavilions.com.** At **16th and Lawrence Sts.** the **Tabor Center,** with 65 stores on three levels, continues to attract visitors. This glass-enclosed galleria is home to some major retailers; a host of unusual items are sold from vendor carts throughout. The third-floor food court will entice you with smells from around the world.

NEARBY

Factory Outlets

Castle Rock Factory Shops, 20 miles south of Denver, provide a bargain hunter's paradise. Many of the best-known brands are represented at 130 stores. Complete with a small playground for the kids and a large food court, this makes an excellent, scenic side trip. Take Meadows Pkwy. (Exit 184) off Interstate 25; **303-688-4494; www.primeoutlets.com.** If you are heading north from Denver on Interstate 25, consider the similar **factory shops in Loveland.**

Wildlife

Rocky Mountain Arsenal National Wildlife Area

The U.S. Army and the U.S. Fish and Wildlife Service have teamed up to offer what is, perhaps, the unlikeliest combination of visual attractions. This enormous tract of federally owned land in north Denver offers photo opportunities of one of the foulest toxic-waste cleanup areas in the country and an uncanny number of species of Colorado wildlife. Mule deer, coyote and a large assortment of birdlife, including owls and bald eagles, call the arsenal home for at least part of the year. Observation blinds add to the experience. For information about the wildlife bus tours, contact the **U.S. Fish and Wildlife Service; 303-289-0232; www.r6.fws.gov/refuges/arsenal.**

Zoo

Denver Zoo (City Park)

Denver's zoo has consistently been one of the city's most popular attractions, with more than 1 million visitors each year. Generous donations by Denver residents have helped the zoo to continue offering better (not necessarily bigger) exhibits throughout the years. More than 4,000 animals representing 715 species make their home here. Include a visit to the Dall sheep mountain and to the Northern Shores exhibit where you can view polar bears and sea lions swimming underwater (this is one of the best areas to be during feeding time). Don't miss the 22,000-square-foot Tropical Discovery area, complete with hundreds of creatures such as monitor lizards and venomous snakes, surrounded by rain forests, rivers and swamps. The outstanding Primate Panorama provides an uncanny look at animals such as lemurs and lowland gorillas in

An orangutan watches humans in the primate area at the Denver Zoo. Photo courtesy of the Denver Zoo.

replications of their natural habitat. Check out the new Komodo Dragon exhibit—the world's largest. Kids will love a ride on the small train. Be sure to visit the animal nursery, where there is usually a newborn receiving special attention. Many of the animals are fed late morning to midafternoon. The zoo is open daily 10 A.M.– 5 P.M. Oct.–Mar. and 9 A.M.–6 P.M. the rest of the year. Fee charged. **E. 23rd St. between York St. and Colorado Blvd.; 303-376-4800; www.denverzoo.org.**

Where to Stay

Accommodations

Denver presents an overwhelming number of lodging opportunities to vacationers. First of all, you need to decide which part of the city to stay in: downtown, uptown, the Tech Center area, near the new airport or near Interstate 70 for a quick exit to the nearby mountains. Then there is the question of price and style. The **Brown Palace** is the best-known Denver hotel—with good reason. For a nonstop row of inexpensive motels, take a cruise down **E. Colfax Ave.** (it's not the best part of town). You can still find a comfortable night's stay at major hotels near Denver's former airport, Stapleton. You can also find most chain motels and hotels by heading south to the **Denver Tech Center** (Interstate 25 and Belleview). Other possibilities include a number of new high-rise hotels, major chain and discount accommodations, bed and breakfast inns and a couple of youth hostels.

We have gone into some depth in picking a range of places to stay in the central area. If, however, you are just passing through or want to stay in a different part of town, the **Denver Metro Convention and Visitors Bureau** can help you make a selection: **303-892-1112; www.denver.org.** Consider the following unique recommendations.

Hotel Teatro—$$$$

Across from the award-winning Denver Performing Arts Complex in the old 1910 Tramway Tower, this 116-room luxury hotel is perfect for well-heeled theater patrons, high-rolling business travelers or couples out on a splurge. Ties with the theater are obvious in the hotel's name as well as the decor. The Teatro is decorated with props from past productions at the Denver Center Theater Company. Though the building is historic, the amenities are 21st century right down to the digital speaker phones and data ports. The contemporary rooms create a welcome, polished ambience. In addition to a night at the theater, consider a trip to **Kevin Taylor's ($$$$),** the hotel's high-quality restaurant. Be sure to consider one of the hotel's enticing packages. **1100 14th St., Denver, CO 80202; 1-800-WYNDHAM; 303-228-1100; www.wyndham.com.**

Lumber Baron Inn—$$$$

Located prominently in the Potter Highlands Historic district, just a stone's throw north of downtown Denver, this relatively upscale B&B ranks as one of the top romantic stays in the metro area. And the enormity of renovation work that owners Walter and Maureen Keller have put into this 1890 mansion is staggering! Choose from one of five beautifully decorated suites, including the Honeymoon Suite with its sizable whirlpool bath recessed in a corner turret. The attention to details, from the lovely antiques spread throughout the 10,000 square feet to the elaborate ceiling wallpaper, really adds to the enjoyment of this place. Each morning, breakfast is served in the dining room, on the porch or in your room, depending on your preference. No smoking; highly recommended. **2555 W. 37th Ave.; 303-477-8205; www.lumberbaron.com.**

Brown Palace Hotel—$$$ to $$$$

When the Brown opened in 1892, one year before the silver panic, it put the "Queen City" on the map. The hotel was such a monument to economic good times it helped create the expectations necessary for Denver to survive and flourish into the future. A stunning example of Victorian architecture, the Brown's triangular exterior is built of Colorado red granite and Arizona sandstone; hand-carved Rocky Mountain animals lie in wait above the arched seventh-floor windows. Though the hotel was originally built on the edge of the city, Denver has grown up around the Brown Palace, and the hotel now enjoys a downtown location.

The magnificent interior lobby leaves lasting impressions on visitors. Six stories of wrought-iron balconies rise to a stained-glass ceiling; the spacious ground floor retains an intimate feel with red sofas and overstuffed chairs, arranged in small groups in the center of the room. Daily from 12–4 P.M., the lobby hosts an elegant tea, served with sandwiches, scones and truffles.

Over the years many famous guests have stayed at the Brown. Dwight D. Eisenhower used the hotel for his presidential campaign headquarters in 1952. The biggest hubbub the hotel has ever seen was in 1964 when the Beatles stayed at the Brown during their visit to perform at Red Rocks. Five thousand screaming fans crowded the streets to catch a glimpse of their favorite musicians. Alas, when the Fab Four arrived, almost none of their fans was aware of the secret back entrance to the hotel.

Each of the 230 rooms and 25 suites has its own unique personality, featuring a window view and the finest furnishings. Unlike some historic hotels, the Brown Palace is not tattered around the edges. Rather, it is a solid, immaculately kept hotel. Many of the bathrooms are decorated in an art deco style and all come with toiletry baskets and thick terry-cloth robes.

The Brown is also home to some of Denver's best-known restaurants. Dine at the publike **Ship Tavern,** with replicas of American clipper ships. Wear a coat and tie to the formal dining room, the **Palace Arms.** It's decorated in a Napoleonic theme and contains a set of dueling pistols thought to have belonged to Napoleon. The classy setting of **Ellyngton's** is popular for breakfast and lunch, including its well-known Sun. champagne brunch. **321 17th St., Denver, CO 80202; 1-800-321-2599; 303-297-3111; www.brownpalace.com.**

Castle Marne—$$$ to $$$$

Among Denver's fine historic bed and breakfast inns, Castle Marne deserves special mention. Built in 1889, this immense stone structure prominently occupies its corner lot at 16th Ave. and Race St., drawing the admiring attention of passersby. The home was designed by the famous eclectic architect of the time, William Lang, designer of the Molly Brown House (see the Museums and Galleries section). Today the restored home features hand-hewn rhyolite stonework, balconies and an impressive four-story turret that dominates the exterior; inside, attention is drawn to the fine woodwork, numerous original ornate fireplaces and the main stairway. Nine rooms of varying sizes (all with private baths, three with private whirlpool baths) are nicely decorated with antiques and artwork. The third-floor landing features a butterfly display in honor of former owner John Mason, the first curator of the Denver Museum of Natural History. Full formal breakfast each morning in the dining room. Complimentary afternoon tea daily. **1572 Race St., Denver, CO 80206; 1-800-92-MARNE; 303-331-0621; www.castlemarne.com.**

Loew's Giorgio Hotel—$$$ to $$$$

From the outside the Giorgio looks amazingly like Darth Vader—you can almost hear it breathe. Don't let the ultramodern exterior put you off—inside you will find exquisite northern Italian decor with pleasant, immaculate surroundings. Country-villa styling accents the 183 guest rooms and 20 suites. Complimentary continental breakfast and access to the well-appointed Sporting Club are included. The elegant **Tuscany Restaurant** features very good northern Italian cuisine. Prices drop considerably on the weekends. The dark one stands at **4150 E. Mississippi, Denver, CO 80246; 1-800-345-9172; 303-782-9300; www.loewsgiorgio.com.**

The Oxford Alexis Hotel—$$$ to $$$$

When completed in 1891 (one year before the Brown Palace), the Oxford Hotel "sported the latest in gadgets and technology as well as Gilded Age opulence." Located across from Union Station, the Oxford stood for years as a standout luxury hotel that catered mainly to train travelers. Since a major restoration in 1983, the hotel has maintained its original richness along with all the modern-day conveniences.

Designed by architect Frank E. Edbrooke, this five-story brick building has had quite a history. The interior, furnished with the finest oriental rugs, woodwork, marble floors and frescoed walls, reflected the profitable silver mining days Colorado was enjoying at the time. Private water closets, along with electric and gas lighting, amazed guests. The Oxford also boasted the first elevator in Denver. During the 1930s the Oxford was remodeled and transformed into an art deco showpiece. Skid row crept into lower downtown Denver in the 1960s and 1970s, and the Oxford deteriorated into a run-down flophouse. But many Denverites remember the Oxford for the great jazz, folk music and melodramas that packed the place in the evenings during those hard times.

But today, 80 classy rooms, the mezzanine and lobby are furnished with antiques. Rooms range from comfortable singles to palatial suites. In the lobby, Baby Doe Tabor's piano sits near the front door, and a fireplace beckons. With **McCormick's Fish House and Bar** you don't even need to leave the building for dining and nightlife. Be sure to visit the **Cruise Room,** a restored art deco bar that opened in the 1930s. Wall carvings, expressing drinking cheers in many languages, were created to celebrate the end of Prohibition. Health club access for a small fee. Special weekend packages offered for couples. **1600 17th St., Denver, CO 80202; 1-800-228-5838; 303-628-5400; www. theoxford.com.**

Holiday Chalet—$$ to $$$

If you're looking for a unique, historic and generally comfortable place to stay without spending a fortune, this lodge fits the bill. Built in 1896 as a private residence for the Bohm family, it still retains much of its original charm. The Holiday Chalet is immaculately kept. The many stained-glass windows spread throughout add colorful touches; a Waterford crystal chandelier graces the front entrance, and sunny bedrooms all have odd little corners. Each of the 10 rooms comes with a kitchenette, telephone and color TV. You'll get used to the pink decor in no time. You may hear some street noise from Colfax Ave., but thanks to 18-inch walls, you certainly won't hear your neighbor snoring. Another reason to stay is because innkeeper Margot Hartman makes you feel right at home—in the same house where she spent many years growing up. **1820 E. Colfax Ave., Denver, CO 80218; 1-800-626-4497; 303-321-9975.**

Denver International Youth Hostel—$

This hostel is indeed inexpensive—you are required, however, to do a chore before you leave. Check-in must be between 8 and 10 A.M. or 5 and 10:30 P.M.; doors are locked the rest of the time. There are about 30 beds available as well as kitchen, bathroom facilities, laundry and game room. Located just east of downtown Denver. **630 E. 16th Ave., Denver, CO 80203; 303-832-9996; www.denverhostel.com.**

Melbourne International Hotel and Hostel—$

Conveniently located downtown, this hostel provides private rooms as well as standard dorm rooms. Each private room has a refrigerator and some have their own baths. A full kitchen and laundry facilities are available. A great place to swap tips with other budget travelers. Check-in 7 A.M.–midnight; call ahead if checking in after 7 P.M. **607 22nd St., Denver, CO 80205; 303-292-6386; www.denverhostel.com.**

WEST OF TOWN

Only minutes west of Denver, the quaint and cozy **Cliff House Lodge Country Inn ($$$ to $$$$)** lies tucked away in the small town of Morrison, just where the foothills of the Rockies begin. This sandstone Victorian lodge, built in 1873 by George Morrison, the town's founder, serves largely as a romantic getaway for Denver couples. Both the lodge rooms and cottages are furnished with antiques. Gourmet breakfast served each morning. Walking distance to shops and restaurants and only minutes from Red Rocks Park, at **121 Stone St., Golden, CO 80465; 303-697-9732; www.cliffhouse lodge.com.** Farther up in the hills in Evergreen, the **Highland Haven Creekside Inn ($$$ to $$$$)** provides a perfect mountain retreat in its 16 rooms, cottages and suites still within striking distance of Denver. Snuggled against an enormous rock outcropping surrounded by towering blue spruce and pines, this Evergreen landmark keeps drawing loyal guests back year after year. Most of their accommodations have a fireplace, TV, VCR and kitchen; all include private baths. Breakfast is served each morning on the porch of the original "Pioneer Cabin." **4395 Independence Trail, Evergreen, CO 80439; 303-674-3577; www.high landhaven.com.**

Where to Eat

Dining in Denver has never been the same since Louis Ballast invented and patented the cheeseburger at his Denver drive-in restaurant in 1944. The following list of eating places reflects the favorites of longtime Denverites as well as some more offbeat eateries. Whether you're in the mood for fine French cuisine, raucous western dining or an exotic Indian meal, these places are worthwhile. For a more complete listing of restaurants throughout the metro area, pick up a free copy of *Westword* newspaper; **www.west word.com.** Check **www.uswestdex.com** or **www.denver.citysearch.com** for a more complete list of restaurant ideas and reviews.

American

The Buckhorn Exchange—$$$ to $$$$

Virtually everyone of any importance in the Old West has eaten here, including Teddy Roosevelt and Buffalo Bill Cody. It looks much as it did then, complete with over 500 elk, deer, mountain sheep and other animal heads mounted on the walls. This is Denver's oldest continuously operated restaurant, first serving the wild and woolly public in 1895. After all those years, you can be assured that this place is part museum. The Buckhorn features buffalo, elk and alligator appetizers or the inevitable Rocky Mountain oysters (you needn't worry about shelling this particular variety). Their bean soup is legendary, as are the steaks. Your Denver cousin is almost obligated to take you here. If you just want to stop by for a drink, head to the upstairs bar, one of Denver's friendliest. Open for lunch Mon.– Fri. 11 A.M.–2 P.M. Dinner is served Mon.–Fri. 5:30–10 P.M., Sat. 5–11 P.M., and Sun. 4–9 P.M. Located in an obscure off-downtown neighborhood at **1000 Osage St.; 303-534-9505.** The RTD light rail makes a stop here.

The Buckhorn Exchange, Denver's oldest restaurant, with some of its 500 "residents" mounted for display on the surrounding walls. Photo courtesy of the Buckhorn Exchange.

Coney Island in nearby Aspen Park. Photo by Dean Winstanley.

Denver Chop House and Brewery— $$$ to $$$$

Housed in the old Union Pacific Railroad's "Head House" just a baseball's throw from Coors Field, the interesting and expansive Chop House draws an equal number of folks for its seven handcrafted microbrews and its quality food. The consistently crowded place exudes the mood of a luxurious railcar with rich dark wood and brass touches throughout. Many patrons shuffle no farther than the bar area for an ale and something from their excellent bar menu. Favorites include the lobster pot pie and enormous onion rings the size of hula hoops, stacked high on a spindle. Main entrées include seafood and poultry, but the steaks, Iowa pork chops and other meaty dishes are the standouts. Open for lunch and dinner daily, 11 A.M.–11 P.M.; until midnight Fri.–Sat.; bar menu until 1 A.M. **1735 19th St.; 303-296-0800.**

El Rancho—$$$ to $$$$

Since 1948 people have been pulling off Interstate 70 at El Rancho restaurant as a matter of tradition. Dinner always begins with a relish tray followed by a basket of homemade cinnamon rolls, salad, soup, entrée and chiffon pie or ice cream. Entrées include rock lobster, buffalo steak, roast prime rib or Rocky Mountain trout. Don't be discouraged if there is a short wait— just pull up a comfortable chair in one of the lounge areas and have a cocktail. The views from nearly everywhere in El Rancho are spectacular and, in winter, any or all of the seven fireplaces may be burning. Open daily; call for hours. Located 18 miles west of Denver on Interstate 70 at the Evergreen Pkwy. (Exit 252); **303-526-0661.**

The Fort—$$$ to $$$$

The Fort is one of the most popular places near the metro area to go for a special occasion, especially when out-of-town visitors show up. Views of Denver from the dining room are wonderful. The restaurant is a reproduction of Bent's Fort, one of the first trading posts in the Colorado Territory (see the **Southeast Plains** chapter). The atmosphere of Colorado's early days permeates this large restaurant—all employees dress in frontier period clothing. And they get into character: when we visited, one waitress dressed as an Indian maiden whacked the cork out of a champagne bottle with a tomahawk. Even so, the most unique thing about the Fort is the food. Owner Sam Arnold has diligently researched frontier recipes for food and drink, updated for modern tastes. The fare is made exclusively with ingredients from the American Southwest. Before dinner try some buffalo sausage, Rocky Mountain oysters or buffalo tongue. Entrées include large steaks as well as buffalo, quail, elk and fish. Specialty drinks with names such as the Hailstorm, Jim Bridger and Bear's Blood conjure up images from the early days. Rumor has it that former Russian president Boris Yeltsin, at a dinner of the Summit of Eight here some years ago, found the available booze very much to his liking. Reservations recommended. Open Mon.–Fri. 5:30–10 P.M., Sat. 5–10 P.M., Sun. 5–9 P.M. West of Denver just off Hwy. 285. **19192 Hwy. 8, Morrison; 303-697-4771.**

Denver Buffalo Company—$$ to $$$

This place has become a Denver dining landmark. Centrally located, it's popular with businesspeople as well as groups of friends. The Southwestern theme works well, from the wonderful Native American art on display to the main attraction—buffalo dishes. All buffalo is raised here in Colorado. It's served in a wide assortment of dishes from prime rib to Italian buffalo sausage. Menu highlights also include salads, pasta dishes and fresh fish. Be sure not to fill up on too many jalapeño corn bread muffins—they are irresistible. The sprawling building also houses a trading post with woolen clothing, leather goods, jewelry and native handicrafts; an art gallery; a coffeehouse; and a popular deli, which features internationally acclaimed Buff-Dogs, buffalo pastrami, jerky and more. The main restaurant is open for lunch Mon.–Sat. 11 A.M.–2:30 P.M.; dinner Mon.–Thurs. 5–9 P.M., Fri.–Sat. till 10 P.M., closed Sun.; deli open 7 A.M.–7 P.M. **1109 Lincoln St.;** restaurant **303-832-0880** or trading post **303-832-0884.**

The Buck Snort Saloon—$ to $$$

In its out-of-the-way location in a narrow canyon near the town of Pine, the Buck Snort has no equal as a backwoods mountain tavern/restaurant. Shoot a game of pool in the front room or have a beer on the back deck, which hangs out over a rocky stream. The Buck Snort's reputation far outpaces its available room—especially on Sat. nights, when live music keeps the place jumping. Menu items include the half-pound Buck Burger, smothered burritos and their wurst sandwich. Save room for their homemade pie. If you are anywhere close to Pine Junction on Hwy. 285 (some 32 miles southwest of Denver), pull off and make your way 6 miles south to Pine on County Rd. 126. From Pine, head up Sphinx Park Rd. for 1.5 fairly rough miles. Negotiating the steep canyon road should be enough to keep you from drinking too much at the saloon. Open 4 P.M. until the last person leaves Wed.–Fri., noon–midnight Sat.–Sun. Closed Mon.–Tues. **15921 Elk Creek Rd., Pine; 303-838-0284.**

Bonnie Brae Tavern—$ to $$

You wouldn't expect great pizza at a tavern with a Scottish name, but the name is based on its location in the Bonnie Brae neighborhood, not the food. Established in 1934 by Carl Dire, this popular spot is now run by his two sons, Mike and Hank. Ever popular with singles, families and University of Denver students, the tavern offers what many consider the best pizza in town. It is a simple place with comfortable, low-slung booths, allowing everyone a good look around the room. A superb minestrone soup and regular specials of American and Italian food help round out the menu. You can expect a wait at this local favorite. Open 10:30 A.M.–10 P.M. (until 9 P.M. Sun.); closed Mon. **740 S. University Blvd.; 303-777-2262.**

D.C. Deli Cafe—$ to $$

This new place continues to garner raves, especially from Denver transplants once hailing from the East Coast (where delis are thick as flies). Check out the interesting Washington, D.C., memorabilia as you make your choice from their 76 sandwiches. Many of the sandwiches feature D.C.-appropriate names such as the Lady Bird smoked turkey or the Truman Mushroom Bomb. The deli excels with its baked goods, including pies and pastries such as the enormous cinnamon roll. Breakfast items feature omelettes; for lunch consider one of their tasty salads to go with a sandwich. We hope this place sticks around for a long time. Open Mon.–Thurs. 7:30 A.M.–10 P.M., Fri.–Sat. till 10:30 P.M., Sun. 9 A.M.–4 P.M. **275 S. Logan; 303-765-5705.**

My Brother's Bar—$ to $$

For years My Brother's Bar has served as a gathering spot for good friends and lovers of hamburgers. With its exposed brick walls, well-worn wood floors and pressed-tin ceilings, this place is nothing fancy—just comfortable. With no TVs or loud music (classical music rules here, including occasional performances), you'll find no distractions from your meal and conversation with friends. The small menu, listed on the wall, features a variety of delicious burgers, including a buffalo burger. The sandwiches are creative and worth a try; a personal favorite is the spicy turkey olé, made with a mixture of turkey, cream cheese and jalapeño peppers. Beer lovers will appreciate the large assortment of fine beers on tap. Great patio seating in summer. Open Mon.–Sat. 11 A.M.–1:30 A.M.; closed Sun. **2376 15th St.; 303-455-9991.**

Wazee Lounge and Supper Club—$ to $$

The Wazee has been around for years, remaining a fond favorite with many Denverites for its atmosphere, beer selection and what just might be the best pizza in Denver. Find a place at one of the numerous tables or at the great bar and have a good time. In addition to pizza, the Wazee also serves sandwiches and salads. This is a classic. **Corner of Wazee and 15th St.; 303-623-9518.**

Coney Island—$

Located along Hwy. 285 about 20 miles southwest of Denver, the Coney Island is hard to miss. Just look for the giant pink hot dog with all the trimmings. Walk inside this hot dog and order up (you guessed it) a hot dog, Coney Island or corn dog. Hamburgers, fries and ice cream are also available. Picnic tables out on the sundeck provide the best seating at this unusual place. It's worth a visit if you're in the neighborhood. Like we said, you can't miss it. If you have an aversion to greasy food, however, keep driving. Located in **Aspen Park; 303-838-4210.**

Breakfast

Dozens—$ to $$

This fun place, located in a comfortable Victorian house with wood floors and high ceilings, specializes in breakfast items (especially egg dishes). The creative menu items all have a Denver or Colorado theme. Choose from a large selection of omelettes, scrambled egg dishes or something lighter such as waffles or fresh fruit. Try one of their fresh-baked goods. Lunches feature sandwiches, but you can also order breakfast items. A full bar is available. Hours are 6:30 A.M.–2:30 P.M. daily. Dozens has two locations. Both are great, but the downtown restaurant has more atmosphere. **13th St. and Cherokee St.; 303-572-0066.** Also at **2180 S. Havana in Aurora; 303-337-6627.**

Jake's Diner (Golden)—$ to $$

Nothing fancy about this place, to be sure, just good, filling breakfasts at cheap prices. Choose from over a dozen breakfast entrées or just dig into one of their gigantic cinnamon rolls. **17695 S. Golden Rd.; 303-278-9805.**

Continental

Tante Louise—$$$ to $$$$

In a couple of unassuming houses linked together on Colfax Ave. and Cherry St. resides one of the city's better restaurants. Certainly it must be the coziest and perhaps the most romantic restaurant in Denver, with small tables in quaint nooks off the winding passageways and large tables beside roaring hearths. The decor has an Old

World charm; the quality of food will have you returning often. Tante Louise, nearing its third decade in business, has always had rave reviews for its fine French cuisine. The prices here are somewhat lower than at the other Denver restaurants of this quality, and the extensive wine list (over 600) is reasonably priced. Open Mon.–Sat. 5:30–10 P.M. **4900 E. Colfax Ave.; 303-355-4488.**

Wellshire Inn—$$ to $$$$

An old English Tudor mansion on the grounds of the Wellshire Municipal Golf Course is home to this appealing restaurant. Unobstructed views of the course and the mountains have made it a favorite among Denverites. One-hundred-year-old imported tapestries and paneling, in addition to leaded stained glass and Tiffany lamps, lend an air of sophistication to the atmosphere. The food has an interesting contemporary continental focus. Renowned chef Michael Carins ensures an excellent dining experience. This is also a good choice for Sun. brunch from 10 A.M. to 2 P.M. (menu rather than buffet). Open for breakfast Mon.–Fri. 7–10 A.M.; lunch Mon.–Sat. 11:30 A.M.–2:30 P.M. Dinner is served Mon.–Thurs. 5–10 P.M., Fri.–Sat. until 11 P.M., Sun. 5–9 P.M. **3333 S. Colorado Blvd.; 303-759-3333.**

Le Central—$ to $$$

Le Central deserves a mention for its great French food and affordability. Their blackboard menu changes daily and features creative variations on pork, beef, chicken and fish. Although new dishes occasionally miss the mark, the restaurant has a strong and loyal following. Thankfully (for some of us) the able wait staff stands at the ready to translate the French explanations of the daily entrées. Enjoy the comfortable, pleasant French country atmosphere while sipping on one of their many modestly priced French wines. Lunch served Mon.–Fri. 11:30 A.M.–2 P.M.; dinner Mon.–Sat. 5–10 P.M. and Sun. till 9 P.M.; brunch Sat.–Sun. 11 A.M.–2 P.M. **112 E. 8th Ave.; 303-863-8094.**

Indian

India's—$$$ to $$$$

After a stint as a pilot in the Indian air force, Kris Kapoor did the most logical thing he could think of—he opened a restaurant in Denver. And what a restaurant it is. India's is a special place for both vegetarian and meat-eating lovers of fine Indian food. Authenticity reigns, from the sitar music and extensive list of regional entrées to the stainless steel plates on which they are served. Those uninitiated into this exotic cuisine will appreciate the menu explanations and descriptions and waiters who take care to gauge your personal spice meter. Highlights include delicious lamb dishes, especially the spicy Boti Masala. Or try the Ticca Jehangir, a delicious blend of tandoori chicken and shrimp. To top off your meal try one of their fruit lassis, a cool, thirst-quenching combination of yogurt and fruit ice that can be found all over India. Full bar. Open for lunch (**$$**) Mon.–Fri. 11:30 A.M.–2:15 P.M. and Sat. 12–2:15 P.M.; dinner Sun.–Thurs. 5:30–9:30 P.M. and Fri.–Sat. 5:30–10 P.M. Reservations highly recommended. At Tamarac Square, **3333 S. Tamarac Dr.; 303-755-4284.**

Italian

Barolo Grill—$$$

You don't have to get dressed up to feel at home in this casual and very popular Italian eatery. The intimate setting works regardless of whether the occasion is romance or a birthday party. Owner Blair Taylor's menu features authentic items. As a matter of fact, he and his staff regularly close up shop and journey to the Old Country for training and new ideas for the restaurant. The trips pay off as evidenced in menu standouts from antipasto to the fabulous duck to the pastas. Did we mention their amazing Italian wine selection? Enjoy. Open for dinners Tues.–Sat. 5:30–10:30 P.M. **3030 E. 6th Ave.; 303-393-1040.**

Carmine's on Penn—$$ to $$$

Tucked away on a south Denver residential street, Carmine's continues to be one of the area's most popular family-style Italian restaurants. What it lacks in fancy decor it more than makes up for with friendly, in-your-face service and outstanding menu items. Start off with a fantastic Caesar salad or the tasty house salad along with rolls topped with parmesan, garlic and olive oil. Entrées are listed on a chalkboard and are prepared for at least two. Meals range from chicken, shrimp, fish and veal, but the excellent pasta dishes are perhaps the favorite. Although this can be quite a romantic place, kids are welcome, too. Open Tues.–Sun. 5:30–10:30 P.M. Closed Mon. **92 S. Pennsylvania St.; 303-777-6443.**

Little Pepina's—$$ to $$$

Good, plentiful, flavorful Italian food. This kind of food makes you feel fulfilled while you're eating and for a long time afterward. They serve gourmet Italian fare as well as classics (all meals come with soup, salad and side of pasta). The only reason not to visit is if you're on a low-carbohydrate diet. This popular restaurant is located in northwest Denver, the original home of Denver's Italian immigrants. Open for lunch Tues.–Fri. 11:30 A.M.–2 P.M.; dinner Sun.–Thurs. 5–10 P.M. and Fri.–Sat. till 11 P.M. **3400 Osage St.; 303-477-3335.**

Pagliacci's—$$ to $$$

You can't miss this restaurant at night, and if you've seen the opera *I Pagliacci,* you'll know why the owners have a lighted neon clown on top of the building. Traditional family-style Italian food has been offered here since 1946. A large wall mural creates the atmosphere of rooftop dining overlooking an Italian city. Featuring homemade pasta and sauces, this busy place is a true classic. Each meal includes all the homemade minestrone and garlic bread you can eat. The food is tasty, plentiful and an excellent value. Extremely professional service. Dinner served Wed.–Sat. 5–10 P.M., Sun. 4:30–8:30 P.M. Closed Mon.–Tues. **1440 W. 33rd Ave.; 303-458-0530.**

Pasquini's—$ to $$

Simply put, the food at this place is awesome; so is the loud, friendly atmosphere. Located alongside busy S. Broadway, Pasquini's and its energetic staff crank out some mighty fine pizza, calzones and submarine sandwiches. Everything is characterized by fresh, noticeable spices. The garlic/butter-drenched bread sticks are to die for. Grab a chair at one of the few tables or at the one on the sidewalk where you can watch the cars whiz by while waiting for your food. After (or during) your meal stop in at the Blue Luna Room upstairs for some blues, rock or other live music. Open Mon.–Wed. 11 A.M.–midnight, Thurs.–Sat 11 A.M.–2 A.M., Sun. 4 P.M.–midnight. **1310 S. Broadway; 303-744-0917.** Also located at **1336 E. 17th Ave.; 303-863-8252.**

Mexican / Tex-Mex

Blue Bonnet Cafe and Lounge—$$ to $$$

Denverites flock to this popular restaurant to put their names on a waiting list for a coveted table. While waiting for a table, order a margarita at their small bar or from a patio table (weather permitting). Once seated, choose from a reasonably priced selection of Tex-Mex items, including a number of house specials such as the El Burro giant burrito and the chili relleno dinner. While waiting for your food, order from a sizable selection of Mexican beers, listen to the jukebox and peruse the management's collection of flattering newspaper articles that line one wall. Open Mon.–Thurs. 11 A.M.–10 P.M., Fri.–Sat 11 A.M.–11 P.M., Sun. noon–9 P.M. **457 S. Broadway; 303-778-0147.**

Morrison Inn—$$ to $$$

Located west of Denver at the foot of the mountains in the small community of Morrison, the inn specializes in Mexican food and good times. You'll see the adobe-colored building with green awnings and trim on Main St. Favorite meals include spinach enchiladas, fajitas and pork barbacoa. Don't expect authentic Mexican food—but you should be ready for incredible taste sensations. A major point in the inn's favor is that no pre-mix is used for the custom-made margaritas. They're great! Open Sun.–Thurs.

11 A.M.–10 P.M. (11 P.M. in summer), Fri.–Sat. 11 A.M.–11 P.M. Located in the middle of Morrison. **301 Bear Creek Ave.; 303-697-6650.**

La Cueva—$ to $$

For almost 30 years the same family has been carefully preparing tasty and surprisingly low-fat dishes at this excellent Mexican cantina. Though the dining room is small, it is impeccably clean and the service exceptional. Everything on the menu is prepared from scratch. Although you will find many familiar items on the menu, the chili rellenos and crispy chicken flautas are standouts. So are the Mexican desserts and, of course, the margaritas. Open Mon.–Fri. 11 A.M.–9 P.M. **9742 E. Colfax Ave.; 303-367-1422.**

Las Delicias—$ to $$

If you are one of those people on a continual hunt for an inexpensive and authentic Mexican cafe, then be sure to come here. Unless you are fluent in Spanish, don't even try to pick up the banter between the service staff; even the jukebox offers only Spanish tunes. This is not a contrived place in the least. The real reason to come here is the food—mouth-watering burritos, tacos and enchiladas will keep you utterly happy. "Las D" is a favorite with the downtown crowd for lunch. Full bar available. Open daily 8 A.M.–9 P.M. **439 E. 19th Ave., 303-839-5675; Las Delicias II, 7610 Conifer Rd., 303-430-0422;** in **Parker** at **19553 E. Main St., 303-840-0325;** also at **4301 E. Kentucky Ave., 303-692-0912.**

Tacos Jalisco—$

With music from a Spanish-language radio station blasting through the restaurant and a location in one of northwest Denver's Hispanic neighborhoods, it's no surprise this restaurant serves up some of the most authentic Mexican food in town. Slip into a booth or table seat at this clean, spacious place and peruse the lengthy menu. Breakfast includes huevos rancheros or mixed with chorizo. Other standouts include the carnes adovada plate, the green chili and the burrito made from anything from chicken to tongue. As incongruous as it may seem, this eatery even received a mention in highbrow *Bon Appetit* magazine. Open Tues.–Thurs. 9 A.M.–9 P.M., Fri.–Sat. till 10 P.M., Sun. till 8 P.M., closed Mon. **4309 W. 38th Ave.; 303-458-1437.**

Other Mexican/Tex-Mex Places

If you get a craving for specific items, here are a few standouts. For terrific margaritas, happy-hour specials on drinks and Tex-Mex food, try **The Rio Grande (1525 Blake St.,** just off of the 16th Street Mall; **303-623-5432). Las Margaritas (1066 S. Gaylord St., 303-777-0194)** is also well known for outstanding margaritas as well as its chicken mole dish. Chili rellenos don't get much better than the way **Benny's Restaurant y Cantina** has been preparing these tasty creations for years. Try Benny's at its original location **(301 E. 7th Ave., 303-894-0788)** or the newer location in **Glendale (4510 E. Virginia, 303-394-1404).** And for green chili (and tamales) with a significant kick, try the authentic and bargain-priced concoction served up by **Chubby's #7,** just north of 8th Ave. **on Santa Fe.**

Lower in fat than mainstream Mexican restaurants and twice as speedy, trendy burrito mills ("wrap" joints) proliferate throughout the Denver area. Get in line, place your order and watch an assembly line process with an efficiency that would make any Japanese manufacturer envious. Numerous **Chipotle Mexican Grill** and **Qdoba Mexican Grill** locations are a good bet **($ to $$),** as are other worthy competitors that continue to spring up.

Asian

Sushi Den—$$$ to $$$$

Known as one of the finest sushi establishments regionally, if not nationally, this see-and-be-seen place lives up to the hype. Well-dressed patrons entrust their pricey vehicles to the valet out front and make their way into this techno-style, trendy place, notable for its concrete walls and track lighting. Sushi Den imports its fish directly from Japan, one of very few places in the country that can claim that feat. Menu standouts abound, from shumai appetizers to the daily sushi specials to the sukiyaki. Open at 11:30 A.M. for lunch Mon.–Fri. and at 4:30 P.M. for dinner Mon.–Sat., 5 P.M. on Sun. Expect a wait for a table. **1487 S. Pearl St.; 303-777-0826.**

For more affordable sushi and Japanese cuisine try **Kokoro ($)** (in **Arvada** at **5535 Wadsworth Bypass; 303-934-2200,** or **south Denver** at **2390 S. Colorado Blvd.; 303-692-8752),** or **Tokyo Joe's ($)** at many metro locations, including **1700 E. Evans Ave.; 303-722-7666.**

Little Shanghai Cafe—$ to $$$

It's difficult to say why more Denverites don't mention Little Shanghai as one of their favorites; in our opinion, it definitely ranks right up there. Amid very attractive and comfortable tables and booths, the excellent wait staff hustles with precision to keep the various dishes flowing steadily to the customers. Sit back and sip on a cold Tsing-Tao beer while considering the fairly extensive menu. Specialties include seafood dishes and an excellent, spicy Kung Pao triple delight. The Chinese dumplings are some of the best we've had in Denver. Lunch specials daily. Open Mon.–Fri. 11 A.M.–10 P.M., Sat.–Sun. till 11 P.M. **460 S. Broadway; 303-777-9838; 303-722-1292.**

New Orient—$ to $$$

Tucked away in an unassuming location in a strip shopping center, this terrific little place specializes in Vietnamese cuisine with Amerasian creations that blend the East and West. The honey-crisp chicken is a perfect example: lightly fried and then stir-fried with snow peas, broccoli and carrots in a spicy honey sauce. Other standouts include the Vietnamese lemongrass bouillabaisse, chock-full of fresh seafood. Be sure to start off with one of their excellent spring rolls. Lunch served Tues.–Fri. 11 A.M.–2:30 P.M.; dinner Tues.–Thurs. 5–9:30 P.M., Fri. until 10:30 P.M., Sat.–Sun. noon–10:30 P.M. **10253 E. Iliff Ave., Aurora; 303-751-1288.**

T-Wa Inn—$ to $$$

A section of S. Federal Blvd. has been transformed into a strip of Vietnamese shops and restaurants. This was one of the first Vietnamese restaurants in town. The food reflects a delicate balance of tastes, borrowing from both Chinese and French cuisines and featuring many traditional specialties. T-Wa boasts an extensive menu of exotic hot-and-spicy dishes and wonderful seafood. Order something from the excellent selection of appetizers. It has very moderate prices for the quantity and quality of food. Open for lunch and dinner daily 11 A.M.–10 P.M.; Sat.–Sun. until 9:30 P.M. **555 S. Federal Blvd.; 303-922-4584.**

Tommy's—$ to $$

This small Thai restaurant serves up delicious and surprisingly inexpensive fare. But perhaps the best of all is a plate of addictive Phad Thai, a concoction of rice noodles stir-fried with shrimp, chicken, bean sprouts and onion. If you try it you'll definitely be back for more. Also stop in for Tommy's daily lunch special. Open Mon.–Fri. 10:30 A.M.–10 P.M., Sat. noon–10 P.M.; closed Sun. **3410 E. Colfax Ave.; 303-377-4244.**

Seafood

Jax Fish House—$$ to $$$$

This hugely popular LoDo spot fills up quickly after work hours, and with good reason. Jax serves up some of the freshest seafood in town. Just ask the patrons at the fresh bar near the entrance, all busily slurping down oysters on the half shell or peeling shrimp with a practiced motion. Relax in the noisy but attractive dining area and peruse the chalkboard for daily specials and a good feel for what's freshest. Or try one of their menu specialties such as the "damn good crab cakes" or the mahi mahi tostada. If you're with a group, consider the seafood platter that includes a variety of tasty items that's large enough to feed four. The narrow outside patio fills up quickly during good weather. Open daily at 4 P.M. On the **corner of Wazee and 17th St.; 303-292-5767.**

South American

Cafe Brazil—$$$

A true dining highlight in Denver, this small ethnic eatery excels on a number of fronts: atmosphere, service and cuisine. Chefs/owners Tony and Marla Zarlenga have created a perfect little slice of Rio right in their two-room restaurant. Chili and coconut permeate many of the terrific dishes. Appetizers include some of the best calamari around. Entrées (try the seafood) all include black bean soup and salad as well as herbed rice and lightly sautéed veggies. More adventurous eaters may want to try the Brazilian national dish, feijoadas. Be sure to save room for dessert. Impressive wines from Argentina and Chile; reservations highly recommended. Open Tues.–Sat. 5–10 P.M. **3611 Navajo St.; 303-480-1877.**

Sabor Latino—$$ to $$$

If you're in the mood for something a bit different, stop by Sabor Latino and taste some excellent South American cuisine. Dishes from Chile and the Caribbean are the best at this small north Denver restaurant. Try the tasty empanadas, a turnover filled with onions, meat and spices. Other dishes worth a try are the ceviche, Pastel de Choclo (corn pie) and the flan custard for dessert. The weekend paella-for-two special is absolutely delicious and includes a bottle of Chilean wine. Your hostess, Maria, is one of the most charming you'll find anywhere. Open Mon.–Sat. 11 A.M.–2:30 P.M. and 5–9 P.M.; closed Sun. **4340 W. 35th Ave.; 303-455-8664.**

Vegetarian / Health

The Harvest Restaurant and Bakery— $ to $$

What used to be a small Boulder restaurant, called the Good Earth, has changed names and flourishes both there and in Denver. Featuring vegetarian and meat dishes, the Harvest stresses freshness and will not serve food containing additives. Breakfast items include buttermilk pancakes and omelettes. You can't really go wrong for lunch, or dinner either—especially if you enjoy a homemade roll or muffin with a steaming bowl of soup or a fruit shake or smoothie for dessert. Service is fast and the prices are still reasonable. If you're dining alone, you may wish to eat at the community table, where single diners can enjoy a meal together. Open Tues.–Sat. 7 A.M.–10 P.M., Sun.–Mon. 7 A.M.–9 P.M. **430 S. Colorado Blvd.; 303-399-6652.**

WaterCourse—$ to $$

From a nondescript location one block south of the state capitol, the WaterCourse serves up topnotch vegetarian food, perhaps the best in town. Chef Dan Landes continues to put out creative vegetarian foods. Even meat-eaters find themselves setting aside their carnivorous cravings for a booth at WaterCourse to pound down a breakfast burrito, a flavorful veggie burger or a serving of the Thai peanut stir-fry. The young, friendly staff provides good service and conversation to the eclectic clientele that ranges from shaved-headed vegans to "suits" from the nearby state capitol. Open for breakfast and lunch Mon.–Fri. 6:30 A.M.–3 P.M., opens 8 A.M. Sat.–Sun. **206 E. 13th Ave.; 303-832-7313.**

Services

Visitor Information

Denver Metro Convention and Visitors Bureau—The visitor center's knowledgeable staff can answer all your questions about attractions, events, shopping, etc. Open in winter Mon.–Fri. 8 A.M.–5 P.M., Sat. 9 A.M.–1 P.M. Summer hours are Mon.–Fri. 8 A.M.–5 P.M. **1555 California St., Denver, CO 80202; 1-800-233-6837; 303-892-1112; www.denver.org.** There is also a center at **1668 Larimer** in the **Tabor Center; 303-892-1505.** Open Mon.–Fri. 8 A.M.–5 P.M.; a concierge desk is available in the Tabor Center Mon.–Fri. 10 A.M.–7 P.M. and Sat. noon–5 P.M.

Greater Denver Chamber of Commerce—1445 Market St., Denver, CO 80202;

303-534-8500; 303-892-1112; www. denver chamber.org.

Websites—For more information about the Mile High City, try the impressively broad **www.denver.citysearch.com, www.qwest dex.com, www.westword.com,** and **www. insidedenver.com.**

Transportation

Cultural Connection Trolley—This easy-to-spot red and green bus makes runs between some of Denver's best museums and attractions including the Denver Art Museum, Botanic Gardens, zoo and others. Buses run on the half hour; $3 for daily pass. 9:30 A.M.–5:30 P.M., May–Labor Day. **303-299-6000; www.rtd-denver.com.**

Metro Taxi Company—24-hour service; **303-333-3333.**

RTD (Denver metro area bus and light rail service)—For maps and route information: **303-299-6000; www.rtd-denver.com.**

Yellow Cab—24-hour service; **303-777-7777.**

Estes Park

Since its settlement over 130 years ago, the Estes Park area has captured the hearts and imaginations of naturalists, photographers and mountaineers from around the world. If you have been here, the logic is obvious—the setting is a classic. Located in the northern Front Range of the Colorado Rockies, the town of Estes Park commands a mountain view to the surrounding craggy peaks of the Continental Divide. Looming nearby is 14,255-foot Longs Peak, one of the most majestic and best-known mountains in the country. Estes Park serves as an eastern sentinel to the immensely popular Rocky Mountain National Park and a conduit for more than 3 million annual park visitors.

Most people coming to this area spend as much time as possible exploring the beautiful high alpine country of the national park and backcountry of nearby Roosevelt National Forest, returning to town in the evening for accommodations and meals. As you can imagine, Estes Park can become quite crowded in summer.

Yet, even at the height of the tourist season, after an early evening rain when the low clouds hang around Lumpy Ridge with its strange rock

formations, the valley takes on an eerie, almost primordial feel. If you have the option, get a better feel for Estes Park by visiting in the off-peak months of May and Sept., or in winter when it's blissfully quiet. In fall, sounds of bugling elk fill the valley; some of these fascinating giants even wander onto the golf course.

People have definitely made their presence known in this incredibly beautiful area of the state. Growth problems, such as building encroachment on the national park boundary and occasional air pollution concerns, have rallied many locals to take action and plan appropriately. With its growing self-awareness the area is coming to grips with the complementary role it plays to the wonders of Rocky Mountain National Park.

History

For centuries before Anglos arrived, Native Americans came to the Estes area from great distances. It's a place that was considered sacred to the Indians—artifacts indicate, at least by some

---

Getting There

From Denver head north on Interstate 25 for about 35 miles and turn west (left) on Hwy. 66. Proceed 16 miles to Lyons and then another 20 miles northwest on Hwy. 36 to Estes Park. The 71-mile drive takes about one and a half hours. An alternate route is via Boulder on Hwy. 36 (the Boulder Turnpike). From Boulder head north on Hwy. 36 to Lyons and then northwest to Estes Park. From the west, Estes Park can be reached via Trail Ridge Rd. (summer only), which crosses the Continental Divide from Grand Lake.

accounts, that Old Man Mountain, located on the west end of town, was a Vision Quest site for braves seeking good fortune for their people. In addition, Arapahos supposedly climbed Longs Peak to set traps for bald eagles. Arapahos laid claim to the territory, but when settlers arrived, Utes were occupying the area.

By the time Joel Estes and his family homesteaded the valley in 1860, most of the Indians were long gone. And visitors were few until 1864, when the challenge of climbing Longs Peak attracted William Byers, editor of the *Rocky Mountain News*. Byers and his two companions stayed with the Estes family while attempting to climb the peak. Byers was so enamored of the scenery, he wrote a story in the *News* and proclaimed the area Estes Park, in honor of his host. The Denver newspaperman returned in 1868 and conquered the peak with his companion, Maj. John Wesley Powell (the one-armed explorer of the Colorado River). Byers, of course, wrote another story about his adventure, which prompted many hunters, mountaineers and tourists to come themselves. Griffith Evans, the new owner of the Estes homestead, soon found himself operating a lucrative makeshift hostel. By 1871 Evans added cabins and opened a full-scale dude ranch.

The following year Lord Dunraven (the fourth Earl of Dunraven, Viscount of Mount Earl and Adare), an Irish nobleman and avid hunter, entered the scene. Impressed with the excellent hunting, Dunraven decided he liked the Estes Park area so much he had to own it—all of it. As a foreigner he was forbidden from homesteading, but Dunraven wasn't going to let little things like laws stand in his way. Through third-party purchases and other shifty methods he gained control of more than 15,000 acres for his private hunting sanctuary.

Though he tried, Dunraven couldn't keep the people away. Famous landscape artist Albert Bierstadt was captivated by the area, and his evocative paintings brought in even more people. As an increasing number of settlers streamed in and homesteading opportunities diminished, newly arrived ranchers and homesteaders began contesting the earl's land claims. Dunraven eventually had to give in, leasing large tracts of his beloved land to ranchers.

In 1905 the town of Estes Park was platted on John Cleave's land at the confluence of Fall River and the Big Thompson River. Cleave, echoing sentiments of many locals over the years, sold out and moved away, saying he "couldn't stand to see the danged place overrun by tenderfeet tourists."

At about the same time, a man of vision (and inventor of the Stanley Steamer), F. O. Stanley, arrived. He had been diagnosed with tuberculosis, but the dry mountain air seemed to cure him. In 1907 he went into partnership to buy Dunraven's remaining land and built the famous Stanley Hotel (see the Where to Stay section). The hotel opened in 1909 and was booked solid the entire first summer—partly because the inventor used his fleet of Stanley Steamer Mountain Wagons to bring his guests to the hotel from the railhead at Lyons. With his flowing white hair and beard, Stanley became known as the Grand Old Man of Estes Park. He made large contributions to the town and was instrumental in reintroducing herds of elk.

When Congress established Rocky Mountain National Park in 1915, Estes Park was well on its way to becoming a center for visitors to the area. Today Rocky Mountain National Park (see the Major Attractions section) is the most visited attraction in Colorado.

Major Attractions

Rocky Mountain National Park

Rocky Mountain National Park, which straddles the Continental Divide for 40 miles, is without question the showpiece of Colorado's public recreation lands. Each year millions of visitors make their way through the park to see some of the most spectacular high mountain scenery in the Rockies. Its eastern side is characterized by steep, glaciated valleys and cirque lakes, carved out by the ice floes that once dominated the surroundings. On the western side of the

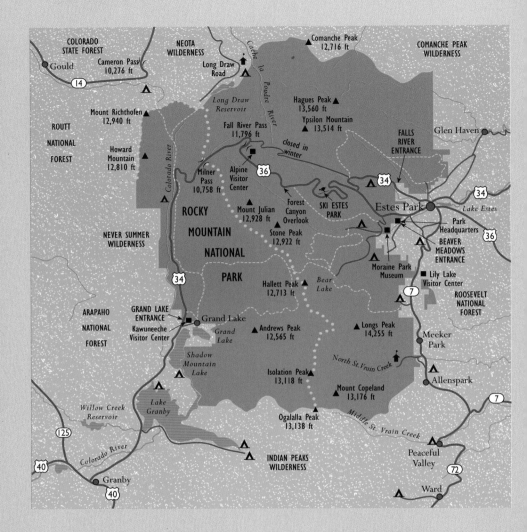

COLORADO
STATE FOREST

NEOTA
WILDERNESS

Comanche Peak
12,716 ft

COMANCHE PEAK
WILDERNESS

Gould
Cameron Pass
10,276 ft

14

Long Draw
Road

Long Draw
Reservoir

Hagues Peak
13,560 ft

Mount Richthofen
12,940 ft

Fall River Pass
11,796 ft

Ypsilon Mountain
13,514 ft

ROUTT

NATIONAL

FOREST

Howard
Mountain
12,810 ft

closed in
winter

FALLS
RIVER
ENTRANCE

Glen Haven

34

34

Milner
Pass
10,758 ft

Alpine
Visitor
Center

36

Forest
Canyon
Overlook

SKI ESTES
PARK

Estes Park

Lake Estes

36

Park
Headquarters

ROCKY

MOUNTAIN

Mount Julian
12,928 ft

Stone Peak
12,922 ft

BEAVER
MEADOWS
ENTRANCE

NEVER SUMMER
WILDERNESS

NATIONAL

Moraine Park
Museum

PARK

Hallett Peak
12,713 ft

Bear
Lake

7

Lily Lake
Visitor Center

34

ROOSEVELT
NATIONAL
FOREST

ARAPAHO

NATIONAL

FOREST

GRAND LAKE
ENTRANCE

Grand Lake

Kawuneeche
Visitor Center

Grand
Lake

Andrews Peak
12,565 ft

Longs Peak
14,255 ft

Meeker
Park

Shadow
Mountain
Lake

North St. Vrain Creek

Allenspark

Isolation Peak
13,118 ft

Mount Copeland
13,176 ft

7

Willow Creek
Reservoir

Lake
Granby

Ogalalla Peak
13,138 ft

Middle St. Vrain Creek

125

Colorado River

Peaceful
Valley

40

INDIAN PEAKS
WILDERNESS

72

Granby

Ward

40

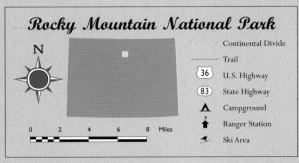

Rocky Mountain National Park

N

- - - - Continental Divide
- - - - - Trail

36   U.S. Highway

83   State Highway

△   Campground

⚑   Ranger Station

⛷   Ski Area

0   2   4   6   8   Miles

Exploring Rocky Mountain National Park's backcountry in winter. Photo by Dean Winstanley.

Continental Divide, the land is more gentle, with lush pine forests covering much of the terrain. But the park's 78 peaks over 12,000 feet make up the most dramatic feature. The loftiest of these is Longs Peak (14,255 feet), which dominates the Front Range skyline and is visible from more than 100 miles away. The park serves as a sanctuary for many species, including elk, deer, bears, bighorn sheep, mountain lions, otters and raptors such as bald and golden eagles, hawks and peregrine falcons.

Getting There

From the east, Rocky Mountain National Park can be reached via Hwy. 34 or Hwy. 36 from Estes Park. Once inside the park, Trail Ridge Rd. (summer only) crosses the Continental Divide 50 miles to Grand Lake on the Western Slope.

Park rangers estimate that 85 to 95 percent of the visitors to the park see it from the car window. The leisurely but dramatically beautiful drive over Trail Ridge Rd. is a must. For those who are looking for something a bit more active, multi-day backpack trips into the park's remote areas or an all-day hike up one of the many mountain peaks provide the challenge.

History

In the early 1900s a conservationist movement in Estes Park developed, spearheaded by naturalist and writer Enos Mills. Heavy impacts on the natural resources from individuals and businesses in what is now Rocky Mountain National Park galvanized a push to protect this uniquely beautiful area from further damage. Many preservationists were happy when the federal government set aside a large part of the land as a national forest, but others felt that wasn't enough. Another movement to create a national park began, despite opposition from Forest Service officials who thought they were the best public stewards. Some private landowners also posed opposition, fearing they would lose their property. On Jan. 26, 1915, President Woodrow Wilson ended all the debate by signing a bill creating Rocky Mountain National Park.

Controlled development of the park really started in 1920 when Fall River Rd. opened, helping visitors gain better access to the beautiful areas. By the 1950s the incredible popularity of the park began to work against it—overcrowding and serious damage to the vegetation (especially the high alpine tundra) were apparent. As a result of all this, protective restrictions were imposed, still leaving ample room for all visitors to enjoy the park. Today this beautiful area remains much as it was when Joel Estes first settled here in the 1860s. With proper management officials hope to keep it that way.

Visitor Information

If you have questions about the park or its regulations, stop in at one of the visitor centers. **Beaver Meadows Visitor Center** is located just inside the east boundary of the park on

Hwy. 36. Visitors entering the park from the west side at Grand Lake can stop in at **Kawuneeche Visitor Center** just inside the park boundary. You may also want to stop at the **Alpine Visitor Center,** located at the top of Trail Ridge Rd. Information on both the national park and adjacent Roosevelt National Forest is available at **Lily Lake Visitor Center,** 8 miles south of Estes Park on Hwy. 7. It's open Memorial Day to Labor Day. For additional information any time of year, contact **Rocky Mountain National Park Headquarters, Estes Park, CO 80517-8397; 970-586-1206; www.nps.gov/romo.** For information about the west side of the park, see the **Grand Lake** chapter.

RECREATION
Biking

Mountain Biking—Since off-road biking is not allowed in the park, the mountain bike trail possibilities are limited to the existing roads. For a challenging dirt road, see the Old Fall River Rd. write-up under the Scenic Drives section below.

Bicycle Touring—Touring on the roads in Rocky Mountain National Park provides some of the most spectacular high mountain scenery you'll find anywhere. There are quite a few challenging uphill stretches, so you should be in good physical shape for most of the rides. Most routes are heavily traveled by cars. **Bear Lake Rd.** is a strenuous 10-mile tour that climbs 1,500 feet. For information about the road, see the Scenic Drives section. **Trail Ridge Rd.,** the 50-mile road between Estes Park and Grand Lake, is one of the toughest and most rewarding bike tours in Colorado. It crosses over the Continental Divide at 12,183 feet and provides incredible high alpine scenery. If you pedal the entire distance, you'll probably be too tired to return the same day. Stay a night in Grand Lake and return the next day. See the Scenic Drives section for more information about Trail Ridge Rd.

Fishing

Successful fishing within Rocky Mountain National Park is fairly sporadic but still possible.

Some of the prime spots require hiking, but there are several lakes and streams alongside the roads. Some of the lakes have paved pathways around them to enable access for disabled anglers. It would be wise to pick up a copy of the park rules. One important rule allows only flies and lures; many stretches of water are catch-and-release only, with barbless hooks required. Of special note is the growing population of the greenback cutthroat trout, which must be released immediately if caught.

Big Thompson River—Surrounded by high peaks, this river ambles northeast through the park before flowing to the town of Estes Park and eventually onto the plains. On its upper reaches, you'll find mainly brook trout, with a few browns and rainbows thrown in for good measure. Most of the trout are fairly small, 8- to 10-inch fryers. From Estes Park drive west on Hwy. 36 to the Beaver Meadows Entrance Station. At the first intersection after the entrance, turn left (south) on Bear Lake Rd. After 1 mile turn right (west) onto Moraine Park Campground Rd., which follows the Big Thompson for 2.7 miles to the Fern Lake trailhead. You can either fish the water along the road or follow the rough trail up into the higher country.

Peacock Pool—Plan a day's outing for this combination hiking/fishing trip. Once you complete the 5-mile hike to this little lake, chances are you'll catch many smallish (8-inch) brook trout. The "pool" is filled by a splashing waterfall in a picture-perfect setting at the base of Longs Peak. The hike, beginning at the East Longs Peak trailhead, is not a cakewalk, so don't attempt it unless you're in pretty good shape. About 4 miles up the trail a spur leads to Peacock Pool (11,360 feet in elevation), offering tremendous views along the way. If you want to complete the hike to **Chasm Lake**—another 1.5 miles from Peacock Pool—you may be able to catch a large cutthroat in that lake's very deep water under the diamond face of Longs Peak. To get to the East Longs Peak trailhead from Estes Park, head 9.2 miles south on Hwy. 7 and turn right at the sign.

Sprague Lake—This shallow, picturesque lake at the east edge of the park yields many pan-sized brook trout. Because it's right next to the road and has a trail all the way around its shore, the lake is popular. To get there from Estes Park, drive west on Hwy. 36 to the Beaver Meadows Entrance Station. At the first intersection after the entrance, turn left (south) and continue on Bear Lake Rd. for about 6 miles.

Thunder Lake—Once again the fishing may not be spectacular, but the scenery makes up for it. Fishing here is reasonably good for rainbow and brook trout. For more information see the Thunder Lake/Wild Basin entry below, under the Hiking and Backpacking section.

West Rocky Mountain National Park—For information about fishing near the park's western boundary, see the Fishing section of the **Grand Lake** chapter.

Hiking and Backpacking

Getting into the backcountry is what Rocky Mountain National Park is all about. Most of the park is accessible only by hiking trails. Backcountry permits are required for any overnight stays. These permits, as well as maps and information, can be picked up at the **Backcountry Office** next to **Beaver Meadows Visitor Center** near Estes Park or at **Kawuneeche Visitor Center** near Grand Lake. Reserve your permit by writing the **Backcountry Office, Rocky Mountain National Park, Estes Park, CO 80517,** or by showing up in person. Reservations can be made between Mar. 1 and May 15 by calling **970-586-1242** or writing the Backcountry Office. No pets are allowed on trails, and in most places camping is allowed in designated areas only. **Sprague Lake Accessible Camp** is a back-country camping area accessible to wheelchairs; **970-586-1242.**

Bridal Veil Falls—Those who are not looking for a particularly steep and strenuous experience will enjoy this fantastic 6-mile round-trip hike with views south to Lumpy Ridge and a plethora of wildflowers in summer. Peregrine falcons and bighorn sheep can often be seen as well. Hikers are rewarded by beautiful 30-foot falls at the end of the trail. To reach the trailhead from Estes Park, head northwest on Devils Gulch Rd. toward Glen Haven. After about 4 miles, bear left on McGraw Ranch Rd., a dirt road marked with yellow gate poles. Proceed on the main branch of this road for 2.2 miles to the Cow Creek/North Boundary trailhead. Begin hiking up the Cow Creek Trail.

Dream Lake Trail—Heading west from Bear Lake, this trail climbs gently up to three lakes—Nymph, Dream and Emerald. It's a popular and easy hike that can be done in a couple of hours. The distances are short (a half-mile to Nymph, 1 mile to Dream and just under 2 miles to Emerald) and the scenery, dominated by Hallett Peak, is magnificent. To reach Bear Lake from the Beaver Meadows Entrance Station on Hwy. 34, head west about 2 miles and then south on Bear Lake Rd. for another 8 miles.

Fern Lake/Odessa Lake Trail—There are two routes into these lakes, but no matter which trail you take, the scenery is incredible. Perhaps the best starting point is from the trailhead at Bear Lake, which is 1,300 feet above Fern Lake and provides a downhill hike for most of the way. To find the trailhead at Bear Lake, walk up Flattop Trail for about 1.5 miles. At a trail junction you'll find a sign pointing the way to Fern and Odessa Lakes. From Bear Lake it's about 4.7 miles to Fern Lake. Along the way you'll pass over a saddle between Joe Mills and Notch-top Mountains. The trail, which hugs the mountainside, climbs up to 10,500 feet and affords magnificent views of surrounding peaks offset by deep valleys. From Fern Lake it's another 3.8 miles to the Fern Lake trailhead (located 2.7 miles west on Moraine Park from Bear Lake Rd.). If you have someone to pick you up (or take the shuttle bus in summer), you can start at one trailhead and finish at the other. For directioins to the Bear Lake trailhead, see the Dream Lake Trail write-up above.

Flattop Mountain/North Inlet Trail—If you feel like taking a long hike, you can follow this trail all the way (18.5 miles) to Grand Lake. From Bear Lake climb west about 2.5 miles to the summit of Flattop Mountain (12,324 feet). This mountain is aptly named, having the roomiest summit of any in the park. From there it's a relatively easy 16-mile, downhill hike southwest along North Inlet Trail through pine forests to Grand Lake. This hike (at least the hike to the summit of Flattop) is very popular in summer, so expect to see some other folks. After crossing over the Continental Divide and beginning your descent to Grand Lake, you'll be in pretty remote country until the last few miles. For directions to the Bear Lake trailhead, see the Dream Lake Trail write-up above.

Longs Peak—This peak has inspired poets, painters and assorted adventurers since explorers first sighted it in the mid-1800s. The challenge of reaching the summit is as exciting today as it was when the 14,255-foot peak was scaled in 1868 by William Byers and John Wesley Powell. It's not only the tallest and most dominant peak in the park, it's also the northernmost 14er in Colorado.

Following are two hikes up the peak. If you plan to climb Longs Peak, it's recommended that you start very early and try to be off the summit by noon to avoid the all-too-common afternoon lightning storms. Both hikes are considered difficult and are not recommended for novices or people with medical conditions. If you want to make it an overnighter, there are a few places to camp along the way, but remember that you need a camping permit.

North Longs Peak Trail is reached from the Glacier Gorge trailhead, just before reaching Bear Lake on Bear Lake Rd. It's the longer of the two routes, but it's also less crowded. Start hiking south on **Loch Vale Trail.** After a mile take the left fork and climb southeast for 5 miles until the trail joins East Longs Peak Trail at the 11,900-foot summit of Granite Pass. From there it's another 2.5 miles to the summit. The round trip takes about 17 hours. To reach the trailhead, drive up Bear Lake Rd. to Glacier Gorge Junction. The marked trailhead is on the left.

East Longs Peak Trail, by far the most popular route up the peak, starts at the Longs Peak

Hiking along the Narrows near the summit of Longs Peak. Photo by Dean Winstanley.

trailhead and climbs 8 miles and 4,850 vertical feet to the summit. The first 6 miles to the Boulderfield ascend through thick pine forests and aspens to treeline, where fantastic views of the area are possible, especially of Longs Peak's magnificent 1,675-foot east face. From the Boulderfield the trail climbs to the Keyhole, where the route traverses a steep ledge system across the west face. From there the trail heads up the Trough, then across a dizzying ledge system called the Narrows and finally up the Homestretch to the summit. The route from the Keyhole to the summit is marked with yellow and red bull's-eyes. The round trip from the ranger station at the trailhead takes about 14 hours. To get to the trailhead from Estes Park, head south 9.2 miles on Hwy. 7 to the turnoff for Longs Peak Campground. Turn right and drive about a mile to the trailhead parking lot.

Thunder Lake/Wild Basin—The 7-mile hike to Thunder Lake can be a moderately difficult outing if you decide to do it all in one day. The main trail follows the St. Vrain River, where you'll be treated to lots of waterfalls and cascades. The upper part of the trail moves through the trees to 10,500 feet, breaking out onto promontories overlooking the valley and the Continental Divide—this scenery is all post-card material. Try fishing in the lake and the stream below it for rainbow and brook trout in the 10-inch range.

The hike to Thunder Lake takes 4 to 5 hours, and the return trip takes about 3 and a half hours. To get to the trailhead, take Hwy. 7 south from Estes Park about 13 miles. Turn right and drive a quarter-mile to Wild Basin Lodge. Just past the lodge, turn right and go through the entrance station. The trailhead is 2 miles ahead.

Tonahutu Creek—See the Hiking and Back-packing section of the **Grand Lake** chapter.

Horseback Riding

High Country Stables—Two-hour, half-day and all-day rides are available at High Country's two locations within the park. Both are located close to Estes Park, at Sprague Lake and at Moraine Park. Numbers change from year to year so call **Park Information** at **970-586-1206.**

Museums

Moraine Park Museum—Located in the historic Moraine Park Lodge with great views out on the park, this museum is worth a stop. The main attractions are the creative hands-on inter-active displays, describing the glaciation and other geologic history of the park. Kids love it. Open late Apr.–mid-Oct. Located 2.5 miles southwest of Beaver Meadows Visitor Center on the Bear Lake Rd.

Scenic Drives

Bear Lake Road—From the Beaver Meadows Entrance Station, it's a 10-mile drive up this heavily traveled, winding road to Bear Lake at 9,475 feet. Along the way you'll have a chance to see deer, elk and other wildlife as well as views of the surrounding peaks. If you just want

A dramatic view looking down from Trail Ridge Road, America's highest continually paved road, which crosses the Continental Divide at 12,183 feet. Photo by Wendy Newman.

to look at the scenery, take one of the shuttle buses, which leave from Glacier Basin Camp-ground about halfway up the road. At the end of the road, Bear Lake Trail takes you a couple hundred yards to the pine-clad shores of the lake. Chances are you've seen a picture of the often-photographed Bear Lake with its unforgettable mountain backdrop.

Old Fall River Road—This was the first auto route over the Continental Divide in this part of the state, and it played a big part in the park's tourist boom of the early 1920s. The first 2 miles are paved and open to two-way traffic. After that, it's a narrow, one-way gravel road (uphill only!), which climbs 9 miles west before joining Trail Ridge Rd. at the 11,796-foot Fall River Pass along the Continental Divide. The route is described by park officials as a "motor nature trail," so stop often to enjoy the scenery as the terrain turns from subalpine forest to alpine tundra. The route doesn't offer the spectacular vistas of Trail Ridge Rd. but does provide shelter from the harsh wind and closer contact with the wilderness. A very popular loop trip is to drive up Old Fall River Rd. and return on Trail Ridge Rd. (both roads closed in winter). To reach Old Fall River Rd. from Estes Park, drive west on Hwy. 34 to the Fall River Entrance Station. Proceed 2 miles from the entrance and turn right onto Old Fall River Rd. Along the way be sure to stop and investigate the enormous alluvial fan and its scattered debris that resulted from the Lawn Lake flood in 1982. Trailers and RVs over 25 feet long are prohibited from driving the road due to narrow switchbacks.

Trail Ridge Road (Hwy. 34)—No question about it, a drive over Trail Ridge Rd. is a must for any visitor to the park. You'll see an incredible amount of scenery in a short span of time. The narrow, winding 50-mile ribbon of asphalt stretching between Estes Park and Grand Lake is the highest continuous paved highway in the United States. More than 200 men braved the elements to build Trail Ridge Rd., which opened in 1932. The landscape transition along the way is remarkable. Heading west the road climbs through meadows, spectacular mountain valleys and over the Continental Divide on a 13-mile stretch of alpine tundra that's similar to the Arctic. Near the summit on the east side, Forest Canyon Overlook provides dramatic bird's-eye views down on a classic glaciated U-shaped valley and glacial cirque lakes. Forest Canyon Lakes are home to some of the park's black bears. From the 12,183-foot summit, the road drops down the Western Slope of the Continental Divide along the North Fork of the Colorado River through Kawuneeche Valley. Along the drive are numerous pullouts and informational signs, which provide excellent information about the changing ecosystems. Near the top you'll find the **Alpine Visitor Center** and the Trail Ridge Store, **970-586-9308.** The center has exhibits on this fragile tundra environment; knowledgeable rangers are on duty to answer your questions. Plan on spending 3 to 4 hours on the way to Grand Lake. The road is usually open from late-May to mid-Oct., depending on snow conditions. To get to Trail Ridge Rd. (Hwy. 34), enter the park at either Beaver Meadows or Fall River and follow the signs.

Skiing (Cross-Country)

The best cross-country skiing in the Estes Park area is in the national park. Due to inconsistent and blowing snow, ski conditions change quickly in this area. Before heading out on a backcountry trip, be sure to check avalanche conditions at one of the visitor centers. The rangers can also give you a number of good trail ideas.

Novices will enjoy the easy trails around **Glacier Basin Campground.** The main trail leaves the campground and heads southwest on easy terrain for 1 mile to **Sprague Lake.** There are also a multitude of trails in and around the campground. Glacier Basin Campground is located about 5 miles up Bear Lake Rd. Skiers must park on the west side of the road and walk across to the east side to begin skiing.

Black Lake offers a moderately difficult 9.5-mile round trip that takes you into some of the most spectacular country in the park. The trip starts at the Glacier Gorge Junction parking lot and follows the signs southwest toward Alberta Falls and the Loch. Just past the intersection of Icy Brook and Glacier Creek, turn south and follow Glacier Creek to Mills Lake. After passing Mills and Jewel Lakes, continue along the creek through the forested drainage. When you break out of the trees, proceed up the open slope to Black Lake. The view from the lake looks out to Longs Peak to the east, McHenrys Peak to the west and Chiefs Head Peak to the south. This trail is for intermediate to advanced skiers. Glacier Gorge Junction parking lot is located about 9 miles up Bear Lake Rd.

For rentals and information see the Cross-Country Skiing and Snowshoeing entry under the Outdoor Activities section.

Snowshoeing

This is perhaps the best way to get around the park in wintertime because you don't have to rely on perfect snow conditions. If trail conditions are marginal, attach a pair of light, aluminum snowshoes to your pack and set off on a day hike. When needed, just strap on the shoes. It's a fantastic way to get into the backcountry and away from the crowds.

Although just about any area of the park can be reached by snowshoes in winter (avalanche conditions permitting), the bulk of trail activity occurs in the **Bear Lake** area. At 9,500 feet, Bear Lake lies about 10 miles from the main park entrance at Beaver Meadows. The park keeps the road plowed throughout the winter. From Bear Lake, a number of short, 1-mile-or-less trails lead to **Dream** and **Nymph Lakes,** as well as other destinations. From the trailhead at Glacier Gorge parking lot about 8.5 miles up Bear Lake Rd., trips up to **Loch Vale** (2.3 miles) and **Black Lake** (5 miles) provide terrific scenery and a bit more challenge.

No matter which trail you choose, your best bet is to check with the rangers at the **Beaver Meadows Visitor Center,** just inside the park; open daily 8 A.M.–5 P.M. They can provide trail ideas, maps, snow conditions and other valuable information. The park also offers ranger-led snowshoe tours lasting from 2 hours to a half day. Call ahead for dates and times; **970-586-1223.**

At least a half dozen places in Estes Park rent snowshoes and poles. **Outdoor World,** open daily at **156 E. Elkhorn Ave.,** is a safe bet; **970-586-2114.** Another place to try is **Colorado Wilderness Sports,** at **358 E. Elkhorn Ave.; 970-586-6548.**

Camping

During the summer, reservations for **Moraine Park** and **Glacier Basin Campgrounds** can be made by calling **1-800-365-CAMP.** The other campgrounds are on a first-come, first-served basis. No hookups or showers are available at campgrounds in the park. All charge a fee. Check the park newspaper for scheduled campfire programs and guided nature walks. Camping is also available in the backcountry (see Hiking and Backpacking in this section for more information).

Aspenglen Campground (54 sites, closed in winter) is located 5 miles west of Estes Park off Hwy. 34 just past the Fall River entrance to the park. **Glacier Basin Campground** (150 sites, closed in winter) is located 9 miles west of Estes Park. Enter the park on Hwy. 36 and turn south on Bear Lake Rd. **Longs Peak Campground** (26 sites, open year-round) is set up for tents only. It's located at the East Longs Peak trailhead. To get there from Estes Park, drive south on Hwy. 7 for 9.2 miles and turn right (west) to the Longs Peak Ranger Station. Follow the road 1 mile to the campground. **Moraine Park Campground** (247 sites, open year-round) is located 3 miles southwest of Beaver Meadows Visitor Center. Drive west into the park, turn left on Bear Lake Rd. and proceed 1.3 miles to Moraine Park Campground Rd. Turn right and proceed to the campground. **Timber Creek Campground** (100 sites, open year-round) is located 7 miles inside the west entrance to the park near Grand Lake.

Festivals and Events

Rooftop Rodeo and Western Week

mid-July Estes Park celebrates its western heritage with the Rooftop Rodeo and Western Week. The main draw is the rodeo, which has cowboys competing for various titles. Other events include a parade, a mountain man rendezvous and an arts and crafts fair. This annual rodeo has been going on for more than 60 years, so you can be assured there will always be one next year. For information call **1-800-44-ESTES.**

Rocky Grass Festival (Lyons)

late July Time-traveling backward into the tie-dyed haze of the 1960s becomes easy at this terrific annual festival, even if the participants seem to sport more gray hair each year. Next to the St. Vrain River, a permanent stage brings nationally acclaimed bluegrass musicians together for three days of jamming in a superb outdoor setting. A veritable marketplace springs up with international food sellers and arts and crafts.

There's no better place to buy a toe ring, a microbrew or a veggie wrap. Because this show is limited to 3,500, it sells out earlier each year. **303-823-0848; www.bluegrass.com.**

Longs Peak Scottish-Irish Festival

mid-Sept. Long, long ago in Scotland, clan members competed in curious contests of strength and stamina to prove themselves as capable soldiers. The ways of the Celts have crossed the Atlantic, and now this annual event in Estes Park provides a weekend of fun and sport. The traditional sporting events include the hammer throw and the caber toss—a caber, by the way, is a tree trunk, averaging 19 feet in length and 120 pounds. Other activities include Scottish bagpipe and drum-major competitions, a highland dance, a parade and sheepdog contests. The highlight of the celebration is the Tattoo, a performance of light and sound that has evolved over 300 years. This festival draws people from all over Colorado and the Rocky Mountain region. Call **1-800-90-ESTES** or **1-800-44-ESTES; www. scotfest.com.**

Outdoor Activities

Biking

Estes Park offers a number of on- and off-road opportunities, and the local highways offer scenic routes (provided you don't mind cars). Dirt roads and trails in Roosevelt National Forest make for some enjoyable rides. For ideas, see the Four-Wheel-Drive Trips and Main Attractions sections. Opportunities in Rocky Mountain National Park are limited to roadways.

Rentals and Information

For information and maps for rides in **Roosevelt National Forest,** contact their office in Fort Collins at **1311 S. College; 970-498-2770; www.fs.fed.us/arnf.** Or try the Estes Park office at **970-586-3440. Colorado Bicycling Adventures** can set you up with all the equipment you'll need to take off and do some exploring. Guided mountain bike tours available

as well. **184 E. Elkhorn Ave., Estes Park, CO 80517; 970-586-4241; www.colorado bicycling.com.** Rentals are also available at **Estes Park Mountain Shop, 358 E. Elkhorn Ave.; 970-586-6548.**

Fishing

Several opportunities for angling lie just outside of Estes Park. If you are interested in fishing within Rocky Mountain National Park, see the Major Attractions section. The local fishing authority is Scot Ritchie at **Scot's Sporting Goods.** He can direct you to the hot spots, provide lessons and guided trips as well as set you up with tackle. Located 1.5 miles west of Estes Park on Hwy. 36 at **870 Moraine Ave., Estes Park, CO 80517; 970-586-2877.**

Big Thompson River

After gaining strength in Rocky Mountain National Park, the Big Thompson River flows through spectacular Big Thompson Canyon on its way to the plains. There is a good-quality section of river (flies and lures only) starting about 5 miles downstream from Lake Estes. The best spot on this stretch is 8 miles downstream from the lake, just below a place called Grandpa's Retreat. To help nurture the primarily pan-sized rainbow and brown trout that call this stretch home, the Colorado Division of Wildlife and the National Forest Service have created several deep holes. The Big Thompson lies parallel to Hwy. 34 for much of its length, and small parking areas are located along the shoulder. This good stretch of water extends 5 to 9 miles down a heavily traveled, steep-walled canyon. The Forest Service recently developed and installed a barrier-free fishing ramp for wheelchairs. It's hard to visualize today, but in 1976 a disastrous flood roared through this area, killing many people.

Lake Estes

Located on the east side of town, between Hwys. 34 and 36, Lake Estes offers an easy-to-get-to spot for anglers who may not have time to search out more secluded areas. The Colorado Division of Wildlife regularly stocks the lake with 8- to 12-inch rainbows. Though the fishing pressure is heavy, an occasional lunker-sized German brown is caught. For best results use worms or salmon eggs on No. 8 and No. 10 hooks. Mepps lures at a quarter of an ounce or less are also effective. The **Lake Estes Marina** sells fishing tackle and rents boats by the hour. **1770 E. Big Thompson Ave.; 970-586-2011.**

Marys Lake

Marys Lake is like Lake Estes in almost every way except for its location. Try fishing the lake's inlet where the fish tend to congregate and feed. Take Hwy. 36 to the west end of Estes Park to Marys Lake Rd. (it's the only stoplight). Turn left and drive 1.5 miles to the small lake.

Four-Wheel-Drive Trips

For more information and maps contact the **Roosevelt National Forest** at 1311 S. College, Fort Collins, CO 80524; 970-498-1375; www.fs.fed.us/arnf. Or try the Estes Park office at **970-586-3440.**

Johnny Park Road

This drive offers great views of Big Elk Meadows, North St. Vrain Creek drainage, Mt. Meeker and Longs Peak. From Estes Park, head 10 miles south on Hwy. 7 and turn left onto Big Owl Rd. (County Rd. 82). Continue to the junction with Johnny Park Rd. (Forest Rd. 118). The road eventually comes out at Hwy. 36 just north of Pinewood Springs.

Pierson Park Road

This 10-mile drive can be taken in a loop from Estes Park. Drive 10 miles south on Hwy. 7 and turn left into the Meeker Park area. After 1.5 miles take another left onto Twin Sisters Rd. Look for the Pierson Park sign. This road takes you through a beautiful valley bordered by Twin Sisters Peaks to the west and House Rock, Pierson Mountain and Lion Head to the east.

Pole Hill Road

From Estes Park drive 3 miles southeast on Hwy. 36 to the top of Park Hill. Turn left onto

Pole Hill Rd. (Forest Rd. 122) at the sign for Ravencrest Chalet. Drive another mile and enter Roosevelt National Forest. There are numerous loop options with a variety of terrain in this area. One short circle tour starts when you take the first left after entering the national forest. You'll pass an observation platform in this area referred to as the Notch. The platform affords excellent views of the Estes Valley, the Mummy Range to the north and Flattop Mountain and Hallett Peak west along the Continental Divide.

Tours

American Wilderness Tours—With six-wheeled trucks that look like they could go anywhere, these folks will take you to spots you may never see otherwise. Open daily during the summer season only. **875 Moraine Ave., Estes Park, CO 80517; 970-586-4237; www.estesparkco.com.**

Golf

Estes Park Golf Club

Low scores are hard to come by on this difficult mountain course, although it's only 6,000 yards long. Grainy greens make putting a real challenge. Be sure to keep in mind the location of Fish Creek while putting—the ball will invariably break that direction. The views are tremendous. In early fall, elk wander onto the course and even on the greens, where their divots may need some attention. Located about 2 miles south of downtown Estes Park on Hwy. 7. **1080 S. St. Vrain Ave., Estes Park, CO 80517; 970-586-8146.**

Lake Estes Executive Course

This relatively flat nine-hole course provides views of the mountains to the west and Twin Owls to the north. Open all year, this challenging course requires complete concentration: water is a big factor, including the par-3 ninth hole, which crosses over the Big Thompson River. Next to Lake Estes on Hwy. 34. **E. 690 Big Thompson Ave., Estes Park, CO 80517; 970-586-8176.**

Hiking and Backpacking

Granted, the scenery from Estes Park is hard to beat, but you owe it to yourself to get out on a trail and escape the crowds, to see elk munching grass in an alpine meadow or the burst of wildflowers as you round a corner. Trails in **Rocky Mountain National Park** (see the Major Attractions section) and nearby **Roosevelt National Forest** cover the spectrum from easy day hikes to challenging high alpine backpacking trips. The Roosevelt National Forest headquarters can provide maps and more information about hiking opportunities in the area; **1311 S. College, Fort Collins, CO 80524; 970-498-1375; www.fs.fed.us/arnf.** Their local number is **970-586-3440.**

For topographic maps, equipment and information, talk with the folks at **Estes Park Mountain Shop** at **358 E. Elkhorn Ave., Estes Park, CO 80517; 970-586-6548.**

Crosier Mountain Trail

This moderately difficult 8-mile round-trip hike starts at 7,200 feet and ends at the 9,250-foot summit of Crosier Mountain. From the summit and various vantage points along the trail, you'll have fantastic views of the Continental Divide to the west in Rocky Mountain National Park. On your way to the summit you'll pass through lush aspen groves and meadows with ruins of settlers' homesteads. Keep an eye out for mule deer and take the time to enjoy the abundant and beautiful wildflowers. To get to the trailhead from Estes Park, take Devil's Gulch Rd. northeast about 8 miles (about a mile beyond Glen Haven). There will be a large gravel cut on the right (south) side of the road. Pull in and park. The trailhead is just up the hill from a gate (please close).

Lily Mountain Trail

Lily Mountain is a fairly easy 1.5-mile hike near Estes Park. The trail starts at 8,800 feet, climbing 986 vertical feet to the summit. Along the way you'll have numerous opportunities for incredible views down to the Estes Valley. From the summit enjoy the panorama of the Mummy Range to the northwest, Longs Peak to the south

and the Continental Divide to the west. Many boulders near the top provide challenging scrambling, if you like that kind of thing. The well-marked trail makes an ideal half-day trip. To reach the trailhead from Estes Park, take Hwy. 7 about 6 miles south. Just before mile-marker 6 there is a small turnoff on the right and a parking area by the trailhead sign.

Lion Gulch Trail

This fairly easy trail starts at 7,360 feet and climbs 1,000 feet, taking you into Homestead Meadows, where remains of homesteaders' ranches dating back to 1889 dot the valley floor. Some ranch houses, corrals, outhouses and other log buildings are still standing. The trails that crisscross the area are readily accessible after you've made the 2.5-mile trip to the meadows on Lion Gulch Trail. You can easily spend an entire day exploring the ruins and perhaps pondering what it would have been like to live in these buildings in the early days. The area is an excellent spot for a picnic and the views won't disappoint you. To reach the trailhead from Estes Park, head southeast on Hwy. 36 to mile-marker 8. The trailhead is on the right side of the road.

Rocky Mountain National Park

See the Major Attractions section.

Horseback Riding

Aspen Lodge Livery

Enjoy open country rides on a 3,000-acre ranch and trips into Rocky Mountain National Park and the Roosevelt National Forest. Riding lessons, breakfast and dinner rides, among other activities, are also offered. **970-586-8133.**

Elkhorn Stables

Located just west of downtown, they specialize in breakfast steak-fry rides. Reservations requested. **650 W. Elkhorn Ave.; 970-586-5225.**

High Country Stables

See the Horseback Riding entry in the Main Attractions section.

Sombrero Ranch Riding Stables

Offers 1- and 2-hour rides, breakfast and dinner trips and pack trips. Only a couple of miles east of Estes Park on Hwy. 34. **970-586-4577.**

Llama Trekking

Keno's Llama and Guest Ranch

Keno's offers llama hikes to the summit of Teddy's Teeth for a great view. Not only will you be treated to exotic companionship, but you'll learn about the history and the flora and fauna of the Estes Park area. Mainly geared for lunch hikes. Call ahead for reservations. **P.O. Box 2385, Estes Park, CO 80517; 970-586-5994.**

Skiing

CROSS-COUNTRY SKIING AND SNOWSHOEING

See the Skiing (Cross-Country) and Snow-shoeing entries in the Main Attractions section.

Rentals and Information

Colorado Mountain School—The school can supply any equipment you need. The people there also lead backcountry tours and offer snow courses. **351 Moraine Ave., Estes Park, CO 80517; 970-586-5758; www.cmschool.com. Estes Park Mountain Shop**—In addition to equipment and information, this shop offers guided backcountry tours. **358 E. Elkhorn Ave., Estes Park, CO 80517; 970-586-6548.**

Seeing and Doing

Museums and Galleries

Estes Park Area Historical Museum

Explore the heritage of Estes Park and the surrounding area at this local museum. Exhibits include a shiny Stanley Steamer automobile and numerous smaller displays describing the noteworthy people who settled Estes Park. Of note is the photo of the Joel Estes family taken in 1859 showing Estes and 6 of his 13 kids. Out in

back next to an old homestead cabin is the original Park Headquarters building, which houses a changing exhibit. Admission fee charged. Open Mon.–Sat. 10 A.M.–5 P.M., Sun. 1–5 P.M., May–Oct. Check for winter hours. **200 4th St. (at Hwy. 36), Estes Park, CO 80517; 970-586-6256; www.estesnet.com/museum.**

MacGregor Ranch Museum

This historic ranch museum contains ranch equipment, household items from the years 1870 to 1950 and more than 50 paintings by western artists. Check out the collection of antiques, china and silver. Marked walking trails wind around the ranch property. Admission is free. Open Tues.–Sat. 11 A.M.–5 P.M., Memorial Day–Labor Day. Located half a mile north of Estes Park on Devil's Gulch Rd. at **180 MacGregor Ln., Estes Park, CO 80517; 970-586-3749.**

Moraine Park Museum

See museums in the Major Attracations section.

Nightlife

Lonigan's Saloon

Although there are several places in Estes Park that offer live music on weekends, the owners of Lonigan's recruit some of the best jazz, blues and rock and roll bands from all over the state. Dark and smoky, this venerable bar has been around for a very long time. Swing by their location at **110 W. Elkhorn Ave., 970-586-4366.**

Stanley Hotel Fine Arts Concert Series

The Stanley presents a year-round series of theater and fine arts performances in a great setting. See the Where to Stay section for more information on this historic hotel. **333 Wonderview Ave.; 1-800-976-1377; 970-586-3371.**

Scenic Drives

Lyons Loop

After you've driven across Trail Ridge Rd., other scenic drives pale in comparison. Even so, if you

The serene, contemplative setting for St. Malo in Allenspark, near Estes Park. Photo by Wendy Newman.

are interested in a beautiful 60-mile loop trip from Estes Park, consider this drive to Lyons and back. There are two fine restaurants along the way—the **Fawn Brook Inn** in the town of Allenspark and **La Chaumière** in the community of Pinewood Springs (see the Where to Eat section). You may want to start out in the glow of late afternoon and stop for dinner as darkness descends.

The scenery is equally spectacular going either direction on the loop, but you'll start out south on Hwy. 7 under the craggy summits of Battle Mountain, Mt. Meeker, Longs Peak and Horsetooth Peak. By far the most impressive are 14,255-foot Longs Peak and 13,911-foot Mt. Meeker. You'll pass the Twin Sisters and a variety of lower peaks that lie to the east. After Allenspark, Hwy. 7 takes an eastern tack and enters a canyon with steep rock walls. The South St. Vrain Creek will be your traveling companion along this part of the drive. More spectacular scenery is in store as you hit Lyons and take Hwy. 36 back to Estes Park.

A highly recommended option, especially in autumn, is located to the south of Allenspark: the Peak to Peak Highway (now a designated Scenic and Historic Byway). To link up with this scenic highway, turn right (south) on Hwy. 72, 4 miles east of Allenspark. For detailed information see the Scenic Drives section of the **Boulder** chapter.

Old Fall River Road

See the Major Attractions section.

Trail Ridge Road

Absolutely don't miss this one! Closed in winter. See the Major Attractions section.

Tramway

Aerial Tramway

This tram will take you to the summit of 8,896-foot Prospect Mountain, which is virtually surrounded by the town of Estes Park. From the top you'll have great views of Longs Peak and the Continental Divide. Souvenir shop and a snack bar available while you are captive atop the mountain. Fee charged. Open mid-May–mid-Sept. **420**

E. Riverside Dr., Estes Park, CO 80517; 970-586-3675.

Where to Stay

Accommodations

Estes Park sports a multitude of lodging choices, ranging from the historic Stanley Hotel to a Holiday Inn and right down to the most rustic of log cabins. Bed and breakfast choices in Estes are staggering—honeymooners, anniversary couples and others flock here regularly just for this reason. The **Estes Park Chamber Resort Association** is very helpful in narrowing down the lodging choices for you; **1-800-44-ESTES; 970-586-4431; www.estesparkresort.com.** Here are a few that have something special going for them:

Wind River Ranch—$$$$

Owners Rob and Jere Irvin have worked hard to preserve the history of this 110-acre ranch homesteaded in 1876. This is a place where you can get away from the crowds and enjoy the stunning scenery in an unstructured, relaxed atmosphere. Take in the views of Longs Peak and Mt. Meeker from atop a trail-wise horse or from the ranch's heated pool and hot tub. Log cabins create a rustic ambience without neglecting the modern comforts. The comfortable main lodge room, with its large stone fireplace, beamed ceilings and wall-lined bookshelves, is a great place to relax and chat with other guests. Full meals included in the price. Minimum stay of three days. Open from June through Sept. 10. The ranch is located 7 miles south of Estes Park on Hwy. 7 at **5770 Hwy. 7, Estes Park, CO 80517; 1-800-523-4212; 970-586-4212; www.windriverranch.com.**

The Aspen Lodge—$$$ to $$$$

This fine four-season guest ranch and convention center offers comfortable cabin or modern western-style lodge accommodations as well as terrific views out to Longs Peak. And the facilities are perfectly suited to folks who are looking for seemingly endless activities. Choose from horseback riding, swimming, hiking, tennis and children's programs in summer; wintertime features cross-country skiing and sleigh rides. Enjoy the athletic club facilities and hot tub any time of year. Meals included if you wish. Located 8 miles south of Estes Park on Hwy. 7 at **6120 Hwy. 7, Longs Peak Rt., Estes Park, CO 80517; 1-800- 332-MTNS; 970-586-8133; www.aspenlodge.com.**

Glacier Lodge—$$$ to $$$$

Twenty-eight cabins at this resort are nestled along the banks of the Big Thompson River— some are so close to the river you can fish from their front porches. Many of the cabins have fireplaces and all are equipped with full kitchens. Other cabins are located up on the hill; groups can stay in a lodge room. Glacier Lodge lives up to its western atmosphere, offering horseback rides, fishing and western cookouts. There is also a heated swimming pool. Kids love the Soda Saloon, where they can meet others of the same age. Minimum four-day stay in summer; closed in winter. **2166 Hwy. 66, Estes Park, CO 80517; 1-800-523-3920; 970-586-4401; www.glacierlodge.com.**

RiverSong Bed and Breakfast Inn— $$$ to $$$$

Situated on 27 wooded acres alongside the Big Thompson River, the RiverSong is truly an excellent place to get away with someone special. In addition to stunning views from the living room up to the Continental Divide and Hallet Peak, the owners, Gary and Sue Mansfield, really make guests feel at home. And Gary is a wealth of information on area hiking trails, flora and fauna. Take a walk on one of the many hiking paths on the property. Retire to a room decorated with antique furniture, or perhaps one with a private sauna and a huge sunken bathtub. Consider staying in the Cowboy's Delight—a large rustic room in the carriage house with its own deck, wood-burning stove and queen-size four-poster bed. One room even has a unique shower that resembles a waterfall.

Delicious, full breakfasts are included. Reservations are essential. **P.O. Box 1910, Estes Park, CO 80517; 970-586-4666; www.romantic riversong.com.**

The Stanley Hotel—$$$ to $$$$

At its grand opening in 1909, this venerable hotel, built by inventor F. O. Stanley, was said to rival anything of its size in the world. Guests were transported by Stanley Steamer from the railhead in Lyons and arrived to ornate decor, a golf course, stables and other luxurious features—spectacular accommodations for the time. At its ideal hilltop perch, the hotel is now listed on the National Register of Historic Places. Over the years the hotel has played host to many notables, including Stephen King, who drew upon its ambience and history for the setting of his horror classic *The Shining.*

Today, despite numerous ownership changes and financial difficulties, the Stanley still attracts guests to its mixed bag of room styles and price ranges. Wherever possible, the rooms have been completely redone with original furnishings—some with canopied, four-poster beds and claw-foot bathtubs. The corner rooms provide magnificent views of the mountains and town. Dine in the MacGregor Room and Dunraven Grille. Be sure to ask about the evening and Sun. afternoon concert series. Two-night minimum stay on summer weekends. **333 Wonderview Ave., P.O. Box 1767, Estes Park, CO 80517; 1-800-976-1377; 970-586-3371; www.stanley hotel.com.**

Taharaa Mountain Lodge—$$$ to $$$$

This luxurious bed and breakfast will spoil your soul with its enormous fireplace, high log-beam ceilings and overall cozy mountain lodge atmosphere. Enjoy a complimentary cocktail and gaze at the surrounding mountains from your private deck (some of the most spectacular views in the area), or relax in the outdoor spa. Ken and Diane Harlan take turns preparing breakfast and you can rest assured it's filling and delicious. The lodge and its 3 suites and 9 lodge rooms contain the best traits and treasures from the couple's world travels. Two-night minimum stay during summer and fall. **3110 S. Hwy. 7, P.O. Box 2586, Estes Park, CO 80517; 1-800-597-0098; 970-577-0098; www. tahaara.com.**

YMCA of the Rockies (Estes Park Center)— $$ to $$$$

This resort, sprawling over 860 forested acres, continues to provide a wonderful setting for group meetings, reunions and generally exceptional memories for families who want to spend some time together. Children and adults alike can choose from a variety of scheduled activities—drop off the kids for swimming, roller skating, basketball, tennis, horseshoes, volleyball, miniature golf, horseback riding and hay-rides, to name just a few. In winter there's always ice skating, snowshoeing and cross-country skiing. A rental shop can take care of all your equipment needs. Also available at this "town" are a church, restaurant, grocery store, library, museum and gift shop.

Most of the 220 cabins have fireplaces and all have refrigerators, stoves, telephones and at least one full bedroom. Some 565 lodge rooms, catering primarily to groups, offer motel-style accommodations. Low-priced YMCA temporary memberships are granted for the duration of your stay. Book far in advance! **Estes Park Center/ YMCA, 2515 Tunnel Rd., Estes Park, CO 80511-2550; 970-586-3341;** Denver metro area **303-448-1616; www.ymcarockies.org.**

Cascade Cottages—$$ to $$$

These small, spartan cabins, located on 40 acres along Fall River, lie just inside the park and are a great option for those who want to escape the crowds and high prices of Estes. Some of the 15 cabins were built back in the 1920s and have been in the Davis family for over 50 years. All units have heat, bath and kitchen facilities. Open Memorial Day–Labor Day. Most cabins are reserved a year in advance. Summer address is **Fall River Rd., Estes Park, CO 80517.**

Wintertime contact is **P.O. Box 781070, Wichita, KS 67278; 316-687-6126.**

Other Lodging

Couples looking for nice, quiet getaways will appreciate **The Anniversary Inn ($$$ to $$$$).** This quaint log home, built in 1890, offers three rooms with private baths and a Sweethearts Cottage with a fireplace and private whirlpool bath. Enjoy a leisurely breakfast on the enclosed veranda while looking out the windows at deer that make their way onto the wooded property in early morning. **1060 Marys Lake Rd., Moraine Rt., Estes Park, CO 80517; 970-586-6200.** Or try a relaxing stay in one of the four rooms at the **Black Dog Inn Bed and Breakfast ($$$ to $$$$).** Rooms include antiques, with other features varying from fireplaces to a hot tub on the Mummy Mt. Room's deck. Breakfasts are a highlight. **650 S. St. Vrain Ave., P.O. Box 4659, Estes Park, CO 80517; 970-586-0374; www.blackdoginn.com.** For a family getaway try the **Creekside Suites ($$$ to $$$$)** in a cozy spot along Fall River. Enjoy the fully equipped one- or two-bedroom riverfront units with decks, fireplaces and kitchens. The outdoor gazebo houses a hot tub that will keep you warm regardless of the weather. **1400 David Dr., Estes Park, CO 80517; 1-800-349-1003; 970-577-0068; www.creeksidesuites.com.**

Camping

Rocky Mountain National Park

See the Major Attractions section.

Roosevelt National Forest

Olive Ridge Campground (56 sites, fee charged) is open all year. Located 13 miles south of Estes Park on Hwy. 7. For reservations, call **1-877-444-6777.**

Private Campgrounds

Estes Park Campground—This campground has 65 sites and hot showers, but there are no electrical hookups. It also has a fairly quiet location with views of nearby mountains. Open late May–early Sept. To get there from Estes Park, head west on Hwy. 36 and then left for 3 miles on Hwy. 66. **P.O. Box 3517, Estes Park, CO 80517; 970-586-4188.**

National Park Resort—In addition to **cabins and motel rooms ($$ to $$$),** this place at the edge of Rocky Mountain National Park has RV hookups and numerous terraced tentsites spread out among the ponderosa pine on a mountainside with views into the park. Showers are available as well. Open May 1–Sept. 30. Located 4 miles west of Estes Park at **3501 Fall River Rd., Estes Park, CO 80517; 970-586-4563.**

Spruce Lake RV Park—This RV-only campground is open Apr.–Oct. with 110 sites. Amenities include a rec room, swimming pool, laundry room, etc. Lake and stream fishing are also available. **1050 Marys Lake Rd., P.O. Box 2497, Estes Park, CO 80517; 970-586-2889.**

Where to Eat

The Fawn Brook Inn—$$$$

Located in the sleepy village of Allenspark, this gourmand's delight is also known for its fine service, intimate atmosphere and excellent views. Sit back in the quaint rustic setting and enjoy a glass of wine or a European beer. Select from a menu that specializes in German preparation of veal, lamb, steak and duck. Start out your meal with a crock of soup. While you're waiting for a table, relax in front of the stone fireplace. Reservations recommended. Open Tues.–Sun. May 1–mid-Oct. Open weekends-only the rest of the year. Call for hours and reservations. In Allenspark, 15 miles south from Estes Park on Hwy. 7; **303-747-2556.**

Andrea's of Estes—$$$ to $$$$

This intercontinental establishment, owned by the Liermann family, is indeed a pleasant addition to the Estes Park area. The restaurant, known for its extensive menu, also boasts a comprehensive wine list that will complement any of the entrées, whether it's one of the elk preparations, ostrich filet (don't miss it) or the homemade spätzle. Vegetarians will enjoy the delectable black bean cakes. Another highlight, weather permitting, is the rooftop beer garden where you can knock back a cold one and take in the wonderful views. Open Thurs.–Sun. 11 A.M.–8 P.M. during winter; hours vary in summer. **145 E. Elkhorn Ave.; 970-586-0886.**

La Chaumière—$$$ to $$$$

The rather plain exterior of this small restaurant successfully disguises the interior's quaint European decor and excellent food. La Chaumière specializes in French cuisine and will impress you with masterful entrées such as grilled lamb with rosemary sauce and baked shrimp stuffed with blue crab; specials change nightly and the entire menu changes every week or so. Surprisingly affordable Sun. dinner specials feature six courses for a set price. Be sure not to skip the excellent desserts, including homemade ice cream. Reservations recommended. Open Tues.–Sat. at 5:30 P.M.; Sun. at 1 P.M. (2 P.M. in winter). Located 12 miles southeast of Estes Park on Hwy. 36; **303-823-6521.**

The Dunraven Inn—$$ to $$$

The Dunraven Inn continues to draw loyal patrons, some looking for a beer at the bar and others seeking the fine Italian cuisine. House specialties include lasagna, eggplant parmigiana marinara and chicken cacciatore. A great selection of Italian wines is available. The walls of the lounge are covered with Mona Lisa wallpaper and dollar bills—tacked up with personal notes by customers. Reservations recommended. Dinner is served Sun.–Thurs. 5–10 P.M., Fri.–Sat. 5–11 P.M. **2470 Hwy. 66; 970-586-6409.** For less expensive family-style Italian with outside seating available, try **Mama Rose's ($$),** in downtown Estes at **338 Elkhorn Ave.; 970-586-3330.**

The Baldpate Inn—$$

It's hard to praise the Baldpate Inn enough as a special place to eat. It has all the ingredients: delicious food, charm, a fascinating history and incredible views from the porch. Lois Smith, the owner and chef, is a cooking and baking machine in summer, producing incredibly delicious homemade soups, corn bread, pies and cakes that complement the all-you-can-eat salad bar. This cozy log building, built back in 1917, gets its name from a famous mystery novel of the time—*Seven Keys to Baldpate.* The connection with the novel (which subsequently became a Broadway play and movie) led people to begin leaving keys at the inn or sending them (15,000 to date). Restaurant hours are 11:30 A.M.–8 P.M. daily in summer and 4–7 P.M. in Oct.; closed the rest of the year. Reservations for the restaurant and a fairly rustic, though charming, 12-room inn **($$$ to $$$$)** and three cabins are highly recommended. **4900 S. Hwy. 7, P.O. Box 4445, Estes Park, CO 80517; 970-586-6151; www.baldpateinn.com.**

Notchtop Baked Goods and Natural Foods Cafe—$ to $$$

This welcome addition to Estes dining features healthful, tasty food in a relaxed atmosphere. For breakfast, order hot muffins from the bakery or enjoy a leisurely meal at a cafe table or booth. Lunches feature fresh-baked breads, homemade soups and salads. A creative mix of entrées for lunch and dinner include grilled chicken and black bean quesadillas and marinated shrimp on rice. Great appetizers as well. Beer (great microbrews) and wine available; live music on weekend nights. Open daily at 7 A.M. In the Upper Stanley Village shopping center at **459 E. Wonderview; 970-586-0272.**

Ed's Cantina and Grill—$ to $$

Locals flock to Ed's year-round for good food and quick, friendly service for a reasonable price. Start off the morning with a traditional breakfast or one of the Mexican-style specialties; lunch and dinner items also focus on Mexican dishes, but burgers, sandwiches and salads also hold their own. Others head to Ed's to quaff a cold beer at the bar and catch a game on the large TV. Open 7 A.M.–9 P.M. daily. **362 E. Elkhorn Ave.; 970-586-2919.**

Donut Haus—$

No frills, just awesome homemade donuts and baked goods. The tasty goodies at this tiny shop are definitely not for the diet-conscious. Open 5 A.M.–4 P.M.; closed Wed. **342 Moraine Ave.; 970-586-2988.**

Services

Visitor Information

Estes Park Central Reservations— This office can help you book limited accommodations. **481 W. Elkhorn Ave., Estes Park, CO 80517; 1-800-762-5968; 970-586-4402.**

Estes Park Chamber Resort Association— Well staffed with knowledgeable volunteers, this information center is open daily. **500 E. Big Thompson Ave., Estes Park, CO 80517; 1-800-44-ESTES; 970-586-4431; www.estesparkresort.com.**

Online—For a great source of information about Estes Park, check **www.estes-park.com.**

Transportation

Estes Park Shuttle and Mountain Tours— This company provides transportation to and from Denver transportation hubs. **875 Moraine Ave., Estes Park, CO 80517; 1-800-950-3274; 970-586-5151.**

Fort Collins and West

In a fine location between the northeastern plains and the Colorado Rockies, Fort Collins residents enjoy a balanced and relaxed lifestyle. Because the Fort Collins economy has always been tied to farming and ranching on the eastern plains, the city lacks some of the drama and excitement of Colorado's well-known mining boomtowns. On the flip side, more than 100,000 people have chosen to call Fort Collins home, because despite steady growth, it has always maintained the soul of a small town.

The city's downtown area is not much larger than that of some midwestern towns with one-third the population. Restored in the early 1980s, Old Town provides a natural linkage for small shops, galleries, restaurants and pubs. Highlighted by a quiet pedestrian mall and ample outdoor cafe seating, Old Town's many businesses reside in spruced-up brick buildings dating from the 1880s.

Thanks to a student contingent numbering 20,000 at Colorado State University (CSU), Fort Collins has a youthful edge, especially evident at university-sponsored programs and sporting events. Of course, the diverse nightlife offerings could be the major beneficiary of this

demographic reality. It may account for the large number of successful microbreweries in the area. True to the town's farming roots, CSU still has a highly touted agricultural program, along with other diverse curriculum offerings. Linking high-tech research with agriculture has been a boon to the area economy. Nearby Loveland with its bronze foundries, public art program and a nationally known Valentine remailing program may also be worth a short stop.

Though Fort Collins provides plenty to do, it is more aptly described as a gateway for vacationers rather than a vacation destination in itself. The town provides easy access to some of Colorado's finest recreation lands, which are often overshadowed by nearby Rocky Mountain National Park. Many visitors never hear about the Red Feather Lakes area or the beautiful, granite-walled Cache la Poudre Canyon (a Colorado Scenic and Historic Byway) just west of Fort Collins. The Cache la Poudre River barrels out of the mountains through Roosevelt National Forest and its four wilderness areas. Together these lands provide diverse opportunities for hiking, fishing, camping, rafting and cross-country skiing. Outside of the wilderness areas, miles of excellent mountain bike trails

Getting There

Fort Collins is located 60 miles north of Denver on Interstate 25 (45 miles south of Cheyenne, Wyoming). The mountainous area to the west of Fort Collins is accessible almost solely from Hwy. 14. **Denver International Airport** is well served by shuttle vans to Fort Collins. Contact **Airport Express** in Fort Collins for reservations and information at **970-482-0505. Greyhound Bus Lines (1-800-231-2222)** makes frequent trips between Denver and Fort Collins.

lure you into the backcountry. Fort Collins uniquely draws together the best attributes of the mountains and plains.

History

The name of the city notwithstanding, there is no military base here. In fact, there hasn't been a fort in Fort Collins since the 1860s.

The mountainous area west of modern-day Fort Collins was well known to Indians, fur traders and trappers who passed through and camped under tall cottonwoods, long before any permanent settlement was established. Traders and Indians peacefully coexisted in the Cache la Poudre area. The Cache la Poudre ("hide the powder") River receives its name from a party of French trappers who stashed their heavy barrels of gunpowder at the river's edge to make traveling through deep snow less burdensome. In 1844 life there was so good for one trader that he described the area, with its mild climate, rugged landscape and teeming buffalo herds, as "the loveliest spot on earth."

In the late 1850s gold discoveries in the Rockies prompted a number of fortune hunters to pour into the Cache la Poudre area. Few people found any gold to speak of, but some of the discouraged prospectors set up farms and ranches. In 1864 two companies of the 11th Ohio Volunteer Cavalry manned a short-lived army post that was called Camp Collins, in honor of Col. William O. Collins, commander at Fort Laramie, Wyoming. This encampment was set up to protect the Overland Trail and the few farms and ranches nearby, but it was soon abandoned simply because it wasn't needed. Fort Collins got its start in 1872 when lots were offered for sale in an agricultural colony modeled after the successful Union Colony at Greeley, just to the east. No ruffians applied, as the lots were sold only to temperate people of "high moral character."

The survival of Fort Collins was not assured in its early days, as it had a population of only a few hundred people. In Sept. 1879 the Agricultural College of Colorado opened its doors to five students. Experiments at this land-grant institution resulted in improved farming and ranching techniques. In the early 1900s the state's sugar beet industry and other agricultural pursuits helped the young town continue a slow but sustained growth. The agricultural college eventually grew into highly respected Colorado State University, the engine that still links the area's past with its future potential. Over the past 15 years, Hewlett-Packard, NCR and other high-tech companies have come to understand the many benefits of locating here.

Festivals and Events

New West Fest

mid-Aug. Fort Collins celebrates its birthday with a huge party that is becoming northern Colorado's largest event. A hodgepodge of musical entertainment and other acts take to stages around the town, and you can be a member of the audience for free. Endless lines of booths offer artsy-craftsy items and lots of tempting, sweet-smelling food. The festival attracts tens of thousands of people over a long summer weekend. **1-800-274-3678; 970-482-5821; www.ft collins.com.**

Sculpture in the Park

mid-Aug. The town of **Loveland** (a dozen miles south of Fort Collins) has long been a haven for sculptors. Each summer 200 of these artisans come to Benson Park to sell and display their work for thousands of visitors. Prices range from $400 to $60,000, which makes the nominal admission fee seem like a real bargain. The park also contains a large number of permanent sculptures. From Hwy. 287 head west on 29th St. and follow the signs. For additional information: **970-663-2940; www.sculptureinthe park.com.**

Fort Collins Flying Festival

late Sept. This spectator event features everything from kite flying to hot-air balloon races.

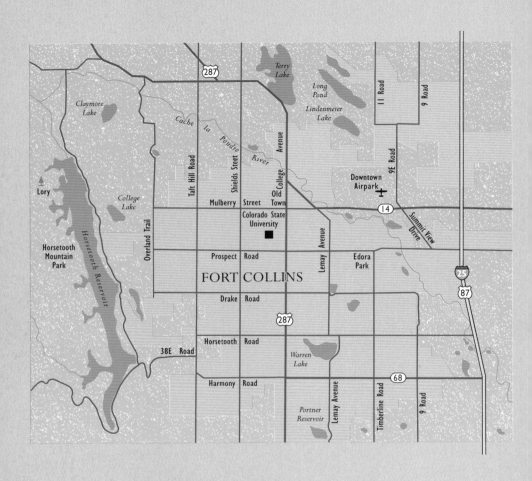

FORT COLLINS

US 287 · Terry Lake · Long Pond · Lindenmeier Lake · 11 Road · 9 Road · Claymore Lake · Cache · la · Poudre · River · College · Avenue · 9E Road · Lory · College Lake · Taft Hill Road · Shields Steet · Mulberry · Street · Old Town · Downtown Airpark · 14 · Summit View Drive · Horsetooth Mountain Park · Overland Trail · Colorado State University · Prospect · Road · Lemay · Avenue · Edora Park · 25 · 87 · Drake · Road · 287 · Horsetooth · Road · 38E Road · Warren Lake · Harmony · Road · Lemay Avenue · Timberline Road · 68 · 9 Road · Portner Reservoir · Horsetooth Reservoir

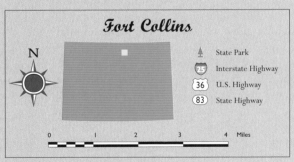

Fort Collins

N

▲	State Park
25	Interstate Highway
36	U.S. Highway
83	State Highway

0   1   2   3   4   Miles

Horsetooth Mountain Park and Lory State Park provide excellent mountain biking and horseback trails. Photo by Bruce Caughey.

Since the Fort Collins area is known for excellent wind currents, this is a perfect place for all kinds of aerial sports; **1-800-274-3678; 970-491-3388.**

Outdoor Activities

Biking

MOUNTAIN BIKING

A wide range of scenic mountain bike routes can be accessed in the Roosevelt National Forest west of Fort Collins. For trail ideas stop by the **Canyon Lakes Ranger District Offices, 1311 S. College Ave., Ft. Collins, CO 80524; 970-498-2770; www.fs.fed.us/arnf.** Another excellent possibility is the Colorado State Forest, a network of gravel and four-wheel-drive roads that wind together in many loop combinations. Within the forest you can bike from yurt to yurt on the **Never Summer Nordic Yurt System** (see the **North Park** chapter).

Lory State Park and Horsetooth Mountain Park

This mountain park, on the western side of Horsetooth Reservoir, and adjacent Lory State Park provide miles upon miles of terrific mountain biking trails. The rolling landscape provides a perfect escape only 15 minutes from the urban trails of Fort Collins. With more than 30 miles of trails, just behind the red sandstone hogback, riders have a great opportunity to explore a lovely area that encompasses the short-grass prairie as well as thick ponderosa forest. As a recognized equestrian area, be sure to share the trail with horseback trail riders.

Try the 1.9-mile-long **Overlook Trail,** which connects with other tougher trails and offers sweeping views. The 6-mile-long **Foothills Trail** also offers a moderate introduction to the area and gorgeous views of the reservoir as it parallels the shoreline much of the way. For more information contact **Lory State Park: 970-493-1623; www.coloradoparks.org.** Also see the Parks and Recreation Areas section.

BICYCLE TOURING

An extensive bike trail system winds its way through Fort Collins, connecting many points within the city. Bicycle shops in town carry a supply of "Tour de Fort," a free map with 56 miles of local bike trails, and all city buses are equipped with bike racks, so great one-direction rides are possible. Try the snaking trail that runs alongside the Cache la Poudre River in north Fort Collins (see the Scenic Drives section). Not only is it relatively flat and very scenic but it is accessible from several points in the city.

Rentals and Information

If you want to rent a mountain, touring or tandem bike, try **Lee's Campus Cyclery,** at the south end of town at **931 E. Harmony Rd.; 970-226-6006; www.leescyclery.com.** Another good bet is **Recycled Cycles, 4031-A S. Mason; 970-223-1969; www.recycled cycles.com.**

Fishing

The Fort Collins area presents an unusual combination of stream trout fishing and warmwater lake fishing. In addition, an abundance of tributaries, small lakes and beaver ponds in the high country west of Fort Collins have trout. This water often presents challenging, uncrowded fly-fishing for smallish (8- to 10-inch) brook trout or cutthroat. Stop by any local fishing store for information about current conditions. Fly-fishers interested in guided trips, equipment and advice should check in at **St. Peters Fly Shop, 202 Remington St.; 970-498-8968; www. stpeters.com.** Or check out the **Division of Wildlife** at **www.wildlife. state.co.us.**

Big Thompson River

See the **Estes Park** chapter.

Cache la Poudre River

The Poudre offers long stretches of accessible water along its journey east from the high reaches of Rocky Mountain National Park. Much of the river parallels Hwy. 14 as it flows east toward Fort Collins. Though the Poudre has a predominant brown and rainbow trout population (averaging about 11 inches), it's also home to a number of ugly whitefish which are actually strong fighters and surprisingly good to eat.

Fly-fishing is the most effective way to take Poudre River trout, but you can do well with lures, worms or salmon eggs. One warning for bait anglers and encouraging news for fly-fishers: the Poudre has two Wild Trout sections in which bait is not allowed. These well-marked sections are located between miles 28.1 and 31.4 and between miles 35.1 and 40.2. Others are farther upstream near the town of Rustic.

The Poudre River is scenic, easy to reach from Fort Collins and, as a result, heavily fished. There are campgrounds, picnic grounds, resorts and frequent turnoffs along Hwy. 14. Try fishing the Poudre in the area near **Long Draw Reservoir** where the river comes out of Rocky Mountain National Park. To get there from Fort Collins, head 10 miles northwest on Hwy. 287 and then 53 miles west on Hwy. 14. Turn left (south) on Long Draw Reservoir Rd. (Forest Rd. 156). The best times to fish the Poudre are prior to runoff in the spring or after mid-July. If you take only one fly along to fish the Poudre, make sure it's a Hare's Ear nymph (size 8 to 14 hook).

Horsetooth Reservoir

See the Parks and Recreation Areas section for fishing information.

Laramie River

In the Chambers Lake area, the Laramie can be good fishing for small brook and cutthroat trout. The narrow stream flows north through the Laramie River Valley and eventually into Wyoming, with many beaver ponds along the way. To get there from Fort Collins, drive northwest on Hwy. 287 for 10 miles and then west on Hwy. 14 for 52 miles. Turn right (north) on Laramie River Rd. (County Rd. 103).

Red Feather Lakes

Red Feather Lake is only one of 14 lakes in the Red Feather region, about 50 miles northwest of

Fort Collins. Six of the lakes are open to public recreation, with fishing as the main attraction. The fishing can be good whether you're in a boat or fishing from the shore. You can use flies, lures or bait, except on Parvin Lake, which is restricted to flies and lures only. Red Feather Lakes can be reached from Fort Collins by taking Hwy. 287 northwest for 22 miles. Turn left onto Red Feather Lakes Rd. (the old North Park freight trail) at the Forks Cafe and continue about 25 miles to the lakes. Red Feather Lakes are also accessible from Poudre Canyon (Hwy. 14) via County Rd. 69 at Rustic. At Goodell Corner, turn left onto County Rd. 162 and continue to the lakes.

Watson Lake / Poudre River

Watson Lake, which has plenty of parking and some picnic tables, is stocked regularly with trout. The Poudre flows by Watson and is also stocked. Fishing pressure on both Watson Lake and this section of the Poudre River is pretty heavy. If you come up empty, however, you can always stop by the hatchery on the way out and see thousands of trout. Watson Lake is about 8 miles northwest of Fort Collins. To get there take Hwy. 287 a mile past La Porte and, at the junction, turn left onto Rist Canyon Rd. (at a marked turn for the Bellvue Fish Hatchery). Continue about a mile to the lake.

Four-Wheel-Drive Trips

Green Ridge Trail

This scenic, moderately difficult 17-mile round-trip drive includes several narrow and challenging sections of road. The drive starts at about 9,400 feet and passes Lake Laramie and Twin Lakes before ending at Deadman Rd. (10,200 feet). Just before reaching Deadman Rd., the trail goes through thick stands of lodgepole pine to Nunn Creek Basin. To the west from Nunn Creek Basin are sweeping views of the Medicine Bow Range. To reach Green Ridge Trail, take Hwy. 14 up Poudre Canyon for 52 miles. Turn right on Laramie River Rd. (County Rd. 103) and drive about 1.5 miles to

the Lost Lake parking lot. The trail, marked with a sign, starts at the north end of the parking lot.

Kelly Flats

This rugged, moderately used road has steep hills and some challenging stream crossings—good ground clearance is a must. The 9-mile round trip leads to the top of Wintersteen Mesa, which provides a panorama of Poudre Canyon and parts of Rocky Mountain National Park to the south. Continue west to Manhattan Rd., which runs north and south between the town of Rustic and Red Feather Lakes. To reach the road, take Hwy. 14 west up Poudre Canyon for 20 miles to Kelly Flats Campground. Turn right off Hwy. 14, just past the campground, and head north. The first 1.5 miles is a steep climb that drops off into a drainage, then climbs for another 2 miles before leveling off in a grassy meadow. At the end of the road, return to Poudre Canyon via County Rd. 69.

Golf

Collindale Golf Course

This fine 18-hole course is the first choice of locals. Characterized by many mature cottonwood trees, a number of creeks and carefully maintained fairways, Collindale is open all year, weather permitting. The greens are usually very fast. So that you don't end up breaking your fairway wood across your knee on the very first hole, be forewarned: there is a large hidden lake to the front right of green No. 1. **1441 E. Horsetooth Rd.; 970-221-6651.**

Mariana Butte Golf Course

Rated by *Golf Digest* as one of the top five new public courses in the nation when it opened in 1993, Mariana Butte is a standout. Located just 4 miles from Loveland, this reasonably priced course offers spectacular views in every direction—Longs Peak and the Rockies to the west, the Devil's Backbone rock formation to the north and the sprawling Colorado plains to the east. Pro shop **970-663-3483;** tee times **970-669-5800; www.marianabutte.com.**

Ptarmigan Golf and Country Club

You can be sure of having a memorable and challenging round at this Jack Nicklaus–designed course. In true Nicklaus fashion, the course follows the natural contour of the rolling terrain rather than trying to dominate it. And it's tough. Long water hazards, lots of trees and monstrously large sand traps come into play on just about every hole. One of the sand traps is as expansive as a California beach, complete with a grass island in the middle. The back nine is considerably more hilly than the front. Call two days in advance for a tee time unless you're a member. Located southeast of Fort Collins, just east of the Windsor exit off Interstate 25. **5416 Vardon Way; 970-226-6600.**

Hiking and Backpacking

Within the Roosevelt National Forest to the west of Fort Collins, four wilderness areas—Cache la Poudre, Neota, Comanche Peak and Rawah—provide terrain ranging from easy, low-altitude hikes to multi-day backpack trips. Two of the most spectacular areas are Rawah and Comanche Peak with pine forests, alpine tundra, barren rock formations, high peaks, cirque lakes and moraines, trout streams and an abundance of wildlife. Both have extensive, interconnecting trail systems.

For details about the wilderness areas and other parts of Roosevelt National Forest, contact the **Canyon Lakes Ranger District Offices, 1311 S. College Ave., Ft. Collins, CO 80524; 970-498-2770; www.fs.fed.us/arnf.** They can supply you with pamphlets and maps of the forest area. In summer, two Forest Service visitor centers can give you tips: at the **Arrowhead Lodge,** 3 miles west of Rustic on Hwy. 14, and at the **old ranger station** in the Red Feather Lakes area on Dowdy Lake Rd. *Open Space and Trails Guide,* a pamphlet offered free of charge by the city of Fort Collins, shows short hikes in town and the foothills. Further information, maps and rental equipment may be picked up seven days a week at **The Mountain Shop, 632 S. Mason; 970-493-5720; www.the mountainshop.com.**

Browns Lake Trail

This beautiful 4-mile (one-way) hike in the Comanche Peak Wilderness Area, at altitudes between 10,000 and 12,000 feet, illustrates up close what the term *treeline* means. Though much of the trail is rather barren, it eventually drops down to Browns Lake in a heavily wooded area. In summer many colorful wildflowers line the trail. To reach the trailhead, head up Poudre Canyon on Hwy. 14 for 26 miles to Pingree Park Rd. (Forest Rd. 131) and turn left. Take Pingree Park Rd. 4 miles and keep right at Crown Point Rd. (Forest Rd. 139) for another 12 miles. The trail is on the left.

Cache la Poudre Wilderness

This small wilderness area ranges in altitudes from 6,000 to 8,600 feet, but it does not have the overwhelming beauty of some of the higher mountain areas. The trade-off is that the steep, rugged terrain is seldom traveled. The maintained **Mt. McConnel Trail** is a 5-mile loop climbing through juniper, fir and pine to the summit. Once there, eat lunch at the flat rock while enjoying the views. Other parts of the wilderness are accessible, if you don't mind bushwhacking. Your efforts will be rewarded with solitude, thick forests and a chance to glimpse some of Colorado's more exotic fauna—bear, mountain lion and the endangered peregrine falcon. The South Fork of the Cache la Poudre River flows through the west central part of the wilderness, so there is a chance for fishing as well. From Fort Collins head northwest on Hwy. 287 for 10 miles and then west on Hwy. 14 for 22 miles to Mountain Park Campground. The wilderness area is south of the river (you'll see the Mt. McConnel trailhead).

Greyrock Trail

Greyrock is perhaps the best known and one of the most often recommended day hikes in the Fort Collins area (on weekends you may want to try someplace else). It's a fairly steep 3-mile (one-way) hike, but the reward comes at the 7,500-foot summit where you'll have views west to higher mountains and east to the plains and

Fort Collins. You might even catch sight of a bobcat or a black Abert's squirrel. Local hikers rate Greyrock as a much better experience during spring or fall, when it is less crowded and cooler, than in summertime. The Greyrock trailhead is located 9 miles west up Poudre Canyon on Hwy. 14. A parking lot is provided opposite the trail, which begins by crossing a footbridge. You might consider **Meadows** and **Dadd Gulch Trails,** a couple of longer but extremely scenic options within the same area.

Lory State Park

More than 30 miles of hiking trails attract many people to this nearby park, only 20 minutes from Fort Collins. The elevation is low enough that you can hike all year, though there are a few snowstorms in winter. One suggested hike is **Arthur's Rock.** Trail maps are available at the park entrance. See the Parks and Recreation Areas section for directions.

Mirror Lake

The trail to this high alpine lake at 11,000 feet takes you through a beautiful section of Rocky Mountain National Park. It's a tough, 7-mile hike over steep terrain through pine and fir to the glacial moraine that holds Mirror Lake. You'll also pass a waterfall on the way. There are two forks along the trail: at the first fork, head right, and keep left at the second one. To reach the trailhead from Fort Collins, head northwest on Hwy. 287 for 10 miles and then west on Hwy. 14 for 53 miles. Turn left on Long Draw Reservoir Rd. (Forest Rd. 156). Continue for 8 miles and look for the parking area on the left side of the road. The trail begins by following Corral Creek.

Rawah Lakes Trail

This 10-mile hike into the heart of the Rawah Wilderness Area makes a great overnighter. It's a fairly steep hike, climbing 2,100 feet through aspen and pine forests, eventually giving way to spruce and fir. From Rawah Lakes there are spectacular views of surrounding peaks in the Medicine Bow and Mummy Ranges. The lakes

even yield an occasional trout. To reach the trailhead from Fort Collins, drive 10 miles northwest on Hwy. 287 and then 52 miles west on Hwy. 14. Turn right (north) on Laramie River Rd. (County Rd. 103). Continue about 12 miles to the trailhead near Rawah Ranch. Start hiking west.

Horseback Riding

Double Diamond Stables

Located within Lory State Park west of town, Double Diamond has guided trail and dinner rides; they also provide hayride parties and guided tours. **970-224-4200.**

Sno-Cap Stables

These stables also offer guided trips and mountain horses for hunting and fishing expeditions. Sno-Cap Stables can be found at Livermore, about 35 miles northwest of Fort Collins on Hwy. 287. **970-482-4784.**

Ice Skating

Edora Pool Ice Center

Skate year-round at this excellent indoor arena. Rentals, changing room, lessons and a snack bar. **1801 Riverside Dr.; 970-221-6679.**

Parks and Recreation Areas

Boyd Lake State Park

With major improvements of late, you won't find a more modern water-sports facility in northern Colorado. With a sandy beach and more than 1,700 surface-acres of seasonally warm water, it's the perfect destination for boating, fishing, sailing and more. Well-designed camping facilities (see the Camping section), picnic areas, a playground and a trail system round out the activities at this family-oriented park. From U.S. 34 near Loveland, turn north onto Madison Ave., then follow the signs. **970-669-1739** (office); **970-663-2662** (Boyd Lake Marina); **www.colorado parks.org.**

Carter Lake Park

Located between Loveland and Berthoud (south of Fort Collins), this 2,100-acre park has long been a favorite of boaters, water-skiers and anyone who enjoys fishing. Also horseback riding, and picnic and camping places. Fee charged. For more information contact the **Larimer County Parks Department: 970-679-4570; www.co. larimer.co.us/parks.**

Edora Park

A wide selection of activities entice visitors to Edora Park, home to arguably the premier disc golf course of northern Colorado. Beware the water hazards at this free Frisbee course, which—like the park—remains open daily from 6 A.M. to 11 P.M. Other attractions include a BMX track, picnic tables, horseshoe pits, tennis courts and walking/biking paths. It can be reached from the Spring Creek Trail section of the Fort Collins bike route and by traveling three blocks east from the intersection of Stuart St. and Lemay Ave. **970-221-6640.**

Horsetooth Reservoir

Named after a nearby rock that looks vaguely like a horse's tooth, this body of water just west of town attracts hordes of people for water recreation as well as hiking, mountain biking and horseback riding. Many dirt roads and trails wind through the land surrounding Horsetooth Reservoir, providing scenic, hilly tours. Horsetooth Mountain Park and Lory State Park, adjacent to the reservoir, offer wide stretches of public land. Horsetooth Reservoir has almost 4,000 acres of water and attracts people from much of northern Colorado. There are picnic and camping areas as well as several marinas. Horsetooth can get crowded at times with swimmers, boaters, water-skiers and jet-skiers.

Horsetooth Reservoir is the first choice of many anglers in this area who come for kokanee salmon, various species of trout (including Mackinaw up to 30 pounds), bass and walleye. You can fish Horsetooth by boat, but because the shoreline drops off quickly, it's possible to fish very deep water from the bank. The problem is that most of the shoreline is composed of large boulders and smaller rocks that make moving around kind of tough. Horsetooth has a reputation of being either hot or very slow. Fish can be taken with lures or bait.

More information about Horsetooth is available from the **Larimer County Parks Department; 970-679-4570; www.co.larimer.co. us/parks.** To get to the reservoir from downtown Fort Collins, drive west on virtually any road until you reach Overland Trail Rd. at the edge of town. Turn left (south) and drive to County Rd. 42C at the south end of town. Then turn right (west) and continue to the reservoir.

Lory State Park

Lory State Park borders the west side of Horsetooth Reservoir in an area between the prairie and foothills. The transitional environment is remarkably rugged and scenic, featuring rolling hills, tall grasses, wide sculpted valleys and sharply uplifted rock formations to the west. With its close proximity to town, the park attracts people for its 30 miles of hiking trails, backcountry camping, rock climbing, picnicking, horseback riding **(Double Diamond Stables; 970-224-4200)** and terrific mountain biking. An easy gravel road travels through the center of the park. Fishing in the coves from the west shore of Horsetooth Reservoir can be quite good. In winter, after a snowstorm, it's an ideal place for cross-country skiing.

Visitors frequently spot deer, rabbits and many birds; occasional sightings of prairie rattlesnakes, bears and bobcats occur as well. To reach the park from town drive west to Overland Trail Rd. Turn right (north) and continue past W. Vine Dr. and Lake Lee on the right. Turn left (west) onto Bingham Hill Rd., marked by a sign, to Lory State Park. Turn left again at the T intersection leading 3 miles to the park entrance. Stop by the new visitor center for information, maps and advice. They also offer interpretive programs, such as ranger-led walks. Six backcountry campsites, located along the Timber Trail, are accessible from the Arthur's Rock trailhead starting about 2 miles from the Arthur's Rock parking lot. Sites are available on a first-come, first-served basis; fee charged. **708 Lodgepole Dr., Bellvue, CO 80512; 970-493-1623; www.coloradoparks.org.**

River Floating

For river floating in the Fort Collins vicinity the choice is obvious—the **Cache la Poudre.** It's a hot spot for both rafters and kayakers. The river starts high in Rocky Mountain National Park and works its way 25 miles northeast before turning abruptly east. For the next 40 miles the Poudre twists down a deep canyon that it has scoured out of the granite. Spilling onto the plains, it loses its fight and flows gently into the South Platte River.

Kayakers are attracted to the Poudre because of its serious whitewater stretches. The problem is that the river can only be run in short sections, due to water diversions and a number of boulder-clogged rapids. The Poudre Canyon stretch can easily be scouted from Hwy. 14, which follows alongside; a number of picnic areas and campgrounds provide easy access. If you are going to arrange your own raft or kayak trip, be sure to check with the Forest Service or an outdoor shop in Fort Collins about avoiding the dangerous sections. If you want to leave the worries to an experienced guide, then contact one of the following:

A1 Wildwater Inc.—Half-day and full-day runs depending on your abilities and interests. Wildwater also offers other trips around the state. Trips run from May into Aug. Call for reservations and details. **317 Stover St., Ft. Collins, CO 80524; 970-224-3379; www.a1 wildwater.com.**

Rocky Mountain Adventures—This outfitter specializes in half-day family runs down the Poudre on paddle rafts. Reservations are a must. **1117 N. Hwy. 287, Ft. Collins, CO 80524; 970-493-4005; www.shoprma.com.**

Skiing

CROSS-COUNTRY SKIING AND SNOWSHOEING

Although Fort Collins is a long way from the major downhill skiing areas, locals get their skiing fix on a multitude of cross-country ski trails. Opportunities abound. Whenever there is enough snow, skiers take to nearby areas, such as Fort Collins City Park or Lory State Park. But cross-country skiers and snowshoers from Fort Collins most often head for the high country. Cameron Pass is perhaps the most popular area. For information and maps stop by the **Canyon Lakes Ranger District Offices, 1311 S. College Ave., Ft. Collins, CO 80524; 970-498-2770; www.fs.fed.us/arnf.**

Backcountry Trails

Blue Lake and Long Draw Trails—Blue Lake is a moderately difficult 6.5-mile trail offering very diverse terrain, from steep, uphill sections to level glides through meadows. The trail climbs steadily uphill from 9,500 feet to 10,800 feet. Panoramic views of the Mummy Range and Rocky Mountain National Park await you at the lake, but there is plenty of scenery along the way. To reach the trailhead from Fort Collins, drive 10 miles northwest on Hwy. 287 and then 53 miles west on Hwy. 14 to the trail parking lot. The trail begins on the left side of the highway, east of Long Draw Reservoir Rd. (Forest Rd. 156). Beginner and intermediate skiers enjoy Long Draw Trail, which begins at the same trailhead. This gradual trail parallels Long Draw Reservoir Rd., actually joining the road at Box Canyon.

Never Summer Nordic Yurt System—Cross-country skiers interested in comfortable huts on a multi-day backcountry trip definitely should check out Never Summer Nordic Yurt System (see the **North Park** chapter for information).

Zimmerman Lake Trail—This very popular, well-marked trail is moderately difficult. It climbs a mile and a half up along an old logging road to Zimmerman Lake. Once at the lake, you can enjoy plenty of off-trail skiing. Winter is indeed a great time to be at the lake—the views of the Medicine Bow Range and Poudre Canyon are spectacular. This high-altitude trail starts at 10,000 feet and climbs to almost 10,500 feet. To reach the trail from Fort Collins, head

The free-flowing Cache la Poudre River attracts kayakers for its steady mix of calm and whitewater. Photo by Bruce Caughey.

northwest on Hwy. 287 for 10 miles and then west on Hwy. 14 for 58 miles. The parking lot is on the left, just past Joe Wright Reservoir.

Groomed Trails

Beaver Meadows—More than 20 miles of maintained, varied trails, some of which are groomed, wind through this resort. Located northwest of Red Feather Lakes, the Beaver Meadows trails are on national forest and private land. Their ski shop provides rentals and lessons. In addition to cross-country skiing, there are a variety of other winter activities as well as accommodations (see the Where to Stay section). To reach Beaver Meadows from Fort Collins, drive northwest on Hwy. 287 for 22 miles and turn left on the Red Feather Lakes Rd. Drive to Red Feather Lakes and turn north on Creedmore Rd. Proceed 6 miles to the Beaver Meadows sign. For more information: **970-482-1845; www.beavermeadows.com.**

Rentals and Information

The Mountain Shop—This shop rents equipment for any kind of cross-country skiing and snowshoeing, whether it is for groomed trails or backcountry telemarking. **632 S. Mason; 970-493-5720; www.themountainshop.com.**

Seeing and Doing

Brewery Tours

The explosion of craft brewing in Fort Collins can be seen in the shadow of a behemoth called Budweiser. This college town manages to hold its own with a delightful mix of microbrewery and brewpub experiences, alongside a fascinating glimpse at big-time corporate brewing. Without a doubt, stop in to take the low-key tour and sample the variety of excellent brews at **New Belgium Brewing Company (500 Linden; 970-221-0524; www.newbelgium.com).** On weekdays at 2 P.M. you'll see the brewery in full action. The well-appointed tasting room has goblets of a mouth-watering array of tastes, including their famous Fat Tire brand. Pick up a six-pack, a half-gallon growler or a keg. Down the road, try the up-and-coming **Odell Brewing Company (800 E. Lincoln; 970-498-9070;**

www.odells.com). Their popular and hoppy-tasting 90 Shilling ale finishes clean. For a smaller, warehouse-style brewing operation, stop in at **H. C. Berger Brewing Company (1900 E. Lincoln; 970-493-9044; www.hc berger.com).** Try their Ault and a Chocolate Stout. For a night out with food and a game of pool, head straight to the long, brick room at **Coopersmith's Pub and Brewing Company** (see the Where to Eat section).

Head to the outskirts of Fort Collins to find **Budweiser,** the fastest-producing brewery in the world, with a top capacity of 2,200 cans of beer per minute. The brewery's hospitality center offers free hour-long tours of the huge facility, including a stop at the **Clydesdale Hamlet,** where you can get a close-up look at these 2,300-pound horses. Your tour ends with a glass of ice-cold beer inside a window-enclosed room looking out over the manicured grounds to the mountains. The gift shop will gladly take your money for that mug, towel or T-shirt. In summer you may have to wait up to an hour; it's better to arrive before noon. Located north of Fort Collins (Exit 271 from Interstate 25) **on Busch Dr., P.O. Box 20000, Ft. Collins, CO 80522; 970-490-4500; www.budweiser.com.**

Museums and Galleries

Colorado State University

Contact the information desk at Lory Student Center for information about the campus art galleries that feature a variety of media styles. Free and open to the public. From I-25 take the Prospect Rd. exit. Drive west on Prospect Rd. for about 5 miles. Turn right (north) on College, and look for the campus on your left. **970-491-6444; www.colostate.edu.**

The Fort Collins Museum

This rather small museum specializes in Fort Collins history, but also features an extensive collection of Folsom points—the most outside of the Smithsonian Institution in Washington, D.C. These prehistoric spear points were collected in the 1920s and 1930s at the Lindenmeier site, near the Wyoming border north of Fort Collins. The museum complex also includes restored and preserved buildings. Open Tues.–Sat. 10 A.M.–5 P.M., Sun. 12–5 P.M. **200 Mathews St.; 970-221-6738.**

Historic Buildings

An interesting tour of the town's historic buildings is highlighted by the **Avery House** at **328 W. Mountain Ave.** This elegant Victorian home also hosts many special events, including a Christmas open house in early Dec., when Victorian-style Christmas wrapping paper, ornaments, notepaper and cookies are for sale. For more information on the Avery House and other historic buildings, call **970-221-0533.**

Swetsville Zoo

It's amazing what can happen when people have a little time on their hands. In this case Bill Swets created Puff the Two-Headed Dragon, Harry the Hitchhiker, Penny the Dimetrodon and about 70 other sculptures out of old car parts, farm machinery and scrap metal. On the outskirts of Fort Collins, these creatures rear up from the surrounding farmland like a weird mirage. Anyone can come by to enjoy these fantasy creatures for free ("donations are appreciated," Swets says). In addition, miniature steam railcars ply a three-quarter-mile route beside the Poudre River. Located just south of Fort Collins, on the east side of Interstate 25 at the Harmony Rd. exit (265). **4801 E. Harmony Rd., Ft. Collins, CO 80525.**

Nightlife

Bas Bleu Theatre Company and Art Gallery

With only 49 seats, this could be the ultimate in intimate theater! Despite recent financial struggles, this one-of-a-kind salon theater continues to offer high-quality, community-based events several nights per week and most weekends. The appealing interior reveals exposed brick; archways separate the small art gallery from the seats. Warning: this has become a very popular haunt and fills up quickly. The ideal Old Town location offers easy access to bars and restaurants. Call ahead for reservations and current schedule. **216 Pine St., Ft. Collins, CO 80525; 970-498-8949.**

Coopersmith's Pub and Brewing Company

This is the cream of Fort Collins brewpubs. See the Where to Eat section.

Lincoln Center

As the city's performing and visual arts complex, Lincoln Center plays host to live theater, concerts, the Fort Collins Symphony, Larimer Chorale and art exhibits. Some of the more unique features include a mini-theater, with its intimate stage, and the Terrace, a sculpture and performance area complete with flower gardens and plants. **417 W. Magnolia St.; 970-221-6735;** box office **970-221-6730; www.ft collins.com.**

Mishawaka Inn

Located about 25 miles from Fort Collins, this bar and restaurant really gets shaking on weekends to live country rock music. The old place was built in 1901 with the help of convict labor. Nationally known acts often play on summer weekends. You might also want to stay for a juicy steak or rainbow trout. Sometimes the view from the deck includes bighorn sheep that come down to drink in the Poudre River. Open Nov.–Feb. Thurs.–Sun., Mar.–Oct. seven days a week. To get there from Fort Collins drive 10 miles northwest on Hwy. 287 and then 15 miles west on Hwy. 14. **13714 Poudre Canyon Hwy.; 970-482-4420.**

Scenic Drives

Poudre Canyon

This 101-mile trip along a designated Scenic and Historic Byway will take you into beautiful mountainous country west of Fort Collins. Start by heading northwest for 10 miles out of Fort Collins on Hwy. 287 and turn west on Hwy. 14. This highway proceeds into a narrow, rocky

canyon next to the Cache la Poudre River. As you're driving upriver, you can almost feel the intense force of the water, especially during spring runoff. The exceptional Poudre is the last free-flowing river along the Front Range, hence the bumper stickers reading, "Don't Damn the Poudre." Today the age-old conflict of growth versus environment remains. The Poudre is Colorado's first National Wild and Scenic River.

Take twisting and turning Hwy. 14 through Poudre Canyon, keeping your eyes peeled for Rocky Mountain bighorn sheep, deer and elk along the route past resorts, campgrounds and interesting geologic formations cut by thousands of years of wind and water erosion. One mile past the summit of Cameron Pass, stop for a few moments to appreciate the dramatic rocky tops of the Nokhu Crags, which lie at the tip of the Never Summer Range. The road continues to skirt the northern edge of Rocky Mountain National Park, allowing tremendous mountain views before coming in sight of the flat expanse of North Park (see the **North Park** chapter). This scenic trip ends in the center of the park at the town of Walden.

Where to Stay

Accommodations

Most national chains have motels here—Holiday Inn, Ramada Inn, Motel 6 and several others are located in a convenient conglomeration at the intersection of Hwy. 14 and Interstate 25 (at the main Fort Collins exit). In the mountains west of town, however, a number of cabins and resorts provide a special atmosphere along the banks of the Poudre River and in more secluded areas such as Red Feather Lakes.

Bed and Breakfasts

As elsewhere in Colorado, the bed and breakfast choices are multiplying rapidly. In Fort Collins consider a night at the elegant **Mariposa on Spring Creek ($$$),** where the airy atrium hot tub with its jungle of plants makes for a memorable visit. Six comfortable guest rooms with private baths and a buffet-style breakfast round out your stay. Spa packages are available, as well as day spa treatments. **706 E. Stuart St., Ft. Collins, CO 80525; 1-800-495-9604; www. mariposaspa.com.** Another popular choice in Loveland (12 miles south of Fort Collins) is the turn-of-the-century **Lovelander Bed and Breakfast Inn ($$$ to $$$$)**—an elegant choice with 11 rooms. Enjoy freshly baked cookies and a steaming cup of tea on arrival, and dessert delivered to your room before bedtime. All this and you still get to wake up to a memorable gourmet breakfast. **217 W. 4th St., Loveland, CO 80537; 1-800-459-6694; 970-669-0798; www.lovelander.com.** The **Elizabeth Street Guest House ($$ to $$$)** offers an experience akin to being welcomed into a friend's home, with plentiful antiques, old quilts, handmade items, leaded windows and oak woodwork. The three comfortable rooms each have their own sink, but two share a bathroom. It's in a great location near campus, and you can even take the owners' dog Louie for a walk. **202 E. Elizabeth St., Ft. Collins, CO 80524; 970-493-2337.**

Sylvan Dale Ranch—$$ to $$$$

This working ranch draws you into the actual operation: stack hay or brush the horses. You are free to participate as much as you want. All of the accommodations have private bathrooms; nine cottages are also available. Enjoy the luxury of the heated pool or play a set of tennis. Stay over July 4th weekend and you can get involved in the cattle drive. There are no telephones or TVs here. The Jessup family has been operating this ranch for more than 40 years. For an extra charge you can sign up on the full American plan and savor wonderful, country-style meals. In the summer, you need to book a minimum six-night stay. During off-season (Labor Day through Memorial Day), the ranch offers a "bunk and breakfast" arrangement. Groups of up to 12 should consider renting Mama J's Guest House. Kids love the activities and the change of being out in the country. Located 7 miles west of Loveland (15 miles south of Fort Collins on

Hwy. 287). **2939 N. County Rd. 31 D, Loveland, CO 80538; 970-667-3915; www. sylvandale.com.**

Beaver Meadows Resort Ranch—$$ to $$$

This ranch/resort is well known for its cross-country skiing and easy access to 20 miles of marked trails, some of which are groomed. Along the backcountry trails, you are invited to stop in a warming hut for snacks and spirits. During the summer Beaver Meadows features horseback riding, mountain biking, a kids' fishing pond and, for more serious anglers, fishing in the North Fork of the Poudre River. Accommodations are in condos, mountain homes or cabins; all come equipped with kitchens. If you don't feel like cooking, stop by the restaurant (open daily). Live entertainment on Fri. and Sat. nights. No minimum stay, but weekly packages are offered. Located 55 miles northwest of Fort Collins in the Red Feather Lakes area. **100 Marmot Dr., Unit 1, Red Feather Lakes, CO 80545; 970-881-2450; www.beavermeadows.com.**

Camping

Boyd Lake State Park

Check out 148 paved pull-through campsites located on a grassy knoll dotted with trees near the lake. The easily accessible sites can accommodate tents, pickup campers, trailers and motor homes. Each site has a picnic table and grill. See the Parks and Recreation Areas section for more information. Reserve sites at **1-800-678-2267** or **www.reserveamerica.com.**

Colorado State Forest

See the **North Park** chapter for information.

Lory State Park

See the Parks and Recreation Areas section for information about the 6 backcountry tentsites.

Roosevelt National Forest

The Poudre River has a cache of campgrounds conveniently located just off Hwy. 14 west of

Fort Collins. Access to the stream from each of these campgrounds is easy, but the campsites often fill up by early afternoon and even earlier on weekends and holidays. Reservations are accepted for **Mountain Park, Dowdy, West Lake** and **Chambers Campgrounds** by contacting **1-877-444-6777** or **www.reserveusa.com.** All the following listed campgrounds charge a fee.

Seven campgrounds are bunched together within about a 15-mile stretch between Poudre Park and Kelly Flats. The first is **Ansel Watrous Campground** (19 sites), which is about 23 miles west of Fort Collins. **Stove Prairie Campground** (9 sites) is 3 miles farther west. Three more miles west is the **Narrows Cooperative** campground (9 units). **Mountain Park Campground** (45 sites) is 3 miles down the road, followed by **Kelly Flats Campground** (23 sites) 2 miles farther. Still rolling west on Hwy. 14, 49 miles west of Fort Collins you will arrive at **Big Bend Campground** (9 sites). Travel another 4 miles to **Sleeping Elephant Campground** (15 sites).

Four public campgrounds are located in the vicinity of Red Feather Lakes. To get there from Fort Collins drive 22 miles northwest on Hwy. 287 to the Forks Cafe. Turn left and drive 30 miles west on Red Feather Lakes Rd. **Dowdy Lake Campground** (62 sites) is located 1.5 miles east of Red Feather Lakes Village on Forest Rd. 218. **West Lake Campground** (29 sites) is 1 mile east of the village on Forest Rd. 200. To reach **Bellaire Lake Campground** (26 sites) take Forest Rd. 162, 3 miles south of the village toward Rustic. **North Fork Poudre Campground** (9 sites) is located 7 miles west of Red Feather Lakes Village on County Rd. 162.

From Fort Collins, drive 10 miles northwest on Hwy. 287 and then 52 miles west on Hwy. 14; then turn right on Laramie River Rd. (County Rd. 103)—there are two campgrounds along this road. **Tunnel Campground** (49 sites) is another 7 miles north on Laramie River Rd. And **Brown's Park** (28 sites) is 14.5 miles north near Glendevey.

A couple other campgrounds are located on the northern edge of Rocky Mountain National Park. To reach **Long Draw Campground** (25 sites) drive 10 miles northwest of Fort Collins on Hwy. 287 and then west on Hwy. 14 for 53 miles to just past Chambers Lake. Then turn left onto Long Draw Rd. (Forest Rd. 156) and continue 9 miles to the campground. Continue another 4 miles on Forest Rd. 156 and you'll arrive at **Grand View Campground** (8 tentsites).

Private Campgrounds

Ft. Collins Mile High KOA—With a swimming pool, full hookups and tentsites available, this campground gets plenty of use. About 10 cabins are also available. To get there drive 10 miles northwest of Fort Collins on Hwy. 287, just opposite the turnoff for Hwy. 14. **6670 Hwy. 287N, P.O. Box 600, La Porte, CO 80535; 970-493-9758; www.koa.com.**

Glen Echo Resort—The Glen Echo offers rustic and modern cabins with kitchenettes; also 77 RV sites; no tenting. Located in Poudre Canyon with good fishing available. To get there drive 41 miles west of Fort Collins on Hwy. 14. **31503 Poudre Canyon Dr., Bellvue, CO 80512; 970-881-2208.**

Where to Eat

Austin's American Grille—$$ to $$$$

The melding of a clean, contemporary, cutting-edge restaurant in a historic building in Old Town works well in this instance. The restaurant's interior and outdoor patio with red umbrellas set the mood for intimate conversation. The people-watching doesn't get much better. Sit back, enjoy the formal but not stilted service and dig into some of the house favorites: fresh grilled salmon, apple-smoked pork tenderloin or roasted chicken. Appetizers include grilled portobello mushrooms and wonderful iron-skillet corn bread. End your meal with decadent crème brûlée or key lime pie. Open Sun.–Thurs. 11 A.M.–10 P.M., Fri.–Sat. until 11 P.M. **100 W. Mountain Ave., Fort Collins; 970-224-9691.**

Bisetti's—$$ to $$$

As soon as you enter this small, family-owned Italian restaurant, the fresh smell of garlic, basil and oregano make you think of Old World, time-tested recipes. Empty Chianti bottles hang from every conceivable spot—you may want to empty one yourself while eating a meal of fettuccine, rigatoni, manicotti or pasta pesto. All pasta is made fresh daily on the premises, and you can really tell the difference. You can't leave without trying a slice of Bisetti's house specialty: cheesecake. Open for lunch Mon.–Fri. 11 A.M.–2 P.M.; dinner Sun.–Thurs. 5–9 P.M., Fri.–Sat. until 10 P.M. **120 S. College Ave.; 970-493-0086.**

Charco Broiler—$$ to $$$

Feel like having a slab of steak cooked to perfection over an open flame? Fort Collins locals go straight to the Charco Broiler's lived-in setting. You'll know why it's crowded nearly all the time as soon as your meal arrives. Try to save some room for a slice of homemade pie. This is also a good choice for your basic American breakfast and bottomless cup of coffee. Open Mon.–Thurs. 6 A.M.–11 P.M., Fri.–Sat. 6 A.M.–midnight, Sun. 11 A.M.–10 P.M. **1716 E. Mulberry** (Hwy. 14, east of Fort Collins); **970-482-1472.**

Rio Grande—$$

Scoring high on the local's approval meter and low (for a Mexican restaurant) on the calorie/cholesterol meter is the Rio Grande. This restaurant features fresh ingredients and is known for its standout black beans, fajitas and other Tex-Mex specialties. Since the restaurant doesn't take reservations, you may have to wait. Kids' menu available. Many come here just for the Mexican beers or strong margaritas, which won't disappoint. Lunch served Mon.–Fri. 11 A.M.–2 P.M., Sat.–Sun. till 2:30 P.M. Dinner served 5–9 P.M. daily. Downtown at **143 W. Mountain Ave.; 970-224-5428.**

Young's Cafe—$ to $$$

Don't let the name fool you. Young's is much more than an ordinary cafe. With outstanding Vietnamese cuisine, this restaurant has a loyal following. The atmosphere is elegant, and carefully prepared meals tease tastebuds you never knew existed. The house specialties are highly recommended as are their Vietnamese "creations," in which you select your favorite seafood or meat to go with a special sauce. Young's is also a good choice for vegetarians and places a strong emphasis on fresh ingredients. Lunch is a bargain. Carry-out is available. Open Mon.–Thurs. 11:30 A.M.–9:30 P.M., Fri.–Sat. until 10:30 P.M., Sun. 4:30–9:30 P.M. In the Crystal Gardens at **3307 S. College Ave.; 970-223-8000.**

Coopersmith's Pub and Brewing Company—$ to $$

The real reason to eat at Coopersmith's is to be able to wash down your food with one of the brewpub's beers. In a unique restored building with exposed brick walls and a wonderful patio area, Coopersmith's serves up creative pub

Coopersmith's Pub in Old Town Fort Collins is the place to go for fresh-brewed beer and a game of pool. Photo by Bruce Caughey.

food. It also has an excellent pool hall, with bar and grub, located just across the walking mall from the main entrance of the primary restaurant. Menu items include everything from grilled mahi sandwiches to salads to a bratwurst simmered in ale. The cheese and artichoke dip is decadent and worth every calorie. Of five beers brewed in large tanks on the premises, our favorite was the subtly sweet Nut Brown Ale. The beer may take a while for Bud drinkers to get used to, but it's worth the effort. Happy-hour prices 4–6 P.M. daily. Nonbeer drinkers may be interested in trying one of the brewery's homemade sodas: root beer, ginger ale or cream soda. Open Mon.–Sat. 11 A.M.–2 A.M., Sun. until midnight. **#5 Old Town Square; 970-498-0483.**

Joe's Fireside Cafe—$ to $$

This local favorite lives up to its claim of "breakfast and lunch with a touch of class." The eclectic menu encompasses traditional and out-of-the ordinary selections, while the comfortable interior reflects the care and concern of the owner. Breakfast items like stuffed French toast or the hip Vegi Bene are delightful and generous choices. Aside from the standard cup of java, you'll always find a fresh-brewed gourmet coffee choice—and your cup will never be empty thanks to the attentive staff. Lunch specials add variety to the regular menu items. Though you'll likely encounter a wait, Sun. brunch at Joe's will leave you smiling. Open Tues.–Sun. 6:30 A.M.– 2 P.M. **238 S. College Ave.; 970-482-2233.**

Vern's Place—$

If you are anywhere near La Porte, stop in for a tank of gas and one of Vern's famous cinnamon rolls. Located 9 miles northwest of Fort Collins just off Hwy. 287. **4120 W. County Rd. 54G, La Porte, CO 80535; 970-482-5511.**

NEARBY
Bruce's—$ to $$$

East of Fort Collins, in the almost empty town of Severance, a totally unique dining experience awaits. Fort Collins residents often make a special trip here when entertaining out-of-town guests. For information on Bruce's, see the Where to Eat section in the **Northeast Plains** chapter.

Services

Visitor Information

Fort Collins Chamber of Commerce—225 **S. Meldrum St., Ft. Collins, CO 80521; 970-482-3746; www.fortcollinschamber.com.**

Fort Collins Convention and Visitors Bureau—If you're going to be around the area for a few days, be sure to contact these helpful folks. **3545 Prospect Rd., Ft. Collins, CO 80525; 1-800-274-FORT; 970-482-5821; www.ftcollins.com.**

Transportation

Buses—**Transfort,** the Fort Collins bus system, serves most of the major areas of the city from 6:30 A.M. to 6:30 P.M. Buses are equipped with bike racks. **6570 Portner Rd.; 970-221-6620.**

Taxi—Shamrock Taxi, 970-224-2222.

Trolley—It doesn't go very far, or very often, but if you're in Fort Collins from May to Sept., check out the trolley. It runs from City Park to W. Mountain Ave. and back, from noon to 6 P.M., Sat., Sun. and holidays, weather permitting. Small fee charged.

Georgetown and Idaho Springs

About 30 miles west of Denver, Interstate 70 drops down from Floyd Hill and makes its way along Upper Clear Creek through one of the oldest historic areas in the state. Gold strikes in 1859 brought thousands of fortune hunters to this high mountain valley rimmed by soaring rocky peaks.

Even if you are just driving through, views from the highway suggest a deeply entrenched mining legacy. Old mine shafts and tailing piles on nearby mountainsides and the long-established towns of Georgetown, Idaho Springs and Silver Plume all serve as reminders of the days when throngs of optimistic miners scoured the area.

Although Idaho Springs was the first settlement in the valley, Georgetown and Silver Plume evoke the most vivid historical images. Once the third-largest town in Colorado, Georgetown is full of impeccably restored Victorian homes and buildings, making it an exceptional National Historic District.

History also accompanies you on a trip along the refurbished Georgetown Loop Railroad. This engineering wonder snakes its way up to nearby Silver Plume, offering a ride as memorable today as it was 100 years ago.

With easy access to these towns along Interstate 70, many skiers and summer visitors stop in Georgetown and Idaho Springs for a look around or to have a meal at one of the many fine restaurants. But don't let the accessibility lead you to believe the area is overdeveloped— lots of remote country surrounds the valley, and it's common to catch a glimpse of a bighorn sheep among the rocky crags. Visit the "Watchable Wildlife" viewing station along the Interstate 70 frontage road at Georgetown Lake— you can spend time looking for bighorns

without having to worry about rear-ending the car ahead.

Ghost towns and old mine ruins are scattered throughout the canyons and mountains in the Georgetown and Idaho Springs area. Many old mining roads, including Waldorf Rd. and the precipitous Oh My God Rd., cut through backwoods sites once teeming with miners. Another road not to be missed is Mt. Evans Road, one of the world's highest paved roads. It climbs 14 miles up 14,264-foot Mt. Evans, providing views of wildlife, the plains and surrounding mountain ranges that are hard to match.

Encompassing most of this area, heavily used Arapaho National Forest attracts many outdoor

---

Getting There

Idaho Springs is located 32 miles west of Denver on Interstate 70. A more scenic route is up Lower Clear Creek Canyon from Golden on Hwy. 6, which follows the old Colorado Central Railroad bed. Georgetown is located 14 miles west of Idaho Springs along Interstate 70.

enthusiasts, especially for its great hiking, mountain biking, cross-country skiing and snow-shoeing. In winter many cross-country skiers converge on the area and fan out on the snow-covered roads and trails. Loveland Ski Area, 10 miles west of Silver Plume on Interstate 70, attracts many day skiers, especially from Denver, with its relatively inexpensive lift tickets, variety of terrain and light powder snow.

History

In January 1859 George Jackson, a prospector on a hunting trip, made his way to what is now Idaho Springs. The story goes that as he trudged through the snow over a hill, he saw haze in the distance that he believed to be smoke from an Indian camp. What he found instead were natural hot springs. More importantly, just up the valley near the confluence of Clear Creek and Chicago Creek, he found some rocks that he thought contained gold.

Returning the next spring, Jackson and a few comrades panned and placered $1,500 in gold the first week. Soon, thousands of miners and merchants poured into the site known as Jackson's Diggins. Eventually the name was changed to Idaho Springs, due largely to the importance of the hot springs, which later lured many visitors for medicinal purposes.

Shortly after Jackson's big discovery, two brothers, George and David Griffith, made a historic strike. After leaving their home in Kentucky and heading west to Denver in 1858, the two brothers followed the masses up to Central City. Since most of the good mining claims were taken, they set off to explore Upper Clear Creek Canyon upstream from Jackson's Diggins. Quickly they struck rich gold ore, established their claims and built a cabin. Other miners followed, and before long the mining camp was named Georgetown, after the elder Griffith brother.

Although Georgetown miners were initially drawn to the gold, by the mid-1860s it was apparent that silver ore abounded in the mountains around Georgetown and its sister mining camp, Silver Plume, 2 miles up the valley. Soon more silver was being produced here than in any other district in the world until the great Leadville strike in 1878. It's estimated that more than $200 million in silver was mined near Georgetown during these early days.

Georgetown boomed and by the 1870s had more than 5,000 residents. Unlike other mining towns in Colorado, Georgetown was settled by families with relatively upstanding morals. Many fine and substantial homes were built, showing off a variety of architectural styles popular in that era.

Georgetown was very proud of its volunteer fire department, which kept the town from burning down (the fate of most other towns during this period). Thanks to the fire department's commitment, more than 200 of Georgetown's original buildings still stand today.

As mines in the valley and surrounding mountains grew in number, locals anxiously awaited the Colorado Central Railroad, which eventually reached Georgetown in 1877. But it was not until 1884 that the famous Georgetown Loop Railroad, stretching from Georgetown to Silver Plume, was finished (see the Major Attractions section). When the Argentine Central Railroad was built from Silver Plume to the mines up near Waldorf, silver ore could be more economically shipped to the mills and smelters.

When the silver market crashed in 1893, most of the mines around Georgetown and Silver Plume closed, and the mining population began to dwindle. Although some mines continued to produce gold, copper and other minerals, the boom days were over.

By 1910 the 22,000-foot Argo Tunnel was completed from Idaho Springs under the mountains to Central City. The Argo connected many existing tunnels and provided easy access between the two mining towns. In 1913 the Argo Gold Mill was completed in Idaho Springs. The finest mill of its kind in the country, it supplied much of the gold for the Denver Mint.

Due to increased mining costs, most of the area's mines are closed these days. Plenty of gold and silver still remain in the hills around Idaho

Springs and Georgetown, but until mining becomes more profitable, the minerals will remain underground.

Major Attractions

Georgetown Historic District

What separates Georgetown from many other historic mining districts in Colorado is the sheer number of old Victorian homes still standing and the heartfelt dedication of its citizens to preserving and restoring these buildings. The Georgetown Society (a local historical preservation group) has spearheaded the painstaking restoration of many homes, buildings and shop fronts. Visitors need only walk or ride through the streets of town to get a feel for the way things were a century ago.

Many buildings in town are on the National Register of Historic Places, including two museums, the **Hamill House** and the **Hotel de Paris** (see the Museums and Galleries section for details). One of the finest examples of resi-dential architecture is the **Maxwell House,** stunningly painted in shades of pink and cream. It is, however, a private home. Stop by the Episcopal church, which houses the oldest pipe organ in the state. You can still see the bell tower that blew off with the roof in a big wind of 1867, the year the church was built.

Pick up a historical buildings map at the **Community Center on 6th St.** (across from the post office) and take a self-guided walking or driving tour; also, visit the website **www. historicgeorgetown.org.**

Georgetown Loop Railroad

If you want to get from Georgetown to Silver Plume, everyone knows that the 2-mile stretch of Interstate 70 will whisk you there in a matter of minutes. But what's the fun of that? If you climb aboard the Georgetown Loop narrow-gauge railroad the trip to Silver Plume takes on a whole new meaning. This historic 3-mile stretch of tracks, once called the "Scenic Wonder of the West," was quite an engineering feat when built more than a century ago.

Steam engine on the Georgetown Loop Railroad. Photo by Bruce Caughey.

History

During the booming silver mining days in Upper Clear Creek Canyon, getting the ore down out of the mines to the mills by wagon was extremely difficult. A railroad line to the upper end of the valley was greatly needed. Building a railroad to Georgetown presented the usual construction problems, but extending the tracks to Silver Plume was a real nightmare. The situation seemed insurmountable—Silver Plume was only 2 miles away but stood a full 700 feet above Georgetown. Conventional railroad locomotives would not be able to climb the 6 percent grade.

An engineer for the Union Pacific Railroad, Jacob Blickensderfer, spent a couple of years studying the problem. His innovative solution required building a system of curves and bridges that would reduce the average grade to 3 percent. The planned route included three hairpin curves and four bridges. At Devil's Gate, the valley's narrowest spot, the track looped over itself by a 300-foot-long bridge that passed 75 feet above the track below. The Georgetown Loop was completed in 1884. From Silver Plume, tracks were laid on up the valley to Greymont and Bakerville.

After silver prices crashed in 1893, the railway shifted its focus to tourists. The engineering feats of the Georgetown Loop were known throughout the world, and soon as many as seven trains a day made the trip between Georgetown and Silver Plume. Passengers seeking further adventure opted for a trip up from Silver Plume to Pavilion Point on the Argentine Central Railroad.

Later, as automobile routes were built into the mountains, train travel began losing its glamour. In 1939 the railroad tracks on the Georgetown Loop were torn up and sold for scrap. But the story has a happy ending. Thanks to help from the Colorado Historical Society and generous benefactors, the Georgetown Loop was restored and reopened in 1984, 100 years after its inception.

Facts

Today the Georgetown Loop Railroad offers trips from the station at the west edge of Georgetown to the restored Silver Plume Depot up the valley. Both depots offer free slide shows and ticket servicing. The Silver Plume Depot also has a number of railroad exhibits. Trips on the railroad begin from either end. The round-trip ride takes about an hour, but we recommend you stop along the way to take a tour of the 1870s **Lebanon Mine,** accessible only by train (for a small additional charge). Put on a hard hat and enter the old silver mine with a guide who will fill you in on its history and explain early mining techniques.

The train makes frequent daily runs from mid-May through mid-Oct. The Lebanon mine tour is available Memorial Day–Labor Day. For information contact **Georgetown Loop Railroad, Old Georgetown Station, 1106 Rose St., P.O. Box 217, Georgetown, CO 80444.** For reservations call **303-569-2403** or in Denver at **303-670-1686; www.georgetown loop.com.**

Festivals and Events

Christmas Market

first two weekends in Dec. The Christmas season gets into full swing at Georgetown's Christmas Market in Strousse Park. Food booths offer home-baked goods from many nations of the world, and homemade crafts are also on display. Folk singers, dancers and carolers provide the entertainment. The shops in town are decorated for the occasion. Open 10 A.M.–dusk. Contact **Historic Georgetown Inc.; 303-569-2840; 303-569-2111; www.georgetown colorado.com.**

Outdoor Activities

Biking

MOUNTAIN BIKING

Plenty of hiking trails and old mining roads provide exciting mountain bike rides in the Clear Creek area. Check the Four-Wheel-Drive Trips,

Hiking and Backpacking and Scenic Drives sections for ideas, or stop in at the **Clear Creek Ranger District Office,** one block south of Interstate 70 on Hwy. 103, in Idaho Springs. **P.O. Box 3307, Idaho Springs, CO 80452; 303-567-3000.**

If you are interested in a guided, downhill ride on the Mt. Evans Highway, Guanella Pass or another local route, consider contacting **Trails and Rails Downhill** in Georgetown, at the Old Georgetown Station, **1106 Rose St.; 1-800-691-4386; 303-569-2403; www.trails andrails.com.**

Barbour Forks

Situated just south of Idaho Springs, Barbour Forks provides a fine, somewhat challenging ride up through a high valley and meadows. Eventually you'll reach a ridge (4.7 miles from Idaho Springs) that offers views down into Devil's Canyon. To reach the trail from Idaho Springs, head south on Soda Lakes Rd. past Indian Hot Springs for 3 miles and then up Forest Rd. 194 for 1.7 miles.

Devil's Canyon

This excellent 3-mile ride winds up into the Arapaho National Forest. The canyon, site of a fire a number of years ago, is currently filled with small saplings. To reach this dirt road from Idaho Springs, head south for 10 miles on Hwy. 103 and turn left after the curve at Ponder Point onto Forest Rd. 246. Road open June 15– Dec. 15.

Fishing

There are many places to fish in the Georgetown and Idaho Springs area but, overall, the fishing is not much to speak of. Mine runoff has made fish in some of the streams unfit to eat; overfishing has also taken its toll. Following are some of the better opportunities.

Fall River Reservoir

This is not a bad place to catch brook, brown and cutthroat trout, but the reservoir is very heavily fished. To reach the reservoir, take the

Fall River Rd. exit on Interstate 70 (about 2 miles west of Idaho Springs). Follow the road 5.5 miles and turn left onto the dirt road just at the base of a steep switchback. Follow the dirt road 3 miles, keeping to the right.

Georgetown Lake

Located at the east end of Georgetown along Interstate 70, Georgetown Lake is well stocked with rainbow and cutthroat trout. Though the pressure is heavy, fishing can be rewarding.

Silver Dollar Lake

To reach this high mountain lake from Georgetown, head 8.5 miles south on Guanella Pass Rd. just beyond Guanella Campground and turn right at the sign to Silver Dollar Lake Trail. The rough road climbs steeply for a mile to the trailhead for Silver Dollar Lake. The hike into the lake is about a mile, and fishing can be good for cutthroat trout.

Four-Wheel-Drive Trips

St. Mary's Glacier to Central City

The backcountry between Silver Lake (near St. Mary's Glacier) and Central City is a great place for jeeping, but a few words of advice are necessary. Many four-wheel-drive roads crisscross the area, and a patchwork of private mining claims prevents access to many of them. Be sure to have a topographic map of the area and follow the brown Forest Service markers.

When you get up on the high alpine meadows, don't create your own road—this kills the fragile plant life and promotes erosion, requiring decades for recovery. This 10-mile (one-way) drive offers beautiful alpine scenery, wildflowers, historic mines and old cemeteries.

To reach the road from Idaho Springs, head west on Interstate 70 for about 2 miles and get off at the Fall River Rd. exit. Drive 9 miles to the end of Fall River Rd. at Silver Lake. Turn right and after a short distance turn left on Forest Rd. 175 up a hill to Yankee Hill. Stick to this route for about 4.5 miles and you'll reach Pisgah Lake. Another mile past the lake brings

A view up lofty Mount Evans from across Summit Lake. Photo by Brad Buckner.

you to the junction with Forest Rd. 273.1. Turn left here and proceed 2 miles to Bald Mountain Cemetery. From the eastern end, turn left (north) and follow the road to Boodle Mill just west of Central City.

Hiking and Backpacking

The territory covered in this chapter offers an excellent array of alpine hikes. Although a large number of hikers from Denver invade this area in summer, the scenic beauty overrides the sometimes crowded trails. A vast majority of the land lies within Arapaho National Forest, including a large part of the 74,000-acre Mt. Evans Wilderness Area south of Idaho Springs. Many of the hikes around Idaho Springs, Georgetown and Silver Plume are accented by old ghost towns and mining sites. We must caution you to not explore the old mines (they are extremely dangerous).

For hiking ideas and information about Arapaho National Forest, visit the **Clear Creek Ranger District Visitor Center,** one block south on Hwy. 103 from Interstate 70 in Idaho Springs, **P.O. Box 3307, Idaho Springs, CO 80452; 303-567-3000; www.fs.fed.us/arnf/ccrd/vvc.htm.**

Chicago Lakes Trail

This 4-mile trail, which leads up to Chicago Lakes in the Mt. Evans vicinity, gets quite a bit of hiking traffic, but it scores a nine on the scenic meter. The trail begins at heavily used Echo Lake. It winds around to the south end of the lake, where badly trampled ground makes it difficult to follow the main trail—look for blazes on the trees. From the lake the trail heads southwest for 1.7 miles to Idaho Springs Reservoir and then up through the Chicago Lakes Burn, where 400 acres went up in flames in 1978. Though the trees are not much to look at, the wildflowers are beautiful. Eventually you reach the spectacular Chicago Lakes Basin, which is surrounded by the looming cliffs of the Mt. Evans massif.

To reach the trailhead at Echo Lake, drive 14 miles south from Idaho Springs on Hwy. 103 and park just outside Echo Lake Campground. Walk across the Mt. Evans Hwy. (Hwy. 5) and look for the trailhead under the power lines.

Grays and Torreys Peaks Trail

These twin peaks, called the Ant Hills by the Ute Indians, are anything but. Standing 14,270 feet and 14,267 feet, respectively, Grays and Torreys were at one time as well known as Longs Peak and Pikes Peak. When Georgetown and Idaho Springs were booming back in the late 1800s, it was very fashionable to hike the 4.5-mile trail to the summit of Grays and traverse the half-mile ridge over to Torreys. Even Victorian ladies, delicate creatures that they were, would adjust their skirts and ride horses sidesaddle up the mountains.

These days the beautiful hike, with spectacular views from the top of the peaks, is still very popular. Beginning at 11,200 feet, the trail crosses Quayle Creek and heads up the valley to the southwest, eventually beginning a steep ascent up Grays Peak. Be sure to take a camera, as this is an excellent area to spot mountain goats.

To reach the trailhead from Georgetown, head west on Interstate 70 for 6.5 miles and get off at Bakerville (Exit 221). From Bakerville proceed south up Stevens Gulch Rd. for 4 miles to the parking area near Stevens Mine.

Herman Gulch Trail

Each day thousands of people whiz by this trailhead alongside Interstate 70 with no idea that a beautiful, secluded valley lies just a short hike away. This fairly steep 2.5-mile trail climbs almost 2,000 feet up through thick stands of pine, eventually coming out into an alpine meadow where wildflowers (especially columbine) grow abundantly in mid-July. The trail heads up to Herman Lake at 12,000 feet, which is a good place for lunch. If you still have the drive, climb the saddle above the lake for views south to the east portal of the Eisenhower Tunnel.

To reach the trailhead from Georgetown, head west on Interstate 70 for 9.5 miles to Exit 218. Park on the north side of the highway; trailhead is near the highway department sandpiles.

Mt. Bierstadt Climb

This 14,060-foot peak, Mt. Bierstadt, deserves mention for its spectacular high-altitude beauty and easy accessibility (the trail to the summit is a mere 2.5-mile climb). From the top of Guanella Pass the mountain and its long jagged north ridge tower to the east. It's an impressive sight and quite often you'll find a painter or two sitting by the road, getting the scene down on canvas. Routes to the summit of Mt. Bierstadt are numerous, but take this hard-earned advice—stay on the boardwalks to avoid the boggy meadow and a bushwhack through wet willow bushes. You don't want to be soaking wet during the climb. After getting around most of the bushes and the bog, head southeast up to the gradual ridge and then to the summit.

To reach the trailhead at the summit of Guanella Pass Rd., drive south 11 miles from Georgetown. Actually begin the hike about 200 yards down from the summit (north).

Mt. Evans (Rest House Trail and Summit Lake Trail)

Yes, we know, you can drive to the summit, but that's not quite as rewarding as doing it the old-fashioned way. This 12-mile (one-way) route from Echo Lake Campground (across from Echo Lake Lodge) to the summit is challenging, beautiful and, at times, even eerie. The trail winds through a number of burn areas complete with charred pine trees, which can make parts of the hike look like a forest out of *The Wizard of Oz.*

From Echo Lake Campground, begin hiking southeast on Rest House Trail (Trail 57). This 6.5-mile section of the trail crosses over a couple of ridges before entering an area of forest near Lincoln Lake that burned in 1968. After 5 miles you'll reach a fork in the trail—the right fork leads 1 mile to Lincoln Lake. This lake lies just below Mt. Evans Rd. (6 miles up from Echo Lake Campground).

Meanwhile, back at the fork, continue on the left trail another 1.5 miles to the remains of the Mt. Evans Shelter House, which burned in 1962. There are a number of good campsites in this area, but be sure to bring a stove, as firewood is scarce. From here you'll need to head right, connecting with the Summit Lake Trail (Trail 82), which climbs 4.7 miles to Summit Lake at 12,830 feet. The last 2 miles of this stretch can be wet and sloppy in early to midsummer, so consider yourself forewarned. From Summit Lake you'll have to scramble the remaining distance (less than a mile) on a very steep talus slope to the summit unless you want to hitch a ride along the road.

To reach the trailhead at Echo Lake Campground, drive 14 miles south from Idaho Springs on Hwy. 103.

Pavilion Point

This is more of a historic walk than an actual hike. A short trail (1 mile, tops) follows a section of the old Argentine Central Railroad bed to Pavilion Point. When the railroad was built in 1905 to transport ore from the Argentine Mining District at Waldorf down to Silver Plume, it was the highest steam railroad track in the country and remained so until it was dismantled in 1920. Hordes of visitors would board at Silver Plume and ride up to Pavilion Point for picnics and memorable bird's-eye views down to Silver Plume and Georgetown. (For information about the Argentine Central Railroad, see the Waldorf Rd. write-up in the Scenic Drives section.)

These days a stone chimney is all that remains of the pavilion, but in summer, with good timing, you can look down on the Georgetown Loop train as it chugs up the valley to Silver Plume.

To reach the trail from Georgetown, drive south on Guanella Pass Rd. for 2.5 miles to Waldorf Junction (Forest Rd. 248). Turn right and proceed 1.2 miles to the fourth switchback and park your car. The unmarked trail heads off to the north. An alternate route begins in Silver Plume on the south side of Interstate 70. After heading under the highway bridge, turn right, park and continue walking on the frontage road for a couple hundred yards. The road turns south up the old Argentine Central rail bed for a gentle 3-mile walk to the old pavilion site.

St. Mary's Glacier

See the Fall River Rd. description in the Scenic Drives section.

Skiing

CROSS-COUNTRY SKIING AND SNOWSHOEING

When snow falls on the mountains and in the valleys around the Georgetown and Idaho Springs area, summertime jeep roads and hiking trails are transformed into wonderful trails for cross-country skiing and snowshoeing. The Forest Service has done a good job marking many trails and providing information and maps for skiers and shoers. Snow conditions and trail ideas are available at the **Clear Creek Ranger District Office,** open daily. **P.O. Box 3307, Idaho Springs, CO 80452; 303-567-3000;** some information available at **www.fs.fed. us/arnf/ccrd/vvc.htm.**

Backcountry Trails

Butler Gulch—This 3-mile trail (one way) leads up into a snow-covered bowl just below the Continental Divide. Due to its quick access from Denver, many skiers come here on weekends.

The trail begins next to the Henderson Mine property up the Jones Pass Rd. After about a quarter-mile, take the left fork over a good bridge and start your climb through the forested valley. The skiing along most of the trail is fairly easy, but there is a steep, narrow section about halfway up that can be a bit tricky for beginners. When you reach a series of switchbacks, the pine trees begin to thin out. Once up in the high open area you can choose your own trail, but be sure to stay clear of the avalanche chutes along the steep walls to the left. Return on the same trail or choose your own route down through the steep, dense forests along the gulch.

To reach the trailhead from Idaho Springs, head west on Interstate 70 to the Hwy. 40 turn-off. From Empire, drive along Hwy. 40 about 7.5 miles to the Henderson Mine turnoff on the left. Proceed about a mile and a half along this road to the ski parking area next to the mine.

Loveland Pass—If you don't want to spend time skiing uphill, consider a few runs down Loveland Pass. This is a great place to practice telemark turns. You need to shuttle cars between the pass and Loveland Valley Ski Area. From the summit of the pass, pull off to the right side of the road and ski along the contour to the west into a wide-open bowl and start skiing down the steep drainage heading north. After a half-mile, you'll run into Hwy. 6. Cross the road and continue skiing down the drainage on easier terrain, where you'll meet up with the runs at Loveland Valley Ski Area. You can't beat the price.

Waldorf Road—Located just 2.5 miles south of Georgetown on Guanella Pass Rd., this 7-mile trail leads along Forest Rd. 248 to the old ghost town of Waldorf. This is a fantastic beginner to intermediate route. For information see the Scenic Drives section.

DOWNHILL SKIING AND SNOWBOARDING

Loveland Ski Area

Nestled just below the Continental Divide 12 miles west of Georgetown on Interstate 70, Loveland is primarily a day ski area. The majority of visitors come from the Denver metro area and enjoy Loveland's excellent, reasonably priced skiing without the extraneous trappings of a major resort. Two connected ski areas—the easy, rolling **Loveland Valley** and the larger, more challenging **Loveland Basin**—provide a wide variety of terrain and snow conditions. Snowboarders love the wide-open chutes and rolls found above treeline as well as the snowboard park.

Loveland Valley is connected to the main base at Loveland Basin by the long Chair 5. It's an excellent place for novices and is very popular with families. Six lifts service Loveland Basin, whisking skiers up to mostly intermediate and advanced runs. The diversity of runs—including glade skiing, bowl skiing and steep bump runs—provides a big part of Loveland's appeal.

With a top elevation of 12,700 feet, the area has become well known for its fluffy powder. Most of the runs have a protected northern exposure, but some of the snow on the south-facing slopes can turn into heavy slop after a few hours in the sun. Winds often kick up, blasting snow off some of the higher slopes (this is the Continental Divide, after all). The recent addition of Chair 9 carries passengers higher than any other quad lift in the world. Loveland is also quite well known for its long season, running from mid-Oct. to mid-May. Base facilities include an expanded restaurant as well as a bar, nursery/day care, rental shop and ski school. **P.O. Box 899, Georgetown, CO 80444; 1-800-736-3SKI; 303-569-3203;** in Denver **303-571-5580; www.skiloveland.com.**

St. Mary's Glacier

Those who just can't quite pack enough skiing into eight months bring their rock skis up to St. Mary's Glacier in the summer. Mary holds claim to being the southernmost glacier in North America, a tidbit that all geographers should be sure to file away for future use. Skiing St. Mary's is for the hearty and knowledgeable, and for good reason. The three-quarter-mile trail to the glacier is rocky and uphill; "snow" maintains the consistency of ice or sun-softened slush. Unless your turns are precise and your edges freshly sharpened you could end up tangled on the rocks below the snow line. For directions, see Fall River Rd. in the Scenic Drives section.

Seeing and Doing

Cemeteries

Alvarado Cemetery

Take time to visit the old Alvarado Cemetery, 3.5 miles east of Georgetown on the Interstate 70 frontage road. Ornate Victorian-era tombstones dot this burial ground, including that of Louis Dupuy, founder of the Hotel de Paris.

Hot Springs

Indian Springs Resort

After a long day on the ski slopes, some skiers returning to Denver on winter weekends avoid the traffic jam by stopping in at Indian Springs until the traffic dies down. Indians, who first used the springs, had a unique arrangement— the springs were a no-man's-land where all tribes could enjoy the hot water. Supposedly after George Jackson found the springs in 1859, local miners enjoyed the luxury of soaking after their long workdays. By the late 1860s the first resort development began. Touted as the Saratoga of the Rocky Mountains, Indian Springs attracted quite a few famous visitors, including Walt Whitman and Teddy Roosevelt.

Today this sprawling, recently renovated (and greatly improved) retreat offers a number of spa experiences. The swimming pool (set at about 90° F) is covered by a translucent bubble and sur-rounded by a botanic garden of ferns, palms and other tropical plants and flowers—a bizarre but soothing sight in winter. Downstairs, private hot mineral baths and the geothermal vapor caves are accessible from the men's and women's locker rooms. For an extra price, try a massage, facial or a dip in Club Mud, an 8-foot-square by 1-foot-deep pool of mud. Hey, it's supposed to be good for you!

Overnight accommodations are available in the 130-year-old lodge, though not recommend-ed. These lodge rooms **($ to $$)** are dingy and the bathrooms are located down the hall, but if you're just too relaxed after a soak it may not matter. Much newer and more comfortable motel-type units across the road **($$ to $$$)** offer larger rooms, private bathrooms, TVs and other creature comforts. Indian Springs has a lounge and restaurant **($ to $$$),** serving break-fast, lunch and dinner 7 A.M.–9 P.M. daily.

The complex, located about 100 yards up Soda Creek Rd. from Miner St. in Idaho Springs, is open 7:30 A.M.–10:30 P.M. year-round. **302 Soda Creek Rd., P.O. Box 1990, Idaho Springs, CO 80452; 303-567-2191;** in Denver **303-989-6666; www.indianspringsresort.com.**

Mine Tours

The Edgar Experimental Mine

In the 1870s this hardrock mine produced large amounts of silver, gold, lead and copper. Today it

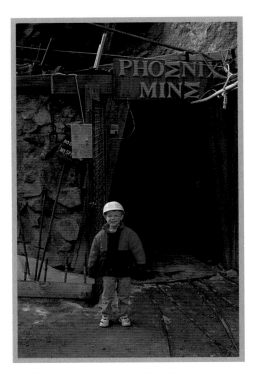

Awaiting a tour into the bowels of the Phoenix Mine near Idaho Springs. Photo by Dean Winstanley.

serves as a research area and classroom facility for future mining engineers from the Colorado School of Mines in Golden. Students use the lat-est in high-tech mining equipment to gain the valuable experience they'll use after graduation. For a small fee, the general public can take a tour lasting 45 minutes to an hour. Open May–Aug., Tues.–Sat. 9 A.M.–4 P.M. During the rest of the year, reservations are necessary. From Idaho Springs head north for a quarter-mile on 8th St. and follow the signs to the mine. **365 8th Ave., P.O. Box 1184, Idaho Springs, CO 80452; 303-567-2911.**

Lebanon Mine Tour

This fascinating tour is accessible only by the Georgetown Loop Railroad. See the Major Attractions section for details.

The Phoenix Mine

This place is a must-see, giving you a glimpse into an actual working hardrock mine—though on the scale of a one-man operation. What really makes this tour is the owner, Al Mosch, and his handpicked relatives who lead tours through the mine, discussing history and mining techniques. Visitors may even get the chance to swing a pickax themselves. Al captivates the crowd with his stories; however, public employees be warned—he doesn't like "bureaucrats." Be sure to touch the "lucky bucket." Open daily 10 A.M.– 6 P.M. Located 1 mile west of Idaho Springs on the Interstate 70 frontage road, and then south on Trail Creek Rd. for three-quarters of a mile. **P.O. Box 3236, Idaho Springs, CO 80452; 303-567-0422; 303-567-4382.**

Museums and Galleries

Argo Gold Mill and Museum
Opened for business in 1913, the Argo Gold Mill processed rich ore from mines in the area, much of it delivered via the 22,000-foot Argo Tunnel. The mill was shut down in 1943 and has since been added to the National Register of Historic Places. Currently it processes tourists

instead of ore. A section of the old mill with much of its original machinery intact is open for self-guided tours (for a rather hefty price). Mining relics, such as ore cars and parts of a stamp mill, are strewn about the grounds. Adjacent to the mill, gunfights (don't worry folks, they're only blanks) take place four times daily at a re-created Old West town.

For an additional charge, you can take a jeep tour up a nearby mountain to the Double Eagle Gold Mine. Open daily 10 A.M. to sundown; hours varying or nonexistent during winter. Located in **Idaho Springs** on the north side of Clear Creek at **2350 Riverside Dr.; 303-567-2421.**

George Rowe Museum
Located in an old schoolhouse built in 1894 and used until 1959, this museum contains a number of interesting historical artifacts as well as a completely restored old-time schoolroom. Highlights include historic photos, clothes and a hand-pump fire wagon purchased by the town after a major fire in 1884. The museum is worth

The 1894 schoolhouse that houses the George Rowe Museum in tiny Silver Plume. Photo by Dean Winstanley.

a look if you're in town. Local history books and other information are available here. Open daily Memorial Day–Labor Day 10 A.M.–4 P.M. and weekends in Sept. Fee charged. **95 Main St., Silver Plume; 303-569-2562.**

Georgetown Galleries

The restored buildings lining the streets of Georgetown house many shops and galleries. **Saxon Mountain Gallery (410 6th St., P.O. Box 112, Georgetown, CO 80444; 303-569-3186)** was opened by the late Bill Alexander, nationally known for his impressive watercolors of mountain snow scenes (especially downhill skiers). The gallery has a large display of his prints and paintings, along with artwork by over 40 other regional artists. **Georgetown Gallery (614 6th St., Georgetown, CO 80444; 303-569-2218)** is a cooperative with works from various Colorado artists and craftspeople. It features watercolors, oils and pastels as well as pottery.

Hamill House

Completed in 1879 this elegant Victorian mansion was home to William Hamill, a local silver magnate, politician and civic leader. At the time it was considered one of the finest homes in the state. Although today it's missing a bit of the original furniture, the exquisite interior serves as a reminder of just how much money some of the mine owners made. Marble fireplaces, walnut and maple woodwork, a curved-glass conservatory and diamond-dust mirrors show off the superb craftsmanship of the era. Be sure to pay a visit to the elegant three-seat, cupola-covered outhouse. Catch a glimpse of how the upper crust used to live. A fee is charged. Summer hours (Memorial Day–late Sept.) are 10 A.M.–4 P.M. daily; closed Jan.–Apr. **305 Argentine St., Georgetown, CO 80444; 303-569-2840; www.georgetowncolorado.com.**

Hotel de Paris

Perhaps the most famous of Georgetown's grand old buildings, the Hotel de Paris served for years as the social center of town and was the talk of the nation. The hotel was built in 1875 by Louis Dupuy, "the mysterious Frenchman," so called because locals disagreed over just who he was, where he came from and, perhaps more importantly, what, if anything, he might be hiding about his past. But evidence suggests he was a French army deserter. Guests at this magnificent two-story hotel were attracted by discussions about art and literature with Dupuy, who was a philosopher and a scholar as well as a gourmet cook. But without a doubt, this plush hotel's main attractions were the fine furnishings, the cuisine and the French wines.

Today the hotel has been faithfully restored by the National Society of Colonial Dames of America, and tours are offered. The stone and stucco building is complete with cast-iron decorations and pressed-metal trim. The original furnishings and decorative art objects fill the hotel. The formal dining room and well-equipped kitchen with its antique stove and accessories highlight the tour. Open daily, late May–late Sept., 10 A.M.–5 P.M.; in winter open Sat.–Sun. only. Closed Jan.–Apr. Located at Griffin St. and 6th St. in Georgetown, **409 6th St.; 303-569-2840; www.georgetown colorado.com.**

Silver Plume Depot

This is the restored, original depot for the historic Georgetown Loop Railroad. It serves as a ticket office for the train and has a number of original rooms, including a telegraph office. The rail yard displays a number of engines and cars. There is also a gift shop and a free slide show about the train. For more information see the Major Attractions section. The depot is located on the south side of **Interstate 70 at Exit 228 (Silver Plume).**

Nightlife

Plume Saloon

Locals crowd into this extremely rustic nightspot for a bite to eat and a drink to take the edge off. Over the mantelpiece of the stone fireplace hangs a portrait of Frances Willard, president of the Women's Christian Temperance Union at the turn of the century. Devilish locals are fond of toasting her as they quaff their drinks. Open year-round Wed.–Sun. from 4 P.M. "until they kick you out," which is usually around midnight. Located next to the Brewery Inn in **Silver Plume; 776 Main St.; 303-569-2277.**

The Red Ram

Though The Red Ram's main attraction is its main-floor burger and Mexican food restaurant **($ to $$),** live music plays most weekend nights in the subterranean and highly historic Rathskeller pub. Descend the stairs into this dark, smoky place, which lends itself to relaxation and knocking a few back. Good beer selection. Open daily at 11 A.M. In **Georgetown** at **606 6th St.; 303-569-2300.**

Tommyknocker Microbrewery and Pub

Although Tommyknocker boasts a full restaurant **($$ to $$$)** on one side of its Miner St. location in historic Idaho Springs, the fresh microbrews are undoubtedly the main attraction. The bar side with its high ceilings features pool tables, sports TVs and live music on weekends. Choose from a variety of beers brewed on the premises, some of which have garnered awards at the Great American Brew Fest. Favorites are the Tommyknocker Red Eye Lager and the Maple Nut Brown Ale. Not a bad place to cool your heels after a day in the great outdoors. Open daily 11 A.M.–10 P.M.; bar open until 2 A.M. **1401 Miner St., Idaho Springs, CO 80452; 303-567-2688; www.tommyknocker.com.**

Scenic Drives

Fall River Road (St. Mary's Glacier)

Drive up this 9-mile road along the Fall River through aspen and pine. Enormous rock outcroppings hang from the valley walls. About 7.5 miles up the road is a turnoff to the ghost town of Alice. If you continue ahead on Fall River Rd. for about a mile, you'll see the trailhead for the short half-mile hike to St. Mary's Glacier. A beautiful lake awaits as well as the glacier. To reach Fall River Rd. from Idaho Springs, head west on Interstate 70 for about 2 miles and look for Fall River Rd. (Exit 238).

Guanella Pass Road

Guanella Pass, a Scenic and Historic Byway, is a perennial favorite and for good reason. Pine forests and shimmering aspen line the road most of the way. At the 11,669-foot summit, the above-treeline view east to Mt. Bierstadt is quite a sight. The road is open year-round, weather permitting, but the best time to go is in early fall when the aspen are turning.

Begin the trip from Georgetown by driving south on Guanella Pass Rd. (Hwy. 118). Be sure to pick up the brochure at the Georgetown Information Center that provides historic and other insights about the Guanella Pass route. It's about 12 miles to the summit. From here you drop south over the pass about 15 miles to the intersection with Hwy. 285 at the town of Grant. Along the way you'll find a couple of campgrounds and plenty of trailheads, including many into the Mt. Evans Wilderness Area.

Loveland Pass

The pass is located 11 miles west of Georgetown on Interstate 70. Instead of driving through the Eisenhower Tunnel, turn left onto Loveland Pass Rd. (Hwy. 6) for a fantastic drive over the top of the Continental Divide. See the Scenic Drives section of the **Summit County** chapter for more details.

Mt. Evans Road

This has to be one of the most underrated attractions in Colorado. The paved Mt. Evans Rd., part of the Mt. Evans Scenic Byway, snakes its way 14 miles to the summit of Mt. Evans (14,264 feet). Although only 35 miles from Denver, this road remains unknown to many city dwellers.

Mt. Evans was first named Mt. Rosalie by the landscape painter Albert Bierstadt, in honor of his wife. In 1863 he was also the first person on record to climb the peak. In 1870 the peak was renamed in honor of the second governor of the

Colorado Territory. A primitive road was built up the mountain in the late 1920s and was improved for regular passenger cars in 1939. The road begins at Echo Lake, 14 miles south of Idaho Springs on Hwy. 103. It climbs up to tree-line after about 3 miles and eventually leads to Summit Lake, where you'll find a rest room, fishing and a short trail to a dramatic overlook of the Chicago Lakes. If you continue on the road from Summit Lake, a tight series of switchbacks will lead you to a parking area just below the summit. Along the way you'll probably catch a glimpse of a bighorn sheep or mountain goat—the Mt. Evans herd is one of the largest in the state. You may also see Denver University's observatory and cosmic ray research lab.

The 360-degree view from the summit is something you'll just have to see for yourself. Be sure to watch out for approaching lightning storms and get to your car if you spot one. Mt. Evans Rd. (Hwy. 5) is open in summer only; the stretch up to Summit Lake is usually open by Memorial Day, with the final stretch to the summit open by July 4. Small fee charged, by the Forest Service. For information check with the **Clear Creek Ranger District Office (303-567-3000; www.fs.fed.us/arnf/ccrd/uvc.htm)** or the **Idaho Springs Visitor Center (303-567-4382; www.clearcreek county.com).**

Oh My God Road

Although there are a couple of steep drop-offs, this drive up Virginia Canyon isn't nearly as intimidating as the name implies. The 9-mile road connects Idaho Springs with Central City and is open year-round to all vehicles. Mine shafts and building remnants dating back to the 1860s can be seen along the road. There are superb views to the south across Clear Creek Canyon to Chief Mountain and Squaw Mountain. Once over the top of the hill, descend through the remains of the Russell Gulch townsite and into Central City.

This drive begins in Idaho Springs at the intersection of Canyon St. and Placer St. and heads north on Virginia Canyon Rd. Stay on the main road or you may have the same nightmare that one unlucky visitor had—he drove off on a side road and plunged his new Blazer into an abandoned mine shaft! For a self-guided map, stop in at the **visitor center** (open daily) in **Idaho Springs** at **2200 Miner St.**

Waldorf Road

Although this road is probably not bad enough to require four-wheel drive, your vehicle should have good ground clearance (RVs can forget it). Located near Georgetown, the road leads up to the old ghost town of Waldorf, which was quite a booming silver and gold mining area when rich ore was found in the 1860s. Just southwest of Waldorf, a stage route crossed over 13,207-foot Argentine Pass, providing transportation to the early mining camps in Summit County.

In 1905 Edward John Wilcox, owner of the prosperous Waldorf Mining & Milling Company, built a 16-mile stretch of railroad track connecting mines in the area with Silver Plume in the valley far below. The Argentine Central Railroad ended up making much more on tourism than it ever did hauling ore. Until it ceased service in 1920, it was the highest railroad in the world. Part of the road to Waldorf follows along the old rail bed. Not much is left of the town, as scavengers have stripped the buildings down to the foundations, but with a vivid imagination you can picture what life must have been like for the hundreds of miners who lived there.

To reach Waldorf from Georgetown, head south on Guanella Pass Rd. for 2.5 miles and turn right at the hairpin curve onto Waldorf Rd. (Forest Rd. 248). Continue about 6 miles to Waldorf.

Wildlife

Georgetown Wildlife Viewing Area

The first of its kind in the state, this is truly one of your surest bets for a close-up view of Colorado's state animal—the bighorn sheep. Of the 6,000 bighorn sheep roaming the state, the herd near Georgetown numbers over 350. Early and late in the day are the best time for viewing;

Mountain goats are year-round residents on the slopes of Mount Evans. Photo by Gene Schmidt.

from Nov. to Jan. be sure to listen and watch for rams clashing horns in a battle for the herd harem. The viewing station, fully equipped with viewing scopes, is located next to Georgetown Lake along Interstate 70 on old Hwy. 6. To reach it from the interstate, take the Georgetown exit (Exit 228).

Where to Stay

Accommodations

Although motels and cabin rentals are available throughout the Georgetown and Idaho Springs area, bed and breakfast inns have really started to proliferate. And with so many historic buildings in the county, it only makes sense. In Idaho Springs, the **Miners Pick Bed and Breakfast ($$$ to $$$$)** offers three comfortable rooms, all with queen-size beds and private baths. Built in 1895 this inn also features a comfortable fireplace sitting room and a common room with a TV/VCR; full breakfast served in the formal dining room. **1639 Colorado Blvd.,**

P.O. Box 3156, Idaho Springs, CO 80452; 1-800-567-2975; 303-567-2975.

Georgetown offers the greatest variety of B&Bs. The intimate **Alpine Hideaway ($$$$),** with its bird's-eye view of town and up-valley, is a bit pricey, but its two elaborately designed and decorated rooms provide a fantastic romantic getaway. Each room features a gas fireplace and whirlpool bath; gourmet breakfast baskets are placed at your door each morning. **P.O. Box 788, Georgetown, CO 80444; 1-800-490-9011; 303-569-2800.**

If you want to stay in Silver Plume, **The Brewery Inn ($$$)** is the place (it's also the only place). This Victorian bed and breakfast was built in the 1890s on the site of the old Boche Brewery. The old spring pump house, which was the water source for the brewery, still operates, and the water flows by the house, under the gazebo in the back-yard and down to nearby Clear Creek. The first-floor suite has a private bath; three upstairs rooms all share a bathroom. **P.O. Box A, Silver Plume, CO 80476; 1-800-500-0209; 303-569-2284.**

For a more complete listing of lodgings, check local websites at **www.idahospringstourism. com** or **www.georgetowncolorado.com.** Other standout B&Bs, as well as some other unique lodging opportunities, are described below.

Georgetown / Baehler Resort Service—$$$ to $$$$

Perhaps the most intriguing lodging possibility in Georgetown is to rent a historic Victorian home. Working through the Georgetown Resort Service, choose from 12 of Georgetown's fine homes, ranging from gingerbread Victorians to Swiss-style chalets to cozy miners' cabins. A minimum stay of two nights is necessary, and some require a stay of one week. Reservations are required. This can be a great mountain rendezvous for two, but family reunions, celebrations and large meeting groups are also encouraged. If you are interested, Odette Baehler, the charming proprietor of the service, provides a wealth of historical information and is available to give tours of town and the immediate area. **P.O. Box 247, Georgetown, CO 80444; 303-569-2665.**

St. Mary's Glacier Bed and Breakfast—$$$ to $$$$

In a spectacular mountain setting, this hand-hewn log inn makes you feel as if you are light-years away from the Denver area (instead of just an hour or so). The furnishings fit the casual yet classy mood of the inn. Drop-dead views of the surrounding mountains from the inn's hillside location are a highlight and available from many of the rooms and common areas. The great room features a wonderful river-rock fireplace. The seven guest rooms all feature private bathrooms; as you might have guessed, the Honeymoon / Anniversary suite is perfect for romance. The beds are covered with hand-sewn quilts and there are artistic touches everywhere. Meet with other guests in the attractive lower-level dining rooms for a hearty breakfast. Kitchen is open for guest use; indoor hot tub available. **336 Crest View Dr., Idaho Springs, CO 80452; 303-567-4084; www. coloradovacation.com / bed / stmary.**

Indian Springs Resort—$$ to $$$

See the Hot Springs section for details.

The Peck House—$$ to $$$

James Peck was a successful Chicago merchant who came west in the Pikes Peak gold rush of 1859. A year later he built the Peck House as his private home in the little town of Empire. It wasn't until 1872 that Mrs. Peck opened her doors to overnight guests, and soon the home became a regular stagecoach stop for travelers over Berthoud Pass. As the oldest hotel in Colorado, the Peck House still carries on in a grand Victorian tradition.

A wide veranda stretches along the front of the building, with views across the valley. Inside, the mood is created by a large parlor with comfortable antique furniture, historic photos, red velvet curtains and plenty of books available to guests. The owners, Gary and Sally St. Clair, have done a tremendous job in catering to all of your wants. A hot tub and downstairs ski lockers are a couple of nice touches. Eleven (some rather small) rooms, all with private baths, are elegantly appointed with period antiques. Let it be known, however, that the undersized antique beds don't suit everyone. The Peck House is well known for its fine dining and Sun. brunch (see the Where to Eat section). Located along Hwy. 40, 2 miles from Interstate 70. **83 Sunny Ave., P.O. Box 428, Empire, CO 80438; 303-569-9870; www.thepeck house.com.**

Camping

Arapaho National Forest

Many of the campground sites in this area can be reserved by calling **877-444-6777** or going on-line to **www.reserveusa.com.** All the listed sites charge a fee. From Georgetown there are two national forest campgrounds up Guanella Pass Rd. Drive south on Guanella Pass Rd.

(Forest Rd. 118) about 4 miles to **Clear Lake Campground** (8 sites). Another 4 miles south is **Guanella Campground** (18 sites).

About 8 miles west of Empire on Hwy. 40 toward Berthoud Pass is **Mizpah Campground** (10 sites). Southwest of Idaho Springs are two other campgrounds. From Idaho Springs drive southwest on Hwy. 103 to the intersection with Forest Rd. 188. Turn right onto Forest Rd. 188 and proceed to **West Chicago Creek Campground** (16 sites), 9 miles from Idaho Springs. If you continue on Hwy. 103 for 14 miles from Idaho Springs you'll reach **Echo Lake Campground** (18 sites).

Private Campgrounds
Indian Springs Resort—Full hookups right next to the hot springs pool (as well as the road). Located 100 yards up Soda Creek Rd. from Idaho Springs. **302 Soda Creek Rd., P.O. Box 1990, Idaho Springs, CO 80452; 303-567-2191; in Denver 303-989-6666; www.indianspringsresort.com.**
Mountain Meadow Campground—This place offers plenty of RV hookups and tentsites. Located about 2 miles west of Empire on Hwy. 40. **P.O. Box 2, Empire, CO 80438; 303-569-2424.**

Where to Eat

The Peck House (Empire)—$$ to $$$$
The ambience of the Peck House, built in 1860, is only part of the dining experience—the fine food is the real attraction. This restaurant serves up lunch, dinner and a well-attended Sun. brunch. Within the Victorian confines of a cozy inn (see the Where to Stay section), the ground-floor dining room is set with red linen tablecloths, and a crackling fire is often burning. Chef/owner Gary St. Clair prepares a tasty menu of steaks, fowl and seafood selections; nightly specials during our visit included baked, stuffed rainbow trout. Also offered is an extensive wine list. On Sun. the champagne brunch

features menu items such as quail and eggs, eggs Benedict and salmon Napoleon. In summer try the pleasant covered porch with mountain views. Open Sun.–Thurs. 3–9 P.M., Fri.–Sat. until 10 P.M., Sun. brunch (summer only) 10 A.M.–2 P.M. **83 Sunny Ave., Empire, CO 80438; 303-569-9870; www.thepeckhouse.com.**

Buffalo Bar (Idaho Springs)—$ to $$$
Located in a brick building on Miner St. that's been a watering hole since 1885, the Buffalo Bar reeks of history (except for the large-screen TVs). The layout is very inviting, with its wooden bar and mirror, exposed brick, high ceilings and the buffalo head on the wall. The Buffalo Bar opens its doors early in the morning when it starts serving its famous breakfast, which includes smoked trout and eggs, breakfast burritos and numerous omelettes. The lunch and dinner menus are extensive, ranging from burgers to baby back ribs to Mexican dishes. The highlight, however, has to be the numerous buffalo entrées from buffalo sausage to buffalo meatloaf to buffalo fajitas. Open 7 A.M.–10:30 P.M. daily. **1617 Miner St., Idaho Springs, CO 80452; 303-567-2729.**

Beau Jo's (Idaho Springs)—$ to $$
Beau Jo's is probably better known for its pizza than any other restaurant in Colorado. Many folks flock to Beau Jo's for their famous "mountain pies," a Colorado version of the Chicago deep-dish pizza. In the early 1970s this Idaho Springs restaurant got its start with a seating area for 15 customers; today they can seat 600 and have opened many locations along the Front Range. One reason for their huge success is the creative pizzas they prepare with a mind-boggling array of choices. Select from five thicknesses of crust (made with sesame wheat, whole wheat, white or butter white), numerous sauces and over 30 toppings. The thick-crust mountain pies come with honey to use on the leftover crust for dessert. Beau Jo's also serves sandwiches, but to order one would be a sin. The restaurant has a comfortable

wood decor and a wild napkin-art display near the entrance. Open Sun.–Thurs. 11 A.M.–9 P.M., Fri.–Sat. until 10 P.M. **1517 Miner St., Idaho Springs, CO 80452; 303-567-4376;** in Denver **303-573-6924;www.beaujos.com.**

The Happy Cooker (Georgetown)—$ to $$

Located in an old, restored Victorian home set back off 6th St., the Happy Cooker serves up some of the tastiest and most creative breakfast and lunch items around. This upbeat place is decorated with turn-of-the-century antiques, and the walls are covered with artwork for sale from the Georgetown Gallery. Menu favorites are quiches, Belgian waffles, homemade bread and soups. If you are on your way to the ski slopes, stop in for a hearty breakfast and a cup of tea. During good weather the patio is a fantastic place to enjoy a meal. Open 7 A.M.–5 P.M. daily. **412 6th St., Georgetown, CO 80444; 303-569-3166.**

Petra Cafe (Georgetown)—$ to $$

Paintings grace the walls and warming sunlight permeates this quaint, comfortable little cafe. The Petra features outstanding homemade breakfasts and lunches and is particularly notable for its baked goods. Breakfast entrées range from heavier omelettes to lighter fare. Lunches include creative sandwiches, homemade soups, stews and fresh salads. Outdoor courtyard seating available, weather permitting. Open 8 A.M.–4 P.M. daily year-round. **507 Taos St., Georgetown, CO 80444; 303-569-2443.**

KP Cafe (Silver Plume)—$

Historical eras blend and wholesome food permeates the KP. Occupying one of the historic mining buildings on Main St., this restaurant is reminiscent of a soda shoppe from the 1940s or 1950s. Open for breakfast and lunch, the KP offers a changing menu selection that usually includes omelettes and burgers and sandwiches. The vegetarian specialties are excellent. Try their Machu Picchu Burrito, loaded with black beans, quinoa and jack cheese. Also worth noting are their homemade soups and pies. If you

try the KP, don't expect fast food. Open Wed.–Sun. 10 A.M.–5 P.M. On the **corner of Main St. and Silver St., Silver Plume, CO 80476; 303-569-2054.** If you would rather load up on fresh baked goods and friendly conversation, stop in across the street at the **Sopp & Truscott Bakery.** This charming place offers fresh-baked bread, cookies and pastries.

2 Brothers Deli (Idaho Springs)—$

Promising "rescue from the pangs of hunger," this newly established gem delivers. It's an equally suitable choice whether you want to hang around for a while at a table or grab something quick on your way to the ski slopes. Although they offer great sandwiches, homemade soups, pizza and salads for lunch, the breakfast "wraps" are hugely popular. Open Sun.–Thurs. 6 A.M.–6 P.M., Fri.–Sat. until 7 P.M. Located across from the Tommyknocker brewpub. **1424 Miner St., Idaho Springs; 303-567-2439.**

Services

Visitor Information

Georgetown Community Information Center—Open Memorial Day–Labor Day; located across from the post office. **601 6th St.; 1-800-472-8230; www.georgetown colorado.com.**

Historic Georgetown Inc.—This group is involved in the historic preservation of Georgetown. They offer information about tours and events. **305 Argentine, P.O. Box 667, Georgetown, CO 80444; 303-569-2840; www. historicgeorgetown.org.**

Idaho Springs Visitor Information Center and Museum—For information on Idaho Springs, stop by the visitor center at **2600 Miner St.** Or contact **P.O. Box 97, Idaho Springs, CO 80452; 303-567-4382; www. idahospringstourism.com** or **www.clear creekcounty.com.**

Silver Plume Information—In the summer months, information is available at the **George Rowe Museum** in Silver Plume at **95 Main St.; 303-569-2562.** Also try the **Silver Plume Town Hall** at **360 Main St., Silver Plume, CO 80476; 303-569-2363.**

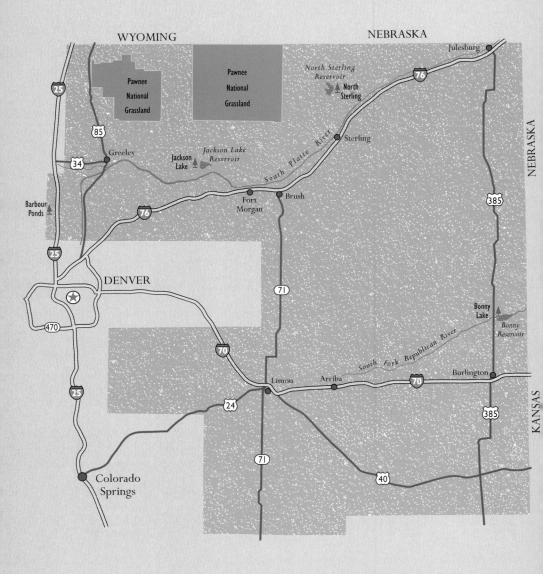

WYOMING   NEBRASKA

Pawnee
National
Grassland

Pawnee
National
Grassland

North Sterling
Reservoir

North
Sterling

Julesburg

76

Sterling

85

Greeley

Jackson Lake
Reservoir

Jackson
Lake

South Platte River

34

Barbour
Ponds

76

Fort
Morgan

Brush

NEBRASKA

385

25

DENVER

71

Bonny
Lake

Bonny
Reservoir

470

70

South Fork Republican River

25

Limon

Arriba

70

Burlington

24

40

385

71

Colorado
Springs

KANSAS

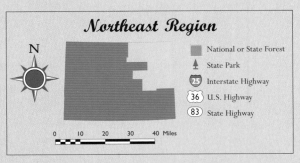

Northeast Region

N

National or State Forest

State Park

Interstate Highway

U.S. Highway

State Highway

0   10   20   30   40 Miles

Northeast Region

*Much of the Northeast Plains continues to be used as cattle and sheep range.
Photo by Bruce Caughey.*

Northeast Plains

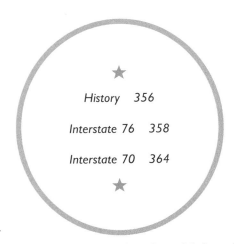

The image of Colorado's plains, dominated by immense rolling grasslands, plotted dirt roads, irrigated fields, oil pumps and an occasional town, has its problems. While the plains don't match the vision of Colorado most people hold, they have their own brand of subtle beauty. A fascinating history can be found along the routes of trappers, traders and homesteaders in the northeast plains; several towns preserve this history in excellent museums. Other attractions are usually passed, but they provide the essence of the "Other Colorado." Consider a ride on the turn-of-the-century carousel in Burlington, which will make you appreciate the craftsmanship of another era.

One of the major influences in the settlement of the northeast plains has always been the accessibility of water flowing down from the Rocky Mountains. The South Platte, the largest and most crucial river in northeastern Colorado, marked a route for explorers and proved to be life-sustaining to settlers. Along with the multitude of irrigation lands stemming from the main channel, it provides the backbone to much of the region's agricultural production. In its own right, however, the South Platte wasn't very impressive—especially compared to the Mississippi. In *Roughing It,* Mark Twain called the South Platte "a melancholy stream straggling through the center of the enormous flat plain, and only saved from being impossible to find with the naked eye by its sentinel rank of scattering trees standing on either bank. . . ." Despite a premium on water, several large warmwater reservoirs, such as those at North Sterling State Park and Bonny State Recreation Area, attract anglers, boaters and campers to the area.

Homesteads more than a century old can be recognized by sudden, dense clumps of trees on the barren prairie. Some homesteads thrive today, while many others have faded or disappeared altogether. Most residents of northeastern Colorado still work on large farms and ranches. It's these people, more than the landscape, that make this corner of Colorado an interesting place. Close-knit communities are situated along historic migration routes, now paved highways. Their strong sense of community is demonstrated at high school football games or town festivals. While driving along, keep your eyes peeled for the many antiques stores tucked away in little towns—you might find a keepsake memory.

A vast diversity of bird life also draws people to northeastern Colorado. Audubon Society members enjoy gazing quietly into binoculars and identifying species, while hunters prefer bagging low-flying pheasants and species of waterfowl. No one, however, will pull a trigger at frequently sighted white pelicans or blue herons.

History

When Maj. Stephen Long passed through Colorado's northeastern plains in 1820, he proclaimed that the region "would never be fit for human habitation other than by the nomad races." He also said it "should forever remain the unmolested haunt of the native hunter, bison and jackal." We're sure the predominant Arapaho and Cheyenne Indians who lived on the plains would have agreed, but by the 1820s traders and trappers began trickling through in search of beaver; soon trading posts were springing up along the South Platte corridor. At one time there were four trading posts (Fort Lupton, Fort Vasquez, Fort Jackson and Fort St. Vrain) within a 15-mile radius. These well-fortified posts did a thriving trade with Anglos as well as Indians, especially when inhibitions loosened after a few swigs of potent "Taos Lightning."

Just when trading had almost dried up, the 1859 gold strikes in the Colorado mountains lured a new wave of people across the plains. The vast majority were passing through, but some discouraged miners settled near the South Platte River, taking advantage of the fertile bottomland.

Almost coinciding with the gold strikes, the short-lived Pony Express established a mail stop in Julesburg, in the far northeastern corner of the state. It wasn't until 1862, however, that mail was carried regularly along the South Platte route to the burgeoning town of Denver. A transcontinental railroad was the next big step. Union Pacific rails reached Julesburg from the east in 1867, causing a population explosion and earning this wild town a description as "wickedest city in the West." Four thousand gamblers, speculators, prostitutes, outlaws and road agents poured into Julesburg, forming a ramshackle village that featured 22 saloons and five dance halls. At this stage of development, there was no law and order—murder by six-shooter occurred at the least provocation. Though the first railroad across America stopped in Julesburg, it passed for the most part above present-day Colorado.

The influx of new settlers wreaked havoc on the Indians' way of life, especially their hunting. The Indians began to strike back as a last resort when the herds of buffalo were depleted. The inevitable conflict culminated on Nov. 29, 1864, with the Sand Creek Massacre (see the History section of the Southeast Plains chapter), where Colorado volunteer troops massacred many women and children, without true provocation. A year later at the Battle of Summit Springs (at a site between Sterling and Akron), the final important Indian battle took place, in which a large band of Cheyenne were defeated by state troops and their Pawnee allies.

With the Indians removed and the arrival of trains to Colorado, cattle barons were at their zenith. John Iliff was the biggest of them all, owning much of the northeastern part of the state. Sheep ranching was to follow, but cattlemen never liked the woolly beasts—one line of a poem said, "A sheep just oozes out a stink, that drives a cowman to drink!" Or was that just an excuse?

In the spring of 1870 the Union Colony agricultural cooperative, under the steadfast direction of Nathan C. Meeker, founded a town named after Meeker's boss, Horace Greeley (owner of the *New York Tribune*). This group of greenhorn easterners came west with inflated expectations of paradise—including waterfalls, which were not to be found on the barren prairie of northeastern Colorado. Water, however, was plentiful, and the town of Greeley was platted at the confluence of the South Platte and Cache la Poudre Rivers. With the help of irrigation canals, the fertile soil produced successful crops. The newcomers had their share of problems, but liquor wasn't one of them—Meeker had brought only temperate colonists. One of the enforced rules of the young town was, "Thou shall not sell liquid damnation within the lines of the Union Colony." This rule prompted the success of several small establishments that sold booze just outside the city limits.

One nagging problem in Greeley was the trampling of crops by roaming cattle; settlers solved it by stringing up a 50-mile-long fence around the crops. Their neighbors scoffed at them, saying the fence was erected to keep out "godless" cowmen. But it worked and the town achieved unprecedented agricultural success. Just when things were going well, Meeker was forced by money matters to leave Greeley and take a job at the White River Indian agency in northwestern Colorado—and in 1879 he was murdered by Ute Indians who didn't appreciate his efforts to transform them into farmers. The

Meeker Massacre caused the entire tribe to be removed to distant reservations (see the History section in the Meeker chapter).

In retrospect it seems not much has changed in terms of the plains economy: crops are more diverse and methods for planting and harvesting have been modernized, but agriculture and ranching remain the mainstays. Though a flurry of activity in the 1970s caused oil wells to sprout up, much of the prehistoric-looking machinery now lies dormant.

Interstate 76 and Interstate 70

Since the Northeast Plains is not a destination as such, we have organized this chapter based on attractions along the major interstate highways, focusing on interesting diversions along the way. The main arterial roads passing through the Northeast Plains from the east are Interstate 76 and Interstate 70. Most people will be coming into the state on these roads.

If you happen to be traveling from west to east, work through the chapter backward.

Interstate 76

This highway leads into the extreme northeast corner of Colorado from Nebraska, ending in north Denver in about 200 miles. Just inside the Nebraska border you'll come to Julesberg, home to the **Northeast Colorado Information Center.** For further information, call the Travel Region office at **1-800-777-9075** or the **Sedgewick County Chamber of Commerce** at **970-474-3504.** However, we are fudging the borders a bit to let you know about a beautiful diversion just before coming into Colorado from the east.

Ogallala, Nebraska

Lake McConaughy

The North Platte River used to meander through this sparse farm and ranch land before Kingsly Dam was completed in 1941. But the river was never as enticing as man-made

Lake McConaughy, which boasts 105 miles of gorgeous, white sand beaches. Attracting legions of recreationists from as far away as Denver, Lake McConaughy makes you feel as though the coast has been transplanted in mid-America. Enough shoreline prompts everyone to stake a claim and break out the toys: volleyball, Frisbee, inflatable raft, catamaran, windsurfer or water skis. Cool breezes come off the long, slender reservoir, and groves of cottonwoods provide comfortably shaded camping spots. Don't forget your fishing gear—this lake has produced record catches of striped bass, coho and kokanee salmon, walleye and tiger muskie. Many folks simply come here equipped with lawn chair and cooler for some "power lounging."

Located 30 miles over the Nebraska border from extreme northeastern Colorado, Lake McConaughy is definitely worth a detour. For more information contact **Ogallala/Keith County Chamber of Commerce, P.O. Box 628, Ogallala, NE 69153; 1-800-658-4390; www.ci.ogallala.ne.us.**

Sterling

The small town of Sterling, in the midst of irrigated farm country, remains a good place to pull off the road for a quick meal at one of a dozen fast-food places on Main St. or to spend the night at one of many American Automobile Association–rated motels. While driving about, keep your eyes open for "living trees" sculptures. These detailed works of art include a clump of giraffes, a mermaid and a golfer. As for outdoor recreation, four golf courses here provide diversions for duffers. North Sterling State Park (see write-up in this section) and Prewitt Reservoir provide good warmwater fishing and boating; campsites, especially at North Sterling, can be found at water's edge. If you're just dying for a break from the surrounding scenery, drive north on N. 7th Ave. to County Rd. 70 and then west for 8 miles to Chimney Canyons, with its 250-foot chalk cliffs. For more information on Sterling, stop in at the **Overland Trail Museum's Visitor Information Center** (see entry below for directions).

North Sterling State Park

This park has become the destination of choice for many campers, boaters and bird-watchers, who come from miles around to enjoy the 3,000-acre reservoir with its many inlets and coves tucked up against the bluffs. It features plentiful campgrounds (141 sites; fee charged) especially suited for those who appreciate convenience and amenities such as hot showers, flush toilets and laundry facilities. Best of all, North Sterling has a sandy swimming beach that is great for kids. The water level can fluctuate with irrigation needs, but usually stays high enough for the boat ramps to function. The fishing also attracts many for the array of warmwater species, including walleye, bass, bluegill and tiger muskie. Thanks to the freedom from city lights, many astronomers come to the area to enjoy the night sky. The park has a visitor center and offers ranger-led interpretive programs. From Main St. in Sterling, turn north on N. 7th Ave. and follow the signs 12 miles to the reservoir. **970-522-3657; www.coloradoparks. org.** Campground reservations are recommended on holidays and weekends from Memorial Day through Labor Day. Contact **1-800-678-CAMP** or **www.reserveusa.com.**

Overland Trail Museum

Take a look inside this excellent regional museum, named for the well-trod route pioneers followed on westerly journeys. The grounds offer shaded picnic tables and an outdoor display of several types of prairie grasses, identified by small markers. This stone museum, housed inside a reproduction of Fort Sedgewick (established on the Overland Trail in the early 1860s to quell Indian problems), features a branding-iron collection and examples of horse-drawn machinery. Check out the one-room schoolhouse and geological and wildlife displays. Lots of interesting stuff can be found here—and it's free. Open Apr. 1–Oct. 30, Mon.–Sat. 9 A.M.–5 P.M., Sun. 10 A.M.–5 P.M.; open Nov. 1-Mar. 30, Mon.–Sat. 10 A.M.–4 P.M., closed Sun. Located conveniently at the intersection of Interstate 76 and Hwy. 6 just east

of Sterling; **970-522-3895; www.sterling colo.com.**

T. J. Bummer's—$ to $$

A slice of Americana pervades the atmosphere at this Sterling standout. T. J. Bummer's has become known over the years for its quality food and friendly service. Jammed with antiques and offbeat collectibles, the place features a Mobil gas pump converted to a fish tank, an old-style Crescent radio receiver from Sears and movie posters from the 1930s and 1940s. Locals stop by Bummer's regularly, and many road-weary travelers make it a point to stop here whenever traveling I-76. Breakfast can be ordered all day. If you enjoy breakfast burritos, don't even think about skipping their award-winning green chili. Sandwiches and burgers highlight the lunch menu, while dinner brings on excellent baby back ribs, prime rib, pepper steak and chicken-fried chicken breast. Top it all off with a slice of home-baked pie or some strawberry shortcake. Open daily 5:30 A.M.–9 P.M. **203 Broadway St., Sterling; 970-522-8397.**

GinJer Snap Ranch gives visitors a sense of the ranching history of the Plains. Photo by Bruce Caughey.

Brush

In the 1860s John Iliff and Jared Brush contracted to sell beef to army troops; thus began a cattle empire reaching from Julesburg to Greeley. In the early 1900s farmers were given incentives to plant sugar beets. Today the beets are such an important crop that the high school football team goes by the name Beetdiggers. With its wide, tree-lined streets Brush still serves as a key agricultural and ranching center. If you are passing through Brush on July 4th weekend, stop in for the Brush Rodeo. The long tradition of rodeo continues as 450 top amateur cowboys and cowgirls compete. Other events include wild cow milking and a 5-kilometer run. On Independence Day the town comes out for a pancake breakfast, a parade and a fireworks display. Free camping (with hookups and picnic tables) at the Brush City Campground; a motel or two can be found in town.

Elk Echo Ranch Country Bed and Breakfast—$$$

You won't find a realtor asking you to consider a 2,000-acre lot in the 'burbs, but there is such a place in Stoneham, where this B&B is located on 2,000 acres of rolling grasslands between Greeley and Sterling. This unique and wholesome lodging opportunity brings to mind a simpler time. The owners welcome you to their elk and buffalo ranch; guests can take complimentary tours to see the animals. Enjoy one of four spacious, well-appointed rooms (the kids can sleep nearby in the tepee) with private bathrooms in their log house, which features large common areas and a wraparound deck. Dinner served by reservation only, but be sure to request your favorite pie, which Noreen will make from her grandmother's cookbook. **47490 WCR 155, Stoneham, CO 80754; 970-735-2426.**

GinJer Snap Ranch (near Akron)—$$ to $$$

For a chuck wagon supper (Fri.–Sat. at 6 P.M.) or an overnight stay in this one-room bed and breakfast, you'll enjoy the warm, western hospitality of Ginger and Jerry Allen. Walk by the buffalo and draft horses to a small gift shop, where you can buy everything from handcrafted country furnishings to tumbleweeds (quantity discounts). At the chuck wagon supper, you can load up your tin plate with simmering barbecued chicken or beef, beans and fresh corn bread. The cowboy food fits the bill before the engaging, often humorous western music show begins (starring such acts as the Pointless Sisters or the Sand Creek Riders). After supper, guests clamber onto hay bales set on a wagon behind strong draft horses and head out for a campfire and roasted marshmallows. The entire evening builds camaraderie in the group of 50 to 80 people and lasting memories among loved ones. "This is where life slows down," Jerry says. Furnished by a local antiques store, their bed and breakfast option comes with a full kitchen, separate living area, private bath and outdoor hot tub. A reasonably priced overnight stay always comes with dinner and breakfast. Call for reservations and directions at **1-877-777-9095; www.ginjer snapranch.com.**

Drovers Restaurant—$ to $$

Because of its 1950s prices, genuinely friendly waitresses and a unique setting amid thousands of penned-up cattle, it's worth going a few miles out of your way to Drovers. Sit at the counter or find an unoccupied table. Most of the clientele comes in from outlying ranches to do some business or to meet with friends over a cup of coffee (it only costs a quarter) and a slice of lemon meringue or cherry pie. The menu varies from traditional breakfasts to burgers, barbecued beef sandwiches and T-bone steaks. Open Mon.–Sat. 5 A.M.–8 P.M., Sun. 8 A.M.–2 P.M. **28601 Hwy. 34; 970-842-4218.** Across the hallway from the restaurant is the sale barn: if you're lucky, you can witness a spirited cattle auction (lasting from noon into the night). It's a bit like visiting another planet, if you come from the city.

Fort Morgan

As the Morgan County seat, this agricultural and ranching center serves as a small but important hub with several worthwhile diversions. Downtown Fort Morgan has a few standard motels for those wishing to spend the night. In late June, the reason to come to Fort Morgan is the Glenn Miller Festival, celebrating the music of a hometown favorite (he attended high school here). More than 500 gather to shuffle, sway and sing along to the popular big-band favorites. For information call **1-800-354-8660.**

Fort Morgan Museum

The displays in this tidy museum cover the history of Morgan County. Permanent exhibits include information on the life of Glenn Miller and an old soda fountain from the Hillrose Drugstore. Unfortunately, cold drinks or ice cream are not served at the fountain any longer. (However, in Akron, 32 miles west of Fort Morgan, you can visit a similar working fountain right on Main St.) Also displayed is a collection of Plains Indian artifacts. A large room is reserved for traveling exhibits that change every two to three months. Open year-round, Mon.–Fri. 10 A.M.–5 P.M.; also open Tues.–Thurs. 6–8 P.M. and Sat. 11 A.M.–5 P.M. **404 Main St., Ft. Morgan, CO 80701; 970-867-6331; www.ftmorganmus.org.**

Jackson Lake State Park

Just northeast of Fort Morgan is Jackson Reservoir, known for its excellent warmwater fishing. Along the western shore you'll find a boat launch and clean, sandy swimming beaches; the warm water makes for ideal waterskiing and windsurfing conditions. Jackson Lake offers wind-protected picnic tables with grills and 180 shoreline campsites with showers, toilets and drinking water (fee charged). To reserve a campsite: **303-470-1144** in Denver; **1-800-678-CAMP; www.reserveusa.com.** On the way to the lake, stop in at the very local Squeek's Corner in Goodrich for a hand-patted hamburger and a slice of cherry pie.

Pawnee Buttes

These two 300-foot-tall sandstone towers provide relief to a landscape virtually devoid of unique features. Once called White Buttes, these primitive monuments rise from the expanse of the Pawnee National Grasslands, having withstood the erosion that affected the surrounding landscape. Get out of your car and take a walk (mountain bikes no longer allowed) on 4-mile Pawnee Buttes Trail. It's like revisiting the Old West while letting your senses adjust to the solitude and comfort of the prairie. Silence is interrupted only by the wind and a surprising number of songbirds and raptors. Stories of rattlesnakes hold some truth, so be aware of where you sit down for a break or a picnic. The best times to visit Pawnee Buttes are in spring and fall when the scorching heat isn't so intense, or in early morning or evening when shadows lengthen and a colorful sky brings added contrasts to the sandstone monoliths.

To reach the trailhead from Fort Morgan, drive north on Hwy. 52 for 25 miles to Raymer. Turn left onto Hwy. 14 and continue about 10 miles to County Rd. 390. Turn right, proceed north for 14 miles and then turn right again onto County Rd. 112. Drive east for 6.5 miles to a T intersection where you'll take a left on a marked road leading shortly to the Pawnee Buttes Trail. The parking area is located next to a large windmill. For more information contact the **Pawnee National Grasslands Office** on the north side of Greeley at **660 O St., Greeley, CO 80631; 970-353-5004; www.fs.fed.us/rz/arnf/png.**

In the Mood Coffeehouse and Theatre

On a side street, in a former church hall, is this little gem that delights travelers. Run by Perry Roberts, a former interviewer of rock-and-roll musicians for a TV station, and his wife, Jeri, the place is friendly and unassuming. Pull up a chair or sit back on a couch and enjoy a latte, cappuccino or Italian soda and a decadent pastry or ice cream. Local ranchers said this place would never work, because they don't provide a bottomless cup of Folgers, but they seem to be doing just fine, thank you. If you time it just right, you may catch a community theater production. Open Mon.–Thurs. 7 A.M.–10 P.M., Fri. until midnight, Sat. 9 A.M.–midnight. **307 E. Kiowa Ave.; 970-867-7378.**

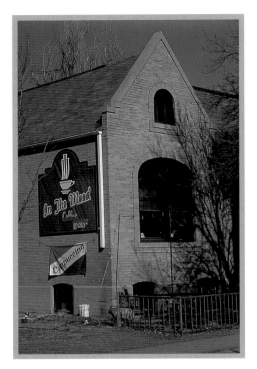

Fort Morgan, the high school home of band leader Glenn Miller, is also home to the In the Mood Coffeehouse. Photo by Bruce Caughey.

Greeley

Founded by the Union Colonists in 1870, Greeley has enjoyed steady, sustained growth. Today it's the largest town in this part of the state, with a population of 70,000. The town's wide streets are shaded by trees, many of which were planted by settlers in the 1870s; cattle and crops are still the moving forces behind the town's economy. History is perhaps the reason to come to Greeley. James Michener lived here while writing *Centennial.* You can visit several excellent museum collections in town.

Centered in Greeley, the University of Northern Colorado is well known for its education and music programs. The town has a top-notch performing arts center—**Union Colony Civic Center, 970-356-5000**—that hosts plays and concerts. Its schedule includes an impressive lineup of local and national talent.

Another Greeley attraction is the Denver Broncos training camp. You can watch practices and scrimmages each July and Aug. as the Broncos prepare for yet another NFL season.

The Independence Stampede, a massive Fourth of July Rodeo and Western Celebration (they claim it's the "world's largest"), attracts more than 400,000 people to this small town for rodeo, live country and classic rock music and lots of great food. Book way in advance if you want to stay in town during the affair. At almost all other times you can find a room at a number of hotels and motels and enjoy a selection of restaurants and bars. For more information contact the **Greeley Convention and Visitors Bureau,** inside the old train depot at **902 7th Ave., Greeley, CO 80631; 970-352-3567; www.greeleycvb.com.**

If you enjoy swing music, don't miss a chance to get "in the mood" at the annual **Glenn Miller Festival.** Miller was a onetime resident of Fort Morgan and the town throws this bash in his honor in late June. Now is your chance to dance the night away to the only sanctioned orchestra bearing the famous bandleader's name. For information and tickets, call **1-800-354-8860.**

Centennial Village Museum

Centennial Village vividly tells Plains history through the chronological reconstruction of 25 buildings from the years 1860 to 1920, most moved here from other places and restored. Take a walk around the well-manicured grounds and the various homes constructed of rock, wood, adobe and sod; you really do get the feeling of an early settlement. Highlights include the wagon house (built in 1917; predecessor to the modern-day Winnebago) and a Swedish-American Stuga home. At the end of the tour, a firehouse and a blacksmith's shop prove especially fascinating for kids. Open mid-Apr. to mid-Oct., Tues.–Sat. 9 A.M.–4 P.M., with slightly longer hours during the peak summer season. A ticket here also includes a visit to the Meeker Home Museum (see next entry). **1475 A St., Greeley, CO 80631; 970-350-9224.**

Meeker Home Museum

Nathan Meeker, founder of the Union Colony at Greeley, was a fascinating man. You can visit his well-preserved, two-story adobe home that has survived the past 100-plus years in good stead. Filled with many of the Meeker family's personal artifacts, it gives an excellent idea of life in the 1870s. If you want to learn every conceivable detail about Meeker's life, you'll find the information here. For casual visitors, however, the personal tour can be too in-depth and, therefore, lengthy. As it stands now, the museum is open Memorial Day to Labor Day, Tues.–Fri. (and the first Sat. of each month) 1:30–5:30 P.M. **1324 9th Ave.; 970-350-9221.**

Fort Vasquez

Built in 1835 by a few hard-core mountain men, Fort Vasquez capitalized on the trade routes along the South Platte River. Twelve-foot-high adobe walls contained rifle ports and two corner towers. An ill-fated attempt was once made to ship 700 buffalo robes and 400 buffalo tongues from Fort Vasquez to St. Louis via the South Platte River. After 69 days of pushing, pulling and occasionally floating a flat-bottomed boat, the tired crew arrived in St. Louis, bearing the hard-earned information that the South Platte was not a navigable stream.

Fort Vasquez crumbled to the ground many years ago, but the WPA reconstructed an identical structure in the 1930s. Today the State Historical Society runs a visitor center next to the fort, with information and displays on the fur trade and Plains Indians, and staffers knowledgeable about the history of the area. Walking around Fort Vasquez provides a glimpse of frontier life—except for the cars zooming by on the nearby highway. Open daily from Memorial Day to Labor Day, Mon.–Sat. 9:30 A.M.–4:30 P.M., Sun. 1–5 P.M. The rest of the year, Wed.–Sun. 9:30 A.M.–4:30 P.M. Located 17 miles south of Greeley (1 mile south of Platteville) on Hwy. 85; **970-785-2832; www.oldstuff.org/fort-vasquez.**

Nightlife

Adjacent to the popular Lucky Star restaurant, known for its huge portions of non-Healthmark-type of food, is the popular night club called **Romances,** which features live Spanish-style music on weekends. Located 3 miles north of Greeley on **Hwy. 85 in Lucerne; 970-351-8000. Bruce's** (see the Where to Eat listing) features live country music on weekends. Or maybe you just feel like a microbrew and a game of pool; in that case, head to the **Union Colony Brewery** (the name itself would have given the town's nondrinking founders a start!) at **1412 8th Ave.; 970-356-4116.** The college crowd goes straight to the **State Armory** at **614 8th Ave.; 970-352-7424.**

WHERE TO STAY

Plenty of motels are spread throughout Greeley, including most of the national chains. For above-average accommodations with lots of amenities and a Southwestern feel, try reserving a room at the **Ramkota Inn ($$$ to $$$$), 701 8th St., Greeley, CO 80631; 970-353-8444.** You might also try the small corporate-style **Greeley Guest House ($$$$),** which offers 19 spruced-up rooms in a suburban setting. **5401 O St., Greeley, CO 80634; 1-800-314-3684.** Or for a unique night's lodging, try one of the following two places:

Sod Buster Inn Bed and Breakfast—$$$$

This 1997 vintage octagonal inn somehow manages to blend into the historic area of central Greeley, not far from the campus of the University of Northern Colorado and the downtown shopping district. The open interior design of the Sod Buster features a massive main-floor great room, with plush couches and a dining area, and 10 lovely guest rooms (9 are upstairs). The 360-degree, wraparound veranda and its many rocking chairs provide opportunities for guests to mingle. The decor blends classic country, American folk art and antiques, giving the place a classy but somewhat feminine feel with many welcome features. Innkeepers Bill and LeeAnn Sterling provide a warm but not overbearing welcome, as does their distinctive canine: Mamie, a happy-go-lucky bulldog. Bill cooks a terrific full breakfast (such as egg casserole, sausage, corn bread, fruit, juice and coffee) at two set times in the morning. You really cannot go wrong here. **1221 9th Ave., Greeley, CO 80631; 1-888-300-1221; 970-392-1221; www.colorado-bnb.com/sodbuster.**

Elk Echo Ranch Bed and Breakfast—$$$

Located about 30 miles north of Brush on 2,000 acres, this ranch provides close-up views of an elk herd, and accommodations verging on plush. See the section on the town of Brush.

WHERE TO EAT

Potato Brumbaugh's—$$ to $$$

Named after a character in James Michener's *Centennial,* this longtime restaurant still draws excellent reviews from locals for its fine food and classy atmosphere. This is one of the few places in northeast Colorado where you'll find linen tablecloths and napkins; Brumbaugh's also features pewter hot plates. Specialties include their slow-roasted prime rib and steaks, but you can also order prawns, lobster and several good chicken dishes. Some lighter meals are also available. Open for lunch Mon.–Fri. 11:15 A.M.– 2 P.M.; dinner Mon.–Sat. 5–10 P.M. Located in a circular building in the Cottonwood Square Shopping Plaza at **2400 17th St., Greeley; 970-356-6340.**

Bruce's—$ to $$$

Located in Severance, about 10 miles north of Greeley, this restaurant has an unusual theme. Bruce's specialty is Rocky Mountain oysters— also known as bull fries, swinging steaks and prairie oysters. In a *Rocky Mountain News* story, co-owner Betty Schott was quoted as saying: "Come to Severance and have a ball." Tender turkey oysters, steaks and seafood are also served. You can get a juicy hamburger for almost the same price as at a fast-food joint. The former

Severance Recreation Hall has a casual feel, with four long tables, each seating about 20 people, and booths running down both sides of the room. On weekends live country and western bands play from 8 P.M. to closing. Open Mon.– Thurs. 10 A.M.–10 P.M., Fri.–Sat. 10 A.M.– 2 A.M., Sun. 10 A.M.–midnight. In **Severance; 970-686-2320.**

Alberto's—$ to $$

This casual, family-style Mexican restaurant draws people for its array of spicy menu options. Have a burrito your way: handheld, smothered, deluxe or supreme (complete with sour cream and guacamole). If you like your green chili hot, really hot, go ahead and order it. Otherwise consider a half-and-half blend or mild green chili. Other menu offerings include stuffed sopapillas, enchiladas, sizzling fajitas and even menudo. Try to avoid looking at the menu's unappealing photographs of the food, because it really is good when it arrives. Dine in or take out. Mon.–Thurs. 10:30 A.M.–8 P.M., Fri.–Sat. 10:30 A.M.–9 P.M. **2605 W. 11th St., Greeley; 970-356-1417.**

Margie's Java Joint—$

Voted Greeley's coolest coffee shop, just off the University of Northern Colorado campus, this funky place draws a diverse clientele for its pastries, sandwiches and gourmet coffee drinks. Part bookstore, part art gallery, part coffee shop, Margie's eclectic atmosphere and reasonable prices might be just right for you. Pull up at one of the mismatched Formica tables and get philosophical. Open Mon.–Fri. 7 A.M.–10 P.M., Sat. 8 A.M.–10 P.M., Sun. 8 A.M.–9 P.M. **931 16th St.; 970-356-6364.**

Interstate 70

Interstate 70 is the most heavily used route into Colorado, entering from Kansas in the east-central part of the state. Along the way many restaurants and lodges are available to weary travelers. The highway passes several interesting and historic places as it makes a beeline west. A more scenic route to Denver and the mountains is to follow **Hwy. 86** from west of Limon via the towns of Kiowa, Elizabeth, Franktown and Castle Rock.

Burlington

The first thing to do when arriving at Burlington is to stop at the **State Welcome Center,** just off Interstate 70; **719-346-5554; www.burlingtoncolo.com.** The center, staffed by volunteer travel counselors, can help you plan your Colorado vacation, and you can pick up armloads of brochures from around Colorado. Burlington offers many fast-food restaurants and inexpensive motels.

Bonny State Recreation Area

About 22 miles north of Burlington on Hwy. 385, Bonny boasts great warmwater fishing (including good-sized walleye) in the reservoir, windsurfing, boating and bird-watching in a pleasant setting. Four campgrounds (more than 200 sites, fee charged) can be found among the cottonwood trees on the lakeshore. The campgrounds can accommodate tents, trailers and motor homes. Only 35 sites have electrical hookups, but **Foster Grove** and **Wagon Wheel Campgrounds** do offer showers. To reserve a campsite: **303-470-1144** in Denver; **1-800-678-CAMP; www.reserveusa.com.** For more information on the recreation area, check out **www.coloradoparks.org.**

Kit Carson County Carousel

Climb onto one of several life-size horses or the more exotic camel, zebra, giraffe, deer or lion at this fully restored, hand-carved wooden merry-go-round. You can observe the incredible detail of the snake curling around the giraffe's neck and the various prancing positions of each animal at this designated National Historic Landmark. These proud animal figures march to the music of a 1909 Wurlitzer Monster Military Band Organ—one of only two of this particular vintage in existence today. Small admission for a ride and tour. Open from late May through mid-Sept. afternoons and evenings. Located on the **County Fairgrounds in Burlington; 719-348-5562.**

Old Town

This collection of 1900s-era buildings, with rooms full of antiques and exhibits, re-creates a historical atmosphere. Tour guides explain the implements of the blacksmith, harness and newspaper shops. The spacious grounds also feature a western saloon, where you can witness cancan shows and staged gunfights—but you can't buy a beer. Craft demonstrations are continuous. Be sure to take a wagon ride from Old Town to the Kit Carson County Carousel (see previous entry). In a large red barn with a 45-foot-high roof, a troupe performs melodramas for the whole family. The melodramas are staged from June through mid-Aug. at 7 P.M. nightly (except Mon.); they are free of charge with a tour ticket. Old Town is open daily: Memorial Day–Labor Day 9 A.M.–6 P.M.; the rest of the year 9 A.M.–5 P.M., Sun. noon–5 P.M. **420 S. 14th St., Burlington, CO 80807; 719-346-7382; www.carousel.org/kcc.**

Genoa

Genoa Tower

If you're into two-headed calves and oddball things from Grandma's attic, then you'll probably get a kick out of the Genoa Tower. Like a bad commercial, it makes itself known from the interstate. Actually, after a long drive across the high plains, this is a good place to stretch your legs. The owner, Jerry Chubbuck, will ramble on about his haphazard collection of stuff, including Indian artifacts, hundreds of branding irons, antique guns, mutated animals—the list goes on and on. Check out the remains of the prehistoric mammoth he discovered. However, locals warned us not to believe everything we encountered; of course, the jackalopes are authentic! The rock tower got a mention in "Ripley's Believe It or Not" due to a claim that you can see into six states from its perch— NOT! Modest admission fee. Open Labor Day to Memorial Day "most every day" from 8 A.M. to 8 P.M.; call ahead in winter due to shorter hours. Located in Genoa (east of Limon), **just off Interstate 70 at Exit 371; 719-763-2309.**

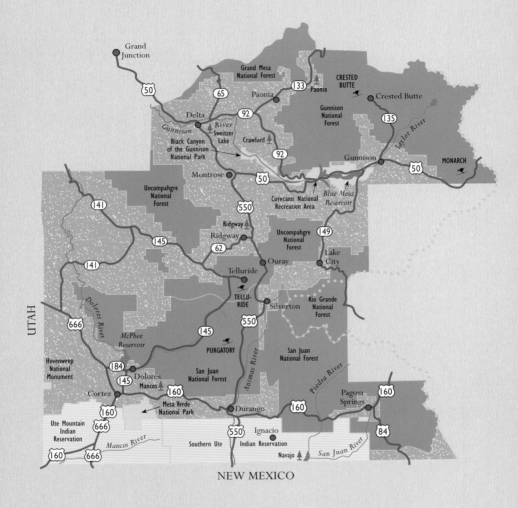

Grand
Junction

50

Grand Mesa
National Forest

133 Paonia

CRESTED
BUTTE

Crested Butte

65

Paonia

Delta

92

Gunnison
National Forest

135

Gunnison River

Sweitzer
Lake

Crawford

92

Gunnison

Taylor River

50

MONARCH

Black Canyon
of the Gunnison
National Park

Montrose

50

550

Curecanti National
Recreation Area

Blue Mesa
Reservoir

Uncompahgre
National
Forest

141

145

Ridgway

62

Ridgway

Uncompahgre
National
Forest

149

Lake
City

141

Ouray

UTAH

Dolores River

Telluride

TELLU-
RIDE

Silverton

Rio Grande
National
Forest

666

McPhee
Reservoir

145

550

Hovenweep
National
Monument

184

PURGATORY

San Juan
National Forest

Animas River

San Juan
National Forest

Piedra River

Pagosa
Springs

160

Dolores

Mancos

160

Cortez

145

Mesa Verde
National Park

Durango

160

84

Ute Mountain
Indian
Reservation

160

666

550

Ignacio

Southern Ute
Indian Reservation

160

666

Mancos River

Southern Ute

Navajo

San Juan River

NEW MEXICO

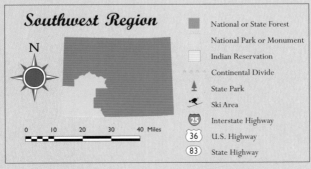

Southwest Region

N

National or State Forest

National Park or Monument

Indian Reservation

Continental Divide

State Park

Ski Area

25 Interstate Highway

36 U.S. Highway

83 State Highway

0   10   20   30   40 Miles

Southwest
Region

The strange, eroded volcanic Dillon Pinnacles cast a beautiful spell on the landscape.
Photo by Bruce Caughey.

Black Canyon Country

Black Canyon Country has often been regarded as an area overlooked by vacationers and tourists. For the most part this remains true, but with the recent designation of the Black Canyon of the Gunnison as a national park, you can be certain coming years will bring at least a modest increase in visitors. In addition to being home to one of the most spectacular canyons in the nation, this region boasts many other attractions, including great hiking and fishing, seemingly endless views of the San Juan and the West Elk Mountains and the fertile, fruit-growing North Fork Valley.

It is the Black Canyon, however, that continues to draw the most attention. While the heart of the canyon is 2,900 feet deep, it is as narrow as 1,100 feet in places—a testimony to the river's patient carving of this gorge. At some points, the canyon is so narrow you cannot see

Getting There

From Denver, Black Canyon Country can be reached several ways. The quickest is to head 250 miles west on Interstate 70 to Grand Junction, and then south on Highway 50 for 40 miles to Delta. A scenic alternative from Denver is to head south (left) off Interstate 70 at Glenwood Springs onto Highway 82 and drive 12 miles to Carbondale. At Carbondale, turn onto Highway 133 (and onto the West Elk Scenic and Historic Byway), which takes you up the beautiful Crystal River Valley past Redstone, over McClure Pass and down into the Upper North Fork Valley above Paonia. The **Montrose County Airport** *offers frequent flights from Denver and, just before landing, passengers get an incredible view into the Black Canyon.*

the river from the rim. But the mighty Gunnison's presence is always heard—the sheer walls of schist and gneiss provide amazing acoustics to amplify the roaring rapids below.

The park also has abundant wildlife; an encounter with a black bear, porcupine, golden eagle or peregrine falcon can be just as memorable as the vistas. For those determined to experience the canyon on a more intimate level than the overlooks, the park has numerous (but strenuous and sometimes treacherous) trails to the canyon bottom. The trout fishing within the secluded confines of the canyon can be some of the best in the state. The canyon cuts a 53-mile-long path before reaching open country, and eventually the waters merge with the Colorado River at Grand Junction.

Just north of the park are the wide-open expanses of the North Fork Valley, where fertile soils and good weather contribute to the success of numerous fruit orchards. Driving up Highways 92 and 133 in the summer and early fall, you pass many fruit stands. Depending on the season, you can nibble on cherries, peaches, plums, nectarines, pears and apples while you visit this region.

The small rural towns of Hotchkiss, Paonia and Crawford have sweeping views of the West Elk Wilderness, a mountain paradise for back-country hikers seeking more solitude than is found at the adjacent Maroon Bells or nearby San Juan Mountains.

To the west of the Black Canyon lies the Uncompahgre Plateau and the large towns of Montrose and Delta, which offer numerous restaurants and a range of overnight accommodations. Whether you are just passing through or focusing on an adventure at the Black Canyon, this region has a great deal to offer.

History

Into the 1880s Ute Indians hunted plentiful game and foraged in the area around the Black Canyon and the North Fork Valley. The Ute Council Tree, an ancient cottonwood still standing in Delta, served as an important meeting place for the tribe.

Most likely the first Europeans in the area were Friars Dominguez and Escalante, who passed through in 1776. Hwy. 92, between Delta and Hotchkiss, is lined with numerous historical markers where the two men camped. Trappers entered the area in the 1820s but did not leave much of a record of their findings. French trapper Antoine Roubidoux built a trading post just west of Delta in 1830 and named it Fort Uncompahgre (see the Museums section). Roubidoux was successful until the Utes burned down the trading post in 1844.

By 1880 Anglo desire for the mineral-rich country of the nearby San Juans became too great—soon the Utes were pushed off their land, which included Black Canyon Country, and forced to live in the arid confines of reservations in the Four Corners area. Following the miners were cattle ranchers and farmers, who quickly began to settle the land from Montrose north to Delta and up the North Fork Valley. The original ranchers moved their herds from Gunnison to the hills just north of Crawford, which is still a cattle town—and the home of rock-and-roll singer Joe Cocker. A trip along Hwy. 92 near Crawford may still be interrupted by a cattle drive.

Early settlers introduced fruit trees to the North Fork Valley. For years the produce of the valley consistently won competitions at the World's Fair. A vicious frost in 1912 killed many orchards in Hotchkiss, but the fruit trees in Paonia, 10 miles up the valley from Hotchkiss, were spared because of the area's "million-dollar wind," which blows in early morning and late afternoon and prevented serious frost damage. Today Paonia is famous for its sweet cherries as well as pears, peaches, apricots, plums and grapes. Paonia once made it into "Ripley's Believe It or Not" for having more churches per capita than any other place in the country.

Major Attractions

Black Canyon of the Gunnison National Park

Wallace Hanson, a U.S. geologist who surveyed the Black Canyon in the 1950s, had this to say:

> Several Western canyons exceed the Black Canyon in overall size. Some are larger; some are deeper; some are narrower; and a few have walls as steep. But no other canyon in North America combines the depth, narrowness, sheerness and somber countenance of the Black Canyon.

The Gunnison River travels 53 miles through the Black Canyon, but only about 14 miles of the river are within the national park boundaries—but it's the most remarkable stretch of the canyon, where it is at its deepest and narrowest. Today the river continues to scour out its course, but at a minuscule rate—approximately the width of a human hair each year.

While the area was recently promoted from national monument to national park and will no doubt see an increase in visitors, don't expect the Black Canyon to turn into a crowded sightseeing mecca like the Grand Canyon or Yosemite.

For one thing, the comparatively small size of the park may deter some from visiting for more than a day. In addition, the landscape is extreme—rolling hills in some places, but sheer vertical walls in others. While much of the terrain may be ideal for rock climbers, backcountry hikers and solitude-seeking anglers, it will also restrict many visitors to the rim overlooks.

The Park Service plans to improve campgrounds, dining facilities and trail maintenance, but has decided to keep the canyon's North rim "primitive," with only dirt roads and a small campground. Thus the North Rim will provide a wholly separate experience from that of the South Rim.

Geology

The deep chasm of the Black Canyon looks out of place. With towering mountains off in the distance and rolling hills covered with Gambel oak in the foreground, the gorge has the appearance of a strange, enormous crack in the earth's crust. The canyon's geologic history helps explain its creation. Sixty-five million years ago, a great bulge in the earth's surface, known as the Gunnison Uplift, steadily vaulted upward. About 30 million years later, the West Elk Mountains and San Juan Range spewed volcanic debris on the area. The ancient Gunnison River began cutting a course, and initially the process of eroding the soft volcanic rock was easy. But once the river reached the underlying core of the Gunnison Uplift, it had to slowly cut into this harder rock. Over time, the Black Canyon of the Gunnison—a deep, thin crack through this dense layer—was eventually created.

History

The Ute Indians infrequently entered the Black Canyon of the Gunnison. Calling the area *Tomichi,* meaning "land of high cliffs and plenty water," they preferred to stay on the rim. Game was plentiful, and the Utes hunted buffalo and deer by driving them into traps or over small cliffs. On the North Rim, some of these old traps and pits can still be found.

The imposing walls of the Black Canyon of the Gunnison National Park. Photo by Bruce Caughey.

The first Anglo documentation of the canyon came in 1853 from an expedition led by Capt. John Gunnison, who was looking for a transcontinental railroad route. Years later, surveyor Ferdinand Hayden deemed the canyon impenetrable. In the 1880s local residents explored an intriguing possibility: diverting some of the water from the Gunnison River to irrigate the arid Uncompahgre Valley to the west via a tunnel through the canyon's rock. The project would be a massive undertaking; first they would need an accurate survey of this "impenetrable" canyon.

With this in mind, William W. Torrence and four other local men set out in Sept. 1900 to float the canyon. They headed downriver in two wooden boats packed with food, surveying equipment and survival gear. On the first day, one of the boats rammed a rock and sank. By the end of three weeks, the expedition had traveled only 14 miles. Eventually halted by an impassable rapids, the men abandoned the boat and climbed nearly 2,000 feet up the cliff faces to safety.

Torrence was determined to return. The following year, he and Abe Lincoln Fellows set out in two primitive rubber rafts. In a section known as the Narrows, they encountered an enormous rapids that wrapped around a bend. They decided that their only choice was to jump into the river and let the rushing waters carry them along. Both survived, and they were able to make it all the way through the canyon. The trip provided enough information to proceed with the diversion-tunnel project, which began in 1904. Despite complications that kept progress slow—dense rock, staggering heat, scalding hot springs, dangerous pockets of gas—the tunnel was completed in 1909. President Taft presided over the opening ceremony.

In 1933 President Hoover declared the most spectacular 12 miles of the canyon a national monument. Three dams—Blue Mesa, Morrow Point and Crystal—were built upstream of the monument, and now constitute the Curecanti National Recreation Area. In Oct. 1999 the national monument became Black Canyon of the Gunnison National Park.

Getting There

To reach the South Rim of the Black Canyon from Montrose, head east on Hwy. 50 for 6 miles and turn left (north). Take this road 6 miles to the park entrance station, where a fee is charged. The North Rim can be reached from Hotchkiss by heading southeast on Hwy. 92 for 13 miles to Crawford Reservoir. Take a right (west) at the sign and continue 11 miles to the entrance station. This road is mostly dirt, and meanders quite a bit, so be sure to look for signs. The North Rim is closed in winter.

RECREATION
Camping

The **South Rim Campground** is being renovated to accommodate heavier RV traffic. Selected sites on Loop A and Loop B will be large enough for RVs, while Loop C will remain for tents only. For those who enjoy listening to the river while they doze off to sleep, the small yet beautiful **East Portal Campground** has 10 walk-in sites and 5 drive-in sites. This campground is at the end of the East Portal Rd., which is restricted to vehicles 22 feet or less in length. The **North Rim Campground** has 13 campsites. A fee is charged at each campground; sites are available on a first-come, first-served basis.

Fishing

Fishing within Black Canyon of the Gunnison National Park can be exceptional. Difficult access and remote stretches of water mean the river has not been overfished. However, hiking trails to the bottom of the canyon are treacherous. If you want to set up camp in the canyon, you will have to carry everything down steep trails covered with loose rock. Instead, you may choose to drive the long, winding road down to the East Portal, where the fishing below Crystal Reservoir is also considered good. (Vehicles longer than 22 feet are prohibited on the East Portal Rd.)

Much of the Gunnison River downstream of the park to its confluence with the North Fork is Gold Medal trout water, meaning the Colorado Division of Wildlife considers this stretch to have some of the best fishing in the state. The gorge is habitat for wild trout (not stocked). However, much like the Black Canyon upstream, part of the reason for the terrific fishing is that the gorge is so remote. You can get there by backpacking or via a float trip down the river. Be sure to check regulations before fishing.

Hiking and Backpacking

Into the Canyon—Before hiking into the canyon, keep in mind that the routes are extraordinarily steep, with loose rock and exposed ledges, and that they are not well marked. You must register with the National Park Service before traveling below the rim (this includes gung-ho day-trippers). If you have the route-finding skills and the stamina to hike to the base of the canyon, you will be rewarded with an outstanding experience. If you think the canyon is impressive from the rim, wait until you're looking up from the bottom of it!

From the **South Rim,** the **Gunnison Point Trail** descends 1,800 feet in 1 mile and is accessible via the Oak Flat Trail. Of all the South Rim routes to the canyon floor, this is most popular. The primitive **Tomichi Trail** leaves from near the South Rim Campground and descends 1,800 feet in about a mile. If solitude is most important to you, perhaps you should try the **Warner Point Trail,** which drops 2,600 feet to access some of the most remote terrain in the canyon.

From the **North Rim,** the aptly named **S.O.B. Draw** drops 1,800 feet from the North Rim Ranger Station, down through poison ivy–lined chutes. **Long Draw** begins at the Balanced Rock Viewpoint and also descends about 1,800 feet in a mile. **Slide Draw** drops 1,600 feet from the Kneeling Camel overlook.

For specifics on any of these routes, inquire at the visitor center or ranger station. Keep in mind that once you drop below the rim, you enter the **Black Canyon of the Gunnison Wilderness Area.** Within this area, no mechanized vehicles are allowed—and that includes bikes. **On the Rim**—Numerous trails meander along the edge of the canyon, providing a good introduction to the various ecosystems of the park. In the winter, many of these trails are great for snowshoeing. On the **South Rim,** the **Oak Flat Trail** leads to a forested platform just below the rim, where an outstanding viewpoint enables you to look down on the ribbon of river below. The **Rim Rock Trail** is a good introduction to the Black Canyon. The trailhead is located near Loop C of the South Rim Campground, where you'll find pamphlets to guide you along the nature trail.

On the **North Rim,** the **Deadhorse Trail** leads into a rarely visited corner of the park. Beginning at the Kneeling Camel overlook, this trail travels 2.5 miles upstream to wonderful views of the canyon. The 3.5-mile **North Vista Trail** begins at the North Rim Ranger Station and travels to Exclamation Point (above the incredibly sheer face of the Painted Wall) and beyond.

Scenic Drives

In the Park—The roads running along both the South and North Rims provide excellent views of the canyon and the neighboring mountain ranges. **South Rim Dr.** has 12 pullouts with views from Tomichi Point and a spectacular view across the canyon to Painted Wall, where you may see climbers making an ascent. The **East Portal Rd.** also provides beautiful sights, although you will have to keep your eyes on the road with all the curves and switchbacks. The shorter, unpaved **North Rim Dr.** also offers great views.

Visitor Center

Located on the South Rim, the newly refurbished visitor center at the Black Canyon features educational exhibits and an auditorium that shows a fascinating video on the canyon's geology, ecology and history. Open year-round. **970-249-1915; www.nps.gov/blca.**

Festivals and Events

The Ute Indian Museum Cultural Day

early July This intriguing festival celebrates the heritage and culture of Native Americans, including a showcase of traditional Indian dances (in 2000, the festival included the national champion hoop dancer). Food vendors, museum tours and activities for all ages are offered. At the Ute Indian Museum just off Highway 550 in south Montrose. **970-249-3098; www.history.co.us/ute-indian.**

The Council Tree Pow Wow

late Sept. This spectacular celebration of Native American dance, heritage and culture is centered around the 185-year-old Ute Council Tree, a cottonwood that still stands along the Gunnison River at Confluence Park in Delta. Experience Native American culture through clothing, crafts and dancing. **970-874-7566; www.deltacolorado.org/powwow.**

Harvest Celebrations

July, Aug. and Oct. In Paonia, July brings **Paonia Cherry Days,** with a parade, crafts, talent show and plenty of cherries and cherry pie for everyone; **970-527-3886.** The **Olathe Sweet Corn Festival** crops up in early Aug. Try to catch this slice of Americana, where people pack in for boiled and roasted corn, a big-name concert and numerous races. It all kicks off with a pancake breakfast before corn takes center stage; at the **community park in Olathe; 970-323-6006.** Cedaredge also has a harvest festival: **Cedaredge Apple Days,** in Oct., with booths and games and, of course, apples; **970-874-8616.**

Outdoor Activities

Biking

MOUNTAIN BIKING

Mountain biking is making its presence known in this part of the state in a big way. With the 142-mile **Tabeguache Trail** connecting Montrose with Grand Junction, and the 128-mile **Kokopelli's Trail** from Grand Junction to Moab, Utah, the sport now has a number of great rides spreading over the Colorado and Uncompahgre Plateaus (see the **Grand Junction** chapter for information on these and other rides). Just west of Montrose the Uncompahgre Plateau offers hundreds of miles of excellent mountain bike routes. For detailed information about area trails, check with the **Paonia Ranger District Office; 970-527-4131; www.fs.fed. us/r2/gmug.**

Fishing

Crawford State Park

This state park a mile south of Crawford on Hwy. 92 offers good fishing in **Crawford Reservoir** for 10-inch rainbows and some warmwater species. The catfish here can be enormous—some over 15 pounds. Some live-bait restrictions. The state park also offers campgrounds, boat ramps and a swimming beach. Entrance fee charged. **970-921-5721; www.coloradoparks.org.**

Curecanti National Recreation Area

This area encompasses over 40,000 acres, including Blue Mesa, Morrow Point and Crystal Reservoirs. Fishing here can be excellent, whether from the shore or from a boat. For more information, see the Major Attractions section of the **Gunnison and Crested Butte** chapter.

Gunnison Gorge

This Gold Medal stretch of the Gunnison River below the national park has seen some effects of the devastating "whirling disease" that can afflict its rainbow trout population. Nonetheless it remains one of the premier stretches of water for anglers. Brown trout reach anywhere from 18 to 22 inches in length, and if you are fortunate enough to catch a rainbow, they can exceed 4 pounds. For access information on this portion of the Gunnison, see the Hiking and Backpacking section. You might also consider running the gorge with a rafting/fishing guide, such as Gunnison River Expeditions (see the River Floating section).

The Gunnison River also has great fishing farther downstream, just before it meets the North Fork. To access this stretch, drive 14 miles east of Delta on Hwy. 92 to a sign marked "Gunnison Forks Wildlife Management Area River Access." Turn right and head south for a mile to the confluence of the North Fork and the Gunnison. Cross the North Fork on a footbridge and access a 4-mile stretch of the Gunnison between the North Fork and the Smith Fork. Check regulations and expect to share much of this stretch with other anglers.

Hiking and Backpacking

Even with the nearby national park, hiking opportunities entice you into the surrounding backcountry. Be sure to consult a good topo map, and for more information, contact the **Paonia Ranger District Office** at **970-527-4131; www.fs.fed.us/r2/gmug.**

Black Canyon of the Gunnison
National Park Trails

See the Major Attractions section.

Gunnison Gorge Wilderness

This recently designated wilderness area encompasses some of the last pristine canyon country in Colorado. While the fishing and river floating are excellent on the Gunnison River, the hiking can be choice as well. Four trails lead from the west rim of the gorge into the wilderness area, where recently introduced bighorn sheep and river otters dwell. From Montrose, head north on Highway 50 for 6 miles and turn right on Falcon Rd. Proceed 3.6 miles to Peach Valley Rd. and turn northeast. From here on you will need four-wheel drive to access the remote roads that branch off Peach Valley Rd. to the trailheads.

The **Chukar Trail** is accessed off the first road on the right after leaving Falcon Rd. The access road leads for 10 miles to the trailhead. The trail drops 500 feet in a mile to the river below, and is often used by outfitters to pack-mule their rafts and gear in for a float trip down

Roadside corn at the Olathe Sweet Corn Festival. Photo by Doug Whitehead.

the gorge. Another 2.1 miles down Peach Valley Rd. brings you to a road that heads right for a mile and a half to the **Bobcat Trail,** which drops 800 feet in a mile to the river. The third access road, 1.4 miles farther along Peach Valley Rd., winds 2 miles to the **Duncan Trail.** This trail drops 900 feet over a 1-mile distance into the canyon, crossing very steep terrain. Follow Peach Valley Rd. another 2 miles to reach the final access road that brings you in 2.5 miles to the **Ute Trail.** Of the west rim routes, this trail is the longest, dropping for 1,200 feet over a 4.5-mile stretch.

West Elk Wilderness

This 176,000-acre wilderness is not heavily visited—perhaps because it has few alpine lakes and because the West Elk Mountains are relatively modest in elevation, never reaching 13,000 feet. The wilderness is exceptionally pristine and beautiful, but many routes are long and strenuous. Mechanized vehicles, including bicycles, are prohibited in the wilderness area.

Soap Creek Trail—A much longer route travels the length of Soap Creek for a total of 15 miles one way. Starting at either the end of County Rd. 709 (just off Hwy. 12 east of Paonia) or County Rd. 721 (accessed off Hwy. 92 near the Blue Mesa Dam), this trail traverses the heart of the wilderness and intersects numerous trails that lead to such scenic destinations as Castle Pass, Soap Basin and Sheep Lake. However, the trail meanders quite a bit, and passes by private property on the north end of the route.

Three Lakes/Beckwith Pass Trail—This trail doesn't enter the wilderness area, but does provide impressive views into the West Elk Range from Beckwith Pass. Included on the hike is access to Lost Lake, Lost Lake Slough and Dollar Lake. The hike to Beckwith Pass is 5 miles round trip, with an elevation gain of a mere 300 feet, while the jaunt to the lakes is a 3-mile loop. To reach the trailhead, drive northeast out of Paonia on Hwy. 133 to Hwy. 12 (just below Paonia Reservoir). Continue on Hwy. 12 until you see signs for the Lost Lake Campground. The trailhead is at the end of the campground road.

Float fishing in the Gold Medal waters of Gunnison Gorge. Photo by Bruce Caughey.

Horseback Riding

Bar X Bar Ranch at Saddle Mountain
The ranch offers horseback rides into the surrounding areas. They are very flexible about destination and duration of trips, although there is a 2-hour minimum time for any excursion. Located near Crawford. **970-929-6260.**

Whistling Acres
Whether or not you are staying at the Whistling Acres Guest Ranch (see the Where to Stay section), this ranch offers wonderful horseback trips into the surrounding countryside, which includes the West Elk Wilderness. Two-hour trips to multi-day excursions are available. Inquire about their guest-involved cattle drive. A few miles outside of Paonia. **1-800-346-1420; www.whistlingacres.com.**

River Floating

The Gunnison River
The run through the Black Canyon, especially the segment within the national park, is highly coveted by expert kayakers. While three dams upstream have limited the flow considerably since the times when Torrence and Fellows surveyed this stretch, the river is nonetheless dangerous and for experts only. For those who do attempt it, remember to register with the park service, and portage around all drop-offs exceeding 25 feet in height.

Downstream from the Black Canyon, the Gunnison Gorge is a wonderful run for kayakers and rafters alike. No roads enter this pristine stretch of canyon that is home to a variety of birds, including great horned owls, golden eagles, prairie falcons and red-tailed hawks. Several trails lead down to the river in the gorge, but most people heading in for a float trip use the relatively short but steep Chukar Trail (see the Hiking and Backpacking section). The best take-out point is at a campground near Hwy. 92 where the North Fork meets the Gunnison.

Below Delta, after meeting with the Uncompahgre River, the Gunnison cuts through the maroon and purple Morrison strata, eventually reaching the exposed red sandstone of Dominguez Canyon. Within the canyon walls are many unusual rock formations—one resembles the profile of Richard Nixon. This 39-mile stretch between Delta and Whitewater is fairly calm, but extraordinarily beautiful.

Outfitters
Dvorak's Kayak and Rafting Expeditions—Offers multi-day expeditions on the Gunnison and other Colorado rivers. **1-800-824-3795; www.vtinet.com/dvorak.**
Gunnison River Expeditions—Hank Hotze began running river trips down the Gunnison in the 1970s and has been been doing it for longer than any other outfitter in the area. The main stretch he runs is the Gunnison Gorge, which combines great rafting, Gold Medal fishing and

plentiful wildlife. **P.O. Box 315, Montrose, CO 81402; 1-800-297-4441.**

Seeing and Doing

Fish Hatchery

Hotchkiss National Fish Hatchery

Located 3 miles southwest of Hotchkiss (1 mile south of the small town of Lazear), the Hotchkiss National Fish Hatchery is a main supplier of trout for reservoirs in western Colorado and parts of New Mexico. The public can tour the facility year-round, 7:30 A.M.–4 P.M. daily, free of charge. From Hotchkiss head west on Hwy. 92 for 2 miles and turn left (south) to Lazear. **970-872-3170.**

Museums

Delta County Historical Museum (Delta)

Located in a restored firehouse, the Delta County Historical Museum has a hodgepodge of displays ranging from dinosaur bones dug up on the Uncompahgre Plateau to Delta's first jail. There is a detailed description of a bank robbery that went horribly wrong in town, as well as a huge collection of pressed butterflies from around the world. Open May–Sept., Tues.–Fri. 10 A.M.–4 P.M., Sat. 10 A.M.–1 P.M. **251 Meeker St.; 970-874-8721.**

Fort Uncompahgre (Delta)

This replica trading post may look a bit out of place, but walking inside is a step back in history to the pioneer days of the early 1800s. With guides dressed in buckskin coats for an authentic feel, Fort Uncompahgre is a great place to see firsthand what life inside a trading fort was like. There is even a blacksmith shop with its double bellows. Every year the fort hosts an encampment, but the place is set up primarily to educate visitors about life during the trapping era. Open year-round, Mon.–Fri. 6 A.M.–9:30 P.M., Sat. 8 A.M.–8:30 P.M., Sun. noon–5:30 P.M. At the east end of **Gunnison River Dr. in Confluence Park; 970-874-0923.**

Montrose County Historical Museum (Montrose)

In the original Denver & Rio Grande Depot, this museum focuses most of its attention on early-day settlers. With numerous exhibits on the local history of farming, the museum also has a railroad caboose for touring and a complete collection of Montrose newspapers dating back to 1896. A homesteader's cabin and country store can be seen outfitted with original furnishings. Open May–Oct.; hours vary. **11 N. First St.; 970-249-2085.**

Pioneer Town (Cedaredge)

Another authentic look at pioneer life can be found in Cedaredge, where the Coalby Store, Girling Mercantile, Lizard Head Saloon and Cedaredge Town Jail are all collected together in Pioneer Town. With antiques, clothes and memorabilia from the past 100 years, this museum is certainly worth a stop. Signs direct you from Hwy. 65. Open May–Sept., Mon.–Sat. 10 A.M.–4 P.M. and Sun. 1–4 P.M. For more information: **Surface Creek Valley Historical Society, P.O. Box 906, Cedaredge, CO 81413; 970-856-7554.**

Ute Indian Museum (Montrose)

If you have time for only one activity in Montrose, then make it a stop at the Ute Indian Museum. Dedicated to Ouray, chief of the Uncompahgre Utes, and his wife, Chipeta, this fascinating museum provides a wealth of information about one of America's most diverse tribal nations. With artifacts (many of which belonged to Ouray and other tribal leaders), interactive displays, videos, photos and dioramas, the museum will inform even the most knowledgeable about traditional Ute culture. The museum occupies the grounds of what used to be Ouray and Chipeta's farm, and Chipeta's grave lies next to the building. A small fee is charged for entry. Open year-round, though you may want to call for hours. Located on the southern end of town, where Chipeta Dr. and Hwy. 550 meet. **17253 Chipeta Dr., Montrose, CO 81401; 970-249-3098; www.history. state.co.us/ute-indian.**

Nightlife

Montrose Pavilion

You probably wouldn't expect an excellent arts facility in a town the size of Montrose, but after years of effort and numerous donations, Montrose now has a fine arts center. Plays, music and lectures can all be found here on various nights. Open year-round. Just south and east of the center of town. **1800 Pavilion Dr., Montrose, CO 81401; 970-249-7015.**

Scenic Drives

Black Canyon of the Gunnison

See the Major Attractions section.

Escalante Canyon

Located northwest of Delta, this starkly beautiful and historic canyon drive is worth a look. From Hwy. 50 the well-marked road follows Escalante Creek up toward the Uncompahgre Plateau. Within easy access are a couple of rocks with Ute petroglyphs and an area where dinosaur digs have been conducted. Many old homesteads remain in the area. One in particular is very interesting: Capt. Smith's cabin. In 1907 Capt. H. A. Smith—at the age of 67—moved into the canyon and built an unusual stone house. One wall was built into a solid slab of rock while the other three walls were made from rough-cut stones. This former Union army officer was a skilled stonemason who claimed to have learned his techniques from Indians. In the cabin, a 6-foot-long sleeping area was cut into the rock, as well as a small niche for a bedside pistol.

To reach Escalante Canyon, head northwest from Delta on Hwy. 50 toward Grand Junction and turn left onto County Rd. 650. Follow the road down to the Gunnison River and across the bridge. There are a number of side trips you can make from there. A well-marked signpost gives directions and information about the different sites. For more information about this area, contact the **Delta Chamber of Commerce; 970-874-8616; www.deltacolorado.org.**

Kebler Pass

See the **Gunnison and Crested Butte** chapter.

Scenic Highway 92

From the town of Hotchkiss, this route travels through open valleys, dense aspen copses and gorgeous views of the Black Canyon and the West Elk Mountains. At certain points on the 52-mile road, you can even see the jagged peaks of the Uncompahgre Wilderness Area near Lake City. The road ends at Hwy. 50, after crossing over Blue Mesa Dam. You can make it a loop trip by taking Hwy. 50 west through the beautiful Cimarron Valley to Montrose, and then north to Delta and east back to Hotchkiss.

Where to Stay

Accommodations

Both Montrose and Delta offer plenty of hotels and motels along Hwy. 50. If you need lodging information, contact the Chamber of Commerce numbers listed in the Services section at the end of this chapter. The unique places to stay listed below are well worth a visit.

Whistling Acres Guest Ranch (Paonia)— $$$$

If you have your sights set on *experiencing* the West rather than just seeing it, you may want to spend some time at the Whistling Acres Guest Ranch. This working cattle ranch has been catering to guests for 16 years. It offers activities for the whole family, including hiking, biking, horseback riding, hayrides, nightly entertainment, cookouts and even dance lessons. You can fish for rainbows and cutthroat on a private stretch of Minnesota Creek or take a private tour of the Black Canyon, which is only half an hour away. In winter, Whistling Acres offers snowmobile tours and cross-country skiing. All activities are included in the price of your stay. In the summer, the ranch also has a bed and breakfast (activities not included), allowing a total of 32 guests to stay at the ranch at one time. To reach Whistling Acres, drive 3.5 miles out of Paonia on 2nd St. (which becomes O 50 Dr.) and look for the red and white barn. **P.O. Box 88; Paonia, CO 81428; 1-800-346-1420; www.whistling acres.com.**

Leroux Creek Inn (Hotchkiss)—$$$ to $$$$

In a beautiful setting on the edge of Grand Mesa, this wonderful adobe bed and breakfast inn provides a tranquil setting for a pleasant and memorable stay. With only four rooms, the owners have time to spend with each guest and to impart their caring and knowledge of the area. The first thing we noticed were the high-quality materials used throughout, especially wood and tile. The tasteful decorations and large common areas make it an especially pleasant setting, but outside on the large deck it's the far-reaching views that will remain etched in your memory. Enjoy a large breakfast adjacent to the open kitchen with soft music in the background. You will undoubtedly connect with other guests who will feel as fortunate as you to have found this special place. Mountain bikes and a library provide other diversions. Wheelchair-accessible bedroom and bath. **1220-3100 Rd., P.O. Box 188, Hotchkiss, CO 81419; 970-872-4746.**

Uncompahgre Bed and Breakfast (Montrose)—$$$ to $$$$

If you are in the Montrose area and looking for something more than just a bedroom and cable TV, we highly recommend the Uncompahgre Bed and Breakfast. Richard and Barbara Helm have converted an old schoolhouse into a spacious and comfortable place to spend the night. Each of the seven bedrooms has 12-foot-high ceilings, private bathroom, television and a unique sense of history (some rooms used to be classrooms). One bedroom even has its own whirlpool bath. Enjoy a nice evening or early-morning walk to the nearby Uncompahgre River, or simply relax on the porch and marvel at the Sneffels Range to the south. Richard and Barbara are very hospitable and have been in the bed and breakfast business for 13 years. Kids are welcome. Located 5.5 miles south from the edge of Montrose. **21049 Uncompahgre Rd., Montrose, CO 81401; 1-800-318-8127; 970-240-4000; www.travelguides.com/home/uncompahgre.**

Cedars' Edge Llamas Bed and Breakfast (Cedaredge)—$$ to $$$

Located at the base of Grand Mesa, this quaint bed and breakfast has some of the best views in all of western Colorado. On a clear day, the North Rim of the Black Canyon, Mt. Sneffels, Dallas Divide and even Lizard Head Peak can all be seen from each room's sundeck. Owners Ray and Gail Record not only run a bed and breakfast but also raise some two dozen llamas for breeding. Two of the guest rooms occupy the upstairs of Ray and Gail's large, solar-heated home. Each bedroom features a private bathroom, comfortable furnishings and a private deck. Two rooms in a separate guest house with a lovely enclosed patio are offered only in the summer. A full breakfast is served either in your room or, weather permitting, outside on your private deck. The Records are warm and pleasant hosts who have lived in the area for a long time—ask them about ideas for outdoor activities. Children welcome. Located 5 miles north of Cedaredge on Hwy. 65. **2169 Hwy. 65, Cedaredge, CO 81413; 970-856-6836; www.llamasbandb.com.**

Camping

Black Canyon of the Gunnison National Park

For information on camping on the North and South Rims of the Black Canyon, see the Major Attractions section.

Crawford State Park

Located a mile south of Crawford on Hwy. 92 at Crawford Reservoir. You'll find 61 improved sites at this recently renovated state park, which is especially suited for RVs; fee charged. Open all year. For reservations: **1-800-678-CAMP; 303-470-1144; www.reserveamerica.com.**

Gunnison National Forest

Some sites can be reserved in Gunnison National Forest at **1-877-444-6777** or **www.reserve usa.com. Smith Fork Picnic Ground** offers dispersed camping with minimal facilities and no fee. To reach it, head southeast from Hotchkiss on Hwy. 92 to Crawford and turn left onto Forest Rd. 712. Proceed 7 miles east to the picnic ground. **Erickson Springs Campground** (18 sites, fee charged) is located in the upper North Fork Valley. From Paonia head northeast on Hwy. 133 for about 12 miles and turn right on County Rd. 12. Proceed 6 miles to the campground. Near Erickson Springs Campground is **Lost Lake Campground** (15 sites, no fee). To reach it, proceed another 7 miles up County Rd. 12 from Erickson Springs, to Forest Rd. 706. Turn right and proceed 2 miles to the campground, which receives heavy use in summer. **McClure Campground** (19 sites, fee charged) is located on McClure Pass, 12 miles north of Paonia Reservoir on Hwy. 133.

Paonia State Park

Located about 16 miles northeast of Paonia on Hwy. 133 at Paonia Reservoir. There are 16 sites; fee charged.

Private Campgrounds

Crystal Meadows Ranch—Attractions include a gorgeous location at the base of Kebler Pass, close proximity to the North Fork, Anthracite Creek and Paonia Reservoir, all the amenities for RV campers, laundry and shower facilities and a great restaurant. From Hotchkiss, drive 17 miles northeast on Hwy. 133. Located just off the highway on County Rd. 12. **30682 County Rd. 12, Somerset, CO 81434; 970-929-5656.**
Delta/Grand Mesa KOA Campground— One of the best-equipped RV campgrounds in the area, with complete hookups and tentsites. Showers, store, swimming pool and close proximity to the Gunnison River make this a reat RV park. Located a mile east of Delta on Hwy. 92. **1675 Hwy. 92, Delta, CO 81416; 970-874-3918.**

Gunnison River Pleasure Park—The clear advantage to staying at this campground is its prime location: right where the North Fork meets the Gunnison. They have a small boat ramp for those floating the river, as well as cabins, tentsites and RV sites (no hookups). There is a restaurant; hours vary from day to day. To get there, drive 14 miles east of Delta on Hwy. 92, and 1 mile south on 28.10 Ln. **970-872-2525.**
The Hangin' Tree RV Park—With 25 RV sites with hookups, tentsites, showers and laundry, the Hangin' Tree is your best bet for a private campground in the southern end of Black Canyon Country. Located 2 miles south of Montrose, across the highway from the Ute Indian Museum. **17250 Hwy. 550 S., Montrose, CO 81401; 970-249-9966.**

Where to Eat

Mad Dog Ranch Fountain Cafe (Crawford)—$$ to $$$$

The Mad Dog is a unique dining experience for a variety of reasons. For one, it is owned by celebrity resident Joe Cocker, and this rock-and-roll singer's gold records are on display. The full-service restaurant features an old-fashioned soda fountain plus an espresso bar. Breakfast offerings range from giant cinnamon rolls to grits. Dinners include perfectly cooked pizzas and tasty barbecue. On warm summer days, check out the tables on the back patio. The Mad Dog offers special dinner menus Wed. and Sat., when they bring out the good china for guests. Be sure to check out the soup and salad bar. Open daily 7 A.M.–9 P.M. in summer, 8 A.M.–7 P.M. in the off-season. On Hwy. 92 in downtown Crawford; **970-921-7632.**

Camp Robber Cafe (Montrose)— $$ to $$$

This pleasant little family restaurant has a simple and friendly atmosphere, plus a beautiful collection of nature photography on the walls. The menu ranges from buffalo burgers to angel hair pasta. Either way, save room for the San Juan mud pie. Open for lunch 11 A.M.–3 P.M., dinner 5:30–9 P.M., and Sun. brunch 9 A.M.–2 P.M. **228 E. Main St.; 970-240-1590.**

The Glenn Eyrie Restaurant (Montrose)—$$ to $$$

As one local put it, "the Glenn Eyrie is about the only place in Montrose refined enough for the high school students to go to on prom night." Sophisticated yet comfortable and homey, the Glenn Eyrie has an extensive menu of palate-pleasing foods. From crab-stuffed Colorado trout to game platters, the Glenn Eyrie will certainly have enough options for you to entertain (as well as an extensive wine list). In summer, dinners are served outside on the lawn as well as in the formal setting inside. Open Tues.–Sat. 5–9 P.M. **2351 S. Townsend Ave.; 970-249-9263.**

The Red Barn (Montrose)—$$ to $$$

The enormous plastic bull overlooking Hwy. 50 from the Red Barn's facade is an indicator that the restaurant specializes in everything beef. However, the Red Barn also has great salads, several chicken and fish platters and an appealing dessert menu. The authentic feel of the Red Barn's interior—with its wooden walls and low lighting—lends itself to a comfortable, down-home atmosphere. A great place to kick back and feast after a long trip floating the Gunnison or camping in the San Juan Mountains. Open Mon.–Sat. for breakfast 6–11 A.M., lunch 11 A.M.–3 P.M., dinner 3–10:30 P.M., plus Sun. brunch 9 A.M.–3 P.M. **1413 E. Main St.; 970-249-9202.**

Zack's Trading Post (Hotchkiss)—$$ to $$$

Zack's is a great place to go for a down-home meal. Serving steaks, burgers, chicken and ham, the restaurant also has six different kinds of pie for dessert. Pull up a chair in the large and lively dining area. Many customers rely on the excellent take-out barbecue. Breakfasts are also served. Open Mon.–Sat. 6:30 A.M.–9 P.M., Sun. 6:30 A.M.–8 P.M. In winter, Zack's closes at 8 P.M. At the east end of **Bridge St.,** just past the junction with Hwy. 133. **970-872-3199.**

Little's Restaurant (Paonia)—$$

Over the past few years, Little's has stopped serving lunch and put more effort into dinners. They've added a more expansive wine list and included more variety of game and seafood. The result is a bit more upscale than the old Little's, but after 22 years in business, some things have not changed—such as the tropical room (including a waterfall), the library and the outstanding open patio. Open for dinner Tues.–Sat. 5–10 P.M. Just west of Paonia on Hwy. 133; **970-527-6141.**

The Boardwalk (Crawford)—$ to $$

With its home-cooked meals—at very reasonable prices—and funky charm, the Boardwalk deserves special mention. This restaurant serves great breakfasts and dinners, including inexpensive T-bone steaks. Homemade baked goods, including their special wheat bread, are served with all meals. Dinners come with potato or rice, and salad bar or vegetable of the day. Fresh bread and rolls are also served. Hours vary by season, so call ahead. Located on the main street in Crawford; **64 Hwy. 92; 970-921-4905.**

Highway 92 Fruit Stands

What is a trip down Hwy. 92 in the summer and fall without a bag of fresh fruit to snack on? All along this stretch of highway are numerous orchards, along with fruit stands selling their produce. A fruit stand that has been selling cherries and apples to locals and visitors for 22 years is **Koke's,** located just west of Paonia on Hwy. 133. The orchard itself has been in the family for 105 years! As far as snacks go, nothing beats the fresh cherries, apples, peaches, nectarines, plums and pears of this region. **970-527-3357.**

Services

Visitor Information

Cedaredge Chamber of Commerce—The office is part of the town hall complex in the center of town. **970-856-6961.**

Delta Chamber of Commerce—301 Main St., Delta, CO 81416; 970-874-8616; www.deltacolorado.org.

Hotchkiss Chamber of Commerce—P.O. Box 158, Hotchkiss, CO 81419; 970-872-3226.

Montrose Chamber of Commerce—Stop by the excellent visitor information center at the Ute Indian Museum at the southern end of town, just off Hwy. 550. 17253 Chipeta Ave., Montrose, CO 81401; 970-249-3098. Or check the visitor center in town at 1519 E. Main St., Montrose, CO 81401; 1-800-923-5515; 970-249-5000; www.montrose.org.

Montrose Colorado Visitors and Convention Bureau—433 S. 1st, P.O. Box 335, Montrose, CO 81402; 1-800-873-0244; 970-240-1429; www.visitmontrose.net.

Paonia Chamber of Commerce—P.O. Box 366, Paonia, CO 81428; 970-527-3886.

Cortez

Extreme southwest Colorado is marked by a unique juxtaposition of terrain, as the soaring peaks and lush forests of the San Juans give way to the desert canyons and high mesas of the Colorado Plateau. Once home to thousands of Anasazi—a Navajo word meaning "ancient ones" or "ancient enemies"—this entire area was alive with Anasazi settlements. The National Park Service is now using the term "Ancestral Pueblo People" to refer to the ancient inhabitants of this part of the state.

This beautiful corner of Colorado continues to be an important location for exploration, excavation, study and interpretation of these remarkable people who vanished mysteriously from Colorado about A.D. 1300. Despite the rash of forest fires in 2000 that scarred Mesa Verde National Park and the Ute Mountain Tribal Park, the Anasazi history survives intact.

Anyone interested in learning more about the culture of the Anasazi should plan on spending a lot of time in the Four Corners area. Most visitors blast their way directly to Mesa Verde National Park, which has an international reputation as a World Heritage Cultural Site. Spending a day or an afternoon at Mesa Verde is an absolute must; however, many other lesser-known sites and museums encourage a larger

range of archaeological and personal discovery. Consider lingering in the area for a few days to understand more about the Anasazi far off the beaten track.

At the hub of activity, Cortez (population 8,000) provides a welcome base. Though a traditionally sleepy agricultural center, Cortez is awakening to a tourism boom. Today an array of lodging and dining possibilities awaits visitors, but during the peak summer season rooms can get booked solid. Ties to Native American cultures also run deep in Cortez. During summer evenings you can listen to stories and flute songs by a Ute Mountain Indian, watch an Indian dancer or see a Navajo sand painter at work (see Cortez Center in the Major Attractions section).

The surrounding area is as diverse as it is beautiful, offering a wide range of outdoor experiences. You'll never be far from the outline of Sleeping Ute Mountain (9,884 feet), which lies to the southwest of Cortez. Enshrouded in Ute legend, the prominent slopes of this mountain clearly show the outline of a sleeping Indian with his arms folded across his chest.

Just 11 miles north of Cortez, the hamlet of Dolores takes a position near McPhee Reservoir. This reservoir provides a number of recreational opportunities, from waterskiing to fishing to

Getting There

Located in southwestern Colorado near the Four Corners—where Utah, Colorado, Arizona and New Mexico converge—Cortez acts as a gateway to traffic coming into the state from the south on Hwys. 160 and 666. From Denver (377 miles to the northeast), Cortez can be reached via Interstate 25 south to Walsenburg and then west on Hwy. 160. Cortez also has a small airport with daily flights from **Denver International Airport.**

canoeing. The reservoir's constant supply of irrigation water means that pinto beans and a few other crops can better survive the long, dry summers, but the pristine Dolores River Canyon and a multitude of Anasazi sites have been lost forever. However, a legal settlement before the dam was built required the removal and preservation of Anasazi artifacts from the flooded area. As a result visitors can now view a fascinating collection of artifacts at the Anasazi Heritage Center (see the Major Attractions section).

Prehistory

Thousands of years before the arrival of the pueblo-dwelling Anasazi, nomadic hunter-gatherers roamed southwestern Colorado in search of food. These nomadic people left little behind and, consequently, what is known about them today is sketchy and speculative. Archaeologists agree, however, that near the time of Christ, people began settling in what is now the Four Corners states including southwest Colorado's mesa lands. Instead of roaming far afield for their food, they started building shallow pit houses and cultivating beans, corn and squash in the rich red soil of the valleys. These early inhabitants did not make pottery but instead wove exquisite, coiled baskets, which were often found perfectly preserved in their dwellings. Archaeologists were moved to name these people Basket Makers. Only a handful of sites in Colorado date to this Anasazi period (Basket Maker II).

By A.D. 550 (Basket Maker III) the Anasazi also learned how to make pottery and experienced dramatic cultural advancements. Soon the bow and arrow replaced the primitive atlatl spear thrower, and the Anasazi began relying on stored food to get them through the winter. Settlements from this period consist of single-family farms with small storage rooms scattered around a single pit house. Many very large pit structures called "great kivas" were built. Evidence suggests that these impressive round rooms and other smaller kivas were used for religious and social purposes. Many Colorado sites, including some near Mesa Verde and the Dolores River Valley, can be traced to this period.

Around A.D. 750 (the Pueblo I period) the Anasazi started coming together in multifamily villages. In some cases several hundred families lived in close proximity to one another. But by A.D. 900 those who had been living together in large villages at higher elevations began to disperse to other areas in the Southwest.

Between the years A.D. 1000 and 1300 (Pueblo II) the Anasazi reached their peak in terms of architectural, political and economic advancements. Many rich and varied cultural traits can be traced to this period. Mesa-top homes built of stone and masonry replaced the subterranean pit houses. Cotton weaving and fire-resistant pottery also improved the quality of life. The entire Anasazi region was connected by a network of roads. A complex, integrated lifestyle can be seen in the region's "great kivas" (Lowry Pueblo and Chimney Rock in Colorado) and "great houses" (best exemplified by Chaco Canyon National Park, New Mexico).

By A.D. 1200 (Pueblo III) the Anasazi gradually sought refuge beneath overhanging cliffs, including the ones we know as Mesa Verde. Reasons for this move are unclear, but the settlements appear to be built in easily defensible positions. Many archaeologists believe these ancient people wanted to be closer to a water source; some of the walled compounds dating to this period enclose natural springs. Other groups near Mesa Verde chose to remain closer to their fields by living atop the mesas. For the first time many Anasazi built towers, which can now be seen in the area straddling the Utah-Colorado border at Hovenweep National Monument. This final period of development featured fine pottery craftsmanship.

By A.D. 1300 the Anasazi had deserted Mesa Verde and the Four Corners area for reasons that have never been fully explained. It was not a spontaneous exodus but rather a gradual migration over the course of many years. Like gypsies, the Anasazi spread out in small groups, eventually losing their cultural identity. The generally accepted theory is that the Anasazi left because of a prolonged drought. Evidence also suggests that a cooling of the climate, a lack of burnable wood and soil depletion after hundreds of years of intensive farming may have contributed to their abandonment of the area. After their departure, the Anasazi cliff houses and mesa-top communities stood empty. Nearly 200 years passed before the area was inhabited again, this time by Ute tribes.

Major Attractions

Mesa Verde National Park

The most dramatic introduction to the ancient Anasazi culture imaginable can be found at this park. With its twisting canyons, panoramic views and outstanding archaeological remains, Mesa Verde continues to fascinate visitors from the United States and abroad. Thanks to fire-fighting efforts, the renowned ruins managed to survive wildfires that scorched large tracts of public land during the summer of 1996 and again in 2000. Despite their fury, the fires didn't damage any of the park's magnificent sights; in fact, they uncovered many artifacts that otherwise might never have been seen. As one of the largest archaeological preserves in America, Mesa Verde has more than earned its status as a World Heritage Cultural Site.

History

During the period between A.D. 1190 and 1300, advances in masonry skills enabled the Anasazi to build huge 100- to 200-room cliff houses, some four stories high. Hundreds of years after the Anasazi disappeared, Ute Indians moved into the Mesa Verde area. They knew about the empty cliff dwellings but kept away, believing the ancient cities to be haunted. Spanish explorers and settlers looked around the area for many years before trappers, prospectors and settlers entered the region, but they never saw the ruins.

Abandoned for almost 600 years, the interconnected settlements at Mesa Verde were finally rediscovered in December 1888. While looking for stray cattle during a snowstorm, ranchers Richard Wetherill and Charlie Mason stumbled upon Cliff Palace, the largest site in Mesa Verde, with more than 200 rooms and 23 kivas. In the 1890s many people flocked to the area to collect artifacts.

In 1906, after persistent lobbying by some Coloradans, Congress passed a bill creating Mesa Verde National Park. It was this unusual foresight that helped create the first park in the country set aside exclusively for the preservation of archaeological artifacts.

Getting There

The entrance to the park is located 10 miles east of Cortez on Hwy. 160, halfway to Mancos. From there a narrow paved road snakes its way up the mesa to the south for about 15 miles to the Far View Visitor Center. From there you will need to make some decisions about tour times and locations.

Facts About the Park

A ticket policy regulates tours of the major ruins at Mesa Verde. Because these tickets are set for specific times and places, it's best to go straight to Far View Visitor Center to obtain them (you may want to arrive before 9 A.M.). The ruins are located in two main areas—Chapin and Weatherill Mesas—so you will need to decide where to begin.

The highly popular Cliff Palace, as well as the dramatic dwellings at Spruce Tree House and Balcony House, entice most visitors directly to Chapin Mesa. Only a fraction of the park's visitors make the twisting 12-mile drive from the Far View Visitor Center to Weatherill Mesa. Once there you board a small tram, which drives to various trailheads for ranger-guided walks. The most dramatic ruin and primary attraction on Weatherill Mesa is Long House, Mesa Verde's second-largest cliff dwelling, once home to 150 Anasazi.

The well-maintained park is designed with facilities to make your visit comfortable. Due to the large number of visitors each year and the

Dusk casts shadows across the kivas of Mesa Verde. Photo by Bruce Caughey.

potential damage to the artifacts and the environment, straying off the trails is forbidden. Some sites close during the winter months. **Mesa Verde National Park, CO 81330; 970–529-4465; www.nps.gov/meve.**

Archaeological Museum

A visit to the Archaeological Museum begins to unravel the fascinating history of the Anasazi Indians. Allow enough time to take in this museum before going to look at the major cliff dwellings. In addition to a bookstore, it contains many Anasazi exhibits and artifacts. Open daily May–Sept. 8 A.M.–6:30 P.M. The rest of the year, 8 A.M.–5 P.M. Free admission.

Lodging and Camping

Though close enough to Durango and Cortez to be a day trip, consider staying overnight and waking in the early morning to the intense colors of the rock walls. There are two options for staying in the park.

Rooms at the comfortable **Far View Lodge ($$$)** feature balcony views of the park and the far-off mountains. The lodge also has a restaurant and a lounge. Reservations are highly recommended. Closed from mid-Oct. to mid-Apr. For reservations and information: **Far View Lodge, Mesa Verde, P.O. Box 277, Mancos, CO 81328; 970-529-4421; www.visitmesaverde.com.**

Located 4 miles from the park entrance, **Morefield Campground** (490 sites, fee charged) offers the only camping in the park. Sites are on a first-come, first-served basis. Nearby is a general store, gas station, gift shop, snack bar and laundry and shower facilities.

Visitor Center

Fifteen miles from the park entrance, the Far View Visitor Center offers information, maps, tickets for tours and modern Southwestern Indian exhibits. Open May–Sept., 8 A.M.–5 P.M. daily.

Other Anasazi Culture Sites

In addition to the spectacular cliff dwellings at Mesa Verde, several other sites provide a more complete understanding of the Anasazi culture—without the frustration of crowds. Gaining a more complete picture of what this peaceful culture was all about takes patience and curiosity.

Anasazi Heritage Center

Since 1988 this fine archaeological museum has provided an excellent basis for understanding the ancient Anasazi culture. Ironically, the controversial McPhee Reservoir project is the reason the Anasazi Heritage Center exists at all. Artifacts were removed from the reservoir area before it was flooded.

In 1977 the Dolores Archaeological Program got under way, discovering 1,600 Anasazi sites, only 125 of which were extensively excavated, sampled and tested. The museum houses more than 2 million artifacts from these digs, with some of the most outstanding pieces displayed for the public. The "discovery" section of the display room gives people a chance to learn about the Anasazi through hands-on experience: you can grind corn, examine grains with a microscope and watch a weaver using a loom. Traveling exhibits (some from the Smithsonian) change at least yearly. Be sure to see the eerie three-stage hologram depicting what these ancient people looked like. Open year-round, modest admission fee. Open 9 A.M.–5 P.M. daily. Follow the signs as you approach the town of Dolores. The center is located just west of town. **27501 Hwy. 184, Dolores, CO 81323; 970-882-4811; www.co.blm.gov/ahc.**

Take a moment to look at the **Dominguez** and **Escalante** ruins located a half-mile from the museum and named for the Franciscan friars who passed through the area in 1776. They were the first to document Anasazi ruins in Colorado.

Cortez Center

The University of Colorado initiated this non-profit center in 1987 to help preserve the Anasazi heritage of the Cortez area. The facility has a museum displaying artifacts from Yellow Jacket and other nearby sites. In summer the museum hosts free evening sessions on a range of subjects, including archaeology, astronomy, art and Native American culture. Adjacent to the center, the **Bufort Wayt Cultural Park** has Native American families-in-residence. Activities include craft demonstrations, Native foods, storytelling and dancing on summer evenings during the week. Open Mon.–Sat. 10 A.M.–9 P.M. in summer; Mon.–Fri. 10 A.M.–5 P.M. the rest of the year. Free admission. **25 N. Market St., Cortez, CO 81321; 970-565-1151; www.cortezculturalcenter.org.**

Crow Canyon Archaeological Center

People from all walks of life come together here for an intensive week of digging, sweating and learning under the guidance of archaeologists. After some classroom training, participants lay out grids and remove dirt inch by inch with trowels, chisels, toothbrushes, buckets and brooms. Crow Canyon also offers a less intensive summer day program that includes examining artifacts, throwing a spear with an atlatl and taking a tour of the laboratory and a working site. Weaving, jewelry making and other classes are offered in the off-season. All full participants receive one week of lodging (shared quarters) and meals. **Crow Canyon Archaeological Center, 23390 County Rd. K, Cortez, CO 81321; 1-800-422-8975; 970-565-8975; www.crowcanyon.org.**

Hovenweep National Monument

Established as a national monument in 1923, Hovenweep (a Ute word meaning "deserted valley") stands as one of the most impressive Anasazi ruins in the Four Corners area. Although the culture of the Hovenweep people was similar to that at Mesa Verde, the structures at Hovenweep are different—characterized by stone towers, some as high as 20 feet.

Looking out across the inhospitable landscape at Hovenweep, it's hard to imagine that prior to A.D. 1300 the inhabitants planted terraced fields in this dry, rocky landscape. Near the end of their habitation here, they moved from smaller scattered pueblos to larger settlements at the heads of canyons. It is thought they did this to protect their water sources and fend off invaders.

Facts About the Monument—Hovenweep National Monument straddles the Colorado-Utah border west of Cortez. There are six main sites—**Square Tower** and **Cajon Ruins** in Utah, and **Holly, Hackberry Canyon, Cutthroat Castle** and **Goodman Point Ruins** in Colorado. Square Tower Ruins stands as the best preserved of the six sites and the only one reachable by car. The others involve a hike. But if you enjoy desert canyon hiking, Hovenweep should not be missed. At sunset the shadow-encrusted lighting on the square, oval and circular towers makes for great photos.

For those staying in the Cortez area, try a scenic driving loop with stops at Hovenweep and Lowry Pueblo (see write-up below). From Cortez head southwest of town for 3 miles on Hwy. 666 and turn right on McElmo Canyon Rd. Drive up this beautiful slickrock canyon over the border into Utah, following the signs to Hovenweep. After 39 miles you arrive at the monument headquarters, where the ranger station, the campground and Square Tower Ruins are located. After spending all the time you want here, drive northeast 25 miles, back into Colorado. This road brings you near Lowry Pueblo and back to Hwy. 666, 20 miles northwest of Cortez. Along the way you have panoramic views of many Four Corners landmarks—Sleeping Ute Mountain, Mesa Verde Plateau and the La Sal Mountains in Utah. Be sure to inquire locally about road conditions because these rough dirt roads can be impassable after storms.

For more information about Hovenweep, contact the park superintendent at **Mesa Verde National Park, CO 81330; 970-529-4465; www.nps.gov/hove.**

Lowry Pueblo

Lowry Pueblo, located northwest of Cortez, was built about A.D. 1000 and inhabited by 100 Indians. From its first excavation in 1928 to its declaration as a National Historic Landmark nearly 40 years later it has proved fascinating for visitors and archaeologists. Lowry's great kiva, one of the biggest yet discovered in the American Southwest, remains a fantastic sight. Picnic tables and rest rooms are the only amenities; no rangers on duty. To reach Lowry Pueblo from Cortez, drive northwest on Hwy. 666 for 20 miles to the town of Pleasant View. Turn left (west) and proceed 9 miles to the site.

Ute Mountain Tribal Park

A great sense of discovery accompanies you while walking down a dusty trail with your Ute escort in this isolated setting just south of Mesa Verde National Park. Undeveloped and relatively undisturbed, the extraordinary Anasazi cliff houses, kivas and storerooms seem to gain a spirit and importance of their own. Recent fires spared the Anasazi heritage of the park, but burned the cabin of Chief Jack House, the last traditional chief of the Ute Mountain Utes.

The Ute Mountain Tribal Park was set up by the tribe to preserve the culture of the Anasazi. It encompasses more than 125,000 acres along a 25-mile stretch of the Mancos River, and you'll find a strong emphasis placed on experiencing Anasazi ruins within a natural setting. No developed amenities exist in the backcountry. You must therefore come prepared and have the stamina to handle at least a few hours of backcountry hiking. Half-day to four-day guided backpacking trips are also available. The fee for this unforgettable experience is nominal. For more information, contact Veronica Cuthair at the **Ute Mountain Tribal Park, Towaoc, CO 81334; 1-800-847-5485; 970-565-9653; www.utemountainute.com.**

Overnight Camping

Primitive campsites are available in the tribal park, down by the banks of the Mancos River. To be allowed to camp overnight in the park, you'll need a permit. Check with the tribe for details. For those of you with willpower, there is a new RV park at the casino (see the Gambling section).

Tour Information

Guided tours can usually be booked from June 1 into autumn—on a more limited basis as the weather cools down. The tribe asks that visitors

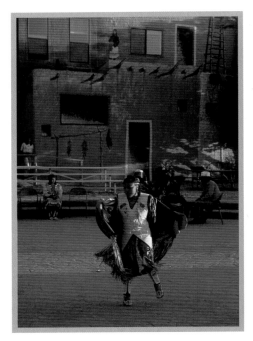

Traditional Native American dancing occurs on summer evenings at the Cortez Center. Photo by Bruce Caughey.

A Ute guide climbs to Eagle's Nest Ruins at Ute Mountain Tribal Park. Photo by Bruce Caughey.

to the park make reservations at least three days in advance. Be sure to call and reconfirm your tour and what time it begins.

Outdoor Activities

Biking

MOUNTAIN BIKING

Less known than its neighbors at Moab, Utah, and Grand Junction, Colorado, the plateau and canyon country surrounding Cortez is begging to be discovered. Stop by **Kokopelli Bike and Board** for trail ideas, rental and repair, **at 30 W. Main St., Cortez, CO 81321; 970-565-4408.** The **Cortez Welcome Center** in Cortez also has information and maps on rides in the vicinity: **928 E. Main St., Cortez, CO 81321; 970-565-4048.** Or check in at the **Dolores Ranger District Office, 100 N. 6th St., P.O. Box 210, Dolores, CO 81323; 970-882-7296; www.fs.fed.us/r2/sanjuan.**

Cannonball Mesa

This fairly easy 10-mile circle tour combines great scenery with the opportunity to explore Anasazi ruins. To get to the trailhead, drive 3 miles south of Cortez on Hwy. 666 to the intersection of McElmo Canyon Rd. (at the M&M Cafe). Turn right and travel precisely 20.4 miles west to an unmarked county road that heads off on your right. Park immediately at the cattleguard at a sign reading "Keep Vehicle on the Road," and begin your ride on the well-marked trail. After riding 1.5 miles north, take a left fork onto a road that switchbacks up Cannonball Mesa. After 2 miles on top of the mesa, take the right fork, which eventually ends at Cannonball Mesa Ruin and offers excellent views over McElmo Canyon.

Fishing

Disappointment Creek

Need we say more?

Hovenweep National Monument. Photo by Dean Winstanley.

Groundhog Reservoir

Some anglers seem to have forgotten about 670-acre Groundhog Reservoir, but the fishing can be excellent for 12- to 14-inch trout—especially from a boat. The reservoir has an assortment of brown, brook, rainbow and cutthroat trout. Cabins and boats available for rent; a convenience store near the lake also sells tackle. To reach the lake from Dolores, take 11th St. (which turns into Forest Rd. 526) north for 27 miles until the road splits. Take the right fork and continue 5 miles on Forest Rd. 533 to the reservoir.

Lower Dolores River

Even though the Dolores has been through a major dry spell, it can still produce rainbow, cutthroat and brown trout (not too many lunkers, though) along its Gold Medal waters. Please observe rules for the 12-mile stretch downstream from the dam to Bradfield Bridge: flies and lures only, catch-and-release. Whatever your opinion of McPhee Reservoir, fish seem to thrive in the nutrient-rich tailwaters from the dam. And, because of the controlled water flow, the river no longer totally dries up in late summer. From Cortez head north on Hwy. 666 for 21 miles to just beyond Pleasant View, then turn right (east) onto County Rd. DD. Drive 1 mile to County Rd. 16, then 3 miles north to an access road for Bradfield Bridge. Once there take Lone Dome Rd. (County Rd. 504), which follows along the Dolores River for 12 miles southeast to the dam. You'll find a couple of campgrounds in the Lone Dome area.

McPhee Reservoir

Filled completely for the first time in 1987, McPhee Reservoir is now one of the largest bodies of water in the state. The sloping, timbered shoreline creates an interesting vista and the fishing can be superb. However, it can also be a bit inconsistent due to severe water level fluctuations. The Colorado Division of Wildlife has been very active in stocking this reservoir with trout. While this is the main thrust of the stocking program, large- and smallmouth bass, bluegills and crappies can be found in abundance. This could become one of the best lakes in the state for catching kokanee salmon. At McPhee, fishing is better from a boat, so you may want to stop by **McPhee Marina** for boat and tackle rentals and a bite to eat. At the upper end of the lake are two boat ramps. See the Camping section for more information about staying overnight near the lake. To reach McPhee from Cortez drive 8 miles north on Hwy. 145, then 4 miles northeast on Hwy. 184. There is a marked access road from there.

West Fork of the Dolores River

Angling for small rainbow, brown and cutthroat trout is normally quite good on the West Fork. Some 8 miles of the river are posted against fishing, but there is still plenty of public water. The small stream is paralleled for 30 miles by a well-maintained gravel road in an exceptionally beautiful, thickly wooded area in the San Juan Mountains. The drive is incredible in late Sept. when the scrub oak and aspen change colors. To reach the West Fork of the Dolores River from the town of Dolores drive 15 miles northeast on Hwy. 145 to a marked turnoff for Dunton Rd. (Forest Rd. 535). The road follows the stream for 30 miles, ending up back on Hwy. 145 north of the town of Rico.

Golf

Conquistador Golf Course

This 18-hole public course offers great views of the surrounding peaks and mesas in the Cortez area. Greens fees are reasonable. The course is open from mid-Mar. to mid-Nov. Located in northeast Cortez just off Hwy. 145. **2018 N. Dolores Rd., Cortez, CO 81321; 970-565-9208.**

Hiking and Backpacking

Hiking near Anasazi sites in the canyons and along the mesas in the Cortez area is hard to beat. Hiking trails at Mesa Verde, Hovenweep and the Ute Mountain Tribal Park take you through juniper and piñon pine and over slickrock to Anasazi ruins. See the Major Attractions section for more information.

From Hwy. 145, east of Dolores, excellent and seldom-used high country lies waiting to be explored. Fourteen-thousand-foot peaks, fields of wildflowers, abandoned mine buildings and abundant wildlife characterize the alpine country of the San Juan and Uncompahgre National Forests accessible from the Upper Dolores River area. For more information, contact the helpful folks at the **Dolores Ranger District Office, 100 N. 6th St., P.O. Box 210, Dolores, CO 81323; 970-882-7296; www.fs.fed.us/r2/sanjuan.** Other great hiking areas lie east of Cortez, closer to Mancos.

Calico/Fall Creek/Winter Trail Loop

This 14-mile loop begins at the new Calico trailhead, above the small town of Dunton. Calico Trail climbs southwest, following a ridge between the Dolores River and the West Fork of the Dolores. Along the route you have spectacular 360-degree views of the surrounding mountains. The trail begins in a vast mountain meadow and rises through Engelmann spruce and subalpine fir before reaching treeline and, eventually, the summit of 11,866-foot Papoose Peak. The trail then drops down to the intersection with Fall Creek Trail, 6 miles from the trailhead. Turn right and follow Fall Creek Trail for 4 miles to a cutoff trail above Dunton that takes you onto Winter Trail to complete the loop. Winter Trail is an old wagon road used to move supplies between Rico and Dunton in the early 1900s. Mail was delivered over this road in winter by skiing mailmen. The 4-mile trail climbs sharply the first mile and then levels off for the remainder.

To reach the trailhead from Dolores drive east on Hwy. 145 for 12.5 miles and turn left onto West Fork Rd. (Forest Rd. 535). Drive about 25 miles to an area called the Meadows above Dunton, then turn right onto Forest Rd. 471. Drive to the trailhead.

Geyser Spring Trail

This easy 1.25-mile trail ends up at a small pool of water fed by the only true geyser in the state of Colorado. The frequency of eruptions varies, but one usually occurs about every half hour. It's not exactly Old Faithful, but the geyser bubbles for about 15 minutes, emitting a strong-smelling sulfur gas. The trail begins 2.2 miles south of Dunton. From Dolores drive east on Hwy. 145 for 12.5 miles and turn left onto Forest Rd. 535. Follow this road for 23.3 miles (a half-mile beyond Paradise Hot Spring, which is closed to the public) and look for the trailhead on the right. The gradual hike up to the geyser takes you through aspen forests and small meadows.

Mesa Verde Trails

Five short designated hiking trails can be found in Mesa Verde National Park. For more information, see the Major Attractions section.

Navajo Lake Trail

Navajo Lake Trail, which begins about 2 miles north of Dunton on Forest Rd. 535, takes you into the heart of the Lizard Head Wilderness. From the trailhead, follow the trail 5 miles up steep switchbacks through open meadows and forests to Navajo Lake in Navajo Basin. This is the source of the headwaters of the West Fork of the Dolores River. Navajo Basin is also a good place to be if you like to climb 14ers—El Diente, Mt. Wilson and Wilson Peak are all within striking distance. This is the most heavily used area in the West Dolores area—so if you don't want to run into other hikers, try another area.

Ute Mountain Tribal Park Trails

A Ute Indian guide must accompany you on any hikes into the park. For more information on the Anasazi ruins see the Major Attractions section.

River Floating

Dolores River

With its sandstone canyons and Anasazi artifacts, the Dolores features more of a desert Southwest feeling than do most of the other major rivers in Colorado. Plan an early trip (mid- to late Apr. through June), perhaps an overnighter, because the Dolores peaks sooner than almost any other

river in the state. The actual river-running season is only three to four weeks each year. Some recent lean water years suggest that you should be sure to check on current flow conditions.

The Upper Dolores, a 37-mile stretch from Rico down to the town of Dolores, drops an average of 50 feet per mile through shady pine forests and ranch property. Kayaks are the best bet for this section.

Aside from the already apparent reduction of water flow on the desert canyon section of the Dolores, other long-term effects of the McPhee Reservoir remain to be seen. Running this 171-mile section of the river can be done in one week, but a lot of people choose leisurely weekend snippets. Highlights of this section include Ponderosa Gorge, Dolores Canyon (offering wild rapids including the famous Snaggletooth, which many prudent rafters choose to portage), Little Glen Canyon, Slick Rock Canyon, Paradox Canyon, Mesa Canyon and Gateway Canyon. For up-to-date flow information or other questions about the river, check with the **Bedrock Store, Bedrock, CO 81411; 970-859-7395; www.doloreswater.com.**

Outfitters

Dvorak's Kayak and Rafting Expeditions—One of the state's most respected outfitters, offering extended day trips down the Dolores; **1-800-824-3795; www.dvorakexpe ditions.com.**

Skiing

CROSS-COUNTRY SKIING AND SNOWSHOEING

Many wonderful ski-touring options are available in this extreme southwest corner of the state. In the transition zone between alpine and desert, many suitable trails exist. The **Cortez Welcome Center** will be glad to provide you with more information. **928 E. Main St.; 970-565-4048.** For more trail ideas, contact the **Dolores Ranger District Office, 100 N. 6th St., P.O. Box 210, Dolores, CO 81323; 970-882-7296; www.fs.fed.us/r2/sanjuan.**

Backcountry Trails

Dunton—A hot soak would be just the thing after a day of cross-country skiing. Thanks to new owners, the Dunton Hot Springs are again open for group accommodations and soaking (see the Where to Stay section). Dunton still offers excellent intermediate touring with wide-open views.

Just above Dunton the road is not plowed. A mile after setting out on skis, you'll reach the fork of Forest Rds. 611 (left) and 535 (right). The left fork leads up through aspen and eventually a meadow, coming out at Groundhog Stock Driveway, 2 miles from the fork. This is a good area for telemarking. The right fork (Forest Rd. 535) leads up past Burro Bridge Campground, over Burro Bridge and past the Navajo Lake trailhead. After about 5 miles, the trail leads into high meadows with good views of Mt. Wilson, Wilson Peak and El Diente Peak to the northeast. This route is not for beginners.

The trailhead is located 12.5 miles east of Dolores on Hwy. 145 and then 20 miles up West Fork Rd. (Forest Rd. 535). Take note, the West Fork Rd. into Dunton can be very slippery—four-wheel-drive vehicles are suggested. Check road conditions before the trip.

Lizard Head Pass—A bit farther up Hwy. 145 from Dolores (47 miles) is 10,250-foot Lizard Head Pass, which attracts heavy snows. With open meadows and great views of surrounding peaks (especially Lizard Head Peak to the north), this is an especially popular area with nordic skiers. From the summit of the pass there are a number of directions in which to ski. Try the south side of the highway and ski southwest for 2 miles down fairly easy slopes, in and out of trees. On the north side of the highway, many advanced skiers head north toward Lizard Head Peak and the Lizard Head Wilderness Area for some great tree skiing. Trails can be difficult to follow in winter, so topographic maps and a compass are recommended. Be sure to stay clear of avalanche-prone areas.

Mesa Verde National Park—Inside the park the eastern loop of Ruins Rd. is not plowed in winter. Although it's usually only skiable for a few days after a snowfall, it can be one of the most memorable ski tours you'll ever take. Like the men who first discovered Mesa Verde during a snowstorm in 1888, you'll be awed by the haunting dwellings at Cliff Palace and other sites along the way. The east loop is an easy 6-mile ski trail. Be sure to check on snow conditions at the park before driving up there. If they give you the thumbs up, drive 10 miles east from Cortez on Hwy. 160 to the park entrance and turn right (south). Drive 20 miles to the intersection of Ruins Rd. Please park well off the road. For more information about skiing, contact the park superintendent at **Mesa Verde National Park, CO 81330; 970-529-4465; 970-529-4475; www.nps.gov/meve.**

Groomed Trails

Mancos–Chicken Creek Area—Head out on 32 miles of groomed track in this gorgeous location east of Cortez. The main trail plugs along for 20 miles, offering several loops and a spur trail for varied abilities. It's all free! From Cortez drive 17 miles east on Hwy. 160 to Mancos. Turn north on Hwy. 184 and continue to Chicken Creek Rd. (County Rd. 141), which leads 3 miles to the parking area and trailhead.

Seeing and Doing

Gambling

Ute Mountain Casino

This thriving complex lies just 11 miles south of Cortez on Hwy. 160/666. The large, ground-floor gambling complex houses 400 slots as well as video poker; for small stakes you can also try the live blackjack and poker games. Up to 500 frothing bingo players sometimes pack a special back room to vie for prizes as large as $10,000. With no alcohol served (free pop and coffee) and no drunken brawls, this casino takes on a much more wholesome atmosphere than most. A restaurant called **Kuchu's** serves food except in the earliest morning hours. The casino itself seems to fly in the face of important beliefs of the Ute Indians. But with extremely high unemployment and few available jobs in the Tribal Park, it serves a useful purpose. Open 8 A.M.– 4 A.M. daily. **1-800-258-8007; 970-565-8800; www.utemountaincasino.com.**

Museums and Galleries

Anasazi Museums

See the Major Attractions section.

Galleries and Shops

A proliferation of Indian pottery shops and the like has sprouted on the main streets of Cortez. Some of them offer carefully worked Indian crafts, while others have cheap (but often pretty) imitations. A gallery of note is the **Ute Mountain Pottery Plant,** located on the Ute Mountain Reservation 12 miles south of Cortez on Hwy. 160 S.; **970-565-8548; www.ute mountainute.com.**

Scenic Drives

Cortez/Hovenweep Loop

See Hovenweep in the Major Attractions section.

Mancos Valley Stage Line

This memorable, real-life stagecoach line in Mancos offers a range of options for people who want to feel the real West where it counts—the seat of your pants! After a very bumpy ride on a coach pulled by a team of horses, you will have a story to tell your friends. The Bartels family offers 1-hour lunch or dinner tours. For information and reservations, contact **4550 County Rd. 41, Mancos, CO 81328; 1-800-365-3530; 970-533-9857; www.thestagecoach.com.**

San Juan Skyway

See the Scenic Drives section of the **Durango** chapter for information about this remarkable 236-mile route.

Where to Stay

Accommodations

For the most part, lodging opportunities in Cortez are predictable, but in the outlying country, you'll find many opportunities for more unusual accommodations. The main street through Cortez is lined with motels ranging from mid-level to low end, including several with Indian themes such as the Arrow Motel and Tomahawk Lodge. A good bet is the renovated **Holiday Inn Express, 2121 E. Main St., Cortez, CO 81321; 1-800-626-5652; 970-565-6000.** During summer it's highly recommended to make reservations in advance because lodging gets surprisingly tight. For more assistance, contact the **Cortez Welcome Center, 928 E. Main St., P.O. Box 968, Cortez, CO 81321; 970-565-4048.**

Blue Lake Ranch—$$$ to $$$$

Located near Hesperus, this plush B&B is worth a little driving time. See the **Durango** chapter for details.

Dunton Hot Springs—$$$ to $$$$

Featuring natural hot springs, dining and a chapel near the Dunton Falls (perfect for weddings), this place has it all. But right now, they only open for groups. Check in and enjoy their eight log cabins, three-bedroom house, bunkhouse, and two tepees. **P.O. Box 818, Dunton, CO 81323; 970-882-7474; www.duntonhot springs.com.**

Bauer House Bed and Breakfast— $$ to $$$

During the warmer months, try out the 1890s vintage Bauer House with its Victorian feel right in the middle of Mancos. A National Historic Landmark, its solid brick and stone construction makes it look as if its next 100 years are guaranteed. It offers three tastefully decorated bedrooms with private bathrooms and a larger third-floor suite with room for 10. Outside, the sweeping yard, complete with a putting green (you can also play a game of bocce ball or croquet), provides the perspective to fully appreciate the building's wonderful architecture. Interior common areas feature exposed wood and the original hardware, all lovingly restored by owner Bobbi Black, who received a Colorado Historical Society grant to fix up the porches and the gorgeous bay window. Full breakfast in the dining room. **100 Bauer Ave., P.O. Box 1049, Mancos, CO 81328; 1-800-733-9707; 970-533-9707; www.bauer-house.com.**

Kelly Place—$$

Located on 100 acres in beautiful McElmo Canyon about 10 miles west of Cortez, Kelly Place not only offers unique, affordable lodging but also involves visitors in the archaeology and early history of the area. Operated primarily for group visits, Kelly Place also opens its doors to occasional overnight guests. Smack dab in the middle of Anasazi country, the Kelly property offers a hands-on approach, helping guests acquire an appreciation for Anasazi prehistory. Ten simple rooms each sleep up to 6 people and have their own bathroom. Two smaller cabins and one large cabin (jetted tub!) offer some privacy and time for quiet reflection. Groups of up to 24 people can be accommodated. Kelly Place accepts reservations only. **14663 County Rd. G, Cortez, CO 81321; 970-565-3125; www. kellyplace.com.**

Jersey Jim Lookout Tower—$

For solitude, space and a four-state, 360-degree view, make early reservations at Jersey Jim, a former fire lookout tower near Mancos. The sun setting behind prominent Sleeping Ute Mountain absolutely can't be beat. But Jersey Jim isn't for those who balk at a bathroom down the hall—here you'll encounter an outhouse down a 55-foot ladder! The crude but functional pulley system helps you bring up your essentials: food, water and bedding. Once inside the small square room (windows all around), limited luxuries include a propane-powered heater, lamp and refrigerator; a double bed, chairs and a few other sticks of furniture round out the furnish-

ings. The space is comfortable for couples, though an occasional family of four rents the tower. Open June 1–late Sept. Jersey Jim Foundation at **P.O. Box 1032, Mancos, CO 81328; 970-533-7060.**

Camping

Anasazi Areas

Mesa Verde National Park—See the Major Attractions section.

Ute Mountain Tribal Park—See Ute Mountain Tribal Park in the Major Attractions section.

Mancos Lake State Park

Mancos Lake State Park (26 sites, fee charged) offers superb views of the La Plata Mountains. They also have two very nice yurts that you can reserve for a more cushy experience. Reserve at **1-800-678-CAMP** or **www.reserveamerica. com.** Take Hwy. 184 just northeast of Mancos and then follow the signs for 5 miles to the park. By the way, you'll find free camping right in Mancos at **Boyle Park.**

San Juan National Forest

Some campsites in San Juan National Forest can be reserved at **1-877-444-6777** or **www. reserveusa.com.** All the sites listed below charge a fee. To reach **McPhee Reservoir Recreation Complex** (73 sites), head west from Dolores on Hwy. 145 for 5 miles and turn right at the reservoir entrance; drive 1 mile to the campground. **House Creek Campground** (58 sites) can be reached by driving about 1 mile east from Dolores on Hwy. 145 and turning left onto Forest Rd. 526. Drive 6 miles and turn left onto Forest Rd. 528 and proceed 5 miles to the campground.

Three campgrounds have opened up along the Dolores River below McPhee Reservoir. For the protection of wildlife the road is closed Dec. 1–Mar. 31. From Cortez head north on Hwy. 666 for 21 miles to just beyond Pleasant View, then turn right (east) onto County Rd. DD. Drive 1 mile to County Rd. 16, then 3 miles north to an access road for Bradfield Bridge.

Bradfield Campground (22 sites) is a half-mile below the bridge. Four miles up the Dolores from Bradfield Bridge is **Cabin Canyon Campground** (11 riverside sites); another 5 miles upriver brings you to **Ferris Canyon Campground** (6 sites). This access road follows up along the Dolores (southeast) for a total of 12 miles from Bradfield Bridge to the dam.

There are a number of campgrounds east of Dolores. **Mavreeso Campground** (14 sites), **West Dolores Campground** (13 sites) and **Burro Bridge Campground** (15 sites) are located up the beautiful West Fork Rd. (Forest Rd. 535) along the West Fork of the Dolores River. To get there, head east from Dolores on Hwy. 145 for 12.5 miles and turn left onto Forest Rd. 535. Mavreeso, West Dolores and Burro Bridge Campgrounds are 5, 7 and 24 miles up the road, respectively. From the junction of Hwy. 145 and Forest Rd. 535 (12.5 miles east of Dolores), continue east on Hwy. 145 for 41 miles to **Cayton Campground** (27 sites), up near Lizard Head Pass.

Heading east on Hwy. 160 from Cortez, there are a few campgrounds. **Transfer Campground** (12 sites) is 9 miles north of Mancos on Forest Rd. 561. It's less than a mile walk from here to the West Mancos River. **Target Tree Campground** (51 sites) is along Hwy. 160, 7 miles east of Mancos. About 16 miles east of Mancos off Hwy. 160, take Forest Rd. 571 to **Kroeger Campground** (11 sites) near the La Plata River.

Private Campgrounds

Cortez KOA Campground—Plenty of RV hookups, laundry facilities, showers and so forth. Located just east of Cortez on Hwy. 160. **27432 E. Hwy. 160, Cortez, CO 81321; 970-565-9301; www.koa.com.**

Dolores River RV Park—Situated along the Dolores River, 2.5 miles east of Dolores on Hwy. 145, this place has hookups, tentsites and everything else you could possibly need. **18680 Hwy. 145, Dolores, CO 81323; 970-882-7761; www.edonnet.com/dolores.**

Priest Gulch Ranchcamp—Located 35 miles northeast of Cortez on Hwy. 145. Full hookups and tentsites. Laundry, store, playground and other amenities. **27646 Hwy. 145, Dolores, CO 81323; 970-562-3810; www.priest gulch.com.**

Ute Mountain Tribal Park—Now you can camp next to the Ute Mountain Casino. For more information see the Gambling section under Seeing and Doing.

Where to Eat

Dusty Rose Cafe (Mancos)—$$ to $$$
The Dusty Rose has attracted a loyal following thanks to its carefully prepared northern Italian cuisine. In a romantic, intimate yet still casual setting, you can enjoy veal, chicken, shrimp and pasta dishes. In addition, they serve breakfast and lunches that will fill you up and get you back on the road. In warmer months try the patio. Take a glance at the wine list, which features a choice selection of Italian wines among others. Open from 5:30 P.M. daily; Sun. brunch 8 A.M.–2 P.M. Hours may vary so call ahead. Reservations accepted. **200 W. Grand; 970-533-9042.**

Main Street Brewery (Cortez)—$$ to $$$
If you could list one hot spot in the area, this would be it. With its long bar, colorful and whimsical murals, wood floors and pressed-tin ceiling, the atmosphere draws you inside. When you belly up to the bar or find a table in the separate restaurant area, consider trying one of their homemade brews. My personal favorite is their amber ale, but the porter came in a close second. If they have the Schnorzenboomer (a new style made completely by accident) on tap, give it a try. The menu includes individual pizzas, salads, sandwiches, burgers and a few choice entrées. The appetizers run the gamut from wings to stuffed mushrooms to Rocky Mountain oysters. Open 3–10:30 P.M. in summer, and 4–10 P.M. the rest of the year; bar hours may be longer. Located in the middle of town at **21 E. Main St.; 970-564-9112.**

Nero's Italian Restaurant (Cortez)— $$ to $$$

Small, intimate (you might even say a bit cramped), Nero's still has some of the best Italian around. With wonderful aromas in the air, and candlelight at the tables, sit back and enjoy a glass of Italian wine as you look over the menu. The clam sauce makes a statement, but you could also check out the seafood, chicken and many other pasta dishes. Check out the deck seating as well. Open from 4:30 nightly in summer; closed on Sun. the rest of the year. **303 W. Main St.; 303-565-7366.**

Line Camp (Dolores)—$$

Considering all you get for your dining dollar, Line Camp is an excellent choice for the entire family. Get here early and pitch some horseshoes, play volleyball, fish in the Dolores River (license required) or look around the small museum. Dinner is served promptly at 7 P.M. inside a large open-air pavilion. After a tasty homemade supper that includes cake and coffee or lemonade, the entertainment begins. A 1-hour western show with live music and comedy from The Trailhands brings the entire audience along for a good time. Open Memorial Day to Labor Day; reservations required. Located 9 miles northeast of Dolores **on Hwy. 145; 970-882-4158.**

Francisca's (Cortez)—$ to $$

Excellent Mexican food is served at reasonable prices at Francisca's. Try the stacked enchiladas, stuffed sopapilla, chili rellenos or a chimichanga. For those not hungry for Mexican food there are a few burgers and steaks. When we asked the owner, Pedro, if we could take a menu for reference, he immediately thought we were spies from another restaurant—his food probably is the best! Thanks to a couple of large white gazebos and many hanging plants, the restaurant always feels like an outdoor patio in summer. Open Mon.–Sat. 11 A.M.–10 P.M. **125 E. Main St.; 970-565-4093.**

M&M Truckstop and Restaurant (Cortez)—$

With rows of Phillips 66 gas pumps out front, this full-service restaurant is a great place for sandwiches, burgers, steaks and the house specialty: Navajo tacos. But their best meal of the day is undoubtedly breakfast (served 24 hours a day). The coffee starts coming just as soon as you find a seat and the service is fast and friendly. In this part of the state, refried beans are an option with your eggs, and pancakes are piled five high. When we asked people in town where they go for breakfast, there was a unanimous reply, "M&Ms." Open 24 hours a day, seven days a week. **7006 Hwy. 160; 970-565-6511.**

Services

Visitor Information

Cortez Welcome Center—This should be your first stop when coming into Cortez. Helpful volunteers have information about the immediate area as well as all points in Colorado. **928 E. Main St., P.O. Box 968, Cortez, CO 81321; 1-800-346-6525; 970-565-4048; www. dlg.oem2.state.co.us/fs/welcome.**

Dolores Visitors Center—Stop by and check out the Galloping Goose Museum and speak with someone about the area inside the replica of the Dolores Railroad Depot, originally built in 1900. It's located in the town center at Hwy. 145 and 5th St. If you need information by mail, contact the Dolores Chamber of Commerce at **201 Railroad Ave., Dolores, CO 81323; 970-882-4018; www.doloreschamber.com.**

Mesa Verde–Cortez Visitor Information Bureau—Be sure to tune your radio when you get near Mesa Verde to AM 1610. **P.O. Drawer HH, Cortez, CO 81321; 1-800-253-1616.**

Montezuma County information—**www. swcolo.org.**

Ute Mountain Tribal Park Visitors Center— All trips into the park depart from here. Small museum on the premises. Located **22 miles south of Cortez on Hwy. 666** at the junction with Hwy. 160.

Durango

Tucked between reddish sandstone bluffs, Durango occupies a spectacular position in the wide Animas River Valley close to the sharply uplifted peaks of the San Juans. It's southwest Colorado's largest town, with a steadily growing population of more than 14,500. Thanks to its location, history and undeniable charm, Durango could be the perfect place to base a trip to the Four Corners area.

An aura of 19th-century prosperity is embedded in this town, which once had visions of surpassing Denver as the wealthiest city in the state. Durango has managed to preserve many of its important historic landmarks; the town encompasses two National Historic Districts as well as the famous Durango & Silverton Narrow Gauge Railroad. A journey upriver to Silverton on the restored train is practically required. Another absolute must-see is Mesa Verde National Park, just 37 miles away (see the **Cortez** chapter for details).

The Animas River, originally known as El Rio de las Animas Perdidas (the River of Lost Souls), flows right through the middle of town, adding another alluring element, especially to rafters, kayakers and anglers. More than 2 million acres of the awesome beauty of the San Juan National Forest can be found just beyond the town limits. Vallecito Lake, with 22 miles of

wooded and secluded shoreline, serves as a popular water sports playground (see the Fishing section).

As one of the world's top mountain biking centers, the Durango area offers hundreds of miles of backcountry trails and a fanatical local population. Local riders have taken home medals at the World Mountain Bike Championships and have competed in the Olympic Games. Backpackers and hikers who want to avoid bikes should consider a trip into the Weminuche Wilderness, where bikes are strictly forbidden. Summer highlights absolutely include golfing, hiking, fishing or taking a drive along the San Juan Skyway. With views like you'll find all around Durango, however, a simple picnic lunch might be the best part of your vacation.

The changing seasons prove this to be a region of infinite variety. In late Sept. brilliant stands of aspen contrast with the reddish soil and barren, snow-dusted summits. Soon the snow begins to pile up, making winter a time for heading to Durango Mountain Resort, 30 minutes to the north. This low-key resort offers a true Colorado experience for those who are in search of a great ski mountain. Few destinations

Getting There

To reach Durango from Denver, take Hwy. 285 southwest to Monte Vista (or take the quick shortcut on Hwy. 112 to Del Norte) and then head west on Hwy. 160. It's a very scenic 333-mile drive. The other route requires going south on Interstate 25 to Walsenburg and then west to Durango via Hwy. 160. You can find daily flights to Durango, with the majority connecting in Denver or Colorado Springs.

feature better cross-country skiing than the abundant national forest lands in the Durango vicinity.

If all this sounds too good to be true, you can be sure that during the peak summer season you may encounter a scramble for rooms and rather congested traffic in the center of town. The crush of visitors can be a little distracting, but it also ensures lodging, dining and high-caliber shopping—in the form of 15 factory outlet stores as well as local shops and galleries. And because Durango is surrounded by mountains, it's never a problem to find solitude. Underneath it all Durango is a stable town, with a good mix of residents who certainly benefit from tourism but don't live solely for it.

History

In 1868 the U.S. government granted Chief Ouray and the Ute Indians a tract of southwestern Colorado that encompassed nearly a quarter of the territory. Almost as soon as this huge tract of land was assigned, rich gold and silver strikes in the San Juan Mountains drew a legion of miners into the area. Terms of the 1868 treaty should have provided governmental protection to the Utes against the intruding prospectors. The mood of the day, however, ensured only the miners' "destiny," and by 1873 Ouray had relinquished 6,000 square miles of mineral-rich land.

The Meeker Massacre of 1879 in northwestern Colorado (see the Meeker chapter) provided the excuse to remove the Southern Ute Indians to a reservation in southern Colorado and New Mexico. This removal coincided conveniently with the early growth of a railroad center named Durango.

A great need for efficient transport of the tons of ore generated by the mines prompted the Denver & Rio Grande Railroad to extend its tracks from the eastern plains to the Animas River Valley. The logical location for a new railroad center was the small farming community of Animas City (2 miles north of present-day Durango). But the town declined the railroad's offer, refusing to have its solitude destroyed. By snubbing the railroad, Animas City sealed its destiny as one more western ghost town. A group of investors formed the Durango Trust to provide money for a new townsite and railroad center. In 1880 Durango sprang into being, with the railroad providing the basis for prolonged future growth.

By 1881 the mining boom was in full swing in the nearby mountains, and so were the related problems of public drunkenness, prostitution and gambling. Not far from Durango's thriving saloons and brothels were the spires of one lonely church. Most of the growing pains, however, subsided as Durango came into its own. The largest industry of the decade was the smoke-belching smelter that refined the rich ore transported from the nearby mines.

When mine production began to wane in the early 1900s, Durango fell on hard times. Over the years, though, large numbers of cottage industries and small retail shops have flourished as the local economy has shifted to tourism and education. The latter came in 1956 with the founding of Fort Lewis College atop a high mesa near town. The college has had little trouble attracting students to its prime location at the base of the San Juan Mountains.

Major Attractions

Durango & Silverton Narrow Gauge Railroad

During the summer season in Durango (early May to late Oct.), the tranquility of town is broken by the lonesome blast of a steam locomotive whistle. You can't miss it—this marvelous sound becomes part of your psyche during any stay. For almost as long as Durango has existed, the smoke-belching locomotive and bright yellow passenger cars have been making a 45-mile trip north to the well-preserved mining town of **Silverton** (see the **Silverton** chapter). Each year more than 210,000 passengers pile on board the daily trains to enjoy a trip that hugs hair-raising cliffs while crossing and recrossing the raging Animas River. To experience the unique beauty and history of the San Juans, nothing beats a trip along these tracks.

History

In the fall of 1881 the Denver & Rio Grande Railroad broke ground for a stretch of track linking the remote mining boomtown of Silverton to the eastern plains. The route was completed the following summer and used for shuttling passengers and supplies. More important, it transported an estimated $300 million in gold and silver out of this rich mining town. In 1921 the D&RG emerged from receivership as the Denver & Rio Grand Western (D&RGW). In the late 1960s the tracks between Antonito and Durango were abandoned, cutting off Durango and Silverton from the rest of the D&RGW rail system. A new owner renamed it the Durango and Silverton Narrow Gauge (D&SNG) and completely refurbished the train, including open and closed coach cars and the old Alamosa parlor car—built in 1880 as a first-class, 28-passenger car equipped with an ash wood bar.

Everyone had a scare in the winter of 1989 when fire consumed the D&SNG roundhouse with all operable locomotives inside. The engines sustained fairly major damage but were saved by a major restoration effort. The roundhouse has since been completely rebuilt.

Further Information

A round trip on the D&SNG takes 8 hours (3 hours getting to Silverton, 2 hours in town and 3 hours back to Durango). To accommodate visitors in wheelchairs, one train each day is equipped with lifts (reservations necessary). Many passengers, young and old alike, who have ridden the full-day round trip suffer from "track burnout." Although most people do make the round-trip journey in one day, and fully appreciate the trip, we should note some options. You can stay a night or two in Silverton before returning to Durango. The D&SNG also offers bus transportation between the two towns, making it possible to take the train one way and to return via Hwy. 550 over scenic Molas Pass. Daily 45-minute yard tours are an option for

those who cannot spend an entire day on the train.

Reservations

Reservations for a trip on the D&SNG are strongly recommended. Advance purchases must be made 30 days prior to the date of the train's departure, but you may be able to buy tickets just by showing up (the more time in advance, the better). When the train sells out, sign up on the waiting list; we're told some people are able to get on board at the last minute. **479 Main Ave., Durango, CO 81301; 970-247-2733; www.durangotrain.com.**

RailCamp

Billed as a "wilderness recreational vehicle," RailCamp functions as an RV on train tracks to bring small groups into Cascade Canyon near the remote Weminuche Wilderness Area of San Juan National Forest. It is offered for people who wish to camp out (and perhaps do some fishing) far away from civilization, while still enjoying the comforts of home. RailCamp is a beautifully refurbished boxcar equipped with sliding glass doors, four bunk beds, a bath, running water, a kitchen with a propane stove, refrigerator, utensils and cooking necessities. What, no cable TV? RailCamp rents by the week (Mon.–Fri.) from late May through late Sept. Reservations are required. **479 Main Ave., Durango, CO 81301; 970-247-2733.**

Wilderness Access

The D&SNG train makes daily stops to trailheads leading into the Weminuche Wilderness Area at Needleton and Elk Park. Backpackers may get on and off the train at these points. See the Hiking and Backpacking section.

Winter Train Travel

From late Nov. through the first of Apr. (excluding Dec. 25), a steam locomotive departs from Durango and travels 26 miles to the wilderness of Cascade Canyon. The 5-hour round trip, with a stop at Cascade Station and return through snow-covered terrain, is tough to match.

Mesa Verde National Park

Mesa Verde National Park, site of the world's largest Anasazi cliff dwellings, lies within an hour's drive west of Durango via Hwy. 160. Whatever your itinerary, don't miss it. Check the Major Attractions section in the **Cortez** chapter for detailed information on this World Heritage Site and other Anasazi culture sites.

Festivals and Events

Iron Horse Bicycle Classic

Memorial Day weekend   World-class cyclists find themselves pitted in a grueling 47-mile road race against the Durango & Silverton Narrow Gauge train. This unique tribute to the long history of the train also includes several other touring and mountain bike races. **970-247-0312.**

The Durango & Silverton Narrow Gauge train plies a scenic—and historic—route along the Animas River. Photo by Bruce Caughey.

Animas River Days

last weekend in June   Whitewater enthusiasts from around the country converge on Durango for a weekend of competitions on the Animas River. Watch as participants maneuver canoes, rafts and kayaks through specially designed courses. One highlight is the all-out race down a swift 4-mile stretch. In addition, there are several instructional clinics. **970-259-3893.**

Durango Pro Rodeo

mid-June to late Aug.   Every Tues. and Wed. night, get a dose of the real West at the **La Plata County Fairgrounds.** Saddle bronc riding, bull dogging, roping and trick riding are only part of the evening's activities: a western barbecue begins at 6 P.M., the rodeo starts at 7:30 P.M. Then every Labor Day weekend the **Ghost Dancer Rodeo** attracts Indian riders from throughout the western United States. **25th and Main Ave. in Durango; 970-247-1666.**

Colorfest

mid-Sept. to mid-Oct.   The Four Corners area celebrates the arrival of autumn's colors with a variety of events. Each year when the aspen turn gold and red, Colorfest happenings fill the calendar. The area's brilliant colors highlight a vintage automobile show, workshops, art shows, fishing contests, raft races, hang gliding and more. **970-247-0312; www.durango. org.**

Outdoor Activities

Biking

MOUNTAIN BIKING

The Durango area has become well known as a world-class hub for mountain biking. Mountain bike enthusiasts find trail possibilities endless, the terrain varied and perfect for the sport. If you didn't bring a bike, don't sweat it—several local shops offer rentals, tour recommendations and maps. You might also check in with the **San Juan National Forest Office, 15 Burnett**

Kayakers race down the Animas River slalom course right in the heart of Durango. Photo by Bruce Caughey.

Ct., Durango, CO 81301; 970-247-4874; www.fs.fed.us/r2/sanjuan.

Colorado Trail

For more experienced riders, a great two-day ride in the San Juan National Forest leaves from Little Molas Lake, climbing 1,700 feet in the first 10 miles. The single track ventures above timberline for long stretches before dropping back down Hotel Draw—a good place to camp for the night. The next day you can complete the final 36 miles (6–10 hours) back into Durango. Many loop trips can be taken from the main line of the Colorado Trail—just be sure to take a detailed map and to be prepared for the weather. See the Hiking and Backpacking section for more information on the Colorado Trail. To reach the trailhead from Durango go north on Hwy. 550 for 41 miles.

Hermosa Creek Trail

This has become one of the more popular day-long rides in the Durango area. It's a fairly advanced 21-mile ride with a couple of bridge crossings and a 2,000-foot decline in elevation. The rough trail passes through beautiful wooded terrain near Hermosa Creek—bring your fishing equipment along. Most people prefer a one-way route. This requires leaving a car at the lower trailhead located 11 miles north of Durango on Hwy. 550 and a mile up County Rd. 201. The upper trailhead where you will begin the ride is near Durango Mountain Resort, 28 miles north of Durango on Hwy. 550. From the ski area parking lot, stay right and follow the signs west on Forest Rd. 528 to Sig Creek Campground. Continue for 2 miles past the campground and turn left on a road that leads to the trailhead. Be sure to take a map along.

La Plata Canyon Road

A maze of dirt roads dotted with remains of old mining camps provides a great day of mountain biking. For more information see the Four-Wheel-Drive Trips section.

Lime Creek Road

Just north of Durango Mountain lies perhaps the best moderate ride you'll ever find. The 12-mile trail follows an old stagecoach route through incredible aspen groves and great views of the Needles. Leave a car at the lower trailhead near Durango Mountain Resort and the ride will be almost exclusively downhill. Otherwise you may want to do a longer loop ride via Hwy. 550 from the ski area. The upper access point can be found on Hwy. 550, just 4 miles south of Molas Pass.

Durango Mountain Resort

Take your bike up the specially equipped chairlift before setting out on more than 36 miles of marked trails that wind through spruce- and aspen-covered slopes. All abilities can enjoy the range of trails that set out from nearly 10,000 feet in elevation. Rentals available at the base area. **970-247-9000.**

BICYCLE TOURING
Animas Valley Loop

This easy, relatively flat 30-mile ride follows the path of the Animas River (a shorter 15-mile route can also be taken if you loop back at Kimo's Store). Leave Main Ave. in Durango and head east on 32nd St. to a stop sign. Turn left onto E. Animas Rd. (County Rd. 250) past prime ranch land to the northern end of the ride at Baker's Bridge. Remember the cliff-jumping scene in *Butch Cassidy and the Sundance Kid*? It was filmed right here. Continue past the one-lane bridge on the only serious uphill pull and ride until you meet Hwy. 550. Head south on Hwy. 550 down to Hermosa, where you will turn right and catch County Rd. 203 just after the railroad crossing. Note: 6 miles before reaching Durango, you'll come to Trimble Hot Springs (see the Hot Springs section). It's a perfect place to stop for a soak before continuing into town.

Rentals and Information

Hassle Free Sports—The knowledgeable people at this shop rent mountain bikes on a per-day basis, with discounts for longer terms. Open Mon.–Sat. 8:30 A.M.–6 P.M. **2615 Main Ave.; 970-259-3874.**

Mountain Bike Specialists—Not only does this store offer rentals and trail information, but they also arrange half-day to multi-day bike tours.

Ask about tours to Anasazi ruins. **949 Main Ave.; 970-247-4066.**

Fishing

Because of its central location to many trout streams and high mountain lakes, Durango captures the interest and attention of people who enjoy fishing. We have noted the better public-access fishing areas, but several private lakes and streams may also be fished by arrangement with outfitters and guest ranches in the area. For further information and supplies, call on **Duranglers Fly Shop, 923 Main Ave., Durango, CO 81301; 970-385-4081; www. duranglers.com.**

Animas River

This is a highly fished river, but rest assured that large trout (including a former state-record brown trout) are pulled from inside the Durango city limits. You can try a novel fishing trip by taking the D&SNG train to Elk Park or Needleton and then fishing the Animas and its many drainages before catching the train back to town. Generally, however, the best fishing is south of town, on intermittent calmer stretches of public water, all the way down to the Southern Ute Indian Reservation.

Dolores River

This has been called the best public-access trout stream in the state. It is worth the trek from Durango to fish the water between the McPhee Reservoir (10 miles north of Dolores) north to Bradfield Bridge. See the Fishing section of the **Cortez** chapter for more information.

McPhee Reservoir

See the Fishing section of the **Cortez** chapter.

Piedra River

See the Fishing section of the **Pagosa Springs** chapter for more information.

Vallecito Reservoir

The surrounding snowcapped peaks of San Juan National Forest help attract visitors to this heavily used reservoir. Spring and fall are the best times to catch good-sized trout and kokanee salmon. Documented catches of northern pike surpass 4 feet in length—you may not want to dangle your toes in the water! There are several boat ramps and docks along the 22-mile shoreline. Boat rentals and fishing supplies are available. Located 23 miles northeast of Durango, Vallecito Reservoir provides campgrounds, motels and lodges. The **Wit's End Guest Ranch and Resort (970-884-4113)** offers many deluxe cabins as well as restaurant meals in its historic lodge. Now with the Orvis-endorsed fishing shop and more cabins located at Wit's End Streamside, it's better than ever. Call the **Vallecito Lake Chamber of Commerce** for other options: **970-884-9782.** Take County Rd. 240 east out of Durango. Stay to the right on 240 at the junction with County Rd. 243. Turn left on County Rd. 501 and continue along the Los Pinos River to the lake.

Four-Wheel-Drive Trips

Durango is close to Silverton and Ouray, often touted as the greatest jeeping area in the world. Serious jeepers can take day trips on these scenic and treacherous roads by heading north out of Durango on Hwy. 550 over Molas Pass to Silverton. See the Four-Wheel-Drive Trips section of the **Silverton** chapter for more information. The area immediately surrounding Durango is not known as a jeeper's mecca, but there are some interesting ghost towns and old mining roads nearby.

Durango Ghosts

A great day trip combining remnants of old mining towns and a far-reaching view of the La Plata Mountains is up La Plata Canyon, just west of Durango. Head west on Hwy. 160 to the town of **Hesperus,** then north on La Plata County Rd. The road is paved up to the small community of **Mayday,** near the site of **Parrott City.** Once a gold placer camp and miner's supply town, Parrott City was the county seat in 1876. A cluster of old white-frame buildings with red trim stands out on the west side of the main street.

The first is the old saloon brought down from La Plata City by Billy and Olga Little. Twenty-seven bullet holes were found in the wall behind the bar—must have been a pretty wild place on Sat. nights!

From Mayday / Parrott City the road turns to dirt and is rough going without a four-wheel-drive vehicle. Four miles up the road is what's left of **La Plata City,** a former mining camp. You will pass the old schoolhouse on the west side of the road. Continue to the end of the road at the 12,000-foot mountain summit for great views of the La Plata Mountains, Junction Creek Canyon, the Animas River Valley and Durango.

Golf

The Cliffs Golf Course at Tamarron

Doubtless one of Colorado's finest courses, the Cliffs lies etched in a once-wild cross section of thick ponderosa woodland beneath the sharp 10,000-foot Hermosa Cliffs. Guests and members staying at Tamarron have first choice of tee times on this classic 18-hole course, which features 72 bunkers, eight water holes and stunning views along its entire 6,885 yards. Nonlodging golfers cannot reserve advance tee times, making play in the peak summer season close to impossible. Expensive greens fees but worth it. Located 18 miles north of Durango on Hwy. 550; **40292 Hwy. 550 N.; 970-259-2000; www.sheraton.com.**

Dalton Ranch and Golf Club

Opened in July 1993 this Scottish links course on the outskirts of Durango provides plenty of challenge. Though the course is fairly new, tall trees line some of the fairly flat fairways, and views to cliffs in the surrounding Animas River Valley bring about a sense of permanence. "There are absolutely no easy holes!" exclaimed one local when queried. Indeed, sand or water hazards come into play on every hole. Fairly reasonable greens fees; pro shop; semiprivate; nonmembers need to reserve within 48 hours of tee time. Located 6 miles north of Durango on Hwy. 550. Turn right on Trimble Ln. across from the hot springs. **589 CR 252, Durango, CO 81301; 970-247-7921; www.dalton ranch.com.**

Hillcrest Golf Course

This well-kept 18-hole course offers a far-reaching view of the La Plata Mountains. On the Fort Lewis College mesa, east of town; **2300 Rim Dr.; 970-247-1499.**

Hiking and Backpacking

Few places compare to the beautiful Durango area for experiencing Colorado's outdoors. Whether a half-day hike in the La Plata Mountains near town or a weeklong trip deep into the Weminuche Wilderness Area, satisfaction is barely a step away. During normal years snow cover remains in the San Juans at the higher elevations (above 11,000 feet) until July. Many folks take backcountry trips in early fall when the aspen are turning color—a spectacular time to see the San Juans, but be prepared for snow. Maps, brochures and advice about hiking in the Durango area can be obtained at local sporting goods stores, at the **Durango Resort Association Visitor Center** at **111 S. Camino del Rio** or down the street at the **San Juan National Forest Office, 15 Burnett Ct.; 970-247-4874; www.fs.fed.us/r2/sanjuan.**

Animas Overlook

This half-hour, interpretive nature walk offers terrific views over the entire Animas Valley. It's perfect for families with young children or those wanting a picnic site with a grill. Wheelchair accessible. To reach the trailhead, head west on 25th St. from north Main Ave. in Durango and into the San Juan National Forest. Continue 8 miles from where the pavement ends to the well-marked trailhead.

Colorado Trail (Junction Creek)

For hikers interested in exploring the southwest end of the 469-mile Colorado Trail, which stretches all the way to Denver, this is the place. To reach the trailhead, head west on 25th St.

from north Main Ave. in Durango. At a cattle guard about 3.5 miles up the road is the San Juan National Forest boundary. Proceed from here about 100 feet and look for the trailhead on the left. This well-maintained trail heads up into some of the most beautiful high country surrounding Durango. For more information about the Colorado Trail, check in at the San Juan National Forest Office in Durango. You can get complete maps at the Forest Service office as well as at local sporting goods stores.

Goulding Creek Trail

Another good day hike, the Goulding Creek Trail is especially nice in Sept. and Oct. when the aspen groves are shimmering gold. It's a moderately difficult 6-mile round-trip hike that climbs up above Hermosa Cliffs near Tamarron. Three miles up the trail is a spot that offers a view into the secluded Hermosa Creek Roadless Area, one of the best elk summering grounds in southwestern Colorado. The trail begins 17 miles north of Durango on the west side of Hwy. 550, a half-mile north of the main entrance to Tamarron Resort.

Twin Buttes

From the top of Twin Buttes (7,737 feet) the view of the surrounding La Plata Mountains is beautiful. It is an easy 4-mile round-trip hike that can often be done in winter, depending on snowfall. To reach the trailhead, take Hwy. 160 to a road 1.3 miles west of the Animas River Bridge (south end of Durango). Turn right and follow the road as it winds north and then west to where it starts climbing a steep hill. You can park there and begin the walk.

Weminuche Wilderness Area

Deep valleys, jagged peaks, beautiful blue lakes and raging rivers characterize the Weminuche. Named for the band of Ute Indians that once inhabited the area, the Weminuche was granted wilderness designation by President Ford in 1975, making it the largest wilderness area in Colorado. Following are some ways to gain trail access to the area:

Chicago Basin, in the heart of the Weminache Wilderness, provides incredible mountain views. Photo by Dean Winstanley.

Via Purgatory Campground—Located 26 miles north of Durango on Hwy. 550. On the east side of the highway, Cascade Creek Trail begins, crossing Purgatory Flats before dropping 4 miles down to the Animas River. From there you can hike another 7 miles upriver on the Animas River Trail to Needleton for access to the wilderness area. Many people find the 8-mile round-trip hike down to the river and back a good day trip.

Via the Narrow Gauge Railroad—One of the most exciting backpacking adventures possible is a trip into the Weminuche Wilderness via the narrow gauge railroad. Starting each day from both Durango and Silverton, as many as 20 to 40 backpackers ride the train to and from the isolated stops at Elk Park and Needleton. From these locations they begin their trips up the extensive trail system. The quick transition from the civilized world of the train to primitive wilderness is striking. One minute you are surrounded by laughing, shouting passengers drinking Pepsi and eating potato chips; the next minute they have traveled on and you are left standing by the train track, miles from the nearest road, with no sounds but the crashing water of the Animas River and the wind in the pines. **Needle Creek Trail,** starting in Needleton, heads up into the breathtaking Chicago Basin, home to Mt. Eolus (14,084 feet), Sunlight Peak (14,059 feet) and Windom Peak (14,087 feet). **Elk Creek Trail** begins in Elk Park and climbs east up into the Elk Creek River Valley and eventually to the Continental Divide.

Backpacking into the Weminuche Wilderness via the narrow-gauge railroad has become very popular. Unfortunately, signs of heavy use are apparent. The Forest Service has been forced to consider limiting use of the area. By practicing no-trace camping (using gas stoves instead of fires, packing out all trash and staying on designated trails), visitors can ensure that this plan of action does not become a reality. For Durango & Silverton Narrow Gauge Railroad information, see the Major Attractions section.

Via Vallecito Reservoir—Both the Vallecito Trail and the Pine River Trail are heavily used and provide access to the Weminuche Wilderness

Area. They are fine for both day hikes and extended trips. This is a popular access for horseback riders. See the Camping section for directions.

Horseback Riding

RAPP Guide Service

For a custom-designed itinerary and a personal and historical perspective, consider hiring this trusted outfitter for a trip into the San Juan National Forest, Ute Mountain Tribal Park or Weminuche Wilderness Area. **47 Electra Lake Rd., Durango, CO 81301; 970-247-8923; www.subee.com/rapp.**

Southfork Riding Stables

Six miles east of town at **28481 Hwy. 160; 970-259-4871; www.durangohorses.com.**

River Floating

"Water is God in southwestern Colorado," said Walt Werner, former ranger with the U.S. Forest Service in Durango. Diverting the water is necessary in this arid landscape, but this "progress" has certainly taken a toll on the natural flow of area rivers. Despite a more controlled spring runoff, the swollen rivers still offer some exceptional runs.

Animas River

Many a kayaker and rafter has wondered if the River of Lost Souls wasn't a name conjured up for those crazy enough to float the 28-mile stretch of the **Upper Animas.** From Silverton down to Rockwood, the river drops an average of 85 feet per mile, offering water that is isolated and beautiful, rugged and dangerous. At Tacoma the river enters a boxed-in, churning chasm lasting 3 miles. Floating this section would have an effect on your body not unlike what the average carrot experiences going through the puree cycle in a Cuisinart.

Closer to Durango, beginning near Trimble Hot Springs (6 miles north of Durango off Hwy. 550), a tranquil 10-mile stretch of the river drops only 5 feet per mile. This section is best for canoes and those who shuddered while reading the previous paragraph. Right in town a kayak course entices those who like running gates. Downstream from Durango, the **Lower Animas** has some good rapids but is a bit more sedate. Especially exciting for novices and intermediates, it winds its way 20 miles south through the Southern Ute Indian Reservation (permits required).

Piedra River

Intersecting Hwy. 160 between Durango and Pagosa Springs, this is a river that more and more serious whitewater enthusiasts are discovering. See the River Floating section of the **Pagosa Springs** chapter for more information.

Outfitters

Durango Rivertrippers—Promising "miles of smiles," these folks offer safe trips for the family. Located at **720 Main Ave., Durango, CO 81301; 970-259-0289; www.durangorivertrippers.com.**

Mountain Water Rafting—Experienced and highly regarded. **108 W. College Dr., Durango; 970-259-4191.**

Skiing

CROSS-COUNTRY SKIING AND SNOWSHOEING

Due to the abundant snowfall in the San Juans, the ski season here is lengthy, but avalanche danger can run high. Backcountry skiers and snowshoers should use good judgment. To find the best snow consider the higher elevations to the north of Durango off Hwy. 550. See the Hiking and Backpacking section for more trail ideas.

Backcountry Trails

Haviland Lake—After a recent snow, consider the several easy routes that take off from Haviland Lake Campground, 17 miles north of Durango via Hwy. 550. Beginners can practice by skiing around the unplowed campground on gentle terrain. A 3-mile route follows a roller-coaster trail on an old wagon road from the campground. The marked route eventually comes out on Forest Rd. 166 (Chris Park Rd.). Look for a historical marker at this point before you complete the loop to Haviland Lake Campground. Another marked 2-mile loop begins just after turning off Hwy. 550 toward Haviland Lake. The trail heads into the forest to the right (south) just before you reach Forest Rd. 166, which leads to Chris Park Campground. **Molas Pass**—See the **Silverton** chapter.

Groomed Trails

Durango Mountain Resort Ski Touring Center—In a great location in the San Juan National Forest, more than 15 kilometers of trails accommodate all abilities. Instructors, rental equipment; small trail fee. Located across the highway from Durango Mountain Resort on **Hwy. 550; 970-247-9000; www.ski-purg.com.**

Ski Rentals and Information

Pine Needle Mountaineering—Anything you want to rent. **835 Main Ave.; 970-247-8728; www.pineneedle.com.**

DOWNHILL SKIING AND SNOWBOARDING

Durango Mountain Resort

Almost invisible off Hwy. 550 between Durango and Silverton lie the numerous and enticing runs of Durango Mountain Resort. An average of 300 inches of dry powder snow and abundant sunshine come together for unusually good conditions. Durango Mountain features an excellent mix of runs, heavy on the intermediate, and a generous vertical drop of 2,029 feet. More than some areas, Durango Mountain is geared to families. Experts, however, will find more than enough surprises on steep, narrow runs that challenge nerves and reaction time.

Located 28 miles north of Durango, the area features a convenient base village, which, though small, provides ample lodging, a few restaurants and close proximity to the lifts. The smallness of what used to be called Ski Purgatory is certain to change with new ownership and a larger base complex called Durango Mountain Resort. Right now, though, **Cascade Village,** a condo and

lodge development, is your best bet. It's located 1 mile north of the ski area; **1-800-525-0896; 970-259-3500.** Many people, however, prefer staying in Durango, enjoying the shops, restaurants and choice of accommodations. Area lodges often provide bus service to Durango Mountain. You may want to ask about the Total Ticket, a package that offers options to exchange one day of a multi-day pass for a different activity. **P.O. Box 666, Durango, CO 81302; 1-800-962-4077; 970-247-9000; www.ski-purg.com.**

Snowcat Skiing

You can have the thrill of your life by climbing onto a snowcat and making fresh tracks, Dec.–May, in an area that includes 35,000 acres of rugged terrain. Check with **San Juan Ski Co.; 970-259-9671; www.sanjuanski.com.**

Seeing and Doing

Alpine Slide

It's similar to an icy luge course, but there's not a snowflake to be seen. Summertime brings out riders of all ages who climb inside plastic toboggans and plunge down the mountainside on dual tracks, banking countless curves before finally coming to a breathless halt at the bottom. Time to head up the chairlift again. Note: ride in the morning to avoid possible afternoon thunderstorms. Located at Durango Mountain Resort, 26 miles north of Durango **on Hwy. 550; 970-247-9000; www.ski-purg.com.**

Gambling

Sky Ute Casino

The Southern Utes operate a gambling parlor with high-tech, bill-eating slot machines, poker and blackjack tables. The $5 limit hopefully will keep you from losing your shirt. Wine and beer are served in the adjacent dining room only; in the casino you'll have to stick to nonalcoholic beer, pop or mineral water. You'll find an RV campground, plus 36 **lodge rooms ($$$)** with queen-size bed or two double beds, TV and phone. Located a half hour southeast of Durango in Ignacio; **1-800-876-7017; 970-563-3000; www.skyutecasino.com.**

Hot Springs

Trimble Hot Springs

Main attractions at Trimble Hot Springs are the Olympic-sized outdoor pool, a smaller outdoor pool with massage jets and two private tubs. The source water, heated far beneath the La Plata Mountains, emerges through a fault at Trimble at a piping hot 119° F before being mixed to a more tolerable temperature. Though the locker rooms are small and a bit dingy, you'll get the benefit of a lovely landscaped park with picnic tables, outdoor grills and a volleyball court. Open in summer 7 A.M.–10 P.M. daily; 8 A.M.–11 P.M. in winter. Admission fee. Located just 6 miles north of Durango via Hwy. 550. **6475 County Rd. 203, Durango, CO 81301; 970-247-0111.**

Museums and Galleries

Animas School Museum

Time stops as you enter an early-20th-century schoolroom furnished with small wooden desks, heavy blackboards and a faded 46-star flag. Can you name the last four states to join the Union? Upstairs find a photographic history of Animas City and Durango. Check out the artifacts from the Basket Maker Anasazi Indians and opium pipes found below a once-active Chinese laundry in the area. Anyone interested in the history of Durango and skiing in the area will enjoy spending some time here. Kids love the Sadie Sullivan doll collection. Open May–Oct., 10 A.M.–6 P.M., closed Sun. **31st St. and W. 2nd Ave.; 970-259-2402.**

Durango Arts Center and Children's Museum

With wide-ranging art exhibit space and a community theater downstairs, and a hands-on children's museum upstairs, this center has become an important hub in the Durango community. Art exhibits rotate throughout the year and the little Gallery Shop entices visitors with its eclectic collection. Check out their programs year-round. **802 E. 2nd Ave., Durango, CO 81301; www.durangoarts.org.** Reach the **Arts Center** at **970-259-2606,** the **Children's Museum** at **970-259-9234** and the **theater** at **970-247-0136.**

Southern Ute Indian Cultural Center

Only 25 miles southeast from Durango lies the world of the Southern Utes. The history, culture and art of the Ute Indians, as well as 700-year-old Anasazi remains, are all on display in this small but interesting collection. Wonderful artistry is especially evident in the Ute bead and leather work, some from the 19th century. Open Mon.–Sat. 9 A.M.–6 P.M., Sun. 10 A.M.–3 P.M. Adjacent gift shop. Located right in the center of **Ignacio; 970-563-4649.**

Nightlife

Bar-D Chuckwagon

If you're looking for an evening of family fun and frontier-style food, the Bar-D has it all. "It's hokey and it's fun—a great place to take the kids or people from out of state," says one Durango local. After supper the Bar-D Wranglers take to the stage with songs, stories and comedy. You can also ride the Bar-D train and browse the half dozen gift shops. Open nightly Memorial Day–Labor Day. Reservations suggested. Located 9 miles north of Durango **on County Rd. 250; 1-888-800-5753; 970-247-5753; www.durango.com/bard.**

Diamond Circle Theatre at the Strater Hotel

Hiss the villain and cheer the hero during a Victorian melodrama presentation. The whole family will enjoy this entertainment in a period setting of red velvet curtains, checkered tablecloths and brass chandeliers. During a break in the show, the actors and actresses serve refreshments from the bar. **699 Main Ave.; 970-247-4431.**

Steamworks Brewing Company

Try their Steam Engine Beer, another craft brew from the on-site vats. Designated drivers should stick to their awesome root beer and cream soda. The airy room gets busy during the afternoon and evening and they feature occasional rock bands on weekends. Full menu, including an excellent Cajun boil. **801 E. 2nd Ave.; 970-259-9200.**

Scenic Drives

San Juan Skyway

It's difficult not to use superlatives when describing this drive through time. You'll see high mountain lakes, deep valleys, rocky summits, virgin wilderness and colorful plateau country with its desert canyons and weirdly eroded buttes. Man-made impressions come in the form of Anasazi cliff dwellings, historic mining towns and ski areas.

This 236-mile, nationally designated (one of two "All American" roads in the state) route can be packed into one day or stretched into a much longer trip. You may easily start this circle tour at any point marked by columbine road signs. Our description begins in Durango. Please flip to the appropriate sections in the book for an in-depth look at major destinations along the way.

Before getting into specifics on the route, credit should be given to Otto Mears, pioneering road builder of the San Juans. Mears, born in Russia in 1841, emigrated to San Francisco with his parents as a teenager. After the outbreak of the Civil War he joined the First California Volunteers and served his adopted country with Kit Carson in the Indian campaign. By 1867 Mears settled in Colorado's San Luis Valley but was faced with the problem of getting his product (flour) to lucrative markets. Never one to sit back and brood, Mears set out to build a toll road over Poncha Pass. His most impressive accomplishment was completing 450 miles of roads over forbidding mountain passes in the San Juans, including Red Mountain and sections of this scenic byway.

From **Durango,** driving north on Hwy. 550, the route roughly parallels the D&SNG route through the Animas Valley. However, the auto route splits off and heads over Coal Bank and Molas Passes. Both passes top out at over 10,000 feet, revealing delicate alpine beauty beside the crests of the Needles Mountains.

The well-preserved Victorian town of **Silverton,** end of the line for the D&SNG Railroad, is the first destination. Hwy. 550 then continues its northerly course over Red Mountain Pass (11,075 feet), before descending into **Ouray.** This twisting stretch over the Million Dollar Highway into the soul of the San Juans will rivet your attention.

Ouray, one of the most popular destinations on the route, features many natural hot springs. If your neck muscles are tightening up from all of this driving, it's obviously time for a soak. From Ouray continue north on Hwy. 550 to the small town of **Ridgway** and turn left (southwest) on Hwy. 62. Soon the view is beautifully transformed by the 13,000- and 14,000-foot peaks seen from Dallas Divide. A left turn on Hwy. 145 leads you southeast toward **Telluride.**

Beautifully situated at the base of a towering box canyon, the historic mining town of Telluride is an easy place to linger for days. Continue southwest from Telluride on Hwy. 145 and enjoy the striking views of Wilson Peak and Mt. Wilson. Keep your bearings past magnificent Trout Lake and over Lizard Head Pass, as the road winds past little **Rico.** Rocky peaks give way to high, reddish bluffs as you approach the small town of **Dolores,** site of the Anasazi Heritage Center and McPhee Reservoir.

Continue south down Hwy. 145 to **Cortez,** located at the epicenter of Anasazi culture and Mesa Verde. From Cortez, Hwy. 160 makes its way east past **Mancos** and Hesperus to complete the scenic loop back to **Durango.**

Vallecito Reservoir

The rocky crags of the San Juan National Forest serve as a beautiful backdrop to Vallecito Reservoir (see the Fishing section), and the 23-mile drive isn't too shabby either. Take County Rd. 240 east out of Durango. Stay to the right on 240 at the junction with County Rd. 243. Turn left on County Rd. 501 and continue along the Los Pinos River to the lake.

Soaring

Durango Soaring Club

The tow plane eases off the grass runway—with you and your experienced pilot not far behind, encased in the glider's glass cockpit. At altitude you are cut loose to ride the thermals and look out over the Animas River Valley. It's an unforgettable experience. Located 2 miles north of Durango on Hwy. 550. **970-247-9037.**

Where to Stay

Accommodations

For inexpensive and moderate motel accommodations simply follow Main Ave. to the north end of town. Both sides of the street offer ample lodging choices, but in the summer, prices creep higher than you might expect and neon "No Vacancy" signs begin flickering in early evening—the town does sell out in high season. In winter, however, it's usually no problem finding a room. In addition to economy accommodations you'll also find a Holiday Inn, a Comfort Inn, a Hampden Inn and a couple of Best Westerns. For a quick rundown of local options: **1-800-GO-DURANGO; www.durango.org.** Here are more ideas for a memorable night's stay in the Durango vicinity:

Apple Orchard Inn—$$$ to $$$$

The soothing sounds of trickling water can be heard from the bedrooms at each of six small cottages. Inside, under a high, wood-beamed ceiling with a fan swirling slowly overhead, you can lay back atop a cushy bed and totally relax. Each luxury cabin provides plenty of privacy, as they spread out around the perimeter of a 4.5-acre impeccably landscaped area behind the main inn. A porch swing on the veranda outside each cabin entices the lucky inhabitants to come outside to enjoy the serene setting. The only welcome interruption: the sounds and sight of

Durango's main attraction, the Durango and Silverton Narrow Gauge train as it passes by a few times daily. The inn also features four tastefully decorated rooms in the main house. John and Celeste Gardiner certainly know how to make you feel welcome and at home. After training in Europe, Celeste is simply a fabulous cook. You can enjoy breakfast in the main-floor dining room or outside under an umbrella, while watching the hummingbirds flit around the feeders. You just won't want to leave this place. **7758 County Rd. 203, Durango, CO 81301; 1-800-426-0751; 970-247-0751; www.appleorchardinn.com.**

Blue Lake Ranch—$$$ to $$$$

To soothe the soul and plunge into pure relaxation, consider taking a break amid the sculpted gardens of this exclusive 100-acre retreat. Located down the road from Hesperus, Blue Lake Ranch occupies a lonesome, flower-covered plain with fabulous views of the La Plata Mountains. Owners Shirley and David Alford have an innate sense of how to make people feel comfortable. The main house has a European feel with special touches such as wall glazing. Without feeling the slightest bit contrived, each of the four rooms has a mood of its own. The immense Garden Room, with expansive views, has a working fireplace and a king-size bed covered with a lace spread. Push aside French doors, walk outside and enter another private area—this one created by an ingenious mix of trees, shrubs and flowers. "I'm obsessed with gardening," David Alford admits. Be sure to allow plenty of time to hang out on the deck (in an Adirondack chair or in the hot tub) and enjoy this special setting—the peacocks won't mind. With the addition of five casitas, Blue Lake has spread out from the main house and now provides more private, impeccably clean lodging options with unbeatable views. There are several other possible arrangements: a comfortable three-bedroom "cabin" with a large deck overlooking Blue Lake, a "cottage in the woods" or, perhaps, the very private "river house" a half-mile away. No smoking; call for reservations and directions; discount in winter. Highly recommended. **16919 Hwy. 140, Hesperus,**

CO 81326; 1-888-BLUELAKE; 970-385-4537; www.frontier.net/~bluelake.

The General Palmer Hotel—$$$ to $$$$

This hotel, built in 1898 and named for the cavalry general who was farsighted enough to push for railroad service into southern Colorado, successfully blends Victorian elegance with modern conveniences. Enjoyable personal touches include chocolates by the bed and a toiletry basket in the bath. Complimentary fresh muffins are served with juice and coffee each morning in the meeting room. **567 Main Ave., Durango, CO 81301; 1-800-523-3358; 970-247-4747.**

The Leeland House and Rochester Hotel—$$$ to $$$$

These two unique, restored bed and breakfasts exist across the street from each other in a prime, close-to-downtown location. Owned by the same family, each provides a memorable night's stay. Staying at the Rochester provides endless conversation starters as you wander around glancing at an array of movie posters and memorabilia. *Condé Nast Traveler* magazine once named the Rochester as the flagship hotel for capturing the western essence of Colorado. The Leeland House maintains a more whimsical decor while providing genuine warmth and comfort in its suites, which now feature small gas fireplaces. Complimentary full breakfast for both properties served at the common dining area at the Rochester Hotel or in its beautifully landscaped garden. **721 E. 2nd Ave., Durango, CO 81301; 1-800-664-1920; 970-385-1920; www.rochesterhotel.com.** Tip: try eating next door to the Rochester at the **Cypress Cafe ($$ to $$$),** which features healthful Mediterranean-style food and a comfy patio.

Tamarron Sheraton Resort—$$$ to $$$$

This three-story lodge built of stone sits perched on a sandstone bluff overlooking its well-known 18-hole golf course. Larger than you might expect, the rooms allow for excellent views. Townhouses with a number of options, some with full kitchens, may also be rented. This self-sufficient resort offers visitors a choice of several restaurants and boutiques. Take advantage of the health spa, tennis courts, indoor/outdoor pool and the excellent golf course. Tamarron is also an ideal place to stay in winter because it's close to the Durango Mountain Resort. Off-season prices can be very attractive. Located 18 miles north of Durango on Hwy. 550. **40292 Hwy. 550 N., P.O. Box 3131, Durango, CO 81302-3131; 1-800-678-1000; 970-259-2000; www.sheraton.com.**

The Strater Hotel—$$$

Some 100 years ago at the seemingly exorbitant cost of $70,000, Henry H. Strater built the hotel that was to become his legacy. Durango was in need of a first-class operation to demonstrate that the burgeoning community was worthy of the title "Denver of the West." The 93 rooms are tastefully decorated in restored antiques; each is different and has its own bath. Despite modern amenities, the authentic Victorian feel of the red brick hotel is retained by antique walnut furniture, lace curtains and old-time light fixtures. Located within shouting distance of the comfortable hotel lobby are **Henry's Restaurant,** the **Diamond Belle Saloon** and the **Diamond Circle Theatre** with its outstanding melodrama. Room rates vary according to season. **699 Main Ave., Durango, CO 81301; 1-800-247-4431; 970-247-4431; www.strater.com.**

Durango Hostel International—$

Okay, so it's slightly rundown. But this AYH-approved house is the cheapest place to stay in town and the absolute best place to meet travelers from around the world. Open 7–10 A.M., 5–10 P.M.; doors closed at all other times. You'll find the hosts by going around to the back entrance. **543 E. 2nd Ave., Durango, CO 81301; 970-247-9905.**

Camping

San Juan National Forest

For reservations, contact **1-877-444-6777** or **www.reserveusa.com.** A fee is charged at all

The 93 rooms at Durango's Strater Hotel reflect a turn-of-the-century elegance. Photo by Bruce Caughey.

the campgrounds listed below. The closest to Durango is **Junction Creek Campground** (34 sites), located about 4 miles from town. Head west on 25th St. from north Main Ave. and follow the road up into the national forest.

Lemon Reservoir—Located 17 miles northeast of Durango. Follow County Rd. 240 out of town. Turn north on County Rd. 243 and follow it to the reservoir. There are **three campgrounds** (total of 62 sites): two located north of the reservoir and one on the east shore.

North toward Durango Mountain—Traveling north out of town on Hwy. 550 leads you to **Haviland Lake Campground** (45 sites), just north of Tamarron. Stay on Hwy. 550 north for another 7 miles to reach **Purgatory Campground** (14 sites). For a more remote location try **Sig Creek Campground** (9 sites), situated 28 miles northwest of Durango on Hermosa Park Rd. From Hwy. 550 turn into the ski area and stay right above the parking lot. Just follow the signs.

Vallecito Reservoir—This popular area 23 miles northeast of Durango can be reached by taking County Rd. 240 out of town. Stay to the right on 240 at the junction of County Rd. 243. Turn left on County Rd. 501. Vallecito Reservoir boasts **five campgrounds** (total of 111 sites) by the reservoir, plus **Vallecito Campground** (80 sites) just to the north on Vallecito Creek.

Private Campground

KOA Kampground—For folks looking for electrical and water hookups, showers and the like, the KOA Kampground is located 5 miles east of Durango city limits at **30090 Hwy. 160, Durango, CO 81301; 970-247-0783; www. koa.com.**

Where to Eat

Ariano's—$$$

The owner and chef, Vince Ferraro, has created a menu loaded with northern Italian specialties. He assured us that his pastas and ravioli are made fresh daily in the restaurant. Milk-fed veal, ginger shrimp, steaks and specials round out the menu.

Bring a huge appetite because the portions are anything but skimpy. An extensive Italian wine list complements the full bar. In the words of one longtime Durango resident, "If I could go to any restaurant in Durango, it would definitely be Ariano's." Open nightly from 5 P.M. **150 E. College Dr.; 970-247-8146.**

Ken and Sue's Place—$$ to $$$

An upbeat, casual atmosphere can be found at this excellent Durango hangout. Yes, Ken and Sue are the involved owners and that makes all the difference. For lunch try the main-plate salads, sandwiches or a plate of pasta. Dinner brings on specialties such as fusilli pasta with grilled chicken, filet mignon with gorgonzola butter or Aunt Lydia's meatloaf. The friendly service, good food and prices will assure you that this restaurant will be a destination of choice for a long time. Open for lunch weekdays 11 A.M.–2:30 P.M. and dinner each night from 5 P.M. **937 Main Ave.; 970-259-2616.**

Kennebec Bakery and Cafe—$$ to $$$

This light and airy restaurant in the unlikely location of a former motel's courtyard has been turning heads for its excellent contemporary American cuisine. The owner worked in catering in Durango for 20 years before making the plunge with this restaurant. Cream-colored walls with inlaid stone set an upscale tone, but the prices are reasonable. With fresh pastries, crab and spinach omelettes topped with hollandaise sauce, and a killer breakfast burrito, the first meal of the day could be their best. They have wonderful lunches, including salads, pasta and burgers, and more elaborate dinners. Full bar available. Open 7 A.M.–3 P.M. and 5–9:30 P.M. Small and friendly. You won't regret taking the 15-minute westerly drive from Durango on Hwy. 160. **4 County Rd. 124, Hesperus; 970-247-5674.**

The Ore House—$$ to $$$

Nothing too fancy graces the menu of Durango's most popular steak house, but we can almost guarantee you will want to savor each bite. All of the beef at the Ore House is aged in an on-premises cooler and hand-cut daily; try a generous rib-eye cut or a 16-oz. T-bone steak. Also offered are fresh seafood items ranging from scallops to Australian lobster. The decor is rustic with barn-wood walls and old mining implements throughout. Consistently voted "best steak house" in a local restaurant poll. Good wine cellar. Bar opens at 5 P.M.; restaurant open 5:30–11 P.M. nightly. **147 E. College Dr.; 970-247-5707.**

Lady Falconburgh's Barley Exchange—$ to $$$

With 20 beers on tap and more than 100 micro, import and domestic bottled beers, you won't go thirsty here. Walk downstairs to this surprisingly light and airy restaurant, with a large square bar as its command center. It feels like a classic English pub in some respects and the hearty, affordable food hits the spot. Comfortable and classy with lots of wood and exposed brick—but it can get a little loud inside. Check out the burgers, sandwiches, appetizers, pasta and salads for lunch or dinner. Open daily 11:30 A.M.–2 A.M. **640 Main Ave.; 970-382-9664.**

Carvers Bakery Cafe/Brewery—$ to $$

An odd cohabitation of a bakery and brewpub under one roof makes you wonder if this schizo place is any good. It's definitely worth a try. In the morning pick up a loaf of bread, giant pastry or bagel for take-out. You may want to take a seat (weekend waits are common) to enjoy a steaming cup of coffee with your favorite egg dish—the eggs, chorizo and hash browns couldn't be better. The solid breakfasts are the highlight, but Carvers also offers a creative selection of lunches and dinners. In the evening slip around to a small back room to sample their various beers, brewed on the premises in large vats. Open Mon.–Sat. 6:30 A.M.–10 P.M., Sun. 6:30 A.M.–1 P.M. **1022 Main Ave.; 970-259-2545.**

Steamworks Brewing Company—$ to $$

See the Nightlife section.

The Durango Diner—$

A sure sign of value is the large number of locals rubbing elbows at the long counter in this unpretentious diner. Huge portions are served as you catch up on the latest goings-on around town. Hash browns are a standout favorite of the house; large peeled potatoes are shaved onto the grill and may be smothered with melted cheddar cheese and green chilis. Other breakfast specialties include flapjacks, biscuits and gravy and omelettes. Lunch items are added to the menu and served until closing at 2 P.M. Open Mon.–Sat. from 6 A.M., Sun. from 7 A.M. **957 Main Ave.; 970-247-9889.**

Griego's—$

The only drive-in Mexican restaurant in Durango is housed in a former A&W franchise. The likeness is obvious until you bite into a burrito, taco or combination plate. Order anything smothered in green chili. But keep in mind that no alcoholic beverages are served to help you cool down. Top off your authentic meal with a homemade sopapilla dipped in honey. Open Mon.–Sat. 10 A.M.–9:30 P.M. **2603 Main Ave.; 970-259-3558.**

Services

Visitor Information

Durango Area Chamber Resort Association—Stop by this excellent visitor center right in the midst of a riverside park on the Animas River. The National Forest Service also staffs a booth here. **111 S. Camino del Rio, P.O. Box 2587, Durango, CO 81302; 1-800-525-8855; 970-247-0312; www.durango.org.** To reserve a room in town, try the **central reservations** number: **1-800-GO-DURANGO.**

Vallecito Chamber of Commerce—P.O. Box 804, Bayfield, CO 81122; 970-884-9782; www.coloradovacation.com/vallecito.

Day Care

Peter Pan Pre-School—750 E. 4th Ave., Durango, CO 81301; 970-247-5954.

Transportation

You'll find buses in and around Durango for a small fee. Sightseers may want to take a 1-hour historic Durango mini-tour. Check with your hotel/motel for more information or call **970-259-LIFT.** A new, open-air trolley plies Main Ave. in Durango in the summertime, 6:30 A.M.–10 P.M. daily.

Gunnison and Crested Butte

The Gunnison area is quintessentially western, its character having been molded by Indians, miners, ranchers and railroads. Located in the fertile Gunnison Valley at the confluence of the Gunnison River and Tomichi Creek, Gunnison is one of the most purely outdoor-oriented destinations in this book. The snowcapped Elk Mountains and Taylor Park lie to the north; to the east you'll see the Sawatch Range and the Continental Divide. West of Gunnison, Curecanti National Recreation Area, which encompasses Blue Mesa Reservoir, and the spectacular Black Canyon of the Gunnison continue to be major draws.

Gunnison serves as an ideal jumping-off point for vacationers. With 1.6 million acres of the Gunnison National Forest surrounding the

Getting There

Gunnison—Located 196 miles southwest of Denver, Gunnison can be reached on Hwy. 285 and Hwy. 24 to Poncha Springs, then west over Monarch Pass on Hwy. 50. Monarch Pass can be slow going in the winter. Getting to Gunnison by air is easy. In winter daily direct flights are available from major cities as well as connecting flights from **Denver International Airport** and **Colorado Springs Airport.**

Crested Butte—Located 30 miles north of Gunnison on Hwy. 135. It takes about 40 minutes to make the trip from Gunnison to Crested Butte. When weather permits, be sure to consider the scenic route to Crested Butte over Cottonwood Pass (see the **Upper Arkansas Valley** chapter). Van service between Gunnison and Crested Butte is available.

town, finding a remote backcountry escape is no problem. Prime hiking, mountain biking, skiing and hunting can be found in abundance. More than 750 miles of trout streams and a number of productive reservoirs attract legions of avid anglers every year. In addition, exploring the back roads and ghost towns in the Gunnison area can constitute a whole vacation in itself.

Gunnison locals appear proud of the fact that chilling winter temperatures in the Gunnison Valley are often the coldest in the country. Up at Crested Butte, about 30 miles north of town, the temperatures are a bit warmer and the skiing is hot. During winter exceptional powder snow challenges downhill skiers on a wide variety of terrain, including some of the best extreme skiing in North America. For snowcat skiing, guests are again flocking to Irwin Lodge for a compelling mix of backcountry terrain at an elevation of 10,700 feet.

Crested Butte is widely considered the mountain biking capital of the planet; you will see more bikes there than cars when the snow melts. In summer high mountain meadows burst into a barrage of colors as wildflowers reach and maintain their apex. Fall brings another welcome change when mountainsides of golden aspen come into the picture. As long as you are willing to treat the fragile surroundings with the utmost respect, laid-back Crested Butte locals seem perfectly willing to share their version of paradise.

Driving up the pastoral valley from Gunnison to Crested Butte, you experience a memorable feeling of isolation and natural beauty. Vast stretches of ranch land dominate the immediate surroundings, while four nearby wilderness areas and the Gunnison National Forest occupy the higher elevations. Emerging in an alpine basin, you'll be awed by the scene: Mt. Crested Butte and other high, rocky peaks, virtually encircling the century-old mining town of Crested Butte.

With humble beginnings primarily in coal mining and supplies, the old town has maintained much of its original western simplicity. Crested Butte has an understated personality that doesn't aspire to become like its more glamorous neighbor, Aspen. Brightly painted false-fronted business establishments and weathered miners' shacks make up the bulk of the town's buildings. The National Historic District designation helps to preserve Crested Butte's intriguing history while ensuring extra scrutiny for any proposed renovation or new construction. The main thoroughfare, Elk Ave., offers a large number of shops, restaurants and bars housed creatively in old buildings. Unlike some ski resorts, dining out here doesn't require an increase in your credit card limits.

The old and the new come together at Crested Butte without colliding, thanks in part to the 3-mile distance between the old town and the modern ski resort at Mt. Crested Butte. This short distance has alleviated many conflicts by separating the luxury condos and multilevel hotels from the historic district. Each locale complements the other without crowding or creating aesthetic confrontations. Most accommodations are located conveniently at the base of the ski slopes at Mt. Crested Butte. A frequent shuttle plies the route between the resort and the old town, allowing you to leave your car parked for the duration of your stay.

History

As early as the mid-1600s the Gunnison area was a primary Ute hunting ground for buffalo, deer and other game. In 1853 a famous expedition, led by Capt. John W. Gunnison, passed through the area in an attempt to find a suitable transcontinental railroad route. Gunnison and his men had a very successful expedition until they reached Utah, where all but four members of the party were brutally killed by a band of Paiute Indians. Capt. Gunnison was shot with 15 arrows before his arms, tongue and heart were removed. The least that could be done was to name a town after the man.

After the Ute treaty of 1868, an Indian agency in the Gunnison area opened at Los Piños. Under the treaty, the Utes had to move west, vacating the Gunnison valleys. It wasn't long before settlers began arriving. Some prospectors pushed their luck by venturing into the Elk Mountains of Ute territory, usually with severe consequences. But rich mineral strikes farther to the west in the San Juan Mountains put pressure on the Utes to renegotiate the treaty, further reducing their territory. The resulting Brunot Treaty in 1873 forced the Utes to cede more land to the United States and relocate in the Uncompahgre area to the west.

In 1874 the town of Gunnison got its start when farmers and cattle ranchers settled in the valleys. Five years later miners struck rich gold and silver deposits and the Gunnison area came to life. Gold and silver strikes up Tomichi and Quartz Creeks, in Taylor Park and in the Elk Mountains spurred the growth of many mining towns such as Pitkin, Tincup and Gothic. With the mining boom in full swing, Gunnison became a very important place to come for supplies and a little hell-raising. The town also became a crucial transportation center. Demand from mining towns in the area and from cattle ranchers eager to send their stock to outside markets prompted both the Denver & Rio Grande Railroad (D&RG) and the Denver South Park & Pacific Railroad (DSP&P) to extend service to Gunnison in the early 1880s.

Autumn casts an amber glow over the Blue Mesa Reservoir near Gunnison. Photo by Bruce Caughey.

In 1893, as in so many other mining areas across the state, the demonetization of silver proved catastrophic. Many became ghost towns immediately, while others lingered on, dying slow deaths. The town of Gunnison, with its cattle industry and role as supply center for the area, emerged unscathed from this period of economic upheaval. So did another nearby town—Crested Butte.

During the mining boom of the early 1880s, Crested Butte provided its rich neighbors with supplies and cut lumber. Soon Crested Butte residents discovered they were living on top of a huge deposit of high-grade coal. In 1881 the Denver & Rio Grande Railroad connected Crested Butte to the outside world and within three years was transporting 1,000 tons of coal per month.

Coal fueled the economy in Crested Butte, and by the 1890s the young town boasted 1,000 residents, 13 saloons and one minister. As the boomtowns in the nearby Elk Mountains began to wither away, Crested Butte became a company town under the guiding hand of Colorado

Fuel & Iron (CF&I). The town prospered until 1952, when the Big Mine finally closed. In 1953 *The Denver Post* published a fallacious article on Colorado's "newest ghost town."

Only 10 years later many skiers began challenging the slopes of Mt. Crested Butte (12,162 feet). Resort developers were on target when they started cutting runs and building a planned community at the base area. The ski industry resuscitated Crested Butte at just the right moment, allowing the delightful town to escape "ghost town" classification.

Major Attractions

Curecanti National Recreation Area

Blue Mesa Reservoir and much of the **Black Canyon of the Gunnison** are encompassed by Curecanti National Recreation Area and its breathtaking scenery. A series of dams have altered the natural path of the Gunnison River on its course through the ancient Precambrian stone of the Black Canyon. Blue Mesa Dam, at the head of the Black Canyon, created the first and largest of three reservoirs. It has transformed the semiarid landscape into an area especially well suited to boating, fishing and windsurfing.

Downstream from Blue Mesa you'll come across the dramatic beauty of **Morrow Point** and **Crystal Reservoirs;** the mixture of jutting rock and calm water in the abyss of the canyon is as close as Colorado can come to the Norwegian fjords. Below Crystal Dam the Gunnison River flows freely through the deepest and narrowest section of the Black Canyon of the Gunnison. This area has been preserved as a national park (see the Major Attractions section in the **Black Canyon Country** chapter).

History

The namesake of Curecanti is former Ute Chief Curecata, who was known for directing the Ute Bear Dance with his twin brother, Kanneatche. The Ute Indians once hunted wild game in the dry hills around the Gunnison River, staying away from the Black Canyon. When trappers and traders began exploring the area in the mid-1800s, the rugged canyon terrain was still viewed as an obstacle. Nonetheless, in 1882 the Denver & Rio Grande Railroad somehow completed its narrow-gauge "Scenic Line of the World" through the upper part of the canyon, which left lasting impressions on its passengers. In 1899 English author Rudyard Kipling wrote the following description about the passage:

We seemed to be running into the bowels of the earth at the invitation of an irresponsible stream. The solid rock would open up and disclose a curve of awful twistfulness. Then the driver put on all steam, and we would go round that curve on one wheel chiefly, the Gunnison River gnashing its teeth below.

The route climbed out of the canyon in the vicinity of Crystal Reservoir and continued to Cimarron and Montrose. The railroad operated until 1949. Today the track bed lies submerged by Morrow Point and Blue Mesa Reservoirs.

Facts About the Recreation Area

Blue Mesa Reservoir is 20 miles long, offering a wide expanse of clear water for sailing, windsurfing and fishing. Narrow arms reach out from the main body of water, making boat exploration the best way to get into remote areas. The two other smaller reservoirs are more difficult to reach, but the beauty of the canyon makes it worth a hike. Hwy. 92 follows the northern rim of the Black Canyon, offering several dramatic overlooks down to Morrow Point and Crystal Reservoirs. Several hiking trails wind their way down to water level; only hand-carried watercraft are allowed on the smaller reservoirs.

Elk Creek Marina

Tackle, gas, a convenience store, boat rentals and tours can all be found here. Located off Hwy. 50 on the north shore near the midpoint of the **Blue Mesa Reservoir; 970-641-0707; www.bluemesalake.com.**

Visitor Information

Elk Creek Visitors Center—A good place to begin your visit to the recreation area is at the park headquarters/visitor center. Several exhibits, a slide presentation and printed information tell the story of the Curecanti area. Rangers will inform you of any interpretive programs and of the area's many recreational possibilities. Open from mid-May to late Sept., 8 A.M.–6 P.M. Located on the north side of Blue Mesa Reservoir off Hwy. 50. For more information contact **Curecanti National Recreation Area, 102 Elk Creek, Gunnison, CO 81230; 970-641-2337; www.nps.gov/cure.**
Other Information—Check in at the Lake Fork, Cimarron and East Portal information centers and talk to the ranger on duty.

Fishing

Curecanti National Recreation Area provides excellent fishing on **Blue Mesa, Morrow Point** and **Crystal Reservoirs.** Blue Mesa is by far the largest, most popular and accessible (the other reservoirs require a hike), with 96 miles of shoreline. It accommodates heavy use from both bank and boat anglers. Shore fishing can be especially great when the water level is low. More than 30 streams flow into Blue Mesa, providing numerous channels and inlets. Thanks to an aggressive stocking program, kokanee salmon are the most frequent catch, although rainbow, brown, Mackinaw and brook trout are frequently caught. In winter many anglers snowmobile out onto the ice; Iola Basin remains a favorite for ice fishing.

Hiking

A number of hiking trails leave the roadside and twist their way down inside the Black Canyon. The half-mile **Neversink Trail,** at the eastern tip of Blue Mesa Reservoir, goes through a lush bird habitat. Several other trails leave the north side of the reservoirs from Hwy. 92 and offer dramatic views.

For a water-level view of Morrow Point Reservoir and the Curecanti Needle, try **Curecanti Creek Trail.** This 2-mile trail rapidly descends 1,000 feet from the rim of the Black Canyon of the Gunnison down to the water level of Morrow Point Reservoir. It would be wise to save some time and energy for the walk back up. The well-maintained trail crosses bridges and even has a few steps in places. The route follows the path of turbulent Curecanti Creek, which looks more like a waterfall than a creek due to the steep grade. Once at the bottom, the view up the canyon walls and across the water to Curecanti Needle is fantastic. There is room for a couple of tents on a sandy bank at the bottom of the trail. Fishing is usually good in the deep water where Curecanti Creek flows into the reservoir. To reach the trail, drive west on Hwy. 50 to the base of Blue Mesa Dam. Turn onto Hwy. 92 and continue west for approximately 10 miles to the well-marked trailhead.

A stunning 2.5-mile trail, the **Dillon Pinnacles Trail,** begins somewhat inauspiciously at a bend in the road right before Hwy. 50 crosses over the reservoir about 10 miles west of the Elk Creek Visitors Center. It winds up the mesa, to just beneath weirdly eroded volcanic tuff formations with sweeping views over the reservoir and to the San Juans in the distance. It can get a bit windy up there, but you can find some protected groves of trees to have a picnic or just lay back and enjoy all nature has to offer.

Morrow Point Reservoir Boat Tours

From within the deep canyon walls you will find a new appreciation for the beauty of the Black Canyon. On the 40-person tour boat, an interpreter relates the history of the lake as you ride toward a water-level view of the Curecanti Needle. Before embarking on a boat tour, you must first take a mile-long hike (including 232 stair steps) down Pine Creek Trail. For reservations and more information call the **Elk Creek Marina; 970-641-0402; www.blue mesalake.com.**

Water Sports

Sailing, motorboating, windsurfing and even sea kayaking are popular activities on Blue Mesa Reservoir. Many boat ramps are situated around Blue Mesa for easy entry into the water. Windsurfers prefer the warmer waters of the Bay of Chickens. Morrow Point and Crystal Reservoirs are limited to hand-carried craft due to the canyon walls. Fluctuating water levels at the two smaller reservoirs cause some boating hazards. Check with rangers at any visitor center for information and advice.

Camping

A number of developed campgrounds are situated, for the most part, around the perimeter of Blue Mesa Reservoir. The major campgrounds are at **Elk Creek, Lake Fork, Cimarron** and **Stevens Creek.** For a smaller, less developed area, try camping among the cottonwoods at **Red Creek** or **Gateview** or among the pines at **Ponderosa Campground.** All campgrounds are first come, first served. There are more than 350 sites; all charge a fee. For information on camping closer to the Black Canyon see the Major Attractions section of the **Black Canyon Country** chapter.

Festivals and Events

Fat Tire Bike Week

late June The genesis of this Crested Butte celebration took place in 1975 when a few locals decided to ride one-speed Schwinn clunkers over 12,705-foot Pearl Pass to Aspen. Of course, today's riders have high-tech, made-for-mountain bikes to assist them. Fat Tire Bike Week mingles a range of pro racing events with tours for riders of all abilities. The **Pearl Pass Classic** in mid-Sept. sees a boisterous reenactment of the first ride more than 25 years ago. **970-349-6438; www. visitbutte.com.**

Wildflower Festival

early July You don't need to be a wildflower expert to enjoy the brilliant colors that explode in the alpine valleys around Crested Butte each summer. A transcendent combination of science and nature creates a long and spectacular season. Glacier lilies, bluebells, pale yellow columbines, larkspur, lupine and scarlet gilia might be seen around any bend in the trail. For information on photography workshops, guided walks and other activities: **1-800-545-4505; www.visitbutte. com/wildflowers.**

Cattlemen's Days

mid-July Gunnison cuts loose each year during Cattlemen's Days, the state's oldest rodeo, celebrating the ranching heritage of the area. Held annually since 1901, the rodeo features stock shows, horse races, a barbecue and pro rodeo events. If you want to get a good feel for the area and its people, work this event into your schedule. **Gunnison County Chamber of Commerce; 970-641-1501; www.cattlemens rodeo.gunnison.com.**

Arts and Music Festivals

summer Each summer Crested Butte attracts an extra dose of culture during its special arts events. The popular **Crested Butte Music Festival** (Aug.) takes place at the recently expanded Center for the Arts at the Town Park. In addition, you may want to visit during the

Festival of the Arts (early Aug.), when Elk Ave. is lined with some 160 booths in a juried show featuring photography, pottery, paintings and more. Food court, jugglers and music spice up the affair. **1-800-545-4505.**

Outdoor Activities

Biking

MOUNTAIN BIKING

It's tough to overstate the importance of mountain biking in Crested Butte. With only one paved road leading into town, it's obvious why the locals' favorite mode of travel is sturdy mountain bikes. Single-track trails and jeep roads provide varied terrain for all abilities. Because Crested Butte has so many backcountry trails, fewer conflicts exist among hikers, horseback riders and mountain bikers. In summer a specially equipped chairlift can take you up Mt. Crested Butte for a great ride down.

Aspen via Pearl Pass

Advanced riders love this rough, high-altitude ride over Pearl Pass (12,705 feet). If you have the stamina to consider a steep (at times) 39-mile, one-way ride, then keep reading. To get to the road over Pearl Pass, take Hwy. 135 south from Crested Butte for 2 miles to the Skyland turnoff. Go left and follow Brush Creek Rd. for 6 miles to a fork in the road. Take the right fork up Middle Brush Rd. to the stream crossing. The trail proceeds just downstream from that point. After the Dead End sign, follow along the old road grade before merging back up with Middle Brush Rd. After passing some rolling meadows, the ride pushes on to the summit of the pass. From there it's mostly downhill to the townsite of Ashcroft, where the pavement begins for the final 13 miles to Aspen.

Cement Creek Trails

A country dirt road passes 12 miles through the valley next to Cement Creek. You can take this road all the way to the base of Italian Mountain or turn off on one of the many trails snaking up the sloping valley walls. Walrod Gulch is a steep four-wheel-drive road. For single-tracking on a rough trail, try Trail 409, leading the way to Farris Creek Rd. and a loop back to Crested Butte. For access to Cement Creek, see the Hiking and Backpacking section.

Crested Butte to Marble

You can't use this route until mid- to late summer due to the heavy snowpack. It's a long 22-mile ride unless you have arranged for someone with a vehicle to pick you up in Marble. Maybe you like long rides? Anyway, this arduous route passes through Gothic (which in itself is a great 7-mile one-way trip), over 10,707-foot Schofield Pass, past the Devil's Punchbowl, on through the pristine ghost town of Crystal, finally ending in Marble. Once in Marble you can either turn around and return to Crested Butte or ride an exhausting loop over McClure and Kebler Passes. Should the journey appear too daunting, turn left just beyond Schofield Pass to Paradise Divide and ride through Schofield Park up toward Cinnamon Mountain. From the Continental Divide the spectacular views of the Ruby Range provide ample reward. Then head downhill toward Crested Butte via Washington Gulch or Slate River Rd.

Gothic Trails

Several excellent trail possibilities converge on the ghost town of Gothic, just 7 miles north of Crested Butte. Forest Service Trail 401 is one of the favorites. It leaves from Gothic and soon heads above timberline with views of Baldy, Gothic and Crested Butte Mountains along its 6-mile route to the top of Schofield Pass. Loop back to Gothic on the jeep road. Catch the trail a half-mile upstream from Gothic at the Judd Falls trailhead or via a spur from Avery Peak Campground.

Rentals and Information

Before heading out on a fat-tire bike excursion, check with one of the many mountain bike shops for trail maps, advice and rentals. Here are a couple ideas:

The Alpineer—Great for rentals and trails advice. **419 6th St., P.O. Box 208, Crested Butte, CO 81224; 970-349-5210; www. alpineer.com.**

The TuneUp—**222 N. Main St., Gunnison, CO 81230; 970-641-0285; www.tuneup@ westelk.com.**

Fishing

No question about it: the Gunnison and Crested Butte area is one of the top fishing destinations in Colorado. Stop by local sporting goods stores or the Chamber of Commerce and pick up a free copy of the detailed *Gunnison Country Angling Guide.* You can also check out the Division of Wildlife site at **www.wildlife.state.co.us.** If you need advice or tackle, drop in at **Gene Taylor's Sporting Goods, 201 W. Tomichi Ave., Gunnison; 970-641-1845.**

Blue Mesa Reservoir

See the Major Attractions section.

East River

Unfortunately, much of the East River below its headwaters at Emerald Lake (see next entry) flows through private land. Permission to fish some of the best stretches requires an okay from landowners. Some good public water can be found adjacent to the Roaring Judy Hatchery, 13 miles downstream on Hwy. 135. The water above and below the hatchery bridge is designated Wild Trout water. You have an excellent chance of hooking a large rainbow, brown, brook or cutthroat on this section. Only flies are permitted; catch-and-release all trout over 12 inches.

Emerald Lake

This high country lake at an elevation of 10,445 feet is best known for its rainbow trout and a beautiful location just below Schofield Pass. The fishing can be a bit sporadic, though the trip is worthwhile. Located at the headwaters of the East River, Emerald Lake can be reached by heading north from Crested Butte for 9 miles to Gothic. From there head on up the Schofield

Pass Rd. (Forest Rd. 317) for 4.5 miles to Emerald Lake. Great picnic spot!

Gunnison River

At the town of Almont, where the East and Taylor Rivers join, the Gunnison River is born. Stretches of this legendary trout stream are easily considered some of the very best in the state. For 3 miles downstream from Almont, you will find plenty of good fishing in public water. Beyond that point the river flows through mostly private property until it passes the Neversink Picnic Area a couple of miles below the town of Gunnison. Neversink down to the inlet of Blue Mesa Reservoir is a popular public fishing area. The length of the free-flowing section below Neversink fluctuates between 5 miles and a half-mile, depending on the water level of the reservoir. Try a weighted Hare's Ear, a Stonefly or a Woolly Worm in the deep pools near the banks; Mepps and Rapala lures are favorites.

As you follow downstream, the Gunnison flows into a series of three reservoirs: **Blue Mesa, Morrow Point** and **Crystal** (see the Major Attractions section). The **Lower Gunnison River** below Crystal Reservoir is difficult to reach but worth it. Below this final reservoir, the Gunnison surpasses all other rivers in the state for sheer numbers of trout per mile. See the **Black Canyon Country** chapter for more information on this Gold Medal water.

Roaring Judy Ponds

Don't be too skeptical about your chances of pulling trophy-sized fish from a couple of small ponds beside the East River. Alan Schneider, a student at Western State College in Gunnison, pulled a record 30-lb., 8-oz. brown trout from one of the ponds in Mar. 1988. The ponds are connected by drainages to the hatchery, but the local wildlife officer swears the record-breaking fish did not come from there. At any rate, the ponds are fed by warm spring water and do not freeze during winter. Fishing for small rainbows is generally quite good. From Crested Butte head about 13 miles south on Hwy. 135. At the Roaring Judy Hatchery, cross over the East River and follow the signs.

Slate River

Between the historic town of Crested Butte and the ski mountain lies Slate River Rd., which parallels its namesake. Turn left and follow the river for 4 miles to the junction of Oh-Be-Joyful Creek. Here you'll find a nice 5-mile stretch of public water and good fishing for rainbow, brown and brook trout. If you continue upstream for another 1.5 miles on the four-wheel-drive road, you'll find more public water at the townsite of Pittsburg.

Taylor Park Reservoir

If a beautiful location is any consideration, you should definitely try fishing here. And the tremendous views are not all: you can catch ample numbers of good-sized rainbows, browns, Mackinaws and even kokanee salmon at this superb Colorado fishery. Located in the shadow of the jagged Sawatch Range, the enormous Taylor Park Reservoir is best early or late in the day. If you are fishing from the shore, your best bet will be to try in early spring when the fish seek out shallow, ice-free water. Rental boats, fishing supplies and licenses can be found at the Taylor Park Marina; call ahead for information and advice on current fishing conditions. To reach the reservoir from Almont, drive 22 miles up the Taylor River on Forest Rd. 742. **970-641-2922; www.taylorparkmarina.com.**

Taylor River

Runoff from the Elk and Sawatch Mountains is stored in Taylor Park Reservoir (see entry above) and escapes ice-cold from the bottom of the dam. Above the reservoir the Taylor teems with rainbows, brooks and browns to 10 inches. Forest Rd. 742 follows the Taylor upstream for 22 miles. Below the reservoir difficult wading requires concentration, because the river bottom consists of smooth, round rocks and sudden, deep pools. Be sure to watch for private property markings. Even so, more than half of the water remains open to the public, and nine Forest Service campgrounds lie next to some of the best stretches. Fishing for browns, brooks and rainbows can be good with large nymphs and select lures. Try throwing a line in the large pools near the bridge just below Taylor Park Dam.

Four-Wheel-Drive Trips

Schofield Pass
See the **Redstone and Crystal River Valley** chapter.

Taylor Pass
For a highly scenic trip over to Aspen and the Roaring Fork Valley you might try this treacherous route. It's rough, rocky and steep at best and can be snow-covered into the summer, so be sure to get updated conditions from the National Forest Service. Taylor Pass, at about 12,000 feet, was built as an important supply route to the booming Aspen area in the 1880s. Now the connection is insignificant, but the views north to the Roaring Fork Valley and Hunter–Fryingpan Wilderness Area are far-reaching. Did we forget to mention the tremendous view south into Taylor Park?

To reach the pass from Gunnison, head north on Hwy. 135 for 11 miles to Almont and then turn left on County Rd. 742, which heads up the Taylor River. Follow the road to Taylor Park Reservoir. A mile or so beyond Lakeview Campground, turn left, following the reservoir shoreline and heading upriver all the way to Dorchester Campground. The road gets rough from here. Once to the summit of Taylor Pass, follow Express Creek to Ashcroft in the Castle Creek Valley. Head down the road about 15 miles to Hwy. 82 near Aspen. For a scenic return to Gunnison, turn left on Hwy. 82 and proceed to Carbondale, then head up the Crystal River over McClure and Kebler Passes (see the Scenic Drives section) to Crested Butte and back to Gunnison.

Tincup Pass
If you want to cross over the Sawatch Range on this early stagecoach route, see the Four-Wheel-Drive Trips section of the **Upper Arkansas Valley** chapter.

Golf

Crested Butte Country Club
Designed by Robert Trent Jones Jr., this fine 18-hole course has been judged among the top mountain courses in the nation. Enjoy the spectacular mountain views from its position at the base of Mt. Crested Butte. If you're able to stay out of the numerous sand traps, you may be able to enjoy the scenery. Besides a pro shop and a restaurant, the Crested Butte Country Club features a full health club with indoor tennis and racquetball facilities. **Country Club Dr. #1, Mt. Crested Butte, CO 81224; 970-349-6129.**

Dos Rios Golf Club
Located in a great setting, this semiprivate club at the confluence of the Taylor River and Tomichi Creek provides far-reaching views. Water is the key to this course—it comes into play on 17 holes. Especially tough is the relatively young front 9, which still needs some maturity. Open to the general public in summer. Moderate greens fees. Pro shop, carts and club rentals. Located 2 miles west of Gunnison, just south off Hwy. 50; **970-641-1482.**

Hiking and Backpacking
Deep canyons, lush meadows, streams, lakes and ghost towns can be easily found in **Gunnison National Forest** and nearby wilderness areas. Narrowing down the long list of hiking possibilities is especially difficult, simply because there are good trails crisscrossing virtually the entire county. Huge quantities of public land can be easily accessed from both Gunnison and Crested Butte. For maps and more information, visit the **Gunnison District Forest Service Office, 216 N. Colorado St., Gunnison, CO 81230; 970-641-0471; www.fs.fed.us/r2/gmug.**

Cement Creek Trail
A veritable trail system leads away from different points along Cement Creek and into the mountains of this little-known mountain valley. The one we have chosen is an excellent, short

hiking loop that begins on Trail 409, only a mile up the Cement Creek Valley. The trail leads quickly uphill toward a large rock outcropping with a couple of deep caves. Just above the caves, the trail splits in two. The left branch of the trail continues uphill to an aspen-cloaked ridge and a number of longer trail possibilities. The right fork leads east across the forested mountainside, eventually reaching Walrod Gulch. Walrod is a seldom-driven four-wheel-drive road that heads back down to Cement Creek a couple of miles upstream from your starting point.

Cement Creek is located 7 miles south of Crested Butte off Hwy. 135. Turn east onto Cement Creek Rd., which leads up the valley to a number of trail access points and a shaded campground. Trail 409 begins directly across from the Cement Creek Guard Station, 1 mile from Hwy. 135.

Copper Creek and Conundrum Trails

These trails have it all: beautiful scenery, a ghost town, natural hot springs and, consequently, heavy use. If your goal is to get away from other humans, try someplace else. Don't underestimate these strenuous backcountry hikes. An overnight stay is the best way to experience Conundrum Trail. It's also quite possible to hike the approximately 6 hours to Conundrum Hot Springs one day and on to Aspen the next. To reach the trail, drive to Crested Butte Ski Area and continue 7 miles north to the ghost town of Gothic (see the Scenic Drives section). A half-mile upstream from Gothic catch the Judd Falls/Copper Creek trailhead. After the overlook to the falls and a short rest on the bench dedicated to Judd, follow about 8 miles northeast up Copper Creek Trail to a junction just before Copper Lake. The right fork is Conundrum Trail; the left fork heads over East Maroon Pass with spectacular views over the Maroon Bells. See the Hot Springs section of the **Aspen** chapter for more information.

Curecanti Creek Trail

See the Hiking section under the Major Attractions section.

Forest Service Trail 401

This trail leaves from north of Crested Butte—at Gothic—and soon offers tremendous above-timberline views along its 6-mile route to the top of Schofield Pass. Leave a car near the end of the hike and you can make it a one-way trek. For more information see the Gothic Trails write-up in the Mountain Biking section (you can expect to see a lot of bikes on this route).

Mill Creek Trail

This 1.5-mile trail cuts between steep valley walls and through a thick conifer forest before ending in a grassy meadow at the edge of the West Elk Wilderness Area. The watery sounds of Mill Creek provide a soothing background for a picnic or a nap. Bring along your fishing pole, too.

For serious backcountry exploration of the West Elk Wilderness Area, the Mill Creek Trail provides a little-used access. The trail continues from the wilderness boundary into a scenic area, with views to the volcanically formed Castles and to West Elk Peak (13,035 feet). A 14-mile route takes you over Storm Pass (12,440 feet), which is steep going on both sides. On an autumn hike you'll be able to enjoy the changing colors, but wear bright clothing and beware of hunters. From Gunnison drive 17 miles north up the Ohio Creek Valley on County Rd. 730 to the Mill Creek turnoff. Turn left and follow Mill Creek 4 miles on a fairly good dirt road (Forest Rd. 727; two-wheel-drive vehicles are fine) until reaching a dead end where the trail begins.

Mt. Crested Butte

Take the chairlift to the top of Mt. Crested Butte and hike down the mountain or vice versa. With well-marked trails, picnic areas and incredible views you won't be disappointed. Good for families with older children; **1-800-544-8448; www.crestedbutteresort.com.**

Timberline Trail

Enjoy superb views of Taylor Park Reservoir while hiking on a level contour averaging over 10,000 feet in elevation, just beneath the snow-streaked peaks of the Sawatch Range. This is a perfect trail for extended trips. The trail is fairly easy and passes many small but fishable lakes and streams along its route. Timberline Trail traverses several roads and has a number of marked access points. From Taylor Park Reservoir take Cumberland Pass Rd. southeast to the ghost town of Tincup. Follow E. Willow Creek Rd. 2 miles east to Mirror Lake. The trailhead begins just below Mirror Lake Campground. Another good idea would be to pick up Timberline Trail as it crosses Cottonwood Pass Rd.

Horseback Riding

Fantasy Ranch

Custom horseback adventures can be arranged for all abilities and time frames. Try a "get acquainted" ride or a breakfast or dinner ride. Their specialty is a three-day ride over Pearl Pass to Aspen. Three locations in town and on the outskirts. **P.O. Box 236, Crested Butte, CO 81224; 970-349-5425; www.fantasyranch outfitters.com.**

Just Horsin' Around

Join Bernie Brown on a narrated tour through historic Crested Butte on a carriage, sleigh or coach depending on your desire and the season. Wonderful dinner sleigh rides, too. Reservations necessary. **2nd and Whiterock Ave., P.O. Box 3791, Crested Butte, CO 80224; 970-349-9822.**

River Floating

The character of the rivers flowing into the Gunnison Basin has been altered forever by several monolithic reservoirs. Nonetheless, excellent stretches still entice rafters and kayakers for short runs. A couple of river outfitters in the area will take you on a quiet family float or a whitewater odyssey.

Lower Gunnison

This stretch of water below the national park will take you into remote sections of the Gunnison Gorge. See the **Black Canyon Country** chapter.

Taylor River

The water rushing out of Taylor Park Reservoir tumbles downstream through the deep canyon. The fast water is ideal for experienced kayakers who can handle Class II to Class V water. The path of the river is followed by Hwy. 306; many developed campgrounds and access points can be found along its entire run from the dam to Almont. The dam tends to lengthen the season by holding water back during runoff and slowly releasing it into the fall.

Upper Gunnison

One mile downstream from Almont, open canoes, rafts and kayaks put in for the fairly gentle trip downriver. The wide river flows unobstructed through the town of Gunnison, all the way to the fringe of Blue Mesa Reservoir. The only rapids in this mild stretch result from the spring thaw. The river passes through a rural

Extreme skiing at Crested Butte Mountain Resort captures the imagination of adventurers. Photo by Tom Stillo, courtesy of Crested Butte Mountain Resort.

setting of pasturelands and country homes. Unfortunately for river enthusiasts, the free-flowing water doesn't last long enough. Beginning 5 miles below the town of Gunnison, large dams force the water into reservoirs for the next 45 miles.

Outfitters

Scenic River Tours—703 W. Tomichi Ave., Gunnison, CO 81230; 970-641-3131.
Three Rivers Resort and Outfitting— in Almont; 970-641-1303; www.3rivers resort.com.

Skiing

CROSS-COUNTRY SKIING AND SNOWSHOEING

Whether you are into telemarking or just gliding along in solitude, any number of trail choices entice you into the backcountry. Mt. Crested Butte is known for its throngs of devoted telemark skiers. Several broad alpine valleys leading from Crested Butte provide safe and easy passage. More adventuresome skiers can test their limits on the ridges and slopes. For maps and further information, contact the **Gunnison District Forest Service Office, 216 N. Colorado St., Gunnison, CO 81230; 970-641-0471; www.fs.fed.us/ r2/gmug.**

Backcountry Trails

Gothic—Tracks are set each year to the ghost town of Gothic (see the Scenic Drives section). It's an easy 7-mile tour from Crested Butte, with tremendous views along the way. Ski tracks usually continue beyond Gothic and into the upper valley.
Pearl Pass—Skiing over Pearl Pass to Aspen has long been a favorite of experienced skiers. This route is strenuous, isolated, dangerous and exceptionally beautiful. The Braun Hut System allows for a warm overnight stay during the long trek (see the **Aspen** chapter). Check with the folks at the **Alpineer** in Crested Butte for more information. **970-349-5210.**

Groomed Trails

Crested Butte Nordic Ski Center—Located in the downtown historic district, this complete facility offers rentals, lessons, advice and 20 to 30 kilometers of maintained track. Open daily. **2nd and Whiterock Ave.; 970-349-1707; www.alpineer.com.**

Snowshoe Tours

Every day at 10 A.M., a $2^{1}/_{2}$-hour snowshoe tour is offered high on Crested Butte Mountain. Tours depart from the Crested Butte Ski and Snowboard School and include a pass, guide, snowshoes and even a snack. It's a great way to see the backcountry, and perhaps even take a break from skiing on a long vacation. **970-349-2251; www.crestedbutteresort.com.**

Ski Rentals

The Alpineer—Good equipment and sound advice can be found here. **419 6th St., Crested Butte, CO 81224; 970-349-5210; www.alpi neer.com.**

DOWNHILL SKIING AND SNOWBOARDING
Crested Butte

Soaring above its namesake town, Mt. Crested Butte appears as an intimidating pinnacle. It's only after you take your first chairlift ride that the mountain begins to reveal its true diversity. Just enough gentle, rolling terrain makes this a wonderful place to learn the sport. With more than half the groomed trails rated blue, the area is especially suited to intermediate skiers. This a great place to perfect your turns before even thinking about extreme skiing. As much as anything, the views to the Elk Mountains and beyond make this a wide-open experience, and one that you can enjoy most of the year without the hassles of lift lines.

Without a doubt, only true experts can take advantage of the entire mountain. As one local said, "Crested Butte has all the expert terrain that a sane person needs." Experts flock to the double black diamonds of the North Face, which offer some of the best "steep and deep" powder anywhere. Untamed and ungroomed, this 400-acre preserve provides a place for radical skiers to find some adventure—that means chutes, powder bowls, cliffs and glades. In spring 2001, Crested Butte hosted the 10th annual U.S. Extreme Skiing Championships in grand style. The North Face ventures very close to a helicopter skiing experience. A unique early-season and late-season promotion provides free lift tickets for all skiers staying at participating lodges. Ask about this. Another great promotion that lasts for the rest of the ski season is that kids ages 5 to 16 pay their ages to ski. **Crested Butte Mountain Resort, 17 Emmons Loop, P.O. Box A, Crested Butte, CO 81225; 1-800-544-8448; 970-349-2333; www.crestedbutteresort.com.**

Irwin Lodge

We are happy to report that Irwin Lodge again offers its remote brand of snowcat skiing to its guests. For more information about the lodge and its 2,100 feet of vertical drop, see the Where to Stay section; **1-888-GO-IRWIN; www.go irwin.com.**

Seeing and Doing

Museums

Crested Butte Heritage Museum and Mountain Biking Hall of Fame

This small museum on a Crested Butte side street will surprise you with its depth and quality of historical exhibits, photos and artifacts. The Mountain Biking Hall of Fame comes as an added bonus—check out the origination of the sport while learning more about its pioneers and heroes. Open year-round 11 A.M.–4 P.M. on weekdays; until 6 P.M. on weekends (by appointment only during "mud season"). Some evening hours during ski season. **200 Sopris St.; 970-349-1880.**

The Pioneer Museum in Gunnison

One thing to be said about this museum is that there are a lot of big exhibits. Big, you ask? Yeah,

big. How about the first post office in Gunnison, a schoolhouse built in 1909, the Denver & Rio Grande Railroad depot, Narrow Gauge Railroad Engine #268 and the old Mears Junction water tank. The Pioneer Museum also displays old photos, furniture and other artifacts that sufficiently convey pioneer life in the valley. Open Memorial Day–Labor Day, Mon.–Sat. 9 A.M.–5 P.M., closed Sun. Located at the east end of Gunnison **on Hwy. 50; 970-641-4530.**

Nightlife

Center for the Arts

Local theater group performances in addition to music, dance and an art gallery display take place at this cultural mainstay in Crested Butte Town Park. With its casual, intimate feel the center has become the community meeting place. For program information contact **970-349-7487; www.visitcrestedbutte.com.**

Idle Spur

This popular Crested Butte hangout features a spacious log-encased room, long bar, varieties of freshly brewed beer and unpretentious atmosphere. It all seems to fit perfectly in this town. Occasional live music during peak times; lunch and dinner served (see the Where to Eat section). **226 Elk Ave., Crested Butte; 970-349-5026.**

Kochevar's

It's tough to beat Kochevar's for a lively crowd. And besides, with pool tables, dartboards and a shuffleboard table, there is something for everyone. This place enjoyed a long history of illicit entertainment—the upstairs was once a notorious bordello. Bar menu served. **127 Elk Ave., Crested Butte, CO 81224; 970-349-6745.**

Parks

Crested Butte Town Park

Visible as you enter town and virtually sandwiched **between the arts and visitor centers,** this park features a large playground and covered picnic area. It also provides four tennis courts, basketball, baseball and a permanent sand volleyball court.

Gunnison Town Park

You'll find an attractive, grassy park for picnicking and a small playground behind the **visitor center** at **500 E. Tomichi Ave.**

Scenic Drives

Alpine Tunnel

The Alpine Tunnel, constructed by the Denver South Park & Pacific Railroad (DSP&P) in 1881, is an engineering marvel. The 1,800-foot-long tunnel was bored through the Continental Divide in a race with the Denver & Rio Grande Railroad to provide railroad service to the Gunnison area. Working conditions were miserable, and the labor turnover was rumored to have totaled more than 10,000 men. Once completed, the tunnel proved very expensive to maintain, prompting the DSP&P to abandon the line in 1910. Even though the west portal of the tunnel caved in a number of years ago, remnants of many buildings and a water tower remain along the drive. Just above the water tank is what's left of Woodstock, a train workers' boardinghouse destroyed in an 1884 avalanche that killed 13 people.

To reach the Alpine Tunnel from Gunnison, head east on Hwy. 50 for 12 miles to Parlin. Turn left, heading north up along Quartz Creek Rd. to Ohio City and then Pitkin. About 3 miles beyond Pitkin, the marked road to the Alpine Tunnel turns off to the right. Follow this rough dirt road about 10 miles up to the west portal of the tunnel. A passenger car with good ground clearance can make the trip.

Black Canyon of the Gunnison

See the **Black Canyon Country** chapter.

Cottonwood Pass

See the **Upper Arkansas Valley** chapter.

Cumberland Pass / Taylor Park Loop

For a firsthand look at Gunnison area history and some outrageous scenery, take this drive. You'll visit Quartz Creek, Tincup and Taylor Park mining districts, all of which brought settlers into the area in the late 1870s. Cumberland Pass, at just over 12,000 feet, is one of the highest dirt roads in the state and can be easily driven in a passenger vehicle.

The loop starts from Gunnison and can be done in one day, but you may want to take a few days and camp along the way. Head east on Hwy. 50 from Gunnison for 12 miles to Parlin, then north on Quartz Creek Rd. The first big area of interest is along Quartz Creek. **Ohio City** and **Pitkin** were centers for two large silver strikes in 1879 and 1880. Cumberland Pass Rd. begins climbing north out of Pitkin to its orange-colored summit. Built as a pack trail in 1880 to connect Tincup with the Quartz Creek camps, the pass has seen a lot of use over the years. From the summit you can look out on the massive, steep mountains of the Sawatch Range to the east and beyond Taylor Park to the north.

When you've seen enough, head down the pass to **Tincup.** Now a peaceful summer residence for a lucky few, Tincup was once a rough mining town that saw seven sheriffs killed within a period of a few months. The origin of Tincup's name is not completely clear, but many believe it comes from one of the original miners here who sifted through the gold-flaked gravel of the stream with his tin cup. People began prospecting here as early as 1859, but things didn't get hopping until 1879 when Tincup became the leading silver producer in the area. (From Tincup you have the option of heading over the Sawatch Range on rugged Tincup Pass Rd.; see the Four-Wheel-Drive Trips section of the **Upper Arkansas Valley** chapter.)

Continuing north from Tincup, the road leads to **Taylor Park Reservoir** in Taylor Park. There are plenty of campgrounds in the area and the trout fishing in the creeks and reservoir can be great. From the reservoir follow the Taylor River southwest through Taylor Canyon, eventually intersecting Hwy. 135, 11 miles north of Gunnison at Almont.

Gothic

A trip to Gothic is easily worth the minimal effort it takes to get there. Located 7 miles north of Mt. Crested Butte, this silver camp once boasted a population of thousands. Rich pockets of silver created much excitement but small returns. In 1880 the town received a visit from President Grant, who wanted a firsthand look at some Rocky Mountain mining camps. By 1885 the Sylvanite Mine could no longer stay open and Gothic began to wither away. Several of the old buildings remain, and the area receives use in warmer months from students of the Rocky Mountain Biological Laboratory. Gothic serves as a jumping-off point for many popular hikes in the Maroon Bells–Snowmass Wilderness Area. To reach Gothic drive to Mt. Crested Butte and continue north on scenic Forest Rd. 327 above the East River.

Kebler Pass

In fall this ultimate foliage drive is highlighted by mountainsides of golden aspen. A graded dirt road winds past alpine meadows covered with wildflowers and dense forests; the West Elk Mountains and the Raggeds rise all around. With an elevation of about 10,000 feet, Kebler Pass never rises above treeline, but the views are far-reaching at times. About 7 miles after reaching the summit, a left turn onto Forest Rd. 706 will land you at Lost Lake. The road can be rough but is passable by all vehicles. Lost Lake is ideal for a lazy afternoon picnic or an overnight stay at the small campground.

To reach Kebler Pass from Crested Butte, take County Rd. 12 from the west end of town. The road continues for about 24 miles before intersecting Hwy. 133 at Paonia Reservoir. From here you can take a right and drive over McClure Pass (8,755 feet) before dropping into the beautiful Crystal River Valley.

Lake City

The 55-mile drive south to Lake City on Hwy. 149 gets progressively more beautiful after you pass through the barren hills near Blue Mesa Reservoir. Soon the San Juan Mountains introduce themselves dramatically as the road continues beside the Lake Fork of the Gunnison. Situated in the narrow river valley is the small town of Lake City, named for its setting only 2 miles from spectacular Lake San Cristobal. The area is better known for the grotesque antics of cannibal Alferd Packer. For more information see the Lake City section in the **Creede and Lake City** chapter.

Where to Stay

Accommodations

CRESTED BUTTE AREA

Crested Butte offers a wide choice of accommodations, from spiffy condos to a variety of bed and breakfasts. If you want to stay in a deluxe hotel on the mountain check out the **Sheraton Hotel ($$$ to $$$$)**. It features an outdoor/indoor pool and the **Woodstone Grille** restaurant, with its roaring hearth, heavy wood beams and generally cozy dining experience; **6 Emmons Rd., Mt. Crested Butte, CO 81225; 1-888-223-2469; www.crestedbutte resort.com.** Check out the **Club Med** that has opened in the former confines of the 257-room Marriott Hotel. One of only three Club Med North American resorts, they offer inclusive, family-friendly winter vacations. Contact them at **500 Gothic Rd., Crested Butte, CO 81225; 1-800-544-8448; www. clubmed.com.**

Crested Butte Reservations, 1-800-215-2226, can help you find a hotel room or condo in town or at the mountain. At **Almont**—halfway between Gunnison and Crested Butte—you'll find a large number of cabin rentals favored by anglers and rafters. A good bet would be **Three Rivers Resort ($$$); 970-641-1303; www.3riversresort.com.**

Irwin Lodge—$$$$

This 22-room, self-contained lodge has roared back into operation and again offers unparalleled year-round activities. The lodge itself may be nothing to write home about, but the supreme location creates your own mountain hideaway. Only 12 miles from Crested Butte, it feels like another world. Most guests tend to spend their time in the lodge's great room, which features a family-style restaurant, a bar, games and television. Best known for snowcat skiing, the lodge makes it possible for guests to average between 10,000 and 16,000 vertical feet of skiing on an average day. The skiing experience at Irwin is open to only 44 skiers/snowboarders each day, which means you are guaranteed incredible powder stashes even days after a major snow. And they do get major snow here: an average of 30 feet per year. The snowcats are divided up by ability level, so you can find the terrain that fits your style, though it is primarily geared to intermediate and expert skiers. The lodge rents fat-boy and parabolic skis. Winter recreation options also include snowmobiling, cross-country skiing and showshoeing. The only way to reach Irwin Lodge in winter is via snowcat, snowmobile or skis on a 10-mile route. In summer you can drive right to the lodge. Summer activities include horseback riding, guided nature hikes, peak ascents, biking and fly-fishing. They can arrange to have a masseuse come in to work out those inevitable kinks or you can retreat to the popular hot tub. Child care available. Most summer weekends are booked for weddings. **1-888-GO-IRWIN; www. goirwin.com.**

Crested Butte Club—$$$ to $$$$

Reserve one of the eight bedrooms at this exclusive inn and you will enjoy modern comfort and Victorian style during your entire stay. This National Historic Landmark, built in 1886 as the Croatian Social Club, has more than its share of history. The inn's false front belies the plush interior. All of the spacious rooms at the club are filled with high-quality antiques or reproductions—each features a sitting area with a fireplace. The romantic Royal Suite, our favorite, includes a whirlpool bath for two and a cleverly hidden TV. The Presidential Suite is dominated by a brass chandelier, which casts a romantic glow over a four-poster bed. All of the elegant rooms also feature conveniences such as deluxe private bathrooms with his-and-her pedestal sinks, copper claw-foot tubs, cable TV with remote control and phones. Guests have free access to the on-site athletic club with weight machines, indoor lap pool, climbing wall, whirlpools and steam rooms; guests receive discounts on spa services such as massages. You'll love the dark wood, intimate feel and friendly atmosphere of the entryway, where they have an eclectic little bar—as a guest, you get a free drink. Continental breakfast served each morning. No smoking; children discouraged; some minimum stay requirements. **512 2nd St., P.O. Drawer 309, Crested Butte, CO 81224; 970-349-6655; www.visitcrestedbutte.com/ cbclub.**

The Pioneer—$$$

In the midst of the beautiful Cement Creek Valley, you can return to pioneer roots by staying the night in one of eight clean, comfortable cabins. Known to some as Star Valley Ranch, the Pioneer features four cabins with three double beds each and four smaller cabins with two double beds each. Inside the cozy cabins you'll find a fully equipped kitchen, bathroom with shower and down comforters on all the beds. The cabins are heated by propane heaters and feature either a fireplace or antique woodstove. Outside each of the cabins, which are spaced to create a sense of privacy, you can gather at the fire ring and have a meal outside at your picnic table. You won't find a lot of extras here, but you will find one of the prettiest places in the land, reasonable rates and ready access to activities such as fishing, hiking, cross-country skiing and snowshoeing. This valley turns into a carpet of gold in the fall, yet few people venture here. Located up **Cement Creek Rd., Crested Butte, CO 81224; 970-349-5517.**

Christiana Guesthaus Bed and Breakfast— $$ to $$$

A casual atmosphere pervades this inexpensive 21-room, European-style ski lodge. Built with smallish rooms (with private baths), it's a good thing there are many comfortable common areas to enjoy. English owners Rosie and Martin Catmur ensure fresh-baked goods, cereals and fruit are served at a hearty continental breakfast. Perhaps the best feature of the lodge is the 12-person outdoor hot tub and wood deck offering great views to Mt. Crested Butte. **621 Maroon Ave., P.O. Box 427, Crested Butte, CO 81224; 1-800-824-7899; 970-349-5326; www. visitcrestedbutte.com/christiana.**

The Nordic Inn—$$ to $$$

At the base of the ski mountain this 25-room, Norwegian-style lodge aptly reflects the warmth of the owners. Each room has two double beds, cable TV and a private bathroom. The common room really shines. Chairs are grouped around the fireplace, providing a relaxing après-ski environment. **P.O. Box 939, Crested Butte, CO 81224; 970-349-5542; www.nordic inncb. com.**

Crested Butte International Hostel— $ to $$

Loree and Ward Weisman have traveled the world, staying in many hostels along the way. They took the features they enjoyed most and built their own place right in downtown Crested Butte. This hostel represents the best lodging value for your money in Crested Butte—and perhaps the entire state. "We wanted people to be pleasantly surprised," Loree says. Guests will be happy to find less-crowded dorm rooms than at most hostels. Four rooms are for couples, and an upper-floor apartment is geared to families. The hostel provides bed, blankets and pillows; sheets can be rented for a small charge or you can use your sleeping bag. The great room, with its couches, television, fireplace and kitchen, becomes the meeting place for a mix of guests of all ages. At the coin-operated laundry next door, you can dry your ski gear and wash the mud off your mountain biking clothes before walking to nearby bars and restaurants. The large male and female bathrooms are exceptionally clean, and designed to stay that way. They also offer public showers if you are camping in the area and want to wash up. The hostel is closed during the middle of the day. **615 Teocalli Ave., P.O. Box 1332, Crested Butte, CO 81224; 1-888-389-0588; 970-349-0588; www.crestedbutte hostel.com.**

GUNNISON AREA

The Inn at Arrowhead—$$$ to $$$$

In a beautiful, secluded location between Cimarron and Lake City, you will find this exclusive preserve, surrounded by vast stretches of public forest land. This inn combines the best attributes of a plush hotel with the activities of a dude ranch. Those who appreciate a quiet setting with just-out-the-door access to cross-country skiing, hiking, horseback riding, mountain biking and fishing will love this place. Snow-mobiling is big here, too—some guests like to ride to Lake City for the day. The first-class rooms in the contemporary, solidly built lodge all have Southwestern touches, fireplaces, private baths and ample space. Check out the sundeck balcony with its hot tub. Downstairs you'll find a large-screen TV, bar and an excellent restaurant (breakfast included in the room rate). Call for directions and reservations. **21401 Alpine Plateau Rd., Cimarron, CO 81220; 1-800-654-3048; 970-249-5634; www. commerceteam.com.**

The Mary Lawrence Inn—$$$

This nice inn located in a prime location just off the Western State College campus has been through a series of owners, but still offers the best bed and breakfast accommodations in town. Jeanette McKinny has taken over as innkeeper of the huge, colorful, stately house, which was built in 1885. It really does look like a bed and breakfast from the minute you drive up. Its Victorian-style common areas provide natural warmth. Once you duck into the rooms, you'll find some touches that work beautifully and some that seem, well, a tad odd as all seven rooms are quite individually decorated. If there are room options, you may want to wander around and find the one that fits your mood. After a good night's sleep, you'll be served a full breakfast in the common dining room. The back porch leads to a small yard and wood deck. Children welcome; no smoking. **601 N. Taylor, Gunnison, CO 81230; 970-641-3343.**

Lazy K Resort—$$ to $$$

If you feel like a getaway, with the convenience of an in-town location, the Lazy K may be your best bet. The two-bedroom cabins and condominiums are spread out among 18 acres of shade trees, landscaped grass, a small stream and a little pond. The decor may be a little dated, but the setting makes up for it. Each cabin comes with a fully equipped kitchen, cable TV, phone and wood-burning fireplace. Visit the **Silver Sage Restaurant and Lounge** on the premises for a hearty meal with friendly service. **1415 W. Tomichi Ave., Gunnison, CO 81230; 1-800-748-2295; 970-641-5174.**

Water Wheel Motel—$$ to $$$

There are 52 rooms at this comfortable motel. All the rooms have air-conditioning and cable movies. Tennis court and exercise room. Take Hwy. 50 west of town for 1.5 miles. **P.O. Box 882, Gunnison, CO 81230; 970-641-1650.**

Camping

Curecanti National Recreation Area

See the Major Attractions section.

Gunnison National Forest

For reservations in Gunnison National Forest: **1-877-444-6777** or **www.reserveusa.com.** All the following public campgrounds in this section are in Gunnison National Forest.

Crested Butte Area

Cement Creek Campground (13 sites, no fee) can be reached by heading 7 miles south of Crested Butte on Hwy. 135. Turn east onto Cement Creek Rd. and travel 4 miles up the valley to the shaded campground. **Irwin Campground** (32 tent and trailer sites, no fee) enjoys a beautiful location; take Hwy. 2 for 7 miles

Crested Butte's Soupçon remains a top choice for consistent fine dining. Photo by Bruce Caughey.

west of Crested Butte to the Lake Irwin turnoff and proceed north on Forest Rd. 826. **Gothic Campground** (4 sites, no fee) is another half-mile up the road.

Lake Fork of the Gunnison

Campgrounds south of Hwy. 50 get much less use than areas to the north. To reach Red Bridge and The Gate Campgrounds, drive 25 miles south on Hwy. 149 from the eastern end of Blue Mesa Reservoir to a turnoff with a sign noting that **Red Bridge Campground** (12 sites, no fee) is 2 miles away. Keep an eye peeled for bighorn sheep during the short drive. Another 5 miles from Red Bridge, down a rough dirt road through a narrow canyon, is **The Gate Campground** (8 sites, fee charged).

Ohio City and Pitkin Area

North of Hwy. 50 along Quartz Creek on the way to Ohio City and Pitkin, beneath the summit of Cumberland Pass (see the Scenic Drives section), you'll discover five small campgrounds (fee charged). They are **Comanche** (6 sites), **Gold Creek** (6 sites), **Middle Quartz** (7 sites), **Pitkin** (22 sites) and **Quartz** (10 sites).

Taylor River Area

North of Gunnison a dozen popular campgrounds can be found from Almont, upstream on Taylor River Rd., to Taylor Park Reservoir. Well known among trailer and RV campers, these areas fill up early; fee charged. The camping areas are scattered along the shaded riverbanks and up above the reservoir.

Private Campground

KOA Gunnison—Get comfortable at this cushy campground near the Gunnison River. One mile west of Gunnison on Hwy. 50, turn south and follow the signs for a half-mile. **970-641-1358; www.koa.com.**

Where to Eat

CRESTED BUTTE

The small, historic district of Crested Butte has a surprising number of excellent restaurants that have been here for years. They usually stay open year-round, excluding the spring mud season and late fall when many close for a few weeks.

Soupçon—$$$$

High expectations should accompany you upon entering this small log cabin on a back alley behind Kochevar's (see the Nightlife section). Once inside, you will join a few others for exceptional French food. The casual atmosphere belies the careful preparation in the kitchen. The menu encompasses innovative poultry, lamb, beef and fish entrées. On our visit a sampling of appetizers included duckling mousse, escargots Monaco and fresh scallops in caviar cream. This smoke-free restaurant is open nightly 6–10 P.M. Reservations are a must. **2nd St. and Elk Ave.; 970-349-5448.**

Le Bosquet—$$$ to $$$$

This fine French restaurant serves consistently excellent food with polished service. Even though it moved from its quaint Elk Ave. location, it still remains a favorite for a special meal in an elegant setting. The featured entrées come with complex and creative sauces. Some examples of the tempting dishes offered are grilled duck breast in a minted raspberry sauce, elk filets in a Bordelaise sauce, veal with a Roquefort basil sauce and fresh salmon with a ginger glaze. A selection of appetizers and salads is also available. Le Bosquet features a very eclectic wine list organized by the place where the grapes are grown, so you might need a little help finding that perfect cabernet. Reservations requested. Luncheon menu 11:30 A.M.–2 P.M. during summer; dinner served nightly from 5:30 P.M. In Majestic Plaza at **6th and Bellview; 970-349-5808.**

The Slogar Bar and Restaurant— $$ to $$$

For a very reasonable set price, with child portions available, we can promise you'll find some of the best family-style fried chicken in this hemisphere. It comes served with sweet and sour cole slaw, mashed potatoes and chicken gravy, warm biscuits with honey butter and sweet corn. Top it off with some home-style vanilla ice cream. If for some reason you are not in the mood for fried chicken, you can also order a steak dinner served family style. Open daily 5–9 P.M. Located on a quiet corner at **2nd and Whiterock Ave.; 970-349-5765.**

Donita's Cantina—$$

At the slightest craving for Mexican food, you should head straight to Donita's. Your hunger will be satisfied with enormous portions of spicy fare. If you're not very hungry, order à la carte. Specials of the house include beef or chicken fajitas; dinner quesadillas with shredded beef, chicken or veggies; and camarones (Gulf shrimp) sautéed in butter and garlic. Everything, including the sauces and salsa, is made fresh daily. The margaritas are excellent. Open seven nights a week 4:30–9:30 P.M. **330 Elk Ave.; 970-349-6674.**

Karolina's Kitchen—$$

Though the restaurant is newer, the Kochevar building has enough history to fill this book. Take a look around the dining room at the various antique contraptions, including a still that was used to provide jugs of moonshine during Prohibition. Large sandwiches, salads and home-made soups make up the bulk of the menu. Also served: pork chops, peel-and-eat shrimp, knock-wurst and sauerkraut and a 24-oz. rustler's T-bone **($$$$)**. Open daily 11 A.M.–midnight. **127 Elk Ave.; 970-349-6756.**

Idle Spur and Crested Butte Brewery—$ to $$$

This award-winning microbrewery also serves up great food. The large dining room, with a river-rock hearth on one side and high log rafters overhead, is a perfect place to hang out and quaff a few. The Idle Spur serves tender steaks, barbe-cued ribs, half-pound burgers and large salads. Specialties include chili-rubbed pork chops, grilled Pacific salmon, smoked trout and fajitas. Children's menu available. Open at 11 A.M. daily until late at night. **226 Elk Ave.; 970-349-5026.**

Ruby Mountain Bakery—$

Select from a long list of wonderfully fresh-baked goods for a quick take-out or enjoy a leisurely cappuccino inside or at the perfect little patio. Hot breakfasts feature specialty omelettes, cornmeal pancakes and a jumbo breakfast bur-rito. Lunch items include quiches, a great Italian sausage sandwich, homemade soups and salads. First opened in 1974, this place has changed its name, but the quality and friendliness still get raves from locals. Yes, it gets hectic during the winter rush, but the food is worth the wait. Open daily at 7 A.M. **308 Elk Ave.; 970-349-1291.**

GUNNISON AREA
The Trough—$$$

As you may have gathered by the name, this is the place in Gunnison to pig out during the long summer months. This spacious, rustically tasteful restaurant and bar is known for monstrous slabs of prime rib, steak and beef ribs. But you can also sample fresh seafood, pork Hawaiian and surf and turf. The not-so-ugly-duckling is served with the Trough's special orange glaze. Open year-round for dinners only, 5:30–9 P.M. One and a half miles west of Gunnison **on Hwy. 50; 970-641-3724.**

Garlic Mike's—$$ to $$$

This Italian eatery has attracted rave reviews from Crested Buttians as well as Gunnison locals. It's a casual place with a spotless open kitchen and, as you might imagine, plenty of hanging garlic cloves and mouth-watering aro-mas. Pull up a table or booth with a red-checked tablecloth and sit back for a delicious traditional Italian meal. You can tear into a hearty plate of pasta or, if you prefer, a beef, poultry or seafood dish. Start out with a traditional antipasto or minestrone. In summer be sure to inquire about eating out on the riverfront patio. Hours vary seasonally; call ahead for dinner reservations. Located about 2 miles north of Gunnison **on Hwy. 135; 970-641-2493.**

Mario's Pizza—$ to $$

Mario's serves great pizza on white or whole wheat, thick or thin crust. You'll probably end up with enough left over for breakfast. The kitchen also prepares pasta dishes, calzones and a long list of reasonably priced sandwiches. Eat in the restaurant or take advantage of free delivery. Open seven days a week 11 A.M.–11 P.M. **213 W. Tomichi Ave.; 970-641-1374.**

The Sidewalk Cafe—$

With breakfast and lunch items at reasonable prices, the seats are usually filled at this attrac-tive little cafe. Lots of windows, plants and an outdoor wooden deck add considerably to the meal. For breakfast, egg dishes as well as "giant" pancakes are the specialties; sandwiches and bur-gers for lunch. Open Mon.–Fri. 5 A.M.–3:30 P.M., Sat. 5 A.M.–2 P.M., closed Sun. **113 W. Tomichi Ave.; 970-641-4130.**

Steaming Bean—$

This comfortable hangout near Western State College provides a perfect setting to waste a little time. With a "lounging patio," excellent espresso and coffee drinks, pastries and art exhibits. Open daily with early-morning, daylight and evening hours. **120 N. Main St.; 970-641-2408.**

Services

Visitor Information

Crested Butte Reservations—Central reservations for all types of lodging, air travel, lift tickets, etc. **1-800-215-2226; 1-800-544-8448.**

Crested Butte Chamber of Commerce Visitors Centers—Located at the four-way stop as you enter town, or at a smaller Mt. Crested Butte branch at the bus stop. Terrific places to gather information and advice about the area. **601 Elk Ave., Crested Butte, CO 81224; 1-800-545-4505; 970-349-6438; www. visitcrestedbutte.com.**

Gunnison County Chamber of Commerce—Right next to the Town Park you'll find a helpful visitor center with information and advice on the entire area. **500 E. Tomichi Ave., P.O. Box 36, Gunnison CO 81230; 1-800-323-2453; 970-641-1501; www.gunnison country.com.**

Day Care

Butteopia Children's Program—They will take care of kids from ages 6 months to 6 years while you are on the slopes. A babysitting referral list is available. Located in the **Wetstone Building, Crested Butte, CO 81224; 970-349-2209.** Or check **Stepping Stones** in town, where drop-ins are welcome; **705 7th St., Crested Butte, CO 81224; 970-349-5288; www.crestedbutte resort.com.**

Transportation

Alpine Express—Door-to-door ground transportation between the Gunnison Airport and Crested Butte. **1-800-822-4844.**

Ouray

To get out and see the rugged, beautiful country around Ouray, the town's former mayor, Bill Fries (better known as country and western singer C. W. McCall), lays out three possibilities: "You can hike it if you've got the legs, ride it if you've got the horse and jeep it if you have the nerve." One look at the mountains around town and you'll know what Fries is talking about.

Ouray remains a relatively quiet little Victorian community of 700, wedged tightly into a nook of the Uncompahgre River Valley. It's also a good escape from the increasing exclusivity of nearby Telluride. To the east and the west of Ouray, colorful rock walls shoot hundreds of feet skyward; to the south, the famous Million Dollar Highway clings to a cliff high above the river, snaking its way 3,300 vertical feet up to 11,008-foot Red Mountain Pass. This gravity-defying road makes up the most famous, and most nerve-wracking, stretch of the 236-mile San Juan Skyway, one of the western United States' Scenic and Historic Byways (see the Scenic Drives section of the Durango chapter).

Ouray's roots go back to the discovery of gold and silver deposits in the 1870s. Hardrock miners have left behind more than 10,000 tunnels, cuts and abandoned shafts within a 10-mile radius of Ouray. Dozens of old wagon roads lead to many of the mines, giving rise to another of Ouray's more recent claims to fame: fantastic

jeeping. Drives over narrow, rough roads such as Engineer Pass, Imogene Pass and Black Bear Pass are not soon forgotten.

Summer is the big tourist season for Ouray, and a number of curio and souvenir shops on the main street suggest as much. Many colorful homes from the late 1800s have been carefully preserved; as a result, the town is a designated National Historic District. Hiking and camping in the nearby Uncompahgre National Forest are big draws. During the winter, when a heavy blanket of snow covers the San Juans, some shops in Ouray close and the day-to-day pace winds down. But winter is a great time to be in Ouray. Ice climbers flock here from all over the country to try the challenging crystalline walls at Ouray Ice Park. Cross-country skiing and snowshoeing on Red Mountain Pass are hard to beat, especially when followed by the activity Ouray is perhaps best known for—soaking in a hot springs pool. The town's many hot springs (see the Hot Springs section) are soothing any time of year, but in winter, when steam rises from the water, it's just a bit more relaxing.

Just 10 miles downriver from Ouray, the Uncompahgre Valley widens and the San Juan Mountains serve as a dramatic backdrop. At 6,985 feet, here lies the historic ranch supply

Getting There

Ouray is located 320 miles southwest of Denver. Travel west on Interstate 70 to Grand Junction, then south on Hwy. 50 to Montrose. Continue south on Hwy. 550 past Ridgway to Ouray. Another more scenic, though slightly longer route is via Hwy. 285 south from Denver to Poncha Springs and then west on Hwy. 50. At Montrose head south on Hwy. 550 to Ouray.

and railroad center of Ridgway. This small town has a determined survival instinct despite many lean years and a 1950s plan to build a dam that would have submerged it. Today though, thanks to the opening of nearby Ridgway State Park and a developer-induced real estate boom, Ridgway is thriving.

Aside from avoiding the crowds and high accommodation prices at Telluride, skiers now have another reason to stay overnight in Ouray. Anyone doing so can get ski tickets to Telluride Resort for half price. Both Ouray and Ridgway offer plenty of great lodging. Bed and breakfast inns and a number of accommodations featuring hot springs are the clear standouts. And believe us, in this gorgeous area of the state you'll want to spend more than a day.

History

Long before prospectors led their heavily laden mules into Ouray, the Ute Indians cherished this spot on the Uncompahgre River for its hot springs. The town's namesake, Chief Ouray, spent much time here.

Mineral strikes in the Ouray area began in 1875. Although most of these early mines produced silver, one mine, called the Mineral Farm, yielded large chunks of gold, which were said to have been extracted from the ground using nothing more than hoes and shovels. The very first building in town was a saloon that did a hopping business. As with other mining settlements in the San Juans, Ouray was hampered in its growth by its isolated location and the astronomical cost of transporting the ore. This problem was solved when Otto Mears built a cliff-hanging toll road (now called the Million Dollar Highway) up the wall of Uncompahgre Canyon to Red Mountain Pass south of town, connecting Ouray with Silverton. Wagons replaced mules for transporting ore, and Ouray began to boom. The first railroad arrived in Dec. 1887, further reducing shipping costs. Ouray became a crucial trading and transportation center for the surrounding mining camps and even

then was attracting tourists. One of the town newspapers, the *Solid Muldoon,* was widely read and frequently quoted around the state. Its unusual format and sarcasm prompted even Queen Victoria of England to send for a subscription!

When the silver crash hit in 1893 and many mines closed, Ouray lost its stride. But in 1896 an Irishman by the name of Thomas Walsh put Ouray-area mining back on track. Walsh, who discovered gold in discarded rock from local silver mines, bought up a number of claims near Yankee Boy Basin, west of Ouray, and named them Camp Bird. The mine went on to make Walsh a fortune—enough to buy his daughter, Evalyn, the famous (but cursed) Hope diamond. The diamond's curse proved true as personal tragedy landed full force in Evalyn's lap for the remainder of her life.

Although mining, once the economic mainstay of the area, is all but history, tourism and relocated city folk keep the economy perking along as more people learn of the beauty and serenity that can be found in this wonderful part of the state.

Festivals and Events

Ouray Ice Festival

third weekend in Jan. This exciting event is as much fun for the spectators as for the participants. Each winter Ouray hosts ice climbers who converge on Ouray Ice Park for an array of activities. Watch experts practice their monkey hangs and make their way up unbelievably tough routes. If you are a novice, consider taking up the sport during the festival—the lessons are free. **303-258-7616; www.ouray icepark. com.**

San Juan Spring Round-Up

mid-May Enjoy this springtime gathering of cowboy poets, storytellers and musicians that provides an entire weekend of western fun. Located in Ridgway, the activities also include songwriting workshops plus art, craft and food booths in the town park. The main evening performances are followed by dancing to live country music. For more information contact the **Ridgway Chamber of Commerce; 1-800-220-4959; www.ridgwaycolorado.com.**

Ouray Jeep Jamboree

late Sept. Maybe you'll feel a bit better about heading out on Ouray's many four-wheel-drive roads as part of an organized caravan. During the peak of fall colors, this annual event provides a large number of outdoor adventures for individuals, families and groups. Call **530-333-4777** to register, or the Ouray Chamber Resort Association at **1-800-228-1876; www.ouray colorado.com.**

Outdoor Activities

Biking

MOUNTAIN BIKING

Many old mining roads with beautiful scenery await your tracks. See the Four-Wheel-Drive Trips section for more ideas. A terrific ride for the entire family is **River Rd.** (City Rds. 23 and 17), a relatively flat 10-mile dirt road from Ouray to Ridgway through the Uncompahgre Valley. In Ouray, take 7th Ave. west and head north just after crossing the river. For maps and information about area trails, talk with Bill Leo at **Ouray Mountain Sports, 722 Main St.; 970-325-4284.** If you are starting from the Ridgway end, bike rentals are available at **Ridgway Outdoor Experience; 970-626-3608.**

BICYCLE TOURING

In addition to the various highways in the area, try a paved section of the Uncompahgre River-Way, a 3-mile trail from Ridgway Town Park north to Ridgway State Park. Once inside the state park you'll find an additional 4 miles of paved trails. Plans are for the RiverWay to eventually extend 65 miles, connecting Ouray to the towns of Montrose and Delta.

Scaling one of the many wintertime routes in Ouray Ice Park. Photo courtesy of Ouray Chamber Resort.

Fishing

Ridgway State Park

See the write-up under the Parks section.

Silver Jack Reservoir

Located northeast of Ouray, Silver Jack provides pretty good fishing for rainbow, particularly in the spring and fall. No motorized boats are allowed on the water. Take Hwy. 550 for 2 miles north from Ridgway, turning east on Owl Creek Rd. (County Rd. 10). Continue about 20 miles over scenic Owl Creek Pass to Silver Jack. The reservoir catches water from the West, Middle and East Forks of the Cimarron River, all of which can be good for brook, cutthroat and rainbow trout.

Four-Wheel-Drive Trips

"Ouray is to jeepers what Oahu is to surfers," states a newspaper article tacked to the wall of a local jeep tour office. And how true it is. For visitors to Ouray, especially those coming for the first time, a jeep trip on the network of old mining roads is a must. Via these exciting roads, often cut into cliffs with sheer drops of hundreds of feet, the area's mining history comes to the forefront. For those with steady nerves nothing can compare with the excitement, beauty and history of a trip over Black Bear and Engineer Passes.

Three of the area's most dramatic drives are covered in other chapters of the book: The incredible **Engineer Pass,** part of the Alpine Loop Scenic and Historic Byway, is covered in the Four-Wheel-Drive Trips section of the **Creede and Lake City** chapter. **Imogene Pass,** a nail-biter crossing over to Telluride, is covered in the Four-Wheel-Drive Trips section of the **Telluride** chapter. Details on **Ophir Pass** and the dizzying **Black Bear Pass** can be found in the **Silverton** chapter.

Corkscrew Road

Drive south from Ouray on Hwy. 550 up to Ironton just before the summit of Red Mountain Pass. Turn left and follow the road south as it starts up Corkscrew Gulch. The narrow road winds up to the summit, which is covered with the same rocky red soil as nearby Red Mountain. From the summit you can return on the same road or work your way east and then south near the ghost town of Gladstone and along Cement Creek Rd. (County Rd. 110), ending in Silverton. Return to Ouray on Hwy. 550.

Yankee Boy Basin / Governor Basin

This is one of the most scenic and memorable drives in the area, as it goes by mines, towering mountains and fields of wildflowers. The road begins just south of town on Camp Bird Rd. (County Rd. 361). Follow the road southwest up the valley through aspen and pine. After about 4 miles the road takes a frightening curve along a ledge blasted out of the canyon's rock wall. Another mile up the road, the famous Camp Bird Mine can be seen on the left (see the History section). Less than 2 miles farther up

the road, a left fork heads over Imogene Pass to Telluride (see the Four-Wheel-Drive Trips section in the **Telluride** chapter). Stay right and proceed up past the old townsite of Sneffels and another fork in the road appears. The left road heads off into Governor Basin, site of the well-known Virginius Mine. The dramatic spires of St. Sophia Ridge are just to the southwest. On the main road follow the steep, winding road up past Twin Falls and into immense Yankee Boy Basin. In summer this wildflower-covered basin is transformed into a riot of color. Mt. Sneffels lies directly to the north and can be climbed via the ridge on its east side. Note: much of the area along this entire road is privately owned and camping is prohibited.

Rentals and Tours

Colorado West Jeep Rentals and Tours— Tag along on a guided tour of the back roads or rent your own jeep. **701 Main St., Ouray, CO 81427; 1-800-648-5337; 970-325-4014.**
San Juan Adventures—Offering guided 4x4 tours and Jeep Wrangler rentals for trips into the surrounding mountains. Located at **450 Main St., Ouray, CO 81427; 1-877-325-0120.**
Switzerland of America Jeep Tours and Rentals—Providing jeep rentals for a day or week. This company also offers guided jeep tours, rafting, horseback rides and balloon rides. **226 7th Ave., P.O. Box 780, Ouray, CO 81427-0780; 1-800-432-5337; 970-325-4484; www.soajeep.com.**

Golf

Fairway Pines Golf and Country Club

Proximity to Ridgway + mesa-top location = unsurpassed views. The only conceivable downside to this challenging championship 18-hole course is that the sweeping, panoramic views of the San Juan Mountains can be a bit distracting as you're leaning over a tricky 6-foot putt. And concentration you'll need. The holes (each individually named) meander along the mesa among stately ponderosa pines, piñon and juniper. Rated by *Golf Digest* as one of the top 13 courses in Colorado. Open Apr. through early Nov., weather permitting. Fairway Pines offers a driving range, restaurant, pro shop and other expected amenities. Call ahead for a tee time. **117 Ponderosa Dr., Ridgway, CO 81432; 970-626-5284; www.fairwaypines.com.**

Hiking and Backpacking

Rugged trails, wide-open mountain meadows, towering peaks, aspen glades, beautiful waterfalls and crashing streams can all be found near Ouray. Uncompahgre National Forest encircles town. Mountains rise to the west, leading into the Mt. Sneffels Wilderness. To the east, the Uncompahgre Wilderness offers hikes in valleys lightly used by other hikers. South of town, trails climb up into the heart of the old mining country. Many shafts, buildings and even an occasional aerial tram indicate the extent of activity that took place here 100 years ago. As in other areas of the San Juans, use caution and *please* stay out of the mines!

A good map of hiking trails in the Ouray area can be picked up at the visitor center next to the Ouray Hot Springs Pool. Topographic maps and rental equipment for camping can be obtained at **Ouray Mountain Sports, 722 Main St.; 970-325-4284.** For additional information stop by the **Ouray Ranger District Office** (also the area Bureau of Land Management office), **2505 S. Townsend Ave., Montrose, CO 81401; 970-240-5300; www.fs.fed.us/r2/gmug.**

Bear Creek National Recreation Trail

This is one of our all-time favorite trails. It begins south of town and heads east up along Bear Creek, on an old road that was built by miners with diggings in the area. The trail cuts into the steep canyon's rock wall high above the raging water. Mining history is so pervasive along the trail that you almost expect to see a miner coming around the next corner leading a burro weighted down with a load of ore. Volcanic intrusions are also visible from the trail.

After some initial switchbacks, the trail traverses high above the creek. Grizzly Bear Mine is

visible after 2.5 miles and Yellow Jacket Mine after 4.2 miles. At Yellow Jacket Mine the trail forks, the left heading up to American Flats where you can take Horsethief Trail northwest, eventually ending up north of Ouray near the Bachelor-Syracuse Mine. The right fork heads up Bear Creek for 3 miles to the summit of Engineer Pass. From here you can turn around or try to bum a ride from a jeeper.

Parents should think twice about taking this trail with small children—the drop-offs to the creek along the first few miles of the trail are substantial, so why tempt fate? To reach the trailhead, from Ouray drive 4 miles south on Hwy. 550 to the first tunnel. The trail begins on top of the tunnel.

Blue Lakes Trail

This 4-mile trail to Blue Lakes leads into the beautiful Mt. Sneffels Wilderness and can be approached from two directions. Perhaps the most popular route is from Dallas Divide. From Ouray drive north to Ridgway and turn left onto Hwy. 62. Proceed about 5 miles and turn left onto East Dallas Creek Rd. (County Rd. 7). Go almost 9 miles to the gate at the trailhead and begin hiking south. A sign marks the trailhead.

The other approach is just south of town on the road to Camp Bird Mine. You can drive up to the mine with a regular passenger car, but if you have a four-wheel-drive vehicle it's possible to continue an additional 3 miles up into Yankee Boy Basin. From there hike up the basin to the northeast for 2 miles to the lakes. This route requires a difficult crossing of Blue Lakes Pass.

Box Canyon Falls and Park

Off Hwy. 550 just southwest of Ouray, short trails lead to dramatic views of this torrential 285-foot waterfall. And the view of town from the 1900s-era steel bridge spanning a narrow gap high above the waterfall is wonderful. The city owns the land and access to this unusual geologic showpiece. Don't miss it, and bring your camera. On-site facilities include a new visitor center, covered picnic tables and rest rooms; no overnight camping; small fee. Open officially from mid-May to mid-Oct., but trails to the falls are kept open in wintertime. For more information call **970-325-4464.**

Portland Trail

This terrific family hike winds its way 1.75 miles (and about 1,000 vertical feet) up through elderly ponderosa pines for an up-close and personal overlook of the classic amphitheater basin just southwest of Ouray. From the overview area, you may continue on, meeting up with the Upper Cascade Falls Trail (see next entry) for a loop hike. Views from the moderately steep Portland Trail are outstanding. To reach the trailhead from town, head south on Hwy. 550 to the Amphitheater Campground turnoff. Turn here and then take an immediate right on the dirt road. Continue about 500 yards to the trailhead on the left side of the road.

Upper Cascade Falls Trail

Beginning at Amphitheater Campground just south of town, this trail (No. 213) heads 2.5 miles and 1,500 vertical feet up a series of switchbacks. The last half-mile traverses the rock walls east of town, eventually crossing over Cascade Creek just above the falls. Just beyond the falls are the remains of the Chief Ouray Mine's boardinghouse and machine shop. The last mile or so is very steep, but the views down onto town and of the surrounding mountains are worthwhile. To reach the trailhead, drive south on Hwy. 550 to the entrance to Amphitheater Campground. A sign marks the trailhead.

Wetterhorn Basin Trail

Located in the heart of the Uncompahgre Wilderness, Wetterhorn Basin Trail is a 5-mile hike that stays above treeline most of the time. The wide-open views to Wetterhorn Peak (14,015 feet) and Coxcomb Peak (13,656 feet) make this hike worth the effort. To reach the trailhead from Ouray, head north on Hwy. 550 a couple of miles past Ridgway and turn right on Owl Creek Pass Rd. After crossing the summit of Owl Creek Pass, turn right on Forest Rd. 860 and proceed 5 miles to the trailhead (you will need a four-wheel-drive or high-clearance pickup truck for the last 1.5 miles).

Ice Climbing

Ouray Ice Park

When the many waterfalls in the Ouray area freeze in winter, out of the woodwork appear droves of that strange breed of winter recreationist, the ice climber. Converging on the Ouray area, these serious thrill-seekers search for an iced-over waterfall and, with pterodactyl-like axes in each hand and ice screws on their belts, start their ascents. It's exciting to watch. By far the best place to watch or participate is at the Ouray Ice Park, just a 3-minute walk from town. When the temperatures plummet, a collection of catwalks, nozzles and pipes creates an enormous wall of ice, stretching more than 120 feet up the vertical sides of Uncompahgre Gorge. Perfecting the creation each winter, local climbers have established approximately 45 routes up this frozen monster. Beginners to expert ice climbers will definitely find a route to suit their abilities. This may be the best place in the country to learn this adrenaline-pumping sport. Give it a shot. **P.O. Box 1058, Ouray, CO 81427; www.ourayicepark.com.**

If you are interested in ice climbing instruction, contact **San Juan Mountain Guides, P.O. Box 825, Ouray, CO 81427; 970-325-4925; www.ourayclimbing.com. Above Ouray Ice and Tower Rock Guides** offers highly experienced guides as well as a climbing school; **450 Main St., Ouray, CO 81427; 1-888-345-9061; www.towerguides.com.**

Ice Skating

A 75- by 160-foot lighted skating rink is set up each winter at **Rotary Park,** just north of Ouray on Hwy. 550. Skates may be rented at the Ouray Hot Springs Pool or at the Box Canyon Falls Visitor Center. Rink hours: 8 A.M.–10:30 P.M. **970-325-4638.**

View of the "Amphitheater" from the Portland Trail near Ouray. Photo by Dean Winstanley.

Parks

Ridgway State Park

Located just a few miles north of Ridgway next to Hwy. 550, this terrific state park is widely considered the jewel of 'em all. Offering a wide array of recreation activities as well as sweeping views southward to the San Juan Mountains and Sneffels Range (including 14,150-foot Mt. Sneffels), the park has quickly turned into one of the area's main attractions.

With the 1,000-acre reservoir as the centerpiece, water sports are perhaps the main activity. Reservoir amenities, including a boat ramp, marina with rental boats and even a fish cleaning station, add to your day on the water searching for the lunker browns and plentiful rainbows, many in the 14- to 18-inch range. Fishing for browns is especially good just below the reservoir on the Uncompahgre River (catch-and-release only). And the hugely popular swimming beach also attracts many to the water as well. If you would like to get out on the water, no problem—the marina rents paddleboats, kayaks and other watercraft.

Three recreation sites at the park (Dutch Charlie, Dallas Creek and Pa-Co-Chu-Puk) offer activities from hiking and biking trails to picnicking to guided interpretive programs. The visitor center is worth a stop for information and displays on the area's wildlife, habitat and geology.

The 268 first-class campsites (including wheelchair-accessible sites) at Ridgway State Park, spread out among three locations, are popular, especially in summer. Shower buildings, laundry facilities and RV hookups contribute greatly to this popularity. At the Dutch Charlie area, **Dakota Terrace Campground** (79 sites) lies within walking distance of the swim beach and marina; **Elk Ridge Campground** (110 sites) occupies higher ground, providing better views of the surrounding mountains. Recent additions at Dutch Charlie include three popular yurts—circular Mongolian-style tents—each equipped with propane heaters, skylights and other comfortable features. **Pa-Co-Chu-Puk Campground,** located just below the dam, offers 81 sites along the Uncompahgre River as well as a number of walk-in tentsites. For campsite and yurt reservations: **1-800-678-CAMP** or **www. reserve america.com.** For other information, contact **28555 Hwy. 550, Ridgway, CO 81432; 970-626-5822; www.colorado parks.org.**

Skiing

CROSS-COUNTRY SKIING AND SNOWSHOEING

The magnificent backcountry skiing around Ouray is becoming better known each year. West of town toward the Mt. Sneffels Wilderness, a number of fine trails offer good views and very few people. The basins around Red Mountain Pass provide an almost limitless amount of ski terrain. As one Ouray local puts it, "Backcountry skiing around Red Mountain Pass is like playing on a 1,000-hole golf course—every hole is different, so just tee off and enjoy." If you are unfamiliar with the area and want to try skiing on Red Mountain Pass, be sure to inquire locally about avalanche danger or go out with an experienced guide. You can also call **970-247-8187** for current **avalanche information** in the San Juan Mountains. For information and rentals try **Ouray Mountain Sports, 722 Main St.; 970-325-4284.** They offer a large assortment of cross-country skis, boots and poles, including telemark equipment, and snowshoes.

Backcountry Trails

East Dallas Creek Trail—This easy trail heads south, winding its way up 7 miles to the northern boundary of the Mt. Sneffels Wilderness. The lofty summit of Mt. Sneffels (14,150 feet) is laid out in front of you while you ski in through piñon, juniper and eventually spruce and fir forests. Private property lines the road for the first 5 miles, so stay on the trail. To reach East Dallas Creek Trail from Ouray, head north on Hwy. 550 for 10 miles to Ridgway and turn left on Hwy. 62. Drive about 5 miles, turn left again onto County Rd. 7 and follow the signs to Uncompahgre National Forest. Start skiing where the plowing stops.

Miller Mesa Trail—A good route for beginners to intermediates, Miller Mesa Trail rises above Ridgway, providing views of both the Sneffels Range and the Uncompahgre Valley. The trail heads south and then east up the mesa for 5 miles. From Ouray drive north on Hwy. 550 to Ridgway and turn left on Hwy. 62. At the west end of Ridgway turn left onto County Rd. 5, marked by a sign to the Girl Scout Camp. After a quarter-mile, turn right and drive about 5 miles to Elk Meadows. Park where the plowing stops.

Red Mountain Pass—At the summit of the pass many people choose to ski the trees on the west side of the road. However, on the east side, U.S. Basin offers what one local termed "the best backcountry skiing with road access in the country." In an isolated and dramatic setting near the basin, Chris and Donna George run the unique **St. Paul Lodge.** Chris, an avalanche expert, offers cross-country ski lessons along with his rugged accommodations. For more information about the lodge and other skiing opportunities on Red Mountain Pass, see the St. Paul Lodge write-up in the Where to Stay section of the **Silverton** chapter.

Groomed Trails

Red Mountain/Ironton Park—On a shelf 4 miles below the top of Red Mountain Pass, the Ouray County Nordic Council has developed a marked trail system perfect for beginner and intermediate skiers. Nine miles south of Ouray on Hwy. 550, three trailheads leave the highway on a number of connecting loop trips. Trails wind through a historic mining area with signs identifying important sites. Local merchants carry a trail map to the area, or send a stamped, self-addressed envelope to the **Ouray County Nordic Council, P.O. Box 468, Ouray, CO 81427; 970-325-4932.**

Seeing and Doing

Ballooning

In Ridgway contact **San Juan Balloon Adventures; 970-626-5495; www.sanjuan**

balloons.com. **Switzerland of America Jeep Rentals** is the best bet in Ouray at **1-800-432-5337; 970-325-4484; www.soajeep.com.**

Hot Springs

The healing waters of the area's natural hot springs were well known to Chief Ouray for their spiritual and medicinal qualities. After Chief Ouray and the Utes left the area, the town became known for its "radioactive" hot springs. Don't worry, the water isn't really radioactive, but geothermal waters continue to boil to the surface from deep inside the earth. You can't walk up Canyon Creek for a soak in a natural hot pot any longer, but three lodges in town **(Wiesbaden, Box Canyon Lodge** and **Best Western Twin Peaks)** have **hot springs facilities;** the large town pool offers an outdoor soak with spectacular views. Nine miles downriver in Ridgway, Orvis Hot Springs features a more natural environment.

Orvis Hot Springs

The highlight at this funky place has to be the large outdoor bathing suit-optional pool with its sandy bottom, perfect temperature and unobstructed views of the surrounding mountains. If you are interested in soaking in hotter water (on the verge of scalding), ease into the smaller stone tub. Inside you'll find four private tub rooms as well. Most families prefer splashing around in the wonderfully constructed indoor pool (bathing suits required). Six spacious but simple overnight **lodge rooms ($$)** share two bathrooms. Tentsites available for a small fee. Hot springs free to overnight guests. Open to the public daily 9 A.M.–10 P.M. Fair warning: this place gets very crowded on weekends and holidays. Located 9 miles north of Ouray on Hwy. 550 (1.3 miles south of Ridgway). **1585 County Rd. 3, Ridgway, CO 81432; 970-626-5324.**

Ouray Hot Springs Pool

Life somehow makes sense while you're soaking in this hot spring's shallow 104° F pool and gazing up at the surrounding peaks. You'd be hard-pressed to find a better view from a hot springs pool in Colorado. The enormous pool is rigidly separated out for different uses, and the young lifeguards are eager to enforce the rules. For swimming laps or cooling off, negotiate your way over the concrete steps to the largest of the numerous pool sections—all are separated by interior walls. In winter, large snowflakes fill the air and steam billows off the water, creating a mystical atmosphere. The hot springs entrance fee is good for the whole day. Rubber kayaks and other water toys are available for rent. Also available is a workout room, lockers, picnic tables, a playground and a running track. Open 10 A.M.–10 P.M. daily in summer; noon–9 P.M. in winter. Located on the north end of town **just off Hwy. 550; 970-325-4638.**

Twin Peaks (Best Western)

See the Where to Stay section.

Wiesbaden Hot Springs

See the Where to Stay section.

Mine Tour

Bachelor–Syracuse Mine Tour

A surefire way to get a feel for what brought people to the San Juan area more than a century ago is to take a tour of the Bachelor–Syracuse gold and silver mine. Featured in *National Geographic,* this top-notch mine tour allows you to ride the "trammer" 3,350 feet back into this hardrock mine, first worked in 1884 by three bachelors. Closed after the huge decline in silver prices in the early 1980s, the mine now offers daily tours during the summer months.

During the fascinating hour-long tour, you stop at a work site where the guide (a real miner) describes the hardrock mining process, from drilling dynamite holes to hauling ore out of the mine by trammer. Be sure to bring a coat, as the temperature in the mine is a brisk 52° F. The mine site also offers a gift shop, gold panning and the "miner's outdoor cafe." A fee is charged.

Open daily mid-May to mid-Sept.; closed July 4; hourly tours. To reach the mine, drive a mile or so north from Ouray on Hwy. 550. Turn right onto County Rd. 14 and follow the signs. **P.O. Drawer 380, Ouray, CO 81427; 970-325-0220.**

Museums and Galleries

Ouray County Museum

This special place provides a great opportunity to gain a historical perspective of Ouray and the San Juan area. Victorian-era items rekindle the town's heyday: narrow-gauge train memorabilia, mineral specimens from local mines and even a piano with worn ivory keys from the Gold Belt Theatre.

Upstairs you'll find several re-created hospital rooms, a general store and a legal office. Downstairs a simulated hardrock mine and blacksmith shop are displayed next to the assayer's office. The museum is located inside the former St. Joseph's Hospital, built in 1887. Open 10 A.M.–5 P.M. daily in summer; 1–5 P.M. Sun.; reduced hours in winter. Admission fee. **420 6th Ave.; 970-325-4576.**

Scenic Drives

Dallas Divide

This 25-mile stretch of road between Ridgway and Placerville is one of the most photographed in Colorado. From the top of the 8,970-foot divide, views to the Sneffels Range (high point: 14,150-foot Mt. Sneffels) and Uncompahgre and Wetterhorn Peaks are stunning. To reach Dallas Divide from Ouray, head north on Hwy. 550 to Ridgway, turn left onto Hwy. 62 and continue for about 10 miles.

Million Dollar Highway

Try as you will, there is absolutely no better vantage point for an auto trip deep into the San Juans than the Million Dollar Highway. This road winds up a glacial valley past once-thriving mines to the 12,217-foot summit of **Red Mountain Pass.** Towering peaks, elephantine mountain slopes, sheer cliff walls and thick stands of aspen and pine dominate the scenery.

The road was the result of Otto Mears's foresight. He understood that most counties were too poor to build roads to provide crucial economic links between the mining towns. Mears took it upon himself to build this road to connect Ouray with Ironton Park in 1883, and in time completed the route over Red Mountain Pass to Silverton. The narrow road had a tollgate located atop Bear Falls, which charged $3.75 per vehicle and 75 cents per horse. (A mile and a half south of Ouray is a turnout to view the 227-foot waterfall.)

Debate continues over the origin of the name Million Dollar Highway. It is true that gold tailings were used in the original construction, but certainly not a million dollars' worth. Though the highway is said to have originally cost $40,000 per mile to build, a million-dollar price tag for the entire project would be too high. Another possibility involves a woman who traveled the road by stagecoach back in its early days. She exclaimed, "I wouldn't go back over that road for a million dollars!" Lastly, the most probable and least colorful explanation is that it cost approximately $1 million to improve the road for automobile use.

The stagecoach is long out of service, but the Million Dollar Highway remains a breathtaking adventure. Take the 22-mile drive south on Hwy. 550 out of Ouray to the top of Red Mountain Pass, which eventually drops into historic Silverton. The entire paved route is easily completed in a passenger car. During the early-summer runoff or after a heavy rainfall, you'll be treated to spectacular waterfalls along the way.

San Juan Skyway

This National Scenic and Historic Byway encompasses the most beautiful part of southwest Colorado. The Million Dollar Highway is just a part of the 236-mile route. For more information see the Scenic Drives section of the **Durango** chapter.

The irresistible Ouray Hot Springs Pool. Photo by Joel Kramer, courtesy of Ouray Chamber Resort Association.

Where to Stay

Accommodations

With its abundance of large Victorian homes and steady stream of visitors, Ouray may be the perfect place if you are interested in operating a bed and breakfast. Here are a few of the top choices that are open year-round:

The **Manor ($$$)** is a centrally located and beautifully renovated Georgian Victorian hybrid with a place on the National Register of Historic Places. Your hosts will make your stay a pleasant one. Their charming, three-story house features seven individually decorated guest rooms with private baths. **317 2nd St., P.O. Box 1165, Ouray, CO 81427; 1-800-628-6946; 970-325-4574.** So you want southern hospitality and a generous breakfast to start your day? Joyce and Mike Manley offer eight rooms at **The Damn Yankee Inn ($$$ to $$$$),** their well-appointed, extremely comfortable chalet-style B&B with all the conveniences. All rooms have private entrances and bathrooms (telephones and cable TV, too). Check out the incredible view of the surrounding peaks from the third-floor sitting room. **100 6th Ave., Ouray, CO 81427; 1-800-845-7512; www.damnyankee inn.com. Mainstreet Bed and Breakfasts ($$$)** includes two lovingly renovated houses filled with antiques and offering a surprising number of rooms with private baths for couples and families. Between the houses you'll find a courtyard with a gazebo, hot tub and children's playground. A couple of highlights: the romantic Lilac Room with its private deck and incredible view of Twin Peaks; and the Oak Creek Suite, which features a sunroom, kitchen and private deck. Families—up to six members—might also want to consider renting the self-sufficient Southwestern style Chipeta Cottage out back. All are open May 15–Oct. 15. For reservations contact the **Mainstreet B&Bs, P.O. Box 641, Ouray, CO 81427; 970-325-4871;** in winter **602-266-9202.**

San Juan Guest Ranch—$$$$

Set in the Uncompahgre Valley just 4 miles north of Ouray, this small ranch is steeped in western

Chipeta Sun Lodge and Spa in Ridgway. Photo by Dean Winstanley.

tradition. The intimacy of the ranch is its highlight, where your friendly hosts are Scott and Kelly McTiernan. Scott and his family have been opening up their beautiful place to guests for over 20 years. Located in the midst of working ranches, the San Juan fits in well with the rest. All of the buildings appear weathered and well used from the outside but comfortably modern from within. Nine comfortable rooms of varying sizes and motifs keep guests happy. Horseback riding on spectacular trails in the San Juan Mountains is the underlying emphasis. You'll also be treated to a jeep tour and a soak in the Ouray Hot Springs Pool. Consider staying here for a fall photo workshop or for cross-country skiing in winter. Meals included. **2882 City Rd. 23, Ridgway, CO 81432; 1-800-331-3015; 970-626-5360; www.sjgr.com.**

China Clipper Inn—$$$ to $$$$

Tucked one block off the main drag in Ouray, this palatial inn excels on a number of fronts. The entire 7,800-square-foot inn was custom-built specifically as a bed and breakfast. Your host, Earl Yarbrough, has lavishly and tastefully decorated each of the seven rooms with antique reproductions and artwork, many with an Asian theme. Some rooms offer features such as fireplaces, bay windows and sundecks. The Asian theme continues into the backyard patio area with its Japanese garden and hot tub. Although a library is open to all, many guests simply find a chair on the covered front porch for views of the surrounding mountains. Full breakfast served in the elegant dining room. No kids. **525 2nd St., P.O. Box 801, Ouray, CO 81427; 1-800-315-0565; 970-325-0565; www.chinaclipper inn.com.**

Chipeta Sun Lodge and Spa—$$$ to $$$$

Enjoying a leisurely breakfast in the solarium with its absolutely stunning views of the Uncompahgre Valley and surrounding San Juan Mountains is reason enough to recommend a stay at this unique bed and breakfast inn. The beautiful, two-story adobe Chipeta takes full advantage of its endless windows not only for views but also for passive solar heating. Twelve guest rooms (some with balconies), all with views, private baths and Southwestern decor, provide an excellent night's sleep. On the third floor you'll find a hot tub located in an adobe turret. Recent additions include eight comfortable suites with kitchenettes. Be sure to also check out the spa facilities that include an outdoor lap pool, weight room/aerobic machines, indoor therapy spa, massages, facials and on and on. Your hosts, Lyle and Shari Braund, provide pleasant conversation and local insights, especially ideas for hiking, biking and skiing the endless trails in the area. **304 S. Lena, Ridgway, CO 81432; 1-800-633-5868; 970-626-3737; www.chipeta.com.**

Best Western Twin Peaks—$$ to $$$

Though the rooms are pretty standard motel fare, this place gets a mention for its three on-site pools. Choose from the indoor hot-springs whirlpool, an outdoor hot-springs waterfall soaking pool and the outdoor heated swimming pool. Rooms vary in size but each has cable TV and a small refrigerator. Other attractions include large grassy areas and a playground. Open Apr.–Oct. **125 3rd Ave., P.O. Box 320, Ouray, CO 81427-0320; 1-800-528-1234; 970-325-4427; www.bestwestern.com/twinpeaks.**

St. Elmo Hotel—$$ to $$$

Built in 1898 as a boardinghouse for miners, the St. Elmo's turn-of-the-century ambience is tastefully preserved in each of the nine uniquely furnished rooms. Period antiques, touches of polished brass and stained glass are in abundance throughout the hotel. Continental breakfast included. **426 Main St., P.O. Box 667, Ouray, CO 81427; 970-325-4951; www.stelmohotel.com.**

The Adobe Inn—$$

Although better known for its Southwestern restaurant (see the Where to Eat section), the well-named Adobe Inn serves as a good value for overnight stays as well. Three rooms (with shared baths) are available, with either bunk beds

or a king-size bed in a room with views up the valley. Continental breakfast is served each morning. **251 Liddell Dr., Ridgway, CO 81432; 970-626-5939.**

Orvis Hot Springs—$$

See the Hot Springs section.

Wiesbaden Hot Springs Spa and Lodgings—$$

Follow a stairway from the glass-enclosed lobby into the geothermal wonders of a hot mineral water vapor cave below. Guests receive free, unlimited use of the vapor cave, hot mineral outdoor pool, sauna and universal weight room. Available for guests at reduced fees is a private outdoor tub and services such as professional massage, reflexology, acupressure treatment and facials. The rooms surrounding the courtyard are fairly standard, though some are equipped with kitchenettes; rooms in the main lodge building take on fanciful designs. For a special retreat ask about renting the rustic cabin on the hill above the lodge. Its small porch offers a spectacular panorama of the surrounding mountains. The Wiesbaden offers special winter discounts. Facilities also open to the general public. **P.O. Box 349, Ouray, CO 81427; 970-325-4347; www.geocities.com/wiesbadenspa.**

Camping

Ridgway State Park

For information on this excellent camping area, see the Parks section.

Uncompahgre National Forest

About half of the campsites listed here can be reserved at **1-877-444-6777** or **www.reserveusa.com.** A fee is charged at all listed sites. Just a mile south of Ouray on Hwy. 550 is the turnoff for one of the most popular national forest campgrounds in the state, **Amphitheater Campground** (30 sites). With fantastic views of the Sneffels Range and the Uncompahgre Valley, people don't want to leave—but there is a seven-day limit. The other campgrounds in the

Ouray area are located quite a few miles northeast, near Silver Jack Reservoir. Drive about 2 miles north of Ridgway on Hwy. 550 and turn right on Owl Creek Pass Rd. (County Rd. 10). After crossing the pass, follow the road north along the Cimarron River to **Silver Jack Campground** (60 sites) at Silver Jack Reservoir, about a 20-mile drive. Continuing north on Forest Rd. 858 for 1 mile brings you to **Beaver Lake Campground** (11 sites). Another half-mile north is **Big Cimarron Campground** (12 sites).

Private Campground

KOA Ouray—Located away from town in a quiet, attractive setting, KOA Ouray offers RV hookups, tentsites, cabins, a store, hot tub and even jeep rentals. Pine trees throughout. Open during summer only. To reach the campground from Ouray, drive 4 miles north on Hwy. 550 and turn left onto County Rd. 23. **Box J, Ouray, CO 81427; 970-325-4736.**

Where to Eat

Bon Ton Restaurant—$$$ to $$$$

Carefully prepared northern Italian cuisine is the specialty of this highly regarded restaurant. The inception of the Bon Ton Restaurant dates back to the 1880s. The long history is still evident in the Victorian atmosphere of its intimate surroundings. Cut-glass booth dividers and exposed brick walls create personal spaces for all diners. You won't be disappointed by indulging in a rich pasta entrée. House specialties include beef Wellington and a selection of veal dishes. Try out the Bon Ton's Sun. champagne **brunch ($$)** beginning at 9:30 A.M.; dinner is served each evening from 5 P.M., and from 5:30 P.M. in winter. Reservations are recommended. **426 Main St., Ouray; 970-325-4951.**

The Adobe Inn—$$$

Joyce and Terre Bucknam serve up some of the most delicious and creative Mexican food you'll find anywhere. Southwestern decor and South American music add rich atmosphere as you look out the windows at the surrounding mountains. Entrées (most everything is homemade) include enchiladas served six different ways and superior chimichangas. Each dinner comes with chips and salsa, refried beans and tomal en elote (corn casserole). The Adobe Inn also has excellent margaritas and a selection of Mexican beers. Dinner served 5:30–9:30 P.M.; bar opens at 5 P.M. Open year-round. **651 Liddell Dr., Ridgway, CO 81432; 970-626-5939.**

The Piñon—$$ to $$$

A private collection of western art adds greatly to the atmosphere at The Piñon, which features fine dinners prepared with fresh ingredients. To start off, try the fantastic tomato basil soup or small Caesar salad. Daily specials such as cajun shrimp tacos are recommended as well as regular highlights including stuffed chicken with cheese and angel hair pasta or steaks and prime rib. Open in summer 5–9:30 P.M.; Mexican dishes are served upstairs at the bar 11 A.M.–9 P.M. daily. **737 Main St., Ouray; 970-325-4334.**

Buen Tiempo—$ to $$

Buen Tiempo's new location and dynamite Southwestern/Mexican cuisine came as a welcome discovery on a recent trip to Ouray. Once tucked away on a side street, this excellent restaurant now commands a prominent location next to the historic Belvedere Hotel on Main St. Exposed brick walls, wooden floors, fanciful lighting and colorful Southwestern decor set the mood. (Be sure to ask about the dollar bills stuck on the ceiling.) Start off with one of the numerous specialty margaritas. Lunch specialties include the Southwestern "Ceazar" salad, offered with salmon, chicken breast or prime rib. The voluminous dinner menu includes fantastic spinach enchiladas and outstanding carne adovada. Provided that you have *buen tiempo,* head out to the attractive patio for views to go with your meal. The Buen is open for lunch 11:30 A.M.–2:30 P.M.; dinner 4:30–

10 P.M.; winter hours more abbreviated. Located in Ouray at **515 Main St., Ouray; 970-325-4544.**

Pricco's—$ to $$

The exposed brick walls, airy skylight and attractive ambience provide a classy yet casual feel at this popular lunch and dinner spot. The historic Pricco building has been around since the late 1800s. For lunch try a hoagie sandwich, Philly cheese steak or homemade soup topped off with a fresh dessert. Dinner standouts include pasta dishes as well as steak, chicken and seafood. Beer and wine are served. Open for lunch 11 A.M.–4 P.M. from Memorial Day to mid-Oct.; dinner served 5–8 P.M. **736 Main St., Ouray; 970-325-4040.**

San Juan Mountain Bakery & Deli—$

For a quick tasty bite or a steaming cup of coffee, stop by this great little place in Ridgway across from the town park. For breakfast choose from pastries, bagels and other specialties like their biscuits and gravy or breakfast burritos; lunch favorites include grilled burgers and ribs, or deli sandwiches on fresh-baked bread. Although there are a couple of tables inside, head out to the sundeck if weather permits. Open Mon.–Sat. 6 A.M.–3 P.M. **520 Sherman Rd., Ridgway; 970-626-5803.**

Silver Nugget Cafe—$

Each mountain town has a cafe that attracts a local crowd. In Ouray, the Silver Nugget fits the bill with its friendly service and country-style food. Choose from generous breakfast, lunch and dinner items as well as homemade pie. Open year-round 7 A.M.–8:30 P.M. daily May–Oct.; closed in winter. **940 Main St., Ouray; 970-325-4100.**

Services

Visitor Information

Ouray Chamber Resort Association—An excellent visitor center is located next to the Ouray Hot Springs Pool at the north end of town. **Box 145, Ouray, CO 81427; 1-800-228-1876; 970-325-4746; www.ouraycolorado.com.**

Ridgway Area Chamber of Commerce—Stop by their visitor center, place a call or visit their website. **150 Racecourse Rd., Ridgway, CO 81432; 1-800-220-4959; 970-626-5181; www.ridgwaycolorado.com.**

Pagosa Springs

An author who visited Pagosa Springs in 1924 called the area a "Shangri-La . . . a great retreat from the speakeasies, jazz and stock market of the real world." Today the stress factors of the "real world" are somewhat different (except for the stock market), but the sentiments still ring true.

Pagosa, a Ute word meaning "healing waters," gets its name from the hot mineral springs that were long coveted by the Indians. Pagosa Springs uses geothermal water to heat many of its buildings. In recent years a local entrepreneur has built a cluster of surrealistic-looking steaming pools at river's edge, finally taking full advantage of this natural occurrence for pure enjoyment (see the Hot Springs section).

The San Juan River crashes down from the Continental Divide to the northeast, making its way through Pagosa Springs and then down to Navajo Reservoir on the New Mexico border. A city park right in the town center features a pleasant riverwalk in addition to a playground and picnic area. The strongest plus of Pagosa Springs, however, has to be its exceptional mountain views and easy backcountry access.

San Juan National Forest near Pagosa Springs offers many outdoor recreational opportunities, including some great mountain bike and horseback rides. The fishing and hunting are outstanding. Countless hiking trails crisscross their way through low valleys and up into the high country of the Weminuche Wilderness and

along the Continental Divide. In winter, the rolling, forested hills are ideal for cross-country skiing. Wolf Creek Ski Area has reached legendary status for its short lift lines and heavy snowfall, quite often the deepest of any Colorado ski area. The fascinating Anasazi ruins at Chimney Rock (see the Anasazi Ruins section in this chapter) provide yet another major draw to the area.

Once again Pagosa Springs has entered a real estate boom phase, and land-sale offices litter the town's entry points offering "incredible bargains." Somehow this low-key, one-stoplight town still remains generally unaffected by the surge of newcomers.

Most people familiar with Pagosa Springs still think of it as a place they pass through on their way to somewhere else. If you want to spend a vacation visiting exceptional museums and enjoying a hopping nightlife, Pagosa is not the place. But to escape hectic schedules—and, for that matter, hectic vacation spots—keep Pagosa Springs firmly in mind.

History

In 1859 when Capt. J. N. Macomb, a surveyor for the U.S. government, arrived at Pagosa Springs, he described the location as "the most

Getting There

Pagosa Springs is situated along Hwy. 160 in the southwestern part of the state, 60 miles east of Durango. From Denver, Pagosa Springs is 265 miles southwest via Interstate 25 south to Walsenburg, then west on Hwy. 160 over Wolf Creek Pass.

Bathers relax in the mineral waters of Pagosa Hot Springs. Photo by Bruce Caughey.

beautiful hot springs in the world. There is scarcely a more beautiful place on the face of the earth." The Utes and Navajos probably agreed with these sentiments, as they sporadically fought with each other for control of the springs. The largest spring (Great Pagosa) measured 75 feet across, and even today its water emerges from the rocks at a scalding 153° F. More than one Indian brave attempted to show his courage by trying to swim across this seething cauldron; the results were grim.

But Native American possession of the springs was short-lived, as Anglo settlers, miners and lumberjacks began crowding into the area. In 1878 Fort Lewis was established to deal with the growing controversies between the settlers and the Utes. In 1891 the town was established and the Utes were pushed aside. Not long after, the Denver & Rio Grande Railroad arrived when it extended service to the nearby San Juan mining district. Ranches and lumber mills sprang up. At one time the Pagosa Springs area was the largest lumber-producing area in the state, but it didn't take long before much of the good timberland was destroyed by logging.

Although a number of spas were started, none really took hold. A travel brochure from the early 1900s pushed the town as "a wonderful place to recuperate." Perhaps the image of dozens of sickly people sitting in the hot springs kept vacationers away. Though the springs have never achieved the fame of those at resorts such as Glenwood Springs and Ouray, they are finally being recognized for their potential commercial success.

Outdoor Activities

Biking

MOUNTAIN BIKING

Located in the midst of rolling terrain cut by miles of jeep roads and single-track hiking trails, Pagosa Springs has become a popular mountain bike destination. The San Juan Forest Association publishes a booklet of recommended rides throughout the national forest (available at shops, bookstores and the **Pagosa Ranger District Office,** which can be found at the **corner of 2nd and Pagosa St.; 970-264-2268**).

To talk face-to-face with an expert on rides in the area, stop by **Juan's Mountain Sports.** In addition to free advice, you'll find quality rental bikes, maps and guided tours for all abilities. **155 Hot Springs Blvd., Pagosa Springs, CO 81147; 1-800-955-0273; 970-264-4730; www.juansmountainsports.com.**

Red Ryder Loop

Try this 16-mile loop ride beginning at the Red Ryder Rodeo Grounds at the east side of Pagosa Springs on Hwy. 84. Head north on Hwy. 84 before turning right on Hwy. 160, then continue 3 miles toward Wolf Creek Pass to the graveled Fawn Gulch Rd. Turn right and continue uphill for about a mile past two cattle guards. Just past the second cattle guard, turn right on an unmarked two-track dirt road. The road leads generally downhill through Willow Draw on a southerly course, with stunning views of the San Juan Mountains. You may need to ford Mill Creek. After crossing turn right onto the gravel Mill Creek Rd. and ride east (downhill!) into town.

Fishing

Echo Lake

"It's the most underrated lake in Colorado," says one Pagosa resident. The lake is well stocked with rainbow trout, largemouth bass and yellow perch. Many big ones have been taken from the deep, unassuming lake. Trout take lures, flies and the surefire worm; bass rise to surface lures; catfish respond to cut bait. Echo Lake is known to have good ice fishing for trout and bass. Located 4 miles south of Pagosa Springs on Hwy. 84.

Lake Capote

Good-sized rainbow and cutthroat trout are regularly pulled from this spring-fed lake on the Southern Ute Indian Reservation. Fishing the lake does not require a Colorado fishing license, but you must obtain a permit from the tribe (four-fish limit). Lake Capote is regularly stocked with catchable trout in the 12- to 14-inch range. At the lake there are boat rentals, a store and a campground with 25 sites (fee charged). Lake Capote is located 17 miles west of Pagosa Springs at the junction of Hwys. 160 and 151.

Navajo Reservoir

The northern third of Navajo Reservoir is located in Colorado, while the remainder of this large body of water lies in northern New Mexico. The reservoir, located within a state park, contains both warmwater and coldwater species. Millions of rainbow trout, kokanee salmon and largemouth bass have been stocked since the dam was dedicated in 1962. Pike, catfish, crappie and perch can also be caught. To fish the Colorado side of the reservoir, only a Colorado license is required. If you cross the border to fish, you'll need a New Mexico fishing license. **Navajo State Park** near Arboles has a visitor center, campground (71 sites, fee charged, flush toilets) and a large boat ramp/marina with rentals available. The reservoir can be reached by taking Hwy. 160 west from Pagosa Springs for 17 miles and then going south on Hwy. 151 for 35 miles.

Piedra River

With its headwaters in the Weminuche Wilderness and its lower waters on the Southern Ute Indian Reservation, the Piedra River has 40 miles of excellent trout water in between. The upper tributaries that flow into the Piedra are quite good for small cutthroat trout. Below these upper tributaries, in the stretch of water from First Fork down to Lower Piedra Campground (just north of Hwy. 160), only artificial flies or lures may be used. Try gray and brown nymphs below the surface or the current hatch on top. Travel upstream (north) from Hwy. 160, 22 miles west of Pagosa Springs. Turn right and follow Forest Rd. 622 just east of the river into a box canyon. The farther upstream you go, the better the fishing.

San Juan River

Ten miles north of Pagosa Springs, the East and West Forks of the San Juan River join. Working downriver from here you'll find many stretches of public water, loaded with small rainbow and brown trout. The river flows through Pagosa Springs; below town there are rumored to be larger trout. Eventually the San Juan flows into the Southern Ute Indian Reservation and Navajo Reservoir.

North of Pagosa Springs, the **West Fork of the San Juan** can be reached by driving a mile on a rough dirt road from West Fork Campground (see the Camping section) to Born's Lake. From there a trail follows the river for a dozen miles up into the Weminuche Wilderness. Stretches of the river flow through a canyon with deep pools and some hard-to-reach places. When the river calms down in July after runoff, the fishing really picks up. The **East Fork of the San Juan** flows out of **Crater Lake** (good fishing for cutthroat) and is paralleled for most of its 10-mile run by Forest Rd. 667. To reach Forest Rd. 667, take Hwy. 160 for 10 miles northeast of Pagosa Springs and turn right. The East Fork has mostly pan-sized rainbow. **Quartz Creek** flows into the East Fork about 8 miles upstream from East Fork Campground and is paralleled for 5 miles by a rather steep trail. The creek is known for fairly large cutthroat trout.

Golf

Fairfield Pagosa

West of Pagosa Springs at the plush Fairfield Pagosa Resort, you'll find the 18-hole **Pines** and nine-hole **Meadows** courses. At an elevation of 7,300 feet, both courses lie in a beautiful setting among the pines. Watch your hook: the Meadows has 6 holes bordering water. The golf course recently changed its policy and now is open to the public. The fees are reasonable considering the excellent course design, impeccable greens and wonderful views. Golf shop, lounge, carts and lessons. Fairfield Pagosa Resort is 3.5 miles west of Pagosa Springs **on Hwy. 160; 970-731-4755.**

Hiking and Backpacking

For information, maps and trail ideas in the Pagosa Springs area, stop in at the **Pagosa Ranger District Office** at the **corner of 2nd and Pagosa St., P.O. Box 310, Pagosa Springs, CO 81147; 970-264-2268.** They have wilderness maps available. If you are interested in getting more in-depth information about hiking possibilities in the Weminuche Wilderness Area, consider picking up a copy of the fine *Backpacking Guide to the Weminuche Wilderness Area,* by Dennis Gebhardt (Basin Reproduction Co., 1976), available at bookstores in Pagosa.

Fourmile Creek Falls

This easy 3-mile hike (one way) follows Fourmile Creek up between Pagosa Peak and Eagle Mountain, both over 12,000 feet. The falls, which plunge more than 150 feet, are on the left. From there you can take the trail up another 4 miles to Fourmile Lake. After about 2 miles there is a fork in the trail; the left fork continues to the lake and the right fork goes on to Turkey Creek Lake and over the Continental Divide into the Creede area. To reach Fourmile Creek Falls Trail from Pagosa Springs, head north out of town on Fourmile Rd. (Forest Rd. 645) and drive about 14 miles to the trailhead.

Poison Park Trail

Poison Park Trail, located near Williams Creek Reservoir, gets pretty heavy horse traffic, but it leads into the spectacular Weminuche Wilderness, where you can branch off in many directions. Talk to the folks at the Pagosa Ranger District Office for trail ideas via Poison Park Trail. The wilderness has few equals for extended backpacking trips. Towering peaks, crystal-clear mountain lakes, wildflowers and thick forests await. To reach Poison Park Trail from Pagosa Springs, head west 2.5 miles on Hwy. 160 and turn right on Piedra Rd. Drive 22 miles and turn right on Williams Creek Reservoir Rd. (Forest Rd. 640). Drive in a few miles and turn left on Forest Rd. 644 and follow it to the end. The Poison Park Trail heads off to the northwest.

Treasure Pass

Treasure Pass is located up near the summit of Wolf Creek Pass, but the trail can be tricky to locate—be sure to bring a map and compass.

Wildflowers and alpine views are incredible. To reach the trailhead from Pagosa Springs, head northeast on Hwy. 160 to the summit of Wolf Creek Pass. A trail heads south to the top of a bowl. From there Treasure Mountain is on the right. You need to head for the saddle on the left side of Treasure Mountain. From the saddle you can return to Hwy. 160 on Wolf Creek Rd. (Forest Rd. 725) or continue southwest on Treasure Mountain Trail for about 4 miles and take the right fork onto Windy Pass Trail, which continues for 3 miles to Hwy. 160 near Treasure Falls. If you choose this route, a car shuttle or hitchhiking is necessary unless you want to hike back up the pass to your car.

Horseback Riding
San Juan National Forest north of Pagosa Springs is beautiful country for horseback riding. There are a number of outfitters who can take you out for an hour-long trail ride or a 10-day pack trip.

Astraddle a Saddle
Eight miles west of Pagosa Springs, this outfit offers trail rides, wagon rides, barbecue dinners and even a Clydesdale-drawn sled in winter. **970-731-5076.**

Pat Parelli International Study Center
This school imparts natural riding techniques in a variety of formats (including getaway weekends and even a 30-day experience). Recently opened in a gorgeous setting near Pagosa. For program information call **970-731-9400.**

Wolf Creek Outfitters
Working out of the Bruce Spruce Ranch, Wolf Creek Outfitters provides mainly short rides on an hourly basis, but they also offer full-day and overnight pack trips. Located 15 miles northeast of Pagosa Springs **on Hwy. 160; 970-264-5332.**

River Floating

Piedra River
Increasing numbers of whitewater enthusiasts are discovering this river, which intersects Hwy. 160 between Durango and Pagosa Springs. The Piedra offers challenging, steep rapids as well as tame, meandering sections. The difficult 20-mile section of the Upper Piedra begins at the Piedra Rd. Bridge 10 miles north of Pagosa Springs on Piedra Rd. This stretch ends at Hwy. 160. This narrow, deep river runs through canyons with steep rock walls that can make portages impossible. The Upper Piedra, recommended for upper intermediate and expert kayakers, peaks early and should be run in May and June. The Lower Piedra, a 10-mile section, is navigable by rafters, kayakers and canoers of all abilities. It winds its way through cottonwood trees and ranches, dropping 20 feet per mile before reaching Navajo Reservoir.

San Juan River
The headwaters of the San Juan River are just northeast of Pagosa Springs. By the time the river gets to town, there is enough water during runoff for kayaking and raft trips. Inner-tubing is also possible, but the water is very cold. The San Juan River is not particularly difficult to float and is very relaxing.

Outfitters
Pagosa Rafting Outfitters—These folks offer trips down the San Juan, Piedra, Animas, Conejos and Rio Grande for a half day to three days. **970-731-8060; www.pagosasprings. riverrafting.com.**

Skiing

CROSS-COUNTRY SKIING AND SNOWSHOEING
Pagosa draws many cross-country skiers and snowshoers to its varied winter terrain. Just out of town, mellow, fairly level trails please novices. On the other end of the spectrum, backcountry skiers enjoy challenging, steep trails, excellent snow conditions and inspiring views—especially in the Wolf Creek Pass area. Rentals are available at the Pagosa Pines Touring Center (see the Groomed Trails write-up in this section). For maps and avalanche information, contact the

Pagosa Ranger District Office on the **corner of 2nd and Pagosa St.; 970-264-2268.** Also, for backcountry rentals and advice, check in at the **Ski and Bow Rack** at the east end of Pagosa Springs; **970-264-2370.**

Backcountry Trails

Chimney Rock—This fairly easy, 3-mile ski up to the Chimney Rock Archaeological Area can be an excellent place to see elk, deer, peregrine falcons and even a bald eagle or two. To reach the trailhead, drive 17 miles west from Pagosa Springs on Hwy. 160 to Hwy. 151 and turn left. Drive about 3.5 miles and look for the snowed-in road up to Chimney Rock on the right. It may be hard to find a place to park off the road. The snowed-in road winds its way up through pine and aspen, eventually terminating just below the summit of Chimney Rock. Make your way up to the summit from here. Please look at the Anasazi ruins but don't climb around on them or remove any artifacts. For more information about Chimney Rock see the Anasazi Ruins section.

Williams Creek Reservoir—This beautiful, fairly easy trail winds its way through pines and meadows with mountain views all around. To reach the trailhead from Pagosa Springs, drive 2.5 miles west on Hwy. 160 to Piedra Rd. and turn right. Follow Piedra Rd. for 22 miles to Williams Creek Reservoir Rd. and park the car. Begin skiing on the snowed-in road. You will pass Williams Creek Campground and then Teal Campground after about 2 miles. From here it's another 3 miles up to Cimarrona Campground.

Wolf Creek Road—This 4-mile trail is not for beginners. From the summit sign at the top of Wolf Creek Pass on Hwy. 160, look to the south. You should see an open bowl. Begin skiing toward its summit (11,600 feet) through the trees. Be sure to stay to the right, as the left side can be struck by avalanches. From the summit, traverse down, heading south and slightly west. On your left is the Continental Divide and to the right is Treasure Mountain. You need to get to the saddle between them. Once at the saddle, you are on Wolf Creek Rd. From here turn right

and ski 2.5 miles back to Hwy. 160, about 2 miles below the pass. Hitch a ride or leave one car here and one at the trailhead. Topographic maps are highly recommended.

Groomed Trails

Pagosa Pines Touring Center—Located on the golf course at the Fairfield Pagosa Resort west of town is a well-maintained 12-kilometer trail system. Perfect for beginners to intermediates, the trails offer clear views of the Continental Divide. The touring center rents and sells cross-country equipment. Fee charged. Open from Nov. 1 to the end of Mar. Head west on Hwy. 160 from Pagosa Springs for 3 miles and turn right onto Piñon Causeway just past the Fairfield Lodge. Continue on to Pines Club Pl. and look for the clubhouse on the right. **P.O. Box 2050, Pagosa Springs, CO 81147; 970-731-4141.**

DOWNHILL SKIING AND SNOWBOARDING

Snowcat Skiing

The expert terrain at the Water Fall and Alberta Creek areas at Wolf Creek Ski Area can be accessed only by snowcat. The deep powder is tough to beat, and only a few skiers at a time are lucky enough to be in the area. A snowcat will shuttle you out from the bottom of the sparse pine forest. Sign up at the top of the Treasure Triple Chairlift. Snowcat skiing is not included in the price of a lift ticket. Contact **Wolf Creek** at **P.O. Box 2800, Pagosa Springs, CO 81147; 1-800-SKI-WOLF; www.wolfcreek ski.com.**

Wolf Creek Ski Area

The newspaper snow reports provide ample proof: Wolf Creek has the highest average snowfall in the state. The ski area receives about 38 feet—or 456 inches—of snow in a normal year! There is no better place to learn to ski powder, because the mountain rarely gets "skied off." Besides great snow Wolf Creek still features one of the least-expensive lift tickets in the state. The base area sits at 10,600 feet, atop the

Continental Divide, and rises to 11,775 feet at the summit, and experts can find some extreme chutes and bowls. As one of the oldest in Colorado, Wolf Creek has had a rope tow in place since 1938. Expansion has been gradual and now the area features six lifts and 1,581 acres of terrain. Even though the vertical drop at Wolf Creek is nothing spectacular, the skiing is. And there is more than enough skiing for all abilities.

Wolf Creek is remote, with no resort development at the base—just a cafeteria, bar and rental/repair shop. If you want to stay in the area, the closest pillow is in Pagosa Springs or on the other side of the pass at South Fork. Wolf Creek is located about 20 miles northeast of Pagosa Springs on Hwy. 160. The kids' ski program is centered at the Wolf Pup Center between the Magic Carpet and Nova chairlift. For more information contact **P.O. Box 2800, Pagosa Springs, CO 81147; 1-800-SKI-WOLF; www.wolfcreekski.com.**

Seeing and Doing

Anasazi Ruins

Chimney Rock Archaeological Area

Chimney Rock, with its towering structure and mountain setting, ever so slightly resembles Machu Picchu, the lost city of the Incas. Occupied 1,000 years ago by as many as 2,000 Anasazi, Chimney Rock was supposedly the northernmost outpost of the Chaco Canyon Anasazi, who were mostly concentrated to the south in New Mexico. The Anasazi at Chimney Rock were farmers who lived in pueblo villages on ridges along the Piedra River and on the high mesa tops. The most impressive remnants of this ancient culture are the large pueblo ruins located just below the two rock pinnacles at the summit.

Chimney Rock Archaeological Area came into being in 1970 when the federal government set aside more than 3,000 acres under the watchful eye of the National Forest Service. The area is also home to the peregrine falcon, which is protected in its natural habitat. Other wildlife, including elk and deer, also thrive here. Visitors are allowed to enter the site only with guided tours. From May 1 to Sept. 15 (weather permitting) rangers lead four walking tours each day lasting about 2 hours each. The tour includes walks to two main sites and a Forest Service fire lookout. Tours begin at the Chimney Rock entrance, 17 miles west of Pagosa Springs on Hwy. 160 and about 3.5 miles south on Hwy. 151. Small fee for those over the age of 12. For more information about the tours contact **970-264-2268.**

Hot Springs

Spring Inn

In a prime location next to the San Juan River, in a mystical, made-to-look-natural setting, you can soak in 15 outdoor pools ranging from 95 to 111° F. The natural spring water has a high mineral content that many locals swear has certain healing qualities. The tubs interconnect, so that you can find one with just the right temperature, size and view. With lounge chairs and tables spread out on the deck, you could spend hours and hours here in the warmer months. You can soak for free as a guest of the Spring Inn (see the Where to Stay section) or pay for privileges. Located just across the bridge **on Hot Springs Blvd.; 1-800-225-0934; www.pagosasprings. net/springinn.**

Museums and Galleries

Fred Harmon Art Museum

This museum captures the lifework of one man from Pagosa Springs, Fred Harmon. Not everyone remembers his comic strip, "Red Ryder and Little Beaver," but at one time the strip appeared in more than 750 newspapers on three continents. Later, Red Ryder and his buddy Little Beaver were seen in films. Fred Harmon was a gifted artist who never had any formal training. In his later years, Harmon devoted his life to capturing the spirit of the West with oil on canvas. Small fee charged. Open Mon.–Sat. 10:30 A.M.–5 P.M., Sun. 12–4 P.M. Two miles west of Pagosa Springs **on Hwy. 160; 970-731-5785; www.harmonartmuseum.com.**

San Juan Historical Museum

Inside this false-fronted museum building, you'll be treated to an array of historical knickknacks. The many displays include items such as Angora goat chaps, worn saddles, a one-horse open sleigh and an old barber's chair; there is also a re-created blacksmith shop and a schoolroom (circa 1900). Since the historical society is located in the same building, chances are you will be able to talk with a knowledgeable person about the area. No fee, but donations are accepted. Open Memorial Day–Labor Day, Mon.–Sat. 10 A.M.–5 P.M. **1st St. and Pagosa St.; 970-264-4424.**

Nightlife

As we mentioned, Pagosa Springs certainly doesn't conjure up images of flashy nightlife. However, if you get the urge to drink a couple of cold ones, **Hogs Breath** features "foot-stompin'" country and rock music on weekends in a classier environment than the name implies. This place also has a solid menu for lunch and for dinner (ribs, Mexican, steaks) and a comfortable, long wooden bar. Open 11 A.M.–2 A.M. daily. **Just off of N. Pagosa Blvd.; 970-731-2626.**

Wildlife

Echo Mountain Alpacas

Get a glimpse of these camel relatives up close by taking a 1-hour tour Tues.–Sat. at 1 P.M. Visitor center with alpaca fleece, yarn and finished goods. **678 Dichoso St., Pagosa Springs, CO 81147;** call ahead to confirm tours at **970-731-2729.**

Rocky Mountain Wildlife Park

As the clock ticks toward the end of your vacation, the realization sets in—the only wildlife you've seen on this vacation has been roadkill. The Rocky Mountain Wildlife Park, essentially a zoo, might just be the place for you to actually get a look at some wildlife. Open daily 9 A.M.–6 P.M.; feedings usually take place at 4 P.M. in summer and 2 P.M. in winter. Located 5 miles south of Pagosa Springs **on Hwy. 84; 970-264-5546.**

Where to Stay

Accommodations

Echo Manor Inn—$$$ to $$$$

Echo Manor Inn, referred to as "the castle" by the locals, looks out of place in Pagosa Springs. It's so unusual that many people driving by actually slam on their brakes and stare at the extraordinary structure. Maureen Widmer has transformed the interior into an oddly juxtaposed collection of treasures. Though the sprawling inn is not for everyone (certainly not young children!), you can't help but be amazed at the European antiques, Waterford crystal, Delacroix paintings, porcelain dolls, stuffed animals and much more crammed into the nooks and crannies of the house. Take off your shoes (house rule), relax and take a meandering look around the vast collection; Maureen's stories create a better sense of why they have all this stuff displayed. In each of the eight superclean bedrooms, guests will find feminine decorative touches and handmade quilts. Extended families, groups and couples seeking some additional space may consider reserving one of the three Courtyard Suites—the main 1,400-square-foot suite can accommodate up to 16 people. Upon returning from Disneyland, the first owner began building additions on the original A-frame, inspired by Fantasyland. The sunny breakfast room offers gorgeous views to the Continental Divide. Be sure to make time for the hot tub on the back porch. Meet the fluffy house dog, Phoebe. No smoking inside. Located 3 miles south of Pagosa Springs on Hwy. 84 on the left side of the road across from Echo Lake. You can't miss it. **3366 Hwy. 84, Pagosa Springs, CO 81147; 970-264-5646; www.echomanor.com.**

Spring Inn—$$$ to $$$$

This comfortable 50-room motel has a huge advantage over the rest: guests have free unlimited use of the 15 outdoor mineral pools located next to the San Juan River (see the Hot Springs section). This ultimate amenity provides a relaxing end to a day exploring the area. Massage and exercise facility nearby. With the addition of a new building featuring larger suites, guests can enjoy a kitchenette and enough room for a family of four. Comfortably decorated and clean, this is a good choice conveniently located in town. Prices vary by season. Located just across the bridge on Hot Springs Blvd., **P.O. Box 1799, Pagosa Springs, CO 81147; 1-800-225-0934; 970-264-4168; www.pagosasprings.net/springinn.**

Davidson's Country Inn—$$$

Staying at Davidson's will provide a simple, country experience particularly well suited to families. The three-story log inn has 10 individually decorated rooms with country touches and a Christian motif that will appeal to many. Except for the Mountain Man Room (with a waterbed and a glass rifle case), the rooms are of the dainty sort. There's also a two-bedroom cabin on the property. Kids will love the solarium filled with pint-size toys; anyone can make use of the pool and ping-pong tables, horseshoes and table games. Box lunches for anyone heading out on a hike or a fishing trip. Full homemade breakfast included; no smoking. Located 2 miles northeast of Pagosa Springs on Hwy. 160. **P.O. Box 87, Pagosa Springs, CO 81147; 970-264-5863; www.coloradolodging/davidsons.com.**

Pack Saddle Ranch Bed and Breakfast—$$$

The Pack Saddle Ranch Bed and Breakfast ranks, appropriately, somewhere between a western dude ranch and a cozy B&B. Enjoy the warm environment created by wood walls and a stone hearth, with a jar of cookies always tempting guests. With 26 acres of land and horses, it's easy to get out and explore the surroundings. Kids love the sprawling lawn and games such as horseshoes, badminton and Frisbee. For breakfast dig into offerings such as pumpkin pancakes or quiche along with juice, coffee and fresh fruit. The Pack Saddle has two interior guest rooms, plus an exceptional late-1800s miner's cabin that was moved onto the property. A separate bunkhouse sleeps 10. No smoking inside; kids welcome. This family caters to your needs, whether you want to board your horses or have a nice dinner. Outdoor hot tub, too. **24910 Hwy. 160, Bayfield, CO 81122; 1-888-706-3482; 970-731-3282; www.packsaddleranch.com.**

Pagosa Lodge—$$$

Anyone visiting Pagosa Springs will inevitably hear about or see the sprawling Fairfield Resort just west of town. It functions primarily as a retirement community interspersed with time-share condominiums and sprawling executive-style homes, but the complex also features the 100-room Pagosa Lodge. The resort is particularly suited to families, as it provides a large number of activities. A fine 27-hole golf course, indoor swimming pool, small game room, tennis facilities and many other diversions make it tempting to never leave the grounds during your stay. If you like the self-enclosed, all-inclusive type of resort vacation, you'll like the Pagosa Lodge. Comfortable if not luxurious accommodations are complemented by a natural setting beside Piñon Lake and incredible views to the San Juans. Try the Great Divide restaurant on the premises. Located 3.5 miles west of Pagosa Springs on Hwy. 160. **P.O. Box 2050, Pagosa Springs, CO 81147; 1-800-523-7704; 970-731-4141; www.pagosalodge.com.**

Camping

Navajo State Park

Seventy-one campsites await you at Navajo Reservoir; fee charged; showers. From Pagosa Springs drive 17 miles west on Hwy. 160 and turn left on Hwy. 151. Proceed about 15 miles, turn left on County Rd. 982 and drive 2 miles. For reservations contact **1-877-444-6777** or **www.reserveamerica.com.**

Echo Manor, the fantasylike bed and breakfast outside Pagosa Springs. Photo by Bruce Caughey.

San Juan National Forest

Camping opportunities are numerous in the San Juan National Forest around Pagosa Springs. A fee is charged at each of the campgrounds listed below. For reservations contact **1-877-444-6777** or **www.reserveusa.com.**

Blanco River Campground (6 sites) is located 13 miles south of Pagosa Springs on Hwy. 84 and 2 miles east on Forest Rd. 656. **East Fork Campground, Wolf Creek Campground** and **West Fork Campground** (between 25 and 28 sites each) are located about 12 miles northeast of Pagosa Springs on Hwy. 160 heading toward Wolf Creek Pass. **Bridge Campground** (19 sites) is 17 miles northwest of Pagosa Springs on Piedra Rd. (Forest Rd. 631). Another 2.5 miles up the road brings you to **Williams Creek Campground** (66 sites). **Teal Campground** (16 sites) and **Cimarrona Campground** (21 sites) are a couple more miles up Piedra Rd. Heading west on Hwy. 160 from Pagosa Springs to the Piedra River and then north a mile on Forest Rd. 621 brings you to **Lower Piedra Campground** (17 sites; no drinking water).

Private Campgrounds

Bruce Spruce Ranch—Located 16 miles northeast of Pagosa Springs on Hwy. 160, this place offers cabins and a trailer park. Closed in winter. **P.O. Box 296, Pagosa Springs, CO 81147; 970-264-5374.**

Elk Meadows Campground—Located 5 miles east of town, Elk Meadows entices visitors by its alluring invitation, "Sleep to the sound of the ol' San Juan River!" We wondered, "What about the sound of the ol' Hwy. 160?" Open from June to Nov. **P.O. Box 238, Pagosa Springs, CO 81147; 970-264-5482.**

Pagosa Riverside—Open year-round and located in a nice setting just 1.5 miles east of Pagosa on Hwy. 160. **P.O. Box 268, Pagosa Springs, CO 81147; 970-264-5874.**

Where to Eat

The Greenhouse—$$ to $$$

With its beautiful views and ample portions, this restaurant is always worth a visit. The menu covers the gamut from moist barbecued ribs to Chateaubriand for two served at tableside. You won't go away hungry: every dinner starts with a relish tray, bread, soup and salad. The Greenhouse also features nightly dinner specials. Arrive early and enjoy a spectacular sunset from the enclosed patio area. Cocktails served in the dining room or in the separate bar area. Call for reservations. Open nightly 4–10 P.M. Located just north of Pagosa Springs on **Piedra Rd.; 970-731-2021.**

JJ's Upstream—$$ to $$$

Located right on the San Juan River, this restaurant has taken the town by storm with its creative menu and careful approach to the entire dining experience. In summer, the deck seating with lights on the water rushing by makes sense, but the inside is nice, too, with high ceilings crosshatched with wooden beams. The interior booths create a nice sense of intimacy for couples and small groups. Dinner entrées range from pan-fried trout to slow-cooked pork ribs and pistachio lamb chops. You'll find owner/chef James in the kitchen, and his creativity can be seen in the well-presented food. Full bar and small bar seating area. Open for lunch and dinner daily from 11:30 A.M.; Sun. brunch. Just east of downtown Pagosa Springs at **356 E. Hwy. 160; 970-264-9100.**

Old Miner's Steakhouse—$$ to $$$

The weathered barn-wood walls create the feeling of a mine shaft, and privacy is guaranteed by low lighting and tables that are tastefully partitioned from one another. Even the waiting room is something special. The food gets rave reviews.

Charbroiled steaks dominate the menu, but you'll also find seafood, pork and chicken dishes. The menu promises "Grub served with hot bread and your 'pickins' from the salad bar." No alcohol or smoking. Open for lunch Mon.–Fri. 11:30 A.M.–1:30 P.M., dinner Mon.–Sat. from 5:30 P.M., call for winter hours. Three and a half miles northeast of Pagosa Springs **on Hwy. 160; 970-264-5981.**

The Elkhorn Cafe—$

Though this slightly tattered restaurant might not be for everyone, we think you'll appreciate the good-but-basic Mexican food. Located downtown, this one-room Mexican restaurant opens early, serving both Mexican and American entrées. For breakfast try the huevos rancheros or the green chili cheese omelette. Lunch and dinner specialties include the Elkhorn stuffed sopapilla and the combination plate. Select from several varieties of Mexican and American beer. The Elkhorn opens Mon.–Sat. at 6 A.M., Sun. at 7 A.M., and closes at 9 P.M. daily. **438C Main St.; 970-264-2146.**

Services

Visitor Information

Pagosa Springs Area Chamber of Commerce—The Chamber occupies a spiffy facility next to the San Juan River. Stop by for information and advice on the entire area. Located across the bridge from the only stoplight in downtown Pagosa Springs. **P.O. Box 787, Pagosa Springs, CO 81147; 970-264-2360; www.pagosa-springs.com.**

Silverton

The ornate Victorian buildings in Silverton are a true reflection of the millions of dollars in gold and silver extracted from the surrounding mountains during the mining heyday of the late 1800s. This small, isolated town, designated a National Historic Landmark, appears as if it were frozen at the turn of the century thanks to the opulent, many-windowed Grand Imperial Hotel, the ostentatious gold-domed courthouse, false-fronted buildings, magnificent Victorian homes and small, restored miners' cabins. Silverton once played host to as many as 32 gambling halls, saloons and what were affectionately known as the Blair St. "sporting houses."

Sealed off in a high mountain valley at 9,318 feet, Silverton exists solely due to its proximity to the rich gold and silver mines in the San Juan Mountains. Now that mining no longer plays a part in the area economy, the town has dwindled to 500 hardy souls who live in this movie-set world, surrounded by four towering peaks (Kendall, Anvil, Boulder and Sultan). The two major auto routes into Silverton require crossing spectacular, sometimes treacherous Red Mountain or Molas Passes. In the midst of hundreds of square miles of the San Juan, Uncompahgre and Rio Grande National Forests, isolation and

Getting There

*Silverton is located 343 miles southwest of Denver. Those arriving from the southwest should take Hwy. 550 north from Durango for 49 miles over Coal Bank and Molas Passes. Many people who visit Silverton do so by riding the Durango & Silverton Narrow Gauge Railroad from Durango (see the Major Attractions section of the **Durango** chapter). From Ouray it is an unforgettable 22-mile drive over Red Mountain Pass on the Million Dollar Highway (see the Scenic Drives section of the **Ouray** chapter).*

supreme natural beauty make Silverton an excellent springboard for hiking, mountain biking and other backcountry trips. Perhaps the most popular pastime is jeeping to ghostly mining camps as well as to nearby towns such as Ouray, Telluride and Lake City.

In summer the historic Durango & Silverton Narrow Gauge Railroad pulls into Silverton several times a day, enabling its passengers to poke around town for a couple hours. The spawning of T-shirt, candle and curio shops attests to the forced speed of most purchases by the train crowd. Understandably the locals are glad to have the train travelers as a captive audience during high season, but it's a love-hate relationship. As one restaurant worker put it, "We've got four trains and two thousand people and two hours to get rid of them." Two hours is really not enough time to get acquainted with Silverton. If you arrive on the train, consider spending a night or two. The town and its residents take on a more genuine and relaxed personality after the last train of the day departs for the journey back to Durango. Besides, to get a complete picture of the area's rich history, you should do some further exploring.

With its rugged terrain and rocky soil, San Juan County does not contain even 1 acre of tillable land. Rhubarb is the one garden crop that survives a growing season rumored to last only 14 days—and not 14 in a row. Winter is unquestionably the longest season—it's a beautifully quiet time when Silverton goes into semi-hibernation and the town takes on a pristine feel. Although most of the town's shops, lodging establishments and restaurants close, just enough businesses remain open to keep things interesting. Many people don't realize that Silverton lies close to some of the best cross-country and downhill skiing anywhere; many others like to snowmobile. An added plus: the quick 24-mile trip south to Durango Mountain Resort (see the Durango chapter) rarely sees any winter traffic.

History

The commonly accepted legend is that Silverton got its name from early miners who bragged, "We may not have gold here, but we have silver by the ton." The first attempt at prospecting came in 1860 when Charles Baker led a party of men over the Continental Divide to the site of Silverton. Despite meager finds, he kept returning to the Upper Animas River vicinity (referred to at that time as Baker's Park). After a short stint in the Confederate army, Baker returned to the area in 1865, only to be killed by Ute Indians.

Once the exclusive domain of Utes, land including all of San Juan County was officially granted to them in an 1868 treaty. Gold fever set in a few years later and, despite the treaty, a steady stream of miners poured into the area. A short, bitter struggle for the land ensued, and the Utes, under the direction of Chief Ouray, soon surrendered 3 million acres of mineral-rich mountains to the U.S. government.

With the "Indian trouble" resolved, Silverton boomed in a hurry. Settlement began in earnest in 1875 when a crude mountain road connected Durango and Silverton. That same year a news-paper known today as *The Silverton Standard and The Miner* printed its first issue. Soon Otto Mears connected Silverton to his system of toll roads in the San Juans, including the route from Silverton to Ouray over the Million Dollar Highway. Since transportation of supplies, mail and tons of high-grade ore was crucial for the town's survival, everyone celebrated when the Denver & Rio Grande Railroad pulled into Silverton in 1882. Over the next decade Silverton's population grew to more than 2,000 residents and the young town became the terminus of three other railroads. From 1880 until the end of the century, nearby mines took minerals worth millions every year from the surrounding mountains.

Growing pains accompanied the early years. Vigilante groups took care of law enforcement and did fairly well at keeping the local peace. After a police force evolved, it was sometimes used as a tool for ethnic suppression. White merchants, tired of the proliferation of Chinese businesses, called on the police to "raid the Mongolians." In 1891 a Chinese Endeavor Society was formed to "convert the Chinese and to induce them to handle soiled linen and red checks with more Christian charity," according to an article in *The Silverton Standard*.

The silver crash in 1893 and, later, the nationwide financial panic of 1907 effectively stopped the growth of the town. Mining was still the bread-and-butter industry, but tourism and occasional moviemaking gradually entered the fray. However, since the Sunnyside Mine shut down operations in 1991 after 117 years of operation, the "mining town that wouldn't quit" now must rely primarily on tourism for sustenance. Today Silverton remains a snapshot of another era.

Major Attractions

Durango & Silverton Narrow Gauge Railroad

Riding the Durango & Silverton Narrow Gauge Railroad is the best way to relive the history of

Animas Forks, one of the San Juan Mountains' most scenic and historic backcountry "ghost" towns. Photo by Dean Winstanley.

the area. On its 45-mile route to Durango, the vintage steam-powered train passes through some of the most beautiful terrain imaginable. Package trips include one-way ridership with bus return, and layovers in Durango or Silverton. See the Major Attractions section of the **Durango** chapter for more information. Call **970-247-2733** in Durango for information and reservations; **www.durangotrain.com.**

Festivals and Events

Silverton Jubilee

last weekend in June This enjoyable, down-to-earth folk festival has really become a wonderful reason to make the journey to Silverton. Sit back and enjoy a weekend of bluegrass and other American folk as well as samplings of traditional sounds from various

nations. Free workshops on technique and instrument crafting are interesting as well. For reservations and information contact **Silverton Arts Council** at **P.O. Box 185, Silverton, CO 81433; 1-800-752-4494; www.silverton festivals.org.**

Gunfight

summer Each day at 5:30 P.M., the notorious corner of Blair St. and 12th St. is the stage for the reenactment of a Wild West gunfight. Running around shooting blanks at each other, the actors have as much fun as the visiting crowd.

Hardrockers Holidays

mid-Aug. Loud blaring rock music? No, it's not that kind of "hardrockers." Rather, this event draws gold and silver miners from across the state to prove their mettle (so to speak) in events ranging from machine drilling to mucking. It's fascinating to learn more about what goes on deep in the mines. **1-800-752-4494.**

Brass Band Festival

3rd weekend in Aug. Since 1981 musicians from around the world have converged on Silverton to make music at the Great Western Rocky Mountain Brass Band Festival. Melodic strains of John Philip Sousa's music fill the thin mountain air. Outdoor concerts held in Memorial Park are free (donation bucket) and open to the public. **1-800-752-4494.**

Outdoor Activities

Biking

MOUNTAIN BIKING

For the most part there are only two directions for mountain bikers to go from Silverton—up or down. Advanced riders will be put to the test on single tracks and jeep roads in the area. But casual riders will still enjoy the county roads in the area, such as Cunningham Gulch (see the Highland Mary Lakes Trail write-up in the Hiking and Backpacking section).

Trails

One lengthy and challenging loop tour from Silverton involves riding over **Ophir Pass** and on to Telluride. Spend the night there and cross over **Imogene Pass** to Ouray the next day. You might want to spend a day recovering and soaking in the hot springs pool before considering a route back to Silverton. Consult the Four-Wheel-Drive Trips section for information on this and other routes in the area.

Fishing

Fast currents and high mineral content prevent good angling in the streams near Silverton. The Durango area offers a number of fishing possibilities only a short distance away. High lakes near Silverton, however, are hopping with small but feisty trout. Just 6 miles south of Silverton on Hwy. 550 you'll find three popular lakes: **Molas, Little Molas** and **Andrews.** Another area abounding with small alpine lakes can be reached by taking Hwy. 550 northwest for 2 miles and then going 5 miles southwest on Forest Rd. 585. At South Mineral Campground a good trail follows the South Fork of Mineral Creek to **Ice Lake, Little Ice Lake, Fuller Lake** and **Island Lake.** The fishing for cutthroat is usually good. Since access is on foot, the fishing pressure remains minimal. You can also take Forest Rd. 815 (four-wheel drive) from the campground for about 2 miles to **Clear Lake,** also a good place to catch cutthroat trout.

Four-Wheel-Drive Trips

Silverton was the first mining area worked in the San Juan boom of the late 1800s. As a result, it's connected by a web of incredible jeep roads to other mining towns, including Lake City, Creede, Ouray and Telluride.

The Alpine Loop Backcountry Byway

Engineer and Cinnamon Passes, located northeast of Silverton, connect with both Ouray and Lake City. The historic sites of Animas Forks (about 12 miles from Silverton and accessible via passenger car), Mineral Point, Rose's Cabin, Capitol City and Sherman lie along the way. High alpine views of the surrounding peaks and basins attract a large number of jeepers each

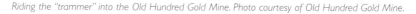

Riding the "trammer" into the Old Hundred Gold Mine. Photo courtesy of Old Hundred Gold Mine.

year. To reach these two roads from Silverton, head east from town on County Rd. 110 (eventually turning into County Rd. 2) along the Animas River. For more information see the Four-Wheel-Drive Trips section in the **Creede and Lake City** chapter.

Black Bear Pass

This is one of the most frightening and dangerous passes in the state and perhaps in the country. Still interested? Black Bear Pass Rd. begins near the summit of Red Mountain Pass (between Silverton and Ouray on Hwy. 550) and heads west up to the 12,840-foot summit of Black Bear Pass; visible to the north is the old Black Bear Mine. The road was built to deliver ore from the mine to Ouray and Silverton via the Million Dollar Highway (see the Scenic Drives section of the **Ouray** chapter). From the summit of Black Bear Pass, the knife-edged road gets rougher and the views get better. The switchbacks descending the mountain are so tight that they require three-point turns. Easing the clutch out without slipping forever over a rocky cliff requires total concentration—this is the point where passengers tend to get out and direct from the road. Below the worst of the switchbacks, the road arrives at the top of Bridal Veil Falls. This is a good place to stop, collect your thoughts and let your adrenaline level return to normal. From the falls drive down the remainder of the road past the Liberty Bell Mine and into Telluride. From Telluride return to Silverton via Imogene (or Ophir) Pass or drive around to Ridgway and Ouray on the highway.

Corkscrew Road/Cement Creek

See the Four-Wheel-Drive Trips section in the **Ouray** chapter.

Ophir Pass

As far as four-wheel-drive roads go, Ophir Pass can be a bit hairy in spots. From the 11,750-foot summit, enjoy great views of the peaks around Red Mountain Pass to the east. To the west a spectacular view awaits of Mt. Wilson, Wilson Peak and El Diente Peak as well as the deep Ophir Valley. A toll road was built by Otto Mears over Ophir Pass in 1881, connecting Telluride with Silverton.

To reach the pass road from Silverton, drive 5 miles north on Hwy. 550 toward Red Mountain Pass and turn left onto the Ophir Pass Rd. Follow the road as it drops down over a bridge before climbing about 4 miles to the pass. From the pass the road descends sharply on a shelf road that cuts across a massive rockslide. It eventually enters a forest of spruce, fir and aspen just above the town of Old Ophir. Before reaching Old Ophir, you may want to visit the old cemetery up the hill on the right. Old Ophir, 3.5 miles from the pass, was once a thriving mining town. Today people still live there, braving the monstrous avalanches that thunder down steep chutes and pummel the valley floor in winter. About 2.5 miles below Old Ophir you will arrive at the remains of New Ophir, established mainly as a stop for the Rio Grande Southern Railroad next to the Ophir Loop. From here you can return to Silverton by heading north on Hwy. 145 to Telluride and over Imogene Pass, or just continue northwest around to Ridgway, Ouray and over Red Mountain Pass.

Stony Pass

The road over Stony Pass was built as a crucial supply route between Silverton and settlements to the east in the San Luis Valley. This very rough road crosses over the Continental Divide, dropping into the Rio Grande drainage at the headwaters of the Rio Grande. It passes by Rio Grande Reservoir and eventually comes out on Hwy. 149 on the Silver Thread Scenic and Historic Byway between Creede and Lake City. To reach the road from Silverton, head east on Hwy. 110 to Howardsville. In its day Howardsville was quite a town; it was once the county seat, and the residents supported many saloons, a livery stable and a meat market. Turn right at Howardsville and up Cunningham Gulch (County Rd. 4). Drive about 2 miles and look for Stony Pass Rd. on the left. The pass summit is another 3 miles.

Rentals and Tours

San Juan Backcountry—These folks provide guided four-wheel-drive tours of varying lengths on the surrounding roads. **1119 Greene St., P.O. Box 707, Silverton, CO 81433; 1-800-4X4-TOUR; 970-387-5565; www. silver ton.org/sanjuanbackcountry.**

Silver Summit Jeep Rentals—Choose from a large selection of Jeep Cherokees and Wranglers. **640 Mineral St., P.O. Box 656, Silverton, CO 81433; 1-800-352-1637; 970-387-0240; www.silverton.org/silver summit.**

Triangle Service Station Jeep Rentals— Open-top Jeep Wranglers and four-door Jeep Cherokees rent for full or half days. **864 Greene St., Silverton, CO 81433; 1-877-522-2354; 970-387-9990; www.silverton. org/trianglejeep.**

Hiking and Backpacking

Silverton is surrounded by vast stretches of BLM land as well as three national forests: to the north the Uncompahgre, to the west the San Juan and to the east the Rio Grande. No matter which direction you choose, high mountains, raging rivers and ghost towns await, providing great hiking and backpacking. The area on the Continental Divide to the east of town provides excellent hiking on rolling hills once you're up on top. For hiking information try the **visitor center, P.O. Box 565, Silverton, CO 81433; 1-800-752-4494,** on the west end of town, but your best bet is to stop at the **San Juan National Forest headquarters** in Durango at **15 Burnette Ct., Durango, CO 81301; 970-247-4874; www.fs.fed.us/sanjuan.**

The Durango & Silverton Narrow Gauge Railroad offers a unique service to hikers by making stops along a remote section of the Animas River (see the Hiking and Backpacking section of the **Durango** chapter).

Continental Divide Trail

Silverton is an excellent jumping-off point for hikes in the Weminuche Wilderness Area. South of town the Weminuche straddles the San Juan and Rio Grande National Forests, providing access to miles of trails and dozens of rugged peaks. Many sheep graze here, so be sure to treat your water. The Continental Divide runs through the wilderness area. A trail along the divide opens up many possible trips. To reach the Continental Divide Trail, follow the directions to Highland Mary Lakes (see below). From Highland Mary Lakes, hike southeast and then south along the divide. About 4 miles south on the divide, a trail switchbacks down into the Elk Creek Valley to the right (west). There is a mine shack just down from the divide that makes a fine place to spend the night. If you follow the trail down Elk Creek for 9 miles, you'll end up in Elk Park, where you can catch the train back into Silverton.

Many hiking trails take off from the Continental Divide Trail (see the Hiking and Backpacking section of the **Creede and Lake City** chapter). Obtain some topographic maps (the Storm King Peak, Howardsville, Rio Grande Pyramid and Needle Mountains quadrangles) to devise your own route.

Highland Mary Lakes Trail

This fine day hike takes you into the upper reaches of Cunningham Gulch, a heavily mined area with many fascinating relics still in place. Near the trailhead the famous Highland Mary Mine can be seen high up on the right. The trail heads due south, climbing up along Cunningham Creek for 2.5 miles to the lakes. To reach the trailhead from Silverton, drive east for 5 miles to Howardsville, then turn right on Cunningham Gulch Rd. Proceed about 4.5 miles to the end of the road. Along the drive you will see many mine sites complete with aerial trams and rusty cables hanging hundreds of feet above the valley floor.

Ice Lake Trail

Beginning at South Mineral Creek Campground, this trail climbs west up the valley for 3 miles to Ice Lake. Along the way you will see a waterfall, ruins of old mining camp buildings and fields of wildflowers. Just north of Ice Lake is U. S. Grant Peak. A nice side trip is Island Lake, about a half-mile northeast of Ice Lake. Some people try to reach the island in the center of the lake by hopping over the ice floes that remain until late summer, but this is not recommended. To reach the trailhead from Silverton, drive 2 miles northwest on Hwy. 550 toward Ouray and turn left onto Forest Rd. 585. Proceed 5 miles, until just past the campground, and look for the trailhead climbing into the forest on the right.

Molas Pass Trail

Although only a 3-mile hike, this trail drops over a thousand feet on its way down to Elk Park, along the Animas River. It's very steep and you should have on a good pair of tightly laced boots to prevent blisters. The trail begins beside Molas Lake, about 5 miles south of Silverton on Hwy. 550. Park at the lake. As the trail drops through spruce and fir forests it provides intermittent views of the rocky west wall of the river valley. Stunning views southeast to the Grenadier Range in the Weminuche Wilderness Area highlight this hike. Once down to the river, the trail runs parallel to the water and then crosses a bridge. Just downriver from here along the train tracks is a fine camping area. Be sure to bring along a stove and leave no traces. The train stops here each morning on its way to Silverton if you want to catch a ride.

Ice Skating

Kendall Mountain Recreation Area

Head over to the Town Rink at Kendall Mountain on the south edge of town. Skating is free and rental skates are available at the town's visitor center.

Skiing

CROSS-COUNTRY SKIING AND SNOWSHOEING

No question about it, the Silverton area is a great place to strap on skinny skis and head into the backcountry. Numerous trails extend into nearby valleys and basins from town. The terrain can be quite difficult and avalanche-prone, but knowledgeable and experienced skiers have unlimited routes. Mountaineering skiing is an especially appropriate method here. Anyone wishing to learn more about avalanche safety should consider a three-day workshop at **Silverton Avalanche School.** The course is attended by ski-patrol members, highway workers and recreational skiers. For more information contact the **Silverton Chamber of Commerce; 1-800-752-4494; 970-387-5654; www. silverton.org.**

Backcountry Trails

Molas Pass—The top of Molas Pass (10,910 feet) allows for unimaginably beautiful views to the rocky spires of the Needles and to the summit of Snowdon Peak (13,077 feet). Many easy backcountry routes can be taken across rolling hills that were cleared by a forest fire over a century ago. Sparse groves of lodgepole pine and spruce are the result of a reforestation effort. Skiers wanting to sample a few short downhill runs can find many opportunities in deep, untracked powder. The avalanche danger is low in most of the area. A number of routes leave from points along Hwy. 550, near the top of the pass. Little Molas Lake is a bit over half a mile from the highway. The route begins on the west side of Hwy. 550, just before reaching the summit of Molas Pass, some 6 miles south of Silverton. Andrews Lake Rd. is an easy climb from the left side of the highway, about a mile after crossing Molas Pass. The snow-covered road reaches Andrews Lake in a half-mile; more challenging terrain lies beyond the lake. One route makes a steep ascent to the top of a knoll (11,290 feet) from the west end of Andrews Lake.

Ophir Pass—Intermediate and advanced skiers may want to ski up the eastern side of the pass (a 1,700-foot gain in elevation) and return on the same route from the 11,789-foot summit. A ski down the other side to the town of Ophir would be foolish because of high avalanche danger. As it is you'll be crossing several avalanche slide paths; the 9-mile route should not be attempted during avalanche warnings. To reach the Ophir Pass Rd. take Hwy. 550 northwest for 4.6 miles to a marked forest road (No. 679) on the left.

Red Mountain Pass—See the Where to Stay section for information on the St. Paul Lodge. Also see the Skiing section of the **Ouray** chapter.

South Mineral Creek—This easy half-day excursion involves skiing along a level forest road in a wind-protected valley. Oftentimes there are tracks leading the way. The area is fairly safe, but some avalanche danger exists. You should inquire about snow conditions before setting out. Head northwest on Hwy. 550 for 2 miles and park at the head of the valley. Forest Rd. 585 leads about 5 miles southwest, ending at South Mineral Campground.

Groomed Trails

Durango Mountain Resort Ski Touring Center—See the Skiing section of the **Durango** chapter.

DOWNHILL SKIING AND SNOWBOARDING

Durango Mountain Resort

This respected downhill resort is situated midway between Durango and Silverton. Staying in Silverton would be a pleasant alternative while skiing Durango Mountain. For more information see the Skiing section of the **Durango** chapter.

Kendall Mountain Recreation Area

Open Fri.–Sun., this small, local area provides a perfect place to teach the kids how to ski. With one small lift and only 150 vertical feet of drop, ticket prices are minimal. Sledding, cross-country skiing and ice skating available, too. Just south of town on 14th St.

Seeing and Doing

Hot Springs

The Ouray hot springs are only a short distance away, although the route can be treacherous

A long-abandoned mining cable car near Silverton. Photo by Dean Winstanley.

in winter. See the **Ouray** chapter for more information.

Museums

Old Hundred Gold Mine Tour

Pull on a yellow rain slicker (you'll need it) and a white hard hat before lurching into a damp mining tunnel. A railcar takes you 1,500 feet underground into an actual 1960s mining operation. The continuously dripping water gives you a sense of the miserable working conditions. Our guide explained a variety of mining techniques and pointed out ore veins as we walked inside the dimly lit tunnel. The entrance fee seemed a bit much for the hour-long tour—indeed, our guide commented, "The only thing we mine now is tourists." Located 5 miles east of Silverton on Hwy. 110 (turn right at Howardsville on City Rd. 4 and follow the signs). Open daily from early May to late Oct. **P.O. Box 430, Silverton, CO 81433; 1-800-872-3009; 970-387-5444; www.minetour.com.**

San Juan County Historical Museum

Located in the old San Juan County Jail, this museum provides historical information and interesting relics from surrounding mining camps. The jail operated from 1902 to 1931, serving as home to the sheriff and his family (one of the sheriff's babies was born in the women's cell). Open 9 A.M.–5 P.M. daily from Memorial Day through mid-Oct. Small fee. Located next to the courthouse on **1559 Greene St.; 970-387-5838.**

Nightlife

A Theatre Group

This community-based theater group has a loyal following. Climb the stairs to the historic Miners Union Theatre (above the old Miner's Union Hall) and, for a reasonable admission fee, you too can catch a live performance. Thanks to an intimate and historic setting you almost feel a part of the amateur action on stage. Though evening performances are the norm, call ahead

for summer and off-season schedules. Curtain time is 7 P.M. **1069 Greene St., Silverton, CO 81433; 1-800-752-4494; 970-387-5337.**

Scenic Drives

Because Silverton is locked in a high valley, you can't drive anywhere from the town without encountering heart-stopping views. The **Million Dollar Highway** is a beautiful and historically fascinating drive (see the Scenic Drives section of the **Ouray** chapter). The outstanding trip along the **San Juan Skyway** can be taken in part or whole from Silverton (see the Scenic Drives section of the **Durango** chapter).

Where to Stay

Accommodations

St. Paul Lodge—$$$$

From the summit of Red Mountain Pass, a cross-country ski trail works its way up to the rustic confines of the St. Paul Lodge at 11,400 feet. Since 1974 Chris and Donna George have been housing groups of skiers in an old tipple house, originally built in the 1880s over the main shaft of the St. Paul Mine, where the ore was cleaned and loaded into carts. Using an eclectic hodge-podge of recycled materials, including lumber from abandoned mine buildings and solid oak paneling from a Denver church, the couple has created a warm environment for up to 22 skiers at a time. The lodge is not for everyone: "I don't need slick California skiers that want to run 20 kilometers of track and drink martinis," George said with a wry smile. For the most part it's rough and basic. Small dormitory rooms and an indoor outhouse can turn off some people, but the lodge also features a redwood sauna and hot showers. Enjoy kerosene light, woodstove heat and unique access to some of the best high alpine skiing anywhere.

The rustic lodge provides ski touring equipment as well as tours guided by Chris, an avalanche expert and former Outward Bound instructor. Chris swears he can "teach you to telemark in 20 minutes." This ski technique is extremely useful for the terrain and conditions in U.S. Basin and on McMillan Peak. Choose from gentle routes as well as steep, wide-open slopes. A stay at the lodge includes three meals a day; Chris is a trained chef. Lodge open in winter only; weekly rental of the comfortable **"Pioneer" cabin ($$$)**, which sleeps six, is available in summer. **P.O. Box 463, Silverton, CO 81433; 970-387-5494; 970-387-5367.**

Grand Imperial Hotel—$$$ to $$$$

Built in 1882, the Grand Imperial is a fine example of Victorian architecture, and the rooms are comfortable if not grand. All rooms facing the outside offer excellent views. For a special occasion reserve one of the large, classy corner suites with arching windows. The floral print wallpaper, antique reproductions and gravity flush toilets really send you back to the hotel's heyday. Though the hotel is not yet up to the standards of its historic cousins in downtown Durango, it's worth considering. Look around the gorgeous lobby, with its fine leather couches, pressed-tin ceiling and portrait of the town sweetheart, Lillian Russell, over the piano. Adjacent to the lobby is the **Gold King Dining Room ($ to $$$)**, a good value for breakfast, lunch and dinner, and the **Hub Saloon** featuring a stunning back bar made of heavy cherry wood columns with intricate carvings and even a bullet hole. Open year-round. **1219 Greene St., P.O. Box 67, Silverton, CO 81433; 970-387-5527.**

The Wyman Hotel and Inn—$$$ to $$$$

The rooms with their private baths, quilt-covered queen-size beds and other creature comforts at this renovated and sizable historic building are a treat after a hard day of play. Each of the 17 tastefully decorated rooms come equipped with a VCR, and you may choose a couple of movies each night from a video library. Breakfast and afternoon tea included. **1371 Greene St., P.O. Box 780, Silverton, CO 81433; 1-800-609-7845; 970-387-5372; www.thewyman.com.**

Villa Dallavale Historic Inn—$$$

Located across from the train station, this comfortable bed and breakfast inn originally served as a rooming house and then a grocery store for 47 years. Innkeeper Gerald Swanson was the store's butcher, as a matter of fact. Born and raised here, Gerald serves as a terrific source for history and things to do in the area. After an extensive renovation, the seven comfortable bedrooms feature private baths, TVs and large beds. Some antiques and historic family photos grace each room. Though the walls are a bit thin, most everything else makes for a pleasant stay. Full breakfast is included. **1257 Blair St., Silverton, CO 81433; 970-387-5555.**

Teller House Hotel—$$

This inexpensive and enjoyable lodging alternative is located atop the Front Porch Flower Shop. Once a boardinghouse for hardrock miners, the Teller House still has a lot of character. Full breakfast at the bakery is included in the price of your room. The nine fairly simple rooms (four with private bath) are situated around the outside of the upper floor, with windows facing both inside to a common area and out. Breakfast served in the Kendall Tea Room behind the flower shop downstairs. **1250 Greene St., Silverton, CO 81433; 1-800-342-4338; 970-387-5423.**

The Silverton Hostel—$

As the name may indicate, this is the cheapest place to stay in the area. Located along historic Blair St. near the train station, the hostel offers basic dorm rooms or private rooms, kitchen facilities and a common area to meet other guests. No frills but a decent, low-cost option. **1025 Blair St., Silverton, CO 81433; 1-888-276-0088; 970-387-0155.**

Camping

One of the most beautiful areas to camp near Silverton is **South Mineral Campground** (23 sites, fee charged). To get there head northwest on Hwy. 550 for 2 miles and then southwest on Forest Rd. 585 for 5 miles. To reach **Sig Creek Campground** (9 sites, fee charged) take Hwy. 550 for 21 miles southwest of Silverton and then proceed 6 miles west on Forest Rd. 578.

Private Campground

Silverton Lakes Campground—Just northeast of town, not far from the Animas River, is this full-service campground. Hookups, groceries, laundry and hot showers are available. **P.O. Box 126, Silverton, CO 81433; 970-387-5721.**

Where to Eat

Handlebars—$$ to $$$

For ambience and consistently good food, Handlebars is our choice for best restaurant in town. Step into this cozy restaurant and saloon and warm up by the fireplace, which is built in a mining ore cart. Gaze at the game trophies and endless memorabilia covering the walls. The lunch and dinner entrée choices are plentiful, but highlights are the homemade soups, salads, hearty sandwiches and excellent ribs and steaks. Down-home western fare dominates the menu, including Rocky Mountain oysters for the adventuresome. Open daily May–Oct. 31, 10:30 A.M.– 9 P.M.; bar stays open until midnight. **117 E. 13th St.; 970-387-5395.**

The Pickle Barrel—$ to $$$

Built in 1880 as the Sherwin and Houghton General Store, this historic brick building has been a favorite local hangout since 1971. Run by Fritz Klinke and Loren Lew, the Pickle Barrel is a great spot for lunch, featuring deli sandwiches and burgers. More elaborate dinners include a creative selection of dishes from a menu that changes weekly. Full bar with microbrews on tap. Open daily Apr.–Oct., 11 A.M.–3 P.M. Tues.–Wed. for lunch and 11 A.M.–9 P.M. Thurs.–Mon. for lunch and dinner. **1304 Greene St.; 970-387-5713.**

Avalanche Coffee House—$

If you want to catch up on the town gossip or just hunker down any time of the year with a steaming cup of coffee, head over to the Avalanche Coffee House. Located along historic Blair St., this cozy little cafe serves a wide variety of coffee drinks along with tasty homemade soups, pastries, breads and bagel sandwiches. Be sure to check out the wonderful local art on the walls, as well as the racks of coffee mugs arranged for local patrons (complete with their names). A welcome addition to Silverton's dining scene. Open daily 7:30 A.M.–4 P.M. in winter; until 5 P.M. in summer. **1067 Blair St.; 970-387-JAVA.**

Services

Visitor Information

Silverton Chamber of Commerce—Stop by the chamber headquarters for some advice on how to spend your time in Silverton. Be sure to ask for a historical walking tour map. Open year-round. **P.O. Box 565, Silverton, CO 81433; 1-800-752-4494; 970-387-5654; www. silverton.org.**

The Silverton Standard and The Miner— Since 1875 this local newspaper has been telling people what's happening in Silverton. Pick up a copy at the newspaper office, and also check out their excellent selection of books and magazines. Ask to see their Hoe Cylinder Press, which dates back to 1830. **1257 Greene St., P.O. Box 8, Silverton, CO 81433; 970-387-5477.**

Telluride

Whether you are looking for a plush ski vacation and nights out at fine restaurants or a week of backpacking in the high mountains of the San Juans, we highly recommend Telluride. Squeezed into a box canyon along the San Miguel River, Telluride could easily be the most beautiful spot in Colorado. Surrounding this growing Victorian town of more than 1,600 full-time residents are lofty, jagged peaks—many approaching 14,000 feet in elevation.

The mining legacy of Telluride is one of great wealth and prosperity—$60 million in gold and silver was mined in the first 30 years alone. But slowed by steadily declining profits in the 1900s, the mines began closing one by one. Today abandoned mine shafts and buildings lie scattered throughout the nearby mountains, and Telluride's focus has completely shifted to year-round tourism, especially world-class skiing.

Some locals claim that Telluride's skiing really started back in the mining days. On payday at the Tomboy Mine, located 3,000 feet above Telluride, the Finns and the Swedes would beat their coworkers to the brothels in town by

Getting There

*The shortest (327 miles) route from Denver to Telluride is via Hwy. 285 to Poncha Springs; then drive west on Hwy. 50 to Montrose, south on Hwy. 550 to Ridgway, west on Hwy. 62 to Placerville and southeast on Hwy. 145 to Telluride. Several routes via Interstate 70 take about the same amount of time. The **Telluride Regional Airport,** 5 miles west of town, is serviced year-round, as is **Montrose County Airport** 68 miles away. Many flights into Telluride arrive via Denver and Phoenix with connections worldwide; winter nonstop flights arrive from many major cities. Rental cars and taxi transport are available from the airport into town.*

skiing down from the site. Today skiers take advantage of 1,050 pristine acres of slopes at Telluride Ski Area—including the Plunge, the longest, steepest mogul run in the United States.

During summer the surrounding Uncompahgre National Forest offers some of the state's best and most beautiful opportunities for exploring nature. Supreme hiking and mountain biking trails and hundreds of miles of bone-jarring jeep roads justify spending an extended period of time here. An additional summer drawing card is the town's numerous festivals. The excellent Bluegrass, Jazz, Wild Mushroom, Film and Hang Gliding Festivals, among others, attract many people who come for the event and leave infatuated with the area.

Telluride is very concerned about its future. Because of its obvious appeal, debates rage on between developers and those wanting slow growth. You'll hear talk about million-dollar real estate deals and movie stars—indeed, most workers have been forced to find more affordable digs down-valley in places like Sawpit and Placerville. Nearly everyone who lives in the area, from an unemployed miner to a commuting worker to John Naisbitt, visionary author, has his or her own vision of the town's future.

Some of the pressure to build in historic Telluride has been siphoned off by the rapid pace of development 5 miles away at the sleek Mountain Village. Already the site of many high-end lodges, condos and homes, the ski-in/ski-out Mountain Village also features an 18-hole championship golf course and a gondola connection to town. (For information about this free, 13-minute gondola trip, see the Seeing and Doing section.)

In the meantime, Telluride somehow retains its very authentic Victorian charm. Downtown Telluride has been declared a National Historic District, and any building plans in that area are closely scrutinized by an architectural review committee. Though land values have risen out of the realm of ordinary incomes and people are quick to make comparisons to Aspen, Telluride has managed to avoid becoming another mega-resort.

History

A handful of eager prospectors first climbed into Telluride from over the towering mountains to the east in 1875. Their efforts were rewarded when they found rich deposits of gold and silver, causing a rush to the area. Successful mines include the Liberty Bell, the Union, the Tomboy, the Pandora and the Gold King.

In 1876 J. B. Ingram discovered through careful research that two adjacent mines had overextended their claims by 500 feet. He filed a claim and set up shop between the two mines, naming his the Smuggler. The Smuggler was sitting on a rich silver vein. Ingram went on to expand his operation, which eventually became one of the richest mines in the state.

Isolation plagued Telluride through the 1880s. The high cost of transporting ore to faraway smelters and mills prevented an all-out mining boom. A solution appeared in 1890 when Otto Mears's amazing pathfinding skills brought the Rio Grande Southern Railroad into town, connecting the mines with the outside world. The boom was interrupted briefly in 1893 when the silver market crashed. But rich gold strikes soon brought the town back to life.

From the beginning Telluride had a reputation as a hell-raising mining town, with an infamous gambling and red-light district on Pacific Ave. By 1891 the 4,000 residents supported 26 saloons and 12 bordellos. Supposedly this immoral section of town and the harsh natural conditions prompted warnings of "to-hell-u-ride" to people bound for this area. Decent people turned a blind eye to the decadence; bordellos were fined $250 weekly, which is said to have almost single-handedly financed the town government!

During the 1890s Telluride prospered. In 1895 the New Sheridan Hotel was built, rivaling the finest hotels in Denver with its accommodations and gourmet dining. But at the turn of the century, the boom days began to wane. Decreasing profits from mining, coupled with labor problems, brought the mining industry in Telluride to its knees, never to fully recover. Most of the mines as well as the Bank of Telluride had closed by 1930, and the population dwindled to 500.

Telluride was saved from becoming a complete ghost town when the Idarado Mining Company bought up the existing mines in the area in 1953 and connected all of the mines with a 350-mile network of tunnels. One tunnel extends 5 miles through the mountains to a point just south of Ouray. Idarado mined millions of dollars worth of copper, lead, zinc, silver and gold before closing in 1978.

During the slow decline of mining in the area, the idea of turning Telluride into a ski resort was kicked around by a few locals. In 1945 a rope tow was constructed at Town Park, but it operated for only two years. It was brought back to life in 1958, when $5 season passes were offered. But in 1971 when ground was broken for the Telluride Ski Area, no one could have predicted the success that would follow. Continued prosperous times are on the horizon for a town that *The Denver Post* once called "doomed."

Festivals and Events

Every summer a diverse procession of festivals attracts people to the area—many are yearly events with loyal followings. For more information and a complete schedule of events, contact **Telluride Visitor Services: 1-888-783-0257; www.gotelluride.org.**

Telluride Bluegrass Festival

mid-June   *Esquire* magazine proclaimed that "Telluride has established itself as the country's premier progressive bluegrass event," and after experiencing a few of them we have to agree. Each summer the town gears up for its biggest event (10,000 visitors at last count), which runs Thurs. through Sun. Since 1973 the country's best bluegrass and mainstream musicians have been performing at the festival. Amateur mandolin, banjo, flat-picking guitar and band contests begin on Wed. and run through Fri. morning. The main acts play Thurs.–Sun. night.

All concerts take place at Town Park. On the weekend some of the musicians play until the wee hours of the morning at local bars and even at some area campgrounds. Workshops for those interested in everything from banjo picking to clogging are offered. **1-800-624-2422; www.bluegrass.com.**

Telluride Jazz Celebration

early Aug.   The outdoor stage in Telluride's Town Park provides a 360-degree view of the scenery—a perfect accompaniment to a weekend of cool jazz. Since 1976 the festival has attracted both well-known and somewhat obscure musicians in mostly mainstream, traditional jazz styles. After the sun sets, the music comes indoors to local bars and area theaters. **1-888-783-0257; www.gotelluride.org.**

Telluride Hang Gliding Festival

late Aug.   Just as the chill of fall enters the high country, professional hang gliders send more chills through the crowd by performing high-altitude acrobatics. There are also competitions between some of the top-ranked hang gliders in the world. It's a quiet and colorful time of year to come to Telluride for this incredible spectator event. **1-888-783-0257; www.gotelluride.org.**

Telluride Film Festival

early Sept.   Whether you are a filmmaker or a film lover, this late-summer event will appeal to your cinematic tastes. Since 1974 the film festival has been attracting attention as a lesser-known American counterpart to Cannes. Free showings of premieres and foreign films take place nightly in an outdoor theater. Animation and innovation are topics at daily seminars, and private showings around town are hot tickets. **603-433-9202; www.telluridefilmfestival.com.**

Outdoor Activities

Biking

MOUNTAIN BIKING

From Telluride you can leave town on a mountain bike and enter another dimension in about 5 minutes—a dimension without cars, houses and people. The terrain is perfect for riders of all abilities and there is even a hut-to-hut system available for an extended ride from Telluride to Moab, Utah (see San Juan Hut Systems in this section).

Bear Creek Trail

A quick morning or evening ride up to Bear Creek Falls can be taken right out of town. See the Hiking and Backpacking section for more information.

Bikepath Trail

Bikers, joggers and in-line skaters flock to this paved trail running parallel to Hwy. 145 between the west end of town and Society Turn, about 2.5 miles down-valley. It's a great way to acclimate and get out on the road without fighting auto traffic. Arguably an even better option is to ride along the unpaved, "crusher fine" **San**

An elated attendee at the Telluride Bluegrass Festival. Photo by Dean Winstanley.

Miguel River Trail that follows the river through town from Town Park, also ending at Society Turn.

Ophir Pass

Known to many as a great four-wheel-drive shortcut from Telluride to Silverton, the Ophir Pass road also offers an interesting road for mountain bikes. But be prepared for riding on a sometimes steep, scree-covered road. See the Four-Wheel-Drive Trips section in the **Silverton** chapter for more information.

San Juan Hut Systems

This tour-de-force mountain bike trek has proven to be the ultimate adventure for those fit enough to appreciate seven days of riding through beautifully diverse backcountry. The 206-mile ride starts in the high mountain terrain near Telluride, gradually working down to the Uncompahgre Plateau and eventually into Utah's

canyon country, ending at Moab. And spending each night in a provisioned hut takes a weighty burden off your mountain bike.

Advanced mountain bikers can leave the main route and take single tracks over more difficult terrain. But the route is geared for intermediate riders as well. The huts are located far enough apart for a good 5 hours of riding each day—they're basic, yet have everything you'll need, including ample food, wool blankets, a sleeping pad and woodstoves. You might also think about doing a two- or three-day stage of the route. **San Juan Hut Systems, Box 1663, Telluride, CO 81435; 970-728-6935; www.sanjuan huts.com.**

Rentals, Tours and Trail Information

Paragon Ski and Sport—213 W. Colorado Ave.; 970-728-4525. Also at **Mountain Village** at **970-728-0992.**

Telluride Sports—150 W. Colorado Ave.; 1-800-828-7547; 970-728-4477; www.tellu ridesports.com.

Fishing

The fishing around Telluride can be good, and when the conditions are right it can get downright hot. You may want to take a guided trip or enroll in fly-fishing school. For information contact **Telluride Outside, P.O. Box 685, Telluride, CO 81435; 1-800-831-6230; 970-728-3895; www.tellurideoutside.com.** Another fine option for guided fly-fishing adventures and schools is the Orvis-endorsed **Telluride Fly Fishing and Rafting Expeditions at 970-728-4477 ext. 107.** Here are a few additional ideas to check out on your own:

Dolores River

This Gold Medal river can be one of the state's best, depending on the release levels from McPhee Reservoir. See the Fishing section of the **Cortez** chapter.

Kids' Fishing Pond

Kids 12 and under can fish in the pond at the Town Park located at the east end of town. They

Mountain biking with Mount Wilson in the background. Photo by Doug Berry, courtesy of Telluride Visitors Services.

love it and can usually catch trout on whatever bait they use.

San Miguel River

This fast-moving river yields trout up to about 12 inches. While catching trout in the San Miguel below Telluride, remember that the water has become mineralized from all of the mining operations: we recommend that you catch and release all fish. After heavy summer rains, the river becomes a useless, muddy flow; when the water is clear, try fishing in the morning and evening with small, brightly colored dry flies. Fishing with black caddis and Hare's Ear nymphs is also recommended. The San Miguel River below the town of Norwood offers poor fishing.

Woods Lake

Nestled at the base of three 14,000-foot mountains (Mt. Wilson, El Diente Peak and Wilson Peak), Woods Lake enjoys a spectacular location away from major roads. Only artificial flies and lures are permitted. The lake is well stocked and an occasional native brook or cutthroat can be caught. To get to Woods Lake take Hwy. 145 northwest for 10 miles (just beyond the town of Sawpit). Turn left and head south on Fall Creek Rd. (Forest Rd. 618), which winds its way to Woods Lake in 9 miles.

Four-Wheel-Drive Trips

Those with courage (in some cases, stupidity) and a reliable four-wheel-drive vehicle can navigate the historic mining roads around Telluride.

Black Bear Pass

Black Bear Pass is etched into the west side of Ingram Peak at the east end of the valley above Telluride. Visible from town, the road zigzags up what seems to be a vertical wall. Locals strongly urge that only experienced drivers attempt this dangerous road. Black Bear is a one-way road that begins near the summit of Red Mountain Pass and heads west, eventually ending in Telluride. See the Four-Wheel-Drive Trips section of the **Silverton** chapter.

Imogene Pass

Built in the 1870s to transport ore from the Tomboy Mine over to Ouray, Imogene Pass is a tough route. The view from the summit makes the drive worthwhile, except for vertigo-prone passengers. From the north end of Oak St. in Telluride, turn right onto the pass road (Forest Rd. 869). As the road climbs, it offers a great view of Telluride and the east end of the valley, including Ingram Falls, Black Bear Pass Rd. and Bridal Veil Falls.

Five miles up the road you'll arrive at the Tomboy Mine site. When the Tomboy was in full operation during the late 1890s, hundreds of men living at the mine camp enjoyed such unusual luxuries as tennis courts, a bowling alley and a YMCA. Today the Tomboy is nothing but ruins. Above the mine it's another 1.5 miles of tough switchbacks to the summit at 13,509 feet. During labor disputes early this century, National Guardsmen erected Fort Peabody on the summit of Imogene Pass and manned it through the winter of 1903–1904.

On the other (east) side of the pass, the road winds down a steep section into Imogene Basin. From the pass it's about 11 miles to Ouray. For more information about the Ouray side of the pass, see the Four-Wheel-Drive Trips section in the **Ouray** chapter. From Ouray you can return to Telluride via Ridgway and Dallas Divide or over another jeep road such as Ophir Pass.

Ophir Pass

This exciting four-wheel-drive road can be reached just south of Telluride. Head south on Hwy. 145 for about 10 miles and turn left to the pass on Forest Rd. 630. The road is very narrow and vehicles traveling uphill have the right-of-way. For more information about the pass from

the Silverton side see the Four-Wheel-Drive Trips section in the **Silverton** chapter.

Tours and Rentals

Telluride Outside—Take a full-day or half-day trip on some of the wild roads near Telluride. Trips depart daily in the summer. Rentals are also available for half or full days. **301 Society Dr., P.O. Box 685, Telluride, CO 81435; 1-800-831-6230; 970-728-3895; www. tellurideoutside.com.**

Golf

Telluride Golf Club

This 6,733-yard, par 71 championship course at the Mountain Village will challenge your senses and your patience (it's still a bit rough). The 18-hole course winds amid massive homes while offering stop-in-your-tracks views to the surrounding peaks. Watch out for deer and elk on the fairways. The signature on this course may be the unique high tee on the par-3 17th hole. Your ball will fly 15 percent farther at this elevation (close to 10,000 feet) than sea level, so remember to club down. Open to the public with the exception of certain weekend tee times. Located in **Mountain Village** at **970-728-6366; www. telski.com.**

Hiking and Backpacking

It's difficult not to use superlatives when talking about hiking and backpacking opportunities in the Telluride area. Just out of town, beautiful forests and high alpine basins covered with wildflowers await. But by all means, stay out of the mine tunnels—they can be death traps!

West of Telluride, **Lizard Head Wilderness Area** in Uncompahgre National Forest straddles the San Miguel Mountains. It's characterized by many glacial cirque lakes, roaring streams, spruce and fir forests and several 14,000-foot peaks.

The **Telluride Visitors Center**, at **700 W. Colorado Ave.**, has very good information concerning trails in the area. Topographic maps, rental equipment and information can be found at **Telluride Sports, 150 W. Colorado Ave.; 1-800-828-7547; 970-728-4477; www.telluridesports.com.**

The nearest Forest Service office for the Telluride area is located 33 miles northwest on Hwy. 145: **Norwood Ranger District Office, 1760 Grand Ave., P.O. Box 388, Norwood, CO 81423; 970-327-4261.** Consider picking up a copy of the helpful and highly readable *Telluride Hiking Guide,* by Susan Kees. It offers dozens of hiking ideas throughout the Telluride area.

Bear Creek Trail

This beautiful 2-mile hike starts in town and leads south, uphill to an impressive waterfall. The trail through this deep valley offers great views of the surrounding craggy peaks. At one point it crosses over an avalanche slide area, showing vividly why cross-country skiers avoid the valley in winter. The trailhead begins at the south end of Pine St.

Bridal Veil Falls

This short, steep hike can catch the unacclimated by surprise. If you are new to the high altitude, take it slow and easy. From Telluride drive up to the end of the box canyon and begin hiking up the jeep road. Views of Ingram Falls on the left and Bridal Veil Falls—Colorado's longest at 365 feet—on the right make this a highly recommended 1-mile hike. At the top of the falls, hanging over the impressive cliff, is the restored old Smuggler-Union hydroelectric plant. This National Historic Landmark, built in 1904, is a private residence; though the views back down the valley to Telluride are stunning, please stay clear of the building.

Hope Lake Trail

From the Hope Lake trailhead, this gradual 3-mile hike leads up to 12,500 feet. Many families like this hike, which offers impressive views. Fishing is usually poor. Hope Lake is located above Trout Lake and was built as a reservoir for the Ames hydroelectric plant. To reach the trailhead from Telluride, head south about 12 miles on Hwy. 145 to Trout Lake. Turn left onto Trestle Rd. (Forest Rd. 626) and drive 1 mile to the intersection with Hidden Lake Rd. (Forest Rd. 627). Turn left again and drive to the parking area 2.5 miles up the road.

Jud Weibe Memorial Trail

For a relatively gentle 2.7-mile loop hike right from town, why not try the Jud Weibe Trail? Starting from the north end of Aspen St., cross over the Cornet Creek Bridge and turn west to begin this popular hike. Eventually you will meet up with Butcher Creek, where the trail angles back to the east, climbing to some sites offering spectacular views of the La Sal Mountains in Utah, the ski area, Bridal Veil Falls and area mountains. Bring your camera. After an elevation gain of 1,200 feet, the trail eventually drops down to a water storage tank near the Tomboy Rd. Once on Tomboy Rd., follow it back down to town.

Silver Pick Basin / Navajo Basin Loop

This exciting backpacking trip is marked with old mine buildings, snowfields and rugged mountains. The trail (No. 408) begins on the north side of Lizard Head Wilderness Area and heads south into Silver Pick Basin. It climbs out of the forest and up into a rocky area where old mining claims dot the mountainside.

At the top of the basin a saddle allows access to Navajo Basin to the southwest. From the saddle, Wilson Peak, Gladstone Peak, Mt. Wilson and El Diente Peak loom from left to right. Wilson Peak is a fairly easy climb but the others are very difficult. If you decide to attempt El Diente (it's possible to climb Wilson and El Diente in one day), be sure to wear a helmet and go up carefully with some friends. Just below the south side of the saddle is an old building that many hikers sleep in.

If you drop down from the saddle into Navajo Basin and follow the drainage west, you will come to Navajo Lake. This is the most popular camping site in the wilderness area, so don't expect to be alone. If you camp, do so at least 100 feet from the lake and streams and use a

*Dramatic Bridal Veil Falls and the power plant.
Photo by Dean Winstanley.*

the falls and then climbs up to 13,000 feet at a divide between Bear Creek and Bridal Veil Creek. From Telluride follow the trail from the south end of Pine St. up to the falls and look for the Wasatch Trail (No. 414) on the right. It climbs steeply for the first mile to La Junta Basin and then gradually climbs to the divide. Follow the trail northeast as it drops down to Bridal Veil Creek, then follow the trail down past Bridal Veil Falls and back into town.

Horseback Riding

Telluride Sports

This outfit offers 1- and 2-hour cowboy breakfast and dinner rides. Ride with Roudy, a cowboy you won't soon forget. **1-800-828-7547; 970-728-4477.**

Telluride Outfitters

Another reliable outfit for 1-hour, 2-hour, half-day and all-day rides into the surrounding national forest. **970-728-9366.**

River Floating

San Miguel River

Much like the Upper Dolores, the San Miguel River flows west out of the San Juans, cutting a deep valley and exposing red rock walls. From Telluride the river meanders west for about 3 miles before plunging 400 feet in a half-mile, then flowing into the South Fork. From here down to the bridge at Naturita (54 miles) the floating can be good May–June, depending on the runoff. At high water this section of the San Miguel can be dangerous due to huge waves. Be careful.

Outfitters

Telluride Outside—Experienced river guides lead one- to six-night trips on the San Miguel, Gunnison, Dolores and Colorado Rivers. They can also cook a pretty mean river meal. **301 Society Dr., P.O. Box 685, Telluride, CO 81435; 1-800-831-6230; 970-728-3895; www.tellurideoutside.com.**

stove. Below the lake the trail splits. The left fork (Navajo Lake Trail) heads toward Dunton and Woods Lake (see the Hiking and Backpacking section of the **Cortez** chapter). The right fork climbs northwest and then down to another fork. From this new fork, head to the right on Elk Creek Trail, which will take you back to the start of the loop.

To reach the trailhead from Telluride, head northwest on Hwy. 145 for about 7 miles and turn left onto Big Bear Rd. (Forest Rd. 622). Follow the road south for 5.5 miles and begin hiking up the jeep road to the wilderness area boundary.

Wasatch Trail

Starting from town, this 15-mile loop trail is one of the most scenic in the Telluride area. Many people hike it in a day, but it also makes a good overnighter. The trail follows Bear Creek up to

Skiing

CROSS-COUNTRY SKIING AND SNOWSHOEING

In winter, the Telluride area is transformed into a superb nordic and backcountry skier and snowshoer's destination. But a word of caution: with its heavy snows and steep mountains you need to be knowledgeable, aware and prepared for avalanche danger.

Backcountry Trails

Lizard Head Pass—See the **Cortez** chapter. **San Juan Hut Systems**—Take off from Telluride on old mine roads and backcountry trails for 7 miles a day with a cozy mountain hut waiting at the end. Or, just reserve one of the huts and make loop trips back to your home base. The five huts in this system extend between Telluride and Ouray. The trails, designed for intermediate to expert skiers, wind through spectacular territory in Uncompahgre National Forest with views of the Sneffels Range. All skiers should have a basic knowledge of changing mountain weather conditions and preparedness. The basic huts all have wood-stoves, a wood supply, bedding and food. **117 N. Willow St., P.O. Box 1663, Telluride, CO 81435; 970-728-6935; www.sanjuan huts.com.**

Groomed Trails

Telluride Nordic Center—About 50 kilometers of groomed trails meander through aspen groves and open meadows with fabulous views to the nearby peaks. This center offers terrain that varies from easy to moderately challenging in a number of areas: on the mile-long Town Park Trail, 5 miles on the valley floor, at the golf course in the Mountain Village and up in the Prospect Basin area. Guided backcountry trips, telemark skiing and skating are all options. In **Mountain Village** at **970-728-1144.**

Rentals, Lessons and Information

There are numerous places to rent skis and snowshoes in town. All of the shops in town and at the Mountain Village should have current knowledge of avalanche conditions in the area. Lessons are available at **Town Park; 970-728-7260.**

DOWNHILL SKIING AND SNOWBOARDING
Telluride Helitrax

Nothing compares with the exhilaration of cutting down through virgin powder in remote basins. Getting away from ski lifts, though, requires climbing into a Helitrax helicopter—an alternative for people with very deep pockets. **970-728-3895; www.tellurideoutside.com.**

Telluride Ski Area

It takes some determination to get to Telluride, but once there you'll be greeted by short lift lines and some of the best conditions imaginable. The skiing and boarding is great, and the views to the 14,000-foot summits of the San Miguel Mountains, the odd rock of Lizard Head Peak and the distant La Sal Mountains in Utah will halt you in your tracks. Telluride Ski Area has a wide reputation for having some of the longest, steepest, nastiest bump runs in the country. It's all true, but there is also a gentle, more sunny side to the mountain that towers over town. The back side of Telluride, with its southern exposure, is a paradise for nonexpert skiers.

But Telluride is still the consummate expert mountain. The shaded front side of the mountain usually offers soft snow since it hardly ever melts and refreezes. The Spiral Stairs run has a 40-degree slope near the top and keeps going for what seems like forever. From the expert front side, the dramatic view down into town and around the edge of the box canyon will take your breath away—as if that's what you need at 11,000 feet! If the tremendous 3,145-foot vertical drop of the mountain isn't long enough, there are walk-up runs from the top of Gold Hill (400 acres of additional expert skiing). Someday the steep slopes of Gold Hill and Prospect Basin, known to a select group of expert skiers, will be serviced by lift.

The ski mountain is accessible both from town and from the Mountain Village. **Telluride**

Ski Resort, 565 Mountain Village Blvd., Telluride, CO 81435; 1-800-525-3455; 970-728-7517; www.telski.com.

Seeing and Doing

Gondola

One thing you really must do while in Telluride is ride the gondola that runs between town and the European-style Mountain Village, where most of the ski lifts are. Why? Because the views are spectacular and the ride is free—the only free gondola in North America. The 13-minute ride provides an opportunity to access hiking and biking trails in summer, as well a chance to explore what Mountain Village has to offer. Open daily during the summer and ski season, 7 A.M.–11 P.M., until midnight on weekends.

Hot Springs

See the **Ouray** chapter.

Museums and Galleries

Telluride Historical Museum

Take some time to wander around this recently refurbished local museum that brings Telluride's early days back to life. The museum's innovative life-size sculpted figures re-create the stories and characters that shaped Telluride's colorful past. Each room depicts a different scene or stage in history, including Native American discovery of the valley, the boisterous mining days and the world's first commercial generation of AC power, in 1891 at the nearby Ames hydroelectric plant. A vast and eclectic collection of artifacts distributed among the scenes creates a realistic and accurate picture of the past. Small fee. **217 N. Fir St.; 970-728-3344; www.telluride museum.com.**

Nightlife

Fly Me to the Moon Saloon

This is the most consistent venue for live music in Telluride. It's also the best place to see the local, blond-haired Rastafarian/Dead Heads in action. Downstairs in a narrow underground room is a stage, a spring-loaded dance floor that absorbs shocks from frantic dancing and a well-stocked bar. The bands usually play danceable rock, reggae or blues. During ski season or large festivals, Fly Me to the Moon can get packed. Cover charge when there is a live band. **132 E. Colorado Ave.; 970-728-6666.**

Last Dollar

This local hangout is a good place to go for a cold beer and a game of pool or darts. A stone fireplace keeps things warm in the winter months. Open nightly until 2 A.M. Located at the **corner of Pine St. and Colorado Ave.; 970-728-4800.**

Leimgruber's Bierstube and Restaurant

Great après-ski spot with Bavarian atmosphere. See the Where to Eat section.

The Limeleaf at Swede-Finn Hall

This historic miners' social hall packs 'em in for après ski, billiards and great food, especially the do-it-yourself Mongolian grill and appetizers. Grab a seat or a pool cue and order from what is arguably the best tap-beer selection in the Telluride area, running the gamut from European imports to Colorado microbrews. Simple decor but a relaxing, inviting atmosphere. Open 4 P.M.–12:30 A.M. **472 W. Pacific Ave.; 970-728-2085.**

Sheridan Bar

There is no better place to imagine how Telluride looked and felt at the beginning of the 20th century. After all, in 1889 Butch Cassidy made his very first unauthorized bank withdrawal only a block away. Located just off the lobby of the New Sheridan Hotel, this bar is a happening spot for locals and visitors. This casual place has a stamped-tin ceiling, well-worn hardwood floors and a massive, cherry wood back bar. Open daily until 2 A.M. during the summer; reduced hours in winter. **231 W. Colorado Ave.; 970-728-3911.**

Ophir Needles from Alta Lakes Road. Photo by Dean Winstanley.

Sheridan Opera House

This marvelously restored theater provides frequent entertainment year-round, ranging from raves to repertory theater to nationally known musicians. **110 N. Oak St.; 970-728-6363; www.sheridanoperahouse.com.**

Scenic Drives

Alta

Located a short 12 miles from Telluride, Alta provides great views of Ophir Needles to the south, Lizard Head Peak, Mt. Wilson and Wilson and El Diente Peaks to the west. The development of the rich Gold King Mine in 1877 enabled the mining community of Alta to boom into the 1890s. Mining in the Alta area produced gold, silver, copper and lead and continued sporadically until the mid-1940s. Today a few buildings remain, including the old boardinghouse for Gold King miners. The site is privately owned by a mining company, but visitors are allowed as long as you stay out of the buildings and don't destroy anything.

To reach Alta from Telluride, head south on Hwy. 145 for about 5 miles to Boomerang Rd. (Forest Rd. 632) on the left. From here continue 4 miles to Alta.

Last Dollar Road

This dirt road travels past old ranch properties with weathered buildings and provides excellent views to the west end of the Sneffels Range. Last Dollar Rd. heads north from Telluride and comes out near Dallas Divide on Hwy. 62. The road traverses Hastings Mesa and is a good shortcut between Telluride and Ouray. Passenger cars can drive Last Dollar Rd. when it's dry, but it would be a good idea to inquire locally before heading off. To reach the road from Telluride, drive west 3 miles and look for Last Dollar Rd. (Forest Rd. 638) on the right.

Lizard Head Pass

Lizard Head Pass is only about 15 miles from Telluride, but a lot of spectacular scenery is packed into this short drive. Heading south on Hwy. 145 takes you by the town of Ophir (about

10 miles from Telluride). This was the location of the legendary Ophir Loop, an impressive 100-foot-high trestle for the Rio Grande Southern Railroad. The railroad, built by Otto Mears, connected Telluride with the smelters in Durango and the rest of the outside world via Lizard Head Pass.

Continuing on the highway from Ophir for another 3 miles takes you to Trout Lake, one of the most beautiful settings in the state. Towering above the lake to the south are Yellow Mountain, Vermillion Peak and Sheep Mountain. Although the lake is privately owned, fishing is allowed.

Trout Lake was built as a reservoir for the historic power plant downriver at Ames, which in 1891 generated the world's first commercial AC power. At the south end of the lake, an old, rickety Rio Grande Southern Railroad trestle appears ready to topple any day. See it while you can.

From Trout Lake continue on Hwy. 145 up to the summit of Lizard Head Pass for views west to the Upper Dolores River Valley and north to the eerie-looking Lizard Head Peak. From the top of an already tall peak, this 400-foot spire of crumbly rock is an inspiring sight as well as what many rock climbers consider to be the most difficult technical climb in the state.

San Juan Skyway

Telluride is but one stop on this 236-mile nationally designated "All American" road. For more information about this dramatic route, see the Scenic Drives section of the **Durango** chapter.

Where to Stay

Accommodations

Telluride has a lot to offer when it comes to accommodations. If you would like to stay in a historic hotel or guest ranch, there are a number of choices. The plush 177-room **Wyndham Peaks Resort and Golden Door Spa ($$$$),** an imposing first-class hotel at Mountain Village,

offers spa facilities, spectacular views and round-the-clock service. Its new 137-room lodge is also top-notch. **1-800-WYNDHAM; 970-728-6800; www.wynd ham.com.**

A cache of excellent bed and breakfast inns are available in and near town. A worthwhile moderate-cost lodging option is the **Oak Street Inn ($$$).** The rooms have shared baths and scant elbow room, but if you are primarily here to ski your brains out, who cares? No breakfast. **134 N. Oak St., P.O. Box 176, Telluride, CO 81435; 970-728-3383.** The owners at the **San Sophia ($$$$)** are wonderful and we can heartily recommend their lodging: 16 rooms with all the trimmings; covered hot tub on the porch, with views to the ski mountain; full breakfasts. **330 W. Pacific Ave., P.O. Box 1825, Telluride, CO 81435; 1-800-537-4781; 970-728-3001; www.sansofia.com.**

For reservations at condominiums or any other lodging, budget to luxury, call **Telluride Central Reservations: 1-888-783-0257; 970-728-4431.** A booking option for high-end stays is Elevation Management, which offers luxury one- to six-bedroom accommodations. **1-888-728-8160; 970-728-8160; www.elevation-management.com.**

Hotel Columbia—$$$$

For our money, the best all-round full-service hotel with friendly staff and great location (right at the gondola building) has to be the Columbia. Owned and operated by Marty and Jeff Campbell, two longtime Telluride residents, the hotel offers 21 luxurious European-style rooms, each with a fireplace, private bath, TV, phone and overstuffed chairs. Most also feature balconies. In addition to the two plush penthouse suites, highlights include the rooftop exercise room and a 360-degree view from the hot tub. Don't miss a meal at the COSMO-politan restaurant, located on the main floor (see the Where to Eat section). **300 W. San Juan Ave., P.O. Box 800, Telluride, CO 81435; 1-800-201-9505; 970-728-0660; www.co lumbiatelluride.com.**

Pennington's Mountain Village Inn—$$$$

This deluxe bed and breakfast at the Mountain Village offers 12 spacious guest rooms and takes advantage of its spectacular ridge-top perch. Inside, the French country decor looks right out of a glossy decorator magazine, but innkeepers Michael and Judy McClean put a warm, human touch on the place. Common areas include a formal sunken library/lounge, a window-encased whirlpool-bath room and an elaborate downstairs game room. Gorge yourself on a large, full breakfast served in the sunny dining room or, if you prefer, in your own bedroom. Call for reservations. **100 Pennington Ct., P.O. Box 2428, Telluride Mountain Village, CO 81435; 1-800-543-1437; 970-728-5337; www.penningtonsinn.com.**

Skyline Guest Ranch—$$$$

Eight miles south of Telluride off Hwy. 145, Skyline Guest Ranch sits on what could be the most beautiful property in the Colorado Rockies. Nestled at 9,600 feet in a mountain meadow, the ranch faces towering peaks, most notably Mt. Wilson and Wilson Peak (both over 14,000 feet) just to the west. Summer wildflowers cover the meadows with every color under the sun. In fall colorful aspen compel visitors to snap roll after roll of pictures. Wintertime transforms the ranch's 160 acres into a cross-country skier's paradise.

Longtime owners and hosts, the Farny family go out of their way to help guests get the most out of their stay—whether it's climbing a mountain or just lounging around the ranch. The easygoing atmosphere encourages everyone to get to know one another. Up the hill from the main lodge is a lake stocked with cutthroat and rainbow trout. A string of horses allows you to ride to your heart's content. After a day of hiking you can relax with a cold beer or head to the sauna and the outdoor hot tub. The ranch offers nightly **sleigh-ride dinners ($$$$)** that are open to the public (see the Where to Eat section).

Accommodations at the ranch include 10 smallish guest rooms in the main lodge and half a dozen private cabins nearby. Exquisite meals, included in the package price, are served in the main lodge. Those staying in the cabins can opt to cook their own meals. Open June–Oct. and mid-Dec.–Apr. A weeklong minimum stay is required in summer. In winter, rates are figured on a daily basis. **P.O. Box 67, Telluride, CO 81435; 1-888-754-1126; 970-728-3757; www.ranchweb.com/skyline.**

Bear Creek Bed and Breakfast—$$$ to $$$$

Several special features set this small, mountain-style contemporary bed and breakfast apart: the large upper rooms have walls of windows with unbelievable mountain views; even if your room doesn't feature such a view, the rooftop deck provides a dramatic 360-degree panorama; the convenient Colorado Ave. location close to the town park is perfect for summer festivals and the sauna, steam room and rooftop hot tub make great places to relax after a day on the slopes. While Bear Creek doesn't have the street appeal or historic charm of some accommodations, its personalized approach will please many. Each of the nine well-appointed rooms has a private bath, cable TV and daily maid service. **P.O. Box 2369, Telluride, CO 81435; 1-800-338-7064; 970-728-6681; www.bearcreektelluride.com.**

New Sheridan Hotel—$$$ to $$$$

In 1895 two enterprising men, Gus Brickman and Max Hippler, decided to stop their search for riches in the mountains around Telluride and build a fine hotel for the town. The hotel's place in history was assured when, in 1902, perennial presidential hopeful William Jennings Bryan made a speech from a large wooden stage erected at the front of the landmark three-story hotel. But as the mining town declined, the hotel followed, eventually closing in 1925. The resilient hotel reopened years later, and after extensive renovations is back in the limelight.

The 32 guest rooms range from the merely comfortable to plush suites, with expansive views and period antique furniture. Some rooms are not equipped with private baths, but the "club" baths are clean and numerous enough. All rooms have color TVs and phones. Continental breakfast included. Just off the first-floor lobby, check out the historic Sheridan Bar and Sheridan Opera House (see the Nightlife section). **231 W. Colorado Ave., P.O. Box 980, Telluride, CO 81435; 1-800-200-1891; 970-728-4351; www. newsheridan.com.**

Mountainside Inn—$$ to $$$

This attractive no-frills place lies wedged between the ski mountain and the river on the west end of town. Scattered throughout four refurbished buildings you'll find a hodgepodge of studios with kitchenettes, motel-style rooms and suites that vary wildly in price. Regardless of the room sizes, all accommodations are attractive and clean. The Mountainside also provides an outdoor hot tub by the river. This place offers some of the best lodging deals in town. **333 S. Davis, P.O. Box 2288, Telluride, CO 81435; 1-888-728-1950; 970-728-1950; www.tel luridemm.com/mtnsd.html.**

Camping

Town Park Campground, on the east end of Telluride, is very popular in the summer. It has 47 sites (5 are primitive), rest rooms and shower facilities. During summer festivals sites are taken quickly. The campground's location in the trees along the San Miguel River and its proximity to town make it a great spot. No RV hookups; fee charged. Open mid-May through mid-Oct.; no reservations. For information call **970-728-2173.**

Uncompahgre National Forest

Sunshine Campground (15 sites, fee charged), 8 miles southwest of Telluride on Hwy. 145, has a larger-than-life view west to Mt. Wilson and Wilson Peak in the Lizard Head Wilderness Area. Two miles farther southwest on Hwy. 145

is **Matterhorn Campground** (24 sites, fee charged) and what is certainly one of the most spectacular views of any national forest campground in the state.

On Hwy. 145 between Sunshine and Matterhorn Campgrounds, Boomerang Rd. (Forest Rd. 632) heads east for 3 miles to **Alta Lakes,** where there are some places to camp. Camping at **Woods Lake** (fee charged) is also possible. It's located 17 miles west of Telluride; drive northwest on Hwy. 145 past Sawpit and turn left on Fall Creek Rd. (Forest Rd. 618). Follow the road south to Woods Lake. Primitive campsites are also available along **Illium Valley Rd.** (Forest Rd. 625) just west of Telluride. The road can be reached from Telluride by driving northwest on Hwy. 145 for about 5 miles. Look for the turnoff for Illium Valley Rd. on the left.

Where to Eat

Skyline Guest Ranch—$$$$

If you're not up for one of Telluride's trendy restaurants, consider a more traditional evening out in the Colorado Rockies at Skyline Ranch's wintertime sleigh-ride dinner. Though not cheap, the food is terrific and you'll definitely make some memories as the draft horses pull your sleigh along a trail in this beautiful part of Colorado. Reservations a must. For information about the ranch, see the Where to Stay section.

La Marmotte—$$$ to $$$$

La Marmotte receives consistently high praise from its toughest critics: the locals. It's a special place for classic and country-style French cuisine. Owners Bertrand and Noelle Lepel-Cointet have hit on a restaurant formula that works well. La Marmotte is located in the old-town icehouse down in the warehouse district. Exposed brick and weathered wood dominate the decor of this small, intimate place. The menu offers entrées ranging from duck to pork tenderloin. A fine selection of French and California wines can be ordered. Reservations recommended. Open year-round 6–10 P.M. nightly. **150 W. San Juan Ave.; 970-728-6232.**

COSMOpolitan—$$ to $$$$

Located in the Hotel Columbia with fantastic views out to the gondola and ski mountain, Chad Scothorn's COSMO has developed a huge following for its highly creative cuisine and pleasant atmosphere. Reasonably priced breakfasts feature homemade beignets, waffles and omelettes; fanciful pizzas and salads highlight lunches. Dinner appetizers include mussels in red curry sauce; entrées change periodically but feature innovative preparations of roast chicken breast and seared yellowfin tuna. Don't skip the wonderful desserts. Deck seating; impressive wine list. Open daily for dinner 4–10 P.M. Ask about their decadant six-course, four-wine dinners in the Tasting Cellar. **300 W. San Juan Ave.; 970-728-1292.**

Eagle's—$$ to $$$

Eagle's attracts as many folks to its bar as it does for the great dining. Natural stone and hand-hewn wood flourishes provide a comfortable atmosphere. Start off with a tasty teriyaki beef skewer or shrimp quesadilla before diving into the entrée selections—highlights include feta cheese pizzas, baby back pork ribs and fresh seafood. Full bar with microbrews on tap. Open 11:30 A.M.–11 P.M. daily; bar stays open later. **100 W. Colorado Ave.; 970-728-0886.**

Honga's Lotus Petal—$$ to $$$

Local girl makes good: after starting out selling juices and salads from a pushcart years ago, Honga, a Korean transplant by way of Boulder, recently opened this very successful restaurant. Why is it so successful? Honga's presentation and wide range of terrific Asian dishes would be hard to top in any locale. Items range from sushi platters to Thai-style curries to Balinese specialties. The restaurant uses only the freshest ingredients available, and prices are surprisingly

reasonable. Be sure to check out the tearoom, which offers dozens of varieties of teas. The odds are high that you will love this place. Open daily; call for hours. **133 S. Oak St.; 970-728-5134.**

Leimgruber's Bierstube and Restaurant—$$ to $$$

Christel Leimgruber brings a genuine warmth and lively spirit to her Bavarian restaurant. Raised in East Berlin, Leimgruber made it across the border to the West just two years before the construction of what used to be the Berlin Wall. She has brought the Old World to Telluride, and local support has been tremendous. The small restaurant, with its friendly service, alpine cuisine and terrific beer, keeps people coming back. Entrées include bratwurst, wienerschnitzel, pork tenderloin with winekraut, chicken and pasta dishes. In addition to a wide selection of Pauliner on tap (Christel is one of the largest importers in North America), choose from a selection of wines and liquors by the glass. Bavarian music and a collection of beer steins give the restaurant a distinctly European feel. There is also deck seating. Leimgruber's gets packed and wild for après ski. Open daily for lunch 11:30 A.M.–2 P.M. and dinner 4–10 P.M. **573 W. Pacific Ave.; 970-728-4663.**

Sofios—$$ to $$$

Mexican food with a Southwestern slant fills the menu at this busy two-story eatery. Enchiladas, burritos and tacos come in traditional and jazzed-up versions. Smaller appetites may order à la carte (**$**) from the varied menu. Sofios also serves egg dishes, pancakes and waffles for breakfast. Breakfast served daily 7:30–11:30 A.M. (noon on Sun.), dinner 5:30–10 P.M. **110 E. Colorado Ave.; 970-728-4882.**

South Park Cafe—$ to $$$

Proving once again that Telluride is not just another mountain town, we offer South Park Cafe. Yes, you can order pizza, arguably as good as that of the restaurant's predecessor, Eddie's. But keeping with the trends, South Park also features fresh Pacific seafood dishes. Menu examples that are helping this place develop a loyal following include grilled scallops with crimini mushrooms, seared sashimi and crab-encrusted snapper with papaya relish. Other options include pasta dishes, sandwiches, heaps of appetizers and decadent desserts. Although the inside seating is cozy and attractive, try for a seat on the terrific sundeck, weather permitting. Open for lunch 11:30 A.M.–3 P.M., dinner 5:30–9 P.M.; pizza served anytime. **300 W. Colorado Ave.; 970-728-5335.**

Blue Jay Cafe—$ to $$

Located down-valley between Sawpit and Placerville, this low-key restaurant can provide a welcome escape from the glitz and higher prices of Telluride. Burgers, sandwiches and great New Mexico green and red chili highlight home-cooked food. Full bar, outside patio seating. Open 8 A.M.–2 P.M. for breakfast and lunch (breakfast served until 2 P.M.); 6–9 P.M. for dinner; closed Wed. Alongside **Hwy. 145; 970-728-0830.**

Fat Alley—$ to $$

Nothing fancy at this place—just reasonable prices and great barbecue. Favorites include the barbecued chicken, pork shoulder sandwich and the potato and black bean sauté. Counter service; beer available. Open daily 11 A.M.–10 P.M. **122 S. Oak St.; 970-728-3985.**

Baked in Telluride—$

Mouth-watering baked goods including croissants, donuts, bagels and brownies keep people coming back to this full-service bakery. There is also fast counter service for deli sandwiches and pizza by the slice. Find an outside bench on the small covered porch or bring your food up on the first gondola ride in winter. Also a few inside tables. Open 5:30 A.M.–10 P.M. daily. **127 S. Fir St.; 970-728-4775.** You can also try

Rose's Market and Deli ($ to $$) for excellent baked goods, deli sandwiches, fresh soups—great stuff for picnics. Open 8 A.M.–9 P.M. daily. **700 W. Colorado Ave.; 970-728-3124.**

Between the Covers—$

Since 1974, this establishment has been providing a terrific selection of books, maps and magazines. Over the years it has expanded to also offer the best place in town to grab a fresh cup of coffee or a latte. Make your way past towering bookshelves to the back of the store to find the small cafe, with views to the ski mountain. Open daily at **224 W. Colorado Ave.; 970-728-4504.**

Services

Visitor Information

Telluride Central Reservations—This is the only number that covers all of Telluride, from events tickets to ski tickets to lodging. **1-888-783-0257; 970-728-4431.**

Telluride Visitors Center—Be sure to stop in at this center at the west end of town for advice, happenings and loads of printed information. They also have a touch screen with 24-hour computerized information. **700 W. Colorado Ave., Box 653, Telluride, CO 81435; 1-888-783-0257; 970-728-4431; www.gotelluride.org.**

Telluride Daily Planet—The local newspaper. **www.telluridegateway.com.**

Transportation

Galloping Goose—Providing free shuttle service around town from 7 A.M. to 11 P.M. daily; down-valley shuttles available for a small fee. **970-728-5700.**

The Gondola—See write-up in the Seeing and Doing section.

Telluride Express—Chartered bus/van transportation to and from the Telluride, Montrose, Cortez and Grand Junction airports can be arranged 24 hours in advance by calling **1-800-800-6228** or **970-728-6000.**

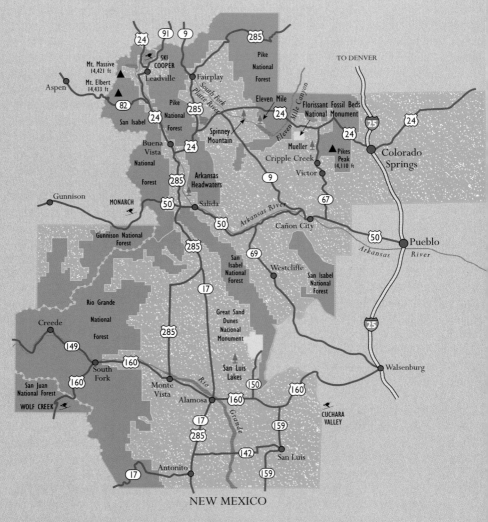

South Central Region

South Central Region

The sun sets on the Sangre de Cristo Mountains. Photo by Bruce Caughey.

Cañon City

Cañon City doesn't claim to stand alone as a vacation destination. But the small, historic town, with a burgeoning population, truly enjoys a great location in the midst of spectacular natural surroundings. The Royal Gorge has long been the best-known attraction in the area, bringing in more than half a million visitors each year. Some 1,000 feet deep and 8 miles long, the gorge is an awesome sight, especially when viewed from the world's highest suspension bridge: examples of nature and human engineering at their best. Past visitors should notice a marginal improvement in scenery around the gorge as tacky billboards touting area attractions have become somewhat less ubiquitous.

Rafting might be the perfect way to experience the beauty of the Arkansas River and the area's fascinating geology. A float trip might be a mellow family excursion or a rough ride through the intense rapids within the gorge itself. A number of little-known mountain parks in the surrounding foothills and thousands of acres of national forests make Cañon City a perfect setting-off point for hikers, mountain bikers and sightseers. A recent added attraction is a 24-mile round-trip train ride alongside the Arkansas River and through the gorge. To get a feeling for the historical importance of gold in the mountains to the north, spend at least a half day on the Gold Belt Tour (see the Scenic Drives section), which leads you to Cripple Creek, among other interesting stops. The area's renowned dinosaur finds have spawned a museum in town.

Cañon City's residents enjoy a protected, natural setting that buffers the town from harsh weather. Historic Main St. preservation projects include renovating sidewalks and lighting, a clock-tower replica and a pedestrian-only side street. But Cañon City is best known as the home of the state penitentiary. In fact Cañon City and Florence, its neighbor just to the east, together lay claim to 13 state and federal correctional facilities. No doubt it's the foundation of

the area economy. For a fascinating and disturbing way to get a feel for life on the inside, stop by the Territorial Prison Museum. Aside from all the stone walls and guard towers, Cañon City remains a quiet town with an intriguing history.

History

A favorite camping area for Ute Indians, Cañon City also served as a war line between the mountainous domain of the Utes and the territory of the eastern plains Indians. Sporadic tribal fighting kept permanent settlers away in the early 1800s. Several U.S. Army explorations headed

Getting There

Cañon City is located 115 miles south of Denver (38 miles west of Pueblo). To get there from Denver, drive south on Interstate 25 for 68 miles to Colorado Springs. Angle southwest on Hwy. 115 for 36 miles, then turn right (west) on Hwy. 50 for the last 11 miles into town.

by Lt. Zebulon Pike and Maj. Stephen Long passed through the area. Their travels in the early 1800s helped chart the territory acquired in the Louisiana Purchase of 1803.

It was the gold rush that eventually brought settlers to Cañon City in 1859. People came not for mining per se, but to build a trading center for supplies and provisions needed by miners in the mountains to the west. The town grew quickly and within two years 900 people lived here.

In 1868 Golden and Denver were vying to be named the territorial capital. Just as the heated political battle appeared deadlocked, Cañon City lined up the support of a block of southern Colorado legislators to name Cañon City as the capital. Even though Cañon City had no possibility of winning, it now had enough clout to make a deal. Soon Denver was named the capital and, in return, Cañon City was given the chance to build the territorial penitentiary. The secure prison walls began keeping prisoners from the general population in 1871, five years before Colorado became a state.

In the early 1900s Cañon City was a prime location for moviemaking. Spectacular scenery provided the backdrop for local cowboy Tom Mix, the hero of many silent Westerns. But the spotlight was short-lived. Grace McCue, a popular leading lady of the times, drowned in the Arkansas River during filming, and the tragedy provoked damage suits that forced the Colorado Motion Picture Company into bankruptcy. Other films such as *Cat Ballou, White Buffalo* and *The Duchess and the Dirtwater Fox* have been made nearby.

Cañon City had the dubious honor of being state headquarters for the Ku Klux Klan in the mid-1920s. The Klan published a small newspaper and eventually controlled many county and civic offices as well as the school board. They even operated a Klan bank in the St. Cloud Hotel for five years. Thankfully, the hateful ideals of the Klan were short-lived.

In addition to tourism, the prison system's steady growth has provided residents with jobs over the years without depriving them of small-town status. Most residents will tell you that having the prison actually makes it one of the safest towns in the country. In addition, its mild climate and lack of many big-city problems have made Cañon City a favored place to retire.

Major Attractions

Royal Gorge Bridge and Park

For 3 million years the Arkansas River cut through solid granite to form this spectacular 1,053-foot-deep chasm. Known to early explorers as the Grand Canyon of the Arkansas, the Royal Gorge has astonished travelers for generations. Today a historic bridge spans the gorge, providing visitors with a dramatic view down to the river below. Despite the amusement park development at the site and steep entrance fees, the gorge remains a magnificent sight. The tourist development at the gorge and bridge is operated by a private concessionaire under contract from the Cañon City government.

History

In 1806 Lt. Zebulon Montgomery Pike camped near the eastern portal of the canyon, but his scouting party determined that it would be impossible to get through the gorge. It took 70 years and the promise of profits from the silver boom to inspire the railroads to chisel a way through the narrow canyon. When the Leadville silver rush was in full force, two railroad companies started laying tracks in different sections of the gorge, and a bitter right-of-way struggle ensued. There was room in the narrow canyon for only one track, and both companies desperately wanted the route. By 1878 the "war" between the Denver & Rio Grande (D&RG) and Santa Fe Railroads escalated to the point of gunfire and sabotage. Somehow, no one was ever killed. Ultimately a lease through the gorge was granted to the D&RG by the courts.

In 1929 the world's highest suspension bridge was built across the Royal Gorge 1,053 feet above the Arkansas River. The bridge is still the best way to get an unobstructed view of the river—that is, unless you attach yourself to an extralong bungee

A compelling ride on the rails now awaits beneath the span of the Royal Gorge Bridge. Photo by Ron Ruboff.

cord and hurl yourself over the edge, as four daredevils did in 1980. The bridge is a tourist attraction; although it qualifies as a major engineering feat, it really doesn't take you anywhere.

Facts About the Bridge and Park

Besides the impressive bridge, other reasonable ways to experience the gorge include the aerial tramway, the steep-incline railway to the bottom or a 26-minute multimedia slide presentation. Young children seem to enjoy the tunnel play area, the carousel and the mini-train. You will find restaurants and, of course, curios by the armload. Open during daylight hours year-round. **719-275-7507; www.royalgorgebridge.com.**

It doesn't cost a thing if you simply want a view of the gorge and bridge from afar. Drive along the road toward the north rim entrance booth. Pull a U-turn in the parking lot, park off to the side and walk the short trail overlooking the rim. The view is a little sweeter without the entrance fee.

Getting There

The gorge is located 8 miles west of Cañon City, off Hwy. 50. You may want to stop inside the park (but before the entrance gate) for a picnic lunch at one of the many tables provided. Don't mistake the Royal Gorge Scenic Railway for the actual park.

Festivals and Events

Music and Blossom Festival

1st weekend in May The biggest event in Cañon City attracts thousands to a colorful spring get-together. For more than 60 years residents and visitors have gathered to celebrate the cherry and apple blossoms in the surrounding orchards. High school marching bands come from across the country to parade down historic Main St. alongside many floats. The weekend features an art show, car show, craft fair, rodeo and carnival rides. For more information call **719-275-2305.**

Outdoor Activities

Biking

MOUNTAIN BIKING

Mountain biking is the best way to go in this area due to rough road conditions on most of the scenic routes. The Scenic Drives section provides many routes near Cañon City that are perfect for sturdy two-wheelers. Serious riders should consider participating in the annual MS/150 Go for the Gorge tour in mid-July. Here's a terrific easy ride:

Tunnel Drive

This short ride winds through three tunnels in what was originally intended to be a water project. Convict labor blasted through solid granite to create this interesting road that dead-ends overlooking the Arkansas River only a short distance from the Royal Gorge. Catch Tunnel Dr. opposite the penitentiary on the west end of town. Tunnel Dr. begins near the banks of the Arkansas as Hwy. 50 rounds a large bend and heads north. This road was formerly open to cars.

Fishing

Want to hear the latest on fishing in the Cañon City area? **No Boundaries Sports** carries on the tradition of providing the latest in fishing gear and local information. They also stock climbing and rafting equipment. **311 Main St.; 719-275-3685.**

Arkansas River

It's possible to catch trout within the Cañon City limits, but the best fishing on the Arkansas is west of town. Actually, for a great day of fishing on the Arkansas, head to the Gold Medal trout water below Salida (see the Fishing section of the **Upper Arkansas Valley** chapter). Large brown trout can be pulled from the roily water. The river is not wadable, forcing most people to approach from the highway side.

Texas Creek

Twenty-six miles west of Cañon City, Texas Creek flows into the Arkansas River. Next to the creek, Hwy. 69 follows south into the high country along the east side of the Sangre de Cristo Mountains. This road provides access to a number of small streams and lakes. Fishing can be good for brown trout in Texas Creek.

Golf

Shadow Hills Golf Course and Country Club

This mature, 18-hole course provides great views and, as the name implies, lots of rolling hills. Two sets of tees help to make the "back nine" marginally different from the front. The course is open to the public with some exceptions. Advance tee times required. Located just south of town on 4th St. **1232 County Rd. 143; 719-275-0603.**

Hiking

Cañon City is a good area for short hikes and picnics. **Red Canyon Park, Temple Canyon** and the **Royal Gorge** provide miles of trails for easy walks. Close to town you might try walking along the 4-mile-long riverwalk (access along the Arkansas River from Mackenzie or Raynolds Ave.). The Tunnel Dr. Trail (see the Biking section for directions) has been extended to 2.5 miles into the gorge. Plans are being made to connect the riverwalk and Tunnel Dr. For longer, more strenuous backcountry trips, see the Hiking and Backpacking section in the **Wet Mountain Valley** chapter.

Horseback Riding

Lajitas Stables

Guided riding trips through the Royal Gorge area provide access to thousands of backcountry acres. Trips are offered from 1-hour to all day (including lunch), all at reasonable rates. Trail rides can be adjusted to your riding ability (or inability). Open mid-May through Sept. Just east of the Royal Gorge turnoff at the Fort Royal complex along Hwy. 50. **1-888-734-1445; 719-275-4055; www.lajitasstables.com.**

River Floating

Arkansas River

Along with the Royal Gorge Bridge, the biggest draw to the Cañon City area is the Arkansas River with its scenic canyons and treacherous rapids. The river is very accessible to rafters and kayakers as Hwy. 50 snakes alongside all the way to Salida, 44 miles upriver. Downriver from Salida to the Royal Gorge entrance, the river travels through the Arkansas River Canyon, past cottonwoods and rock walls, offering a few rapids but nothing extraordinary. Thanks to the Arkansas Headwaters Recreation Area, the put-ins and parking along this part of the river are vastly improved. But don't let ease of access lull you into a false sense of security. Unless you know what you're doing, be sure to take out above Parkdale or you will end up entering the Royal Gorge! At Parkdale begins a 7-mile stretch of churning, sometimes dangerous rapids, enclosed within towering rock walls. If you are not an expert, sign up with an outfitter. For information about the Upper Arkansas River from Salida upriver to Granite, see the River Floating section of the **Upper Arkansas Valley** chapter.

Outfitters

Upriver, along Hwy. 50 from Cañon City to Salida, nearly 100 raft outfitters offer guided trips down the river. Outfitters are open for business from May through Sept., but the fastest water is during the spring runoff.

Echo Canyon River Expeditions—Established in 1978, Echo Canyon offers half-day, full-day and overnight trips. **45000 Hwy. 50 W., Cañon City, CO 81212; 1-800-748-2953; www.echocanyonrafting.com.**

River Runners—For nearly 30 years, River Runners has provided trips through Browns Canyon and the Royal Gorge areas of the Upper Arkansas River. Highly reliable. **11150 Hwy. 50, Salida, CO 81201; 1-800-332-9100; www.riverrunnersltd.com.**

Wilderness Aware—The guides at this award-winning outfit get you downriver safely, and provide information about the flora, fauna and geology while on half-day and full-day trips down the Arkansas. They also run multi-day trips on other rivers of the state. **P.O. Box 1550 WS, Buena Vista, CO 81211; 1-800-462-7238; 719-395-2112; www.inaraft.com.**

Seeing and Doing

Amusements

Buckskin Joe Frontier Town and Railway

You won't miss the signs for Buckskin Joe on the drive to the Royal Gorge. It's a re-creation of an Old West town, made of 100-year-old log buildings from ghost towns around the state. Used frequently as a movie set, it has a print shop, blacksmith shop, livery stable, barn and H.A.W. Tabor's general store. Gunfights 11 times daily—if you're "lucky" you might even catch a hanging. Many shops, a few saloons and the Gold Nugget restaurant (try the buffalo burger). Admission charged. Open May–Sept. 9 A.M.–dusk. **P.O. Box 1387, Cañon City, CO 81215; 719-275-5149; www.buckskinjoes.com.**

Gold Panning

Stop by or call the Bureau of Land Management (BLM) office to learn about recreational gold panning or sluicing opportunities near town. **3170 E. Main St., Cañon City, CO 81212; 719-269-8500.**

Museums

Cañon City Municipal Museum

This museum features displays of Indian artifacts and big-game trophies. Anson Rudd's small stone house, built in 1860, is just behind the museum; inside find furnishings of the late 1800s. Free. Open daily, May–Aug. 8 A.M.–5 P.M., Sept.–Apr. 1–5 P.M. In the municipal building at **6th St. and Royal Gorge Blvd., Cañon City, CO 81212; 719-269-9018.**

Colorado Territorial Prison Museum

Under the shadow of guard towers at the Colorado State Penitentiary, a pathway leads through a steel gate to cell house 4 that used to hold many of the state's women prisoners. Now it holds only the tragic remnants of prison life in Colorado. This museum leaves a lasting impression with its convict attire, disciplinary paraphernalia, historical photos and display cases of homemade, but lethal, "shivs." A long hallway leads between dozens of cell doors; each one exhibits a different aspect of prison life. The gift shop sells a variety of convict-made arts and crafts. Open daily in summer 8:30 A.M.–6 P.M.; in winter, Fri.–Sat. 10 A.M.–5 P.M. **1st and Macon Ave., P.O. Box 1229, Cañon City, CO 81215-1229; 719-269-3015; www. prisonmuseum.org.**

Dinosaur Depot

Open since 1995, this museum highlights the area's renowned dinosaur finds. Just as the nearby Garden Park Fossil Area gives testament to another world some 145 million years ago, this museum provides a perfect introduction to the many dinosaur species that once lived here. In the Depot's fossil preparation laboratory watch a stegosaurus being prepared for exhibition. Interpreters explain the dinosaur exhibits, adding a personal touch. Check the dinosaur trackway in the plaza just outside. Tours of the Garden Park Fossil Area include a recent discovery of a dinosaur trackway near Skyline Dr. From mid-May until Labor Day the Depot is open daily 9 A.M.–5 P.M.; shorter winter hours. **330 Royal Gorge Blvd., Cañon City, CO 81212; 1-800-987-6379; 719-269-7150; www.dinosaurdepot.com.**

Indian Museum in the Holy Cross Abbey

In the unlikely location of a Benedictine abbey, Father William, a monk since 1939, showed us around the small basement Indian museum with its collection of axes, arrowheads, pots, wicker and other items. He told us of the days when 92 monks roamed the old Tudor gothic–style building. Across the green is a gift shop with some interesting religious items for sale. Open 9 A.M.–4 P.M. in summer; shorter winter hours. Located 2 miles east of town **on Hwy. 50; 1-888-588-8631; 719-275-8631; www.holycrossabbey.com.**

Railroad Tour

Royal Gorge Route

Passenger service is again available along the historic Denver & Rio Grande rail route. You will marvel at the spectacular ride through the Royal

The Indian Museum lies in the unlikely basement location of the Holy Cross Abbey. Photo by Bruce Caughey.

Gorge, either in the comfort of climate-controlled coaches or in one of two open-air observation cars. The 24-mile round trip lasts 2 hours and travels right beside the crashing, churning whitewater of the Arkansas River at the base of the gorge. A snack bar and rest rooms are available on the train. Tickets prices may seem steep at first, but you get your money's worth from this unique adventure. Avid rail buffs can pay extra for a seat in the engine cab. Trains depart the renovated Sante Fe Depot three times daily May–Oct., weekends-only in winter. **401 Water St., Cañon City, CO 81212.** Reservations: **1-888-724-5748; 303-569-2403; www.royalgorgeroute.com.**

Scenic Drives

Gold Belt Tour

This designated National Back Country Byway pulls together the area's best scenic drives into an eventful 3-hour to 3-day circle tour. This tour threads a path between the eerie rock walls of **Phantom Canyon** to the former mining boom-towns of **Cripple Creek** and **Victor,** returning along the confining, one-lane Shelf Rd. or via the meandering High Park Rd. Stop by the **Cañon City Chamber of Commerce** for a brochure; **403 Royal Gorge Blvd.; 719-275-2331.**

From Cañon City, travel east on Hwy. 50 for 8 miles to the Hwy. 67 cutoff (option: turn off on Hwy. 115 just east of Cañon City to visit the quiet, tree-lined streets of Florence). **Phantom Canyon Rd.** goes north, following the railroad line—which began somewhat inauspiciously in 1894; the second day of operation was greeted with a massive train wreck. Soon, though, three trains daily made the winding journey from the gold mines at Cripple Creek and Victor down to the ore reduction mills in Florence. As you drive into the mine-scarred hamlet of Victor, a 4,500-foot elevation gain, you'll feel the history of the area (see the **Cripple Creek and Victor** chapter).

If you're skittish about heights take **High Park Rd.** from 9 miles northwest of Cripple Creek through rolling hills, ending with a fabulous view of the Royal Gorge Bridge. The recommended route back to Cañon City, however, requires traversing a narrow shelf perched high above a streambed. To reach the well-marked **Shelf Rd.,** head west off Hwy. 67 just south of Cripple Creek. The narrow road passes by the Shelf Rd. Climbing Area, where thrill-seekers cling to limestone cliffs.

Also of interest is Red Canyon Park (see the write-up in this section) and the **Garden Park Fossil Area.** While you can't see much at Garden Park today, excavations have yielded complete skeletons of camarasaurus, allosaurus, diplodocus and other dinosaurs now on display at the Smithsonian Institution as well as at the Carnegie, Denver and Cleveland Museums of Natural History. The Garden Park Paleontology Society has ambitious plans for a regional Dinosaur Discovery Center. For information, contact the **Cañon City Chamber of Commerce; 1-800-876-7922; 719-275-2331; www.canoncitychamber.com.**

Oak Creek Grade (County Road 143)

Heading southwest from Cañon City, this scenic, mostly dirt road leads toward the Wet Mountain Valley. Drive along through sparse woods before the Sangre de Cristo Mountains open up before you in an incredible panorama. Crestone Needles, Kit Carson Peak and Humboldt Peak are among the 14ers you'll see. Stay right at the major forks and you'll end up visiting Silver Cliff/Westcliffe in the Wet Mountain Valley (see the **Wet Mountain Valley** chapter). To reach County Rd. 143 from Royal Gorge Blvd. turn south on 4th St. and cross over the Arkansas River.

Phantom Canyon Road

See the Gold Belt Tour write-up above.

Red Canyon Park

Red sandstone rocks shoot up the valley in dramatic formations. The contrast of immense red rocks against the lush green of the pines makes this beautiful park well worth the short drive from Cañon City. Hiking trails provide access to more secluded portions of the park. Several picnic areas with grills and tables. To get there, head north on Field Ave. until you reach the park 12 miles north of Cañon City.

Skyline Drive

This one-way lane threads its way along the narrow spine of the hogback northwest of Cañon City. Look down on the town and prison from 800 feet above. The 3-mile drive was built by convict labor in 1906. Chances are good you've never seen a road like it before. To reach Skyline Dr., head west on Hwy. 50 out of town. About 3 miles after the highway turns north, you'll see the sign for Skyline Dr. Turn right (east) and continue on up the hill.

Where to Stay

Accommodations

Best Western Royal Gorge Motel—$$$

This 68-room motor inn has a trout pond and outdoor heated pool (not one and the same). The gazebo-covered whirlpool bath is a perfect place to soak weary muscles. While it's your basic motor inn, all rooms are spotless and well maintained, with air-conditioning, cable TV and movies. Catch a trout in the pond and have it cooked up at the on-site restaurant. They even furnish the fishing pole. One mile east of downtown Cañon City **on Hwy. 50; 1-800-231-7317; 719-275-3377; www.bestwestern.com.**

St. Cloud Hotel—$$$

The St. Cloud Hotel was built in Silver Cliff in 1883. After the silver rush ended, the entire hotel was dismantled and moved, reopening on July 4, 1886, at its present location on Main St. in Cañon City. The hotel eventually closed, but after many years standing empty, it was completely restored in 1997 and now offers 35 nonsmoking rooms. While the hotel makes you feel right at home, with modern conveniences mixed in with antiques, its deluxe rooms don't qualify as luxurious. Even so, the range of room sizes is appealing and, thanks to a genuine turn-of-the-century ambience, this place remains our first choice in town. The comfy beds tend to dominate the smaller rooms. Downtown at **631 Main St., Cañon City, CO 81212; 1-800-405-9666; 719-276-2000; www.stcloudhotel.com.**

Cañon Inn—$$ to $$$

The remodeled Cañon Inn boasts 152 rooms with queen- and king-size beds. Thirty poolside rooms vie for your reservation; the outdoor heated pool is open year-round, as is an airy solarium with six large hot tubs. If that's not enough, try the putting green or switch on cable TV in your air-conditioned room. There are two dining rooms, and the lounge features live acoustic entertainment on weekends. Reduced winter rates. Two miles east of downtown Cañon City **on Hwy. 50; 1-800-525-7727; 719-275-8676; www.canoninn.com.**

Camping

Although very few designated campgrounds exist on public land near Cañon City, you can find excellent car campsites along the Gold Belt Tour (see the Scenic Drives section).

San Isabel National Forest

Oak Creek Campground is located 15 miles southwest of Cañon City. For directions see Oak Creek Grade in the Scenic Drives section. Six sites; no drinking water; no fee.

Private Campgrounds

Indian Springs Ranch—This 2,500-acre working ranch is a beautiful place to camp out and explore the 450-million-year-old fossil area. Don't miss the outlaw cabin of "Wild Bill" McKinney. Heated pool, showers, hookups and unlimited backcountry tentsites. On Phantom Canyon Rd. 6 miles off Hwy. 50. Open Apr.–Sept. **P.O. Box 405, Cañon City, CO 81215; 719-372-3907.**

Royal Gorge KOA Kampground—Full and partial hookups with tentsites. Signs will direct you from Royal Gorge Rd. west of town. **719-275-6116.**

Royal View Campground—Many secluded tentsites and 31 RV hookups. Go 1.5 miles west of the Royal Gorge exit on Hwy. 50. **719-275-1900.**

Where to Eat

Oak Creek Grade
General Store / Steakhouse—$$$

On a scenic back road between Westcliffe and Cañon City, you can find great food and western entertainment. See the Where to Eat Section of the **Wet Mountain Valley** chapter.

Merlino's Belvedere—$$ to $$$

Opened in 1946, this restaurant has a solid reputation that goes far beyond the borders of Cañon City. All Italian dishes come from family recipes—try the ravioli, cavatelli, manicotti or spaghetti and you won't be disappointed. If you are not in the mood for fresh pasta, order from a long list of steak, seafood or chicken dinners. Sandwiches and soup are available Open

Mon.–Thurs. 5–9 P.M., Fri.–Sat. 4:30–9 P.M., Sun. noon–8 P.M. Expect a wait (sometimes lengthy) if you show up at the dinner hour. Reservations available for groups of 12 or more. **1330 Elm; 719-275-5558.**

St. Cloud Bar and Grille—$$ to $$$

The St. Cloud offers a good mainstream menu featuring rib-eye steaks, salmon and pasta, plus a full-service bar. During the dinner hour a pianist often entertains, helping to bring elegance back to the historic surroundings of the St. Cloud Hotel. Lunches tend to be slanted to inexpensive sandwiches and salads. Open daily for lunch 11 A.M.–5 P.M.; dinner Sun.–Thurs. 5–9 P.M. and Fri.–Sat. until 10 P.M. Downtown at the St. Cloud Hotel, **631 Main St.; 719-276-2000.**

Janey's Chili Wagon—$ to $$

Janey Workman came to Cañon City in 1967 with $750 in her pocket and dreams of opening a restaurant. Her tenacity and "rags-to-riches" success earned her a profile in the *National Enquirer*. Despite three different locations over the years, she has developed a loyal clientele for her excellent, homemade Mexican cuisine. The Chili Wagon's current home is practically a local landmark. Try the massive El-Burrito or a combination plate with your choice of Janey's tasty red or green (or half red and half green) chili. The restaurant is light and airy with neon accents around the doorways. Full bar; carry-out available. Open Tues.–Sat. 11 A.M.–8:30 P.M., closed Sun.–Mon. **807 Cyanide; 719-275-4885.**

The Owl Cigar Store—$

This old bar/restaurant has a simple formula for success: a good selection of cold beer, pool tables and a little hamburger grill behind the bar. "Ask anybody, they're the best hamburgers in town," said our helpful bartender/cook. The best part is that the burgers cost about a buck. They also serve up old-fashioned shakes and malts. The Owl has been in the same family for decades and remains a great place to unwind after a long day on the road. Eat in or take out. Open Mon.–Sat. 8 A.M.–8 P.M. **626 Main St.; 719-275-9946.**

St. Cloud Coffee House and Bakery—$

Stop in for a home-baked goodie for breakfast or midday fare. The St. Cloud Coffee House has become a favorite spot to relax and read the paper while enjoying a cappuccino or latte. Open Mon.–Sat. 7 A.M.–2 P.M. Downtown next to the St. Cloud Hotel, which is at **631 Main St., 719-276-2000.**

Waffle Wagon Restaurant—$

Go where the locals go for a full breakfast. Homemade biscuits and gravy, breakfast burritos, pecan and blueberry waffles and egg dishes are among the choices at this crowded restaurant. Open Wed.–Sun. 6 A.M.–1 P.M. **1304 Royal Gorge Blvd.; 719-269-3428.**

Services

Visitor Information

Cañon City Chamber of Commerce—The Chamber office, in the historic former home of Gov. James Peabody, has lots of ideas about what to see and do. **403 Royal Gorge Blvd., Cañon City, CO 81212; 1-800-876-7922; 719-275-2331; www.canoncitychamber.com.**

Florence Chamber of Commerce—117 S. Pikes Peak Ave., Florence, CO 81226; 719-784-3544.

Colorado Springs

When Katharine Lee Bates wrote "America the Beautiful," she was looking out upon Colorado Springs, and the "purple mountain majesties" in the anthem refer to the perch that inspired her: Pikes Peak. It's quite a legacy to live up to, but Colorado Springs and its famous mountain manage to do so beautifully.

Colorado's second-largest urban center, with half a million residents, sits on a high plateau right in the shadow of the 14,110-foot peak. Crammed into the area you'll find a lion's share of the state's most popular attractions. In addition to Pikes Peak are the red sandstone towers of Garden of the Gods Park, Seven Falls, the popular Cave of the Winds and scenic Cheyenne Canyon. But nature doesn't get all the credit: the Pikes Peak area is also home to the U.S. Air Force Academy, the renowned Broadmoor Hotel, quaint Manitou Springs (with its luxurious, restored historic inns), the Olympic Training Center and the country's only mountain zoo. Nearby are Florissant Fossil Beds National Monument and the mining-town relics of Cripple Creek (now a gambling boomtown) and Victor.

This concentration of human-made and natural treasures and the city's central location make Colorado Springs one of America's most popular vacation destinations. In that lies a pair

of warnings—squadrons of people in touring formation sweep through each summer, and there's plenty of fool's gold in them thar hills. Some of the scores of area attractions, though amazingly popular, stretch the imagination in terms of audacity and sheer cheesiness. For example: cliff dwellings have been moved here 350 miles from their natural home, and the North Pole now rests at the foot of Pikes Peak.

But Colorado Springs does have it all. And with a little forethought and a bit of extra effort, ways can be found to see the worthwhile sights far from the mad-dashing crowd.

Getting There

Colorado Springs is located 65 miles south of Denver on Interstate 25. The town is a major bus hub; **TNM&O Coaches (719-635-1505)** *serves Colorado Springs with frequent runs to Denver. The* **Colorado Springs Airport (www.flycos.com),** *in the far southeast corner of town, handles more than 100 direct flights per day and is served by 10 major carriers.*

History

Years before Zebulon Pike spotted his namesake peak in 1806, the Ute Indians hunted the area below what they called "The Long One." Pike first saw the peak from near present-day Las Animas, where he recorded, "it appeared like a small blue cloud." Pike tried to christen it Grand Peak or Blue Peak, but his name stuck.

In 1859 the mountain gained its enduring place in history thanks to the gold rush: thousands of fortune hunters headed west in Conestoga wagons with "Pikes Peak or Bust" emblazoned on the sides. Although in those early years most of the gold actually was found 100 miles to the north, near Central City, Pikes Peak proved to be a magnet for would-be millionaires.

That same year, prospectors staked out a town named El Dorado (now known as Colorado City) at the base of the Ute Pass Trail. Wedged between Colorado Springs and Manitou Springs, this area served as the territorial capital of Colorado before Denver's rise.

The city of Colorado Springs was conjured up by a love-struck general for his thankless queen in the early 1870s. The general was William Jackson Palmer, a Civil War hero who founded several southern Colorado cities as part of his Denver & Rio Grande Railroad empire. Colorado Springs was to be the posh resort home for his blue-blood bride, Queen Mellen, complete with a castle of her own. But she stayed at the estate only a year, running home to the safe civility of the East and, later, of England.

Palmer's vision was to make the town a genteel place for well-to-do people. The name Colorado Springs was chosen by an early publicist because of its "rich eastern spa sound," as historian Marshall Sprague put it. The actual springs referred to are the ones at Manitou Springs.

The city soon became better known as "Little London" because of the number of Englishmen and other tea drinkers brought in by Palmer. The resort didn't really take off until a second gold rush in 1891, this time closer by in Cripple Creek (see the Cripple Creek and Victor chapter). By 1900 the population of the region had swelled to over 50,000. Over the next 10 years, thanks to tycoons who had invested in Cripple Creek mines, Colorado Springs was the richest city per capita in the country.

Guided and goaded by tycoons such as Spencer Penrose, founder of the Broadmoor Hotel, Colorado Springs thrived for the next few decades as a tourist and retirement center. During World War II the military's omnipresence began. In 1942 Camp Carson, now Fort Carson, was built, followed quickly by Peterson Air Force Base and later by the North American Aerospace Defense Command (NORAD). In 1955 Colorado Springs struck gold again, this time by landing the U.S. Air Force Academy. It's one of the state's most popular tourist attractions. Today the area is home to almost as many generals as the Pentagon, with more space-related agencies—including the U.S. Space Command, which oversees all space-based defense activities—than anywhere else in the world.

Major Attractions

Air Force Academy

The U.S. Air Force Academy, training center for America's future Air Force officers, receives more than a million visitors annually, making it one of Colorado's top attractions. The academy's beautiful location is one reason why in 1954 it was chosen over 580 other proposed sites around the country. Although much of the stunning 18,500-acre campus at the foot of the Rampart Range is off-limits, most of the facilities are free and open to the public. An easy way to see the grounds is to take a self-guided tour using the "Follow the Falcon" brochure available at the **Barry Goldwater Visitors Center.** This facility, open daily in summer 9 A.M.–6 P.M. and until 5 P.M. in winter, features an enormous gift shop, displays about cadet life and films on the history of the air force; **719-333-2025.**

A short nature trail from the visitor center leads to the chapel, which is not to be missed. The soaring 17-spire **Cadet Chapel** is an engineering and architectural masterpiece that took five years to design and four years to build. Tours are given daily 9 A.M.–6 P.M. in summer and until 5 P.M. in winter. Just below the chapel is the great square where you can see Colorado's version of the changing of the guard. At 11:35 A.M. Mon.–Fri. during the academic year, most of the 4,000 cadets parade across the square to lunch. Many visitors to the academy enjoy the planetarium (program schedule is available at the visitor center). The campus is also a game refuge, so watch for deer and wild turkeys by the road.

Golf
Retired or active military are invited to play the two excellent and challenging 18-hole courses at the academy. The Blue is a Robert Trent Jones Jr. course with long, narrow fairways, and the Silver is a mountainous course with shorter holes demanding a bit more precision. Call one day in advance for tee times. **719-333-2456.**

Hiking
The academy offers a number of scenic hiking trails around the grounds as well as access to the adjacent **Pike National Forest** located in the foothills just to the west. Stop in at the visitor center for maps and information about the 12-mile **Falcon Trail,** the relatively flat 14-mile **Santa Fe Trail** and the shorter hike to **Stanley Canyon Reservoir.**

Getting There
The South Entrance can be reached from Colorado Springs by heading north on Interstate 25 to Exit 150B (Academy Blvd.). The North Entrance is located a few miles farther north on Interstate 25 at Exit 156B. **Visitor Services Division, HQ USAFA/PAV, 2346 Academy Dr., USAFA, CO 80840-9400; 719-333-2025; www.usafa.af.mil.**

Garden of the Gods
Red sandstone formations that jut out at wild angles, thousand-year-old juniper trees, twisting needles of rock sculpted by wind—all these make this Colorado Springs city park truly a "garden fit for the gods."

Dedicated in 1909, the 1,350-acre park at the foot of Pikes Peak has since become a Registered National Landmark. And although it sounds like a cliché, a trip here really should not be missed. Many visitors take a quick drive through the park—maybe with a stop to pretend to hold up Balanced Rock—then leave and think they've seen it all. The best approach is to start out at the newly built and impressive

Garden of the Gods Visitors Center. Then be sure to park your car and take a walk on one of the many trails, several of which are usable by wheelchairs. Take time to watch the technical climbers who can usually be found negotiating the treacherous Over the Rainbow route on Gateway Rocks. Those tempted to try some rock scrambling of their own should be warned that climbing in the park (unless you obtain a permit) is prohibited, and rangers definitely enforce the rules. Picnicking and guided horseback riding are also popular (see the Horseback Riding section).

Geology
A half day in Garden of the Gods is probably the equivalent of a semester of geology. About 300 million years ago, Frontrangia, part of the ancestral Rocky Mountains 30 to 50 miles west of the modern-day Rockies, stopped growing. Ancient rivers began to carry rocks and debris from the shrinking mountains, spreading them out over the Colorado Springs area in hundred-foot-thick alluvial fans. Balanced Rock and Steamboat Rock are evidence of these deposits. A great sea covered Colorado for the next 150 million years; then, about 60 million years ago, the Rockies began to rise again. As a massive dome grew at the site of Pikes Peak, it vertically tilted the horizontal rock layers along its edges. Wind and water finished the job, stripping away the less resistant rocks while carving the tougher ones into the towers and spires that make up Garden of the Gods.

The formations are as whimsical as their names: Three Graces, Kissing Camels, Weeping Indian, Rocking Chair. An early publicist for the area, W. E. Parbor, lost his job when he dubbed one formation "Seal Making Love to a Nun." The name was changed to Seal and Bear.

Getting There
The south entrance to the Garden of the Gods can be reached by taking Hwy. 24 west from Interstate 25 to the Ridge Rd. exit; the northeast entrance is reached from Interstate 25 by heading west on Garden of the Gods Rd. (Exit

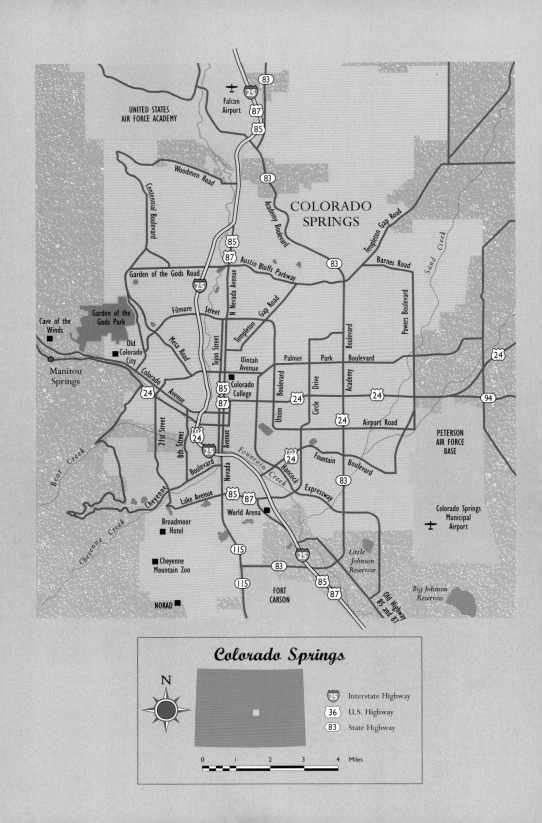

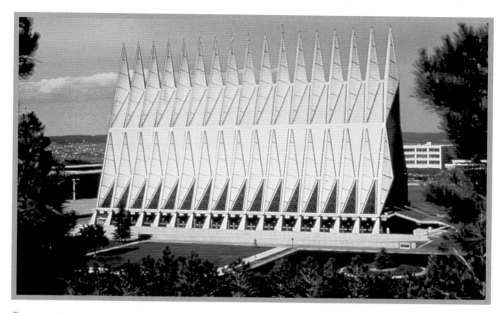

The unusual chapel at the U.S. Air Force Academy in Colorado Springs. Photo courtesy of the Colorado Springs Convention and Visitors Bureau.

146) to 30th St., turning left and proceeding about a mile.

Trading Post

Built in the late 1920s to resemble the home of Pueblo Indians, the post is the largest gift shop in the Pikes Peak region. It includes a Southwest Indian art gallery with paintings, rugs, crafts, pottery and jewelry. Patio dining in summer, serving buffalo burgers and wood-fired pizza. Located near Balanced Rock on the west edge of the park. Open daily 8 A.M.–8 P.M. in summer, 9 A.M.–5:30 P.M. in winter. **1-800-874-4515; 719-685-9045; www.co-trading-post.com.**

Visitors Center

Located at the east entrance to the park on 30th St., this state-of-the-art information center should not be missed. In addition to excellent interpretive displays covering the gamut from local geology to bird life, a theater (small fee) provides a fantastic 12-minute multimedia feature that makes the geology of the Garden of the Gods interesting and understandable. Nature talks and walking tours can also be arranged

here. The classic Colorado view from the center balcony out to the Garden of the Gods, with Pikes Peak in the background, alone is worth a visit. Two gift shops and a cafeteria. Hours are 8 A.M.–8 P.M. in summer; 9 A.M.–5 P.M. in winter. **1805 N. 30th St., Colorado Springs, CO 80904; 719-634-6666; www.gardenof gods.com.**

Pikes Peak

Pikes Peak, at 14,110 feet, is America's Mountain, the best-known peak in the country. This isn't because it's the highest (30 other peaks surpass it in Colorado alone) or the most beautiful, but because it rears out of the plains apart and alone, dominating the landscape around it. Those who take the time to reach its summit are rewarded on clear days with dramatic and unobstructed views of many mountain ranges and the eastern plains.

History

A small expedition headed by Lt. Zebulon Pike came to within 15 miles of the summit on Nov. 27, 1806, when Pike declared, "I believe no human being could have ascended to its pinnacle." The first ascent came just 14 years later, by Dr. Edwin James, a botanist with the Long expedition. In 1929 a Texan, Bill Williams, pushed a peanut to the top with his nose. He wore out 170 pairs of pants during the 20-day trek. Today there's a cog railroad and a toll road to the summit.

A whale was reported on the summit in 1923. When journalists investigated, they found a 40-foot wooden frame with a notorious public relations man inside spraying seltzer through a blowhole.

Today die-hard runners race up and down the peak every Aug. in one of the most rigorous marathons on the planet. It's also the nation's second-oldest marathon. In winter a local club trudges up through the snow to set off midnight fireworks marking the New Year.

Facts About Pikes Peak

The view from the summit is well worth the trip. From there you can look straight down on Colorado Springs, see Denver 70 miles to the north, the Spanish Peaks and spiny Sangre de Cristo Mountains to the south and the snow-capped Sawatch and Mosquito Ranges to the west. The summit itself is windswept and barren, except for the summit house, and anywhere from 10 to 30° F colder than Colorado Springs. Take a coat. The summit house features a gift shop, snack bar and incredibly good hot chocolate and donuts. Ask one of the workers to tell you stories about living on the summit (especially during lightning storms).

Getting There

To reach the Pikes Peak Hwy. from Colorado Springs, head west for 10 miles on Hwy. 24. At the town of Cascade, look for the marked exit to the left.

Hiking the Peak

Of the several hiking routes to the summit of Pikes Peak, **Barr Trail** is the most commonly used. The trail, about 13 miles one way, starts just off Ruxton Ave. above Manitou Springs, near

the cog railway station. Fred Barr built the trail between the years 1921 and 1923 with a pick, shovel and dynamite. The trail has made Pikes Peak one of the state's longest but easiest 14ers, and its most ascended. Probably the best way to make the hike is a two-day trip with a stopover at the **Barr Camp** 6.8 miles up. Here you'll find two well-equipped cabins as well as lean-tos and tentsites. Meals can be provided as well. To book sites in advance, contact **Barr Camp, P.O. Box 6283, Colorado Springs, CO 80934; 719-635-4742; www.questadventuresinc. com.** For a one-day trip, it's possible to take the cog railway or hitchhike to the summit and hike down. A shorter and, perhaps, more remote and scenic route is possible from the northwest side of the peak via the Crags (see the Hiking and Backpacking section of the **Cripple Creek and Victor** chapter). For information on other routes, call **719-578-6640** 8 A.M.–5 P.M. Mon.–Fri.

Pikes Peak Cog Railway

Zalmon A. Simmons decided to build a cog railroad up Pikes Peak after a painful ride to the top on a mule. His goal, says historian Marshall Sprague, was no less than "to alleviate the suffering of the soft-bottomed human race." The railroad, which first made it to the top in 1891, is still a quick and easy way up the mountain. Swiss-made diesel trains have long since replaced the old angled steam engines, but one relic still sits at the station. Trains depart regularly from the depot for the 3-hour round trip. Reservations are advised. Open Apr.–Nov., but trains don't always make it all the way up in Apr. and May because of snow. **515 Ruxton Ave., Manitou Springs.** For fares and other information, contact **P.O. Box 351, Manitou Springs, CO 80829; 719-685-1045; 719-685-5401; www.cograilway.com.**

Pikes Peak Highway

Although Pikes Peak has been tamed by a highway, the 38-mile round-trip road itself is anything but tame. The drive includes 156 often harrowing turns along a nearly 7,000-foot climb. The original carriage road was built in 1868–1888 and the first car reached the summit in 1901. The present highway, built in 1915–1916, provides awesome panoramas of the Continental Divide. You might even spot bighorn sheep, deer or elk. The road is paved for the first 7 miles and is currently being upgraded the rest of the way to the summit. Open, believe it or not, to the summit most of the year. Toll fee is charged. For information call **719-385-7325** or **719-684-9383.** For an adventurous descent along the highway via a mountain bike, consider a guided trip with **Challenge Unlimited.** They run early morning and sunset rides from the summit. **1-800-798-5954; 719-633-6399.**

Pikes Peak International Hill Climb

For information on this spectacular car race to the summit of Pikes Peak, see the Festivals and Events section.

Cave of the Winds

Although it's rather pricey and has sacrificed something to commercialization, such as a nightly laser light show that illuminates the scenic canyon and colored lights that enhance the formations' natural beauty, those who have not been down in a cave may still find the Cave of the Winds worth visiting. Discovered by children in 1880, the mile-long cavern gets its name from winds that used to blow through it. Alas, the magical sound has since been silenced by the need for a new entrance.

The cave is known for its dazzling samples of stalactites and stalagmites. (Okay, which one hangs from the ceiling?) A 60-foot-long, 40-foot-wide, 35-foot-tall room was added to the tour in 1988, lit by 10,000 more watts of colored lights.

The 40-minute guided tour on paved walkways can make you feel a bit like you're on a conveyor belt, and the teenage guides (no, not geologists or spelunkers) with their canned spiel provide less-than-adequate answers to anything more than superficial questions about caves. One alternative may be the lantern tour, sans the colored lights and other unnatural additions:

slightly more expensive, it's offered on weekends only. For a true taste of spelunking, make reservations for the so-called "wild tour" of the Grand Caverns. This is a muddy 2 1/2-hour plunge into the deepest pockets of the cave. Located 6 miles west of Colorado Springs off Hwy. 24 above Manitou Springs. Open 9 A.M.–9 P.M. in summer; 10 A.M.–5 P.M. in winter. **P.O. Box 826, Manitou Springs, CO 80829; 719-685-5444; www.caveofthewinds.com.**

Cheyenne Mountain Zoo

Clinging to the side of Cheyenne Mountain, this zoo's setting has to be one of the greatest. What the zoo lacks in size it makes up for in unique animal habitats. It's also a bastion for endangered species, more than 50 of which are represented among the zoo's more than 650 animals. These include orangutans, snow leopards, Mexican gray wolves, lowland gorillas, black-footed ferrets and a huge collection of giraffes. Some of the better exhibits are the birds of prey and the monkey house.

Just above the zoo stands the **Will Rogers Shrine of the Sun,** a tribute to the famed American humorist as well as the final resting place for Spencer Penrose, developer of the Broadmoor Hotel. Admission to the zoo also includes the shrine, which is worth a quick drive. Open daily 9 A.M.–5 P.M. To reach the zoo from Interstate 25, head south on Nevada Ave. Turn right on Lake Ave. and proceed to the Broadmoor. Then turn right and follow signs on Mirada Rd. up to the zoo. **4250 Cheyenne Mt. Zoo Rd., Colorado Springs, CO 80906; 719-633-9925; www.cmzoo.org.**

Glen Eyrie

Colorado Springs' own castle, Glen Eyrie, is a well-kept secret mainly bypassed by most summer visitors. Privately owned by the Navigators, a Christian group, Glen Eyrie is primarily a conference center but offers limited tours (for a fee), afternoon tea and even overnight stays.

Built by Gen. William Palmer in 1904 for his wife, the Tudor-style castle testifies to Palmer's European tastes and high standards of

A classic view of Pikes Peak towering over the Garden of the Gods in Colorado Springs. Photo by Dean Winstanley.

architecture. It includes 24 fireplaces, some of which were brought over from cathedrals and castles in Europe. Ironically, Mrs. Palmer, who spurned the nest when it was merely a wooden home, never saw the castle. The estate was practically a city unto itself, with greenhouses, stables, nine reservoirs, a dairy, schoolhouse, pool, bowling alley and Turkish bath. Listed on the National Register of Historic Places, the castle sits amid many of the same stunning rock formations found in Garden of the Gods. No drop-ins. Contact: **P.O. Box 6000, Colorado Springs, CO 80934; 1-800-944-GLEN; 719-634-0808; www.gleneyrie.org.**

Manitou Springs

Colorado Springs was named for the mineral springs that are actually located in Manitou Springs. Ute Indians used this area on the west edge of Colorado Springs as one of their favorite hunting grounds. They probably used the springs for their medicinal value. Manitou is in fact an Indian word meaning "Great Spirit," but the town's name actually comes from a reference to a spirit in Longfellow's poem "Hiawatha."

Manitou Springs became nationally known in 1877 for "the water cure," said to remedy almost any illness. Later, as hospitals began to take over its role, this Victorian town evolved into a tourist center and has been designated a National Historic District. The 26 springs (9 of which have been restored) still bubble, and samples are available in many restaurants and stores.

Today Manitou Springs is home to artists, craftspeople and even a couple of witches' covens. Many knickknacks, antiques and original works of art can be found in the quaint shops crammed into a few blocks. There's also a charming outdoor arcade, including what has to be one of the few penny arcades left in the country.

Most visitors to the Pikes Peak area end up in Manitou Springs because of its proximity to many of the most popular attractions. If you do find yourself here for a day, get off the main road and walk through the Queen Anne homes that crawl up either side of the canyon. For lodging and restaurant information see the Where to Stay and Where to Eat sections.

Miramont Castle

Stair-stepping up Mt. Manitou is the eccentric castle that Father Jean Baptiste Francolon had built for his mother and himself in 1895. The name Miramont means "look at the mountain." The structure is a fantastic (though a bit run-down), rambling hodgepodge of nine different styles of architecture, from Byzantine to Romanesque. Inside the 46 rooms, a Victorian Life Museum, a miniature model of Colorado Springs in the 1888 "Little London" days and, as sort of an added bonus near the end, a model railroad display highlight the tour. The castle was built by Francolon after he was sent to Manitou to avail himself of the mineral waters for his health. Over the years it has been a sanatorium run by the Sisters of Mercy and an apartment complex in which banisters and furniture are said to have been used by apartment dwellers as firewood before the castle was added to the

En route to Pikes Peak's summit in style. Photo courtesy of Manitou and Pikes Peak Railway Co.

National Register of Historic Places in 1977. Today it is operated by the Manitou Springs Historical Society. Admission fee charged. Open daily Memorial Day through Labor Day, 10 A.M.– 5 P.M.; tea room and soda fountain, 11 A.M.– 4 P.M.; Sept.–May, 12–3 P.M. daily; weekends-only in Jan. **9 Capitol Hill Ave., Manitou Springs, CO 80829; 719-685-1011.**

Seven Falls

Billed as "The Grandest Mile of Scenery in Colorado," the concentration of beauty in Seven Falls and South Cheyenne Canyon is both a blessing and a curse. Indian tribes used to trap animals in the box canyon by stampeding them into its dead end. Although truly spectacular, it can still feel like a trap as some 300,000 visitors a year cram into this area.

Seven distinct but connected falls splash 300 feet down a black granite wall and are accessible by two sets of stairs. One set leads to Eagles Nest platform, which offers a good view of the falls; another goes to a mile-long trail ending at an overlook of the city. Eagles Nest is accessible via elevator by those unable or unwilling to attack the stairs. For another great view of the falls, consider going up North Cheyenne Canyon, rather than South Cheyenne Canyon, and walking up the never-crowded Mt. Cutler Trail. It's an easy 2-mile round trip and it's free.

Located at the west end of Cheyenne Blvd. in southwestern Colorado Springs. Open daily 8 A.M.–11:15 P.M. May 15–Sept. 15; 9 A.M.– 4:15 P.M. the rest of the year. Admission fee charged. **P.O. Box 118, Colorado Springs, CO 80901; 719-632-0741; 719-632-0752; www.seven falls.com.**

U.S. Olympic Complex

Each year this 35-acre complex plays host to thousands of athletes training for the Olympics in the thin mountain air of Colorado Springs. The complex, home to 18 of the 41 national governing bodies for amateur athletics, is the headquarters of the U.S. Olympic Committee. The attractive facilities house 14 sports teams that you can watch train. The visitor center features a gift shop and an Olympic video. One-hour tours of the complex are offered on the hour in winter and every half hour in summer. Open year-round Mon.–Sat. 9 A.M.–5 P.M., Sun. 10 A.M.–5 P.M. **1 Olympic Plaza, 1750 E. Boulder St., Colorado Springs, CO 80909; 719-578-4618; 719-578-4644; www.olympic-usa.org.**

Festivals and Events

Aside from the highlights listed below, you can get an update of weekly events by calling **719-635-1723.**

Pikes Peak International Hill Climb

July 4th Every summer race-car drivers take to the highway in the Race to the Clouds. It's the second-oldest auto race in the world and certainly one of the most grueling. Bobby and Al Unser, Mario Andretti and Rick and Roger Mears have all won the event. The best vantage points include Devil's Playground or Crystal Creek; Halfway Picnic Grounds and Glen Cove aren't bad either. Many people drive up the night before and stake out a camping site near the best viewing areas. There is a charge for both camping and the race. For more information contact **Pikes Peak International Hill Climb Association, 135 Manitou Ave., Manitou Springs, CO 80829; 719-685-4400; www.ppihc.com.**

Pikes Peak International Raceway

weekends in summer Pikes Peak International Raceway (PPIR) is arguably the finest auto-racing venue in Colorado. This super-speedway located 12 miles south of Colorado Springs on I-25 has done a terrific job attracting high-profile drivers and at least one NASCAR and Indy-class car event each summer. Races held June through Sept. **1-888-511-PPIR; 719-382-7223.**

Pikes Peak or Bust Rodeo

early Aug. As the state's largest outdoor rodeo, this event attracts the country's best professional cowboys and cowgirls. The city kicks things off with a free pancake breakfast downtown and a parade. At **Penrose Stadium.** Information: **1-800-DO-VISIT; 719-635-1632.**

International Balloon Classic

Labor Day weekend More than 125 hot-air balloons take off from **Memorial Park** at sunrise each of the three days, making for spectacular photo opportunities. Accompanied by parachuting displays and other aerial events, the classic has become one of the most prestigious ballooning events in the country, increasing in popularity every year. Worth waking up for. **719-471-4833; www.balloonclassic.com.**

Colorado Opera Festival

summer Many of the country's best directors and artists are in residence in Colorado Springs for this annual summer series. Operas are usually (but not always) in English and range from rare to contemporary. **719-473-0073; www.colo-opera.org.**

Athletic Competitions

Several national and international events are hosted yearly in the Colorado Springs area, many at the **Olympic Training Center.** Call for schedules, **719-578-4644.** For top-notch college hockey at the terrific **World Arena,** score some tickets to see the **Colorado College Tigers** Division I team: **719-389-6111; 719-576-2626; www.worldarena.com.** Visit an **Air Force Falcons** college football game along with all the famous pageantry; tickets available at **1-800-666-8723** or **719-472-1895.** If you love baseball, check out a **Colorado Springs Sky Sox** game, the AAA farm team for the Colorado Rockies. For that special occasion, you can watch the game from a hot tub! **719-591-SOXX.**

Outdoor Activities

Biking

MOUNTAIN BIKING

With Colorado Springs' close proximity to the mountains, there are plenty of scenic and challenging rides in and around town as well as just west in the Rampart Range. Mountain bike rentals are available at **Team Telecycle** in **Woodland Park** at 719-687-6165. Also at **Criterium Bike Shop,** a terrific place for maps, trail ideas, other information and repairs; north end of town at **6150 Corporate Center Dr.; 719-599-0149.** Maps and information about trails in the Pike National Forest can be obtained at **Pikes Peak Ranger District Office, 601 S. Weber St., Colorado Springs, CO 80903; 719-636-1602; www.fs.fed.us/r2/psicc/pp.**

Gold Camp Rd. and trails branching off from it offer many popular rides of varying difficulty. Gold Camp and a number of other roads listed in the Scenic Drives section make for worthwhile scenic rides. **Rampart Reservoir** shoreline provides popular rides (see the Fishing section), though some sections are for advanced riders.

In town try the trails (specifically the old jeep trail) that run through **Palmer Park.** It can be accessed in town just off Maizeland Rd. between Chelton Rd. and Academy Blvd. Much work has been done to provide an excellent paved trail along Monument Creek **(Monument Trail)** that connects to the gravel-topped **Santa Fe Trail** at the north end of town. From there, continue north through the Air Force Academy and eventually El Paso County. Also consider a ride through the Garden of the Gods on either the paved roads or single-track trails.

Fishing

Elevenmile Canyon and Reservoir
See the **South Park and 285 Corridor** chapter.

Manitou Lake
Locals suggest using salmon eggs and worms to land rainbow trout at this ideal family spot. U.S. Forest Service fee charged. Seven miles north of Woodland Park on Hwy. 67.

Rampart Reservoir
This out-of-the-way reservoir provides 10 miles of excellent shoreline for fishing. The difficulty of getting to this reservoir means the angling is usually uncrowded. Ice fishing prohibited. Fee charged. Rampart Reservoir is located 8 miles east of Woodland Park on Rampart Range Rd.

Golf

Air Force Academy
Two beautiful 18-hole courses are open to active and retired military only. See the Major Attractions section for information.

Broadmoor Golf Club
The courses at the Broadmoor are considered by many to be some of the finest in the state. This is where Jack Nicklaus got his start with a win in the U.S. Amateur. The three 18-hole courses provide three good reasons to stay at the Broadmoor Hotel, since they're reserved for members and hotel guests only. Pines and scrub oak dot the rolling fairways, which all have Cheyenne Mountain as their backdrop. Greens fees are moderately expensive if you are a guest and pricey for friends of hotel guests. Tee times are available for the general public on the South Course the day ahead only. Cart required. **719-634-7711; www.broadmoor.com.**

Patty Jewett Golf Course
Built in 1898 this 27-hole course was the first set of links west of the Mississippi. The tall trees, mature greens and views to Pikes Peak make Patty Jewett one of the best public courses in Colorado Springs. **900 E. Española St.; 719-385-6938.**

Pine Creek Golf Club
This 18-hole public course, located on the high prairie grasslands about 10 miles northeast of downtown, offers fantastic views of Pikes Peak and the mountains to the west. Over 70 sand traps provide a formidable challenge; so does the strong wind, which tends to pick up later in the day. Full facilities. Take Exit 151 (Briargate) from Interstate 25, just north of town, and follow the signs about 3 miles east. **9850 Divot Trail; 719-594-9999; www.pinecreekgolfclub.com.**

Spraying a "rooster tail" during the July 4th Pikes Peak International Hill Climb. Photo courtesy of the Pikes Peak Hill Climb Museum.

Hiking and Backpacking

Colorado Springs' city and county mountain parks are full of great hikes. The treks range from hour-long strolls to two-day climbs up Pikes Peak. The **Colorado Springs Convention and Visitors Bureau, 1-800-DO-VISIT,** provides a reasonably good list of hiking trails in the area. For more detailed information about hikes in nearby Pike National Forest, contact **Pikes Peak Ranger District Office, 601 S. Weber St., Colorado Springs, CO 80903; 719-636-1602; www.fs.fed.us/r2/psicc/pp.**

Bear Creek Regional Park

Five miles of easy trails, with access for the disabled. An ecologist's dream, the park also contains a nature center at the west end that can guide and educate. Nature center open 9 A.M.–4 P.M. Tues.–Sat. Bear Creek Rd. off of Lower Gold Camp Rd. in west Colorado Springs. **719-520-6387; www.coloradosprings.com.**

The Crags

See the Hiking and Backpacking section in the **Cripple Creek and Victor** chapter.

North Cheyenne Canyon Park

Start your visit to this scenic and historic canyon at the **Starsmore Discovery Center** with its fantastic interpretive displays, climbing wall and nature hikes. Kids will love it. Trail maps and books available. Open Mon.–Sat. in summer 9 A.M.–5 P.M., opens at noon on Sun.; limited days and hours in winter. To reach Cheyenne Canyon, head west on Cheyenne Blvd. from Colorado Springs. **2120 S. Cheyenne Canyon Rd.; 719-578-6146; 719-578-6147; www. coloradosprings.com.** Here are a few trail ideas in the park:

Mt. Cutler Trail—See the Seven Falls entry in the Major Attractions section.

North Cheyenne Canyon Trail—This 5-mile loop has an easy grade, passes three springs and provides widespread views of the canyon and down to Colorado Springs. The trail begins just past the entrance to the park, on the left side of the road.

St. Mary's Falls Trail—This 4-mile round-trip trail begins at the top of Helen Hunt Falls and leads to St. Mary's Falls. Cross the bridge and follow the path on the far side of the stream. Expect a half day there and back. Bring a lunch and enjoy great glimpses of Colorado Springs.

Pikes Peak

See the Pikes Peak entry in the Major Attractions section.

Horseback Riding

Academy Riding Stables

This stable rents horses for 1- and 2-hour guided tours through Garden of the Gods—a good way to avoid the many carloads of visitors. Riders must be at least 8 years old. Reservations urged. **4 El Paso Blvd., Colorado Springs, CO 80904; 719-633-5667; www.arsriding.com.**

Riding Stables at the Broadmoor

Explore the trails on Cheyenne Mountain with views to the city. Offers 1- to 2-hour guided rides; carriage and hayrides available also; no one under 7 years old. **719-448-0371.**

Ice Skating

Colorado Springs World Arena

This enormous facility houses two ice rinks. Skate rentals available. Call for hours. **3205 Venatucci Blvd.; 719-477-2153; www.worldarena.com.**

Skiing

CROSS-COUNTRY SKIING AND SNOWSHOEING

Mueller State Park and the Crags

The best cross-country skiing in the Pikes Peak area lies about 30 miles away at the Crags and Mueller State Park. See the Outdoor Activities section in the **Cripple Creek and Victor** chapter.

Rampart Reservoir

Located about 8 miles east of Woodland Park on Rampart Range Rd. The 13-mile Lakeshore Trail around the lake makes for a good day of cross-country skiing. Although it's possible to drive all the way from Colorado Springs to the reservoir on Rampart Range Rd., the dirt road is often blocked in winter. It is wiser to take Hwy. 24 west to Woodland Park and then backtrack 8 miles to the reservoir.

Rentals and Information

Mountain Chalet—This shop in downtown Colorado Springs rents touring equipment and can point skiers in the right direction. **226 N. Tejon St.; 719-633-0732; www.mtchalet.com.**

Seeing and Doing

Amusements

North Pole / Santa's Workshop

Most people probably don't realize it, but the North Pole isn't on some remote ice floe above the Arctic Circle; it's perched conveniently on the flank of Pikes Peak. It's always Christmas at the region's only amusement park, where you'll find brightly garbed elves, reindeer, plenty of rides, magic shows, Christmas gift shops and of course Santa himself (real beard). Kids who still believe love the place. Open mid-May through Christmas Eve. Summer hours 9:30 A.M.–6 P.M. Closed Thurs. in May, and closed Wed.–Thurs. Sept.–Dec. Located 10 miles west of Colorado Springs on Hwy. 24 at the entrance to the Pikes Peak Hwy. **719-684-9432; www.santas-colo.com.**

Museums and Galleries

American Numismatic Museum

Numismatic is probably a word only coin collectors know, and this is a museum probably only coin collectors will love. Operations for the American Numismatic Association are headquartered here, so this is the big time of coin collecting. The museum houses one of the most extensive collections of coins, paper money, tokens and medals in the United States. Open Mon.–Fri. 9 A.M.–4 P.M. Free entrance. **818 N. Cascade Ave., Colorado Springs, CO 80903-3279; 719-632-2646.**

Colorado Springs Fine Arts Center

This marvelous facility is housed in an art deco masterpiece built in 1937 and listed on the

National Register of Historic Places. A museum, theater, library, art school and shop make up the Colorado Springs Fine Arts Center. Of specific note is the **Taylor Museum for Southwest Studies,** which houses a fabulous collection of Native American works and Hispanic art including its well-known collection of santos. Six traveling exhibits are showcased annually. Theater activities include repertory theater, three film series and various performances. In summer enjoy lunch at **The Warehouse** on the balcony looking out to Pikes Peak (see the Where to Eat section). Fee charged. Open Tues.–Fri. 9 A.M.–5 P.M., Sat. 10 A.M.–5 P.M., Sun. 1–5 P.M. **30 W. Dale; 719-634-5581.**

Manitou Cliff Dwellings Museum

If you want to see Indian cliff dwellings in their natural setting, you'll have to go to Mesa Verde in southwestern Colorado. None of the cliff dwellers lived within 350 miles of Manitou Springs. The 40-room dwelling here is a reconstruction of prehistoric Basket Maker apartment houses under a convenient sandstone overhang above Manitou. It was built in 1906 after the stones were hauled from a private ranch near Mesa Verde. This pales in comparison to the real thing. Gift shop/museum housed in re-created Taos Pueblo adjacent to the cliff dwellings. Admission fee charged. Open 9 A.M.–8 P.M. in summer; 9 A.M.–6 P.M. in May and Sept.; 10 A.M.–4 P.M. Mar.–Apr. and Oct.–Dec.; weekends-only in Jan. and Feb. **1-800-354-9971; 719-685-5242; www.cliffdwellingsmuseum.com.**

Manitou Springs

For information on this terrific art area just west of Colorado Springs, see the Major Attractions section.

May Natural History Museum

The giant Hercules beetle by the highway welcomes visitors to one of the world's outstanding collections of arthropods. Bugs, that is. Some 8,000 of them are on display, collected by James May over a period of 63 years. The entire collection includes more than 100,000 critters.

Don't miss the tarantula locked in a death grip with a hummingbird, and the Colombian beetles so big they are said to have knocked people over with speeds of 40 miles per hour. The center also has 5 miles of nature trails and a new Museum of Space Exploration. Take the Hercules turn off Hwy. 115, 9 miles south of Colorado Springs. Admission fee charged. Open daily 8 A.M.–6 P.M. May–Sept. 30; by appointment other times of year. **710 Rock Creek Canyon Rd.; 719-576-0450.**

McAllister House

Maj. Henry McAllister, "born friend" of Colorado Springs founder Gen. William Jackson Palmer, came out to Colorado Springs in 1872. He built the first brick house in Colorado Springs. After one of the area's infamous chinook winds blew a train off its tracks, McAllister ordered 20-inch-thick walls to withstand all the elements. His unique house opened as a museum in 1961. Guided tours give a taste of Colorado Springs in its "Little London" era. Summer hours 10 A.M.–4 P.M. Wed.–Sat., noon–4 P.M. Sun.; winter hours 10 A.M.–4 P.M. Thurs.–Sat. Admission fee. **423 N. Cascade Ave.,** near downtown; **719-635-7925; www.oldcolo.com/hist/mcallister.**

Old Colorado City

Once the territorial capital, Colorado City today boasts a quaint collection of old buildings housing many art galleries, restaurants and clothing stores. Browse the businesses along W. Colorado Ave.; even if you don't buy anything it's worth a visit. One notable stop is **Michael Garman Galleries.** Dominated by "Court and Darby Street," a miniature 24-foot-long city scene, the studio contains other of Garman's unique urban miniatures and realistic figures. A variety of pieces are for sale at reasonable prices. **2418 W. Colorado Ave.; 719-471-1600; www.michaelgarman.com.**

Pioneer's Museum

To see the way Colorado Springs was, visit this museum in the old El Paso County Courthouse.

The building, which is on the National Register of Historic Places, is worth the stop in itself. Inside, among other things, is the house and furnishings of writer and poet Helen Hunt Jackson. Other tidbits of Pikes Peak history include historic photos (such as William Henry Jackson photos), antique toys and Indian artifacts. Changing exhibits attract many locals. Open 10 A.M.–5 P.M. Tues.–Sat. Free admission. **215 S. Tejon St.; 719-385-5990.**

ProRodeo Hall of Fame

This well-designed hall of fame and museum is a monument to the legacy of the American cowboy. A visit begins with two multimedia shows: one on the history of the Old West, another that re-creates the feel of being a cowboy. After that, Heritage Hall traces the development of cowboy gear. The Hall of Champions showcases the trophies, belt buckles and other paraphernalia of the rodeo greats. Where do Brahma bulls retire? Right here at the mini-rodeo arena—at least one especially mean-looking one has. Open daily 9 A.M.–5 P.M. year-round. Admission fee. Take Exit 147 west off Interstate 25; **719-528-4761; www.prorodeo.com.**

Western Museum of Mining and Industry

Before heading to the mining country up around Cripple Creek and Victor, think about stopping by this gem of a museum. Visitors can learn how the mines were worked and what to look for when sightseeing. See a host of mining machines in operation and learn how to pan for gold. Tours include a multimedia show, a blacksmith shop and a reconstructed mine. Admission fee. Open 9 A.M.–4 P.M. Mon.–Sat., closed Sun. Take the Gleneagle Dr. exit (156A) off Interstate 25 at the North Entrance to the Air Force Academy; **719-488-0880.**

World Figure Skating Hall of Fame and Museum

Displays memorabilia of skating champions, including the Broadmoor's own Peggy Fleming, and a history of the sport. The museum includes what is billed as the largest and finest collection of skating art in the world and also has a gift shop. Free admission. Open Mon.–Sat. 10 A.M.–4 P.M. **20 First St.; 719-635-5200; www.usfsa.org.**

Nightlife

Cruising

Depending on your mood, Nevada Ave. on Fri. and Sat. nights could be a good place to take a drive back in time. Or it could be a place to avoid at all costs. The approximately 10-block-long section of the parkway that cuts through downtown has to be one of the last great cruising strips in the West. Hundreds of "cherried-out" cars, from vintage Chevys to low riders and the latest sports cars, extend bumper to bumper along Nevada Ave. Most cruisers drive a loop that starts around Colorado Ave. to the south, eventually wrapping around the statue of Gen. Palmer to the north. But if you are in a hurry to get somewhere, take Cascade Ave. or Interstate 25.

The Golden Bee

Walking into the Golden Bee, the curators like to say, is like pulling on a familiar sweater—you feel right at home. This authentic English pub was brought over from London and reassembled in the basement of the International Center at the Broadmoor Hotel. Infectious piano tunes and a wide variety of English ales (often ordered by 38-oz. yards) make this small room one of the best nightspots in Colorado Springs. The entire pub sings along to the ragtime piano music, often led by at least one anxious, musical patron. The record for polishing off a full yard stands at about 7 seconds. Warning: waiting in line is often part of visiting the Bee. Pub menu and complimentary cheese and crackers. Open 11:30 A.M.–2 A.M. daily. Across from the Broadmoor at **1 Lake Ave.; 719-577-5776; www.broadmoor.com.**

The Iron Springs Chateau

The emphasis is on audience participation at this comedy melodrama. Things get under way at

6 P.M. with an all-you-can-eat meal of barbecued beef and country-fried chicken. The curtain goes up at 8:30 P.M., with ample opportunity for cheers and jeers. A rousing sing-along olio and dancing in the lounge round out an entertaining night. Open Tues.–Sat. in summer, Fri.–Sat. in winter; dinner served 6–7 P.M. Reservations necessary. In Manitou Springs across from the Cog Railway Station at **444 Ruxton Ave.; 719-685-5104; 719-685-5572.**

Jack Quinn's Ale House and Pub

Smack dab in the center of downtown Colorado Springs sits this terrific Irish pub. Decorated in dark wood and other authentic flourishes, Quinn's serves Irish food **($$)** as well as great varieties of libations, including Guinness stout on tap. Live music on weekends. Open 11 A.M.–2 A.M. Mon.–Sat., from noon on Sun. **21 S. Tejon St.; 719-385-0766.**

Loonies Comedy Corner

Local and national stand-up comics perform here Wed.–Sun. nights. Call for reservations. **1305 N. Academy Blvd.; 719-591-0707.**

Meadow Muffins

With walls covered in memorabilia, Meadow Muffins continues to be a Colorado Springs institution attracting a young crowd. Its dance floor features pop and rock; new theme every night. Microbrews, cheap beer and free popcorn. Mon.–Sat. 11 A.M.–1:30 A.M., Sun. 11 A.M.–midnight. **2432 W. Colorado Ave.; 719-633-0583.**

Phantom Canyon Brewing Company

Phantom Canyon continues to draw raves from microbeer connoisseurs for its excellent brews. Located in the historic Cheyenne Building downtown, this spacious, attractive brewpub offers a selection of five fresh brews, characterized by a lean toward hoppiness. Other drinks are available, of course, as well as an impressive menu of pub favorites and a full selection of other entrées and appetizers. Food served Sun.–Thurs. 11 A.M.–10 P.M., until midnight Fri.–Sat.; light menu until 2 A.M. Mon.–Sat. **2 E. Pikes Peak Ave.; 719-635-2800.**

Pine Gables Tavern

Classic rowdy mountain bar that is well known for its live rock and roll, cheap beer and great Bloody Marys. Located about 10 miles west of Colorado Springs off Hwy. 24 at **10530 Ute Pass Ave., Green Mountain Falls; 719-684-2555.**

Scenic Drives

Cripple Creek and Victor

The three scenic drives described below lead from Colorado Springs to the historic mining towns of Cripple Creek and Victor. A combination of two of them makes for a great 70-mile round trip.

Gold Camp Road—Teddy Roosevelt traveled by train along Gold Camp Rd. back at the turn of the century. But even without the tracks the scenery is just as stunning. The sometimes harrowing drive is open late spring to early fall. It's quite a show in late Sept. when the aspen are turning. Due to a tunnel cave-in, you'll have to start your journey by detouring west up Old Stage Rd. located near the Broadmoor Hotel on the way to Cheyenne Mountain Zoo. On the way to Cripple Creek the dirt road wraps around Cheyenne Mountain, with views of Colorado Springs, then plunges through several tunnels still etched with the soot from Short Line (of Monopoly fame) locomotives. Since the road is often in poor condition and very narrow, the 30-mile trip can take hours. RVs and trailers are not recommended.

Highway 67—This is the most traveled and fastest route to Cripple Creek, but that doesn't mean the drive is any scenery slouch. After winding up Ute Pass to the town of Divide on Hwy. 24, take Hwy. 67 south through great stands of aspen and a one-way tunnel. You might consider this paved route for a speedy return trip.

Through Florissant—This route works best for stops at **Florissant Fossil Beds National Monument.** Take Hwy. 24 to Florissant, turn south on County Rd. 1 for a couple of miles and look for the monument entrance on the right (west). About 5 miles past the monument the road turns to dirt, climbs up past Mt. Pisgah and then descends into the Cripple Creek basin. For more information about the fossil beds, see the Major Attractions section of the **Cripple Creek and Victor** chapter.

High Drive

A quick, cliff-hugging drive with a tremendous panorama of the Broadmoor, Cheyenne Canyon and Colorado Springs. Drive up North Cheyenne Canyon to the end of the pavement at the Gold Camp Rd. crossroads. Follow the signs to the right for High Dr. or Lower Gold Camp Rd., both of which eventually feed into Hwy. 24 without ever really having left the city.

Pikes Peak Highway

See the Pikes Peak entry in the Major Attractions section.

Rampart Range Road

The scenery along this road starts off auspiciously in Garden of the Gods and never really quits. The rough road actually goes north through Pike National Forest and all the way to Hwy. 67 northwest of Castle Rock, but the Woodland Park turnoff is usually far enough for the shock absorbers of most vehicles (and riders). Beware of boulders in the middle of this roller-coaster, washboard dirt road. Taking Hwy. 24 back to Colorado Springs from Woodland Park makes for an adventurous half-day trip.

Where to Stay

Accommodations

Colorado Springs is home to plenty of well-known first-rate hotels. There's also a healthy representation of national bargain chains, campgrounds, dude ranches and cabin-type motels. But without question, Colorado Springs and Manitou Springs score highest for their proliferation of outstanding bed and breakfasts and

historic inns. It's easiest to find a bed by calling the **Colorado Springs Convention and Visitors Bureau** at 1-800-DO-VISIT during business hours Mon.–Fri. 8 A.M.–5 P.M. (weekends also in summer); **www.coloradosprings-travel.com.** Below are some of the more interesting and indigenous places to stay in the area.

The Broadmoor—$$$$

A destination in itself—worth visiting even if you're not staying. This exceptional resort at the foot of Cheyenne Mountain is one of only a few in America to be awarded Mobil's five-star rating. The complex contains three hotels, three championship golf courses, 16 tennis courts, a carriage museum, several excellent restaurants (see the Where to Eat section), three spring-fed pools, a shooting grounds, a "Fifth Avenue" row of shops and a new, first-rate health spa. Separating the modern Broadmoor West from the two older hotels is an idyllic lake graced by a variety of waterfowl. One of the most pleasant ways to spend an hour in Colorado Springs is to stroll around the shoreline path—and you don't have to be a guest. A casino originally stood where the main hotel now stands. After it burned down, Spencer Penrose, who had made his fortune in gold and copper, bought the property in 1916 and opened the luxury resort two years later.

Room rates include free access to the spa's indoor pool, sauna and aromatherapy room, among others. For an additional charge, enjoy a relaxing massage, facial or numerous other soothing treatments. Staying here can be an expensive proposition, ranging from just over $100 a night to $1,000. The off-season winter rates, however drop 30 to 40 percent. Check out their package deals. **1 Lake Ave., Colorado Springs, CO 80906; 1-800-634-7711; 719-634-7711; www.broadmoor.com.**

Cheyenne Mountain Conference Resort—$$$$

Check out the weekend packages and the views west to Cheyenne Mountain and surrounding mountains at this 221-room resort. An 18-hole

The beautiful and elegant The Cliff House in Manitou Springs. Photo by Dean Winstanley.

golf course, fitness center, three swimming pools and a nearby lake with fishing and sailing provide you with plenty to do. Its **Mountain View Dining Room** provides excellent food and views out to Cheyenne Mountain. **3225 Broadmoor Valley Rd., Colorado Springs, CO 80906; 1-800-428-8886; www.graylyn.com/cmcr.**

The Cliff House—$$$$

The smashing overhaul of this palatial old hotel has not gone unnoticed: The Cliff House has garnered many awards for its work (and the price tag for transforming this place was staggering). Choose from 56 unique, luxurious rooms and suites spread throughout this four-story inn, originally built in 1873 as a hotel and stage stop. My favorites are the fourth-floor turret suites at either end of the inn. Room fees include afternoon tea in the main-floor common areas or outdoor porch and breakfast in **The Cliff House Dining Room** that also serves outstanding dinners **($$$$)**. **306**

Cañon Ave., Manitou Springs, CO 80829; 1-888-212-7000; 719-685-3000; www.thecliffhouse.com.

Rockledge Country Inn—$$$$

The Rockledge, another of Manitou Springs' historic gems, commands a terrific hilltop location just above town. Built in 1912, this 9,000-square-foot beauty blends English Tudor with western ranch style. Each of the guest suites will spoil you with king-size beds with feather comforters, entertainment centers, fireplaces and spas in some rooms, good views and other features. Owner Hartman Smith has achieved a masterpiece in the recent renovation of this place. In addition to the full breakfasts, including such items as smoked trout quiche, candlelight dinners may be arranged in advance. An award-winning, outstanding place for a romantic getaway. **328 El Paso Blvd., Manitou Springs, CO 80829; 1-888-685-4515; 719-685-4515; www.rockledgeinn.com.**

Antlers Adam's Mark Hotel—$$$ to $$$$

Located in downtown Colorado Springs, the Antlers provides 292 rooms for those who want a downtown location. Rooms and suites come with turndown service and cable TV, data port and other things business travelers may need. Other amenities include a health club, indoor pool and whirlpool. Downstairs, the Antlers Grille and Judge Baldwin's Brewing Company provide food and entertainment. **4 S. Cascade Ave., Colorado Springs, CO 80903; 719-473-5600; www.antlers.com.**

Hearthstone Inn—$$$ to $$$$

This country inn, listed on the National Register of Historic Places, is actually two sister Victorians in a row of similar mansions on serene Cascade Ave. near downtown Colorado Springs. Inside are three floors with 25 sumptuous, sometimes eccentric rooms. Each chamber has its own theme (and price), such as the Gable Room, the Author's Den and the Billiard Room. All but two rooms have baths or showers, some have antique fireplaces and one boasts its own breakfast terrace. But none has a TV or telephone, as it should be in this 19th-century setting.

Half the fun of staying at the Hearthstone is exploring the other rooms. Puzzles, games and a piano in the homey lobby encourage guests to revive the art of conversation. Just behind the inn is Monument Valley Park, with a jogging trail, tennis courts and swimming pool. The gourmet breakfast is easy to miss at 8 A.M., but don't. **506 N. Cascade Ave., Colorado Springs, CO 80903; 719-473-4413; www. hearthstoneinn.com.**

Holden House—$$$ to $$$$

This restored 1902 Victorian offers all the comforts of home without any dishes to do. Sallie and Welling Clark have filled (more like jammed) the home with family heirlooms, including a tremendous quilt made by Sallie's great-grandmother. You'll find two guest rooms and a suite upstairs in the main house, two carriage-house suites out back and the Independence

bungalow overlooks town. The four bedrooms Two Sisters (two with shared bath) are appointed with antiques and fresh flowers. The "Honeymoon Cottage" out back, which used to be an old wagon shop for the town livery stable, has its own fridge and sink. Your hosts, Wendy and Sharon, used to be in the catering business so rest assured, you'll have plenty to eat, especially at breakfast. Both Wendy and Sharon are enthusiastic about Manitou and the surrounding area and can be a great source of information about where to go and what to see. **10 Otoe Pl., Manitou Springs, CO 80829; 1-800-2SISINN; 719-685-9684; www.twosis inn.com.**

American Youth Hostel—$

The Colorado Springs AYH shares facilities with Garden of the Gods Campground near Manitou Springs. Each of the 12 cabins has four bunk beds. No rest rooms in cabins, but campground facilities are accessible. It's a good idea to call ahead. Swimming pool and hot tub. Open May–Oct. only. **3704 W. Colorado Ave., Colorado Springs, CO 80904; 719-475-9450.**

OTHER BED AND BREAKFASTS

On the higher end consider a night at the luxurious **Old Town Guest House ($$$ to $$$$)** in Old Colorado City. Though newly built, this three-story brick building blends in fairly well with its historic neighbors. Eight plush rooms provide varying features from unique furnishings to hot tubs on private balconies. Breakfast the indoor/outdoor

26th St., Colorado

1-888-375-4210; 719-632-

nline.com/co/oldtown.

y at an impressively renovated

me, consider **Room at the Inn**

$$). It's a special place, from the orig-

d and tile in the home's five rooms, to

period antiques, to the distinctive turret.

o rooms also in carriage house; wood deck

with whirlpool bath; full breakfast. **618 N. Nevada Ave., Colorado Springs, CO 80903; 719-442-1896; www.roomattheinn.com.** The impressive views, elegance and history of **Cheyenne Canyon Inn ($$$ to $$$$),** an enormous old Mission-style mansion, are matched only by the Herculean effort that went into its renovation. Choose a night's stay in one of the 10 guest rooms or the romantic (and separate) **Le Petite Chateau,** with its own fireplace and outside deck hot tub. Before digging into your enormous breakfast consider an early morning walk on trails in North Cheyenne Canyon Park, adjacent to the inn. **2030 W. Cheyenne Blvd., Colorado Springs, CO 80906; 1-800-633-0625; www.cheyenne canyoninn.com.** Located along the Pikes Peak Hwy., the **Black Bear Inn ($$$)** provides a comfortable mountain lodge atmosphere. The nine guest rooms offer queen-size beds, TVs, phones and private baths. Full breakfast; outdoor hot tub. **5250 Pikes Peak Hwy., Cascade, CO 80809; 719-684-0151; www.blackbearinn pikespeak.com.** Farther west, in Woodland Park, consider a night at the **Woodland Inn Bed and Breakfast ($$ to $$$).** With 12 wooded acres, six comfortable guest rooms and full breakfasts, this place also stands out for its very affordable balloon ride packages for guests. **159 Trull Rd., Woodland Park, CO 80863; 1-800-226-9565; 719-687-8209.**

Camping

Pike National Forest

For information, maps and campground vacancies, stop by the **Pike's Peak Ranger District Office, 601 S. Weber St., Colorado Springs; 719-636-1602; www.fs.fed.us/r2/ppsicc/ pp.** If you want to make reservations for a campsite at least 10 days in advance, contact **1-877-444-6777** or **www.reserveusa.com.** The campgrounds listed below charge a fee.

North of Woodland Park via Hwy. 67 are several good campgrounds. The first, 5.8 miles north of Woodland Park, is **South Meadows Campground** (64 sites). Another mile up the road is **Colorado Campground** (81 sites). Farther up the road are **Painted Rocks Campground** (18 sites) and **Trail Creek Campground** (7 sites). They're usually filled by early afternoon in summer.

Private Campground

Garden of the Gods Campground— Conveniently located near the south entrance to Garden of the Gods, this RV heaven includes 300 campsites, with heated pool, whirlpool bath and grocery store. Tours available. Open Apr. 15– Oct. 15. **3704 W. Colorado Ave.; 1-800-345-8197; 719-475-9450.**

Where to Eat

Charles Court at the Broadmoor—$$$$

This elegant restaurant decorated in the style of an English country manor is perhaps the Broadmoor's best and Colorado Springs' most exclusive. The continental and Southwestern food is superlative, but the prices are even more stunning. Charles Court is in the modern Broadmoor West with a wonderful lake view. If for no other reason, sup at Charles Court for the awesome wine selection (650 choices!) and the knowledge displayed by the wine steward. He does everything to educate you about your bottle short of producing the vintner in person. We were told that over 100,000 bottles of wine are stored in the Broadmoor wine cellar. Sun. brunch is unsurpassed in the Colorado Springs area. Reservations recommended. Dinners served Mon.–Sat. 6–9 P.M.; hours for breakfast and lunch vary. Coat and tie required, dresses or suits for women. **1 Lake Ave.; 719-577-5774.** If you want romance and a chance to show your dance moves, consider the **Penrose Room** instead. Recently remodeled, the Penrose specializes in French cuisine from its perch atop the Broadmoor's South Tower. Reserve this for a very special occasion. **1-800-634-7711; 719-634-7711.**

The Briarhurst Manor—$$$ to $$$$

The Briarhurst Manor continues to be one of the top choices in town for a special dinner. In 1975 European-trained and highly recognized chef Sigi Krauss opened for business, serving excellent continental cuisine. The impressive stone manor, built in 1876, allows dinner to be served in its various intimate rooms and occasionally on the sprawling patio. It is difficult to isolate certain dishes as standouts but the Colorado rack of lamb, roasted with garlic and thyme and then baked, is exquisite. Stop by at the end of Aug. when up to 2,000 people per day visit the Briarhurst's Oktoberfest celebration out on the lawn. Make sure you dress up for dinner; reservations suggested. Open Mon.–Sat. 5:30–9:30 P.M. **404 Manitou Ave.; 719-685-1864.**

Craftwood Inn—$$$ to $$$$

This fine restaurant is the place in town to go for three main reasons: romantic atmosphere, fine selection of wild game dishes and creativity. Located in a beautiful English Tudor-style home built in 1912, the Craftwood Inn offers a warm atmosphere with a stone fireplace in one room and soft music playing throughout. Cris Pulos, the talented chef and owner, has put together an incredible menu. Start off your meal with an unusual appetizer such as black bean ravioli or artichoke hearts wrapped with venison. Entrée choices include variations on fish, poultry and, especially, meat. Wild game specialties range from grilled Colorado boar and sautéed caribou to mixed game bird including pheasant sausage. Vegetarians should not shy away—the salads are tasty as well as the veggie platter served with wild rice. Desserts are exceptional and also difficult to choose from. We recommend the

prickly pear sorbet or the jalapeño white chocolate mousse. Full bar. Open Mon.–Thurs. 5–8:30 P.M., Sat.–Sun. 5–9 P.M. In Manitou Springs at **404 El Paso Blvd.; 719-685-9000.**

Flying W Ranch—$$$

This working cattle and horse ranch north of Garden of the Gods is part restaurant, part tourist attraction. Keep a tight rein on your travelers checks, pardner, as you visit 14 different museum buildings and gift shops. All kidding aside, it can be a lot of fun, especially for out-of-state visitors and families. All meals include the campfire western show featuring the Flying W Wranglers, a cowboy band that's been around since the 1950s. Chuckwagon suppers are held mid-May–mid-Sept. Dinners are served inside during the winter months. Dinner served 7:15 P.M. with show at 8:30 P.M. daily during summer, dinner and show at 6:45 P.M. Fri.–Sat. in Sept. Reservations are necessary. Take Garden of the Gods Rd. west off Interstate 25 to 30th St. and turn right. Follow the signs. **3330 Chuckwagon Rd.; 1-800-232-3599; 719-598-4000; www.flyingw.com.**

Zeb's—$$$

Named after Zebulon Pike, this restaurant lives up to its name with Pikes Peak-sized portions. Prime rib is a sure bet, as are the well-known barbecued baby back pork ribs, which are baked during the day, then put on the grill at night. Dinner is served with a great view of the mountains. Open Sun.–Thurs. 6–10 P.M., Fri.–Sat. 5:30–11 P.M. **945 S. 8th St.** in south central Colorado Springs; **719-473-9999.**

Blue Star—$$ to $$$

With cuisine that's a far sight more creative than you'll find at many local spots, the Blue Star draws loyal clientele for its constantly changing menu that primarily features dishes of the Pacific rim, Mediterranean and Southwest. Choose an item or two from the tapas menu to start things off. Then dive into entrées such as grilled chicken orange cous cous salad or the smoked pheasant soft tacos with sweet roasted red pepper curry sauce. Happy hour daily 4–7 P.M. (Beer aficionados wanting to just kick back with a good brew may want to pay a visit next door first to a terrific microbrewery, the **Bristol Brewing Company**.) The Blue Star is open for lunch and dinner Mon.–Fri. 11:30 A.M.–9 P.M.; for dinner Sat. 4 P.M.–midnight, Sun. 4–9 P.M. **1645 S. Tejon; 719-632-1086.**

Mission Bell Inn—$$ to $$$

This venerable and still popular Mexican restaurant in Manitou Springs is named for the immense iron bell and thick oak front door that were moved to it from an old mission in Mexico. The Masias family has been operating this colorfully decorated restaurant since 1962. Along with the standard Mexican fare such as chalupas, flautas and enchiladas, try a norteño (a smothered, stuffed green pepper), which is quite good. Open Wed.–Sun. 5–9 P.M., closed Mon. In Manitou Springs at **178 Crystal Park Rd.; 719-685-9089.** For another Mexican mainstay, try **Henri's ($ to $$$)** in **Old Colorado City** at **2427 W. Colorado Ave.; 719-634-9031.** Another popular, more spacious place is **Old Santa Fe Mexican Grille ($ to $$),** open daily 11 A.M.–10 P.M. at **2165 Academy Pl.; 719-597-8806.**

The Warehouse—$$ to $$$

The Warehouse wins the trifecta of praise at its downtown location. First, the renovated, turn-of-the-century building provides a wonderful, artistic ambience, offering artworks and gallery shows. Second, the **Palmer Lake Brewing Company** is located here, featuring six of its handcrafted brews on tap. Finally, the food, including upscale Colorado cuisine, is wonderful. For lunch choose from a creative list of appetizers, salads, pastas and entrées. Dinner is highlighted by entrées such as pepper seared pork medallions, grilled buffalo sirloin and shrimp and scallop sauté. The lengthy martini list and dessert options are also notable. Highly recommended. Open Mon.–Fri. 11 A.M.–midnight, Sat. 4 P.M.–midnight, closed Sun. **25 W. Cimarron; 719-475-8880.**

Giuseppe's Old Depot—$$

Recently rebuilt after a devastating fire, Guiseppe's is back better than ever. This restored Denver & Rio Grande train station, originally built in 1887, specializes in spaghetti, pizza and other Italian dishes. Great salad bar, too. Families love this cavernous place. Relax at the comfortable tables and watch the freight trains go by. Meals arrive on plates rimmed with train track. Kids who are into model trains go ape. Open Sun.–Thurs. 11 A.M.–9 P.M., Fri. and Sat. 11 A.M.–midnight. **10 S. Sierra Madre; 719-635-3111.**

Adam's Cafe—$ to $$

Repeatedly chosen by *Springs* magazine readers as the best natural food restaurant, Adam's should not be missed for a number of reasons. This cozy little cafe in Manitou is best known for its excellent breakfasts (Fri.–Sun.), delicious homemade soups and salads and regional Southwestern, Mediterranean and northern Italian entrées. The daily seafood special is popular as well. The atmosphere is relaxed, with hanging plants, artwork and soft music in the background. Don't miss their tasty gourmet desserts. Open Mon.–Thurs. 11 A.M.–3 P.M. and 5–9 P.M.; Fri.–Sun. 8 A.M.–3 P.M. **110 Cañon Ave.; 719-685-1430.**

Dale Street Cafe—$ to $$

Located in an old home north of the downtown area, this small cafe serves up truly fine lunches and dinners with a European flair. When weather permits, sit at one of the tables in the front yard and peruse the fine wine and beer list. Standout menu items include salads (Caesar, spinach, etc.), pasta dishes and a number of Mediterranean pizzas, which are just light enough to leave room for a slice of their superb key lime pie. Open Mon.–Thurs. 11:30 A.M.–9 P.M., Fri.–Sat. 11:30 A.M.–9:30 P.M., closed Sun. **115 E. Dale St.; 719-578-9898.**

Juniper Valley Ranch—$ to $$

For 50 years, the Parker family has been serving up their family-style dinners at this fourth-generation homestead. And little has changed since the early days, especially the menu. Choose from baked ham or all-you-can-eat skillet-fried chicken dinners with all the fixin's. The old red-mud homestead house and ranch decor are a real throwback. Reserve well in advance as this is a remarkably popular place. Open Fri.–Sat. 5–9 P.M., Sun. 1–8 P.M. Closed Nov.–early Apr. Located 12 miles south of Fort Carson **on Hwy. 115** on the east side of the road; **719-576-0741.**

Panino's Restaurant—$

Though far from fancy, Panino's is somewhat of a tradition in Colorado Springs. The late Tony Frasca introduced his panino—his thin-crust pizza sandwich that's stuffed with Italian meats, cheese, veggies and other goodies—to the Springs years ago at the N. Tejon St. location. The rest is history. They also serve up subs, pasta, pizza and salads. Open Mon.–Sat. 11 A.M.–9 P.M. Three locations: **604 N. Tejon St., 719-635-7452; 1721 S. 8th St., 719-635-1188; 750 Village Center Dr., 719-227-8300.**

OTHER DINING RECOMMENDATIONS

Saigon Springs ($$ to $$$) offers a reasonably priced and complex Vietnamese menu. Outstanding egg rolls. Exotic food contrasts with the drab location. Mon.–Thurs. 11 A.M.–9 P.M., Fri.–Sat. 11 A.M.–9:30 P.M. **3408 N. Academy Blvd.; 719-597-1175.** For larger-than-life burgers in a campy 1950s-like decor, try **Conway's Red Top ($ to $$).** The burgers have won boucoup local awards year after year; the malts are unforgettably rich and thick. Red Top has three locations, but the S. Nevada Ave. restaurant is the one with the 1950s ambience. Open Sun.–Thurs. 11 A.M.–8 P.M., Fri.–Sat. 11 A.M.–9 P.M. **1520 S. Nevada Ave.; 719-633-2444. Michelle's ($ to $$)** is famous for its homemade ice cream, which the Micopolous family has been offering for years at this old-time soda fountain. Also try the frozen yogurt, sandwiches and gourmet burgers. Open Sun.–Thurs. 9 A.M.–11 P.M., Fri.–Sat. 9 A.M.–midnight. **122 N. Tejon St., 719-633-5089,** or in the **Citadel Mall** on **Academy Blvd.,**

719-597-9932. Heaps of rib-stickin' and inexpensive breakfast food featuring omelettes and down-home specials awaits at the **North End Diner ($ to $$).** Very relaxed and popular; lunches served also. Open Tues.–Sat. 5 A.M.–8 P.M., Sun.–Mon. 5 A.M.–4 P.M. **3005 N. Hancock; 719-442-1833.**

Cafes

Coffee drinkers and lingerers will like the places listed here. **Boulder Street Coffee Roasters,** a popular spot just north of the downtown area, offers pastries, bagels and desserts along with great coffee. **332 N. Tejon; 719-577-4291. Pikes Perk,** at three locations in town, provides comfortable couches as well as a full line of jolting coffee and tea drinks and bakery items. **Manitou Bakery and Cafe** offers outstanding baked goods, quiches and daily lunch specials. **729 Manitou Ave.; 719-685-5808.**

Sunday Brunch

Sun. brunch in Colorado Springs is a chance for truly decadent all-you-can-eat spreads that are guaranteed to put on a few pounds. **The Lake Terrace at the Broadmoor ($$$)** (see the Where to Stay section) serves an exquisite spread, perhaps the best in town, 9:30 A.M.–1 P.M. Be sure not to miss their bananas foster! Another choice, with great views out toward Cheyenne Mountain, is the well-named **Mountain View Dining Room** at the **Cheyenne Mountain Conference Resort ($$$)** (see the Where to Stay section).

Services

Visitor Information

Colorado Springs Chamber of Commerce—P.O. Box B, Colorado Springs, CO 80901; 719-635-1551; www.cscc.org.

Colorado Springs Convention and Visitors Bureau—Provides information and brochures during regular business hours. **104 S. Cascade**

Ave.; 1-800-DO-VISIT; 719-635-7506; www. coloradosprings-travel.com.

Manitou Springs Chamber of Commerce—Walls of brochures and someone to talk to about Manitou. **354 Manitou Ave., Manitou Springs, CO 80829; 719-685-5089; www.manitousprings.org.**

Pikes Peak Country Attractions Association—**354 Manitou Ave., Manitou Springs, CO 80829; 719-685-5894; www. pikes-peak.com.**

More Colorado Springs Information— www.coloradosprings.com.

Transportation
Pikes Peak Tours—Daily sightseeing tours, airport transport and related services. **1-800-345-8197; 719-633-1181; www.colorado grayline.com.**

Springs Transit—City bus service. For fares and schedules call **719-475-9733.**

Yellow Cab Taxi Service—**719-635-9907.**

Creede and Lake City

A diverse and beautiful 75-mile stretch of Hwy. 149—the Silver Thread Scenic and Historic Byway—strings together the three communities of South Fork, Creede and Lake City. In addition to proximity, these towns have other things in common: millions of acres of public lands, hundreds of miles of productive trout streams and a far-reaching network of breathtaking two- and four-wheel-drive roads. Both Creede and Lake City have been named National Historic Areas.

The Uncompahgre, Rio Grande, Gunnison and San Juan National Forests as well as several wilderness areas provide enticements for people who like to explore the backcountry without crowds. If you have the time, take a hike to the stunning formations at the Wheeler Geologic Natural Area. In winter, after the hunters have left, locals reclaim a sense of solitude. Very few visitors come through Creede and Lake City after the snow has fallen, but cross-country skiing, snowshoeing and snowmobiling remain excellent ways to enjoy the surroundings.

Many alpine lakes and the popular Rio Grande and Lake Fork of the Gunnison Rivers lure anglers to the area. Jeep roads connect with

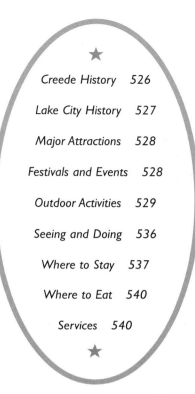

Getting There

Creede is located between South Fork and Lake City on Hwy. 149 about 300 miles southwest of Denver. The easiest route from Denver is to take Interstate 25 south for 160 miles to Walsenburg, then head west on Hwy. 160 for 120 miles to South Fork. Turn right onto Hwy. 149 for the remaining 22 miles to Creede. A more scenic route from Denver is via Hwy. 285.
Lake City is located 53 miles northwest of Creede on Hwy. 149; it's also 55 miles southwest of Gunnison via Hwy. 149.

the destinations of Silverton, Telluride and Ouray. Your regular passenger car can also take you to some pretty incredible scenery: Lake San Cristobal, Slumgullion Earthflow and the Silver Thread itself to name a few.

Isolated and strikingly picturesque, Creede lies nestled in a compact side canyon of the Rio Grande Valley. With few of the trappings of a full-service resort, Creede is a place that snaps you back to the wide-open mining history of a century ago. Historic St., lined with galleries, shops and a few restaurants, leads directly into a sharply cut ravine behind town. Continuing into the ravine, this road works its way to the town's original settlement, which is now called North Creede, soon arriving at the mines that have pulled out 80 million troy ounces of silver in the past century. Outside of Creede, in the Upper Rio Grande Valley, a large number of rental cabins and guest ranches cater to visitors.

Creede is in no danger of becoming a ghost town even though its active mining era has passed. A dramatically beautiful environment and low-key atmosphere have drawn a unique brand of people together who choose to call Creede home. They make the town a special place, without the cookie-cutter sameness so evident in some areas. A perfect example of Creede's resourcefulness lies in the town's nationally acclaimed repertory theater (see the Major Attractions section for details).

Northwest of Creede, Lake City sports a distinct history (including one of Colorado's most bizarre chapters) yet remains a charming little community. The colossal peaks of the San Juan Mountains dwarf this diminutive town to even smaller proportions. Unlike Creede, more than a handful of 14ers tower nearby.

Tucked into a grassy canyon at the confluence of Henson Creek and the Lake Fork of the Gunnison, Lake City remains a Colorado original that relatively few Coloradans know about. In the 1920s and 1930s, when Lake City was on the verge of becoming a ghost town, a rash of visitors from the south discovered its air-conditioned summer weather at 8,663 feet. Many Lake City visitors are Texans and Oklahomans who have been coming here for generations.

Since the late 1800s South Fork (to the southeast) has developed primarily as a logging and lumbering community, though it has grown to serve the needs of visitors. Located at the foot of Wolf Creek Pass, and due to its proximity to year-round recreational possibilities, it offers a decent mix of restaurants and motels. South Fork and Pagosa Springs (see the Pagosa Springs chapter) are the two most convenient places to stay while skiing the deep powder at Wolf Creek Ski Area atop the Continental Divide.

Creede History

"Holy Moses!" shouted Nicholas C. Creede when he discovered the area's first silver lode in 1889. Within a few months, the Holy Moses, Ethel, Amethyst and Last Chance Mines were producing fantastic quantities of high-grade ore. A latecomer to the silver boom, the new town of Creede was soon attracting 300 newcomers a day and nearing a population of 10,000. During

this time a mass of humanity became locked in a struggle for huge stakes. With land selling for exorbitant prices, some new arrivals built shanties on wooden supports laid across Willow Creek; later, outhouses were built across the creek, which "flushed" away the sewage. This reckless growth contributed to Creede's reputation for nonstop nightlife. In 1892 Cy Warman penned a famous poem about the town—the last verse reads, "It's day all day in the daytime, and there is no night in Creede."

Soapy Smith, a strongman con artist from Denver, ran nearly all of the gambling in town from his Orleans Club. Smith once claimed he found a petrified man in the mud near town at Farmer's Creek. He cleaned it for display at the Vaughn Hotel and charged a quarter admission. Soon enough, however, the so-called "Solid Muldoon's" cement skin began to flake off, and the scam was forced to move to a new location. Smith eventually resurfaced in Skagway, Alaska, where he was gunned down in 1898.

Boomtown status attracted a special breed of men and women whose names have survived the passage of time. Bat Masterson was the marshal of Creede for a short while. Bob Ford was another of Creede's residents—famous only because he killed Jesse James with a shot to the back. Ford operated a saloon in Creede until Ed O'Kelly gunned him down with a double-barreled shotgun. Champagne, wine and song flowed freely at Ford's funeral. He will be forever remembered in a ballad as "the dirty little coward." The flourishing trade of ladies of the night had a queen named Slanting Annie. Calamity Jane and her friend Poker Alice Tubbs were a couple of other well-known locals.

Though Creede was once the leading producer of silver in the state, the repeal of the Silver Act in 1893 caused the area economy to collapse. Boom had turned to bust in less than five years. On top of that came flash floods and catastrophic fires in 1892, 1895, 1902 and 1936 that destroyed many of the town's grand old buildings.

Even with all this adversity, the town has always managed to rebuild and, over the years, it has attracted an eclectic bunch of locals. For a

A solitary whitewashed church etches the sky in Lake City. Photo by Kirstin Bebell.

while a volatile combination of hippies and rednecks flocked to the area—very gradually the distinction has become blurred. Today the town is a relaxed haven for writers and artists as much as for retirees and outdoor types.

Lake City History

Many years before Creede hit its heyday in the late 1880s, this San Juan mining camp had already gone through a few booms and busts. After 1874 when the Utes ceded most of the San Juan territory, rumors of gold inspired prospectors to come into the Lake City area. When Enos Hotchkiss made a major strike in 1874, a rush of prospectors started arriving. Within two years the young town of Lake City had a population of 1,000 and supported two banks, five blacksmith shops, seven saloons, two breweries, the *Silver World* newspaper and four Chinese laundries. The first church on the Western Slope of Colorado was built at Lake City in 1876. Today this pretty, white-framed church still stands at 5th St. and Gunnison Ave.

Because it was difficult to get ore out of this hard-to-reach valley, Lake City's initial boom died down by 1880. The town experienced periods of exaltation and discouragement until 1889, when the Denver & Rio Grande Railroad laid 38 miles of track from Sapinero (north of town) to Lake City. The railroad became a stabilizing force in the economy for years to come.

Compared with other mining towns, Lake City stayed a rather calm place to live. There were a few lynchings and, of course, the requisite bordello district (called Hell's Acres), but most hoodlums moved on to other camps.

One particularly gruesome exception to law and order occurred the winter before Lake City was established. In January 1874, when Alferd Packer and some companions showed up at a Ute encampment near present-day Delta, they were warned not to continue because of deep snow and severe weather. Though Packer knew nothing of the San Juans, he claimed expertise, and five eager prospectors hired him as their guide. They set out on the dangerous passage into the snow-covered mountains with only enough provisions to last 10 days. Six weeks later Packer showed up at the Los Piños Indian agency 76 miles northeast of Lake City—all alone, with a beard and long hair but appearing well fed.

He claimed to have endured the below-zero weather by eating rose pods and roots. Packer then stupidly turned down something to eat and soon went on a drinking binge in Saguache, paying for drinks with money from several wallets. This suspicious behavior raised a few eyebrows, especially when Native Americans, walking along the same trail Packer had taken, found strips of human flesh. It wasn't until late summer that five partially decomposed bodies were discovered a few miles south of Lake City on the northeast side of Lake San Cristobal (the area is now called Cannibal Plateau). Four of the men had been murdered in their sleep with an axe to the head and the fifth, found nearby, was shot to death. Chunks of flesh had been cut from the men's chests and thighs.

Packer sensed something was awry and managed to escape from detention in a Saguache jail. Nine years later he was discovered in Wyoming living under the assumed name of John Schwartz. On April 13, 1883, Packer was sentenced to hang at the Lake City courthouse. The embellished version of the sentencing has presiding Judge Melville Gerry shouting, "Packer, ye man-eatin' son of a bitch, they was seven dim-mycrats in Hinsdale County and ye eat five of 'em, God damn ye! I sentins ye to be hanged by the neck until ye're dead, dead, dead. . . ."

Gallows were constructed, but because of a technicality, Packer's trial was declared unconstitutional. He was given a new trial, convicted of manslaughter and sentenced to 45 years of hard labor at the Cañon City Penitentiary. However, as his last act, Colorado Gov. Charles Thomas pardoned Packer, who was released after serving only 5 years. He died of natural causes in 1907 and is buried in Littleton under the misspelled name Alfred Packer.

A fenced area with an interpretive sign and five small white crosses marks the incident, a couple miles southeast of Lake City on the Silver Thread (Hwy. 149), just north of the highway, between mile-markers 69 and 70.

Major Attractions

Creede Repertory Theater

Since 1966 the old Creede Opera House has been a perfect setting for popular musicals, historical dramas and light comedies. The plays take place in an 1892 vintage building, which first opened as the Rio Grande Hotel. Impeccably restored, the Creede Theater now commands its place as the town's centerpiece, seating 243 patrons in its intimate confines. Performances take place on a rotating schedule throughout the summer. It's a fun evening for people who come from miles around to enjoy the energy and excitement of the show. Since performers expand their repertoire as the season progresses, you can see six plays performed in four days by late summer. The nonprofit theater recruits performers from across the country, last year drawing more than 700 auditions for a mere 40 jobs. Patrons have a chance to meet the actors after each performance. Other events take place during the year, including musical groups and several children's plays in the 60-seat upstairs theater. Reservations necessary; many plays are sold out early. On Main St. in downtown Creede. **P.O. Box 269, Creede, CO 81130; 719-658-2540; www.creederep.com.**

Festivals and Events

Creede Repertory Theater

mid-June to Labor Day   See the above listing for details about this one-of-a-kind theater.

Days of '92

4th of July weekend   Creede's Main St. turns into an open market as vendors sell jewelry and crafts. Everyone turns out for the parade complete with a kazoo band (more marchers than spectators), and soon afterward the mining contests get under way. Fiercely competitive hard-rock miners test their skills in events such as single-jack drilling, machine drilling and hand mucking. At the end of the festivities, an impressive fireworks display lights up the sky. For more

A magical reflection on Lake San Cristobal captures the natural beauty of the surrounding peaks. Photo by Bruce Caughey.

information, call the Lake City Chamber of Commerce at **719-658-2374; www.lakecity co.com.**

Lake City Arts and Crafts Festival

3rd Tues. in July Since 1976 this juried arts fair has featured an ever-increasing number of arts and crafts, which are on display in the town park. It's the perfect time of year to enjoy the cool mountain air while wandering leisurely among the many booths while talking to artists and artisans. A nice variety of styles and interests are represented and the location cannot be beat. Call the Lake City Arts Council at **970-944-2706.**

Outdoor Activities

Biking

MOUNTAIN BIKING

The Creede area offers more good terrain for biking than you could ever explore in an entire summer of riding. Consider some of the roads in the Four-Wheel-Drive Trips and Scenic Drives sections. In particular, the Bachelor Historic Tour offers a number of trails that take off from the main road, such as the **Rat Creek Trail.** The seldom-traveled but badly eroded road to the stunning formations at Wheeler Geologic Natural Area is another option (see the Hiking and Backpacking section). Quality rental bikes, trail ideas and maps are available at **San Juan Sports** on **Creede Ave.; 719-658-2359.**

Due to the spectacularly high mountains surrounding Lake City, mellow biking routes are sparse. A couple of ideas: **Camp Trail** entices expert bikers, while the **Colorado/Continental Divide Trails** at Spring Creek Pass are suited for those with intermediate skills. Please remember to stay on the trail to help prevent erosion. For rentals in Lake City, stop in at **San Juan Mountain Bikes** (behind the bakery) at **925 Ocean Wave Dr.; 970-944-2274; www.san juanmountainbikes.tripod.com.**

Fishing

We've noted the better possibilities, but you can choose from literally hundreds of miles of streams and dozens of brimming lakes and reservoirs in this spectacular part of the state. For local conditions, stop by the **Ramble House** on **Creede Ave.; 719-658-2482.** Talk with Alton Cole and take a look at his excellent selection of flies and lures. Or check in at the **Rio Grande Angler,** also on **Creede Ave.; 719-658-2955.**

High Country Lakes

Fern Creek Trail (see the Hiking and Backpacking section) leads into the Weminuche Wilderness west of Creede. After a few miles, the trail comes out at **Little Ruby Lake** and **Ruby Lake. Fuchs Reservoir** is also in the area, but as the water level fluctuates considerably, anglers should look primarily to Ruby Lake, the deepest and most consistent body of water. Here the catch generally results in good pan-sized rainbow and brook trout. You can take refuge in a few tumbledown cabins on the lakeshore. If you continue up the trail toward the Continental Divide, you will reach **Trout Lake.** This high lake can be good for cutthroat trout, especially in midsummer and fall.

Lake Fork of the Gunnison

The Lake Fork headwaters begin in the mountains far above Lake San Cristobal. Some good public fishing for smallish rainbow and brook trout can be found in a mile-long stretch 1.5 miles below Lake San Cristobal. The water, accessible from Hwy. 149, offers some nice riffles for dry fly-fishing. This little-known area receives relatively light use.

Within Lake City town limits, some good holes attract many anglers in the summer months. The water is stocked, and occasionally some very large trout are pulled out on nymphs, flies and lures. Below Lake City the river flows through mostly private property until reaching Gateview. Below Gateview, at Red Bridge Campground, the river is entirely public, offering some prime trout water. With waders this 30-foot-wide stream can be easily fished. Along the stretch between Gateview Campground and Blue Mesa Reservoir, the water and the bank are strewn with debris from the reservoir, making the area unattractive and difficult to fish.

Lake San Cristobal

The second-largest natural lake in Colorado, Lake San Cristobal was formed about 800 years ago when the Slumgullion Earthflow blocked the valley. It is rimmed by high, snowcapped peaks, and in fall the area becomes a golden carpet of aspen. Primarily rainbows and browns prowl the depths, but every now and then someone pulls out a 20-pound Mackinaw. In spring, just as the ice recedes from the banks, you'll have your best shot at catching one of these hogs. Bank fishing and boat casting are both popular at this crowded, easy-to-reach destination. The mossy upper end of the lake is the best place to fly-fish from the bank. Many people do very well by throwing lures or baiting with eggs, cheese or worms. To get there drive 2 miles south of Creede on Hwy. 149, turn right on County Rd. 30 and proceed 1.5 miles to the lake.

Rio Grande

The Rio Grande's runoff usually calms down in early July. Twelve miles east of Creede (6 miles west of South Fork), a 15-mile stretch of Gold Medal water, beginning at Collier Bridge, entices anglers. Many lunker trout can be caught on flies and lures. The land along this stretch is mostly public; please observe and obey posted signs. The water is easily wadable, with many of the larger trout staying low near the banks.

Rio Grande Reservoir

Thirty miles west of Creede, this long reservoir offers good fishing for trout from both boats and shore. Skewer a worm and wait for a tug on your line while enjoying the scenery. The northern shore is traced by Forest Rd. 520, while the steep southern shore serves as the boundary for the Weminuche Wilderness. Several campgrounds and picnic areas are nearby. From Creede, drive west on Hwy. 149 for 21 miles and then turn left on Forest Rd. 520, which reaches the reservoir in 9 miles.

Rio Grande Tributaries

Since the waters in Rio Grande Reservoir are used as irrigation for the valley below, the reservoir itself provides relatively poor fishing. However, a wide variety of fishing challenges can be found in many of the Rio Grande tributaries.

Starting at the west end of Rio Grande Reservoir, a trail follows **Ute Creek** into the Weminuche Wilderness. This small creek offers a chance at small cutthroat; larger brookies inhabit the higher elevations. About 6 miles from the reservoir, Ute Creek forks into **West, Middle** and **East Ute Creeks;** trails follow each tributary to popular high country lakes with good-sized cutthroat and rainbow trout. Just below the east end of Rio Grande Reservoir, **Little Squaw Creek** flows down from the Weminuche Wilderness, entering the Rio Grande at River Hill Campground. This creek is small but boasts a population of large cutthroat trout. There is no good trail along the lower portions, but you can fight your way upstream. **Squaw and Weminuche Creeks,** at the east end of the reservoir, are available for those willing to take a hike. To the west of the reservoir flows **Pole Creek,** an excellent fishing area accessible by four-wheel-drive vehicle.

Road Canyon Reservoir

Just 5 miles east of Rio Grande Reservoir, this smaller fishery offers a chance for big fish—meaning up to 6-pound rainbow trout and 2-pound brookies. The long, western shore of Road Canyon Reservoir is easily accessible for bank fishing. Boats at wakeless speeds are allowed. Road Canyon Campground is located at the southwest end of the reservoir. Follow the directions to Rio Grande Reservoir (see above) and you'll pass Road Canyon Reservoir 4 miles after turning off Hwy. 149.

South Fork of the Rio Grande

The South Fork of the Rio Grande converges with the Rio Grande at the community of South Fork, 22 miles southeast of Creede. A major tributary of the Rio Grande, the South Fork is paralleled for many miles by Hwy. 160. The stream is pretty good for brown, rainbow and brook trout. A trail from Big Meadows Campground (14 miles southwest of the town of South Fork) follows the upper reaches of the South Fork to some small lakes near the Continental Divide.

Four-Wheel-Drive Trips

More than most parts of Colorado, this mountainous, mineral-rich district provides great four-wheel-drive routes. Lake City is a natural hub for other San Juan mining towns—Silverton, Telluride and Ouray, to name a few. If you have time for just one adventure, don't miss the Alpine Loop National Back Country Byway, which goes over Engineer and Cinnamon Passes.

Alpine Loop

This spectacular 49-mile round trip, dedicated as a National Back Country Byway, is only one of the many four-wheel-drive routes in the area. From this loop trip various forays into the San Juans provide enticements off the main route. This particular drive can be taken just as easily in either direction, but we will start out by heading west over Engineer Pass. From the south end of Lake City, a green sign directs you toward Engineer Pass. The road soon climbs uphill alongside Henderson Creek, reaching a T intersection at **Capitol City** after 9 miles. This ghost town was named in an attempt to compete with Denver for the state capital—good thing it lost! Turn left and drive 4.5 miles over fairly rough road to **Rose's Cabin,** which is a good place to shift into four-wheel drive. Bear right here at the sign indicating Ouray/Silverton (unless you want to make a detour to Silverton) and in a half-mile take another right. This road leads above treeline to the summit of **Engineer Pass** (13,100 feet), which offers fantastic views of the San Juans.

The main road then drops over the other side of the pass and comes around the west side of Engineer Mountain before descending into a valley. (A couple of miles after the pass, Mineral Point Rd. leads off to the right for 7 miles to the Million Dollar Highway—Hwy. 550—just south of Ouray.) Some 5.5 miles after the summit, you arrive at a marked turnoff for **Cinnamon Pass,** a moderately steep jeep road that breaks off to the left. This road goes over the pass and then winds downhill, passing many mine ruins along the way and reaching Lake City in 24 miles. Back at the marked turnoff for Cinnamon

Pass, consider going straight (past the ghost town of Animas Forks) for 13 miles to Silverton.

Bachelor Historic Tour

This fairly easy four-wheel-drive route (or a somewhat dicey drive for vehicles without decent clearance) takes you over the ruts and rocks on a narrow, historic route into the aspen-covered hills. Begin by driving north from Creede's Main St. into the narrow canyon for a 17-mile circle tour. The first notable sight is Creede's firehouse—or should we say fire cave?—blasted 120 feet back into a solid rock wall and, right next door, the Creede Underground Mining Museum (see the Museums and Galleries section). A half-mile after setting out, the road splits. Take the left fork up West Willow Rd. Very soon after the fork, on your left, is the stone foundation to the **Humphry's Mill,** which was a large gravity ore concentrator. The road follows the creek up to the **Commodore Mine,** which tapped a huge amethyst silver vein, along a steep 2.5-mile stretch called the Black Pitch. When the road practically doubles back on itself at the **Midwest Mine,** be sure to stay left. Keep left again as the road crosses Willow Creek.

The road eventually passes the **Bachelor** townsite. Now only a deserted meadow with a few foundations, it was once home to 1,000 people. In 1893 the town boomed with mines such as the Bachelor, the Spar, the Cleopatra and the Sunnyside and as many as a dozen saloons. The views from the road down to the Rio Grande Valley are tremendous. On the way back to Creede you'll pass the **Sunnyside Cemetery** with gravestones dating back to the 1880s. You can pick up a detailed booklet of the entire route at the opening of the route (donation suggested).

East Willow Creek Loop

The beautiful aspen-cloaked mountains north of Creede are strewn with mine remnants. Drive through this area on an easy four-wheel-drive road that makes a 7-mile loop. Drive north on Main St. into the sharp ravine at the end of town.

After 0.6 mile, turn right at the fork leading to North Creede. Thousands of miners lived here in 1890, but today North Creede is home to only a few hardy souls who love its isolation and beauty. Follow the road up the west wall to the vicinity of the top-producing Solomon–Holy Moses vein. Both sides of the road are littered with old mine buildings and shafts. The road switches back down to West Willow Creek; a hiking trail leads up into the unspoiled Phoenix Park area. Take West Willow Rd. back down to Creede or continue past the Midwest Mine to Bachelor (see the preceding write-up, on the Bachelor Historic Tour).

Stony Pass

This stunning ride over a rough road provides incredible views as you angle toward the Continental Divide among 13,000-foot peaks. To reach Stony Pass Rd., drive west from Creede on Hwy. 149 for 21 miles. Turn left onto Forest Rd. 520, which passes Rio Grande Reservoir and circumvents Pole Creek Mountain (13,716 feet) on the 30-mile route to the summit of Stony Pass. Once there, enjoy the views before continuing down the other side. The road eventually leads down Cunningham Gulch, ending at a T intersection at County Rd. 110. A left turn will land you in the National Historic District of Silverton (see the Four-Wheel-Drive Trips section of the **Silverton** chapter for more information on the history of this area and for connecting routes). The trip to Silverton takes about 4 hours. A right turn on County Rd. 110 takes you through Animas Forks and over Cinnamon Pass to Lake City. Return to Creede on Hwy. 149.

Rentals

Cannibal Outdoors—Specializing in a wide variety of outdoor activities (see the River Floating section), the folks here will drive you around the beautiful high country surrounding Lake City. **P.O. Box 803, Lake City, CO 81235; 1-877-CANNIBAL; 970-944-2559; www.cannibaloutdoors.com.**
Cottonwood Cove—This South Fork business offers jeep rentals. **719-658-2242.**

Roots of an ancient pine. Photo by Dean Winstanley.

Hummer Adventure Tours—For those looking for an adventure in the wide-bodied, rugged vehicle known as the Hummer, call this outfit, run through Lake City's Rocky Top Lodge at **970-944-2780.**

Lakeview Outfitters—Located in Lake City, they'll rent you a jeep for journeys along any county-maintained roads in the area. **1-800-456-0170; 970-944-2401.**

Hiking and Backpacking

Sandwiched by Rio Grande National Forest and the La Garita and Weminuche Wilderness Areas, Creede and Lake City offer a slew of remote hiking options, including multi-day hikes along the high reaches of the Continental Divide, climbs up five nearby 14ers of varying difficulties or shorter day hikes. Since wilderness areas in this vicinity receive relatively little use, it isn't difficult to get away from crowds. It is horse country, though, and you will find traces wherever you go. For additional information on hiking in the area, consult the **Gunnison, Crested Butte, Ouray** and **Silverton** chapters. For more trail information contact the **Creede Ranger District, P.O. Box 270, Creede, CO 81130; 719-658-2556.** For topographic maps, advice and supplies, stop by **San Juan Sports** on **Main St.** in **Creede; 719-658-2359.**

Continental Divide Trail and Colorado Trail

This trail section is in the Weminuche Wilderness. Along this 80-mile length of the Continental Divide Trail from Stony Pass to Wolf Creek Pass, you'll find some incredibly beautiful backcountry. But this underused area offers a special set of considerations for avid hikers. For one thing, most of the trail is above treeline, leaving hikers susceptible to lightning strikes. Pick up topographic maps, because the trail can be difficult to find—especially between Stony Pass and Weminuche Pass—and you may need to change your route at the last minute. Despite all the necessary precautions, this is a prime route that we highly recommend. There isn't enough room here to detail the passage along the Continental Divide.

Fern Creek Trail

This may not be the most beautiful trail in the wilderness, but its destination at the shores of Little Ruby Lake, Fuchs Reservoir and Ruby Lake is enticing. As an added bonus, the fishing can be quite good at Ruby Lake and the reservoir. At Ruby Lake some people make use of a couple of drafty, abandoned cabins for overnight shelter. Often used as a stock driveway, the 3.5-mile Fern Creek Trail climbs steadily to the lakes. In early summer, fields of wild iris take over the grassy meadows, providing a pretty purple haze. To reach the trailhead from Creede, take Hwy. 149 west for 17.5 miles to Fern Creek Rd. (Forest Rd. 522). Turn left and drive for about 2 miles to the trailhead.

Rio Grande Pyramid

In 1874 when the Wheeler survey party came through the area, William Marshall called the then-unnamed Rio Grande Pyramid "one of the handsomest and most symmetrical cones in Colorado." It hasn't changed much since then. A hike to the 13,821-foot summit is an invigorating experience. In a day it's a daunting 20-mile round-trip hike with a 4,500-foot elevation gain. In two days you'll be able to stop and smell the flowers: columbine, Indian paintbrush and alpine sunflowers, among others. Many picture-perfect campsites can be found at the midpoint near Weminuche Pass.

The trail begins at Rio Grande Reservoir and reaches the summit of Weminuche Pass after about 5 miles. From the pass, which sits atop the Continental Divide, continue south for a mile to a split in the trail. Take the right fork up Ricon de La Vaca ("Valley of the Cow"). In a short while the trail emerges above treeline, with an awesome view to the landmark Rio Grande Pyramid and, just south of the summit, the window—a 150-foot-deep cut in the ridge. Shepherds used to call it the devil's gateway. Stay on the trail until it veers sharply south away from the peak. From here the trail disappears, but the obvious route up the east flank of the peak is squarely in front of you. From the top it's hard to imagine a better view of the San Juans.

To reach the trailhead from Creede, drive west on Hwy. 149 for 21 miles and then turn left on Forest Rd. 520, which leads to Thirtymile Campground (at the eastern end of Rio Grande Reservoir) after 9 miles. Trail 818 heads west along the southern shore of the reservoir before turning south to Weminuche Pass.

Wheeler Geologic Natural Area

Reminiscent of Bryce Canyon, Utah, the unusual rock formations at Wheeler Geologic Natural Area will fascinate you with their variety and beauty. The oddly beautiful geology has been created by wind and water erosion of piles of volcanic tuff (ash). Outcast Ute Indians used the area as a hideout, camping among the eerie rock spires, canyons and domes. Once designated a national monument, this remote site could not be reached by passenger car, so its designation was changed in 1933. The site can be reached on foot in 3 to 4 hours over a gentle 7-mile trail. To reach the trailhead, drive east of Creede on Hwy. 149 for 7.3 miles. Turn left on Pool Table Rd. (Forest Rd. 600) and proceed 10 miles to a sign marking what's left of Hanson's Mill. Park your car at the trailhead and a sign will direct you to the hiking path. A quarter-mile after setting out, take the left (west) fork and continue for a mile down to East Bellows Creek. Ford the small creek and pick up the trail on the other side. In 4 miles the trail rejoins the jeep road leading to the formations.

Horseback Riding

Cottonwood Cove

This is the best place to head if you're considering a guided ride near Creede. **HC33, South Fork, CO 81154; 719-658-2242.**

Freeman's

If you prefer riding without a guide, call these folks at **719-658-2454;** 18 miles west of Creede on Hwy. 149 as you head toward Lake City.

Lakeview Outfitters

Located just south of Lake City and run in conjunction with Lakeview Resort, the outfitters will guide you on a 2-hour ride. They also rent watercraft that you can take onto Lake San Cristobal. **P.O. Box 1000, Lake City, CO 81235; 1-800-456-0170; 970-944-2401.**

Vickers' Ranch

This outfit offers guided rides near Lake City and also rents cabins; **P.O. Box 969, Lake City, CO 81235; 970-944-2249.**

River Floating

Rio Grande

The Rio Grande begins its nearly 2,000-mile journey to the Gulf of Mexico above Rio Grande Reservoir in the mountains west of Creede. The water exits the dam and rushes into a narrow canyon accessible only by boat. The fishing in this 5-mile stretch is excellent and there are many secluded campsites along the way. Since the river drops fairly rapidly, rafters will find good Class III and Class IV rapids. After it emerges from the canyon, the water flattens out in the wide Rio Grande Valley. The best put-in for a trip into the canyon is a couple of miles below Rio Grande Reservoir at River Hill Campground (see the Camping section). Take out at the Fern Creek Rd. Bridge.

The most popular of runs lies down below Wagon Wheel Gap, southeast of Creede. Good fishing and a few rapids make this float down to South Fork a memorable one. Good places to put in along Hwy. 149 include Phipps Bridge and Goose Creek Rd. Bridge. Soon after setting out, beware of the steel bridge with rather closely spaced supports (dangerous to rafters). Otherwise, enjoy the ride!

Outfitters

Cannibal Outdoors—This Lake City outfitter will guide you on a float trip or wild Class IV whitewater. Fishing, jeep tours, mountain bike tours and guided peak ascents are also among their specialties. **P.O. Box 803, Lake City, CO 81235; 1-877-CANNIBAL; 970-944-2559; www.cannibaloutdoors.com.**

Mountain Man Rafting Tours—Take a guided float down the Upper Rio Grande or just rent all the gear you need and go by yourself. This established company is run locally by Greg Coln—you can trust his advice and experience. **P.O. Box 11, Rio Grande Meadows, Creede, CO 81130; 719-658-2663; 719-658-2843; www.mountainman tours.com.**

Skiing

CROSS-COUNTRY SKIING AND SNOWSHOEING

When the snow falls, most of the people in the Rio Grande Valley are long gone. The higher elevations always have enough snow and, at times, even the valley floor can be a good place to ski or snowshoe. For trail and avalanche information, contact the **Creede Ranger District, P.O. Box 270, Creede, CO 81130; 719-658-2556.**

Backcountry Trails

Hinsdale Haute Route—The Lake City area offers a variety of popular trails for skiers of all abilities. This route takes you to a yurt, a backcountry hut where you can spend the night. The trail is usually skied often enough to leave tracks for those of intermediate ability. Leave from the Lake City Post Office and head south on Hwy. 149 for 15.6 miles. The trail follows the West Fork of Cebolla Creek for 1.5 miles before reaching the yurt. To reserve use of the Wilson Yurt or other backcountry yurts, call the office of the **Hinsdale Haute System** at **970-944-2269.**

Spar City Trail—This well-marked, 5-mile loop is one of the best tours in the valley. Working its way on an easy grade to the ghost town of Spar City, this trail is usually well packed, except after recent storms. In 1892 300 people lived in Spar City while working the nearby silver mines. The town once had a host of buildings, including a jail, a dance hall, a newspaper office (the *Spar City Candle*), a sawmill and a lumberyard. On the way to the townsite, the trail offers great views to the Bristol Head Cliffs before heading deeper into a mixed forest of pine and aspen. To reach the trailhead, drive south and west of Creede on Hwy. 149 for 7 miles to Sevenmile Bridge (at Marshall Park Campground). Turn left and continue to the trailhead.

West Willow Canyon—Beginning at the northern edge of Creede, this 11-mile loop trip heads up to the townsite of Bachelor. The scenic route follows a road over varying terrain, which is not recommended for beginners. If you want an even more difficult and longer trip, head up past the Equity Mine and to the Continental Divide. This route follows a jeep trail up West Willow Creek from a sharp switchback at the northern extreme of the loop. To reach the trailhead go north from Creede until the road is no longer plowed (see the Scenic Drives section for specific information).

Guided Tours

Lost Trails Ranch—Bob Getz will take you on guided backcountry ski tours in the Weminuche Wilderness above Rio Grande Reservoir. He also specializes in winter survival courses. Reservations required. **6638 W. 7 North Rd., Del Norte, CO 81132; 719-852-3543.**

Rentals and Information

San Juan Sports—Before setting out into the backcountry, stop by this full-service shop for trail ideas, topographic maps and the latest on avalanche conditions. The shop stocks rentals for summer and winter backpacking, winter skiing and snowshoeing and summer biking equipment. **On Creede Ave.; 1-888-658-0851; 719-658-2359.**

DOWNHILL SKIING AND SNOWBOARDING

Wolf Creek Ski Area

Located about halfway between Pagosa Springs and South Fork at the summit of Wolf Creek Pass along Hwy. 160 (see the Skiing section of the **Pagosa Springs** chapter).

Seeing and Doing

Museums and Galleries

Creede Underground Mining Museum

What makes this underground experience so compelling is not that it goes into a real mine (it doesn't), but that a true hardrock miner takes you through. Chuck Fairchild, our miner/guide, explained the evolution of mining tools and techniques used over the past century inside a large U-shaped tunnel that resembles a real mine. During our 1-hour tour (shorter tours available for children), our small group gained a better understanding of the pains, joys and dangers of going inside for a shift. The exhibits and personal approach make this museum a true learning experience. Bring along a sweater or light jacket: the underground temperature remains at a constant 55° F. Gift shop; fee charged. Open daily in summer 10 A.M.–4:30 P.M.; fall hours 10 A.M.–3 P.M., closed Sun.; limited hours in winter. From Creede take Main St. north into the ravine at the end of town; the museum is **adjacent to the underground firehouse; 719-658-0811.**

Hinsdale County Museum in Lake City

The Stone Trade Palace built in 1877 now serves as a repository for many treasures from Lake City's colorful history. Included in the interesting exhibits are a barber's chair from 1874, a huge blacksmith bellows and the requisite display on the notorious cannibal Alferd Packer. Small fee. Open daily with shorter hours on Sun.; off-season times may vary considerably. **At Silver and Second Sts., Lake City; 970-944-9515.**

Galleries

Artisans must be attracted to the picturesque natural setting of Creede and Lake City. The number of galleries per capita is astounding. Without making too many judgments, here are a few of the best. On Main St. in Creede check out **Baskay, Quiller, Abbey Lane** and **Rare Things** galleries. In Lake City, stop by **Higher Elevations,**

The balcony of the Creede Hotel overlooks Creede's historic Main Street. Photo by Kirstin Bebell.

Gwendolyn's and **Nice Woodworks.** Both towns are great places to stroll around and poke into stores no matter what they carry.

Nightlife

Creede Repertory Theater

See the Major Attractions section.

Tommy Knockers

If you're looking for a place to relax and wet your whistle, head to this smallish, lively bar just east of Main St. Owners Jennifer, Jeremy and Brian cater to locals and guests and encourage patrons to write their name on a dollar bill to have it posted on the mirror—a reminder of the Wild West when a miner could pay for his next drink in advance by marking his money with his name. **107 Wall St., Creede; 719-658-0138.**

Scenic Drives

Silver Thread

The 75-mile drive on Hwy. 149 from South Fork through Creede to Lake City enjoys proper recognition as an official Scenic and Historic Byway. The journey, once a stage route, takes in many interesting natural and man-made sites along its beautiful route. The paved road crosses the Continental Divide at Spring Creek Pass before heading over 11,361-foot Slumgullion Pass with a close-up view to the odd-looking earth flow. Most unique natural features and places of historical significance have interpretive signs and are covered elsewhere in this chapter.

Where to Stay

Accommodations

The Rio Grande Valley is home to a number of guest ranches and lodging establishments. Many families from Texas, Oklahoma and other southern states flock to the higher elevations of southern Colorado during the summer to escape the oppressive heat of their homelands. No matter where you're from, an extended stay is recommended. Right in the town of Creede the choices are extremely limited; South Fork hosts a number of motels and is a convenient home base while skiing at Wolf Creek Ski Area. For a more complete listing of accommodations, contact the **Creede/Mineral County Chamber of Commerce** at **719-658-2374** or the **Lake City Chamber of Commerce** at **970-944-2527**.

The Inn at Arrowhead—$$$ to $$$$

Because the only way to this deluxe inn from Lake City requires navigation of a four-wheel-drive road, we have included it in the Where to Stay section of the **Gunnison and Crested Butte** chapter.

Old Carson Inn (Lake City)—$$$ to $$$$

If you want to experience the peace, solitude and nature that makes this area so special, Old Carson Inn should be your first choice. The seven rooms at this gorgeous hewn-log inn provide a comfortable and dramatic setting for your entire stay. Each tastefully decorated bedroom features a country theme and is named after a historic mine in the area. Beautiful mountain photographs, ample books and attractive quilts and antiques complete the decor. Be sure to spend some time on the spacious deck and in the outdoor hot tub. Innkeepers Clay and Bettina Wormington serve huge family-style breakfasts in the log dining room and are happy to light a fire in the wood-burning stove or in the outdoor campfire ring on cold nights. **P.O. Box 144, Lake City, CO 81235; 1-800-294-0608; 970-944-2155; www.oldcarsoninn.com.**

Wason Ranch (Creede)—$$$ to $$$$

Just 2 miles southeast of Creede on the banks of the Rio Grande, Wason Ranch rents modern cabins of various sizes. The ranch owns 4 miles of riverfront property with excellent fishing (guests only) for good-sized German browns. Cabins come equipped with kitchenettes, furnishings and baseboard heat; larger three-bedroom cottages down by the river come with fully loaded kitchens, fireplaces and, most important, unobstructed views out picture windows. In summer, guided river trips are available; in winter, the ranch hosts a large number of

skiers and snowmobilers. Very reasonable prices; discounts for longer stays. For reservations contact Rod and Marilyn Wintz, **P.O. Box 220, Creede, CO 81130; 719-658-2413.**

The Blessings Inn (Creede)—$$$

This inn is a delightful option for people who enjoy personal service in a distinctive and convenient setting. With aspen paneling and candies to welcome you, this bed and breakfast feels homey and relaxing. The inn was recently remodeled by Randy and Liz Sawatzky, and four upstairs bedrooms, with private baths, are comfortably and tastefully furnished. The bedroom on the main floor provides easy access and a chance to catch the heavenly smells wafting in from the kitchen. The inn is also home to a cafe, although breakfast is only for guests of the inn. It's worth staying for lunch or dinner and trying out the house specialties of blackened chicken followed by a decadent slice of homemade pie. **466 S. Main, P.O. Box 219, Creede, CO 81130; 719-658-0215.**

Creede Hotel (Creede)—$$ to $$$

In 1890 there were 100 places to stay right in Creede. Though the number has dwindled considerably, you can still stay the night comfortably, especially at the Creede Hotel, where each of the rooms and other accommodations reflects the personality of this charming little town. On the second floor of the hotel are four rooms with a quaint yet comfortable assemblage of period furniture and private bathrooms. The two front rooms access a terrific streetside balcony overlooking Creede Ave.—a great place to relax before heading downstairs to the excellent restaurant for dinner (see the Where to Eat section). Across the creek behind the hotel is a charming old home divided into three lodging units, all with private baths; you will also find a peaceful cabin with two bedrooms, a kitchen and a bathroom, and a two-bedroom cottage with a full kitchen and bathroom. A full breakfast at the hotel (included) may include an egg and sausage casserole, salsa eggs or creamy oatmeal with homemade muffins. Open in summer only; if you want to stay in winter, call ahead and see if the owners might be around. **P.O. Box 284, Creede, CO 81130; 719-658-2608.**

Wolf Creek Ski Lodge and Motel (South Fork)—$$ to $$$

This small motel offers easy access to the slopes at Wolf Creek. The owners are friendly and the rooms clean—what more do you want? Okay, they've got a hot tub, too. Their good restaurant serves up breakfast and dinner. **Box 283, 31042 W. Hwy. 160, South Fork, CO 81154; 719-873-5547.**

OTHER LODGING

The Old Firehouse No. 1 ($$$) is a classy B&B featuring four upstairs rooms furnished carefully in antiques or reproductions, each with a private bathroom. Full breakfast. **P.O. Box 603, Creede, CO 81130-0603; 719-658-0212.** For basic cabin rentals on a mile of private river access, a restaurant, bar and horse outfitting, inquire at the **R. C. Ranch ($$), P.O. Box 370, Creede, CO 81130; 719-658-2253.** Down the road near Lake City try the **Rocky Top Lodge ($$$$)** with its clean and comfortable non-smoking cabins and modern log condos, usually offered as a package deal that includes meals. **P.O. Box 232, Lake City, CO 81235; 970-944-2780.** You'll need an early reservation to stay at one of the 20 popular cabins at **Vickers' Ranch ($$$ to $$$$),** but you'll enjoy the private water along the Lake Fork and the beautiful setting. **P.O. Box 969, Lake City, CO 81235; 970-944-2249.**

Camping

To make a reservation at a national forest campground contact **1-877-444-6777** or **www.reserveusa.com.** All the following campgrounds charge a fee, with the exception of the three that are noted.

Gunnison National Forest

South of Lake City, not far from Lake San Cristobal, are a couple of prime campgrounds. Drive 2 miles south of Lake City on Hwy. 149, turn right at County Rd. 30 and continue 6 miles

to reach **Williams Creek Campground** (25 sites). Continue another 4.5 miles to **Mill Creek Campground** (22 sites) with an incredible view up the valley to some high 13ers.

Slumgullion Campground (21 sites) is located 6.5 miles southeast of Lake City on Hwy. 149. From just west of the campground, Forest Rd. 788 heads northwest from Hwy. 149 to a number of campgrounds. After turning, drive 2.5 miles to **Deer Lakes Campground** (12 sites). In another 4.3 miles you'll come to **Hidden Valley Campground** (6 sites, no fee). Continue another 1.5 miles to **Spruce Campground** (8 sites) and soon after, **Cebolla Campground** (5 sites).

Big Blue Campground (11 sites, no fee) is located 10 miles north of Lake City on Hwy. 149, then 10 miles northwest on rough Forest Rd. 868.

Rio Grande National Forest

There are several nice campgrounds near the town of South Fork. To reach **Beaver Creek Campground** (20 sites) and **Upper Beaver Campground** (12 sites) drive 2.5 miles southwest from South Fork on Hwy. 160. Turn left on Forest Rd. 360 and continue for 3 and 4 miles, respectively. From Upper Beaver Campground drive another 2 miles on Forest Rd. 360 to **Cross Creek Campground** (9 sites).

Five miles southwest of South Fork on Hwy. 160 is **Highway Springs Campground** (11 sites). **Park Creek Campground** (10 sites) is 9 miles southwest of South Fork on Hwy. 160. Ten miles northwest of South Fork on Hwy. 149 is **Palisade Campground** (13 sites).

Closer to Creede, a number of campgrounds await. **Marshall Park Campground** (15 sites) is 6 miles southwest of Creede on Hwy. 149. To reach **Rio Grande Campground** (4 sites) from Creede drive 10 miles southwest on Hwy. 149.

A grouping of campgrounds is located farther southwest of Creede via Hwy. 149. To reach **Silver Thread Campground** (11 sites) drive 23 mile southwest of Creede on Hwy. 149; turn right on Forest Rd. 510 and continue for

0.3 mile. **North Clear Creek Campground** (22 sites) is another 1.8 miles up Forest Rd. 510. **Bristol Head Campground** (11 sites) is 24.5 miles southwest of Creede on Hwy. 149.

To get to **Road Canyon Campground** (5 sites, no fee), drive 21 miles southwest of Creede on Hwy. 149 and turn left on Forest Rd. 520. The campground is located on the southern end of Road Canyon Reservoir. Another 3.5 miles down Forest Rd. 520 will take you to **River Hill Campground** (20 sites). Continue another 1.5 miles to **Thirtymile Campground** (33 sites) on the eastern end of Rio Grande Reservoir. **Lost Trail Campground** (7 sites) is on the northwestern end of the reservoir another 5.5 miles down Forest Rd. 520.

Private Campgrounds

Castle Lakes Campground Resort—On the edge of a lake reflecting gorgeous mountain scenery, this wooded campground offers tent and RV sites, one- and two-bedroom fully equipped units and a lodge with a general store, laundry, showers and movies. From Lake City head 2 miles south on Hwy. 149, turn right on County Rd. 30 and turn right into the campground 3.5 miles past Lake San Cristobal. **P.O. Box 909, Lake City, CO 81331; 970-944-2622. Riverbend Resort RV Park**—Just over 50 tent and RV sites are available, some with full hookups. This park is located along a 1-mile stretch of the South Fork of the Rio Grande. To get there from South Fork, drive 3 miles southwest on Hwy. 160. **P.O. Box 129, South Fork, CO 81154; 719-873-5344. Woodlake Campground**—Shaded, grassy campsites and RV hookups. It also offers fishing on its private stretch of river. Located 2.5 miles south of Lake City on Hwy. 149. **P.O. Box 400, Lake City, CO 81235; 970-944-2283.**

Where to Eat

In Lake City you may wish to eat at the **Crystal Lodge** 2 miles south of Lake City on Hwy. 149 or stop in—especially for breakfast—at the comfortable **Lake City Cafe, 310 Gunnison Ave., 970-944-2733.** Many of the restaurants in Lake City and Creede close during the off-season. While vacationing near Creede, check out **The Blessings Inn and Cafe** (see the Where to Stay section) or try the following:

The Bristol Inn—$$$

Located in an out-of-the-way corner of the woods southwest of Creede, the Bristol Inn has a loyal following. The casual yet elegant atmosphere complements the kitchen, where only the freshest ingredients are used; the homemade bread is made from fresh stone-ground flour. Chicken, beef and fish entrées are served with a professional flair, even though tips are not accepted. From Mother's Day through the end of Sept. the restaurant is open for dinner Wed.–Sat. 5–9 P.M.; their famous Sun. buffet 11 A.M.–3 P.M. should not be missed. The restaurant also houses an art gallery, so you'll be able to browse before or after your meal. Reservations strongly recommended. Located 18 miles **southwest of Creede** on Hwy. 149; **719-658-2455.**

Creede Hotel—$$

With no set menu and only limited entrée selections each evening, you can be assured the chef uses the freshest quality ingredients. Special dishes include grilled tamari honey chicken and mouth-watering lasagna. The healthy meals provide comfort for vegetarians and others. This small, homey restaurant tends to fill up before plays next door at the Creede Repertory Theater. In summer don't miss a chance to eat on the outside deck as the sun settles over the valley and casts an otherworldly glow on your surroundings. For further information about the historic Creede Hotel, see the Where to Stay section. **Creede Ave.** in downtown Creede; **719-658-2608.**

Services

Visitor Information

Creede/Mineral County Chamber of Commerce—Operates a friendly visitor center during peak seasons right on Creede Ave. **P.O. Box 580, Creede, CO 81130; 1-800-327-2102; 719-658-2374; www.creede.com.**

Lake City Chamber of Commerce—Follow the signs to a visitor center that the Chamber shares with the U.S. Forest Service. **P.O. Box 430, Lake City, CO 81235; 1-800-569-1874; 719-944-2527; www.lakecityco.com.**

South Fork Chamber of Commerce— P.O. Box 116, South Fork, CO 81154; 1-800-571-0881; 719-873-5512; www.south fork.org.

Cripple Creek and Victor

Although not known to many Americans these days, the gold-hearted mining town of Cripple Creek was once a household word throughout the country. The Cripple Creek district produced more than $600 million in gold—more than any other single geological deposit on earth. That's over $12 billion in today's dollars. The streets in Cripple Creek are literally paved with gold—gold ore, that is. A very low grade.

Cripple Creek sits in the crater of an extinct volcano, which created the goldfields. And the gold isn't gone. Some local miners say 80 percent of the gold in the area is untapped. Today international companies own most of the claims, and increased activity (especially open-pit mining) is easily seen today.

Although the immediate area around Cripple Creek is scarred by mine remnants and nearly barren of trees, it's ringed by tremendous mountains, including Pikes Peak to the northeast and the Sangre de Cristo Range to the southwest. Nearby, Mueller State Park provides a gorgeous wooded setting with some of the region's best hiking, cross-country skiing and wildlife viewing. Another thing to do in Cripple Creek is mingle among its ghosts and mine skeletons to get a sense of its glorious past. But a word of

caution: most of the mine shafts in the district are death traps. Stay on the roads and designated trails.

After relying on its gold mining history to attract tourists, Cripple Creek is currently caught up in the throes of a much more recent rush—legalized gambling. Colorado voters gave the go-ahead in 1990 for businesses in Cripple Creek (as well as Central City and Black Hawk) to offer limited-stakes gaming (maximum $5 bets). Since the first casinos opened the following year, the town's character has changed dramatically. Depending on whom you talk with, gambling has either rejuvenated the local economy while preserving the integrity of Cripple Creek's historic buildings or it has driven out longtime townsfolk with spiraling property values and crowded streets.

Although the visitors and locals place the historical mining focus on Cripple Creek, most of the gold mining actually took place at nearby Victor; its hills and yards are perforated with famous mines like the Ajax, the Independence and the Portland. The town bears the name of early settler Victor Adams, but its most famous resident was Lowell Thomas, one of the world's

Getting There

From Denver, drive 65 miles south on Interstate 25 to Colorado Springs and then west for 25 miles on Hwy. 24 to the town of Divide. From Divide, drive south (left) on Hwy. 67 for 20 miles to Cripple Creek. Since gambling began in Cripple Creek, traffic on Highway 67 has increased dramatically as have DUI arrests. If you have time, you may want to consider one of the alternative routes listed in the Scenic Drives section.

first radio news commentators. Victor, once known as the "City of Gold," remains much more like it was originally than does Cripple Creek. And since gambling began, Victor has become a quiet place to escape the often frenzied casino atmosphere of Cripple Creek.

History

According to a local miner, Cripple Creek was named the day an early settler's son fell off the house they were building and broke a limb. That same day a calf broke its leg jumping over a high-banked stream nearby. The settler's comment: "This sho is some Cripple Creek."

It took drunken cowpoke and erstwhile rancher Bob Womack (known as "Crazy Bob") to transform a barren cow pasture he called "Poverty Gulch" into "the world's greatest gold camp." There was no reason for people to believe his claims of riches: the geology was all wrong, and the man drank himself into a stupor regularly.

The beginning of the country's last major gold rush was delayed even further by false reports. In 1884 two charlatans salted a vein with gold in Cripple Creek. Hundreds of prospectors rushed to the area, only to discover the hoax after about a month of digging. In 1891, however, Womack finally convinced a few people to believe him, and gold fever rose faster and higher than ever before. Unfortunately, Womack was left out: soon after finding his first gold, he got drunk again and sold his claim for $500 and a case of whiskey. The mine went on to produce hundreds of thousands of dollars of the precious metal.

Within a year of the find, 2,500 people were living in Cripple Creek. The rush made millionaires out of at least 30 people, and the town got a taste of fame. The Wright brothers won an auto race from Cripple Creek to Colorado Springs, and Groucho Marx delivered groceries between Cripple Creek and Victor for a while. Boxer Jack Dempsey even lived in Cripple Creek, mining during the day and boxing at night.

In April 1896 fire broke out in a Cripple Creek dance hall and burned down most of the town. Another blaze five days later nearly finished the job, leaving 5,000 people homeless. Within days the town was rebuilding, with brick this time. Three years later an eerily similar fire destroyed 12 blocks and 200 buildings in Victor.

By 1900, 25,000 people lived in Cripple Creek, making it the state's fourth-largest city at the time. The district boasted 150 saloons (70 on notorious Myers Ave. alone), 90 doctors, 34 churches and 15 newspapers (priorities were in order). Myers Ave. was also home to plenty of "pleasure palaces."

As gold prices fell, the boom declined as quickly as it had surged. By 1912 most of Cripple Creek's 475 mining companies had folded. Eight years later only 40 of the original 500 mines were working. Bob Womack, the spark of the rush, died penniless in Colorado Springs.

The beginning of gold mining in the town of Victor had ironic origins. Two promoters, Frank and Harry Woods, advertised the town in 1893 by saying that on every lot was a gold mine. The promotional gimmick turned out to be true as homesteaders began pulling gold out of their backyards. When grading for a hotel, Frank and Harry discovered an 18-inch vein and decided to build a mine there instead. Within a year, the Gold Coin Mine was turning out $50,000 a month. Frank, who had a penchant for luxury, built stained-glass windows in the mine's shaft house, lined it with marble and laid down carpeting.

Lowell Thomas, the author, radio announcer and lecturer, began his journalism career as a paperboy for the *Victor Record* and went on to travel the world. The Lowell Thomas Museum at 3rd and Victor tells his story and is worth a brief stop.

Major Attractions

Florissant Fossil Beds National Monument

Palm trees in Colorado? Once upon a time— about 34 million years ago—yes. Also thriving

A petrified sequoia stump at Florissant Fossil Beds National Monument. Photo courtesy of Florissant Fossil Beds National Monument.

in the Florissant area were enormous redwoods, a thousand species of insects including tsetse flies common to South Africa, giant katydids and an incredible variety of plants and animals. Thanks to a once-raging volcano field nearby and tons of ash, these remnants of the late Eocene epoch have been preserved better than any other ancient ecosystem in the world.

The fossil bed formed when volcanic eruptions sent lava and mud into the Florissant Basin, creating a large lake. Continued eruptions sent more ash and dust over the lake, taking insects, leaves and fish to the bottom with it. Over a 500,000-year period the sediment formed shales. Mudflows eventually covered and protected these future fossil beds, and recent erosion led to their discovery.

Facts About the Monument

Florissant ("flowering" or "blooming") was named for the abundant wildflowers in the area. Stop by the visitor center for an introduction to spotting fossils. The Petrified Forest Loop (1 mile) is the best. Don't miss the Trio (three petrified

redwood trunks sharing a root system) and Rex Arborae ("King of the Forest"), a petrified stump 14 feet tall and 74 feet around. Scientists guess the tree once towered 250 to 280 feet—one of the biggest sequoias ever found. Admission fee. Interpretive walks and talks take place hourly in the summer. Open daily in summer 8 A.M.–7 P.M.; during the rest of the year 8 A.M.–4:30 P.M. **P.O. Box 185, Florissant, CO 80816; 719-748-3253; www.nps.gov.**

Getting There

To get to the fossil beds, take Hwy. 24 west from Colorado Springs for 35 miles to Florissant. Turn south on County Rd. 1. The monument entrance is about 2.5 miles up the road on the right (west). From Cripple Creek, head northwest on County Rd. 1 for 16 miles to the monument entrance.

Near the Monument

After learning about excavation techniques at Florissant Fossil Beds, travel about 1.5 miles north on Teller County Rd. 1 to the **Florissant**

Fossil Quarry. This privately owned property borders the national monument and offers the opportunity to dig your own fossils. Environmental education programs are available, too. Small fee. Open in summer 10 A.M.–4 P.M. and by appointment. **P.O. Box 126, Florissant, CO 80816; 719-748-1002; 719-748-3275.**

Gambling

Since its legalization in 1990, limited-stakes gambling has definitely become the town's number one attraction and has brought with it many changes. Past visitors who have yet to see the "new" Cripple Creek may be a bit taken aback by the town's metamorphosis—historic buildings lining Cripple Creek's Bennett Ave. sport new faces, interiors and flashy signs; live music, hordes of optimistic (and beaten) gamblers and lot after lot of cars all contribute to the town's neo-boom. Nearly 20 gambling establishments have sprung up along or near Bennett Ave., with others either under construction or in the planning stages. As Cripple Creek struggles to balance its history with the abrupt gambling rush, the policies are still evolving. For instance, children are no longer permitted to enter most casinos, hotels or restaurants. The transition continues.

Casinos

After visiting enough of them, you'll notice that the casinos begin to blend together. Rows of slot and video poker machines, a few blackjack tables and full bar service generally appear everywhere; other attractions such as live music, in-house restaurants, TV sports and ice cream shops/arcades for the kids are evident as well. However, some of the casinos have begun to develop reputations for certain features. A few of the highlights are listed below. Most of the casinos are open 8 A.M.–2 A.M. daily with shortened hours Sun.

Bronco Billy's Sports Bar and Casino— Along with gambling, Bronco Billy's is known for its numerous TVs airing sports programs. Locals also tout the food at the "historic" Home Cafe, which serves standard fare along with daily specials and a 99-cent breakfast. **233 E. Bennett Ave.; 719-689-2142.**

Double Eagle Hotel and Casino—One of the newer establishments along Bennett Ave., the Double Eagle offers a little bit of glitz and glamour, including plenty of modern hotel rooms. **442 E. Bennett Ave.; 719-689-5000.**

Gold Rush Hotel and Casino—The rather spacious Gold Rush provides the Golden Grille Restaurant boasting mesquite specialties. **209 E. Bennett Ave.; 1-800-235-8239.**

Imperial Hotel and Casino—One of the most historic places in town, the immense Imperial establishment offers a multilevel gaming parlor and a popular lunch/dinner buffet. An extensive seafood buffet **($$)** is available on Fris. and worth a few trips through the lengthy buffet line. Rooms are also available at the historic hotel (see the Where to Stay section). **123 N. 3rd St., P.O. Box 869, Cripple Creek, CO 80813; 1-800-235-2922; 719-689-7777.**

The Virgin Mule—One of the last independently owned casinos that have managed to stay open, this small casino offers dollar beers and originality. A live-in cat named Spike may even give you some good luck. Antique crystal chandeliers light up the atmosphere as you try your hand at the slots. **269 E. Bennett Ave.; 719-689-2734.**

Parking

You'll find plenty of free lots scattered through town. If you don't want to drive to Cripple Creek, many tour companies provide buses and vans from Colorado Springs. For more specifics on transportation, see the Services section at the end of this chapter.

Mueller State Park

Located just off Hwy. 67 between Cripple Creek and Divide, Mueller State Park provides an exciting addition to outdoor recreation in the Pikes Peak region. Mueller, with its approximately 6,000 acres of pine-covered hills, mountain meadows, streams, ponds and dramatic Pikes Peak granite formations, such as the enormous

Dome Rock, attracts a large number of visitors. Thanks to protection when the property was a private ranch, wildlife here is thick. You can see plentiful elk, bighorn sheep, mule deer, eagles and hawks and even an occasional bear, bobcat or mountain lion.

Camping

Mueller boasts 132 campsites, including 110 with electric hookups and 22 walk-in tentsites. Rest rooms, hot showers and laundry facilities available; fees vary. For reservations call **(303) 470-1144** from Denver or **1-800-678-CAMP** or **www.reserveamerica.com.**

Trails

The park's extensive network of recreation trails—over 90 miles of them—provides access into remote parts of the park for hikers, mountain bikers, horseback riders, cross-country skiers and snowshoers. Spectacular views of Pikes Peak and the Sangre de Cristo Range await you along many trail sections. Pick up a trail map at the entrance station or park headquarters. For access to some of the more remote trails in the southern section of the park, drive to the day use area 8 miles north of Cripple Creek via Hwy. 67 and County Rd. 61 (Fourmile Rd.).

Other Information

Mueller is located 15 miles north of Cripple Creek along Hwy. 67. At the park entrance, turn west. Information and trail maps can be obtained at the entrance station or at the impressive visitor center, which features interactive exhibits and informative wildlife displays. Interpretive hikes and slide shows are offered during the summer season. **P.O. Box 39, Divide, CO 80814; 719-687-2366; www.coloradoparks.org.**

Festivals and Events

Donkey Derby Days

last weekend in June As the major event of the summer, Cripple Creek's Donkey Derby Days packs in tourists for a parade, donkey races, live music and other activities. **1-877-858-GOLD; 719-689-3315.**

Fall Aspen Leaf Tours

last two weekends in Sept. and first in Oct. For those of you without four-wheel-drive vehicles, check out the popular Fall Aspen Leaf Tours. Free jeep rides on the surrounding roads provide excellent views of the nearby mountains and the golden aspen. **719-689-2169.**

Outdoor Activities

Biking

MOUNTAIN BIKING

See the Scenic Drives section and Mueller State Park write-up in the Major Attractions section for ideas.

Fishing

For information on nearby fishing opportunities at Eleven Mile Canyon, Eleven Mile Reservoir and Spinney Mountain Reservoir, see the **South Park and 285 Corridor** chapter.

Hiking and Backpacking

For information and ideas, contact the Pikes Peak District of **Pike National Forest** at **719-636-1602** or **www.fs.fed.us/r2/psicc.** Here are some good possibilities:

The Crags

Located on the northwest slope of Pikes Peak, this is a relatively undiscovered hiking area. Trails spread out over the back side of Pikes Peak and through the immense granite formations that give the area its name. From Cripple Creek, head north on Hwy. 67 about 14 miles and turn right (east) onto County Rd. 62 (Forest Rd. 383). Drive 3.5 miles to the trailhead at the end of the turnaround near the Crags Campground.

To reach the Crags from Colorado Springs, head west 25 miles on Hwy. 24 to Divide and turn left onto Hwy. 67. Drive 4.3 miles and turn left onto County Rd. 62 (Forest Rd. 383).

Backcountry pond at Mueller State Park. Photo by Dean Winstanley.

Mueller State Park

Mueller provides 90 miles of excellent trails. For details, see the Major Attractions section.

Pikes Peak (via the Crags)

On a clear day, the 6.5-mile hike up Pikes Peak from the Crags Campground is one of the most scenic in the state (and much easier than Barr Trail on the east side of the mountain). This trail climbs 4,100 vertical feet through pine and aspen, across an alpine bowl covered with wildflowers and on to the rocky upper reaches of the peak. Once you make your way out of the trees, enjoy the stunning views of the Spanish Peaks to the south, Mt. Evans to the north and the several mountain ranges in between.

This is a great route up the peak, but it requires a topographic map and careful attention along the way. From the Crags Campground (see the Camping section), start up the trail to the Crags. After about 200 yards, you will come to a spot where the creek on the south side of the trail forks. Here you must leave the Crags Trail and cross the closer of the two creeks (so that you are in between the two), and follow the old logging road up to the southeast. After about 1.5 miles the road comes to an old area just below treeline where there are many stumps. Just after the trail swings north, be looking for a trail going off to the right and take it. Eventually you climb up over a saddle to timberline where you have a view of the summit to the southeast. Continuing on you reach the Pikes Peak Hwy. at a place called Devil's Playground, named for the way lightning bounces off the rocks when it hits in the vicinity. From here, cross the road and make your way to the top.

The Vindicator Valley Trail

Hike, bike or horseback ride this loop trail as it wraps around gold mines. Interpretive signs tell the facts while you explore the past. Begin your journey at one of two trailheads: Goldfield City Hall in Cripple Creek or follow the signs on Teller County Rd. 81 as you head south toward Victor.

Skiing

CROSS-COUNTRY SKIING AND SNOWSHOEING

The Crags

The Crags continues to be one of the best areas to go near Cripple Creek for good winter touring trails, from beginner to advanced. For information, see the Hiking and Backpacking section or contact the Pike National Forest at **719-636-1602** or **www.fs.fed.us/r2/psicc.**

Florissant Fossil Beds National Monument

Open to the public year-round, the national monument provides miles of easy terrain for cross-country skiers. The visitor center provides trail maps and even loans out snowshoes. For more information, see the Florissant Fossil Beds National Monument write-up in the Major Attractions section.

Mueller State Park

Ninety miles of trails. For more information, see the Major Attractions section.

Seeing and Doing

Museums and Historic Tours

Cripple Creek District Museum

All historic mining towns should have a museum like the Cripple Creek District Museum. The museum houses tons of antiques and paraphernalia from the boom days. Rooms in the main three-story building have specific themes such as mining and assaying. Be sure to inspect the fascinating 3-D engineers' map of the Portland Mine. Two other buildings house a natural history collection and an assay office where someone is usually on hand to demonstrate how ores are tested. Open daily, Memorial Day–Sept., 10 A.M.–5 P.M.; open weekends the rest of the year, 12–4 P.M. At the west end of Bennett Ave. **Box 475, Cripple Creek, CO 80813; 719-689-2634.**

Ghost Walk and Cemetery Tours

Sensational stories from your local guide provide you with a true appreciation for the self-proclaimed "World's Greatest Gold Camp." Stroll through Cripple Creek and hear tales of the old days, including several accounts of spirits that just can't seem to leave it behind. Seasonal tours begin at 5 P.M. and 8 P.M. Cemetery tours,

which include a strenuous hike, are by appointment only. Both tours meet in the Palace Hotel lobby; fee charged. **1-877-858-4653; www. cripple-creek.co.us/ghost.html.**

Molly Kathleen Mine

Ride the "skip" down 1,000 feet into the Molly Kathleen Mine for a taste of the subterranean insides of a hardrock mine. Although it looks touristy from the outside, don't be put off: miners lead this full-fledged tour through the inner workings of an actual mine, which clearly demonstrates why people flocked to Cripple Creek in the first place. The Molly operated from 1892 until 1961. Open daily May–Oct., 9 A.M.–5 P.M. Admission fee charged. The Molly's just north of town off Hwy 67. **P.O. Box 339, Cripple Creek, CO 80813; 719-689-2466.**

Nightlife

With the explosion of gambling in Cripple Creek, the casinos and bars are where you'll find most of the action. You can find everything from live music to comedy at the casinos (see the Major Attractions section).

The Butte Opera House

Live theater and melodramas once again bring a little culture to Cripple Creek at the newly renovated opera house. Movies and concerts are also on the bill and are a welcome alternative to the casinos. **1-877-858-GOLD.**

The Crystal Canyon

One of the only establishments without gambling, the Crystal Canyon serves cheap beer and offers live bands, karaoke and pool tournaments. Open Tues.–Sat. 11 A.M.–2 A.M., Sun.–Mon. 4 P.M.–2 A.M. **401 E. Bennett Ave.; 719-689-9633.**

Railroads

Cripple Creek & Victor Narrow-Gauge Railroad

Ride this train and get a literal feel for the Old West—by the seat of your pants. The narrow-gauge tracks of the Old Midland Terminal Railroad take you on a 4-mile round trip past some great mountain scenery, historical sites and mines. Along the way you'll hear a bit about Cripple Creek's history, in which narrow-gauge trains played a huge role. Fifty-five locomotives used to stop here daily, hauling ore out and passengers in. The ride's great fun for kids. Open Memorial Day–mid-Oct., 10 A.M.–5 P.M. The train leaves every 45 minutes from Midland Station at the end of Bennett Ave., next to the Cripple Creek Museum, at the north end of town. **P.O. Box 459, Cripple Creek, CO 80813; 719-689-2640.**

Scenic Drives

Cripple Creek/Victor

From Cripple Creek make sure to drive to Victor along Hwy. 67, which goes past some of the larger mines in the region. Also consider driving half of this 12-mile round trip via **Range View Rd.** This dirt road leaves Cripple Creek just north of the Molly Kathleen Mine, climbs around Battle Mountain and connects with Diamond Ave. in Victor.

Gold Camp Road

This beautiful and historic back road follows the path of the railroad, which used to connect Cripple Creek with Colorado Springs. An excellent drive during the warmer months. See Gold Camp Rd. in the Scenic Drives section of the **Colorado Springs** chapter.

Phantom Canyon

This section of the Gold Belt Tour, a Scenic and Historic Byway, begins in Victor and snakes its way through a narrow canyon to the south along an old stagecoach line. See the Scenic Drives section of the **Cañon City** chapter.

Shelf Road

Like Phantom Canyon, Shelf Rd. (part of the Gold Belt Tour) is an old stagecoach road that runs between Cripple Creek and Cañon City. The scenery along the way is wonderful, but beware of the casino employees that use this road as a shortcut and tend to take the curves a

little haphazardly. For information, see the Scenic Drives section of the **Cañon City** chapter.

Where to Stay

Accommodations

The Imperial Hotel—$$$ to $$$$

One of Cripple Creek's original brick hotels, the Imperial stands as a reminder of the town's mining boom days. Most of its furniture dates to the rich Victorian period, as do the antiques and paintings. Some rooms include private claw-foot tubs while other guests must rely on bathrooms down the hall. The Imperial also offers a three-level gaming parlor in the adjacent building. Reservations recommended. **123 N. 3rd St., P.O. Box 869, Cripple Creek, CO 80813; 1-800-235-2922; 719-689-7777.**

The Victor Hotel—$$$

Built in 1899 and operated for years as a bank, this historic bed and breakfast provides a quiet getaway. With many of the other original buildings in various stages of dilapidation, the Victor Hotel, flush from its $1.25 million renovation, stands out like a rich cousin. From the fine period decor in the lobby to the 30 comfortable rooms, the dollars have worked magic. Ride up to your room in the original cage elevator. The rooms represent a tasteful blend of old and new—exposed brick and original steam registers blend with queen-size beds, private baths, cable TV and phones. **4th St. and Victor Ave., Victor, CO 80860; 719-689-3553.**

The Hotel St. Nicholas—$$ to $$$$

Innkeepers Noel and Denise Perran and Kurt and Susan Adelbush have nicely renovated this old hospital that was once crowded with injured gold prospectors. The refurbished inn is perched on a hilltop offering a panoramic view of the mountains and a glance at the hectic activity in downtown Cripple Creek. Soak in the rooftop whirlpool bath after a hard day of playing slots or blow off some steam in the sauna. If those amenities don't help, retreat to the Boiler Room Tavern for a cold beer. Cable TV, guest telephones and free shuttle to the gaming establishments (if you actually want to venture away from this cozy brick hotel). **303 N. 3rd St., P.O. Box 1459, Cripple Creek, CO 80813; 1-888-786-4257; 719-689-0856; www.cripple-creek.co.us/stnick.html.**

The Last Dollar Inn—$$ to $$$

Named after the thirteenth largest mine in the district, this century-old bed and breakfast offers six elegant rooms of various sizes. One of the largest is the Linda Goodman room, a spacious Victorian haven named after the astrologer (and previous owner). Each room has a private bath. Although Goodman has passed away, several of her collectibles bedazzle the house, such as the magnificent stained glass window of St. Francis of Assisi. Rick and Janice Wood serve a gourmet breakfast that will happily wake you from your slumber. They know Cripple Creek history and will be great sources for helping you find places off the typical tourist path. **315 E. Carr Ave., Cripple Creek, CO 80813; 1-888-429-6700; 719-689-9113.**

Camping

Pike National Forest

The Crags—The **Crags Campground** (17 sites, fee charged) is on the west side of Pikes Peak. Take Hwy. 67 north from Cripple Creek for 13.5 miles (or 4.3 miles south from Divide). Turn onto Forest Rd. 383 (County Rd. 62). Drive 3.5 miles to the campground. Reservations can be made at **1-877-444-CAMP** or **www.reserveusa.com.**

State Park

Mueller State Park—For details on Mueller's 132 campsites, see the Major Attractions section.

Private Campground

Lost Burro—A bit rustic, the Lost Burro offers RV hookups, tentsites, rest rooms, showers and picnic tables. Located 4 miles northwest of Cripple Creek on County Rd. 1. **P.O. Box 614, Cripple Creek, CO 80813; 719-689-2345.**

Where to Eat

Although scads of casino restaurants have popped up claiming to offer the full spectrum of culinary "specialties," casino dining is a bit inconsistent. For ideas about casino dining see the casino write-ups in the Major Attractions section.

Zeke's—$ to $$$

Although once known wide and far for its crusty (some would say grungy) mining bar atmosphere, Zeke's has changed a bit. The atmosphere is about the same but an expanded menu (including burgers, sandwiches and good barbecue) and outside patio seating have smoothed the edges. They still serve the house specialty, chili. Like many buildings in Victor, this one has a colorful history; it was once expanded to incorporate an area formerly used as a house of ill repute. Open year-round 10 A.M.–2 A.M. (until midnight on Sun.), serving breakfast, lunch and dinner. **108 S. 3rd St., between Victor and Portland Aves. in Victor; 719-689-2109.** While in Victor, you may want to also try **It's Someplace Else ($ to $$$).** It's in a building that's a little more polished than others in town and offers hefty helpings of burgers, pizza and hospitality. **306 Victor Ave.; 719-689-9922.**

Services

Visitor Information

Cripple Creek Welcome Center—P.O. Box 430, Cripple Creek, CO 80813; 1-877-858-GOLD; 719-689-3315; www.cripple-creek.co.us.

Victor Chamber of Commerce—P.O. Box 83; Victor, CO 80806.

Day Care

Gold Town Learning Center—Open 7 A.M.–2 P.M. seven days a week. Will entertain children 12 months to 12 years. **719-689-3473.**

Transportation

City of Cripple Creek Shuttle—Runs 6 A.M.–3 A.M. daily, serving stops every half hour. **719-689-3753.**

Ramblin' Express—Offers transportation to Cripple Creek from Colorado Springs and Woodland Park, including limousine service if you hit it big. **719-590-8687.**

Leadville

In 1880 Leadville was the second-largest city in Colorado, bursting with a population of more than 30,000. Today a quiet mountain community of 3,500 maintains Leadville's profound sense of history in a low-profile atmosphere. Although the last of the working mines (the Little Johnny) closed down a couple years ago, residents have managed to preserve and protect many of the town's opulent Victorian-era buildings. Few places rival Leadville, designated a National Historic District, for the preservation of Colorado's mining heritage.

One of the most highly mineralized areas in the world, Leadville has produced gold, silver, zinc, molybdenum, manganese and turquoise. Just east of town, hundreds of mines at California Gulch and Carbonate, Fryer and Iron Hills provided the source of Leadville's livelihood for many decades. The town's mining fortunes have long since disappeared, but more than a handful of local museums have rescued the legacy of the area's mining history.

Stopping off in Leadville for an hour or two hardly cracks the door on this town's past. Try booking a room in one of many historic accommodations. Staying a couple days (or longer) allows a chance to fully enjoy the town and its intensely beautiful surroundings.

Located at 10,152 feet near the headwaters of the Arkansas River, Leadville is hemmed in by the Sawatch Range to the west and the Mosquito Range to the east. Colorado's two highest peaks, Elbert (14,433 feet) and Massive (14,421 feet), absolutely dominate the view from town. The

Colorado Trail tracks along the base of these peaks and other trails wind to their summits—literally at the top of Colorado (see the Hiking and Backpacking section). Fishing, mountain biking and camping opportunities also help make this area a sort of outdoor paradise.

Though anything but a winter resort, Leadville lies at a ski crossroads: you can be on the slopes at Ski Cooper in 20 minutes and at six other major downhill areas in less than an hour. Cross-country skiers appreciate the expanse of well-suited terrain—especially near the summit of Tennessee Pass, where the U.S. Army trained its elite 10th Mountain Division ski troops during World War II.

For a quiet, less expensive and historical change of pace, Leadville makes an ideal vacation base.

History

Leadville's history is mirrored by the twists and turns of H.A.W. Tabor, who came west with his wife, Augusta, during the Pikes Peak gold rush of 1859. After many years of chasing his fortune from one Colorado gold camp to another, Tabor eventually settled in Oro City (2.5 miles from

---

Getting There

Leadville is located 103 miles southwest of Denver. To get there take Interstate 70 west to Copper Mountain (Exit 195). Turn south on Hwy. 91 and continue 24 miles to Leadville.

present-day Leadville), where he hoped somehow to strike it rich. Not long before Tabor arrived, Oro City had boomed when gold deposits were discovered in California Gulch in 1860. But the deposits were not big producers and a heavy black sand made it difficult to isolate the gold ore.

It wasn't until 1875 that William Stevens and his partner, A. B. Wood, a metallurgist, reworked some of the abandoned mines and discovered that the heavy black sand clogging the gold sluicing operations contained a high silver content. Working quietly to discover the source, Stevens and Wood staked out claims that eventually netted them millions. After this initial success, miners began prospecting to the north and west on Iron and Carbonate Hills. But when George Fryer discovered a rich body of ore on what is now called Fryer Hill, Leadville sprang to life.

Tabor, sensing that Oro City was losing ground to Leadville, moved down the road a couple of miles to this fledgling town. Soon after he opened the doors of his general store, he grubstaked two poor German prospectors with little money or mining experience in return for a one-third interest in their claim on Fryer Hill. As luck would have it, the two miners soon hit a 30-foot-thick silver vein, some 28 feet below the surface. A month later their Little Pittsburg Mine was producing $50,000 worth of ore per month for each of the three partners.

Tabor became the talk of the state and was soon commissioned to purchase a claim for a Denver wholesaler. Hearing of Tabor's commission, a man named Chicken Bill salted one of his unproductive claims with silver dust and duped Tabor into buying the mine. Tabor didn't get paid for the "worthless" claim. Although he was the laughingstock of the town, somehow he felt lucky enough to continue mining at the site. He hired a group of miners to deepen the shaft and soon discovered the famous Chrysolite lode. In less than two years, the former stonecutter was Leadville's first multimillionaire.

By 1880 Leadville had gone from a camp of 200 to a rip-roaring city of 30,000. The mines were producing nearly $12 million of silver a year, and trains regularly made their way to the valley. As the area flooded with fortune hunters, a quarter-mile of saloons, brothels, wine-theaters and gambling halls sprang up along State St. (now Second St.), giving Leadville an uninhibited atmosphere. The *Leadville Herald-Democrat* described a chaotic street scene:

> On all sides was a conglomerate mass of diversified humanity—men of education and culture, graduates of Harvard and Yale and Princeton, mingling with ignorant and uncouth Bull-whackers . . . representatives of the better element in all the callings of life—hopelessly entangled in throngs of gamblers, burro-steerers, thugs, bullies, drunkards, escaped convicts, dead beats and the "scum of the earth" generally.

It wasn't long before Tabor and the other bonanza kings attempted to civilize the city with gracious Victorian homes, hotels and even the Tabor Opera House. Many who got their start in Leadville are well remembered today, such as Meyer Guggenheim and Marshall Field. Sidewalks lined the gaslit streets, and Harrison Ave. was paved with black slag. The mountains around Leadville were left treeless from the frenzied construction of mine shafts as well as the extraction of charcoal for the smelters and city buildings.

In the scandal of the era, H.A.W. Tabor divorced his stoic wife, Augusta, to marry the young divorcee, Elizabeth "Baby Doe" McCourt, who shared his passion for a flamboyant lifestyle. He married Baby Doe in a lavish Washington, D.C., ceremony attended by President Chester Arthur.

The glory days ended in 1893 when the Sherman Silver Purchase Act was repealed. The price of silver plummeted during the ensuing panic and Leadville's glory days were over.

Tabor's fortunes continued to mirror those of Leadville as he lost virtually everything he owned. Though he eventually moved to Denver and pushed his way into political office as high as U.S. senator, Tabor died a penniless postmaster in 1899. While on his deathbed, he told Baby

Unknown gold panner in Colorado's early days.

discovered, the Climax Mine near Leadville accounted for as much as 80 percent of the total world production of this steel-hardening mineral.

In 1942, 15,000 men in the U.S. Army's 10th Mountain Division were stationed at Camp Hale, 18 miles north of Leadville just over Tennessee Pass. In white camouflage uniforms, the army troops practiced alpine combat maneuvers before heading to Europe for battle. Camp Hale was nicknamed Camp Hell by men forced to endure the high altitude, harsh weather and rigorous training regimen. Near the summit of Tennessee Pass, a 20-foot-high slab of granite is etched with the names of nearly 1,000 of these men who lost their lives in World War II. A number of their fellow veterans went on to make a huge impact on the ski industry in Colorado. Locally, Ski Cooper is a direct result of efforts by former 10th Mountain members.

Festivals and Events

Boom Days

first weekend in Aug. During Leadville's main summer bash, you'll have no trouble imagining what the town was like during the real silver boom. The streets once again fill with tough-looking hardrock miners, dancing girls, brass bands and burros. The weekend kicks off with a parade down Harrison Ave. and ends with a burro race over Mosquito Pass. In between check out mining events such as hand mucking (loading broken rock by hand) and jackleg drilling (drilling with a jackhammer). The Lions Club sets up a traditional beer garden every year. **719-486-3900.**

Leadville 100

mid-Aug. Each year this grueling 100-mile footrace heads up into the Sawatch Range, crossing above 12,000-foot elevations at times. It takes a rare breed of runner to somehow enjoy this brutal annual event. Hundreds of spectators join hundreds of runners for the exciting 4 A.M.

Doe to "hang on to the Matchless," the mine that he believed would make her rich again. For 36 years Baby Doe lived in a cabin next to the Matchless Mine above Leadville, until she froze to death one winter evening. With the irony of a Greek tragedy, only Tabor's first wife, Augusta, who preferred to live simply, died a millionaire.

Just before the turn of the century, James J. Brown (husband of the *Titanic* heroine, "unsinkable" Molly Brown) sank a deep shaft into the Little Johnny Mine just east of the city and discovered a huge gold vein. This discovery revitalized Leadville enough for it to be established as a permanent mining town.

Up until 1900 zinc was thought to be a worthless by-product that had clogged the silver sluicing operations. After the turn of the century its value became known and much of the metal was taken from the abandoned silver mines. Lead and manganese deposits were also worked profitably. A huge body of molybdenum was discovered in 1918 at Fremont Pass. Until fairly recently when synthetic replacements were start. Most runners return to Leadville 20 to 30 hours later. A 100-mile mountain bike race is offered as well. **719-486-3900.**

Outdoor Activities

Biking

MOUNTAIN BIKING

The Leadville area is recognized as a premier location for mountain bike enthusiasts. The maze of old mining roads right around town provides a limitless area for exploring. Some particularly good roads are just east of town on heavily mined **Fryer Hill.** Or try an extremely tough ride up and over **Mosquito Pass,** ending in South Park (see the Four-Wheel-Drive Trips section). Riders who want to find single-track trails might set off from the western side of Tennessee Pass on a number of marked cross-country ski trails. Here are a couple of favorites:

Downtown Leadville after a winter snow.
Photo by Dean Winstanley.

Turquoise Lake Trail

This fairly easy 6.5-mile trail winds along the beautiful, forested shoreline of Turquoise Lake. Start at any of the campgrounds or picnic areas along the perimeter of the lake and complete a loop trip back to your cooler. See the Fishing section for directions to the lake.

Weston Pass

From the beginning of Weston Pass Rd. ride 10 gradual miles to the top of the pass. Turn around or continue on to South Park. For more information and directions see the Scenic Drives section.

Rentals and Tours

Bill's Sport Shop—A small selection of good rental mountain bikes and local topographic maps. Ask Paul Copper (Leadville native) for advice on local trails. **225 Harrison Ave.; 719-486-0739; www.toski.com/bills.**

Fishing

Despite runoff from the heavily mined mountains near town, many excellent fishing opportunities exist near Leadville. The Arkansas River, beginning about 20 miles south of Leadville, provides excellent fly-fishing for brown trout. See the Fishing section of the **Upper Arkansas Valley** chapter for more information. For tackle and fishing information, stop by **Buckhorn Sporting Goods** at **616 Harrison Ave.; 719-486-3944.**

Crystal Lakes

Stocked with rainbow and cutthroat, these lakes are usually hopping with feeding trout in early evening. From the shore, small dry flies are effective on top; many anglers cast hardware into the middle where larger trout swim the deep water. This easy-access fishing area is only 3.5 miles south of Leadville on Hwy. 24.

Halfmoon Creek

Directly beneath the tallest peaks in Colorado, Halfmoon Creek offers many pools and eddies to the diligent angler. It is stocked with rainbow trout, but browns and brookies can also be caught. To reach Halfmoon Creek travel west on Hwy. 24 for about 2 miles. Continue west on Hwy. 300 instead of following Hwy. 24 around a wide bend in the road. Stay on Hwy. 300 for a mile before turning south on Halfmoon Creek Rd. (Forest Rd. 110). After a couple of miles the creek parallels the dirt road for 4 miles to Halfmoon Campground. Upstream from Halfmoon Campground, a jeep road parallels the creek, eventually narrowing into a trail. It is possible to hike all the way up to North Halfmoon Creek, which is also good for small brook trout.

Turquoise Lake

At nearly 10,000 feet in elevation, this large lake offers some of the best fishing in the Leadville area, only 3 miles west of town. Good fishing combined with a beautiful location make it a heavily used recreation area; eight campgrounds are located around the lake. Fishing from a boat or from the shore will yield brown, rainbow and cutthroat trout. There are other species in the lake, including stocked kokanee salmon. Turquoise Lake is known for its excellent ice fishing. Hiking trails lead from Turquoise Lake to high alpine lakes, including a couple of good producers just inside the Holy Cross Wilderness: **Galena Lake** and **Bear Lake.** To reach Turquoise Lake, drive west on 6th St. to the edge of town. Turn right (northwest) on Turquoise Lake Rd. and continue 3 miles.

Twin Lakes Reservoir

So, you want to catch a Mackinaw (lake trout) in the 30-pound range? Twin Lakes, at the foot of Independence Pass, will give you the chance. But you can keep only one and it must exceed 20 inches. In addition to large lake trout, Twin Lakes Reservoir is stocked with rainbow and cutthroat trout. Although shore fishing can be good, many anglers prefer trolling for Mackinaw; boat ramps are located on the north side of the lake. Several picnic and camping areas make this lake an extremely popular destination. From Leadville follow Hwy. 24 south for 14 miles until reaching Hwy. 82. Turn right and head west on Hwy. 82, which follows along the north shore. Be sure to stop off Hwy. 82 between the lakes, at the visitor center and power plant. There you can get information on the area and see an interesting scale model of the water storage system.

Four-Wheel-Drive Trips

There are untold numbers of four-wheel-drive roads in the mountains around Leadville. This is a great place to explore because the mines have left so many visible traces.

Hagerman Pass

This fairly mild road manages to slip through a gap along the Continental Divide between Leadville and Basalt. Just to the west of the summit, a four-wheel-drive vehicle is needed for a rough stretch, but lower elevations on both sides of the pass can be negotiated by most passenger cars. The views from the open summit stretch back to Leadville and the Arkansas Valley; you can't help but enjoy the western view down to Ivanhoe Lake and the Upper Fryingpan Valley. (Bring your fishing pole!) See the Fishing section of the **Aspen** chapter for information.

The historic route plunges into the impressive Sawatch Range along the defunct Colorado Midland Railroad bed. Along the way you can stop off to see two tunnels, bored so the trains could make their way to Aspen and the Roaring Fork Valley. One tunnel is near a parking lot; the other requires a 2.5-mile hike. In 1886 trains began passing through Hagerman Tunnel, bored out of solid rock at 11,500 feet. Due to high maintenance costs, the Carlton Tunnel was constructed 800 feet lower in elevation.

From Leadville drive west on 6th St. to the edge of town. Turn right on Turquoise Lake Rd. and follow along to the dam. Check your odometer, and 3.5 miles west of the dam turn left on a marked side road, which continues over the pass. The easy hiking trail to the abandoned Hagerman Tunnel is marked, below the summit on the east side of the pass.

Mosquito Pass

At 13,188 feet the road over Mosquito Pass is the highest through road in North America. Built as a wagon road in 1879, it connected Leadville with the mining camps of South Park. Heavy traffic over the pass was short-lived as trains arrived the following year. Today this difficult four-wheel-drive road offers great views of many Colorado mountain ranges as well as countless mining remains.

At the summit a stone marker commemorates the mail-carrying Father John Dyer, known as the "snowshoe itinerant." In the late 1800s he not only held services for many mining camps but also carried the mail over several high passes on 10-foot wooden skis. Every Aug. during Boom Days, a 23-mile pack burro race takes place on Mosquito Pass.

From Leadville take 7th St. east from Harrison Ave. The road leads into the Fryer Hill mining district as it follows Evans Gulch up toward the pass. Stay on the main road past the Matchless Mine. About 4.5 miles after starting out, Mosquito Pass Rd. breaks off to the left. From here, the road leads 18 miles over the summit and down to the town of Fairplay. Instead of returning on the same route, come back to Leadville via Weston Pass, located 5 miles south of Fairplay on Hwy. 285 (see the Scenic Drives section).

Golf

Mt. Massive Golf Club

The folks here say this golf course is the highest in the world. The well-maintained greens are located near the base of Mt. Massive (14,421 feet). Since this nine-hole course is surrounded by a thick forest of lodgepole pines, it is not uncommon to see deer and elk wander onto the links. Located 3.5 miles west of town on Turquoise Lake Rd. (County Rd. 4); **719-486-2176.**

Hiking and Backpacking

The Leadville area offers some of the most spectacular mountain terrain imaginable—and hiking is perhaps the best way to get out and enjoy it. The town is surrounded on three sides by San Isabel National Forest, including Colorado's two highest peaks to the west: Mt.

Elbert (14,433 feet) and Mt. Massive (14,421 feet). At lower elevations a web of trails meanders through ponderosa forests, wildflowers, meadows and crumbling remnants of the mining boom. Several other great hikes near the Leadville area are discussed in the **Vail Valley** and **Upper Arkansas Valley** chapters. For trail information and maps, contact the **Leadville Ranger District Office, 2015 N. Poplar St.; 719-486-0749; www.fs.fed.us/r2/psicc/ leadville.** For topographic maps and outdoor equipment try **Bill's Sport Shop** at **225 Harrison Ave., 719-486-0739,** or **Buckhorn Sporting Goods** at **616 Harrison Ave., 719-486-3944.** Recreation and topo maps also available online at **www.leadville.com.**

Colorado Trail

Passing just to the west of Leadville, the 469-mile Colorado Trail offers access to spectacular scenery: thick woods, trout streams and historic mining areas. Consider leaving a second car at a pickup point near the trail and taking a one-way backpacking trip for a few days. The stretch near Leadville between Tennessee Pass and Twin Lakes is absolutely gorgeous. A side trip up Mt. Elbert or Mt. Massive can be easily taken from the Colorado Trail.

Interlaken Trail

This 2-mile, one-way trail leads due west along the gentle shoreline of the eastern Twin Lake, eventually reaching the ghost town of Interlaken; the round-trip hike takes about 2.5 hours. True to its name, Interlaken—a few cabins and other boarded-up buildings—lies directly between the Twin Lakes. From Leadville take Hwy. 24 south for 14 miles until reaching Hwy. 82. Turn right and head west on Hwy. 82 for about 3 miles to the tip of the eastern lake. Just before crossing a bridge, turn left on a gravel road that passes below the dam and intersects shortly with the Colorado Trail.

Leadville National Fish Hatchery

Beginning near the teeming cement fish tanks of this hatchery is a nature trail with 15 numbered stations along its 1-mile route. The easy walk takes about an hour and is in a beautiful area near the base of Mt. Massive. At a midpoint between the three Evergreen Lakes is a picnic area. Pick up a trail guide at the visitor center. To reach the hatchery take Hwy. 24 west of Leadville for 2 miles to Hwy. 300. Turn right (west) and drive a couple more miles to the historic hatchery, built in 1889.

Mt. Elbert

A hike up Colorado's tallest peak (14,433 feet) requires a degree of strength, stamina and common sense. This is a popular hike that can be done in one day. The first part of the hike is heavily wooded and provides the best chance for sighting mule deer and other wildlife. After you leave the trees behind, colorful alpine tundra takes over the ground. Please stay on the trail, as this plant life is easily damaged. In early summer the trail passes over snowfields close to the top. When you make it to the summit, the views are astounding in all directions.

North Mt. Elbert Trail begins at an elevation of 10,100 feet and climbs 4.5 miles to the summit. Although the shortest route, it's steeper than the South Trail. To reach the trailhead from Leadville, head west on Hwy. 24 for about 2 miles. Continue west on Hwy. 300 instead of following Hwy. 24 as it turns south around a wide bend. Stay on Hwy. 300 for a mile before turning south on Halfmoon Creek Rd. (Forest Rd. 110). Continue 6 miles on the dirt road to Halfmoon Campground. The trail leaves from just above the campground parking area.

South Mt. Elbert Trail is longer but receives more use thanks to its more gradual incline. The trail begins at 9,600 feet and climbs 5.5 miles to the summit. The trailhead is located at Lake View Campground near Twin Lakes (see the Camping section).

Yet another approach to the summit of Mt. Elbert is on **Black Cloud Trail.** Least used of all the routes, this is a truly beautiful way to the top. Even if you don't have the urge to conquer a 14er, this can be an excellent short hike—just return when you feel like it. The trail gains nearly 5,000 feet in 5.5 miles, but the steady uphill pull is rewarded by the view from the top. To reach the trailhead travel south on Hwy. 24 for 14 miles to Hwy. 82. Turn right and drive past Twin Lakes to a half-mile beyond Twin Peaks Campground. The trail leaves from the north side of the highway.

Mt. Massive Trail

Even though Mt. Massive is 12 feet shorter than Mt. Elbert, its trail is quite a bit longer—from Halfmoon Campground it is 6.4 miles to the summit, with an elevation gain of almost 4,500 feet. This long day hike is fantastic if you're in good shape. The trail begins on the Colorado Trail and tracks north along the base of the peak for 3 miles. At a marked junction with Mt. Massive Trail you take the left fork and head sharply uphill toward treeline. Once above the trees, views to Leadville and Mt. Elbert are incredible. It gets even better once you are on the summit! To reach the trailhead see the entry on North Mt. Elbert Trail. Both hikes begin just above Elbert Creek Campground.

Horseback Riding

Leadville Stables

What could be better than having a friendly Leadville native take you on a guided horseback ride through the historic mining district? Take a one-day, two-day, half-day or longer trip with an expert on the area. The breakfast rides feature hot biscuits and sausage gravy. Located at the northern edge of town. **131 N. Hwy. 91; 719-486-1497; 719-486-0739; www.bills sports.com.**

River Floating

The Upper Arkansas River is renowned for giving rafters thrilling whitewater rides. A slew of outfitters make the run, but most are based downriver near the towns of Buena Vista and Salida. The Upper Arkansas River, including Browns Canyon, is discussed in detail in the River Floating section of the **Upper Arkansas Valley** chapter, as are ideas for outfitters.

Skiing

CROSS-COUNTRY SKIING AND SNOWSHOEING

Leadville lies at the center of a cross-country skier's paradise. Miles of backcountry trails weave through the lower reaches of the Sawatch Mountains. In addition, groomed trail systems leave from the base of Ski Cooper on Tennessee Pass and from the Colorado Mountain College campus. All in all, the snow conditions at this altitude are excellent, as are the views. For maps and information about trails and avalanche conditions in San Isabel National Forest, contact the **Leadville Ranger District Office, 2015 N. Poplar St.; 719-486-0749; www.fs.fed.us/r2/psicc/leadville.**

Backcountry Trails

Leadville National Fish Hatchery—A marked system of looping trails for various abilities leads away from the fish hatchery at the base of Mt. Massive. The area is stunning in its natural beauty. A good half-day trip is on the Highline Trail Loop or the more difficult Kearney Park Loop. More information is posted at the hatchery. To get there see the Hiking and Backpacking section.

Silver City Trail—Skiing through Leadville's historic mining district is one of the best ways to get a feeling for the lifestyle of the miners. Back when the mines were operating year-round, however, men working the mines in winter never saw the sun. Today miles of unplowed mining roads weave past the abandoned mine buildings that litter the countryside. Dangerous pits and holes abound off the roads. A map with a key to the markers on the "routes of the silver kings" is available at the **Greater Leadville Area Chamber of Commerce, 809 Harrison Ave.; 719-486-3900.**

Tennessee Pass—Just west of the summit of Tennessee Pass on Hwy. 24, a number of trails head off into the woods. Some of the trails follow the old Denver & Rio Grande Railroad beds. The **Mitchell Creek Loop** begins on the fairly level grade of a railroad bed for 2.5 miles

before getting a bit tougher. The entire loop is slightly over 7 miles long. More difficult tours include the **Powder Hound Loop** and the **Treeline Loop.** Views of old mine buildings accompany nearly every tour. This is the area where the 10th Mountain Division trained before heading off to Europe in World War II. All of the trails are marked; maps are available from the **Leadville Ranger District Office, 2015 N. Poplar St.; 719-486-0749.**

10th Mountain Trail Association Hut System—Over 300 miles of trails stretch into the beautiful backcountry between Leadville, Aspen, Vail and Summit County with 22 huts along the way. It's a great way to experience the backcountry in the Leadville area any time of year. Huts in the Leadville area include the Skinner Hut near Hagerman Pass, Uncle Bud's Hut north of Turquoise Lake, 10th Mountain Division Hut near Tennessee Pass and the Belvedere Hut a couple of miles off of Hwy. 91 about 4 miles from Leadville For detailed information about overnight hut accommodations see the Skiing section of the **Aspen** chapter or contact the association at **979-925-5775; www.huts.aspen.co.us.**

Twin Lakes Trails—A number of trails lead off from Twin Lakes, 22 miles southwest of Leadville. You might ski across the frozen lakes to the ghost town of Interlaken or head up Independence Pass on the road that closes for winter. From Leadville take Hwy. 24 south for 14 miles until reaching Hwy. 82. Turn right and head 8 miles west on Hwy. 82.

Groomed Trails

Piney Creek Nordic Center—If you're looking for the quieter, more reflective experiences found via cross-country skis or snowshoes, the Piney Creek Nordic Center is the perfect place. Twenty-five kilometers of maintained trails leave from the base of Ski Cooper on Tennessee Pass. Many of the trails are loops of varying length and difficulty. From the Piney Creek trails, the panorama of Mt. Elbert, Mt. Massive and lofty peaks stretching north into the Holy Cross Wilderness has to be one of the most outstanding high country sites in Colorado. Reasonable trail fees make the terrain accessible to all skiers. Cross-country and snowshoe rentals and instruction can be arranged at the nordic center. For those interested in telemark skiing, 302 acres of lift-served slopes at the ski mountain are perfect (telemark clinics and rentals available). Located 10 miles north of Leadville on Hwy. 24; **719-486-1750.** For a unique ski-in dining experience in a yurt along the Continental Divide, see the **Tennessee Pass Cookhouse** write-up in the Where to Eat section.

Rentals and Information

Bill's Sport Shop—This place has equipment, maps and advice for cross-country skiers and snowshoers. Open 9 A.M.–5:30 P.M. daily. **225 Harrison Ave., Leadville, CO 80461; 719-486-0739; www.toski.com/bills.**

Nordic Inn—For rentals and information/advice about the Twin Lakes area, stop in here. **Twin Lakes, CO 81251; 1-800-626-7812; 719-486-1830; www.twinlakesnordic inn.com.**

Piney Creek Nordic Center—The nordic center offers excellent telemark and cross-country equipment. See entry above for information.

DOWNHILL SKIING AND SNOWBOARDING

About 20 minutes from Leadville, you can be on the slopes at **Ski Cooper.** Although it's a terrific, low-key alternative to the big ski resorts, you may be happy to know that in under an hour you can reach **Copper Mountain, Breckenridge, Vail, Beaver Creek, Keystone** and **Arapahoe Basin.**

Ski Cooper

This small but venerable ski area is yet another result of efforts by 10th Mountain veterans. Perched atop Tennessee Pass, Ski Cooper offers a fairly even mix of trail difficulty for skiers, snowboarders and telemarkers. Certainly not one of the glittery ski resorts, Cooper still draws loyal crowds by catering to families, offering relatively inexpensive tickets and learn-to-ski packages

and uncrowded slopes. Since the base elevation is at 10,500 feet, the snowfall (260-inch average) is normally dry and powdery and all-natural.

Four lifts service the 365 skiable acres with a 1,600-foot vertical drop. Powder hounds with the desire and available cash should seriously consider backcountry skiing opportunities with **Chicago Ridge Snowcat Tours.** Full-day and half-day tours from Ski Cooper deposit you on the Continental Divide for fresh powder runs through 2,500 acres of tree-covered slopes and open bowls. Ski Cooper is located 10 miles north of Leadville on Hwy. 24. Ski school, rentals, day care (2 to 7 years), restaurant. **719-486-2277; 719-486-3684; www.ski cooper.com.**

Seeing and Doing

Museums

"The Earth Runs Silver," a multi-image slide show with narration, is a good place to get an overall view of Leadville before heading to your museum of choice. Shows are held at the **Fox Theater** in summer at **115 W. 6th.** For tickets and information stop by **809 Harrison Ave.; 719-486-3900.**

Healy House and Dexter Cabin

The Healy House, an elaborate Victorian built in 1878, was originally a single-family residence but served as a boardinghouse from 1897 to 1902. Five of the residents in 1898 were female schoolteachers. In those days schoolteachers were required to wear seven undergarments at all times and take examinations twice a year. For their troubles they were paid $40 per month; $30 was for the rental of cramped quarters in the Healy House.

Dexter Cabin looks like any primitive log cabin until you get inside. The builder of the small structure was James Dexter, who made a pile of money in mining and investments. Dexter Cabin was never used as a residence; rather, it was for members of an exclusive poker club. The cabin's interior, furnished with the finest woods,

Cutting through the powder at Ski Cooper. Photo courtesy of Ski Cooper.

is an example of pure luxury. The museum complex is open from Memorial Day to Labor Day, 10 A.M.–4:30 P.M. daily; shorter hours in May and Sept. Fee charged. For an added historical treat, inquire about the summertime live per-

formances by local actress Melva Touchette as Baby Doe Tabor. Performances of her two-act, one-woman show take place at 7 P.M. in the Healy House and should not be missed. **912 Harrison Ave.; 719-486-0487.**

Heritage Museum

Inside this former library (built in 1904) you'll find mining implements, dioramas of mining activity, a scale model of the Ice Palace and placards describing the exciting history of the area. Upstairs are museum exhibits from Leadville's heyday as well as a gallery featuring the work of Colorado artists. Small admission fee. Open 10 A.M.–6 P.M. May through Oct.; winter visits by appointment only. **102 E. 9th St.; 719-486-1878.**

Matchless Mine

The headlines around the country screamed "Queen of Colorado's Silver Boom Perishes" and "Baby Doe Freezes to Death While on Guard at Matchless Mine." It was a tragic end to the life of Baby Doe Tabor, second wife of mining magnate H.A.W. Tabor. On his deathbed H.A.W. Tabor whispered to Baby Doe, "Hang on to the Matchless." Baby Doe moved into a shack at the mine and became a recluse. She died in squalor

The renovated Tabor Grand Hotel building speaks to Leadville's mining heyday. Photo by Bruce Caughey.

in 1935 after a 36-year vigil. The Matchless has been preserved, and tours of the property are given, including the exterior workings of the mine. Follow E. 7th St. east of town for 1 mile to the mine entrance. Small admission fee. Open June–Labor Day 9 A.M.–5 P.M.

National Mining Hall of Fame

There couldn't be a more appropriate place for a national mining museum than Leadville, Colorado. Housed in a four-story Victorian shell of the former junior high school, the large museum serves as a showcase for mining methods and technologies (including reclamation of old mining sites), both historical and futuristic. It's a great place to learn about the hardships and engineering feats of miners. The highlight is a fascinating walk-through replica of an actual working underground hardrock mine. The Smithsonian's mineral exhibit demonstrates that wealth can be found in many colors. Walk through room after room of idle heavy equipment, exhibit cases and colorful murals telling the story of mining in the United States. Upstairs, individuals who have "achieved lasting greatness in mining" are commemorated on plaques. Fee charged; gift shop. Open May–Oct., daily 9 A.M.–5 P.M.; Nov.–Apr., Mon.–Fri. 9 A.M.–2 P.M. **120 W. 9th St., P.O. Box 981, Leadville, CO 80461; 719-486-1229; www.leadville.com/miningmuseum.**

Nightlife

Silver Dollar Saloon

Very few saloons in Colorado are well into their second century of operation. The Silver Dollar is one of them. The first drink was pushed across the bar in 1879 when it opened under the name Board of Trade. The stunning white oak back bar with inlaid diamond dust mirror was shipped by wagon from St. Louis, Missouri. There is also an oak windbreak as you enter the bar; some say it was placed there to protect men from the prying eyes of their wives. During Prohibition the bar remained active, with a trapdoor mounted beneath the bar for quick disposal of moonshine.

Today, strangely, the bar touts itself as an "Irish Pub." **315 Harrison Ave.; 719-486-9914.**

Railroads

Leadville, Colorado & Southern Railroad

In 1988, after a 50-year silence, a passenger train once again began arriving and departing from Leadville. Pulled by a strong locomotive, the open passenger cars on the standard-gauge railroad provide expansive views during the entire traverse up to treeline. Stephanie and Ken Olsen found the bargain of a century when they purchased two 1,750-horsepower engines, eight flatcars, five cabooses, 13 miles of track and a roundhouse for $10—less than it costs for a ticket to ride the train today. However, they have poured a lot of money, sweat and effort into the operation to make it a worthwhile venture. The train departs daily from the Leadville depot, Memorial Day through Oct. The ride takes about $2^1/_2$ hours, including a short break at the water tower. Reduced rates for children. **326 E. 7th St., P.O. Box 916, Leadville, CO 80461; 719-486-3936; www.leadville-train.com.**

Scenic Drives

Independence Pass (Hwy. 82)

During the summer and fall, this beautiful drive leads to Aspen over a narrow, twisting road. For more information see the Scenic Drives section of the **Aspen** chapter.

Routes of the Silver Kings

Driving among the decaying wooden mine structures and piles of yellowed tailings is a fascinating way to get a true picture of the once-booming industry. Good dirt roads thread their way between famous mines on **Fryer Hill** and **California Gulch.** Several round-trip auto tours leave from Leadville and climb into the mountains. Along the roads numbered route markers are placed at points of historical interest. Each marker corresponds with a description in a booklet that can be purchased at the **Greater Leadville Area Chamber of Commerce,**

809 Harrison Ave.; 1-800-933-3901; 719-486-3900; www.leadville.com.

Weston Pass

This old wagon road, which crosses the Mosquito Range south of Leadville, connects the Upper Arkansas Valley with South Park. The dirt road will shake your car, and a high-clearance vehicle wouldn't hurt. Following the South Fork of the South Platte River, the road winds its way up to an elevation of 11,921 feet. The route goes between Weston Peak (13,572 feet) to the north and Marmott Peak (13,326 feet) to the south. To reach Weston Pass Rd. from Leadville take Hwy. 24 for 6 miles south to the marked turnoff. Turn left and drive 10 miles to the pass. From here, continue down to Hwy. 285 south of Fairplay.

Where to Stay

Accommodations

Aside from the places described in detail below, you may also want to try one of these quaint bed and breakfast inns: **Apple Blossom Inn ($$$ to $$$$)** offers four rooms and hearty breakfasts in a handsomely renovated 1879 home built by a local banker; **120 W. 4th St., Leadville, CO 80461; 1-800-982-9279; 719-486-2141; www.colorado-bnb.com/abi.** The **Ice Palace Inn ($$$),** built from wood used for the 1894 Leadville Ice Palace, provides three rooms with private baths; **813 Spruce St.; Leadville, CO 80461; 1-800-754-2840; 719-486-8272; www.icepalaceinn.com.**

Delaware Hotel—$$ to $$$$

By 1886 the Delaware Block was completed, with 50 upstairs offices and bedrooms. Named for the first owners' home state, the hotel originally featured the conveniences of steam heat and hot and cold water but had only four bathrooms for the entire complex. The exterior similarities between the Delaware and renovated Tabor Grand/Vendome Building across the street can be attributed to a common architect, George E. King. For a long time the venerable Delaware operated as the Crew Beggs Dry Goods Company, but it has been back in service as a hotel for quite some time.

Climb the stairway from the renovated lobby area and you'll get a feel for this classy, historic hotel. Each room at the Delaware is slightly different, with uneven floors and furniture from the late Victorian period; some have the nice touches of exposed brick and brass beds. All have plush carpet and private bathrooms. With the exception of the suites, the rooms are on the small side—shall we say cozy? The two-room suites are a bargain for four people—a personal favorite was the suite tucked into the western corner on the third floor with a gorgeous mountain view. Hot tub on the main floor. A night's stay in any room at the Delaware includes a full breakfast. **700 Harrison Ave., P.O. Box 960, Leadville, CO 80461; 1-800-748-2004; 719-486-1418; www.delewarehotel.com.**

Leadville Country Inn—$$ to $$$$

Maureen and Gretchen Scanlon (a mother/daughter team) run this textbook example of a successful bed and breakfast in a beautifully restored 1893 Queen Anne Victorian and its carriage house. Each of the nine rooms features a private bathroom. But only Maggie's Room has an antique copper tub laid into a polished wooden frame, just right for a long soak. Maggie's king-size bed provides for a picture-perfect view out to Colorado's highest peaks. A favorite room is Sophie's Attic with its private entrance, richly textured walls, four-poster bed, antique loft and a decadent bathroom with a whirlpool bath for two. The antiques that decorate each of the inn's rooms are remarkable—Gretchen used to operate an antiques store. A full breakfast can be taken in the large common room or, if you prefer, in your bedroom. Did we forget to mention the gazebo and outdoor hot tub? **127 E. 8th St., Leadville, CO 80461; 1-800-748-2354; 719-486-2354; www.leadvillebednbreakfast.com.**

Mt. Elbert Lodge—$$ to $$$

Located at the base of Independence Pass, a few miles west of Twin Lakes, this historic establishment comes as a welcome surprise. The rustic but comfortable lodge features five tidy bed and breakfast rooms, some with shared baths. Three housekeeping cabins (one suited for honeymooners) are nicely situated along Lake Creek; three cabins sit across the road, at the Black Cloud Trail, which climbs north to the summit of Mt. Elbert. This affordably priced place is perfect for families and folks interested in getting out into the backcountry. Open year-round; reservations are needed well in advance for peak summer season. **P.O. Box 40, Twin Lakes, CO 81251; 1-800-381-4433; 719-486-0594; www. mount-elbert.com.**

Nordic Inn—$$

Constructed in 1879 as a stagecoach stop, the Nordic Inn enjoys a pristine mountain location in the tiny community of Twin Lakes (year-round population, 20). Summer or winter (cross-country ski rentals available) the Nordic Inn finds itself amid the stunning San Isabel National Forest, offering basic accommodations to those who love the outdoors but don't necessarily feel like camping out. This funky former brothel and historical landmark provides smallish rooms, most of which share baths. The German-style restaurant downstairs is available for breakfast, lunch or dinner (see the Where to Eat section). Adventuresome souls may wish to reserve a room during the annual Hooker's Ball in mid-Oct. (costumes required). Closed in mud season: early spring and late fall. Located 22 miles south of Leadville on Hwy. 82. **6435 Hwy. 82, Twin Lakes, CO 81251; 1-800-626-7812; 719-486-1830; www.twinlakesnordicinn.com.**

Camping

San Isabel National Forest

Eight campgrounds (368 campsites) are situated around the perimeter of Turquoise Lake. This heavily wooded area offers hiking, fishing and boating. The **Belle of Colorado Campground,** on the east end of the lake, is the only walk-in campground and is limited to tents. All campgrounds charge a fee and have water and toilets. Turquoise Lake is located 3 miles west of Leadville. Many of these campgrounds, as well as others in the national forest, may be reserved by calling **877-444-6777.**

South of Leadville, under the towering summits of Mt. Elbert and Mt. Massive, are the nicely wooded **Halfmoon** (24 sites) and **Elbert Creek** (17 sites) **Campgrounds.** A fee is charged at both. Since a trailhead for climbing Elbert and Massive takes off from the area, use is heavy, especially on weekends. To reach the campgrounds travel west from town on Hwy. 24 for about 2 miles. Continue west on Hwy. 300 instead of following Hwy. 24 as it turns south around a big bend. Stay on Hwy. 300 for a mile before turning south on Halfmoon Creek Rd. (Forest Rd. 110). Continue 6 miles on the dirt road to the campgrounds.

In the Twin Lakes area there are five large campgrounds; all charge a fee. From Leadville follow Hwy. 24 south for 14 miles until reaching Hwy. 82. Turn right and head west on Hwy. 82, which skirts the north side of the reservoir. After 3 miles you'll reach **Dexter Point Campground** (26 sites) beside the lake. Another 2 miles down Hwy. 82, turn right onto Forest Rd. 125 and continue to **Lake View Campground** (59 sites). As the name suggests, the view to Twin Lakes is beautiful. Past Lake View Campground you can proceed west along Hwy. 82 to **White Star** (64 sites), **Perry Peak** (26 sites) and **Twin Peaks** (37 sites) **Campgrounds.**

Private Campground

Sugar Loafin' Campground—Not far from Turquoise Lake, this scenic campground offers full RV hookups and tentsites. Amenities include hot showers, laundry, a grocery store and, listen up, ice cream socials! Located 3.5 miles west of Leadville on County Rd. 4; **719-486-1031.**

Where to Eat

Tennessee Pass Cookhouse—$$ to $$$$

For special occasions, consider a nighttime ski, snowshoe or snowmobile trip up through the trees to the Tennessee Pass Cookhouse. A guide from the Piney Creek Nordic Center leads you 1 mile by headlamp to this romantic getaway—a gussied-up yurt, serving elegant, all-inclusive meals for a set price. Antique wood tables, fancy throw rugs, soothing music and a warming fireplace are highlights along with the fantastic full-course meal. Menus change seasonally but may include grilled elk tenderloin with blueberry, sage and port wine, oven-roasted chicken with wild mushroom jus, baked salmon in teriyaki and other entrées. Lunches and summertime dinners are available as well. During daylight hours, the high mountain panorama from the porch is matchless. Reservations needed. Located at the Piney Creek Nordic Center at Ski Cooper. **719-486-1750; 719-486-8114; www.tennesseepass.com.**

Nordic Inn—$ to $$$

The alpine setting in the town of Twin Lakes is the inn's main draw and, simply, it cannot be matched. A wall of small windowpanes in this cozy restaurant opens up to one of the finest mountain views imaginable. The warm wooden interior of this historic stagecoach stop, especially with a roaring fire, can really fit the bill in winter. You'll find standards for breakfast and lunch. German dinner specialties include jaeggerschnitzel and sauerbraten; there are also pork and poultry dishes and a voluminous bottled beer selection. Open daily 7 A.M.–11 A.M. for breakfast, 11 A.M.–3 P.M. for lunch and 5–9 P.M. for dinner; lunches in winter for guests only. Open sporadically in spring and autumn. For information on the inn see the Where to Stay section. Located 22 miles south of Leadville on Hwy. 82. **Twin Lakes, CO 81251; 1-800-626-7812; 719-486-1830.**

Casa Blanca—$ to $$

Consistently good food, quick service and reasonable prices at this small, spare Mexican restaurant continue to draw raves from locals. Be sure to grab one of the window tables if you can. Owners Cleo and Tony Mascarenaz do a terrific job with the crispy chili rellenos as well

as large combination dinners. You can order à la carte, too. Good selection of Mexican beers; they also serve wine. Open Tues.–Sun. 11:30 A.M.–8 P.M. Closed Mon. **118 E. 2nd Ave.; 719-486-9969.**

The Grill Bar and Cafe—$ to $$

With its full bar and large dining area the Grill is certainly the liveliest Mexican restaurant in town. And the food's good, too. Slip into one of the red vinyl booths, order up a drink, eat some chips and choose from a wide selection of Mexican entrées. Stuffed sopapillas are the specialty and are highly recommended, especially smothered with green chili. Restaurant open 4–10 P.M. weekdays; 11 A.M.–10 P.M. weekends. Bar stays open longer if there is a crowd. Located off the main drag at **715 Elm St.; 719-486-9930.**

Steph and Scott's Columbine Cafe—$ to $$

Every Colorado mountain town seems to have a down-home cafe where the locals hang out. In Leadville it's the Columbine Cafe. Breakfasts and tasty desserts (especially pie) are probably the main draws. Breakfast specialties include eggs Benedict, biscuits and gravy and creative potato dishes such as the Denver potato skillet. Lunches feature many sandwiches, po-boys and Buddha's spicy Cajun burger, named after the resident pooch. Buddha is said to be a veteran of a Grateful Dead tour covering all 50 states and 105 shows. Be sure to check out the specials on the chalkboard. Pleasant atmosphere and very friendly staff. Open 6 A.M.–3 P.M. daily. **612 Harrison Ave.; 719-486-3599.** If you are craving a great cup of Joe or a latte, head across the street to the **Cloud City Coffee House** at **711 Harrison Ave.; 719-486-1317.**

Services

Visitor Information

Leadville/Lake County Chamber of Commerce—809 Harrison Ave., P.O. Box 861, Leadville, CO 80461; 1-800-933-3901; 719-486-3900; www.leadville.com.

San Luis Valley

High in the mountains of southern Colorado lies an often overlooked, oval-shaped treasure—the San Luis Valley. Its rich and fascinating cultural heritage and extensive history combine with natural surroundings as beautiful as any in the state, making the region worth considering for an extended stay. Ranging in elevation from 7,000 feet on the valley floor to the lofty 14,345-foot summit of Blanca Peak, the geography is impressive. At 125 miles long and 50 miles wide, it's one of the largest valley basins in the United States. To the east and south, the valley is bounded by the mighty Sangre de Cristo (Blood of Christ) Range, which is dominated by the Sierra Blanca Massif. Nestled up against these mountains are the ever-shifting Great Sand Dunes, perhaps the most unusual (and popular) geographical feature in the valley. To the north and west, the valley is enclosed by the San Juan, La Garita and Conejos-Brazos Mountains. The Rio Grande River originates in the nearby mountains and flows southeast through most of the valley on its way to New Mexico.

Long a frontier between New World colonial settlements, the valley has a history spiced with Indian, Anglo and, particularly, Spanish influences. The Hispanic culture is etched deeply in the valley even today; examples surface frequently in Spanish architecture (such as the Catholic churches), arts and crafts, local folklore and the Castilian dialect, which has changed little since the 16th century. Most of the towns, rivers, peaks and valleys have Spanish names.

The people in the San Luis Valley are some of the friendliest in the state. You'll find few pretensions and a relaxed attitude toward everyday life. Set in the approximate center of the valley, Alamosa is the area's largest community and is home to Adams State College. It has served as a main shipping point for valley products (including well-known valley potatoes) to outside markets since its founding in 1878, when the Denver & Rio Grande Railroad arrived. From Alamosa, communities in the valley spread out in all directions.

North of Alamosa, situated against the jutting Sangre de Cristo Range, lies the intriguing little settlement of Crestone. Originally a stage stop and mining area, the town has long been a summer getaway. More recently it has become a haven for a community of spiritualists. Apparently, Crestone was once a sacred Indian site

Getting There

Alamosa is located 212 miles from Denver via Interstate 25 south to Walsenburg, then west on Hwy. 160 over La Veta Pass. The San Luis Valley can also be reached via Hwy. 285 from the Upper Arkansas River Valley to the north. Buses service some towns in the valley with more frequent stops in Alamosa. **United Express** flies into the **Alamosa Municipal Airport** from Denver. Call **1-800-241-6522** for information and reservations.

where lines of planetary energy are said to converge. Many groups, from Tibetan monks and Zen Buddhists to New Agers, have been snapping up real estate in the area.

West of Alamosa lie Monte Vista and Del Norte, both early stage stops and trading towns that serve as agricultural centers today. To the east, the Fort Garland Museum remains a vivid example of life in frontier Colorado.

The vibrant Hispanic community of Colorado's oldest town, San Luis, evokes an atmosphere reminiscent of John Nichols's *Milagro Beanfield War*. Located in the southern part of the valley at the foot of 14,047-foot Culebra Peak, this town has one of the last commons (vegas) in the country outside of the Boston area. The San Luis vega, an 860-acre tract of land, is used by the entire community for grazing and crops. Culturally, the people of San Luis and the neighboring villages composed mostly of adobe-style structures seem more connected to New Mexico than to Colorado.

West of San Luis, the small town of Manassa was settled by Mormons who thought the local Indians were descendants of Manasseh, son of Joseph. It's also the birthplace of former heavyweight boxing champion Jack Dempsey (a.k.a. the "Manassa Mauler").

At the extreme south end of the valley near the New Mexico border lies Antonito, home to the depot of the Cumbres and Toltec Scenic Railroad, offering one of the most beautiful and historic narrow-gauge railroad trips in the country. Antonito was a railroad town built to house Anglos who were less than willing to assimilate into the much older and established Hispanic settlement of Conejos, just north of town. Our Lady of Guadalupe Church in Conejos is considered to be the oldest in the state, although residents of nearby San Acacio beg to differ.

History

The Ute Indians controlled the San Luis Valley for hundreds of years before Europeans ever set foot in the area. Called the Blue Sky People by other tribes, the Utes followed herds and hunted throughout this territory.

Although some speculate that Spanish explorer Francisco Coronado entered the San Luis Valley in 1540, the first recorded European visit to the valley was by another Spaniard, Don Diego de Vargas, in 1694. Eighty-five years later the governor of New Mexico, Juan Bautista de Anza, passed through the San Luis Valley on a vengeful search for Comanche Indians who had raided northern New Mexico settlements. De Anza noted both the Rio Grande and Cochetopa Pass, a well-traveled crossing over the Continental Divide in the northwest section of the valley.

In the winter of 1806–1807, Lt. Zebulon Pike and his men came west into the valley at the sand dunes before making their way south to what Pike thought was the Red River of Texas. They built a stockade nearby, raised the American flag and settled in for the remainder of the winter. However, Pike, the Inspector Clouseau of American explorers, had made a major navigational error—what he thought was the Red River was really the Rio Grande. He had raised the American flag on Spanish soil. It was not long before a detachment of Spanish troops arrived, arrested Pike and his men and escorted them to Santa Fe and then all the way down to Chihuahua. Pike and his men were eventually released at the U.S. border with the promise that they would never set foot in Mexico (New Spain) again.

In the first half of the 1800s Mexican government officials were anxious for settlers to populate what was then the Mexican frontier. They awarded large sections of land (known as land grants), much of it in what is now northern New Mexico and southern Colorado, to men who planned to develop the area. However, it was not until after the Mexican War that the first permanent settlement appeared in the valley. In 1851 a group established the town of San Luis. A number of Hispanic settlements soon followed the lead of San Luis. By that time the United States had gained possession of southern Colorado, and one of the responsibilities that beset the new government was protecting these frontier settlements from marauding Utes and other Indians from the south. In 1852 Fort Massachusetts was built, then replaced six years later by Fort Garland, which helped stabilize the valley until being abandoned in 1883.

Rich mineral strikes in the valley at Summit-ville and Kerber Creek and in the San Juan mining district to the west helped bring about a rail connection with the Front Range by way of La Veta Pass in 1878. Alamosa, a railroad town and former stage stop, literally sprang up in a few days when most of the buildings were shipped in by flatcar as the railroad arrived. Aptly named, Alamosa means "cottonwood grove" in Spanish. A particularly large tree by the Rio Grande served as the town gallows; early train passengers were occasionally greeted by a corpse swinging from this giant cottonwood.

During the 1880s much of the valley along the Rio Grande was irrigated by canals, turning the naturally arid land into rich farmland espe-cially suited to growing potatoes. Today the valley is used primarily for farming and ranch-ing. And as unlikely as it seems, this arid valley sits on top of a deep, enormous aquifer. Seeing the aquifer as vital to the valley's agriculture, residents have successfully banded together to prevent outsiders from pumping the water out and using it to irrigate lawns in the suburbs of far-off cities.

Major Attractions

Cumbres and Toltec Scenic Railroad

The wail of the whistle, hiss of the steam and pungent aroma of coal smoke make this narrow-gauge train irresistible. An added bonus is the lush, rolling countryside and inspiring rock for-mations along the way. The Cumbres and Toltec, America's longest and highest narrow-gauge railroad, begins its 64-mile journey to Chama, New Mexico, from the small burg of Antonito, Colorado. Its serpentine path takes you along the dramatic Toltec Gorge of the Los Piños River and up to the 10,015-foot summit of Cumbres Pass,

On the Cumbres and Toltec Scenic Railroad. Photo by Dean Winstanley.

used by the Spanish to enter the San Luis Valley as early as the 16th century. From the summit the train drops down a steep 4 percent grade into Chama. Along the way the train crosses the Colorado–New Mexico border seven times. This scenic railroad, now a National Historic Site, should not be missed if you are spending any time in the San Luis Valley.

History

Tracks between Antonito and Chama were orig-inally laid down in 1880 by the Denver & Rio Grande Railroad to connect their line to the pro-ductive mining camps of southwestern Colo-rado. After the gold and silver mining petered out in the San Juans, the need for the train fiz-zled, and eventually the route was discontinued. In the late 1960s a determined group from Colorado and New Mexico set out to fix the track. Volunteer gangs and train crews worked more than 2,000 hours fixing tracks and clearing

Great Sand Dunes National Monument. Photo by Steve Trimble, courtesy of the National Parks Service.

obstacles. In September 1970 the refurbished track from Antonito to Chama was opened, and the train made its run.

Facts About the Train

The Cumbres and Toltec Scenic Railroad is jointly owned by the states of Colorado and New Mexico. The train runs daily from Memorial Day weekend through mid-Oct. The trip to Chama takes all day, stopping at the halfway point (Osier), where lunch is served for an extra charge. Afterward, many people take the train that returns to Antonito, while others push on to Chama and return to Antonito by van (the return takes about an hour and a half).

Reservations are highly recommended. Overnight lodging packages in either Chama or Antonito can also be arranged. Group rates are available, and the caboose can be reserved for special parties. **P.O. Box 668, Antonito, CO 81120; 719-376-5483.** In Chama, **P.O. Box 789, Chama, NM 87520; 505-756-2151.**

Great Sand Dunes National Monument

Like a piece of the Sahara Desert grafted onto the side of the snowcapped Sangre de Cristo Mountains, Great Sand Dunes National Monument looks out of place—almost inappropriate. Never ceasing to amaze visitors, the 39 square miles of dunes rise as high as 750 feet and are one of the state's most popular places during summer. Thanks to the hard work of valley residents, the Great Sand Dunes were proclaimed a National Monument by President Hoover in 1932. Congress acted in 2000 to redesignate the dunes as a national park in the near future.

The beckoning power of the dunes is amazing. Many find an overpowering desire to conquer the sand when they reach the dunes parking area. During the midst of tourist season, visitors dressed in Bermuda shorts wade across Medano Creek and scamper all over the dunes, lost in their own thoughts about Lawrence of Arabia and the French Foreign Legion. From the top of the dunes, spectacular views of the San Juan Mountains to the west and the Sangre de Cristos to the east transfix visitors even by moonlight.

Providing all of the information you need for a stay at the monument, the newly renovated visitor center has exhibits explaining the natural and human history of the area. Ask about walks, talks and campfire programs with rangers in the summer months. There is also a good bookstore here. Hours vary.

Getting There

From Alamosa head east on Hwy. 160 for 14 miles to Hwy. 150. Turn left (north) and drive 16 miles to the monument entrance. The monument can also be reached from Hwy. 17 north of Alamosa by driving east from Mosca. **Great Sand Dunes National Monument, 11999 Hwy. 150, Mosca, CO 81146; 719-378-2312; www.nps.gov/grsa.**

Geology

There are many colorful explanations as to why the sand dunes exist. The real reason is that water and wind scour the surrounding mountains, breaking much of the rock down into sand. The sand is blown or carried by rivers down into the valley. Once in the valley, prevailing winds carry the sand northeast to where the Sangre de Cristos rise 5,000 feet from the valley floor. Acting as a natural trap, these mountains create such a high barrier that the wind loses its punch, dropping the sand and thus forming the dunes.

Camping

Piñon Flats Campground (88 sites) is the only camping area within the monument. It's open year-round on a first-come, first-served basis. Fee charged. In winter, water is available at one loop. **Great Sand Dunes Oasis Campground and RV Park,** located just outside the park entrance, offers hookups, showers and other amenities; **719-378-2222; www.alamosa.org.** Additional camping (51 sites) is available at **San Luis Lakes State Park,** about 10 miles west of the park entrance on Sixmile Rd. (see the Wildlife section).

Four-Wheel-Drive Trips

Medano Primitive Rd. follows Medano Creek up along the edge of the dunes for a few miles. Four-wheel-drive vehicles can follow the road but are not allowed to drive off it. Because the sand creates traction difficulties, air needs to be let out of the tires; this prevents most from continuing over Medano Pass to the Wet Mountain Valley (east). Near Piñon Flats Campground there is an air hose for refilling tires. Open May–Sept. Check with visitor center for conditions. Trips are offered by the **Great Sand Dunes Oasis Campground and RV Park,** located just outside the monument entrance; **719-378-2222; www.alamosa.org.**

Hiking and Backpacking

The sand dunes' location next to the Sangre de Cristos makes for some unique hiking and backpacking opportunities. Permits are free but required for all backcountry camping within the park. Pick them up at the visitor center. No backcountry fires. For additional information contact the visitor center.

Along Medano Creek—Flowing out of the Sangre de Cristos from the east, Medano Creek makes its way down a canyon and runs into the dunes. The creek then angles left, paralleling the edge of the dunes all the way past the picnic area and campground, eventually disappearing into the dry soil of the San Luis Valley. When you approach Medano Creek during spring and summer you will notice a rather unusual phenomenon—waves come down the creek about every 30 seconds. These "bores" are created by sand buildup on the bottom of the creek, forming antidunes. The water pressure builds up, the antidunes break and water comes gushing downstream. A primitive road follows the creek upstream along the dunes and then up into Rio Grande National Forest, passing numerous old log cabins along the way. Eventually the road reaches Medano Pass, where views back down to the dunes are spectacular, as are those of the Wet Mountain Valley to the east.

Mosca Pass—A 3.5-mile trail heads up to the summit of Mosca Pass, providing great views of the San Luis Valley and the Wet Mountain Valley. The trail follows Mosca Creek up through juniper and piñon pine. Look for the trailhead on the east side of the road just beyond the visitor center.

On the Dunes—By day, dune trekking is hot and thirsty work, so bring lots of water, and don't forget shoes, sunscreen and a hat. Many people don't realize how vulnerable they are up on the dunes. The dunes occasionally endure violent thunder and hailstorms: proof positive is on display at the visitor center, where you can see exhibits of sand that has been fused into big globs by lightning.

Festivals and Events

Crane Festival

mid-Mar. Each spring as hundreds of bird species make their way north on the valley's main flyway, many outside observers converge on Monte Vista to witness the flurry of avian activity at the nearby Alamosa–Monte Vista National Wildlife Refuges. Guests of honor are the thousands of sandhill cranes and extremely rare whooping cranes. Many activities take place in town, including wildlife art exhibits, wetland educational seminars, photo contests and a banquet. Free buses leave Ski-Hi Park each morning at 7:30 for the wildlife refuge. There is a reason that this area is referred to as "The Valley of the Cranes." **1-800-835-7254; www.r6.fws.gov/alamosanwr.**

Sunshine Festival

1st weekend in June This annual celebration draws large crowds to Monte Vista for a weekend of fun and, hopefully, summer sun. Well over 100 booths are set up through Chapman Park on the banks of the Rio Grande, offering everything from delicious food to arts and crafts. This is a good chance to see some of the valley's weavings and other handicrafts. Live music and dancing throughout the weekend. **719-852-2731; www.home.amigo.net/slvic.**

Castles and Kites Festival

end of June Bring a kid out to Colorado's biggest sandbox to fly kites, build sand castles and have other fun. At Great Sand Dunes National Monument; **1-800-BLU-SKYS.**

Ski-Hi Stampede

end of July Claiming to be Colorado's oldest pro rodeo, this three-day event has been a tradition since 1921. Rodeo competition is accompanied by parades, a chuckwagon dinner, a carnival and a country and western concert. All events take place at Ski-Hi Park. **2345 Sherman Ave.; 719-852-2055.**

Outdoor Activities

Biking

MOUNTAIN BIKING

With an enormous amount of public land in the area, mountain biking continues to grow in popularity. Some good trails can be found in the southwestern section of the Rio Grande National Forest (west of Antonito in the Cumbres Pass area and up the Conejos River). Other national forest riding ideas include the road into La Garita Arch (see the Scenic Drives section), Taylor Gulch and Saguache Park near Saguache, Limekiln near Del Norte and Zapata Falls near the Great Sand Dunes (see Los Caminos Antiguos write-up in the Scenic Drives section).

For more information, including an excellent mountain biking book, contact **Rio Grande National Forest Headquarters, 1803 W. Hwy. 160, Monte Vista, CO 81144; 719-852-5941; www.alamosa.org/rgnf/rgnfhome.htm.** Another excellent trail information source is Eric Burt at **Kristi Mountain Sports.** Kristi also rents mountain bikes and carries all accessories. **7565 W. Hwy. 160, Alamosa, CO 81101; 719-589-9759; www.slvoutdoor.org.**

Fishing

It would be like opening a can of worms to effectively cover all of the noteworthy fishing holes in the San Luis Valley area. Okay, the pun is weak, but it's true given the large number of fishable streams, lakes and reservoirs in the valley. For up-to-date fishing conditions as well as an excellent booklet on fishing opportunities in the valley, contact area visitor centers or the San Luis Valley Office of the **Colorado Division of Wildlife, 722 S. County Rd. 1, Monte Vista, CO 81144; 719-587-6900; 719-852-4783; www.dnr.state.co.us/wildlife/fishing/index.asp.** Or stop by **Alamosa Sporting Goods** for ideas at **1114 Main St.; 719-589-3006.**

Conejos River

Meaning "rabbits" in Spanish, this river flows southeast through the Conejos Valley from Platoro Reservoir (good fishing, boat rentals available) to Antonito, eventually merging with the Rio Grande southeast of Alamosa. The best and most scenic water is in Rio Grande National Forest and can be reached via Hwy. 17 and Forest Rd. 250 about 18 miles west of Antonito. The Conejos can reach a width of 50 feet and is best fished with chest waders. On the upper Conejos you'll catch good-sized brown trout for the most part; the lower areas east of Antonito are flanked by cottonwoods and can be good for rainbows, browns and even an occasional northern pike. After runoff this stream clears up, providing excellent fly-fishing (many stretches are restricted to flies and lures only). When it is running murky your best bets are nymphs. Many productive tributaries flow into the upper Conejos from the west and southwest. Trails provide good access to **Elk Creek** and the **South Fork of the Conejos** and on up to high lakes near the Continental Divide.

La Jara Reservoir

Several small streams flow into La Jara Reservoir, helping it maintain a population of small, pan-sized brook trout. Motorboats are allowed on the rather large reservoir and provide the best way to get around. No rentals; primitive campsites. La Jara Reservoir is located 13 miles south of Alamosa on Hwy. 285.

Rio Grande

The Rio Grande, at 1,887 miles long, is the second-longest river in the country and a diverse river system, offering good fishing during its flow through Colorado. The stretch from just above the town of South Fork downstream to Del Norte has been given Gold Medal designation. Only one-third of this 22.5-mile stretch is open to the public. It can be the inspiration for a good float trip, with large brown trout feeding near the banks. Current restrictions on this stretch of the river include a limit of two fish 16 inches or over and fishing by flies and lures only. For more information about this stretch, see the Fishing section in the **Creede and Lake City** chapter. Farther downriver, between Monte Vista and Alamosa, a large population of northern pike (16- to 32-inch range) provides a lot of excitement if offered the right lure. They like the slow water near weeds and other obstructions.

Sanchez Reservoir

Fishing at this reservoir, 5 miles south of the town of San Luis, has improved markedly in recent years, most notably for 30- to 40-pound northern pike. Check out the freezer at Alamosa Sporting Goods at 1114 Main St. for a firsthand look at some recent catches. There are also some sizable walleye and yellow perch, but the trout are few and far between. Boat ramp available; primitive camping by the shore.

Four-Wheel-Drive Trips

Although the valley is not well known for four-wheel-drive roads, there is a worthwhile route in Great Sand Dunes National Park (see the Major Attractions section). Also, see the **Creede and Lake City** chapter for some great nearby routes.

Golf

Cattails Golf Course

This reasonably priced 18-hole public course in Alamosa has developed into a nice option for golfers in the San Luis Valley. Located in a pleasant, largely treed area along the Rio Grande. Full

Looking across San Luis Lake to Blanca Peak. Photo by Jon Koshak, courtesy of Colorado State Parks.

golf services; restaurant and lounge. Located just north of Alamosa on State St. **719-589-9515.**

Hiking and Backpacking

Surrounding the valley, Rio Grande National Forest boasts a diverse landscape of 14,000-foot peaks, rolling hills, river canyons and thick forests of pine and aspen. The Continental Divide forms the western edge of the forest, with San Juan National Forest just over the divide. Access to the South San Juan Wilderness Area is fairly easy from the Rio Grande side of the divide. For more information about trail possibilities, contact **Rio Grande National Forest Headquarters, 1803 W. Hwy. 160, Monte Vista, CO 81144, 719-852-5941;** the **Conejos Peak Ranger District Office, 15571 County Rd. T5, La Jara, CO 81140, 719-274-8971;** the **Del Norte Ranger District Office, 13308 W. Hwy. 160, Del Norte, CO 81132, 719-657-3321;** or the **Saguache Ranger District Office, 46525 Hwy. 114, Saguache, CO 81149, 719-655-2553.** Obtain online information on each

of these districts at **www.alamosa.org/rgnf/ rgnfhome.htm.**

Blanca Peak

The Mt. Blanca Massif, located in the Sangre de Cristo Range northeast of Alamosa, is the dominant feature in the San Luis Valley. Without many foothills around it, the mountain shoots up thousands of feet from the valley floor, providing a view that has held valley residents and visitors spellbound for centuries. At 14,345 feet, Blanca Peak is Colorado's fourth tallest.

The actual climb up the peak is rated moderate, but the trail takes a bit of effort to reach. Unless you have a good four-wheel-drive vehicle and a full day, you will need to camp along the way. From Alamosa head east on Hwy. 160 for 14 miles and turn left (north) on Hwy. 150. Proceed about 3.2 miles to a dirt road heading off to the right (east), up into the mountains. Turn onto the dirt road and drive about 1.5 miles northeast to a parking area. Passenger cars should park here—the road ahead is not maintained and is extremely punishing even for four-wheel-drive vehicles. From the parking area it's about 4.5 miles up to Lake Como. From Lake Como the easy trail crosses alpine tundra to Blue Lakes and then to Crater Lake, just a half-mile above Blue Lakes. From Crater Lake the trail starts climbing a rocky slope up to the saddle between Ellingwood Point and Blanca Peak. From the saddle head straight up to the 14,345-foot summit of Blanca Peak. Hike early to avoid afternoon thunderstorms.

Crater Lake

The sweeping panoramas and colorful wild-flowers along this 3.5-mile trail, which crosses west over the Continental Divide from the southern Rio Grande National Forest, are hard to beat. The trail (No. 707) begins on the side of Forest Rd. 380, about a mile south of Elwood Pass, and climbs up through Douglas fir before reaching treeline after about three-quarters of a mile. Another half-mile brings you to the 12,200-foot summit of the divide. The scenery here is *big.* Two options await: first is to descend the west side to Crater Lake where rainbow and cutthroat trout await; second is to head south on the Continental Divide Trail across the immense alpine meadow. The Divide Trail eventually leads you to the beautiful South San Juan Wilderness Area and the New Mexico border. To reach the trailhead from Monte Vista, head south for 12 miles on Hwy. 15 and turn west onto Forest Rd. 250 for 32 miles to Forest Rd. 380. Continue west another 7 miles to the trailhead.

Crestone Trails

To explore the northeastern part of Rio Grande National Forest in the Sangre de Cristo Range, the town of Crestone is the best jumping-off point. From town head north for a mile, then northeast on the dirt Forest Rd. 950 past North Crestone Campground and begin hiking up along the creek. After a couple of miles there is a fork in the road. The left fork heads up to Groundhog Basin and Venable Pass for views of the San Luis Valley and east down into the Wet Mountain Valley. The right fork (Trail 744) turns

southeast and heads about 3 miles up to North Crestone Lake. To the south 13,900-foot Mt. Adams blocks the view of Crestone Peak and Crestone Needle, two of the most treacherous 14,000-foot peaks in the state.

Great Sand Dunes National Monument

For information about hiking on the dunes, up Medano Creek to Medano Pass and up Mosca Pass, see the Major Attractions section.

Stations of the Cross Shrine

See the Religious Shrines section.

Skiing

CROSS-COUNTRY SKIING AND SNOWSHOEING

Cumbres Pass

From Antonito, Hwy. 17 snakes its way 39 miles over La Manga and Cumbres Passes to the New Mexico border, offering some good areas to cross-country ski. The adequate snowfall and pretty scenery entice skiers from northern New Mexico and southern Colorado. The terrain between the two passes is perfect for ski touring, made especially good as a result of a forest fire in 1879 that left the area open and now dotted with spruce trees. Avalanches can be a problem, so use extreme care. Trujillo Meadows is an excellent area to focus on; see the Camping section. For maps and trail information, contact the **Conejos Peak Ranger District Office, 15571 County Rd. T5, La Jara, CO 81140; 719-274-8971.**

Rentals and Information

Kristi Mountain Sports rents cross-country skiing and snowshoe equipment. **7565 W. Hwy. 160, Alamosa, CO 81101; 719-589-9759; www.slvoutdoor.org.**

DOWNHILL SKIING AND SNOWBOARDING

For information on the nearby Wolf Creek Ski Area, see the **Pagosa Springs** chapter.

Swimming

Splashland

This is a great place to cool off after a trip to the Great Sand Dunes. Though it resembles a regular pool found in Anytown, USA, Splashland is actually fed by geothermal water. This water flows continuously through the pool, providing a complete changeover every 8 hours. Showers, rental suits and towels are available. Wading pool for the kids. Small fee. Opens in mid-May with limited hours. Regular hours are Tues., Thurs., Fri. 10 A.M.–9 P.M.; closed Wed.; Sat.–Sun. 12–9 P.M. One mile north of Alamosa on Hwy. 17. **719-589-6307; www.bewellnet. com/splashland.**

Seeing and Doing

Hot Springs

Mineral Hot Springs Spa

Recently renovated, this historic facility provides soothing soaks as well as massages, herbal wraps and other treatments. In addition to the original bathhouse and "tower pool," two outdoor geothermal pools are available as well as private indoor tubs. Weather permitting, flop into a deck chair and catch some rays. This is a welcome addition to San Luis Valley soaking opportunities. Locker rooms, snack shop and other facilities. Located 12 miles north of Moffat on Hwy. 17. **719-256-4328; www.mineralhot springs.com.**

Sand Dunes Swimming Pool

Whether it's after a hot day on the dunes or in midwinter, a visit to this new pool facility will be soothing and memorable. Plunge off either diving board into this clean swimming pool where water temperatures vary between 98° and 102° F. Wonderful views east to the Sangre de Cristos and the Great Sand Dunes add to the experience. Baby pool, covered picnic tables, snack bar and shower rooms ensure the whole family will enjoy this place. Open daily Feb.–Nov. 10 A.M.–10 P.M.; closed Thurs.; Dec.–Jan. 1–8 P.M. Follow

the marked sign 1 mile north of Hooper on Hwy. 17 to 1191 County Rd. 63. **719-378-2807.**

Valley View Hot Springs

During weekdays this series of natural mineral pools provides a relaxing soak to anyone interested (members-only on weekends). Locals in the valley rave about it, but the bashful should be warned: bathing suits are optional and seem to be the exception rather than the norm. Valley View Hot Springs is located in the upper end of the valley, northeast of the now-defunct Mineral Hot Springs. At Valley View's prime location against the west slope of the Sangre de Cristo Range, you can soak in the developed pool or hike up the mountainside to four smaller natural rock pools. Overnight accommodations **($)** are available in dorm rooms, private cabins or tent and RV sites. From Alamosa, drive 50 miles north on Hwy. 17 to where it meets Hwy. 285. At this junction turn right on the dirt road and head east for 8 miles. Small fee charged. Open 9 A.M.–10 P.M. daily. **P.O. Box 65, Villa Grove, CO 81155; 719-256-4315; www.vvhs. com/soak.**

Museums and Galleries

It seems as if the valley has always had its fair share of museums. Now the number of art galleries is growing rapidly. Many of the traditional arts and pioneer Spanish crafts of the San Luis Valley are in danger of dying out. Do your part to preserve this priceless aspect of the valley's cultural heritage by visiting a gallery or two. In addition to traditional arts and crafts, many galleries carry contemporary works or a blend of new and old. Pick up a copy of the *San Luis Valley Guide to the Arts* at any visitor center for a complete listing of the galleries and studios. Listed below are a few of the notable museums and galleries.

Fireworks Gallery (Alamosa)

This gallery run by Carol Mondragon and Mike Cavaliere shows striking paintings, pottery, jewelry and other fine collectibles, mostly from local artists, including photographer J. D.

Marston. Recent emphasis focuses more on folk art, including wonderful Oaxacan wood sculptures. Carol, herself a fine potter, admits that she has been too busy recently selling other people's work to do enough of her own. Open 10 A.M.– 6 P.M. daily. **608 Main St., Alamosa, CO 81101; 719-589-6064.**

Fort Garland Museum

Twenty-six miles east of Alamosa on Hwy. 160 sits Fort Garland, one of the most famous outposts on the frontier and, for some time now, a museum run by the Colorado Historical Society.

As settlers pushed into the San Luis Valley from the south, protection from the Indians and a strong military presence in the area became priorities of the U.S. military. In 1852 Fort Massachusetts was built a few miles north of the present site of Fort Garland but was replaced by Fort Garland just six years later.

During the Civil War, Union soldiers from Fort Garland were sent south into New Mexico, where they had a bloody battle with Confederate troops at Glorieta Pass. The Union side won, and their victory essentially eliminated any serious threat to the American West by the rebels.

Following the Civil War, only a volunteer regiment was retained at the fort. Kit Carson commanded the fort in 1866 but left only a year later. The fort continued to play a crucial stabilizing role in Colorado's history until 1883, by which time the Utes had been relocated to reservations in southwestern Colorado and northeastern Utah.

Today the reconstructed fort is a worthy place to visit to get a feel for Colorado history. Anglo, Indian and Hispanic artifacts fill the many rooms, much as they did during the days when the fort was considered the Siberia of U.S. Army outposts. One visitor to the fort in the 1860s said he was "struck with commiseration for all the unfortunate officers and men condemned to live in so desolate a place." Be sure to check out the recently added Buffalo Soldiers exhibit.

Open Apr. 1 to Labor Day, 9 A.M.–5 P.M. daily; in winter 8 A.M.–4 P.M. Small fee charged. **P.O. Box 368, Hwy. 159, Fort Garland, CO 81133; 719-379-3512; www.coloradohistory. org/fort-garland.** Check with the folks at Fort Garland for directions to **Pike's Stockade,** a replica of the makeshift abode Lt. Zebulon Pike and his men wintered at during their ill-fated exploration of the area in 1806–1807.

J. D. Marston Photography Gallery (Crestone)

Although you will no doubt run across J. D.'s outstanding work at galleries in the valley, his own gallery is certainly the best one-stop opportunity. His outstanding black-and-white nature photos won the prestigious Ansel Adams Award. Color works available as well. Call for gallery hours and directions. **719-256-4162; www.jd marston.com.**

Jack Dempsey Museum (Manassa)

The pride of this community shows itself in the Jack Dempsey Museum, a one-room log cabin sitting near the spot where this former world heavyweight boxing champ grew up. Boxing mementos and pictures donated by locals and the Dempsey family are on display. Be sure to take a look at the old postcards (of the jackalope and fur-bearing trout variety) that have been on the display rack since the place opened in the mid-1960s. Open Memorial Day–Labor Day, Mon.–Sat., 9 A.M.–5 P.M. **406 Main St., P.O. Box 130, Manassa, CO 81141; 719-843-5207.**

Rio Grande County Museum and Cultural Center (Del Norte)

The Del Norte museum houses some fine historical relics. A highlight is the display of Indian rock art as well as a recently added exhibit (including artifacts) on John Charles Frémont's fourth and final expedition in the winter of 1848–1849, entitled "Of Ice and Men." Looking for a railroad route, the party froze and starved to death just north of Del Norte in the La Garita Mountains. Throughout the summer months, regional and local artists are in residence; every two weeks lectures are given on the valley's wildlife and social history. Open May–Sept.,

Mon.–Sat. 10 A.M.–5 P.M.; open the rest of the year Mon.–Fri. 11 A.M.–4 P.M. **580 Oak St., P.O. Box 430, Del Norte, CO 81132; 719-657-2847.**

Saguache County Museum

If you are passing through Saguache, you should visit this museum, at a site that is on the National Register of Historic Places. The museum houses a little of everything, including what is said to be one of the largest Indian arrowhead collections in the country. The museum is sprawled out in the old town jail and the schoolhouse next door. The jail cell holds the Alferd E. Packer display, in honor of this notorious cannibalistic Coloradan who was held briefly in Saguache in 1874. Small fee. Open Memorial Day–Labor Day, 10 A.M.–5 P.M. daily. Located 35 miles north of Monte Vista. **Hwy. 285, Saguache, CO 81149; 719-655-2557.**

San Luis Museum, Cultural and Commercial Center

Hispanic culture of southern Colorado comes to life in this excellent museum in Colorado's oldest town. The building's 17th-century New World Spanish architecture blends with solar technology as an example of old ways coming together with new. The museum contains a wonderful collection of santos (Hispanic religious items), including wood carvings and, most notably, a morada (where the Penitentes gathered for meetings and worship). Downstairs the award-winning exhibit La Cultura Constante de San Luis vividly conveys the Hispanic culture of southern Colorado, especially that of the San Luis Valley. Open Memorial Day–Labor Day Mon.–Fri. 8:30 A.M.–4:30 P.M., Sat.–Sun. 10 A.M.–4 P.M.; open Mon.–Fri. 8 A.M.–4:30 P.M. the rest of the year. **402 Church St., P.O. Box 619, San Luis, CO 81152; 719-672-3611.**

Religious Shrines

Stations of the Cross Shrine

Nothing has more properly marked the deep faith of the people of San Luis than the Stations of the Cross. Laid out along a 1.4-mile round-trip path winding its way up the mesa at the edge of town, the shrine features 14 spectacular, nearly life-size bronze statues (created by local sculptor Huberto Maestas) that depict the suffering and death of Jesus Christ.

On the mesa top, the final depiction of Christ's crucifixion commands an impressive position with a view down on the town, the valley and across to nearby Culebra Peak (14,047 feet). While on the mesa, stop in for some quiet time and reflections at the recently completed La Capilla de Todos los Santos chapel. The trailhead for the shrine is located at the corner of Hwy. 142 and Hwy. 159 in San Luis. For information call **719-672-3685.**

Scenic Drives

Alamosa–Monte Vista National Wildlife Refuges

See the Wildlife section.

Stations of the Cross Shrine in San Luis. Photo by Dean Winstanley.

Cochetopa Pass

Used by Indians, mountain men and early settlers as an easy crossing of the Continental Divide, Cochetopa Pass can be driven today by passenger cars. Cochetopa (an Indian word meaning "buffalo crossing") rises to 10,022 feet, crossing to the west, then eventually branching north to Gunnison or southwest over Los Piños Pass to Lake City. Capt. John Gunnison crossed Cochetopa Pass in 1853 on his expedition to search for a transcontinental railroad route. The Los Piños Indian agency was established on the west side of the pass in 1868 and for years served as the central government post for dealing with the Utes. To reach Cochetopa Pass from Alamosa, drive 17 miles northwest on Hwy. 160 to Monte Vista, then head north on Hwy. 285 for 35 miles to Saguache. From Saguache head west on Hwy. 114 (North Pass Rd.) until you see the sign for the Cochetopa Pass turnoff on the left. Open in summer only.

La Garita Arch

This 5-mile (one-way) drive up Forest Rd. 660 provides great views of the surrounding rolling hills, wildlife viewing (especially antelope) and something for geology buffs, too. La Garita Arch, located at the end of the road, is an enormous eroded hole in a lava dyke (over 100 feet tall). The maintained dirt road and surrounding trails also make an excellent mountain bike trip. Head northeast from Del Norte on Hwy. 112 for 3 miles and then left at the La Garita Ranch sign and continue north for about 6 miles. You'll see Forest Rd. 660 on the left (west) side of the road.

Los Caminos Antiguos Scenic and Historic Byway

Los Caminos Antiguos, which means "the ancient roads," explores the rich cultural heritage of the San Luis Valley by retracing the settlement of the valley and its unique blend of Native American, Hispanic and Anglo cultures.

The 170-mile route begins on the New Mexico border on Hwy. 17, roughly following the route of the **Cumbres and Toltec Scenic Railroad** (see the Major Attractions section)

over Cumbres Pass. It's a beautiful drive, especially in the fall when the aspen turn. The road passes through rolling hills and the Conejos River Valley for 39 miles to the town of **Antonito.** Just north of Antonito on Hwy. 285 you'll pass by **Conejos** (1 mile off the road), site of Colorado's oldest church. A bit farther north, turn right (east) at **Romeo** and continue through the towns of **Manassa** and **San Acacio** to Colorado's oldest town, **San Luis.** From here, head north on Hwy. 159 to **Fort Garland** for a tour of the museum (see the Museums and Galleries section).

If you still have the stamina, head west on Hwy. 160 for 12 miles and then north on Hwy. 150 toward the Great Sand Dunes National Monument. After 10.5 miles a road on the right heads 4 miles up to **Zapata Falls,** offering great views out to the valley. A short trail leads to the 60-foot-high falls. Continuing a few miles north on Hwy. 150 leads you to **Great Sand Dunes National Monument** (see the Major Attractions section). The tour makes its final turn and heads about 15 miles west on Sixmile Ln. to Hwy. 17, 14 miles north of Alamosa. Birders may want to stop along Sixmile Ln. for a visit to **San Luis Lakes State Park.** Information about the drive are available at local visitor centers.

Southern Rio Grande National Forest

The highly scenic 57-mile backcountry drive through the valleys and mountains of the southern Rio Grande National Forest is worth the late-summer washboard bumps and dust. Early summer when the wildflowers are in bloom, or autumn when the aspen turn, would be the best times to head down here. The first section of this route begins at Antonito and follows the Conejos River west along Hwy. 17 for 20 miles to Forest Rd. 250. From here turn right and follow the river up the Conejos River Valley, lined by tall mountains and impressive cliffs. The fishing along this section of the Conejos is excellent (see the Fishing section). After 23 miles up Forest Rd. 250 you'll reach the old town of **Platoro** where you'll find the reservoir and a number of lodges, including **Sky Line Lodge** (stop here for one of their Golden Bonanza cheeseburgers). In winter the road is not plowed beyond this point. In summer, however, continue over **Stunner Pass** and stay left on Forest Rd. 380 when you approach Stunner Campground. From here the road climbs up near the Continental Divide and eventually continues down to Hwy. 160, a few miles west of South Fork.

Wildlife

Alamosa–Monte Vista National Wildlife Refuges

Birders will be glad to know that the San Luis Valley is an incredibly rich bird habitat. Canals and marshland near the Rio Grande make this area a popular place for many migratory birds, such as whooping cranes, sandhill cranes, avocets and teals. In winter many hawks, bald eagles and golden eagles make their home here.

The U.S. Fish and Wildlife Service, which oversees two large tracts of land, offers self-guided drives through both refuges year-round. Headquarters are located at the Alamosa refuge, 3 miles east of Alamosa on Hwy. 160 and 2 miles south on El Rancho Ln. The Monte Vista refuge is located 6 miles south of Monte Vista on Hwy. 15. For more information contact **Refuge Manager, Alamosa–Monte Vista National Wildlife Refuges, 9383 El Rancho Ln., Alamosa, CO 81101; 719-589-4021; www. r6.fws.gov/alamosanwr.**

Colorado Alligator Farm

Though it is starting to get a bit rough around the edges, the alligator farm remains a must-see. Viewing alligators and other warmwater squirmers in a 7,500-foot-high mountain valley is not just a novelty—it's downright bizarre! How do they survive? As proprietor Erwin Young explains, geothermal water flows from the ground at a constant 87° F, providing a perfect environment for this unique Colorado livestock.

You'll be led back to at least one of the large aquarium buildings to see firsthand what Erwin and his employees are raising. Many fish species, including the Rocky Mountain white tilapia, swim in the tanks and through the many canals.

Outside in a large lagoon you'll find gator central. Separated from you by only a low chain-link fence, almost 100 alligators sun on the banks and lie in the water waiting to be fed. And when they are fed (pellets made from vegetable protein) their enthusiasm is frightening.

This place offers boat rides and fishing for largemouth bass, catfish and tilapia; fish and gator meat available for sale. Recent additions of other exotic reptiles and a lonely ostrich are a bit superfluous and disturbing. For an additional fee, get your picture taken while holding one of the gators. Open daily 7 A.M.–7 P.M. in summer; 10 A.M.–3 P.M. the rest of the year. Located north of Alamosa between Mosca and Hooper on Hwy. 17. **P.O. Box 1052, Alamosa, CO 81101; 719-589-3032; www.gatorfarm.com.**

San Luis Lakes State Park

Opened in the spring of 1993, San Luis Lakes provides spectacular views of the nearby Sangre de Cristo Range and the Great Sand Dunes. Even nonbirders will be amazed at the variety of birdlife, which ranges from grebes to great blue herons. Many birds can be seen at San Luis Lake, even with boaters plying the waters. To increase your chances for sightings you may want to drive or walk north to Head Lake or a couple of other small bodies of water; be sure to ask if the ranger is leading any nature hikes. This north area is closed to vehicles during duck nesting season (mid-Feb. through the end of Aug.). San Luis Lakes has a campground with electric hookups (51 sites), water and a shower building. Small fee. Located 8 miles east of Mosca on Six Mile Rd. **P.O. Box 175, Mosca, CO 81146; 719-378-2020; www.coloradoparks.org.**

Where to Stay

Accommodations

Alamosa is by far the largest town in the valley and serves as a major intersection for traffic heading to all points on the compass. So naturally there are quite a few motels to choose from. For

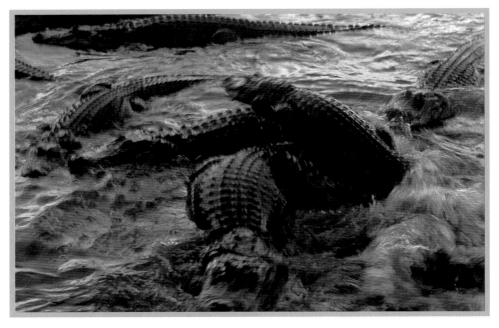

Feeding time at the Colorado Alligator Farm. Photo by Dean Winstanley.

more information contact the **Alamosa Chamber of Commerce; 1-800-BLU-SKYS; 719-589-3681.**

Great Sand Dunes Lodge—$$

If proximity to the Great Sand Dunes National Monument is important but you want to avoid spending a night at a campsite, this place is your best option. Though not fancy, the lodge rooms (each with two queen beds, air conditioning, phones, etc.) are comfortable and clean. Each features a private patio with views to the dunes and the Sangre de Cristo Mountains. Located adjacent to the Great Sand Dunes Oasis Campground just outside the entrance to the National Monument along Hwy. 150. Restaurant, gift shop and convenience store on site. Open Apr. through Oct. **7900 N. Hwy. 150, Mosca, CO 81146; 719-378-2900; www.gslodge.com.**

Conejos River Guest Ranch (Antonito)—$$$

Located along the scenic Conejos River about 10 miles west of Antonito on Hwy. 17, Conejos

River Guest Ranch is a scenic, quiet place. The owner, Jana Nall, has done an admirable job of renovating and redecorating the ranch, part of which is 100 years old. Each lodge room has its own private bathroom and decor theme; some have better views than others. The housekeeping cabins are a bit more rustic. There is plenty to do at the 14-acre ranch, including fishing along the ranch's private section of the river, horseback riding (extra charge), horseshoes or just sitting on the sundeck taking in the scenery. Lodge guests receive a full country breakfast. You may also want to try the ranch for a steak or trout dinner **($$ to $$$).** Open May–Dec. **25390 Hwy. 17, P.O. Box 175, Conejos, CO 81129; 719-376-2464; www.conejosranch.com.**

The Cottonwood Inn and Gallery (Alamosa)—$$$

This charming bed and breakfast is a bright spot for travelers to the valley. Innkeeper Julie Mordecai opened for business in the summer of 1988 after painstakingly refurbishing this fine old corner-lot home. The handsome wood trim, local art and tasteful antiques all accent the comfortable feel inside. Four rooms are available, two with private baths. In addition, three larger, attractively decorated apartment-style accommodations provide more privacy. Julie is knowledgeable about the San Luis Valley and can offer good advice. Wholesome, full breakfasts are made from local products and are guaranteed delicious: Julie also operates a small cooking school at the inn. The Cottonwood doubles as a small art gallery; much of the art throughout the house is for sale, as are the local crafts on display. Call for details on their weekend workshops. **123 San Juan Ave., Alamosa, CO 81101; 1-800-955-2623; 719-589-3882; www.cottonwoodinn.com.**

El Convento Bed and Breakfast (San Luis)—$$$

Built in 1905 as a school and then used as a convent, this restored building is open for business as an intriguing bed and breakfast. El Convento ("the convent") offers four upstairs bedrooms with kiva fireplaces in two of the rooms. Thick adobe walls, 10-foot-high ceilings and hand-carved furniture give the place a homey, roomy feel. Downstairs is Centro Artesano, where local artisans practice and sell their works. A delicious homemade breakfast is served in the dining room each morning. For a quiet, slightly different overnight experience in the state's oldest town, try a night at El Convento. **512 Church Pl., San Luis, CO 81152; 719-672-4223.**

Monte Villa Inn (Monte Vista)—$$ to $$$

Monte Villa Inn offers spotless (though somewhat drab) rooms for reasonable prices. Built in 1929 this restored, 35-room hotel features rooms with king-, queen- and double-size beds, each room a little different in size and color. Be sure to ride the original cage elevator. Downstairs there is a coffee shop/dining room (see the Where to Eat section) and lounge. **925 1st Ave., Monte Vista, CO 81144; 719-852-5166.**

Movie Manor (Monte Vista)—$$ to $$$

Ever enjoyed a drive-in movie from the comfort of your own motel room? We didn't think so. George Kelloff's Movie Manor is Americana gone crazy. "It's the only one of its kind in the world," George beamed. So unique is it that it was included in a PBS special. Two and a half miles west of Monte Vista, Kelloff's Drive-In has been showing movies on its big screen since 1955. Back in the early days, when the Kelloff family lived over the snack bar, George and his wife would tuck the kids in and scoot their beds over to the window so they could see the movie. As George explained, "I started thinking, hey! Why not build a motel at the back of the drive-in so everybody can do this?" The rest is history.

The first addition to this two-story motel was completed in 1964 and it has been added on to more than once since then. The rooms are comfortable and every window looks out at the big screen. A movie speaker is built into the ceiling and it's free with the room. Movies are not shown in winter. There is also a lounge and a dining room on the premises. If unique is what you seek, look no further. **2830 W. Hwy. 160, Monte Vista, CO 81144; 1-800-771-9468; 719-852-5921; www.coloradomotelvacation/movie.com.**

Conejos River AYH Hostel (Antonito)—$

Located along the Conejos River west of Antonito, this budget accommodation offers a dorm-style hostel with a kitchen and common area. Gas grill and picnic tables outside. **3591 County Rd. E2, Antonito, CO 81120; 719-376-2518.**

Willow Spring Bed and Breakfast (Moffat)—$

Located in the don't-blink-or-you'll-miss-it burg of Moffat, the Willow Spring offers a low-key, quiet night's rest. The large two-story brick inn, built in 1910 as the Forbes Hotel, provides four rooms with sinks; bathrooms are at the end of the hall. The inn is surrounded on three sides by enormous old narrow-leaf cottonwood trees. Inside, family antiques and an enormous kitchen stand out. Full homemade breakfasts are provided each morning by innkeepers Jim and Harriet

Campbell. **P.O. Box 500, Moffat, CO 81143; 719-256-4116.**

Camping

Great Sand Dunes National Monument
See the Major Attractions section.

Rio Grande National Forest
In the southwestern section of the national forest are a number of campgrounds. Many of these campsites can be reserved by calling **1-877-444-6777.** A fee is charged at these campgrounds, except for the four that are noted as having no fee.

Forest Rd. 250, the major access road to this area, heads west along the Alamosa River 12 miles south of Monte Vista from Hwy. 15. Thirteen miles up Forest Rd. 250, just past Terrace Reservoir, is **Alamosa Campground** (10 sites, no fee) at 8,600 feet. Another 21 miles up the road is **Stunner Campground** (10 sites, no fee) at 10,000 feet.

From Antonito head west into Rio Grande National Forest on Hwy. 17 for 13 miles to **Mogote Campground** (41 sites) at 8,300 feet. Two miles farther west is **Aspen Glade Campground** (34 sites). Six miles farther up Hwy. 17, Forest Rd. 250 heads off to the right (northwest), reaching **Elk Creek Campground** (44 sites, 16 without picnic table or fireplace) at 8,700 feet. Five more miles up Forest Rd. 250 is **Spectacle Lake Campground** (24 sites). Another mile will bring you to **Conejos Campground** (16 sites). **Lake Fork Campground** (19 sites) is yet another 9 miles up Forest Rd. 250, at 9,500 feet. **Mix Lake Campground** (22 sites) at Platoro Reservoir is another 5.5 miles up the road; boats are available.

Near the top of Cumbres Pass (about 35 miles west of Antonito on Hwy. 17), turn right onto the Trujillo Meadows Rd. and proceed about 4 miles to the **Trujillo Meadows Campground** (50 sites); boat ramp.

Two miles south of Monte Vista on Hwy. 15, and then right on Forest Rd. 265 for 13.5 miles, will lead you to **Rock Creek Campground** (13 sites, no fee) and **Comstock Campground** (8 sites, no fee).

From the Del Norte Ranger Station, head about 9 miles west on Hwy. 160 and turn north on Embargo Creek Forest Access Rd. for 12 miles to **Cathedral Campground** (33 sites).

Up in the northeastern part of the valley near Crestone is **North Crestone Campground** (14 sites). From Crestone head 1.5 miles northeast on Forest Rd. 950. This is a great place to watch for bighorn sheep. They have been reintroduced to various parts of Rio Grande National Forest and are doing well. Look for them up on top of the rocky canyon walls.

San Luis Lakes State Park
See the write-up in the Wildlife section.

Private Campgrounds
Blanca RV Park—This park has 26 full hookup sites and 6 tentsites; showers and a laundromat also available. Located at the east end of the town of Blanca. **719-379-3201.**

Great Sand Dunes Oasis Campground and RV Park—Offers RV hookups, primitive cabins, showers and other services, including four-wheel-drive trips into the park. Located just outside the entrance to Great Sand Dunes National Park. **719-378-2222; www.alamosa.org.**

Where to Eat

Dos Rios (Monte Vista)—$$ to $$$
This sizable place, located 2 miles north of town, draws in folks from area towns and farms for hearty meals and terrific Mexican food. Although the decor is unremarkable, the menu stands out for its sheer size and interesting entrées. Mexican standouts include a variety of vegetarian options, halibut Vera Cruz and the tasty flauta encantada. Sandwiches, steaks and other traditional down-home food available as well. Full bar. Open Tues.–Sat. 11 A.M.–9 P.M. **1635 N. Hwy. 285; 719-852-0969.**

Colorado Profile—Penitentes

One of the most fascinating and mysterious sects of the Christian faith once thrived in southern Colorado, playing an integral part in the history and culture of the Hispanic communities. The Penitentes began as an offshoot of Catholicism in 13th-century Europe that honored St. Francis of Assisi. Members practiced self-flagellation as a way to prove their devotion, but eventually the practice died out everywhere in Europe except for Spain. It is commonly believed that when the conquistadors came to New Mexico, the Penitentes (los Hermanos) came with them. Beginning about 1810 in the isolated communities of northern New Mexico, the Penitentes thrived and eventually spread north into southern Colorado. Since many of the small villages did not have a regular priest, the Penitentes filled a spiritual void and satisfied a desire for ritual.

Many men in the communities joined los Hermanos and met at their moradas or lodges. Self-torture was a part of their practice, but more important, the men quite often helped bind together the community, taking on charitable work that no one would do. The Penitentes continued to obey the Catholic Church, adhering to all of its precepts except during Holy Week. During this time, the brothers dressed in black hoods and white breechcloths and reenacted Christ's capture, trial and crucifixion. Whipping themselves with cactus leaves, they climbed a hill on which one of the members was tied (and, some say, even nailed) to a cross and left there until he fainted. Because of the high number of injuries and the mock crucifixions, the Catholic Church finally outlawed the Penitentes. The Penitentes did not disband but instead became secretive and did not allow outsiders to visit their moradas or witness their rituals.

Well into the 1900s there were still hundreds of practicing moradas spread throughout southern Colorado. Today, however, these numbers have dwindled to just a few, but many deserted moradas can still be seen in and around the small Hispanic villages of southern Colorado.

Monte Villa Inn (Monte Vista)— $$ to $$$

Good steaks, Mexican food and fettuccine are the highlights. The comfortable dining room is open year-round and usually has a number of locals eating there (a good sign). Full bar. Open Tues.–Sat. 5–8:30 P.M. The coffee shop is open 6 A.M.–5 P.M. **925 1st Ave.; 719-852-5166.**

True Grits (Alamosa)—$$ to $$$

Somewhat of an institution in Alamosa, True Grits is considered by many to be *the* place to go for a great steak. And the decor is what you'd expect: spacious, somewhat smoky and dark, with country music in the background, brown wood everywhere and pictures of John Wayne staring at you from the walls. Along with nightly specials, the dinner menu continues the Wayne theme with the Sons of Katie Elder filet mignon, Rooster Cogburn country-fried steak, the Little Pilgrim children's meals and so forth. Lunch offers slightly lighter fare. Full bar with margaritas as the house specialty. This place does the Duke proud. Open 11 A.M.–10 P.M. daily. At the corner of Hwys. 17 and 160. **100 Santa Fe Ave.; 719-589-9954.**

Emma's Hacienda (San Luis)— $ to $$

Keep in mind that even though you can count the places to eat in San Luis on one hand, Emma's standout Mexican food would get rave reviews no matter where it was located. In business since 1949, Emma still occasionally oversees the restaurant. Menu notables include Emma's Special (a little of everything), enchiladas and the S.O.B. burger smothered with green or red chili. Try a slice of homemade pie for dessert. It seems fitting that in this laid-back town the restaurant should keep nonspecific hours. But it's usually open for business 10 A.M.–8 P.M. **355 Main St.; 719-672-9902.**

Buffalo herd at Zapata Ranch. Photo by Dean Winstanley.

St. Ives Pub and Eatery (Alamosa)— $ to $$

Almost everything in this cafe and pub is as green as the Notre Dame leprechaun. Very popular, the St. Ives serves up fantastic burgers, sandwiches and salads. It is open and airy with rough-hewn wood walls. Full bar. Open Mon.– Sat. 11 A.M.–11 P.M., closed Sun. **719 Main St.; 719-589-0711.**

Taqueria Calvillo (Alamosa)—$ to $$

With marvelous Mexican food, this establishment draws raves from valley locals. Choose from a large variety of items, or spring for the house specialty: the Mexican buffet. Open Tues.–Sat. 11 A.M.–8 P.M., Sun. 11 A.M.–3:30 P.M., closed Mon. In Alamosa just west of the intersection of Hwys. 17 and 160. **119 Broadway; 719-587-5500.**

Ute Cafe (Fort Garland)—$ to $$

Not fancy by any stretch of the imagination, this small roadside cafe serves up a tasty menu that is equally divided between American standards and items from south of the border. Grab a counter seat or table near the window and enjoy. The Ute serves breakfast, lunch and dinner items, any of which can be highlighted with the homemade red or green chili. The adventuresome may want to try the Italian-tinged "half breed," which includes a side of spaghetti with green chili. Top it all off with a slice of homemade pie or a honey-slathered sopapilla. Open 6:30 A.M.–9 P.M. in summer, 7:30 A.M.–4 P.M. in winter, closed Sat. Located along the north side of Hwy. 160 in **Fort Garland; 719-379-3553.**

Bauer's Campus Pancake House and Restaurant (Alamosa)—$

This no-frills breakfast hangout serves up good pancakes, waffles, gigantic cinnamon rolls and egg dishes smothered in green chili. If you're looking for a latte, you've come to the wrong place. Locals meet for breakfast and sit around for an hour or two, chatting at their tables as the ceiling fans slowly rotate above. Lunch menu highlighted by burgers and sandwiches. Open daily 5 A.M.–1:30 P.M. **435 Poncha Ave.; 719-589-4202.**

Milagro's Coffeehouse and Cafe (Alamosa)—$

Stop by Milagro's, just off Main St., for a coffee or latte. In addition to java, they offer simple breakfast and lunch items from the board, including bagels, pastries, soups, salads and quiche. Not your traditional San Luis Valley establishment, Milagro's also serves as a used-book store, gallery and community information center. Open 7 A.M.–7 P.M. daily. **510 Hunt; 719-589-9299.**

Services

Visitor Information

Alamosa Visitor Center—This center provides printed information and advice from the staff. **Cole Park, Alamosa, CO 81101; 1-800-BLU-SKYS; www.alamosa.org.**

Del Norte Chamber of Commerce—1160 Grand Ave., P.O. Box 148, Del Norte, CO 81132; 719-657-2845.

Monte Vista Chamber of Commerce—1035 Park Ave., Monte Vista, CO 81144; 719-852-2731; www.home.amigo.net/slvic.

San Luis Valley Visitor Center—947 1st Ave., Monte Vista, CO 81144; 719-852-0660.

San Luis Visitor Center—P.O. Box 9, San Luis, CO 81152; 719-672-3355.

South Park and 285 Corridor

At the center of Colorado, the high grassland basin of South Park and its surrounding peaks has for years remained relatively undiscovered. Displaying its beauty in a different way than mountain resorts, the entire 30- by 40-mile park has been largely devoid of commercialism. Partly due to this lack of development, people historically drove through the South Park region without slowing to enjoy the scenery and outdoor activities. This phenomenon has changed, however, as the area is experiencing unprecedented growth.

Fairplay, the largest town in South Park, appeals to many with its obvious ties to history. At an elevation of almost 10,000 feet, this one-time gold mining camp is now home to only 500 permanent residents. Of particular interest is the South Park City Museum, a reconstructed 19th-century mining town. Some 30 buildings, containing more than 50,000 historic objects, were carted here from around Colorado. Fairplay also has two historic hotels, several local restaurants and a patrol car with a very active radar gun (the speed limit is 25).

Around the perimeter of the park, the Mosquito, Park and Tarryall Mountain Ranges offer unlimited terrain for hiking, mountain biking and cross-country skiing. Hundreds of thousands of acres are set aside for public use in Pike National Forest, including Lost Creek and Buffalo Peaks Wilderness Areas. The aspen-cloaked mountains are dotted with ghost towns

and weathered remnants of gold mines; when exploring away from designated roads or trails, beware of open shafts and pits. At the base of several 14,000-foot peaks north of Fairplay, the Bristlecone Pine Scenic Area boasts 1,000-year-old trees growing in beautiful wind-twisted forms. Gushing tributaries from the surrounding mountains form the headwaters of the South Platte River, then find their way to the valley floor, which is laced with miles of streams and many reservoirs. Anglers consider these waters some of the finest in Colorado, and much of it is accessible to the public.

Hwy. 285 leads to South Park from Denver. Originally established by Ute Indians, this route has been used by covered wagons, the narrow-gauge Denver South Park & Pacific Railroad (DSP&P) and cars. Today this smooth, paved road plies a winding route past the communities of Bailey, Shawnee and Grant before angling southwest over Kenosha Pass (10,001 feet) and dropping into South Park. The area included in this chapter, from Bailey to the top of Kenosha Pass, we refer to as the 285 corridor. This time-honored route follows the North Fork of the South Platte River up through a pine-clad valley on its southwestern voyage. The memory of the

Getting There

The town of Fairplay, situated in the northwest corner of South Park, is located 80 miles southwest of Denver on Hwy. 285.

far-reaching view into South Park from the summit of Kenosha Pass will stick with you for years.

History

Long before Spanish explorers came to South Park, Ute Indians were ensconced in the area. Plentiful game provided the Utes easy hunting for deer, elk, antelope and buffalo. Other tribes learned about the fine hunting and came to South Park. Because the area was worth fighting for, frequent skirmishes erupted.

One notable battle, in the spring of 1852, pitted the Utes against the Comanches for control over the park. Although the Comanches won the bloody battle, witnessed by frontiersman Kit Carson, the Utes never fully relinquished South Park. It wasn't long, though, until the Anglos wrested control over the park from all tribes.

Trappers were attracted to the park, primarily for beaver but also for the boundless game. It wasn't until the gold rush in 1859, however, that settlement of towns began. In July of that year, a few straggling prospectors crossed Georgia Pass and started prospecting north of present-day Como at the north end of the park. Their gold pans revealed an exciting strike and, within two weeks, hundreds of prospectors were staking out claims. After only a couple of months, the town of Tarryall ("Let's tarry, all," said one early miner) was in place and all of the claims had been taken. Disgruntled late arrivals dubbed the town Graball and founded a new town called Fair Play on the banks of the South Platte River. Prospecting fell into a deep freeze with the arrival of winter. But by the summer of 1860, 11,000 miners were swarming over the surrounding hills and establishing gold camps with names like Buckskin Joe, Hamilton, Montgomery and Sacramento.

South Park was known to many as "Bayou Salado" because of its plentiful natural salt springs. In 1864 the Colorado Salt Works, located just north of Antero Junction on Hwy.

285, started evaporating brine into usable salt. During its three years of operation, the works produced up to 4,000 pounds of salt per day for use in refining gold ore and on many dinner tables.

Silver Heels is a name that conjures up images of South Park's heyday. As the legend goes, Silver Heels was the most beautiful woman ever seen at Buckskin Joe—a dance-hall girl whose beauty went far beneath her skin, to the depths of her soul. When a terrible smallpox epidemic broke out, the people who had not contracted the disease left immediately. Silver Heels, however, stayed behind to help stricken miners, and eventually she too became sick. When the epidemic had run its course, she mysteriously disappeared. Many years later, a silent woman was seen visiting the cemetery in Alma, paying her respects to victims of the disease. She always wore a veil over her face, it was said, to hide pockmarks; the townsfolk seemed to know who the mystery lady was. Grateful miners honored her by naming the beautiful Mt. Silverheels (13,822 feet) in her memory, sometime before 1870.

By 1879 the Denver South Park & Pacific Railroad finally completed the route from Denver to Como. A tent city with more than a thousand residents sprang up at the Como terminus of the railroad, where a roundhouse was built. From Como people often transferred onto a stagecoach to complete the trip west over Mosquito Pass to the booming town of Leadville. Eventually the rail line was completed over Boreas Pass to Breckenridge and on to Leadville. In the 1880s Como became known for its coal reserves, and lumbering began in the vast forests around South Park. Ranchers fenced in the prime grazing land, and it wasn't long before large herds of sheep and cattle flourished.

The trains provided exciting weekend excursions for people from Denver as well as a means to move goods. But due to limited demand, the railroad was abandoned in 1938. Without the train Como began to decline, while the rest of South Park remained aloof from much of the development happening in other parts of the

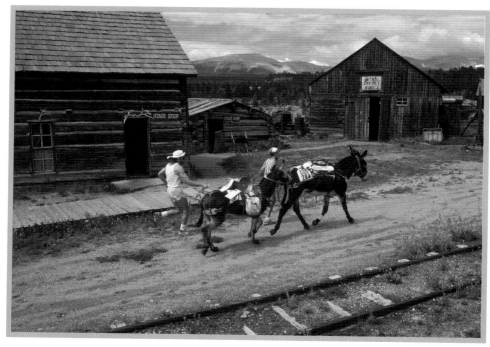

Burro race in South Park. Photo by Gary Nichols.

state. That has changed. With mixed blessings South Park is now growing fast.

Festivals and Events

Burro Days

last weekend in July You don't want to miss the "world championship" pack burro race. This fun event has contestants racing to the top of Mosquito Pass (13,188 feet) and back to Fairplay. Determined men and women are pitted not only against the pass but also against the iron wills of their burros. Food booths, arts and crafts displays, parade and dancing. **Park County Tourism Office, Box 220, Fairplay, CO 80440; 719-836-4279.**

Mountain Man Rendezvous

summer Modern-day mountain men converge on South Park each summer to hone skills such as axe throwing, black powder shooting and flint

knapping. In keeping with the styles of the early 1800s, participants wear heavy buckskin jackets instead of Gore-Tex and sleep in primitive tents and tepees. A traders row completes the strange visual picture of the rendezvous. Three rendezvous take place in South Park each summer: **Bayou Salado Rendezvous in Fairplay, 719-477-0538; Rocky Mountain College Rendezvous near Jefferson, 303-841-4432;** and **Como Mountain Man Rendezvous,** call Booshway Jack Portice at **719-836-2403.**

Outdoor Activities

Biking

MOUNTAIN BIKING
With varied terrain in South Park and the surrounding mountains, this area attracts many mountain bikers. Since there are no places to rent bikes, though, you must bring your own.

Mining roads and hiking trails provide hundreds of miles of possibilities throughout the area. For more information and a free copy of *Take a Ride in the Park,* an excellent mountain bike trail guide, contact the **South Park Ranger District Office** at the junction of Hwys. 285 and 9, **P.O. Box 219, Fairplay, CO 80440; 719-836-2031; www.fs.fed.us/r2/psicc.** Take a close look at the Four-Wheel-Drive Trips and Hiking and Backpacking sections for other trail ideas. Here are a few ideas to challenge all skill levels:

Boreas Pass Loop

This popular and historic ride retraces the old Denver, South Park & Pacific Railroad route up to 11,480-foot Boreas Pass, then loops back down Old Boreas Wagon Rd. to the Gold Dust Trail and County Rd. 50. It's a moderately difficult 13-mile loop with expansive views and many reminders of the mining/railroad days. To reach the trailhead, drive 3 miles northwest of Como on County Rd. 33 to County Rd. 50 and then west to Forest Rd. 801. Turn right and proceed 1.7 miles to Forest Rd. 33.2A. The trailhead begins here. Begin by riding 1.3 miles up Forest Rd. 33.2A to the Boreas Pass Rd. (County Rd. 33), turn left and follow the road 3.8 miles to the summit. From here either return by the same route or try returning via the Old Boreas Wagon Rd. For specifics on the return route, consult the *Take a Ride in the Park* mountain bike guide available in Fairplay at the South Park Ranger District Office.

Buffalo Creek Area

Just southeast of Bailey on County Rd. 68, this area has been developed as a mountain bike trail system by the U.S. Forest Service. The area's 11 rides range from 1 to 10 miles in duration and provide an interesting mix of terrain. For more information about the rides, including how the two fires in the area have impacted recreation opportunities, contact the **South Platte Ranger District Office** east of Conifer on Hwy. 285; **303-275-5610; www.fs. fed.us/r2/psicc.**

Fishing

The South Park Area truly does offer some of the finest public-access mountain fishing in Colorado, if not the Rocky Mountain West. Up-to-date fishing reports are available at **303-291-7538** and **www. dnr.state.co.us/wildlife/fishing.** Listed below are some of the flat-water and river highlights.

Eleven Mile Canyon

Plenty of brown and rainbow trout inhabit the tumbling waters of the South Platte River in this narrow, scenic canyon about 40 miles west of Colorado Springs. This regularly stocked river comes out of Eleven Mile Dam and flows northeast through the canyon for 10 miles. Since the water flow exiting the dam fluctuates, so does the quality of the fishing. To reach Eleven Mile Canyon drive to Lake George along Hwy. 24 and look for the canyon turnoff on the south side.

Eleven Mile Reservoir

Located within Eleven Mile State Park 11 miles southwest of Lake George, this reservoir is known for its bountiful rainbow and brown trout, kokanee salmon, pike and perch. The

Brown trout from a South Park stream. Photo by Gary Nichols.

largest kokanee (up to 5 pounds) in Colorado are often caught at Eleven Mile Reservoir. Eleven Mile's 3,400 surface acres provide good results from both boats and shore. Ice fishing is popular in winter. From Lake George along Hwy. 24, look for the road sign to the reservoir on County Rd. 92 at the west edge of the town. Ironically, the reservoir can't be reached from Eleven Mile Canyon. The reservoir's address is **4229 County Rd. 92, Lake George, CO 80827; 719-748-3401; www.coloradoparks.org.** Rental boats, guide services, tackle, etc. are available at **11 Mile Sports** on the north shore of the reservoir; **1-800-725-3172; 719-748-0317.**

Jefferson Lake

At the headwaters of Jefferson Creek northwest of Kenosha Pass, this popular lake provides quality fishing. Early and late in the day, fly-fishing for rainbows can be excellent from the northeast side. Many boaters ply the water for Mackinaw, brook and rainbow trout. Jefferson Lake receives heavy fishing pressure but is also frequently stocked. From the small town of Jefferson in the northwest corner of South Park, head north and west on County Rd. 35. After a couple of miles, turn right (north) on County Rd. 37, which leads to the campgrounds and to the lake within Pike National Forest.

South Platte River

Each fork of the South Platte offers a variety of fishing. The headwaters lie northwest of Fairplay in the Mosquito Range. Most of the land surrounding the South Platte as it runs through the park is private. (The best public fishing is actually in the Deckers area and below Cheesman Reservoir.) For some good public water closer to South Park, try fishing the Middle Fork of the South Platte below the Montgomery Reservoir outlet (on Hwy. 9 north of Fairplay). With the Division of Wildlife acquisition of 28 river miles above Hartsel, the Middle and South Forks of the South Platte River constitute the longest Gold Medal trout stream (42 miles) in the state. This means you'll have a much improved chance for catching big fish. The **Middle Fork** flows south

from the reservoir to Fairplay between piles of river rock displaced by dredging operations but can still be good for small rainbow and brown trout. The **South Fork** of the South Platte merges with the Middle Fork just below the town of Hartsel in the center of South Park, creating the South Platte River. The **North Fork** of the South Platte flows east from Kenosha Pass toward Denver. Located right next to Hwy. 285, the river is heavily fished with fair results.

Spinney Mountain State Park

Once you've battled a feisty cutthroat trout at Spinney, you'll keep returning. As a matter of fact, Spinney Mountain is famous for its trophy-sized cutthroat, especially in the spring as ice recedes from the shoreline. The South Fork of the South Platte fills the 2,500-acre reservoir, and the land upstream from Spinney Mountain is now open to the public; downstream can also be good. Flies and lures only. Three boat ramps and picnic area available. Open May–Nov. From Fairplay, drive 18 miles south on Hwy. 9 to Hartsel and east on County Rd. 59 for 10 miles to the entrance point. **719-748-3401; www.coloradoparks.org.**

Tarryall Creek

On the east side of South Park, Tarryall Creek exits from Tarryall Reservoir. A challenging and often good stretch of water for brown and rainbow trout exists above the reservoir. A few miles of public water above the confluence with the South Platte are designated Wild Trout water. Though the creek is fairly narrow, the fish often grow to lunker sizes. To reach the creek from Jefferson (northeast corner of the park), take County Rd. 77 southeast for about 20 miles.

Four-Wheel-Drive Trips

Mosquito Pass

At 13,188 feet, this classic four-wheel-drive road is the highest road over a pass in North America. It leads west over the Mosquito Range to Leadville, through an area saturated in mining history. For details see the Four-Wheel-Drive Trips section of the **Leadville** chapter.

Webster Pass

A narrow, rough road leads up beautiful Hall Valley from the east side of Kenosha Pass. After passing Handcart and Hall Valley Campgrounds, the road gets extremely rough and steep as it heads through thick groves of aspen to the summit of Webster Pass (12,108 feet). Try this four-wheel-drive tour in autumn and you'll be treated to quite a show. On the opposite side of the pass, the former wagon road switchbacks down to Montezuma (see the **Summit County** chapter for more information). To reach the road from the town of Grant, drive 3 miles southwest on Hwy. 285 and right on County Rd. 60.

Hiking and Backpacking

The varied terrain of the mountains around South Park is perfect for weekend backpacking trips and short walkabouts. Miners have left traces of their work all around, but instead of appearing as ugly scars, this kingdom of abandoned mines and mining camps leaves most hikers with a profound sense of history. If you visit in fall, a barrage of colors, unequaled on Colorado's eastern slope of the Continental Divide, will make your backcountry experience even better. For more information on hiking and backpacking, including the Lost Creek and Buffalo Peaks Wilderness Areas, contact the **South Park Ranger District Office,** at the junction of Hwys. 285 and 9, **P.O. Box 219, Fairplay, CO 80440; 719-836-2031.** Or try the **South Platte Ranger District Office along Hwy. 285** east of Conifer at **303-275-5610.** Information on both districts is available at **www.fs.fed.us/r2/psicc.**

Colorado Trail

From South Park and the 285 corridor, it's easy to reach the Colorado Trail. The moderately steep trail offers hikes as long or short as you wish through beautiful and surprisingly uncrowded terrain. Plan a two- or three-day backpacking trip by leaving a vehicle at a pre-arranged point along the trail. A good access point lies just south of the town of Bailey on Forest Rd. 560 near Wellington Lake. Another easy place to start or stop a hike is at Kenosha Pass Campground on Hwy. 285. From Kenosha Pass the well-defined trail heads west past the Jefferson Creek Recreation Area and then over Georgia Pass toward Breckenridge. Several campgrounds are near the route; primitive camping can be done anywhere except in the Jefferson Creek area, where designated campgrounds are the rule.

Limber Grove Trail

This nice, relatively gentle and family-friendly 3-mile round-trip hike heads into the woods only to emerge on a rocky slope near treeline. The trail leads to one of the best areas for viewing gnarled bristlecone and limber pine groves. Some of the bristlecone trees date back 1,000 years, and the views of the Mosquito Range and South Park are tremendous. Limber Grove Trail begins across the road from Horseshoe Campground about 9 miles southwest of Fairplay (see the Camping section for directions).

Lost Creek Wilderness Area

Within the Tarryall Range to the east of South Park, the Lost Creek Wilderness Area offers spectacular scenery with easy access. The wilderness is known for its unearthly rock formations and grottos. As the name implies, the creek disappears for a mile or so as it works its way under a rocky hill. There's an excellent trail system, including a 25-mile loop, which circles through the southern section of the wilderness. Lost Creek is a very popular area and can get quite crowded in the summer. Since most of the trails are below 10,000 feet, you can hike in early spring and well into the fall. Here are a few of the trailheads:

From Hwy. 285, 1 mile northeast of Jefferson, turn east onto Lost Park Rd. (County Rd. 56). The dirt road leads to Lost Park Campground in 20 miles. The campground serves as a trailhead for the **Brookside-McCurdy Trail** (No. 607) and the **Wigwam Trail** (No. 609). Ranchers have grazing rights around this section of the wilderness, so you'll probably see some

Autumn along the Colorado Trail. Photo by Dean Winstanley.

cattle. Be sure to purify your drinking water. Another trailhead can be reached by driving southeast from Jefferson on Tarryall Rd. (County Rd. 77) for about 20 miles to Tarryall Reservoir. Continue another 4 miles to the **Ute Creek Trail** on the left (northeast) side of the road. The trailhead is marked, and there is a parking area. Still another 5 miles along County Rd. 77 brings you to the **Twin Eagles trailhead,** which also provides access into the wilderness area.

Perhaps the most popular access to the wilderness area is **Goose Creek Trail.** This section of the wilderness area features some of the most beautiful rock formations. Fishing for small trout along Lost Creek is not bad either. It can be reached by continuing about 11 miles southwest on County Rd. 77 from the Twin Eagles trailhead to Forest Rd. 211. Turn left (northeast) on Forest Rd. 211 and follow it 12 miles to Forest Rd. 558. Turn left and continue about 1 mile to the trailhead.

Mts. Democrat, Lincoln and Bross

Bagging three 14ers in a long day of hiking is ambitious but entirely possible in the Mosquito Range towering just above Alma. And for that reason you will undoubtedly encounter many hikers in the area. The mountains' proximity and connecting saddles make it relatively easy to climb all three together. All in all, the elevation gain is about 3,600 feet on the 6-mile loop trail. Of course, hiking to the summit of the first mountain (14,148-foot Democrat) is enough for many hikers. The trail to Democrat leads northwest from Kite Lake, which is above treeline, passing some exposed mining shacks on the way to the summit. From the top, views to the Sawatch, Gore, Tenmile and Elk Ranges are tremendous.

If you are still energetic enough to continue, walk back down to the saddle between Democrat and Lincoln. The trail leads 2 miles northeast to the summit of Lincoln (14,286 feet), passing Mt. Cameron along the way. Mt. Cameron is a mountain in its own right, but it's actually considered a part of Mt. Lincoln. From Lincoln head back down to Cameron and then hike 1 mile southeast to the broad summit of Mt. Bross (14,169 feet). Hiking down the scree slope from Bross to Kite Lake can be a bit tricky but very doable.

To reach the trailhead from Fairplay, follow Hwy. 9 northwest for 7 miles to the town of Alma. In Alma turn left on Buckskin Gulch Rd. (County Rd. 8) that breaks away from Main St. in the center of town. Follow the rough dirt road 7 miles up Buckskin Gulch to Kite Lake. Don't try this last bit in a passenger car if it has been raining. High-clearance vehicles are better suited to this road in all types of weather. The road passes many old mines along the way to the trailhead at Kite Lake.

Horseback Riding

American Safari Ranch

Located in the wide-open northern part of South Park, this operation provides a wide variety of activities, including pony rides for the kids (at least 6 years old), breakfast rides, chuckwagon barbecue dinners and hay rides. **P.O. Box 128, Fairplay, CO 80440; 719-836-2431.**

Hiking into the Lost Creek Wilderness Area. Photo by Dean Winstanley.

Skiing

CROSS-COUNTRY SKIING AND SNOWSHOEING

Many avid cross-country skiers are discovering the wealth of trails in the South Park area. With groomed and backcountry trails, this is fast becoming a touring oasis. For more information on backcountry skiing, contact the **Park County Tourism Office** on **Main St. in Fairplay** at **719-836-4279,** or the **South Park Ranger District Office in Fairplay** at the intersection of Hwys. 285 and 9; **719-836-2031; www.fs.fed.us/r2/psicc.**

Backcountry Trails

Boreas Pass—Stretching between Como and Breckenridge, the Boreas Pass Rd. peaks out at 11,481 feet. It's a popular cross-country route. Follow the signs west from Como on County Rd. 33 and drive as far as the road is plowed before setting out on skis. See the Skiing section of the **Summit County** chapter for more information about the pass summit and west side of the pass.

Bristlecone Pine Scenic Area—This 7-mile round trip is a backcountry highlight. Allow about 6 hours round trip, over varied terrain, to complete this beautiful and historic tour. There is little avalanche danger as the trail follows a road to nearly 12,000 feet in elevation—a gain of 700 feet. The trail passes mining sites from the 1860s, ending on a ridge among bristlecone pine trees. To reach the trail from Fairplay, drive 7 miles northwest on Hwy. 9. Turn left (west) in Alma at the Texaco station and continue on County Rd. 8 for 3 miles to the Paris Mill. The road isn't plowed beyond this point. Begin skiing here, taking the first road on the right (Forest Rd. 315) beyond the Paris Mill.

Tie Hack Trail—This 5.5-mile ski loop is well marked by Forest Service blazes. It follows a fairly difficult route that is best skied after a snowstorm. Tie Hack Trail is steeped in history: the trail follows an old stage road to the defunct mining camps of Sacramento and Horseshoe, passing through aspen groves and wide-open meadows. Several stretches of downhill cruising help make this a fun tour. By the way, tie hacks were men who cut timber and worked it into usable railroad ties. To reach the trailhead from Fairplay, drive south on Hwy. 285 for a quarter-mile to County Rd. 18, marked by a Forest Access sign. Turn right (west) and drive 3.5 miles to the trail, which follows a jeep road from the right side of the road.

Groomed Trails

Fairplay Nordic Center—Even though South Park can get very windy, the Fairplay Nordic Center enjoys a protected setting with 22 kilometers of groomed trails. In fact, it is on the lee side of a ridge and the wind sometimes drops powder on the trails, even on sunny days. This relatively unknown touring center offers lessons and rentals throughout the winter. Ask about bed and breakfast ski packages. To get to the center, turn north on Fourth St. in Fairplay (at the Fairplay Country Store) and continue north for four blocks to Bogue St. Turn left and continue 1.8 miles. **P.O. Box 701, Fairplay, CO 80440; 719-836-2658.**

Rentals and Information

Fairplay Nordic Center—The only place to rent skis without having to go over Hoosier Pass. Talk with owner Gary Nichols about backcountry skiing routes and avalanche conditions (see preceding entry).

Wheelchair Recreation

Wilderness on Wheels

For people confined to wheelchairs, this is a totally accessible outdoor area designed for special needs. A mile-long wooden boardwalk, wide enough to allow two wheelchairs to pass, has been constructed along the banks of Kenosha Creek. Campsites, prime fishing spots and a nature trail are just the beginning. Campsite reservations can be made by calling ahead; no fee is charged. Rest room and shower facilities are available. In addition, a 7-mile trail to the summit of Twin Peaks (12,300 feet), with accessible rental cabins along the way, is nearly complete. Located 15 miles west of Bailey on Hwy. 285. For more information including volunteer opportunities, contact **303-751-3959; www.coloradopros.com/wow.**

Seeing and Doing

Museums

South Park City

South Park City puts history in context. More than 30 buildings from crumbling mining towns in the area have been moved to this central location where a period town, circa 1870–1900, has been re-created. Filled with room settings, dioramas and exhibits, this museum vividly shows how life was a century ago. Open since 1959 the museum offers a simple trapper's cabin, a mercantile, the South Park Lager Beer Brewery, the old Bank of Alma and a stage stop from the top of Mosquito Pass. Other displays include heavy equipment used in hydraulic and hardrock mining and a narrow-gauge engine with several cars and a caboose. A slide show on the history of South Park is shown daily on the half hour from 10:30 A.M. to 3:30 P.M. at the stone brewery building.

Definitely not a tourist trap. Admission fee charged. Open May 15–Oct. 15, 9 A.M.–5 P.M. (till 7 P.M. Memorial Day–Labor Day). Follow the signs from the center of Fairplay; **719-836-2387; www.southparkcity.org.**

Scenic Drives

South Park is a natural for leisurely scenic drives. In addition to following directions to the excellent routes listed below, consider picking up the detailed brochures on area drives available in Fairplay at the **U.S. Forest Service Office** and **Park County Tourism Office.**

Boreas Pass/Hoosier Pass

The connecting routes between the mines in South Park and Summit County provide both history and beauty. Hwy. 9 over Hoosier Pass can be taken right out of Fairplay to Breckenridge; Boreas Pass is a graded dirt road heading north from Como with spectacular scenery on the route to Breckenridge. For more information on Boreas Pass, see the Scenic Drives section of the **Summit County** chapter.

Bristlecone Pine Scenic Area

This short (but rough) drive leads into one of the few areas in Colorado where ancient, wind-twisted bristlecone pines can be seen. This type of tree is believed to be the world's oldest living thing—one tree in Nevada is thought to be 4,500 years old. New branches grow only on the leeward side of trees, as new buds are quickly blown off the windy side. The trees somehow survive at exposed elevations as high as 12,000 feet. This scenic area, at the foot of 14,169-foot Mt. Bross, can be seen from a car. From Fairplay drive 7 miles northwest on Hwy. 9. Turn left (west) in Alma on County Rd. 8 and continue 3 miles up Buckskin Gulch until reaching Forest Rd. 315. Continue up 315 to Windy Ridge.

Guanella Pass Scenic and Historic Byway

For an exciting drive with a beautiful view of Mt. Bierstadt from the summit, head north on Guanella Pass Rd. from Hwy. 285 at Grant. For details see the Scenic Drives section of the **Georgetown and Idaho Springs** chapter.

Weston Pass

This road, which crosses the Mosquito Range, can get pretty rough, but it should be okay in the family car as long as it has high clearance. Originally an Indian trail, the road became a wagon route crossing the 11,945-foot pass in 1860. The road still provides exceptional scenery and colorful wildflowers during summer as well as access to trails into the Buffalo Peaks Wilderness Area. On the west side of the pass, it descends south of Leadville. To reach Weston Pass Rd. from Fairplay, drive 5 miles south on Hwy. 285 to the marked turnoff. Take a right on County Rd. 5 and begin the odyssey.

Where to Stay

Accommodations

Glen Isle on the Platte—$$$ to $$$$

For 100 years Glen Isle has been a rustic retreat. Thankfully, few changes have been made to the outward appearance of Glen Isle over the years. And the surefire hospitality of Barbara Tripp, who's been serving as the resort host for more than half a century, is as strong as ever.

Nineteen cabins for 2 to 10 people are available, as well as 14 comfortable lodge rooms with bathrooms down the hall. During the summer season, Glen Isle operates as a resort with breakfast and activities during the week. You may want to check out the chuck-wagon dinner on Sat. night. Kids love fishing in the private pond (an ice rink in winter), and the resort is hemmed in by plenty of national forest terrain. For families this is a low-priced alternative to guest ranches; the minimum stay is two nights. Reserve early for summer visits. In winter, only cabins are open. Charming gift shop. Located just 2 miles west of Bailey on Hwy. 285. **P.O. Box 128, Bailey, CO 80421; 303-838-5461.**

Ute Trail River Ranch—$$$

For a rustic, back-road mountain cabin escape, this place may be worth a visit. Located along the Tarryall River (good fishing on the property) and near hiking and mountain biking trailheads, Ute Trail River Ranch offers eight cabins. Three better-equipped winterized cabins come with private baths and kitchenettes. The other summer-only cabins are a bit more spartan, some with wood stoves and shared bath facilities. Kids under 5 years old stay free. On County Rd. 77 about 3 miles southeast of Tarryall Reservoir. **21446 County Rd. 77, Lake George, CO 80827; 719-748-3015; www.owa.com/tarry all/ute.html.**

Hand Hotel—$$ to $$$

Although originally constructed in the 1930s along historic Front St., this charming B&B with its 11 distinctly different (though somewhat

Fairplay Nordic Center. Photo by Gary Nichols.

diminutive) guest rooms transports you back to the 1800s. The plush lobby includes chairs and couches situated around a large mantel as well as a plethora of wildlife trophies mounted on the walls. Each guest room features antiques as well as a small, private bathroom. Enjoy your continental breakfast from the enclosed breakfast room off of the back with its picture windows and outstanding views. **531 Front St., P.O. Box 1059, Fairplay, CO 80440; 719-836-3595; www.handhotel.com.**

Como Depot—$$

The restored Como Depot used to fill up with guests when the narrow-gauge train made its runs from Denver to South Park in the early 1900s. After the train stopped service, the hotel shut down until 1978, when it was reopened by Jo and Keith Hodges (Como's first business in 25 years). Four upstairs rooms are simple, clean reminders of the past. One room sleeps three to four guests and has a fireplace. Three rooms share a bathroom down the hall, equipped with a claw-foot bathtub. It's nothing fancy, but this friendly place exudes the colorful history of Como. The downstairs restaurant has a good reputation among locals (see the Where to Eat section). Closed Nov.–Mar. **Como Depot, Box 110, Como, CO 80432; 719-836-2594.**

Fairplay Hotel—$$

Twenty-one basic rooms are spread out on the upper floor of the historic Fairplay Hotel. About half of the rooms come with a private bathroom. A comfortable lobby area has couches situated around a stone mantel adorned with a huge elk trophy; the sometimes noisy Silver Heels Lounge offers big-screen TV and drinks. **500 Main St., Box 639, Fairplay, CO 80440; 719-836-2565.**

Camping

Pike National Forest

Many of the Forest Service campgrounds are available for reservations. A camping fee is charged except at the campgrounds that are noted as having no fee. Reservations: **1-877-444-6777** or **www.reserveusa.com.**

Beginning on the east side of Kenosha Pass on Hwy. 285 at the town of Grant, take Guanella Pass Rd. (County Rd. 62) north. After 2.5 miles you'll reach **Whiteside Campground** (5 sites). Another 2.5 miles up the road is **Burning Bear Campground** (13 sites). Continue 2 miles to reach **Geneva Park Campground** (26 sites).

Take Hwy. 285 west of Grant for 3 miles to the Hall Valley turnoff. Head northwest on rough and narrow County Rd. 60 for 5 miles to **reach Handcart Campground** (10 sites). Virtually at the same point on the road **is Hall Valley Campground** (9 sites). After the campgrounds this road gets even rougher as it leads over Webster Pass (see the Four-Wheel-Drive Trips section).

Popular **Kenosha Pass Campground** (25 sites) is at the top of Kenosha Pass on Hwy. 285, between Grant and Jefferson.

On Hwy. 285 west of Kenosha Pass, turn northwest on County Rd. 35 at Jefferson. Continue 2 miles and turn right (north) on County Rd. 37. After 1.5 miles you'll come to a succession of campgrounds. The first one is **Lodgepole Campground** (35 sites), followed by **Aspen Campground** (12 sites) and **Jefferson Creek Campground** (17 sites). Bring your fishing pole along and try your luck at Jefferson Lake. If you continue on County Rd. 35 for 6 miles from Jefferson, you will reach **Michigan Creek Campground** (13 sites).

From 1 mile northeast of Jefferson along Hwy. 285, head southeast on County Rd. 56 for about 20 miles. This will take you to the edge of the Lost Creek Wilderness Area and **Lost Park Campground** (10 sites, no fee).

From Como, take Boreas Pass Rd. (County Rd. 33) northwest for 7 miles to a turnoff for **Selkirk Campground** (15 sites, no fee).

Beaver Creek Campground (3 sites, no fee) is located 4 miles north of Fairplay on Forest Rd. 659.

To reach **Kite Lake Campground** (7 sites, no fee) from Fairplay, follow Hwy. 9 northwest for 7 miles to Alma. In Alma turn left on County Rd. 8 that breaks away from Main St. across from the Texaco station. Follow the rough dirt road 7 miles up Buckskin Gulch to Kite Lake, which is above treeline. The road is especially rough for the last mile. You may want to walk, unless you have a jeep.

From Fairplay you can easily reach **Fourmile Campground** (14 sites) and **Horseshoe Campground** (7 sites). Drive south on Hwy. 285 for 1.5 miles, turn right (west) on County Rd. 18 and continue for 7 miles.

Five miles south of Fairplay on Hwy. 285 is a turnoff for Weston Pass Rd. (County Rd. 5). Turn right (southwest) and drive 11 miles to **Weston Pass Campground** (14 sites). Fifteen miles south of Fairplay on Hwy. 285, take a right turn (west on County Rd. 76) and drive for half a mile to **Buffalo Springs Campground** (17 sites, no fee).

From the town of Lake George along Hwy. 24 in the southeast part of the park, head south on Forest Rd. 245 to **Eleven Mile Canyon.** This scenic canyon has six campgrounds with a total of 91 campsites (fee charged). The road in the canyon is slim and twisting, so large trailers and RVs are advised to stay near the entrance. Great fishing.

From Lake George, you may also access a number of terrific campsites by driving northwest on County Rd. 77, which eventually reaches Hwy. 285 at Jefferson after 42 miles. Drive 12.5 miles along County Rd. 77 to **Spruce Grove Campground** (28 sites). Great access to Lost Creek Wilderness Area; huge rocks, some walk-in sites. Another 1.5 miles north along County Rd. 77 takes you to **Twin Eagles Campground** (9 sites) and trailhead.

State Parks

Eleven Mile State Park—The 350 campsites can be reached from Hwy. 24 at the west end of Lake George. Turn left off County Rd. 92 and drive 11 miles. Fee charged. Some sites available on the reservoir shore; showers, laundry facilities are available. Reservations available: **1-800-678-CAMP; 303-470-1144** from Denver; **www.reserveamerica.com.**

Where to Eat

Como Depot—$ to $$

Gather around the fireplace at this local favorite and enjoy a down-home meal. This historic hotel in the town of Como has a relaxed setting and decent mountain food. The menu provides anything from a simple quarter-pound hamburger to 14 ounces of prime rib or a salmon steak. Try their Mexican specialties and chili that's "not for wimps." Tasty breakfast entrées and homemade pies are popular, too. Open Thurs.–Mon. 8 A.M.–8 P.M. In Como; **719-836-2594.**

Crow's Foot—$ to $$

This popular restaurant lies at the foot of Crow Hill along Hwy. 285 in the town of Bailey. Once you discover it, you'll be back. The meandering interior features a Southwestern decor with dried red chilis and art. Menu items range from breakfast enchiladas to high country burritos and fajitas. You can smother your meal with five different kinds of chili, including the four-alarm Angel Fire Southwestern chili; with its smattering of habañeros this could be the hottest in the state. American dishes also have a place on the lengthy menu. All lunch and dinner entrées are served with soup or salad and choice of potato. Check out the terrific pie selection as well. Open 7 A.M.–10 P.M. daily. At Park Plaza in Bailey, **60629 Hwy. 285; 303-838-5298.**

Fairplay Hotel—$ to $$

This has long been the restaurant of choice for a filling breakfast before heading out for a day of skiing. The cozy dining room of the hotel has a warm ambience. Breakfast is the standout here: omelettes, eggs, home fries and, especially, gigantic cinnamon rolls. For lunch try a burger, fried chicken or a bowl of homemade soup. Dinners include reasonably priced fish, chicken and beef dishes. Open Sun.–Thurs. 7 A.M.–9 P.M.; until 10 P.M. Fri.–Sat.; closes 1 hour earlier in winter. **500 Main St., Fairplay; 719-836-2565.**

Mountain Shadows Inn—$ to $$

Boasting "food that tastes so good, you'll think it's your mama's cookin'," this place is definitely 100 percent down-home. It's been packing locals in for years (maybe 70 or so) for pretty standard fare in heaping portions. This goes for the kids' menu, too. Breakfast highlights include gigantic cinnamon rolls (each one could feed two people), biscuits and gravy and omelettes; lunch and dinner items include burgers, sandwiches, fried chicken, steaks and some seafood for the more adventurous. Try the homemade pies and soups. You won't leave hungry. Open Mon.–Fri. 6 A.M.–9 P.M.; until 10 P.M. on weekends. In Lake George at **38321 Hwy. 24, Lake George; 719-748-3833.**

Rhoda's Front Street Cafe—$ to $$

Fine, creative food in Fairplay? We hope this classy place will thrive, perhaps by drawing tourists over Hoosier Pass from Breckenridge. Soft colors and local watercolor paintings grace the walls of the cafe's two rooms. Breakfasts are fairly standard but the creativity comes out in lunch and dinner items such as the soup du jour, grilled portabella sandwich, pastas and steak. Daily specials highlight the menu—the Southwestern-style chicken lasagna is delicious, as is the crème brûlée dessert special. Open in summer Wed.–Sun. 11:30 A.M.–9 P.M. for lunch and dinner; breakfast Sat.–Sun. 8:30–11:30 A.M.; in winter open Fri.–Sun. only. **435 Front St., Fairplay; 719-836-7031.**

Services

Visitor Information
Park County Tourism Office—P.O. Box 220, Fairplay, CO 80440; 719-836-4279.

Upper Arkansas Valley

Throughout the earlier years of its settlement, the Upper Arkansas Valley, stretching 45 miles north from Salida to the small town of Granite, hosted people "just passing through." Early on, wagon roads and rail lines crisscrossed the valley, providing routes over the Continental Divide to the west, over Poncha Pass to the south, across Trout Creek Pass to South Park and alongside the Arkansas River. Today things have changed—for a variety of reasons, the Upper Arkansas Valley has evolved into one of Colorado's best outdoor destinations.

The Arkansas River, one of the longest in North America, flows through the entire valley before entering Upper Arkansas Canyon on its way to the eastern plains at Pueblo. And the river continues to attract huge numbers of rafters and kayakers (well over 130,000 per year) who seek the thrill of shooting some great rapids. River runs through the Numbers, Browns Canyon and the Royal Gorge have helped the Arkansas to become the most popular river floating area in the country.

Along the western edge of the valley, the lofty Sawatch Mountain Range angles skyward, providing a memorable view, especially to first-time visitors. More 14,000-foot peaks are packed into this small area than anywhere else in North America. The Sawatch, within San Isabel National Forest (and the Collegiate Peaks Wilderness Area), offers fantastic recreational possibilities, especially if you like to climb peaks. Monarch, at the southern end of the range, is a fine small ski and mountain snowboard area.

Mining history can be relived by a visit to one of the many ghost towns in the region. Though some require a four-wheel-drive vehicle, many others can be reached in the family car. But the ghost towns are not the only places to get a sense of the Upper Arkansas Valley history. Salida, in the southern end of the valley, still reflects its railroad legacy. The turn-of-the-century brick buildings in downtown Salida make up a very large National Historic District with interesting art galleries and some notable restaurants. This town of 5,700 residents, along with smaller Buena Vista (half of Salida's population), located 25 miles up-valley, offers the majority of accommodations, restaurants and other services. Buena Vista (called *Byoonie* by the locals) enjoys quick access to the Sawatch Mountains and put-in spots for popular river runs.

History

Before settlers entered the scene, the Upper Arkansas area was the domain of Native American

---

Getting There

Buena Vista is located 117 miles southwest of Denver via Hwy. 285. Another approach from the east is up the Arkansas River from Pueblo to Salida—a 97-mile trip on Hwy. 50 that includes a beautiful canyon section.

tribes, especially the Utes. Semipermanent Ute villages were located along the Arkansas River near Buena Vista. Farther upriver were the Comanche. After the Indians obtained horses, allowing them to travel much farther to hunt, habitation in the valley declined. Lt. Zebulon Pike, who passed through the area in 1806, found an old Indian camp in which he believed 3,000 natives had once lived. By the time settlers entered the area in the 1860s, few Indian villages were in evidence, though curious, friendly Utes made occasional visits.

It was mining that first drew large numbers of settlers to the Upper Arkansas. In 1860 gold was discovered at Kelly's Bar near Granite, 20 miles upriver from Buena Vista. Eager to strike it rich, placer miners spread out along the Arkansas and up the side valleys and gulches. Though some decent mines were worked in the 1860s and 1870s, this area paled in comparison to strikes upriver at Oro City, near present-day Leadville. By the 1880s better roads and improved mining techniques contributed to successful mines throughout the area, including those up Clear Creek and Chalk Creek Canyons. Vibrant mining towns like Winfield, Vicksburg and St. Elmo grew and prospered in these two canyons.

Meanwhile, down along the Arkansas River, hay farmers and ranchers moved in. By the end of the 1870s cattle grazed throughout the valley. Buena Vista grew as a supply town for the mines and ranches as well as a transportation center for those making their way upriver to Leadville (Oro City). By 1880 Buena Vista had grown large enough to be voted the new county seat. Townsfolk in Granite, the prior county seat, did not take kindly to the news, refusing to relinquish the county records. Buena Vista residents took matters into their own hands by sneaking into the courthouse in Granite late one night and stealing all the county records. The next day, county business went on as usual, but from Buena Vista.

The railroads finally came to the Upper Arkansas Valley in 1880, when Gen. Palmer's Denver & Rio Grande Railroad made its way upriver to South Arkansas (later named Salida).

Mount Princeton, one of the most prominent features in the Upper Arkansas Valley. Photo by Buena Vista Chamber of Commerce.

This town grew quickly as a rail hub and smelting and supply center. From Salida the Denver & Rio Grande extended tracks up the valley through Buena Vista and on to Leadville. They also ran a line up Poncha Pass and over Marshall Pass to the Western Slope near Gunnison. Shortly thereafter, the Denver South Park & Pacific Railroad arrived in the valley. Its major achievement was the Alpine Tunnel at the upper end of Chalk Creek, which was bored through the Continental Divide in a race with the Denver & Rio Grande to reach Gunnison. When the Colorado Midland Railroad reached the valley in 1887, both Salida and Buena Vista were rip-roaring towns. Buena Vista was especially rowdy, with 36 bars and a "hanging" judge, who was responsible for stringing up outlaws. Two of Colorado's most notorious madams operated in these towns. Cockeyed Liz ran her "palace of joy" in Buena Vista for years until marrying at the age of 40. Laura Evans, who lived to the ripe old age of 90, ran a bordello in Salida from 1896 until 1950.

With the demise of the mining industry and railroads, most area residents make their living ranching, farming or in tourism-related businesses. The latter has become extremely important, especially with the incredible growth of commercial rafting on the mighty Arkansas River during summer months. Dedicated in 1990, the Arkansas Headwaters Recreation Area helps floaters, anglers and other visitors to the valley enjoy the river to its fullest.

Festivals and Events

FibArk

mid-June   FibArk (meaning First in Boating on the Arkansas) brings visitors to Salida for a long weekend of music, crafts, a bed race, a parade and boat races including a whitewater rodeo. The featured event is the 26-mile kayak and raft race from Salida down to Cotopaxi, touted as the oldest and longest whitewater race in North America. Some nuts even swim this stretch of the river! **1-877-772-5432; 719-539-7997; www.peaksnewsnet.com/fibark.**

Salida Art Walk

weekend in late July   This festival sheds light on why Salida has developed into a terrific art center. More than 40 galleries, restaurants and shops participate, with all-day events Sat. and Sun. Check out one of the evening receptions to meet and view the works of artists and craftspeople at the numerous galleries in historic downtown Salida. All are within a five-block area. **1-877-772-5432; www.salidaartwalk.org.**

Outdoor Activities

Biking

MOUNTAIN BIKING

The Upper Arkansas area has quickly become extremely popular among mountain bikers. One reason for this is the diversity of terrain. Trails through the hills on the east side of the valley tend to be a bit mellower than those that wind into the lofty Sawatch Range to the west. For maps and other trail ideas, visit the **Salida Ranger District Office, 325 W. Rainbow Blvd., Salida, CO 81201, 719-539-3591,** or one of the shops listed in this section. Pick up a free copy of the area's mountain bike trail guide at any of the visitor centers.

Alpine Tunnel Trail

For a scenic and relatively mellow ride up to the old Alpine Tunnel, see the Tunnel Lake Trail write-up in the Hiking and Backpacking section.

Midland Trail

This highly recommended intermediate trail runs for about 14 miles between Trout Creek Pass and the outskirts of Buena Vista. For the most part, the trail follows the grade of the long-defunct Midland Railroad. Along the way you'll see remnants of the railroad days and enjoy great views west to the Sawatch Range. If you choose to travel only one way, start at the Trout Creek Pass end. To reach the trailhead from Buena Vista, head east on Hwy. 285/24 for about 9 miles to County Rd. 309. Begin riding here. After 1.4 miles, turn left onto County Rd. 376.2. After about 3 more miles turn left onto Shields Gulch Rd. (County Rd. 315). Proceed for just over 2 miles and turn right onto the Midland Trail. After a few miles you'll hit a one-lane road that you take west until you see the Barbara Whipple Trail on the left. This trail descends to the bridge over the Arkansas at Buena Vista's Recreational River Park.

Monarch Crest Trail

This trail is not meant for beginning or intermediate riders, but advanced mountain bikers can be rewarded with what many consider to be one of the finest rides in Colorado. At the summit of Monarch Pass on Hwy. 50, start up the one-lane dirt road just east of the Monarch Tram gondola tower. About a third of a mile up the road, turn onto Trail 531. From here you can climb to the Continental Divide, where you can ride with spectacular views of surrounding mountain ranges. The ride eventually takes you to Marshall Pass and down to Poncha Springs for a 5-hour, 28-mile ride. For more information about this ride, contact the Forest Service office in Salida or one of the bike shops listed in this section.

Rainbow Trail

Beginning up at the Continental Divide, southwest of Poncha Springs, the well-maintained Rainbow Trail (No. 1336) stretches 100 miles along the north and east side of the Sangre de Cristo Range, ending in the Wet Mountain Valley. The trail travels through a wide variety of terrain from flat open meadows to steep, forested stretches. Many side trails lead off from the main one, providing unlimited exploring if you're up for it. Access points to the trail are numerous; many lie along Hwy. 50, southeast of Poncha Springs. Visit the Forest Service office in Salida for maps.

Rentals and Information

Absolute Bikes—This full-service shop provides full- and half-day bike rentals. They are helpful and really know their stuff. Open daily near the river. **330 W. Sackett Ave., Salida; 1-888-539-9295; 719-539-9295; www.abso lutebikes.com.**

HeadWaters Outdoor Equipment—Rentals and excellent information about where to ride. **228 N. F St., Salida, CO 81201; 719-539-4506; www.americaadventure.com.**

The Trailhead—Supplies, trail ideas, maps and rental mountain bikes. **707 N. Hwy. 24, Buena Vista, CO 81211; 719-395-8001; www.trail headco.com.**

Fishing

The Upper Arkansas Valley has long been known for its excellent fishing. Countless anglers have reeled in lunker browns and other trout from stretches along the Arkansas River. The multitude of streams and lakes in the mountains to the west has yielded ample numbers of smaller brookies, cutthroat and rainbows. Many of these can only be reached by hiking trail or four-

wheel-drive road. Tributaries along the Arkansas and high lakes provide worthwhile fishing. If you plan to fish in the area, your best bet is to consult with locals for up-to-date information on where the fish are biting. Upriver (13 miles north of Buena Vista on Hwy. 24), **Arkansas Valley Anglers** can meet a variety of your fishing needs from fly-fishing lessons to overnight float fishing trips; **1-800-370-0581; www.fly fishingcolorado.net.** In Salida, try the highly regarded **ArkAnglers.** These folks run float or wade trips, fly-fishing school and rentals out of their fly shop at **7500 W. Hwy. 50; Salida, CO 81201; 719-539-4223.** You might also try contacting the **Division of Wildlife: 303-291-7538; www.wildlife.state.co.us/fishing.** Listed below are some of the better spots.

Arkansas River

The Arkansas is still one of the best rivers to land a brown or rainbow trout in the 10- to 12-inch range, especially during the spring caddis fly hatch. During this hatch, which usually lasts from three to four weeks, fly-fishers should try the elk hair caddis. Snow runoff from mid-May through the end of July normally inhibits good fly-fishing, but you might try spin casting with a Mepps or Panther Martin. Also, those planning to fish during runoff should be warned that this is when the Arkansas is thick with rafters and kayakers. In Aug. (or when the river flow finally drops below 600 cubic feet per second), decent fly-fishing can return, with anglers successfully using black woolly buggers, pheasant tail nymphs and grasshopper patterns.

Generally speaking, you'll find good fishing on the Arkansas all the way from Granite down through Texas Creek. Some of the better access spots include the lower section of Browns Canyon (Hecla Junction), Ruby Mountain (via Fisherman's Bridge) and the 7.5-mile section from the bridge below Salida down to Badger Creek. This last stretch is flies and lures only; anglers can keep only two fish over 16 inches. The Arkansas Headwaters Recreation Area brochure includes a great map of the public access points, all of which are well signed.

Clear Creek Reservoir

Though the level of this 400-acre reservoir fluctuates greatly, making for inconsistent fishing, the Division of Wildlife stocks plenty of rainbows, browns and brookies. Fish from shore or launch a boat from the north shore ramp. Clear Creek Reservoir is located 16 miles north of Buena Vista on Hwy. 24 and then 1 mile west on Clear Creek Canyon Rd. (County Rd. 390). Upriver from the reservoir, above Winfield, four-wheel-drive vehicles and hikers can reach upper Clear Creek to fish for cutthroat.

Cottonwood Lake

Located off the Cottonwood Pass road, this small wooded lake at 9,600 feet offers bank fishing for rainbows up to 2 pounds. No motorboats allowed. Wheelchair-accessible fishing dock and trail. Head west from Buena Vista on County Rd. 306 for about 12 miles and turn left at the sign.

Twin Lakes Reservoir

Home to huge Mackinaw and other trout. See the Fishing section in the **Leadville** chapter.

Four-Wheel-Drive Trips

Aspen Ridge / Bassam Park

Located in the rolling Arkansas Hills on the east side of the Arkansas River, this route runs 30 miles north-south between Buena Vista and Salida. With thick stands of aspen trees and occasional views west to the magnificent Sawatch Range, this drive wins our recommendation (especially in autumn). Much of the route, including the popular picnic area at Bassam Park, is accessible by regular passenger cars, but if you travel the entire way you'll need a four-wheel-drive vehicle.

To reach the road from Salida, head northwest on Hwy. 291, 1 mile past the traffic light at First and F Sts. Turn right onto County Rd. 153, cross the river and turn right on County Rd. 175 (Ute Trail). About 7.5 miles from the highway, bear left onto County Rd. 185. A few miles down the road you'll pass through Calumet, an old Colorado Fuel & Iron Company town and mine. When you reach the intersection after 20 miles turn left and proceed 4 miles to Bassam Park, where it joins up with County Rd. 187. Keep going north on County Rd. 187 until reaching the junction with County Rd. 307 after a total of 29 miles. Turn left and proceed 1.4 miles to Hwy. 285/24 (at the Trout City Inn), about 7 miles east of Johnson Village.

Tincup Pass

Stretching from St. Elmo over the Continental Divide to the ghost town of Tincup, this rugged road provides sweeping views from its 12,154-foot summit. To the west the West Elk Mountains are an impressive backdrop to Taylor Park. Before the Denver South Park & Pacific Railroad built the Alpine Tunnel under the divide, Tincup Pass was an important stagecoach and freight supply route for settlements such as Gunnison and Tincup on the Western Slope.

To reach this road from St. Elmo (see the Scenic Drives section), cross the bridge in town and turn left. Tincup Pass Rd. starts climbing through a thick aspen forest and eventually opens into an enormous bowl before reaching the pass 8 miles up the road. Enjoy the fantastic views from the summit or take a 1.5-mile hike up 13,124-foot Fitzpatrick Peak. From the summit of the pass descend about 7 miles, past Mirror Lake to Tincup. For information about Tincup, see the Scenic Drives section of the **Gunnison and Crested Butte** chapter. From Tincup an interesting return trip to the Upper Arkansas area is over Cottonwood Pass. Drive north from Tincup to Taylor Park Reservoir and then east over Cottonwood Pass (see the Scenic Drives section) to Buena Vista.

Golf

Collegiate Peaks Golf Course

This nine-hole course offers great views of Mt. Princeton and other mountains in the Sawatch Range. Large cottonwood trees dot the course, with a creek and several small lakes coming into play. To reach the course from the center of

Buena Vista, turn west at the stoplight and continue 1.3 miles. Turn right at the green-and-white sign for the golf course. **28775 Fairway Dr., P.O. Box 533, Buena Vista, CO 81211; 719-395-8189.**

Salida Golf Club

Built in the 1920s, the nine-hole course at the Salida Golf Club offers a challenging round to even the best golfers. With narrow fairways on many of the holes, accuracy is necessary to avoid the thick, troublesome roughs. The par-3 eighth hole is particularly difficult with a pond guarding its elevated green. West-facing tees provide wide views of the Sawatch Range (particularly Mt. Shavano). **404 Grant St., Salida, CO 81201; 719-539-1060.**

Hiking and Backpacking

If you enjoy putting on a pack and getting out into the backcountry (especially high alpine country), the Upper Arkansas Valley region is for you. When you get your first glimpse of the towering Sawatch Range, you'll know why. There are many trails, from easy mile-long jaunts to long, steep ascents of 14,000-foot peaks. In the Upper Arkansas area, a dozen 14ers are easily accessible, but not necessarily easy to climb. They are La Plata Peak, Huron Peak, Missouri Mountain, Mt. Belford, Mt. Tabeguache, Mt. Shavano, Mt. Antero and the Collegiate Peaks—Mt. Oxford, Mt. Yale, Mt. Princeton, Mt. Harvard and Mt. Columbia. If you plan to hike in the high country, remember to get an early start to avoid the frequent afternoon thunderstorms.

Information for hiking trails can be obtained at the **Salida Ranger District Office, 325 W. Rainbow Blvd., Salida, CO 81201; 719-539-3591. The Trailhead** supplies trail maps, equipment rental and information at **707 N. Hwy. 24, Buena Vista, CO 81211; 719-395-8001; www.trailheadco.com.** Also try **HeadWaters Outdoor Equipment** at **228 N. F St., Salida; 719-539-4506; www.americaadventure.com.**

Brown's Creek Trail (Mt. Antero)

This 11-mile trail begins in the valley at 9,000 feet and climbs west along Brown's Creek, even-

View from within the Sawatch Range, climbing toward the Mount Tabeguache summit. Photo by Dean Winstanley.

tually reaching the summit of 14,269-foot Mt. Antero. It provides outstanding scenery, from mountain meadows and spruce forests to the far-reaching views from the summit of Mt. Antero. Except for the final push up the peak, the trail climbs gradually. To reach the trailhead from Hwy. 285 between Buena Vista and Poncha Springs, head west on County Rd. 270 for 1.5 miles and then straight on County Rd. 272 for 2 miles. At the intersection turn left and proceed 1.5 miles to the trailhead.

A much shorter route up Mt. Antero can be accessed via a four-wheel-drive road that begins on Chalk Creek Rd. (County Rd. 162). From Nathrop drive west up Chalk Creek about 11 miles and turn left on Baldwin Gulch Rd. This rocky road takes you about 6 miles, up near the gem field, about a mile south of the Mt. Antero summit.

Colorado Trail

The 469-mile Colorado Trail, stretching from Denver to Durango, makes its way through the

Upper Arkansas area, skirting the eastern edge of the Sawatch Range. Terrain varies from relatively low-altitude sections through ponderosa pine groves to high alpine meadows. Access to the trail is possible from numerous roads that head west from Hwy. 285 (between Poncha Pass and Buena Vista) and from Hwy. 24 (north of Buena Vista).

Fitzpatrick Peak
A fairly steep 1.5-mile hike leads to the summit of this 13,124-foot peak, offering fantastic 360-degree views to most ranges in southern and central Colorado, including the far-off San Juans. The trail begins at the summit of Tincup Pass and heads off to the southwest, where the summit of the peak is visible. For information about Tincup Pass, see the Four-Wheel-Drive Trips section.

Ptarmigan Lake Trail
Beautiful Ptarmigan Lake at 12,132 feet is a popular destination for hikers. Fishing at the 11-acre lake has been very good for small cutthroat. Views of the surrounding peaks are perhaps the biggest attraction. The moderately difficult 3.3-mile trail climbs about 1,500 vertical feet. The Forest Service asks that you camp and collect firewood well away from the lake. To reach the trailhead from Buena Vista, drive about 14 miles west on Cottonwood Pass Rd. (County Rd. 306). The trailhead is on the left side of the road.

Rainbow Trail
See the Biking section.

Tunnel Lake Trail
This trail traverses the Continental Divide beginning at the east portal of the Alpine Tunnel (see the Scenic Drives section in the **Gunnison and Crested Butte** chapter). The 7.5-mile trail begins at the Hancock townsite, an old settlement that serviced area mines and housed Alpine Tunnel workers. Hike 3.5 miles along the old railroad grade to the caved-in portal of the Alpine Tunnel. This easy section of the trail provides great views of the surrounding valleys and

mountains. On top of the tunnel (another half-mile), the trail (No. 1439) heads north through alpine meadows and willow fields. The wildflowers in midsummer are awesome! Alpine Lake can be seen below. The trail intersects Tincup Pass Rd., 4 miles above St. Elmo. To reach the trailhead, turn left (south) off County Rd. 162 onto County Rd. 295 just before reaching St. Elmo. Continue about 5.5 miles to the ghost town of Hancock.

Horseback Riding
With a rich ranching history in the valley and a vast amount of nearby public land, horseback riding is very popular in this part of the state.

Mt. Princeton Riding Stables and Equestrian Center
Located just a couple of miles up Chalk Creek Rd., these folks offer trail rides up into the nearby Sangre de Cristo Range. One-hour rides, half-day and sunset rides—you name it, they provide it. **13999 County Rd. 162, Nathrop, CO 81236; 719-395-6498; www.colorado trailrides.com.**

River Floating
Of the many large rivers originating in Colorado, none is run by more rafters, kayakers and canoers than the Upper Arkansas River. With its easy access and abundant stretches of rapids, the river receives heavy use. When the spring runoff begins, river rats flock to the area; scores of outfitters offer exciting float trips throughout the summer.

Upper Arkansas River
Forty-seven miles of the Upper Arkansas, from Granite down to Salida, provide a full range of water. Running parallel to Hwy. 24 between Granite and Buena Vista, the infamous Numbers rapids, rated Class IV, are too treacherous for many river runners. Below Buena Vista, at Ruby Mountain and Fisherman's Bridge, boaters put in for the most popular river run in the state—Browns Canyon. From Ruby Mountain, the first 2 miles are relatively mild until the river drops

into the granite canyon with Class III and IV rapids. Boulder fields abound during low water; they are transformed into standing waves at high water. Most rafters and kayakers conclude this exciting section by taking out at Hecla Junction to avoid the nasty Seidel's Suckhole (a churning spot a half-mile downriver that flips many boats). Below Seidel's Suckhole the river flows 12 miles to Salida, offering less hair-raising water.

Below Salida the river enters the narrow Arkansas River Canyon and eventually the exhilarating Royal Gorge, 44 miles downstream. Along the way are numerous put-ins and even a campground at Five Points (between Texas Creek and Parkdale). For information about this part of the river, see the River Floating section of the **Cañon City** chapter.

River users got a boost in 1990 with the dedication of the **Arkansas Headwaters Recreation Area.** In the works for a number of years, the recreation area represents a partnership between state and federal agencies that has helped beef up facilities and access along the river for recreational purposes. This linear park extends 148 miles, essentially from Leadville to Pueblo. Along the way you'll find numerous river access points, changing rooms and camping and picnic sites.

Boaters should check with the recreation area for any requirements. Private property occupies 60 percent of the land along the river, so please respect landowners' rights. Maps of the river showing put-in and take-out spots are available at many river companies in the valley and at the Chamber of Commerce visitor centers in Salida and Buena Vista. For an excellent mile-by-mile description of the river including geology, wildlife and a compelling history, pick up *The Upper Arkansas River,* by Frank Staub (Fulcrum, 1988). For more information contact the **Arkansas Headwaters Recreation Area Office** at **307 W. Sackett; P.O. Box 126, Salida, CO 81201; 719-539-7289; www.coloradoparks.com.**

Outfitters

Almost 100 licensed commercial river outfitters run the Upper Arkansas River. The outfitters vary in quality and type of service provided.

Although you can check with the Chamber of Commerce offices, the following are a few of the most reputable businesses we know about.

Dvorak's Kayak and Rafting Expeditions— One of the longest-operating outfitters in Colorado, Dvorak's specializes in expedition-type boating. In addition to trips down all major stretches of the Upper Arkansas, they run extended trips on other major rivers in Colorado, other states and internationally. Fishing expeditions and kayak lessons offered as well. **17921-B Hwy. 285, Nathrop, CO 81236; 1-800-824-3795; 719-539-6851; www.dvorakexpeditions.com.**

4 Corners Rafting—Consistently one of the most highly regarded outfitters, these folks offer trips ranging from mellow family floats to adventure-class trips on a wide variety of Upper Arkansas stretches. Half-day, full-day and overnight trips available. **P.O. Box 569, Buena Vista, CO 81211; 1-800-332-7238; www.four cornersrafting.com.**

River Runners—For nearly 30 years, River Runners has provided trips through Browns Canyon and the Royal Gorge areas of the Upper Arkansas River. Highly reliable. **11150 Hwy. 50, Salida, CO 81201; 1-800-332-9100; www. riverrunnersltd.com.**

Wilderness Aware—Not only do the guides at this award-winning outfit get you downriver safely, they provide great information about the flora, fauna and geology. Wilderness Aware runs half-day and full-day trips down the Arkansas as well as many multi-day trips on other rivers of the state. **P.O. Box 1550 WS, Buena Vista, CO 81211; 1-800-462-7238; 719-395-2112; www. inaraft.com.**

Rockhounding

Attention geologists and weekend rock hounds! Rock formations in the Upper Arkansas River area yield a fairly diverse assortment of minerals and gems. Armed with rock hammers, hordes of people scour the mountains and valleys each year, but plenty of specimens still lie unclaimed. Be sure to stay off private land unless you have permission from the landowner. Two popular places to look are Mt. Antero and Ruby Mountain Recreation Site. For information on these and other spots, check with the visitor centers listed in the Services section.

Skiing

CROSS-COUNTRY SKIING AND SNOWSHOEING

Although snowmobiles compete for many of the area's trails, you can find secluded areas away from the whine of their engines. Valley locals and the San Isabel National Forest people have done plenty to accommodate cross-country skiers and snowshoers by marking trails and providing services in the towns. For avalanche information, maps and other assistance, contact the **Salida Ranger District Office, 325 W. Rainbow Blvd., Salida, CO 81201, 719-539-3591; or The Trailhead, 707 N. Hwy. 24, P.O. Box 2023, Buena Vista, CO 81211, 719-395-8001, www.trailheadco.com.**

Backcountry Trails

Cottonwood Pass Road—From the trailhead near Rainbow Lake follow the easy grade of Cottonwood Pass Rd. for 10 miles to the summit at 12,126 feet on the Continental Divide. Pine and aspen line the road up to treeline. On a clear day you'll have views west to Taylor Park, the Elk Mountains and other mountain ranges. To reach the trailhead from Buena Vista, head west on County Rd. 306 for about 9 miles to where the snow plowing ends just past Rainbow Lake at the Avalanche parking lot.

Old Monarch Pass Road—Located just west of the Monarch Ski Area on Hwy. 50, Old Monarch Pass Rd. takes off to the right. The first 1.5 miles to the summit have set tracks. From the summit of the pass, take time to enjoy the spectacular views of the surrounding mountains. The trail descends to the west for 7 miles through pine forests on Forest Rd. 237 to Forest Rd. 888. Be sure to save enough energy for the return trip or get a shuttle.

Tincup Pass Road—The road up to the summit of Tincup Pass at 12,154 feet makes a fantastic ski trip, but it can receive heavy snowmobile traffic on weekends. This intermediate trail starts at St. Elmo. Cross the bridge over Chalk Creek, turn left and begin skiing up the trail through the trees. It's steep for the first half-mile but gradually mellows for the remaining 7.5 miles to the summit. To reach the trailhead from Buena Vista, drive south on Hwy. 285 for about 10 miles and turn right on Chalk Creek Rd. (County Rd. 162). Drive about 15 miles to St. Elmo.

Rentals and Information

Monarch Ski and Snowboard Area—The shop at the ski area rents cross-country, snowshoe and telemark equipment. **719-539-3573.**

The Trailhead—This shop rents everything from telemark skis to gaiters. **707 N. Hwy. 24, P.O. Box 2023, Buena Vista, CO 81211; 719-395-8001; www.trailheadco.com.**

DOWNHILL SKIING AND SNOWBOARDING

Monarch Ski and Snowboard Area

Major ski magazines and other national ski area reviewers have long sung the praises of Monarch. Located along the Continental Divide near the summit of Monarch Pass, the ski mountain is a natural. A basin traps more than 350 inches of light, fluffy powder snow each winter; who needs snowmaking machines? The runs are laid out so you can practically reach any one of the five lifts (including, thankfully, a new high-speed quad) from any place on the mountain. A major attraction is Monarch's diversity of terrain—beginners, intermediate skiers and experts can find challenging runs from the top of all the lifts. This is especially appealing to families: one parent can take the kids down an easy bunny slope while the other hits the mogul run; everyone can meet at the bottom for another ride up the lift. Although the vertical drop is only 1,170 feet, you'll get as much skiing in (if not more) than at a much larger area. Monarch's appeal to many skiers is its laid-back atmosphere. Lift ticket rates are reasonable to boot. The entire mountain is open to snowboarders, with Meadows

Snowboard Park set up specifically for the sport. Die-hard powder hounds with extra cash to spend may want to investigate Monarch Snowcat Tours, which provides excellent backcountry skiing via snowcat.

The day lodge at the base offers a cafeteria and the **Sidewinder Saloon** for après ski. Day care, ski school and rentals are also available. Three miles down the road you can stay at the reasonably priced Monarch Mountain Lodge (see the Where to Stay section). The ski area is 16 miles west of Poncha Springs on Hwy. 50. **1 Powder Pl., Monarch, CO 81227-1100; 1-800-996-7669; 719-539-3573;** snow information at **1-800-228-7943;www.skimonarch.com.**

Rentals

Mt. Shavano Ski and Snowboard Shop— This longtime, reliable shop provides a wide range of rental skis and snowboards. Open daily in winter. Located a few miles west of Poncha Springs at **16101 W. Hwy. 50; 1-800-678-0341; 719-539-3240.**

Seeing and Doing

Fish Hatchery

Mt. Shavano Trout Hatchery and Rearing Unit

Those who enjoy aquariums will love this sizable trout hatchery—where else can you see a million fish at one time? Annually the facility hatches 6 million rainbow, brown, brook and cutthroat trout, kokanee salmon and arctic grayling. After raising the fish to stocking size, they are transferred to other facilities or released in rivers, streams, lakes and reservoirs around the state. Many of these fish end up in southeastern Colorado waterways. That doesn't include, of course, the elusive Colorado fur-bearing trout of the high mountain streams. Open daily 8 A.M.–4:30 P.M. Located half a mile northwest of Salida on Hwy. 291. **7725 County Rd. 154, Salida, CO 81201; 719-539-6877.**

Hot Springs

Cottonwood Hot Springs Inn and Spa

Though it looks as if this offbeat place is perpetually under repair, Cottonwood Hot Springs provides fairly pleasant outdoor soaking opportunities with three large rock-lined pools as well as three-tiered private whirlpool baths. Check out their massage therapy and other treatments. Very basic **lodge rooms and cabins ($ to $$)** available as well. Located along Cottonwood Creek about 5 miles west of Buena Vista. **18999 County Rd. 306, Buena Vista, CO 81211; 719-395-6434; 719-395-2102; www.cottonwood-hot-springs.com.**

Mineral Hot Springs Spa

This terrific, newly opened spa may be worth the 30-mile drive south of Poncha Springs. For information, see the **San Luis Valley** chapter.

Mt. Princeton Hot Springs Resort

Don't miss a soak in one of the two large swimming pools or one of many rock pools down along Chalk Creek. Suits required. Open Sun.–Thurs. 9 A.M.–9 P.M., Fri.–Sat. 9 A.M.–11 P.M. For additional information see the Where to Stay section.

Salida Hot Springs

Hot mineral water is piped from 8 miles away to Salida Hot Springs pool, the largest indoor hot springs pool in Colorado. Built as a WPA project in 1937, this well-maintained facility is worth a stop. Take a swim in the 25-meter lap pool or a hot soak in the 18-inch wading pool or 4-foot-deep shallow pool. Private enclosed hot tubs are available for an additional hourly charge. Summer hours: daily 1–9 P.M. Winter hours: Tues.–Thurs. 4–9 P.M., Fri.–Sun. 1–9 P.M. Located next to the Chamber of Commerce at **Centennial Park, 410 W. Rainbow Blvd., Salida, CO 81201; 719-539-6738.**

Museums and Galleries

Buena Vista Heritage Museum

Located in the old Chaffee County Courthouse, built in 1882, this museum features period clothing displays, a schoolroom and a mining and ranch room with historical artifacts. Railroad buffs will be particularly interested in the scale layout of historic valley sites and the three major narrow-gauge railroads that chugged their way through the Upper Arkansas Valley in the 1880s. Art exhibits offered throughout the summer. Open daily Memorial Day–Labor Day, 9 A.M.–5 P.M. Fee charged. **511 E. Main St., Buena Vista, CO 81211; 719-395-8458.**

Salida Art Galleries

Slowly but surely Salida has emerged as a terrific town for browsing through art galleries. The proliferation of small galleries, shops and studios in historic downtown Salida has helped the town garner national recognition: it was recently near the top of the list in the book *The 100 Best Small Art Towns in America.* Local artwork graces the walls of many local restaurants as well. To get you started, stop by **Cultureclash** at the **corner of F and 1st Sts.,** which features contemporary art and jewelry. Six contemporary regional artists' work can be viewed at the offbeat **ART-tic-u-la-tion, 113 E. Sackett Ave.** At **Mountain Spirit Winery and Gallery, 201 F St.,** sip local, award-winning wine while viewing jewelry, watercolors, pottery and wire sculpture. For more information, contact the Chamber of Commerce: **1-877-772-5432; 719-539-2068; www.salidachamber.org.**

Salida Museum

The Salida Museum is packed with the usual mining, railroad, pioneer and Indian artifacts as well as the unusual. Displayed prominently is a horseskin coat made by an early Salida resident after his favorite horse died: what a tribute! It's worth a visit. Open Memorial Day–Labor Day, 11 A.M.–4 P.M. Small fee charged. Next to the Chamber of Commerce, at **406 W. Rainbow Boulevard.**

Nightlife

Il Vicino

For information about this fantastic microbrewery in Salida, see the Where to Eat section.

Lariat Saloon

Their claim that "We sell and service hangovers" just about says it all. Originally opened in 1885, this rowdy Buena Vista nightspot is a great place to find a cold beer and a bar game, whether it's pool, foosball or shuffleboard. Smoky, packed and popular; occasional live music. **206 E. Main St., Buena Vista; 719-395-9494.**

Salida Steam Plant

Check out the schedule of musical performances and live theater at the Steam Plant. It's a terrific venue for live music and theater. **Sackett and G Sts., Salida; 719-530-0933; www.snobol 4.com/steamplant.**

Victoria Hotel and Tavern

Very popular among Salida locals, the Vic is a great place to unwind and listen to live rock and blues music on weekends. Open daily noon–2 A.M. **143 N. F St., Salida; 719-539-4891.**

Scenic Drives

Clear Creek Canyon Road

A drive up Clear Creek Canyon is highly recommended for its beautiful scenery and history. Beginning in 1867 prospectors made their way up this canyon and surrounding gulches while looking for gold and silver. Known as the La Plata Mining District, many successful mines led to the founding of a number of settlements, including Beaver City, Vicksburg and Winfield, by the 1880s. The largest of these towns was **Winfield,** which had a population of more than 1,500 by 1890. Today quite a few buildings remain at these sites—many are used as summer homes. Winfield Cemetery serves as the final resting place for more than 25 of the early residents, many of whom died from gunfights, avalanches, fire and lightning. The **Winfield School Museum,** open in summer, displays old worn desks and other memorabilia in a historic school building.

Clear Creek Canyon serves as a jumping-off point for trails up many of the 14,000-foot peaks in the area, including Mt. Oxford, Mt.

Belford and Missouri Mountain. To reach the road from Buena Vista, drive about 16 miles north on Hwy. 24 and turn left on County Rd. 390. A few cabins remain at **Vicksburg,** 8 miles up the road. You'll reach Winfield in another 4 miles.

Cottonwood Pass

Before Independence Pass Rd. was built, the route over 12,126-foot Cottonwood Pass served as a vital supply link not only to the mining camps of Tincup and Pitkin in Taylor Park on the west side of the Continental Divide but also to Ashcroft and Aspen via Taylor Pass (see the **Gunnison and Crested Butte** chapter). Built as a toll road in 1880, the road (paved to the summit) climbs through pine forests, aspen groves and eventually into alpine tundra where wildflowers, especially columbine, can be seen flourishing into mid-Aug.

Be sure to stop on the summit for great views in all directions, especially west down to Taylor Park and north to the Three Apostles. There is good camping along the way, with plenty of side roads to explore. Cottonwood Pass Rd. (closed in winter) can be easily driven in a regular car.

To reach the pass from Buena Vista, head west for 28 miles up Cottonwood Creek on County Rd. 306. From the summit continue down the west side 12 miles to Taylor Park Reservoir. At the reservoir return to Buena Vista along the same route or via Gunnison or Tincup (see the Four-Wheel-Drive Trips section) and Cumberland Pass, eventually heading back east over Monarch Pass on Hwy. 285.

Midland Tunnels Road

If you are heading north from Buena Vista, consider taking a scenic alternative to Hwy. 24. This road parallels the Arkansas River on the east side for about 10 miles before rejoining Hwy. 24. From the stoplight in Buena Vista, head east on Main St. for a couple blocks and turn left at the Colorado Transportation Department building. This road takes you north out of town. You'll drive through a series of four rock tunnels, blasted out of the mountainside over 100 years

A yellow-bellied marmot in the high country in early summer. Photo by Dean Winstanley.

ago by the Colorado Midland Railroad. Since the Denver & Rio Grande already had its tracks laid down by the river, the Colorado Midland had no alternative but to blast the tunnels through this narrow section of the valley. A local claims this was the only stretch of railroad track on which one train could be in four tunnels at once. After making your way through the tunnels, be on the lookout for Elephant Rock, which is hard to miss.

St. Elmo

St. Elmo is the typical Old West ghost town. Weathered false-front buildings line the main street, resembling a Western movie set. Originally settled in 1880, St. Elmo served as a supply center and hell-raising Sat.-night town for the mines around the area. The biggest mine, the Mary Murphy, produced millions in gold until closing in 1926. In 1881 the Denver South Park & Pacific Railroad started construction of the Alpine Tunnel just a few miles above town (for information see the Scenic Drives section of the

Gunnison and Crested Butte chapter). By the mid-1880s St. Elmo was home to more than 2,000 residents, but by 1890 its inevitable decline began. A fire in 1890 destroyed the two main blocks in town, including the post office. The postmaster valiantly saved the mail from going up in flames but was harassed for failing to rescue the liquor and cigar supply.

To reach St. Elmo from Nathrop (8 miles south of Buena Vista), head west up Chalk Creek on County Rd. 162. St. Elmo lies about 15 miles up the valley. Along the way you'll notice the white Chalk Cliffs to the right on the south side of Mt. Princeton. A popular legend claims that Spanish conquistadors stashed two bags of gold and silver at the base of the cliffs while being chased by Indians. Many treasure hunters have lost their lives over the years climbing these limestone cliffs looking for the booty. Keep your eyes peeled for the herd of bighorn sheep frequently spotted near the cliffs. The scenery becomes especially striking when the aspen turn colors in fall. In summer, consider a stay in a very rustic **cabin ($)** in St. Elmo. For information, contact the **St. Elmo General Store; 719-395-2117; 719-395-4773; www.st-el mo.com.**

Tramway

Monarch Aerial Tramway

Take a ride up to an observation tower on the Continental Divide for incredible views of the surrounding Colorado mountain ranges. The experience is a bit sedentary but at least your lungs can get a workout at 12,000 feet. Located at the summit of Monarch Pass, the tram runs from May 15 to Oct. 15, daily 9 A.M.–5 P.M. Be sure to peruse the sprawling gift/trinket shop. From Poncha Springs drive west on Hwy. 50 for 16 miles. **719-539-4091.**

Where to Stay

Accommodations

Although the Upper Arkansas area lends itself to the outdoors and camping, a number of lodging opportunities await, including interesting bed and breakfasts. In Salida you may want to check out the **Gazebo Country Inn ($$),** an attractive Victorian home with three spacious guest rooms and backyard hot tub near the downtown area; **507 E. 3rd St., Salida, CO 81201; 1-800-565-7806; www.gazebocountryinn.com.** The **Thomas House ($ to $$)** provides affordable B&B accommodations (six rooms and a hot tub) in Salida as well; **307 E. 1st St., Salida, CO 81201; 1-888-228-1410; 719-539-7104; www.thomashouse.com.** In Buena Vista, consider a night at the **Liar's Lodge ($$ to $$$),** an attractive, newly built log lodge that perches above the Arkansas River, with five rooms, full breakfast and private fishing access; **30000 County Rd. 371, Buena Vista, CO 81211; 1-888-542-7756; 719-395-3444; www.liarslodge.com.** You might want to try the **Meister House Bed & Breakfast ($$$),** a cozy B&B offering six rooms (most with shared baths) in a historic 1880s building; **414 Main St., P.O. Box 1221, Buena Vista, CO 81211; 719-395-9220; www.meisterhouse.com.** In addition, many motels line the main streets in Buena Vista and Salida. The following are what we consider to be the valley standouts.

The Tudor Rose—$$$ to $$$$

With its 37 acres adjacent to public land and comfortable accommodations, the Tudor Rose provides a wonderful bed and breakfast stay. Named for its Tudor-style design, the large inn offers six rooms, most with private baths. Highlights include the Lancaster Room, with its vaulted ceiling and king-size brass bed, and the romantic Henry Tudor Suite, with a private whirlpool bath and four-poster, king-size bed. Guests enjoy the "wolf den" on the main floor while watching videos or listening to music. After a long day of hiking or skiing, slip into the sunken hot tub on the back deck, where you'll find great views of the valley and surrounding mountains. Full breakfast. **6720 Paradise Rd., P.O. Box 89, Salida, CO 81201; 1-800-379-0889; 719-539-2002; www.thetudorrose.com.**

Monarch Mountain Lodge—$$ to $$$

Monarch Mountain Lodge's location just 3 miles down the road from Monarch Ski Area offers quick access to the outdoors and seclusion for those wanting to avoid town. Each of the 98 rooms comes with private bath and TV; if you want to cook your own meals, choose one of the 16 rooms that come with a kitchenette. South-facing balconies look out to the South Arkansas River and the surrounding forest. Additional features include a fitness center with Nautilus machines, racquetball courts, a heated pool and an outdoor whirlpool bath. There's also a restaurant and lounge. Located in Garfield, 13 miles west of Poncha Springs **on W. Hwy. 50, Monarch, CO 81227; 1-800-332-3668; 719-539-2581; www.monarch mountainlodge.com.**

Mt. Princeton Hot Springs Resort— $$ to $$$

Sandwiched between Mt. Princeton and Mt. Antero along Chalk Creek Gulch, this resort has three outstanding features: comfortable accommodations, pretty good dining and, of course, hot springs pools. Early settlers wasted no time in constructing bathhouses by the 1870s. Improvements continued, climaxing with the completion of the imposing Antero Hotel in 1917. This elegant four-story resort, with its large veranda, served as host to the rich and famous until the stock market crash of 1929 prompted a slow decline. A newer lodge has since been built featuring nine rooms and 40 spacious, modern motel units just across the road.

The hot springs are the biggest draw here, including three large outdoor swimming pools, a couple of private indoor hot tubs and numerous rock pools down by the creek. Overnight guests of the lodge have free use of the hot springs; a reasonable fee is charged to others. The restaurant in the main lodge, with its expansive outdoor deck, is popular with locals (see the Where to Eat section). From Buena Vista drive south on Hwy. 24/285 to Nathrop and turn west on County Rd. 162. Proceed 5 miles to the lodge. **15870 County Rd. 162, Nathrop, CO 81236; 719-395-2447; www.mtprince ton.com.**

Vista Court Cabins—$$ to $$$

The cluster of cabins that make up Vista Court allows for privacy at a reasonable price. Each of the eight cabins has a private bath, kitchenette and cable TV. Four of the cabins have two bedrooms. The comfortable lodge with its Southwestern motif features five rooms with private baths and a great railed-in porch for kicking back. Relax in the whirlpool bath on the front lawn while looking off at Mt. Princeton. The owners, Ginger and Grover Horst, have put extensive work into the place and are eager to make your stay enjoyable. A good lodging choice any time of year; great for kids. Located a half-mile west of the traffic light in Buena Vista on Main St. **1004 W. Main St., P.O. Box 3056, Buena Vista, CO 81211; 719-395-6557.**

The Adobe Inn—$$

The Adobe Inn looks a bit out of place in Buena Vista; its distinct Southwestern style is something you'd expect to find in Santa Fe. Paul and Michael Knox remodeled this old building and it barely resembles its former self. A solarium with Mexican tiles, a large adobe fireplace and south-facing windows make for a cozy place to relax and read or chat with other guests. Three guest rooms, each with a private bath, represent the cultures of the Southwest. In an adjacent house, the tastefully furnished wicker and Mediterranean suites provide additional sleeping space for larger groups. Breakfast is served each morning, quite often including eggs with chili, fruit and coffee or Mexican hot chocolate. Located adjacent to the excellent Casa del Sol restaurant (see the Where to Eat section). **303 N. Hwy. 24, P.O. Box 1560, Buena Vista, CO 81211; 719-395-6340; www.bbonline.com/ co/adobe.**

The River Run Inn—$$

When this was built as the Chaffee County Poor Farm in 1892, little did anyone know that one day visitors would flock happily to the River Run Inn's doors (or that it would achieve a listing on the National Register of Historic Places). Inside, seven guest rooms await (three with private baths); a third-floor dorm provides inexpensive accommodations for individuals and groups on a budget. Innkeeper Virginia Nemmers, a former ranch chef, ensures that guests are well fed with a full breakfast and homemade goodies at other times of the day. The River Run Inn sits in the country outside of Salida with fantastic views west to the Sawatch Range. An added feature for anglers—the inn offers private fishing on its stretch of the Arkansas River, with public water on either end. Call for directions. **8495 County Rd. 160, Salida, CO 81201; 1-800-385-6925; 719-539-3818; www.river runinn.com.**

Streamside Bed and Breakfast—$$

Location, location, location—it certainly figures significantly at this quaint B&B located up Chalk Creek Rd. on the way to St. Elmo. Denny and Kathy Claveau offer three comfortable rooms (private baths and queen beds) and streamside lounging as well as a fine breakfast served each morning. Your hosts love the outdoors and are eager to help you choose a perfect day hike or mountain bike ride. Closed during the winter season. **18820 County Rd. 162, Nathrop, CO 81236; 719-395-2553; www.southwestern inns.com/strmside.htm.**

Trout City Inn—$$

Some people take their history very seriously—Juel and Irene Kjeldsen, owners of the Trout City Inn, are two examples. About 10 miles east of Buena Vista, their unique inn sits where the Denver South Park & Pacific Narrow Gauge Railroad had a station, water tank and telegraph office in the 1880s. Today you'll find the reconstructed station and four guest rooms, including two within the train cars that sit out back. Victorian decor and antiques can be found in the depot, where a full breakfast is served each morning by the hosts dressed in period costumes. The Trout City Inn also features a trout

stream and a westerly view to Mt. Princeton, perfectly framed by the valley walls. Great historical information; kids will love it. Open June–mid-Sept. **Box 431, Hwy. 24/285, Buena Vista, CO 81211; 719-395-8433** summer, **719-495-0348** winter.

Camping

Arkansas Headwaters Recreation Area

This recreation area provides excellent camping facilities at five sites along the Arkansas River. Minimum facilities include pit toilets, picnic tables, fire pits. Fees are charged at all sites. Six miles north of Buena Vista, **Railroad Bridge** (14 sites) affords river access. About 5.7 miles south of Buena Vista on Hwy. 285, turn left at Fisherman's Bridge, drive a half-mile, turn right and proceed another 2.5 miles to **Ruby Mountain** (22 sites). This scenic spot down along the Arkansas River offers put-ins for floats down through Browns Canyon. Another 10 miles or so farther south on Hwy. 285, turn left (east) on County Rd. 194 and proceed about 3 miles to **Hecla Junction** (22 sites). This is the main take-out spot for rafters and kayakers coming out of Browns Canyon. About 7 miles downriver from Salida on Hwy. 50 brings you to **Rincon** (5 sites). Near Pine Junction, about 15 miles upriver from Cañon City is **Five Points** (20 sites). For reservations (at least three days in advance): **1-800-678-CAMP; 303-470-1144** in Denver; **www.reserveamerica.com.**

San Isabel National Forest

Reservations can be made at most campgrounds in the forest at **1-877-444-6777** or **www. reserveusa.com.** Fees are charged at all sites.

Driving 7 miles west from Buena Vista along Cottonwood Pass Rd. (County Rd. 306) and then south on County Rd. 344 leads to **Cottonwood Lake Campground** (28 sites), along the shores of beautiful Cottonwood Lake. Another 4 miles west on Cottonwood Pass Rd. leads to **Collegiate Peaks Campground** (56 sites).

From Nathrop (8 miles south of Buena Vista on Hwy. 285), Chalk Creek Rd. (County Rd.

162) heads west to four campgrounds. Driving 7 miles up Chalk Creek Rd. leads to **Mt. Princeton Campground** (17 sites). Another mile up the road is **Chalk Lake Campground** (21 sites). Still another mile up the road is **Cascade Campground** (23 sites). **Iron City Campground** (17 sites) is 15 miles west of Nathrop on County Rd. 162.

Heading west from Poncha Springs on Hwy. 50 toward Monarch Pass will take you to four more campgrounds. Six miles west of Poncha Springs at Maysville, turn right on County Rd. 240 and proceed 4 miles to **Angel of Shavano Campground** (17 sites). Another 6 miles up County Rd. 240 is **North Fork Reservoir Campground** (8 sites). Thirteen miles west of Poncha Springs on Hwy. 50 is **Garfield Campground** (12 sites). Another 2 miles west on Hwy. 50 brings you to **Monarch Park Campground** (38 sites).

O'Haver Lake Campground (30 sites) is located southwest of Poncha Springs. To reach the campground from Poncha Springs, head south on Hwy. 285 for 5 miles and turn right (west) on County Rd. 200 for 2.3 miles and then right on County Rd. 202 for 1.5 miles.

About 20 miles east of Salida on Hwy. 50 and right (southwest) for 3 miles on County Rd. 06 leads to **Coaldale Campground** (11 sites). One mile farther up County Rd. 06 is **Hayden Creek Campground** (11 sites).

If you just want a primitive camp on national forest land, drive up **Clear Creek Canyon Rd.** (County Rd. 390). To reach the road from Buena Vista, head north on Hwy. 24 for about 16 miles and turn left on County Rd. 390 toward Clear Creek Reservoir. Along the road, which continues 12 miles to Winfield, there are plenty of places to camp.

Private Campgrounds

Buena Vista KOA Kampground—Located 2.5 miles southeast of Buena Vista on Hwy. 24, this well-equipped (though a bit arid) RV campground offers, among other things, a large recreation room, hot tub and free movies nightly. Tentsites are also available. **27700 County Rd. 303, Buena Vista, CO 81211; 1-800-562-2672; 719-395-8318.**

Heart of the Rockies RV and Tent Campground—Plenty of RV sites, many with full hookups. Tentsites available. Heated swimming pool, groceries, other activities. Located 5 miles west of Poncha Springs on Hwy. 50. **16105 Hwy. 50, Salida, CO 81201; 1-800-496-2245; 719-539-4051.**

Where to Eat

Antero Grill—$$ to $$$

On a blink-or-you'll-miss-it stretch of Hwy. 285, 16 miles south of Buena Vista, the Antero Grill truly earns the accolades that have been showered upon it by numerous publications and local residents. Serving up "modern American cowboy cuisine," award-winning chef David Woolley draws on Latin, Southwestern and Native American influences, as well as his experience at fine restaurants in Florida and Santa Fe. The New West theme saturates the place, from the cowboy paintings to the denim napkins to the barbwire-shaped swizzle sticks. Fresh ingredients are the rule. Lunch samplings include coffee-barbecue, Navajo fry-bread pizza and country-fried steak with sweet corn mashed potatoes; dinner features aged steaks, the Antero mixed game grill and the standout iron-skillet paella, which defies the conventional logic that you can't get great seafood in the mountains. Indoor seating and a great outdoor patio are within sight of the Arkansas River. Reservations suggested; call ahead for hours. You'll love this place. **14770 Hwy. 285; 719-530-0301.**

Buffalo Bar and Grill—$$ to $$$

From its excellent steaks to the cozy dining room with views to the lofty Sawatch Range, things are done just right at the Buffalo. Owners Larry and Katie Kelly opened this standout steak house after 22 years in Lake Tahoe, where they operated a similar and very successful restaurant. Choose from choice cuts of sirloin, rib eyes or a filet mignon; other entrées include chicken, chops and seafood dishes such as tasty sourdough prawns. Burgers, including buffalo, are available as well. All dinners come with salad or homemade soup, baked potato, vegetables and fresh bread. Save room for the homemade pastries and other dessert items. Bar area; patio seating in summer. Bar opens at 3:30 P.M.; dinner served nightly 5–10 P.M. **710 N. Hwy. 24, Buena Vista; 719-395-6472.**

Casa del Sol—$$ to $$$

Most frequent travelers through Buena Vista eventually discover the outstanding cuisine at Casa del Sol. Since 1974 the Knox family has been offering unusual and select dishes from various areas of Mexico. Everything is made from scratch with prime ingredients, including red chili from the Española Valley of New Mexico and dark chili from Mexico. At a dinner table, tucked away in one of the restaurant's many nooks and crannies, try the rellenos, chicken enchiladas or one of the specialties like chicken mole, pechuga suiza and shrimp quesadillas. Salad and soup come with dinner. If possible, try lunch in the attractive outdoor patio area. Desserts also deserve mention, especially the rum butter nut cake. Limited bar menu. Reservations in summer are a good idea. Lunch served 11:30 A.M.–3 P.M., dinner 4:30–9:30 P.M. Open daily May–Oct. and on weekends in winter. **303 N. Hwy. 24, Buena Vista; 719-395-8810.**

Grimo's—$$ to $$$

A while back, Grimo's opted to remove its rowdy bar area and concentrate on a small, romantic atmosphere for their tasty Italian food. The change works well and the usually packed house attests to that. Hand-hewn wood beams, red tablecloths and a number of other nice touches add greatly to the meal. Start off with a glass of chianti or other choices from the wine list. Veal, chicken and pasta dishes dominate the menu. In addition to baked eggplant parmigiana, Grimo's specialties include pesto dishes, veal and chicken marsala and Steak Sinatra, named in honor of Ol' Blue Eyes. Dinners come with

homemade soup and a tossed salad. Save room for the decadent desserts. Open Tues.–Sat. 4–9 P.M., Sun. 4–8 P.M. At the **junction of Hwys. 285 and 50 in Poncha Springs; 719-539-2903.**

Country Bounty—$ to $$

The consistently full parking lot at Country Bounty is no fluke. Located prominently along Hwy. 50 in Salida, this place serves up enormous portions of down-home cooking. The lengthy menu includes a full spectrum of standout dishes such as traditional breakfast items (like biscuits and gravy), homemade soups, burgers, chicken-fried steak and on and on. Those of you on a diet, consider yourselves warned: Country Bounty is famous for its homemade cobblers and pies, including such specialties as Rocky Road and banana meringue. The service, usually very friendly and efficient, was disappointing on one recent visit. You may want to browse the gift shop that occupies a large portion of the interior floor space. Open daily 6 A.M.–9 P.M. in summer, 7 A.M.–8 P.M. in winter. **413 W. Rainbow Blvd. (Hwy. 50), Salida; 719-539-3546.**

Coyote Cantina—$ to $$

This relaxed, relatively large Mexican restaurant is a welcome addition to the area. The Coyote offers a full range of traditional Mexican dishes, ranging from burritos to rellenos to enchiladas, and they serve them up in huge portions. A variety of sauces from mild to habañero-ish *hot* accompany your meal—it's up to you. Full bar, outside seating (weather permitting). Bring your appetite. Open daily for breakfast, lunch and dinner. Conveniently located **on Hwy. 285 in Johnson Village,** 2 miles south of Buena Vista; **719-395-3755.**

Evergreen Cafe—$ to $$

Take a seat at the counter or find a table at this smallish 1950s-style diner, a longtime favorite in Buena Vista. For breakfast, create your own omelette, try a breakfast crêpe or go for something more traditional. Lunch specialties include "gourmet" burgers, sandwiches, soups and salads; try a slice of their homemade pie. Open daily 6:30 A.M.–2 P.M. in summer, 8 A.M.–2 P.M. in winter. **418 Hwy. 24 N., Buena Vista; 719-395-8984.**

First Street Cafe—$ to $$

A bit off the main drag, the First St. Cafe is worth a stop whether you want a meal or a freshly ground cup of coffee. Located in one of the oldest brick buildings in Salida's historic downtown section, the cafe is decorated with plants and latticed wood paneling. For breakfast try stuffed French toast, a breakfast burrito, an omelette or quiche. Lunch is the most popular meal here for salad bar, sandwiches and stir-fry. Dinners feature steaks, lemon garlic chicken and grilled trout topped with almonds. Great beer selection. Open in summer Mon.–Sat. 8 A.M.–10 P.M., closed Sun.; in winter Mon.–Sat. 8 A.M.–9 P.M., closed Sun. **137 E. 1st St., Salida; 719-539-4759.**

Il Vicino—$ to $$

Every now and then we find a restaurant that really gets us fired up. Il Vicino, in downtown Salida, is such a place. The creative pizzas are fired up as well. Wood-fired, that is. Place an order at the counter for one of these excellent pies, with ingredients running from pepperoni to pesto and pine nuts. Calzones, lasagna, sandwiches and salads round out the menu. But perhaps Il Vicino's greatest claim to fame (depending on your age and point of view) is its selection of truly outstanding ales, including the award-winning Wet Mountain India Pale. All beers are brewed on the premises. Grab a table seat and sample one of the many other ales or their excellent root beer. In case the point was not made—we love this place. Take-out available. Open Sun.–Thurs. 11:30 A.M.–10 P.M.; weekends until 11 P.M. **136 E. 2nd St., Salida; 719-539-5219.**

Bongo Billy's—$

If you find yourself craving a great cup of locally roasted coffee or a latte, head straight to Bongo Billy's. They also offer baked goods for breakfast as well as dessert (try the pies), sandwiches, salads and homemade soups. Indoor seating and outdoor decks available at both locations, though the one in Salida is better. Open Sun.–Wed. 6:30 A.M.–9 P.M., Thurs.–Sat. 6:30 A.M.–11 P.M. **Salida** location on the river at **300 W. Sackett Ave., 719-539-4261; Buena Vista** location at **713 S. Hwy. 24, 719-395-2634.**

Services

Visitor Information

Chaffee County Visitors Bureau—1-800-831-8594; www.vtinet.com/14ernet.

Greater Buena Vista Area Chamber of Commerce Visitors Center—343 S. Hwy. 24, P.O. Box 2021, Buena Vista, CO 81211; 719-395-6612; www.vtinet.com/14ernet.

Heart of the Rockies Chamber of Commerce—406 W. Hwy. 50, Salida, CO 81201; 1-877-772-5432; 719-539-2068; www.salida chamber.org; www.vtinet.com/14ernet.

Wet Mountain Valley

Though the phrase "off the beaten path" gets too much use, it still seems appropriate when describing the Wet Mountain Valley. This beautiful, relatively remote location in the southern part of the state, wedged between the Wet Mountains to the east and the jagged peaks of the Sangre de Cristo Range to the west, remains unknown to many Coloradans. Quite a few people, however, find the valley by accident and end up returning by design. The surrounding San Isabel National Forest gets year-round use by anglers, horseback riders, cross-country skiers and hikers. Steep trails into the Sangre de Cristos on the western side of the valley lead along many streams and to high alpine lakes. Some of the state's most rugged 14,000-foot peaks, including Crestone Needle, await those who want a difficult climbing challenge.

Though cattle ranching and farming are the mainstays, it was the silver boom in the late 1800s that attracted thousands of folks to the valley. Today Silver Cliff, the dominant mining town during the boom days, and nearby Westcliffe, the original rail town in the valley, are the supply centers providing the few services the area has to offer. Rosita and Wetmore provide peaceful hideaways for residents and visitors alike.

Although tourism has made an impact and growth is an issue, many locals cherish the relative lack of development. Many artistic,

individualistic people are attracted here by the beauty and a simple, unadorned lifestyle. One local told us his biggest problem was the noise a herd of elk made while bugling out in his front yard. We should all have such problems.

History

Along with documented facts, many legends animate the early history of the valley. One, concerning a lost gold mine, has turned out to be partially true. Spanish conquistadors, while exploring the region from their territory to the south, discovered a deep cave located high on a mountain in the valley, which they used as a repository. The cave's entrance was reportedly marked with a Maltese cross. In the late 1920s the existence of the cave was officially confirmed. Originally known as La Caverna Del Oro, or Cave of Gold, the name was changed when it yielded nothing of any value, even after a number of speleologists explored the vertical shafts and found evidence of earlier mining. Now it goes by the more mundane name of Marble Cave, thanks to its location high up on Marble Mountain, southwest of Westcliffe.

Getting There

Westcliffe is located 150 miles southwest of Denver. From Denver drive south on Interstate 25 to Colorado Springs and take Hwy. 115 from the south end of town. Drive to Florence and head south on Hwy. 67 and then west on Hwy. 96.

Ute Indians who inhabited the Wet Mountain Valley came into contact with trappers in the first half of the 1800s, but nothing changed much until the 1870s. In 1870 a group of 400 German immigrants arrived in the valley to establish Colfax, an ill-fated agricultural co-op, about 7 miles south of present-day Westcliffe. As it turned out, many of the colonists did not find communal living to their liking. On top of that, the cows reportedly ate garlic, which ruined the cheese!

About the time of Colfax's demise, the silver mining boom hit the valley. In the winter of 1872–1873 Richard Irwin discovered rich silver deposits, and the rush was on to the new camp Rosita. For a short time, Rosita received recognition for being what the *Pueblo Chieftain* called "the liveliest mining town in the territory." Aside from another strike at Querida in 1877, the valley's real glory days began when horn silver was discovered in 1878: these chunks of black, greasy rock from a nearby cliff melted down to 75 percent silver. Thousands of people poured into the area and established the town of Silver Cliff. Many considered it to rival the booming town of Leadville. Silver Cliff was even in the running to be named the state capital.

Hopes soared for the town in 1881 when the Denver & Rio Grande Railroad announced plans to lay tracks from Cañon City up Grape Creek to the area. But, much to the irritation of Silver Cliff residents, the train tracks stopped a mile from town—and as it had done so many other times throughout the state, the Denver & Rio Grande built its own community. Westcliffe became more important than Silver Cliff. When mining activity waned, prosperity in the valley took a sharp downturn and the trains stopped. Ranching and farming then became the dominant industries. When the Denver & Rio Grande Railroad laid tracks to the valley again in 1900, development and prosperity seemed a sure thing. But alas, the railroad continued to lose money and ended service to Westcliffe in 1937, this time for good. Today cattle ranching and hay farming remain important to the area's economy, along with a steadily increasing flow of visitors and those who call the valley home.

Festivals and Events

Jazz in the Sangres

2nd weekend in Aug.   Come to Wet Mountain Valley for a weekend of great jazz performed by some of the best musicians in the Rocky Mountain West, including some nationally known performers. Styles range from fusion to blues to big band. You don't even have to be a jazz lover to have a good time in this spectacular setting. Shows run during the day Sat. and Sun.; performers appear Fri. night at local restaurants and bars. Make sure to book accommodations well in advance, unless you want to camp out in the Westcliffe area. **719-783-9163.**

Wet Mountain Western Days

Labor Day weekend   This festival in Westcliffe celebrates western heritage and lifestyles with music, cowboy poetry, a fiddle contest and historical demonstrations. The weekend includes a parade and the honoring of a Ranch Family of

The dragon breathes real smoke at Bishop Castle in the Wet Mountain Valley. Photo by Bruce Caughey.

the Year. Contact the **Westcliffe Chamber of Commerce: 1-877-793-3170; 719-783-9163; www.custerguide.com.**

Outdoor Activities

Biking

MOUNTAIN BIKING

Wet Mountain Valley offers many places to explore on a mountain bike. On the west side of the valley, jeep roads and national forest trails are everywhere. Unfortunately, there are no decent rental shops, so you've got to strap on your bike. For information inquire locally and refer to the Hiking and Backpacking and Scenic Drives sections.

Fishing

It's not exactly an angler's paradise, but many worthwhile fishing spots can be found in the Wet Mountain Valley area. Streams running down out of the Sangre de Cristos are, for the most part, steep and fast-moving. Most people have luck fishing the beaver ponds along smaller tributaries. For tackle and some advice about where the fish are biting, stop in at the **Sangre de Cristo Fly Shop, 104 Main St., Westcliffe; 719-783-2313.**

Hermit Lake/Horseshoe Lake

See Hermit Pass in the Four-Wheel-Drive Trips section.

Lake Isabel

You can get to heavily stocked Lake Isabel in your car, and some lunker browns in the 15-pound range cruise these waters. A boat ramp is available, but motorized boats are not allowed. Many people try their luck ice fishing here in winter. From Westcliffe, drive east on Hwy. 96 and turn south on Hwy. 165 for 25 miles.

Lakes of the Clouds

To reach three lakes at an 11,200-foot elevation, you'll need a four-wheel-drive vehicle to get within a couple of miles or else you'll be in for a 5-mile hike. Below the lakes are beaver ponds that yield brook and cutthroat trout. The upper lake offers good rainbow and cutthroat fishing; the lower lake has mostly cutthroat. Don't bother with the middle lake because it's too shallow and often has winterkill. To reach the lakes from Westcliffe, head north on Hwy. 69 for about a mile, turn left on County Rd. 171, right on County Rd. 172 and proceed to the Gibson trailhead (about 8 miles).

Middle Taylor Creek

See Hermit Pass in the Four-Wheel-Drive Trips section.

Four-Wheel-Drive Trips

Hermit Pass

From the 13,000-foot summit of this road high in the Sangre de Cristo Range, you'll have beautiful views of the expansive San Luis Valley to the west and Wet Mountain Valley to the east. The road travels up Middle Taylor Creek past beaver dams, Hermit Lake and Horseshoe Lake; all provide decent fishing for brook, rainbow and cutthroat trout. To reach the road from Westcliffe, head west on Hermit Lake Rd. (County Rd. 160) and keep going.

Medano Pass

Once a route used by the Indians and even a few Spanish conquistadors, 9,950-foot Medano Pass Rd. is a spectacular way to cross the Sangre de Cristos. From the summit of the pass, the road drops 6 miles along Medano Creek to **Great Sand Dunes National Monument** (see the Major Attractions section of the **San Luis Valley** chater). When you reach the dunes, it's a 4-mile drive to the visitor center. You may want to let some air out of your tires to help you drive across the sand and then refill at the park's campground. To reach Medano Pass from Westcliffe, drive south on Hwy. 69 for 24 miles and turn right (west) on County Rd. 17. The summit of the pass is 9 miles west of Hwy. 69. Allow at least 2 hours for the trip.

Golf

St. Andrew's Golf Course

Just 3 miles north of Westcliffe, St. Andrew's nine holes sprawl over an agreeable landscape near the base of the Sangres. The gorgeous mountain views are reason enough to play at this almost treeless course, which was patterned after the original Scottish links. Three small willow-lined creeks wind through the entire course. Many are surprised by the quality of the greens—at least since they found the guy who was tromping around in baseball spikes! Inexpensive greens fees; rentals, lessons and driving range. Don't miss the great food in the clubhouse where you can eat inside or on the patio with incredible mountain views. **800 Copper Gulch Rd.; 719-783-9410.**

Hiking and Backpacking

Although Wet Mountain Valley remains undiscovered by many Colorado residents, it's fairly well known among active hikers and backpackers, especially those who like steep, challenging terrain. The Sangre de Cristo Range, which runs along the entire western edge of the valley, matches any mountain range in the state for rugged, high-altitude hikes—Crestone Needle and Crestone, Humboldt and Kit Carson Peaks all top out above 14,000 feet. Among them, only Humboldt is considered a fairly easy climb; the other three have claimed their share of lives over the years. This eastern slope of the Sangre de Cristo Range, and much of the rolling Wet Mountains on the east edge of the valley, lie within San Isabel National Forest. Many well-marked trails crisscross the forests and valleys, but you should take along a good topographic map. For more information, check with the **San Carlos Ranger District Office, 3170 E. Main St., Cañon City, CO 81212; 719-269-8500.**

Comanche/Venable Loop Trail

Although this trail can get crowded in summer, the beauty of the area makes it worth trying. The fairly difficult, 10.5-mile loop begins at Alvarado Campground. Start the hike up the Comanche Trail (No. 1345). You'll climb steeply through the pine and aspen, eventually paralleling Hiltman Creek up to Comanche Lake. The trail then switchbacks up to the crest of the Sangre de Cristo Range, well above treeline. On extended trips many people continue west, down the western slope of the mountains to Crestone Creek. If you're not interested in this option, head north from the crest along the trail, which eventually drops down to Venable Lake and Venable Creek. Be on the lookout for the waterfall along Venable Creek, about 1.5 miles below the lake. Eventually you'll run into Rainbow Trail, a half-mile north of your starting point. There is great camping and pretty good fishing along the entire route. To reach the trailhead from Westcliffe, head south on Hwy. 69 for 3 miles and turn right on Schoolfield Rd. Proceed 7 miles to Alvarado Campground.

Rainbow Trail

This 100-mile-long trail is very popular, with few uphill stretches. For the most part, it traverses the eastern slope of the Sangre de Cristos from Music Pass, about 15 miles southwest of Westcliffe, north by northwest to the Continental Divide near Marshall Pass. Take off for a day hike or a longer trip. There are many places to reach the well-marked trail. One of the easiest accesses from Westcliffe is at Alvarado Campground (see the previous entry for directions). For printed information about the Rainbow Trail, including maps and access points, contact the **San Carlos Ranger District Office** at **719-269-8500.**

Horseback Riding

Bear Basin Ranch

Located on 3,000 acres about 11 miles east of Westcliffe, Bear Basin Ranch offers horseback trips ranging in duration from 2 hours to several days. Trips head into the ranch property, the adjacent San Isabel National Forest and the nearby Sangre de Cristo Range. In addition to horseback trips, owner Gary Ziegler, an accomplished mountaineer, arranges guided climbs of the Crestones. If you want to stay overnight, ask about the rustic **bunkhouse ($)** that sleeps 20. Contact **Bear Basin Ranch, Westcliffe, CO 81252; 719-783-2519; www.gorp.com/ adventure.**

Llama Trekking

Wet Mountain Llamas

This outfit offers reasonably priced llama rental for one day or longer. After a 1-hour orientation, you're ready to pack your "Colorado camel" into the Greenhorn or Sangre de Cristo Mountains. Paul Brown's operation comes highly recommended. **608 County Rd. 295, Wetmore, CO 81253; 719-784-3220.**

Skiing

CROSS-COUNTRY SKIING AND SNOWSHOEING

Cross-country skiing opportunities in the Wet Mountain Valley vicinity abound. Many trails lead up into the Sangre de Cristo Range west of Westcliffe. For information about trail possibilities, contact the **Custer County Chamber of Commerce, 719-783-9163;** the **Sangre de Cristo Mountain Council, 719-783-2487;** or the **San Carlos Ranger District Office, 3170 E. Main St., Cañon City, CO 81212; 719-269-8500.**

Backcountry Trails

Hermit Pass Trail—Many local cross-country skiers wax their skis and head for the 5-mile-long Hermit Pass Rd. A popular jeep route in summer, this road winds its way up Middle Taylor Creek, past Hermit Lake to the summit of the pass, just over 13,000 feet. From the summit, views west into the San Luis Valley and east to Wet Mountain Valley are stunning. To reach the trailhead, head west from Westcliffe on Hermit Lake Rd. (County Rd. 160). Drive to where the plowing stops and begin skiing up the road.
Rainbow Trail—This 100-mile trail provides excellent cross-country skiing with fairly easy

rolling terrain. See the Hiking and Backpacking section.

Seeing and Doing

Cemeteries

Silver Cliff Cemetery

One night in 1882, as four drunken miners were walking by the Silver Cliff Cemetery, they saw blue lights darting around the gravestones. At first no one in town believed the stories of mysterious lights. Eventually many townsfolk also saw them. Over the years locals and visitors alike claim to have seen these lights at the graveyard. The phenomenon even attracted the attention of *National Geographic*. Whether you go to the graveyard at night to look for the ghostly blue lights or roam around during the day to see this Victorian burial site, it's worth a trip. To reach the cemetery from Silver Cliff, head south on the road next to Clever's along Hwy. 96.

Museums and Galleries

Bishop Castle

About 27 miles southeast of Westcliffe, among the thick pine trees of the Wet Mountains, lies one of Colorado's most bizarre attractions. Since 1969 Jim Bishop has been working single-handedly on his colossal stone and iron castle, which so far is a cross between Camelot and the Eiffel Tower. Not many who see it would argue Bishop's claim that the structure, billed as a monument to hardworking people, is the country's biggest one-man physical project. Jim describes it as "building by coincidence rather than design," which makes it more art than architecture. At the moment it consists of three stories of hand-set stone, topped with ornamental iron arches and an assortment of other wrought-iron flourishes. Other features include a 160-foot tower, flying buttresses and a spiral stone staircase to the top. On the front gable is perched a metal dragon whose nose serves as a chimney for a woodstove on the dramatic glass-encased

Having a "feed" at Mission: Wolf. Photo by Dean Winstanley.

third floor, which has hosted weddings and all-night rave parties, according to Bishop. He's the first to admit that the project may never be finished, but he adds, "It ain't important that I get it done; it's important that I'm doing it." Free admission. Visitors are free to explore the castle. To reach Bishop Castle from West-cliffe, drive 16 miles east on Hwy. 96 and turn right onto Hwy. 165. Proceed about 12 miles and look for the signs on the right side of the road. **1529 Claremont Ave., Pueblo, CO 81004; 719-564-4366; www.castlecollect ables.com.**

School House Museum

Enter a re-created 1880s classroom for a glimpse of a typical school day, which used to include a run to the outhouses lined up behind the school. Excellent black-and-white photos trace the history of the area. Open Memorial Day–Labor Day 1–4 P.M. **302 S. 4th St., Westcliffe.**

Silver Cliff Museum

Get a feel for the history of the valley at this small museum. Exhibits are housed in the old

Silver Cliff Town Hall and Fire Station, which operated from 1879 to 1959. The museum is worth a look if you're in the area. Open Memorial Day–Labor Day 1–4 P.M. Located on **Hwy. 96 in Silver Cliff.**

Scenic Drives

Rosita / Junkins Park

For spectacular scenery and a look at historical settlements around Wet Mountain Valley, take time to drive this 40-mile loop. From Westcliffe head east on Hwy. 96 for 16.2 miles and turn right on County Rd. 358, just before the intersection with Hwy. 165. It takes you through Junkins Park with its interesting rock formations and remains of old cabins built by Czechoslovakian settlers. After passing through Junkins Park, you'll drop down a hill to Blumenau, originally settled in the late 1800s by German immigrants. The view of the Sangre de Cristos is fantastic from here. Farther on you'll reach an intersection: County Rd. 347 heads to the right, back to Hwy. 96; County Rd. 328, on the left, leads to the virtual ghost town of Rosita, the original silver mining settlement in the valley. Many old buildings still stand, including the general store and the Wet Mountain Rosita Fire Station. If you continue west from Rosita, you'll drive by Rosita Cemetery on the left. Established in 1870 there are still old tombstones as well as recent ones. From here proceed west to Hwy. 69, turn right and head back to Westcliffe.

Wolves

Mission: Wolf

Though difficult to find, Mission: Wolf rates as a unique attraction. This sanctuary/refuge for wolves sits on 73 forested acres with sweeping views west to the Sangre de Cristos. Kent Weber and Tracy Brooks along with a dedicated staff and volunteers have built large enclosures on the forested land to house approximately 50 pure and crossbred wolves. Most of these animals were raised elsewhere before being taken in as permanent residents. As Kent explains, "Many people who think having a wolf as a pet is a great idea quickly change their minds when they find out the animals can't be domesticated." Visitors are welcome to roam the grounds with a staff member.

The focus of Mission: Wolf is education. Along with a few wolves, Kent and Tracy spend months on the road educating students, teachers and others about the plight of these beautiful, intelligent animals. They stopped by the *Today Show* and have even made an appearance on *Mr. Rogers' Neighborhood*. Arrange a visit by contacting **P.O. Box 211, Silver Cliff, CO 81249; 719-746-2919; www.indra.com/fallline/mw.**

Where to Stay

Accommodations

During the jazz festival and hunting season, most accommodations book well in advance. The rest of the year you shouldn't have any trouble finding a place. For a complete rundown on lodging opportunities, contact the **Custer County Chamber of Commerce, P.O. Box 81, Westcliffe, CO 81252; 719-783-9163;** **www.custerguide.com.** Here are a few good choices:

The Historic Pines Ranch—$$$$

First developed as a guest ranch way back in 1893 by Englishman Reginald Cusack, the Pines enjoys a superb location at the edge of the Sangre de Cristo Range. Catering mainly to families, owners Dean and Casey Rusk provide a number of activities for guests, ranging from horseback rides (including overnight trips) to fishing to square dancing. Modern, well-kept cabins with private baths but no kitchens are the primary accommodations. The ranch is open year-round; in winter, activities shift toward cross-country skiing and sleigh rides. No matter what keeps you busy during the day, unwind in the indoor pool or whirlpool bath. Priority is given to guests who book six-night stays, but shorter early- and late-season visits are encouraged. Mippy's tearoom is a new addition, with fancy traditional tea parties scheduled each week. Excellent family-style meals are offered in the dining hall.

Some may want to reserve time for a secluded cow-camp experience in a separate nearby location. Here you help with the chores, cooking, checking cattle and fences, making repairs and doctoring. With no running water (they haul water in) and no electricity, and lots of time on horseback, you'll gain an understanding of the real West; isolated and beautiful. To reach the ranch from Westcliffe, drive about 1 mile north on Hwy. 69 and then west for about 10 miles on Pines Rd. **P.O. Box 311, Westcliffe, CO 81252; 1-800-446-WHOA; 719-783-9261; www.historicpines.com.**

Main Street Inn Bed and Breakfast—$$$$

Mark and Wanda Johnson have restored this homestead, built in the late 1800s, to its original Victorian charm. From the street you will be drawn to the architectural detail and covered front porch. Inside, beautifully appointed common areas have tasteful and whimsical decor, including a parlor pump organ. You'll find refinished wood floors covered by fine rugs throughout the place. The five comfortable rooms feature a private bathroom and antique furnishings along with a writing table and plush feather bed. The upstairs rooms offer terrific views. Enjoy the resident innkeepers' hospitality and knowledge of the area during a full, yet informal breakfast (served 8:30–10 A.M.). A few things to note: no pets, no smoking, children are discouraged. A minimum two-night stay is required in the summer. **501 Main St., Westcliffe, CO 81252; 1-877-783-4006; 719-783-4000; www.mainstreet bnb.com.**

Courtyard Inn—$$$

Once a plain-vanilla, basic motel, the Courtyard has taken on quite a bit of charm in recent years under its new owners. If you are used to staying in fine inns, however, it doesn't approach that level of luxury. It does feature a pretty, landscaped courtyard with flowers and trees, with benches for quiet reflection. The smallish rooms have folk art touches and feather beds along with the modern conveniences of TV and telephone. Clean and slightly funky, the Courtyard is a good place to pull up for a night or two. On **Main St.** in Westcliffe. **719-783-9616; www.courtyard inn.com.**

Cross D Bar Trout Ranch—$$

See the Camping section.

Alpine Lodge—$ to $$

For a more rustic stay in the Wet Mountain Valley, consider renting one of the cabins at the Alpine Lodge. Located at the base of the Sangre de Cristos, the small cabins have kitchenettes and sleep up to six people. You may want to consider dinner at the excellent lodge restaurant (see the Where to Eat section) for a change of pace. Located 3 miles south of Westcliffe on Hwy. 69, and then 7 miles west on Schoolfield Rd. **6848 County Rd. 140, Westcliffe, CO 81252; 719-783-2660.**

Bear Basin Ranch—$

See the Horseback Riding section.

Camping

San Isabel National Forest

For campground reservations, contact **1-877-444-6777** or **www.reserveusa.com.** All listed campgrounds charge a fee. **Alvarado Campground** (47 sites), in the foothills of the Sangre de Cristo Range, is 10 miles from Westcliffe. From town head about 3 miles south on Hwy. 69 and then west on Schoolfield Rd. **Lake Creek Campground** (11 sites) is 12 miles northwest of Westcliffe on Hwy. 69 and 3 miles west from Hillside.

In the Wet Mountains southeast of Westcliffe are a number of other campgrounds. From Westcliffe drive east on Hwy. 96 and turn south on Hwy. 165 for 18 miles to **Ophir Campground** (31 sites). A couple of miles farther south on Hwy. 165 takes you to **Davenport Campground** (15 sites). Five miles south from Davenport is the **Lake Isabel Recreation Area.** Campgrounds include **Southside Campground** (8 sites), **St. Charles Campground** (15 sites) and **La Vista Campground** (16 sites). **Ponderosa Campground** and **Spruce Campground** have electric outlets and can accommodate large groups up to 120.

Private Campground

Cross D Bar Trout Ranch and Campground—Twenty primitive tentsites and 26 RV sites with hookups are available. Recently added is a three-bedroom, two-bath ranch house, cabins and a "deluxe" Sioux tepee. **2299 County Rd. 328, Westcliffe, CO 81252; 1-800-453-4379; 719-783-2007; www.cross-d-bar-troutranch.com.**

Where to Eat

Oak Creek Grade
General Store/Steakhouse—$$$

Accidentally stumbling onto this place was the best part of a recent trip to the area. Jack Slater and his wife Audrey run an inviting business in an improbable location on a gorgeous stretch of lonely road halfway between Westcliffe and Cañon City. Jack built a hand-hewn log building and attempted to run it as a general store, but it didn't work out. Despite everyone's advice to the contrary and without even changing the General Store sign, Jack tried something different, and the word got out. Now, thanks to warm hospitality, great food and western entertainment, they tend to sell out, especially in summer. You can be assured of a good time, but plan to come here on their terms: Fri. and Sat. nights only, reservations required, no booze served, choice of flame-broiled steak or baked chicken. Kids love this place, too. You will enjoy a terrific western music show (sometimes with the national yodeling champions) and an engaging personal touch. **719-783-2245; www.custerguide.com/ generalstore.**

Alpine Lodge—$$ to $$$

Located among the pines, 10 miles southwest of Westcliffe, the lodge offers good dining in an attractive, rustic atmosphere. Sit by the stone fireplace and look out at the Wet Mountain Valley while enjoying one of the steak or seafood entrées. The Alpine Lodge has nightly specials, including prime rib, all-you-can-eat barbecue and chicken and sirloin marinated in a honey bourbon sauce. A salad bar, sandwiches and homemade soups round out the lighter side of the menu. If you're not counting calories, try a slice of the excellent homemade pie or cheesecake. Open Thurs.–Sun. 5:30–8:30 P.M. Hours have been known to vary, so call ahead. **6848 County Rd. 140, Westcliffe, CO 81252; 719-783-2660.**

Shining Mountains Food and Gifts—$ to $$

This pleasant Southwestern-style cafe is the place to go in Westcliffe for healthful dishes made with fresh ingredients. Owners Margaret and Sheila Davis offer homemade pastries and pies, deli sandwiches, veggie dishes and good Mexican food. The homemade green chili and the Mexican pita are definitely worth a try. When weather permits, the patio is a nice place for a meal or a cold beer. In summer the Southwestern gift shop offers a selection of jewelry, pottery and rugs, among other things. Open summer, Mon.–Sat. 10:30 A.M.–3 P.M., Sun. 11 A.M.–3 P.M.; winter hours vary. **212 Main St., Westcliffe; 719-783-9143.**

Yoder's High Country Inn—$ to $$

If home-style food, fresh-baked pies and specials every night of the week sound good to you, then head to Silver Cliff and join the locals who frequent Yoder's. This has quickly become the place where valley residents head for value and friendly service, but not for a cold beer (alcohol not served). The simple restaurant and family recipes remind you of being a guest in someone's country kitchen. Try the outstanding smoked ribs, pot roast or baked chicken. For a lighter lunch try the salads or a gyros sandwich. Open Mon.–Sat. 11 A.M.–8:30 P.M., until 8 P.M. in winter. Located a block off Main St. at **700 Ohio St., Silver Cliff; 719-783-2656.**

Karen's Gourmet Coffee Cafe—$

Pick from a variety of coffee specials to go or stay for breakfast or lunch. Specials include the popular Reuben sandwich, fresh salads and homemade soups. Don't leave without trying the frozen custard. Open Mon.–Sat. 7:30 A.M.– 4 P.M., Sun. 11 A.M.–3:30 P.M. **104 Main St., Westcliffe; 719-783-2313.**

Services

Visitor Information
Custer County Chamber of Commerce— Located at **3rd and Main St., P.O. Box 81, Westcliffe, CO 81252; 719-783-9163; www. custerguide.com.**

Wet Mountain Tribune—Stop by the newspaper office for area information and a copy of the paper that has been published every Thurs. since 1883. Open daily. **400 Main St., Westcliffe, CO 81252; 719-783-2361.**

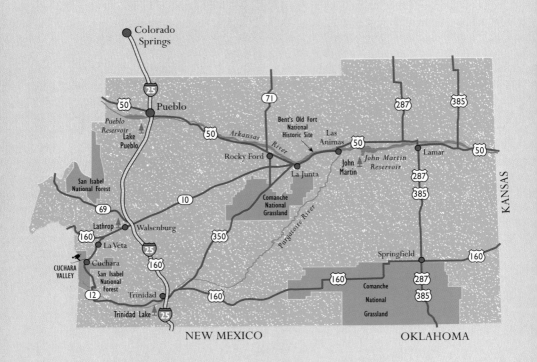

Colorado
Springs

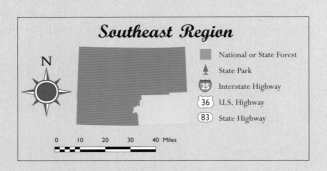

Southeast Region

N

0   10   20   30   40 Miles

	National or State Forest
25	State Park
25	Interstate Highway
36	U.S. Highway
83	State Highway

Southeast Region

Relaxing by the campfire. Photo by Dean Winstanley.

Cuchara Valley

It's surprising that most Coloradans are unfamiliar with this little valley in the southern part of the state. Vacationers, primarily from Texas, Oklahoma and Kansas, have been coming to the Cuchara Valley since the early 1900s, discovering early on what many natives continue to overlook. Nestled between the eastern slope of the southern Sangre de Cristo Range and the looming Spanish Peaks, the Cuchara Valley offers plenty of outdoor beauty along with an interesting history and a mix of Hispanic and Anglo cultures. Originally part of a Spanish land grant, the valley retains a Hispanic feel. In addition, working ranches give Cuchara a western flair. Texas longhorn cattle graze in some of the pastures along the road.

The expansive San Isabel National Forest runs through the central part of the valley, stretching west to east from the top of the Sangre de Cristo Range to the twin Spanish Peaks. These twins dominate the surrounding landscape, towering 7,000 feet above the nearby prairie. The national forest offers a number of outdoor activities, most notably hiking, mountain biking and cross-country skiing. It's also worth jumping in the car for a day on the Highway of Legends Scenic and Historic Byway.

At the northern entrance to the valley, the small town of La Veta serves as sentinel. In addition

to local ranchers, an eclectic though friendly citizenry is largely made up of seniors, alternative lifestyle advocates, artists and expatriate southerners. If you're a golfer, a round at the Grandote Golf Club may cause you to stay longer than you expected. And the diminutive Cuchara Ski Valley, when Mother Nature provides enough snow, also awaits. As an alternative vacation destination, Cuchara Valley lures you with its peace, quiet and stunning scenery.

History

Right from the beginning the Spanish Peaks have been inexorably tied to the history of southern Colorado and the Cuchara Valley. Called *Huajatolla* ("breasts of the earth") by the Plains Indians, these two mammillary peaks were a source of significant religious wonder and, perhaps, mineral wealth. Gold on Aztec shrines in present-day Mexico was said to have come from "a double mountain far to the north." Despite reported sightings of ancient mines on the mountains, no significant mineral strikes have ever been recorded at the Spanish Peaks.

The Mountain Branch of the Santa Fe Trail, which brought settlers across the prairie in the first half of the 1800s, relied heavily on the Spanish Peaks as a landmark. In 1862 the first

Getting There

From Denver, the Cuchara Valley and the town of La Veta can be reached by driving 160 miles south on Interstate 25 to Walsenburg and then turning west on Hwy. 160. Drive about 11 miles and turn left (south) onto Hwy. 12. The town of La Veta is 4 miles down the road at the base of Cuchara Valley.

settlement in the Cuchara Valley sprang up at the present site of La Veta. Col. John M. Francisco, with the help of Henry Daigre and Hiram W. Vasquez, built a fort that took on the name Fort Francisco and later Francisco Plaza. Francisco and his associates started a large sheep and cattle ranch, thereby enticing many sheep ranchers into the area during the next few years. But like the case of many settlements in this part of the country, the real boost came in 1876 when the Denver & Rio Grande Railroad came to town on its way west. Farming and coal mining became the prominent industries for quite a while, but they eventually bowed to the rise of tourism.

Outdoor Activities

Biking

MOUNTAIN BIKING

Over the past few years, mountain biking activity on country roads and Forest Service trails around the La Veta area has proliferated. Opportunities range from challenging single-track trails to loop trips to the Spanish Peaks. Information on National Forest lands can be obtained from the **San Carlos Ranger District Office, 3170 E. Main St., Cañon City, CO 81212; 719-269-8500; www.fs.fed. us/r2/psicc/sanc.**

Fishing

Lathrop State Park

See the Parks section.

Golf

Grandote Golf Club

Named for the Tarahumare Indian prophet who led his people to the Spanish Peaks from the south, this fine 18-hole course commands an excellent view of the nearby Spanish Peaks. Grandote is noteworthy for its combination of reasonable greens fees and high rating. Water hazards, including the Cucharas River and two

lakes, come into play on 10 of the holes. The front 9 is still open, but the back 9, with plentiful aspen and pine, looks much more mature than it really is. Check out the great weekend package rates. Open May 1 to mid-Oct. Cart and club rentals available; full pro shop. **5540 Hwy. 12, P.O. Box 506, La Veta, CO 81055; 1-800-457-9986; 719-742-3123; www.san-gres.com/grandote.htm.**

Walsenburg Golf Club

See Lathrop State Park in the Parks section.

Hiking and Backpacking

The southernmost parcel of San Isabel National Forest encompasses the Spanish Peaks, Upper Cuchara Valley and the mountains immediately to the west, providing relatively undisturbed hiking and backpacking possibilities. The Spanish Peaks Wilderness Study Area protects the two famous mountains that have long helped explorers, pioneers and hikers find their way. Information on the national forest lands can be obtained from the **San Carlos Ranger District Office, 3170 E. Main St., Cañon City, CO 81212; 719-269-8500; www.fs.fed.us/r2/ psicc/sanc.** For a unique backcountry experience, you can go off trail with Bob Kennemer and his professional guides at **Wahatoya Base Camp,** who lead clients on hiking, backpack, snowshoe and cross-country ski outings to pristine places in the La Veta area. Reservations required two weeks in advance. **P.O. Box 589, La Veta, CO 81055; 719-742-5597.**

North Fork Trail

Beginning near Trinchera Peak and angling southeast, this 4.5-mile hike ranges in altitude from 9,800 to 10,800 feet. The trail begins along the four-wheel-drive road to Trinchera Peak near Bear Lake Campground (see the Camping section) and ends at Purgatory Campground.

Peaks/Wahatoya Trail

This highly recommended 10-mile hike takes you along the southern edge of the Spanish Peaks and then north through the saddle

Grandote Golf Club with 13,626-foot West Spanish Peak in the background. Photo by Wendy Newman.

between the two peaks. Be on the lookout for deer and wild turkeys that thrive in this area. Reach the trailhead by taking the Cordova Pass Rd. (see the Scenic Drives section). After crossing over the pass, continue down to the Apishapa Creek Picnic Ground. Look for the trailhead on the left (north) side of the road. It's marked as Apishapa Trail (No. 1324).

West Peak Trail

Starting at about 11,000 feet, this trail is fairly easy up to treeline, then it's a steep rock scramble to the 13,626-foot summit of West Spanish Peak. Be sure to watch for thunderstorms. To reach the trailhead (No. 1390), drive to the top of Cordova Pass (see the Scenic Drives section) and look on the left (north) for the 2.5-mile trail.

Horseback Riding

Dark Horse Outfitters

Trail rides with this small operation, run by Leslie Hicks out of her self-proclaimed Rancho-Not-So-Grande, are highly recommended. Overnight horseback trips also available.

P.O. Box 393, La Veta, CO 81055; 719-742-3652.

Parks

Lathrop State Park

If the summer heat is getting to you, head over to Lathrop State Park. Two lakes, Martin and Horseshoe, attract many area locals for swimming, boating and excellent lake fishing. Both reservoirs are stocked regularly and offer fishing for rainbow trout, wipers, channel catfish, bass, walleye and the legendary (and predatory) tiger muskie. Plenty of "tall" fishing stories are told about these enormous monsters, including tales of muskies chasing boats and swallowing unsuspecting ducks.

Terrain at Lathrop is covered in juniper and piñon pine, with one of the best views to the Spanish Peaks in the area. Ninety-six camping sites (fee charged) are available with full hookups, laundry facilities and showers. For reservations: **1-800-678-CAMP** or **www.reserve america.com.** One of the park's recent additions is the 5-kilometer hard-surface trail that encircles Martin Reservoir.

Lathrop State Park also features a nine-hole golf course, open much of the year. The **Walsenburg Golf Club, 719-738-2730,** overlooks Martin Reservoir and has a clubhouse restaurant, plus cart and club rentals. Lathrop State Park is located about 3 miles west of Walsenberg on Hwy. 160 at **70 County Rd. 502, Walsenburg, CO 81089; 719-738-2376; www.coloradoparks.org.**

Skiing

CROSS-COUNTRY SKIING AND SNOWSHOEING

For those who like to go out on their own, the San Isabel National Forest hiking trails make for good cross-country skiing in the winter. You might try skiing up the **Cordova Pass Rd.** (see the Scenic Drives section), accessed from the summit of Cucharas Pass. Another standout trail in winter is the **Old La Veta Pass Rd.,** originally a narrow-gauge railroad route built in the 1870s. A 3-mile ski up to the summit leads to a number of old buildings, including the depot listed on the National Register of Historic Places. A small fee is charged for access to surrounding private land. To reach the trail (road) from La Veta, take County Rd. 450 northwest for about 3 miles to Hwy. 160 and turn left (west). After 4 miles turn left onto Old La Veta Pass Rd. (County Rd. 443).

For guided tours, check with **Wahatoya Base Camp, 719-742-5597.** Cross-country and downhill ski rentals are also available at **Seasons Sports** in the village of **Cuchara; 719-742-3102.**

DOWNHILL SKIING AND SNOWBOARDING
Cuchara Ski Valley

Although it has experienced financial woes and marginal snows in the past, Cuchara Ski Valley offers an affordable opportunity to ski and take in the spectacular slopeside views of the Spanish Peaks. It's not in the league with powerhouses like Steamboat and Vail, but the area does have its own appeal: small crowds, relatively inexpen-

sive lift tickets and lodging, a general low-key family atmosphere and, of course, the views. Skiers can take advantage of 1,600 vertical feet and four lifts serving mainly beginner and intermediate terrain. A couple of expert runs are thrown in for good measure, including the Burn, a high (though small) bowl. The area caters largely to southerners, spawning such ski trail names as El Tejano (Spanish for "the Texan") and San Antonio. Although Cuchara averages about 250 inches of snow annually, wind is a factor; it can whip the snow off a trail right down to the rock. Night skiing, ski rentals and lessons are available.

The base of the mountain offers shops and a **restaurant ($$ to $$$).** A large condominium complex (open year-round) adjacent to the base area offers the only lodging at the mountain. About 2 miles north of the ski area along Hwy. 12 in the village of Cuchara, the **Cuchara Inn (719-742-3685)** offers quality hotel accommodations. The Cuchara Ski Valley is 12 miles south of La Veta on Hwy. 12. **946 Paradero Ave., Cuchara, CO 81055; 1-800-227-4436; 719-742-3163; www.cuchara.com.**

Seeing and Doing

Museums

Fort Francisco Museum

For such a small town, La Veta has put together an impressive museum that looks back nearly 130 years to the days of the first pioneers. The museum occupies the site of the Francisco Plaza, built in 1862 by the original La Veta settler, Col. John M. Francisco. Some of the original fort structures contain museum displays. The two main buildings have theme rooms focusing on clothing, pioneer ranching, Indian artifacts and furniture. Each room is packed full of an eclectic assortment of items, most of them donated locally. Read through letters written by settlers to the territorial governor in 1873 appealing for protection against the Indians. One letter was written in 1853 to a local attorney from a fellow attorney in Springfield, Illinois—Abraham Lincoln. Allow plenty of time to examine the large collection. Also inspect the blacksmith shop, saloon, post office and schoolhouse that were moved to the grounds from within the area. Admission fee is minimal. Open daily from Memorial Day to Labor Day 9 A.M.–5 P.M. Located in the center of La Veta just off Hwy. 12 (west side).

Nightlife

La Veta Sports Pub and Grub

If you're looking for a local hangout, this is it. Stop in for a beer and a burger and maybe watch a game on the tube; or drop a quarter in the CD jukebox and try some country swing on the small, makeshift dance area. Barbecued ribs available Sat. nights. Open seven days a week, year-round: Sun.–Thurs. 11 A.M.–midnight, Fri.–Sat. 11 A.M.–2 A.M. Near the golf course in La Veta; **923 S. Oak; 1-888-453-3093; 719-742-3093.**

The Yurt

For a much more rustic and positively unique place to shoot some pool and knock back a couple of beers, track down this yurtlike structure. Each fallen aspen log has been cut and hand-sanded. In complete contrast to The Yurt's impressive handiwork, the glow-in-the-dark pool table is the center of most activity. Mind your manners, because Sid (the owner) has two rules, "No pissing and no fighting." That applies to the dogs that roam in and out, too. Live music on the weekends.

Scenic Drives

Cordova Pass

This road, built in 1934, can get rutted out and very bumpy, but it is one of the most beautiful in the area. Traveling just south of the Spanish Peaks, Cordova Pass winds a serpentine course to its summit at 11,000 feet and then 32 miles down to the town of Aguilar near Interstate 25.

After reaching the summit of Cordova Pass Rd. you drive through a tunnel blasted through one of the rock dikes radiating from the Spanish Peaks. Along the way, aspen groves and spectacular, unobstructed views of the adjacent Spanish Peaks vie for your attention. Just up the road a few miles is a well-marked trailhead for a fantastic quarter-mile wildflower identification trail, best seen in July and Aug. A brochure that will help you identify the flowers is available at the Forest Service office in La Veta.

Cordova Pass was originally known as Apishapa Pass. *Apishapa* means "stinky water" in Apache, possibly named after the nearby river, which takes on a strong smell during the dry part of the year.

To reach the pass, drive south from La Veta on Hwy. 12 to Cucharas Pass. Just at the summit, turn left onto Cordova Pass Rd. (Forest Rd. 415). In addition to a picnic area, you'll find a number of good hiking trails along the road (see the Hiking and Backpacking section for some ideas).

Highway 12 South from La Veta

Along this highly scenic route (known as the Highway of Legends), enjoy green pastures with grazing longhorn cattle, aspen and evergreen stands and far-reaching views to the Spanish Peaks and their incredible geology. The two mountains are lava formations that popped up millions of years ago, causing cracks in the sedimentary layers on the surface. Lava flowed into these cracks, causing igneous intrusions. These intrusions, much more resistant to erosion than the surrounding sedimentary layers, remain now as lava dikes, radiating from the two peaks like bicycle spokes from the hub of a wheel. An amazing sight, many of them can be seen from Hwy. 12. Some of these dikes run unbroken as long as 13 miles, rising as high as 100 feet. Some of the better-known dikes along the highway include Devil's Stairstep, the Gap and Profile Rock (the profiles of George and Martha Washington and an Indian).

About 15 miles south of La Veta, the highway reaches the summit of **Cucharas Pass.** From here you can turn left up Cordova Pass (see previous entry) or continue down south, eventually reaching Trinidad (see the Scenic Drives section in the **Trinidad** chapter).

Where to Stay

Accommodations

In addition to the charming accommodations listed below, the town of Walsenburg, at the junction of Hwy. 160 and Interstate 25, offers numerous inexpensive motel rooms. Skiers and summer visitors may want to consider renting a condominium at the ski area (see the Downhill Skiing and Snowboarding section).

Inn at the Spanish Peaks—
$$$ to $$$$

Wooden beams traverse the never-ending ceilings of this Santa Fe-style inn. More of a luxurious B&B than an anonymous inn, this place will comfort you with the see-through fireplace, entertain you with the full private library and entice you with the incredible views of the surrounding Spanish Peaks. Although all three of the suites are decked out with a private balcony, try the Colorado Room. It captures the essence of the area with a hewn-log queen-size bed, split-rail balcony and photographs of colorful Colorado. Full Southwestern-style breakfast served each morning. **310 E. Francisco St., La Veta, CO 81055; 719-742-5313; www.inn atthespanishpeaks.com.**

River's Edge Bed and Breakfast—
$$$ to $$$$

Michael Moore, owner and chef, wants you to "Let time flow by on the banks of the Cucharas River." Just a minute's walk from the small town of Cuchara, this luxurious home offers four rooms and one suite, all decorated in a mountain motif. Enjoy the gourmet breakfast and relax outside while listening to the river babble by. At night you can gaze through the telescope at stars and galaxies you've only dreamed of, or

retreat to your private room for a hard-earned night's sleep in a wonderfully soft bed. **90 E. Cuchara Ave., Cuchara, CO 81055; 719-742-5169.**

Yellow Pine Ranch—$$$

Yellow Pine Ranch guest cabins are nestled between Cuchara and La Veta and easy to miss—but don't. If you're looking for privacy and serenity, relax in one of the nine semirustic cabins scattered among the pine and aspen forests. Handmade curtains and cozy quilts make each cabin unique. Take advantage of the horse livery that operates on the ranch by riding in the neighboring San Isabel National Forest. Or try your fishing luck at the stocked pond. There's also a hayride that will whisk you off after dinner. And later on, you can prop your feet up and toast a marshmallow by the group campfire. Baby-sitting available, too. **15880 Hwy. 12, Cuchara, CO 81055; 719-742-3548.**

Camping

Lathrop State Park

See the Parks section.

San Isabel National Forest

Four San Isabel National Forest campgrounds can be reached from Hwy. 12, starting just 2 miles south of the Cuchara Ski Valley turnoff. Turn right onto Forest Rd. 413, which follows Cucharas Creek up to Bear Lake and Blue Lake, nestled at 10,500 feet on the eastern flank of the Sangre de Cristo Range. The first campground is **Cuchara Campground** (31 sites, fee). Farther up Forest Rd. 413 are **Bear Lake Campground** (14 sites) and **Blue Lake Campground** (15 sites); fees charged at both. There are good views from these campgrounds southwest to 13,500-foot Trinchera Peak. Back on Hwy. 12, continue south over Cucharas Pass down to North Lake and turn right (west) onto Forest Rd. 411. Follow this road about 4 miles to **Purgatory Campground** (23 sites, no water, no fee).

The Fort Francisco Museum in La Veta. Photo by Wendy Newman.

Private Campground

Circle the Wagons RV Park—Located in La Veta, this place has all the amenities. Circle the Wagons is well known in summer for its nightly square dances and cowboy poetry. In addition, small **cabins ($$)** are available. Open year-round. **124 N. Main St., P.O. Box 122, La Veta, CO 81055; 719-742-3233.**

Where to Eat

Timbers Restaurant—$$ to $$$

In marked contrast to a number of cafes and restaurants in the area, the Timbers' upscale dining is geared for well-heeled resort visitors and locals. The cozy atmosphere of this attractive restaurant includes a stone fireplace and high ceiling with hewn-log beams. On a stage at one end of the room sits a guy at a grand piano playing a never-ending medley of show and pop tunes. Timbers serves dinner only, and you will not leave hungry. Entrées include steaks, chicken, pasta and fish such as trout amandine. The fajitas are absolutely great. Full bar. Open 5–10 P.M. daily in summer; limited days in winter. Call ahead. In the village of **Cuchara; 719-742-3838.**

Alys' Fireside Cafe—$ to $$$

Finally there's a terrific place to eat in Walsenburg—and surprisingly it's affordable gourmet fare. Owner and chef Alys Romer left a fast-paced career as a chef and food industry professional, favoring the pace of small-town Colorado. Step off Main St. and into this warm, remodeled restaurant and see firsthand why this place is getting such raves. Lunches boast Dagwood and pesto/roasted pepper sandwiches with homemade breads, the buffalo mozzarella salad and freshly prepared soups. Try the rack of lamb, prime rib or the featured vegetable and pasta dish for dinner. Although the dinner menu changes frequently, you can count on everything being fresh and plentiful. Desserts rate an A+, especially the terrific carrot cake. Open for lunch Mon.–Sat. 11:30 A.M.–2:30 P.M.; dinner Thurs.–Sat. 6–9 P.M.; closed Sun. **606 Main St., Walsenburg, CO 81089; 719-738-3993.**

La Veta Sports Pub and Grub—$ to $$

See the Nightlife section.

Ryus Avenue Bakery—$

The Ryus Avenue Bakery is a bright spot if you hit La Veta hungry. Even if you aren't hungry, one whiff of the baking bread will change your mind. Fresh breads, rolls, pastries and sandwiches are the featured treats at this small shop, as is the excellent coffee and espresso. Be sure to try a slice of homemade pie or perhaps a whole pie for the road. Only open Tues., Thurs. and Sat. 8 A.M.–1:30 P.M. **129 W. Ryus Ave., La Veta; 719-742-3830; 719-742-3926.**

Services

Visitor Information

Huerfano County Chamber of Commerce—400 Main St., Walsenburg, CO 81089; 719-738-1065.

La Veta/Cuchara Chamber of Commerce Visitors Center—131 E. Ryus Ave., P.O. Box 32, La Veta, CO 81055; 719-742-3676; www.ruralwideweb.com/lvcc.htm.

Pueblo

Pueblo, situated along the Arkansas River at the east edge of the Rockies, has come a long way toward shedding its image as a shabby steel-mill town. A number of attractions draw visitors, including more than a million people who annually enjoy Pueblo Reservoir (Lake Pueblo State Park). The reservoir serves as a recreational anchor to the town (see the Major Attractions section). The town's burgeoning Union Avenue Historic District has started to come into its own with antiques shops, galleries and restaurants, some with outdoor cafe seating.

In many ways, Pueblo is a city in waiting, hoping that a $50 million bet on an ambitious riverwalk project will revitalize the community. The city promises a series of retail shops and entertainment venues, and though the project is far from complete, it serves as a symbol for a city pushing hard to redefine itself.

It's still debatable how much of your precious vacation time you may want to spend in Pueblo. But by exiting Interstate 25, you will appreciate how Pueblo's restored Victorian neighborhoods and parks make for an attractive town. At least drive by the immense Rosemount Victorian House Museum, or better yet, stop in for a tour. And for about three weeks each Aug., Pueblo packs them in for the Colorado State Fair.

Pueblo's people leave a lasting impression on any first-time visitor. Community pride, a

natural openness toward visitors and traditional hardworking ethics surface in everything from community projects to friendly conversations in local pubs. A diversity of ethnic groups, particularly Hispanics, populate the town, which is also home to the University of Southern Colorado. Up until the end of the Mexican War in the 1840s, the Arkansas River, which runs through the middle of town, served as the U.S.–Mexico border.

History

Over the years, Pueblo has been a natural crossroads for Indians, Spanish troops, traders/trappers and gold seekers, due to its prime Front Range location on the Arkansas River. Ute Indians long used the area as a camp when they traveled up the Arkansas Valley into the mountains. The first recorded visit to the Pueblo site was by Juan de Ulibarri, a Spaniard who came up from Santa Fe in 1706 looking for escaped Indian slaves.

In 1806 Lt. Zebulon Pike led an expedition into Colorado from St. Louis to "ascertain direction, extent, and navigation of the Arkansas and

---

Getting There

Pueblo is located 110 miles south of Denver on Interstate 25. The town is serviced by **Greyhound Bus Lines, 1-800-231-2222.** Some small commuter lines fly into Pueblo Memorial Airport. **Airporter Inc., 719-578-5232,** provides ground shuttle service between the Denver, Colorado Springs and Pueblo airports.

Red Rivers." As the result of some pretty bad information, Zeb wasn't too successful in finding the Red River (due to the minor fact that it's located in Texas, a few hundred miles to the south). But he did manage to find the Arkansas River and follow it west to the present site of Pueblo. Here he erected a log outpost, said to be the first structure built by settlers in Colorado. From here he set out on an unsuccessful attempt to scale the mountain that bears his name.

In 1822 fur trader Jacob Fowler and his party built a house on the Mexican side (south) of the Arkansas River. Twenty years later Jim Beckwourth, mountain man and "White Chief" of the Crow Indians, helped establish Fort Pueblo as a trading center for mountain men and Indians. The crude fort was relatively peaceful until the Christmas massacre of 1854, when 100 Utes and a few Apaches led by Tierra Blanca were allowed in by a settler drunk on "Taos Lightning." The Indians nearly wiped out the entire settlement, sparing only a young Mexican woman, two children and a man named Romaldo. According to an account described in *The WPA Guide to 1930s Colorado,* Romaldo, plagued with a bullet hole through his tongue, told the story using Indian sign language.

Fort Pueblo remained largely uninhabited for the next few years. According to Lt. E. G. Beckwith, who passed by Fort Pueblo in 1855, mountain men avoided the site entirely, "because it was believed to be haunted by headless Mexican women." Others were concerned about the slightly more substantial threat of additional Indian attacks.

Lured by large gold strikes, prospectors began to enter the area in the late 1850s, establishing Fountain City near Pueblo. In 1860 Pueblo City absorbed Fountain City; it really picked up when the Denver & Rio Grande Railroad rolled into town in 1872. The railroad connection to the gold and silver mines in the mountains, along with access to nearby coal deposits at Trinidad and Walsenburg, made Pueblo the perfect workshop for the mines. Between 1870 and 1880 Pueblo's population grew by leaps and bounds, increasing eightfold to 24,588.

The Colorado Coal & Iron Company, later the Colorado Fuel & Iron Company (CF&I), opened its first blast furnace in 1881. Other companies opened smelters in 1882 and 1888. European immigrants, Mexicans and African Americans responded to a need for workers by making Pueblo their home, thus giving the town a melting-pot image.

Early explorers had conflicting ideas about the agricultural potential of the Pueblo area. Ulibarri, the early visitor from Santa Fe, praised the valley for its beauty and fertility. But Maj. Stephen Long, whose expedition in 1820 brought him through the Pueblo area, had another opinion. He referred to the surrounding land as "dreary and disgusting, almost wholly unfit for cultivation." Ulibarri was closer to the mark, because in the late 1800s farmers moved into the valley in droves. With the help of irrigation, the land east of Pueblo soon became an agricultural center. Ranching got a big boost from Charles Goodnight, a pioneer of the range cattle industry who blazed 2,000 miles of cattle trails from Texas to Wyoming and headquartered his operation near Pueblo. Today Lake Pueblo State Park and the city zoo are located on parts of his ranch.

By 1902 CF&I steelworks was the biggest employer in town, and it continued to be for decades. As recently as the 1940s Pueblo was the second-largest town in Colorado. In 1982, due to an industry downturn, CF&I was forced to lay off 4,000 workers. It was a devastating blow to the Pueblo economy. But in some ways it was a blessing in disguise. By shutting down the smokestacks, shedding its steel-town image and aggressively marketing itself, Pueblo has been successful in attracting new, cleaner industries.

Major Attractions

Lake Pueblo State Park
Situated on the Arkansas River just a few miles west of town, Lake Pueblo State Park enjoys an impressive setting. Semiarid plains surrounded by limestone cliffs and buttes contrast with

Dormant smokestacks have made the Riverwalk a desirable place. Photo by Anne Boutin.

mountain panoramas of Pikes Peak to the north and the Wet Mountains to the west. Completed in the early 1970s, Lake Pueblo (Pueblo Reservoir) is one of the largest bodies of water in the state. Its cool, clean water, excellent fishing and sailing also make it one of the most popular places in the state for recreation.

Facts About the Lake

At high water there are over 60 miles of twisting shoreline. Most of the northern shoreline is accessible by road, whereas getting to most of the southern shore involves a hike or access by boat. You can pay an entrance fee or purchase an annual parks pass. Following are some things to do once you get there.

Camping

The park has more than 400 sites (fee charged). On summer weekends the sites can fill up quickly. For reservations up to 120 days in advance, contact **1-800-678-2267** or **www. reserveamerica.com.** Modern toilets, showers and trailer hookups are available. Camping is offered in the park Apr. 1–Sept. 30, though the Juniper Breaks Campground provides unimproved sites year-round.

Fishing

Most of the boats plying the waters of Pueblo Reservoir are out for a day of fishing. And with good reason. A *Denver Post* article stated that the reservoir "maintains its standing as the best all-around walleye, largemouth bass, smallmouth bass and wiper fishery in the state." People fish here year-round. According to park officials, trout (up to 6 pounds) are best caught in spring and fall. Walleyes strike often in winter; crappie, smallmouth and largemouth bass, white bass and sunfish feed in the spring and summer. Large channel catfish also call these waters home. Tackle and minnows are available at the Northshore and Southshore Marinas.

Swimming

Swimming in the reservoir is not allowed. There is, however, a swimming area located just below the dam. A sandy beach down by the river is

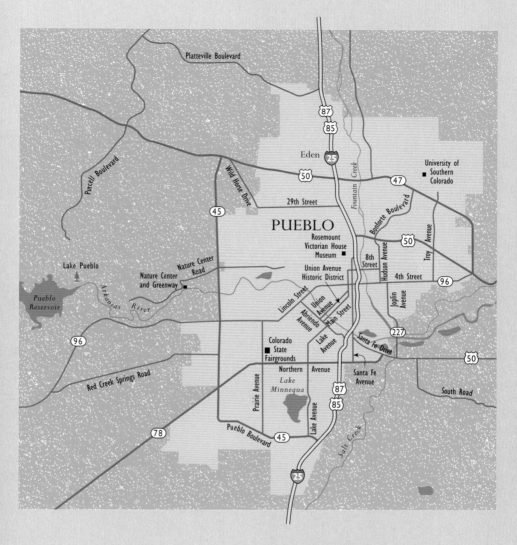

Platteville Boulevard

87
85
Eden
25
50
47
University of
Southern
Colorado

Purcell Boulevard

Wild Horse Drive

29th Street

45

PUEBLO

Rosemount
Victorian House
Museum

Bonforte Boulevard

50
Troy Avenue

Hudson Avenue

8th
Street

4th Street

96

Union Avenue
Historic District

Lincoln Street

Nature Center
Road

Lake Pueblo

Nature Center
and Greenway

Arkansas River

Union
Avenue

Main Street

Abriendo
Avenue

Joplin
Avenue

Pueblo
Reservoir

Santa Fe Drive

227

96

Lake
Avenue

50

Colorado
State
Fairgrounds

Northern
Avenue

Avenue

Santa Fe
Avenue

Red Creek Springs Road

Prairie Avenue

Lake
Minnequa

87
85

South Road

Salt Creek

78

Pueblo Boulevard

45

Lake Avenue

25

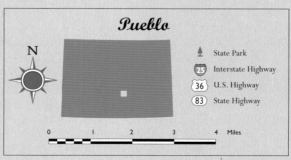

Pueblo

N

⛟ State Park

25 Interstate Highway

36 U.S. Highway

83 State Highway

0   1   2   3   4 Miles

protected by limestone bluffs and shady cotton-wood trees. **Rock Canyon Swim Area** has lifeguards. There is a small fee. For an additional charge give the huge water slide a try and follow it up with some fun in the bumper boat area. Open in summer only, 11 A.M.–7 P.M. daily; **719-561-2111.**

Water Sports

Boat ramps allow easy launching for powerboats and sailboats. Both marinas offer boat slips and boat rentals. Wind at the reservoir is consistently strong in springtime, and the sailboaters and windsurfers love it. If you plan to windsurf, remember that the water in the reservoir comes from snow melt-off—it's really cold in spring-time. Most windsurfers wear a wet suit until at least mid-May. Although windsurfing is allowed all over the reservoir, a special launch area is set aside on the north shore.

If you want to sit back, relax and let someone else show you around, consider a trip on the *Prarie Princess II,* an attractively restored 1955 cruise boat that can accommodate more than 30 people. Promotional materials tout such prestigious previous passengers as Vanilla Ice and Julio Iglesias. Two-hour cruises are available Fri.–Wed., year-round; **719-547-1126.**

Wheelchair Access

The Rock Canyon area, just below the dam, offers accessible fishing, camping and swimming areas as well as a half-mile, level nature trail suited for wheelchairs. In addition, the Analine Fishing Pond offers a dock designed for use by disabled visitors.

Wildlife

A state wildlife area adjacent to the northwest corner of the park serves as home to deer, badgers, bobcats, coyotes, wild turkeys, quail, hawks, golden eagles and bald eagles. On sum-mer weekends, the visitor center offers classes and guided tours focusing on native wildlife. Below the dam to the east are the **Greenway and Nature Center of Pueblo** and the **Raptor Center of Pueblo** (for information on

these centers, see the Parks section). You can hike, bike or in-line skate down from the reser-voir or drive from town.

For More Information

The visitor center at park headquarters, on the south shore, is open daily 8 A.M.–4:30 P.M. year-round. **Lake Pueblo State Park, 640 Pueblo Reservoir Rd., Pueblo, CO 81005; 719-561-9320; www.coloradoparks.org.**

Union Avenue Historic District

A short distance from the yet-to-be-completed Riverwalk, the Union Avenue Historic District has become the center of Pueblo nightlife. The 1889 vintage Union Depot serves as the focal point. The renovated rail depot operates as a kind of community center, hosting weddings and local events as well as housing shops and ser-vices. While this former red-light district might not provide the type of adventure it once did, the few intimate, quirky little drinking holes and restaurants have local character oozing from the seams. While the historic district is still develop-ing, you can wander among the restored brick buildings dating to the turn of the 20th century and choose among some good restaurants and bars.

For live music and a chance to experience "The Best Place in Town to Take a Leak," check out **Phil's Radiator Service and Beer Gar-den.** While Phil's no longer actually provides cooling and flushing services, they're quite adept at pouring cold, cheap beers. If you're lucky, you can catch a Latin-tinged Hank Williams cover band on their tiki-torch-enhanced patio or a game of pool in the converted garage. Open 4 P.M.–2 A.M. daily. **109 E. C St.; 719-584-2671.**

Nick's Italian-American Bistro ($$ to $$$) sports a covered patio with fountains and Christmas lights. They serve up traditional Italian fare on the patio year-round, warming the area with a fireplace in winter. In summer, the patio is packed with primarily older visitors munching on vodka rigatoni and shaking their groove thing to tunes from local bands. Open

Mon.–Thurs. 11 A.M.–10 P.M., Fri.–Sat. 11 A.M.–2 A.M., Sun. buffet brunch 11 A.M.–3 P.M. **310 S. Victoria St.; 719-583-1111.**

Steel City Diner and Bakeshop ($$ to $$$), opened in November 1999 by Richard Warner and Mary Oreskovich, presents masterful cuisine in simple, unpretentious surroundings. From the fresh-baked garlic peppercorn bread served with the meal to the last phenomenal lick of the spoon after a bowl of hand-cranked ice cream, the experience is serious pleasure. Of particular note are the wild mushroom ravioli with hazelnuts and goat cheese and the "unintimidating mixed green salad" (which boasts far more flavor than the name might imply). The gourmet fare, admits Warner, is still seeking a strong local following, so bring lots of friends with you as you visit this fabulous joint across from the Union Depot. **121 B St.; 719-295-1100.**

The Rogue's Gallery and SoHo Bar is one of Pueblo's newest entries into the bar scene. This New York–influenced spot features an upstairs art gallery highlighting photography from local artists and a downstairs bar specializing in martinis. Open Mon.–Thurs. 4–11 P.M., Fri. 4–11 P.M., Sat. 4–11 P.M., closed Sun. **224 S. Union Ave.; 719-545-6969.**

Check out the **Gold Dust Saloon ($ to $$),** a relaxing corner bar with hanging plants, large windows, high ceilings and postered walls. Throw peanut shells on the floor or order a burger and fries from their inexpensive lunch menu, 11 A.M.–3 P.M., or limited bar menu, 3–8 P.M. Open until 2 A.M. Mon.–Sat. **130 S. Union Ave.; 719-545-0741.**

Or try **Magpie's ($ to $$),** where owner Billy Coppola has compiled an unusual beer list for the Tap Room. Also an excellent lunch and dinner spot. Don't skip the Magpie, an enormous cream puff with vanilla ice cream and chocolate sauce. That's the only puff you'll have, because Magpie's is a nonsmoking restaurant and bar. Open for lunch Tues.–Sat. 11 A.M.–2 P.M., dinner 5–8 P.M.; the bar is open until it closes. **229 S. Union Ave.; 719-542-5522.**

Festivals and Events

Colorado State Fair

Aug. Each year Pueblo cuts loose when it hosts the Colorado State Fair. The town had its first annual fair back in 1872 and it has been going strong ever since. Cowboys and city slickers alike crowd into the fairgrounds for the 17-day event, which features stock shows, fiestas, top national rock and country music groups and, of course, a rodeo. It's hard not to have a good time no matter what your interests are. Be sure to make advance hotel reservations, as space gets very tight. The fairgrounds are at the corner of Prairie and Arroya Aves.; **1-800-876-4567; 1-800-444-FAIR; 719-561-8484; www.pueblo. org/visitorsguide/events.**

Chile and Frijole Festival

mid-Sept. Pueblo has a festival that celebrates one of its hottest products: the chili. Local farmers grow 10 million pounds of 'em a year in addition to nearly 7 million pounds of beans (or frijoles). The smell of roasting chilis fills the air at this spicy gathering, as do the sounds of regional music on the streets and at the Sangre de Cristo Arts Center. The festival features an 1840s historical market and is centered on the Hispanic cultural tradition that defines Pueblo. **1-800-233-3446; 719-542-1704; www.pueblo. org/visitorsguide/events.**

Outdoor Activities

Golf

The sun shines 73 percent of the year in Pueblo, making it a great climate for golfing. Compared to many urban and mountain courses, Pueblo offers an absolute bargain on greens fees. The best course in the area is probably the **Walking Stick,** located on the northeast end of town near the University of Southern Colorado, a challenging links-style course with plenty of undulating terrain. **4301 Walking Stick Blvd.; 719-584-3400.** Another well-known course is the **Pueblo West Golf Club,** about

8 miles west of town. To reach it, head west on Hwy. 50 to McCulloch Blvd., then turn left. **251 S. McCulloch Blvd.; 719-547-2280.** In town try **City Park Golf Course,** in City Park at **3900 Thatcher Ave.; 719-561-4946.** The three courses are open all year.

River Floating

The Arkansas River flowing through town is one of the most popular floating rivers in the state. If you're a whitewater aficionado, however, this part of the Arkansas isn't for you, because by the time the river exits its steep mountain canyon and arrives at Pueblo, most of its fight is gone. If you like tranquil water, try the **Nature Center of Pueblo** (see the Parks section). For a more secluded float, head upriver on Hwy. 50 to Swallow's Canyon, just below the town of Portland. This 10-mile stretch of the Arkansas offers a mellow, peaceful float that snakes along through cottonwood groves. Look for blue herons, ospreys and eagles. It's perfect for an open canoe. You can float all the way down into Pueblo Reservoir and get out at the Oasis Marina on the north shore or stop before the reservoir at any one of a number of fishing access roads.

For more challenging rafting and kayaking water located upriver, see the River Floating sections in the **Cañon City** and **Upper Arkansas Valley** chapters.

Seeing and Doing

Museums and Galleries

El Pueblo Museum

Located on what is believed to be the original El Pueblo site in downtown Pueblo, this museum provides plenty of historical information about Pueblo and the Arkansas River. You'll also find some interesting artifacts, including some excavated from the original El Pueblo trading post built in 1842. Other exhibits provide information about the plains and mountain Indian tribes of Colorado. Check out the metal chest armor worn by a Spanish conquistador who visited the area hundreds of years ago. For a glimpse at frontier life prior to 1870, El Pueblo is quite good. Small admission fee. Open year-round Tues.–Sat. 10 A.M.–3 P.M., closed Sun.–Mon. **324 W. First St.; 719-583-0453.**

Fred E. Weisbrod Aircraft Museum

This collection of vintage military aircraft is still getting off the ground. Climb inside and inspect fighters, missiles, research vehicles and support equipment, like the 1942 Ford Refueler. A building in the southwest corner of the grounds houses a B-24 photo display. Located 6 miles east on Hwy. 50 at **Pueblo Memorial Airport, 31475 Bryan Cir.** Open daily 9 A.M.–sunset. For special tours call **719-948-9219.**

Rosemount Victorian House Museum

This palatial 24,000-square-foot Victorian mansion will impress you immediately. Construction of Rosemount was contracted in 1891 for John A. Thatcher, founder of the First National Bank of Pueblo, and was completed three years later. Serving as a monument to the finest designers and craftsmen of the era, Rosemount was built for about $100,000, an extravagant sum at that time. Thirty-seven rooms, 10 fireplaces, dual gas and electric lighting, a 1,500-gallon copper-lined tank in the attic for pressurized water, stunning woodwork throughout—it really has to be seen and experienced to be appreciated.

John Thatcher's son, Raymond, lived in the house until his death in 1968, at which time Rosemount was willed to a private museum foundation. Most of the original furniture and carpets remain. The mansion was named after Mrs. Thatcher's favorite flower. With its obsessively detailed decor, a rose theme appears in almost every room, from ceiling frescoes to patterns on chamber pots. Most impressive is the Steinway player piano (one of only 200 produced) that still plays its original tunes. Even if you are just driving through Pueblo, make time to stop in for an hour-long tour from knowledgeable guides. Open June 1–Sept. 1 Tues.–Sat. 10 A.M.–4 P.M., Sun. 2–4 P.M.; Sept. 1–June 1

A unique vertical display at the Buell Children's Museum in Pueblo. Photo by Anne Boutin.

Tues.–Sat. 1–4 P.M., Sun. 2–4 P.M. The last tour begins at 3:30 P.M. Closed in Jan. The admission fee stings a bit, but there's a discount for seniors and children. Kids under 6 are free. **419 W. 14th St.; 719-545-5290; www.rosemount.org.**

Sangre de Cristo Arts and Conference Center

Located downtown, the arts center includes a permanent western art display, four galleries with changing exhibits and a theater for performing arts. On selected Fris. from 5 to 8 P.M. in summer, live music, food and good times can be had on the front steps. Galleries are free and are open Mon.–Sat. 11 A.M.–4 P.M. The **Buell Children's Museum,** opened in 2000, is impressive proof of Pueblo's commitment to the future. Located next to the Arts Center (where it was formerly housed), the museum is pure eye candy for children and adults. Exhibits include a people-sized kaleidescope, a kite exhibit, kinetic sculpture and hands-on art and computer

areas. The Kid Rock Cafe offers an extensive jelly selection to satisfy your young one's PB&J fix. Bright colors and giddiness abound. The Children's Museum also is open Mon.–Sat. 11 A.M.–4 P.M.; admission is charged. **210 N. Santa Fe Ave., Pueblo, CO 81003; 719-543-0130;** box office **719-542-1211; www.pueblo. org/visitorsguide.**

Nightlife

Gus' Place

Gus' Place is a must for anyone who wants to get a feel for Pueblo's past as well as quaff a cheap beer. The memorabilia on the walls serve as a museum of sorts to the idle CF&I steel mill just a stone's throw from the front sidewalk. For decades, Gus' served as the watering hole of choice for steelworkers coming off shift and looking for a cold one: for three years Gus' held the record in *Ripley's Believe It or Not* for serving more beer per barstool than anywhere else in the world. Nowadays urban professionals pack the place, but just as the mill workers did, they feast on a Dutch Lunch (the only menu item: a do-it-yourself sandwich plate with meat, cheeses and veggies) and a schooner of beer. Open daily 10 A.M.–2 A.M.; until 8 P.M. on Sun. **1201 Elm; 719-542-0756.**

Irish Brewpub and Grille

This funky place, run by two generations of Italians, now brews its own beer. See the Where to Eat section.

Union Avenue Historic District

See the Major Attractions section.

Parks

Mineral Palace Gardens

An ideal spot for a spring or summer family picnic, the Mineral Palace Gardens sports fountains, a duck pond, a community pool with a water slide and diving boards, and well-groomed flower gardens. It's the perfect place to catch some shade from the warm southern Colorado sun. **1600 N. Santa Fe Ave.; 719-545-5319.**

The Riverfront

Trails for hiking and bicycling follow the Arkansas River through Rock Canyon, connecting 16 miles of trails in Lake Pueblo State Park with those in town. The meandering river is lined with tall cottonwood trees and limestone bluffs. This place where Indians used to camp is now a peaceful escape from town.

Greenway and Nature Center of Pueblo— The center, on the banks of the Arkansas River, offers nature trails and year-round events intended to educate children and adults alike about the prairie, desert and river valley ecosystems. It's a perfect place for family picnics at one of many tables. Bicycle rentals are available. Reach the Nature Center on foot by following the river trail just west of Pueblo Blvd. By car, turn west off Pueblo Blvd. just north of the Arkansas River, onto Nature Center Rd. Go past the entrance to the Raptor Center of Pueblo to the end of the road. Open daily, 9 A.M.–5 P.M. **5200 Nature Center Rd., Pueblo, CO 81003; 719-549-2414.**

Raptor Center of Pueblo—One of very few centers in the country that rehabilitates birds of prey and returns them to the wild. Feeding time varies; you'll be glad to know that the center accepts meat donations. Located next to the Greenway and Nature Center of Pueblo. Open daily in summer 9 A.M.–5 P.M.; winter hours vary. **719-549-2327.**

Zoo at City Park—Located just east of Rock Canyon, this is a great place to take the kids. Be sure to check out the eco-center exhibits including a tropical rain forest and the cooler (literally) coastline exhibit with black-footed penguins. The zoo has other regular exhibits as well as a kid's favorite called Happy Time Ranch—a farm re-creation complete with all the barnyard animals. Across from the zoo entrance is a restored carousel, built originally in 1911. After a trip to the zoo and a ride on the carousel, your kids will be so grateful they might even start eating their beets. Small fee. The zoo is open daily 10 A.M.–5 P.M. in summer and 9 A.M.–4 P.M. in winter. **719-561-9664.**

Where to Stay

Accommodations

Aside from two fabulous bed and breakfast inns—the Abriendo Inn and Baxter Inn—lodging in Pueblo is limited to well-known motel/resort chains offering the latest in cable TV hookups and other standard comforts. However, an interesting bed and breakfast—K.K. Ranch—is located in Beulah, 26 miles west of Pueblo, via Hwy. 71.

Abriendo Inn—$$$ to $$$$

Since 1989 the Abriendo Inn has offered what is quite easily one of the finest bed and breakfast experiences in the state. The massive, foursquare masterpiece, listed on the National Register of Historic Places, was built in 1906 for brewery giant Martin Walter and his eight children. Today the entire home is exquisite, from fine antiques in each of the 11 rooms (all have private bathrooms, air conditioners, TVs and telephones) to the woodwork throughout. Owner Kerrelyn McCafferty Trent, a former teacher and interior designer, says she wanted the inn to be elegant but not pretentious—a goal she has achieved. With the completion of three deluxe rooms on the third floor, travelers can enjoy all the perks, including a personal refrigerator, microwave and double-size whirlpool baths. You'll be in awe of the imaginative use of space and angles. The downstairs is highlighted by wooden wainscoting and a beautiful winding, wooden staircase. Breakfast, including freshly brewed coffee and such taste treats as egg sausage soufflé, is served on either of the two porches or in the sunny breakfast room adjacent to the kitchen. Though many guests are business travelers, Abriendo is highly recommended for honeymoons and other romantic getaways. Kids are not encouraged; no pets. **300 W. Abriendo Ave., Pueblo, CO 81004; 719-544-2703. www.abriendo@bed andbreakfastinns.org.**

Baxter Inn—$$$ to $$$$

Located across from the Rosemount Victorian House Museum (see the Museums and Galleries section), the Baxter Inn provides an elegant place of rest for those who appreciate absolute attention to detail. From complimentary lip balm to personal notes left on the pillow of every guest in this five-room historic building, owners Dave and Lois Jones have placed remarkable focus on assuring a memorable stay. The red, rusticated sandstone home was built in 1893 by Charles Kretschmer, and was owned for 50 years by the Catholic Diocese of Pueblo. It gained a place on the National Register of Historic Places due to its first occupant, O. H. P. Baxter, one of the founders of Pueblo. With its carved, golden oak staircase, stained glass windows and extensive collection of antiques, the Baxter is definitely not the place to take your pet (or even rowdy children), but it should suit your taste if you're seeking peace, quiet and immaculate beauty. **325 W. 15th St., Pueblo, CO 81003; 719-542-7002; www.puebloonline. com/baxterinn.**

Pueblo Marriott—$$$

This hotel's 164 guest rooms offer conveniences appreciated by many modern travelers, such as coffeemakers, hair dryers, full-size irons and boards and two-line speaker phones with voice mail and data ports. **110 W. 1st St., Pueblo; 1-800-228-9290; 719-542-3200.**

The Inn at Pueblo West—$$ to $$$

This Best Western Inn is located north of Pueblo Reservoir in the planned community of Pueblo West, 10 miles west of Pueblo. The 80-room inn has a restaurant (popular Sun. brunch 10 A.M.– 2 P.M.) and cocktail lounge. The inn arranges tee times for guests at the nearby Pueblo West Golf Club. **201 S. McCulloch, Pueblo West, CO 81007; 1-800-448-1972; 719-547-2111.**

K.K. Ranch—$$

Retired Navy Capt. Kay Keating runs a delightfully tight ship at the K.K. Ranch in Beulah. The guest house is a quaint, cozy Victorian, brimming with antiques and heated by woodstoves. International guests will feel at home since Keating can get by in Japanese, German and French, learned in her sailing days. What gives K.K. its flair is Capt. Keating's avocation of restoring antique carriages. At the moment she owns 15 of the museum-quality vehicles, including a stagecoach and an eerie-looking hearse. She also restores antique sleighs, which she usually puts out in winter for dashes through nearby Pueblo Mountain Park. Accommodations include three upstairs bedrooms with a shared bathroom. A hearty continental breakfast is served. Call for reservations and directions. **8987 Mountain Park Rd., Beulah, CO 81023; 719-485-3250.**

Where to Eat

La Renaissance—$$$ to $$$$

La Renaissance is definitely a Pueblo dining highlight. Located in a former Presbyterian

Leaded glass doorway at the Baxter Inn in Pueblo. Photo by Anne Boutin.

church built in the 1880s, the restaurant has been in operation since 1974. High ceilings and, of course, lots of stained glass provide a unique interior design element. The menu is primarily continental, offering prime rib, steaks, chicken and tempting seafood entrées. These are five-course dinners, so come hungry. A good selection of imported wines and beers awaits you. The diverse lunch menu contains pasta, sandwiches, seafood and salads. There is also a dessert cart. Compared to restaurants in Denver, La Renaissance is a good value. Lunch served Tues.–Thurs. 11 A.M.–2 P.M., dinner Tues.–Sat. 5–9 P.M. **217 E. Routt Ave.; 719-543-6367.**

Carriage House at Rosemount—$$

This unique little lunch spot, located in the old carriage house at the Rosemount Victorian House Museum, is a great spot to stop for a sandwich or salad. Open Mon.–Fri. 11 A.M.–2 P.M. **419 W. 14th St.; 719-595-0098.**

Irish Brewpub and Grille—$$

Like an old shoe, this friendly place is seriously comfortable, if slightly tattered. For the past four decades the pub has attracted a loyal following. Second-generation owner Ted Calantino (local winner of an annual jalapeño-eating contest) serves up an array of inexpensive appetizers such as alligator sausage, oysters and spicy wings. With seven huge tanks in the refrigerated basement, the pub pours its own beer, including a spicy chili beer. The full menu features steaks, sandwiches, pastas and salads. In summer check out the funky back deck overlooking the alley and parking lot. Open 3 P.M.–2 A.M. daily; food served from 5 P.M. **108 W. 3rd St.; 719-542-9974.**

Ianne's Whisky Ridge—$ to $$$

Operated by a third generation of successful Pueblo restaurateurs, Ianne's is known for its fine Italian food. Their tasty pasta dishes, veal and steaks highlight the menu. This semielegant eatery has the atmosphere of a suburban living room, with its stone fireplace, skylights and gray blue carpeting. In the adjacent bar listen to live jazz on weekend nights and selected weeknights. Open 11 A.M.–10 P.M. daily; bar is open until 2 A.M. **4333 Thatcher Ave.; 719-564-8551.**

Do-Drop-Inn—$ to $$

Ask the locals where the best pizza in town is and you'll get the Do-Drop-Inn for an answer. And it's great! This is a small, very casual down-town bar that also serves up sandwiches and a pretty decent margarita. Belly up to the bar or sit in a booth. Take-out orders are available (add $1 per order). The Do-Drop opens every day at 6 A.M. to serve omelettes and other breakfast favorites. On Fri. and Sat. they're open until 11 P.M.; every other day they're open until 10 P.M. **1201 S. Santa Fe Ave.; 719-542-0818.**

Grand Prix—$ to $$

This place gets the prize for the most randomly selected Mexican restaurant name. As co-owner Sadie Montoya explained, "My grandfather was part French, and since we wanted something a bit different than the typical Sombrero or La Casa, we chose Grand Prix." This family-run local favorite serves up spicy dishes including their popular combo plates, flautas and chili rel-lenos. The same chef has been cooking since opening day back in 1969, an aspect that has

helped maintain a loyal clientele. All of the food is prepared from scratch, including the spicy green chili. The spacious restaurant is highlighted by the long wooden bar and the bizarre collec-tion of liquor decanters placed throughout (be sure not to miss the Elvis statue collection behind the bar). Open Tues.–Fri. 11 A.M.–1 A.M., Sat. 4–11:30 P.M., Sun. noon–8 P.M., closed Mon. **615 E. Mesa Ave.; 719-542-9825.**

Gus' Place—$ to $$

See the Nightlife section.

Union Avenue Historic District Restaurants

See the Major Attractions section.

Services

Visitor Information

Pueblo Chamber of Commerce—Visitor information is available Mon.–Fri. **302 N. Santa Fe Ave., Pueblo, CO 81003; 1-800-233-3446; 719-542-1704.** Or stop by the **Red Caboose Visitor Information Center at Hwy. 50 and Elizabeth St.; 719-543-1742; www. pueblo.org.**

Events Line—Provides a 24-hour recording of events in Pueblo; **719-542-1776.**

Southeast Plains

The southeastern section of Colorado with its miles of windswept plains isn't exactly a garden spot. Jackrabbits and rattlesnakes outnumber tourists by dizzying numbers. These high, somewhat barren plains, however, slope down to the fertile Arkansas River Valley, which is one of the most intensely farmed areas in the state; miles of irrigation canals have made much of it possible. For 150 miles, from Pueblo to the Kansas border, the Lower Arkansas River makes its way east across the plains through fairly lush bottomland dotted with farms and ranches. The area's produce, especially the melons, is some of the best in the country.

What the southeast plains lack in outright tourist appeal is more than made up for by its fascinating history. The Native American, Hispanic and Anglo cultures have all left an indelible imprint on this part of Colorado. The Mountain Branch of the Santa Fe Trail, which brought so many pioneers west from Missouri in the early to mid-1800s, traveled through the heart of the Arkansas Valley before angling southwest at La Junta. Today Hwy. 50 follows the Santa Fe Trail west from the Kansas border through the Arkansas Valley toward the lofty Rockies.

For hearty hikers, naturalists, archaeologists and paleontologists, the immense Comanche National Grassland provides many interesting opportunities, including an impressive variety of birdlife and what could be the longest set of fossilized dinosaur tracks in the world (see the Lamar section).

Along Hwy. 50 you'll find a number of farming and ranching communities that offer accommodations, restaurants and a few attractions worth your time. One big draw to this corner of the state is the excellent bird hunting, especially for geese and pheasants. Springtime and early summer fishing in the warmwater reservoirs can also be worthwhile.

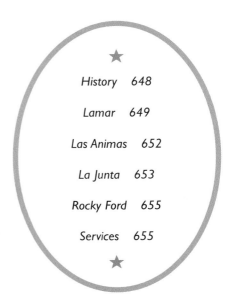

History

After Mexico declared independence from Spain in 1821, the Santa Fe Trail was established as a trade route between St. Louis, Missouri, and Santa Fe, New Mexico. Along the Mountain Branch of the trail (the northern route), near present-day La Junta, Bent's Fort was established in 1833 and for years served as the most important trading center for the American western frontier (see the La Junta section for details on Bent's Old Fort National Historic Site). Along with mountain men and travelers passing by on the Santa Fe Trail, the fort attracted the attention of Plains Indians. From the north side of the Arkansas River, bands of Arapaho and Cheyenne camped near the fort and traded their buffalo robes for food and goods. Other tribes, such as the Kiowa, Prairie Apache and Comanche, camped along the south side of the river, also trading at the fort.

In the late 1840s U.S. troops spent time in the area during the war with Mexico. After the U.S. victory, much land south of the Arkansas River previously claimed by Mexico became part of the United States. With this part of Colorado (at that time the New Mexico Territory) under U.S. jurisdiction and the allure of gold strikes in the Colorado mountains, settlers poured west along the Santa Fe Trail. Because of this huge influx, relations with the Plains Indians inevitably deteriorated.

In 1861 the Treaty of Fort Wise required the Plains Indians to cede much of their land in eastern Colorado. The Arapaho and Cheyenne refused to honor the treaty. After a band of renegades attacked the Hungate Ranch south of Denver in 1864, and settlers called for massive retaliation against the Indians, a group of Arapaho and Cheyenne, under the leadership of Chief Black Kettle, sued for peace. The Indians met with Gov. Evans in Denver and then traveled to Sand Creek, near Fort Lyon, where they were to be under the protection of U.S. troops. Gov. Evans dispatched a battalion of Colorado volunteers to southeastern Colorado, where the Indians were camped. What ensued was one of the most tragic episodes in American history.

The volunteer soldiers, led by Col. John M. Chivington, traveled to Fort Lyon, a few miles northeast of Las Animas, where they were told the location of the Indians. The soldiers traveled north to Sand Creek and, on the morning of Nov. 29, 1864, attacked the Indian camp. Here is Chivington's report on what happened: "I, at dawn this morning, attacked a Cheyenne village of one hundred and thirty lodges, from nine hundred to one thousand warriors strong. We killed Chief Black Kettle, White Antelope and Little Robe, and between four and five hundred other Indians. . . ." Later it was discovered that only about 150 Indians were in the camp. Chivington and his men killed approximately 120—mostly old men, women and children.

Although anti-Indian sentiments ran high during this era, Chivington's act outraged many settlers. The Sand Creek Massacre dealt one of the most serious blows to the Plains tribes in Colorado, who were eventually relocated to reservations in other states. The National Park Service is looking into possible purchase of the area where the massacre occurred and management as a national historic site. For information on the site's status, contact **Bent's Old Fort National Historic Site** at 719-383-5010; www.nps.gov/beol.

By 1870 cattle ranchers began to move into southeastern Colorado. The Chisholm, National and Goodnight Trails brought huge herds of Texas longhorns up from the Lone Star State for summer grazing on the high, grassy plains. Many head were sold to Colorado ranchers. One of the liveliest cattle towns was Trail City, located near the Kansas border. Edward Bowles, a rancher in northeastern Colorado, visited the town as a boy and recalls, "It was the toughest town God ever let live; nothing there but saloons and gambling houses, hotels and corrals." The Santa Fe Railroad arrived in the valley by the mid-1870s and proved to be a crucial link for moving cattle (and, later, produce) to market back east.

Cattle barons ruled this part of the state for a number of years, until encroaching homesteaders changed the balance of power. Farmers eager to carve a niche in this wild country snapped up agricultural land in the Arkansas Valley. Once irrigation canals were in place, land in the valley produced large crops of vegetables and, especially, melons, which became well known throughout the country. Today this part of the state is still dominated by ranching and agriculture.

Highway 50

This chapter describes towns that lie along Hwy. 50, beginning near the Kansas border and then heading west. To reach this area from Denver, head south on Interstate 25 for 110 miles and then east on Hwy. 50.

Lamar

Touting itself as "Goose Hunting Capital of the Nation," Lamar rolls out the red carpet each fall for hunters who arrive from all around the country to hunt a variety of game birds and deer. Each fall, VIPs take part in the Two Shot Celebrity Goose Hunt.

Established in 1886, the town was named after L. Q. C. Lamar, secretary of the interior under President Grover Cleveland. By naming

Mysterious carvings in Picture Canyon in the Comanche National Grassland. Photo by Dean Winstanley.

the town in his honor, early developers hoped to sway the secretary to install the headquarters of the area land office in Lamar. The townsfolk must have successfully tapped into his ego because they got their wish.

In the 1890s Lamar suffered the devastation of a prolonged drought, a major fire and a catastrophic invasion of jackrabbits. The gentle beasts were eating up the farmers' crops, and finally action was taken. More than 100 hunters encircled a large area of land and converged on the horde of rabbits. When the dust cleared, more than 4,700 rabbits had been shot or clubbed to death. The rabbits were then strung up on wire for the whole town to see. This annual harvest went on for a few years until the problem was under control.

Today Lamar serves as a trade center for the region. There are plenty of services for travelers cruising through the area. For more information about the Lamar area, contact the **Lamar Chamber of Commerce, 109A E. Beech, P.O. Box 860, Lamar, CO 81052; 719-336-4379.**

Big Timbers Museum

This museum takes its name from the 25-mile stretch along the Arkansas River where enormous cottonwood trees (some 18 feet in circumference) once lined both banks of the river. Indians, trappers, traders and pioneers traveling the Santa Fe Trail used to camp in Big Timbers, which provided a lush, wooded area in an otherwise barren region. The cottonwoods were later harvested to construct nearby towns. William Bent (of Bent's Fort fame; see the La Junta section) maintained a couple of trading stations here.

Housed in this small museum is a collection of pioneer memorabilia, including a kitchen display, farm implements and period clothing. Interesting collection of historic photos. Free. Open 1–5 P.M. daily. **7515 Hwy. 50, P.O. Box 362, Lamar, CO 81052; 719-336-2472.**

Comanche National Grassland

Flat expanses of short-grass prairie, twisting rocky canyons and scorching heat: all of these ingredients make up the harsh country in the

Comanche National Grassland. Checkerboarded in sections of public land that cover two primary areas (one 50 miles south of Lamar and the other south of La Junta on Hwy. 350), this country was the territory of the Plains Indians until the early 1800s. When ranchers entered southeastern Colorado in the 1870s, they allowed their herds to graze the fragile land. Eventually homesteaders settled in the area and, as required by the federal government, farmed at least 40 acres of their 160-acre tracts. The dry soil was ill suited for cultivation techniques of the times, but the farmers stubbornly persisted. The use of the natural ground cover caused problems that eventually came home to roost in the Dust Bowl days of the 1930s. Beginning in 1938 Uncle Sam began buying back the land to retire it from cultivation.

Though the U.S. Soil Conservation Service has successfully reclaimed much of these grasslands, on the whole they constitute a hot, dry,

Fossilized allosaurus footprint trackway beside the Purgatoire River in Picket Wire Canyonlands. Photo by Dean Winstanley.

fairly inhospitable region visited by relatively few. Archaeologists are an exception. Several prehistoric Indian campsites and rock art provide fascinating clues about early Colorado residents. **Picture Canyon**—near Springfield, south of Lamar—provides an opportunity to view these petroglyphs. In recent years, some amateur archaeologists have hypothesized that strange lines carved in some of Picture Canyon's caves are similar to Ogam writing used by the ancient Celts of Ireland. Others choose to believe Plains Indians used the caves for ceremonies. During the fall and spring equinox, festivals are held that attract visitors to these caves. Call the **Springfield Chamber of Commerce, 719-523-4061,** for information.

The grasslands also hold an appeal for those who enjoy desert hiking and wildlife. Antelope, mule deer, coyotes, badgers, foxes, raccoons and jackrabbits all inhabit the grasslands. The plentiful birdlife includes raptors such as bald eagles, prairie falcons and red-tailed hawks. The endangered lesser prairie chicken can be spotted in spring. These colorful relatives of the grouse strut their stuff while performing a stomping courtship dance—it's quite a sight.

Some years ago the U.S. Army turned over a beautiful canyon area along the **Purgatoire River** to the U.S. Forest Service. Known as **Picket Wire Canyonlands,** this picturesque area south of La Junta is definitely worth a visit because of the wildlife, historic sites and its main attraction: more than 1,300 fossilized dinosaur footprints. These dinosaur trackways are located in the ancient mudflats along the Purgatoire River. Apatosaurus (brontosaurus) and allosaurus prints are found at over 100 trackways. Due to the fragility and significance of these prints, access to the canyon is limited. Ranger-led tours are offered every Sat. in May, June, Sept. and Oct. For information on access, tours and directions, check with the **Comanche National Grassland Office in La Junta; 719-384-2181.**

If you visit the grasslands in summer, be sure to bring drinking water. For information and maps, stop in at the **Comanche National Grassland Office,** 46 miles south of Lamar on

Hwy. 287; **27162 Hwy. 287, P.O. Box 127, Springfield, CO 81073; 719-523-6591.** The northwestern tract is administered out of La Junta; the office is located along Hwy. 50 at **1420 E. 3rd St., La Junta, CO 81050; 719-384-2181; www.fs.fed.us/r2/psicc.**

Queens State Wildlife Area

About 15 miles north of Hwy. 50 on Hwy. 287 sit four of the Plains' finest warmwater reservoir fisheries, all within a 5-mile radius of each other. Throwing a line from a boat on **Nee Noshe, Nee so Pah, Nee Grande** or **Nee Shaw** can yield walleye, perch, crappie, northern pike, channel catfish and bass. Nee Noshe is especially well known for excellent striped bass fishing. Springtime fishing is best here as water levels can drop dramatically by autumn due to irrigation needs. Boat ramps are available at every reservoir except Nee so Pah.

Cow Palace Inn—$$$

Lamar's activities seem to center on this large motel, which caters to goose hunters, vacationers and businesspeople. It also doubles as a popular place for local wedding receptions. One hundred comfortable rooms come with color TVs and king- and queen-size beds. The motel has an indoor pool and a courtyard dining area with many tropical plants. The **restaurant ($$ to $$$)** is known for its excellent steaks and salad bar. **1301 N. Main St., Lamar, CO 81052; 1-800-678-0344; 719-336-7753; www.bestwesterncolorado.com.**

Las Animas

Founded in 1869 at the junction of the Arkansas and Purgatoire Rivers, Las Animas was originally an important cattle grazing area. The largest business was the Prairie Cattle Company, an English outfit that grazed 50,000 head of longhorn in the early 1880s. By 1916 the last major roundup was held. Today Las Animas serves as a trade center for farmers and ranchers.

Accommodations and restaurants can be found in town. For additional information contact the **Las Animas/Bent County Chamber of Commerce, 332 Ambassador Thompson Blvd., Las Animas, CO 81054; 719-456-0453; 719-456-9654.**

Boggsville

In 1862 Thomas Boggs and a number of other local pioneers settled at this site along the Purgatoire River. Until the arrival of the railroad in 1873, Boggsville was a regional center, even serving as the first county seat in Bent County. Boggsville makes for an excellent historical glimpse of life in the 1860s and 1870s. A number of original homes have been re-created or restored, including that of frontiersman Kit Carson. Carson settled in Boggsville in 1867 with his wife and seven children. Call for hours. From Las Animas, head south on Hwy. 101 for 1.8 miles. **P.O. Box 68, Las Animas, CO 81054; 719-456-0822.**

Kit Carson Museum

Housed in a building originally constructed to house German prisoners in World War II, the Kit Carson Museum provides an interesting look into the history of the area. The museum is really a complex of eight historic structures, including the main building, a stagecoach stop, a one-room steel jail, the original Bent County jail, the first Las Animas city jail, a carriage house, a one-room schoolhouse and a blacksmith shop. It's definitely worth a visit. Open Mon.–Fri. 1–5 P.M. from Memorial Day to Labor Day. At **9th and Bent, Las Animas; 719-456-2005.**

John Martin Reservoir State Park

Surrounded by flat, treeless terrain, John Martin Reservoir may not be one of the most scenic bodies of water in the state. But when full it's one of the biggest. Located along the Arkansas River between Lamar and La Junta, the reservoir provides enough water to support an impressive waterfowl population. Bird-watchers can be treated to sightings of white pelicans in summer and bald and golden eagles in winter.

The reservoir also ranks as a pretty good warmwater fishing destination, stocked with channel catfish, largemouth and smallmouth bass, striped bass, crappie, walleye and sunfish. A couple of long, concrete boat ramps at the east end of the reservoir guarantee to get you into the water no matter what the level. Swimming and waterskiing are also popular.

Just below the dam at John Martin's eastern border is spring-fed, warmwater **Hasty Lake,** stocked with rainbow trout, yellow perch, crappie, smallmouth and white bass, channel catfish, walleye and northern pike. Hasty Lake's developed, tree-shaded campground provides showers, RV hookups and other amenities; fee charged. For reservations: **1-800-678-CAMP** or **www.reserveamerica.com.** Located 5 miles south of Hwy. 50 from the town of Hasty (east of Las Animas). For more information: **719-336-3406; www.colorado parks.org.**

Bent's Fort Inn—$$

This comfortable Best Western inn serves as a fine base for exploring the sites of southeastern Colorado or as an overnight stop while blasting through the area. In addition to the well-maintained rooms, you'll find a **restaurant/ lounge ($$)** known for its steaks and Mexican fare. The pool is a welcome oasis during sweltering summer days. **10950 E. Hwy. 50, Las Animas; 719-456-0011; www.bestwestern colorado. com.**

La Estancia Mexican Restaurant—$ to $$

Although there are several Mexican restaurants along the Mountain Branch of the Santa Fe Trail, this one has consistently good authentic fare in a clean and charming atmosphere. Try the carnitas, a filling dish of marinated pork and sautéed onions. There's an outdoor patio for cool evenings. Open Tues.–Thurs. 11 A.M.–2 P.M., Fri.–Sat. 4:30–8 P.M., Sun. 11 A.M.–8 P.M., closed Mon. **625 Carson Ave., Las Animas; 719-456-0225.**

La Junta

La Junta (Spanish for "the junction") was probably named for its location at the convergence of the Santa Fe and Navajo Trails. Hwys. 50 and 350 follow these same routes. Since the Santa Fe Railroad arrived in 1875, La Junta has served as the transportation hub for the lower Arkansas Valley. Today the town is home to the largest airport in southeastern Colorado. Amtrak trains running between Chicago and Los Angeles make daily stops. Produce and cattle are also shipped by train to every part of the country. For its setting on the windswept plains, La Junta is an attractive town, with parks and focal points, such as the Santa Fe Plaza and Otero Junior College. Although its population is predominantly Anglo, the Hispanic influence is apparent. La Junta has a number of places to stay the night, along with a couple of good steak houses and Mexican restaurants. For more information contact **La Junta Chamber of Commerce, 110 Santa Fe Ave., P.O. Box 408, La Junta, CO 81050; 719-384-7411.**

Bent's Old Fort National Historic Site

In 1834 brothers William and Charles Bent and Ceran St. Vrain completed a trading post along the Arkansas River in southeastern Colorado. It quickly became the most important hub for U.S. trade with Mexico (which seceded from Spain in 1821) and the western territories all the way to the Pacific Ocean. Traders moved American-made goods along the Santa Fe Trail from Missouri to Santa Fe, where they traded for Mexican products to be brought back east. Mountain men also showed up to trade beaver pelts in exchange for supplies they needed to survive in the wilds.

The Bent brothers and St. Vrain were also adept at trading with the Plains Indian tribes. Since the fort was located on southern Cheyenne hunting grounds, good relations with this tribe were especially important. To secure harmonious relations, in 1837 William Bent married Owl Woman, the daughter of a Cheyenne holy man.

Outside Bent's Old Fort National Historic Site. Photo by Wendy Newman.

The immensely profitable Bent's Fort thrived until the late 1840s. After Charles Bent was killed in the Taos Revolt of 1847 and a cholera epidemic swept into the area from Missouri a few years later, William Bent abandoned the fort.

Today the immense adobe structure has been reconstructed to look similar to the way it did in the 1840s when it was in its prime. This National Historic Site is furnished with a few antiques and many reproductions of other items. During living history programs, costumed employees provide a wealth of information about the way of life at Bent's Old Fort. This is a highly recommended stop for anyone interested in the settlement of Colorado and the American West. Small fee in summer months. Open daily 8 A.M.–5:30 P.M. June 1–Aug. 31, and 9 A.M.–4 P.M. the rest of the year. Located 8 miles east of La Junta. **35110 Hwy. 194 E., La Junta, CO 81050-9523; 719-383-5010; www.nps.gov/beol.**

Koshare Indian Kiva and Museum

What started as a Boy Scout troop's project in 1933 has grown into a nationally known Indian dance group and an excellent Native American museum. "Buck's Brats," as they were known for years, developed quite a reputation for their authentic Native American dances. Today the Koshare Indian Dance Group, from Explorer Scout Post 230, performs around the country as well as in their kiva at this museum. Though it takes a few minutes to get used to these blond youngsters, they really can dance.

Generous donations have helped finance the attractive museum, which houses $40 million worth of Native American artifacts and art representing tribes around the country. The magnificent Koshare collection is beautifully displayed. If you're interested in Native American culture, dance and history, this is a don't-miss on your itinerary. Open 10 A.M.–5 P.M. daily June–Aug.; 12:30–4:30 P.M. Tues.–Sun. other months. Dance performances Sat. at 8 P.M. June, July and Dec. Call for winter holiday dance times. On the Otero Junior College campus at **115 W. 18th St., P.O. Box 580, La Junta, CO 81050; 1-800-693-KIVA; 719-384-4411.**

Otero Museum

Displays and artifacts of local life from 1875, when the Santa Fe Railroad arrived, until the present are the focus of this interesting historical museum. Exhibits include early grocery store items, farming and ranching equipment, histories of the local sugar beet factories and a Santa Fe Railroad room. The number of artifacts crammed into this place is impressive. Fee charged. Open June–Sept. 1–5 P.M., closed Sun. Located off Anderson St. **between 2nd and 3rd Sts., P.O. Box 223, La Junta, CO 81050; 719-384-7500.**

Picket Wire Canyonlands
For information about this beautiful and interesting area of the Comanche National Grassland, see the Lamar section.

The Finney House—$$
While making your way along Hwy 50, rest your weary soul at the Finney House. Shirley Flock, owner and innkeeeper, has restored this magnificent 1899 Victorian home. Relax beside the koi pond or unwind in the rotunda that serves as a sitting room. There are four sizable rooms available, including one room with a private entrance and full kitchen. The house is adorned with several original stained glass windows and lavished in oak. Despite it's very elegant appearance, you'll feel right at home; accept that Shirley sees to every detail and you don't have to do anything but enjoy it. **608 Belleview, La Junta, CO 81054; 719-384-8758; 719-384-8769.**

Rocky Ford

This small farming community gets its name from early pioneers who crossed the Arkansas River at this safe point in order to avoid quicksand along many other sections of the river. Rocky Ford really should be remembered for being the site of the first community irrigation canal in the Lower Arkansas Valley. In 1874 settler George Swink convinced his neighbors to help dig a ditch. When it was finished, their hard work helped produce fantastic crops. Swink went on to develop the sweet, juicy Rocky Ford cantaloupe, which is known throughout the country. If you are traveling through the area in Aug. or Sept., stop by one of the many roadside produce stands for a taste of this delicious treat as well as other fruit from the valley. Pick up a fruit stand brochure or seek further information at the **Rocky Ford Chamber of Commerce, 105 N. Main St., Rocky Ford, CO 81067; 719-254-7483.**

Arkansas Valley Fair
Held in mid-Aug. to coincide with the melon harvest, this multi-day gathering of Arkansas Valley residents features events such as horse races, livestock shows, a carnival and a rodeo. Special theme days include Fiesta Day, which celebrates the area's Hispanic culture. You'll eat enough on Watermelon Day to keep you away from melons for a year. For more information about this annual event, contact the **Rocky Ford Chamber of Commerce, 719-254-7483.**

Services

Visitor Information
Colorado Welcome Center—Provides one-stop information for this area as well as other destinations in Colorado. **109 E. Beech, Lamar, CO 81052; 719-336-3483; www.state.co.us/data2/fs/wclamar.htm.**

La Junta Chamber of Commerce—110 Santa Fe Ave., P.O. Box 408, La Junta, CO 81050; 719-384-7411; www.lajunta.net.

Lamar Chamber of Commerce—109A E. Beech, Lamar, CO 81052; 719-336-4379.

Las Animas/Bent County Chamber of Commerce—332 Ambassador Thompson Blvd., Las Animas, CO 81054; 719-456-0453.

Rocky Ford Chamber of Commerce—105 N. Main St., Rocky Ford, CO 81067; 719-254-7483.

Trinidad

Located along Interstate 25 a mere 19 miles north of the New Mexico border, historic Trinidad lies under the shadow of nearby Fishers Peak. With a history dating back to the arduous days of the Santa Fe Trail, the Spanish and ranching influence on Trinidad is still palpable today: cobblestones cover the hilly streets of old downtown, designated the Corazon de Trinidad National Historic District. Museums, including the outstanding Baca and Bloom houses at the Trinidad Museum, are also major attractions.

This town of about 10,000 bustled at the turn of the 20th century when it served as a center for nearby coal towns. Though coal mining is practically dormant today, signs of the old days as well as beautiful scenery can be seen along the Highway of Legends—a Scenic and Historic Byway. History, galleries and an influx of residents over the past few years have many locals likening Trinidad to Santa Fe, but on a much smaller scale. Though currently that comparison really seems like a stretch, time will tell if Trinidad can (or really wants to) develop such a reputation.

reached a breaking point on Christmas Day 1867, when a friendly wrestling match turned into a free-for-all riot. Several people were killed during this racially motivated "Battle of Trinidad."

The Trinidad area was a part of the Territory of New Mexico from 1850 until the Colorado Territory usurped the land in 1861. The town grew steadily as a sheep center then a cattle center, until vast deposits of coal were mined from the nearby hills. For decades coal mining was the main source of employment for the people of Trinidad. Locals hope tourism will mean better times ahead.

History

Trinidad's position at the confluence of the Purgatoire River and Raton Creek has always been a favored camping place—first for nomadic Indian tribes, then for trappers and traders. In the 1800s many Conestoga wagons passed through present-day Trinidad, heading south over Raton Pass on the Mountain Branch of the Santa Fe Trail. This pioneer path provided a fairly direct route between Santa Fe and trading centers along the Missouri River. In 1859 Gabriel Gutierrez and his nephew built a cabin, establishing Trinidad's first recorded permanent settlement.

As the town grew, it maintained a tough reputation. Men of Spanish and Mexican descent mingled uncomfortably with those from the eastern states. Fistfights were common, and tension

Seeing and Doing

Museums

A. R. Mitchell Museum of Western Art and Gallery

Arthur Roy Mitchell, a leading western-style painter of our century, painted more than 160 cover illustrations for popular "pulp" Westerns. In his later years he concentrated on painting accurate representations of early western life, gathering many awards for his style and exper-

---

Getting There

Trinidad is located 197 miles south of Denver on Interstate 25.

Bloom Mansion. Photo by Wendy Newman.

archaeology exhibits. The highlight was a diorama of nearby Trinchera Cave, which was occupied for thousands of years by prehistoric humans. Other items include arrowheads and artifacts uncovered in the 1960s at the site of Trinidad Reservoir. The now-defunct archaeology program at Trinidad State Junior College was initiated in 1951 by Hal Chase, a friend and contemporary of Jack Kerouac, William Burroughs and Allen Ginsberg. Chase appears in Kerouac's classic *On the Road* as Chad King. Free Admission. May–early Sept., Mon.–Fri. 10–4 P.M. **Freudenthal Memorial Library, Trinidad State Junior College; 719-846-5508.**

Ludlow Monument

Consider a drive to the Ludlow Massacre site, where one of the nation's bloodiest labor disputes unfolded on Apr. 20, 1914. A battle between striking coal workers and militiamen ended tragically with eight miners and a dozen children dead. This violent story of early American labor action is preserved in a granite monument erected by the United Mine Workers. From Trinidad, take Interstate 25 north 12 miles to the Ludlow exit.

Trinidad History Museum

This fascinating museum represents a decade-long span of tremendous change in the Colorado of the 1870s: from territory to state, from Santa Fe Trail to railroads, from sheep to cattle ranching, from natural gas to electricity, from adobe to brick Victorian. Side by side, the imposing domiciles at the museum (Baca House and Bloom Mansion) allow you to trace this dynamic phase of Colorado history. Elaborate Victorian and Hispanic gardens align the pathway between the houses. Guided tours available. Small fee charged. Open May–Sept., 10 A.M.–4 P.M. daily; off-season by appointment. **300 E. Main St.; 719-846-7217; www.coloradohistory.org.**

Baca House—Built of adobe bricks in 1870 by John Hough, a merchant from Pennsylvania, this house was undoubtedly the finest in Trinidad at that time. It was purchased for $7,000 by Don Felipe Baca in 1873, complete with furnishings

tise. Some 250 of his originals are on display in this large collection of western art. The gallery is also home to many other artists in the same genre. One part of the museum is dedicated to Hispanic folk art of Colorado and New Mexico. Rare bultos (wooden sculptures) and retablos (wooden altar pieces) are displayed in addition to a small replica of a morada—the meeting house of the Penitente brotherhood. The upstairs is dedicated to several visiting artists in residence, resulting in a wonderfully eclectic western art gallery. Gift shop includes jewelry and Southwestern art. Free admission. Open Apr.–Sept., Mon.–Sat. 10 A.M.–4 P.M., closed Sun. and holidays. **150 E. Main St.; 719-846-4224.**

Louden-Henritze Archaeology Museum

It was a pleasant surprise to be given a personal tour through this small but excellent collection of and dishes. Uneven wooden floors are covered by handwoven rugs. Looking out of the second-floor windows you can see the path of the Mountain Branch of the Santa Fe Trail (now Main St.) through distorted hand-rolled glass.

Bloom Mansion—In 1882 the Victorian-styled Bloom Mansion was built next to the Baca House for Frank Bloom, a Colorado cattleman, merchant and banker. The differences between the two are startling. First off, the opulent Bloom Mansion was built for much less than the Baca House, thanks to the establishment of the railroads and the accompanying infusion of cheap labor. Conveniences from the eastern United States were built into the elaborate three-story setting such as the combination gas/electric fixtures in the parlor. Beautiful antiques can be found throughout the mansion's rooms. Behind the house, where a brick barn once stood, you'll enjoy a stroll through a carefully tended historic garden, enhanced by a splashing waterfall.

Santa Fe Trail Museum—Behind the Baca House, the adobe carriage house and sheepherders' quarters contain rooms full of interesting items from Trinidad's early days. Displays include Kit Carson's buckskin coat, a gun collection, a bear trap and many Native American artifacts.

Parks

Trinidad Lake State Park

Only 4 miles west of Trinidad is a pleasant area for water sports, hiking and cushy camping. Trinidad Lake water levels can fluctuate quite a bit, but the reservoir is open for boating and fishing. Annual stocking includes rainbow trout, but warmwater species, including largemouth bass, catfish, walleye and crappie, can also be caught. Hiking trails offer great views of Fishers Peak and the nearby Sangre de Cristos. Consider secluded Long's Canyon for interesting history and viewing blinds for glimpses of migratory birds. Or hike to see geological evidence of the boundary between the Cretaceous and Tertiary periods: stratified layers of rock from each period, with a thin layer of uridium in between. The uridium is believed to have come from the giant meteor that may have wiped out the dinosaurs. Inquire at the visitor center for directions to the site.

Sixty-two developed campsites on the north side of the lake provide flush toilets and showers. RV hookups and tentsites; fee charged. Campground reservations can be made at **1-800-678-CAMP** or **www.reserveamerica. com.** Interpretive programs offered in summer. To reach Trinidad Lake State Park, take Hwy. 12 west of Trinidad for 4 miles. For more information stop by the excellent visitor center or contact **32610 Hwy. 12, Trinidad, CO 81082; 719-846-6951; www.coloradoparks.org.**

Scenic Drives

Highway of Legends

This 120-mile loop is one of the highlights of a trip to the Trinidad area. The highway is well named, with history as a major component of the drive. The route offers a variety of things, including tiny Hispanic communities, geologic oddities, alpine forests and spectacular views of the Sangre de Cristo Range and Spanish Peaks.

To begin the route from Trinidad, drive west on Hwy. 12. About 8 miles out of town you'll see some large black slag piles on the north side of the highway left over from the coal processing at **Cokedale.** Now a National Historic District, Cokedale is perhaps the best-preserved example of the many Colorado coal mining camps that thrived in the early 1900s. On the south side of the highway are the remnants of the coke ovens. As the road makes its way west through the Purgatoire River Valley, you'll travel through many small Hispanic plazas and communities, some of which date back to the 1860s. About 31 miles from Trinidad you'll pass through **Stonewall Gap,** an unusual, narrow opening in an uplifted line of Dakota sandstone. Soon after, Hwy. 12 turns north as it continues to climb through pine and aspen toward Cucharas Pass. Along this stretch you'll pass Monument Lake, which offers fairly decent trout fishing, as well as camping and accommodations at **Monument Lake Resort.**

From 9,941-foot Cucharas Pass, the view northeast to the Spanish Peaks is quite good. The highway drops from here down into the Cuchara Valley, winding its way north to La Veta, Hwy. 50

and Walsenburg. From Walsenburg return to Trinidad by heading south on Interstate 25 for 37 miles. Information on Cucharas Pass and the beautiful Cuchara Valley can be found in the Scenic Drives section of the **Cuchara Valley** chapter. An excellent map of the Highway of Legends containing historical and geological information about places along the way may be obtained in Trinidad at the **Colorado Welcome Center** (see the Services section).

Where to Stay

Trinidad lodging centers on motels. Many motels are easily visible from Interstate 25 as it winds through Trinidad. For specific listings contact the **Colorado Welcome Center** at **719-846-9512** or **www.tsjc.cccoes.edu/welcome.** Here is one unique lodging idea in the area:

Chicosa Canyon B&B—$$$ to $$$$

Tucked away (way away) in a lush canyon 14 miles northwest of Trinidad, this nicely renovated 1870 homestead provides a quiet, relaxing night's stay. Antiques adorn each of the three rooms, and you'll find kiva fireplaces in two of them. A lofty renovated cabin out back that once accommodated cowboys now provides privacy, a refrigerator and incredible Southwestern decor—outfitted with a queen-size bed and two twin beds in the loft. Dogs are welcome for those staying in the cabin. Keena, the innkeeper and former Denver restaurateur, knows her way around her impressive kitchen and provides excellent baked goods, smoothies and full breakfasts. Other highlights: hot tub in the solarium, patio dining and hiking and mountain biking around Chicosa Canyon's 65 acres. **32391 County Rd. 40 Trinidad, CO 81082; 719-846-6193; www.bbonline.co/chicosa.**

Where to Eat

Black Jack's Saloon and Steakhouse— $ to $$$

This is unquestionably the place in Trinidad to go for a steak and your favorite drink. Highlights include an excellent salad bar and an open grill

so you see how well (or medium-well) your steak is going to turn out. Seafood options also please the palette. And don't worry, it's quite alright if you throw your peanut shells on the floor. Open daily 4–10 P.M.; saloon stays open later. In Trinidad's historic district at **225 W. Main St.; 719-846-9501.**

Main Street Bakery and Cafe—$ to $$$

It's hard to miss this one: the aroma will guide you. This place on historic old Main St. has more to offer than the homemade goodies stocked in the pastry case. Specialties include chicken pot pie and foccacia bread stuffed with fresh vegetables and plenty of deli meats; try the panino picante with salami, provolone and roasted red peppers. Full bar to complement your entrée. Mon.–Wed. 7am 3 P.M., Thurs.–Sat. 7 A.M.–9 P.M., Sun. 8A.M.–2 P.M. **121 W. Main St., Trinidad; 719-846-8779.**

Wazubi's Blue Cup Coffee House—$

For a smoothie or gourmet coffee, swing into Wazubi's. Homemade soups and salads also tempt your taste buds. Live acoustic music periodically. Open Mon.–Thurs. 7 A.M.–7 P.M., Fri. 7 A.M.–11 P.M., Sat. 8 A.M.–11 P.M. **269 N. Commercial St., Trinidad; 719-846-8760.**

Services

Visitor Information

Colorado Welcome Center—This is a great source of information on Trinidad and other Colorado destinations. You'll see the signs on Interstate 25. Open daily. **309 N. Nevada Ave., Trinidad, CO 81082; 719-846-9512; www. tsjc.cccoes.edu/welcome.** The **Trinidad Chamber of Commerce** resides here as well; **719-846-9285; www.trinidadco.com.**

Transportation

Trinidad Trolley—Free hourly tours of the downtown historic district begin at the Colorado Welcome Center. Trolley tours run Memorial Day to Labor Day, 9 A.M.–4 P.M. daily.

Index

About the Authors

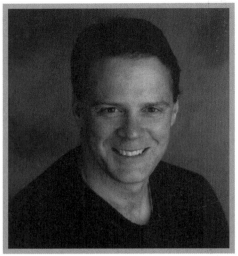

BRUCE CAUGHEY has had a lifelong interest in Colorado and in travel. He has spent time in 27 foreign countries, including a year on the island of Crete, Greece, where he coauthored a hiking guide entitled *Crete: Off the Beaten Track* (Cicerone Press). These days, he can be found hiking, fishing, skiing and biking in the mountains of Colorado, or spending time at his family's cabin near Deckers.

A fourth generation native Coloradan, Bruce is coauthor, with Doug Whitehead, of the best-selling book *Colorado's Best* (Fulcrum), which has been featured weekly on KCNC-TV. Bruce has also contributed to the Rough Guide Series in London. His freelance projects have included special travel coverage for *The Denver Post, Rocky Mountain News, National Geographic Traveler, Frontier Airlines Inflight Magazine,* and on the Internet.

Bruce serves as Communications Director for Douglas County School District and lives in Parker, Colorado. Whenever possible he hits the road with his daughters, Shannon and Julia, on shared Colorado adventures. The girls keep track of their trips with Dad by keeping their own journals and lending their own kid's-eye perspectives to many activities and places in the guide.

Also a fourth generation Coloradan, **DEAN WINSTANLEY** spent his early years piling into the family's International Travelall (the "cornpicker") for family trips to hike, camp, ski, fish and exploring all corners of his beautiful state. Through these early family adventures and his parents, Dean gained a true love and appreciation for the unique natural beauty, history and archeology of Colorado.

After graduating from Colorado College in 1982, Dean spent a number of years teaching English and seeking a much needed "travel fix" through Asia, including working in the People's Republic of China. Upon his return from overseas Dean teamed up with Bruce to write *The Colorado Guide*. Dean has also written about Colorado in *The Denver Post* and on the Internet.

Currently Dean works on outdoor recreation policy and funding issues for Colorado State Parks as the Policy and Special Projects Manager in Denver. Whenever possible he escapes to the mountains with his wife and two children to rejuvenate from life in the (increasingly) big city.